ISBN 978-1-331-05731-4
PIBN 10139206

1 MONTH OF
FREE
READING

at

www.ForgottenBooks.com

By purchasing this book you are eligible for one month membership to ForgottenBooks.com, giving you unlimited access to our entire collection of over 1,000,000 titles via our web site and mobile apps.

To claim your free month visit:

www.forgottenbooks.com/free139206

English
Français
Deutsche
Italiano
Español
Português

www.forgottenbooks.com

Mythology Photography **Fiction**
Fishing Christianity **Art** Cooking
Essays Buddhism Freemasonry
Medicine **Biology** Music **Ancient
Egypt** Evolution Carpentry Physics
Dance Geology **Mathematics** Fitness
Shakespeare **Folklore** Yoga Marketing
Confidence Immortality Biographies
Poetry **Psychology** Witchcraft
Electronics Chemistry History **Law**
Accounting **Philosophy** Anthropology
Alchemy Drama Quantum Mechanics
Atheism Sexual Health **Ancient History**
Entrepreneurship Languages Sport
Paleontology Needlework Islam
Metaphysics Investment Archaeology
Parenting Statistics Criminology
Motivational

LIST OF AUTHORS.

LIST OF AUTHORS

LIST OF AUTHORS

J. G. F. H.	John G. F. Holston, M. D.
S. D. H	Samuel D. Hopkins, M. D.
E. K. H	Ebenezer K. Hunt, M. D.
H. M. H	Henry M. Hurd, M. D.
P. R. I	P. Robertson Inches, M. D.
R. L. I	R. Lindsey Ireland, M. D.
A. B. I	Asa B. Isham, M. D.
B. J	Bettina Jackson.
J. E. J.	Joseph Edward Janvrin, M. D.
S. E. J	Smith Ely Jelliffe, M. D.
S. L. J	Samuel Lawrence Jepson, M. D.
J. W. J.	J. Wilkinson Jervey, M. D.
J. T. J	Joseph T. Johnson, M. D.
F. B. J	Frank B. Johnston, M. D.
F. U. J	Francis Upton Johnston, M. D.
H. E. J	Howard E. Jones, M. D.
O. M. J	Oswald M. Jones, M. D.
O. J	Otto Juettner, M. D.
H. A. K	Howard A. Kelly, M. D.
M. K. K.	Margaret K. Kelly.
G. M. K.	George M. Kober, M. D.
A. K	Adolf Koenig, M. D.
G. N. K	George Noble Kreider, M. D.
D. S. L.	Daniel Smith Lamb, M. D.
C. W. L.	Caroline W. Latimer, M. D.
L. G. L.	Louis G. LeBoeuf, M. D.
C. E. L	Charles E. LeConte
C. A. L	Charles A. Lee, M. D.
D. L	Daniel Lewis, M. D.
J. U. L	John Uri Lloyd, Ph. M.
T. L	Thomas Lothrop, M. D.
G. A. L	Grace Anna Lewis.
A. G. L	Anna Green Loveland.
S. L	Starling Loving, M. D.
L. F. L	Lorenzo F. Luckie, M. D.
J. S. M.	John Sangster MacCallum, M. D.
T. L. M.	Thomas Lawrence McDermott, M. D.
C. C. M	Caleb Clarke McGruder, M. D.
K. A. J. M	Kenneth A. J. McKenzie, M. D.
R. A. M	Robert A. McLean, M. D.
L. S. M	Lewis Samuel McMurtry, M. D.
A. M	Andrew MacPhail, M. D.
M. D. M	Matthew D. Mann, M. D.
J. P. M	James P. Marsh, M. D.
C. M	Clarence Martin, M. D.
F. C. M	Francis C. Martin, M. D.
J. B. M	Joseph Benson Marvin, M. D.
R. J. M	R. J. Massey, M. D.
C. H. M., Jr.	Claudius Henry Mastin, Jr., M. D.
W. H. M	William Henry Mays, M. D.
J. G. M	J. G. Meacham, Jr., M. D.
K. C. H. M	Kate C. H. Mead, M. D.

LIST OF AUTHORS

E. S . . . . Elsworth Smith, M. D.
H. L. S . . . . Henry Lee Smith, M. D.
J. A. S . . . . James A. Spalding, M. D.
A. J. S . . . . Aaron J. Steele, M. D.
W. R. S . . . . Walter R. Steiner, M. D.
C. G. S . . . . Charles G. Stockton, M. D.
L. H. T . . . . Lewis H. Taylor, M. D.
H. L. T . . . . Henry Ling Taylor, M. D.
H. M. T . . . . Hannah M. Thompson.
J. M. T . . . . Joseph M. Toner, M. D.
R. R. T . . . . Richard R. Tybout, M. D.   ·
J. T . . . . James Tyson, M. D.
J. V. D . . . . J. Van Duren, M. D.
J. J. W . . . . James J. Walsh, M. D.
S. B. W . . . . Samuel B. Ward, M. D.
D. W . . . . Davina Waterson.
W. H. W . . . . William H. Welch, M. D.
S. W . . . . Stephen Wickes, M. D.
S. D. W . . . . Sylvester David Willard, M. D.
J. W. W . . . . John W. Williams. M. D.
F. C. W . . . . Frank C. Wilson, M. D.
R. W., Jr. . . . . Robert Wilson, Jr., M. D.
J. M. W . . . . J. McF. Winfield, M. D.
A. B. W . . . . Alfreda B. Withington, M. D.
J. H. W . . . . Julius Hayden Woodward, M. D.
J. J. W . . . . Joseph Janvier Woodward, M. D.
L. F. W . . . . Lemuel F. Woodward, M. D.
L. J. W . . . . L. J. Woolan, M. D.
R. B. W . . . . Ray B. Wright, M. D.
T. R. W . . . . Thomas R. Wright, M. D.
J. A. W . . . . John Allan Wyeth, M. D.
M. W. Y . . . . Marion Wolcott Yates, M. D.
J. Z. . . . . John Zahorsky, M. D.
B. F. Z . . . . Benjamin F. Zimmerman, M. D.

NOTE: The biographies unsigned were either compiled by the Editor or gathered from old books where the name of the writer could not be found.

H

Holyoke, Edward Augustus (1728–1829).
Edward Augustus Holyoke, first president of the Massachusetts Medical Society, was born in Marblehead, Massachusetts, August 1, 1728, and died in Salem, March 31, 1829, thus living to the great age of one hundred years and eight months. His ancestors emigrated from England in 1638 and settled in Lynn, Massachusetts. His father, Edward Holyoke, minister at Marblehead, was born in Boston and graduated from Harvard College in 1705, was elected president of the college in 1737, and presided over its destinies for thirty-two years until his death in 1769. His mother, Margaret Appleton, of Ipswich, was descended from John Rogers, the first Smithfield martyr. Edward Augustus was the eldest son and the second of eight children. When nine years old his father moved to Cambridge to take up his duties of president of the college, and here the boy received his education, finally graduating from the college with the class of 1746.

In 1747 he began to study medicine with Dr. Berry, of Ipswich, and remained with him nearly two years, settling in Salem in 1749 to pass the rest of his life practising there. At first patients were few and far between—a livelihood hard to gain—but in the course of time it was said that there was not a single house in town to which he had not been called as physician.

In business he was most methodical and during a professional life of nearly eighty years was never once at a greater distance than thirty miles from Salem.

Dr. Holyoke was twice married, first to Judith, daughter of Benjamin Pickman, who, with her only child, died in 1756; and second, to Mary, daughter of Nathaniel Viall, a Boston merchant. They had twelve children. Mrs. Holyoke died in 1802, and all but two of the children died before their father.

Dr. Holyoke was below the middle height in stature, tough and wiry in build. In demeanor he was dignified, mild, placid and agreeable.

He was essentially a family practitioner and was not ambitious for public distinction. However, he was instrumental in organizing the Massachusetts Medical Society and was its first president (1782–84), also the first person to receive from Harvard College the honorary M. D. This was in 1783. In 1815 Harvard conferred upon him her LL. D. He was president at various times of the American Academy of Arts and Sciences.

His health was good until the last years of his life. He habitually gave much time to theological inquiries, especially during the last forty years of his life, and he was a constant observer of the external rites of Christianity.

Dr. Holyoke's practice was based

on four drugs, mercury, antimony, opium and quinine. He did little surgery and during his entire practice is said never to have witnessed the amputation of a limb. He was preceptor to thirty-five medical students and was thus a prominent factor in medical education in the days before the schools. In a long personal letter to John F. Watson, Esq., of Germantown, written on his hundredth birthday he says: "My health is good. That is, I have a good appetite and sleep as well as at any period of my life, and, thanks to a kind Providence, suffer but little pain except now and then pretty severe cramps; but my mental faculties are impaired, especially my memory for recent events."   W. L. B.

Mass. Med. Society Transactions, vol. iv.
Sermon by John Brazer, 1829.
Hist. Har. Med. School, T. F. Harrington, vol. i.
As to Founding of Mass. Med. Socy., Bost. Med. and Surg. Jour., vol. civ.

Homans, John (1836-1903).

John Homans, a pioneer ovariotomist in New England, was born in Boston, November 26, 1836. His grandfather, of the same name, was a graduate of Harvard College, 1772, and an army surgeon during the War of Independence. His father, also John, was a graduate of Harvard College, 1812, who practised medicine in Boston.

John Homans the third graduated from Harvard College in 1858 and received his M. D. from her Medical School in 1862. The same spirit which inspired his grandfather in 1776 impelled him, at the outbreak of Civil War, to offer his services to the government. He was at that time house surgeon in the Massachusetts General Hospital, and had not yet taken his medical degree. In January, 1862, he was commissioned assistant surgeon in the United States Navy, and served on the gunboat "Arostook" during the search for the disabled United States steamship "Vermont," in Hampton Roads, and later on the James River, during McClellan's campaign. He was at the battles at Fort Darling, Virginia, and at Malvern Hill. In November, 1862, he was given a commission as assistant surgeon in the regular army. He was at New Orleans, and later, on the staff of Gen. Banks, took part in the disastrous Red River expedition. Those of his friends who were fortunate enough to have heard his informal accounts of that ill-advised expedition and of the search for the "Vermont" will not soon forget them. As side-lights upon much that passes for history, they were instructive as well as entertaining. Subsequently he was ordered to Washington, and held various surgical appointments in connection with the Army of the Shenandoah. He was surgeon-in-chief of the first division of the Nineteenth Army Corps, was present at the battles of Winchester and Cedar Creek, and ultimately became medical inspector on the staff of Gen. Sheridan. He resigned the army from May, 1865, after an eventful career of a little over three years. He immediately went to Europe for study and travel, spending most of his time in Vienna and Paris. In November, 1866, he returned to Boston and began to practise, being appointed successively surgeon to the Boston Dispensary, the Children's Hospital, and in August, 1868, to the Carney Hospital. His second ovariotomy was done there in April, 1873, and he became consulting surgeon ' in 1880. It was here that he did many ovariotomies and demonstrated that the operation was not as serious as imagined. He developed an antiseptic technic and trained the sisters in charge of the operating-room with great care. Later he transferred his activities to St. Margaret's Hospital, where ovarian tumors from all over New England and the provinces came for operation. Many times Dr. Homans paid the patient's expenses out of his own pocket. Between 1872 and 1900 Dr. Homans performed six hundred and one. He was among the first to open the abdomen for abscess of the appendix. It was considered a great honor by the medical student of the time to be selected as one of his operative assistants at St. Margaret's. As an operator he was fearless and painstaking though somewhat excitable when in a tight place. Trouble for the assistants was sure to follow when he began to hum "I dreamt I dwelt in marble halls." He was no respector of persons and would have his joke no matter what happened. He was a surgeon to out-patients at the Massachusetts General Hospital from 1879 to 1882, and visiting surgeon from 1882 to 1889, when he was retired on account of age limit.

He did comparatively little writing, his publications being "Three Hundred and Eighty-four Laparotomies for Various Diseases," 1887, and various papers for the medical journals. Homans was clinical instructor in the diagnosis and treatment of ovarian tumors in the Harvard Medical School after 1881, and member of the American Surgical Association.

He died in his home in Boston, February 7, 1903 in his sixty-sixth year, after a short illness, leaving a widow, three sons and three daughters. One son of the same name followed the profession of medicine in Boston.

W. L. B.

Boston Med. and Surgical Journal, vol. cxlviii.
Bulletin Har. Med. Alumni Association, April, 1903.

Honyman, Robert (17— -1824).

Robert Honyman, Revolutionary surgeon and physician, was born in Scotland about 1752 and educated at Edinburgh University from which he graduated in medicine and entered the British Navy, but resigned and emigrated to America, settling in Louisa

County, Virginia, in 1774. He espoused the cause of his adopted country when the Revolution began, and fought as a private, being soon promoted to the rank of regimental surgeon. After the war he resumed his work, an extensive one, in Louisa and Hanover Counties, and continued to practise until his death.

He is said to have been a profound student and scholar, and a great reader, and to have possessed a marvelous memory. He read more and remembered more of what he read than any man in Virginia. At the age of sixty he is said to have begun the study of Italian as he desired to read that also.

In the earlier years of his practice when all inflammatory diseases showed a highly sthenic type, he used heroic treatment and did not spare the use of the lancet. Later on, when their type became more asthenic, he abandoned the use of the lancet and resorted to free emesis followed by a stimulating treatment.

He was stern in deportment and violent and demonstrative in his resentments. If any one questioned or complained of his bill, under no circumstances would he visit him again. The following extract from his will which is recorded at Hanover Court House, is of interest: "I also give and bequeath to my son, my thermometer, my diploma of doctor of physic, and also a human rib, which will be found in a small trunk in my chest, with my earnest request that he will carefully keep the said rib, which is of James V., King of Scotland, and transmit it carefully to his descendants."

He married Mildred Brown, a woman of rare beauty and accomplishments, and was the progenitor of some distinguished men.

He died in 1824, leaving a large fortune amassed by his practice, and is said to have written and published numerous articles.

R. M. S.

Hood, Thomas Beal (1829-1900).
The son of a Dr. James Hood, he was born on March 19, 1829, in Fairview, Ohio.

In 1840 he went to Brownsville, Ohio, and remained there about three years as help in a store. His father, who had loaned considerable money in the so-called "wild lands" of Illinois, sent him early in the winter of 1849 into Brown, McDonough and Schuyler Counties, Illinois, to foreclose the mortgages. He settled mortgages, ousted squatters and compromised litigations and returned home with several thousand dollars in gold concealed in his belt. Then he went to Baltimore to attend lectures in the Medical Department, University of Maryland, but returned home to Gratiot, Ohio, before gradnation he began to practise medicine with his father. In 1850 he married Margaret, daughter of Samuel Winegarner, but she died a few mohths afterwards. A little later he began practice at Columbus, Ohio, where in June, 1854, he married Mary Hyde, widow of Dr. Eliphalet Hyde and daughter of William G. Boggs.

He graduated M. A. in 1874 at Ohio Wesleyan University and took his M. D. in 1862 at the Western Reserve University, Cleveland, Ohio. In 1861 he went to Cleveland, appeared before the Faculty, Medical Department Western Reserve College and passed examination, and on November 6 was appointed assistant surgeon seventy-sixth Ohio Volunteers. He left Newark with the regiment February 6, 1862, and ten days later was in the battle of Fort Donaldson. He was mustered out October 13 and resumed practice at Newark, Ohio, and in 1867 was appointed assistant in the provost marshal general's office, Washington, under direction of Surg. (afterwards surgeon-general) Jedediah H. Baxter.

Dr. Hood was professor of anatomy 1870-71, practice of medicine 1877-91, diseases of nervous system 1892, and dean of medical faculty 1881-1900,

Howard Medical School. He died on March 15, 1900.   D. S. L.

Lamb's History of Medical Department, Howard University, D. C.
Minutes of Medical Society, D. C., March 21 and 28, 1900.
Trans. Medical Society, D. C., v, 1900,
National Medical Review, 1900-1901, x.

Hooper, Franklin Henry (1850-1892).
Franklin Henry Hooper, laryngologist, son of Robert C. Hooper, was born in Dorchester, Massachusetts, on September 19, 1850. He was educated in Europe and matriculated at Harvard Medical School in 1876. Afterwards he spent several years in European clinics and in Vienna, specially at that of Schroetter, making laryngological studies. On returning to Boston he was immediately appointed assistant in throat diseases at the Massachusetts General Hospital and afterwards aurist at the Boston Dispensary, becoming eventually professor of laryngology at the Dartmouth Medical College and instructor of the same at the Harvard School.

In addition to his recognized ability as diagnostician he owed much to his bold use of anesthesia in the removal of adenoids. His famous experiments upon the innervation of the larynx, with special reference to the functions of the recurrent laryngeal nerve, made his work of special value.

The disease from which he himself suffered began on his tongue in 1884, and in 1891 there appeared small epithelial growths. A portion of the tongue was removed but in 1892 the glands of the neck became affected and he died after much suffering, cheerfully borne, on November 22, 1892.

His writings included:
"Experimental Researches on the Tension of the Vocal Bands, etc.," 1883.
"A Case of Cavernous Papilloma of the Vocal Bands," 1884.
"Concerning the Positions of Paralyzed Vocal Bands," 1886.
"Effects of Varying Rates of Stimu-

lation on the Action of the Recurrent Laryngeal Nerves," 1888.

"The Mechanical Effects of Adenoid Vegetions in Children," 1889.

"Multiple Papilloma of the Larynx in Young Children," 1891.

Boston Med. and Surg. Jour, 1892, vol cxxvii.

Hooper, William Davis (1843-1893).

He was born on August 28, 1843, at "Beaver Dam," Hanover County, Virginia—now historic ground, the locality having been the scene of one of the most desperately hard fought battles of the "seven days fights around Richmond," that of Mechanicsville or Ellison's Mills.

His father dying when he was only seven years of age, his mother removed to Richmond, where he was educated in the schools of that city. He then found employment in the drug-store of Mr. Hugh Blair, of Richmond, where he acquired an excellent knowledge of chemistry and pharmacy. On the outbreak of Civil War he entered the army (Confederate) as a hospital steward and was assigned to duty in the dispensary at Camp Lee, afterwards Howard Grove Hospital, a position for which his experience particularly well fitted him. While thus serving he began to study medicine as a government student in the Medical College of Virginia, at Richmond, and, graduating with the highest honors, received the prize offered for the best original essay, in the spring of 1865.

At the close of the war, within a few weeks after his graduation in medicine, he settled in Liberty, now called Bedford City, in Bedford County, Virginia. He possessed a thorough knowledge of medicine and surgery, and was quick, almost unerring, in diagnosis, making him a high authority, and calling into requisition his services as a consultant in distant parts of the state. In 1873 he went abroad and traveled in Europe, visiting many of the largest hospitals in England and on the Continent, adding much to his store of professional knowledge. In June, 1875, he repeated his visit to Europe.

He married in June, 1875, Miss Kelso, of Bedford County. They had only one child, a son, who died before his father.

In December, 1892, the latter was for the fourth time attacted by "grippe," and never really recovered. In June he was taken suddenly ill, his strength failed very rapidly and he died on July 31, 1893.

He made numerous contributions to medical literature. The following are the titles of some:

"Report of a Case of Extra-uterine Pregnancy; Removal of the Fetal Skeleton by Abdominal Incision—Recovery." ("Transactions Medical Society of Virginia," 1872.)

"Relation of the So-called Ague to Malarial Fever," ibid., 1874.

"Intestinal Obstruction of Twelve Days' Duration." ("Virginia Medical Monthly," vol. ii.)

"Remarks on Aspiration, with Report of a Case." ("Transactions Medical Society of Virginia," 1876.)

"Irritation of the Ganglion of Remak." ("Virginia Medical Monthly," vol. xii.)

"Gun-shot Injury of the Brain. Breech-pin of Gun Imbedded in Cerebral Substance for Three Months without Producing Constitutional Symptoms." ("Transactions Medical Society of Virginia," 1887.)

"Report· on Addresses in Medicine, with a Description of a New Method of Treating Ulcerated Bladder with Prostatic Enlargement." ("Transactions Medical Society of Virginia," 1888.)

R. M. S.

Trans Med. Soc. of Va, 1893.

Hopkins, Lemuel (1750-1801).

This eminent consulting physician, renowned for his skill in treating tuberculosis, a satirist and poet of some repute in his day, was born in Salem Society (now Naugatuck) on June 19, 1750, the second son of Stephen Hopkins, Jr., and Patience, his second wife. Of his boyhood we know nothing save that he was of a slender constitution and was then troubled with a "cough, hoarseness, a pain in the breast and the spitting of blood." On his mother's side he was descended from a consumptive parent and family and he had that form of body which had been observed to indicate a pre lisposition to consumption." After being given a good classical education by his father, who was a farmer in easy circumstances, he began the study of medicine under the distinguished Dr. Jared Potter of Hallingford. Subsequently he removed to Litchfield and studied under Dr. Seth Bird. In 1776 he began practice in that town and served for a short time during this year, as a volunteer soldier in the Revolutionary Army. He removed to Hartford in 1784 where he resided until his death.

In Hartford he soon made quite a name for himself. He employed "the cooling treatment in fevers, the puerperal especially, and wine in fevers since called typhus"—methods which were then thought madness and some of his cases became the subject of much newspaper discussion. With large features, bright staring eyes and long ungainly limbs, which gave him an uncouth figure, he presented marked eccentricities of character and very brusque manners, yet with it all won the confidence and friendship of his patients. He kept at this time a medical school or a "room full of pupils" as he called his students, and among them Dr. Elisha North of Goshen and New London probably became the most prominent.

His great specialty was tuberculosis, which is charmingly considered in the two manuscript treatises on "Consumption" and on "Colds," which are now in my possession. They revealed a knowledge far ahead of that time and prove Hopkins to be a rival with Rush for honors in treating the great white plague. He believed this disease was curable in its early stages and sometimes in the far advanced, and lamented the fact that physicians were apt to treat this disorder with a dull formal round of inert or hurtful medicines. Fresh air and good food were factors employed in his treatment of these cases.

He appreciated the fact that a neglected cold might bring on this disease.

On account of his associations with a little coterie of literary men who were designated as "the Hartford Hits," he became a familar household name, especially in his native state, as a man of letters. This group, composed of Hopkins, Joel Barlow (Barlow later allied himself with the party of Jefferson), Timothy Dwight, David Humphreys, John Trumbull, Richard Alsop and Theodore Dwight, were strongly Federalistic in their principles and fervent in their sentiments, before the adoption of the Constitution, in favor of a strong centralized government. They were ardent supporters later of Washington's administration and strove to win the adherence of others by ridiculing the Democrats and their measures in poems which had great popularity in the newspapers of that period and were subsequently published in book form. Possessed of keen dry wit, Hopkins was peculiarly well fitted for these tasks. His other literary productions are seen especially in the poems "The Hypocrite's Hope," "The Cancer Quack" and "Ethan Allen," which may be consulted in Everest's "Poets of Connecticut" or Smith's "American Poems."

Hopkins was made an honorary member of the Massachusetts Medical Society in 1791; seven years earlier he had received the honorary degree of M. A. from Yale. He was one of the founders of the Connecticut Medical Society.

On March 24, 1901, he was very sick indeed with his cough and was "bled repeatedly notwithstanding the opposition of his friends, yet lived to resume somewhat his practice."

Some days after, he was brought home ill from a patient's house, and on April 14 he died.   W. R. S.

The Johns Hopkins Hosp. Bull., Jan., 1910 (W. R. Steiner).
Bronson's Hist. of Waterbury, 1858.
Anderson's Hist. of Waterbury, 1896.

Horner, Gustavus B. (1761-1815).

He was born in Charles County, Maryland, on January 27, 1761, and went as a boy to the local schools, afterwards studying medicine with Dr. William Brown of Alexandria, Virginia.

When fifteen he entered the Continental Army as a private soldier, and served as such until made a surgeon's mate in February, 1878.

When the war ended he settled at Warrentown, Virginia, and very soon had good practice, especially as a surgeon, before his death being called upon to do practically all the big operations in a large surrounding territory.

At one time his health became delicate, and as recreation he took to politics, and served in the State Legislature and was several times a presidential elector.

Regarded as an authority in his community, his opinion in all questions in medicine and surgery was final.

He married and left children, and several of his descendants were prominent physicians. In the winter of 1814-15 there prevailed in Eastern Virginia an unmanageable and fatal epidemic of a disease variously termed *pneumonia vera, pneumonia biliosa, pneumonia typhoides, bilious fever, typhus fever* and *catarrhal fever,* but which was, judging from the descriptions of it, probably a malignant type of epidemic influenza, in which he became much interested. He saw a great many cases and devised a treatment of a very depleting nature for the disease. Contracting the disease himself he insisted that he would personally try his own course of treatment, which was carried out, but he died on the first of January, 1815.   R. M. S.

Horner, William E. (1793-3853).

William E. Horner was the son of William and Mary Edmunds Horner and born on June 3, 1793, in Warrenton, Fauquier County, Virginia. His grandfather, Robert Horner, was a merchant who had emigrated from England to Maryland before the Revolution, and had later moved to Virginia. Several of Horner's relatives on both sides of the family were physicians.

Horner was a delicate child, so light in weight that "his rude companions would frequently snatch him up unceremoniously, greatly to his annoyance, and, in spite of his struggles and resistance, run off with him in bravado to display their greater strength."

When twelve years old, Horner went to school in Warrenton under Charles O'Neill, clergyman. The teacher was neither deep nor thorough. In consequence, Horner was more or less hampered in his subsequent career.

In 1809, Horner began to study medicine under Dr. John Spence, an Edinburgh graduate, and during this period attended two sessions at Pennsylvania University. In his studies he showed a special partiality for anatomy. The following extract from a letter to his father written in May, 1811, shows his feelings at this time:

"The books you sent to me gave great satisfaction. Instead, however, of satisfying my present anxiety to become well acquainted with the structure of the human body, they have excited in me an enthusiastic zeal to commence practical anatomy. A man, with the assistance of maps may obtain a tolerable knowledge of countries, but it is only by traversing them that he becomes the geographer in reality. In like manner it is with the anatomist, for no anatomical plates can give him that confidence as to induce him to undertake a surgical operation, or give him as good an idea of the subject of dissection."

In 1813 Horner continued his medical studies in Philadelphia. In July, 1813, a year before taking his M. D., Horner was commissioned surgeon's mate in the Hospital Department of the United States army. In the following September he was attached to the ninth Military District north of the Highlands, New York. Jackson gives an interesting picture of Horner at this period:

"Let us pause and survey his position at this time. He had just reached his twentieth year, of slender form (his weight about one hundred pounds), his pay, some thirty or forty dollars per month, and rations. He has donned his uniform, made after the regulation of the surgeon and physician-general, Dr. James Tilton, of Delaware. Whatever may have been the professional excellences of the surgeon and physician-general, his sartorial qualifications were not very brilliant. The dress was coal-black, which, from the readiness it shows dirt, was found in the service of the hospital and camp the most unfit that could have been selected.

"The coat was single-breasted, with standing collar, a gold star on each side, short-waisted and pigeon-tailed; the nether garments were tight. Picture the slight frame of the new-fledged surgeon's mate thus arrayed.

"At first it was thought very fine, but it was soon found to attract an attention in the streets that did not consist of admiration; and when he arrived in camp it had acquired for the surgeons, from their fellow-officers and soldiers, the soubriquet of "Crows." In a short time, the offspring of the physician and surgeon-general proved an abortion. The surgeons, in disgust, threw it aside, and each dressed after his own fashion."

Horner joined the army on the Niagara frontier September 25, 1813. He at once had orders to take charge of the transportation of seventy-three invalids from Lewistown to Greenbush. There was considerable difficulty in transportation, and while on the Mohawk near Little Falls the boats used in transporting the invalids grounded.

After delivering up his command at Greenbush, Horner went to Philadelphia, attended the medical course at the University during the winter and graduated in April, 1814. He then returned to the Niagara frontier as surgeon. He had severe experiences during the campaign, for the attack on Fort Erie, on the fourth of July, and battle of "Chippewa," on the fifteenth, filled the wards of the hospital with wounded. Between sixty and seventy fell to the share of Dr. Horner. The battle of Bridgewater, on the twenty-fifth of July, in which the British

were defeated, swelled his list to one hundred a n d seventy-five wounded and sick.

Notwithstanding his incessant occupation with very inadequate assistance in dressing the wounded and prescribing for the sick, he kept notes and records of his cases, many of them of great interest. The results were published in the "Medical Examiner" in 1852.

After the conclusion of peace, Horner resigned from the army and went to Warrenton, Virginia, where he practised for a short time. He soon tired of this. "Flesh and blood," he writes, "could stand it no longer; often have I paced with rapid and disordered steps my little office, agitating in the most painful state of mind my future fortunes."

After some indecision as to what to do, Horner finally decided to remove to Philadelphia. He had received a small legacy from his grandmother, which he converted into cash before he left. On arriving in Philadelphia in the winter of 1815–16 he attended lectures at the university and devoted much time to reading works on medicine and to dissection. His enthusiasm for anatomy had meanwhile attracted the attention of Caspar Wistar, at that time professor of anatomy at the University of Pennsylvania. In March, 1816, Wistar offered Horner the position of dissector at a salary of five hundred dollars. The offer was at once accepted. The connection formed with Wistar ripened into personal friendship and warm regard.

On the death of Wistar in 1818, John Syng Dorsey, nephew of Philip Physick was appointed to the chair of anatomy. Dorsey appointed Horner as his demonstrator and placed the dissecting class with all its emoluments in his hands. Dorsey died soon after his appointment and the chair of anatomy passed to Dr. Physick. Physick continued Horner as demonstrator on liberal terms and in 1820 he was made adjunct professor of anatomy and appointed professor when Dr. Physick resigned in 1831.

In 1820 he married Elizabeth Welsh of

WILLIAM E. HORNER.
(By permission of Dr. A. Hubbell.)

Philadelphia, and his family life was very happy.

Horner devoted himself closely to his teaching, to the development of the museum of anatomy, started by Wistar, and to scientific study. He also established a medical practice of considerable magnitude, and was a successful surgeon. During the cholera invasion of 1832, Horner was made a member of the Sanitary Board of the city. He made a special study of the lesions produced by cholera in the mucosa of the intestines and showed by means of microscopic study of specimens injected with water that especially severe injuries are suffered by the epithelial layer. He published an account of his method of study and the results in 1834 in the "American Journal of the Medical Sciences." He was one of the first medical men in the country to make practical use of the microscope.

Horner's chief attention, however, was given to the study of anatomy rather than pathology. He was untiring in the preparation of specimens and at his death his collection is said to have rivalled those of some of the better museums in Europe. He bequeathed all his specimens, together with his instruments and apparatus connected with the dissections to the medical department of the university, a donation valued at some eight or ten thousand dollars. It formed the larger part of the collection known as the Wistar and Horner Museum, subsequently housed in the Wistar Institute of Anatomy at Philadelphia.

His chief claim as an original investigator rests upon the discovery of the muscle which he called the "tensor tarsi" and which is frequently called the muscle of Horner. He was led to this discovery because the common account of the apparatus for lachrymation did not seem to him to explain fully the phenomena of that function. He accordingly sought for and found a special muscle situated on the posterior surface of the lachrymal ducts and sacs. His discovery was accepted as such by a number of European anatomists, but others pointed out that the muscular apparatus described by Horner had previously been described by others, though not exactly as Horner described it; several indeed have denied the existence of the muscle as an independent structure. He is, in any case, justly entitled to credit for calling attention to the structure and pointing out its physiological bearings. Horner's original articles on the subject appear in the "London Medical Repository" for 1822 and in the "American Journal of the Medical Sciences" for 1824.

Horner also investigated the anatomical basis of the peculiarly intense odor of the negro and found that the glands of the axilla in the black race exist in much larger numbers and are much more greatly developed than the white. ("American Journal of the Medical Sciences," vol. xxi p. 13).

Horner in addition made contributions on the musculature of the rectum, and on a fibro-elastic membrane of the larynx which he called the "Vocal or Phonetic Membrane."

As a teacher, "Dr. Horner was not fluent, copious in language, nor had he any pretentions to elocution, but he was a very excellent teacher of anatomy. His plan was, to a certain extent, novel. He composed a text-book, which was a most complete but concise treatise on "Anatomy."

"It was written in strict reference to the course of study pursued in the University of Pennsylvania, and was kept in as compendious a state as possible, so that there should be no unnecessary loss of time in reading it."

Horner was throughout life deeply religious. In 1839 he united with the Roman Catholic Church, and in 1841 was active in the establishment of St. Joseph's Hospital. He labored against considerable physical disabilities, as he suffered from an affection of the heart. In 1840 he visited Europe in company with Joseph Leidy, and returned much benefited in health. He soon, however, began to suffer again. Finally, in January, 1853, he had to abandon his lectures.

Jackson gives an interesting account of Horner's fortitude while awaiting the end.

"He was lying on a couch; Dr. Henry Smith and myself sitting on each side. Dr. Horner was suffering some pain, a new symptom that had just commenced. He demonstrated with his finger the different regions of the trunk, enumerating the organs they contained, and the state of each, and indicated the exact seat where he then suffered the most. This was done with the interest and earnest manner of a demonstration to his class. I was so struck with it as to call the attention of Dr. Smith to this display of the 'ruling passion strong in death.' 'Look! here is the anatomist dissecting his body—making a postmortem before he is dead.' The remark so amused Dr. Horner that he laughed heartily, in which we joined him. At the end he said: 'Well, I have not had so good a laugh for a long time.' This occurred on the third day before his death."

The direct cause of death was an entero-peritonitis, on March 13, 1853.

His chief writings were:

"Edition of Wistar's Anatomy," Philadelphia, J. E. More, 1823.

"The United States Dissector or Lessons in Practical Anatomy," first edition, 1826, fourth edition edited by Henry H. Smith, Philadelphia, 1846.

"A Treatise on Pathological Anatomy," 1829, three editions published.

"A Treatise on the Special Anatomy of the Human Body," published in two volumes, 1826, eighth edition, Philadelphia, 1851.

"A Plate of the Fetal Circulation" (about 1828).

Horner contributed numerous articles to various medical journals, especially to the "Philadelphia (American) Journal of the Medical Sciences."

In addition to those referred to in the text, the following partial list of the more important papers of Horner was submitted to Jackson by Dr. H. H. Smith soon after Horner's death.

1. "Case of Lumbar Abscess, attended with Artificial Anus, opening from the Colon into the Groin." ("Philadelphia Journal of Medical and Physical Sciences," vol. i, 1820.)

2. "On the Treatment of Ruptured Tendo Achillis, with a Plan of Treatment." (Ibid., vol. xxi.)

3. "Cases of Congenital Hydrocephalus, in which the Brain was Tapped" ("American Journal of the Medical Sciences," vol. iv, 1829.)

4. "Case of Ozema Cured by the Use of Chloride of Lime." (Ibid., vol. vi, 1830.)

5. "Ligature of the Primitive Carotid Artery (in a Court-room)." (Ibid., 1834.)

6. "Amputation at Shoulder-Joint, with a Description of a New Instrument for Tying Deep-seated Arteries." (Ibid, vol. i, new series, 1841.)

7. "Experiments in the Vascular Connection of the Mother and Fetus." (Ibid., vol. xii.)

8. "On the Direct Communication of the Pulmonary Air Vesicles with the Pulmonary Veins." (Ibid., vol. v, new series.)

9. "Cases of Aneurysm, Showing the Importance of Placing a Ligature above and below the Sac." (Ibid., vol. i, new series, 1841.)

10 "Case of Aneurysm of the Femoral Artery; also of the Brachial." (Ibid., vol. iv, 1842.)

11 "Excision of the Upper Jaw-bone without incising the Cheek." ("Philadelphia Medical Examiner," vol. vi, new series, 1850.)

12 "Case of Lacerated Perineum, with an Account of an Operation for its Relief." ("American Journal of Medical Sciences," vol. xx, new series, 1850.)

13 "Extirpation of the Parotid Gland." ("Medical Examiner.")

14 "Surgical Apparatus invented or modified; a valuable modification of Dessault's splint for fracture of the femur, in which the counter-extension is made by the upper end of the inner splint, now generally employed at the St. Joseph's

Hospital." Written out, but not published.

15 "A Sternum Dilator for Aiding in Injecting Subjects." ("American Journal of Medical Sciences," vol. iii, 1828.)

16 "A Bandage Machine or Roller." (Ibid., vol. i, 1827.)

17 "Instruments for Dilating Stricture through the Perineum."

C. R. B.

William E. Horner, M. D., a discourse delivered before the faculty and students of the University of Pennsylvania, Oct. 3, 1853, by Samuel Jackson, M. D., Philadelphia; T. K. and P. G. Collins, Printers, 1853.

Gross, Lives of Eminent Amer. Phys., Phila., 1861.

Boston M. and S. Jour., 1849–50, xli.

N. Jersey M. Reporter., Burlington, 1854, vol. vii.

Horr, Oren Alonzo (1834–1893).

Here was a remarkable man, an excessively earnest worker in medicine, one born a physician. He first saw the light in Waterford, Maine, October, 1834, was educated at three academies, and graduated from Bates College in the class of 1858.

He studied medicine at the Medical School of Maine, then in New York, and returned to the Medical School of Maine, from which he graduated in 1861. He first practised in Norway, Maine, married Elizabeth Kingman, and in 1863 moved to Minot. In September of that year he was appointed assistant surgeon of the one hundred and fourteenth United States Negro Regiment, and went with it to Texas, remaining there through the war.

While with his regiment he made great advances as a surgeon, and became an adept in autopsies. Hard work brought on poor health, but by 1870 he was practically well and began again practising at Lewiston, Maine, where he stayed for the rest of his life. Doctor Horr was long an active member of the Maine Medical Association, an earnest supporter of the Central Maine Hospital.

In 1886 he made a prolonged stay in Europe, investigating recent advances in medicine. In a short biography it is difficult to characterize so popular a physician. He was a constant attendant at medical meetings, a keen debator, and a first rate clinician. His medical papers were instructive, well built, well thought out and well written. Few men could write better than Dr. Horr upon "Croup," "Extirpation of the Ovaries," and "Plaster of Paris in Surgery" ("Transactions Maine Medical Association," 1879.) In the midst of his career he was cut short, May 28, 1893, by septicemia, contracted from an autopsy in a criminal case.

J. A. S.

Trans. Maine Med. Assoc., 1893.

Hosack, Alexander Eddy (1805–1871).

The elder Hosack seems to have been so anxious for his little son Alexander Eddy to become a student that it is said he "neglected no opportunities that could afford facilities to enlighten his mind." Unfortunately the boy Alexander, born in New York City in April, 1805, was at nineteen "so enfeebled in constitution by close application to books" that his attention for some time had to be turned to the restoration of health. Dr. Aydlott and a Mr. McFarlan "watched over the early mental growth" of Alexander, and by 1823 he had recovered health and graduated M. D. at the University of Pennsylvania with a thesis on "Senile Catarrh." For the following three years he stayed in Paris, working under Dupuytren, returning to New York with a keen interest in his work and a mind well calculated to weigh fairly all new theories. One fact is worthy of record: He was the first in the city of New York to anesthetize with ether, his first experiments being an amputation, stone, and removal of two breasts. He also introduced Syme's operation for exsection of the elbow into the States. In 1823 he invented an instrument for the purpose of rendering the operation for staphylorrhaphy more complete in its minutiæ and was rewarded by universal praise from his confrères. Hosack operated twenty-three times for stone; tied the two carotids for encephaloid tumor and in one instance cut the portio dura. He gave special attention to the removal of tumors in the urinary passages of the female and amputated the urethra with signal success and permanent cure. He had also an excellent method for curing popliteal aneurysm by compressing the femoral artery.

Among his contributions of value must be named:

"Observations on the uses and Advantages of the Actual Cautery," 1831.

"A Memoir on Staphylorrhaphy," 1833.

"On Sensitive Tumors of the Female Urethra." 1839.

"Three Operations for Encephaloid Tumors of the Antrum and Superior Maxillary Bone."

"Twenty-three Cases of Lithotomy by a Peculiar Operation."

Disting. Living New York Surgeons, S. W. Francis. N. Y., 1866.
Med. and Surg. Reporter, vol xiii., Phila., 1865.

Hosack, David (1769–1835).

David Hosack was one of those who live for tomorrow, who doggedly advocate and carry out reforms for which they themselves get neither thanks nor profit. He brought the same keen interest to bear on a new town sewer as on a new view of disease or a new plant for his botanical garden.

He was born on August 31, 1769, at number 44 Frankfort Street, New York, the son of Alexander and Jane Arden Hosack and the eldest of seven children. His father came from Moray, Scotland, and came over as an artillery officer under Gen. Sir Jeffrey Amherst and was at the re-taking of Louisburgh. His mother was of English-French descent.

When about thirteen young David went to school under the Rev. Alexander McWhorter of Newark, New Jersey, then for a short time to Dr. Peter Wilson of Hackensack and finally, in 1786, to Columbia College, New York, beginning to study medicine with Dr. Richard Bayley, a New York surgeon, in 1788, graduating B. A. from Princeton in 1789.

His next important step was his marriage to Miss Catharine Warner, and another, removing to Virginia because he thought it would become the capital of the United States. But the call of a metropolis was too strong and he came back in 1792 and in that same year, seeing the necessity for studying in the European hospitals, he left his wife and baby with his parents and spent two years in Edinburgh and London, meeting Robert Burns and all the celebrities of that day, listening to learned divines on Sunday and getting all he could during the week from men like Munro Black, Gregory, Duncan in Edinburgh, and in London consorting mainly with those who, like himself, were genuine botanists.

During his winter in London, by the concurrence of Sir Joseph Banks and other scientists, his "Observations on Vision" was published in the "Transactions of the Royal Society" and the author thanked. He took full advantage of his stay, doing anatomical dissections under Dr. Andrew Marshall and studying chemistry and mineralogy and visiting the hospitals. A tedious journey of fifty-three days in the Mohawk, varied only by an outbreak of typhus on board, brought him again to New York, where he settled down to practise, helped somewhat by friendships made on board. The professorship of botany in Columbia College was offered him in 1795, and in the autumn of that year he and the other young doctors had plenty of opportunity to distinguish themselves because yellow fever of a malignant type broke out. Also at this time he took care of Dr. Samuel Bard's patients for a while so well that a partnership was offered and accepted, for it was a great compliment to Hosack.

Having lost his wife and child, he married on December 21, 1797, Mary, daughter of James and Mary Darragh Eddy, and had nine children. Success attended him, particularly in his observation and treatment of yellow fever. He became a strong advocate of contagion and was the first to pursue sudorific and mild treatment. Such faith was put in his judgment that he was often asked by the board of health to investigate diseases.

"He was an excellent botanist and mineralogist; the author of three volumes, of "Medical Essays," of numerous articles in the medical journals and of a "Life of De Witt Clinton and Hugh Williams." His love of botany induced him to found the Elgin Botanic Garden—a piece of land about twenty acres at Hyde Park on the Hudson, with at one time under cultivation nearly 1,500 species of American plants besides exotics. He also founded the Humane Society—one branch for the recovery of persons nearly drowned and another for the relief of the indigent poor; the City Dispensary was remodelled, and he instituted medical lectures to policemen.

It was a matter of wonder to his friends how he managed to do as much, but Hosack knew the value of odd moments and always read or made notes when a little spare time came. The "Medical and Philosophical Register," (1810) started and was also edited by him in conjunction with Dr. John W. Francis, and he managed to complete his mineralogical collection begun in Edinburgh and present it to Princeton College.

Dr. Hosack felt that after fifty years of practice he would be justified in retiring to his pretty country house at Hyde Park, Duchess County. He had married his third wife Magdalena, widow of Henry A. Coster and with her kept up a fine old-fashioned hospi-

tality, welcoming alike famous men and shy ambitious students. Three times, in spite of his busy life and large family, he adopted into his household and trained a poor but clever young man, one of them being Delale, who became superintendent of the Jardin des Plantes, Montpellier.

In December, 1835, he seemed to have a presentiment of coming illness, apoplexy or paralysis, and began to try and write with his left hand. On the eighteenth he had an apoplectic stroke from which he never rallied and died on the twenty-second at the age of sixty-four.

"Although Hosack originated no new surgical procedures he was an excellent surgeon and introduced several good things from Europe. Up to this no American had tied the femoral artery for aneurysm. Hosack did so in 1808, and introduced the method of treating hydrocele by injection. He insisted in operations upon the importance of leaving wounds open to the air in order to check hemorrhage—a method advocated later by Astley Cooper and Dupuytren."

Dr. Hosack held the chair of materia medica in Columbia College, 1797; that of surgery and midwifery in the College of Physicians and Surgeons of New York, 1807, and there, afterwards, the chair of the theory and practice of physic and clinical medicine.

His writings embraced nearly every subject and science, and fill two columus of the Surgeon-General's Library Catalogue, Washington, D. C.

D. W.

Med. in Amer., J. G. Mumford, 1903, Phila.
Amer. Med. Biog., S. D. Gross, 1861, Phila.
Autobiography, S. D. Gross, 1887, Phila.
Boston Med. and Surg. Jour., 1868-9, vol. lxvii.
Mass. Med. Soc., Boston, 1868, vol. xi.
American Med. Biog., Williams.
A portrait in the Surg.-Gen. Lib.,Wash., D. C

Hosmer, Alfred (1832-1891).

Alfred Hosmer was born in Newton Upper Falls, Massachusetts, September

11, 1832. His mother moved to Walpole, New Hampshire, when he was a boy, and there he gained his preparation for Harvard College, graduating with the class of 1853. Entering the Harvard Medical School, he graduated in 1856. After serving as house pupil in the Massachusetts General Hospital he went abroad and studied medicine in Paris for nearly a year, returning to settle in Watertown, Massachusetts, where he spent his life practising.

On June 6, 1860 he married Helen Augusta Stickney, of Watertown.

He was a fellow of the Massachusetts Medical Society from 1856 until his death from cerebral apoplexy, May 14, 1891, also president of the Society in 1882. Among other offices held he was president of the Obstetrical Society of Boston, of the Middlesex South Medical Society, first president of the Massachusetts Medico-Legal Society, post surgeon at the United States Arsenal at Watertown, and fellow of the American Academy of Arts and Sciences. He contributed several papers to the "Boston Medical and Surgical Journal," among them "A Peculiar Condition of the Cervix Uteri which is found in Certain Cases of Dystocia."

Outside his medical activities he was an ardent Christian.

W. L. B.

Bos. Med. and Surg. Jour., vol. cxxvi.

Houghton, Douglas (1809–1845).

Douglas Houghton, a scientific explorer, was born in Troy, New York, September 21, 1809. His American progenitors migrated from Bolton, Lancashire, England, and settled in Boston, Massachusetts. His father was a lawyer in Troy, New York, but in 1812 he moved to Fredonia, Chatauqua County, New York, where Douglas's early education was obtained at home and in Fredonia Academy. In 1829 he graduated from Rensselaer Polytechnic Institute, Troy, New York, and in 1829 assisted the professor of

chemistry and natural history in the same school. Meantime he had been studying medicine, and in 1830 was licensed to practise by the Chautauqua County (New York) Medical Society. On the recommendation of Prof. Eaton he gave a course of scientific lectures in Detroit. This made him hosts of admirers and friends, so that he settled in Detroit and began medical practice with unusual success. He practised dentistry as well as medicine and surgery. The writer saw a tooth filled more than fifty years before by Dr. Houghton, as good as when introduced. In 1831–32, as physician to H. R. Schoolcraft's expedition to the headwaters of the Mississippi and the copper region of Lake Superior, Dr. Houghton gathered materials for two reports to the Secretary of War. One gave a list of species and localities of plants collected; the other discussed the existence of copper deposits in the geological basin of Lake Superior. These reports gave him a wide reputation as a scientist of unusual ability. In 1837 a small appropriation was made for a geological survey of Michigan and Dr. Houghton made state geologist, also in 1839, professor of chemistry, mineralogy and geology in the University of Michigan, being the second professor appointed. (He never taught regularly in this chair, Dr. S. H. Douglas doing the work.) In Michigan there have been named after him a city, a county, a lake, and in Detroit a public school. Dr. Houghton is described as five feet five inches tall; feet and hands small and delicately formed; a large well developed head; prominent nose; eyes blue, sheltered under light but massive eyebrows, bright and at times merry.

He married on September 11, 1833, Harriet Stevens, of Fredonia, New York, who with two daughters survived him.

On October 13, 1845, writes a friend named Peter McFarland, Dr. Douglas Houghton left Eagle Harbor, Lake

Superior, in an open sail boat, for a camp about ten miles distant that contained a geological surveying party to which he desired to give instructions ere leaving for the winter. His work kept him in the camp till after dark, when a storm threatened that proved to be snow accompanied by a very high wind. There were four rowers, the doctor holding the rudder, his faithful dog, Meemee, a black and white spaniel, being at his feet. The violence of the storm increased and the waves rolled higher and higher; on rounding a point they could see the light at the harbor. "Pull away, my boys, we shall soon be there; pull steady and hard." But an enormous wave capsized the boat and all went under. The doctor was raised from the water by his trusty friend Peter McFarland. "Cling to the keel, doctor," he cried. "Never mind me," said Houghton, "go ashore if you can; be sure I'll get ashore all right without aid." Very soon the boat was righted and all clambered on board, but another large wave capsized it again. They were now but two hundred yards from shore, but all were about exhausted from cold and fatigue. Two of the five men managed to reach shore, but three, including Dr. Houghton, sank and did not rise.

L. C.

History University of Mich., Ann Arbor, Univ. Press, 1906.
Appleton's Cyclopedia of Amer. Biography.
Boston Med. and Surg. Jour., vol. iii.
Mich. Pioneers and Historical Collection, vol. xxii.
Life by Alvah Bradish, Detroit, Raynor and Taylor, 1889.
A portrait by Alvah Bradish is in the University of Michigan Library.

Howard, Edward Lloyd (1837–1881).

Edward Lloyd Howard, physiologist and medico-jurisprudentist, was born in Baltimore, January 14, 1837 under the "Star Spangled Banner," for his maternal grandfather was Francis S. Key, who wrote this, and his father's father was Col. John Eager Howard,

who distinguished himself at the Battle of Cowpens during the Revolution.

The boy received a liberal training at home by means of private tutors and in 1857 he began to study medicine under Dr. Charles Frick, later attending the University of Maryland, where he took his medical degree in 1861.

Excited by the great riot in the streets of Baltimore, which occurred on April 19, 1861, Dr. Howard at once, without one day of medical practice intervening, enrolled himself as a private in the Maryland Guard. All through the war he served, on the Confederate side, first as a combatant, then in a surgical capacity. When Lee surrendered at Appomattox Court House, Dr. Howard was paroled and returned to Baltimore.

In 1868 he was appointed lecturer on anatomy in the Baltimore College of Dental Surgery and in 1869 became there professor of the same subject. A year later, in connection with Dr. Thomas Latimer, he founded the "Baltimore Medical Journal." In 1872 he was appointed lecturer on physiology in the Baltimore College of Physicians and Surgeons, and in 1873 professor of anatomy and clinical professor of nervous diseases in the same institution. In 1874 he relinquished these chairs for the chair of physiology. Always a deep student of matters connected with legal medicine, he was, in 1872, appointed secretary of the section on "Psychology and Medical Jurisprudence" of the American Medical Association. He wrote a few papers on lego-medical subjects, the most important of which is "The Legal Relations of Emotional Insanity," which he read before the Society in 1874, and was appointed, in 1874, a committee of one to engineer the passage of a law establishing a State Board of Health in Maryland which he did successfully in the same year.

Dr. Howard was a fluent and copious talker, and was fond of society, in which he was very popular indeed. At the same time, he was a hard student, a profound and original thinker. As a writer he could hardly be excelled, and the matter is a cause of regret that he wrote so very little. His friends all speak of a "fatal habit of procrastination" which caused him to be forever putting off much work of a medico-literary character. He was a great lover of nature, of music, and of poetry. Sunsets and sunrises were almost objects of worship to him, and he used to go long distances in order to find some spot from which a glorious sunrise could be observed to especial advantage. His favorite lines (and the fact is characteristic of the man) were those of Wordsworth:

Here you stand,
Adore and worship when you know it not;
Pious beyond the intention of your thought;
Devout above the meaning of your will.

He came to his death by drowning, September 5, 1881.

T. H. S.

Trans Am. Med. Assn., 1882 (J. Morris).
Tr. Med. and Chir. Fac. Maryland, Balt., 1882 (T. S. Latimer).

Howard, Richard L. (1809-1854).

Richard L. Howard, a prominent physician and teacher in Columbus, Ohio, was born in Andover, Vermont, in the year 1809. The details of his early education are unknown, but he took his medical degree from the Berkshire Medical Institute, at Pittsfield, Massachusetts, in 1831. Removing to the West, he first settled in Windham, Portage County, Ohio, but after a brief stay in this place, removed to Elyria, in Lorain County, where he practised for about eight years. In 1844 he came to Columbus, Ohio, and in that city remained until his death. In 1847 Dr. Howard accepted the chair of surgery in the Willoughby Medical College, then just removed to Columbus, and when this college was merged into the Starling Medical College he retained the same position in the new building.

On the death of his colleague, Dr. John Butterfield, in 1849, Dr. Howard succeeded to the editorship of the Ohio Medical and Surgical Journal, which he continued to conduct with eminent success until 1853, when signs of failing health compelled him to resign his editorial duties. He died of double pneumonia in Columbus, January 16, 1854.

He was president of the Ohio State Medical Society in the year 1850, and was always interested in the progress of the medical profession. He is said to have been the first physician in Columbus to devote his entire time to surgery, and the first in Central Ohio to employ chloroform for purposes of anesthesia.

An introductory lecture before the medical class of the Starling Medical College in 1849 is the only product of Dr. Howard's pen which his biographer has been able to discover.

H. E. H.

Ohio Med. and Surg. Journal, vol. vi (1853-4), and the Columbus Medical Journal, vol. xxix 1905).

Howard, Robert Palmer (1823-1889).

Robert Palmer Howard was dean of the medical faculty of McGill University from 1882 until his death in 1889, and began his studies in the faculty with which his name was so intimately associated in the year 1844, graduating four years later. In 1856 he was made professor of clinical medicine, and on the death of Dr. Holmes in 1860, became professor of the theory and practice of medicine, a chair which he continued to occupy until his death. In 1856 he was elected physician to the Montreal General Hospital and was twice president of the Canadian Medical Association, president of the College of Physicians and Surgeons of Quebec, and vice-president of the Association of American Physicians.

Thus all the honors in the gift of the profession came to him; but they indicate only slightly the place which he held in the hearts of his students during the thirty-year period of his teaching. His great merit is that from the beginning of his influence over McGill Medical Faculty, he was, and continued to be, an ardent believer in experimental methods in medicine, and lost no opportunity of encouraging research in pathology and physiology. It was under his fostering care that McGill Medical School attained to its greatness.

Dr. Howard had an aptitude for the practice and teaching of medicine. His lectures and clinics are yet remembered. He was of a grave demeanor but won from his students affection and admiration. Their interests were near his heart and he strove for their welfare in personal matters as well as in the wider field of education. In all legislation touching medical training, he was forward and labored earnestly to obtain a General Medical Council for Canada. Howard was one of the first among the older physicians to make a systematic record of his cases and of the conditions observed in them. He was the first to lecture on appendicitis. His store of knowledge was made public freely. His contribution upon "Rheumatism" in Pepper's "System of Medicine" is a good indication of his range of knowledge and style. In William Osler's "Practice of Medicine" frequent mention is made of his cases, and the book is dedicated to him. A. M.

Howard, William Travis (1821-1907).

William Travis Howard, gynecologist, was the son of William A. Howard, an architect, and born in Cumberland County, Virginia, on January 12, 1821. As a lad he went to Hampden Sidney and Randolph Macon Colleges then studied medicine under the eccentric genius John Peter Mettauer, the doctor who is reputed never to have left off a tall stovepipe hat on any occasion. Howard graduated from Jefferson Medical College in 1842 and settling first

in North Carolina moved in 1866 to Baltimore to become professor of physiology in the University of Maryland, taking in 1867 the chair of diseases of women and children and becoming emeritus professor in 1897. He was also for many years visiting surgeon to the Hospital for the Women of Maryland, consulting surgeon to the Johns Hopkins Hospital and the Hebrew Hospital.

Although best known as a gynecologist, he never lost his interest in general medicine, in which field his attainments were of a very high order. For the younger men, he was a most valuable consultant, aiding them with his acute diagnostic powers and broad knowledge of therapeutics. He was a diligent and thoughtful student, all his life keeping ahead of the times. He invented a modification of Tarnier's forceps and also the Howard speculum.

The University of Maryland gave him her LL. D. in 1907. He was also a founder of the American Gynecological Society and its president in 1884, occupying the same positions with regard to the Baltimore Gynecological and Obstetrical Society and being president of the Medical and Chirurgical Faculty of Maryland in 1902. He was not a great writer; his chief papers were:

"Rupture of the Uterus with Laparotomy," 1880.

"Encysted Tubercular Peritonitis which Presented the Characteristic Phenomena of a Unilateral Ovarian or Parovarian Cyst," 1885.

"Two Rare Cases of Abdominal Surgery," 1885.

He died after a few days' illness from the effects of ptomain poisoning, at Narragansett Pier, on July 31, 1907.

Tr. Am. Gyn. Soc., 1808, vol. xxxiii (W. E. Moseley).
The Med. Annals of Maryland, E. F. Cordell, 1903.

Howe, Appleton (1792-1870).

Appleton Howe, a founder of the Norfolk District Medical Society and its president for three years, was born in Hopkinton, Massachusetts, November 26, 1792.

He graduated from Harvard College in 1815 and from the Harvard Medical School in 1819 and studied as a private pupil under Dr. John C. Warren. Admitted as a fellow of the Massachusetts Medical Society in 1823, he founded the Norfolk District Medical Society, a branch of the Massachusetts Medical Society, in 1850. On completing his medical studies he settled for the rest of his life in South Weymouth.

He married twice, first to Harriet, daughter of Eliphalet Loud in 1821, then to Eliza, daughter of Joseph Loud, in 1850. His first wife died childless, but by his second he had two children.

Howe held office in the state militia between 1822 and 1840 and was major general of Division, and in 1840–1841 he represented his district in the State Senate.

He was a man of decided opinions and as a practitioner he exhibited good judgment, being neither timid nor rash. In his religious views he held to the great facts and principles of divine revelation with a tenacious grasp, and was a liberal supporter of public worship, yet from a strange self-distrust he never publicly united with the Christian church.

He died of cardiac disease at his home in Weymouth, October 10, 1870, aged seventy-eight years.

W. L. B.

Ebenezer Alden in Bos. Med. and Surg. Jour., vol. lxxxiii.

Howe, Samuel (1801–1876).

Samuel Howe, the first to train the blind and deaf mutes in America, was born in Boston in 1801, nine years before the Harvard school removed from Cambridge. That was the year which saw the establishment in practice of Jackson and John C. Warren, and the new vaccination of Jenner intro-duced to these shores. There was little wealth in Howe's family, and the little there was dwindled sadly during the war of 1812; for his father, Joseph N. Howe, a ship owner and maker of cordage, trusted the federal government for naval supplies, and it failed him. The unhappy merchant was brought nearly to ruin, and his family grew up in poverty. In spite of this there was money supplied for sending one of the boys to college, and Samuel was selected. He went to Brown University and graduated in 1821 when twenty, a mature age for graduation in those days.

After leaving Brown he returned to Boston and studied medicine with Jacob Bigelow at the same time attending the lectures in the Harvard school, and the clinics at the Massachusetts General Hospital, finding as instructors Jackson, J. C. Warren, Parkman, and Ingalls. Such men could appreciate a promising student, and were foretelling an unusual future for Howe, when suddenly he astounded them and the Boston community by announcing that he was going to Greece. No one encouraged him except one eminent man—Gilbert Stuart, the artist, now growing old, who faltered that his heart also was in the venture if only the times were still young for him. He helped Howe to go, and Howe worked out there through the insurrectionary times when Greece fought against Turkish rule. In 1832 he settled down in Boston and began his best known work, the education of the blind.

He was fortunate enough to secure the sympathy and support of Dr. John D. Fisher, a young man, one year his own junior—himself a philanthropist and with a private fortune. With Fisher's aid Howe took up the problem of teaching the blind and began his studies by visiting Europe again to investigate the Valentine Haüy methods then employed in Germany and France.

Howe was no dreamer. He was a

man of affairs; a sane humanitarian; a tempered enthusiast. New working machinery was necessary; he created it, instructing his assistants so thoroughly that later, when the Sydenham School was established in England, a corps of Howe's former pupils were secured as teachers. He invented a novel form of raised letters for the books of the blind; and the first product of his press was a Bible which was published in 1843—a book half the size, and produced at half the cost, of the Scriptures for the Blind then recently brought out in England.

To test upon himself continued blindness he went about for weeks with his eyes bandaged and used books for the blind.

His best known subject was Laura Bridgman, the famous blind deafmute, whom he found at Hanover, New Hampshire, brought to Boston, when she was a child of eight, and educated at the Perkins Institute. Dickens describes the girl. For forty-three years Howe was superintendent of the Perkins Institute. He asked but was refused permission to work at the Hartford Asylum, but emerged triumphant from opposition in the founding of the Massachusetts School for Feeble-minded Children.

In 1869 Howe had an experience which took him back to the scenes of his youthful crusade of forty years before. The Cretan insurrection of '66 was becoming an international problem. Greece was taking sides with Crete against Turkey. Howe organized a relief expedition to feed and clothe the destitute people, loaded a ship with supplies, visited Crete, and saved thousands from starvation. Then he visited the Greek mainland, and learned to his delight that he was not forgotten there. He returned with added honors to America, and promptly was called to further public work. There was serious talk of annexing the islands of the sea. Santo Domingo was their first object, and thither went Howe with other forlorn commissioners, by direction of Pres. Grant. The object was a failure, as we know.

Howe came home, but went back later to the island, seeking health and forwarding a commercial enterprise. This expedition was a double failure, and our philosopher returned to Boston a broken man. His end was near. Much buffeting and novel strivings do not conduce to a peaceful old age. He died with little more ado, in his seventy-fifth year, on the ninth of January, 1876.

He married Julia Ward, author of the famous "Battle Hymn of the Republic," written in camp in 1861, and sharer in all his philanthropy. When travelling with her as a bride in England, they spent some time at a house where a young daughter, Florence, asked Dr. Howe's opinion as to whether it "would be a dreadful thing" to devote her life to nursing? The Crimean War and Florence Nightingale's work showed his wisdom in encouraging her. In May, 1910, the two women who met as girls celebrated respectively their ninetieth and ninty-first birthday.

J. G. M.

From Boston Medicine One Hundred Years Ago and a Notable Physician of the Last Century, by J. G. Mumford, M. D., Johns Hopkins Hospital Bulletin, May, 1907.

Hoy, Philo Romayne (1816–1892).

Philo Romayne Hoy, who did much for his State as a natural scientist, was descended from an old Scotch family Hawey, one of whom fought at Flodden and was sold to an English family but eloped with his master's daughter to Ireland. Three of his male descendants escaped from a difficulty with a public officer by coming over to the United States in 1756, and from these came the father of Philo, Cap. William Hoy, who gave his boy the best local education he could and let him study medicine under Dr. Alexander McCoy. The student graduated from the Ohio Medical College of Cincinnati and six years later began to practise in New Haven, Ohio, and afterwards in Racine, Wisconsin, first marrying Mary Elizabeth Austin, who died in 1872 leaving three children, Albert Harris, who became a doctor; Jenny Rebecca and Philo Romayne.

The new country to which he came was comparatively unknown as far as its natural resources were concerned, and Hoy went to work to make a complete collection of flora and fauna, especially of native woods, shells and fossils. He welcomed all the naturalists who came to see him and corresponded pleasantly with such men as Agassiz, Henry, and Kirtland. His collection went to Racine, the interests of whose college he had done so much to promote.

His writings were chiefly in the "Transactions of the Wisconsin Academy of Science." "How did the Aborigines of This Country fabricate Copper Instruments?" vol. iv; "Who built the Mounds?" vol. v; "Who made the Ancient Copper Implements?" vol. v, etc., and, in vol. i of the "Geology of Wisconsin," "A Catalogue of Wisconsin Lepidoptera;" "A List of Noctuidæ in Wisconsin," and A Catalogue of Cold-blooded Vertebrates."

His name has been perpetuated in making him godfather to some three or four fossils and four fauna (the arthoceras Hoyi, etc.). There are many American doctors bound up with the natural history of the States in the same way ,though dust has gathered over the connection and few now know aught connected with the names. Paris made Hoy a member of the Entomological Society of France, and he was also naturalist on the United States Survey and a fellow or member of the leading academies of science in America.

He contrived, though continuing a large practice, to gather one of the largest local natural history collections, believing a local one to attain ever increasing value in view of the destruction of forests and increase of inhabitants leading to the extermination of many species.

He was a man who was alive all over; all men, all sciences were eagerly studied and, although not so well after a severe chill in 1890, there was no physical intimation of his sudden death two years later, leaving none but the pleasantest memories behind. D. W.

Wisconsin Acad. Sci., vol. ix.
Personal Commun. from his daughter.

Huger, Francis Kinloch (1773-1855).

Francis Kinloch Huger was born in Charleston, South Carolina, September, 1773, the son of Maj. Benjamin Huger and Mary Esther Kinloch. He was sent to England to school when he was eight years old, and returned to Carolina on a brief visit in 1791. He completed his education and studied medicine under the distinguished surgeon, John Hunter, of London, and in 1794 was engaged as surgeon on the Medical Staff of the English Army in Flanders, under the Duke of York. Leaving the army he went to Vienna for study and there met Dr. Eric Bollman, a Hanoverian physician, who, in October, 1794, informed him of the plan to liberate Lafayette who was then confined in the fortress of Olmutz, and Dr. Huger volunteered to assist in the rescue.

Dr. Bollman, through making acquaintance with the surgeon of the fortress, was enabled to lend French books to Lafayette and to indicate invisible writing. By this means of communication the plot for the rescue was perfected. While out riding with two guards, on November 8, 1794, Lafayette alighted and gradually drew the officer who had him in charge away from the high road. Suddenly he grasped the hilt of the officer's sword and drew it and the two friends galloped to his assistance. In the scuffle the officer was slightly wounded and Lafayette's coat was stained with blood. Lafayette unfortunately misunderstood the directions of his friends to proceed to Hoff where a servant and horse awaited him. He was arrested at the village of Zagorsdorf as a suspicious person, identified and returned to Olmutz. Dr. Huger was surrounded and captured near the scene of the rescue and treated with the utmost rigor by his captors. Dr. Bollman was arrested at the frontier and both remained in prison eight months. Lafayette was in prison for three years after this event, but was not informed of the liberation of his friends.

In 1795 Dr. Huger entered the University of Pennsylvania to complete his medical education and graduated in 1797.

In 1798, war with France being threatened, he was commissioned a captain in the United States Army, and in 1812 he was commissioned colonel and served in the war against England until 1815. He died in Charleston in February, 1855, in his eighty-second year.

In the reception room of the Château Lagrange, the home of Lafayette, on one side of the chimney was, or is, a portrait of Dr. Huger. There is also a memorial medallion in the Medical Laboratory in the University of Pennsylvania.   D. W.

Figures of the Past, Joseph Quincy, Boston. Old Penn Weekly Review, Oct. 30, 1909

Hun, Edward Reynolds (1842–1880).

Edward Reynolds Hun, eldest son of Dr. Thomas Hun, was born in Albany, New York, on April 17, 1842 and graduated from Harvard College in the class of 1863, receiving his professional diploma from the College of Physicians and Surgeons in New York City, 1866. After several months of study abroad he went into private

practice in Albany, and not long afterwards accepted the position of special pathologist of the New York State Lunatic Asylum at Utica. His experience there led to his publishing a translation of Bouchard's tract on "Secondary Degenerations of the Spinal Cord," which appeared in the "American Journal of Insanity" for January and April, 1869; a paper on the "Pulse of the Insane," in the same journal for January, 1870; a paper on "Hematoma Auris," in the number for July, 1870; and one on "Labio-glosso-laryngeal Paralysis," in the issue for October, 1871. He also presented to the Medical Society of the State of New York, at its annual meeting in 1869, a complete, valuable, and well illustrated paper on "Trichina Spiralis."

The large amount of work he did in connection with St. Peter's, the Albany and the Child's Hospitals, the Orphan Asylums and the like, together with his ever-increasing private practice, compelled him to relinquish his connection with the Asylum at Utica. On the reorganization of the faculty of the Albany Medical College, in 1876, he accepted the chair of diseases of the nervous system, which he filled up to the time of his death.

Dr. Hun was an indefatigable worker, never sparing himself night or day in the care of the sick, and the annals of the Albany County Medical Society, together with the papers before mentioned, bear ample evidence of the interest he took in the literary and scientific departments of his profession. He was a member of the New York Neurological Society, and of the Medical Society of the State of New York.

In 1874 he married the daughter of John B. Gale, of Troy. His widow with four children survived him.

In 1876 he was thrown from his carriage, while returning from a professional call in the country, receiving injuries to his head and chest. He was unconscious for several hours, but his convalescence was fairly rapid and apparently complete. After a time, however, his general health began to fail; obscure and ill-defined trouble with his brain followed; and in 1879 he was compelled, temporarily as it was hoped, to give up his practice. In spite of every care there was not the permanent improvement which his friends had hoped, and death came to him quite suddenly on March 14, 1880, in the thirty-eighth year of his age.

S. B. W.

Med. Am Albany 1882. iii.
Tr. on Soc. N.Y. Syracuse 1881. (S.B.Ward)

Hunt, Harriot Kezia (1805-1806-1875).

Harriot Kezia Hunt, the first woman to practise medicine in America, was a Bostonian, pedigreed, born and bred, the daughter of Joab Hunt and Kezia Wentworth. She was born in 1805. When her father died in 1827 his estate was found to be encumbered and self-support became necessary. A private school started by herself and sister brought money but she felt it was not her vocation. The case of her sister during a protracted illness drew her attention to medicine; she procured medical books and pursued investigations for herself with the conviction that much of the ordinary practice was blind and merely experimental. In 1833 she entered the family of a Dr. and Mrs. Mott. The doctor left the care of most female patients to his wife; this care Miss Hunt shared, and by the opportunity thus afforded, supplemented theoretical knowledge by clinical observation. In 1835 she opened a consulting-room and assumed the responsibility of practicing without a medical diploma— reprehensible, but a course justified by subsequent events, for when in 1847 Miss Hunt requested permission to attend lectures at the Harvard Medical School— stating "that after twelve years' practice which had become extensive, it would be evident to them that the request must proceed from no want of patronage, but simply from a desire for such scientific knowledge as could be imparted by their professors"—her request was promptly refused. After the graduation of Elizabeth Blackwell at Geneva in 1849, "Miss Hunt thought the times might be more favorable and in 1850 repeated her application at Harvard. In mobile America great changes of sentiment can be effected in three years—five out of the seven members of the faculty voted that Miss Hunt be admitted to the lectures on the usual terms. But, on the eve of success, Miss Hunt's cause was shipwrecked by collision and entanglement with that of another of the unenfranchised to privileges. At the beginning of the session two colored men had appeared among the students and created by their appearance intense dissatisfaction. When, as if to crown this outrage it was announced that a *woman* was also about to be admitted, the students felt their cup of humiliation was full and in indignation boiled over in a general meeting. The compliant faculty bowed their heads to the storm, and to avoid the obloquy of rejecting under pressure a perfect reasonable request, advised the female student to withdraw her petition. This she did, and the majesty of Harvard, already endangered by the presence of the negro, was saved from the futher peril of the woman. Miss Hunt returned to her private medical practice which, though unsanctioned by law and condemned by learning, steadily increased and with such success that she became widely known."

In 1853 the Womans Medical College of Philadelphia, gave her the honorable M. D. In 1856 she wrote "Glances and Glimpses" an autobiographic dealing with her social and professional life.

A. B. W.

Dr. Chadwick, International Review, Oct., 1879.
Mary P. Jacobi, in "Woman's Work in America."
Rev. H. B. Elliot, in "Eminent Women of the Age," 1872.

Hunt, Henry Hastings (1842-1894).

This charming and attractive man was born in Gorham, Maine, July 7, 1842, fitted for college at the Gorham Academy, and graduated from Bowdoin with high honors in 1862. He immediately enlisted as hospital steward in the Fifth Battery of Light Artillery of Maine, and served through the war.

He afterwards studied medicine at the Portland School for medical instruction, graduating at the Medical School of Maine in 1867. He then took post-graduate courses at Philadelphia and began to practice at Gorham until 1882, then finding the wear and tear of country practice too hard he moved to Portland, where he rapidly obtained a choice of clientage.

In 1884 he was chosen to the chair of physiology in the Medical School of Maine, but resigned in 1891, owing to poor health. He was a member of the Maine Medical Association, of the American Medical Association, and a visiting physician to the Maine General Hospital for many years. In 1887 he married Miss Gertrude Jewell, of Buffalo.

Henry Hunt was a type of the best class of physicians, studious, tireless, patient. His opinion was always prized. As a medical writer, Dr. Hunt showed great mastery for his subject, together with taste and skill in authorship, so that it was a matter of regret that he had not time oftener to prove his capabilities in that direction. Perhaps the best of his papers was one on "Diphtheria," (1886).

For several years before his death, Henry Hunt knew that he was a victim of an incurable disease due to an injury of the spinal cord.

His frequent sufferings, to which he jokingly referred as "just old fashioned rheumatism" were severe, but he kept at his work till about three months before his death.

He died November 30, 1894, and one does not see people today cry as they did at his funeral.

J. A. S.

Trans. Maine Med. Assoc., 1894.

Hunt, Thomas (1808–1867).

Thomas Hunt was born in Charleston, South Carolina, May 18, 1808 and died in New Orleans March 20, 1867. Of good lineage, his early education was under the accomplished scholar Bishop England, his studies being directed to law, but his readings embraced all branches of literature and science. His love of the classics adhered to him through life and his proficiency in Greek was profound. Selecting medicine as his profession, he received his M. D. from the University of Pennsylvania in 1829 then went to Paris, but was soon recalled by the death of his father and entered at once into practice. At the age of twenty-three he lectured on anatomy and operative surgery and taught practical anatomy. When the Amelia was wrecked off Folly Island in 1832, he distinguished himself, along with Dr. Warren Stone, a passenger on that vessel, by his treatment and management of the cholera which attacked the unfortunate crew and voyagers.

In 1833 he removed to New Orleans, again to face cholera and to render himself prominent in the warfare against, and conquest of, this disease. He was soon elected surgeon to the Charity Hospital, but held the office for a short while as it interfered with larger plans. He entered actively into the enterprise of establishing the Medical College in Louisiana. The introductory lecture on anatomy he delivered in 1834 and the existence and growth of the university were largely due to Hunt. He held the chairs of anatomy and physiology, pathological anatomy and practice, physiology and pathology and special pathology; was dean of the faculty and at the time of his death president of the University of Louisiana, also surgeon to the Marine Hospital, New Orleans.

He wrote a good deal on dermatology, his pamphlets going through three editions; these included:

"Practical Observations on Certain Diseases of the Skin generally pronounced Incurable," London, 1847.

"Memoir of the Medicinal Uses of Arsenic." 1849.

The professional life of Dr. Hunt extended over thirty-eight years, thirty-four of which were spent in New Orleans.

J. G. R.

N. O. Med. and Surg. Jour., 1867.

Hunt, William (1825-1896).

The son of Uriah and Elizabeth Shreve Hunt, he was born September 26, 1825, at 106 North Fourth Street, Philadelphia, a descendant of a long line of Quakers who came over here about 1680. He went as a lad to a Friend's School, then began to study medicine under Dr. George B. Wood and graduated at the University of Pennsylvania in 1849. He married, in 1856, Rebecca T., daughter of Richard Price, and had three children, William, George and Margaret.

A genial, busy intellectual man this William Hunt; helping to form the University Biological Club and the Surgical Club where members met to display specimens and partake , at first, of such mild refreshments as "crackers, cheese and ale." He wrote a good deal too and was for many years on the staff of the "Annual of the University Medical Sciences, " and with Dr. T. G. Morton compiled a "History of Surgery in the Pennsylvania Hospital." The "Pennsylvania Hospital Reports" were edited by him and Dr. J. DaCosta and he did the same for Holmes's "System of Surgery," (the American edition) besides contributing to the "International Encyclopedia of Surgery."

But the writing, the operating and the pleasant entertaining of friends came to an end when he was severely injured by being run over in 1887, and although he worked at intervals the results of the accident ended in his death on April 17, 1896, at his home in Philadelphia.

Among his appointments and writings may be noticed: resident physician, Pennsylvania Hospital; demonstrator of anatomy, University of Pennsylvania; surgeon to the Episcopal Hospital; assistant surgeon, United States Army; fellow of the College of Physicians; president, Philadelphia Academy of Surgery ; honorary fellow, American Surgical Association, etc.

"Clinical Notes and Reflections;" "Diabetic Gangrene;" "Ossification of the Crystalline Lens;" "The History of Toxemia;" "Unusual Surgical Cases;" "Traumatic Rupture of the Urethra," etc., etc.

Tr. Coll. of Phys. of Phila., vol. ix, 1897. Hist. of the Penn. Hospital, 1895.

Hunter, William (1729?-1777).

William Hunter was born 1729 in Scotland and educated under the elder Monro at Edinburgh, afterwards studying with great assiduity both at Edinburgh and Leyden.

He came to Rhode Island about 1752, gave lectures on anatomy, on the history of anatomy, and comparative anatomy, at Newport, during the years 1754-56, these being the first lectures given on the science in New England, if not in America. He was soon appointed by the colony of Rhode Island surgeon to the troops sent by them to Canada, and afterwards returned to Newport. He married the daughter of Godfrey Malbone.

Independent of his lectures, his literary contributions in behalf of his profession were principally letters addressed to his London namesakes. He was a most eminently successful practitioner, as well as operator and obstetrican.

He was a very handsome man, his manners courtly and amiable, his opinions liberal. His medical library was the largest in New England at his day, and contained most of the standard Greek and Latin authors of antiquity, as well as the modern works of his own time. The latter were mostly dispersed by the accidents of the Revolutionry War; what remained of the former were distributed to individuals and medical institutions by his only son the Hon. William Hunter.

According to the "New York Medical Repository" his manuscript lectures are said still to be in existence.

He died at Newport, 1777.

Thacher, American Med. Biog.

Huntington, David Low (1834-1899).

David Low Huntington, army surgeon, graduated in arts at Yale, in medicine at the University of Pennsylvania in 1857. In 1862 he entered the regular army as assistant surgeon and served mostly in the West. He was medical officer on the staff of Gen. Grant, medical director of the army of the Tennessee and accompanied Sherman on his famous march to the sea. Huntington was present in many battles of the war and rendered valuable service at Champion Hills, Vicksburg, Missionary Ridge, Resaca, Dallas, Kenesaw Mountain, etc. After the war he was stationed at different army posts east and west, and from 1875 to 1880 was surgeon in charge of the Soldiers' Home at Washington from 1880 to 1887, working in the surgeon-general's office. After the death of Otis, Huntington completed the remaining volumes of the well known "Medical and Surgical History of the War." The last volume was published in 1883. During the last years of his military service Huntington was in charge of the Army Medical Museum and Library. After his retirement in 1898 he travelled in Europe for his health, when death suddenly overtook him at Rome, December 20, 1899.

A. A.

Yale Alumni Weekly, Jan. 31, 1900. J Am. M. Ass Chicago, 1900, xxiv. Med. Rec , N. Y., 1899, lvi, 969.

Hurd, Anson (1824–1910).

Anson Hurd, surgeon in the Civil War, was born in Twinsburg, Summit County, Ohio (the Western Reserve of Connecticut) December 27, 1824, of Revolutionary ancestry, the names Hurd, Brainard and Brooks being prominent in New England history. He was one of fourteen children, educated at Twinsburg Academy and the Ohio Wesleyan University at Delaware, Ohio, where he received his academic degree in 1849.

His medical studies were under Dr. William Blackstone of Athens, Ohio. In 1852 he received his M. D. from Starling Medical College and began practice in Oxford, Indiana, whence he was sent for several terms as member of the State Legislature and was active in early public affairs. He contracted tuberculosis and in 1856 after consulting the leading diagnosticians in New York he took a pony,

blanket and lariat and spent a year a pioneer in outdoor life, sleeping on the ground, under the stars, and travelling over the Staked Plains of Texas.

Returning to Indiana he was commissioned surgeon in the fourteenth Indiana Volunteer Infantry.

In 1865 he settled in Findlay where he lived throughout his remaining years.

Hurd received honorary degrees from the Ohio Medical College, the Columbus Medical College and the Kentucky School of Medicine. And his papers included: "Plaster of Paris in Treatment of Fractures," 1872. "The Identity of Diphtheria and Membranous Croup," 1873. "Extra-uterine Pregnancy with Report of Cases,"1878- "Puerperal Eclampsia with "Cases," 1873, of which the association ordered 1,200 extra copies printed for its members. "Suturing the Severed Tendo Achilles in Open Wound," 1875, the fourth case reported at that time. These were some of his most valuable contributions to medical literature.

Dr. Hurd married, in 1853, Amanda Cell. Of their three children one, Huldah survived him.

Dr. Hurd was a man of genial disposition, and while brusque in manner this peculiarity was really to conceal his philanthropy.

G. C. M.

Hurd, Edward Payson (1838–1899).

Dr. Hurd was born at Newport, Canada, August 29, 1838, where his father, Samuel Hurd, was post-master, justice of the peace, and county treasurer.

The boy studied at Eaton Academy, at St. Francis College, Richmond, Quebec, and in 1861 entered McGill Medical School, where he graduated in 1865 with highest honors, winning the Holmes gold medal.

For one year he held the position of "dresser" and teacher at McGill, until his marriage, December 1, 1866, to Sarah Elizabeth Campbell, of Newburyport, Massachusetts.

For four subsequent years he practised

at Danville, and at Smithfalls in Canada, where he had a large country practice. Two daughters, Kate Campbell and Mabeth, were born in Canada, and for the sake of their education he moved to Mrs. Hurd's old home at Newburyport, where in 1872 a son, Randolph Campbell, was born. Of these three children the elder daughter and the son became doctors.

In 1883 he was one of the organizers of the Anna Jacques Hospital and a member of its staff as long as he lived. His office practice brought him much surgery, as he was harbor physician for many years, and was often obliged to amputate frozen feet or crushed hands, or to sew up long scalp wounds by flickering gas light, assisted only by one of his children. His success was excellent, because he was a quick operator and used plenty of hot water even before the modern rules of antisepsis had been formulated.

For many years Dr. Hurd was city physician, doing strenuous work for trifling pay because of his love for the poor. He was for two years president of the Essex North District Medical Society; member of the Massachusetts Medical Society, and also of the Climatological Society, and of the Société de Médecine Pratique de Paris, France.

After 1882 Dr. Hurd contributed regularly to the "New York Medical Record" and the "Boston Medical and Surgical Journal" and other medical publications. His writings from 1885 until his death in 1899 are outlined in the following list of translations interspersed with articles for the medical journals:

1855, Translated from the French: "Clinical Therapeutics," by Dujardin-Beaumetz, with special introduction by the author.

1886, "Diseases of the Lungs," by Germain Sée, with introduction.

1886, "Diseases of the Stomach and Intestines," Dujardin-Beaumetz.

1886, "Diseases of the Heart," two volumes, Dujardin-Beaumetz.

1886, "Infectious Diseases," by Carl Liebermeister, two volumes (from the German).

1887, "Diseases of the Liver," Dujardin-Beaumetz.

1888, "Diseases of the Kidneys," Dujardin-Beaumetz.

1888, "Diseases of the Nervous System," by Prof. Charcot, with special preface by the author.

1889, "Appendicitis and Perityphlitis," by Dr. Charles Talamon.

1889, "The Bacterial Poisons," by Dr. Gamaleïa.

1889, "A Treatise on Diphtheria," by Dr. H. Bourges.

1890, "A Treatise on Fractures," by Prof. A. Désprés.

1891, A brochure on "Sleep, Insomnia and Hypnotics."

1892, Translated "Antiseptic Therapeutics," by E. L. Trouessart.

1893, Translated "New Medications," two volumes, by Dujardin-Beaumetz.

From 1893 until his death he constantly wrote for medical journals. During these years he was professor of pathology and dermatology at the College of Physicians and Surgeons, Boston, and delivered courses of lectures in both these subjects every year. He never took any vacation, and his recreation consisted in the study of Greek and Latin authors and French poets. Every Sunday afternoon, when possible, he devoted a couple of hours to reading aloud with a friend the stirring Homeric poems, or lighter verse from Horace.

He died of pneumonia February 24, 1899, aged sixty-one.

K. C. H. M.

From an Autobiography in "History of Essex County," Massachusetts.

Hutchison, Edwin (1840-1887).

There is a piece of very concrete biography embodied in St. Elizabeth's Hospital at Utica, New York, a biography in short of one who in spite of personal ill-health and short years was long remembered for his ability as an ophthalmologist and as founder of the hospital mentioned.

The son of one Holmes Hutchinson of Utica, he was educated in James Lombard's School, the Utica Academy and at Yale, afterwards studying medicine in the Long Island Medical School and graduating M. D. from the New York College of Physicians and Surgeons in 1866. Like most young men at that time he went to the war and was successively surgeon to the third Maryland Volunteer Infantry and the one hundred and thirty-seventh New York Volunteers, taking charge in the latter of Gen. Geary's hospital under Gen. Sherman in his famous march through Georgia.

At the close of the war he settled down in New York and became known for his surgery, especially in eye disease, though his right forearm, through an early accident, was almost immovably fixed.

Very much he recognized the need of a hospital for proper treatment of those who could pay and those who could not, so, along with his friend Dr. J. E. West, an embryo hospital was established, to grow gradually larger and attract students because of its founder's skill.

In 1866 he married Miss Christine Rosswog and found time to write valuable articles on his specialities to the "American Journal of Insanity" and the "New York State Medical Transactions." But during the last four years of his life he had to go south every winter and succumbed at last to kidney disease in the hospital he had founded. Only a few days before his death he joined the Roman Catholic church though reared as a Protestant. "I loved him dearly" writes his biographer "for he had an amiability, a tenderness, a love of all things beautiful—rare among men."

Trans. Med. Soc. New York, 1888 (Dr. T. H. Pooley).

Hutchison, Joseph Chrisman (1827–1887).

Joseph Chrisman Hutchison was born in old Franklin, Missouri, February 22, 1827, the son of Nathaniel Hutchison, M. D., a native of Armagh, Ireland, and of Mary Chrisman, of Farquier County, Virginia. He graduated from the University of the State of Missouri, at Columbia, and in 1848 received his M.

D. from the University of Pennsylvania, after a partial course in Jefferson Medical College.

For a few years he practised medicine in Missouri, but in 1853 removed to Brooklyn, with the interests of which, medical, sanitary, and educational, he became closely and actively identified. In 1854 he had charge of the cholera hospital in Brooklyn, and the successful treatment of cholera patients was in a large part due to his skillful, and well organized efforts. His constant interest in the medical work of the city was manifested in the various positions of public medical trust held, as attending surgeon to the Brooklyn Hospital, surgeon-in-chief of the Orthopedic Dispensary, etc.; and the numerous hospitals to which he was attached as consulting surgeon show the confidence of their medical officers in him.

With all his professional work, he found time to contribute to medical literature the results of his clinical observations, in clear, concise, and well digested articles, always of a practical character, and bearing evidence of being written from the bedside rather than the study. One of the last papers prepared by him was on "Transfusion," read before the New York Medical Association in 1884. He held membership in many societies, local, national, and international and also added to his other labors that of teacher, having held the position of lecturer on the diseases of women from 1854 to 1856, inclusive, in the University of the city of New York, and from 1860 to 1867 that of professor of operative and clinical surgery in the Long Island College Hospital. His talents found abundant use also in departments closely connected with medical practice. From 1873 to 1875 he was health officer of Brooklyn. He was also the author of a work on Physiology and Hygiene, long in use throughout the country.

The suffering and distress that are incident to a weak and failing heart and pulmonary edema were borne with a patience and bravery that are the outcome of a life-long self-control and a reliance on power that is more than human; but the end was quite painless, on July 17, 1887, in Brooklyn.

N. Y. Med. Jour., 1887, xlvi.
Med Rec., N Y., 1887, xxxiii.
Tr. N. Y. Med. Ass., 1887, iv (J. D. Rushmore (port.).
N. Eng. Med. Monthly, 1884-5, iv (port.).

Hutchinson, James Howell (1834-1889).

Born at Cintra, Portugal, where his father was engaged in business, he was brought to the United States at an early age and educated in this country. At the University of Pennsylvania in 1854 he received his B. A. and graduated in medicine from the same university in 1858, afterwards serving as resident physician at the Pennsylvania Hospital, and then going abroad to study in the schools of Paris and Vienna. While in Europe he devoted much attention to skin diseases, and his friend and biographer, Dr. John Ashhurst, states that he was "probably more familiar with modern dermatology than any of his contemporaries." Dr. Hutchinson began practising medicine in Philadelphia in 1861 and, successful from the first, he acquired a large private practice besides many honorable professional positions. During the Civil War he served for a time as acting assistant surgeon United States Army and was one of the physicians to the Children's Hospital, the Episcopal Hospital and the Pennsylvania Hospital, to which institution his grandfather had also been physician. He was a member and eventually president of the Philadelphia Pathological Society, elected to the College of Physicians of Philadelphia in 1863, and was also a member of his county and state medical societies and of the Association of American Physicians.

Dr. Hutchinson was noted for the correctness and dignity of his style, saying just what he meant in few but well chosen words, and rigidly avoiding all flowery excrescences and ambiguities of language. He never inflicted upon the profession or the public an independent volume, but he edited—and well edited—two reprints

of Dr. Bristowe's "Practice of Medicine;" contributed elaborate articles, which have already become classical, on typhoid, typhus, and simple continued fevers, to the "System of Medicine," edited by Dr. Pepper and Dr. Starr; and was a valued contributor to the "Transactions of the College of Physicians." For more than a year he was the editor of the "Philadelphia Medical Times," in its early days. The skill with which he edited Dr. Bristowe's work was fully recognized by its author who, when the second American edition was about to appear, wrote to Dr. Hutchinson expressing his "sense of the care and trouble . . . bestowed" on the first reprint.

Dr. Hutchinson married Ann Ingersoll and had six children. One, James P. Hutchinson, after graduating in medicine devoted himself to the practice of surgery.

. F. R. P.

Memoir by John Ashhurst, Jr., from the Transactions of the College of Physicians of Philadelphia, 1890, 3 series, vol. xii
Med. News, Phila., 1890, vol. lvi.

Hyatt, Elijah H. (1827-1898).

Elijah H. Hyatt, expresident of the Ohio State Medical Association, was born in Wayne County, Ohio, in 1827 and died at his home in Delaware of apoplexy, December 24, 1898. He was first educated in the public schools and at an academy near Wooster from which he graduated, later from the Ohio Wesleyan University in 1852, and from Starling Medical College, Columbus, in 1856. He served in the Civil War as captain and surgeon. In 1861 he married Eliza Ely and had three daughters. At the close of the war he began to practise in Delaware, Ohio, soon establishing an enviable reputation as physician and surgeon. From 1875 to 1892 he filled the chair of materia medica and therapeutics in the Columbus Medical College. Dr. Hyatt enjoyed a wide reputation as an able surgeon and teacher and took an active interest in public questions and was highly honored as a citizen.

In 1873 he married Miss Sarah Johnson and had two more children, Frank Hastings, and Wendell Gaillard, the latter studied medicine.

J. N. B.

Hyndman, James Gilmour (1853–1904).

James Gilmour Hyndman was born in Cincinnati, Ohio, September 12, 1853 and died in that city September 18, 1904. He was the son of a certain William Graves and Barbara Gilmour Hyndman, natives of the north of Ireland, who came to America in their early childhood. Hyndman received his education in the public schools, and graduated from Woodward High School in 1870, when seventeen.

He began to study medicine under Dr. James L. Whittaker and in 1872 entered the Cincinnati Hospital as interne and remained in that capacity for two years, in 1874 graduating from the Medical College of Ohio, having served as interne. In the same year he began to practise and in July became assistant editor and in 1875 co-editor of "The Clinic," a journal then published by the Medical College of Ohio, Dr. J. T. Whittaker being editor.

In 1875 he was made physician to the dispensary and assistant to the chair of physiology in the Medical College of Ohio, and among other appointments had that of assistant to the chair of theory and practice, 1875; lecturer on laryngology and physical diagnosis, 1877; professor of chemistry, 1879; chair of laryngology, 1894.

He was a most excellent teacher, and for several years he was consulting laryngologist to the German Hospital of Cincinnati. Dr. Hyndman was a ripe scholar and one of the translators of "Ziemssen's Cyclopedia of Medicine."

On June 20, 1883, he married Mary E. Mitchell, daughter of Samuel M. Mitchell of Martinsville, Indiana, but they had no children. Hyndman died in Cincinnati, September 18, 1904, of appendicitis.

A. G. D.

Greve's Centennial History of Cincinnati.
Stone's Biography of Eminent Physicians and Surgeons

I

Ives, Ansell **W.** (1787–1838).

Born at Woodbury, Connecticut, on the thirty-first of August, 1787, he was the third child of a struggling farmer who had to let the boy be apprentice to a farmer till he was nineteen, when, having qualified himself to keep an elementary school, he taught for several years with credit to himself and advantage to his employers. Continning at the same time, with the greatest zeal, his plan of self-instruction, he soon found himself sufficiently advanced to commence the study of a profession; and having chosen that of medicine, entered himself a student with Dr. North, a physician of New London. On removing to Fishkill, in the State of New York, he continued his studies with Dr. Barto White, and completed them in the office of Dr. Valentine Mott, graduating in the College of Physicians and Surgeons of the University of New York in the year 1815. He contributed largely to our medical journals; and some of his papers, especially that on "Humulus Lupulus," gained him much credit, both at home and abroad. He republished, with notes and additions, "Paris's Pharmacologia," and "Hamilton's Observations on the Use and Abuse of Mercurial Medicines," and also a description of the "Epidemic Influenza," which prevailed in the northern and eastern states in the year 1815; indeed, his whole time was spent in improving his own mind, or making himself useful to his fellow-men.

Dr. Ives was well formed, his manners prepossessing, and he had a fund of humor and anecdote which made his company acceptable to his associates. He enjoyed a fine share of health, until he was attacked in February, 1837, with neuralgic pain about the left hip, which gradually increased in duration and violence until his sufferings, for hours together, were almost beyond endurance. About five months from the attack the hip and thigh began to enlarge, which they continued steadily to do with augmented pain till February 2, 1838, when death relieved him from his agony. On dissection a large tumor was found on the left ileum, extending downwards u n d e r the left gluteus muscle.   F. U. J.

From Amer. Jour. Med. Sci., 1838, vol. xxii·
The same biog. is in William's Amer. Biog.·
1845.

Ives, **Eli** (1778–1861).

Eli Ives was born in New Haven, February 7, 1775, son of Dr. Levi Ives, a physician of large practice in New Haven. He entered Yale College in 1795, graduating in 1799, and then spent fifteen months as the rector of the Hopkins Grammar School, at New Haven. While thus teaching, he took up the study of medicine under his father and Dr. Eneas Munson, Senior, and later went to Philadelphia to attend the lectures of Rush, Wister and Barton, at the University of Pennsylvania. In 1802 he returned and began the practice of medicine, being made a member of the Connecticut Medical Society on May 4, 1802. Three years later he again went to Philadelphia to attend the lectures there, but did not remain long enough to graduate. In October, 1811, the honorary degree of M. D. was conferred upon him by the Connecticut Medical Society.

He was prominent among those who established the Yale Medical School, being on all the committees of conference and practically at the head of the movement so far as the medical society was concerned. On the opening of the school in November, 1813, he became the professor of materia medica and kept the position until 1829, when he was transferred to the chair of the theory and practice of medicine. This professorship he filled until 1852, when he took the chair of materia medica again, retaining it until his death nine years later, but being for the last eight years professor emeritus. He is described by Dr. Henry Bronson, who was once his private pupil, as "tall and spare, of a weak organization, with a pleasant countenance and mild blue eye, unceremonious and unpretending, familiar and agreeable in manners and plain in dress." He was not an eloquent instructor, but gave a good practical course. In his knowledge of botany he was ahead of his time, and, at the opening of the medical school, established, on grounds adjoining the college, a botanical garden for the benefit of his classes, which was not properly seconded as an enterprise and so perished from neglect. He gave special attention to indigenous vegetable remedies in his extensive practice, and is said to have been one of the first to employ chloroform, having prescribed it

by inhalation as well as by stomach, in 1832, a year after its discovery by Samuel Guthrie, of Sackett's Harbor.

He was a member of the first convention which framed the United States Pharmacopœia in 1820, and, at the second convention in 1830, was made the president. For three years, from 1824–1827, he was vice president of the Connecticut Medical Society. When the American Medical Association met in New Haven in 1860, he was chosen its president. He served, also, as the candidate for lieutenant-governor on the anti-Masonic ticket in 1831, and acted for many years as the president of the Horticultural and Pomotogical Societies. He married on September 17, 1805, Maria Beers and had three sons, who took up the study of medicine, and one daughter who married a physician. He died on October. 8, 1861. A portrait of him is preserved in the family. It was reproduced for his memoir in the "Proceedings of the Connecticut Medical Society for 1867."   W. R. S.

Proceedings Connecticut Medical Society, 1864–1867.
Bacon's "Some Account of the Medical Profession in New Haven."

J

Jackson, Abraham Reeves (1827–1892). Abraham Reeves Jackson, one of the older members and ex-presidents of the American Gynecological Society, died November 12, 1892, of a stroke of paralysis, due to cerebral hemorrhage. His appearance and work showed him as in the fulness of his powers. But the finger of Providence had touched him two years before, and although the touch was a light one, he knew its meaning. Yet he strode on cheerfully, and said nothing of it, except to a friend. The fatal touch came while still on duty.

He was born June 17, 1827, in Philadelphia. His early education was obtained in the public and high schools. After graduating at the Central High School of Philadelphia, in 1846, he began the study of marine engineering, but soon decided that medicine would offer a more congenial career. His admiration in early boyhood for the character and personality of his family physician had much to do with his partiality for the profession. He graduated from the Medical Department of the University of Pennsylvania in 1848, and forthwith began his life's work at Stroudsburg, Pennsylvania. Here he practised for twenty years, with the exception of two spent in the service of his country—1862 to 1864—as assistant medical director of the Army of Virginia. In 1870 he moved from Stroudsburg to Chicago, and immediately assumed the position in the profession for which his natural endowments and careful preparation had fitted him. In 1871 the character of the man was displayed in the successful establishment of the Woman's Hospital of Illinois, of which he was the first surgeon-in-chief. After this he limited his practice entirely to gyne-

cology, with constantly increasing influence and renown. His last year was the most successful and remunerative of his life.

In 1872 he was elected lecturer on gynecology at Rush Medical College, and held the position until 1877, when he resigned. In 1882 he established and incorporated, with the aid of two colleagues, the College of Physicians and Surgeons of Chicago, and was its president and professor of gynecology until removed by death.

He was a charter member of the Chicago Gynecological Society, and its president in 1883. From 1889 until his death he occupied the position of president of the Association of Acting Assistant Surgeons of the United States Army; honorary member of the Detroit Gynecological Society, and corresponding member of the Boston Gynecological Society.

His writings were numerous, and always conservative in tone and original in thought. They carried his name wherever medicine is read, and were honored with the stamp of authority, both abroad and at home.

It is pleasant to remember that, in addition to his labors and honors and responsibilities, his life contained much that was enjoyable. He was the companion of Mark Twain in the famous trip made by the "Innocents Abroad," and was the original of the very original doctor, whose jokes are the best in the book. He was funny, but never vulgar; witty, but never sarcastic and personal.

He married in 1850 Harriet Hollinshead, of Stroudsburg, by whom he had two daughters. He was left a widower by her death in 1865, and in 1871 married Julia Newell, of Janesville, Wisconsin, who survived him. With her he made a trip around the world in 1890, which constituted their last romance, preserved in the memory of one who was capable of enjoying such talented companionship.

In 1877, while operating upon an infected patient, he inoculated his finger, and never fully recovered from the effects of the disease. In 1889 new symptoms made their appearance in the form of an attack of aphasia. November 1, 1892, symptoms again appeared, and were followed the next day by the attack of apoplexy from which he died.

He was honored in his own country and left the world better than he found it. He fought a good fight. We give him his niche among our immortals, feeling that in honoring him we honor ourselves.

Among his writings are:

"Remarks on Intrauterine Polypi," 1876.

"The Ovulation Theory of Menstruation," 1876.

"Vascular Tumors of the Female Urethra," 1878.

"The Treatment of Sterility," 1879.

H. T. B.

Tr. Amer. Gyn. Soc., vol. xxviii, 1893 (port.).

Jackson, Hall (1739–1797).

Dr. Clement Jackson, of whom we know hardly anything of value towards the formation of his biography, was practising in Hampton, New Hampshire, when his son Hall was born November 11, 1739. The father, either to enlarge the bounds of his practice or to better educate his children, moved to Portsmouth, New Hampshire, in 1749. His son, after receiving the ordinary common school education of those days, had also a special education in the classics by a local clergyman. He then entered his father's office and rode about with him seeing cases and studying medicine and investigating the action and compounding of drugs until he had acquired sufficient knowledge to

begin practice. Before entering into practice he went to Europe and completed his medical education under the best masters of the day, being remarked for his skill in surgery, an art which was by no means so extensively or so fearlessly practised in those days. While in London he received honorable notice for an ingenious invention by which he extracted from a gun-shot wound a bullet which had baffled the skill of the attending surgeons.. . . .

Returning home well equipped, he opened first a pharmacy as a sort of focus for practice, and as a source of income until he should gain enough patients to become self-supporting. This pharmacy he handed over ultimately to a son named John. From 1760 to 1775 he remained constantly in Portsmouth identifying himself with the community, gaining an excellent reputation and marrying the widow Mary Dalling Wentworth.

With the outbreak of the Revolution he came at once to the front and after the Battle of Lexington rode post haste to Boston to do his share in taking care of the wounded and in preparing for further medical and surgical work in the army which was soon to be recruited from the various New England States.

Returning to Portsmouth in a few days, he enlisted a company of men and was elected both their captain and surgeon, and these he continued drilling persistently, until news arrived of the battle of Bunker Hill, when he forthwith packed his chaise with all available instruments, drugs and lint, set off early in that June morning, and twelve hours later was amid the wounded whom he found in a most deplorable condition. In the two days that had elapsed since the battle, the Massachusetts surgeons had attended to their wounded in some reasonable fashion, but nothing had been done for those from New Hampshire. Three physicians belonging to the New Hampshire troops were indeed on the field, or wherever the wounded had been transported, but they were all young and inexperienced, and had never performed a single operation, to say nothing of the capital operations now demanded, and even with the best of skill they were most amazingly unprovided with even such necessary trifles as surgical needles or sutures.

Jackson began his work at once, though twilight had set in, worked nearly all night long with the aid of lanterns, and during the next day and the one following performed fortyeight operations, extracted a large number of bullets, and did one amputation at the hip-joint on a soldier by the name of Hutchinson. When a week and a day later this poor fellow died, Hall Jackson said that the only thing that killed him was his name, so deeply indignant were the patriots then with the name of Hutchinson, as borne by a detested governor.

When this imperative work was done, it next became a vital question of a permanent hospital for the sick and convalescents of the twenty-five thousand troops soon collected around Boston. In this great work Jackson did yeoman service. In addition to these labors, he was about the only surgeon about competent for medical consultations and many a day in such work with Dr. Benjamin Church he spent in riding out to Waltham, Watertown, and Medford, to visit several of the officers of high rank who had been wounded at the battle or had fallen ill later on from their heroic exposure in the service of their country. For four months Jackson remained in the camp on Winter Hill, with the exception of a few days when he suffered intensely from so severe an inflammation of the eyes that he was obliged to give himself complete rest, and gradually became weary of working without pay of any sort, not even of rations for himself or his horse. There he was, paying out of his own purse

twelve dollars a week for his board and lodgings and seven dollars a week for the care of his horse. Nor would human nature let him forget that while so occupied in a wasting business, he had left three rival physicians at home, of whom he says in one of his very few letters extant, "Cutter, Brackett and Little are eating up my patients daily." The most galling thing, however, to him was the selfish behavior of many of the so-called patriots in Boston. "I am utterly disgusted with some of those damnable patriots and their glorious cause of liberty, which they are constantly flaunting in our faces. If liberty consists in killing the wounded, starving the sick and letting them languish in the hospitals on bad salt pork for their only meat, I do not want to be much farther employed in such a glorious cause."

Despite his discouraged state of mind, neither Gen. Lee nor Gen. Sullivan would hear of his abandoning the sick to inferior physicians and it was not until October that he was able to return home for needed rest and then to make up for time lost to his patients and practice.

Ultimately, the New Hampshire Assembly honored Dr. Jackson with the thanks of the province, paid him fifteen pounds a month and proper rations for himself and his horse and elected him surgeon to the New Hampshire troops in the Revolutionary Army. In return for these favors he enlisted a body of men and drilled them into a company of heavy artillery with four guns from a fort in Portsmouth harbor. In the next year he was surgeon-in-chief in Col. Pearse Long's regiment and after that probably retired from active service and paid attention to his private practice.

The rest of Dr. Jackson's life was spent in active medical work. He was a first rate surgeon, and regarded as clever as an obstetrician; he paid a good deal of attention to couching of cataracts, and with the needle had remarkable results in curing the blind. He was elected an honorary member of the Massachusetts Medical Society in 1783, and in 1793 received the honorary degree of M. D. from Harvard College. He took great interest in small-pox inoculation.

His life was terminated, like many others of our profession, by an accident occurring while on his rounds of duty. In September, 1797, while "turning out" for another carriage his own was overturned and he was thrown and suffered a fractured rib. Fever soon ensued and September 28, 1797 he died. Hardly any other medical name in New Hampshire stands out brighter than that of Hall Jackson, for he was kind to the poor, charming in manners, genial in society, skillful in every branch of medicine which he practised, and above all an honest patriot.

J. A. S.

"The Graves we decorate," Portsmouth, New Hampshire, 1907." "Letters by Whipple, Thornton and Hall Jackson," Philadelphia, 1889.

Jackson, Samuel (1790–1872).

He was born March 22, 1787, the year in which the College of Physicians, Philadelphia, was founded, and graduated from the medical department of the University in 1808, having received his college education also at the University. His thesis was on "Suspended Animation." He was a student of Dr. Hutchinson, and after Dr. Hutchinson's death, of Dr. Wistar. He did not begin practice until about 1815, when he severed his connection with the drug business, of which he had assumed charge in 1809 on the death of his brother. He rapidly became prominent and in 1820 when the yellow fever prevailed in Philadelphia he was chairman of the Board of Health. He rendered signal service not only fighting the disease fearlessly and valiantly, but publishing import-

ant papers in the "Philadelphia Journal of Medical and Physical Sciences." He himself had an attack of the fever and regarded it of local origin, due to filth and putrescent animal and vegetable matter.

His writings, chiefly opening lectures at the University and biographies of colleagues, occupy some two columns in the catalogue of the Surgeon-General's Library at Washington. His best work was his "Principles of Medicine founded on the Structure and Functions of the Animal Organism" (1832), the first of its kind published in America.

Jackson was seventy-six years of age when he delivered his last course of lectures at the University in the session of 1862–63, which I attended. He had the appearance then of being a very old man—older than he seems in the bronze tablet which we in 1910 erected to his memory in our University. He was so feeble that he leaned on the arm of an assistant as he walked to his desk, whence he delivered his lectures sitting. There was, however, no lack of spirit in his message. With his bright eyes beaming, his face full of enthusiasm, and his white hair streaming over his shoulders, he was truly picturesque. Leaning forward, he narrated with great animation the happenings of the day in physiology as they appeared to the eyes of the great French physiologists, Claude Bernard, Milne Edwards and Brown-Séquard. For at that day the French were the acknowledged leaders in physiological science.

He became professor of materia medica in the College of Pharmacy in 1821 as the colleague of Prof. George B. Wood. Jackson's introduction to medical teaching was in the Philadelphia Hospital, in whose wards he served from 1822 to 1845, and attracted many students to his lectures. At that day the subjects of practice of medicine and the institutes of medicine were united under one professorship. Institutes of medicine was a term which in its broadest significance covered almost the entire subject of medicine except anatomy, surgery and materia medica, but practically was a synonym for physiology. In 1827 Dr. Nathaniel Chapman was the professor of practice and institutes, but finding the subject too extensive, Jackson was appointed assistant and delivered the course on Institutes. In 1835 a chair of institutes was established and Jackson elected to it, resigning in 1863 after twenty-eight years' incumbency. He died April 4, 1872, nine years after his resignation, aged eighty-two years.

J. T.

Old Penn., vol. viii, 1910. Address by James Tyson, M. D.
The Life and Character of Samuel Jackson, Phila., 1872 (J. Carson).
Boston Med. and Surg. Jour., 1850, vol. xli
Tr. Med. Soc. Penn., Phila., 1897, vol. xii (J. L. Stewart).

James, Frank Lowber (1841–1907).

For eighteen years Frank Lowber James edited the "National Druggist," besides devoting much time to the study of microscopy. At one time he also edited the "St. Louis Medical and Surgical Journal." He was a scientist, journalist and soldier; travelled extensively in many lands, and held the degree of doctor of philosophy from the University of Munich. Born in Mobile, he was sent abroad to complete studies in chemistry, for which he had shown natural proclivities, and became a pupil of Baron Justus von Liebig, and also a member of his household. At the beginning of the war, James returned and entered the Confederate Army in the Nitre and Mining Bureau. He had special charge of the explosives and torpedo work in Mobile Bay, for which distinguished service he was outlawed and a price set on his head by the Federal Government. He was captured, taken to New Orleans, tried before Gen. Butler and sentenced to death, but escaped prison and wandered in the Orient for many years, until the death sentence expired of inanition. Then he went to Memphis and was associated with

Albert Pike, and later with James M. Keating, on the old "Appeal" newspaper, finally removing to St. Louis, where he lived for the rest of his life. He was a Government expert in the "embalmed beef" investigation. It was while carrying out a series of scientific investigations that an insect flew into his right eye, causing loss of sight in that member. He died on May 19, 1907, of erysipelas.

The Med. Herald, Sept., 1907.
St. Louis Med. and Surg. Jour., 1894, vol. lxvii.

James, Thomas Chalkley (1766–1835)

Thomas Chalkley James was born in Philadelphia, August 31, 1766, and was the youngest son. The ancestors of Dr. James were originally from England, and on both sides were connected with the Society of Friends. His father, Mr. Abel James, was for many years one of the leading merchants in Philadelphia.

James was well educated after the manner of Friends, especially at their school, under the superintendance of Robert Proud, the historian of Pennsylvania. James studied medicine under the direction of Dr. Adam Kuhn, a disciple of Linneus, whose opinion always carried weight among his medical brethren, and who had the honor of educating some of the first physicians of our country. In 1787, at the age of twenty-one, he received the certificate of bachelor in medicine from the University of Pennsylvania.

When in London, in 1790, he found his countryman and fellow student, Dr. P. S. Physick, a pupil and an assistant of the celebrated Mr. John Hunter, pursuing his studies in St. George's Hospital. By Physick's advice, Dr. James · entered (May 30, 1791) as a house pupil of the Story Street Lying-in Hospital under the care of Drs. Osborne and John Clarke, the two leading obstetric teachers in London. There he had soon the pleasure of receiving as companion, his friend Dr. J. Cathrall, who was also with him at Canton. The winter of 1791–2 was spent in London chiefly in attending lectures, and also as an attendant at St. George's Hospital.

After much deliberation respecting the relative advantages of spending a winter in Edinburgh or Paris, and after consulting by letter his friends on this side of the Atlantic, he finally followed the example of Drs. Physick and Cathrall, and went to Edinburgh in the spring of 1792. Here he remained and attended the lectures during the succeeding winter, in company with Hosack of New York.

It does not appear that Dr. James graduated at Edinburgh in imitation of his friends, Dr. Wistar and Physick, being content with the honors of his own university in Philadelphia, then in its infancy. In the month of June, 1793, Dr. James, accompanied by Dr. Ryan, arrived at Wiscasset, in the then district of Maine. They reached Philadelphia a short time only before the terrible and then unknown epidemic, the yellow fever, visited this city. Dr. James had hardly time to receive the congratulations of his anxious friends, when the fatal scourge appeared, bringing dismay and terror even to the boldest spirits.

He married Hannah Morris (a lady connected with one of the first families in Pennsylvania, "eminently adapted by her mild, but decided character, her judicious, yet cheerful disposition to meet the peculiarities of Dr. James's character").

In 1802, November 27, James, in conjunction with the late Dr. Church, commenced his first regular course of lectures on obstetrics.

The first course of lectures on midwifery in the University of Pennsylvania was commenced by James in November, 1810. In 1807 (January 26) he was appointed physician to the Pennsylvania Hospital, as successor of Dr. J. Redman Coxe, and on the twenty-fifth day of June, 1810, was translated

at his own request to the station of obstetric physician. The duties of this appointment he continued to discharge with scrupulous attention and punctuality until the twenty-sixth of November, 1832. He was elected fellow of the College of Physicians and Surgeons on the sixth of October, 1795. On the fourth of September, 1810, he gave the details of a case of premature labor, artificially induced by himself, in the case of a contracted pelvis, after the expiration of the seventh month, with the gratifying result of safety to mother and child. This was the first record, we believe, in this country, of the scientific performance of this operation.

On the seventh of August, 1827, he read a paper on extrauterine pregnancy, in which he seemed anxious to establish the opinion from the historical detail of cases, that ventral or abdominal pregnancy never originally occurred; that tubal or uterine pregnancy had previously existed in cases where the child was found in the cavity of the abdomen, the tube or uterus having been ruptured or ulcerated so as to allow the escape of the fetus from its original location into the peritoneal cavity. His reasoning from the anatomy and functions of the parts concerned, from the mode in which the fetus is sustained, and especially from the facts on record was ingenious and powerful; but facts subsequently detailed seem to confirm the opposite opinion, however improbable, that the ovum may be deposited in the peritoneal surface and there be developed with its contents, in some instances, even to the usual period of utero-gestation.

With Hewson, Parrish and Otto, he edited the "Eclectic Repertory" which for eleven years gave medical men important abstracts from foreign journals and books and also original papers.

But about the year 1825 the result of uninterrupted mental and bodily exertion began to be manifest in museu-lar tremor and impairment of utterance, and Dr. P. Dewees became his assistant. At last, ten years later, he had also to curtail his practice after twenty-five years valuable service to the Pennsylvania Hospital. He died on the fifth of July, 1835.

H. L. H.

Amer. Jour. Med. Sci., Phila., 1843, u. s., vol. vi life of W. P. Dewees, (H. L. Hodge).
Lives of Eminent Amer. Phys., Phila., S. D. Gross, 1861
Hist. of Med. Depart. of the Univ. of Penn., J. Carson, 1869, Phila.

James, William (1842–1910).
Born in New York, on January 11, 1842, of devout and independent parentage, throughout life his studies were much disturbed by ill health. In his youth he attended a Lycée in France and afterwards the University of Geneva, there gaining an unusual command of French. His German he acquired a few years later at the University of Berlin. In 1862–64 he was in the Lawrence Scientific School; then for four years in the Harvard Medical School, from which, two years later, he received the degree of M. D. He also studied with Agassiz in the Cambridge Museum.

The progress of his mind can be traced in the successive topics of his teaching. In 1873 he became an instructor in anatomy at Harvard; but soon, finding greater interest in physiology, he accepted an assistant professorship in that subject, in 1876. For the next three years, in addition to teaching physiology, he offered a course on the theory of Evolution in the Department of Philosophy. In 1880 he abandoned physiology altogether, becoming in that year assistant professor, and in 1885 professor, of philosophy. He now gave himself enthusiastically to psychology, and under his energetic guidance a psychological laboratory was established here. But after the publication of his treatise on psychology, in 1890, his interest in it declined, and he turned more towards the history of philosophy and the theory of knowledge. In 1892 he resigned the directorship of the laboratory, and after 1897 was never willing to offer a psychologic course. Religion and metaphysics claimed him, and his last years were devoted to the elaboration of a comprehensive philosophy in which the portion known as "Pragmatism" has occasioned wide discussion. His scientific equipment lent him authority, while his remarkable literary gifts secured for him a wider hearing than that accorded to any other living philosopher. His name has been chiefly associated with his persuasive exposition of the doctrine of "Pragmatism," by which the value of any assertion that claims to be true is tested by its consequences, i.e., its practical bearing upon human interests and purposes—a doctrine which he derived from C. S. Peirce at Cambridge (Massachusetts) in the early "seventies." Of the permanent value of this doctrine it is difficult to speak. But there can be no question of the impetus which he lent to the study of psychology by a combination of qualities which placed him among the foremost thinkers of his time.

Whether readers agreed with his books or dissented, all perceived that they vitalized their subjects. Several obliged a kind of new departure of human thought in their respective fields, the most notable being "The Principles of Psychology," 1890; "Talks to Teachers on Psychology," 1899; "The Varieties of Religious Experience," 1902; and "Pragmatism," 1907. Perhaps four short papers should also be mentioned: "The Feeling of Efforts," 1880; "The Dilemma of Determinism," 1884; "Is Life Worth Living?" 1895; "The Will to Believe," 1896.

The honors received by Prof. James were many and great. He was a member of the National Academy in America, France, Italy, Prussia, and Denmark; was a doctor of letters at Padua and Durham, of laws at Harvard,

Princeton and Edinburgh, of science at Geneva and Oxford. He delivered a course of Lowell Lectures in Boston, of Gifford Lectures in Edinburgh, of Hibbert Lectures in Oxford. He was one of the founders, and always a chief supporter, of the Society for Psychical Research, a subject which profoundly interested him. More than once he was president of the American Psychological Association and of the Boston Natural History Society.

Records of the Faculty of Arts and Sciences, Harvard, October 18, 1910.
Harvard Univ. Gaz., 1910, vol. vi.

Jameson, Horatio Gates (1778–1855).

This surgeon was born in York, Pennsylvania, in 1778, the son of Dr. David Jameson who had emigrated to Charleston, South Carolina, in 1740 in company with Dr. Hugh Mercer.

Horatio studied medicine under his father and began practice at the early age of seventeen. After living in Somerset County, Pennsylvania, Wheeling, Adamstown, Pennsylvania, and Gettysburg he arrived in Baltimore in 1810 and attended lectures at the College of Medicine (University of Maryland), and graduated M. D. in 1831, his inaugural thesis being "The Supposed Powers of the Uterus." For some years he combined the business of druggist with that of medicine. During the War of 1812 he was surgeon to the United States troops in Baltimore for which service his widow received a pension.

He was physician to the City Jail for several years; from 1814 to 1835 he was surgeon to the Baltimore Hospital; from 1821 to 1835 he was consulting physician to the Board of Health.

In 1827 he joined with Drs. Samuel K. Jennings, William W. Handy, James H. Miller, Samuel Annan, and John W. Vethake in founding the Washington Medical College, which college in 1839 obtained a charter conferring University rank, but it never succeeded in founding any other department and was suspended in 1852. In 1830, by special invitation, he visited Europe and read a paper on the "Non-contagiousness of Yellow Fever" before the Society of German Naturalists and Physicians at Hamburg. He was the first American to attend these meetings and the only delegate present from the new world on this occasion. In 1832 he was appointed superintendent of vaccination and improved the virus in use by repassing it through the cow. He also had charge of the cholera hospitals established during the terrible epidemic of that disease.

In 1835 he accepted a chair in and presidency of the Ohio Medical College at Cincinnati, but his wife's ill-health caused him to return to Baltimore after one session. In 1854 he removed to York and thence after a brief stay, to Philadelphia where he wrote and published his book on "Cholera." It is interesting to note that he had found the treatment of this disease more successful as it was milder and more simple. During a visit to New York for the purpose of disposing of this work he was taken suddenly ill and died August 24, 1855, at the age of seventy-six. His remains were brought to Baltimore for interment. His last written article was published in the "American Journal of the Medical Sciences" for October, 1856.

Dr. Jameson was well built, erect, his face was florid, healthy and clean-shaven, and free from wrinkles; his eyes were dark brown, piercing and surmounted by bushy eyebrows. He wore heavy gold spectacles and was very neat in his attire, and was noted for his mechanical ingenuity.

In the "American Medical Recorder" for January, 1829, there is an account of a remarkable trial held in the Baltimore City Criminal Court in the spring of 1828. It was the result of a suit brought by Dr. Jameson against Dr. Frederick E. B. Hintze for defamation of character. The trouble arose from the attempt to establish a second medical school in Baltimore and the envy and ill-will thereby engendered. The report gives interesting details of some of Jameson's great and original operations. The cases mentioned are: 1. Extirpation of upper jaw, with preliminary ligation of the carotid artery, 1820. It was the first time the operation had ever been performed and was a complete success, the patient being in good health at the time of the trial. 2. A case of lithotomy in which a hard fibro-cartilaginous tumor just within the neck of the bladder produced a grating sensation on passing the catheter simulating that caused by a stone in the bladder. 3. Removal of a scirrhus of the uterus, the first done in America. 4. A large tumor of the neck in which an exploratory trocar was introduced. 5. Attempted ovariotomy, etc. The result was that Hintze was fined and Jameson completely vindicated.

From 1829 to 1832 Dr. Jameson published a quarterly journal entitled the "Maryland Medical Recorder," and in this and the "American Medical Recorder" his numerous papers and reports of operations appeared. In 1817 he published two lectures on "Fevers in General," pp. 48, and a work, "American Domestick Medicine," pp. 161 (second edition 1818). His work on cholera has already been mentioned, "A Treatise on Epidemic Cholera," Philadelphia, 1854, pp. 286.

He was twice married, first in 1797 to Catherine Shevell, of Somerset County, Pennsylvania, by whom he had nine children. She died in 1837 and late in life he married a widow Ely, who survived him but had no children. His sons were all physicians and died early leaving no descendants.

E. F. C.

Cordell's Med. Annals of Maryland, 1903 (port).
Am. Med. Recorder, Phila., 1829, vol. xv.

Jay, John Clarkson (1807–1891).

John Clarkson Jay, son of Peter Augustus Jay and grandson of John Jay, died at his home, "Rye," at Rye, Westchester County, November 15, 1891, in his eighty-four year, the immediate cause being senile gangrene. He graduated from Columbia College in 1827, and the College of Physicians and Surgeons, New York, in 1830, and served in New York Hospital the usual term. Upon his marriage with Laura Prime, daughter of Nathaniel Prime, a well-known banker, he left his practice and for a short time engaged in the banking business, but soon retired from both business and professional pursuits to live at his country seat, "Rye," where 400 acres gave him ample occupation.

Jay was well known in the scientific world as a specialist in conchology. His wonderful collection of shells, for many years the most noted in the United States, is now owned by the American Museum of Natural History, and is known as the Jay Collection. These shells were gathered during the expedition to Japan under the command of Commodore Matthew C. Perry. They were submitted to Dr. Jay, who wrote articles on them which appeared in the government reports. He was also the author of "A Catalogue of Recent Shells," published in 1835; "Description of New and Rare Shells," and of later editions of his "Catalogue," in which he enumerated about 11,000 well-marked varieties and about 7,000 well-established species.

Dr. Jay was for many years a trustee of Columbia College and for ten years a trustee of the College of Physicians and Surgeons. He was actively interested in founding the Lyceum of Natural History, now the New York Academy of Sciences, and was its treasurer from 1836 to 1843. One son, Dr. John C. Jay, Jr., and four daughters survived him.

Med. Record, New York, 1892-3, vol. xxx

Jeffries, John (1796–1876).

John Jeffries, son of Dr. John Jeffries, a distinguished physician of Boston, was born in 1796 and graduated at Harvard in arts in 1815, and in medicine in 1819. Together with Dr. Edward Reynolds he founded the Massachusetts Charitable Eye and Ear Infirmary in 1824, and for eighteen years was one of its surgeons. He had a large general practice, but ophthalmic surgery was his speciality.

He was one of the first honorary members of the American Ophthalmological Society.

On July 16, 1876 he died in the eighty-first year of his age.

H. F.

Trans. Am. Ophth. Soc., vol. ii, Hubbell's "Development of Ophthalmology, Boston Med. and Surg. Journal, 1876, xcv,

Jenkins, John Foster (1826–1882).

In Falmouth, Massachusetts, lived the Hon. John Jenkins with his wife Harriet and on the fifteenth of April, 1826, came the first of their nine sons, John Foster, who as a boy went to the Roxbury High School, the Union College of Schenectady and the University of Pennsylvania, taking his M. D. there in 1848. From May, 1849 to 1856 he practised in New York City then went to and remained in Yonkers, marrying in 1854 Miss Elizabeth Siccard David, and having two children, John Foster and Mary Siccard. Among other appointments he held was the presidency of the Medical Society of the State of New York and the vice-presidency of the New York Obstetrical Society.

He spent two long holidays in Europe visiting clinics, attending Society meetings and ransacking old bookshops for his beloved library. When at home the demands of a large obstetric and general practice did not leave much time for reading or writing, but three good papers were given to the medical world: "Puerperal Mania; has it any Connection with Toxemia?" 1875; "Relations of War to Medical Science," 1863, and an exhaustive monograph giving 178 cases of "Spontaneous Umbilical Hemorrhage," its frequency,

pathology and treatment being well considered. His "Tent Hospitals," too, written when general secretary of the United States Sanitary Commission, was a valuable aid in military sanitation.

A "break-down" seems almost an inevitable sequence in a doctor's life, especially from renal or cardiac disease. Jenkins was no exception, and four years before his death in October, 1882, his health from the former cause necessitated frequent rest.

Of Dr. Jenkins as a book lover one of his biographers writes: He spent many an hour wading through catalognes in search of new treasures, though sorely perplexed for space for his ponderous tomes of classic medical literature. Five days were occupied by Bangs & Company in 1883 selling the 1,800 lots of his library. It brought scholars and librarians from all over the country. The owner had probably spent not less than $10,000, but the books only fetched $3,940.

D. W.

Memorial Sketch, by Dr G. J. Fisher, in Tr Med. Soc. of the State of N. York, 1884.

Jenks, Edward Watrous (1833–1903).

Edward Watrous Jenks, gynecologist and obstetrician, was born at Victor, New York, where his father had long kept a general store, but in 1843 the family removed to LaGrange County, Indiana, where Jenks, Senior, had large tracts of land. Here he laid out the town of Ontario and established the LaGrange Collegiate Institute, in which E. W. Jenks received his general education and in 1853 began his medical training at the University of New York, continuing it at Castleton Medical College, Castleton, Vermont. He began practice at Ontario, Indiana, continuing there till his removal to Detroit in 1864, excepting two years spent at Warsaw, New York, and one winter at Bellevue Hospital, Medical College of New York, where he received his *ad eundem*, M. D.

When Dr. Jenks settled in Detroit,

1864, medical matters were in a plastic state. Since the early fifties abortive efforts had been made to utilize its clinical material for the medical department of Michigan University and he soon solved the problem by founding the Detroit Medical College. He married Miss Darling, of Warsaw, in 1859, but she died childless shortly after moving to Detroit. In 1867 he married Miss Joy, daughter of the Hon. J. F. Joy, of Detroit, by whom he had two children, Mattie and a son, Nathan, who became a physician in Detroit.

Jenks died of pneumonia, on the cars between Detroit and Chicago, March, 1903.

Among his many appointments and memberships he was:

In 1866 a founder of the Michigan State Medical Society, its president in 1873; a founder of the Detroit Academy of Medicine, vice-president in 1869, president in 1871; a founder of the Detroit Gynecological Society in 1879, president in 1888; a founder of the American Gynecological Society; a founder of the Detroit Medical Library Association; honorary member of the London Obstetrical Society, 1884; member Maine State Medical Society, 1875. Jenks was a founder and editor of the "Detroit Review of Medicine and Pharmacy, 1866–69; a founder of the Detroit Medical College in 1868, its president and professor of obstetrics from 1868 to 1880; in 1879 professor of obstetrics and diseases of women and children at Bowdoin College, Maine; in 1879 professor of gynecology, Chicago Medical College; in 1892 professor of gynecology, Michigan College of Medicine and Surgery, Detroit; from 1865–80 gynecologist to Harper's Hospital, Detroit; 1868–80 gynecologist to St. Mary's Hospital, Detroit; 1875–80 gynecologist to the Woman's Hospital.

Papers:

"Pelvic Cellulitis." ("Detroit Review of Medicine and Pharmacy," vol. iv.)

"Causes of Sudden Death in Puerperal Women." Address in Obstetrics.

("Transactions of American Medical Association," vol. xxix, 1878.)

"Fibrous Tumors of the Uterus." ("Transactions of Amercian Medical Association," vol. xxvi.)

"Ovariotomy." (Ibid., vol. xxix.)

"Elephantiasis Arabum." ("Detroit Review of Medicine and Pharmacy," vol. x.)

"Menstruation without Ovulation." ("Transactions of Michigan State Medical Society," Lansing, 1870.)

"Atresia of the Genital Passages of Women." ("Chicago Medical Journal and Examiner," September, 1880.)

"Report of a Successful Case of Cesarean Section After Seven Days' Labor." (Reprint "American Journal of Obstetrics," New York, 1877, p. 8.)

"Treatment of Puerperal Septicemia by Intrauterine Injections." ("Transactions of American Gynecological Society," vol. iv.)

"Perineorrhaphy With Special Reference to Its Benefits in Slight Lacerations and a Description of a New Method of Operating." ("American Journal of Obstetrics," New York, 1879, vol. xii.)

"Relation of Goitre to Pregnancy and Derangements of the Generative Organs of Women." (Reprint "American Journal of Obstetrics," New York, 1881.)

"On Postural Treatment of Tympanitis Intestinalis, Following Ovariotomy." (Ibid., July, 1878.)

"Disease of the Vagina and Vulva." ("Pepper's System of Practical Medicine," Philadelphia, 1886, vol. iv, pp. 367–404.)

"Perineo-vaginal Restoration." ("American Journal of Obstetrics," New York, 1893.)

"On a New Mode for Operating for Fistula in Ano." (Reprint, "Transactions of American Gynecological Society," Boston, 1883, vol. ii.)

L. C.

Representative Men in Mich., West. Biographical Co., Cincinnati, O., 1878, vol. i.

Jervey, James Postell (1808–1875).

He was born at Charleston, South Carolina, December 4, 1808, and obtained his early education at Charleston College, which he left before graduation to study medicine. He graduated in medicine from the Medical College of South Carolina in 1830, after which he studied for two years in Paris. Conspicuous for good scholarship from his earliest school days, Dr. Jervey won distinction at the Medical College of South Carolina, taking, at the end of his course, in 1830, the silver cup awarded for the best Latin thesis.

Soon after his return to Charleston in 1832 an outbreak of cholera occurred. Volunteer physicians were called for by the city to take charge of cases isolated in an emergency hospital on Folly Island and Dr. Jervey responded and remained at his post until all danger was passed. During the session of 1851–52, and thereafter for several sessions, Dr. Jervey delivered courses of lectures upon comparative anatomy and medical jurisprudence at the Medical College of the State of South Carolina. These lectures were marked by the daily attendance of many of the faculty; and in 1852 the students themselves adopted resolutions "to express to Prof. L. Agassiz, M. D., and to James Postell Jervey, M. D., the high appreciation of their lectures delivered before them during the winter."

Dr. Jervey practised in Charleston until 1861. He was then given a commission as surgeon in the Confederate States Army and for some time was in charge of the hospital at Summerville, South Carolina. At the close of the war he moved to Pohowatan County, Virginia, where he lived until 1873 when he returned to Charleston.

Sympathetic and eager in relieving every form of suffering, and an excellent raconteur, he was a welcome guest in social, literary and professional circles.

Dr. Jervey married in 1832, Miss Emma Gough Smith, daughter of Dr. Edward Darrell Smith, professor of chemistry in the South Carolina College of Columbia. They had twelve children, of whom seven lived to maturity. One son, Henry Dickson, and one grandson, J. Wilkinson, Jervey, followed the medical profession.

J. W. J.

Jerome, James H. (1812–1884).

James H., Jerome son of Horace and Nancy Reed Jerome, was born at Cochecton, Wayne County, Pennsylvania, September 28, 1812. His general education was obtained at the common schools and Ovid Academy, Michigan, and during this time he learned the trade of a hatter which he followed till 1834, afterwards beginning to study medicine with Dr. Moses Tompkins at Hecla, New York. In 1837, passing the examination of the New York State Censors, he received legal authority to practise. At once he began work at Trumansburg, New York, soon acquiring a good reputation as physician and surgeon. During the intervals of his medical college courses Dr. Jerome acted for one season as prosector for Dr. Willard Parker. In July, 1855, he was elected professor of anatomy and physiology in Geneva Medical College. In 1858 he resigned and was appointed physician-in-chief of the Marine Hospital Service in the port of New York with a salary of $5,000. His salary being held up by a complication of practical politics, he resigned to resume practice at Trumansburg, New York. In 1865 he removed to Saginaw, Michigan, and became engrossed in land deals, lumbering and farming, but always retained a lively interest in medical societies. Immediately after beginning practice he joined the Tompkins County (New York) Medical Society; September, 1847, he organized at Oswego, New York, the South Central New York Medical Association and was its president in 1851. He was a founder of the Saginaw County Medical Society; a founder of the third epoch of the Michigan State Medical Society and its president. In 1855 Hobart Free College gave him her honorary M. D. Dr. Jerome was a man of vigorous intellect, keen perceptions, retentive memory and independent character.

In 1838 he married Lizette Atwater of Perry, New York. and had eight children. Mrs. Jerome died in 1863, and in 1865 he married Calista Allen.

He died at his home in Saginaw, August 8, 1884, from a protracted illness of inflammation of the liver.

Papers:

"The Treatment of the Michigan Insane." ("Transactions of Michigan State Medical Society," vol. i.)

"Domestic Sanitation." ("Transactions of Michigan State Board of Health, " 1881.)

L. C.

Representative Men in Mich., West. Biographical Co., Cinn., O., 1878, vol. viii.

Jewett, Charles (1842–1910).

Charles Jewett, a New York gynecologist, was born in Bath, Maine, on September 27, 1839, and at his death, from apoplexy, when seventy-one years old was still in active practice at the Long Island College Hospital. His A. B. was from Bowdoin College and his M. D. from the College of Physicians and Surgeons, NewYork.

Although a busy man he found time to do a little writing and to edit the "Practice of Obstetrics." Three of his books were: "Childbed Nursing," "Outlines of Obstetrics" and "Essentials of Obstetrics."

In 1866 he married Abbie E. Flagg and a son, Dr. Harold F., and a daughter, Alice Hale, survived him.

Jewett was a clever and popular man and had many appointments. Among them he was a member of the American Academy of Medicine; American Gynecological Society and British Gynecological Society; president of the Medical Society of the State of New York; gynecologist and obstetrician to the Long Island College Hospital; consulting obstetrician to Kings County Hospital; consulting surgeon to St. Christopher's Hospital; consulting gynecologist to Bushwick, Swedish and German Hospitals and Bushwick and Eastern District Dispensaries, Brooklyn; professor of obstet-

rics and gynecology in Long Island College Hospital, and co-editor of "American Gynecology" 1902.

D. W.

Jour. Am. Med. Assoc., vol. lv, 1910.
The Am. Gyn. Soc., Album, 1901.

Jewett, Theodore Herman. (1815–1878).

Dr. Jewett was born at South Berwick, Maine, March 24, 1815. His ancestors were of Danish and French descent, and he was the son of Capt. Furber and Sarah Orne Jewett. His childhood was spent in Portsmouth, New Hampshire, the family returning to South Berwick in 1823, when the father decided to settle on land.

Theodore was a student from childhood and entered Bowdoin at the age of fifteen, graduating with the class of 1834. While there he was a great favorite, studious and quiet and highly thought of by his classmates. He studied privately with Dr. William Berry of Exeter, New Hampshire, with Dr. Winslow Lewis, of Boston, both of whom predicted great success for him, and also attended medical lectures at Dartmouth and Harvard, and finally (1840) took his degree at the Jefferson Medical College in Philadelphia. He hoped, at this time, to study in Europe, and to settle in a larger city, but his health was delicate, a brother had just died from tuberculosis, and his father begged the son would stay at home, so he spent his life in South Berwick, always hoping that opposition to his original plans would cease. To an ambitious man like Jewett, it was a lonely life, far from the circle of his professional friends of whom he was so fond.

He worked thoroughly and well, and soon became known and appreciated as an excellent physician. He had wonderful tact in diagnosis, and in discovering appropriate remedies.

He never tired of living and he never grew old. For many years he was a most satisfactory lecturer on obstetrics in the medical School of Maine. During the Civil War he was surgeon of the Enrollment Board at Portland, and was once president òf the Maine Medical Association. His presidential address, delivered in 1878, was a remarkable and cultivated essay on the "Practice of Medicine." He also wrote a large number of papers for the Maine Medical Association such as, for instance, upon "Spinal Meningitis," "Ovariotomy," and "Belladonna in Congestion of the Brain."

Jewett married in March 17, 1842, Caroline Frances Perry, of Exeter, New Hampshire, daughter of Dr. William Perry, and had three daughters, among whom was the celebrated authoress, Sarah Orne Jewett.

He died suddenly at the Crawford House, in the White Mountains, September 20, 1878, from heart disease which he had for a long time concealed from his family, until at last obliged to give up work.

Living in a small country village, Dr. Jewett did a large service to medicine; practising in a larger field, he would undoubtedly have obtained world-wide renown and fame in his cherished profession.

J. A. S.

Trans. Maine Med. Assoc. 1879, vi.

Johnson, Charles Earl (1812–1876).

He was born March 15, 1812, at "Banden," the colonial home of his family near Edenton, North Carolina.

He graduated from the University of Virginia and had his medical education at the University of Pennsylvania where he was a private pupil of Prof. Samuel Jackson.

He practised in his native county until 1840, when he removed to Raleigh and soon after did good work in an epidemic of fever which occurred in the State capital.

He was one of the founders of the North Carolina Medical Society and its president for two successive years (1856–1857), and an editor of the old "North Carolina Medical Journal." In May, 1861, he was appointed by Gov. Ellis surgeon-general of the North Carolina Troops and during his term of office (1861

–1862) he visited every battlefield in Virginia, taking medicines and supplies for the sick and wounded.

In 1869 Dr. Johnson published an able treatise on "Insanity and its Medico-legal Relations." A notable discussion occurred between him and Dr. S. S. Satchewell in 1854 at a meeting of the State Medical Society. In this Dr. Johnson fully sustained his already growing fame as a debater, and subsequently published his remarks along with a former address under the title of "An Address on Malaria."

He was twice married. His first wife, Emily A. Skinner, died in 1847 leaving four children. His second wife, Frances L. Iredell, with her five children survived him when he died in 1876.

H. A. R.

"Memoirs" of Dr. Johnson by P. E. Hines, M. D., 1876.
Biographical History of North Carolina, Ashe, 1907, vol. ii.

Johnson, Francis Marion (1828–1893)

Francis Marion Johnson was born on a farm near Georgetown, Kentucky, August 27, 1828. His parents, Garland and Theresa Johnson, were of Scotch-Irish descent and pioneers in that county. Being the eldest in a large family he attended school only during the winter and worked in the summer to assist his father, gathering together a few dollars by working extra hours.

The first money he ever earned as a lad was spent for a copy of "Plutarch's Lives" and this old book with its well worn pages is a treasure in possession of his family. Working during the day and studying far into the night, he studied medicine under the old family physician, Dr. Elliott. He graduated from Transylvania University at Louisville, Kentucky.

With a thorough-bred horse which he had raised himself, a few dollars in his pocket and a carpet bag he rode from Georgetown, Kentucky, to Missouri and settled in the little town of Farley in Platte County, a fortunate location, for the country along the Missouri river was full of malaria and a doctor's services in constant demand.

In 1855 he married Mary Jane Limberlake and had four children, three daughters and one son. About this time mutterings of war were heard and Johnson became a surgeon under Gen. Sterling Price. When Lee surrendered, and not till then, did Dr. Johnson return to his desolated home. Penniless, he again started out to retrieve home and fortune, removing to the little town of Platt City where he soon had a good practice. His wife died, and in 1870 he married Julia M. Tillery of Liberty, Missouri. Never having been very robust, he determined to go to a city where work would be easier, so on his fiftieth birthday he went to Kansas City where he remained until his death, January 25, 1893.

Johnson was a thinker and logical reasoner and evolved many ideas which at the time were looked upon as heretical by some of his fellow practitioners. In 1872 he read a paper before the Kansas City District Medical Society in which he maintained a theory of the infectiousness of pneumonia, but met with no endorsement. The wide experience in obstetrics gained in an extensive country practice led him to devote especial attention to that important branch of work and he was elected dean of the college and chosen for the chair of obstetrics in the Kansas City Medical College in 1880, which professorship he held until his death. The clinical obstetrical department which was started during Dr. Johnson's incumbency averaged over eight cases of labor to the student, an unusual record at that date in the West.

Dr. Johnson had a peculiar physiognomy which was masked by a long beard giving him an expression of fierceness which much belied his gentle nature and benevolence.

Shortly before his death Dr. Johnson devised an obstetrical forceps which included the "third curve" of the Tarnier axis traction principle in connection with the long graceful Hodge forceps, which

supplied a principle ingenious and practical. Used with the patient drawn well over the edge of bed or table so that grasp could be effected with only slight engagement, the delivery is facilitated with but slight danger of traumatism as no tension is put upon the perineum.

G. C. M.

Johnson, Hosmer Allen (1822–1891).

Allen Hosmer Johnson, a scientist who helped to found in Chicago the Academy of Natural Sciences and the Chicago Medical College, was born in the village of Wales, Buffalo, October 22, 1822, and a boyhood spent among wild natural surroundings inclined him afterwards to travel circumspectly through Switzerland, California and Colorado, sleeping frequently "under the blue blanket," and learning to love the starlit sky.

When twelve he was at Almont, Michigan, helping to cut a farm out of the woods when Indians and wolves were far more abundant than civilized beings. At nineteen he was at the University of Michigan and showed remarkable talent for languages, not excluding the Ojibway tongue. From this university he held his A. B. A. M. and LL. D., graduating M. D. from Rush Medical College in 1852, and remaining there as professor of materia medica until 1859 when, with others, he founded the North Western Medical School and was a popular member of the faculty until his death, of pneumonia, in the winter of 1891. He married Miss Margaret Ann Seward and had two children, one of whom, Frank Seward, became professor of pathology in the Chicago Medical College.

Dr. Johnson did not contribute much to medical literature though for some years he edited "The Northwestern Medical Journal." The Astronomical Society and the Historical Society which he also helped to found and the Academy of Natural Sciences furnish the best record of his work.

D. W.

Physicians and Surgeons of Chicago, J. M. Sperry, Chic., 1904.

Johnson, Joseph (1776–1862).

Joseph Johnson, physician and historian, the fourth son of William and Sarah Nightingale Johnson, was born in Mt. Pleasant, near Charleston, on the fifteenth of June, 1776. His father William Johnson was one of the leaders of the Revolutionary movement in South Carolina and was imprisoned in St. Augustine, Florida, during a part of the Revolution.

Dr. Johnson went as a lad to schools and the College of Charleston, taking at the latter two medals for Greek and Latin, which are still in possession of some of his descendants. From the College of Charleston he went to the University of Pennsylvania from which he received the degree of doctor of medicine in 1797. His graduating essay was "An Experimental Inquiry into the Properties of Carbonic Acid Gas or Fixed Air; Its Mode of Operation, Use in Disease, Most Effectual Method of Relieving Animals Affected by it." He returned to Charleston where he practised for many years.

He was president of the Medical Society of South Carolina in 1808 and 1809, and practised for about fifty years in Charleston.

On the fifth of October, 1802, he married Catherine Bonneau, the fourth daughter of Francis and Hannah Elfe Bonneau and had fifteen children. Their third child, Francis, became a doctor.

Joseph Johnson died at the house of his twelfth child, the Rev. R. P. Johnson, in Pineville, South Carolina, October 6, 1862, aged eighty-six years.

Among Dr. Johnson's important writings are;

"Oration" delivered before the Medical Society of South Carolina at the anniversary meeting, December 24, 1807, and published at their request.

"On the Properties and Uses of Eufatoria." ("Charleston Medical Journal.")

"Some Account of the Origin and Prevention of Yellow Fever in Charleston, South Carolina." (Ibid., 1849, vol. iv.)

"The Traditions and Reminiscences of the Revolution," published in 1851. This, the most important of his works, is a book of great historical value.

"Observation on the Uses of Hydrocyanic Acid in the Treatment of Pneumonia and Phthsis." "Charleston Medica Journal," September, 1853, vol. viii.)

"The Alleged Connection Between the Phases of the Moon and Quantity of Rain." (Ibid., July, 1854, vol. ix.)

F. B. J.

A short biography may be found in "Eminent and Representative Men of Carolina." Several portaits are in possession of his descendants and one is in the South Carolina Hall at Charleston, South Carolina.

Johnson, Laurence (1845–1893).

Laurence Johnson was born in South Butler, Wayne County, New York, June 7, 1845, and died of pneumonia in New York City, March 18, 1893. His father, the Hon. Thomas Johnson, was a native of Saratoga and of Scotch descent, while his mother's ancestors were from the North of Ireland.

His education until his sixteenth year was gained in the "district school," after which he became a student in Falley Seminary, at Fulton, Oswego County, at that time one of the best academies in the state. Those who knew young Johnson then declared that he was an excellent student, his delight being the study of the natural sciences, especially chemistry and microscopy. In the winter of 1862 he taught a district school. When President Lincoln issued a new call for men, Laurence abandoned his school and enlisted in Company A, Ninth New York Heavy Artillery. His first service was in the defense of Washington. The war being closed, he tendered his resignation, May 9, 1865. His interest in military affairs remained unabated, and in his library is one of the most complete lists of histories of the Civil War to be found in any private or public collection.

He became a student in the Bellevue Hospital Medical College, from which he received the degree of Doctor of Medicine in 1868, and at once began practice in that city. The artistic tendencies of his mind led him to apply to the American Academy of Design for instruction. He was told that if he would make an acceptable drawing of the human foot he would be admitted as a student for a year, with the welcome condition of free tuition. Although he had never received any instruction in drawing, he undertook the task. After many attempts his work was accepted, and he became an enthusiastic student of the Academy. He soon became proficient, and was offered a position as instructor in anatomical drawing, which, however, was not accepted. In his "Medical Botany" the colored plates are from water colors of his own, and they are models of superb execution.

Early in his medical career he was appointed attending physician to the Northwestern Dispensary; in 1875 he became attending physician to Demilt Dispensary, in the department of diseases of the digestive organs, and was also connected for a time with the Hospital for the Ruptured and Crippled. He was a member of the medical staff of the Randall's Island Hospital for several years, a position which he resigned in order to become one of the visiting physicians to Gouverneur Hospital, a position held at the time of his death. The trustees of the University of the City of New York elected him lecturer on medical botany in the Medical School, and afterwards appointed him professor of clinical medicine.

Dr. Johnson was not a prolific writer, but his literary work was of a character which required accuracy and the most painstaking and judicial scrutiny of every detail. His book on "Medical Botany," to which allusion has been made, was in a marked degree original work, and occupies a high rank as a text-book. The American edition of Phillips' "Materia Medica and Therapeutics" was edited by him, and also a "Medical Formulary," one of William Wood & Company's Library of the series of 1881.

His reputation as an expert in medical botany and materia medica led to his selection as one of the members of the Committee of Revision of the United States Pharmacopœia of 1880, a position involving so much attention to the minutest details that it is difficult to understand how a man who had secured so large a practice could have found the time for such a task.

He was president of the Medical Society of the State of New York in 1886 and re-elected in 1887.

He married Ada Rowe of Wayne County in 1872 and a son and daughter survived him.

Tr. Med. Soc. of N. Y., 1894 (Daniel Lewis).

Johnston, Christopher (1822–1891).

Christopher Johnston, surgeon, was of Scotch descent. His grandfather emigrated to Baltimore in 1766 and Christopher was born in that city September 27, 1822, his mother, Miss Elizabeth Gates, daughter of Maj. Lemuel Gates. On the death of his father in 1835 he was adopted by an aunt and was educated at St. Mary's College, Baltimore, afterwards studying medicine with Dr. John Buckler, receiving his M. D. at Maryland University in 1844, and the same year visiting Europe. In 1847 he joined with Charles Frick and others in founding the Maryland Medical Institute, an excellent preparatory school, "organized to elevate the standard of office instruction in accordance with the design of the National Medical Convention." From 1853 to 1855 he was again in Europe studying in the hospitals of Paris and Vienna, and on his return he was appointed lecturer on experimental physiology and microscopy and curator of the Museum at the University of Maryland. In 1857 he resigned this post to take the professorship of anatomy in the Baltimore College of Dental Surgery, where he remained until 1864. The battle of Gettysburg saw Johnston's aiding on the field rendering zealous service to the wounded. On January 1, 1864, he became professor of anatomy and physiology in the University of Maryland, and from 1869 to 1881 he held the chair of surgery as successor to Prof. Nathan R. Smith.

Dr. Johnston early manifested a strong taste for scientific study and research, acquiring great expertness as a microscopist and a skilled artist. One of his earliest papers was on the "Auditory Apparatus of the Mosquito" ("London Quarterly Journal of Microscopical Science," 1855.) He was a frequent contributor to scientific and medical literature, his largest work being that on "Plastic Surgery" ("Ashhurst's International Encyclopedia of Surgery," 1881).

He was slow and careful in his operations, and ingenious in devising expedients. He was the first surgeon in Maryland to remove the upper jaw complete, 1873. (In Jameson's classical operation—1820—the roof of the antrum was left) and to operate for exstrophy of the bladder (1876). He assisted in founding the Maryland Academy of Sciences and the Medical and Chirurgical Faculty, and was consulting surgeon to the Johns Hopkins and other hospitals. The Johns Hopkins University, its museums and laboratories had much of his thought and he bequeathed to it his medical and surgical instruments, his microscopical cabinet, his cabinet of crystals, and his library.

Dr. Johnston's personal appearance was striking with his commanding figure and graceful carriage, his large and classic head. He died October 11, 1891, from an attack of diphtheria contracted in operating.

He married Miss Sallie C. Smith, daughter of Benjamin Price Smith, of Washington, District of Columbia; she died a few years before him. They had four sons; the eldest, Christopher, became professor of oriental

history and archeology in the Johns Hopkins University. E. F. C.

Cordell's Annals of Maryland, 1903 (port.).

Johnston, William Patrick (1811–1876).

He was the son of Col. James and Ann Marion Johnston, and born October 24, 1876 in Savannah. He graduated at Yale, and at Philadelphia studied medicine under Prof. William Horner, and while in the drug store of Samuel Griffith acquired a practical knowledge of materia medica and pharmacy. After graduating M. D. in 1836 at the University of Pennsylvania he was appointed a resident physician at Blockley Hospital, Philadelphia.

In 1837 he was appointed physician to the Philadelphia Dispensary, and took charge of the Southwestern District, but in the autumn he went to Europe till 1840; the greater part of the time being spent in Paris hospitals acquiring a knowledge of special diseases.

His marriage to Miss Hool, of Alexandria, Virginia, induced him to settle, in 1840, in Washington and he was elected professor of surgery in the National Medical College, District of Columbia, but in 1845 was transferred to the chair of obstetrics and diseases of women and children. He joined with the other members of the faculty in establishing the Washington Infirmary. After the close of the war of 1861–5 he resumed his course on obstetrics until he resigned in 1871. He was then made emeritus professor, and on the death of Dr. Thomas Miller, became president of the faculty.

He was one of the originators of the Pathological Society of Washington in 1841 and vice-president of the American Medical Association in 1866. Dr. Johnston was the first physician in Washington to devote special attention to the diseases of women, but he never abandoned general practice.

He died of chronic heart disease October 24, 1876, and two of his sons followed their father's profession. D. S. L.

" In Memoriam, Board of Directors, Children's Hospital, Washington, 1876." Trans. Amer. Med. Assoc., 1878, xxix.
Busey, Reminiscences.

Johnston, Wyatt Galt, (1859-1902). Wyatt Galt Johnston died June 19, 1902, in the forty-third year of his age. He was the son of Dr. J. B. Johnston of Sherbrooke, Quebec, and in December, 1905, married Julia, daughter of the late Michael Turnor of Rugely, England. He received his early education at Bishop's College, Lennoxville, and began to study medicine in McGill University in 1880, graduating in 1884. As a student he showed especial aptitude for pathology and was a constant associate of William Osler. After graduating he was resident medical officer in the Montreal General Hospital for one year and in 1885 he worked in Virchow's laboratory in Berlin, the following year carrying on research into pernicious anemia with Prof. Grawitz at Greifswald, upon a subsequent visit to Germany working at comparative pathology in Munich. Returning to England, he continued his studies at the Zoological Gardens in London. His first university appointment was demonstrator of pathology at McGill, where he did the work unaided for four years. For personal reasons he resigned this post but continued to work in the Montreal General Hospital devoting himself to bacteriology and medico-legal work.

Dr. Johnston's first important public work was a bacteriological study of the water supply of Montreal and of surface water generally. In 1895 he was appointed lecturer in bacteriology in McGill University; bacteriologist for the provincial board of health; and medico-legal expert for the district of Montreal, in 1897 being made assistant professor in public health and lecturer in medico-legal pathology.

His death on June 19, 1902, when only forty-three, was due to septic poisoning acquired in the autopsy room of the Montreal General Hospital in February. He received a second infection in April, when a thrombus appeared in the internal saphenous vein of the left leg. This was followed by extensive coagulation which extended to the iliac veins of both sides and the immediate cause of death was pulmonary embolism.

Prof. Johnston had a full knowledge of the whole literature of pathology and allied subjects, his success laying in his originality, inventiveness, and discovery of the simplest and most direct methods. When any new one was announced he often found a new and a better one. For example, he devised a rapid and convenient method for collecting samples of water at various depths in such a way as to exclude the possibility of contamination and one of distinguishing and counting the various animalculæ found in surface water. He used hard-boiled eggs for the diagnosis for diphtheria. His modification of the Widal reaction for the diagnosis of typhoid fever by means of dried serum is well known.

For twenty years Dr. Johnston was connected with the medical faculty of McGill University and with the Montreal General Hospital. His status among scientific men as a trustworthy investigator in bacteriology, preventive and legal medicine added greatly to the reputation of his university and hospital, but his written work amounted to some fifty short papers. He was a member of the American Medico-Legal Association.

A. M.

Johnstone, Arthur Weir (1853-1905).

Arthur Weir Johnstone, was born at Paint Lick, near Danville, Kentucky, July 15, 1853. His father was the son of the Rev. Alexander Johnstone, a Presbyterian, well known as a man of extreme Calvinistic views, and a strong upholder of antislavery principles.

Arthur's early education was received at the public schools. He then entered Center College, Danville, where he graduated in 1872. After leaving college he joined a corps of United States engineers, which was employed on a triangulation of a portion of the Mississippi.

He began to study medicine with Dr. John B. Jackson, of Danville, a man with a high reputation for learning, then attended one course of lectures at Tulane University, in 1873, and graduated from the University of New York in 1876, after graduation practising in Danville with Dr. A. R. McKee. This arrangement lasted but a short time, when Johnstone returned to New York and studied for three months in Charles Heitzman's laboratory, while taking a course in diseases of the eye with Knapp in his clinic.

He now returned to a country practice, but again only for a short time. His strong inclination had always led him towards surgery, and becoming interested in gynecology, which was at that time rapidly advancing along bold surgical lines, he determined to pursue this as a specialty. To this end he wrote to Lawson Tait, at Birmingham, England, asking him whether he would receive him as a pupil, and on what terms. It happened that Tait was, at that time, prejudiced against Americans, and on receiving Johnstone's letter he remarked to Greig Smith, who was with him, that he would make his fee so large that it would be prohibitive. He wrote Johnstone, therefore, that his terms were $2,000 for a year. To his surprise, Johnstone at once accepted. A personal acquaintance with Johnstone soon sufficed to obliterate all prejudice and antipathy on Tait's part, and he often subsequently referred to Johnstone as his most promising pupil. Johnstone remained with Tait six months, during which time his paper on "Menstruation," which attracted a great deal of attention, was read before the British Gynecological Society, then sitting in Birmingham.

On Johnstone's return he settled once more in Danville, where he started a private hospital, with the intention of building up an exclusively gynecological practice, and he soon secured patients from all parts of the State. He was, I believe, the first person in Kentucky during this period to operate for extra-uterine pregnancy, after making a diagnosis. It was about this time (1886) that he joined the American Gynecological Society.

About three years later Johnstone formed a partnership with that eminent and much-loved old warrior in the surgical world, Dr. Thaddeus Reamy, of Cincinnati. This association, however, was not a happy one and lasted but a year; after its termination, he opened another private hospital of his own. in Cincinnati, near Mt. Auburn.

In 1897 Dr. Johnstone married Ethel Chamberlin, a daughter of Major W. H. Chamberlin.

In September, 1905, Johnstone was taken ill with what he himself at first supposed was a simple attack of colic; Dr. B. R. Rachford and Dr. Marion Whitacre, however, who were immediately called in, made a diagnosis of appendicitis of a severe character. Dr. E. C. Dudley, of Chicago, operated on September 16; on opening the abdominal cavity he remarked that the case was the most desperate one he had seen. During the ensuing night complications arose, and Dr. Dudley had no sooner reached home than he had to hasten back. Upon reopening the abdomen an intestinal obstruction was found with an acute peritonitis, which made the condition hopeless, and Dr. Johnstone survived this operation only two hours, conscious almost to the last, and assuring those around him that the operation had given him his one chance of recovery.

Dr. Johnstone was always a student and an investigator, and his eagerness was both attractive and contagious. Each year saw him seeking fresh knowledge in various schools and post-graduate courses.

The following is a list of some of his contributions to medical literature:

"Experimental and Microscopic Studies on the Origin of the Blood Globules." ("Archives of Medicine," New York, 1881, vi.)

"The Menstrual Organ." ("British Gynecological Journal," 1887–8, ii.)

"Menopause; Natural and Artificial." ("New York Journal of Obstetrics and Gynecology," 1894, iv.)

"The Relation of Menstruation to Other Reproductive Functions." (".American Journal of Obstetrics," New York, 1895, xxxii.)

"The Function and Pathology of the Reticular Tissue." ("American Gynecological and Obstetrical Journal," 1896, ix.)

"The Endometrium in the Cycle of the Rut." (Read before the British Gynecological Society, 1889.)

"Menstruation: Its Necessity and Purpose."

"Comparative Zoology of Menstruation."

"Clinical Importance of the Menstrual Wave."

"Autointoxication from Defective Menstruation."

"Pathological Aspects of Stevenson's Wave."

"Internal Secretion of the Ovary."

"Etiology of Dermoids of the Ovary and of the Testicle."

"The Infantile Uterus."

"The Anatomy of the Uterus in Horizontal Animals, Showing the Necessity of Menstruation in Vertical Classes." (Read before the International Medical Congress at Rome, 1902.)

"The First Centennial of Ovariotomy." ("Surgery, Gynecology and Obstetrics," 1905, i,

H. A. K.

Trans. Amer. Gyn. Soc., 1906, vol. xxxi.

Johnstone, Robert (1805–1847).

Robert Johnstone was born in Goshen, County Longford, Ireland, in January, 1805, and had the usual elementary education available for lads of his day and locality. At the age of fourteen he was apprenticed to Mr. Martin Ford, an apothecary of Tuan, County Galway, for the term of three years, and in 1823 matriculated in Trinity College, Dublin, where he probably took his M. D. in 1827. His diploma as a member of the Royal College of Surgeons of London bears date June 13, 1828, and is distinguished by the autographs of Sir Astley Cooper, John Abernethy and other celebrities. After some hesitation in deciding upon a place for permanent settlement, Dr. Johnstone finally selected the United States and came here with his wife in 1831, settling first in Cleveland, Ohio, then removing for a year to Millersburg, Ohio, and then returning again to Cleveland. Here he soon built up a good practice and was on the high road to success when he was cut off prematurely by an attack of typhus fever contracted from a patient, which terminated his life July 16, 1847.

Dr. Johnstone's taste was for surgery, rather than medicine, though he practised both. On January 29, 1846, he successfully removed, for a medullary sarcoma, the left superior maxillary bone of a child aged four and one-half years, the son of Daniel Solloway of Cleveland.

H. E. H.

A fine portrait of Dr. Johnstone is in the possession of his son Mr. Arthur Johnstone in Cleveland.

Jones, Ichabod Gibson (1807–1857).

Ichabod Gibson Jones was born in Unity, Waldo County, Maine, in 1807 and died at his home in Columbus, Ohio, in 1857.

In 1831 he came from Maine to Worthington, Ohio, where he remained until 1834, when he removed to Columbus, in which city he lived until 1857.

His tastes inclined him to internal medicine and obstetrics, almost to the exclusion of surgery, which he studied only to attain proficiency in the more common operations incident to parturition.

His primary education was obtained in local schools. At the age of twenty he studied medicine with his uncle, Dr. Gibson, of Boston, and then entered New York University from which, when twenty-four, he obtained the M. D. degree, and in 1831 was appointed teacher of practical medicine and therapeutics in the Eclectic School at Worthington, Ohio, a position held until 1834.

He was tall, very slender; had brown hair, irregular features, and a rather erect carriage. To the stranger his manner was austere and his expression rather that of melancholy, incident perhaps to discomfort from dyspepsia, from which he suffered almost constantly for many years prior to his death.

Through his own suffering he became almost a fanatic on the subject of diet, and often restricted his patients so much that some of them said they were in greater danger from starvation than from their diseases.

He was a vigorous advocate for vaccination, which then as now was opposed by many swayed by prejudice on the hope of notoriety. The opposition came mainly from practitioners of his own school, and Dr. Jones joined the regulars in combating it. He believed that the immunity resulting from thorough impregnation of the system with the vaccine virus is permanent, and that when the first operation is properly performed and the virus active, a second is never necessary— a failure of the first is evidence of lack of care in the performance of the operation, or of the inertness of the virus. In 1833 he married Cynthia Kilbourne, a daughter of Col. James Kilbourne, the founder of the village of Worthington. There were four children: Louisa, James Kilbourne, Emma, and Elizabeth.

Dr. Jones died in Columbus, Ohio, in 1857, from cancer of the stomach.

Through his lectures in the Eclectic school he naturally became interested in botany, writing several papers descriptive of indigenous plants and trees, of which the most notable, perhaps, is a description of the grasses of this region; and he prepared an herbarium of the flora of central Ohio, the only complete work of the kind of his time.

He wrote many papers on professional subjects, and in 1853 published a voluminous work on "Practical Medicine and Therapeutics,"[1] differing from ordinary works of the kind only in treatment, as it embraced the doctrines of the Eclectic school.

S. L.

Biographical Sketch, Address to the Old Northwest Genealogical Soc., 1903, by Starling Loving.

Jones, John (1729-1791).

This man of ordinary name was of some extraordinary ability. He lived before the fashion of double-barrelled appellations and Thacher tells in pompous English how when "Some of the physicians of New York entered into a resolution to distinguish themselves by a particular mode of dressing their hair" John walked about plainly coiffed, refusing the "new-fashioned bob" and was cut in consultation for a while. But, nevertheless, this clever young surgeon made his way.

He was born in Jamaica, Long Island, in 1729, his two grandfathers physicians, his father, Evan, one also. The latter married Mary Stephenson of New York and had four sons, John being the eldest, and very fortunate in all good opportunities for learning. First came medical tutelage under the famous Cadwallader of Philadelphia, then, in London he attended the lectures of John Hunter, and studied under Percival Pott; in Paris under the great French reformers, Petit and Le Dran, and in Edinburgh under the

[1] "The American Eclectic Practice of Medicine," Cincinnati, 1853-4.

elder Monro, taking his M. D. from Rheims University in 1751.

It was as a surgeon he became noted after his settling in New York to practise and his chroniclers note of him that he was the first to do the operation of lithotomy in that city, and that so well as to cause a demand for his services in the middle and eastern states of America. James A. Mease, writing of him, says "he had acquired a facility in operating to which few surgeons have arrived. I have seldom known him more than three minutes in a lithotomy and in the duties of an accoucheur. He became distinguished in colonial annals as surgeon to the troops in the French War of 1758 and on his return was made professor of surgery in the medical school of the College of New York. Asthma, his great enemy, was always troublesome and he took another journey to Europe and found living in London fog to give alleviation and no doubt, he also, had great joy in freshening up his mental side in visiting his old surgical masters.

Like most of the profession, he did good service during the war and having to go to Philadelphia, he found his asthma so much better in that place that he stopped there and was made a physician to the Pennsylvania Hospital when Redman resigned in 1780. He attended Franklin in his last illness but in 1791 was himself summoned by death if it can be called a "summons" when the illness is brought about by one of those acts of unselfish carelessness which are done by busy doctors. He died in June from the result of chill and when good hopes were entertained of his recovery, was found dead in bed.

His best work, and that for which he is commonly quoted, is his "Plain, Concise, Practical Remarks on the Treatment of Wounds and Fractures," New York, 1775, reprinted in Philadelphia in the following year with Van Swieten on the "Diseases Incident to Armies and Gunshot Wounds." This little book became the *vade mecum* of continental surgeons during the Revolutionary War. Jones attempted little more in it than to condense the teachings of Pott and Le Dran, but there are a few notes of originality, the most conspicuous being a case of trephining in delirium eighty days after a slight head injury. The dura was opened and drained and the patient recovered.

This book was the first written on Surgery in the United States.

From a sketch in Surgical Memoirs, J. G. Mumford, 1908, and one by Dr. James Mease in Thacher's Medical Biography.

Jones, Johnston Blakely (1814–1889).

Among those who have given life and talents wholly to the good and upbuilding of North Carolina, none did more than Johnston B. Jones, who was born in Chatham County, North Carolina, September 12, 1814. His father, Edward Jones, a native of Ireland, was a lineal descendant of Jeremy Taylor and came to North Carolina when young and attained prominence as a lawyer, serving as solicitor-general to the state for over thirty years.

Johnston Jones received his early education in Raleigh, under a noted educator, Mr. Joseph G. Cogswell, afterwards spending several years at the University of North Carolina but not taking a degree. He began his medical studies in Charleston, South Carolina, but owing to delicate health was advised to go abroad, so, choosing Paris, he studied medicine for two years. During his student days in the French capital he was known as "the handsome American"—in fact, from youth to age he was remarkable for a physical beauty which seemed but the outward expression of the luminous mind within. At the expiration of his stay in Paris he made a six months' tour of Scotland and Ireland, visiting kinsfolk and friends. Soon after his return to America he took his degree in medicine at the Charleston College.

In 1841 he began to practise in the little town of Chapel Hill, the home of the State University, where he remained until 1868, then removed to the city of Charlotte where he practised until his death, March 1, 1889.

He died a poor man so far as worldly goods go, but rich in the respect and love of those who had known his kindness and experienced the benefit of his skill.

He was one of the prime movers in the organization of the North Carolina Medical Society, and always took the deepest interest in its welfare.

His mind was acute, vigorous, original and analytic; and to great professional learning he added extensive and accurate information on many subjects. His patience and sympathy made his services as grateful to the feelings of his patients as his great skill made him useful to his necessities. The wife of a prominent North Carolinian went to Philadelphia, not long after the Civil War, to consult the celebratd Dr. Agnew who, when he learned that she was from North Carolina, said there was one in her own state, Johnston B. Jones, who could surpass him, and added that she would have done well to consult him.

In 1841 he married Ann Stuart, and was survived by two sons and two daughters, one of whom became Dr. Simmons B. Jones of Charlotte, North Carolina.

L. T. R.

"Cyclopedia of Representative Men of the Carolinas," vol. ii (Brant and Fuller, 1892).

Jones, Joseph (1833–1896).

Best known for his writings on "Diseases in the Southern States," Joseph Jones was born on September 6, 1833, in Liberty County, Georgia, the son of the Rev. Charles and Mary Jones Jones. As a lad he had private tuition and five years at the University of South Carolina, Columbia, tak-

ing his A. M. from Princeton College, New Jersey, and his M. D. from the University of Pennsylvania in 1855. The University of Georgia gave him her LL. D. in 1892. The Savannah Medical College chose him as her professor of chemistry in 1858, but three years after he was one year professor of natural philosophy and natural theology in the University of Athens, Georgia, then professor of chemistry in the Medical College of Georgia, Augusta. During the war he was six months in the cavalry and for the rest of the time full surgeon-major in the Confederate Army.

Keen in his studies of disease, he made investigations in most of the southern states, being more in the center of things by his service as professor of chemistry and clinical medicine in the university of Louisiana and as president of the board of health in that state. He had the usual pleasant time given to all sanitary inspectors, especially at the ports. After a continuous battle of four years with the maritime and railroad interests the court voted quarantine to be a legitimate exercise of police rights. The whole life of Dr. Jones was devoted to the thankless task of promoting civic and military hygiene in the city. His writings, too numerous to mention, included "Digestion of Albumen and Flesh," 1856; "Physical, Chemical and Physiological Investigations on Solids and Fluids of Animals," 1856 (his M. D. thesis); "View to Ascertain the Action of Saline Solutions, etc.," 1856; "Observations on the Chemical, Physical and Pathological Phenomena of Malarial Fever," 1859; "Sulphate of Quinina administered during Health, etc," 1861; "Inquiries on Hospital Gangrene," 1869; "Explorations and Researches concerning the Destruction of the Aboriginal Inhabitants of America by Various Diseases, etc.," 1878; "Observations on the Losses of the Confederate Armies from Wounds, etc.," 1861; "Contributions to the Natural

History of Specific Yellow Fever,"
1874; "Medico-legal Evidence relating to the detection of Human Blood presenting the Alterations characteristic of Malarial Fever on the Clothing of a Man," 1876; "Observations on the African Yaws and Leprosy," 1877; "Sanitary Memoirs of the United States Sanitary Commission," New York, 1890; "Medical and Surgical Memoirs;" "Con tributions to Teratology," 1888; "Explorations of the Aboriginal Remains in Tennessee." It can be imagined that such a widely interested man was foremost in founding the Southern Historical Society. He was also honorary member of the Virginia Medical Society; of the Physicians and Surgeons of Philadelphia. and member of the Louisiana Medical Society and of several other societies.

He married, in 1858, Caroline S. Davis of Augusta, Georgia, and two years after her death in 1868, Susan Rayner Polk, daughter of the Bishop of Louisiana. His eldest son, Stanhope, became a doctor but died in 1894. Five of his other children were Charles Colcock, Hamilton Polk, Caroline Mary Cuthbert, Frances Devereux and Laura Maxwell.

D. W.

Jour. Am. Med. Ass., Chicago, 1896, vol. xxvi.

N. Orl. Med. and Surg. Jour., 1895-6, n. s., vol. xxiii.

Tr. Louisiana Med. Soc., N. Orl., 1896.

Tr. Med. Soc. Virg., Rich., 1896.

Jones, Nelson E. (1821–1901).

Nelson E. Jones, son of Henry Jones, was born at "Fruit Hill," Liberty Township, Ross County, Ohio, September 20, 1821. His great grandfather came to America towards the end of 1700.

Nelson was one of nine children, and was from birth a delicate child. As he grew in years, unable to follow the pursuits of the farm, he was encouraged to educate himself for a profession. After finishing at the country school near his home, he attended

Augusta College in Kentucky for a time, but his health compelled him to return home, where he studied by himself until 1844, when he entered Hudson College. Again obliged to quit study on account of sickness, he returned to Chillicothe and entered the office of his family physician, Dr. Wills. In 1845 he graduated from Hudson College, and for a short time was associated with Dr. Kirtland in the practice of medicine in Cleveland, Ohio. Late in the year 1845 he went to Dubuque, Iowa, and afterwards to Jacksonville, then Guttenberg, Clayton County, Iowa. Here was advertised a city settled by the Dutch, and glowing accounts of the prospect attracted him. In this town he had the field to himself, too much so in fact, as the following extract from an old letter will show:

"No beginner in a new field could ask for a brighter outlook. I am busy from morning until night, and often from night until morning; many days I am in the saddle the greater part of the time, as patients sometimes live thirty or more miles apart. There is a loneliness about this life, however, which does not attract me, and, as I wrote you before, there is a young lady in Cleveland that I very much desire to see, so you may expect me before long."

The following June, 1846, he married Virginia Smith, daughter of Anson Smith, of New London, Connecticut. He then moved to Londonderry in Ross County, and afterwards settled in Circleville.

His mind was active and unimpaired to the last, and he passed much of his later years in writing stories of the olden time and of the early days of medicine. He published one small volume called the "Squirrel Hunters of Ohio" and one on the "Nests and Eggs of the Birds of Ohio," illustrated by his daughter and wife.

In nearly the half century of medical study and practice to which he diligently applied himself in Circleville and the adjoining country, he was known as a gifted writer and debater, and the county medical society, which he helped organize and maintain, profited much by his experience and writings.

H. J.

Jones, Ralph Kneeland (1823–1888).

If an abundance of medical instruction be of value to a physician in his practical life, then Ralph Kneeland Jones should have been a successful practitioner of medicine. As such he was generally regarded in the three localities in which he spent his busy life. He was born in Stockbridge, Massachusetts, July 13, 1823, the son of Samuel Jones and Abby Maria Gilbert his wife. He traced his New England ancestry back to Thomas Jones who settled in Guilford, Connecticut, in 1639.

He studied medicine with Dr. Lucius Smith Adams of Stockbridge, and finally took his degree at the Harvard Medical School in 1847. His talents as a student were so marked that he attracted the attention of the faculty, and was immediately upon graduating chosen house pupil at the Massachusetts General Hospital.

When Dr. Jones finished his term of eighteen months in the hospital, he settled eventually to practice at Holme's Hole in Martha's Vineyard, and during his leisure hours he wrote some medical papers, one of which, a very curious "Case of Stone in the Bladder of a Child," was printed in the "Boston Medical and Surgical Journal." He gave considerable attention to uterine diseases and always liked that branch of practice better than general practice. He married Octavia Ann Yale Norris of Tisbury, Massachusetts, who descended from the Mayhews, an old "Vineyard" family, and had four children, one of whom became a doctor.

With a view to giving his children better educational advantages, Dr. Jones

moved to Bangor, Maine, in 1857, and was soon held in high esteem both as a man and as a physician. He became one of the most active members of the Penobscot County Medical Society, and among other papers he composed for its meetings was an excellent article on "Malpractice Suits," and as orator of the Maine Medical Association he delivered a charming address on "The Limitations of Medicine," arguing that therapeutic nihilism was unfit for any one who wished to be considered as a practitioner of medicine.

Dr. Jones had a serious fall upon the icy streets of Bangor in the winter of 1886, and from that time onwards he was far from strong. He attended to his patients as well as he was able, and often worked harder than he should have done. Symptoms of lateral spinal sclerosis became evident in the early summer of 1888, and on the twenty-eighth of August of that year he died. In a quiet way he had labored hard, and done much good as a friend and as a physician.

J. A. S.

Transactions of the Maine Medical Association.
Transactions of the Penobscot County Medical Association.

Jones, Toland (1820–1894).

Son of Thomas Jones, a native of Worcester County, Maryland, and Mary F. Truitt, a native of the eastern shore of Maryland, he was born on a farm in Madison County, Ohio, January 10, 1820, and at the age of twenty entered Denison University, Granville, Ohio, but left before the completion of his course, without a degree. On leaving Denison he studied with Dr. Aquila Toland, of London, and at the end of the customary three years, matriculated in the Medical College of Ohio at Cincinnati with the intention of taking his M. D., but left the college at the close of his first year and practised in London, Ohio. Some years later the M. D. was conferred on him by Cleveland Medical College, Ohio, in recognition of his skill in surgery, the particular event being a successful amputation at the hip-joint.

He was a member of the Madison County Medical Society, and the Ohio State Medical Society.

In 1862 he entered the army as a private soldier in "A" Company, one hundred and thirteenth Ohio Volunteer Infantry, was soon promoted to a captaincy, and before his term of service expired became colonel of the regiment. He took part in the battles of Chickamauga, Chattanooga, Kenesaw Mountain, Atlanta, and Jonesville, marched with Sherman to the sea, and after the war returned to London and resumed practice.

In 1846 he married Frances A. Toland, daughter of Dr. Aquila Toland, and had four children, William Pitt, Imogene, Eva, and Bessie. William Pitt graduated M. A. from Dartmouth College and began to study medicine under his father, but died soon after. His wife and the daughters survived the doctor who died on the sixteenth of February, 1894, at his house in London, Ohio. The cause was uncomplicated lobar pneumonia, which ran a brief course and caused little suffering.

S. L.

Jones, Walter (1745–1815).

Born in Northampton County, Virginia, he was educated at William and Mary College, graduating in 1760 and studying medicine at, and graduating M. D., from the University of Edinburgh, in 1769, the subject of his thesis being "De Dysenteria." He is said to have been held in high esteem by Cullen and his other professors, and was described as "the most shining young gentleman of his profession in Edinburgh, and one who would make a great figure wherever he went." He settled and practised in his native county, and maintained

the highest standing as a physician and scholar, and on April 11, 1777, received the appointment from Congress of physician-general to the hospitals of the Middle Military Department, but held the position only two months, resigning the first of July following. He was elected to and served in Congress in 1797–99, and in 1803–11.

It was said of him by an intimate acquaintance that "for the variety and extent of his learning, the originality and strength of his mind, the sagacity of his observations, and captivating powers of conversation, he was one of the most extraordinary men he had ever known. He seemed to possess instinctively the faculty of discerning the hidden cause of disease, and applying with promptness and decision peculiar to himself the appropriate remedies."

He left one son, Walter, when he died on his plantation in Northumberland County, Virginia, on December 31, 1815.

Medical Men of the Revolution, J. M. Toner
Encyclopedia of Amer. Biography.

Joyce, Robert Dwyer (1828–1883).

Robert Dwyer Joyce was born in Limerick County, Ireland, in 1828. The Joyce family, from which Robert Dwyer Joyce was descended, had established itself not far from the city Limerick, and at the time of the poet-physician's birth was living in Glen Oisin.

Dr. Joyce received his early education at an ordinary country school and Queen's College, Cork, and after teaching for some time studied medicine in the same city. During this period he dipped into poetry occasionally and there was a clear pre-figurement of his future poetic career. In the "Dublin Freeman's Journal." We read of him:

"During the interval between 1857 and 1865 he lived first in Cork and afterwards in Dublin, and supported himself partly by writing and partly by the prizes and scholarships of the college, for he never competed for a scholarship he did not win."

For a time, while in Dublin, he devoted himself to medical practice, as far as it came to him, and to medical study while still continuing to devote himself to literature. For a time he was professor of English literature at the preparatory college of the Catholic University in Dublin.

He seems to have realized that the opportunities open to him in Ireland were rather limited, in his profession at least, and accordingly when about thirty-five he came to this country and settled in Boston, and it was not long before he had a c q u i r e d a good practice, when he set himself once more to the cultivation of literature. His first venture of any ambition was a volume of " Ballads, Songs and Romances." In the meantime he had written a prose work called "Legends of the Wars in Ireland." Some of these charming old poetic legends introduce historical matter of considerable importance. On the other hand some of them reflect his professional interest. "Rosaline, the White" for instance is the kind of pseudo-medical story with which Conan Doyle began his career as a writer of fiction. Joyce's real triumph as a literary man did not come until the publication of "Deirdre, an Irish Epic." About three years after " Deirdre" a second long poem entitled " Blanid" was published. This was his last work. It was published in 1879, when its author was in his fifty-second year, and further works of even higher order were confidently anticipated from him by his friends. Dr. Joyce's health began seriously to fail about the middle of the year 1882. He died peacefully on the evening of the twenty-fourth of October, 1883.

M. K. K.

Abridged from a biography by James J. Walsh, M. D., LL. D.

Joynes, Levin S., (1819–1881).

He was born in Accomac County, Virginia, on May 13, 1819, and at the age of sixteen years graduated A. B. from Washington College, Pennsylvania.

After spending two years at the University of Virginia, he began the study of medicine, first attending lectures at the University of Pennsylvania, and afterwards at the University of Virginia, from which he graduated M. D. in 1839.

He was president of the American Medical Association in 1858 and of the Medical Society of Virginia in 1878–9.

After graduating he went to Europe and spent two and a half years attending lectures, chiefly in Dublin and Paris. Returning to his native county in 1843, he settled there, and the following year removed to Baltimore, from which city he was called to Philadelphia, in 1846, to assume the professorship of physiology and legal medicine in the Franklin Medical College. In 1849 he returned to his own county, and took up practice again. This he continued to do until he was elected professor of the institutes of medicine and of medical jurisprudence in the Medical College of Virginia in 1855. He was elected, in 1856, dean of the faculty, and held these two positions until the end of the session of 1870–1, when, on account of failing health, he resigned. When the Civil War became imminent, he gave his allegiance to his native state, but always a conservative, and, having accepted the position of assistant surgeon in the forces of Virginia, he resigned when the Medical Department of the Confederacy was thoroughly organized.

He was an instructive and accomplished teacher; a perfect encyclopedia of knowledge, his authority on all medical subjects rarely questioned, and never, to the writer's knowledge, worsted in debate.

He was twice married. In December, 1854, to Rosa F. Bayly, of Richmond, who died in 1855, and in June, 1858, to Susan V. Archer, also of that city, who, with one son, survived her husband.

He died at his home on January 18, 1881, of malignant disease of the antrum and surrounding parts.

His writings extended through his whole professional career. The following are some of them:

"Obstetrical Auscultation." ("American Journal of Medical Sciences," January. 1845.)
"Emphysema of the Cellular Tissues in Labor." (Ibid January, 1852.)
"Ancient Superstition." (The Stethoscope." October, 1851.)
"Obstruction of the Intestinal Canal by Worms." (Ibid., January, 1851.)
"The Legal Relations of the *Fetus in Utero.*" ("Virginia Medical Journal," September, 1856.)
"Physiological Position of Fibrine," (Ibid., May, 1859.)
"Hemorrhagic Malarial Fever." ("Richmond and Louisville Medical Journal," March, 1877.)
"Medical History." ("Virginia Medical Monthly," vol. i.)
"Infantile Paralysis." (Ibid., vol. iv.)
These and many others were his contributions, all of which showed the marks of through preparation in the study of the subject and exactness of the manuscript.

R. M. S

Dr. J. N. Upshur's "Medical Reminiscences of Richmond." etc.
Trans. Med. Soc. of Va., 1881, Va. Med. Monthly, February, 1881.

Judd, Gerrit Parmele (1803–1873).

A medical missionary, he was born in Paris, Oneida County, New York, April 23, 1803, a seventh descendant of Thomas Judd, of Kent, England, who came to America in 1634 and was one of the founders of Farmington, Connecticut.

He attended lectures at Fairfield, Herkimer County, New York, from 1820–1825, and also studied with his father, Dr. Elnathan Judd.

He was a member of the Medical Society of the College of Physicians and Surgeons of the Western District, New York.

In 1827, with fourteen associates, he sailed from Boston in the brig "Parthian." This was the second reinforcement of missionaries of the American Board of Commissioners for Foreign Missions to the Sandwich Islands. This 18,000 mile voyage lasted for 145 days. They arrived at Honolulu March 31, 1828. He entered the service of the Hawaiian Government May 10, 1842. The motive which induced him to take this step was a desire to be more useful to the nation for whose welfare he had left his native land; the fact of Mr. Richards being about to visit Europe, the absolute necessity that someone should aid the king and chiefs in conducting their affairs with foreigners, and the impossibility of their procuring any other secular man with a knowledge of the native language to aid them. "My business was to organize the finances in conjunction with Haalilio" and John Ii. Haalilio went with Mr. Richards and took his place in the treasury board. We had to learn book-keeping in the native language and pay off innumerable debts.

"February 25, 1843. The islands were ceded to Great Britain for the time being and until the decision of the British Government could be made known in relation to the demands of Lord George Paulet, Saturday: on the following Tuesday, February 28, by the request of Lord George Paulet I was appointed by the king to be his deputy to act in the British Commission appointed by him for the government of the Islands, viz., R. H. Lord George Paulet, Lieut. Frere, C. F. Makay, G. P. Judd.

"I suffered much from weakness of the eyes and in the course of the year lost entirely the sight of my left eye, while it was almost impossible with the right to see either to read or to write. The blindness proved to be a cataract and liable to affect the other eye at some future time."

The following anecdote is related of him: A number of cannon planted on an extinct crater back of the town of Honolulu were used to fire salutes. On one occasion a cannon exploded, severely injuring a native. Dr. Judd responded to the call for help and with his amputating instruments rode his horse up the face of the crater in order to render aid as soon as possible. This was considered quite a feat as the course chosen had theretofore been considered impossible for a horse.

On his arrival in 1828 at Honolulu, island of Oahu, he began immediately to fill his duties as the attending physician of the mission. He performed many surgical operations which were the first of their kind that had been attempted. At the end of ten years he had thoroughly mastered the Hawaiian language and edited a small book called the "Anatomia" of some sixty pages with nineteen plates illustrating the intricacies of the human body, which he in conjunction with a native had drawn and engraved. This work was remarkable in the number of new Hawaiian words coined, as the ignorance of the Hawaiian in regard to the human body made it impossible otherwise to describe it. The "Hawaiian Spectator" of April, 1838, vol. i, page 13, contains an account written by the doctor of the climate and healthfulness of these islands, as evidenced by his ten years' experience among the natives and foreigners. He points out that owing to the cool sea breezes the temperature never becomes excessive and from the small variation in temperature the islands were certainly healthful.

He married Laura Fish of Clintorn New York State, September 20, 1827, by whom he had nine children, all born in Honolulu.

He died in the coral stone house which he had built in Honolulu and named "Sweet Home," July 12, 1873, of apoplexy.

(Genealogical Record of the Judd Family, the Hastings Family, Record and References in numerous encyclopedias.)
Personal communication from his son

K

Kane, Elisha Kent (1820–1856).

Elisha Kent Kane, explorer, scholar, scientist, was born on the third of February, 1820, in Walnut Street, Philadelphia, the eldest of the seven children born to John Kent, jurist, and Jane Leiper Kane. The spirit of adventure and daring seems to have been in him from his cradle and the embryo scientist was unappreciated by worried schoolmasters and received as a boy that which is often reserved for old savants, a good many hard knocks. He had the free life of a country lad and when sixteen was sent to the University of Virginia, but functional heart trouble interfered considerably with his work. He had the good luck to study natural science under Prof. Rogers, engaged just then on the geology of the Blue Mountains, and accompanied him in his journeyings. An attack of rheumatism and drawing nigh to death was his next campaign, then a determined effort for an M. D. degree, which he took with highest honors from the University of Pennsylvania after studying under Dr. William Harris. Boyish in appearance, not yet twenty-one, he was made resident physician in the Pennsylvania Hospital, Blockley, and found time to explore still further than his colleagues the nature of a new substance found in the renal secretion which M. Nauche of Paris had named Kyestein and announced as a final test in cases of suspected utero-gestation. The result of the Blockley Hospital research was published in the "Medical Intelligencer," March, 1841, but Kane shortly after wrote a thesis on the subject in which, as Dr. Samuel Jackson said, that which was still a matter of controversy was investigated and permanently settled.

In 1843 Kane became assistant surgeon in the United States Navy. He served in China, on the coast of Africa, in Mexico (where he was wounded), in the Mediterranean and on the first Grinnell Arctic expedition in the search for Franklin. The ships met with many disasters and Kane's medical skill did much to help and hearten the scurvy-stricken crew. He also joined the second expedition in 1853 with Dr. Isaac I. Hays as surgeon. The Advance touched at various Greenland points to obtain Esquimaux recruits and finally reached 78° 43′ north, the highest point attained by a sailing vessel. In 1855, after tremendous hardships including desertion by a Danish crew, Kane was obliged to abandon the ship and by indefatigable exertions succeeded in moving his boats and sick some sixty miles to the open sea. He reached Cape York and successfully arrived at Upernavik in August. The explorer and his companions were enthusiastically received here. Arctic medals were authorized by Congress and the Queen's medal presented to officers and men. Kane had the Founders medal of 1856 from the Royal Geographical Society and that of 1858 from the Société de Géographie. The chart exhibiting the discoveries of the expedition was at first issued without Kane's name attached to any land or sea it embraced, but Col. Force, exercising his authority in the distribution of honors, had Kane's Sea printed on a body of water between Smith's Strait and Kennedy Channel.

His health had been terribly broken by hardships endured, and in the hope of recovering he went to England where London fogs did not improve matters. He set out, crippled by rheumatism, on a painful journey to Cuba where his mother and brother joined him, but after a few weeks of pleasure in their company and much pain in his body, this heroic young navigator set out in that ship which sails into the land of shadows and does not return.

Of his marriage there is no public record, but there is extant a curious little volume called "The Love-life of Dr. Kane," containing the correspondence and a history of the acquaintance, engagement and secret marriage between Elisha K. Kane and Margaret Fox (1866). Truly the warm glow of affection in the letters forms a good contrast to any other account of Kane's life story found in his "United States Grinnell Expedition" (1854) or in the second volume in 1856. Yet a third aspect of him, in his home life, may be gained by reading William Elder's "Biography" of him right away from his boyhood's days to that on which men of science and art and rich and poor marched sorrowfully beside the coffin of this good man.

D. W.

Biog. of Elisha Kent Kane, W. Elder, Phila., 1858.
Charleston, Med. Jour., 1857, xii.
Appleton's Cyclopedia of Am. Med. Biog.
The Love-life of Dr. Kane, N. York, 1866.

Kearsley, John, Sr. (1685–1772).

He emigrated from England to Pennsylvania in 1711, and acquired a very large practice in Philadelphia where he had for apprentices Drs. Zachary, Redman, and Bard. Kearsley was prominent in public affairs, serving as a member of the Pennsylvania Assembly. He also possessed considerable ability as an architect, as shown by Christ Church in the city of Philadelphia, designed by him.

In 1750 Dr. Adam Thomson published his pamphlet entitled "On the Preparation of the Body for the Small-pox." Dr. Kearsley attacked Dr. Thomson's conclusions in a publication entitled "Remarks on a Discourse on Preparing for the Small-pox," which in turn was replied to by Dr. Alexander Hamilton, of Annapolis, Maryland, in "A Defense of Dr. Thomson's Discourse."

Kearsley died in 1772, aged eighty-seven, leaving a large part of his property to found Christ Church Hospital, a still flourishing institution for the support of poor widows who are members of the Episcopal Church. F. R. P.

Keating, John M. (1852–1893).

William V. Keating, professor of obstetrics in the Jefferson Medical College, married in 1851 the daughter of Dr. René La Roche, a writer on yellow fever, and in 1852 their son, John M. Keating, was born in Philadelphia.

From the Polytechnic the lad went to the University of Pennsylvania graduating thence in medicine in 1873 and serving afterwards as resident physician at the Pennsylvania Hospital. As physician to the Blockley Hospital and lecturer there on diseases of children he carried on a good work done by his father and was, moreover, gynecologist to the St. Joseph's Hospital. Mothers and Children, how to make them Healthy and Happy, was the chief life-work and pen-work of the genial John Keating, especially in editing the "Archives of Pediatrics" and "The International Clinics," and in working as the president of the Pediatric Society. He was wholly absorbed by his work and a progressive failure of health which necessitated an annual residence and practice in Colorado was undoubtedly brought about partly by his unsparing use of his energies. When his brief yearly visits to Philadelphia came, if he was asked to go to the hospital he used to say the sight of such an institution made him feel "so horribly homesick." At his last visit he seemed so well that everything seemed on the mend, but a slight cold developed into pneumonia and on November 17, 1893, the kindly and courageous doctor died.

His wife was Edith McCall, daughter of Peter McCall of Philadelphia, and he had three or four daughters and a son.

His most important work was his "Cyclopaedia of Diseases of Children" in which he succeeded in associating with himself many of the best known men of America and England and producing a valuable and representative book. Some of his other works were: "The Mother's Guide;" "Mother and Child;" "Maternity;" "A Dictionary of Medicine;" "Diseases of the Heart and Circulation in Childhood."

Dr. Keating was also a fellow of the University of Pennsylvania and the American and British Gynecological Societies.

Trans. of Coll of Phys. of Phila., 3d series, vol. xvi, 1894.
Arch. Pediat., N. Y., 1893, vol. x (port.).
W. P. Watson.
Tr. Am. Pediat. Soc., N. Y., 1894, vol. vi.
Tr. Am. Gynec Soc , Phila., 1894, vol. xix (E. P. Davis).
Internat. Clinic, Phila , 1894, 3 series, vol. iv.

Kedzie, Robert Clark (1823-1902).

Robert Clark Kedzie was born at Delhi, New York, January 28, 1823. His parents were of Scotch descent and when he was a small lad moved to three hundred acres of virgin forest west of Monroe, Michigan. In 1841, with a barrowed capital of twenty-five dollars, he entered Oberlin College, and on graduating, in 1845, taught in Rochester (Mich.) Academy for two years. In 1851 he graduated in the first class of the medical department of Michigan University and settled in Vermontville, Michigan, until he enlisted for the war. In 1861 he entered the army as surgeon of the Twelfth Regiment of Michigan Volunteers. After the battle of Shiloh he was taken prisoner while caring for his wounded, and on release was so ill that he returned home. On his recovery he accepted the chair of chemistry in the Agricultural College at Lansing and in 1863 moved his family there. He was president of the Michigan State Medical Society in 1874; professor of chemistry, Michigan Agricultural College, 1867. Dr. Kedzie was a large man physically, mentally and morally; large head, high brow, firm chin, prominent nose, blue penetrating eyes, quick in movement and speech, his countenance kindly and expression winning. When he began his work at Lansing there was a widespread belief that the waters in flowing wells lined with iron tubing were magnetic

and their exploitation for gain was common. Dr. Kedzie made an exhaustive study of the phenomena and showed that it was due to the earth's magnetism collected on the metal tubing and not in the water.

Magnetic wells for medicinal purposes vanished, to be heard of no more. He demonstrated that the destruction of lives and property due to explosions of kerosene oil arose from improper methods of detecting explosive grades of oil. He showed the Legislature the proper methods and induced them to pass a law enforcing their adoption, and destruction of life and property ceased. He also conducted the studies which proved that sugar beets would grow profitably in Michigan, thus opening the way for a business of many millions yearly. By sanitary conventions under the direction of the Michigan State Board of Health, he induced every community by its leading citizens to study its own sanitary conditions. Later he promoted farmers institutes, now numbering several hundreds, by which chemical science was applied to little communities of farmers, so helping them to larger prosperity, and some thirty-two valuable papers on "Municipal Health" testify to his keen oversight of the public good. In 1850 Dr. R. C. Kedzie married Harriet Fairchild of Ohio. A son, Frank Kedzie, succeeded his father in the chair of chemistry at the Michigan Agricultural College; the father died November 7, 1902, from apoplexy, at Lansing, Michigan. His valuable papers, chiefly state reports, included:

"Magnetic Conditions of Mineral Wells." ("Detroit Review of Medicine and Pharmacy," vol. vi.)

"Poisonous Paper." ("Report of Michigan State Board of Health," 1873.)

"Meteorology of Central Michigan." ("Transactions of Michigan State Board of Health," 1874.)

"Use of Poisons in Agriculture." (Ibid., 1875.)

"Yellow Fever at Memphis."
(Ibid., 1880.)
"Relations of Soil Water to Health."
("Transactions of Pontiac Sanitary
Convention," 1883.)
                                    L. C.

Representative Men in Mich., West. Biographical Co., Cincin., O., vol. vi.

Keerl, Henry (1755–1827).
Henry Keerl was descended from
an old Bavarian family. He was born
in the town of Mainbernheim, thirteen
miles from Würzburg, in the year
1755, the only child who survived
infancy and was educated by a wealthy
uncle. He completed his medical
studies at Göttingen University and
obtained a commission as surgeon in
one of the Hessian regiments, which
were being hired by the British Government of the petty German poten-
tates to aid in subduing the rebellious
American colonies. But it was destined that he should not see his native
land again.
After the defeat of his Col. Von Rall
the privates and non-commissioned
officers were sent for safety to the interior
of Pennsylvania. The officers petitioned to be permitted to accompany
them, but were sent on the sixth of
January, 1777, to Baltimore, where
they were paroled.
Dr. Keerl spent some time traveling
through the country. With a friend
he visited the Carolinas, where family
tradition asserts they "were solicited
to remain and marry among the rich
widows whose husbands had been
killed in the war." But having formed agreeable acquaintances and finding a favorable opening in Baltimore,
he finally settled and practised, about
1782, and in connection with his profession kept a drug, instrument and
glassware store at the "Sign of the
Golden Swan, upper end of Market
Street, New Congress Hall."
He early became a member of the
Medical and Chirurgical Faculty. He
died July 6, 1827. He was twice

married, first to Anna Maria Myers,
of Baltimore, afterwards to Margaret
Kandel, of Frederick, Maryland, and
left numerous descendants. His life
was spent in the habitual practice of
virtue and piety.   E. F. C.

Johns Hopkins Hosp Bull 1905. xvi.
A picture of him is in the possession of
his family.

Keyser, Peter D. (1835–1897).
Peter D. Keyser was born in Philadelphia, February 8, 1835, obtaining
his collegiate education at the Delaware College, graduating as A. B. in
1852, and later as A. M. He studied
chemistry for two years under Dr.
F. A. Genth of Philadelphia, then
spent several years as a medical student
in Germany, and at the beginning of
the Civil War entered as captain of
the ninety-first Pennsylvania regiment,
until after the battle of Fair Oaks,
when he resigned on account of ill
health and injuries and again visited
Europe, studying medicine in Munich,
taking his degree in 1864 at Jena and
subsequently visiting clinics at Berlin,
Paris, and London. In 1865 he entered upon private practice, and became
surgeon in charge of the Philadelphia
Eye and Ear Hospital, which he had
founded. In 1868, 1870, 1871, 1872,
he delivered courses of lectures on diseases of the eye. For many years he
served as ophthalmological surgeon to
the Wills Eye Hospital. He became
professor of ophthalmology in the
Medico-Chirurgical College of Philadelphia in 1889, and dean of the institution. His writings were numerous
and were chiefly clinical contributions.
After a short illness he died March
9, 1897.   H. F.

Medical Record, vol. li, 1897.

Keyt, Alonzo Thrasher (1827–1885).
Alonzo Thrasher Keyt was born
at Higginsport, Ohio, January 10,
1827, the son of Nathan and Mary
Thrasher Keyt. His father was of
Dutch ancestry, his mother of Quaker

stock—a descendant of Edward Penn, of Pennsylvania. A few years after his birth his father removed to Moscow, Ohio. The boy was educated in Parker's Academy in Felicity, Ohio, and in 1845 he began to study medicine with Dr. William Johnston, of Moscow, matriculating at the Medical College, Ohio, in 1847. He had his M. D. in March, 1848, and in 1849 practised at Moscow, Ohio, but in 1850 removed to Walnut Hills, Cincinnati, where he remained until the end of his life, November 9, 1885.

In manner he was sedate, almost grave, slow and deliberate in action, in accordance with the Dutch blood coursing in his veins. He crossed swords, in a lively journal controversy concerning the expediency of creating a vesico-vaginal fistula for cystitis, with the late Prof. Parvin, a master in dialectics and phraseology. The latter had no advantage in style, of expression or cogency of reasoning, although the operation he contended for has become an established one.

In 1873 Dr. Keyt's attention was attracted to the consideration of the graphic method in the portrayal of the movements of the circulation. First, experimentation was commenced with M. Mavy's spring instrument, but it did not take long to discover that the spring did not furnish all the undulations of the blood-column to the slide. To elucidate the problems of the circulation a double instrument was required—one that would take two tracings, the heart and an artery, or two arteries, the one above the other, upon the slide, with a ebronographic trace below, so that the time could be recorded and the difference in time between the two tracings be computed. Such a mechanism Dr. Keyt devised, a cardiograph and sphygmograph combined, which he termed the compound sphygmograph. This invention has stood the test of time and is today the best adapted

for its purpose of any that have been produced.

A scheme was arranged, by means of which lesions of the mitral and aortic cardiac orifices were represented, and their relations to pulse wave velocity. The developments were recorded by the compound sphygmograph, and the results secured have been confirmed by graphic tracings of clinical cases. These experimental researches formed the basis of a series of articles in the "Journal of the American Medical Association" for 1883.

His book "Sphygmography and Cardiography," is an enduring monument to his industry and genius. Between its covers is included more of patient, painstaking effort than is rarely presented to the professon in equal volume.

To him is due the discovery that an abnormal delay of the pulse-wave follows upon mitral regurgitation. The value of this revelation to the practical physician is obvious.

On October 10, 1848, Dr. Keyt married Miss Susannah D. Hamlin of Cincinnati and had seven children.

Dr. Keyt died suddenly November 9, 1885, at Cincinnati, from rupture of a cerebral artery.

His principal writings are included in "Sphygmography and Cardiography," New York, 1887. A. B. I.

Phila. Month. Med. Jour., vol. i, 1889 (A. B. Isham).
There is an oil painting owned by Mrs. Mary H. Isham.

Kidder, Jerome Henry (1842–1889).

He was born in Baltimore County, Maryland, where he spent his boyhood days, then entered Harvard College at the age of sixteen and was graduated bachelor of arts in 1862. He was appointed a medical cadet during the war, and the study of medicine, begun at that time, was continued in Baltimore, and in 1866 he received the degree of doctor of medicine from the University of Maryland. Shortly afterwards he was commissioned an assistant surgeon in the United States Navy in which he served for eighteen years with much distinction. He was promoted to passed assistant surgeon in 1871, and to surgeon in 1876, and resigned his commission June 18, 1884. Dr. Kidder was recognized as one of the most accomplished and efficient surgeons in his corps. He became specially interested in chemical and physical research and he was ordered to join the scientific party sent out by the United States Government to observe the transit of Venus at Kerguelen island, in 1874. On his return to Washington he studied the material which he had collected at the Smithsonian Institution. Dr. Kidder was a contributor to the National Medical Dictionary compiled under the editorial supervision of Dr. John S. Billings. His principal scientific papers have appeared as follows: Those relating to sanitary and kindred subjects, in the reports of the surgeon-general of the navy from 1879 to 1882; the "Proceedings of the Naval Medical Society for 1884;" the "Reports of the Forty-eighth Congress," and the "Report of the Smithsonian Institution for 1884"; on the natural history of Kerguelen island, in "Bulletins Nos. 2 and 3 of the National Museum," published in 1875 and 1876; on fishery matters, in the "Reports and Bulletins of the Fish Commission" subsequent to 1883; and on chemistry and physics in the publications of various scientific societies. He died suddenly from pneumonia in his forty-seventh year. C. A. P.

Bull. Philos. Soc., Washington, 1892, xi.
Minutes Med. Soc., D. C., Apr. 17, 1889.
Nat. Med.-Biog., Phila., 1890.
Bull. Philosophical Soc., D. C., 1892, vol. xi.

Kilty, William (1758–1821).

This Maryland army surgeon, who united in himself the two professions of medicine and law, was born in London, 1758, and received his literary education at St. Omar's College in France. He studied medicine with Dr. Edward Johnson, of Annapolis, and in April, 1778, proceeded to Wilmington, Delaware, where he retained the appointment of surgeon's mate in the Fourth Maryland Regiment (Laffell and Scarff). He was appointed surgeon of the regiment. He was captured at the Battle of Camden, and in the Spring of 1781 returned to Annapolis, where he remained until the close of the war, owing to his failure to obtain an exchange. He then studied law. In 1798 he was authorized by act of Legislature to compile the statutes of the state, and in compliance with this he prepared and published, in 1800, the two volumes known as "Kilty's Laws." He settled in Washington the same year, and in 1801 was appointed by president Adams, chief judge of the Circuit Court of the District of Columbia. Some time after this he returned to Maryland and was appointed by the governor, chancellor of that state in 1806.

In 1818, by authority of the Legislature, he published with Harris and Watkins, a continuation of Kilty's Laws. He died at Annapolis, October 10, 1821.

Kilty seems to have been a man of quiet, unassuming life, and his greatest interest was no doubt in his professional and judicial work. At the same time he was very patriotic and took a deep interest in the welfare of his state and country.

His most important work was his "Report on the British Statutes in Force in Maryland."

Kilty was an original member of the Society of the Cincinnati. Mr. Allan McSherry, a great-great nephew, has a portrait of him made during the Revolution. E. F. C.

See Proceedings of Maryland Bar Association, "The High Court of Chancery and the Chancellors of Maryland," by Wm. L. Marbury, LL.B.; also "Old Maryland," ii, 5, May, 1906.

Kimball, Gilman (1804–1892).

A gynecologist, he was born at New Chester (now Hill) New Hampshire on December 8, 1804, the son of Ebenezer and Polly Kimball, and after a good education began to study medicine at Dartmouth College where he took his M. D. in 1826, starting practice the next year in the town of Chicopee, Massachusetts. Two years in a small town taught him his limitations and, aspiring to be something more than mediocre in surgery he spent one year under Auguste Bérard in Paris, and also went almost daily to the Dupuytren clinic.

Then followed sixty years of fine service to suffering humanity in Lowell, Massachusetts, particularly when chosen surgeon to a hospital erected by mill owners for their operatives In 1842 he succeeded Willard Parker as professor of surgery at Woodstock, Vermont, and held the same chair in the Berkshire Medical Institution at Pittsfield, Massachusetts. Like most surgeons he was glad to be in warfare and accompanied Gen. Butler to Annapolis and Fort Monroe first as brigade surgeon then as medical director and helped greatly in organizing the hospitals until, twice prostrated by malaria, he had to resign.

As early as 1855 he operated for the removal of ovarian tumors, a proceeding then still regarded as too daring by most surgeons. In New England, outside Boston, it had hardly been done at all, so Kimball required a good deal of courage when he set out to rescue the some forty per cent. of women likely to die of the disease. Even before this, in 1853, he was a pioneer in extirpation of the uterus for fibroids. About 1870, writes his friend Dr. F. H. Davenport, he joined Dr. Ephriam Cutter in the treatment of fibroids by electrolysis. Outside of gynecology he did two amputations (one successful) at the hip-joint; a ligation of the internal iliac artery, unsuccessful, the external iliac, the femoral and subclavian arteries, all of which did well.

Kimball only gave up work when his health obliged him so to do a few years before his death. When he died at Lowell on July 27, 1892, his eighty-seven years had not impaired his mental vigor one little bit and his interest in things medical was as keen as ever.

He was twice married; first to Mary, daughter of Dr. Henry Dewar of Edinburgh, Scotland, then to Isabella Defrier of Nantucket, Massachusetts.

His writings were chiefly on: gastrotomy, ovariotomy and uterine extirpation, in the "Boston Medical and Surgical Journal," 1855, 1874 and 1876.

Yale and Williams Colleges gave him their honorary M. D., and Dartmouth her honorary A. M.; he was also a fellow of the College of Physicians and Surgeons of New York; member of the Massachusetts Medical Society and president of the American Gynecological Society. D. W.

Am. Jour. Obstet., N. Y,. 1892, vol. xxvi.
Tr. Am. Gyn. Soc., 1892, vol. xvii.

King, John (1813–1893).

John King is remembered not only in his own state of Ohio, but throughout the country as a famous analytical pharmacologist. New York City was his birthplace on January 1, 1813, and, his parents being well off, their son had time to become a good linguist, to amuse himself with engraving, music and mechanics before he graduated in medicine from Wooster Beach's Medical School, New York. After graduating he devoted many years to practical work as a botanist, pharmacologist and chemist, in 1851 becoming a teacher in the Cincinnati Eclectic Medical Institute and remaining surrounded by enthusiastic pupils there until his death at North Bend, Ohio, in 1893. His eclecticism was akin to an all-embracing catholicism in medicine. He was an omnivorous reader and able to keep in touch with the current German and French medical literature. It was his interest in Virchow's work which prompted his "Manual of Practical Microscopy" (1859). Neither he nor his adoring students thought the lectures ended when the hour struck, but the latter knew that even on Sunday morning he would ask them to meet him and discuss the subject or a kindred, one perhaps from the moral and ethical side.

His greatest effort as a writer was the "American Dispensatory," 1855, which passed through eighteen editions and was recently revised by John Uri Lloyd and Harvey W. Felter. In 1855 he published a text-book on "Obstetrics;" three years later one on "Gynecology." 1866 saw his "Chronic Diseases."

He discovered and introduced podophyllin (1835), macrotin, irisin, independently of William S. Merrell, and introduced into medical practice hydrastis and sanguinaria.

That which made King a power, even beyond the confines of his own school, was his equipoise of character, his tremendously active mind and his universal philanthropy.

Abridged from a biography in Daniel Drake and his followers. Dr. O. Juettner, Cincinnati 1909.
Ann. Eclect. M. and S., Chicago, 1893, vol. iv. (W. C. Cooper).
Eclect. M. J., Cincin., 1891, vol. li. (A. J. Howe).
Chicago Med. Times, 1890, vol. xxii. (A. Wilder).
Eclect. M. J., Cincin., 1894, vol. liv (J. U. Lloyd).
Tr. Nat. Eclect. M. Ass., Orange, N. J., 1894, vol. xxi.

Kinloch, Robert Alexander (1826–91).

Robert Alexander Kinloch, surgeon, was born at Charleston, South Carolina, on February 20, 1826. In 1845 he graduated with distinction from Charleston College. Three years later, he took his M. D. from the University of Pennsylvania, after which two years were spent in the hospitals of Paris, London and Edinburgh. Returning home he began to practice in his native city, but when the war broke out entered the Confederate ranks as surgeon. During his military career he served at various times upon the staffs of Gens. Lee, Pemberton and Beauregard and was also detailed as a member of the medical examining board at Norfolk, at Richmond, and at Charleston. Subsequently he held the position of inspector of hospitals for South Carolina, Georgia and Florida.

Upon the close of the war he resumed practice in Charleston; and in 1866 was elected to the chair of materia medica in the Medical College of the State of South Carolina. Three years later, in 1869, he was transferred to the chair of the principles and practice of surgery, and subsequently to that of clinical surgery, which he occupied at the time of his death. In 1888 he was elected dean of the faculty and continued to serve until he died.

He was a member of the Medical Society of South Carolina, the American Surgical Association, and associate fellow of the Philadelphia College of Physicians.

For a short time he served as editor of the "Charleston Medical Journal," in which he published many of his medical contributions.

Kinloch's chief title to distinction rests upon his work as a surgeon. From the beginning of his career he was self-reliant, bold, and determined, possessed of a rare skill in execution and perfect poise in the face of unforeseen emergencies, qualities which compelled the success of later life. On one occasion when quite a young man he was called upon to remove the inferior maxilla of a patient. It was customary to request some older man to share the responsibility and in this instance Dr. John Bellinger was invited. After waiting an hour for Dr. Bellinger, Dr. Kinloch remarked, "Well, gentlemen, we will proceed with the operation." His surprised friends exclaimed, "What! without

Dr. Bellinger?'' "Yes," replied Dr. Kinloch, "I came to do this operation and I propose to do it."

He was the first in the United States to resect the knee-joint for chronic disease, his operation preceding that of Dr. Gross by three or four months and also the first to treat fractures of the lower jaw and other bones by wiring the fragments, and among the first to perform a laparotomy for gunshot wounds of the abdomen without protrusion of the viscera. In this case thirteen perforations were sutured, one being overlooked and discovered after death.

As a professor and as dean Dr. Kinloch strove to elevate the standards of medical education and chafed under restrictions which he could not overcome. "The standard of the College could and should be elevated. It is painful for me to make such an announcement. It is more painful for me to say that I am powerless to improve the situation" was what he once said.

Dr. Kinloch married Elizabeth Caldwell, of Fairfield County, South Carolina, in 1856, and had four daughters and four sons, of whom two, George and Edward Jenner, studied medicine.

He died of pneumonia following an attack of la grippe on December 23, 1891.

His writings included:

"A New Form of Intra-uterine Pessary," 1875.

"Two Laparotomies on Same Patient; removal of Both Ovaries for Cystic Disease," 1887.

"Drainage of Wounds; Special Reference to Drainage after Urethrotomy," 1891. R. W., Jr.

Med. Rec., N. Y., 1892, vol. xli.
Tr. Am. Surg. Ass., Phila., 1892, vol. x (C. H. Mastin).
Portrait in the Raper Hosp. at Charleston.

Kilpatrick, Andrew Robert (1817–87).

Andrew Robert Kilpatrick, a surgeon of Texas, was the son of the Rev.

James Hall and Sarah Tanner Kilpatrick and born on March 24, 1817 near Chaneyville, Rapides, Louisiana. He first attended lectures at Jefferson Medical College and the Georgia Medical College, taking his M. D. from the latter in 1837. He practised in three or four places and finally settled in Navasota. When only nineteen he proved himself an able obstetrician and in 1868 was professor of anatomy in Texas Medical College.

His chief writings were on the subject of epidemics: "The History of Epidemic Yellow Fever in Woodville, Mississippi," 1844; "Cholera in Louisiana," 1849; "Yellow Fever in Louisiana," 1855; "Yellow Fever in Texas," 1867. He was also associate editor of the "Southern Medical Record" and the "Texas Medical Journal."

He married three times; his last wife, whom he married in 1854, being Mary M., daughter of Joel T. Tucker of St. Landry Parish, Louisiana.

D. W.

Daniel's Texas Med. Jour., Austin, 1887–8, vol. iii.

Kirkbride, Thomas Story (1809–1883).

It needs an exceedingly sane man and one in full self-possession to understand and ease the burden of delusion, the loneliness, the worry of those who are "out of their mind" and have lost the key. A tremendous amount of such help is now given, but Thomas Kirkbride lived in times when the whip, the shackles, and dark cells were not uncommon, and did splendid work in reforming such evils. He was born in Morrisville, Bucks County, in July, 1809, of English descent, his people coming from Kirkbride, Cumberland, England to America with Penn. His father, John, and his mother, Elizabeth Story Kirkbride, belonged to the Society of Friends and brought up the boy in a quiet way, sending him to local schools and giving him plenty of wholesome life on their farm. A few years at Trenton and Burlington,

New Jersey, a clear year of farm work and then he settled down to read medicine with one Nicholas de Belleville, M. D. He graduated M. D., 1832, from the University of Pennsylvania and was immediately appointed resident physician to the Friends Asylum for the Insane at Frankford, and his next appointment of the kind was physician-in-chief for the new department for the insane in connection with Pennsylvania Hospital, in 1840. At that time there were only ten such special asylums in the States and the public conscience had not been aroused to the evils existing. It was a responsible post for young Kirkbride, but he consecrated his whole life to the duty of raising and defending the helpless patients under his care and thousands owed recovered reason to his humane and studious consideration of their woe. The terms "keeper" and "asylum" were changed to "hospital" and "nurse"; restraint was avoided wherever possible and the surroundings made attractive. "Kirkbride's Hospital," as it came to be called, was known as a model institution, one worth visiting by foreign alienists. Dr. S. D. Gross says Kirkbride had a fine physique, a well shaped head, a benevolent face and a gentle voice, which, coupled with determination and promptness, made him beloved and obeyed. So generally were his views adopted that his book on "The Construction and Management of Hospitals" governed largely in the erection of about thirty other institutions.

During his forty-three years of unwearying service 4638 of the 8852 patients were discharged cured or improved—an unprecedented record for that time. One patient, however, nearly cut short Kirkbride's existence by hiding up in a tree and shooting him, the bullet fortunately not penetrating the skull.

The American Medico-psychological Association, then known by the bulky title of "The Association of Medical Superintendents of American Institutions for the Insane," numbers him among its thirteen originators, also as vice-president, and for eight years, president.

He married, in 1839, Ann West, daughter of Joseph R. Jenks, merchant, but she died in 1862 leaving him a son and a daughter. In 1866 Eliza, daughter of Benjamin F. Butler of New York, attorney-general, became his wife and had four children.

In March, 1883, he was seriously ill for nine months with typhoid pneumonia and died peacefully on December 16.

He did not do much writing in a way that would awaken public interest except on his own specialty and a few medical biographies by request of the College of Physicians, Philadelphia. A good oil painting of him by Howard R. Butler is in that College.

He was a member of the College of Physicians, the Philadelphia County Medical Society, the American Philosophical Society; honorary member of the British Medico-Psychological Association, etc., and an LL. D. of Lafayette College Pennsylvania.

The Hist. of the Penn. Hosp. by Morton and Woodbury, Phila., 1895. A portrait of him is in this biography.
Autobiography, S. D. Gross.
Dr. Thomas Story Kirkbride, J. B. Chapin, 1898.

Kirkpatrick, Robert C. (1863–1897).

Robert C. Kirkpatrick at the time of his death was only thirty-four years old. He was surgeon to the Montreal General Hospital, lecturer in clinical surgery and demonstrator of surgery in McGill University, graduating from McGill University in the faculty of arts in 1882, and from the faculty of medicine in 1886. He acted as house surgeon to the Montreal General Hospital, and after a period of study in Edinburgh was admitted a licentiate of the Royal College of Physicians. In 1888 he became superintendent of the Montreal General Hospital in succession to Dr. McClure who had entered the Chinese Medical Mission Service;

in 1891, assistant surgeon. Dr. Kirk-patrick was the first in Canada, and one of the first in America, to repair with success the stomach wall after perforation by ulcer; and he had a good record in the performance of the operation for resection of the bowel, and of gastro-enterostomy. He was also a competent managing editor of the "Montreal Medical Journal." The cause of death was tubercular meningitis.

A. M.

Kirtland, Jared Potter (1793–1877).

Jared Potter Kirtland, an eminent naturalist of Cleveland, Ohio, was born in Wallingford, Connecticut, November 10, 1793. In early life he was adopted into the family of his grandfather, Dr. Jared Potter, a physician of Wallingford. His father, Turhand Kirtland, removed in 1803 to Poland, Mahoning County, Ohio, leaving his son Jared in the home of his grandfather. The boy received his early education in the district and academic schools of Wallingford and Cheshire. Even at this period he is said to have manifested a predilection for the natural sciences, and studied botany and scientific agriculture systematically. In 1811 the death of his grandfather, who left the young Jared his medical library and a sum of money sufficient to pay for his medical education in Edinburgh, enabled him to study medicine with Dr. John Andrews of Wallingford and Dr. Sylvester Wells of Hartford, Connecticut. At this period too he made the acquaintance of Prof. Benjamin Silliman, of Yale College, who took an interest in the bright boy and offered him many facilities for the study of chemistry. Unfortunately the outbreak of the war with England at this time compelled the abandonment of the plan of completing his education in Edinburgh, and in 1813 he became the first medical matriculant in the first class at Yale College. Ill health, however, compelled him

to stop studying awhile, but later he took a course of lectures at the University of Pennsylvania, but subsequently returned to Connecticut and graduated from Yale College in March, 1815. During his attendance at Yale he took special courses in botany from Prof. Ives, and in mineralogy and geology from Prof. Silliman, and devoted some time likewise to the study of zoology. Immediately after graduation Dr. Kirtland began practice in Wallingford, dividing his time between some practice and the study of scientific agriculture, botany and natural history, and five years he practised in Durham, Connecticut. In the same year he married Caroline Atwater, of Wallingford, and had two children. The death of his wife and one of his daughters, which occurred in 1823, was a severe trial which unsettled him for a time and revived a desire to remove to Ohio, and in the same year he settled with his father in the town of Poland. Here, almost in spite of himself, he found an active medical practice forced upon him, though it had been his desire and intention to devote himself to agricultural pursuits. In 1815 he married Hannah F. Toucey, of Newton, Connecticut. At the close of some service in the Legislature, Dr. Kirtland resumed practice in Poland, but in 1837 became professor of the theory and practice of medicine in the Ohio Medical College at Cincinnati, which position he filled for the next five years, and in the following year, having resigned his position in Cincinnati, removed with his family to Cleveland, and accepted and filled until 1864 the chair of the theory and practice of medicine in the newly organized Cleveland Medical College.

Dr. Kirtland was actively interested in the work of the Medical Convention of Ohio, was president of that body in 1839, and a paper from his pen on "Irregular Malarious Diseases and Their Counteractions by means of Strychnine" is preserved in the "Proceedings" of the Convention of 1849. He was equally active in the organization of the Ohio State Medical Society, was, in 1846, its first vice-president, and its president in 1848. Two papers by Dr. Kirtland are also published in the Cleveland Medical Gazette of 1860, the one entitled "On the Use of Podophyllin and Leptandrin as a Substitute for Mercurials in Diseases of the Digestive Organs;" the other, "Parthenogenesis in Bees and Moths." A third paper, "On the Use of Opium in Certain Forms of Nervous Irritability and Coma, Which Frequently attend Typhus fevers," will be found in the "Transactions of the Ohio State Medical Society," 1851.

But in spite of his eminent medical character, it was in the field of the natural sciences that Dr. Kirtland secured his most extended and most enduring fame. Even as a boy he had manifested great interest in botany, natural history and scientific agriculture, and in 1834 he announced in the "American Journal of Art and Science" (vol. xxvi) his discovery of the "Existence of Distinct Sexes in the Naiads," a species of fresh water shell-fish, heretofore believed to be hermaphrodite. This discovery produced a considerable sensation in that day, and was denied by many naturalists, but its truth was finally confirmed by Agassiz and Karl T. E. von Siebold. In 1837 Dr. Kirtland was appointed an assistant to Prof. W. W. Mather in the geological survey of the state of Ohio, authorized by the Legislature, and spent the summer in collecting specimens in all departments of natural history for an extended report upon that subject. This survey was suspended before completion, and the legislature even refused to reimburse to Dr. Kirtland the expenditures which he had made from his own pocket in the performance of his part of the work. He accordingly retained the specimens already procured, and ultimately pre-

sented them to the Cleveland Academy of Natural science, organized in 1845 chiefly through his influence and example. In 1853, in company with Spencer F. Baird and Dr. Hoy, he traveled extensively throughout Ohio, Michigan, Illinois, Wisconsin and even Canada, engaged in the study of the natural history of these states, and in 1869–70, though now seventy-seven years of age, he made a trip to Florida, for similar purposes.

As early as 1840 Dr. Kirtland had purchased a farm on the shore of Lake Erie, about five miles west of Cleveland, and now devoted his declining years to scientific agriculture, the cultivation of fruits and flowers and the management of bees, and his private grounds became one of the show-places of the neighboring city. Even in the art of taxidermy Dr. Kirtland was an expert, and numerous specimens from his hands are found in the museums of both the United States and England.

In 1861 he received from Williams College the degree of LL. D. He was also a regular correspondent of Agassiz, Spencer F. Baird, Joseph Henry, Marshall P. Wilder and numerous other scientists.

Dr. Kirtland died on his farm at Rockport December 10, 1877, at the advanced age of eighty-four years.

An excellent portrait is in Western Reserve Medical College, and a bust by Dr. Garlick may be seen in the Museum of the Western Reserve Historical Society in Cleveland.

H. E. H.

Cleveland Med. Gazette, 1890–91, vol. vi
Nat. Acad. Sci., Wash., 1886, vol. ii.
Cleave's Biographical Cyclopedia.

Kissam, Richard Sharp (1808–1861).

Richard S. Kissam, son of the great lithotomist, was born in New York, October, 2, 1808. In 1824 he entered Union College, Schenectady, and later Washington College, Hartford, Connecticut, in 1827 becoming a student of Dr. Cogswell, and in 1828 attending at the Retreat for the Insane. He graduated at the College of Physicians and Surgeons, New York, in 1830, his dissertation being on Iritis. For several years he practised surgery at Hartford, Connecticut, founded the "Eye and Ear Infirmary" and achieved a widespread reputation as an operator for cataract. In 1834 he removed to New York, taking up the practice of his cousin, Dr. Daniel W. Kissam. The operation of transplantation of the cornea was performed by him in 1838 with at first apparently good results, but failure in a few weeks. During 1844–45 he gave instruction in surgery and was appointed professor of the principles and practice of surgery in Castleton Medical College, but declined the appointment.

Kissam was dignified yet unostentatious, of the most prepossessing manners, scrupulously neat, with a brilliant and sparkling eye, fascinating by his wit and humor in ordinary conversation, or drawing upon the more scientific treasures of his highly cultivated mind as occasion required.

He died November 28, 1861.

H. F.

American Med. Times, Dec. 14, 1861, vol. iii
Trans. A. M. Assoc., vol. xiv.

Kleinschmidt, Carl Hermann Anton (1839–1905).

In a small town called Petershagen, situated on the Weser in North Germany, Carl Kleinschmidt was born in 1839 and educated at the public schools, enjoying the benefit of a gymnastic course at the Royal College, Minden, Prussia. He came to Georgetown, District of Columbia, with his parents in November, 1857, when about eighteen, where he assisted his father in a little store, but continued his studies and soon mastered the English language. His education was first directed towards theology, but his aptitude for medicine and surgery attracted the attention of Dr. John Snyder, of Georgetown, who persuaded his parents to let him study under him, so he entered Georgetown University and he graduated thence in 1862. The war between the States was then actively going on and influence was offered to obtain him a position in the United States Army, but on account of his intimate association with southern people, his sympathies were with them, and he was appointed assistant surgeon in Confederate ranks. He was in most of the bloody conflicts in which the army of Northern Virginia was engaged, with all its hardships and trials and devotion to suffering humanity; he was at Gettysburg with the rear guard during Lee's retreat; at the Wilderness and the terrible series of battles that followed, and finally at Appomattox, after which he walked nearly all the way to Georgetown, arriving destitute of almost everything.

After the Civil War he went abroad and took a course at the Berlin University and returning began active practice in Georgetown.

In 1874 he assisted in the reorganization of the Central Dispensary, and was appointed lecturer on diseases of the eye and ear in the summer course of Georgetown University. In 1876 he was appointed professor of physiology in the medical department of Georgetown University and maintained his connection with it to the end of his life. He was a most excellent teacher and through his omnivorous reading the works of the great German masters were made accessible to the students and the functions of the different organs portrayed in apt language by the lecturer, aided by physiological experiments and by skillful charts and drawings from his own hands.

He was elected president of the Medical Society in 1886, and president of the Medical Association of the District of Columbia 1895–1896. In 1889 Georgetown University conferred upon him the degree of Ph. D. He died in Washington May 20, 1905.

Dr. Kleinschmidt was not a prolific writer. He was the author of a timely address on "The Necessity for a Higher

Standard of Medical Education," Washington, 1878, and an excellent report on "Typhoid Fever" presented to the Medical Society of Washington, District of Columbia, 1894. He also assisted Dr. S. C. Busey and Dr. John M. Toner in the preparation of numerous and valuable monographs. G. M. K.

Knight, Frederick Irving (1841–1909).

Frederick Irving Knight, laryngologist, was born in Newburyport, Massachusetts, May 18, 1841, the son of Frederick and Anne Goodwin Knight. His education was received at the Newburyport High School and Yale College whence he graduated in 1862. Apparently he had already begun to look towards his profession, for he showed unusual interest in the Soldiers' Hospital—it was during the Civil War—and spent so much time in helping to watch and nurse the patients that he was often spoken of as "Doctor" Knight. In 1866 Yale gave him the degree of A. M. Having finished his academic course at New Haven, he entered the Harvard Medical School, from which he graduated in 1866. He then entered the City Hospital of Boston, where he passed the usual time as interne, and upon graduating went to New York City. There he associated himself with Professor Austin Flint, with whom he studied for one year when, declining an offered partnership, he returned to Boston and became the assistant of Dr. Henry I. Bowditch (Harvard, 1828), which partnership was continued for twelve years.

Meanwhile in 1871–1872 Dr. Knight spent a year abroad at Vienna, Berlin and London, under the personal instruction of the best masters of the day.

From the beginning he had devoted his attention to diseases of the chest and the upper air passages, and having perfected his knowledge of these subjects as far as possible he returned to Boston.

In 1872, while in Europe, he was made instructor in percussion, auscultation and laryngoscopy, and on his return established a clinic in New York to include

laryngology, largely limited to teaching methods of examination. In 1879, after seven years of instruction, percussion and ascultation were separated from laryngology and the title of Teacher became that of Instructor of Laryngology. In 1880 Harvard established a voluntary fourth year. Dr. Knight gave a course to the class of that year, consisting of three exercises a week for two months. In 1882 he was made assistant and in 1886 clinical professor. By this time the whole field of disease was covered by systematic lectures, demonstrations and the clinical use of patients.

Although at a period when his mental and physical powers were in every respect at their best, he resigned this position in 1892 in order to allow of the appointment of his friend, Dr. Franklin H. Hooper, who had for some time aspired to attain it. The high-minded unselfishness of this act was great, for Dr. Hooper was hopelessly ill. It was not likely that his life would be prolonged sufficiently for him to occupy the place for any great length of time. It was equally probable that if Dr. Knight resigned the position he would not take it up again.

Dr. Knight was connected at various times with the Boston City Hospital, the Boston Dispensary and the Carney Hospital, but resigned these positions in 1872 to establish a special clinic in laryngoscopy at the Massachusetts General Hospital. He was also consulting physician to the Masaschusetts General Hospital.

While abroad he married in Berlin, October, 15, 1871, Louisa Armistead Appleton, daughter of William Stuart Appleton, formerly of Baltimore, Maryland; one child, Theodora Knight, survived him.

Dr. Knight was one of the founders of the American Laryngological Association. At the first meeting of the Association held in New York City, June 10, 1879, the first scientific contribution presented was the paper of Dr. Knight on "Retro-Pharyngeal Sarcoma."

Dr. Knight was elected third president of the association and in 1880 founded the "Archives of Laryngology," a magazine devoted to the study of diseases of the upper air passages. The editorial staff was composed of four of the leading laryngologists of the time, namely, Louis Elsberg, J. Solis-Cohen, George M. Lefferts and Frederick Knight. Terminated at the end of four years, it remains to-day the most elegant and best edited periodical on laryngology that has ever appeared. Under such management as controlled it and with the vastly increased number of specialists in the field there is no doubt that to-day it would be an acknowledged success.

Dr. Knight was a pioneer in the movement against tuberculosis. Fifteen years ago he became deeply interested in the subject and devoted much time and energy to it.

He was a member of the Amercan Academy of Arts and Sciences, ex-president of the American Laryngological Association and of the American Climatological Association and a member of the Massachusetts Medical Society.

His writings included:

"Paralysis of the Velum Palati in Acute Naso-pharyngitis," 1887.

"Congenital Bony Occlusion of the Posterior Nares," 1887.

"Intubation for Stenosis of the Larynx in a Boy of Twelve," 1892.

"Torticollis Following Removal of Adenoids of the Rhino-pharynx," 1894.

"Three Cases of Laryngeal Neoplasm," 1894.

"The Sequelæ of Syphilis and Their Treatment; Nasal Sequelæ," 1896.

"Three Cases of Obscure Laryngeal Disease; Tuberculosis, Syphilis, Epithelioma," 1897.

D. B. D.

Abridged from a memorial sketch by Dr. D. Bryson Delavan, N. York, 1909 (portrait).

Knight, James 1810–1887).

James Knight was chiefly interested in orthopedic surgery and, struck by the cry-

ing need for an orthopedic hospital in New York, generously gave up his private house for that purpose, and when the society built a suitable place it was placed under his charge.

He was born in Taney Town, Frederick County, Maryland, on February 14, 1810, son of Samuel Knight, a manufacturer of military arms, whose people came from England in 1766.

After seven years at the Baltimore General Dispensary, in 1835 he finally settled and remained in New York, where he became known as a skillful and tender orthopedist. His two volumes, "On the Improvement of the Health of Children and Adults by Natural Means" (1868) and "Orthopedia, or a Practical Treatise on the Alterations of the Human Form" (1874) were well received.

He was member of the Medico-Chirurgical Society of Maryland, the County Medical Society of New York, and fellow of the New York Academy of Medicine.

He died in October, 1887.

D. W.

Stone's Biog. of Eminent Phys. and Surg.

Knight, Jonathan (1789–1864).

Jonathan Knight was born in Norwalk, Connecticut, September 4, 1789, the son and grandson of physicians. At the age of fifteen, he entered Yale College, graduating four years later, in 1808, and then had charge of an academy at Norwich, Connecticut, for two years. At the expiration of this time he was appointed a tutor at Yale. While there the establishment of a medical department was discussed, and Prof. Benjamin Silliman, then professor of chemistry in the college, suggested Knight for the chair of physiology and anatomy. To better equip himself for this position, he spent the winters of 1811 and 1812 in Philadelphia, so that in 1813 he was ready to do the work. This position he held until 1838, when, on the death of Dr. Thomas Hubbard, he was transferred to the chair of surgery, which he held until shortly before his death, thus occupying a professorship in the Yale Medical School for fifty-one years, earning great fame as a successful teacher.

He became, after the death of Dr. Thomas Hubbard, the leading surgeon in Connecticut. Especially was he familiar with the literature of surgery. "Conscientious, forbearing, conservative, perhaps in all that time of his supremacy (which continued until his death), he never did an unnecessary or premature operation" is the tribute paid him by his pupil and successor, Dr. Francis Bacon. He was the first surgeon to cure aneurysms by manual compression. This was done in 1848 by relays of assistants from among his pupils at the medical school, who relieved each other at short intervals. After forty hours' treatment, the aneurysm disappeared.

He was twice president of the American Medical Association, his re-election due to the skillful way in which he presided over its first session, using his common sense, without, as he admitted, much knowledge of parliamentary rules. He died on August 25, 1864 Unfortunately, he wrote little, save two introductory lectures and an eulogium on Dr. Nathan Smith. A portrait by Nathaniel Jocelyn was painted in 1828 and is still in existence. W. R. S.

Proceedings of Connecticut Medical Society, 1864-1867.
Bacon's "Some Account of the Medical Profession in New Haven, 1887.
Kingsley's Yale College, vol ii, 1878.

Kollock, Cornelius (1824–1897).

Cornelius Kollock, who for the last twenty years of his life devoted himself to gynecology and abdominal surgery in the little village of Cheraw, South Carolina, near which he was born in 1824, was well known and consulted in both the Carolinas, and was president of the South Carolina Medical Association in 1887. He was the son of Oliver Hawes and Sarah Wilson Kollock. Student days were passed at Brown University, Rhode Island, and his M: D. taken at the University of Pennsylvania in 1848, after which he studied in Paris for two years in the leading clinics. Then he settled down in Cheraw, which village even when he died had only about one thousand persons in it including five doctors, but a glance at the portrait of Kollock shows he knew his own mind and under what circumstances he could do his best work. The "Transactions of the American Gynecological Society" show the deep interest he took in professional subjects even when seventy years old.

A Christian man of unflinching integrity and courage, skillful in dealing with the diseases and frailties of the little community in which he worked. His death on the sixteenth of August, 1897, caused universal regret.

He married Mary Henrietta Shaw and one son, Charles Wilson, followed his father's profession.

Tr. Am. Gyn. Soc , 1898, vol. xxiii (R. B. Maury) (portrait).
Tr. South. Surg. and Gyn. Assoc , vol xi, 1899 (portrait).

Kreider, Michael Zimmermann (1803–1855).

A pioneer surgeon in Ohio, he was born in Huntingdon, Pennsylvania, the son of Daniel and Salome Carpenter Kreider, and grandson of Michael and Susan Carpenter Kreider; being thus doubly descended from Dr. Henry Carpenter (Zimmermann), a Swiss physician who located in Germantown in 1698. He attended school in Huntingdon, and acquired, for that day in the West, an unusually good education.

On the death of his mother in 1820 the home was broken up and with a younger brother he walked over the Allegheny Mountains and made his home for two years with an uncle in Delaware County, Ohio, in 1822 beginning to study medicine with Dr. Samuel Parsons in Columbus, and in 1825 after an examination, there being no medical schools in the West at that time, was given a license to practise by the State Medical Board, and settled in Royalton, Ohio. In 1841, having retired from political office he took up his practice of surgery with energy and became widely known as a surgeon, probably operating more than any other surgeon in Ohio, outside of Cincinnati.

Of physicians, Dr. M. Z. Kreider stood at the head, and in surgery was head and shoulders above all the others. Far and near he was called upon to perform all the capital operations. He was a self-made man, who by indomitable perseverance and energy attained to his commanding position. He was a very large, broad shouldered man, well proportioned, with a large nose, bright eyes, and a generally keen and alert expression, with strong and rapid movements. Not only a noted physician, but a successful preacher and politician.

He married, first, Sydney Ann Rees, daughter of Gen. David Rees, and had one son, Edmund Cicero, and four daughters. His second wife was Mary Ann Carpenter, his cousin, by whom he had two children. He contributed frequently to the "Ohio Medical Journal" of Columbus and Cincinnati.

In 1853 he suffered a sun stroke while traveling in Michigan and this brought on diabetes which caused his death, July 20, 1855, at the early age of fifty-two.

G. N. K.

History of the Carpenter Family, S. D. Carpenter, M. D., 1907.
History of Huntingdon County, Pennsylvania, 1882.
History of Fairfield County, Ohio, Scott, 1871.
History of Fairfield and Perry Counties, Ohio, 1900.

Kuhn, Adam (1741–1817).

Concerning this young botanist, on the twenty-fourth of February, 1763, the great Linneus sat down to write to Adam Kuhn père, and in fine Latin thus commends his pupil:

"He is unwearied in his studies and daily and faithfully studies materia medica with me. He has learnt the symptomatic history of diseases in an accurate and solid manner. In natural history and botany he has made remarkable progress. He has studied anatomy and physiology with other professors." This was high praise from such a master.

"The boy was born at Germantown near Philadelphia on November 17, 1741. His grandfather, John Christopher Kuhn and his father, Dr. Adam Simon Kuhn, came from Heilbronn, Swabia, to Philadelphia in September, 1733.

"Adam first studied medicine with his father then sailed for Europe in 1761 and arrived at Upsal, by way of London.

"Of Adam Kuhn Dr. Charles Caldwell, cold, cautious, and sarcastic, says: "He was by far the most highly and minutely furnished specimen of old-school medical production I have ever beheld. He wore a fashionable curled and powdered wig; his breeches were black, a long skirted buff or white waistcoat, his coat snuff colored. He carried a gold headed cane and a gold snuff-box; his knee and shoe buckles of the same metal. His footsteps were sternly and stubbornly regular; he entered the sick-room at a given minute and stayed a given time and never suffered deviation from his directions.

"'Doctor, if the patient should desire toast, water or lemonade he may have it?' asked the nurse sometimes. He would turn and reply with oracular solemnity, 'I have directed weak sage tea. Good morning madam.' His lectures, not instructive, were mere commonplace. So far from containing an original thought, no portion of it appeared to be the professor's own."

This was pretty strong, yet he adds, without commendation, that Kuhn came to see him (Caldwell) three times a day when he was ill.

Linneus, following a pretty fancy, named an American plant *Kuhnia* (Kuhnia Eupatorioides) after Adam and when the latter returned to Philadelphia wrote very intimate and graceful letters to him in fine Latin. One has this injunction in it. "I pray and entreat thee send some seeds and plants among which I ardently desire the seeds of the *Kuhnia*, which perished in our garden."

Kuhn went to London in 1764 and studied there a while, and in 1767 was in Edinburgh where he took his M. D. that same year on the twelfth of

June. His thesis, on "De Lavatione Frigida," was dedicated to his friend Linneus. He visited France, Holland and Germany but whether before or after Edinburgh is not very clear. In 1768, after his return to Philadelphia, he became professor of materia medica and botany in the University of Pennsylvania and helped in 1774 in vaccinating a population considerably decimated by small-pox. As a lecturer, in his five or six professorships held, "he was faithful and clear in the description of diseases and in the mode of applying their appropriate remedies, avoiding theoretical discussions." It would be pleasant to know more of Kuhn, but the short-length long-adjectived pompous biographies in old medical journals do not give much. A discreet young physician, "not remarkable for powers of imagination but his talent for observation profound; a lover of music, abstemious in diet, neat in person," says one biographer.

He did not marry until he was thirty-nine, after which it is gratifying to learn "he had two sons, respectable characters," by his wife Elizabeth, daughter of Isaac Hartman of St. Croix.

When seventy-three he "grieved" his patients by giving up practice, and in June, 1817, began to feel conscious that life was ending. After a short confinement of three weeks to the house, but suffering no pain, Adam Kuhn passed away on July 5, in full serenity of mind and heart.

His other appointments included: Physician to the Pennsylvania Hospital, consulting physician, Philadelphia Dispensary, 1786; one of the founders and in 1808. president of the College of Physicians of Philadelphia; professor of the theory and practice of medicine, University of Pennsylvania, 1789, and on the junction of the two medical schools of the College and University, was chosen professor of the practice of physic, 1792–1797.

Of his writings, with the exception of the thesis mentioned, nothing can he traced save a short letter addressed to Dr. Lettsom on "Diseases Succeeding Transplantation of Teeth." He opposed Rush's "Treatment of Yellow Fever" by publishing his own, over initials, in the "General Advertizer" of September 11, 1793.(?)   D. W.

Eclectic Repertory, Phila., 1818, Dr. S. Powell Griffiths.
Stoever's Life of Linneus.
Autobiography of Charles Caldwell, Phila., 1855.
The Botanists of Philadelphia, Harshberger, Phila., 1899.

L

Laird, James M. (1852–1904).

To the mountain ranges and rivers, to one of those valleys drained by the Great Kanawha in Southern West Virginia, there came many years ago a man the stamp of whose character will not soon be effaced and whose name will not soon be forgotten.

James M. Laird was the sixth son of J C. Laird and was born near Kerrs Creek, Rockbridge County, Virginia, October 18, 1852 of a family conspicuous for intellectual traits. His parents intended at one time that he should study for the ministry but after several sessions spent at Washington and Lee University, Lexington, Virginia, he decided to study medicine and took his course at the University of Virginia where he graduated M. D., later spending a year in Bellevue Hospital, New York. This was in 1876. He practised in Fayetteville, West Virginia, and later at Peytona, then went to Montgomery where in 1880 he formed a partnership with Dr. C. I. Lewis, later entering into one with Dr. John C. Wysor. The firm continued in practice together until August 1, 1892, when Dr. Wysor left Montgomery. Dr. Laird married in June, 1889, Miss Margaret M. Hill of Charleston, and she had two sons, James M. and Morris W., and died in October, 1899.

Enjoying a wide range of popularity and practice he was a favorite consultant throughout several counties, coming into the profession not long after the more general adoption of Lister's theories, he was perhaps the first to practice aseptic surgery in the Kanawha Valley.

I have heard him tell of the introduction of aseptic gauze for dressing, how cheesecloth was boiled in an iron pot and then kept in bichloride solution until needed for use.

As a surgeon he was thorough and conservative and while he did no original work and made no contributions to science, he achieved more than a local reputation.

For many years he was a sufferer from valvular disease of the heart and nephritis and died suddenly February 16, 1904 at the Sheltering Arms Hospital, Hansford, West Virginia, several hours after taking an anesthetic for the opening of a deep suppurating gland of the neck.

J. E. C.

Lamson, Daniel Lowell (1834–1894).

Although he might be called by some a "Jack of all trades," this man was also master of many. The son of Edward Preble and Lois Jane Farrington Lamson, he was born in Hopkinton, July 8, 1831. He fitted for college at two academies, studied medicine at the Dartmouth Medical School, and afterwards at the University Medical School of New York, where he took his M. D. March 4, 1857, and settled in Freyburg. Dr. Lamson early became a member of the Maine Medical Association, and was examining surgeon for pensions nearly up to the time of his death. He married September 1, 1858, Henrietta Reede, who died July 17, 1865, and afterwards Mrs. Sarah Matilda Vose Chipman, who survived him.

Dr. Lamson had a lucrative practice, and attended to it faithfully. Despite his mechanical talent, he never neglected a patient for any pet invention. He was highly thought of everywhere within fifty miles of his town, as an excellent and faithful surgeon and physician. He wrote several papers of interest, the best one of them being "Aphasia from Brain Injury," Maine Medical Association, 1882. He was often chosen as visitor to the Medical School of Maine.

Lamson was a born inventor, and had he not adopted medicine as his profession, he would have made his fortune, for with his own hands he invented a working steam engine, a double stitch sewing machine (long before such things were ever patented), and a mowing machine with which he lost a fortune by neglecting to get a patent.

He improved the telephone, and was an expert electrician. For several years he kept the town clock wound up, and in constant repair, climbing the tall tower for that purpose.

He was the leader of the village band, and a teacher of each instrument. He was the originator and took care of all the water works. Besides all this, he invented several surgical instruments, and among them an automatic vaccinator, which is still in use in times of threatened epidemics. He was an ingenious man, and when he died from an apoplectic stroke, February 14, 1894, it seemed as if the whole village ceased to live or breathe. J. A. S.

Trans. Maine Med. Assoc., 1894

Lane, Levi Cooper (1833–1902).

Of English Quaker stock, Levi Cooper Lane was born in Ohio May 9, 1830. His early education was partly private, partly in Farmer's College and Union College, Schnectady, from which latter he received his M. A., and in 1877 his LL. D.

He graduated in 1851 from Jefferson Medical College and in the same year was appointed interne in New York State Hospital on Ward's Island where he remained four years.

In 1855 he entered the navy, but four years later resigned and settled to practise in San Francisco with his uncle, Dr. Elias Samuel Cooper, for whom Cooper Medical College was later named. He at once became identified, as professor of physiology, with the medical department of the University of the Pacific—the first medical school on the Pacific coast and of which Dr. Cooper was the leading spirit. In the following year Cooper died, and this school was discontinued and Dr. Lane called as professor of anatomy to the newly organized Toland Medical College; but in 1870, in association with its old members and some new blood he revived the original school which he entered as professor of surgery. In 1882 he built a fine college building, which he incorporated as Cooper Medical College. To this he added, in 1890, Lane Hall, and in 1894 Lane Hospital, the total gift approximating half a million dollars—money earned by himself in his profession, as he expressed it.

Dr. Lane was a most indefatigable student. His impromptu thesis before the Navy Board was in Latin. German and French were to him familiar tongues and he knew also Greek, Spanish and Italian. For many years it was his custom to devote the early morning hours to reading, investigation and writing. Thus he wrote his scholarly work, the "Surgery of the Head and Neck."

As a surgeon Dr. Lane, following Sir Astley Cooper, never operated on an important case without previously performing the operation on the cadaver. In his knowledge of anatomy and surgery he had not his superior on the coast—probably not his equal.

Not only was he skillful and resourceful but he possessed decided originality. He devised a number of new operations, notably vaginal hysterectomy, which he was the first to perform in America and which he devised as an original procedure, not being aware that the operation had been performed a number of times in France in the early years of the century. He also originated an operation for craniectomy, for microcephalia and devised important changes in hare-lip operations.

Notwithstanding Dr. Lane's active and energetic life, his physical side was far from robust. In early youth he had been asthmatic, and a resultant emphysema had rendered him liable to frequent attacks of bronchitis. He spent some months of the winter of 1882 in Guatemala, in recuperation, and in the middle seventies gave two years of his life to study in Europe where he received the M. R. C. S. (Eng.) degree and the M. D. of Berlin.

In the early seventies he married Mrs. Pauline Cook but had no children. A fine portrait by Toby Rosenthal and a marble bust are in the possession of the college.

Dr. Lane did not seek public position, but was once a member of the City and State Board of Health and president of the State Medical Society.

Among his articles are found:
"Ligations for the Cure of Aneurysm," 1884.
"Rudolf Virchow," 1893.
"Surgery of the Head and Neck," 1898.   H. G, JR.

Am. Med., Phila., 1902, vol. iii.
Brit.-M. J., 1902, vol. i.
Lancet, London, 1902, vol. i.
Pacific Med. J., San Fran., 1902, vol. xlv.

Lang, John (1859–1896).
John Lang was born in Dumbarton, Scotland, first of August, 1859, and took high honors as a student. He held the L. R. C. P., Edinburgh, and the L. F. P. S., Glasgow. At first he was house surgeon at the Eye Infirmary, Glasgow, 1884, then went to China where he stayed seven years, having charge of the Amoy Mission Hospital. On account of ill health he went to Victoria, British Columbia, in 1892, and practised as an oculist, being appointed ophthalmic surgeon to the Provincial Royal Jubilee Hospital, where he did useful work and was held in high repute.

As the result of an accident to the Point Ellice bridge, May 26, 1896, when many persons were drowned, he received severe injuries to his kidneys which a few weeks later proved fatal.   O. M. J.

Larsh, N. B. (1835–1887).
N. B. Larsh, of Nebraska City, Nebraska, was one of the medical pioneers of the state. In 1859 he came to Nebraska City and became at once a factor in the affairs of his city and state as well as in the medical profession. In 1868 he was one of those who organized the Nebraska State Medical Society; in 1870, 71 and 72 he was

superintendent of the State Hospital for the Insane at Lincoln; and in 1872 became president of the State Medical Society.

That he continued active in both public and professional affairs is evidenced by the fact that death (December 22, 1887) was due to an acute congestive disturbance following severe exposure while on a professional call and that at the time he was mayor of Nebraska City.

Larsh was of French parentage and was born January 6, 1835, at Eaton, Ohio. He attended Antioch College, Ohio, and received his M. D. from Miami Medical College in 1857. After spending a short time in Palestine, Ohio, he came to Nebraska City in 1859 where on December 2, 1859, he married Ella S. Armstrong.

Dr. Larsh was one of the most active members of the State Medical Society in its early days. He signed the original constitution as a delegate from Otoe County and was elected president in 1870. He contributed at this meeting a paper reporting a case of pyemia. At the meeting in 1871 in Lincoln he presided and also read a paper reporting a gunshot wound of the abdomen.   H. W. O.

Report of the Committee on Necrology of the Nebraska State Medical Society, 1888. The History of Nebraska.

Latham, H. Grey, (1831–1903).
He was the son of Dr. Henry Latham of Lynchburg, Virginia, and born in that city on March 4, 1831. His father was a distinguished physician, and both he and his son had the honor of being chosen president of the State Medical Society.

Educated in private schools at Lynchburg and the University of Virginia; he studied medicine in the University, graduating in 1851, and did hospital work in Richmond, Baltimore and Philadelphia. He then settled in his native town.

He was a member of the Medical Society of Virginia, and elected president in 1891; an honorary fellow in 1892.

Before studying medicine he was engaged for a time in engineering, being one of the corps of engineers who located the route of the Virginia and Tennessee Railroad. At the beginning of the Civil War he organized the Latham Battery, and in many battles of the first two years of the war he and his men were conspicuous for their bravery. He ruled his men through their devotion to him. About the latter part of 1862 he was commissioned surgeon in the army, and as such served until the close of the war.

He married in 1853 Anna Turner. They had three children, none of whom survived their father.

He suffered for several years from organic disease of the heart, of which he died on May 5, 1903.

His wit was proverbial and he was noted as a toast-master and as a writer of humerons sketches and poetry, and his professional papers are scholarly and full of thought, though not numerous. The title of two are:

"Report on the Advances in Surgery." ("Transactions of Medical Society of Virginia," 1885.)

"A Neglected Medical Function." ("Presidential Address," ibid., 1892.)

R. M. S.

Trans. Med. Soc. of Va., 1903.

Latimer, Henry (1752-1819).

Henry Latimer, army surgeon, was born in Newport, Delaware, in April, 1752, and graduated from the University of Pennsylvania in 1773, completing his medical education at Edinburgh University. He settled in Wilmington, Delaware, but on war breaking out was appointed hospital surgeon and physician.

He was honorably mentioned by Gen. Washington during the war, and in 1813 appointed surgeon-general of the army and discharged in 1815. He was a member of the State Medical Society from its organization, and at one time its president.

As a surgeon in the Continental Army he won distinction and afterwards both as physician and surgeon was considered a man of ability and of high character.

He married early in life, and had five children, and died in Wilmington, December, 1819.

H. M. T.

Historical Encyclopedia of Delaware, 1882.

Latimer, Thomas Sargent (1839-1906).

He was born at Savannah, Georgia, June 17, 1839. Having received a literary training at the Sherwood Academy, York, Pennsylvania, he entered the medical school of the University of Maryland, and graduated M. D. in 1861 and soon after went south and entered the Confederate Army as private, but was soon appointed assistant surgeon, later full surgeon and assistant medical purveyor of the army of Northern Virginia. The war having closed, he remained at Richmond one year, and in 1866 was appointed resident physician to the Baltimore Infirmary, which position he held two years, then began private practice.

Among other appointments he was professor of anatomy in the Baltimore College of Dental Surgery; in 1873, held the chair of surgery, in the College of Physicians and Surgeons; and was appointed, in 1876, to the chair of physiology and diseases of children, and in 1883 professor of the principles and practice of medicine; president of the Baltimore Medical Association, 1872-73; of the Clinical Society of Maryland, 1880-81, of the Medical and Chirurgical Faculty of Maryland, 1884-85, and for many years he held the same office in the Faculty of the College of Physicians and Surgeons. With E. Lloyd Howard he edited the "Baltimore Medical Journal" in 1870-71. In 1873 he was the editor of the "Physician and Surgeon." and was a frequent contributor to the journal literature and wrote sections in Harris' "Principles and Practice of Dentistry" and in Loomis' "Text-book of Medicine." Among his most valuable articles are those on alcoholism, actinomycosis and diseases of children. He died May 16, 1906, from Bright's Disease. He knew that his case was hopeless several years before the end, but he stuck to his work until the last year of his life. Then with that fine sensibility which characterized him, he offered his resignation, but his faculty refused to accept it, and he remained in office until his death.

E. F. C.

Cordell's "Medical Annals of Maryland," 1903, and sketch by his colleague, W. R. Stokes, in "Old Maryland," vol. iv, No. 1, Jan., 1908. There are portraits at the College of Physicians and Surgeons and at the University of Maryland, Baltimore.

Lawrence, Jason Valentine O'Brien (1791–1823).

Lawrence spent six years in study at the University of Pennsylvania, where he received his M. D. degree in 1815, returning at once to New Orleans, and beginning the practice of medicine with Dr. Flood, his step-father. During his study at the University of Pennsylvania, he had acquired a taste for the more scientific aspects of medicine, which caused him, three years after his return, to sacrifice an unusually brilliant prospect of entering upon a large practice at home so that he might return to Philadelphia for further scientific study.

At that period the medical school of the University of Pennsylvania closed its doors in April and was not again opened until the following November. To offer advantages to those desiring to study during this vacation period, Lawrence opened a private school in which he gave a course on anatomy and surgery. This course began in March, had a recess in August, and ended in November. He gave

six lectures a week and these were distinguished for the ease and perspicuity of their style and attracted many students. His school differed from the private courses in anatomy given by numerous practitioners at this time, in that it was more systematically organized, and was open to the public, while the lessons given by others were more in the nature of instruction to private pupils. The school founded by Lawrence existed for many years, and later became known as the Philadelphia School of Anatomy. In 1875 this school was closed, but soon afterwards another school bearing the same name was opened by a former teacher in the school, and was continued until recent years.

In the fall of 1818 Lawrence became assistant to Dr. Gibson, professor of surgery at the University of Pennsylvania, and in 1822 he was also made assistant to Dr. Horner, then adjunct professor of anatomy, and about the same time he was appointed surgeon to the Philadelphia Hospital.

Although if Lawrence had lived, he would probably have established an extensive practice in Philadelphia, his devotion to scientific teaching and study during the earlier years of his life left him little time to work at building up a trade among the wealthy. While he was attending the poor, during an epidemic of typhus fever in 1823 he was stricken with a mortal illness. He was at that time but thirty-two years old.

In 1821 the "Academy of Medicine was formed for the development of scientific medicine." Lawrence was an active member of this academy. He was diligent in scientific investigation, one of his chief pieces of work being the "Study of the Action of Veins as Absorbents." Dr. Chapman, professor of practice and physiology at the University of Pennsylvania became interested in the views brought forward by Magendi, that the veins as well as the lymphatics served as absorbents. He himself disbelieved in the conclusions of Magendi, and at his suggestion a committee of the Academy of Medicine was appointed to make a study of the subject. He gave pecuniary assistance to this committee, which consisted of Dr. Lawrence, Dr. Harlan and Dr. Coates. Over ninety experiments on living animals w e r e performed. Lawrence, not satisfied with this, in the following summer, together with Dr. Coates, performed an additional series of over one hundred experiments. He had begun a third series to determine the method of absorption in the brain, when his work was cut short by death. The results were published in the "Philadelphia Journal of Medical and Physical Sciences," vol. iii, p. 273; vol. v, pp. 108 and 327, and they not only verified but extended Magendi's views.

In New Orleans, Lawrence had exposed himself to yellow fever by making autopsies on putrid bodies. He investigated the subject still further in the epidemic of 1820, and left the most complete record of autopsies which had been made up to this time. He left over 3000 pages of manuscript, much of it for use in a projected work on pathological anatomy, a subject at that time neglected in America. He died in Philadelphia in 1823.

C. R. B.

Prof. W. W. Keeu, History of the Philadelphia School of Anatomy.
For Obituary Notices, see:
Dr. Coates, Phila , Jour. Med. and Phys Sci., 1873.
Eulogium, by Prof. Jackson, ibid.

Lawson, Leonidas Merion (1812-1864).

Leonidas Merion Lawson was born in Nicholas County, Kentucky, September 10, 1812, a son of the Rev. Jeremiah Lawson. He received his early education in the school which afterwards became Augusta College and in 1830 began to study medicine, two years later receiving a license to prac-

tise in the first medical district of Ohio. He removed soon afterwards to Mason County, Kentucky, where he practised until 1837, graduating at Transylvania University, Lexington, Kentucky, in the spring of 1838. In 1841 he removed to Cincinnati, Ohio. In 1842 he founded the "Western Lancet," and continued editor until 1855. In 1844 he commenced a reprint of Hope's "Pathological Anatomy." During the same year he received a call to a chair in Transylvania University, and in 1845 spent several months in the hospitals of London and Paris. On his return he moved to Lexington, Kentucky.

In 1847 he was made professor of materia medica and general pathology in the Medical College of Ohio, which position he held until 1853, when he was appointed professor of the principles and practice of medicine, and in 1856 he returned to the Medical College of Ohio, but in 1860 filled the chair of clinical medicine in the University of Louisiana.

In 1861 he published his treatise on "Phthisis Pulmonalis," a work to which he had given six years of earnest labor, and which was a standard text-book long after its publication.

Lawson married twice. His first wife a Miss Louisa Cailey, of Felicity, Ohio, who died in 1846 leaving three daughters. One of them—Louise—became a noted sculptor, receiving high honors in this country and abroad. She died in 1899.

His second wife was Eliza Robinson, daughter of John Robinson of Wilmington, Delaware; by her he had two sons and five daughters. Dr. Lawson died January 21, 1864.

A. G. D.

Cincin. Lancet and Obs 1864, n. s vii.
Portrait in Surg -gen Lib Wash. D C.

Lawson, Thomas (1795(?)-1861).

This army surgeon after the completion of his medical studies was surgeon's mate in the navy, clearly too young, and promoted to surgeoncy of the sixth Infantry May 21, 1813. Upon the reduction of the army in 1815, retained in the service as surgeon of the seventh Infantry. Upon reorganization of the medical department, 1821, army surgeon senior in grade and so continuing until his promotion as surgeon-general in 1836.

His character was marked not only by administrative ability but by an intrepid bravery which led to his appointment as lieutenant-colonel of a regiment of Louisiana volunteers and to his assignment to the organization and command of a battalion of New York and Pennsylvania volunteers in the Seminole war. He served in every war in which his country was engaged up to his death, excepting the Black Hawk one. When appointed surgeon-general he was acting as medical director of the troops from the north designed for service in the Florida War, so that he did not arrive in Washington until six months after his appointment.

He secured for army medical officers actual military rank, but without command, and enunciated the principle that such officers should be allowed to engage in private practice at their stations when it could be done without interfering with military duty. In 1850 he inaugurated the custom of sending delegates from the army to the American Medical Association, and in 1856 secured an increase of the commissioned medical force, the enlistment of hospital stewards as such, and the authorization of extra duty-pay for soldiers detailed for hospital service. He accompanied Gen. Winfield Scott on his Mexican campaign and received the brevet of brigadier-general for gallantry.

A man of commanding character, he exerted a most effective and beneficient influence in favor of his department. While on a trip for rest and recreation he died of apoplexy at Norfolk, Virginia, May 15, 1861.

J. E. P.

Pilcher, James Evelyn, Journal of the Association of Military Surgeons of the United States, vol. xiv, 1904 (port.).
The Surgeon-Generals of the United States Army, Carlisle, Pa., 1905 (port.).

Lazear, Jesse William (1866–1900).

Jesse William Lazear, of the United States Army Yellow Fever Commission and one who laid down his life in the investigation, was born in Baltimore on May 2, 1886. His early education was received at Trinity Hall, a private school in Pennsylvania. From there he went to the Johns Hopkins University, graduating in 1889; he studied medicine at the University of Columbia and after graduation served for two years at Bellevue Hospital. He then studied for a year in Europe, part of his time being passed at the Pasteur Institute in Paris. On his return he was appointed bacteriologist to the medical staff of the Johns Hopkins Hospital and also assistant in clinical microscopy in the University.

He displayed brilliant promise in research. It was he who first succeeded in isolating the diplococcus of Neisser in pure culture in the circulating blood in a case of ulcerative endocarditis, and he was the first person in this country to confirm and elaborate the studies of Romanovsky and others concerning the intimate structure of the hematozoa of malaria.

In 1900 when the United States Army Yellow Fever Commission was appointed he was made a member and reached Cuba several months before his colleagues. This time he spent in investigating the pathological and bacteriological side of the disease, so that when the commission met he was able to say with confidence that cultures and blood examinations promised nothing of special importance.

He, as well as the other members of the commission, believed in the theory of the transmission of the disease by means of the mosquito. It was, therefore, with a full knowledge of his danger that he allowed a mosquito which was known to have bitten a yellow-fever patient to alight upon his hand and take its fill. Five days later he was taken ill with the disease, but before he would consent to be removed to the yellow-fever hospital he made over to his colleague, Dr. Carroll his notes on mosquito inoculation and told him of his personal experience. For three days he held his own, but then the dreaded black vomit made its appearance, a symptom which he well knew indicated that the case was all but hopeless. Dr. Carroll who visited him at this time said that he could never forget the expression of alarm in his eyes when this symptom was impending. Four days later, on September 26, 1900, he died.

Lazear's early death was a most grievous loss to his profession and to the world at large. He laid down his life before the Yellow Fever Commission had well entered upon their work, so early indeed in its career that his name appears on but one of their published reports. Nevertheless, although his untimely death deprived him of a full share in the brilliant results which they achieved, he did heroic service and Dr. Reed, when speaking of him before the Medical and Chirurgical Society of Maryland, closed his remarks with these words: "It is my earnest wish that, whatever credit may hereafter be given to the work of the American Commission in Cuba, the name of my late colleague, Dr. Lazear, may always be associated therewith."

Dr. Lazear is buried at the Loudon Park Cemetery at Baltimore and a memorial tablet has been erected to his memory at the Johns Hopkins Hospital.

He married and left two children, the younger of whom he never saw.

C. W. L.

The Etiology of Yellow Fever, Reed Carroll and Lazear, Phila., 1900.
J. Am. Med. Ass., Chicago, 1900, vol. xxxv.
Johns Hopkins Hosp. Bull., Balt., 1900, vol. xi.
Science, N. Y. and Lancaster, Pa., 1900, n. s., vol. xii.

Leaming, James Rosebrugh (1820–1892).

On February 20, 1820 there was born at Groveland, Livings County, one James Rosebrugh Leaming, destined to help suffering humanity by his special study of chest affections. In 1845 he studied under Dr. Lauderdale of Genesco; in 1847 matriculated at, and in 1849 graduated from, New York University, immediately after settling down to practise in that city, where his lectures in the New York clinic, of which he was president, were strikingly clear, original and useful. " Beyond all doubt his greatest teaching was with regard to pleural pathology and the interpleural origin of râles. His teaching of the latter met with a storm of opposition, but he lived to see his propositions meet with wide-spread acceptancy in the profession." By common consent Dr. Leaming was credited with an ear, which in its acuteness, was almost without a rival. He will be always regarded as a leading diagnostician of heart and lungs. He was so sure of his own power of detecting the occult features of cases that one of his dying regrets was the inability to sound his own chest. Curiously, his acuteness of observation seemed to extend to his quick knowledge of men, so astonishing was the accurate estimate he formed.

He died on December 5, 1902, after suffering heroically, aged seventy-two.

Among his many memberships was that of the New York Academy of Medicine; the Pathological Society; the Medical Society of the State of New York, and the American Medical Association; and among his noteworthy writings are:

"Cardiac Murmurs," New York, 1868; "Respiratory Murmurs," New York, 1872; "Plastic Exudation within the Pleura, Dry Pleurisy," Philadelphia, 1873; "Contributions to the Study of Diseases of Heart and Lungs," New York, 1884; "Significance of Disturbed

Action and Functional Murmurs of the Heart," 1875.

Tr. N. Soc., N. York, Phila., 1893. (J. L. Corning)
Med. Rec., N. York, 1893, vol. xliii.
Tr. N. York Acad. M. (1893), 1894, n s., vol. x.

LeConte, Joseph (1823–1901).

A geologist and teacher, he was born February 26, 1823, and descended from Guillaume LeConte (LeConte de Nonant, of Normandy) who settled about 1698 at New Rochelle in the state of New York. His father, Louis, had left the North to take up his permanent abode upon a family estate in Liberty County, Georgia, and it was here Joseph was born.

From the University of Georgia he received the degrees A. B., 1841; A. M., 1845; from the College of Physicians and Surgeons, New York, M. D., 1845; from Lawrence Scientific School (Harvard), B. S., 1851; from Princeton, LL. D., 1896. He was a member of the National Academy of Sciences, and various other societies. In Cambridge he studied under Louis Agassiz, and in New York, under Dr. Torrey and Dr. Louis A. Sayre.

He was elected to the chairs of geology and natural history, University of Georgia, 1852; to the chairs of geology and chemistry, South Carolina College, 1856; to that of chemistry in the medical department of the same college, 1857; and those of geology and zoology, University of California, in 1869— which positions he continued to hold until his death. During the Civil War he was chemist of the Confederate laboratory for the manufacture of medicines, 1862-3 and chemist of the Nitre and Mining Bureau, with the rank of major, 1863, until the end of the war.

Dr. LeConte practised as a physician only a few years after graduating M. D., and before taking up his studies under Agassiz. Nevertheless he continued to be interested in medical subjects, publishing a number of papers on such topics; and a book, "Sight," which is an exposition of the principles of monocular and binocular vision. Besides these, he is the author of various books and articles, most of which lie in the domain of natural science. In his own specialty of geology his best work lay along the line of mountain making and structure.

Up to the time of his death he was head of the departments of geology and biology in the University of California, but elected to those of geology and zoology, for in 1869 the term "Biology" had not yet entered scientific nomenclature.

In 1847 he married Caroline Elizabeth Nisbet, daughter of A. M. Nisbet, of Milledgeville, Georgia, and had five children, four of whom survived him, Emma Florence, Sarah Elizabeth, Caroline Eatton and Joseph Nisbet.

It is a peculiar fact that the LeConte family were scientific men from father to son for two hundred years. Dr. Pierre LeConte (born in 1704) was in his day a physician of some note, and since his time there has not been one generation of this family in the male line which has not been represented by scientists and by one or more physicians. This striking example of heredity was noted by Samuel Scudder in his memoir of Dr. J. L. Le Conte, read before the National Academy of Sciences in 1884.

His many scientific publications were mostly confined to geology and physiology. Among those connected with medical science are:

"Science of Medicine," "Medical and Surgical Journal," 1850; "Artificial Production of Sex," "Nashville Journal of Medicine and Surgery," 1866-'67. A series of articles on "Binocular Vision," "American Journal of Science," 1868-'87; "Glycogenic Function of the Liver," "American Journal of Science," 1878-'80; "Genesis of Sex," "Popular Science Monthly," 1879; "Rev. Scientifique," 1880; "Effect of Mixture of Races on Human Progress," Berkeley "Quarter-

LEE S9 LEE

ly," 1880; "Significance of Sex in Evolution," "Science," 1880, "Pacific Medical Journal," 1880; "Ptomaines and Leucomaines, and their relation to disease," "Pacific Medical Journal," September, 1889, "Science," 1889. He also published several books bearing remotely on medicine. Among them are "Sight," an exposition of monocular and binocular vision, 1880; "Evolution; Its Nature, Its Evidences, and Its Relation to Religious Thought," 1888. C. E. L.

The Autobiography of Joseph LeConte, 1903.
Jour. Am Med. Asso., Chicago, 1901, vol. xxxvii.
Tr. Med. Assoc., Georgia, Atlanta, 1902. (W. L. Jones.)
Portrait in LeConte's Autobiography, 1903.

Lee, Arthur (1740–1792).

Arthur Lee was born in the County of Westmoreland, Virginia, on December 20, 1740. He was the sixth son of Thomas Lee of Stratford, the first native Virginian to be appointed governor of the colony. The distinction attained by each of his six sons caused Washington to write in 1771: "I know of no county that can produce a family all distinguished as clever men, as our Lees."

Arthur Lee was educated and took his M. D. at Edinburgh University. On returning to Virginia he settled in Williamsburg, and practised with success for several years. Not liking his profession, however, he gave it up, went to London and began to study law in the Temple.

While there, he rendered most important service to his country in sending to America the earliest information of the plans of the British Ministry. When instructions were sent to Gov. Bernard, Lee communicated their nature to the patriots of Boston.

In 1775 he was in London as agent of Virginia, and presented to the King in August of that year the second petition from Congress. When Jefferson declined the position, Lee was

appointed minister to France, and joined his colleagues, Dr. Franklin and Mr. Deane, at Paris in December, 1776. History deals fully with the dissentions which arose between Lee and his colleagues and which resulted in his return to America. So uuquestioned was his intergrity, he found no difficulty in reinstating himself in the opinion of the public, and in 1784 was appointed one of the commissioners for holding a treaty with the Indians of the Six Nations, a trust which he executed with much honor to himself. In 1790 he was admitted a counsellor of the Supreme Court of the United States by a special order.

He died after a short illness on the fourteenth of December, 1792, at Urbanna, Middlesex County, Virginia.

His published articles were all of a political nature, and consisted of the Monitor's Letters, written in 1769 in vindication of the colonial rights, "Extracts from a letter to Congress, in answer to a Libel by Siras Deane," 1780; and "Observations on Certain Commercial Transactions in France," laid before Congress in 1780.
R. M. S.

Lee, Charles Alfred (1801–1872).

Charles Alfred Lee, son of Samuel and Elizabeth Brown Lee, was born at Salisbury, Connecticut, March 3, 1801. He graduated A. M. at Williams College, Massachusetts.

He began to study medicine with his brother-in-law, Luther Ticknor, M. D., of Salisbury, Connecticut, and graduated M. D. from the Berkshire Medical College, at Pittsfield, Massachusetts, where he held the office of demonstrator of anatomy during the winter session, and instructor in botany during the summer course.

On the twenty-eighth of June, 1828, he married Hester Ann Mildeberge, daughter of John A. and Ann (De Witt) Mildeberge, of New York City, and had nine children, only three of whom, all sons, survived.

When the Northern Dispensary of New York City was being established, Dr. Lee and Dr. James Stewart were among its most active and most efficient promoters.

He accepted the chair of materia medica and general pathology in the Geneva Medical College, New York. After the year 1850, Dr. Lee devoted himself chiefly to teaching various branches of medicine in different medical colleges, among which may be named the University of the City of New York; Geneva Medical College; University of Buffalo, medical department; Vermont Medical College, at Woodstock; Maine Medical School, at Brunswick; Berkshire Medical College; Starling Medical College, Columbus, Ohio. The branches taught by him in these different colleges were: therapeutics and materia medica; general pathology, obstetrics, and diseases of females; hygiene and medical jurisprudence.

In 1850, in connection with his colleagues, Drs. Hamilton, Flint, Hadley, and Webster, he founded the Buffalo Medical School, acting under the charter of the University of Buffalo.

He wrote extensively on a great variety of medical and scientific subjects. His "Physiology for the Use of Elementary Schools" was published by the American Common School Society about 1835 and passed through ten or more editions, much popularizing this important branch of knowledge His "Manual of Geology for Schools and Colleges" was published in 1835. In 1843 he was instrumental in establishing the "New York Journal of Medicine and the Collateral Sciences." In 1845 Dr. Lee brought out an edition of "Principles of Forensic Medicine," by William A. Guy, M. D., with extensive and valuable notes and additions, and in 1848 commenced the most important and laborious professional work of his life—the editing an American edition of Dr. James Copland's "Dictionary of Practical Medicine," issued irregularly in London.

The Dictionary was fifteen years in passing through the press of the Harpers, owing to its slow publication by its author in London. The entire work forms three immense octavo volumes. He also edited and enlarged an English work entitled "Bacchus, an Essay on the Nature, Cause, Effects and Cure of Intemperance," by Ralph B. Grindrod. A. T. Thomson's "Conspectus" of the London, Edinburgh, and Dublin Colleges, and of the United States Pharmacopœia. "Pharmacologia, or, the Theory and Art of Prescribing," by J. A. Paris, M. D.

He wrote, the last years of his life, a work on the "Indigenous Materia Medica of the United States," which is in manuscript and would form a volume of about six hundred pages.

In the spring of 1862, the second year of the war, Dr. Lee visited Europe to collect plans, models, and specifications of the best and most recent naval, civil, and military hospitals of Great Britain and the Continent, for the use of the United States Government. These, with others, were placed in the archives of the War Department at Washington. He wrote for the "American Medical Times," of New York, about fifty elaborate and carefully prepared letters designed to furnish useful information to our army and naval surgeons.

During the war he accepted a situation as hospital inspector and visitor, in the United States Sanitary Commission's employ. He labored efficiently in this field until the close of the war, and in the spring of 1865, soon after the surrender of Gen. Lee's army, the doctor was engaged for several months throughout the South in collecting materials for "Memoirs of a Sanitary History of the War." ("Sanitary Records and Medical History of the War," issued by the United States Sanitary Commission.)

Lee was a member of the New York Academy of Medicine and the New York State Medical Society.

Dr. Lee was taken ill on the thirtieth day of January, with endocarditis, and died after two weeks of suffering. His wife and three sons survived him.

J. M. T.

N. Y. Med. Jour., Ap., 1872, vol. xv.
Boston Med. and Surg. Jour., vol. xlii, 1850 and 1872.
Med. Reg., N. Y., 1872, vol. x.

Lee, Charles Carroll (1839–1893).

Charles Carroll Lee was born in Philadelphia, Pennsylvania, March 24, 1839, and died suddenly from pleurisy in his home in New York City, May 11, 1893. He was descended from the distinguished family of Lees which settled in Virginia in 1641. In 1770 one member of the family settled in Maryland. The Hon. Thomas Sim Lee, Governor of Maryland in 1779, was Dr. Lee's grandfather. His father, the Hon. John Lee, married Harriet Carroll, granddaughter of Charles Carroll, of Carrollton, the last of the signers of the Declaration of Independence to die. It may thus be seen that a long line of distinguished ancestors had undoubtedly left their impress upon the mind and physique of Lee. He graduated from Mt. St. Mary's College, Emmettsburg, Maryland, in 1656, and received his M. D. from the University of Pennsylvania in 1859. His LL. D. was conferred by Mt. St. Mary's College in 1890. He was successively appointed to the position of house physician to Wills, Blockley and Pennsylvania Hospitals and assistant surgeon in the regular army at the begnning of the Civil War. At its close, after being appointed to full surgeon, he resigned and settled in New York City. He was a warm personal friend of Dr. George T. Elliott, and through him was at once introduced to the best circle of medical men in the city and appointed surgeon to St. Vincent's Hospital and to the Charity Hospital soon after he came to New York. After being assistant surgeon in the Woman's Hospital, under Peaslee, he became surgeon early in 1879, after the latter's death, a position held over ten years, when, on account of

laborious private practice, he resigned. When Lee's name was brought up before the Board of Managers for confirmation, Mr. John A. Parsons presiding, one of the lady managers asked in surprise, "Do you know he is a Jesuit?" Mr. Parsons replied, "Why, madam, I always heard he was a surgeon." At the time of his death he was consulting physician to the Charity Hospital, St. Elizabeth's Hospital and the Woman's Hospital.

Lee had often been asked to take a professorship in some of the different medical schools in New York and Philadelphia, but had declined the honor. In 1887, however, he allowed himself to be elected professor of diseases of women in the New York Post-Graduate School, a position held at the time of his death. He was president of the New York Obstetrical Society for two years, vice-president of the New York Academy of Medicine for three years, and at the time of his death president of the Medical Society of the County of New York.

Although not so deft an operator as some, his education, his experience and his therapeutic knowledge rendered him at all times a safe surgeon, and his death-rate was as small as the smallest. As a clinical teacher he always interested his class with a wonderfully graphic and charming description of the disease, or lesion, present in the patient before him. He was ever willing to use new appliances, instruments, and medicines, or to try new surgical operations when such seemed to be improvements, but never simply because they were new. As a presiding officer he was quick, judicious, and gracious. In this position he showed, *par excellence*, the gentleman of the old school, adorned with all the culture and refinement of the best modern society.

As a writer he gave many practical contributions on important subjects. He wrote the article in the "American System of Gynecology" on "Diseases of the Vagina." His subjects were various and showed a breadth of thought and study. Early in his career in New York he wrote an excellent article on "Hematocele." In 1879, in the "Medical Record," we find his helpful paper on "Cystitis"; in 1881, in the same journal, his article on "The Proper Limitation of Emmet's Operation"; and in the "Transactions of the American Gynecological Society for 1884," his excellent article on "Puncture of the Gravid Uterus during Ovariotomy." Later, in the "New York Medical Record" appeared "Puerperal Fever"; while in 1886 he wrote the very scholarly paper in the "International Encyclopedia of Surgery" (New York) on "Ovarian and Uterine Tumors." In 1888 he wrote a thoroughly honest paper on "Hysterorrhaphy in the Treatment of Retroflextions of the Womb," and in the fall of 1891 he read before the New York Obstetrical Society a paper on "The Ultimate Results of the Removal of the Uterine Appendages," which was published in the "New York Journal of Gynecology and Obstetrics" and in the "University Medical Magazine." It was eminently fair and judicious, and no paper ever read by Dr. Lee before the Obstetrical Society gave a better impression of his honesty, his ability, and his judicial mind. In the "Transactions" of the American Gynecological Society," and in those of the Medical Society of the County of New York, of the Obstetrical Society, and of the Academy of Medicine of New York, may be found many pages of his excellent remarks in the discussion of various papers.

Dr. Lee married Helen, daughter of the late Dr. Isaac Parrish, of Philadelphia, in 1863, who, with five children, survived him. One son became a doctor.

H. T. H.

Incidents of my Life, T. A. Emmet.
Am. J. Obstet., N. Y., 1893, xxvii (port.) (R. Waldo).
Boston M. and S. J., 1893, cxxiii.
N. York J. Gynec. and Obstet., 1893, iii (port.) (T. A. Emmet).
Tr. Am. Gynec. Soc., 1893, xviii (H. T. Hanks).
Portrait in the Sur -Gen. Lib., Wash , D. C.

Lefevre, John M. (1857–1907),

John M. Lefevre was a well known and very popular practitioner in the early days of Vancouver, and a member of the Board of Directors of the General Hospital, in which he exhibited a lively interest, also taking a prominent part in the establishment of the new hospital, which was completed shortly after his death in 1907. He held the M. D. and C. M. from McGill University (1879) and the M. R. C. S., England, 1896.

He was surgeon to the Canadian Pacific Railway during construction, and to the Company in Vancouver.

Dr. Lefevre was a good diagnostician and took a keen interest in his professional work. He spent a year among the hospitals of Europe, and before returning presented himself for examination and passed the membership of the Royal College of Surgeons, England.

After a short illness he died, in 1907, aged fifty years.

O. M. J.

Leidy, Joseph (1823–1891).

A friend being asked to introduce him as lecturer protested that he himself rather needed introducing. "Keep your seat, Dr. Hunt, I will introduce myself" called out the speaker of the evening, and he said:

"My name is Joseph Leidy, doctor of medicine. I was born in this city the ninth of September, 1823, and have lived here ever since. My father was Philip Leidy, the hatter, on third street above Vine; my mother, Catherine Mellick, but she died a few months after my birth, and my father married her sister Christina, who was all in all to me, the one to whom I owe all that I am. At an early age I took great delight in natural history, of which I have reason to think I know a little, and a little of that little I propose to teach you to-night."

Anatomist, botanist, paleontologist, zoologist, the "little" summed up by friendly hands at his death amounted to five hundred and fifty-three volumes, papers and communications. After his early education at private schools he

JOSEPH LEIDY.

thought of being an artist, but attendance at a drug-store set him thinking of medicine, and in 1844 he graduated M. D. from the University of Pennsylvania, with a characteristic thesis on the "Comparative Anatomy of the Eye of Vertebrate Animals." In the same year he became prosector in anatomy at the university and demonstrator of anatomy in the Franklin Medical College, 1846. When the chair of anatomy became vacant at the university through the death of Dr. Horner in 1853, Leidy, who had acted as his assistant, was appointed. Thirty at the time, he held it until he was sixty-eight and "the lustre he threw on the university quenched all jealousies by its brightness."

To say that he was always at work would be as natural as to say a lover would be with his mistress; the joy of increasing knowledge overmeasured fatigue. Appointments and honors were multiplied: professor of natural history to Swarthmore College; presidency of the Academy of Natural Sciences; professor of zoology in the University of Pennsylvania; Harvard gave him her LL. D. He was honored by the Lyell medal from the London Geological Society and the Cuvier medal from the Paris Academy of Science. He was, besides, member, active or honorary, of over forty native and foreign societies. At the time of his death he had attained an enviable reputation as a mineralogist and botanist; was among the highest authorities on comparative anatomy and zoology; a distinguished helminthologist and paleontologist.

In 1864 he married Anna, daughter of Robert Harden.

Perhaps his wonderful monograph on "The Fresh Water Rhizopods of North America," the result of laborious research, best shows how loving a student he was, and his drawing and coloring of microscopic objects proved him also a real artist. As an anatomist, "nothing" says his collaborator Dr. Hunt, "could exceed the beauty of Leidy's dissections . . . the

display of the diaphragm, the muscles of the abdomen and chest, the thoracic and abdominal viscera; the clear, concise explanation and exhibition of the human brain. I was with him also during many of his investigations particularly into the comparative anatomy of the liver, the development of the Purkinjean corpuscles in bone and that of the intermaxillary bone. Leidy's wonderful display of temporal bones is now in the museum. His description of the vocal membranes and larynx structures is admirable. His acquaintance with extinct forms of life was equally wonderful.

1846 marked his sure track concerning the origin and action of the *Trichina spiralis* of hog cholera, though the full significance of the parasite in the hog was not all at once apparent. The great German helminthologist Leuckart, Cobbold and others fully acknowledged the discovery as due to Dr. Leidy.

But the weight of his genius stays the pen. How to do justice in a few brief pages. "By his knowledge" says the giant lizard Hydrosaurus Foulkii "I was reconstructed." "By his knowledge of my life in prehistoric days the wonderful changes in my size from less to greater have been shown" echoes the Equus Americanus. Coming more to the human side of Leidy, savants and students, rich and poor and children all eagerly added their share of praise to the gentle-hearted scientist who received correction gladly but bestowed it on amateur scientists so modestly and sweetly that it never discouraged or hurt at all.

Here is one little intimate glimpse. He had a fine *spirituelle* face, curiously resembling pictures of the Saviour, and children noticed this. "One day Leidy was staying with a member of the Academy and the company started out for a walk. The host's little daughter suddenly broke away and ran over the grass in pursuit of a butterfly. After much exertion she caught it and whispered in her father's ear that it was 'for Jesus Christ' and timidly gave it to the doctor."

Early in April, 1891, hard work began

to tell and frequently he had to sit down during half the lecture. The examination tired him greatly and he said jokingly "The old machine is breaking up." On Thursday the twenty-eighth he took to his bed and two days after gradually lapsed into unconsciousness and died.

More fitting and enduring than sculptured bronze or marble are the monuments chosen. On the western slope of the Rockies in Wyoming stands Mount Leidy, so christened by Dr. F. V. Hayden the explorer and geologist. In the Luray caves one of the giant columns was dedicated to him while he still lived. A big party went out for the ceremony and Miss Ally Leidy christened the pillar.

It would be impossible to give all his writings; a tolerably full list is in the Surgeon-general's Catalogue, Washington, District of Columbia, and some of the most important are:

"Researches into the Comparative Structure of the Liver." ("Amercian Journal of the Medical Sciences," n. s., 1848.)

"On the Intimate Structure and Histology of the Articular Cartilages." (Ibid., n. s., 1849.)

"A Synopsis of Entozoa and Some of Their Ecto-Congeners," Philadelphia, 1856.

"An Address on Evolution and Pathological Importance of Lower Forms of Life." ("Therap. Gazette," Detroit, 1886.)

"An Elementary Treatise on Human Anatomy," Philadelphia, 1889.

D. W.

Joseph Leidy. An address by Dr. Wm. Hunt, Phila., 1892.

Universities and their Sons (Penn.), Boston, 1902.

Proc. Am. Phila. Soc. (W. S. W. Ruschenberger), Phila., 1892, vol. xxx.

Med. News, Phila., 1891, vol. lviii.

Med. and Surg. Reporter, Phila., 1891, vol. lxiv.

Science, N. Y., 1891, vol. xvii.

Portrait in the Surg.-Gen. Lib., Wash., D. C.

LeMoyne, Francis Julius (1798–1879).

Originator of cremation in America he was born in Washington, Pennsylvania, September 4, 1798, and was the only child of Dr. John Julius and Nancy McCully LeMoyne; his father, when the French Revolution began, left France on account of his liberal sentiments, with the members of the French Colony, and settled at Gallipolis, Ohio, in 1790; a few years later going to Washington, Pennsylvania.

Francis Julius LeMoyne was educated at Washington College (now Washington and Jefferson College), Washington, Pennsylvania, and graduated at the age of seventeen. He attended lectures for two winters at the University of Pennsylvania, making the trip to Philadelphia both times on horseback, and, graduating in 1823, began active practice in 1824, after serving a year as interne at the Pennsylvania Hospital.

In May, 1823, he married Madelaine Romaine Bureau of Gallipolis, Ohio, whose parents were also members of the French Colony, and had eight children, three sons and five daughters. Dr. LeMoyne was a strong, broad, earnest man; a great reader and a student to the end of his life. He was fearless of criticism and wholly indifferent to popular sentiment; uncompromising on all questions of right or wrong: he often said, "of two evils choose neither."

About 1835 he became deeply interested in the antislavery movement and in education. He was one of the founders of the female Seminary at Washington in 1836, which is still in existence. Later he endowed a chair in Washington and Jefferson College and after the war established a normal school for the colored people at Memphis, Tennessee. Following this he established the Citizen's Library and Free Reading Rooms at Washington, Pennsylvania.

Dr. LeMoyne's last effort in reform was in regard to cremation. He became convinced years before his death that cremation was the proper and sanitary method of disposing of the dead and with that in view he offered to build a crematory in the Washington cemetery, Pennsylvania. However, his offer was declined, so he erected one in 1876 on his own grounds, the first and only in the United States until 1884.

Dr. LeMoyne died October 14, 1879 of diabetes and was cremated.

Of his sons, Frank, born at Washington, Pennsylvania, April, 1839, followed him in the medical profession.   A. K.

Lennox, Richmond (1861–1895).

Richmond Lennox was born in Brooklyn, New York, June 28, 1861. He was educated at the Brooklyn Polytechnic Institute, and graduated at the College of Physicians and Surgeons of New York in 1882. After serving as interne at the Roosevelt Hospital, he spent two years in the study of the eye and ear in Germany, France, and England. On his return to Brooklyn he devoted himself to ophthalmology and otology, was connected with the New York Eye and Ear Infirmary; ophthalmologic surgeon to the Brooklyn Eye and Ear Hospital, and to the Kings County Hospital. He was a member of the American Ophthalmological Society, was recognized as an able operator in eye disease, and did good work in his contributions to literature.

Unfortunately his life was cut short at the age of thirty-four, his death occurring November 14, 1895.   H. F.

Knapp's Archives of Ophthalmology, vol. xxv.

Letterman, Jonathan (1824–1872).

The son of a prominent doctor, he entered after private tuition the Jefferson Medical College, graduated M. D. in 1849 and entered the army as assistant-surgeon in the same year and was immediately assigned to duty in the Seminole War, at the close of which he entered upon a diversified period of service at various frontier stations, with brief respite at Fort Monroe. In 1861 he was assigned to duty with the army of the Potomac, and in May, 1862, was made medical director of the Department of West Virginia. A month prior to his promotion to the grade of surgeon-major he succeeded to the position of medical director of the army of the Potomac. Here he evinced a remarkable grade of administrative

ability, rehabilitating the service of the sick, creating a military medical organization, installing an effective hospital service, also instituting a system of transportation of the wounded in charge of an ambulance corps, making the medical department adequate to the needs of even such great battles as Chancellorsville and Gettysburg. The organization thus created formed the basis of the military medical administration during the remainder of the war. He resigned December 22, 1864, to engage in civilian work in California, and in 1866 published his "Medical Recollections of the Army of the Potomac." He was also a surgeon-general of California in 1868, and a member of the Board of Medical Examiners of the University of California, 1870. He died March 15, 1872.   J. E. P.

Clements, B. A., Journal of the Military Service Institution, 1883.

Levis, Richard J. (1827–1890).

Richard J. Levis, born June 28, 1827, in Philadelphia, graduated from the Central High School, and in 1848 from Jefferson Medical College. He settled in Philadelphia and attained a high reputation as a general and ophthalmic surgeon. In 1859 he was elected surgeon to the Philadelphia Hospital and in 1871 to the Pennsylvania Hospital where he served until 1887. He was also an attending surgeon at Wills Eye Hospital. During the Civil War he was acting assistant surgeon to the United States Military Hospital in Philadelphia. A skillful ophthalmic surgeon, he introduced the well known wire loop still used in certain cases of extraction of cataract. For many years he was clinical lecturer on ophthalmology and aural surgery at Jefferson Medical College and also took up active work at Jefferson Hospital, helping to establish the Philadelphia Polytechnic, where he held the chair of clinical and operative surgery.

He died November 12, 1890.
H. F.

Morton's History of the Pennsylvania Hospital, 1895.

Lewis, Francis West (1825–1902).

Medical annals and medical libraries would be searched in vain for the professional and literary achievements of Francis W. Lewis, son of Mordecai D. and Sarah West Lewis, but the Childrens' Hospital on Twenty-second Street in Philadelphia is a fine monument to a man who gave his best years to lightening the burden of suffering childhood.

He himself when only seven went to Bronson Alcott's School in Germantown, afterwards to Bishop Hopkins' Institute at Burlington, Vermont, graduating from the University of Pennsylvania at eighteen and taking his M. D. there in 1846 and becoming a fellow of the College of Physicians in 1855.

Two years were then spent partly in studying ophthalmics under Sir William Wilde in Dublin and afterwards in work at the Salpêtriere, Paris, a varied experience to end in an appointment of resident physician at the Pennsylvania Hospital.

The cares, two years later, of a large private practice among the Philadelphia poor drew on his strength and he made frequent voyages abroad, but during these and while he was tending sick soldiers in the Satterlee Hospital, Philadelphia, or in the temporary military hospital in Harrisburg he had one cherished hope—that of giving sick children a hospital all to themselves.

Finally, in 1855, aided by Dr. Penrose and Dr. Bache, a small house furnished with twelve beds was opened in Blight Street, Philadelphia, and Dr. Lewis' love for his new work as physician there grew ever greater, though from 1866–68 he had decided to and had given up practising. "Another infant cherubized" he would sigh as a disease-worn child set out to heaven from the hospital and he prized nothing more than his welcome from the children when he went into the wards.

A broad minded philanthropist, a lover of natural science and art, a great reader and a good friend, Dr. West with his two sisters helped onwards the well-being of their native town, but one cold night in February, 1902, a day of severe blizzard, he received his death blow from pneumonia because he would attend the Charity Organization meeting, his death taking place that same month.

Trans. Coll. of Phys., Pa., 1903, vol. xxv.
Universities and their Sons (Penn.) 1902.

Lewis, Samuel (1813–1890).

It takes all sorts of doctors to build up the medical profession and the name of a man who spends his time and money accumulating books curious and useful, ancient and modern, for others which he himself can never hope for time to enjoy is worth recording. Such a one was Samuel Lewis "who possessed a steady and intelligent generosity out of all proportion to the size of an income never more than moderate"—this opinion of him by S. Weir Mitchell.

He was born in Barbadoes, November 16, 1813, and came to Philadelphia with his uncle and guardian the Rev. Prescod Hinds when not quite twenty-one and in the fall of the same year matriculated at the University of Pennsylvania, but after one year went to Edinburgh and matriculated there, first experiencing a severe attack of small-pox owing to non-vaccination while in the Indies, and being given a patient, who had died of the disease, to dissect. After recovery he became dresser to the celebrated Syme, professor of clinical surgery in Edinburgh. After a while he stayed in London then on to Dublin, returning to Edinburgh in 1840 and taking his M. D. there. The same year he went back again to Philadelphia and entered active practice besides helping Dr. Hollingsworth edit "The Medical Examiner." He was closely attached to all medical interests but was most of all anxious to improve the college library and in 1864 presented to it his private library of 2,500 carefully selected volumes, so making the college collection the best in the state. He valued books for their historical association and their utility rather than their rarity, though he loved also a beautiful book. His greatest happiness lay in adding to his gift, until the numbers exceeded 10,000, including an unequalled collection of the School of Salerno. It formed part of his holidays, in Europe, to buy collections adding to the number, and if any friend craved a book, to supply the library with it. Equally generous with his money, he was friend to many in a delicate way and was known always as a faithful and sincere Christian.

In 1890 advancing age began to tell on him and it was also known he had a lesion of the aortic valve. On November 8, after a slight attack, he was able to enjoy his books again, but on the fifteenth slight congestion of the lungs increased and he died, aged seventy-seven years.

He held a fellowship of the College of Physicians, Philadelphia, and was president in 1884, and was also a member of the Royal College of Surgeons, London, 1839, and of the Royal Medical Society of Edinburgh, 1840.   D. W.

Univ. M. Mag., Phila., 1890, vol. iii
Tr. Coll. Phys., Phila., 1890, 3 s., vol. xii.
(S. W. Mitchell, et. al.)

Liebermann, Charles H. (1813–1886).

Charles H. Liebermann was born in Riga, September 15, 1813, his father a military surgeon who died while the boy was a child. His mother belonged to the Radetzkeys who furnished many famous personages in German and Polish history. The doctor's uncle became his guardian and gave the child a good education. He entered Dorpat University, from which he graduated M. A. in 1836 then on to Wilna, where he studied medicine, but after some time returned to Dorpat, and so to Berlin University where he took his M. D. and became a private pupil of Prof. Dieffenbach, serving for some time as his assistant. Dr. Liebermann enjoyed the advantages of the lectures and clinics of the famous ophthalmist von Graefe in his treatment of affections of the eye and also studied physical deformities.

He came to the United States early in 1840 and landed in Boston, but settled to practise in Washington shortly after

his arrival, on the north side of Pennsylvania Avenue, between Ninth and Tenth streets.

Professor Dieffenbach, the originator of the operation for the cure of strabismus, said: "Dr. Liebermann, who has been one of my distinguished pupils and for some time after closing his academical course my associate in the practice of medicine and surgery, was, after myself, the third physician in Europe and the first one in the United States, who, as early as October last (1840), performed the operation for strabismus with complete success."

The medical profession of the United States as well as the politicians saw with some regret the rapid immigration of and the prominent positions given in the professions and public places requiring scientific acquirements, to foreigners. Dr. Liebermann had to contend with a natural objection to foreigners but so well was he equipped, professionally and so discreet and honorable in his intercourse with medical men, that he soon gained not only their high regard but that of the citizens in general. He identified himself as soon as practicable, with the profession of the city by joining the Medical Society of the District, and was its president from 1865 to 1868. He joined the Medical Association of the District in 1843. He was one of the founders of the medical department of the University of Georgetown, and filled the chair of professor of surgery from 1849 to 1853, and again from 1857 to 1861, when he resigned and was elected emeritus professor. He was also a member of the first Pathological Society of Washington, organized in 1841. He had much mechanical ingenuity, which enabled him to succeed in the treatment of cataract, joints and deformities. He was for over twenty years the leading oculist in Washington. He was also a member of the staff and consulting surgeon to the Providence Hospital for a number of years.

He married in 1841 a Miss Betzold, of Alexandria, and had two children, a son and daughter. In 1872 he retired from practice. His mental powers to the last seemed as active and strong as in middle life when he died on March 27, 1886.   D. S. L.

Busey, Reminiscences.
Jour. Amer. Med. Assoc., vii, 1886.
National Intelligencer, 1841.

Linde, Christian (1817–1887).

Christian Linde was descended from the noble Danish family of De Linde-Freidenreich, and was born on that estate near Copenhagen, February 19, 1817. He was educated at the Royal University from which he graduated in 1837, but on account of political troubles while attending the hospitals of the Danish capital, he came to America in 1842 and settled near Oshkosh. Here he intended to found a landed estate and devote a portion of his time to hunting, of which he was passionately fond. This pursuit led him much among the Indians with whom he soon gained fame and influence as hunter and healer. From his blond countenance and numerous deeds of strength and bravery, they called him Muckwa (meaning White Bear). This phase of his life and character is marked by incidents romantic, tragical and humorous sufficient to fill a volume, and in later years he was fond of relating them to his intimates. To illustrate the difficulties of his practice in the early days, it is related that:

During a small-pox scare among the Indians along the lower Fox, he set out on a tour of vaccination accompanied by John L. Williams, famous as the son of the lost Dauphin of France. Despite the doctor's reputation for honesty among the savages, they were still skeptical and at each place visited, they required as a precautionary measure that the operation be performed on his companion. The condition of Williams' arms, as well as feelings, after several days' touring, may be left to the imagination.

But the insistent demands of the settlers for his professional services drew him reluctantly from the woods and streams, and after practising a few years in Green Bay and Fond du Lac, he settled permanently in Oshkosh. He was the first regular surgeon in Northern Wisconsin and during his long career he was called upon to perform many difficult operations. In keeping with his fine sentiments of honor as a man, his professional ideals were the highest. Dr. Linde belonged to the Medical Associations of his country, state and nation, serving as president of the Winnebago County Society, as vice-president of the Wisconsin Society. To these and to various publications he furnished a number of learned papers on surgery. His most brilliant contribution to medical science, however, was the use of animal tendon in surgery. To him belongs the distinction of having discovered its value and first applied it in the treatment of wounds.

Dr. Linde married three times: to Sarah Dickinson, daughter of Clark Dickinson, in 1843; to Sarah Davis, niece of Gov. Doty, in 1852, and to Mrs. Hulda Henning Volner in 1858. Dr. Fred Linde, the only issue of the first marriage, was associated with his father until his untimely death in 1880. Two daughters survived Dr. Linde.

Besides his attainments in medicine, Dr. Linde was a fine classical scholar and linguist, being able to converse in seven languages.

He died at Oshkosh, of senile capillary bronchitis. Stoical in his philosophy of life, during his last hours he discoursed calmly of death, and at the end whispered "How beautiful it is to die!"   M. L. B.

United States Biographical Dictionary for Wisconsin, Reports of Wisconsin Historical Society, Harney's History of Winnebago County.

Lindsly, Harvey (1804–1899),

Harvey Lindsly was born on January 11, 1804 and descended through both parents from English stock, the representatives of which came to this country over two hundred years ago, and settled in New Jersey. He was prepared for college at the Classical Academy in Somerset County, New Jersey, graduated at Princeton, studied medicine in New York and Washington at which latter city he took his medical degree. He was an honorary member of the Rhode Island Medical Society and published numerous articles in the "American Journal of the Medical Sciences" and other medical journals; also in the "North American Review," the "Southern Literary Messenger," and other literary periodicals. For several years, 1839–45, he was professor of obstetrics and subsequently, 1845–6, of the principles and practice of medicine in the National Medical College, District of Columbia. He was president of the Washington Board of Health for ten years and president of the American Medical Association in 1859.

He was the author of an "Essay on Origin and Introduction into Medical Practice of Ardent Spirits," Washington, 1835; "Medical Science and the Medical Profession in Europe and the United States," Washington, 1840; Address before the American Medical Association," Philadelphia, 1859.

He died on April 28, 1889.

D. S. L.

Lamb's Hist. of the Med. Dept. of Howard Univ., Wash. D. C., 1900.

Lining, John (1708–1760).

Born in Scotland in 1708, John Lining emigrated to America in 1730, settling at Charleston, South Carolina, where his skill as a physician gained him a large practice, and his scientific experiments a distinguished reputation abroad as a philosopher as well as a physician. He experimented early in electricity and was a correspondent of Benjamin Franklin. His meteorological observations extending over the years 1738, 1739, 1740 and 1742, which

were communicated to the Royal Society of London, were probably the first ever published. In order to determine the loss or gain in body-weight under varying thermic and meteorological conditions he made a series of experiments extending through one year, carefully comparing the weight of all solids and fluids ingested, with the weight of the perspiration, urine and feces. The account of these experiments was published in the transactions of the Royal Society of London. In 1753 he published an accurate history of the yellow fever, "which was the first that had been given to the public from the American continent."

In 1747 he was named by the General Assembly as one of three physicians who should visit vessels entering the port and certify to the health of the crew.

In 1739 he married Sarah Hill, of Hillsboro, North Carolina, but had no children.

He died on September 21, 1760.

R. W. JR,

History of South Carolina, Ramsay; South Carolina under the Royal Government, McCrady; An Account of the Weather and Diseases of South Carolina, Chalmers; The South Carolina Gazette, Sept. 20–27, 1760.

Linsley, John Hatch (1859–1901).

John Hatch Linsley, the son of Daniel C. and Patty Linsley, daughter of the Hon. John D. Patch, was born at Windsor, Vermont, May 29, 1859, and came early with his family to Burlington. His preliminary education was obtained there in the public schools and his medical one in Vermont University, where he graduated in 1880. He was associated for a short time after his graduation with Dr. S. W. Thayer and later practised himself in Burlington. During these early years he was instructor in laboratory chemistry in the university, and later in histology and pathology.

In 1888 he went to New York, where he was appointed professor of pathology in the Post-graduate Medical School, a position he held for four years until his health compelled him to abandon it. During this time he became enthusiastically interested in bacteriology and spent some time in Berlin in 1890 under Prof. Koch.

Soon after his return from Berlin, Koch's famous discovery of tuberculin was announced and Linsley was sent back to Berlin by the Post-graduate Medical School to secure what information he could in regard to the new serum and he brought back the first bottle of tuberculin used here. Soon after, he translated Fraenkel's standard work on bacteriology, but health, never rugged, broke down at this time and he was compelled to abandon work.

He held relations with the medical department of the University of Vermont during his stay in New York and was later made professor of histology, pathology and bacteriology, which position he held until 1899. In 1891 he returned to Burlington to live, but on account of his health was able to do only a limited amount of teaching and private laboratory work.

In 1897 Linsley proposed to the Vermont State Board of Health to give the people of the state, especially the physicians, an object lesson in the use of the laboratory in preventing disease. An arrangement was made with this Board by which Linsley agreed to examine specimens, from practitioners of the state, of suspected cases of diphtheria and typhoid fever without remuneration for his services. The Board, however, agreed to reimburse him as far as possible for the necessary equipment. The success of the experiment undertaken at his suggestion by the State Board was instantaneous. With characteristic energy, Linsley undertook to interest the Legislature of the state in the usefulness of a State Hygienic Laboratory and, equipped with his microscope and other technical apparatus, proceeded, after the gathering of the next

General Assembly in 1898, to Montpelier. The result was the present State Laboratory of Hygiene, one of the best of its kind in this country, and from the day of its foundation, through Dr. Linsley's efforts, to the present time, one of the most completely equipped in the country, and is his best and most enduring monument, and in it, as director, he did his last and most valuable work, besides writing many papers for state and other societies.

He was married in July, 1880, to Nettie, daughter of Harmon A. Ray of Burlington, and had one son and a daughter, Daniel Ray and Patty Hatch Linsley.

He died of meningitis at his home in Burlington, February 17, 1901.

C. S. C.

Am. Pub. Health Ass. Rep., 1899, Columbus, 1900, vol. xxv (port.).
J. Am. M. A., Chicago, 1897, vol. xxix.
South. Prac., Nashville, 1898, vol. xx.
Tr. M. Soc., Tennessee, Nashville, 1898.

Littell, Squier (1803–1886).

The Littells were among the earliest emigrants to America, the line beginning with George Littell who with his brother Benjamin came from London to Newbury, Essex County, Massachusetts, about 1630. Squier was the third child of Stephen and Susan Gardiner Littell and was born in Burlingtou, New Jersey, December 3, 1803. But both parents died early and the boy was adopted by his uncle Dr. Squier Littell of Butler County, Ohio, and had an education at such schools as the country then possessed, afterwards studying medicine with his uncle dividing time between the farm and his studies.

In 1821 he began to work under Dr. Joseph Parrish of Philadelphia, and three years later graduated at the University of Pennsylvania with a thesis on "Inflammation." Before settling in Philadelphia, he visited Buenos Ayres hoping to get a post there, but failed in this, yet was made a licentiate by examination of the Academy of

Medicine there. Some time after his return to Philadelphia he married Mary, daughter of Caleb Emlen, but she died early leaving him with an infant son and daughter.

On the Wills Hospital being organized in 1834 he was elected one of the surgeons; a fellow in 1836 and afterwards a councillor. Although a general practitioner in every sense, he was best known as an ophthalmist and as a patient and cautious investigator bold in execution when operation was necessary. When no longer young he devoted himself to mastering the difficulties of the ophthalmoscope (then new) and using it daily. His "Manual of Diseases of the Eye" was one of the earliest American books on the subject and was favorably received here and abroad. He also edited "The Monthly Journal of Foreign Medicine."

Although he always practised vaccination, he believed neither in the efficacy of that nor in the malarial origin of disease, not from narrow mindedness, for he had widely read and studied.

He was a staunch churchman and one of the committee to revise the Prayer Book in 1838, also editing some journals of the Episcopal Church.

As he neared his eightieth birthday he began to suffer from an affection of the choroid, and to one so fond of books this was a great trial. Early in the spring of 1886 his strength began to fail and he was found dead in bed on July 4, at Bay Head, New Jersey, where he had gone for his health.

His contributions to medical literature were numerous and of value; they include:

"Diseases of the Eye," 1837.

"Tumors at the Base of the Brain producing Amaurosis," 1838.

"Notes on Secondary Variolous Ophthalmia," 1855.

"Memoir on Granular Ophthalmia (by request) in the Transactions, Congrès d'Ophthalmologie de Bruxelles," 1857.

"Epithelial Cancer of the Colon," 1873.

Memoir, A. D. Hall, M. D. Trans. Coll. Phys., Phila., 1887.

Little, James Lawrence (1836–1885),

Of Scotch-Irish and English forbears, he was born in Brooklyn February 19, 1836, and went to private schools until nearly twenty when books attracted him and he entered a bookstore. But, reading more than selling, particularly the medical works, he soon wanted very much to become a doctor. When a boy he had the same wish and purchased a skull from an old African grave digger for twenty-five cents. But the skull was a gruesome specimen, unprepared and the lad threw it into Wallabout Bay and postponed medicine for a while.

One day Dr. Willard Parker was asked to take in another student. He was going to refuse, but somehow the tall earnest young man applying made an impression and Little was admitted and studied with Parker for two years and graduated at the College of Physicians and Surgeons, 1860, and resigning a position at Bellevue Hospital became junior assistant at the New York Hospital. Little brought enthusiasm and thoroughness. He reported cases for the "American Medical Times;" and devised a method of making and applying plaster--of-Paris splints to supersede the old starch bandage. Eminently painstaking as a lecturer, for one of his class says "Little did not merely tell the men to apply a flax-seed poultice but brought the flaxseed and the cloth and made the poultice before the class." His clinics were besieged by crowds of patients from far and near, and everyone knew when they were being held, by the mud stained buggies of the other practitioners standing near the door. He was the first American surgeon to puncture the bladder with the aspirator for the relief of retention of urine. He simultaneously ligated the subclavian and carotid arteries of the right side for aneurysm of the first part of the subclavian. The operation for stone he had done seventy-seven times with only two fatalities.

He married in June, 1858, Elsie A., daughter of John Charlotte, of New Berne, North Carolina.

Though very patient, he sometimes took good humored ways of checking talkative invalids. "Let me see your tongue," he would say, as they unwound their lengthy woes. But one night a prosy friend came and stayed late. Little was very tired and only half listening when he involuntarily said "Please let me see your tongue" and then became wide awake in trying to explain the request:

He was actively engaged in work on March 31, 1885, and on April 4 he had succumbed to diabetes.

Among the writings which his scanty leisure gave time for are: "The Use of Plaster of Paris in Surgery," 1867; "Median Lithotomy;" "Excision of the Lower Jaw for Osteo-Sarcoma;" "Anchylosis of the Temporo-maxillary Articulation, Treated by Excision of the Right Condyle."

And his appointments and memberships numbered: Lecturer on operative surgery to New York Hospital; professor of surgery, University of Vermont; visiting surgeon, St. Luke's Hospital and afterwards to St. Vincent's. Member of the New York State Medical Society; fellow New York Academy of Medicine.

Brooklyn Med. Jour., vol. xiv, 1900.
Post-graduate, N. York, 1887-8, vol. ii.
Tr. M. Soc., N. Y., Syracuse, 1886. (D. B. St. J. Roosa.)

Little, Timothy (1776–1849).

George Little, the founder of the Newbury (Massachusetts) branch of this family, came from London, England, and was the grandfather, twice removed, of Dr. Timothy Little, now to be delineated. Timothy Little was born in Newbury, October 27, 1776, was educated at Phillips' Exeter Academy,

studied medicine with Dr. Jewell of Berwick, Maine, and was later a member of the Massachusetts Medical Society. He settled first in New Gloucester, Maine, about 1806, and before long enjoyed a large practice. He possessed great reputation as a medical teacher, and often had as many as fifteen students under his instruction at one time. He built up an extensive anatomical museum, composed of dissections made by himself or by his pupils under his direction. The teaching value of these collections is indicated by a vote at an early meeting of the Directors of the Medical School of Maine, in 1821, requesting the loan of the museum to the new institution.

Finding country practice too difficult to endure, Dr. Little removed to Portland in 1826 and practised there until his death.

He married Eliza Lowell of Portland by whom he had five sons, none of whom, however, practised medicine. He early imbibed the views of Swendenborg and often officiated in the local church in the absence of the regular preacher.

Dr. Timothy Little died at Portland, November 28, 1849, his widow surviving him until 1853.   J. A. S.

Communication from Dr. Frederick Henry Gerrish, Portland.
Mss. Transactions, Maine Medical Society.

Litton, Abram (1814–1901).

Abram Litton was born in Dublin, May 20, 1814, and was brought to the States by his parents when he was three years old. In 1831 he graduated from the Nashville university, and at once commenced his life as a teacher. He was made professor of mathematics and natural philosophy in the University of Nashville in 1839, before he went abroad to study. He visited Paris, Berlin, Bonn and Heidelberg, looking for laboratories open for study but found at Giessen, with the great Liebig, the opportunity he sought to perfect himself in the methods of precision.

He spent three and one-half years abroad, and on May 15, 1843, was appointed professor of chemistry and pharmacy in the Medical Department of the St. Louis University. This college was later known as the St. Louis Medical College, or Pope's, and now is recognized as the Medical Department of Washington University. His slender salary was $300, later increased to $600, and finally placed at $1000. He added to this income by his labors in connection with the Geological Surveys of Iowa and Missouri, and by his employment as chemist in the Belcher Sugar Refinery.

The first effort of the Washington University towards advanced education was in starting a scientific school. They sought a professor of chemistry, and endeavored to find him in the East. Judge Treat, a director of the university, conferred with Prof. Horsford, of Harvard, concerning the best available man. He replied, "Why not Litton, of St. Louis?" This aroused their interest in a man eminently qualified for the place, who had labored in their midst for more than ten years as a teacher and as a scientist. Later the Rev. W. G. Eliot asked Dr. Litton to take the professorship, telling him that they wanted to establish a scientific school of high grade in the city, but that they lacked money. Dr. Litton responded to this appeal and offered his services. This was in 1857.

For full forty-nine years, he held his place in the St. Louis Medical College. He resigned in 1892, much to the regret of the faculty, and against their earnest protest. He died September 22, 1901.

Every student must remember the expression of hopeless despair manifested not only in his mobile face, but in his whole body, as some particularly dull boy disappointed his oft-repeated efforts to force comprehension of the facts he so clearly presented. His laboratory was a store house of living truths to him. I remember well the rush he would make down its long stairway, every angle of his bony frame bristling with exclamation points, if sounds of disaster in some beloved experiment reached him.

Though immersed in the fumes of his laboratory and enveloped in the mysteries of the phenomena of the material world, his love of humanity ever kept him in touch with those who came to him for help and advice.

Remarks made in behalf of the Alumni Association of the St. Louis Medical School, by Henry H. Mudd, on the "Life and Character of Dr. Abram Litton and Dr. John T. Hodgen."
There is a portrait in Wash. Univer., Missouri.

Livingston, Robert Ramsey (1827–1888).

Robert Ramsey Livingston, of Plattsmouth, was undoubtedly the most prominent of Nebraska's early physicians. A Canadian by birth, of Scotch-Irish descent, he was born August 10, 1827, in Montreal. His early education was received in the Royal Grammar School in the same city.

Having received the degree of M. D. at McGill University he later attended lectures at the College of Physicians and Surgeons in New York City and for a time after graduation acted as superintendent of the Lake Forest Mining Company near Houghton, Michigan. In 1857 he abandoned this work and came to Plattsmouth.

In 1861, while acting as temporary editor of the "Platte Valley Herald," he received the news that the flag had been fired upon at Fort Sumter. He immediately stopped the press as an edition of the paper was being issued and printed a circular calling for volunteers to serve the Union. As a result of this, Company A of the First Nebraska was organized at Plattsmouth with Livingston as captain (July 12, 1861). In July of the same year he was promoted to the rank of major; in June, 1862, lieutenant-colonel of the First Nebraska Regiment.

Gen. John M. Thayer, who later became governor of Nebraska, always spoke in the warmest terms of the activity and ability of Dr. Livingston. He continued to advance, in the summer of 1863 being promoted to the position of commander of the St. Louis Post and a few months later commander of the district. In the spring of 1865 he was brevet brigadier-general and in July of the same year was mustered out.

He was one of the charter members of both the Nebraska State Medical Society and the Omaha Medical College, having served on the faculty of the latter as professor of the principles and practice of surgery.

In the State Medical Society he was for many years the moving spirit. The circular which called the first convention of physicians together for its organization was written and issued by him. He served in 1872 as its president, also he wrote much of the material in the early volumes of the "Transactions" and one on the "Progress of Surgery" which appeared in the "Transactions" of 1884.

H. W. O.

The J Sterling Morton History of Nebraska, ii (port). The Western Medical Review, vol. l. vi (H. W. Orr).

Lloyd, James (1726–1810).

According to J. M. Toner (Address on "Medical Biography," Philadelphia, 1876) Dr. Lloyd was the first surgeon in America to use ligatures instead of searing wounds with the actual cautery, and to use the double flap in amputation. He also performed lithotomy and was the first in Massachusetts to devote himself wholly to obstetrics. For nearly sixty years he was the great physician and surgeon of New England and a warm advocate of inoculation for the small-pox.

He was the youngest of ten children born to Henry Lloyd, a Boston merchant, son of James Lloyd, who prob-

ably came from Bristol, England, in 1670. James was born on Long Island, state of New York, and educated in Stamford and New Haven, Connecticut. When seventeen he began his medical studies with Dr. William Clark, of Boston, and after five years sailed to London, where he spent two years as dresser at Guy's Hospital. While in London he attended lectures by William Hunter and William Smellie, then returned to Boston primed with all the latest knowledge of midwifery and surgery, and shortly, because of his attainments, acquired a large practice. Having acquired from Smellie's scientific method of teaching obstetrics a new conception of that science as a distinct branch, he practised and taught midwifery in a manner different from any of his predecessors.

Harvard conferred the honorary degree of M. D. on him in 1790. He was also an incorporator of the Massachusetts Medical Society.

Dr. Lloyd died in March, 1810, leaving a son James, who graduated from Harvard College in 1787 and was a United States Senator.

W. L. B.

A Sermon by J. S. J. Gardiner, Boston, 1810.
A Genealog. Dict. of the first settlers of N. E., James Savage, 1860.
Amer. Med. Biog., 1828, James Thacher, M. D. (portrait).
Hist. of Med. in the U. S. to 1800, Francis R. Packard, M. D., 1901.

Lloyd, Zachary (1701–1756).

Born in Boston, Massachusetts, on the fifteenth of November, 1701, he studied medicine with Dr. Kearsley, Sr., in Philadelphia, and in 1723 went abroad to continue his medical studies. He began practice in Philadelphia in 1726 and was one of the Founders of the College of Philadelphia, also assisted to found the Pennsylvania Hospital, serving as one of the members of its first medical staff, and at his death bequeathing to it 350 pounds and a number of books. He was at one time Health Officer of the Port of Philadelphia. He never married, and died on September 26, 1756, while paying a professional call.

Dr. John Jones, who had been his pupil, wrote of him as "A person whose whole life had been one continued scene of benevolence and humanity."

F. R. P.

Locke, John (1792–1856),

John Locke was born in Lempster, New Hampshire, February 19, 1792, the son of Samuel Barron and Hannah (Fussell) Locke; and in 1796 his father moved to Bethel, Maine.

Young Locke's mechanical taste and ingenuity, as well as his love for books, was manifested at an early age, botany being his favorite study, but this he pursued under great difficulties. The books available were the "Pentandria" —the fifth class of plants in the Linnean system—and a small work by Miss Wakefield. In 1816 he met Dr. Solon Smith of Hanover and with him spent two years in further study of botany, while studying medicine also. Before graduating he obtained the position of assistant surgeon in the navy, but after a short and disastrous voyage, resigned and returned to medicine. Although he had never seen a piece of chemical apparatus, his genius led him to construct his own instruments. Chiseling out a mould in a soft brick he made twenty plates of zinc the size of a silver dollar. With as many silver dollars, and cloths wet in brine, he constructed a "Volta's pile" which was a partial success.

He received his M. D., from Yale College in 1818, and that year delivered his first public lectures in Portland, Maine, also in Boston, Salem, and Dartmouth College.

After graduation he began practice, but abandoned it, not from want of patients, but from their neglect to pay. Discouraged, he accepted a position as assistant in a Female Academy in Windsor, Vermont.

In June, 1821, he went West and established a school for girls in Lexington, Kentucky, in 1822 going to Cincinnati, Ohio, where he found a friend, one Ethan Stone, who introduced him to a number of the most influential citizens, with whose assistance he established a school for girls which soon became popular, even famous. Dr. Locke's method of instruction was largely conversational.

In 1835 he was elected professor of chemistry in the Medical College of Ohio but found the place wanting in the necessary means of illustration, so, to meet every possible demand, he visited Europe, and purchased many thousand dollars worth of apparatus. Dr. Locke held this position until the session of 1849–50, when he was displaced, but at the solicitation of friends he resumed and held the chair until 1853. In 1854 he accepted the position of principal in the academy at Lebanon, Ohio. The following year he returned to Cincinnati.

He had a most accurate knowledge of geology, and in 1838 was engaged in a state geological survey of Ohio. His report on the "Geological Structure of the Southwestern Portion of the State," being regarded as a paper of greatest value. Later he was, in connection with David D. Owen, called into the service of the United States, for the survey of the mineral lands of the Northwest, and during his survey his familiarity with electricity and magnetism was very useful in indicating the depth and course of veins of ore.

Dr. Locke invented a number of scientific instruments; among them the thermoscopic galvanometer described in the "American Journal of Sciences," vol. xxxiii. The object was, "to construct a thermoscope so large that its indications might be seen on the lecture table, and at the same time so delicate as to show extremely small changes of temperature," and in volume xxiii of the "American Journal of Sciences" is a description of a microscopic compass invented by him.

His greatest achievement was the invention of the "Electric Chronograph," or "Magnetic Clock." Lieut. Maury, in an official letter to the Hon. John Y. Mason, secretary of the navy, dated National Observatory, Washington, January 5, 1849, says: "I have the honor of making known to you a most important discovery in astronomy, by Dr. Locke, of Ohio." After his observations in magnetism had been published, the English government presented to him a complete set of magnetic instruments.

After his return to Cincinnati in 1855, he broke down completely. For rest he went to Virginia to examine some coal lands, but returned with his infirmities greatly aggravated.

He married, in Cincinnati, October 25, 1825, Miss Mary Morris, of Newark, New Jersey.

He was author of "The Outlines of Botany" (1829); A sub-report on "The Survey of the Mineral Lands of Iowa, Illinois, and Wisconsin," published by Congress (1840); sub-report on "The Geology of Ohio," published by the state (1838); and text-books on botany and English grammar.

He died in Cincinnati, July 10, 1856.

A. G. D.

From an address on the Life and Character of Professor John Locke," by M. B. Wright, M. D., 1857.

Logan, George (1753–1821).

George Logan, son of William and grandson of James Logan, the distinguished friend and secretary of William Penn, was born at Stenton, near Philadelphia, September 9, 1753. He was sent to England for his education when very young, and, on his return, served an apprenticeship with a merchant of Philadelphia. He had early a great desire to study medicine, which he undertook after he had attained to manhood. After spending three years at the medical School of Edinburgh, he travelled through France, Italy, Germany and Holland, and returned to his own country in 1779.

He applied himself for some years to agricultuie, and was active in securing and exchanging seeds and plants with the leading botanists. He married Martha, the fifteen-year old daughter of Robert Daniel, of South Carolina, and she was an equally enthusiastic botanist, writing a treatise on gardening when seventy years of age. He also served in the Legislature. In June, 1798, he embarked for Europe for the purpose of preventing a war between France and America. For this step he was violently denounced by hostile partisans, but he persevered and succeeded in his intentions. He was a Senator from Pennsylvania in the Congress of the United States, from 1801 to March, 1807. In 1810 he visited England—as formerly France—with the same philanthropic desire of preserving peace between the two countries. He was exceedingly grieved at the war which followed, his health gradually declined for some years, and he died April 9, 1821.

Memorials of John Bartram and Humphrey Marshall, William Darlington, 1849.

Logan, Samuel (1831–1893).

Samuel Logan, surgeon, was born near Charleston, South Carolina, on April 16, 1831, a Scotsman his father, his mother a Glover of South Carolina. The boy was educated in his native city and graduated from the South Carolina Medical College in 1853, practising but a few months in Charleston, where he was appointed assistant demonstrator of anatomy in his alma mater. A year later he became professor of anatomy and lectured on surgery in the summer school until the outbreak of the Civil War, when he volunteered his services to the Confederacy.

In 1865 and 1866 he resumed his duties in the chair of anatomy and surgery at the South Carolina Medical College and the following summer became professor of anatomy in the Medical College of Richmond, Virginia, accepting the chair of surgery in the

New Orleans School of Medicine the next year. In 1867 he was dean of that school and professor of anatomy and clinical surgery in the University of Louisiana in 1872. He was peculiarly fitted for teaching and his clinical lectures and operations were of the highest rank. He was one of the editors of Geddings Surgery, published in 1858. Dr. Logan was president of the New Orleans Academy of Medicine in 1872 and of the New Orleans Medical and Surgical Association in 1876 and a member of the South Carolina Medical Society. He married Mary Virginia King, a daughter of a former judge of the Louisiana Supreme Court.

J. G. R.

N. Orl. M. and Surg. Jour., vol. xx, n. s., 1892-3 (portrait).
Proc. Orleans Parish M. Soc., N. Orl., vol. i, 1893, 1894.
Daniel's Texas M. Jour., vol. viii, 1892-3.

Long, Crawford Williamson (1815–1878). The credit of first using ether as an anesthetic, though not of demonstrating it to the medical world, must be ascribed to Crawford W., son of James Long, a lawyer of Danielsville, Georgia, where Crawford was born on the first day of November, 1815.

His paternal grandfather, Capt. Samuel Long, of Pennsylvania, distinguished himself during the Revolutionary War, and was one of Gen. Lafayette's officers at Yorktown.

He matriculated at Franklin College— now the University of Georgia—at a peculiarly early age. After studying for one year at the University of Pennsylvania, he graduated there, then spent a year in New York, and there attained reputation as a skillful surgeon, and though a young man, soon acquired an extensive practice, for his abilities were apparent. In 1841, because of family importunities, he returned to Georgia and began practice in the village of Jefferson. His office became the place of sojourn of the young men of the village who desired a pleasant evening. About that time the inhalation of laughing gas, as an exhilarant, was much discussed. Lecturers on chemistry would sometimes entertain by giving a "nitrous oxide party," during which the participants would become drunk from its inspiration. It was in the winter of 1841 that some young friends importuned Dr. Long to permit them to have a party in his rooms in his office. The physician had no means of preparing nitrous oxide gas, but suggested that sulphuric ether would produce similar exhilaration. The ether was produced; the young men inhaled and became hilarious, some of them receiving bruises. Long noted these bruises were not accompanied with pain, so divined that ether must have the power of producing insensibility, and from this simple observation came the great discovery of anesthesia.

He promptly determined to prove the value of his discovery, and during the month of March, 1842, ether was administered to Mr. James Venable until he was completely anesthetized, then a small cystic tumor was taken from the back of his neck. To the amazement of the patient he experienced no pain. From five to eight other cases, testing the anesthetic power of ether, were satisfactorily dealt with by Dr. Long during the years 1842 and 1843— quite a goodly number when it is remembered that surgical operations were not frequent in the country practice of a young physician more than half a century ago.

Dr. Crawford Long's surgical operations, under ether, were exhibited to medical men and also to persons of the community, as established by affidavits of persons operated upon, and of witnesses to the operations. Says Ange De Laperrière, M. D., of Jackson County: "I do certify that the fact of Dr. C. W. Long using sulphuric ether by inhalation to prevent pain in surgical operations was frequently spoken of and became notorious in the county of Jackson, Georgia, in the year 1843." In May, 1843, Drs. R. D. Moore and Joseph B. Carlton, for many years leading physicians in the city of Athens, Georgia, discussed the trial of Dr. C. W. Long's discovery in a case of surgery before them. They were unfortunately prevented from making the experiment by having none of the fluid at hand. Mrs. Emma Carlton, widow of Dr. Joseph B. Carlton, who died recently in Athens after living here for many years, signed the following: "I do certify that Dr. Crawford W. Long, of Jefferson, Jackson County, advised my husband, Dr. Joseph B. Carlton, a resident of Athens, Georgia, to try sulphuric ether as an anesthetic in his practice. In November or December, 1844, in Jefferson, Georgia, while on a visit to that place, in the office of Dr. Long, my husband extracted a tooth from a boy who was under the influence, by inhalation, of sulphuric ether, without pain—the boy not knowing when it was done. I further certify that the fact of Long using sulphuric ether, by inhalation, to prevent pain, was frequently spoken of in the county of Jackson at this time, and was quite notorious."

It is to be regretted that Long did not at once make known to the world his great discovery of anesthesia. Considered from a present point of view, his delay seems extraordinary. But it must not be forgotten that since that period the world has moved with exceeding rapidity. Sixty-five years ago, for a young medical practitioner in an obscure village, far from contact with centers of thought, removed from railroads, enjoying but modest postal facilities, with no great hospital organizations or medical associations to confirm his professional research, for a modest, diffident, young physician to claim a discovery so startling as anesthesia has proven to be without first securing most exhaustive proof of its worth, would have brought upon him the adverse criticism of his

elders, and possibly the laughter of his colleagues.

Dr. William H. Welch said that Long "is necessarily deprived of the larger honor which would have been his due had he not delayed publication of his experiments with ether until several years after the universal acceptance of surgical anesthesia . . . we need not withhold from Dr. Long the credit of independent and prior experiment and discovery but we cannot assign to him any influence upon the historical development of our knowledge of surgical anesthesia or any share in its introduction to the world at large." A careful examination of the question clearly shows that two and a half years elapsed after the discovery by Crawford W. Long, before Dr. Wells, of Hartford, knew the anesthetic power of nitrous oxide; that four and a half years passed after Dr. Long's initial experiment before Dr. Morton claimed to have the same knowledge. Morton is declared to have received the suggestion from Jackson; the latter claims to have made the discovery about the time Dr. Long made it, but left it to Morton to practically prove it. Hugh H. Young of Johns Hopkins Hospital, in his interesting pamphlet entitled "Long, the Discoverer of Anesthesia," says "The immediate and universal use of anesthesia in surgery is due to the great Boston surgeons, Warren, Hayward and Bigelow."

In 1849 Morton petitioned Congress for a reward as the discoverer, but he was opposed by the friends of Wells and Jackson. The friends of Morton and Wells presented volumes of testimony to the Senate of the United States in behalf of their candidates, but Jackson afterwards acknowledged the justice of Dr Long's cause. For five years Crawford W, Long refused to take any part in the controversy, but he naturally desired to be recognized as the discoverer of anesthesia, and to that effect wrote an article for the "Boston Medical Journal."

Confronted by so formidable an opponent as Dr. Long, the friends of Morton

CRAWFORD W. LONG.

and Wells finally seemed to lose hope, the bill before Congress was allowed to die, and it was never resurrected. In 1877 Dr. J. Marion Sims investigated the claims of Dr. Long to the discovery of anesthesia, and was convinced of their merit. He demanded their recognition by the medical profession, Dr. Long especially desiring the endorsement of the American Medical Association. It was but a short time afterwards that Dr. Long died, on the sixteenth of June, 1878, in the city of Athens, Georgia, for many years the place of his residence. In 1910 an obelisk, given by Dr. L. G. Hardman, was set up in the city of Athens in memory of Long.

He married, in 1842, Caroline, neice of Gov. Swain of North Carolina.

I. H. G.

Abridged from Long and His Discovery, by Dr. Isham H. Goss, Nov., 1908.
Tr. Med. Ass., Georgia, Augusta, 1881, vol. xxxii.
Vir. Med. Mon., Richmond, 1878, v.
There is a portrait in the Surg.-Gen. Lib., Wash., D. C., and in Packard's Hist. of Med in the U. States, Phila., 1901.
Medicine in America, J. G. Mumford, 1903.
A Consideration of the Introduction of Surgical Anesthesia, William H. Welch,1908.

Long, David (1787–1851).

David Long, son of Dr. David Long who came from Shelburn, Massachusetts, was born in Hebron, Washington County, New York, September 29, 1787. He was descended from David Long, who came from Scotland to Taunton, Massachusetts, in 1747. After studying medicine with his uncle, Dr. John Long, of Shelburn, he afterwards graduated M. D. in New York City and came to Cleveland in June, 1810, presumably influenced by a letter written by Stanley Griswold and dated May 28, 1809. This letter is to be found in a scrap book in the Historical Society of Cleveland.

Dr. Long was a surgeon in the western army in the War of 1812. At the time of Hull's surrender it was feared that the frontier settlements would be over-run by Indians. News of the surrender reached Dr. Long when at Black River, at what is now called Lorain. In order to protect

the settlers by bringing them early knowledge of this event, he rode on horseback to Cleveland, a distance of twenty-eight miles, in two hours and fourteen minutes. On another occasion, in a case of great emergency, he rode fourteen and a half miles in fifty minutes, changing horses twice. These incidents show the hardships surrounding pioneer life, and the energy and endurance which Dr. Long brought to overcome them. In 1811 Dr. Long married Julianna Walworth, daughter of Judge Walworth. A son, Solon, died at the age of eighteen, and a daughter, Mary Long Severance, lived in Cleveland until the age of eighty-six, being one of the most influential women in the charities of Cleveland. Dr. and Mrs. Long, in addition to thier own children, adopted several others. He was highly esteemed by the foremost citizens, and his position in the community and church was an influential one. He died in Cleveland on September 1, 1851, of apoplexy.

A short sketch and portrait of Dr. Long were published in the "Magazine of Western History," January, 1886.

D. P. A.

Longworth, Landon Rives (1846–1879).

Landon Rives Longworth was born in Cincinnati, Ohio, December 25, 1846, the second son of Joseph and Anna Maria Rives Longworth. His mother, Miss Anna Maria Rives, was the daughter of Dr. Landon Rives, who was for many years professor of obstetrics in the Medical College of Ohio. In 1863 Landon entered Harvard College and received his A. B. in 1867. In 1868 he went to Europe to study art and worked under Hans Gude, at Carlsruhe, and became a painter of no ordinary merit.

His aim was both to cultivate his art and to bring the enjoyment of it within the reach of the people. He found, however, no encouragement. Discouraged, he sought other fields, in which, with his wealth, he could be of the greatest benefit to humanity. The spring of 1870 found him beginning to study medicine under Dr. Edward Rives, and he matricu-

LONGWORTH 110 LOOMIS

lated in the Medical College of Ohio, but in the fall went to New York, where he entered the College of Physicians and Surgeons. In 1873 he graduated, taking the faculty prize for a thesis on "The Ligature of the External Carotid," which was later published in the "Archives of Scientific and Practical Medicine," May, 1873. After graduation he again visited Germany, going first to Vienna, where he sat under Hebra; studied the ophthalmoscope with Jaeger and Arlt, the laryngoscope with Schrötter and Stoerck, and enjoyed the benefits of the many practical courses in operative surgery. After one term in Vienna he went to Strasburg to study histology. There he entered the laboratory of Waldeyer, and took the courses of V. Recklinghausen, and while there published his "Discoveries of the Nerve Terminations in the Conjunctiva" in the "Archiv. für Microscopische Anatomie" of Max Schultze. Returning home in the Fall of 1874, he was immediately chosen assistant demonstrator in the Medical College of Ohio and lecturer on dermatology and pathologist to the Good Samaritan Hospital. He was adjunct professor of anatomy and clinical surgery in the Medical College of Ohio in 1875 and professor in the same chairs from 1876 to 1879, also pathologist to the Cincinnati Hospital from 1876 until his death. Surgery and dermatology were his specialties, and he rapidly built up a practice but soon after gave it up and devoted himself exclusively to scientific investigation. With characteristic energy he turned his house into a medical workshop, retaining only two rooms for non-medical work—his sleeping apartment and a music room; the latter a place where all the better musicians of the city were in the habit of meeting.

It was in this house that Dr. Longworth began his work on photography, injection, and the electric light. The process of photography of microscopic preparations he developed, by means of a new apparatus, to such an extent that all his results were satisfactory—results that would have been given to the world in a short time, if he had lived, in the form of a work on microscopic anatomy. The methods which he used were described fully in a lecture given by him before the Academy of Medicine of Cincinnati, May 18, 1878, entitled "Hints on Improvements in Micro-Photography." During his last year his whole time was taken up by injecting, and the electric light. He devised a new instrument for injecting, his injection mass being his own invention.

In the last session of the college he used the electric candle for his demonstrations in anatomy, and had just completed the construction of a lantern, by means of which he could throw the images of solid bodies upon the screen, thus enabling him to perform dissections of organs, such as the brain, before a class of 350, showing each and all of them every step, by means of the large picture thrown upon the screen. In his studies on electricity he went so far as to construct a new electric candle, for which he was granted a patent, May 21, 1878.

Dr. Longworth was never married.

On the fifth of January, 1879, he was taken ill with pneumonia, and died on the fourteenth. A. G. D.

From an address by Dr. F. Forchheimer, read at the commencement exercises of the Medical College of Ohio, February 28, 1879.

Loomis, Alfred Lebbeus (1831–1895).

With little money and less health, Alfred Loomis began to practise in New York when only twenty-three. Tuberculosis had run rife in the family and on January 23, 1895, he himself died of it. His parents were Daniel and Eliza Beach Loomis and Alfred was born at Bennington, Vermont, on October 16, 1831, and had barely enough money to carry him through Union College where he took his M. A. in 1856, and his M. D. from the College of Physicians and Surgeons of New York in 1852. It was not long before he gave special attention to chest disease, the art of auscultation and percussion, then developing rapidly, having great attractions for him. In 1864 want of money, war, fire had brought the University of the City of New York to a very low ebb. Loomis brought all his energy as teacher and organizer to diagnose and heal its condition, with the result that the Loomis Laboratory was built and endowed and the property freed of debt. He joined with Dr. Trudeau in making provision for impecunious consumptives and took keen interest in the Hospital in the Adirondacks. His great talent lay in discriminating between the patient and the disease, seeing beyond the morbid process to the man fighting with it for his life. During the three days he himself lay dying, all classes came to beg to do something for him, for few men had exerted so powerful an influence in so many directions.

Among his appointments were: professor of pathology and practice of medicine, University of the City of New York; physician, Bellevue Hospital; lecturer on physical diagnosis, College of Physicians and Surgeons, New York.

His chief written work was "Physical Diagnosis," 1873, and also a volume on "The Diseases of the Respiratory Organs, Heart and Kidneys," 1876, besides papers to leading medical journals.

Med. Rec., N. Y., 1895, vol. xlvii.
N. York Med. Jour., 1895.
Tr. Med. Soc., N. York, Phila., 1895.

Loomis, Henry Patterson (1859–1907).

Henry Patterson Loomis, fellow of the American Climatological Association since 1896, died at his home in New York City on December 22, 1907, of pneumonia, after a short illness, in the forty-ninth year of his age and at the height of his intellectual powers and his professional work. The son of Dr. Alfred L. Loomis, first president of the association, he inherited a name distinguished in the annals of medical science, and an ample fortune which might have robbed a mind less devoted to the pursuit of truth in our calling, of two of the strongest incentives to work. Graduating from Princeton University in 1880, he took his degree in medicine from the New York Medical School in 1883; in 1887 was appointed visiting physician to Bellevue Hospital, and for a number of years was professor of pathology in the University of New York. His demonstrations, supplementing the clinical teaching of his renowned father, were always of great interest to the students. He was one of the first to attempt to clear up the confusion resulting from the application of the term "Bright's disease" to kidney affections, and to insist upon a proper classification based upon anatomical study. His article upon "Diseases of the Kidneys," written in 1896 for the "American System of Practical Medicine," leaves little to be added at this day. But it was in the field of tuberculosis that he sought and gained his highest honors, continuing the work that had been dearest to his father's heart. The Loomis Sanatorium at Liberty, New York, was one of the first institutions to treat tuberculosis "at the right time, and in the right place, and in the right way, until the patient was well" instead of in the old way—until the patient was dead.

In 1896 Loomis was made visiting physician to the New York Hospital, and in 1897 consulting pathologist to the New York Board of Health. Upon the organization of the Cornell University Medical College in New York City in 1898, he was chosen to fill the chair of materia medica and therapeutics. He was an active and talented contributor to medical literature, and especially to the "Transactions of the Climatological Association," his last paper being a very timely "Plea for the Systematic Study of Climatology in the Medical Schools" (1906), which deserves the careful study of every physician.

C. E. N.

Loomis, Silas Lawrence (1822–1896).

Silas Lawrence Loomis was the son of Silas and Esther Case Loomis and born May 22, 1822. When five years old his father died. He taught school in Massachusetts and Rhode Island, 1837–43, in this way being able to work his way through college, graduating in 1844 at Wesleyan University, Middletown, Connecticut. In 1848 he married Betsy Ann Tidd, who died in 1850. The next year he married Abigail Paine. He was appointed in 1857 astronomer to the Lake Coast Survey and in 1860 special instructor in mathematics, United States Naval Academy, Annapolis, and ordered on a cruise at sea. In 1861 he became professor of chemistry and toxicology in Georgetown Medical College, but resigned in 1867. During the war of 1861–5 he was acting assistant surgeon, United States Army; served in the Army of the Potomac on staff of Gen. McClellan, and also in military hospitals in Washington. Associated with others in founding Howard University, he is said to have suggested the university instead of a college and to have organized the medical department. In 1878 he was employed by the United States Department of Agriculture colleeting special statistics of food products of the United States, and estimated the population of the United States in 1880, being in error only by 18,000. He discovered a process for and invented machinery for making textile fiber from varieties of the palm in 1878. He wrote "Normal Arithmetic," 1859, "Analytical Arithmetic," 1860, and "Education and Health of Women," 1882.

His A. M. was from Howard University, his M. D. (1857) from Georgetown. He died on June 22, 1896.

D. S. L.

Appleton's Biog., 1888.
Twentieth Century Biog. Dict.
Lamb's Hist. of the Med. Dpt. of Howard Univ., Wash., D. C., 1900.

Loring, Edward Greely (1837–1888).

Edward Greely Loring, Jr., was born in Boston in 1837 and began his medical studies in Florence, Italy, in 1859, continning them at Pisa. In 1862 he returned to Boston, entered Harvard Medical School, graduated in 1864 and became an externe in the ophthalmic clinic of the Boston City Hospital and the Massachusetts Charitable Eye and Ear Infirmary,

In 1865 he began practice in Baltimore, but in the following year left for New York to be the associate of Dr. C. R. Agnew. He became surgeon to the Brooklyn Eye and Ear Hospital, the Manhattan Eye and Ear Hospital, and later the New York Eye and Ear Infirmary, and a member of the American Ophthalmological Society in 1865. He died of angina pectoris, April 23, 1888.

Loring was a prolific writer, his most notable work being his well known and admirable "Text-book on Ophthalmoscopy" in 1886. By his writings on ophthalmological subjects and by his perfection of the ophthalmoscope (which is still one of the most popular instruments) he did far more than any other one man to place American ophthalmology abreast with that of the world.

H. F.

Trans. Am. Oph. Soc. vol. v, (port.).

Luckie, James Buckner (1833–1908).

Born in Covington, Georgia, July 16, 1833, he was of Scotch descent, his ancestors, emigrating from England and Scotland, and settling in the Carolinas. His father, Judge William Dickinson Luckie, moved to Georgia, where Dr. Luckie spent his boyhood.

Educated in the common schools and in Gwinnet Institute, he began the study of medicine when eighteen with Dr. John B. Hendrick and in the winter of '53 attended his first course of lectures in Augusta, Georgia. The following winter he attended the Pennsylvania Medical College at Philadelphia and graduated in March, 1855. He practised a year in his native county, then in Orion, Alabama. On the outbreak of Civil War he received the appointment of assistant surgeon. Serving in Kentucky, he was made medical purveyor by Gen. Kirby Smith, afterwards Inspector of Hospitals; and served with Graces' Brigade in the Army of Virginia, closing his army career with the surrender of Gen. R. E. Lee at Appomattox.

He settled in Pine Level, Montgomery County, Alabama, but removed in 1872 to Birmingham, Alabama. It was he, with Dr. M. H. Jordan, who fought the terrible epidemic of cholera at this place in 1873, he being the last one to have the disease.

He was a charter member of the Jefferson County Medical Society, served on the Board of Censors, and was counsellor of the State Medical Association.

In his medical carrer he became noted as a surgeon, and, at a time when such a procedure was practically unknown, he successfully set a broken neck, following this he had another successful case of the same. He also did the first successful triple amputation in the United States, and also the second.

The name of his first wife was Imogene Fielder, by whom he had one child, and in 1866 he married Susan Oliver Dillard and had nine, six boys and three girls. Four of the boys studied medicine, but the two oldest died.

Dr. Luckie died at Birmingham, December 11, 1908, age seventy-five.

L. F. L.

History of Jefferson County.
"Coal and Iron in Alabama."
"Anomalies and Curiosities of Medicine," Gould.
Virginia Medical Monthly, October, 1887.
Records National Railway Surgeons, June 28, 1888.
Journal of the Southern Medical Association, Jan., 1909.
Alabama Medical Journal, Jan , 1909

Lovejoy, James Wiliam Hamilton (1824–1901).

James William Hamilton Lovejoy was born December 15, 1824, in Washington, District of Columbia. His father, John Naylor Lovejoy, Jr., was of Georgetown; his mother was Ann Beddo, of Montgomery County, Maryland. He went as a lad to private schools in Washington, and graduated A. B., 1844, A. M., 1847, Columbian College, District of Columbia. After teaching school a few years he studied medicine at the Jefferson Medical College, Philadelphia. After graduation, he returned to Washington and engaged in general practice. He was appointed professor of chemistry in the Georgetown

Medical School, 1851, and became professor of materia medica in 1880; in 1883, professor of theory and practice of medicine; he resigned in 1898 and was appointed emeritus professor. For five years he was dean and ten years president of the medical faculty.

He was active in the management of many charitable institutions, being one of the founders of the Garfield Hospital, and serving as a consultant until death. In 1881 he was elected director and consulting physician to the Children's Hospital. In 1893, when the training school was established in connection with the hospital, he was chairman of the lecture faculty, lecturing here and in the Garfield School for Nurses for several years.

He was a member of the medical Society for forty-seven years, its president in 1876, and corresponding secretary in 1868, also president of the District Medical Association for three years, 1870 to 1872.

On November 24, 1858, he married Maria Lansing, daughter of William A. Green, Brooklyn, New York. She died in 1866, and he, suddenly, March 18, 1901.

D. S. L.

Minutes of Medical Society, D. C., March 20 and April 3, 1901; "Who's Who in America," 1901-2.

Lovell, Joseph (1788–1836).

Joseph Lowell, surgeon-general of the Army, graduated from Harvard in 1807 and studied medicine under Dr. Ingalls, of Boston, entering military service as surgeon of the 9th Infantry in May, 1812, getting the charge of the general hospital at Burlington, Vermont, where in August, 1814, he became hospital surgeon. Upon the formal organization of the army medical department he was in 1818 appointed surgeon-general. He then organized the department and revised and reissued the regulations for its government and in 1821 still further improved and elaborated the organization, giving it the form which it retained up to 1861. In 1834 he instituted the system of examinations for admission to the

medical corps and secured the final abolition of the whiskey ration in the army.
He also administered the affairs of the
medical department in the early part of
the Seminole War, and died October, 17,
1836.   J. E. P.

Pilcher, James Evelyn, Journal of the Asso-
ciation of Military Surgeons of the United
States, vol. xiv, 1904 (port.).
The Surgeon-generals of the United States
Army, Carlisle, Pa., 1905 (port.).

Luedeking, Robert 1853–1908).

Born in the city of St. Louis, on November 6, 1853, Robert Luedeking was a
fine representative of the best type of
American citizen of German extraction.
He graduated from the High School in
1871, studied in Heidelburg for two years
and took his M. D. in Strasburg and after
a year of post-graduate work in Vienna,
returned to St. Louis, where his father
had kept a school for girls until 1854.
To men of science Luedeking was
known as one who early in his career had
done original and brilliant work in pathological anatomy, while his later writings,
laden with the fruits of long experience in
clinical medicine, were read eagerly by
practitioners. He devoted special attention to the diseases of children. The
officers of the Washington University and
the faculty of its medical department
prized him as an able executive officer and
in 1902 Luedeking was chosen dean.

Soon after graduation in medicine and
return to this country, Luedeking entered
the Health Department, and for five years,
from 1877 to 1883, served the city successively as dispensary physician, secretary
of the Board of Health, and for several
periods of a month or two at a time as
acting superintendent of the City and
Female Hospitals. During the prevalence of small-pox in 1881–83 he often
visited the small-pox hospital. His kind
face and manner, his jolly laugh, his unfailing cheerfulness were as valuable to
the officers as his advice and suggestions.

In 1882 he was appointed lecturer on
pathological anatomy in the St. Louis
Medical College (now a part of the Medical Department of Washington Univer-

sity), and the following year to a professorship in the same branch, which position
he continued to hold until 1892, when he
was made professor of diseases of children. This chair he continued to hold
until his death, although in 1895 a professorship of clinical medicine was added
to his duties. He was also chief of the
clinic for diseases of children at the
O'Fallon Dispensary, and instructor in the
children's department of Bethesda Hospital from 1892 on. He was editor of the
"St. Louis Medical Review" in 1884–86.

Some of his chief publications were:
"Untersuchungen ueber die Regener-
ation der Quergestreiften Muskelfasern."
"The Present Status of Serum-ther-
apy."
"Pathology of Pneumonia."
"Concerning the Antistreptococcic
Serum."
"Perforative Inflammation of Meckel's
Diverticulum."
"Cellular Agency in Disease."
"Notes on Diabetic Coma."
"Etiology of Gastric Carcinoma."
"Heredity in Pathogenesis."

Mrs. Luedeking, who survived her husband, was a daughter of S. W. Biebinger,
formerly president of the Fourth National
Bank. The children, two, were both
girls.

Quarterly Bull. Med. D. Dept. of Wash.
Univ., St. Louis, Mo. March, 1908.

Lundy, Charles J. (1846–1892).

Charles J. Lundy of Detroit was in
early life a teacher at a Business College
and received his A. M. degree at the
Notre Dame University (Indiana). His
first course in medicine was taken at the
Rush Medical College, but in consequence
of the great fire he was forced to leave,
and took his final course at the University
of Michigan, graduating in 1872. Returning to Notre Dame as resident physician he remained there for two years.
He then took up post-graduate studies
at Bellevue Hospital Medical College
and engaged in general practice in Detroit. Subsequently he again studied in
New York, devoting himself to the dis-

eases of the eye and the ear, having as his masters Agnew, Webster, Noyes, Callam, and others and returned to Detroit to engage in special practice. He was one of the founders of the Michigan College of Medicine and its professor of diseases of the eye and ear and throat, and later in the consolidated institution the Detroit College of Medicine. He was an able and forceful writer, and his contributions to literature are numerous; some of these are in the Surgeon-general's Catalogue, Washington, District of Columbia. He died May 24, 1892. H. F.

Trans. Mich. State Med. Soc., 1892, vol. xvi.

Lusk, William Thompson (1838–1897). On May 23, 1838. there was born in Norwich County, Connecticut, one William Lusk, obstetrician, a man destined to help a great many other babies comfortably into the world. He went as a student to Heidelburg and Berlin and after graduating at the Bellevue Hospital Medical College he again went to Europe and studied in Edinburgh, Paris, Vienna and Prague. In 1870–1 he lectured on physiology in the Harvard Medical School and became professor of obstetrics to the Bellevue Hospital Medical College, yet found time to most ably co-edit the "New York Medical Journal." Modest even to diffidence it required some persuasion to make him publish his great work on "The Science and Art of Midwifery" (1882), a book which at once took rank as the best text-book. It went through four American editions and has been translated into French, Italian, Spanish and Arabic. He was no less famous as a praetitioner, and his frequent visits abroad to read papers before societies made him widely known among his foreign confrères. He died suddenly, at the height of his fame, on June 12, 1897. "The purity of his life and his steadfastness to duty made him an uplifting influence in the community."

He married, in 1864, Mary Hartwell Chittenden of Brooklyn and had five children. Five years after her death in 1871 he married Mrs. Matilda (Meyer)

Thorn and had one daughter. Two sons, Graham and William G., became respectively professor of physiology in New York University and a New York physician.

Of his numerous articles in the "New York Medical Journal" and other periodicals may be mentioned: "Uremia a Common Cause of Death in Uterine Cancer;" "Inquiry into the Pathology of Uterine Cancer;" "Irregular Uterine Action During Labor;" "On the Origin of Diabetes;" "Cephalotribe and Cephalotripsy;' "Nature and Prevention of Puerperal Fever;" "The Prognosis of Cesarean Operations;" "Recovery of the Singing Voice after Dilatation of the Uterus."

He was president of the American Gynecological Society; State Association, fellow of the New York Academy of Medicine, vice-president of New York Obstetrical Society, member of New York Gynecological Society, professor of obstetrics in Bellevue Hospital Medical College, visiting physician to Bellevue Hospital, editor of "New York Medical Journal," LL. D. Yale, honorable fellow of Edinburgh Obstetrical Society; London Obstetrical Society, corresponding member for the same societies of Paris and Leipsic. From 1861–3 he served in the United States Army, rising to the rank of assistant adjutant-general.

D. W.

Am. Gyn. and Obstet. Jour., N. Y., 1897, vol. xi. (H. C. Coe).
Am. J. Obstet., N. Y., 1897, vol. xxxvi.
Med. News, N. Y., 1897, vol. lxx.
Tr. N. Y. Acad. of Med., 1896-1901. (Austin Flint).
Trans. Amer. Gyn. Soc., vol. xxiii, 1898 (port.).
Memorial Address Dr. Alexander Smith.

Luzenberg, Charles Aloysius (1805–1848). Although a foreigner, Charles Luzenberg, a great surgeon of New Orleans, may be claimed by America, for his father, a military commissariat, left Germany when his son was fourteen and settled in Philadelphia, sparing no expense to complete the fine education the boy had begun in Landau and Weissemberg. Attending the lectures and operations of Dr. Physick brought out still more young Luzenberg's surgical genius, and when he went to New Orleans in 1829, bearing a letter to Dr. David C. Ker of the Charity Hospital, that doctor, after seeing his skill, soon had him elected house-surgeon.

A paper which appeared in the tenth volume of the "American Journal of the Medical Sciences" and the "Révue Médicale" for 1832 proves that if Luzenberg did not first bring into notice what was then a new idea, that is, of excluding light in various variolous disorders to avoid pox marks, he at all events revived it.

Two whole years, 1832–4, were spent studying in European clinics, particularly under Dupuytren, and on his return to New Orleans, full of zeal and schemes for improving surgical and medical procedure, he built the Franklin Infirmary, now the Luzenberg Hospital and there did operations which brought patients from afar to get the benefit of his skill. Among such operations was the extirpation of a much enlarged cancerous parotid gland from an elderly man. This case, reported in the "Gazette Médicale de Paris," 1835, brought a commendation with a resolution of thanks to the author and enrollment as corresponding member of the Académie de Médicine. Soon after, he excised six inches of mortified ileum in a case of strangulated hernia. The patient was put on opium treatment and in thirty-five days the stitches came away and he entirely recovered. One other operation he took special interest in doing was couching for cataract and in this he had brilliant results.

When Luzenberg had his hospital on a permanent basis his next idea was a Medical School. Being influential, and also friends with the state governor, this project, with the help of his medical confrères, was soon embodied in the Medical College of Louisiana with himself as dean, and, *ad interim,* professor of surgery and anatomy. In 1839 he founded the Society of Natural History and the Sciences and to it bequeathed a rich collection of specimens. When the Louisiana Medico-Chirurgical Society was legally incorporated he was, because of his help in forming it, chosen first president. It held brilliant meetings at which the French and English physicians of the state met to exchange views, and it was undoubtedly the spirit of these meetings that caused a college building to be erected for the Medical School, and that started the "New Orleans Medical and Surgical Journal."

One thing he had in hand was never finished—at his death piles of manuscript and a fine collection of literature, old and new, on yellow fever, showed that his contemplated work on the cause and cure of the disease would have been a monument of careful research. The manuscript was in Latin.

A too active life caused premonitions of failing health to go unheeded but in the spring of 1848 actual pain in the precordial region with paroxysms of palpitation and dyspnea totally incapacitated him from work. A thorough change to Virginia was planned but at Cincinnati he could go no further and died there on the fifteenth of July, 1848.

D. W.

Lives of Eminent Amer. Phys. and Surgs., S. D. Gross.
Biographies of Eminent Phys. and Surgs., R. F. Stone.

Lynah, James (1725–1809).

James Lynah, surgeon, was born at Dublin, Ireland, in 1725, where he received both his collegiate and professional education. After graduating in medicine he entered the British Naval Service, and received a surgeon's commission. Rescued from shipwreck in the West Indies, he was taken to Kingston, Jamaica, whence he removed to Charleston, South Carolina, about 1765 or 1766. Settling in the wealthy and cultivated Huguenot settlement of St. Stephen's Parish, he soon acquired an extensive and remunerative practice, but on the outbreak of the Revolution he espoused the cause of the colonies and served at intervals with Marion's corps. He was also surgeon in Col. Joseph Maybank's cavalry regiment, and was "chief surgeon of the Regiment of Light Dragoons" in Col. Daniel Harry's cavalry, in which capacity he was present at the siege of Savannah. When Count Pulaski was wounded in this fight Dr. Lynah, with the assistance of his son and two others, removed him from the line of fire and extracted the bullet on the field. This bullet and a note from one of Count Pulaski's Aides-de-camp is now in the possession of the Historical Society of Georgia.

At the close of the War he removed to Charleston, South Carolina, where his attractive personality and professional skill enabled him to build up a large practice. He was one of the founders of the Medical Society of South Carolina, and at the time of his death held a commission as surgeon-general of the state of South Carolina.

He died of pulmonary tuberculosis in October, 1809, and was buried at Laurel Spring Plantation.

He married in Ireland, and one son, Edward Lynah, who likewise studied medicine, was the sole issue of which there is record.

A fine portrait, by an unknown artist, is in the possession of Mr. J. H. Lynah of Savannah, Georgia.

R. W., Jr.

(Private family record)

Lyster, Henry F. (1837–1894).

Henry F. Lyster, son of the Rev. William N. and Ellen Emily Cooper Lyster, was born in Sanderscourt, Ireland, November 6, 1837. In 1846 the family settled in Detroit, and the boy had his general education in Detroit schools and Michigan University, where he took his A. B. in 1858 and stayed on there at the medical department, obtaining his M. D. in 1860 and beginning practice in Detroit at once, but on the outbreak of war in 1861 he was commissioned assistant surgeon of the Second Michigan Infantry and on July 15, 1862, surgeon of the Fifth Michigan Infantry. He was wounded at the battle of the Wilderness on May 5, 1864; on recovery he returned to his post and was mustered out May 28, 1865. He was surgeon-in-chief of the Third Brigade, First Division, Third Army Corps for some time, also medical inspector and medical director of the Third Corps. Returning to Detroit he continued in practice until disabled by disease. During 1868–69 he was lecturer on surgery at the University of Michigan and during 1888–90, professor of theory and practice of medicine and clinical medicine. He was a founder of the Michigan College of Medicine, president of its faculty in 1879 and professor of principles and practice of medicine and clinical diseases of the chest, 1875–76. In 1873–74 co-editor (new series) "Peninsular Journal of Medicine," and in 1882 assistant editor of "Detroit Clinic," and was a founder of the Detroit Academy of Medicine; of the Wayne County Medical Society; of the Michigan State Medical Society.

Dr. Lyster was about six feet tall and of spare build, dark hair, dark eyebrows and blue, clear eyes. On January 30, 1867, he married Winifred Lee Brent, daughter of Capt. Thomas Lee Brent of the United States Army. Mrs. Lyster with five children survived him, and one son became a physician.

Dr. Lyster died of pernicious anemia on the train between Detroit and Chicago, October 3, 1894.

Papers:

"Amputations Through Condyles of the Femur." ("Detroit Review of Medicine and Pharmacy," vol. i.)

"Anesthetic Treatment of Hare-lip." (Ibid., vol. v.)

"Excision of the Hip-joint for Morbus Coxarius." ("Transactions of Michigan State Medical Society," 1870.)

"The Limitation and Prevention of Typhoid Fever." ("Transactions of Pontiac Sanitary Convention, Michigan State Board of Health.")

"Influence of Mind in the Cure of Disease." ("Transactions of Michigan State Medical Society," 1889.)

"Climate and Topography of the Lower Peninsula of Michigan." (Ibid., 1878.)

"Reclaiming of Drowned Lands." (Ibid., 1879).

"Prevention of Pulmonary Consumption." (Ibid., 1880.)

"Report on Epidemic, Endemic and Contagious Diseases." (Ibid., 1881.)

L. C.

History of Mich. University, Ann Arbor, 1906.
Biographical Cyclopedia of Mich., West. Pub. Co., N. Y. and Detroit, 1900.

M

MacBride, James (1784–1817).

Equally well known as physician and botanist, James MacBride was born in Williamsburg County in 1784. He graduated from Yale in 1805 and afterwards studied medicine. Settling in Pineville, South Carolina, he practised there for many years, but later removed to Charleston where he died of yellow fever in 1817, only thirty-three yet when he had already made a reputation as doctor and scientist. Botany attracted him most and his chief writings on this subject were contributed to the "Transactions of the Linnean Society" and elsewhere. His name has been embodied by Dr. Stephen Elliott in the *MacBridea pulchra*, a genus found in St. Johns, Berkeley, South Carolina, of which but two species are known to exist. Dr. Elliott also dedicated to him the second volume of his "Sketch of the Botany of South Carolina and Georgia" (1824).

Profoundly skilled in his profession and high in the confidence of his fellow-citizens he fell a victim to yellow fever as the result of fatigue and exposure, depriving Charleston of a good citizen and medical botany of a devoted student.

Memorials of John Bartram and Humphrey Marshall, W. Darlington.
Sketch of the Botany of S. Carolina and Georgia. Stephen Elliott.

MacCallum, John Bruce (1876–1906).

Born in Dunnville, Ontario, Canada, June 10, 1876, he was the second son of Dr. George A. MacCallum of that town. After going as a boy to the local schools he went to Toronto where he graduated from Toronto University in 1896. In the autumn of the same year he went to Baltimore to begin studying medicine at the Johns Hopkins Medical School, where he took his M. D. in 1900. While a student there he carried out several investigations on anatomical subjects; the most important of which was that on the architecture of the ventricles of the heart.

During this time, at the end of his third year of study, he began to show alarming symptoms of the lingering illness which caused his death, and his final year was interrupted by a prolonged stay in the hospital. Nevertheless, in the autumn after his graduation he was sufficiently well to accept a position as assistant in anatomy in the University, which he held for a year, during which time he completed other anatomical studies. That summer he attempted to spend in Germany, but was again prostrated by his old illness and compelled to return to Canada where he spent the winter in the woods in the hope of regaining his health. There with no facilities of any sort he completed the translation and editing of Szymonowicz's "Histology." After a stay of two months in Jamaica and another summer on the northern lakes of Ontario, he again felt himself strong and in 1902 went to Denver where he thought to practice. He taught anatomy in the Denver Medical School for a short time, but soon became disheartened and left it all to drift westward to California. There he was invited by Prof. Jacques Loeb to become his assistant in physiology and from his acceptance of this post until his death his work in the new subject was most productive.

In 1905, when he had become assistant professor of physiology in the University of California, he again fell ill and hurried east to Baltimore where he remained some time in the hospital. Afterwards another summer in Canada restored him but little. Nevertheless, the

West called to him and he insisted on returning to Berkeley where he died in February, 1906, apparently from slowly advancing tuberculosis.

This is an outline of his brief life in which each turning was directed by his illnesses. In his harness to the end, he cheerily though falteringly tested the effects of various drugs on jellyfish when from his weakness he could no longer control a rabbit, and the paper on these experiments which his mother wrote at his dictation was published after his death.

He was indefatigable in his interest in his work and worked as an artist with a grasp of his problem. Throughout his crippled life he bore himself with the courage and cheerfulness which stood so well by Stevenson.

His writings include:

"On the Histology and histogenesis of Heart Muscle." ("Anatomical Anzeiger," 1897.)

"On the Histogenesis of Striated Muscle Fibre and the Development of the Human Sartorius." ("Johns Hopkins Hospital Bulletin," 1898.)

"On the Pathology of Fragmentatio Myocardi, and Myocarditis Fibrosa." ("Johns Hopkins Hospital Bulletin." 1898.)

"Contribution to the Knowledge of the Pathology of Fragmentation and Segmentation and Fibrosis of the Myocardium." ("Journal of Experimental Medicine," 1899.)

"On the Muscular Architecture and Growth of the Ventricles of the Heart." ("Johns Hopkins Hospital Reports 1900," vol. ix.)

"Development of the Pig's Intestine." ("Johns Hopkins Hospital Bulletin," 1901.)

"Notes on the Wolffian Body of Higher Mammals." ("American Journal of Anatomy," vol. i, No. 3, 1902.)

"On the Influence of Calcium and Barium on the Flow of Urine" (preliminary communication)." (Ibid., i, No. 10, 1904.)

"Influence of the Saline Purgatives on Loops of Intestine Removed from the Body, Secretion of Sugar into the Intestine Caused by Intravenous Saline Infusion." (Ibid., vol. i, Nos. 13 and 14, 1904.)

"Influence of Calcium and Barium on the Secretary Activity of the Kidney." ("University of California Publications," ii, No. 3, 1904, second communication.)

"Action on the Intestine of Solutions Containing Two Salts, Action of Purgatives in a Crustacean (Sida Crystallina)." (Ibid., vol. ii, Nos. 5–6.)

"On the Diuretic Action of Certain Hemolytics and the Action of Calcium in Suppressing Hemoglobinuria." (Preliminary communicaton). Ibid., ii, No. 10.)

"The Diuretic Action of Certain Hemolytics and the Influence of Calcium and Magnesium in Suppressing Hemolysis" (second communication). Ibid., ii, No. 12.)

"The Action of Pilocarpine and Atropin on the Flow of Urine."

"Action of Saline Purgatives in Rabbits and the Counteraction of their Effects by Calcium" (second communication). Ibid., i, No. 1904.)

"Factors Influencing Secretion." ("Journal of Biological Chemistry," vol. i, 4 and 5, 1906.)   C. R. B.

McCann, James (1837–1893).

About the year 1825 a certain Thomas McCann of Scotch-Irish ancestry married one Sarah Wilson and settled on a farm near Verona, Penn township, Allegheny County, Pennsylvania, and on this farm James McCann was born April 12, 1837. His education was obtained in the public schools in which, at the completion of his course, he served as teacher for one or two years, after which he entered at Cannonsburg, Pennsylvania, but terminated his studies before graduating.

About 1858 or 1859 he went to Pittsburg and for a time was employed at clerical work; later becoming a student of medicine under Dr. John Dickson, before attending medical lectures in the University of Pennsylvania. He did not, however, complete his studies at the University at this time, but entered the Union Army as assistant surgeon of the Fifth Pennsylvania Artillery, in which capacity he first saw service at the battle of Gettysburg, July, 1863. Returning to graduate, he took his M. D. at the University of Pennsylvania, March 23, 1864. In 1893, on the day of his death, the LL. D. was conferred on him by Heidelberg College, of Tiffin, Ohio. Steps towards the conference of the same degree were also taken by the Western University of Pennsylvania, but his death occurred beforehand.

Dr. McCann was a member of the American Surgical Association, of the county, state and national medical societies. He was president of the Allegheny County Medical Society.

While originally a general practitioner Dr. McCann soon gravitated towards surgery and at the time of his death occupied the foremost rank in that branch of medicine in Western Pennsylvania, From the time of the establishment of the West Penn Hospital until he died he filled a position of surgeon on the staff.

In 1885 he was largely instrumental in organizing the Western Pennsylvania Medical College—now the medical department of the University of Pittsburg, where he occupied the chair of principles and practice of surgery from its inception to the time of his death.

In 1862 he married Sarah Boyd and had nine children. His wife died in April, 1883, and in 1889 he married Martha Scott, by whom he had a daughter. His oldest son, Thomas, born April 22, 1863, graduated M. D. at Bellevue Hospital Medical College in 1887 but died of a chronic pulmonary affection in 1903.

Another son, John B., also adopted his father's vocation and settled in Pittsburg.

James McCann died July 13, 1893, at his house No. 928 Penn Avenue, Pittsburg, Pennsylvania. Several years before his death he suffered from septic infection, following an operation on a patient, from which he never fully recovered. The direct cause of death was a cerebellar abscess due it was believed to this infection.

His contributions to medical literature were numerous and continued over a long period. Among them may be mentioned: "Clinical Observations in the Treatment of Severe Railroad Injuries of the Extremities." ("Transactions, American Surgical Association," 1884, vol. ii.)

"Splenectomy for Dislocated or Wandering Spleen; Recovery." (Ibid., 1887, vol. v.)

"Enterectomy for Removal of Sarcoma of Mesentery; Recovery." (Ibid., 1892, vol. x.)

Chapter on "Wounds," in Keating's "Encyclopedia of Diseases of Children."

His portrait is in the assembly room of the Allegheny County Medical Society, in the Pittsburg Free Dispensary. A. K.

McCaw, James Brown (1823–1906).

An army surgeon, he was born in Richmond, Virginia, on July 12, 1823. He came of a race of doctors, being the great-grandson of James McCaw, a Scotch surgeon from Wigtonshire, who came to Virginia in 1771 and settled near Norfolk whose son, James D. McCaw, was a pupil of Benjamin Bell, of Edinburgh, and an M. D. of the University of that city, and returned to Virginia, and practised in Richmond until his death in 1842, and Dr. William R. McCaw was the father of the subject of this sketch.

He was educated·in Richmond schools and studied medicine at the University of New York, graduating in 1844, being a pupil of Dr. Valentine Mott. Then he soon removed to Richmond, his home during the rest of his life.

He was a founder and a charter member of the Medical Society of Virginia, and a member and at one time president of the Richmond Academy of Medicine.

Dr. McCaw was editor, or co-editor, of the "Virginia Medical and Surgical Journal" from April, 1853, to December, 1855, and co-editor of the "Virginia Medical Journal" from January, 1856, to December, 1859; in 1864 he became editor of the "Confederate States Medical Journal," of which only fourteen numbers appeared—the only medical journal published under the Confederacy; in April, 1871, he became one of the editors of the "Virginia Clinical Record," of which three volumes were issued. At the outbreak of the war, in 1861, he was made surgeon-in-charge and commandant of the Chimborazo Hospital at Richmond. This hospital he organized from its very beginning, and made it one of the largest the world has ever known, in which, during the four years of the war, 76,000 soldiers were treated with a remarkable number of recoveries, considering the poor facilities, and scant supplies. He was successively professor of chemistry and practice of medicine in the Medical College of Virginia for many years; served as dean of the faculty for twelve years, and at the time of his death was president of the board of visitors.

"He was," says Dr. J. N. Upshur, "a man of most distinguished presence, magnetic and successful.

He married in 1845 Delia Patteson, of Richmond, and had nine children, of whom six survived him; three sons entered the medical profession. He died in Richmond on August 13, 1906, at the age of eighty-three.

His writings included:

"Remarks on the Uses and Effects of Sulphate of Quinine." ("Stethoscope," December, 1857.)

"Present Condition of the Medical Profession in Virginia." ("Virginia Medical and Surgical Journal," vol. i.)

"Sick Headache." ("Virginia Medical Journal," vol. i.)

"Uterine Hydatids." Ibid., vol. v.

"Belladonna as an Antigalactic." ("Maryland and Virginia Medical Journal," vol. i.)

"The Action of Bismuth." Ibid., vol. ii.)

"Theory of the Heart." ("Richmond Medical Journal," vol. v.)

Transactions of the Med. Soc. of Va., 1906.
"Medical Reminiscences of Richmond during the past forty years." (J. N. Upshur.)
R. M. S.

Maclean, Alexander Campbell (1854–1907).

Alexander Campbell Maclean was born in Belleville, Ontario, Canada, June 22, 1854, a descendant of the clan Maclean of Lochbine. His father, Charles Maclean, was a prominent figure in Scotch politics and for a time Chancellor of the Exchequer of Scotland. His mother, Jane Campbell, was a daughter of Capt. Campbell of Kintia and a niece of the Duke of Argyle, in whose family she spent her girlhood. Maclean was a graduate of the University of Michigan and there took his A. B. He then entered the medical department and graduated in 1877.

Maclean was a member of the Salt Lake County Medical Society and the Utah State Medical Association. After serving as interne in the University Hospital at Ann Arbor he was appointed surgeon to the Iron-Silver mine at Leadville, Colorado, and later surgeon to the Denver and Rio Grande Railroad at the same place. In 1889 he came to Salt Lake City and at once took a prominent position in the profession. He was closely associated with Dr. Hamilton in the organization of St. Mark's Hospital, Salt Lake City, and for years one of the staff. He married May 15, 1883, Susan Mariner of Memphis, Tennessee, and had four children, three sons and one daughter.

He died in Pueblo, Colorado, August 3, 1907, from a mental breakdown following tabes dorsalis.

W. B. E.

Maclean, Donald (1839–1903).

Donald Maclean, surgeon, was born at Seymour, Canada, December 4, 1839. His father, of Edinburgh, Scotland, became totally blind at the age of fifteen, but by the aid of tutors prepared himself for the ministry, only to be rejected because of his blindness. He then moved to the wilderness of Canada, where Donald was born. The boy's education was obtained partly at Oliphant's School, Edinburgh, and partly at Cobourg, Bellville, and Queen's College, Canada. In 1858 he returned to Edinburgh and entered the medical side at the University, in 1862 becoming a licentiate of the Royal College of Surgeons there. Returning to the United States he became assistant surgeon in the army, working in various hospitals at St. Louis, Louisville and elsewhere. In 1864 he was professor of surgery in the Royal College of Physicians and Surgeons at Kingston, Ontario. In 1872, lecturer, and later professor of surgery in the department of medicine and surgery, University of Michigan, resigning this position in 1889 for private practice in Detroit, Michigan. In 1884 he was president of the Michigan State Medical Society; in 1894 president of the American Medical Association. He was honorary member of the Ohio State Medical Society, the New York State Medical Society, and member of the Royal College of Surgeons of Edinburgh, and fellow of the Royal College of Physicians. During the late Spanish War he was surgeon and stationed at Old Point Comfort. When assistant to Syme of Edinburgh, he acquired great dexterity in those operations which made Syme famous. As a teacher he commanded the confidence and . enthusiasm of his pupils. Of spare build, about five feet ten inches high, with sandy hair, smooth-shaven face clear blue eyes, firm elastic step, kindly manner, he was a most attractive personality to his friends and a pillar of strength to the cause he championed. Being a ready writer, forceful speaker, a faithful friend and powerful enemy, he exerted a wide influence. In the controversy between University of Michigan and the Michigan State Medical Society over the introduction of homeopathy into the university, he led the university party. He was a leader in hastening the evolution of the Michigan State Medical Society from a convention with political methods into a society for mutual instruction and fellowship. He married twice. His first wife was a Kingston lady, by whom he had two children; one, a son, Dr. Donald Maclean, Jr., and a daughter. His second wife was

Mrs. Duncan of Detroit. Dr. Maclean died at his home in Detroit, July 24, 1903, from heart failure.

His papers included:

"Cystic Goiter, Complicated by Epilepsy," ("Physician and Surgeon," Ann Arbor, vol. i.)

"Cases of Skin Grafting." (Ibid., vol. i.)

"Malignant Tumor of the Neck." ("Physician and Surgeon," vol. iii.)

"Tumors of the Mammary Gland." (Ibid., vol. iii.)

"Carcinoma Mammæ." (Ibid., 1884, vol. vi.)

"Three Cases of Laparo-Nephrectomy," ("Transactions Ninth International Medical Congress," vol. i.)

"Psoas Abscess." ("Physician and Surgeon," vol. ii.)

"Resection at Shoulder-joint for Caries and Necrosis of Humerus." (Ibid., 1887.)

"Radical Cure of Hernia." ("American Lancet," Detroit, 1887, vol. ix.)

"Excision of Scapula." ("Physician and Surgeon," Ann Arbor, 1883.)

"The Treatment of Fractures in the Light of Modern Histology and Pathology." ("Chicago Clinical Review," 1893).

L. C.

Biographical Cyclopedia of Mich., Detroit, N. Y., 1900. Hist Univ. Mich., Ann Arbor, 1906.

McClellan, George (1796–1847).

George McClellan was born in Woodstock, Connecticut, in 1796, graduated in arts at Yale in 1815, and after studying medicine with Dr. Hubbard of Pomfret, Connecticut, and later with Dr. John Syng Dorsey of Philadelphia, graduated in medicine at the University of Pennsylvania in 1819. He is known best as a surgeon and as a teacher of surgery, but he also practised ophthalmic surgery, in which he acquired considerable fame. In 1821, when only twenty-five years of age, he founded the Institution for the Diseases of the Eye and Ear in Philadelphia. It appears that the institution went out of existence when the

Jefferson Medical College was founded in 1825—in which foundation Dr. McClellan took a leading part. It is interesting to note that Dr. McClellan was sued in 1828 because of a failure in a cataract operation, and the verdict of five hundred dollars was in favor of the plaintiff. According to Dr. Gross "the suit had been instigated by professional enemies."

He died in Philadelphia in 1847.

H. F.

Hubbell's "Development of Ophthalmology."

McClurg, James (1746–1823).

James McClurg, a Revolutionary surgeon, was the son of Dr. Walter Mc-Clurg, a wealthy citizen and noted physician of Elizabeth City County, Virginia, who also served his country as a surgeon in the Virginia State Navy in the Revolution.

The boy James had the best educational advantages of the day and fully availed himself of them at William and Mary College, from which he graduated in 1762. He studied medicine at the University of Edinburgh, where he attracted the attention and commendation of Cullen, Black and other professors. Taking his M. D. from this celebrated institution of medical learning in 1770, his professional studies were then pursued in Paris and London.

Returning to Virginia in 1773, he located at Williamsburg, where he came into competition with such men and practitioners as Arthur Lee, and others of like caliber. In a very short time, however, he made way to the head of his profession in the state, a position which he held for fifty years.

A professorship of anatomy and medicine having been created at William and Mary, he was elected in 1779 to the chair, but it is not known that he ever gave any instruction in these subjects. During the war of the Revolution he served as a surgeon in the earlier years, and later as a medical director, making for himself a great reputation. He was a member of the convention which framed the Federal Constitution in Philadelphia in 1787, but did not sign that document. For many years he was a counsellor of the state also. A member of the Medical Society of Virginia, he was elected its president in 1820 and 1821, though then too feeble to take any part in its proceedings.

When Richmond became the seat of government, Dr. McClurg removed from Williamsburg to that city, and was for the succeeding forty years its leading physician, the latter period of his life being almost entirely given up to consulting practice, a fact that showed well his high standing with both the profession and the laity.

"The Philadelphia Journal of Medical and Physical Sciences" was in 1820 dedicated to "The Elegant Scholar and Accomplished Physician, Dr. McClurg." This shows that his reputation extended beyond the confines of his own state.

No statement of the fact that he was ever married can be found.

He died in Richmond in July, 1823, at the age of seventy-seven, and it may truly be said of him that of the many eminent physicians Virginia has given to our profession, none stood higher than he.

His inaugural essay entitled "De Calore" was regarded as an original and profound production, but was never published. It is said to have contained suggestions from which were thought to have originated some of the opinions afterwards demonstrated by the founders of the French school of chemistry. While residing in London he published a paper entitled "Experiments upon the Human Bile and Reflections on the Biliary Secretions, with an Introductory Essay" (London, 1772), which attracted much attention both on account of its originality and charming and elegant style. He made several contributions to the "Philadelphia Journal of Medical and Physical Sciences."

The collection of portraits in the Library of the Surgeon-general contains one of Dr. McClurg.   R. M. S.

Virginia Med. and Surg. Jour., vol. ii., 1854 (port.).

McCosh, Andrew J. (1858–1908).

Born in Belfast, Ireland, in 1858, Andrew J. McCosh was the son of the Reverend Dr. James McCosh, who came from a professorship in Queens College to be president of Princeton College, now Princeton University.

Although only fifty years old, he was one of the leading surgeons of this country, and, in spite of active practice, had contributed much to the advancement of his profession along the modern lines of scientific research. For twenty years he had been surgeon to the Presbyterian Hospital, and his specialty in his own practice was appendicitis.

He graduated from Princeton in 1877, took the master's degree in 1878, received his degree of doctor of medicine from the College of Physicians and Surgeons in 1880, and then had a two-year post-graduate course in medicine at the University of Vienna. He began practice in New York in 1883. In 1905 Columbia University conferred upon him the degree of LL. D., and Princeton paid him a similar honor a year later.

Dr. McCosh was professor of clinical surgery in the College of Physicians and Surgeons, Columbia University, and a fellow of the American Surgical Association.

Books written by Dr. McCosh, many of which were translated into foreign languages, included "Appendicitis in Children," "Iodoform Poisoning," "Observations on the Results in 125 Cases of Sarcoma," "Remarks on Spinal Surgery," "Four Cases of Brain Surgery," "The Treatment of General Peritonitis," and "Surgical Intervention in Benign Gastric Lesions." He assisted Dr. M. Allen Starr in writing "A Contribution to the Localization of the Muscular Sense."

He died at the Presbyterian Hospital, as a result of an accident, in which he was thrown from his carriage and his skull fractured.

New York Even Post., Dec. 3, 1908

McCreery, Charles (1785–1826).

The following extract is from a letter of Miss Tula Clay Daniel of Hardinsburg, Kentucky, a grand-daughter of Dr. Charles McCreery. She writes: Family records show Dr. McCreery to have been of Scotch-Irish descent. His grandfather moved to this country and settled in Maryland in 1730. His father married Mary McClanahan and Charles, the seventh son, the youngest of nine children, was born June 13, 1785, near Winchester, Clark County, Kentucky. His brother Robert was father of Thomas Clay McCreery, the noted Senator, lawyer, orator from Daviess County, and his brother James the grandfather of Senator James B. McCreery. Dr. McCreery studied medicine under Dr. Goodlet of Bardstown, moved to Hartford, Ohio County, Kentucky, in 1810. In 1811 he married Ann Wayman Crowe, whose parents came from Maryland with their relations, the Tevis family. In Hartford a family of seven children were born to them.

Dr. McCreery did a large practice in Ohio and adjoining counties, making extended rides on horseback and yet found time to deliver lectures regularly in his home to his own as well as other students. His surgical instruments were made under his own supervision by an expert silversmith in Hartford. His chief operation, the one that makes his fame enduring, was the extirpation of the entire collar bone in 1813, the first on record. "New Orleans Medical and Surgical Journal," January, 1850. This operation, done upon a young man, though the bone was said to be scrofulous, was a decided success, the patient making a complete recovery, with perfect use of the arm and living past middle life.

"This bold, delicate and extraordinary operation was executed for the first time in America in 1813 by the late Charles McCreary of Hartford, in this State. The subject of the case, as I learn from Charles F. Wing, Esq., of Greenville, who was intimately acquainted both with the patient and his surgeon, was a youth of the name of Irvin, fourteen years of age, laboring under a scrofulous affection of the right collar bone. A disease of a similar kind existed at the period of the operation in the right leg, from which several pieces of bone were subsequently removed, and which became so much curved and shrunken as to be upwards of two inches shorter than the other. By degrees the part got well, but the disease recurred two or three times afterwards, though it was always amenable to treatment. The loss of the bone did not impair the function of the corresponding limb" (Gross).

The case of Dr. Valentine Mott of New York, performed in 1828, which Dr. Mott supposed was the first operation of the kind done in the United States, and about the wonders of which surgical writers at the time said much, was not a complete removal, for about one inch of the acromial end of the clavicle was left.

Dr. McCreery was a fine historian, a great reader, eloquent speaker, ready writer and close student. The love of his patients for him bordered on idolatry, his name being to them a synonym of kindliest sympathy and readiest helpfulness. His home life was characterized by unusual sweetness and tenderness and an intense appreciation of child nature. He was a well formed, handsome man with fine dark eyes.

Dr. McCreery died of cardiac dropsy, August 26, 1826, at West Point on his return from Shelbyville, where he had gone to bring his two oldest daughters home from Science Hill Academy.

A. S.

President's Annual Address, Kentucky State Medical Society, forty-sixth meeting, James H. Letcher.

McCurdy, John (1835–1890).

John McCurdy, of Youngstown, Ohio, was born in Ireland, January 11, 1835, of Scotch-Irish extraction, his parents coming to this country when he was eight years of age. His father, a physician, receiving his degree from Edinburgh, abandoned the practice of medicine on coming to this country and engaged in stock-raising. John was educated at Jefferson Medical College in 1857 and at Cleveland Medical College in 1858. For more than a year he was house-surgeon to the United States Marine Hospital in Cleveland; then engaged in practice with T. Woodbridge of Youngstown. During the Civil War he served with distinction at the front as assistant surgeon of the twenty-third Ohio Volunteer Infantry, and medical director of the fourteenth Army Corps and acting medical inspector of the Army of the Cumberland. He was twice taken prisoner, spending almost three months in Libby Prison. He was a frequent contributor to medical journals and was one of the founders of the Mahoning County Medical Society, several times its president; and an active member of the Ohio State Medical Society.

J. N. B.

Tr. Ohio State Med. Soc., Toledo, 1890 (port).

McDermont, Clarke (1823–1881).

Born in County Antrim, Ireland, Clarke McDermont immigrated to this country in 1840, and, having had a classical education, was able to become principal of a private school in Lexington, Kentucky.

He began to study medicine under Dr. Dudley, professor of surgery in Transylvania University and the most noted lithotomist in America, in 1849 graduating from the University of New York, and immediately going to Edinburgh and Dublin for post-graduate work. Returning to this country, for a while he assisted Prof. Detmold in his private classes, and in 1852 went to Dayton, Ohio, and associated himself with Dr. Green.

Promptly in the beginning of the War for the Union he was appointed to the surgeoncy of the Second Ohio Volunteer Infantry. In 1862–1863 he served as medical director of the right wing of the Army of the Cumberland, and later was detailed to hospital service in Nashville, Tennessee, and Louisville, Kentucky. In the latter place he had charge of the hospital for sick and disabled officers. In the official report of the battle of Murfreesboro, Gen. Rosecrans commended him for gallantry on the battle-field, and for great humanity in the care of the wounded; in recognition of his services he was brevetted Lieutenant-Colonel, U. S. Volunteers. At the close of the war he was assigned as surgeon to Camp Dennison, until appointed surgeon-general of the state under Governor Hayes.

True to his lineage, he was full of Irish wit and humor, which bubbled to the surface at the most unexpected times; and this, with the keen observation and information which came from reading and travel, made him a charming companion. He died April 7, 1881.

W. J. C.

Macdonald, Alexander (1784–1859).

Alexander Macdonald was born on the Isle of Skye in 1784 and had his professional education at Edinburgh University where he graduated M. D. in 1805. His early intention had been to enter the army, but having met with an accident—a broken leg—he was advised that he would never be able to endure the hardship of marching. He then turned to medicine in the hope that he might be able to join the army as a surgeon. But this he was not destined to do.

Soon after graduation he was appointed surgeon aboard an emigrant ship bound for Charlestown, Prince Edward Island. The captain was a very brutal fellow who ill-used the Highland emigrants in every possible way, and was at constant feud with Dr. Macdonald and Col. Rankin, another cabin passenger, who tried to defend them. The captain made such fiendish threats as to what he would do to Dr. Macdonald on the return trip, when he would not have the Highlanders and Col. Rankin to help him, that the doctor had no desire to accompany this savage captain on the return voyage.

When Dr. Macdonald came to America he had a bill of exchange for 150 pounds, but the conditions of the country were such that he could not get it cashed. At last a man named Bannerman, a fellow countryman, told the doctor that he could get it cashed; the bill was handed over to the volunteer broker and that was the last the doctor ever saw of Bannerman or the money. He was now in a strange land and penniless, and might have been in great distress but for the unstinted kindness he received from the Rev. Alexander Macdonald, of Arisaig, Nova Scotia, whom he had known in Skye.

From Antigonish he went to Jamaica, where he practised for three years. While in Jamaica he had a severe attack of fever, in the delirium of which he tore up his diploma. He returned to Antigonish with the intention of going back to Scotland, but fell in love and married Charlotte the eldest daughter of Daniel Harrington, and never returned to his native land.

When Dr. Macdonald came to Antigonish the roads were mere bridle paths, the bridges were few and poor; when he got into practice he had an immense country to cover; long journeys had frequently to be made, often at night and in the severe storms of winter, and the hardships and dangers were terrible. Many stories are told of the doctor's hairbreadth escapes; how once one stormy winter's night when on horseback journeying to visit a patient some fifty miles distant, he and his horse fell over a snow-covered bluff on the seacoast, a perpendicular height of some sixty feet, killing the horse, and leaving the rider in a dangerous spot, from which he had much difficulty in extricating himself, and only after bravely battling with the storm all night did he again reach his home; another tale relates how, on one occasion, he was nearly carried out to sea by moving ice.

His hardships were, perhaps, increased by his absent-mindedness, and his consequent neglect of comforts in traveling. It is said that on coming home from a distant part of his professional field one cold winter's day, he remarked to his wife, on entering the house, that one of his feet was quite warm while the other was almost frozen. On pulling off his boots it was found that he had put two stockings on one foot and left the other bare. This peculiarity of absent-mindedness led to much practical joking at his expense. On one occasion, some friends, finding his horse ready saddled at his office door, reversed the saddle and awaited results. Out came the doctor, and without noticing what had been done, he mounted and rode away.

But if Dr. Macdonald was absent-minded in unimportant matters, there are no stories of his being so in the treatment of his patients. In addition to a large practice, he filled many public positions. He was a justice of the peace, judge of the Court of Common Pleas, prothonotary surgeon to the Militia, etc., etc. He was a man of high professional attainment and sterling character, and his memory will long live in the county of Antigonish, where he died in 1859.

The well known W. H. Macdonald, M. D. (commonly known as "Dr. Bill") is a son, and Dr. W. Huntley Macdonald, a grandson of Alexander Macdonald.   D. A. C.

McDowell, Ephraim (1771–1830).

Ephraim McDowell was born in Rockbridge County, Virginia, on the eleventh of March, 1771. His ancestors removed from Scotland to the valley of Virginia in 1737. His mother was Sarah McClung and McDowell's father was prominent in political life in Virginia, a member of the Legislature of that state, and in 1782 came as a land commissioner to Kentucky (then a portion of Virginia), and soon after removed his family to Danville.

Ephraim McDowell went as a lad to a school at Georgetown, Kentucky, then to Staunton, Virginia, to study with Dr. Humphreys, and in 1793 to Scotland to attend lectures at the University of Edinburgh. He remained in Edinburgh during the session of 1793–94, but did not receive his M. D. As far as we know, this was not conferred upon him until 1832, when, entirely unsolicited on his part, the University of Maryland gave him her honorary M. D. The Medical Society of Philadelphia, at that time the most distinguished of the kind in this country, sent him its diploma in 1807, two years before he performed his first ovariotomy.

While taking the course at Edinburgh University, McDowell attended the private instructions of John Bell, the most able and eloquent of the Scottish surgeons of his day. That portion of Bell's course in which he lectured upon the diseases of the ovaries and depicted the hopeless fate to which their victims were condemned, made a powerful impression upon his auditor. Indeed, McDowell afterwards stated that the principles and suggestions at this time enunciated by his master impelled him sixteen years afterwards to attempt what was considered an impossibility. In 1795 McDowell returned to his home in Danville, then a small village in the western wilderness, and entered upon the practice of his profession. Being a man of classical education, coming from the most famous medical school of the world, he easily gained the first professional position in his locality, and

EPHRAIM McDOWELL.
(By permission of the American Gynecological Society.)

within a few years became known throughout all the western and southern states as the best surgeon in his entire section of the country. During this time his practice extended in every direction, persons coming to him from all the neighboring states, and he frequently making long journeys on horseback to operate upon persons whose conditions would not permit them to visit him at his home. As far as known, he was in the habit of performing every surgical operation then practised. In lithotomy he was especially successful, and was known to have operated, up to 1828, twenty-two times without a single death. He operated many times for strangulated hernia, and did successfully various amputations and other operations, including tracheotomy.

In 1809, fourteen years after he began practice, he was sent for to see a Mrs. Crawford, living in Green County, Kentucky, some sixty miles from Danville. McDowell found her to be afflicted with an ovarian tumor, which was rapidly growing and hastening to a fatal termination. In the language of Prof. Gross: "After a most thorough and critical examination, Dr. McDowell informed his patient, a woman of unusual courage and strength of mind, that the only chance for relief was the excision of the diseased mass. He explained to her, with great clearness and fidelity, the nature and hazard of the operation; he told her that he had never performed it, but that he was ready, if she were willing, to undertake it, and risk his reputation upon the issue, adding that it was an experiment, but an experiment well worthy of trial." At the close of the interview Mrs. Crawford declared that any mode of death, suicide excepted, was preferable to the slow death which she was undergoing, and that she would submit to any operation which held out even a remote prospect of relief. Mrs. Crawford was forty-seven at the time of the operation, and died on

March 30, 1841, aged seventy-eight years. It was not until seven years afterwards, and when he had twice repeated the operation, that McDowell published an account of it. In 1816 he prepared a brief account of his first three cases, a copy of which he forwarded to his old preceptor, John Bell, who was then travelling on the Continent for his health, and had left his professional correspondence in the charge of Mr. John Lizars. The communication failed to reach Mr. Bell, and another copy of the report was forwarded by McDowell to Philadelphia for publication. The report appeared in the "Eclectic Repertory and Analytical Review" for October, 1816.

Two additional cases completed this report, all three patients making complete and prompt recovery.

Three years later (October, 1819) McDowell reported in the same journal two additional cases. It will be observed that seven years elapsed from the time he first operated until he made his publication, when he was enabled to add two more successful cases. That so long a time should have been allowed to elapse was most probably due to the surgeon's natural aversion to writing. Perhaps the manner in which this report was made did much to provoke the criticism with which it was received. Dr. James Johnson, the very learned editor of the "London Medico-Chirurgical Review," was especially severe and satirical in his criticisms.

How many times during his career McDowell performed ovariotomy is not now certainly known. Dr. Jackson reports him to have made a long horseback journey in 1822 of some hundreds of miles into middle Tennessee, to do an ovariotomy (successful) upon Mrs. Overton, who lived near the Hermitage, Pres. Jackson's house. The only assistants he had were Gen. Jackson and a Mrs. Priestly. The former seems to have been greatly pleased with McDowell, and took him to his house as guest. Dr. William A. McDowell, for five years his uncle's pupil and two years his partner, tells us that up to 1820 his uncle had done seven ovariotomies, six of which he witnessed, and that six of the seven were successful. Dr. Alban G. Smith succeeded Dr. William A. McDowell as partner of Dr. Ephraim McDowell, and while with him Dr. Smith himself twice performed ovariotomy. The younger McDowell states later that he knew of his uncle having during his career operated thirteen times, exclusive of the two cases Dr. Smith operated upon, and of the thirteen eight recovered. McDowell first operated in 1809; in July, 1821, Dr. Nathan Smith, professor of surgery in Yale College, performed ovariotomy at Norwich, Connecticut. Dr. Smith had never heard of McDowell's work and operated in an entirely original way. Dr. Alban G. Smith, previously mentioned, reported his first operation (May 23, 1823) in the "North American Medical and Surgical Journal, for January, 1826.

When we think of one living on the border of Western civilization, in a little town of five hundred inhabitants, far removed from the opportunity of consultation with anyone whose opinion might be of value, and nearly a thousand miles from the nearest hospital or dissecting room, performing a new and untried operation of such magnitude upon the living, before the days of anesthesia, with a full sense of the responsibility and danger, without skilled assistants, our admiration for McDowell's courage and skill rises to its full height.

He possessed an excellent medical library for his day and locality, and was in the habit of purchasing most of the principal new works on medicine. While having a fair knowledge of the classics he gave most of his professional leisure to history and belles-lettres.

At the age of thirty-one, Dr. McDowell married Sarah, the daughter of Kentucky's famous "war governor," Isaac Shelby, with whom he lived happily, and had a family of six children, two sons, and four daughters, only three of these surviving him. Mrs. McDowell was his survivor by ten years. In the later years of his life he removed from the village to a country home, where he spent the later years of his life, still continuing his professional work. He died on the twentieth day of June, 1830, after a brief illness.

Careful reflection upon the operative methods of the "Father of Ovariotomy," as I have endeavored to portray them will demonstrate that, except as to asepsis, but little improvement has been made upon his methods as orginally conceived and carried out.

L. S. M.

Gross, S. D. Origin of ovariotomy; brief sketch of the life and services of the late Ephraim McDowell. Tr. Ky. M. Soc., 1852, Louisville, 1853, ii.

Gross, S. D. Memorial oration in honor of Eph. McDowell, "the father of ovariotomy," Louisville, 1879.

Chesney, J. P. Interesting incidents in the private life of Eph. McDowell. Cincin. M. Report., 1870, iii.

Dedication of the monument to Ephraim McDowell. Cincin. Lancet and Clinic, 1879, n. s., ii.

Gross, S. D. Biography of Ephraim McDowell in his "Lives of eminent American Physicians," Phila., 1861.

Jackson, J. B. Biographical sketch of Ephraim McDowell. Richmond and Louisville M. J., Louisville, 1873, xvi (port.)

Letcher, J. H. Memoir of Ephraim McDowell. Tr. McDowell M. Soc., Evansville, Ind., 1875.

Mc.Murtry, L. S. Necrology. Tr. Amer. Med. Assoc., Phila., 1878, xxix.

Monument to Ephraim McDowell. Its dedication in Danville, Ky., on May 16, oration by Samuel D. Gross. Med. Record, N. Y., 1879, xv.

Mary Y. Ridenbaugh. The Biography of Ephriam McDowell, together with valuable scientific treatises, etc., 8°, New York, 1890.

Biographical sketch. Columbus M. J., 1902.

Heroes of Medicine, Ephraim McDowell. Pract., London, 1897, lviii (port.).

W. L. Lowder. Ephraim McDowell. Med. and Surg. Monitor, Indianapolis, 1901, iv.

The passing of the historic McDowell building at Danville, Ky. Physician and Surgeon, Detroit and Ann Arbor, 1902, xxiv.

McMurtry, L. S. Memorial address. Tr. Southern Surgical and Gynecological Assoc., 1893, Phila., 1894, vi; also, Med. News, Phila., 1894, lxiv.

McDowell, Joseph Nashe (1805–1868). Joseph Nashe McDowell was born in 1805, and came to St. Louis in 1840, from Cincinnati, where he had been associated in the Cincinnati Medical College with Dr. Drake, Gross and other distinguished men; he had no sooner arrived in St. Louis when he set to work with enthusiasm and unceasing industry to organize a faculty of medicine. He worked under the charter of the Kemper College and his college was then known as the Medical Department of the Kemper College but, as we know, was changed to the name of the Missouri Medical College.

Dr. McDowell soon became known throughout the West and Southwest. He was an unusually fluent and eloquent speaker, a natural orator and possessed to a pre-eminent degree that rare and wonderful power of adapting himself to any and all kinds of audiences. He literally revelled in antitheses and climax, and as a vivid word-picturer few could equal him. A perfect master of invective and ridicule, never at a loss to entertain any company, he might be thrown into. Backed by a fund of inexhaustible anecdotes he made parable, anecdote and quaint comparison an effective means to stimulate and fix the memory of his students. It is said that in his medical lectures that he had a story for almost every bone, muscle and nerve in the human body. He was proverbially improvident and careless. He always found it more difficult to keep than to get, for while fortune often indeed aided him a lack of forethought as quickly undid him.

It is said in his early years of residence in St. Louis, he delivered a number of acrid lectures against Jesuitism, because, as it was claimed, the Jesuit Fathers of the St. Louis University had allowed a rival medical school (the St. Louis Medical College) to organize under the charter of their college. After the delivery of the lectures the doctor became so impressed that his life was constantly in danger that he made and wore a brass breast-plate, and always thereafter carried arms.

Dr. McDowell had so constructed his college building as to be a formidable fortress, and his residence on the opposite corner was also planned to resist an assault. Any one who had ever seen this huge, octagon shaped stone building, could readily see that it had been built on such lines. He had early conceived a plan to go across the plains and capture upper California. With this in view he bought from the United States government, for $2.50 each, 1400 discarded muskets, which were stored in his house and in the basement of the college. Through determination, patience and diligence he got hold of quantities of old brass, to make cannon. This proposed expedition to Upper California was to be accomplished by persuading his graduates and others to company him. It is said that several hundred graduates and young men had promised to do so.

It is also related that he purchased a cave in Hannibal, Montana, had it cleaned out and fixed up, built walls of masonry and an iron gate at its entrance. He took a copper vase containing the body of one of his children and suspended it from the roof of the cave. Some time after he had done this some evil disposed and mischievous town loafers broke down this gate and opened the copper coffin. This made the doctor give up the idea of having any such place as a burial place for the dead. Dr. McDowell himself once became very sick and believing himself upon the point of death he called in Dr. Charles W. Stevens, his partner in the practice of medicine, and his son, Dr. Drake McDowell, to his bedside and made them take oath that should he die they would place his body in an alcohol filled copper vase, take it to the Mammoth Cave of Kentucky and have it suspended from the roof of the cave.

When he delivered his class valedictory, it was always an event dear to every medical student of the town, for such was his antipathy to the St. Louis Medical College, or Pope's College, as he called it, owing to the fact that the late Charles A. Pope was dean, that he was sure to say something rich in climax, ridicule and comparison. I remember to have once heard him say at a commencement in his college: "That by the grace of God and the permission of the Pope, I expect to lecture here for the next twenty years to come."

The late Dr. Montrose A. Pallen, who at that time attended the St. Louis Medical College, went to hear one of these valedictories.

McDowell slowly sauntered down the aisle of the amphitheatre with a violin and bow in his hand. Seeing so many students sitting side-ways he commandingly said: "Gentlemen, I pray you, gentlemen, sit straight and face the music." After scraping off a few tunes he very gravely laid down his violin and bow and said: "Gentlemen, we have now been together for five long months and we have passed many pleasant and delightful moments together, and doubtless some sad and perplexing ones, and now the saddest of all sad words are to be uttered, namely, 'Farewell.' We have floated in an atmosphere of physiology, we have waded knee-deep, nay, neck-deep into a sea of theory and practice, we have wandered into the tortuous maze and confusing labyrinth of anatomy; we have wearily culled amidst pungent odors and savored the queer elements of materia medica. We have patiently plodded in the crucible of chemicals. Yes, gentlemen, filled with that weariness at times which could have made us sleep sweetly, or snore profoundly upon a bed of flint, and now, gentlemen, farewell. Here we have made the furrow and sowed the seeds. In after years one of your number will come back to the City of St. Louis, with the snow of many winters upon his hair, walking not on two legs, but on three, as Sphinx has it, and as he wanders here and there upon the throughfares of this great city, suddenly, gentlemen, it will occur to him to ask about Dr. McDowell. Then he will hail and ask one of the eager passersby: 'Where is Dr. McDowell,' he will say: 'What Dr. McDowell.' 'Why, Dr. McDowell, the surgeon.' He will tell him, gentlemen, that Dr. McDowell lies burried out at Bellefontaine. Slowly and painfully he will wend his way thither: there he will find amidst rank weeds and seeding grass a simple marble slab inscribed, 'J. N. McDowell, Surgeon.' As he stands there contemplating the rare virtues and eccentricities of this old man, suddenly, gentlemen, the spirit of Dr. McDowell will arise upon ethereal wings and bless him. Yes, thrice bless him. Then it will take a swoop, and when it passes this building, it will drop a parting tear, but, gentlemen, when it gets to Pope's College, it will expectorate."

He was a remarkable teacher. His influence was profound, no student ever sat before him and listened to his lectures who remained uninstructed. The students from his college were better and more enthusiastically instructed in anatomy than almost any college in the land. Anatomy here became almost a mania. Any college possessing such men teaching anatomy like McDowell, Hodgen, Stevens, and his son John McDowell, certainly was supplied with anatomical teaching material remarkable and effective. His death came on October 3, 1868. Three sons survived him, and two, Drake and John, became well known physicians.

Abridged from a paper by Dr. W. B. Outten in the Med. Fortnightly, Mar. 25, 1908.

MacGowan, Daniel Jerome (1815–1893).

The parents of this medical missionary emigrated from Ulster to North America shortly after the Revolution and their son, Daniel Jerome, for fifty years did good work in China. In the course of his missionary labors be found time to write on the character, institutions, customs and history of the Chinese and of Siberia. These writings attracted the attention of the British Foreign Office and they gave him a responsible post at Wenchow to enlarge the store of historical and scientific knowledge which he had amassed. An expedition to North China when he was seventy-nine proved too great a labor and he died on July 31, 1893.

Med. Rec., N. Y., 1893, vol. xliv.

McGuire, Hugh Holmes (1801–1875).

He was born in Frederick County, Virginia, on November 6, 1801, and was the son of Edward McGuire descendant from Thomas MorMcGuire Lord or Prince of Fermanagh, Ireland, who was born in 1400.

He read medicine with Dr. Robert Barton of Winchester, attended lectures in the University of Pennsylvania, and graduated therefrom in 1822, the subject of his thesis being "Tetanus."

He was a member of the Medical Society of Virginia. Settling in Winchester to practise, he devoted himself specially to surgery and during his life did most of the surgical work in his section. He is said to have been the first Virginian to operate for cataract, doing the couching or needling operation with a needle made under his direction by a mechanic, and the first in America to operate for club-foot. He cut directly down upon the tendons, severing all the tissues covering them—a method which has been revived in recent years. A skillful lithotomist, too, he operated for stone more than thirty times without a death. Thus successful as a surgeon, possessing both judgment and skill, he acquired a national reputation which led to his being called to the chair of surgery in schools in Philadelphia, New Orleans and Louisville—calls declined, however, as he preferred the quieter life of a country town and work among his own people.

When the Medical School of the Valley of Virginia was established at Winchester in 1826, he was made professor of anatomy and physiology and filled the chair until the school was disbanded. Upon its revival in 1850 he became dean and professor of surgery, and so continued to be until it ceased to exist on the outbreak of Civil War, when, despite advanced age, he entered the Confederate Army as surgeon, and served through the entire war.

He married Anne Eliza Moss and two of the sons, Hunter and William P., became physicians. He died at Winchester in 1875.

R. M. S.

An unpublished biographical sketch by J. M. Toner, M. D.
A steel engraving and photographs of Dr. McGuire are in the possession of his son, Dr. W. P. McGuire, of Winchester, Va.

McGuire, Hunter Holmes (1835–1900).

He was born in Winchester, Virginia, the son of Dr. Hugh Holmes, a surgeon of note, and the founder of the Medical College at Winchester, Virginia, and Anne Eliza Moss McGuire, his wife.

First he studied medicine at the Winchester Medical College, graduating in 1855, and in 1856 matriculating at both the University of Pennsylvania and at the Jefferson Medical College, but was soon taken ill and had to return home.

In 1857 he was elected professor of anatomy in the college at Winchester, but desiring greater clinical advantages, he resigned the position after one session and returned to Philadelphia. The intense sectional feeling aroused by the insurrection of John Brown in 1859 lead to the calling of a mass meeting of the Southern students then in Philadelphia, at which it was determined that they should return South. The large majority went to Richmond and entered the College there, the remainder going to New Orleans. Having saved some money from the fees received from his pupils in the quiz classes, he paid the traveling expenses to Richmond of all the students who were unable to pay it themselves. The number of these southern students was some three hundred. Dr. McGuire, who led the move, completed the course of lectures in Richmond and received a second degree. He then went to New Orleans and there established a quiz class, but the secession of South Carolina soon after convinced him that war was inevitable, and he returned home and offered his services to his state.

When Virginia seceded he volunteered as a private soldier in Company F, Second Virginia Regiment, and marched to Harper's Ferry. Soon after he was commissioned surgeon in the Virginia forces, and in May, 1861, he was made medical director of the Army of the Shenandoah, then under the command of Stonewall Jackson. Later, when Jackson organized the First Virginia Brigade, he requested that Dr. McGuire might be assigned him as brigade-surgeon. Thereafter he served as chief surgeon of Gen. Jackson's command until the death of his beloved commander with whom he was on most intimate terms. He was then attached as surgeon to the Second Army Corps under the command of Gen. Ewell, and later became medical director of the Army of Northern Virginia under Lieut.-gen. Ewell. Still later on, he was made ia drector of the Army of the Valley of Virginia, under Gen. Jubal Early, and so continued until the surrender of Gen. Lee.

To him belongs the credit of organizing the Reserve Corps Hospital of the Confederacy, and of perfecting the Ambulance Corps. After the close of the war he was elected to the chair of surgery in the Medical College of Virginia, which had been made vacant by the death of Dr. Charles Bell Gibson. He continued to fill the chair until 1878, when, on account of some disagreements, he resigned. In 1880, however, he was made professor emeritus.

In 1893 he headed a movement to establish in Richmond a medical school having a three years' graded course, there being no such college in that section of the South. The school was incorporated and established under the name of the College of Physicians and Surgeons, but its name was changed two or three years later to University College of Medicine. In connection with the school the Virginia Hospital was established, and Dr. McGuire was made president of both institutions. He was also clinical professor of surgery. He was president of each of the local societies organized in Richmond during his residence there, and was one of the founders of the Medical Society of Virginia, serving for many years as chairman of the Executive Committee, until elected president in 1880–81. He was president of the American Medical Association in 1892, and president in 1875 of the Association of Medical Officers of the

Army and Navy of the Confederate States, president of the American Surgical Association in 1886, of the Southern Surgical and Gynecological association in 1889, and associate fellow of the College of Physicians of Philadelphia. In 1887 the University of North Carolina conferred upon him the title of LL. D., and the same honor came from Jefferson son Medical College.

He married in 1866 Miss Mary Stuart, of Staunton, Virginia, and had nine children. Two of his sons became physicians, Dr. Stuart McGuire, of Richmond, who inherited his father's skill as a surgeon, and Dr. Hugh McGuire, of Alexandria, Virginia, a physician.

Some six months before his death he suffered a stroke of acute bulbar paralysis, and while, for a time, his general condition improved, he never regained the power of articulation. After many weeks of improvements and set-backs, he rapidly grew worse during the week preceding his death, which occurred suddenly on September 19, 1900, at his home near Richmond.

His contributions to medical literature consist chiefly of journal articles and papers and discussions in society meetings. He wrote the article on "Intestinal Obstruction" in Pepper's "System of Medicine," and that on "Gun-shot Wounds" in Holmes' System of Surgery." Most of his articles appeared in the pages of the "Virginia Medical Monthly." The following are some of the articles from his pen:

"The Last Wound of Gen. Jackson." ("Richmond Medical Journal," vol. i.)

"An Operation for Ligation of the Subclavian Artery." ("Virginia Clinical Record," vol. i.)

"An Operation for External Perineal Urethrotomy," Ibid., vol. ii.

"Drainage in Chronic Cystitis." ("Virginia Medical Monthly," vol. i.)

"Three Cases of Gun-shot Wounds of the Pelvis Followed by Stone in the Bladder," Ibid., vol. i.)

"Disease of the Sacro-iliac Joint," Ibid., iv.

"Gun-shot and Other Wounds of the Peritoneum." ("Transactions of the Medical Society of Virginia," 1873.)

Other articles in the latter journal are "The Choice of Anesthetics," "Nervous Disturbances Following Urethral Stricture," and "Cases of Supra-pubic Cystotomy and its Results."

R. M. S.

" Virginia Medical Semi-Monthly," September 21, 1900.
"Transactions of the Medical Society of Virginia," 1900.)
Brit. M. J. Lond., 1900, ii.
Tr. South. Surg. and Gynec. Ass., 1902, Phila., 1903, xv. (port.).

McHenry, James (1753–1816).

James McHenry, army surgeon, was the son of Daniel and Agnes McHenry and born in Ballymena, Antrim, Ireland. He persuaded his father to emigrate to America and the family settled in Baltimore, James studying medicine in Philadelphia under Benjamin Rush. Then came his military life. In 1776 surgeon of the fifth Pennsylvania battalion; then recommended by Congress as hospital surgeon. He was captured by the British at Fort Washington but was exchanged in 1778 and appointed surgeon of the Flying Hospital. Later on, an assignment as secretary to Gen. Washington ended his active medical career, and in 1780 he became nominal aid but really mentor to the Marquis de la Fayette. As a politician he also did good work in the Maryland Senate, Assembly and Convention. His last appointment was the secretaryship of war in Washington's cabinet and afterwards in that of Adams. To him the army owes many radical and enduring reforms, and Fort McHenry, near Baltimore, is named in his honor. It was off here that Francis Scott Key, while prisoner on a British man o'war, wrote "The Star Spangled Banner."

After a long and crowded period of work McHenry went to live in his house near Baltimore and died there on May 3, 1816.

J. E. P.

James Evelyn Pilcher, Jour. Ass. Military Surgeons of the U. S. A., vol. xvi, 1905.
The Surgeons-general of the United States Army, Carlisle, Pa., 1905.
There is a portrait in both these vols.

McKechnie, John (1730–1782).

Fortunately for his life-history, this pioneer and log-cabin physician left behind him a diary containing a good deal of information, medical and biographical, well worth rescuing for a while from the oblivion of more than a century. Dr. John McKechnie was born in Scotland about 1730, studied medicine either at Aberdeen or Edinburgh, obtained a license or a degree in 1752, and practised in his native land for three years. Accomplishing but little in that time he decided to come to America, the land of promise. Embarking on the brig "Crawford Bridge," Curry her captain, he, with sixteen others, left Greenock, Scotland, at 4 p. m. July 26, 1755, and landed all well on board at the end of Long Wharf in Boston, September 12, of the same year, at 7 p. m., as his diary exactly informs us.

It is not known how long he practised medically in the neighborhood of Boston, but it is a fact that wearying of the attempt to make a living as physician or a teacher, he became an official of the Plymouth Land Company with the rank of Lieutenant and the position of a land surveyor. With this Association he remained four years. We find farther traces of his engagement with the Kennebec (Maine) Company in 1760 and later, during which period he surveyed large tracts of land on the Kennebec and Penobscot Rivers. His work was so accurate that it has to this day remained the standard, and farms still pass from owner to owner under the so-called "McKechnie" surveys. While thus occupied he went occasionally on business to Boston, both for the Company as well as for his private affairs, and in one old receipt we find him signing as Lieut. McKechnie. The earliest document styling him "Doctor" McKechnie is dated at Pownalborough in 1764, and concerns the sum of twelve shillings received for services and medicine to a patient.

Some time in the year 1760 he was teaching at Pemaquid, Maine, where he met Mary North the daughter of Capt. North, the commander of the Fort, and married her. Her father officiated at the wedding, although he is said not to have favored the match, either because Dr. McKechnie was too old, or had no settled profession. For the next six years the happy couple moved from place to place as the husband's duties as surveyor, teacher or physician called him. We find him treating a patient for small-pox at Swan's Island in 1764. He followed the usual routine of "blooding" patients, as his old diary shows, and, like other physicians of that time, supplied them with large quantities of drugs. He settled permanently at Bowdoinham, not far from Brunswick the seat of Bowdoin College, in 1764, and, according to all accounts, remained practising there until 1771 when he moved to Winslow, near Fort Halifax, on the east side of the Kennebec River, opposite what is now called Waterville, Maine. At Winslow then, he built his cabin and partitioned off a room for a dispensary of the drugs which were so extensively dealt out to sick people in that era. His practice increased with considerable rapidity, and in four years he built a still larger home, on the other side of the local stream, the Cobossecontee. Having also put a good deal of his earnings into growing timber he enlarged the capacity of his saw mill.

When Benedict Arnold set out on his ill-fated expedition to Quebec, in 1775, his march carried him through Winslow, and some of his soldiers requiring medical care were left in charge of Dr. McKechnie. Among others mentioned in an old diary we find the following cases attended by Dr. McKechnie: Mortification of the hand,

contusion of the shin, toe cut with an axe while hewing a road through the primeval forests, jaundice, camp fever, strangury, deafness resulting from a cold in the head, and finally a bad injury to the hand from the bursting of a musket.

After having been a prominent man in Winslow before the Revolution, he was held in suspicion as a loyalist during that stormy period. Although a man of means (one person owed him for instance a thousand dollars on a note) he was not one of the seven citizens asked to buy ammunition for soldiers enlisting from the settlement in the Revolutionary War, he is said to have had no sympathy with the "Rebels" as he called them and the Sons of Liberty kept him under constant surveillance. Once upon a time they called upon the good doctor to ask just what certain words of his were meant to imply. But taking down his sword which he had worn during his Lieutenancy his only answer was "Gentleman, if at any time I have said anything that you did not understand, I am sorry for it."

He was a faithful physician, travelled long distances for his few patients, grew aged before his time and was worn out in looking after the interests of his practice, his business, and his large family of thirteen children. None of these, however, appear to have taken up their father's practice. The cause of his death, April 14, 1782, is unknown, but he is said to have died suddenly. He was a deeply religious man, as these few titles of books from his library prove: "The Unbloody Sacrifice," "Justification" and "The Four Fold State." Oddly enough, his widow, surviving him, married again, a curious man, who was willing that his wife should be buried beside her first husband, but as for himself he would never consent to be buried in that lot of ground, because a man whom he had hated all of his life was already buried there.

J. A. S.

Waterville, Maine, Centenary, Dr. F. C. Thayer.
Family Papers from Dr. F. H. Mckechnie.

McKeen, James (1797–1873).

Probably one of the ablest physicians ever practising in Maine was James McKeen, son of Joseph McKeen, first president of Bowdoin. Born in Beverly, Massachusetts, November 27, 1797, he graduated at Bowdoin in 1817 and while a student was noted for his scientific zeal and attainments, being considered a careful observer and excellent thinker. He read much about Napoleon and followed him in his marches by pins stuck into the map of Europe. He was fond of astronomy. One night the college president observed a lantern shining on the steps of one of the dormitories. Suspecting some silly trick on the part of the students he crept up to ascertain what was going on, and found young McKeen studying the heavens with a sidereal map; the lantern was to display the positions of the constellations on the map after he had gazed at them in the skies above him.

After graduating from Bowdoin, he studied with Dr. Matthias Spalding of Amherst, New Hampshire, a man very active in vaccination and more than once president of the New Hampshire Medical Society. Later, he studied with Dr. John Ware of Boston, and graduated at the Harvard Medical School in 1820. He then established himself at Topsham, Maine, a small town near Brunswick, Maine, the seat of Bowdoin College, and practised there with great success for more than fifty years.

In 1825 he was chosen professor of obstetrics in the Medical School of Maine, a position occupied honorably to himself and beneficially to his scholars for fourteen years, and was also professor of theory and practice of medicine in the same school.

He was one of the founders and incorporators of the Maine Medical Society, and afterwards of the Maine Medical Association. He wrote several papers; one in 1829 was an essay "On the Influence of the Imagination upon the Fetus in Utero."

Later on, this Society dying out, the Maine Medical Association was established, largely upon his initiative, and of that he was long secretary and second president.

He was a life-long student of medicine. During a yellow-fever epidemic in New York he was so much interested in satisfying his medical curiosity regarding the symptoms and studying the best treatment so as to be ready if it should break out in Maine, that he left Topsham without telling anybody where he was bound, and braved the terrors of a stage-coach journey and all the risks of contagion in New York. No one in our times can have any idea of the terror in those days of epidemics. Public travel was paralyzed for fear of spreading the disease. One very delightful episode of this long journey, so valuable medically to McKeen, was that riding in the coach with him was a man whom he thought the most interesting conversationalist that he had ever met, and who eventually proved to be Daniel Webster on his way to Washington.

Setting out for Europe in 1837, Dr. McKeen was obliged, owing to the unsettled state of financial credit, to take with him eleven hundred dollars in silver coin for his expenses. Arriving in Dublin he took lodgings which he soon found to be disreputable. He accordingly transferred his silver dollars bag by bag of a hundred each to a respectable place, but darkness coming on during his last trip with a single bag he was waylaid by two footpads. He shook off both assailants, but one of them had captured his umbrella. Not intending to lose even that, he chased the rascal and hitting him on the back with the remaining bag of hard cash knocked him end over end. Policemen then came on the scene, and Dr. McKeen was charged with having committed an assault, but fortunately for him he received a quick discharge when the character of the assaulted man was verified by the police.

He had great presence of mind, for occasionally leaving behind him his saddlebags with medicine he pretended to the patient that medicine was of no use on that day, and that dieting would be the proper treatment, thus skillfully hiding his forgetfulness.

Fifty years after graduating from Bowdoin College, he collected the few remaining members of his class at Topsham, and there re-kindled within them the youthful enthusiasm of half a century before. He had a great and a deservedly great career in medicine, and died without long illness on the day after his seventy-sixth birthday at Topsham, Maine, November 28, 1873.

A. S.

MSS. Records, Maine Medical Society.
Transactions, Maine Medical Association.

McKinley, John (1721-1796).

John McKinley, first governor of Delaware, was born in the north of Ireland, February 24, 1721. Nothing is known of his parentage and family aside from the knowledge implied by his having been educated and able to begin at once the practice of medicine when he came to this country.

He was a charter member of the first Delaware Medical Society, which was the third medical society in the United States.

In 1757 he was appointed sheriff of New Castle County under the Colonial Government. He held this office for three years and in 1759 was chosen chief burgess of the small borough of Wilmington. Continuous re-election by his fellow townsmen kept him in this office for fifteen years. In 1777 he became the first governor of Delaware, or "President" of the State, as the title then was.

Dr. McKinley was prompt to take a stand against British oppression, and, like others of his race, became an ardent, outspoken patriot. He was of fearless and decided character, and greatly popular with those who opposed taxation without representation. In September, 1777, just after the Battle of the Brandywine, a detachment of British soldiers appeared in Wilmington, and after looting the governor's house, took him prisoner as a valuable prize. After one year in close captivity he returned once more to his home on the northwest corner of Third and French streets and resumed his practice and other duties. The public library at New York contains a sworn statement by Dr. McKinley as to damage done his property by British soldiers, but it is doubtful if the infant Republic made good his loss.

In the First Presbyterian Church, of which he was a trustee, and which is now used as the building of the Delaware Historical Society, is a large lantern. It is of iron with glass panels, and bears the following inscription:

"The lantern of Dr. John McKinley, of Wilmington, Delaware."

"This lantern lighted the path of that devoted, able physician during his nightly visits to the sick and afflicted, born by his devoted African servant, 'Fortin' when street lamps were unknown."

"There are a few persons still living in Wilmington who bear kindly recollections of master and man."

He left no children: his wife's name was Jane Richardson and they were married about the year 1764.

Dr. McKinley died at the age of seventy-five years on the thirty-first of August, 1796, in Wilmington.

A. R.

Biographical and Genealogical History of the State of Delaware.

MacLaren, Laurence (1817-1892).

Laurence MacLaren was the son of John MacLaren, architect, of Perth, Scotland, who emigrated to Prince Edward Island in 1804, where Laurence was born in 1817 but had his medical education in Edinburgh and took the diploma of the Royal College of Surgeons there. After gradnation he began to practice in Richibucto, New Brunswick, where he remained twenty-five years. Then he removed to St. John, New Brunswick, and continued in active work there until a short time before his death, which took place in September, 1892.

He was especially distinguished as a surgeon, and did a goodly number of important and successful operations, among which we may mention ligature of the common carotid artery and several lithotomies. He was at one time a member of the New Brunswick Medical Council, and for several years was on the staff of the St. John Public Hospital.

His wife was Jane M. Jardine of Liverpool, and they had ten children. Two of his sons studied medicine, and graduated at the university of Edinburgh.

A. B. A.

McLaughlin, James Wharton (1840–1909).

James Wharton McLaughlin is best known for his indefatigable labors in the search for truth in the chemical and biological laboratories, his researches as to the causes of immunity and infection, and especially his discovery of the bacillus of dengue, all of which were published in the medical journals of America and Europe.

Briefly summed up, his record is that he was born on September 7, 1840, and came south just prior to the Civil War, enlisting as a private soldier in Company D, First Kentucky Infantry (C. S. A.), and served through the entire war with Johnson, Jackson, Morgan and Forrest, then settled in La Grange, Texas, studied medicine, and graduated at Tulane, New Orleans, in 1867. He met and married in September, 1867, Tabitha Bird Moore, of Fayette County, and returning to La Grange practised medicine until 1869, then removed to Austin, and died there on November 13, 1909, survived by his wife, three sons, Dr. Bird McLaughlin, of New York; Dr. Cyrus McLaughlin, of California, and Dr. James W. McLaughlin, Jr., of Austin, and three daughters, Evelyn, Minnie and Frances.

He practised for forty years in Austin saving for an interval of eight years when he occupied the chair of practice in the University of Galveston. In 1894 he was president of the Texas State Medical Association and a university regent.

His interest in his work was very keen even to the end. The Mayos of Rochester had extirpated his entire cervical and maxillary glandular system in the desperate hope of arresting the dread cancer, which, beginning on the lip, spread downwards. His paper—his favorite theme—"Theory of Immunity by Wave Interference and Catalysis"—as opposed to that of Ehrlich—had only recently appeared in the "New York Medical Record," and a week before he died he discussed his presidential address for the Texas Academy of Science on the subject of Ehrlich's "Side Chain Theory of Immunity." which Dr. Hilgartner was to read for him. Some of his other papers were:

"Researches into the Etiology of Dengue," 1886.

"An Explanation of the Phenomena of Immunity and Contagion Based on the Action of Physical and Biological Laws," 1890.

"Fermentation, Infection and Immunity," 1892.

"The Bacteriology of Dengue," 1896.
D. W.

From The Texas Medical Journal, Dec., 1909.
Phys. and Surgs. of America, Dr. Watson.

MacLeod, James (1845–1900).

James MacLeod, foremost in securing the passage of the medical law for the province, editor of the "Maritime

Medical News," and president of the Maritime Medical Association, was born at Uig, Scotland, June 13, 1845, the third son of the Rev. Samuel MacLeod. He graduated M. D. from the McGill Medical College, Montreal, and at the time of his death was well known as a prominent surgeon in Charlottetown, Prince Edward Island, and for his work in connection with the two hospitals there. He married Margaret Alma Gates, and died in 1900.

McLoughlin, John (1784–1857).

John McLoughlin, known to Americans as the "Father of Oregon" and to the Indians as the "Great White Chief," was born October 19, 1784, in La Rivière du Loup, Canada, son of John McLoughlin, an Irishman and Angelique Fraser, a Scotch-Canadian, both Roman Catholics. There were seven children, John coming second. He was educated in Canada and Scotland and on his return to Canada joined the Northwest Company, in 1821 being put in charge of Fort William. There he married the widow of a fur trader, Alexander Mackay, and had four children, Eliza, John, Eloisa and David.

He came overland to Fort George (Astotoria) in 1824, then founded and remained in Fort Vancouver twenty-two years. The Indian population of Oregon numbered some 100,000; the state was half as large again as Germany and he had no one on whom to depend save the few subordinates of the company with him, yet, through his strong justice, no wars occurred during his rule and he firmly stopped the sale of liquor to Indians by excluding the sale of it even to the whites.

When the American immigration set in (1843–5) McLoughlin, through sternly observant of his loyalty to the Hudson Bay Company, aided in the usual immigrational distress with food, farming supplies and medical help, often doing all this at his own expense. He founded Oregon City and opened up the country; he adverted a war between the United States and Great Britain; smoothed the way for missionaries and preserved his integrity when endowed with absolute power as chief factor of the Hudson Bay Company west of the Rocky Mountains, yet—the story is too long to give here—he said when near death "I might better have been shot forty years ago. I planted all I had here and the government has confiscated my estates." Worried by mendacity and ingratitude he died a broken-hearted man, at Oregon City, September 3, 1857, and was buried among the Roman Catholics, he having joined their church in middle life.

Dr. John McLoughlin. Frederick V. Holman, 1907.
Marcus Whitman. Myron Eells, 1909.

MacNaughton, James (1796–1874).

One of the founders of the City Hospital, Albany, and surgeon-general of that state, James MacNaughton, who came over to the United States in 1817, lived here some fifty-seven years and became known as a leading surgeon.

He was born on December 10, 1796, at Kenmore, Scotland, and entered Edinburgh University when sixteen. Graduating M. D., four years later he took a ship's surgeoncy and landed at Quebec, afterwards settling in Albany and remaining there the rest of his life, marrying the daughter of a Mr. Nicholas McIntyre who had befriended him on arrival.

When he was appointed professor of anatomy and physiology in the College of Physicians and Surgeons of the western district of New York the number of students increased from 100 to over 230 and the same success attended him when called to the chair of the theory and practice of medicine in Albany College. During the epidemic of Asiatic cholera in Albany, 1832, he was unwearied in his efforts to check the disease and provide hospitals.

He died in Paris of heart disease, while away on a holiday on the eleventh of June, 1874.

Obit. Notice by Prof. W. J. Tucker. Trans. of the Med. Soc. of the State of New York. Med. and Surg. Reporter, Phila., 1874, vol. xxx.

Macneven, William James (1763—1841).

William James Macneven was born at Ballynahowne, County Galway, Ireland, on March 21, 1763. His ancestors were country gentlemen, living on their own estate, which was transmitted in a direct line from father to son.

He was the eldest of four sons and at the age of ten or twelve was sent for by his uncle, Baron Macneven, to receive his education in Germany where he had an excellent one at the college at Prague; subsequently passing through the medical college, and taking the degree of Doctor in Physic at Vienna, in 1874. The same year he returned to Dublin and began to practice.

His intimacy with Lord Edward Fitzgerald, with Jones, O'Connor, and other individuals of note; his entrance as a member of the Secret Society, in which he was joined by Thomas Addis Emmet; his arrest on the twelfth of March, 1798; his confinement in Kilmainham and subsequent removal to Fort George, are among the foremost occurrences most worthy of detail.

After the liberation of the state prisoners from Fort George, he passed the summer and autumn of 1802 in a pedestrian tour through Switzerland, and wrote an account of his journey, called "A Ramble through Switzerland." At the completion of this tour, he visited his relations in Germany.

New resolutions now animated him. The cause of liberty in his own country had sustained a blow, the effects of which paralyzed further effort. He accordingly set sail from Bordeaux for New York in June, 1804, and arrived on the afternoon of the fourth of July in the midst of the rejoicings of the American nation in commemoration of the Declaration of Independence. He lost no time in making known his intentions of becoming an American citizen, fixing upon New York as his permanent home, and immediately entering into practice there. The M. D. was conferred on him at Columbia College.

In 1810 he married Mrs. Jane Margaret Tom, the widow of Mr. John Tom, merchant, of New York, and daughter of Mr. Samuel Riker, of Newton, Long Island. By this marriage Dr. Macneven had a family of several sons and daughters, most of whom died of consumption.

In March, 1838, he was attacked with an alarming illness, and lay some days dangerously sick, but the attack at length terminated in a severe fit of the gout. His professional pursuits were now both irksome and injurious to him, and he determined on retiring to the country. In November, 1840, he received a severe injury of the leg, which, together with a shock from a fall, occasioned him a long and painful illness. From this time his strength gradually failed him, and on July 12, 1841, he died.

Dr. Macneven, at the opening session of the College of Physicians and Surgeons, in 1807, delivered a long course on clinical cases as they occurred in the New York Almshouse, where, with Dr. Hosack, he was an associate physician. In 1808 he received from the Regents the appointment of professor of midwifery. In 1810 a reorganization of the school took place, when Samuel Bard was placed at the head. Dr. Macneven was now chosen professor of chemistry, and, in 1816, while Dr. Francis was in Europe, materia medica was added to his chair. This arrangement continued until 1820, when they were separated, Dr. Mitchell, being assigned that duty with natural history.

He wrote "Pieces of Irish History," and numerous political tracts. His "Exposition of the Atomic Theory," printed in 1820, was received with favor, and reprinted in the "French Annals of Chemistry." As co-editor of the "New York Medical and Philosophical Journal," a work which, made up chiefly of selections, he projected with Dr. Benjamin De Witt in 1812, he wrote several papers on subjects strictly medical. He also published, in 1821, with emendations, an edition of "Brande's Chemistry."

Eminent American Physicians and Surgeons. S. D. Gross.

Macrae, Donald (1839–1907).

In the death of Donald Macrae, which occurred in Council Bluffs, Iowa, on August 14, 1907, Iowa lost one of her highly honored citizens and physicians. Dr. Macrae was called the Father of the Medical Society of the Missouri Valley, having been active in its organization, and its first president in 1888.

He was born at Pollewe in Rosshire, Scotland, October 3, 1839. His father was the Rev. Donald Macrae, minister of Pollewe. He received his education at the University of Edinburgh, from which he graduated with the M. A., subsequently taking his medical degree there in August, 1861. After practicing for a year and a half in the Edinburgh Royal Infirmary, Dr. Macrae accepted a position as surgeon for the Cunard Steamship Company, and crossed the Atlantic seventy-five times during his four years service.

In 1867 Dr. Macrae married Charlotte Bouchette, daughter of Joseph Bouchette, surveyor-general of Canada. Soon afterwards he went to Council Bluffs, arriving in March, 1867, and continued in active practice until illness compelled him to retire a short time before his death. Mrs. Macrae died in March, 1904.

Dr. Macrae was for many years identified with the Omaha Medical College, where, beginning in 1881, he was professor of principles and practice of medicine. In 1877 he was elected president of the Iowa State Medical Society.

The Med. Herald, Sept., 1907.

McRuer, Daniel (1802–1873).

A typical Scotchman with a "burr" in his talk, Dr. McRuer is worth describing. He was born in Knapdale, Argyleshire, Scotland, January 12, 1802, the son of a clergyman, who before the birth of his son had settled in Greenock. His parents left him an orphan at the age of five, but, befriended by relatives, he studied medicine with a surgeon apothecary,

and after obtaining a degree from some source unknown to me, he had sufficient political influence to get the position of surgeon's mate in the English Navy. The vessel on which he was on duty was shipwrecked in South America. He was rescued with others by a passing vessel, and brought safely to St. Johns, New Brunswick, where he practised for a while, but learned to like America and decided to move into Maine, where he practised at Nobleborough and Damariscotta.

At this place, he married Mary Ann Wright, about 1825. When Dr. McRuer wished to become a member of the Maine Medical Society, in the year 1826, his election was refused on the ground that although regularly nominated, he, as a foreigner, had never exhibited any testimonials regarding his qualifications as a practitioner.

He was, however, finally admitted. In 1834 he removed to Bangor, where he practised until his death.

A man of sterling worth, he did great service in the Civil War as an army surgeon; he had also a large consulting practice and did twenty-six ovariotomies in days when that operation was rare and few physicians dared to do it, with perfect result in twenty of them. He was a student, interested not only in medicine, independent and original in thought and language. Of a calm and cheerful nature, he made the best of life, despite the terrible misfortune of his later years, terminating in blindness from glaucoma. He contributed to the pages of the "Boston Medical and Surgical Journal," 1838, 1849 and 1853, papers on "Women's Diseases," "Cod Liver Oil," and "Removal of an Ovarian Tumor." He also wrote a pamphlet of fifty pages on "Ulcerations and Abrasions of the Cervix Uteri."

Having lost his sight, which he was enduring with remarkable cheerfulness, he was next loaded down with physical pain and renewed burdens in the shape of gallstones. Every attack weakened him more and more until he was willing to give in. He died suddenly April 5, 1873, after a hot bath which he had been taking for the relief of the pain caused by the passage of a gallstone. His career was remarkable, saved as he was from shipwreck, far from Scotland, and then rescued to live, honored and renowned in his American home.   J. A. S.

Trans. Maine Med. Assoc., 1873.

McWilliams, Alexander (1775–1850). Of Scotch descent, the first of a family who came to this country having escaped threatened arrest for treason on account of political connection with the party of the pretender, Alexander McWilliams was born in St. Mary's County, Maryland, in 1775. Soon after graduating he entered the navy (1802) as assistant surgeon and afterwards was ordered to sea in one of Jefferson's gun-boats. He served during the Tripolitan War, and was present at the burning of the "Philadelphia." On his return voyage he was taken ill with a continued fever and was left at Gibraltar, remaining there several weeks, finally returning home on the frigate "Constitution" and getting a post at the navy yard, Washington. But this he resigned and commenced private practice, locating himself near the Navy-yard, then the most thickly populated part of the city and seemingly offering the best prospect for a doctor.

He was an honorary M. D., 1841, Columbia College, District of Columbia; an incorporator of the Medical Society, District of Columbia, under both charters; assistant surgeon, United States Navy, 1802–05, and president of the Medical Association, District of Columbia, 1847–50.

Dr. McWilliams was very fond of natural science, more especially of botany, to which he devoted much attention, and often, during the proper

season, neglected his professional work to make excursions in search of new plants and flowers. During the early years of the medical department in Columbia University he was professor of botany, and subsequently published the "Flora of the District of Columbia." He was one of the "Botanic Club" which published, in 1830, the "Prodromus of the Flora Columbiana." He was the first resident to build a conservatory, which he filled with many rare plants. This he superintended and managed in person for his own amusement, without any commercial purpose. Connected with the conservatory was a large aviary, in which he had many rare foreign birds. He was also a good mineralogist, and made a large collection of minerals.

His inventive genius was somewhat remarkable, but unprofitable. He. invented a ship guage to measure the draft of water a vessel would draw and to determine the depth of the water. This was approved by a board of naval officers, but never adopted and consequently he failed to realize any profit from its manufacture. Many models of other inventions were destroyed by a fire in the patent office. He was the first physician to employ adhesive plaster to make extension in case of fractured legs.

At the time of his death, March 31, 1850, he had for some time confined his professional labors exclusively to his duties at the Alms House, of which he was the physician. He was an active thinker on medical subjects even at that advanced age. In a discussion on the relation of typhus and typhoid fever, he maintained their unity.
                              D. S. L.

Minutes of Medical Society, D. C., April 1, 1850.
Busey, "Reminiscences."

Maddin, Thomas La Fayette (1826–1908). Thomas La Fayette Maddin was born in Columbia, Tennessee, September 4, 1826, of Irish ancestry. His parents were the Rev. Thomas Maddin, D. D., and Sarah Moore.

The son was educated in the common schools of Middle Tennessee and North Alabama and his medical education was gained under Dr. Jonathan McDonald, of Limestone County, Alabama, and he graduated from the medical department of the University of Louisville.

Constant overwork in a large country practice in Alabama proved a severe trial to a physical constitution never very stout, and he went to Nashville, Tennessee. The opportunities for medical observation offered him in Alabama were various and extensive, and a number of serious epidemics of typhoid fever gave him large experience in disease.

In 1854 Dr. Maddin commenced private tuition in the various branches of medicine, and erected rooms for that purpose. For several years his classes were large, and his reputation as a teacher great. In 1857 Shelby Medical College was founded as the medical department of a projected university of the Methodist Episcopal Church South, which has since developed into the Vanderbilt University. He occupied for two years the chair of anatomy there, and afterwards that of surgery. At the time of the war, Maddin was in charge of one of the largest of the hospitals established in Nashville by Confederate authorities. During the subsequent years of the war, the large number of wounded quartered in and near the city afforded Dr. Maddin an extensive surgical experience, and he performed a number of interesting operations, notably two for traumatic aneurysm. One of these required the ligature of the external iliac artery, the aneurysmal tumor extending from the inguinal region to a line drawn from the crest of the ilium to the umbilicus. The other was an aneurysm of the left subclavian artery, necessitating the ligature of that artery in its middle third and a number of subsidiary vessels. The delicate operation, which from its difficult and hazardous nature was declared inadmissible upon consultation with Dr. Frank H. Hamilton,

then medical inspector of the army of the Cumberland, was witnessed by that surgeon, who also gave his assistance. It was pronounced by him, resulting as it did in the relief of the formidable tumor, a great surgical triumph. In the circuit of his private surgical practice, Dr. Maddin is also credited with the first successful ovariotomy performed in Tennessee.

In 1867, Dr. Maddin was called to the chair of institutes of medicine in the medical department of the University of Nashville, and after several years' acceptable service therein was transferred, about the time of the alliance of that institution with the medical department of Vanderbilt University, to the chair of theory and practice of medicine and clinical medicine.

Dr. Maddin was a member of the State Medical Society, the County and City Medical Societies, and contributed a number of able papers to their archives, and also to the medical journals of the time. For several years he was co-editor of the "Monthly Record of Medicine and Surgery," published at Nashville.

He died April 27, 1908, at his home, 109 Ninth Avenue South, Nashville, Tennessee.

W. D. H.

Mann, James (1762–1832).

James Mann, surgeon of the United States Army, graduated at Harvard University in 1776 and studied medicine under a Dr. Danforth. For three years he served as surgeon in the Continental Army and in 1812 was appointed hospital surgeon in the United States Army and rendered valuable service as head of the medical staff on the Canadian frontier. He is the author of "Medical Sketches of the Campaigns of 1812,'13, and '14," a most interesting book, which was published in 1816. He died in New York in 1832.

A. A.

Toner, Collect. Med. Biogr., Congress. Libr., Washington.

Manson, Otis Frederick (1822–1888).

A physician and surgeon in the Confederate Army, he was born in Richmond, Virginia, October 10, 1822, and went as a lad to the schools of his native city; studying medicine and graduating from the medical department of Hampden-Sidney College in 1840, at the age of eighteen. He at once settled in Granville County, North Carolina, and soon acquired a large practice.

He was a charter member of the Medical Society of Virginia, member, and later an honorary member, of the Medical Society of North Carolina, and the societies of other Southern states.

At the beginning of the war he went to Richmond at the request of Gov. Vance of North Carolina to look after the health of the troops of the state, and when a hospital for these soldiers was established, he was selected by the governor as surgeon-in-chief. In 1862 he was commissioned surgeon in the Confederate Army and served as such through the war, acting at the same time as a medical adjutant with rank of major for the state of North Carolina.

At the close of the war he settled in Richmond, and in 1867 was elected professor of pathology in the medical college of Virginia, to which chair was added a year later that of physiology. He resigned in 1882, and was made professor emeritus. In 1871–72 he was associate editor of the "Richmond Clinical Record," and for a number of years, president of the City Council.

Throughout his life he was a diligent student, an ardent investigator and a voluminous writer. An able physician devoted to his work and one of marked administrative ability, his organization and conduct of the Moore Hospital won for him the highest praise.

While living in North Carolina he availed himself of the abundant opportunity for studying malarial fevers, and accumulated a very large library, which contained much literature, both American and European, on that subject, and, in consequence, he acquired a remarkable

knowledge of the disease. He was the first American writer to describe "Puerperal Malarial Fever," an honor eventually gracefully accorded him by Dr. Fordyce Barker, who had claimed priority, and was among the first of the leaders who brought the use of quinine sulphate into prominence in the treatment of other diseases than intermittent fever, such as pneumonia, cholera infantum, puerperal fever, etc., in which diseases he advocated its use in large doses. Many of his doctrines and treatments received bitter opposition, but are now generally accepted and practised by Southern physicians. He was an accomplished man in other fields than medicine; pure and refined in his tastes, winning in manners.

He married, in 1841, a daughter of Spottswood Burwell of Granville County, North Carolina, who died in 1871, and had six children. He married again in 1881, as his second wife, Mrs. Helen (Gray) Watson, of Richmond, by whom he had no children.

After some months of feeble health from nervous prostration due to overwork, he died at his home in Richmond from an apoplectic stroke. February 1, 1888.

He was an extensive contributor to medical journal literature, and the following are a few of his contributions:

"Quinine in the Febrile Paroxysm." ("Stethoscope," and "Virginia Medical Gazette," vol. i, No. 2.)

"Puncture of the Bladder Above the Pubes." (Ibid., vol. i, No. 6.)

"On Large Doses of Quinine in Fever and Inflammation." (Ibid., vol. ii, No. 3.)

"Endemic Diseases of the Roanoke Valley and North Carolina." ("Virginia Medical Journal," vol. iv, No i.)

"Excision of the Superior Third of the Humerus." ("Confederate States Medical Journal," vol. i, No. 3, March, 1864.)

"Quinine in Remittent Fever." ("Virginia Clinical Record," October, 1871.)

"Cholera Infantum" ("Virginia Medical Monthly," vol. ii.)

"The Intermittent Form of Malarial Pneumonia." (Ibid., vol. iii.)

"A Treatise on the Physiological and Therapeutic Action of the Sulphate of Quinine," 1877.

"Malarial Hematuria." ("Transactions of the Medical Society of Virginia," 1886.)

At the time of his death he was engaged in the preparation of an exhaustive work entitled "A History of Fevers from the Earliest Times."

A phototype portrait of Dr. Manson illustrates the memorial sketch of Dr. S. S. Satchwell.   R. M. S.

Memorial of Prof. Otis Frederick Manson, M. D., S. S. Satchwell, A. M., M. D. pamphlet. Va. Med. Monthly, March, 1888.

March, Alden (1795–1869).

Alden March, noted as an operator and an inventor of surgical appliances, won his way to fame although handicapped by impecuniosity and adverse circumstances.

An ancedote will best illustrate his want of opportunity and his determination to succeed in his profession. One day, as he was carrying a common soap box, containing some anatomical preparations with which he was making himself thoroughly acquainted by most patient and minute application, a fellow-student remarked to him: "March, it is no use for you to try to make a distinguished man in your profession, since thousands, who have had far better advantages, have tried, and have failed to accomplish their object." He said: "I leave it for others to decide as to the correctness of this prophecy."

He was born in the town of Sutton, Worcester County, Massachusetts, September 20, 1795. His ancestors were of English origin, and settled in Massachusetts, so long since that their descendants became identified with the early history of that state. The name of March first appears in the history of the town of Newbury, Massachusetts (now Newburyport), as early as 1653.

Dr. March spent his early years on his father's farm, working in the busy season and going to school in winter. When nineteen years of age, by the death of his father, the charge of the homestead devolved upon him for about one year. In the winter of 1817 he taught a writing school at Hoosick, Rensselaer County, and also spent a part of the summer in quarrying and cutting slate stone for the roofing of houses.

His brother, Dr. David March, an army surgeon, suggested to him the study of medicine, and under this brother he began to study Latin, Greek and medicine. In 1818 and 1819 he attended medical lectures on anatomy and surgery at Boston, and graduated M. D. at Brown University September 6, 1820. Shortly after receiving his diploma he visited Cambridge, Washington County, where an elder brother resided. While here he performed his first surgical operation, which was for the remedy of that deformity known as hare-lip.

As an operator he was quick, dexterous, cautious, bold and successful. There is no record of his surgical operations during ten years of his professional life. Yet those of which there is record number seven thousand one hundred and twenty-four.

In the "Transactions of the American Medical Association of 1853," on pages 505 and 506, we find in connection with his essay on morbus-coxarius, mention of an invention designed by him, to fulfill a very important indication in the treatment of this disease.

Dr. Bryan, professor of surgery in the Philadelphia College of Medicine, in speaking of Prof. March's essay on improved forceps for hare-lip operation, says: "It embodied so much that is valnable that we think this production of one of the most distinguished surgeons of New York ought to be made to assume a permanent form, and be embodied in the standard works."

In 1860 Dr. March also invented instruments for the removal of dead bone; and, in 1867, employed a new method for removing urinary calculi.

Dr. March, it is believed, delivered the first course of lectures ever given in New

York, on anatomy, with demonstrations and dissections of the recent subject. They were delivered to a class of fourteen students, in the fall of 1821. "The first subjects," he says, "ever dissected for public demonstration, to the medical students in Albany, I procured from Boston, by what might now be called the overland route, by horse power across the Green Mountains, for you will please bear in mind there was no railroad communication at this time. It was then that I prepared arterial anatomical specimens, and formed the nucleus of the museum of the Albany Medical College."

In 1834 he established a Practical School for Anatomy and Surgery, the Albany Medical School being broken up by a disastrous fire which destroyed the building, and with it much of March's valuable anatomical and pathological preparations.

When the Albany Medical College was established in 1838, through March's efforts he was appointed professor of surgery, giving his first course of lectures the ensuing year, 1839, and remaining professor of surgery until his death, a period of thirty-one years.

Although the establishment of surgical clinics has been claimed by another city, yet it is believed Albany was the first to inaugurate this mode of imparting medical instruction; and the honor should be conceded to Dr. March as the first to organize them in this country.

His appointments included: 1825, professor of anatomy, Vermont Academy of Medicine, Castleton; 1827, professor of anatomy, Albany Medical Seminary; 1833, professor of anatomy and operative surgery, Albany Medical School; 1834, professor of surgery, Albany Medical College; 1832 and 1833, president of the Albany County Medical Society; 1857, president of the New York State Medical Society; 1864, president of the American Medical Association, and one of its founders. Honorary member of the Massachusetts State Medical Society, the Pennsylvania State Medical Society, the Connecticut State Medical Society, and the Rhode Island State Medical Society.

The degree of LL. D. was conferred on him by Williams College in 1868; 1869, honorary member of the "Institut des Archivistes de France."

His writings included:
1821, "Upon Dissection of the Human Body."
1834, "Surgical Cases, and Reports of Some of the More Important Surgical Operations."
1849, "Description of Malgaigne's Instrument for Maintaining Apposition in Those Oblique Fractures of the Tibia, in which the Superior Fragment obstinately Tends to Overlap the Inferior," which was published in the "Transactions of the American Medical Association."
1852, Paper on "Strangulated Hernia and Reducible," published in the "Western Lancet."
1853, "An essay on Morbus Coxarius or Dip-disease, and Report of Investigations." Published in "Transactions of the American Medical Association."
1853, "Report of a Case of Backward Dislocation of the Astragalus."
1854, Paper on "Penetrating Wounds of the Abdomen with Punctured Wounds of the Intestines. Penetrating Wounds of the Larynx, and Their Treatment, with Cases for Illustration, and Their Medico-Legal Aspect."
1854, "Report of an Operation for Extirpation of Tumor from the Neck."
1854, "On Clinical Surgery."
1855, "On Improved Forceps for Harelip operation."
1856, "On Four Months in Europe."
1856, "On Encysted Osseous Tumors."
1858, "On Intra-capsular Fracture of the Cervix Femoris, with Bony Union."
1861, "Report of a Case of Compound Comminuted and Complicated Fracture of the Upper Part of Tibia."
1867, "Essay on an Unusual Place of Lodgment and Exit of Biliary Calculus."
1867, "Essay on New Method Employed in Removing Urinary Calculi."
1867, "Essay on the Relations of the Periosteum to Osteogenesis."
Nearly all these essays and reports were read by him before the New York State

Medical Society, and published in the "Transactions."

In 1841, 1848 and 1856 he visited Europe, not only to perfect himself in his profession, but also to investigate, critically, that grave malady morbus coxarius, or hip disease. He says: "I take the position that spontaneous dislocation of the hip (as purely the result of morbid action, unaided by superadded violence) seldom or never takes place; I also propose a mode of treatment by which progressive absorption of the acetabulum and head of the bone may be arrested before the life of the patient is endangered by the progress of the disease."

March married Miss Joanna P., daughter of Mr. Silas Armsby of the town of Sutton, Massachusetts, February 22, 1824. His family consisted of four children, two boys and two girls. Two died in infancy. Henry became a physician.

An intimate friend of his, in speaking of March, senior, as a professor of religion, said: "The crowning glory of Dr. March's character was his consistent Christianity.

About the middle of May, 1869, he felt the symptoms of approaching illness which terminated his life. On the twenty-seventh he visited his daughter, where he became sick and remained all night, expecting to return to his home the following day, but he was not able. He lingered until Thursday, June 17, 1869, when he died.

J. L. B.

Autobiography of Samuel Gross, 1887.
The Late Alden March (W. C. Wey), 1869.
Nat. Med. Jour., Wash., 1870-1, vol. i (J. McNaughton).
Tr. Med. Soc., Co., Albany, 1870, vol. ii.
Tr. Med. Soc., State of N. York, Albany, 1870 (J. L. Babcock).
There is a portrait in the Surg.-Gen. Lib., Wash., D. C.

Marion, Otis Humphrey (1847-1906).

Otis Humphrey Marion was born in Burlington, Massachusetts, in 1847, graduated at Kimball Union Academy in 1869, Dartmouth College in 1873, and Harvard Medical School in 1876, and became house surgeon to the Boston City

Hospital in 1876-77, spending the winter of 1878 studying abroad, and settling eventually in Allston (Boston), Massachusetts.

He served as surgeon of the First Regiment, Massachusetts Volunteer Militia, and introduced into the Massachusetts Militia the system of First Aid to the Injured.

He was medical director of the First Brigade, Massachusetts Volunteer Militia, and surgeon-general of Massachusetts on the staff of former Gov. John L. Bates, with the rank of brigadier-general.

He died of pneumonia, November 27, 1906, leaving a widow, a daughter and two sons.

W. L. B.

Obit. in the current daily press and medical journals.

Markoe, Thomas Masters (1819-1901).

Thomas Masters Markoe, physician and pathologist, was descended from a refugee Huguenot family who had emigrated to the West Indies. His direct ancestor, Peter Markoe, settled in the Island of Santa Cruz, and the doctor's father, Francis Markoe was sent to be educated to the United States and settled in New York, marrying Sarah Caldwell, of Philadelphia, where their son was born September, 1819. He graduated from Princeton, in 1836 and from the College of Physicians and Surgeons, in 1841 becoming an assistant in the New York Hospital while still a student.

In 1842 he became assistant curator in the pathological museum and lecturer on pathological anatomy, while from 1852-92 he was surgeon to the New York Hospital. A professorship in the college of Physicians and Surgeons New York, was given him in 1860, and from 1878-88 he held there the chair of the principles of surgery.

Throughout the war he served as surgeon in the Union Army and afterwards returned to his practice.

His genial personality was much appreciated by the students, and his lectures were interesting even apart from their practical bearing. His telling descriptions of the processes of repair and his "healthy laudable pus" stood out clear and strong in their minds. His writings were not many, but his work on "Diseases of the Bones" (1872) was an authority for many years.

Apart from his busy professional life much of his time was given to other interests. He was trustee of the Astor Library in 1863 and up to 1895 its president, and took, moreover, a lively interest in the museums of Natural History and Art.

In 1850 he married Charlotte Atwell How and had five children; Charlotte How, Thomas Caldwell, Francis Hartman, James Wright and Sallie Caldwell. Francis and James became physicians in New York.

Med. News, N. York, 1901, lxxix.
Post-Graduate, 1900, xv.

Marshall, Moses (1758–1813).

The fame of this expert medical botanist has been somewhat eclipsed by that of his uncle Humphrey (not a doctor) of whom Darlington left studious and loving record in his "Memorials of Bartram and Marshall," but Moses made several long exploring journeys through the wilds of the West and rendered valuable assistance to his uncle in preparing the "Arbustum Americanum."

He was the son of James and Sarah Marshall and the grandson of Abram Marshall who came from Gratton, Derbyshire, England, to Delaware in 1697. He studied medicine under Dr. Nicholas Way of Wilmington but never took any medical degree, none being required at that time for practising in Pennsylvania, but, it being customary to attend a course of lectures, he went to those by William Shippen and Rush. His diary at this time shows medicine not wholly absorbing, for frequent mention is made of a certain Polly Howell and Sally Samson, the latter "behaving for three evenings, especially the last, in a most engaging manner."

Then followed a year or two employed in desultory medical work, including inoculation round about London Grove, Pennsylvania, and in keeping an apothecary's shop "which came to nothing and less." The truth was he had not found his true vocation—botanizing— but his uncle writes to Franklin in 1785, and Moses himself to Dr. Lettsom in London, suggesting a government supported exploration of the western states. In 1786 Sir Joseph Banks wrote to Humphrey Marshall asking for one hundredweight of fresh ginseng roots. Moses spent twenty days in the Alleghanies getting these and charged Lettsom $1.25 a pound. Lettsom and he seem to have carried on a brisk correspondence, especially concerning the "Talinum Teretifolium" hitherto undescribed by botanists. He sends Lettsom three tortoises and some plants, one of which, a polygala, is thus mentioned in a letter:

"Should this prove to be a new genus I had designed the appellation of Lettsomia, with this provision that it might not be unpleasing to thee, and that, in the interim, I should not be able to discover a plant more exalted, conspicuous and worthy." He also asks for a "surgeon's pouch of instruments" to be sent him, and Lettsom hastens to acknowledge the compliment of a floral godchild and encloses ten pounds in case Moses should be out of pocket for seeds asked for. A plant was also named after Moses but many authorities claim the Marshallia for his uncle. Two letters of 1792 have recently come to light which settle the question. Muhlenberg the correspondent, was himself a leading Philadelphian botanist:

"Dear Sir:

"I beg leave to inform you that the new edition of the Genera Linnaei is safely arrived. I am happy to see that the editor, my friend Dr. Schreber, has done what I requested of him. He has given your name to a hitherto undescribed plant that belongs to the Syngensia, which he names the Marshallia. Give my best respects to your uncle, Mr. Humphrey Marshall, and believe me with great esteem, sir,

"Your humble servant,

"Henry Muhlenberg."

In the collection of the Marshall papers in the possession of Gilbert Cope there is the following copy of the reply to this note in the handwriting of Dr. Marshall:

"West Bradford, April 13, 1792.

"Reverend Sir: I have just received yours of the ninth instant, and am much pleased to hear of the arrival of the Genera Plantarum. I am very sensible of the honor done me, through your request, by Dr. Schreber, and think myself but too undeserving. I shall be pleased in your calling on your intended journey, and hope you will consider my uncle's house as a welcome stage, I am, with all due respect,

"Your much obliged friend,

"Moses Marshall."

Marshall's letters speak of many long trips which meant fatigue, danger and expense. His appointment as justice of the peace curtailed these excursions, but he continued exchanging specimens and seeds with European confrères. About 1797 he married Alice Pennock and had six children. After his uncle's death there is not much told of his scientific work and he died on the thirteenth of October, 1813.

D. W.

Sketch by Dr. Wm. T. Sharpless. West Chester Daily News, Nov. 22, 1895.
Memorials of Bartram and Marshall, Wm. Darlington.
The Botanists of Philadelphia. Harshberger.

Martin, Ennalls (1758–1834).

He was born at his home, "Hampden," in Talbot County, Maryland, August 23, 1758, the son of Thomas and Mary Ennalls Martin. At a very early age he was sent to Newark Academy, Delaware, where he did well as a Latin and Greek scholar. In 1777 he was taken to Philadelphia by his father and put under Dr. William Shippen, the anatomist, then surgeon-general of the Continental Army, who assigned him to duty in the apothecary department. As the army was greatly in need of surgeons, particularly for the hospitals, and as young Martin proved himself an unusually apt scholar, he soon received a commission from Congress as hospital surgeon's mate, with the understanding that he was to attend the medical school of Philadelphia, then conducted by the Profs. Shippen, Rush, and Kuhn. He was at once stationed at Bethlehem Hospital, and took his M. B. in 1782. Meanwhile he was appointed demonstrator of anatomy by Shippen, to which work he applied himself with great zeal and became a skilled dissector, sometimes even taking Shippen's place. To show Martin's zeal and faithfulness, it is said that during his five years' service he left his station but twice, once to visit his father, who was an extensive farmer, tanner, and tobacco planter, and again to go on to Saratoga to bring away the sick and wounded after the defeat of Burgoyne.

Having obtained his M. D. he settled in practice at Talbot Court House, afterwards called Easton, although Shippen did everything to induce him to remain in Philadelphia. He was an occasional contributor to the "Medical Repository," then the only medical periodical in the country. He was inflexible in carrying out the treatment which his judgment suggested. It was useless to object, and he was known repeatedly to take a recalcitrant patient by the nose and force the medicine down his throat. His bluntness and brusqueness caused his patients to fear him and his colleagues to apply to him the soubriquet—"Abernethy of Talbot." He was the first to introduce vaccination into Talbot, and by his strong force of will to overcome the prejudice against it.

He was one of the founders and

incorporators of the Medical and Chirurgical Faculty of Maryland in 1799, was its orator in 1807, and became president in 1815, holding the office until 1820 when he declined further election. The subject of his oration was "Fever." He was also the author of "An Essay on the epidemics in the winters of 1813 and 1814 in Talbot and Queen Anne's Counties, Maryland," read at the annual convention of the Faculty in 1815, and was engaged on a work on the diseases of the Eastern Shore of Maryland at the time of his death. He died at Easton, December 16, 1834, at seventy-six, after an active professional life of over fifty-two years. He left a large family. His wife Sarah Haywood Martin, died June 3, 1835, aged sixty-eight. He received the honorary degree of M. D. from the University of Maryland in 1818.

E. F. C.

For sketch and portrait of Dr. Martin, Cordell's Medical Annals of Maryland, 1903

Martin, George (1826–1886).

George Martin, a Philadelphia botanist, was born near Claymont, Delaware County, Pennsylvania, in 1826, going as a boy to the West Town Friends' School and afterwards to the University of Pennsylvania where he took his M. D. about 1847. He first practised at Concordville, Delaware, for some three years then for five at the Fifth Street Dispensary, and then worked with his cousin, John M. Sharpless, at the chrome works of the latter. During the war he helped in the military hospitals in Chester and settled in West Chester about 1866 remaining there until his death there on October 28, 1886 He was a fellow of the college of Physicians of Philadelphia and from 1878 had devoted much time to mycological studies, especially in the examination of the parasitic leaf fungi and only a few days before his death had completed "A Synopsis of the North American Species of Septoria" as a continuation of a series of myological

papers he had already contributed. He was also a zealous botanist and in close association with the leading botanists of the day.

His writings included: "New Florida Fungi." ("Journal of Mycology," i, 97.) "Synopsis of the North American Species of Asterina, etc." (Ibid., i, 133, 145.) "New Fungi." (Ibid., ii, 128.) "The Phyllostictas of North America." (Ibid., ii, 13, 25.)

J. W. H.

The Botanists of Philadelphia. J. W. Harshberger, 1899.

Martin, Henry Austin (1824–1884).

Henry Austin Martin, surgeon, eldest son of Henry James Martin, was born in St. James, London, on July 23, 1824. He came from an old Huguenot family and was cousin to Lord Kingsale.

He came to America when a boy and studied at the Harvard Medical School, graduating in 1845 and settling to practice in Roxbury where he was a leading doctor for forty years.

He was, besides being a very eloquent speaker and finished writer, a very skillful surgeon. During the Civil War he was a medical director, and surgeon-in-chief of the second division of the second (Hancock's) corps.

In 1870 he introduced true animal vaccination into America, and by vast effort and continual writing, succeeded in having that method universally adopted within two years. In 1877 he presented to the American Medical Association a paper on the "Use of Pure Rubber Bandages in Surgery," and Martin's bandage became known throughout the profession. ("Surgical Uses, Other than Hemostatic, of the Strong Elastic Bandage," "Transactions, American Medical Association," Philadelphia, 1877, vol. xxviii.)

He was a great student all his life getting up long before daylight in winter, and always reading or writing several hours before breakfast. One of his hobbies was the collecting of old line engravings, on which he was an authority, and filling his rooms with all that an antiquarian and bibliophile loves to possess.

He married Frances Coffin Crosby, eldest daughter of Judge Nathan Crosby of Lowell, Massachusetts, on August 9, 1848. They had five children, two of whom, Stephen Crosby and Francis Coffin, became physicians.

Dr. Martin died at his home, 27 Dudley St., Roxbury, from diabetes, on December 7, 1884.

F. C. M.

Boston Med. and Surg. Jour., 1885, vol. cxii.
Jour. Am. Med. Assoc., Chicago, 1885, vol. iv. (H. O. Marcy.)
N. York Med. Jour., 1884, vol. xl.

Martin, Henry Newell (1848-1896).

A biologist, Henry Newell Martin was born at Newry, County Down, Ireland, of Irish parentage, on July 1, 1848, the eldest of a family of twelve. His father was a congregational minister, who afterwards became a schoolmaster. The boy's education was acquired chiefly at home and at the age of fifteen he matriculated at the University of London (an exemption as to age being made in his favor) and at the same time became apprentice to a Dr. Mc-Donagh in the vicinity of University College. It was stipulated that his duties as apprentice should not prevent his attending lectures and doing hospital work. It was during his apprentice-ship, in 1867, that the friendship began with Michael Foster, and the latter re-lates that, although Martin was only able to give half the usual time to his course on practical physiology, he learned more than the rest of the students in their whole time. He greatly distinguished himself at University College, taking several medals and prizes. In 1870 he obtained a scholarship at Christ's College, Cambridge, and was appointed demonstrator of physiology. He did much by his personal qualities and bright ways to make natural science popular in that University. He distin-guished himself in Cambridge as he

had in London, gaining first place in the Natural Science Tripos in 1873. While there he took the B. Sc. and M. B., London, gaining in the former the schol-arship in zoology. He proceeded later to the D. Sc. being the first to take that degree in physiology. About this time he began to do research work, his first paper being on the structure of the olfactory mem-brane. In the summer of 1874 he assisted Foster in his course on biology and subsequently acted as assistant to Huxley. Under Huxley's supervision, he prepared a text-book of this course, which appeared under their names with the title "Practical Biology." In 1874 he was made fellow of his college, and was fairly launched upon his career. Shortly after this, the Johns Hopkins University was founded, and in 1876 Martin was invited to be-come the first occupant of the chair of biology. He accepted the offer and thus nearly the whole of his scientific career was passed in America. He came prepared to develop the higher teaching of biologic science and es-pecially to foster the spirit of research, and during his stay in Baltimore (1876-1893) he produced a very marked effect on American science, fully carrying out the great aim of the university which had adopted him. He car-ried on many important investigations, among which may be especially mentioned those on the excised mammalian heart, one of which formed the subject of the "Croonian Lecture" of the Royal Society in 1883. The whole was published by his friends and pu-pils in 1895, under the title "Physiolog-ical Papers." He turned out from his laboratory many trained physiologists, who have maintained the high stand-ard he set. He wrote several text-books, of which his "Human Body," 1881, was most important, becoming very popular. He became a fellow of the Royal Society in 1885; he was also given the honorary M. D. by the Univer-sity of Georgia. He was one of the founders of the American Physiological Society. In 1892 he lost his wife, and his health, which had already begun to fail, gave way rapidly, so that in 1893 he found it impossible to continue his labors, and resigned his chair. He had never acquired American citizenship and he now returned to England, hoping to obtain improvement there and to be able to resume his investigations. But his health gradually failed, and on October 27, 1896, he was carried off by a sudden hemorrhage while living at Burley-in-Wharfedale, Yorkshire. A memorial tablet has been erected to Prof. Martin in Johns Hopkins University which commemorates "his brilliant work as investigator, teacher and author," by which "he advanced knowledge and exerted a wide and enduring influence." There is also an oil portrait of him there. He was somewhat under the ordinary stature and very youthful looking. In 1879 he married the widow of Gen. Pegram, a Confederate officer, celebrated under her maiden name of Heffie Cary as a great beauty and woman of great fascination. She was considerably older than himself. She died in 1892 without children.

E. F. C.

Nature (Lond.), Nov. 19, 1896, and Proc. Roy. Soc., vol. lx, No. 364, Dec., 1896 for sketches by Foster. See Physiological Papers, 1895, and review by Prof. Locke in Science, Jan. 16, 1897. Also Memoir by Prof. Wm. H. Howell, 1908, Johns Hopkins Circular. Cordell's Medical Annals of Maryland, 1903.

Martin, Solomon Claiborne (1837–1906). On the twenty-seventh of March, 1906 the city of St. Louis lost Prof. Solomon Claiborne Martin, dermatologist, of Barnes University. His death, unexpected, did not lack a certain tragic feature, since but an hour before he spoke of feeling it his duty to resume his lectures at the great institution of which he was one of the founders.

He was born in Claiborne county,

Mississippi, October 26, 1837, and went to the University of Michigan, from which institution he graduated in 1859, taking his M.D. from Tulane University in 1865.

During the Civil War he was attached to the staff of Gen. Wirtz Adams' Independent Calvary Corps with the rank of major. Later he served under Gen. Albert Sydney Johnston and was at the side of Gen. Johnston when wounded. After exchanging the sword for the surgeon's lance, Martin spent three years in Europe at the great clinics in Heidelberg, Vienna and Paris. He was a perfect linguist, speaking fluently German and French. The writer first met the deceased through the St. Louis "Medical Era" of which the latter was editor. He contributed a large number of valuable articles to literature. Most of his contributions pertained to dermatology and syphilology. Finding that the "Medical Era" which he edited did not justify the publication of too many editorials on his favorite subjects, the "American Journal of Dermatology and Genito-Urinary Diseases" was established, which afterwards became one of the most popular special magazines in the medical world.

He was married to Miss Anna Rosa Calhoun, of Port Gibson, Mississippi, and in 1870 removed to St. Louis, where he spent the rest of his life. They had five children, the eldest son, Dr. S. C. Martin, jr., succeeded his father as editor-in-chief of the two journals in which he was assisted by his younger brother Dr. Clarence Martin, an army-surgeon.

C. M.

Jour. of Physical Therapy, 1906, vol. i.

Mastin, Claudius Henry (1826–1898). This Alabama surgeon was born in Huntsville, Alabama on June 4, 1826, the son of Francis Turner, planter and Ann Elizabeth Caroline Livert. His paternal grandfather Francis Turner Mastin, came from Wales when

Lord Fairfax came and settled in Maryland. His mother was a daughter of one Claudius Livert, a physician of Lyons.

The boy went to Greenville Academy Huntsville and afterwards to the University of Virginia then studied medicine with Dr. John Y. Bassett, who in those anti-legal dissecting days had a room whereunto in the darkness often the dead body of a negro from some near by plantation burial ground was conveyed up the back stairs by the students. Mastin spent many night hours there over his anatomical studies and easily took his M.D. from the University of Pennsylvania in 1849. He returned to Huntsville, then on to Nashville, Tennessee but eventually attended lectures at Edinburgh University, the Royal College of Surgeons, London and in Paris, finally settling in Mobile, Alabama, to practise with his uncle Dr. Livert.

In 1861 he served as a Confederate states volunteer, afterwards with the regulars as medical director on the staff of Gen. Leonidas Polk until after the battle of Shiloh when he became inspector of the army of the Mississippi under Gen. Beauregard. The war over he returned to Mobile and shewed himself an expert surgeon, doing most of the major operations of his day. His uncle had made a series of experiments upon animals in 1828 using metallic ligatures for ligation of arteries leaving the gold, silver or lead wire to become encysted. Nephew Claudius put the knowledge thus obtained into actual practice upon the human subject, ligating the external iliac with a silver wire for aneurism of the femoral artery at Scarpa's triangle in June 1866. He was thus the first to tie successfully with a metallic ligature a large artery in the human body. Having considerable ingenuity he was the inventor of several instruments: he also wrote many articles chiefly dealing with genito-urinary surgery.

In September 1848, he married Mary E. McDowell of Huntsville, a descendant of Ephriam McDowell the ovariotomist and had two sons and two daughters. He died when seventy-two on the third of October, 1898, after an immediate illness of one week, in active service and full enjoyment of his faculties. He was a man of most striking appearance, tall, erect and with piercing eyes.

He held his LL.D., from the University of Pennsylvania; and was president of the American Surgical Association in 1890-1. His keen interest in the advance of medical science led to his founding the Congress of American Physicians and Surgeons and being a prominent organizer of the American Genito-Urinary Association. He was also a member of the Boston Gynecological Society; of the Southern Surgical and Gynecological Association and of the Central Council of the University of Pennsylvania.

His articles include:

"Inguinal Aneurism; successful ligation of external iliac artery by means of silver-wire," 1866.

"Internal Urethrotomy as a cure for urethral Stricture," 1871.

"Chronic Urethral Discharges," 1872.

"A New Method of Treating Strictures of the Urethra," 1873.

"Subcutaneous division of Urethral Stricture," 1886.

C. H. M.

Family Papers.
Mem. Record of Alabama, vol. ii.
Alabama Med. and Surg. Age. Anniston, 1895-6, vol. viii.
Med. Rec., N. Y., 1898, vol. liv.
Tr. Am. Surg. Ass., Phila., 1900, vol. xviii.
Tr. South. Surg. and Gynec. Ass., 1902, Phila., 1903 (port.).

Matthews, Washington (1843-1905).

Washington Matthews, having lost his mother in early infancy, his father, a physician, brought him while still a child to the United States and settled in Dubuque, Iowa. Young Matthews studied medicine under his father and later attended lectures at the University of Iowa, where he obtained his M.D. in 1864. In the same year, entering the Army of the United States, he served as acting assistant surgeon until the close of the Civil War. In 1868 he was promoted to the rank of captain, and in 1889 to that of major. During a great part of his military life Matthews was on duty at various army posts in the West. Coming in contact with many Indian tribes, he became deeply interested in Indian ethnology and philology, and wrote numerous articles on anthropological subjects, among which may be mentioned "The Human Bones of the Hemenway Collection," "Myths of Gestation and Parturition," "On Measuring the Cubic Capacity of the Skull," etc. A volume of "Navaho Legends" was published in 1896. Matthews died at Washington, April 29, 1905.

A. A.

Watson, Physicians and Surgeons of America, Concord, 1896.

May, Frederick (1775–1847).

Frederick May, was born November 16, 1773, in Boston, Massachusetts, and took his M.B. in 1795; his M.D. in 1811, from Harvard.

He came to Washington in 1795—five years before the transfer of the National government to the City, and he was a pioneer who prepared the way for others.

The third president of the Medical Society, he was re-elected for fifteen successive years, 1833–1848, and then declined a re-election against the unanimous protest of his colleagues. No other president served in that office for so long a period.

When he came to the City it was a mere wilderness, and he was the only practitioner of medicine. He soon succeeded in securing the confidence of the residents, and, as the city increased in population so did he add to his popularity and professional usefulness.

In the year 1823, upon the establishment of a medical school in this city

he was appointed to the chair of obstetrics. In this he distinguished himself as a lecturer, by the soundness of his doctrine, the beautiful and classic style of his lectures. He was an incorporator of the Medical Society of District of Columbia.

During the last year of his life he withdrew from active duty, and died January 23, 1847.

D. S. L.

Minutes of the Medical Society, D. C., January 23, 1847, published in the Boston Medical and Surgical Journal, 1847, xxxvi. Busey, "Reminiscences". Drake's Dict. Amer. Biog., 1872.

May, Frederick John (1812–1891).

The son of Dr. Frederick May, he was born on May 19, 1812, his ancestry was of the early New England colonists and patriots of the Revolution. He graduated B.A. Columbia College in 1831 and shortly after graduation in medicine from Columbia College in 1834 he went to Europe and spent over a year in the leading hospitals of London and Paris, in this way familiarizing himself with all the latest in medicine and surgery. After an extended tour through Europe, the West Indies and the United States, he practised in his native city and joined the Medical Association in 1838, his father then being president. In 1839 he was elected to the chair of anatomy and physiology in Columbia College, District of Columbia and in 1841 was transferred to that of principles and practice of surgery, which position he filled most acceptably until his resignation, in 1858. He was honored about the same time with the professorship of surgery in the University of Maryland, which he filled for two years. He became also a member of the section of physiology and medicine of the National Institute, Washington. In 1858 he was elected to the chair of surgery in the Shelby Medical College, Nashville, Tennessee. He was one of the first surgeons in America to amputate with success at the hip-joint, and the first in Washington to perform ovariotomy. His skill was widely recognized, so that for years most of this kind of practice in Washington fell to his care.

Shortly after the Civil War he removed to New York, continuing however, to spend much time in Washington attending to his real estate and other interests and the whole family returned to live in Washington about 1880. In 1884 he was elected surgeon on the consulting staff of Garfield Memorial Hospital, serving there faithfully and as president of the medical staff for five years, until the necessity for lessening his duties owing to advancing age induced him to resign. He died on May 2, 1891.

D. S. L.

Minutes of Medical Society, D. C., May 4, 1891. Busey's "Reminiscences."

May, James (1798–1873).

This physician was born on April 11, 1798, in Dinwiddie county, Virginia; graduated from the University of Pennsylvania in 1820, and began practice in Christiansville, in the county of Mecklenburg, Virginia. After a few years he removed to Petersburg, and practised in partnership with his brother, Dr. Benjamin May, who was the elder and blind, having become so very soon after he began practice. Nevertheless, " By force of intellect, shrewd, hard sense, courage and will, he forged his way to the front among men who were no pigmies, and he stood easily *unus inter pares*, acquired a good practice and was much sought in consultation.

He was a member of the Medical Society of Virginia. A very hard worker, he was rarely known to have taken a holiday. By frugality and prudence he massed a handsome fortune, but was a man that could not be allured by the seductions of wealth or by it be moved to display or self-indulgence, being always plain in dress, and almost primitive in his tastes

and habits. In those days it was sometimes a custom with the wealthier farmers in Virginia to say to their physicians, when the patient was convalescent, bringing forth at the same time a roll of bank notes or a bag of specie, "Doctor, pay yourself." In connection with this custom, an amusing anecdote is told by the late Dr. J. H. Claiborne of Dr. May. The doctor and he had been attending a valuable negro man, the property of a plain old farmer, and on the occasion of their final visit, the patient having been pronounced convalescent, the farmer brought forth a bag of specie and placing it on a table with the mouth wide open, remarked, "Doctors, pay yourselves." Dr. May had a very large hand, and as he went for the "pay," it looked much larger than usual. The old man noticed it, and his confidence failed him, and just as Doctor Claiborne was about to pay himself, he touched him on the shoulder and said, "Doctor, before you put your hand in that bag, remember there is a God in Heaven looking at you. It was afterwards remarked by the Doctor, "he scared me so that I did not get half my pay."

He died in Petersburg, November 15, 1873, in the seventy-sixth year of his age, after over half a century of practice.

So far as we can discover, he made no contributions to medical literature, save only his inaugural thesis, "Hemoptysis," if this may be termed a contribution.

R. M. S.

Va. Clin. Record, vol. iii.
Seventy-five years in old Virginia, J. H. Claiborne, M.A., M.D., 1904.

Meacham, Franklin Adams (1862–1902).

Chiefly known for his heroic efforts in fighting unsanitary conditions in the Philippines Franklin Adams Meacham was born near Cumberland Gap, Kentucky, October 28, 1862, the son of an army surgeon.

He graduated at Yale and took his

M.D., at the University of Virginia in 1889 and settled to practice in Salt Lake City. But his bent was towards bacteriology and in 1894 he earnestly studied this and surgical pathology at Johns Hopkins University, publishing a number of articles, and on return was made chief-surgeon of the Holy Cross Hospital, Utah.

In April, 1900 (?) he went to Manila and was assigned chief of the health department and afterwards chief medical inspector.

He instituted the campaign against bubonic plague, the extermination of rats, the fungus treatment for the extermination of locusts, the virus inoculation for plague prevention and many other projects.

In the report of the Honorable the Secretary of the Interior for 1902, in connection with the epidemic of bubonic plague in Manila, it was stated: "Especial credit is due to chief Health Inspector Meacham for the ingenuity which he displayed in devising means for the destruction of rats and for the tireless energy with which he devoted himself to securing the adoption of such means."

On March 20, 1902, Asiatic cholera appeared in Manila and Maj. Meacham's efforts from this time up to the date of his death were largely expended in its suppression. He was taken to the hospital, sick, some time in April, although he had been ailing for several weeks before. He was supposed at the hospital to be suffering from gastritis.

I did not see Maj. Meacham when he was sick. It is stated that he had been in bed at the hospital for several days, had got out of bed to walk across the floor and had dropped back dead. This was on April 14. I performed the autopsy and found advanced fatty degeneration of the heart muscle and coronary artery disease. His heart is now preserved in the Pathological Museum of our Laboratory.

He had borne the brunt of the fight against bubonic plague, and from the beginning of cholera had displayed tireless energy in his efforts to combat the new epidemic. Although suffering from a high fever, he had for several days continned to expose himself to the intense heat of the sun by day and had worked in his office until late at night, keeping his colleagues in ignorance as to his true condition. He gave up only when unable to rise from his bed, and died three days later of heart failure, the result of utter exhaustion from long continued overwork. Dr. Meacham was an able administrator, and was endowed with the faculty, as valuable as it was unusual, of discharging disagreeable duties in such a way as to win not only the.respect but the regard of those most injuriously affected. He sacrificed his life in the discharge of duty, and his death was an irreparable loss. I quote from the ministerial report.

Dr. Meacham was married, but his wife was not in the Philippines at the time of his death. She was on her way to the Islands at the time he died and arrived in Manila a few days after, only to learn she was too late.

He was buried in the National Cemetery, Arlington, Virginia, and the class of '87 (Yale) erected a tablet to his memory in the Memorial Vestibule of the University.

Personal Communications from Dr. Richard P. Strong. Department of the Interior, Manila.

Meachem, John Goldsborongh (1823–1896).

The son of the Rev. Thomas and Elizabeth Meachem of Axbridge, Somerset, England, he was born there May 27, 1823. In 1831 his parents came to the United States and the boy was educated at Richmond Academy New York. In 1840, he began to study under Dr. Harvey Jewett at Richmond New York and attended lectures at Geneva Medical College one year, and the following year at Castleton Medical College, from which he graduated in 1843, and began to practice the same year at Weathersfield Springs,

New York, subsequently at Linden, and at Warsaw, New York until 1862 when he came to Racine, Wisconsin, where the remainder of his life was spent.

His professional standing was recognized by the Bellevue Hospital Medical College, whose diploma he received in 1862. In 1861 he was appointed enrollment surgeon by Gov. Hunt of New York, and in 1862–63 had charge of the regimental hospital at Camp Utley, at Racine. He was one of the founders of and a physician to St. Luke's Hospital at Racine for more than twenty years. In 1881, he was president of the Wisconsin State Medical Society. A general practice of over fifty years embraced many dangerous and difficult cases in surgery. His numerous cases of amputations, trephining, and liberal practice in lithotomy, ovariotomy, and other lines of his profession attest both skill and knowledge.

His contributions to medical literature included: " Removal of Two Stones Weiging two ounces, from Bladder of Female," "Ligature of Carotid Artery for Occipital Aneurism," "Medical Education," "Stroma-syphilis," "Fifteen Cases of Puerperal Eclampsia, with one death, Bleeding the Remedy," "Insanity due to Uterine Disease," "Pneumonia and its Treatment." "Lung Diseases as they occur on the shore of Lake Michigan," "Passage of a Needle through the Heart, with Recovery," and an address before the Wisconsin State Medical Society on " Honor to Professional Men," may properly be mentioned as showing both professional skill and professional spirit. These papers were published in the "Transactions of the Wisconsin State Medical Society."

Meachem married in June 1844, Myraette, daughter of Reuben Doolittle. Two daughters, Myraette and Elizabeth, died in their girlhood. One son, John Goldsbrough Meachem, Jr., became a physician.

He died February 1, 1896, from heart disease after an illness of nearly one year; leaving a stainless character as a heritage for his kindred.   J. G. M. Jr.

" The United States Biographical Dictionary and Portrait Gallery of Eminent and Self-made Men," American Biographical Pub. Co., Chicago, 1877, with portrait.
"History of Racine and Kenosha Counties," Wisconsin, 1879.
"Transactions Wis. State Med. Soc," 1896.
Obituary by Solon Marks, M. D.

Meigler, Marie J. (1851–1901).

Marie Meigler, gynecologist, was born in Main Stockheim, Bavaria in 1851, and descended from the old German family, von Rittenhausen. Her father was Francis R. Meigler, a graduate of the University of Wurzburg, who in 1853 came with his family to Illinois.

Marie graduated from Cook County Illinois Normal School, and in 1871 from the classical course, State Normal School, Oswego, New York. She entered the Woman's Medical College, Chicago, in 1876 and obtained her degree in 1879, being valedictorian of the class. There were several of the faculty who although consenting to teach the women did everything to discourage them.

When Marie was a senior her class found a notice on the bulletin board inviting them to take the examinations for interne at Cook County Hospital. Although sure of defeat, the ill-taught girls resolved to face contempt at the competitive examination in order to preserve the "open door" to public office for their successors. They were received by the students in the amphitheatre with shouts and hisses. The chairman of the staff looked inquiringly at the secretary, the secretary responded, " You instructed me to notify the regular colleges, the Woman's College is a regular College." No appointment was received but the members of the faculty ashamed of their work, reformed their ways, and when again Marie competed for the position of interne in the Cook County Hospital, she was told that she did so successfully but was not appointed because a woman—however, a year later a woman did receive the appointment. After gradnating, Marie Meigler became surgical assistant to Dr. William H. Byford. The year 1880 was spent pursuing her medical studies in Zürich. Upon her return she held various positions in her Alma Mater and after Dr. Byford's death in 1890 was appointed his successor to the chair of gynecology.

In 1882 Dr. Meigler was appointed to the staff of the Cook County General Hospital, in 1886 one of the attending surgeons at the Woman's Hospital in Chicago and in 1890 gynecologist to Wesley Hospital. She held the last two positions till the time of her death. In 1895 she was appointed head physician and surgeon of the Mary Thompson Hospital, in this appointment Dr. Meigler received the unanimous support of the Chicago Gynecological Society and a large majority of the members of the medical profession of Chicago. In 1897 she was elected dean of the Northwestern Woman's Medical School, having previously served as its secretary for many years.

For several years she was professor of gynecology in the post-graduate Medical School of Chicago.

Dr. Meigler was a member of the state medical society and Chicago Medical Society. She gained great distinction as a diagnostician and surgeon. At the time of her death the "Gazette Médicale de Paris" referred to her as celebrated for her success in abdominal surgery and said that Europe had no such woman operators of this stamp.

She died of pernicious anemia in California on her fiftieth birthday, May 18, 1910.

Dr. Meigler had editorial connections with the "Woman's Medical Journal of Chicago." She wrote:

"A Guide to the Study of Gynecology," 1892; History of the Woman's Medical College of Chicago," 1893; and in collaboration with Charles W. Earle, "Diseases of the New-born." ("American Textbook of Obstetrics.")　　　A. B. W.

Journal Amer. Med. Assoc. vol. xxxvi.
Les femmes médicins professeurs de Chirugie à l'étranger. Mlle. le Dr. M. J. Meigler (Chicago).
Gazette Medicale de Paris, 1901, 12 Serie.
Woman's Journal, Boston, vol. xxxii.

Meigs, Charles Delucena (1792–1869).

Charles Delucena Meigs was the fifth of the ten children of Josiah Meigs sixth in descent from Vincent Meigs who came from Dorset, England and settled in Connecticut about 1647. Charles was born in the island of St. George, but when two years old, his grandfather was made professor of mathematics and astronomy at Yale and the family migrated to the ruder climate, but in 1801 his grandfather had to superintend the erection of the University of Georgia and the whole family finally settled in Athens, where Charles went to the grammar school and earned French from Petit de Clairvière a cultivated emigré. He graduated at the University of Georgia in 1809 and began that same year to study medicine under Dr. Thomas Fendall, serving as apothecary boy and being sent out to cup and leech by his master. In a letter he says, "I got one course of lectures at the University of Pennsylvania then went home to set up for myself. Everybody called me doctor; I thought so myself.

After his marriage to the daughter of William Montgomery, a large cotton merchant in Philadelphia, he settled first to practice in Augusta, but afterwards went to Philadelphia, quickly obtaining, not practice, but the intimacy and esteem of men like La Roche, Hodge, Bond, Bache and Bell. He was one of the first editors of "The North American Medical and Surgical Journal" and found time to translate and publish Velpeau's "Elementry Treatise on Midwifery" and seven years after he issued his "Philadelphia Practice of Midwifery" a work showing the bent of his mind to be towards obstetrics. Meigs drew special attention to cardiac thrombosis as a cause of those sudden deaths which occur in childbed and which had generally been attributed to syncope. In this connection T. Gaillard Thomas says: "It has been remarked that Meigs just escaped the honor which is now and will be hereafter given to Virchow for a great pathological discovery," and Meigs himself said, "I have a just right to claim the merit of being the first writer to call the attention of the medical profession to these sudden concretions of those concresible elements of the blood in the heart and great vessels." It may be said he did not follow his discovery into detail as regarded secondary deposits of emboli. He does not assert his claim as far as that.

As professor of obstetrics at Jefferson Medical College he worked hard studying every thing connected with his branch, studying German until he was able to read with ease the most important German obstetricians, but in his work on "Woman, her Diseases and their Remedies" (1847) there is an amount of personal experience seldom equalled, brought to bear on every point.

His books, all written in the midst of most fatiguing obstetrical and general medical practice and lecturing were a remarkable example of what the human machine can accomplish. Consistent with his idea that men ought to retire before losing the power of judging their own fitness for duty he sent in his resignation when he was sixty-seven, a resignation unwillingly accepted by the dean, faculty and students, for, to the latter he had in teaching obstetrics so dealt with the science as ever to raise higher and higher the obedience of the classes to the highest law of manly respect for woman and to inspire the purest sentiments of man towards mother, sister or wife. He would portray the responsibilities of the acceoncheur to the public; paint vividly the tragic scenes through which he had to wend his way and throw around them an atmosphere of romance and tenderness.

The doctor's robe cast off he donned that of the bibliophile and eagerly, joyfully, spent his newly acquired leisure at his country house Hamanassett among his old books, adding thereunto other scientific pursuits and never losing touch with the big world outside. Gradually failing health with gastrodynia made him a not unwilling traveller, when, one night, the twenty-second of June 1869, he set out, without waking any more, on his last journey.

His best known publications are:
"Woman, her Diseases and Remedies," 1847.
"Obstetrics, the Science and Art," 1849.
"Treatise on Acute and Chronic Diseases of the Neck of the Uterus," 1850.
"On the Nature and Treatment of Childbed Fevers," 1854.
"A Translation of a Treatise on the Diseases and Special Hygiene of Females," by Colombat de L'Isère

His appointments numbered among others: fellowship of the College of Physieiaus Philadelphia and presidency from 1848–1855. Professor of obstetrics and diseases of women and children in Jefferson Medical School, 1841.

D. W.

Boston Med. and Surg. Jour., 1849, vol. xl.
Proc. Am. Phil. Soc., Phila., 1873, vol. xiii.
Tr. Coll. Phys. Phila., 1872, n. s., vol. iv. (J. F. Meigs.)
Memoir of Dr. Charles D. Meigs.   J. Forsyth Meigs, Phila., 1876.

Meigs, James Aitken (1829–1879).

For his work during nearly a quarter of a century as one of the leading men of the Academy of Natural Sciences, Philadelphia, James A. Meigs is chiefly remembered. He was born in Philadelphia, July 31, 1829, of English and Scotch ancestry and after schoolboy life at Mt. Vernon Grammar School and the Central High School he began to study medicine under Drs. F. G. Smith and J. M. Allen. He matriculated from Jefferson Medical College in 1851 and settling in Philadelphia, practised there until his death. In 1868 he entered the faculty of the Jefferson Medical College with a dissertation on the "Correlation of Physical and Vital Forces" a subject he discussed with masterly ability. He had for a long time made a specialty of the study of physiology and natural sciences and was well fitted for his department. "A ripe scholar, with a command of language the offspring of a tenacious memory and a well disciplined mind he stood before his class the peer of any member of the faculty, wisely confining himself in his teaching as Dunglison had done, to physiology. Like one imbued with his work he carried his class with him and frequently vivisected an animal to impress the lesson. If he had one fault it was a love of detail which made him take two sessions for the ordinary course, but can this be called a fault? "I often urged him" says S. D. Gross "to write an elaborate treatise on philosophy, as no man in America could better grapple with its great problems. He always said he would but died without doing it."

Of the man in his personal life only all that is sweet and tender can be said. Much of his leisure was spent among his beloved books and with his old parents. Mutual love could not have been stronger and he seldom spent an evening from home except for a play, of which he was very fond. One idea he had was to save money enough to gain leisure for teaching and authorship, but his unexpected death came on November 9, 1879 from embolism of the heart or lungs after two or three days invalidism. His fortune of some $200,000 gained chiefly among middle class patients went to his father, who was very proud of his son and frequently went to the class room to hear him lecture. His friends had often urged him to take more time for recreation and literary pursuit but without avail. He seldom absented himself from the city even in the heat of summer; in fact he led what might be called a suicidal life.

His papers on Anthropology are among the best he wrote; they include: "Relation of Atomic Heat to Crystalline Form;" Cranial Characteristics of the Races of Men;" "Hints to Craniographers . . . . . on the Exchange of Duplicate Crania;" "Observations on the Form of the Occiput in the Various Races of Men;" "On the Mensuration of the Human Skull;" "Observations on the Cranial Forms of the American Aborigenes" also his "Correlation of the Vital and Physical Forces."

He held many appointments besides those mentioned, notably; physician to the Howard Hospital; professor of the

institutes of medicine in the Philadelphia College of Medicine; consulting physician to the Philadelphia Hospital at Blockley; member of the biological section of the Academy of Natural Sciences; of the Medico-Legal Society of New York; Societé d'Anthropologie, Paris; and the Anthropological and Ethnological Societies of London.

D. W.

Boston Med. and Surg. Jour., 1879, vol. ci.
Med. Bull. Phila., 1880, vol. ii and iii.
Med. Rec, N. Y., 1879, vol. xvi.
Phila. M. Times, 1879–80, vol. x.
Tr. Coll. Phys., Phila, 1881, 3 s., vol. v.   (H. C. Chapman.)

Mendenhall, George (1814–1874).

George Mendenhall was the son of Aaron and Lydia (Richardson) Mendenhall and was born at Sharon, Pennsylvania May 5, 1814.

In 1844 he went to Cincinnati, Ohio, where he practised until his death.

While he enjoyed a large general practice, his reputation was made in obstetrics, in which he was an authority.

Mendenhall was of quaker ancestry. The family came to America in 1682, and formed a part of William Penn's colony at Philadelphia, one of his aunts, Mary Mendenhall, married Benjamin West, the artist. Dr. Mendenhall had his primary education in a country school; Latin he studied at odd times behind the counter of a country store.

In 1834 he graduated from the University of Pennsylvania and to help in obtaining this coveted education he sold the horse he had ridden over the mountains from his country home.

He was a member of several state and national societies. The only vacations he took were at the times of attendance on the sessions of the American Medical Association. In 1870 he was its president, when it met in Washington. In 1873 his health began to fail, and he went to Europe to recuperate. During his stay in Wiesbaden the honor of membership in the Royal Obstetrical Society of London was given him. During the war between the states he was prominent in the Sanitary Commission, both in the field and at home.

When the Miami Medical College was founded, 1852, Dr Mendenhall was elected professor of obstetrics and diseases of women and children, which position he held until 1857, when the school was united with the Medical College of Ohio, where he became professor of obstetrics and diseases of women and children and professor of obstetrics in 1859. When the Miami Medical College was re-established, in 1865, he was again professor of obstetrics and diseases of women and children there until 1873. He was dean of the Miami Medical College from 1853 to 1857; and again from 1865 to 1873.

Dr. Mendenhall was on the staff of the Cincinnati Hospital from 1858 to 1872. October 7, 1838, he married Elizabeth S. Maule, of Philadelphia and had seven children. Upon his return from Europe in 1873, he was stricken with paralysis, from the effects of which he never recovered, and died in Cincinnati, June 4, 1874. Mendenhall was not well known as an author, but his "Students Vade Mecum," passed through eighteen editions and was for a long time much consulted by students.

A paper on "Vaccination" by Dr. Mendenhall will be found in the Transaction of the Ohio State Medical Convention of 1848; another on "Nitric Acid as an Antiperiodic" in the same Transactions for 1854, and a report on "The Epidemies of Ohio, Indiana and Michigan made to the American Medical Association in 1852.

A. G. D.

From Appleton's Biographical Encyclopedia, and in C. T. Greve's Centennial History of Cincinnati. The Cincinnati Lancet and Observer, vol. xvii (1874), and the Trans. of the Ohio State Medical Society for 1874.

Mercer, Hugh (1725–1777).

An eminent physician, captain in Braddock's war and general in the Revolution, he was born in Aberdeen in Scotland, son of a minister of the Church of Scotland. He studied at the University of Aberdeen and entered the Medical School of Marschall College in 1740, graduating in 1744.

He espoused the cause of Prince Charles Edward the Pretender and was with his army at Culloden, but escaping the fate of so many of his comrades, he sailed from Leith in the fall of 1746 for America. Landing at Philadelphia, he soon set out for the western border of Pennsylvania and settled near Mercersburg, then known as Greencastle. Dr. J. M. Toner says that he founded Mercersburg. Here, until the beginning of the French and Indian war he practised, living the life of a country doctor in a wild, sparsely settled region. Possessing the natural instincts of a soldier, he joined Braddock's army as captain of a company and took part in the ill-fated expedition against Fort Du Quesne. In the assault he was wounded and left behind, but after a perilous journey through the wilderness, he succeeded in joining his comrades. In 1756 he was commissioned captain of one of the companies raised to protect the residents against the Indians and their French allies, his company being stationed at McDowell's Fort, now Bridgeport. Here he also acted as surgeon to the garrison and practised among the people. In one of the numerous fights with the Indians he was again wounded and abandoned, and again made his way over one hundred miles through the forest and joined his command at Fort Cumberland. On this weary tramp he was forced to live on roots and herbs, and the carcass of a rattle-snake, and so closely was he pursued by his foes that he once had to take refuge in the hollow trunk of a tree, around which the Indians rested.

Mercer was again wounded while commanding one of the companies which captured an Indian settlement at Kittanning in 1756. For his services in these Indian wars he received from the Corporation of Philadelphia a note of thanks and a memorial medal.

The summer of 1757 saw him in command of the garrison at Shippensburg, December, promoted to the rank of major and placed in command of the forces of the province of Pennsylvania west of the Susquehanna. The next year he commanded part of the forces under Gen. Forbes in the expedition against Fort Du Quesne, and during this war Mercer made the acquaintance of Washington and a friendship sprung up between them which lead to Virginia becoming the home of the former on the advice of the latter.

Dr. Mercer some time after the end of the French and Indian wars removed to Virginia and settled in Fredericksburg. Here he lived and practised until the beginning of the Revolution. The reputation he gained as a physician and citizen is attested by an English traveller who visited Fredericksburg during the Revolution, an account of which visit was published in 1784. He wrote "In Fredericksburg I called upon a worthy and intimate friend, Dr. Hugh Mercer, a physician of great eminence and merit, and, as a man, possessed of almost every virtue and accomplishment."

The building where the doctor had his consulting room and apothecary's shop is still standing (1908) and is situated on a corner of Princess Ann and Amelia streets.

The beginning of the Revolution found him actively engaged in raising and drilling troops, for, abandoning his large and lucrative practice he entered the service of the colonies as colonel of the third Virginia continentals. In appreciation of his distinguished services he was soon promoted to be a brigadier-general, the date of his appointment being June 5, 1776. Gen. Mercer participated with great distinction in the campaigns of Washington, until refusing to surrender, he was clubbed and bayonetted, and left for dead on the field of Princeton. Despite, however, his seven bayonet wounds of the body and many of the head from the butts of muskets, be was not yet dead, and after the battle was removed to a farm-house, where he was tenderly cared for by Mrs. Clark and her daughter, the wife and child of the owner of the house, and by Maj. Lewis, whom Gen. Washington sent for the purpose. The surgeons who attended him were Dr. Benjamin Rush

and Dr. Archibald Alexander, of Virginia. In spite of every care and attention that could be given him, he succumbed to his wounds, passing away on January 12, 1777. He was buried in Christ Church yard, Philadelphia. Many years later his remains were removed to Laurel Hill Cemetery and a monument erected to his memory by the St. Andrew's Society, of which he had become a member in 1757. This monument was dedicated on November 26, 1840, and bears as part of its inscription these words: "Gen. Mercer, a physician of Fredericksburg, in Virginia, was distinguished for his skill and learning, his gentleness and decision, his refinement and humanity, his elevated honour and his devotion to the cause of civil and religious liberty."

Soon after his death it was recommended that a monument be erected at Fredericksburg and on June 28,1902, an act was passed by Congress directing that the resolution of 1777 be carried into effect.

Mercer married not long after coming to Fredericksburg Isabella Gordon of that town and had a daughter and four sons. A portrait of Mercer is in possession of the Mercersurg (Pa.) Academy, and in the historical paintings of the battle of Princeton by Peale, at Princeton, and by Trumbull at New York, he is given a prominent position.

R. M. S.

Various Encyclopedias of American Biography, Southern Messenger, April, 1838. The Life of Hugh Mercer, John T. Goolrick.

Mercier, Alfred (1816–1894).

Alfred Mercier better known as a writer than a doctor, was born at McDonough, Louisana, June 3, 1816. In his fourteenth year he was sent to France to be educated. In 1842 he published at Paris a volume of poems, the principal of which were "La Rose de Smyrne" and "L'Ermite de Niagara" which were highly praised in the Révue de Paris. He travelled extensively through Europe and made a philosophic study of men and things. In 1848 he wrote a romance for "La Réforme," a prominent literary journal of the day, but on the morning that the first feuilleton was to appear, the commune broke into the office and "pied" the forms.

Originally intended for the bar, his tastes led him into literature; but republican France making small account of letters, he suddenly resolved to study medicine. After he graduated in that science he practised for three years in New Orleads. In 1859 he returned to France, remaining there until the close of the Civil War, when he finally returned to New Orleans resuming practice until the end of his life.

His works of fiction include "Le Fou de Palerme" (1873), "La Fille du Prêtre" (1877), "L'Habitation de St. Ybars" (1881), and "Johnelle" (1891. His style was virile and picturesque, tinged with delicate fancy and indicated true genius and profound scholarship. An ardent lover and complete master of Latin prosody, he solaced his last moments with recitations from his favorite Virgil.

Dr. Mercier died in New Orleans on May 12, 1894.

J. G. R.

Mettauer, John Peter (1787–1875).

A surgeon, he was the son of Francis Joseph Mettauer, one of two brothers, who came to this country with Lafayette, as regimental surgeons, their regiment being quartered after the battle of Yorktown in Prince Edward Country, and when it returned to France the elder Mettauer was persuaded by prominent citizens to remain. He later married Elizabeth Gaulding, a resident of the county, and John Peter was born in 1787. He was educated at Hampden-Sidney College and graduated A. B. in 1806, later in life receiving his A. M. and LL. D. After study at the University of Pennsylvania he received his M. D. in 1809, the subject of his thesis being "Disease." As a student, he was remarkable for his diligence and for being a great reader, ever availing himself of every opportunity of practice and of gaining experience. He, therefore, was a favorite with his

teachers, among whom were such men as Rush, Shippen, Wistar and Physick.

After graduation he returned home and built up a practice, the largest and most arduous, probably, ever had by a Virginia physician before. "Though doomed to labor in the country as a practitioner," he said, "I resolved to continue my studious habits and, if possible, not to fall behind the daily improvements of my profession."

He was a member of the old (antebellum) Medical Society of Virginia, and also of the present society. From 1848 to its discontinuance (about 1860), he was professor of medicine and surgery, clinical medicine and therapeutics, materia medica, midwifery and medical jurisprudence in the medical department of Randolph-Macon College. He also served for a short time as professor of surgery in the Washington University of Baltimore, Maryland.

Of the many able men that Old Dominion has given to the medical profession, Dr. Mettauer was, unquestionably, the most remarkable. By nature a great surgeon, he was also an able physician, and a voluminous contributor to medical literature. His marvelous surgical skill and ingenuity soon obtained for him such a reputation that, despite the fact of his work lying in an obscure country village and before the day of numerous railroads, patients flocked to him from all around some even from abroad. He did in numbers almost, if not every, operation known in his day and it is certain he did 800 operations for cataract; some have put the number far above this. In operations for vesical calculus, his total exceeded Dudley's 225 by 175, making in all 400. His many contributions to surgery which were freely given to the profession in his published articles, should have obtained for him the position he deserves among the world's greatest surgeons, but this has never been accorded him. In medical history he has received scant mention, and yet, to him, unquestionably, belongs the priority of the cure of vesico-vaginal fistula. His first successful operation was

J. Peter Mettauer.

(By permission of Dr. G. B. Johnston.)

done in August, 1838, and preceded Dr. Hayward's by nearly a year, and Sim's by ten. In this operation he used a concoidal speculum, curved scissors and lead-wire sutures. He was a strong advocate of lead-wire as a suture material in all plastic work. He was the first surgeon in Virginia, and one of the first in the United States, to operate successfully for cleft palate, his first operation having been done in 1827.

The most notable of his articles was one entitled "The Continued Fever of Middle Virginia from 1816 to 1829," which shows conclusively that he recognized typhoid fever as a distinct disease, and was familiar with its characteristic lesions. In other papers he advocates new methods of treatment and new uses of remedies, often showing that he was far ahead of his time in his views and practice. Almost every medical journal of Virginia published his papers.

During the whole of his professional life he was a constant contributor to medical journals, though the period of his greatest literary activity was from 1825 to 1845. He contributed articles to almost every medical journal published in this country in his time. Beside his articles he left in addition a large number of manuscripts which are now in the possession of Dr. George Ben Johnston, of Richmond, Virginia.

There was one work on surgery of 3,000 closely written legal-cap pages. Why he never published it was not known. "This work shows," says Dr. Johnston of Richmond, Virginia, "an intimate and enormous knowledge of all the directions that surgery in his time took, and not a little of the choicest fruit of elegant acquaintance with the older literature is scattered here and there throughout the work."

Many young men who desired to study medicine became his private pupils, and the need of assistants and nurses in his enormous work lead to the organization of these students into a medical school in 1837. From that date until 1848, the school was known as Mettauer's Medical Institute, and from 1848 to its discontinuance about 1860, it was a chartered institution, termed the Medical Department of Randolph-Macon College. The sessions of this school were ten months in length, and on its rolls were usually from thirty to thirty-five students. Some of these students graduated, but it is improbable that any went immediately into practice, though the school was recognized by some of the best larger city colleges. In 1848 the faculty consisted of three doctors, John Peter Mettauer and his brother and son, both named Francis Joseph.

There is ample authority for the statement that for forty years Dr. Mettauer had always from forty-five to sixty surgical cases under his care. Not only was his private hospital constantly filled, but also the hotels at Kingsville and Worsham, neighboring villages, and many private residences were often filled with patients awaiting their turn for operation, or just recovering from one.

Dr. Mettauer was an ingenious mechanic, and under his direction many of his instruments were made by his students in the shop of old Peter Porter in Farmville. Some of these instruments are the property of Dr. George Benjamin Johnston. Some are made of iron and others of silver. Some were made by the doctor himself, and others by an old negro in the county who was a skillful artisan in gold and silver.

In appearance he was a man of striking personality, tall well-formed and robust, his forehead was high and intellectual; his eyes piercing black and overshadowed by heavy brows. In his habits he was exclusive, admitting few to intimacy. In versatility, originality and skill he was unsurpassed, and practical common sense ever guided him in his work. In power of endurance and capacity for work he must have been as untirable as it was possible to be. In the latter part of his career, he undertook journeys, requiring several weeks, to operate.

On one occasion he went in his carriage as far as Georgia, and it is said that he received $1000; in that day a stupendous fee. Much of his time was given to work from which he derived neither fame nor fortune and he seems to have placed no value upon money.

He invariably wore a tall stovepipe hat which nothing would induce him to remove, and he wore it everywhere and on all occasions, even at meals and it is said, also when in bed. He never attended service in any church, which was attributed to his unwillingness to remove his head gear, but was more probably due to the fact that he would not take the time from his work. When called upon to testify in court, he always declined to remove it. He even left directions that he should be buried with it on, and that there should be placed in his coffin a number of instruments and the letters of his first wife.

Another of his marked peculiarities was his intense affection for his native locality, which he was twice induced to leave and settle in a city, but he only remained away for a few months on each occasion.

He would never assist in an operation, as he had an insuperable objection to watching another's work. He was also remarkable for the care and detail of his preparation for an operation, being far ahead of his time in this. In the last week of his life he did three successful ones, for cataract, for stone, and an excision of the breast, though then in his eighty-eighth year. "Facile princeps of the medical and surgical profession of the world" was the opinion of him expressed by Dr. Mutter, a Philadelphia surgeon of note, in 1845. He is accredited, said the "American Journal of Medical Sciences" after his death, with more improvements in operations and inventions of instruments to date than any other man.

Dr. Mettauer married four times; to a Miss Woodward of Norfolk; to Miss Carter of Prince Edward County; to Miss Mansfield, of a northern state, and to Miss Dyson, of Norfolk. He had six children, three sons and three daughters. His sons were all physicians, the last of whom was Dr. Archer Mettauer, of Macon, Georgia.

His long and laborious career came to an end in November, 1875. Having been called to a case of morphine poisoning a short distance from his house, he got his feet wet in a tramp through the snow and forgetting himself in his interest in the patient, neglected proper precautions and contracted a cold which developed into pneumonia, and in two days he was dead. A truly heroic death crowned the long and useful life.

Selected with a view of showing the variety of subjects upon which he wrote, the following are a few of Dr. Mettauer's more important contributions to medical literature:

"The Continued Fever of Middle Virginia from 1816 to 1829," inclusive. ("American Journal of Medical Sciences," vol. vi.)

"Experiences with Crusta Genu Equinae in Epilepsy." (Ibid., vol. xvi.)

"On Staphylorrhapy." (Ibid., vol. xxi.)

"Vesico-Vaginal Fistula." ("Boston Medical and Surgical Journal," vol. xxii, "American Journal of Medical Sciences," n.s., vol. xiv; "Virginia Medical and Surgical Journal", vol. iv, "American Journal of Medical Sciences", n.s., vol. xxvii.)

"Extirpation of the Parotid Gland." (Ibid., vol. xviii.)

"Practical Observations on Hypospadias and Epispadias." (Ibid., n.s., vol. iv.)

"Lithotomy." (Ibid., n.s., vol. xii.)

"Perineal Repair." (Ibid., n.s., vol. xiii.)

"Ligation of the Common Carotid Artery." (Ibid., n.s., vol. xviii.) "Prophylactic Treatment of Puerperal Fever," Charleston, South Carolina. ("Medical and Surgical Journal," 1851.) "Scarlet Fever." ("Virginia Stethoscope and Medical Gazette," vol. i, no. 2.) "Contributions to Practical medicine. (Ibid., August and September, 1854.) "Prophylaxis of Traumatic Inflammation." ("Virginia Medical and Surgical Journal," vol. i.) "Operative Surgery." (Ibid., vol. iii.) Volume II, (no. 1) of the "Virginia Medical Monthly" contains an article on the "Prophylaxis of Childbed Fever," which was probably his last published contribution, as it appeared in April, 1875.

The only known likeness of Dr. Mettauer is a small photograph, in the possession of Dr. George Benjamin Johnston, of Richmond, Virginia.

R. M. S.

Tr. Am. Surg. Assoc., 1905. (G. B. Johnston) (port.)

Metz, Abraham (1828–1876).

Abraham Metz, was born in Stark County, Ohio, but early in life lost both parents and was compelled to rely almost entirely upon his own exertions for a living. Nevertheless he was able by dint of perseverance to acquire sufficient elementary education to enable him to teach a district school at the age of twelve and he thus saved money enough to start him in the study of medicine. At the age of sixteen he studied medicine with Dr. Kahler in Columbia County, and soon after attended a course of medical lectures in the Willoughby Medical College. The outbreak of the Mexican War interrupted his studies and he was detailed in the position of acting surgeon. On the close of the war he returned to Ohio. Finally, he was able to attend a course of lectures in the Cleveland Medical College and to graduate there in 1848. Dr.

Metz settled finally, 1848, in Massillon, Ohio, where he made his permanent home. Fortune placed in his care an unusual number of cases of diseases of the eye, and his success with these was such that similar cases flocked to him for treatment and finally enabled him to confine his practice entirely to ophthalmology.

In 1864 he was called to the chair of ophthalmology in the newly organized Charity Hospital Medical College in Cleveland, and he continued to hold this position until his death February 1, 1876.

Dr. Metz was a member of the Ohio State Medical Society and presented to that body reports on the progress of ophthalmology in 1860, 1864 and 1865. He also published a treatise on "The anatomy and histology of the human eye." Philadelphia, 1868.

H. E. H.

Michener, Ezra (1794–1887).

Ezra Michener, botanist, was born in London Grove Township, Chester County, Pennsylvania, November 24, 1794.

His parents were Mordecai and Alice (Dunn) Michener. His early education consisted of nothing beyond the rudiments of reading, writing and arithmetic with a smattering of book-keeping, but he had an innate fondness for plants, though at that time there had been no botanical book for beginners either written or printed in America. After working on the farm until he was twenty-one, he went to Philadelphia to study medicine, graduating from the University of Pennsylvania in 1817. In 1816 he attended the lectures of Dr. Wm. P. C. Barton on botany, but there was still no book for beginners. Shortly after graduation he began to practise near his birthplace, living in a log house, and several years later bought a small farm in New Garden Township, where he lived until his ninety-third year. The grounds about his house were planted with many rare trees, of which he was a great lover, and his coffin was made, by his wish, of boards from the trunk of a tree (Paulownia Imperialis) which he had planted.

He wrote "Conchologia Cestrica" in collaboration with Dr. William D. Hortman and the preface seems to indicate that it was prepared at the suggestion of the Cabinet of Natural Science of Chester County. He also collected an extensive herbarium of Hysterophyta (Fungi), and his collection of the mammalia, birds and reptiles of Chester County form a part of the collection at Swarthmore College.

Barton's "Flora Philadelphiæ" was the first real botanical book Michener had for study, until Darlington published his "Florula Cestrica" in 1826, in which work Michener assisted. Darlington acknowledged his indebtedness to Michener in the collection and preparation of the Shallophyta for his "Flora Cestrica," referring to him as a naturalist of acumen, diligence and indomitable perseverance. He was greatly interested in cryptogams and did much good work in their collection and study. Fifteen books and twenty-three medical reprints stand to his credit, besides numerous articles. One of his books was "A Retrospect of Quakerism." He was an ardent member of New Garden Meeting (Hicksite Friends), and sat at the head of the meeting for many years. On the title page of "Conchologia Cestrica" is the quotation (written) "An undevout philosopher is mad," which was exactly Michener's idea. I knew him as a devout man, rich in knowledge and finding nothing trivial in nature but God in all.

His reputation as an accoucheur was great in his locality. He assisted at my birth and in some families had attended five generations. I called on him the day before his death, July 23, and found this old man of ninety-three ready to show interest in my recent graduation in medicine and desired I should examine him to see how completely all cartilage had ossified, calling my attention particularly to his floating ribs. He asked me to come again and then said, "No,

thee need not, for I shall not be here." He also spoke a little about death and his wish to be through with life.

In 1819 he married Sarah Spencer and had seven children. After her death, he married, in 1844, Mary S. Walton.

Among his correspondents were many of the most eminent scientists of his time, including Darlington, Rothrock, Curtis, Lining, Ravenel and Tuckerman. Agassiz said of him "that he did not belong exclusively to Chester County, Pennsylvania, or America, but to the whole scientific world."

B. M. H.

The Botanists of Pennsylvania, Harshberger. Personal Communications.

Middleton, Peter (———1781).

Peter Middleton, born in Scotland, graduated at the University of Edinburgh, and came to New York, where he was one of the most eminent medical men in the middle of the eighteenth century. In 1750, he assisted Dr. John Bard in making one of the first dissections for the purpose of anatomical instruction recorded in this country. In 1767, he aided in establishing the medical department of Kings College (Columbia University) in New York, in which he was the first professor of pathology and physiology, from 1767 to 1776, and of chemistry and materia medica from 1770 to 1776. He was a governor of Kings College from 1770 to 1780. He published a letter on "Croup" in the "Medical Repository" (vol. ix), and "Historical Inquiries into the Ancient and Present Systems of Medicine," (1769).

C. R. B.

Miles, Albert Baldwin (1852–1894).

A surgeon, he was born in Prattville, Alabama on May 18, 1852. His father, a farmer, removed to Arkansas in 1857 and an uncle living in El Dorado educated the boy and sent him to the University of Virginia.

In 1872 he entered the medical department of the University of Louisiana, in pursuance of a fixed intention to study medicine. He graduated from the University in 1875, being the Valedictorian of his class. In April 1877 he became assistant house surgeon of the Charity Hospital, holding this positiou until 1881, when he accepted the post of house surgeon to the Hôtel Dieu. On April 4, 1882 he was elected house surgeon of the Charity Hospital and held this office until his death in 1894.

From 1875 to 1885 he was demonstrator of anatomy and it is recorded that he never missed a single appointment with his classes. In 1886 he became professor of materia medica and therapeutics, and filled this position until the end of the session of 1892-3 when he was elected professor of surgery, succeeding Dr. Logan.

His simple direct style, made him one of the best lecturers ever connected with the medical department, and his gentle yet strong personality won universal attachment and regard.

As a surgeon Miles possessed the clear mind and steady hand that overcame all emergencies. He had great success with gunshot wounds of the abdomen and wrote several papers on the subject. An easy writer, he, however, contributed comparatively little to medical literature. Among his papers may be mentioned: "Tracheotomy in a case of bronchocele," "Epithelioma and its treatment;" "Report of a case of remarkable control over muscular movements," which were published in the "New Orleans Medical and Surgical Journal."

"A case of gunshot wound of abdomen with sixteen perforations of the ileum and three of the mesentery." ("Philadelphia Medical News.")

In 1894 he read a paper on, "Thirteen cases of gunshot wounds of the abdomen," before the American Surgical Association, this appeared subsequently in the "Annals of Surgery." For several years he was co-editor of the "New Orleans Medical and Surgical Journal;" was a member of the American Surgical Association; vice-president of the Southern Surgical and Gynecological Association and president of the Louisana State Medical Society. His last paper was a "Life of Dr. Warren Stone."

His executive ability was notable and during his régime at the Charity Hospital many improvements were instituted. The ambulance system was largely his plan, his suggestions assisted in the planning of the outdoor clinical buildings, and the new amphitheatre, which he never beheld completed.

To his wisdom is greatly due the founding of the Charity Hospital and the Training School for Nurses, of whose faculty he was first dean.

J. G. R.

N. Orl. M. and S. Jour., n. s., vol. xxii., 1894—1895.
Tr. South. Surg. and Gynec. Ass., 1902, Phila., 1903, vol xv., port.

Miles, Manly (1826–1896).

Manly Miles, physiologist, was born at Homer, Cortland County, New York, July 20, 1826; the son of Manly Miles, a soldier of the Revolution, and Mary Cushman, a lineal descendant of Miles Standish. In 1837 his family moved to Flint, Michigan, where he worked on the farm, to his common school education adding reading and study during spare moments. He was widely known as the "boy with a book," and the boy who never failed to accomplish anything he undertook. In 1850 he graduated M.D. from Rush Medical College, Chicago, and practised in Flint till 1859, when he was appointed by Gov. Wisner assistant state geologist in the department of zoology. In 1860 he was appointed professor of animal physiology and zoology in the Michigan State Agricultural College at Lansing. While in the zoological department of the Geological State Survey he was in constant correspondence with the leading naturalists of the period, as Agassiz, Cope,

Lea, etc, and discovered two new shells, two others being named after him by Lea. His catalogue was by far the most complete of any then compiled. In 1864 the duties of "acting superintendent of the farm" were added to his chair while in 1865 he became professor of animal physiology, practical agriculture and farm superintendent. In 1869 he ceased to teach physiology, devoting his entire time to practical agriculture, being far ahead of his time. In 1875 he resigned to accept the professorship of agriculture in the Illinois State University. Later he moved to Houghton Farm, near Mountainville, New York, and devoted himself entirely to scientific experiments, though afterwards he accepted the professorship of agriculture in the Massachusetts Agricultural College at Amhurst, Massachusetts. In 1886 he returned to Lansing to investigate, study and write till his death. Among his appointments and memberships were: membership of the Michigan State Medical Society; member of the Buffalo Society of Natural Science; of the Entomological Society of Philadelphia, Pennsylvania; fellow of the Royal Microscopical Society; and of the American Association for the Advancement of Science. Dr. R. C. Kedzie, who entered the Agricultural College two years later than Dr. Miles, said: "that he found Dr. Miles an authority among both professors and students, on birds, beasts, reptiles, stones of the fields and insects of the the air." In teaching agriculture Dr. Miles created such enthusiasm among the students that each regarded it a favor to work with him in the fields or ditches—he worked with the boys and filled the work with intellectual enjoyment. He was especially fond of boys who tried to learn something; he liked pets and little children. To his death he retained his habits of investigation and study, though his great deafness rendered his public work difficult. Dr. Miles was the

first professor of practical agriculture in the United States. On February 15, 1851, he married Mary E. Dodge, of Lansing, Michigan, who survived him.

Dr. Manly Miles died at Lansing, Michigan, February 15, 1898, from fatty degeneration of the heart.

His papers included:

"The Microbes of Nitrification." ("Scientific American," vol. xxxii.)

"Energy as a Factor in Agriculture." ("Popular Science Monthly," vol. xli.)

"Progress in Agricultural Science." ("Popular Science Monthly," vol. xxxviii.)

"Heredity of Acquired Characteristics." ("Proceedings of the American Association of Advanced Science," vol. xli.)

"How Plants and Animals Grow." ("Popular Science Monthly," vol. xliii.)

He was a constant writer and advisor of the "American Agriculturalist" and wrote many books on practical agriculture, as "Stock Breeding," "Experiments with Indian Corn," "Silos and Ensilage," "Land Drainage."

L. C.

Popular Science Monthly, April, 1899. Bulletin of the Michigan Ornithological Club, vol. ii, No. 11, Grand Rapids, Mich., April, 1898.

Millard, Perry H. (1848–1897).

Perry H. Millard was born May 14, 1848, in Ogdensberg, New York. He was principal of the High School, but at the end of a year he went to the Rush Medical College at Chicago, where after a three years' course he graduated in 1871 and began to practice in Chicago, but losing everything in the great fire of 1872, he came to Stillwater, Minnesota, the same year. In September, 1880, he spent nine months at Guy's Hospital, London, also two months in Vienna. He was mainly instrumental in getting through the first Medical Practice Act of Minnesota in 1883, and was the *vis a tergo* in establishing the Medical Department of the Minnesota

State University, being dean of the department at the time of his death.

He was best known for his work on the State Board of Medical Examiners. The law of 1887 was made up entirely by Dr. Millard and an attorney of Stillwater, Fayette Marsh. Dr. Millard was chiefly instrumental in getting this law passed by the State Legislature. Dr. Millard was president of the Minnesota State Medical Association and vice-president of the American Medical Association. He was one of the most active organizers and promoters of the Association of American Medical Colleges, and labored earnestly and persistently for the good of the medical profession. He died at John Hopkins Hospital, Baltimore, after a lingering illness, February 1, 1897.

He married in 1874 Caroline, daughter of John R. Swain.

B. F.

Miller, Henry (1800–1874).

In the latter part of the eighteenth century there emigrated from Maryland to Kentucky the parents of Henry Miller. Of German descent, and therefore of that sturdy character which has contributed so much to the best citizenship of this country, they became one of the three original families of the town of Glasgow, in the county of Barren, where on November 1, 1800, Henry Miller was born. His early years were spent in his native village, his companions and associates the descendants of these bold pioneers. Such associations together with the strong German blood in his veins gave him the rugged physique and traits of character for which he was noted. He attended the schools of his native village where he acquired a good knowledge of English and subsequently of Greek, Latin and mathematics. He began to study medicine when seventeen under Drs. Bainbridge and Gist, two Glasgow practitioners. In those days there were few drug stores, and pharmacy and dentistry were

departments of medicine and the physician always kept a supply of drugs in his "shop," also extracting teeth and practising venesection. After two years Miller entered the medical department of Transylvania University at Lexington, Kentucky, and attended his first course of lectures, at the end forming a partnership with his preceptor, Dr. Bainbridge, and practising until the fall of 1821 when he returned to Lexington and attended his second course when he graduated with honors. His inaugural thesis bore such distinct marks of genius and so highly was it esteemed by his brethren that it was published at the time, no ordinary compliment in those days. He returned afterwards to practise in Glasgow and the following year was elected demonstrator of anatomy in his alma mater without even being consulted. He gave up this position at once and went to Philadelphia, making the trip on horseback, in order that he might better equip himself for the place to which he had been elected. On account of some dissensions in the faculty, he soon resigned his position and again returned to Glasgow until 1827, when he removed to Harrodsburg, Kentucky, and practised for nine years. In 1837 the Medical Institute of Louisville was founded with Dr. Miller as professor of obstetrics and diseases of women and children, which chair he retained until 1858. In 1867, nine years after retirement from the University, he was recalled by the creation of a special chair for his occupancy, that of medical and surgical diseases of women. He soon resigned this position, but two years later accepted a similar chair in the Louisville Medical College which he retained until his death, February 8, 1874.

Dr. Miller was widely known abroad as well as at home as an author. In 1849 he published his greatest work, "Theoretical and Practical Treatise on Human Parturition," which ten years later was revised and republished under the title "Principles and Practice of Obstetrics," a work recognized for years as an authority, being regarded as one of the most sound and reliable books in the language. He accepted nothing as true without thorough investigation and most critical study, though his opinions on some points were not accepted at the time, subsequent study and investigation proved their validity. He was a frequent contributor to the various medical journals at the time and his articles carried with them the weight of authority. In 1860 he was elected president of the American Medical Association at its annual meeting in Louisville. He was the first in Louisville and one of the first in the United States to employ the speculum uteri, or to employ anesthesia in obstetric practice in Louisville.

June 24, 1824, Dr. Miller married Clarrisa Robertson, and had seven children, one of whom, Edward, became an eminent surgeon.

A partial list of his writings is given in the "Surgeon-general's Catalogue," Washington, District of Columbia.

B. F. Z.

Richmond and Louisville Med. J., Louisville, 1872, vol. xiii.

Tr. Amer. M. Ass., Phila., 1875, vol. xxvi.

Tr. Kentucky Med. Soc., Louisville, 1875 (L. P. Yandell).

Miller, John (1774–1862).

John Miller was born in the town of Armenia, County of Dutchess, New York, on November 10, 1774. His advantages for early education were very limited; he attended the district school about one year and a classical school in Connecticut about the same length of time, his boyhood being spent in laboring on the farm. He commenced to study medicine with Dr. Miller, an uncle, in Dutchess County, in the year 1793. At the expiration of little more than a year he went to Washington County, New York, and entered the office of Dr. Moshier, of Easton, in that county. While living with Dr. Moshier, young Miller received a severe injury by being thrown from a horse and was unable to pursue his studies more than two years. During his period he returned to his home in Dutchess County. After several months at home he was induced by the advice of Dr. Baird, of New York, to seek an appointment in the then small Navy of the United States. For this purpose, though much against the wishes of his family, he went to New York, where he was presented by Dr. Baird and others, with letters of recommendation to Dr. Benjamin Rush, of Philadelphia. At that time Miller was in poor health, and being tall, more than six feet in height, and thin in body, Dr. Rush was somewhat amused that so ghostly looking a young man should think of going into the navy, and said to him: "Young man, you look better fitted for a skeleton in my office than for a post in the navy." Dr. Rush went with him to visit the President of the United States, and through the influence of Dr. Rush he obtained the place he sought, and was directed to report himself to the surgeon of the United States brig New York, then soon to sail for Tripoli. Upon further acquaintance Dr. Rush advised Miller to resign his post in the navy and proffered him a position in his family and office as a private pupil. This offer he readily embraced, and remained for nearly two years, accompanying the doctor on his rides into the country, and attending the lectures of Dr. Rush and Dr. Shippen at the University of Pennsylvania. From Pennsylvania he returned to Washington County, New York, in 1798, and entered into co-partnership with Dr. Moshier, his former instructor, where he remained until 1801. He was licensed to practise medicine by the Vermont Medical Society in 1800. The law regulating the practice of medicine in New York was not enacted until 1806. On leaving Washington County in 1801, he came into the then town of Fabius, Nonodaga County, now Truxton, Cortland County, New York, and practised there twenty-five years. From his early physical training on the farm he was well prepared for laborious duties in a new country. The country being new, the roads always poor, many times almost impassable, yet he performed an amount of labor almost incredible, frequently riding on horseback thirty, forty and more than fifty miles a day, at all times, by night or by day, through storms and sunshine, with an energy that no obstacle could prevent.

He loved his profession, and while attending to its duties, amid all his incessant labors, he found time to cultivate his mind by reading much of the current professional literature of the day, and his well-balanced mind and retentive memory enabled him to make the best use of what he read. He was elected an honorary member of the New York State Medical Society in 1808. He was the last of that band of physicians, who, in August, 1808, organized the Cortland County Medical Society, and its first vice-president and the oldest living member by ten years.

Having spent the first years of his life in laboring on the farm, Dr. Miller while yet in the vigor of his days, left his profession and turned his attention to agriculture. Notwithstanding he still manifested an interest in its welfare. Dr. Miller early became prominent in public life. His first public office was that of coroner, which appointment he received from Gov. George Clinton, in 1802. He was a justice of the peace from 1812 until 1821, and one of the judges of our county courts from 1817 to 1820.

They had eight children—five sons and three daughters. Mrs. Miller died in 1834, aged 59 years. Of the family only one of the sons and two daughters survived. All of them arriving to mature age, and most of them falling a victim to that destroyer of our race—consumption.

In the temperance cause Dr. Miller took an early and active part. During his days of pupilage he once saw a beautiful child sacrificed in consequence of the intoxication of the physician called to its relief in an hour of suffering. This made a deep and lasting impression on his mind,

and led him at the commencement of his labors as practising physician firmly to resolve to abstain entirely from all intoxicating drinks.

He retained his wonted faculties almost to the last hour of his long life. He actively and usefully lived, he calmly and quietly died, on the thirtieth day of March, 1862, in the eighty-eighth year of his age, leaving behind him abundant evidence of his preparation for, and acceptance through, the grace of our Lord and Saviour, into the rest prepared for the just.

From a biography by Dr. G. W. Bradford, in the New York State Jour. of Med., Aug., 1907, vol. vii.

Miller, Thomas (1806–1873).

Thomas Miller's father, Maj. Miller, came to Washington with his family in 1816, and was attached to the Navy Department. The boy Thomas was born February 18, 1806, at Port Royal and received his early education under the care of the Jesuits at the old Washington Seminary, afterwards known as Gonzaga College. His medical studies were begun with Dr. Henry Huntt. After graduating M. D., in 1829, at the University of Pennsylvania, he practised in Washington, his office being in one of the famous buildings known as "Newspaper Row."

In 1830 he united with six others to form the Washington Medical Institute, for the purpose of giving instruction to students, and in 1832 began a course of teaching in practical anatomy. The same year, also, he was one of the physicians to the Central Cholera Hospital during the epidemic, and in 1833 was one of the original founders of the Medical Association of the District, and at the time of his death, president. In 1833, also, he married the daughter of a lawyer, Gen. Walter Jones.

One of the incorporators of the Medical Society in 1838, he was ever afterwards an active member in furthering its interests. In 1839 he became professor of anatomy in the National Medical College and for twenty years labored as a teacher with distinction and success, on retirement being made emeritus professor and president of the faculty.

In 1841 the Pathological Society was organized, and Miller was its first president. He was, subsequently, one of the attending surgeons to the Washington Infirmary, and one of the consulting staff of Providence Hospital and the Children's Hospital. The people did not then appreciate his efforts to abate nuisances and eradicate local causes of disease. To him is due the credit of abolishing the primitive and unsanitary habits, practices, and customs of a village population, for his untiring zeal in the interests of sanitary reform drove the reluctant municipal authorities to enact ordinances which clothed the board of health with some measure of authority to declare a nuisance and power to abate it. He died on September 20, 1873.

Dr. Miller was the author of "Introductory Lecture on Anatomy," Washington, 1840. D. S. L.

Busey, Reminiscences.
Minutes of Medical Society, September 22, 1837 and September 30, 1874.
Transactions, American Medical Association, 1874, xxv.

Miltenberger, George Warner (1819–1905).

Born in Baltimore, March 17, 1819, this obstetrician was the son of Gen. Anthony Felix Wybert Miltenberger, and educated at the Boisseau Academy, Baltimore, and at the University of Virginia, taking his M. D. at Maryland University in 1840. Soon after he was appointed demonstrator of anatomy in his alma mater. His talents as a lecturer led to the further honor of a lectureship on pathological anatomy in 1847. For several years he had a large quiz class and a surgical service in University Hospital. There he taught almost everything and laid broad and deep the foundations of solid attainments in the various branches of medicine.

In 1852 he succeeded Prof. Samuel Chew in the chair of materia medica and therapeutics, in 1855 becoming dean of the faculty and in 1858 succeeding to the chair of obstetrics. His close application to his professional work was notorious; he did all his reading in his carriage, and enjoyed but little rest or recreation. At one time he had eighteen horses in his service. He gave up all amusements and social pleasures, church services and holidays; for many years he seemed to live only for the good of his patients. He was a ready and pleasing lecturer—never using notes—and impressed his hearers with his honesty, his sincerity, and his mastery of his subject. In 1891 he offered his resignation—for the second time—which was accepted and he became professor emeritus and honorary president of the faculty, having completed his half century in the service of the university from which he had graduated.

Dr. Miltenberger was president of the Baltimore Obstetrical and Gynecological Society in 1885–86; president of the Medical and Chirurgical Faculty of Maryland in 1886–87, and was appointed consulting physician to the Johns Hopkins Hospital on its opening in 1889. On his accession to the chair of obstetrics, his attention was turned to that direction and all his later writings were on that subject, in the "Maryland Medical Journal" and in the "Transactions of the Medical and Chirurgical Faculty of Maryland." On April 30, 1906, a portrait of him was presented by his friends to the Medical and Chirurgical Faculty. His wife, née Neale, died in 1898, and he left no direct descendants. At his death, December 11, 1905, he left a large fortune to his nephews and nieces. E. F. C.

For sketches and portrait see Cordell's Medical Annals of Maryland, 1903, and History of the University of Maryland, 1907.

Miner, Julius Francis (1823–1886).

Julius Francis Miner, surgeon, was born in Peru, Berkshire County, Massachusetts, on February 16, 1823. As a boy he went to two preparatory schools and as a medical student to the Berkshire Medical College, Pittsfield, Massachusetts, and to Albany Medical College, New York, taking his degree from the latter in 1847. While in New York he also took up special surgical and ophthalmological studies. First he practised in New Braintree, Massachusetts, afterwards in Buffalo, being appointed in 1860 visiting surgeon to the Buffalo General Hospital; in 1867, professor of surgical anatomy and ophthalmology; in 1870, professor of special and clinical surgery. His last course of lectures was delivered in 1881–82. When in 1861 he issued the first number of the " Buffalo Medical and Surgical Journal" his idea was to afford a means of communication between the practitioners of the vicinity and his editorship soon made the journal one worth reading.

He was best known as a surgeon. He performed most of the important operations of his day and in more than one instance instituted procedures which have been widely adopted. Four times he successfully performed thyroidectomy, and ligated the external iliac artery for aneurysm; the internal and external carotid and most of the other arteries that require ligation for injury or disease: he removed a spleen weighing over seven pounds, with fatal result; exsected for traumatism and disease of the hip, knee, ankle, shoulder- and wrist-joints; in two cases he removed over four and a half inches of the femur, securing a useful limb. A similar operation was done on the humerus, removing large portions of the shaft for gunshot or other injuries; he removed the entire fibula successfully and the ulna with the elbow-joint, so saving an aim; twice he removed foreign bodies from the opening of the left bronchus; in operating for recto-vaginal fistula he instituted a procedure as successful as it was novel and ingenious. Many of these operations call for boldness and originality even at our stage of development in surgery; nearly- all were specially noteworthy at that time and form a list of major operations equalled by few contemporary surgeons. His operation for ovarian tumor in 1869 will

be regarded as his greatest addition to surgery. (" Buffalo Medical and Surgical Journal," June, 1869.) He had previously (1866), for the first time in the history of ovariotomy, tied separately the vessels of the pedicle, cut the ligatures short and returned the pedicle to the abdominal cavity with success. In an emergency he ligated the radial artery with a pocket knife and an aneurysm needle fashioned from a hairpin. As one said, speaking as a layman: " With nerves of tempered steel, he had a gentle hand, a tender heart, a compassionate nature."

In 1867, while operating upon a charity patient, he pricked his thumb with a spicula of bone and received the infection which eventually ended his life. Iritis and other symptoms followed, but it was not until 1873 that serious results were observed. His lectures in 1881–82 were delivered sitting and at their close he resigned and became emeritus professor. His paper on " Ovariotomy by Enucleation without Clamp, Ligature or Cautery" appeared in the " American Journal of Medical Science," vol. lxiv, 1872. Late in the summer of 1886 I saw him for the last time. Our talk ran on the production of his old friend, the late Austin Flint, and we talked of the ideas he had so well set forth in that address. The end came early on the fifth of November, 1886. He sought in religion as he had sought in medicine, to know the truth, and had found it and faced death with the same cheerfulness with which he had met the weariness of protracted illness.

E. N. B.

Abridged from An Address on the Life and Character of Julius F. Miner, by Dr. E. N. Brush, Phila., 1888.
Buffalo Med. and Surg. Jour., 1886–7, vol. xxvi.
N. York Med. Jour., 1886, vol. xliv.
Med. Press, West. N. York, Buffalo, 1885–6, vol. i.

Miner, Thomas (1777–1841).

An early investigator of epidemic cerebrospinal meningitis, one of the most learned physicians of this day, Thomas Miner was born in Westfield, the northwest parish of Middletown, Connecticut, on October 15, 1777. His father was the Congregational minister in that town and saw to it that he received a good elementary education. Finally Miner was fitted for college under Dr. Cyprian Strong, of Chatham, and graduated in 1796 from Yale, with the degree of A. B. The next three years were spent in teaching in Goshen, New York, which work, however, was sadly interrupted by two attacks of intermittent fever. Returning to Middletown in December, 1799, he began the study of law, only to discontinue it during 1810, on account of a serious attack of rheumatism. In the autumn of 1801, his health permitted him to take charge of an academy at Berlin, where he taught for two years, or until ill health again interfered with his plans. He was able, however, when twenty-five years of age, to study medicine under Dr. Osborne, of Middletown, and continue with Dr. Smith-Clark of Haddam. In the spring of 1807 he began to practice at his father's house, but, in the autumn, removed to Middletown, and finally settled at Lynn, only to remove, in two years, back to Middletown, where he practised until an affection of the lungs and heart suddenly ended, for the great part, his professional career, and left him, at the premature age of forty-one, a confirmed valetudinarian.

Subsequently he practised in consultation, and for two or three years did some literary work for the "Medical Recorder of Philadelphia," engaging himself in making selections, abridgments and translations from the French. In 1823, with Dr. Tully, he published "Essays on Fevers and other Medical Subjects," which received much criticism on account of the doctrines it advanced. Two years later there appeared his admirable account of an epidemic of "Cerebrospinal Meningitis in Middletown," 1823. In it he called the affection typhus syncopatis.

He received the honorary degree of M. D. from Yale in 1819. He was a member of many important committees in the Connecticut State Medical Society,

and in 1832 was made its vice-president. Two years later he was promoted to the presidency, an office which he held for three years. He married Phebe, daughter of Samuel Mather. She died February 5, 1811.

His death at the home of his friend, Dr. S. B. Woodward, in Worcester, on April 23, 1841, was due to complications resulting from an affection of the valves of the heart.

Woodward describes him as one of the most learned physicians in New England —not only in professional attainments, but in foreign languages and theology. He was acquainted with the French, Italian, Spanish and German languages and was often employed by publishers in the country as translator.   W. R. S.

Williams, S. W., American Medical Biography, 1845.

Hazen, Miner C., Centennial History of the Middlesex County Medical Association, in Trans. Conn. Med. Soc., 1892.

Minot, Francis (1821–1899).

Francis Minot, Hersey professor of the theory and practice of physic in the Harvard Medical School, was born in Boston, April 12, 1821, and died in Readville, Massachusetts, May 11, 1899.

He graduated from Harvard College in 1841; from the Harvard Medical School in 1844, and after graduation studied medicine abroad. In 1860 Trinity College, Hartford, gave him her A. M. From 1859 to 1886 he was physician to the Massachusetts General Hospital and from 1886 to the time of his death one of the consulting physicians there. He was instructor in the theory and practice of medicine in the Harvard Medical School from 1869 to 1871 and assistant professor from 1871 to 1874. He was the first clinical lecturer on the diseases of women and children to be mentioned in the announcements of the Harvard Medical School: this was in 1871.

In 1878 he gave the annual discourse before the Massachusetts Medical Society, choosing for his subject "Hints on Ethics and Hygiene." In 1889 he was president of the Association of American Physicians.

He was treasurer of the Massachusetts Medical Society from 1863 to 1875 and was one of the founders of the Massachusetts Medical Benevolent Society. For many years he was a member of the Obstetrical Society of Boston.

Dr. Minot contributed papers on "The Treatment of Acute Pneumonia," "Cases of Pulmonary Consumption Followed by Recovery or Arrest of the Disease," and other topics, to the medical press. He was an excellent teacher and a man of most courteous bearing both in the classroom and at the bedside.

His portrait is in the Boston Medical Library where he is also commemorated by a book fund.   W. L. B.

Bos. Med and Sur. Jour., vol. cxl.

Mitchell, Ammi Ruhammi (1762–1824).

Ammi Mitchell was the son of Judge David Mitchell, who was judge of the Court of Common Pleas for Cumberland County, Maine, and member of the General Court of the Commonwealth of Massachusetts, and was born May 8, 1762, and named after the celebrated Dr. Cutter.

When young Mitchell was nineteen years old he went to Portsmouth and studied medicine with his namesake. While there, our government gave to France a new man of war called the "America" in place of a French ship which had been lost off our coasts. The French government had sent Dr. Meaubec to Portsmouth, to be surgeon of the new ship on her return to France. This gentleman took a great fancy to young Mitchell, and persuaded him to go with him to France as surgeon's mate on the "America." This he did and visited all the places of interest under Dr. Meaubec's patronage, to say nothing of obtaining the best possible opportunities of studying medicine in Paris for a long time.

When Dr. Mitchell returned to North Yarmouth, he could hardly decide to spend his life in so small a place. It happened, however, that while considering whether to settle, one patient came, and before her case was finished, another wanted his services, so that ultimately

Dr. Mitchell passed his life in that town, gaining an extensive practice.

In his practice, Dr. Mitchell had remarkable success, most of which, in those religious days was regarded as due to the fact that he always asked God's blessing on his medicine chest and its contents as well as upon himself, looking heavenward for assistance to the efficacy of the drugs grown on God's earth and sacred soil. He was successful, also, owing to his intense humor. He had an enormous fund of anecdote, which made everybody laugh, and his wit went far to help his cures. He was most energetic in stamping out an epidemic of malignant fever brought in 1807 by a vessel from the West Indies.

At his funeral service, the Rev. Asa Cummings publicly regretted that at times Dr. Mitchell's mirth would run through an audience like contagion, when sobriety of mind would have been much more appropriate. Dr. Mitchell was distinctly a literary man, and not a few papers were written by him, and read before the public, or printed in the newspapers of the day.

Dr. Mitchell died, as it were, in harness, May 14, 1824. He and his horse and carriage were seen going down a hill and an hour later the horse and empty wagon appeared in Dr. Mitchell's yard. Search was made, and the good physician was found dead on the road side, having probably been thrown by a bad place in the road.

People from miles around attended the funeral, and there was much lamentation for the sudden death of their genial, respected, and beloved medical man, who at sixty-four seemed well prepared for many years more of active and generous practice.

He married when twenty-four, and was the father of twelve children.

J. A. S.

Thacher's Med. Biog.

Mitchell, Giles Sandy (1852–1904).

Giles Sandy Mitchell was born in Martinsville, Indiana, May 31, 1852, the son of Samuel M. and Ann Sandy Mitchell. Dr Mitchell attended the public schools of his native place, and graduated from Indiana University, Bloomington, Indiana, in 1873. In that year he went to Cincinnati, Ohio, and began to study medicine under Dr. Thaddeus A. Reamy, attending lectures at the Medical College of Ohio. In 1875 he graduated from that school, and began practice with Dr. Reamy. From 1876 to 1878 Mitchell traveled abroad, visiting many countries in the interest of his medical education, and for his health, and returned in the autumn of 1878. From 1879 to 1884 he was adjunct professor of obstetrics in the Medical College of Ohio, but resigned this position to accept the professorship of obstetrics in the Cincinnati College of Medicine and Surgery, which he held many years. He was for several years professor of gynecology in the Woman's Medical College, and the same in St. Mary's Hospital from April, 1896, until his death. He was a member of the Academy of Medicine of Cincinnati from 1875 (its president in 1891); of the Cincinnati Obstetrical Society; of the Ohio State Medical Society, and the National Association of Obstetricians and Gynecologists. His M. A. was conferred by the Indiana University. Rare skill as an operator placed him in the front rank as a gynecologist, and his genial manner won for him a very large clientèle. During the latter years of life he devoted himself to gynecology.

May 11, 1875, he married Mary A. Reamy, daughter of his partner. She died on April 18, 1876, leaving a son who lived only three months, and on October 22, 1883, the doctor married Esther De Camp, of Cincinnati, who survived him. They had no children by this marriage. Dr. Mitchell died of angina pectoris, May 5, 1904. Though for two years a sufferer from the disease, he died in harness, visiting his patients on the very day of his death.

A. G. D.

Cincin. Lancet-Clinic, 1904, n.s., vol. liii.

Mitchell, John (1680?–1768).

This botanist, the date of whose birth is uncertain, was born, educated and took his M. D. in England, but as there were several scholarly John Mitchells of that time it is difficult to identify his birth. He came over to America about 1700, and lived in Virginia, at Urbanna, on the Rappahannock. The climate and people must have pleased him, for he stayed some forty-seven years, interested in everything scientific, especially botany, and making long excursions to gather plants, but writing also on electricity, yellow fever, politics and publishing a map of the British and French dominions in America which is said to mark an era in the geography of North America. Like most doctors and scientists of that time he kept his interests wide by corresponding with European confrères, especially with Linnaeus who named the partridge vine or chequer berry after him *Mitchella repens*. Every fresh plant seems to have been sent by the American botanists to their acknowledged head in Sweden and the great man always most courteously thanked these friends and ofttimes pupils for remembering him.

Mitchell returned to London about 1747 and became a fellow of the Royal Society, the fruits of his literary solitude in America, being given to the learned Society in several addresses, among them one on "The Preparation and Use of Various Kinds of Potash," and one on "The Force of Electrical Cohesion."

His biographers simply state that "he died in March, 1768." Where buried, no one knows and very few that he is commemorated in the *Mitchella repens*.

His writings included:

"Dissertatio brevis de principiis botanicorum," 1738.

"Nova Plantarum Genera," 1769.

"Essay on the Causes of the Different Colours of People in Different Climates," read before the Royal Society, by Peter Collinson, 1744.

"The Contest in America between

Great Britain and France, by an Impartial Hand," 1757.

"An Account of the Yellow Fever which Prevailed in Virginia in 1737 to 1741 and 1742, in Letters to Cadwallader Colden and Benjamin Franklin," published by Rush in the "Medical and Philosophical Register," vol. iv. Letter concerning the "Force of Electrical Cohesion."

D. W.

Thacher's Amer. Med. Biog.
Amer. Med. and Phil. Register, vol. iv.
Dict. of National Biog.
Contributions to the Annals of Medical Progress (J. M. Toner).

Mitchell, Thomas Duché (1791–1865).

Thomas Duché Mitchell, author and editor, received his early education in the Quaker schools and after a year in the drug store and chemical laboratory of Dr. Edward (?) Parrish, attended three courses of medical lectures at the University of Pennsylvania, from which he graduated. The honorary degree of A. M. was conferred on him by the trustees of Princeton College in 1826.

In 1812 he was appointed professor of vegetable and animal physiology in St. John's Lutheran College and in 1819, published a volume of medical chemistry. From 1822 to 31 he was engaged in the practice of medicine at Frankford, near Philadelphia, while 1826 saw the Total Abstinence Society firmly established by him, he going so far as to deprecate the use of alcohol in the preparation of tinctures.

In 1832 he published an octavo volume of 553 pages on "Chemical Philosophy" on the basis of "The Elements of Chemistry," by Dr. Reid, of Edinburgh, and about the same time his "Hints to Students" appeared, and he became also co-editor of the "Western Medical Gazette," with Profs. Eberle and Staughton, and editor of the "Journal of Medical and Associate Sciences."

Another book came out in 1850, an octavo volume of 750 pages on "Materia Medica," also an edition of "Eberle on the Diseases of Children," to which he added notes and about 200 additional pages. His volume of 600 pages on the "Fevers of the United States" was never published. He was the biographer of John Eberle in "American Medical Biography," by Samuel D. Gross, M. D. As a writer and author he was indefatigable, as a lecturer, clear and impressive. A classical and scientific scholar, a rigidly upright and conscientious gentleman, he died in Philadelphia, May 13, 1865.

A list of his writings is in the "Surgeon-general's Catalogue," Washington, D. C.

A. S.

Boston Med. and Surg. Jour., 1852, vol. xlv ("Cato").

Mitchill, Samuel Latham (1764–1831).

Samuel Latham Mitchill was born in North Hempstead, formerly Plandome, Queen's County, Long Island, New York, on the twenty-ninth of August, 1764. In this village his father, Robert Mitchill, of English descent, was a farmer, of the Society of Friends.

Young Mitchill had his classical education under Dr. Leonard Cutting; his early medical studies with his uncle Latham; and completed them in New York, with the erudite Dr. Samuel Bard, with whom he continued three years—a devoted pupil.

He advanced the scientific reputation of New York by his early promulgation, when first appointed professor in Columbia College, of the Lavoisierian system of chemistry. His first scientific paper was an essay on "Evaporation;" his mineralogical survey of New York, in 1797, gave Volney many hints; his analysis of the Saratoga waters enhanced the importance of these mineral springs. His ingenious theory of the doctrine of septon and septic acid gave origin to many papers, and lent impulse to Sir Humphry Davy's vast discoveries; his doctrines on pestilence awakened inquiry from every class of observers throughout the Union; and his expositions of a theory of the earth and solar system captivated minds of the highest qualities. Speculations on the phosphorescence of the waters of the ocean, on the fecundity of fish, on the decortication of fruit trees, on the anatomy and physiology of the shark, swelled the mystery of his diversified knowledge. His correspondence with Priestly is an example of the delicious manner in which argument can be conducted in philosophical discussion. His elaborate account of the fishes of our fresh and salt waters adjacent to New York, comprising 166 species, afterwards enlarged, invoked the plaudits of Cuvier. Reflections on somnium—the case of Rachel Baker—evinced psychological views of original combination, while the numerous papers on natural history enriched the annals of the Lyceum, of which he was long president. Researches on the ethnological characteristics of the red man of America betrayed the benevolence of his nature and his generous spirit. The fanciful article, "Fredonia," intended for a new and more appropriate geographical designation for the United States, was at one period a topic which enlisted a voluminous correspondence, now printed in the proceedings of the New York Historical Society.

He increased our knowledge of the vegetable materia medica of the United States, and wrote largely on the subject to Barton of Philadelphia, Cutler of Massachusetts, Darlington of Pennsylvania, and Ramsay of South Carolina. He introduced into practice the *sessamum orientale*. With Percival, of Manchester, and other philosophers in Europe, he corresponded lengthily on noxious agents, also seconded the views of Judge Peters on gypsum as a fertilizer. He cheered Fulton when he was dejected; encouraged Livingston in appropriation; awakened new zeal in Wilson, when Tompkins, the governor of the state, had nigh paralyzed him by his frigid and unfeeling reception; and with John Pintard, Cadwallader D. Colden, and Thomas Eddy, was a zealous promoter of that system of internal improvement which has stamped immortality on the name of De Witt Clinton. Jonathan Williams had his co-operation in

furtherance of the Military Academy at West Point; and, for a long series of years, he was an important professor of agriculture and chemistry in Columbia College, and of natural history, botany, and materia medica in the College of Physicians and Surgeons of New York. His letters to Tilloch, of London, on the progress of his mind in the investigation of septic acid—oxygenated azote—are curious as a physiological document. Many of his papers are in the "London Philosophical Magazine" and in the "New York Medical Repository," a journal of wide renown, which he established with Miller and Smith; yet he wrote in the "American Medical and Philosophical Register," the "New York Medical and Physical Journal," the "American Mineralogical Journal," of Bruce, the "Transactions of the Philosophical Society of Philadelphia," and supplied several other periodicals, both abroad and at home, with the results of his cogitations. He accompanied Fulton on his first voyage in a steamboat, in August, 1807; and, with Williamson and Hosack, he organized the Literary and Philosophical Society of New York in 1814. Griscom, Eddy, Colden, Gerard, and Wood found him zealous in the establishment, with them, of the Institution for the Deaf and Dumb. Mitchill's translations of our Indian War Songs gave him increased celebrity; and I believe he was admitted, for this generous service, an associate of their tribes. The Mohawks had received him into their fraternity at the time when he was with the commission at the treaty of Fort Stanwix.

As a physician of the New York Hospital, he never omitted to employ the results of his investigations for clinical appliances. The simplicity of his prescriptions often provoked a smile on the part of his students, while he was acknowledged a sound physician at the bedside.

His first course of lectures on natural history, including geology, mineralogy, zoology, ichthyology, and botany, was delivered, *in extenso*, in the College of

SAMUEL L. MITCHILL.

(By permission of the Surgeon-General, Washington, D. C.)

Physicians and Surgeons, in 1811, before a gratified audience, who recognized in the professor a teacher of rare attainments and of singular tact in unfolding complex knowledge with analytic power.

He was the delight of a meeting of naturalists; the seed he sowed gave origin and growth to a mighty crop of those disciples of natural science. He was, emphatically, our greatest living ichthyologist. The fishermen and fishmongers were perpetually bringing him new specimens; they adopted his name for the streaked bass (perca Mitchilli). When he had circumnavigated Long Island, the lighthouse at Sands Point was called the Mitchill, and the topographers announced the highest elevation of the Neversink Hills as Mount Mitchill.

The records of state legislation and of Congress must be consulted to comprehend the extent and nature of his services as a public representative of the people. He manfully stood by Fulton in all his trials, when navigation by steam was the prolific subject of almost daily ridicule by our Solons at Albany; and when the purchase of the Elgin Botanic Garden, by the constituted authorities, was argued at the Capitol, he rose in his place, and won the attention of the members by a speech of several hour's length, in which he gave a history of gardens, and the necessity for them, from the primitive one of our first parents down to the last institution of that nature, established by Roscoe, at Liverpool. It is probable that no legislative body ever received more instruction in novel information than the eminent philosopher poured out on this occasion; and even the enlightened regents of the university imbibed wisdom from his exposition. With his botanical Latinity occasionally interspersed, he probably appeared more learned than ever.

When Mitchill was quite a young man he would return from church service and write out the sermon nearly verbatim. There was little display in his habits or manners; his means of enjoyment corresponded with his desires, and his

Franklinian principles enabled him to continue superior to want. With all his official honors and scientific testimonials, foreign and native, he was ever accessible to everybody—a counsellor of the young, a dictionary for the learned. Even the captious John Randolph called him the "Congressional Library."

In the prime of his manhood, Dr. Mitchill was about five feet ten inches in height, of comely rather slender and erect form. He possessed an intelligent expression of countenance, an aquiline nose, a gray eye, and full features. His dress at the period he entered into public life was after the fashion of the day, the costume of the times of the Napoleonic consulate: blue coat, buff-colored vest, smalls, and shoes with buckles.

Dr. Mitchill died in New York, on September 7, 1831.

His writings included:

"Remarks on the Gaseous Oxyd of Azote or Nitrogene, etc."

"Observations on the Canada Thistle."

"Catalogue of the Organic Remains," presented to the New York Lyceum of Natural History, 1826.

He was also co-editor of the "Medical Repository" from 1797–1824.

S. W. F.

Abridged from Gross' Lives of Eminent Amer. Phys. (S. W. Francis).
Eulogy on the Life of S. L. Mitchill. F. Pascalis, N. Y., 1831.
Reminiscences of S. L. Mitchill enlarged from Valentine's City Manual (S. W. Francis), N. Y., 1859.

Monette, John Wesley (1803–1851).

John Wesley Monette, who wrote much concerning Mississippi, was born of Huguenot parentage at Staunton, Virginia, April 5, 1803. In his infancy his family settled at Chillicothe, Ohio, where he was educated. In his eighteenth year he completed the course of study prescribed in the Chillicothe Academy.

In the year 1821 his father, Dr. Samuel Monette, removed to the then flourishing town of Washington, the early capital of Mississippi, where he practised. He also directed the studies of his son, who had decided to become a physician. Four years later, March 21, 1825, John Wesley Monette received his diploma from Transylvania University, at Lexington, Kentucky. He immediately returned home and resumed practice, which he had engaged in some time before the completion of his medical course.

On December 10, 1828, he married Cornelia Jane Newman, daughter of George and Charlotte Newman, and had ten children, but only four survived childhood, George N., A. C., Anna, and Maria Louise.

Dr. John W. Monette was a student by nature, and, although he was actively and successfully engaged in an exacting profession, he never lost interest in literary work. He had a large and well selected library, composed principally of works on medicine, history, geography, geology, and theology.

In 1823, shortly after Dr. Monette began the study of medicine, an epidemic of yellow fever broke out in Natchez and was soon conveyed to the town of Washington, which is only six miles distant. This afforded the young medical student an excellent opportunity to study the disease as it appeared in his father's practice. Two years later, soon after his graduation, a more fatal epidemic of yellow fever visited Natchez and Washington, both towns being well-nigh depopulated. This epidemic afforded to Dr. Monette and his life-long friend Dr. Cartwright, their first opportunity to acquire distinction in their profession. In referring to their essays on the subject of yellow fever which were written at that time and subsequently, a contributor to "DeBow's Review" says that they soon placed their reputation among the best contributors to the medical literature of the day. On December 2, 1837, Dr. Monette read before the Jefferson College and Washington Lyceum an interesting paper, entitled "The Epidemic Yellow Fevers of Natchez," in which he suggested the use of quarantines in restricting the disease. This contribu-

tion was published by the Lyceum in its official organ, the "Southwestern Journal." The return of the epidemic in 1839 gave Dr. Monette an opportunity to continue his investigations. He shortly afterwards published a small volume, entitled "Observations on the Epidemic Yellow Fevers of Natchez and the Southwest from 1817 to 1839." When the next yellow fever epidemic broke out in New Orleans in the summer of 1841 Dr. Monette had the pleasure of seeing his quarantine theory put to a test. It is claimed that this was the first time that an attempt was ever made to control the spread of yellow fever by means of quarantine, and that to Dr. Monette is due the credit of originating this method of restricting the disease.

This successful result increased the demand for articles from his pen dealing with the subject of yellow fever. In the winter of 1842–3 he contributed a series of papers on this subject to the "Western Journal of Medicine and Surgery," published at Louisville, Kentucky.

Dr. Monette's other contributions to the science of medicine are numerous and interesting. The "Western Medical Journal" of June, 1827, refers to his use of oil of turpentine as an external irritant, particularly in the treatment of typhus fever, in language that would lead the reader to suppose that he was a pioneer in the use of this now familiar remedy. His other contributions to medical reviews are too numerous and technical to be given in detail.

Dr. Monette's earlier literary efforts outside the field of professional contributions seem to have been directed principally to the subject of natural history. As early as 1824 he prepared a carefully written essay of 201 manuscript pages on the "Causes of the Variety of the Complexion and the Form of the Human Species." In this essay he attempts to show the primitive unity of the human race and to prove that racial differences can be accounted for by the influence of environmental conditions.

It is clear that many principles published by Darwin in 1869, in the widely recognized literary prize of the last century, "The Origin of Species," were stated by Dr. Monette in a hypothetical way thirty-five years earlier. One of these writers based his conclusions on deductive and the other on inductive reasoning.

Although Dr. Monette showed a reverent regard for the Scriptures, he was not inclined to accept them as scientific authorities. He was glad to find his conclusions corroborated by the ancient writer of Genesis, but was not led to his conclusions by an attempt to square his facts with Genesis.

Another paper belonging to the early period of Dr. Monette's literary activity bears the title "Essay on the Improbability of Spontaneous Production of Animals and Plants." This contribution was probably never published and is decidedly interesting even at this time.

The results of his diligent efforts are pathetic. He seemed to be completely enamored of science, but his ideals were so exalted he could not give his consent to publish many of the treatises that he prepared with the greatest care from time to time. The only evidence that remains of his persistent efforts to penetrate the secret of nature is the large batch of manuscripts, now yellow with age, which are prized by his son as a most precious family heritage. Like his great predecessor, William Dunbar, the pioneer scientist of the Mississippi Valley, his name does not appear in the history of American science, yet his services entitle him to distinction in the state of his adoption.

As early as 1833 Dr. Monette entered upon his great literary undertaking—the writing of an elaborate work on the "Geography and History of the Mississippi Valley."

The first volume of this work contains a history of the Mississippi Valley prior to the acquisition of Louisiana by the United States. The second volume, entitled "The United States in the Valley of the Mississippi," contains the first comprehensive history of the Mississippi Valley as a whole during this period. There were few books of value then available upon the history of the Mississippi Valley which are not referred to in the footnotes of these volumes.

Dr. Monette did not live to finish the work on his physical geography, which treatise he seemed to think would be his most important contribution to knowledge. Judging from his manuscripts, this work was well-nigh completed at the time of his death.

Dr. Monette also wrote, from time to time, anonymous articles, humerous or satirical. Among his miscellaneous writings may be mentioned a poem of 250 lines on "Friendship." It was first written in 1823, and, to use the language of the author, was "Inscribed to Hon. A. Covington, the humane, the generous, and the good." It was rewritten and enlarged for the "Natchez Gazette" in August, 1825. Among his other poetical efforts are an "Ode to July 4, 1820" and "A Satirical Poem." Among his anonymous writings are a number of articles on "Empiricism." These were directed principally against the pretensions and practices of the "steam doctors," the disciples of Samuel Thompson, Samuel Wilcox and Horton Howard. Dr. Monette says that the general tenor of the teachings of all these men is the same, viz., "that all diseases proceed from cold, and are curable by capsicum, lobelia, and steaming."

Dr. Monette died in the prime of his life, without reaping the full fruits of his years of unremitting toil. A marble slab in the family burying ground at his old home, "Sweet Auburn," in Washington, Mississippi, bears the simple inscription:

SACRED
TO THE MEMORY OF
JOHN WESLEY MONETTE, M. D.,
BORN APRIL 5, 1803.
DIED MARCH 1, 1851.

F. L. R.

Abridged from an account by Dr. Franklin L. Riley, in the Miss. Hist. Soc. Jour., vol. ix.

Monroe, Hollis (1789–1861).

Monroe, Nahum Parker (1808–1873).

Of Dr. Philip Monroe, father of Hollis, I know only that he practised in Surry, New Hampshire, not far from Keene. He must have been a man of some means for his son Hollis, born in 1789, graduated at the Yale Medical School in 1819, probably attracted by the fame of Dr. Nathan Smith, one of the great minds of American medicine. Hollis went early to Belfast as assistant to a physician who during an epidemic of small-pox had more than he could properly attend to. Arriving there and doing his share as assistant Dr. Hollis Munroe found sufficient patronage to hold him firmly to Belfast the rest of his life. He was fond of botany, first as a study allied to medicine and later on as something interesting for children. From this point of view he lectured often on botany to the schools of Belfast. He was also much inclined to natural history and spoke publicly thereon at the local lyceums, then the center of New England cultivation. He was very fond of talking, but he would not tell stories. You had to talk of something profitable or it had no interest for him.

He was rather of an ascetic cast of mind. He was careless about money in the extreme. Paying his own bills he never seemed to have money beyond. At times he would carry his love of silver to the extreme, bearing about with him pocketsful of the heavy stuff. "You could see it" he said. Once he went to the bank to borrow money and they asked him why he did not spend what he had on deposit in the bank. He replied that he was actually not aware that he had any there. He was a member of the Maine Medical Society and of its successor, the Maine Medical Association, but did not often appear at their public meeting. He rarely wrote medical papers. He devoted himself to his practice and his patients, riding thousands of miles to care for them in all sorts of weather.

He and his brother lived alongside of one another very amicably for several years. In fact it was by Philip's advice that the younger brother settled in Belfast. As for Dr. Hollis he worked hard and late, grew old, caught lung fever after exposure amidst his outlying cases, and died from congestion of the lungs June 21, 1861, aged sixty-one, leaving behind the remembrance of a worthy life in medicine, and a good image of his medical father in New Hampshire.

If Dr. Hollis were reserved and avoiding publicity, his brother Nahum Parker was the reverse; for he shone in the light of publicity and politics all his life. Born January 4, 1808, nineteen years after his brother, the youngest and well beloved child of Philip Monroe, Nahum Parker studied medicine in Belfast with his brother, and graduated at the Albany Medical School in 1839. Moving to Belfast, he was soon helped into abundance of medical work by his brother who had been twenty years in the same field and knew everybody. While Hollis was purely a medical practitioner, Nahum Parker devoted himself as much as he could to surgery, and soon became well known in that branch of medicine. He is said to have been able to do all the operations of the day. In 1848 he married Miss Sarah Ann Johnson, of Belfast, and had two children.

From that time on to the breaking out of the Civil War he was held in high esteem by a large clientèle and by his associates in medicine. With the oncoming of the war he was made surgeon of the Twentieth Maine Regiment, and was present at many battles, including Fredericksburg. After a year of active service, during which he had a serious attack of erysipelas, he was compelled to resign. On returning home he was called to the capital where for a long time he was of the greatest service medically to the troops. He was made surgeon-general of Maine, and among other public offices was a representative to the Legislature, doing good service for medicine there. He was a very distinguished member of the Maine Medical Association.

Although naturally of great strength

and physical endowment, Nahum Parker Monroe was too careless of his health. He gradually failed, moved to Baltimore in 1871, slowly developed schirrus of the stomach and general tuberculosis and died April 23, 1873, aged only sixty-three and at a time when he seemed to have ten years more of active life before him.

It is so unusual for two brothers living side by side to do so well together, and to become both men of so much mark, even if we cannot positively call either of them men of great ability. The medical skill, however, of Dr. Hollis, and the surgery of Dr. Nahum Parker, entitles the Monroes to excellent rank in the history of medicine in Maine.

I like to think of these two excellent physicians practising in Belfast, Maine, as relations, perhaps, of mine. For their grandfather, Philip, a man of roving propensities, descended from William Monroe who escaped from the Battle of Worcester and emigrated to America, settled in Surry, New Hampshire, where he kept the village inn. There is a legend that his first wife was Mary Parker, and if so, then she was an aunt of mine some generations back. This seems more than probable when we recall the fact that her grandson, Nahum Parker, had the same name as my grandfather twice removed, once living in Kittery, Maine. The coincidence of "Nahum Parker" is odd, at all events, meaningless though it may be from a geneological point of view. However, the relationship may be, the first Philip had a son Dr. Philip Monroe, of whom he was so fond that when old Philip died they had inscribed upon his tombstone after his days of birth and death "Father of Dr. Philip Monroe."

J. A. S.

Montgomery, Frank Hugh (1862–1908).

Frank Hugh Montgomery was born at Fair Haven, Minnesota, January 6, 1862, and went as a boy to the St. Cloud (Minnesota) High School and the University of Minnesota.

He graduated M. D. from Rush Medical College, Chicago, in 1888, and went afterwards to the Johns Hopkins Medical School and the hospitals of London, Paris and Vienna.

At the time of his death he was the associate professor of dermatology in the Rush Medical College, Chicago; dermatologist to the Presbyterian, St. Elizabeth, and St. Anthony de Padua Hospitals of Chicago.

He was elected a member of the American Dermatological Association in 1897, and was one of the founders of the Chicago Dermatological Society.

Dr. Montgomery was a collaborator with Dr. J. Nevins Hyde of a "Practical Treatise on Diseases of the Skin" (1895). He made frequent contributions to medical journals on dermatology, perhaps the most important being those on blastomycosis, although all of his writings demonstrated that he was a master in this difficult and intricate specialty, for his knowledge was broad and all of his scientific discussions and articles bear the imprint of scholarly labor and a thorough acquaintance with dermatological literature.

His death, which occurred at White Lake, Michigan, on July 14, 1908, was very tragic. He was drowned while trying to save a companion who had been thrown with him into the water by the capsizing of a sail boat.   J. M. W.

Moore, Edward Mott (1814–1902).

Edward Mott Moore was born at Rahway, New Jersey, July 1, 1814, son of Lindley Murray and Abigail (Mott) Moore, descendants of Samuel and Mary (Isley) Moore, who removed from Newbury, Massachusetts, to New Jersey in 1666. His father was a prominent member of the Society of Friends. The son studied medicine in New York and Philadelphia and graduated M. D. at the University of Pennsylvania in 1838. He served as resident physician at Blockley Hospital, and also at the Frankford Lunatic Asylum until he removed to Rochester in 1840, where he began practice. In 1842 he was called to the chair of surgery in the medical school of

Woodstock, Vermont, and lectured there for eleven years. He held the same chair at Berkshire Medical College, Massachusetts, 1853–54, at Starling Medical College, Columbus, Ohio, 1854–55 and at the Buffalo Medical College, 1858–83. Dr. Moore was distinguished for research and experiments on the heart's action, undertaken in Philadelphia about 1838, with Dr. Pollock, continuing the experiments begun by Dr. Hope, and investigated the following year by a committee of the London Medical Society. In his articles on medical and surgical topics he suggested many original methods of treatment. In one of these he controverted the asservations of the physiologists as to the rationale of the production of the vowel sounds. He was the author of monographs on fractures and dislocations of the clavicle; on fractures of the radius, accompanied with dislocation of the ulna; on fractures, during adolescence, at the upper end of the humerus; and a treatise on transfusion of the blood based on original investigations. Among his appointments, he was president of the New York State Medical Society, one of the founders of the American Surgical Association, succeeded Dr. Gross as its president in 1888. In 1889–90 he helped frame the constitution and was president of the State Board of Health of New York. For nearly fifty years he was at the head of St. Mary's Hospital staff. Dr. Moore married at Windsor, Vermont, November 11, 1847, Lucy R., daughter of Samuel Prescott, of Montreal, Canada, and died in Rochester, New York, March 4, 1902.

His writings included: "Treatment of the Clavicle when Fractured or Dislocated," 1870. "A Luxation of the Ulna not Hitherto Described, with a Plan of Reduction, etc.," 1872. "Gangrene and Gangrenous Diseases," 1882; and with C. W. Pennock, "Reports of Experiments on the Action of the Heart," 1839.

C. G. S.

Boston M. and Surg. J., 1902, vol. cxlvi.
Buffalo M. J., 1901-2, n. s., xli.
J. Am. Med. Ass., Chicago, 1902, vol. xxxviii.
Tr. Med. Soc. N. Y., Albany, 1903 (W. S. Ely).

Moore, John (1826–1907).

John Moore, surgeon-general of the United States Army, was born in Bloomington, Indiana, in 1826, and received his collegiate education at the Indiana State University. In 1848–49 he attended lectures at the Medical School of Louisville, and graduated from the medical department of New York University in 1850, in 1853 being commissioned assistant army surgeon and promoted to captain in 1858. Upon promotion to major, in 1862, he was detailed as medical director of the Central Grand Division of the Army of the Potomac; in the following year he was transferred to the Department of the Tennessee, and in 1864 received the brevet of lieutenant-colonel for gallant and meritorious service during the Atlantic Campaign. In 1865 he was appointed colonel and medical director of Volunteers, receiving during this service the brevet of colonel "for faithful and meritorious service during the war." After serving at various posts he was appointed surgeon-general of the army in 1886, by Pres. Cleveland.

Under the administration of Gen. Moore great advances in army medical work were accomplished. Instruction in first aid was inaugurated in the service by direction of general order No. 86, from the headquarters of the army, November 20, 1886. In 1887, the act organizing a Hospital Corps in the United States Army became a law. The third medical volume of the medical and surgical history of the rebellion appeared during his administration, under the editorship of Maj. Smart. He retired in 1890, and continued to live in Washington up to the time of his death in 1907.

C. A. P.

J. Ass. Mil. Surg. U. S., Carlisle, 1904, xv.

Moore, Samuel Preston (1813–1889).

Samuel P. Moore, surgeon, United States Army, surgeon-general, Confederate States Army, was the son of Stephen West and Eleanor Screven Gilbert Moore, and lineal descendant of Dr. Mordicai Moore who accompanied Lord

Baltimore to America as his physician. He was educated at the schools of Charleston and graduated M. D. from the Medical College of the State of South Carolina in 1834, afterwards appointed assistant surgeon in the United States Army, 1835, serving at many frontier posts in Florida, and with high credit in Texas during the Mexican War, and continued service after being created major at various stations in Missouri, Texas and New York. When South Carolina seceded from the Union, he resigned and settled in Little Rock, Arkansas, whence he was called in June, 1861, to the surgeon-generalcy of the Confederate Army. Under the stress of overwhelming difficulties he organized a medical department for the Confederate armies. In 1863, at Richmond, he organized the Association of Army and Navy Surgeons of the Confederate States and became its first president, and was also active as president in a similar association, established after the close of the war. The useful work was his of finding methods of providing the Confederate troops with medicines from the plants indigenous to the southern states. He inaugurated and directed the publication of "The Confederate States Medical Journal" from 1864 to 1865, and he adopted the one story hospital wards which became so popular in both northern and southern armies. At the close of the Civil War he remained in Richmond, not engaging in active medical practice, but interested in all public affairs, and died May 31, 1889.

J. E. P.

James Evelyn Pilcher, Journal of the Association of Military Surgeons of the United States, vol. xvi, 1905 (port.)
The Surgeon-generals of the United States Army, Carlisle, Pa., 1905 (port.)

Morgan, Charles Edward (1833–1867).

Charles Edward Morgan, a native of New Orleans, Louisiana, was the son of George Morgan, a banker.

A book-worm in childhood, an enthusiastic student of mineralogy at eleven, the possessor of a respectable cabinet of specimens at fifteen, and the author of a work on "Natural Philosophy" at seventeen, he had already achieved much by a jealous hoarding of time.

He gained his baccalaureate degree from Columbia College in 1854, his diploma from the College of Physicians and Surgeons, New York, three years afterwards.

He had seven years in Europe, conscientiously spent in the interest of medicine and the collateral sciences, and on his return to New York in 1864 was given an appointment to service in the Northern Dispensary as one of the attending physicians to the class of skin diseases. Until within a few days of his death, he was revising for the press a work of his own on "Electro-physiology and Electro-therapeutics, including an account of the Electric Fishes." Here he impressed into good service his knowledge of the limner's art, in tracing upon the block many of the cuts.

To illustrate his quiet confidence, it may be worth remarking that about a year before the completion of his self-imposed task, when urged to publish through fear of anticipation, he replied, "I have no fear of that; there are many points considered in my book which no one else will think of."

A contributor to the medical journals, but only to a limited extent, an excellent linguist, a critic in art with a bias for mathematics and the natural sciences, as well as a competent microscopist, science owed much to him.

He died in the thirty-fourth year of his age, of acute diarrhea and hemorrhage of the bowels, after an illness of only five days.

N. York Med. Record, 1867, vol. ii.

Morgan, Ethelbert Carroll (1856–1891).

Ethelbert C. Morgan was born in Washington, February 11, 1856, the son of Dr. James E. Morgan, one of the oldest physicians in the District.

Gonzaga College gave him his preliminary education whence he graduated B. A., June, 1874. Even during boyhood he gave evidence of a mechanical turn of mind, preferring to pass his time in building miniature derricks, railway cars, boats, houses, etc., rather than in sports and out-door play; fond also of chemistry, physics and general experimentation, spending most of his leisure in a very creditable pharmaceutical and chemical laboratory which he had fitted up at his home. He studied medicine in Georgetown University in 1874, 1875 and 1876. In 1876 he entered the medical department of the University of Pennsylvania taking his M. D. there in the spring of 1877. In the same year he visited Europe for the purpose of attending lectures and clinics. He finally became a pupil of the French laryngologist Charles Fauvel and with him took courses in diseases of the upper air passages. In 1878 he left Paris for Vienna pursuing a similar line of studies and for six months he was assistant to Prof. Schnitzler in the Vienna Polyclinic. In 1878 he returned to his native city and for the first two years practised general medicine, but devoted most of his attention to affections of the air passages and ear to which class of diseases he finally limited his practice in 1881. In the same year he was elected surgeon in charge of diseases of the nose, throat and chest in Providence Hospital and professor of laryngology in the medical department of Georgetown University, positions which he held until death. His were the first lectures on laryngology ever delivered in the regular session of any medical school in Washington. In 1881, he was elected a member of the American Laryngological Association; his inaugural thesis "Diphthonia," which paper, together with his classical monograph on "Uvular Hemorrhage" gained for him a most enviable reputation among his fellow members, and in 1888 he was elected president. He held a number of positions in the Medical Association and the Medical Society of the District of Columbia. In 1888 Georgetown University conferred upon him the degree Ph D.

A versatile and clear writer, his scientific work was thorough and of permanent value and he contributed to "Buck's Reference Hand Books" and "Keating's Encyclopedia of Diseases of Children," having prepared the article on "Ozena, Carcinoma, and Sarcoma of the Larynx" for the former and articles on "Epistaxis" in the latter. He was the inventor of a very efficient uvula hemostatic clamp, an atomizer and universal powder blower. But thirty-five when he died, few men of his age attained greater distinction or a larger measure of success.

His success was due to individual merit, scientific attainments, a thorough training, earnest and honest work coupled with unusual professional and business tact and unswerving loyalty to his patients. The writer, although six years his senior, profited by his philosophical mind on more than one occasion, especially when he informed him "If you want good advice go to friends, if you want to borrow money go to strangers, if you want nothing go to your relatives."

He was unmarried and accumulated quite a fortune, a large part of which he left, with characteristic generosity, for the endowment of scholarships and research work in the literary and medical department of Georgetown University.

He died at his home on the evening of May 5, 1891, from consumption, contracted some years before, after an attack of typhoid fever, during his professional duties.

G. M. K.

Morgan, John (1735–1789).

The founder of the first medical school in America was of Welsh ancestry, his father, Evan Morgan, having emigrated from Wales to Pennsylvania, settling in Philadelphia where he became a very successful merchant. John Morgan went to the Academy at Nottingham, in Maryland, kept by the Rev. Samuel Finley. Morgan received the degree of A. B. from the College of Philadelphia in 1757, with the first class that graduated. He then served as apprentice to Dr. John Redman for six years, thirteen months of

JOHN MORGAN.

(By permission of the Surgeon-General, Washington, D. C.)

which he passed as resident apothecary to the Pennsylvania Hospital. Of this period he writes, "At the same time I had an opportunity of being acquainted with the practice of other eminent physicians in this place; particularly of all the physicians of the hospital, whose prescriptions I put up there above the space of one year." After his apprenticeship had expired he spent four years as surgeon to the Pennsylvania troops in the war between the French and English. Dr. Rush speaks of the excellence of his work in this capacity, stating "I well remember to have heard it said, 'that if it were possible for any man to merit heaven by his good works, Dr. Morgan would deserve it, for his faithful attendance upon his patients.'"

In 1760 he went abroad, studying first in London, especially with the Hunters, and then going to Edinburgh. Norris quotes a letter of introduction which Benjamin Franklin, then living in London, gave him to Lord Kames, in which he states that he thinks Morgan "will one day make a good figure in the profession, and be of some credit to the school he studies in, if great industry and application, joined with natural genius and sagacity, afford any foundation for the presage." At Edinburgh he took his M. D. in 1763. His thesis was entitled "De Puopoiesis," and in it he first advanced the view that pus was a secretion formed by the blood-vessels in conditions of inflammation.

From Edinburgh he went to Paris, where he particularly studied anatomy. He read a paper on "Suppuration" before the Royal Academy of Surgery in Paris, and demonstrated the methods employed by the Hunters to inject and preserve anatomical specimens, and subsequently a paper "On the Art of Making Anatomical Preparations by Corrosion" to the Academy, upon the strength of which he was elected a member.

Continuing his travels into Italy, he met Morgagni. Rush, in his account of Morgan states that Morgagni " was so pleased with the doctor that he claimed

kindred with him, from the resemblance of their names, and on the blank leaf of a copy of his works, which he presented to him, he inscribed with his own hand the following words: "Affini suo, medico praeclarissimo, Johanni Morgan, donat Auctor."' This anecdote has had its veracity impugned because the College of Physicians of Philadelphia contains the original books given by Morgagni to Morgan, and by the latter donated to the college, and there is no such inscription to be found on their fly leaves. Dr. George Dock has recently investigated the subject, and his conclusions would seem to warrant our belief in what has ever been regarded as one of the most pleasant legends of early medical history.

The young American received many substantial honors during his sojourn abroad. He was made a member of the Belles-Lettres Society of Rome, and in England was honored by election to the Royal Society as well as by being made a licentiate of the Royal College of Physicians.

During his travels Morgan had thought much of the project of founding a medical school in his native city, and, upon his return in 1765, brought with him a letter from the proprietary, Thomas Penn, to the Board of Trustees of the College of Philadelphia, endorsing his scheme to establish a medical school in connection with the college. Dr. Morgan's project met with immediate approval, and on May 3, 1765, they elected him professor of the theory and practice of medicine in the college, thus establishing the school which still flourishes as the department of medicine of the University of Pennsylvania. On May 30, 1765, Morgan delivered his celebrated address, entitled "A Discourse upon the Institution of Medical Schools in America." He had written this when in Paris, and it had undergone careful scrutiny by Fothergill, William Hunter and Dr. Watson, of London. In it he recommended a very comprehensive preliminary education preparatory to the study of medicine.

Dr. Morgan arrived at home in April,

1765, and in the following month proposed to the trustees of the college his plan for translating medical science into their seminary, boldly urging a full and enlarged scheme for teaching medicine in all its branches. Morgan retained his professorship until his death, when Dr. Benjamin Rush succeeded. As a teacher he was held in the greatest respect and esteem by his pupils. Not only active in the medical school, in 1772 he actually made a trip to the West Indies and collected subscriptions aggregating over £2000 for the advancement of the literary department of the college. He was one of the founders and a very active member of the American Philosophical Society.

Upon settling in Philadelphia to practise he resolved that he would neither compound his remedies nor do any surgical work. He also endeavored to introduce the English custom of presenting the physician with his fee at the time of each visit. In the first two instances he was successful, although he encountered great opposition from the older physicians.

After Dr. Benjamin Church, the first medical director of the Continental Army, had been found guilty of treason and dishonorably discharged, Congress, in October, 1775, appointed Morgan as his successor, and he at once joined the army then in the vicinty of Boston. From the outset he set himself resolutely to bring order out of the chaos which existed in the army Medical Department. Morgan set to work at the root of the matter by instituting rigid examinations for those desiring to enter the medical service, and by exercising the most vigilant supervision over the work of the entire department. The greatest difficulty confronting Dr. Morgan, however, was that of obtaining hospital supplies. The finances of the Continental Army were never in a particularly fine condition; but during Dr. Morgan's career as chief of the medical department they were at a very low ebb. It was the jealousy and insubordination of the regimental surgeons which finally played a large part in causing his dismissal from the post of director-general. On July 17, 1776, Congress passed a law, based on a memorial presented to it some time previously by Dr. Morgan, settling definitely the discipline, pay, and other matters relating to the regulation of the medical service.

The direction of medical affairs in the northern part of New York State was under Dr. Samuel Stringer. Under his management, or mismanagement, things soon fell into a disgraceful state of confusion. Morgan appealed repeatedly to Congress to settle the disputes which were raised by the officiousness and insubordination of Dr. Stringer, and at length Congress appointed a committee to investigate, acting upon the report, with the result that Congress dismissed both Dr. Stringer and Dr. Morgan from their positions. Morgan, in righteous indignation, published one of the most interesting documents in the medical literature of this country, namely, his pamphlet entitled "A Vindication of His Public Career in the Station of Director-General of the Military Hospitals and Physician-in-chief to the American Army," Anno 1776, by John Morgan, M. D., F. R. S., Boston, 1777. What angered him more than any other of the injuries he felt he had received was the appointment on October 9, 1776, of Dr. William Shippen, Jr., as director of the hospitals on the west side of the Hudson river. Dr. Shippen had been director of the hospital of the Flying Camp in the Jerseys, and subject to the authority of Dr. Morgan. Dr. Shippen was ordered to report directly to Congress, thus ignoring Dr. Morgan, through whom such reports had hitherto been made. It is sad to find Morgan blaming his quondam friend and colleague in the establishment of the medical department of the University of Pennsylvania, as the chief author of his overthrow, but he does so in unequivocal language.

A tardy vindication of his conduct in this and another similar affair with Dr. William Shippen, Jr., although it must have afforded Morgan some satisfaction, yielded him no more substantial benefit. What added to his chagrin was the fact that on April 11, 1777, his rival Shippen was appointed to succeed him in the post of director-general and physician-in-chief of the army, and Morgan withdrew to a great extent from active contact with public affairs. He had been elected physician to the Pennsylvania Hospital in 1773, and he continued to serve on its staff until 1783, when he resigned under somewhat peculiar circumstances, though the minutes of the hospital stating his action add that it was "to the grief of the patients, and much against the will of the managers, who all bore testimony to his abilities, and great usefulness to the institution."

Morgan possessed an ample fortune. He is said to have been the first man in Philadelphia who carried a silk umbrella. He had a collection of valuable works of art, but that, together with his fine library, was destroyed by the enemy, partly at Bordentown, New Jersey, and partly at Danbury, Connecticut, to which places they had been removed to secure them from the very fate they met.

In 1765 he married Mary, daughter of Thomas Hopkinson, who died in 1785. They had no children. Dr. Morgan died on October 15, 1789, and both he and his wife are buried in St. Peter's churchyard, Philadelphia.

In addition to his writings already referred to he published the following:

"The Reciprocal Advantages of a Perpetual Union between Great Britain and her American Colonies" (1766), before the Revolution, and "A Recommendation of Inoculation According to Baron Dimsdale's Method" (1776).

He also contributed to the "Transactions of the American Philosophical Society" the following:

"An Account of a Pye Negro Girl and Mulatto Boy;" "On the Art of Making Anatomical Preparations by Corrosion;" and an article "On a Snake in a Horse's Eye, and of other Unnatural Productions of Animals."   F. R. P.

Early History of Medicine in Philadelphia. Phila. Jour. of the Med. andPhysical Sciences, 18²0.

Med. Library and Historical Journal, March, 1906.

N. Am. Med. and Surg. Jour., Phila., 1827, iv.

Phila. J. Med. and Phys. Sc., 1820, i (B. Rush).

Morehouse, George Read (1829-1905).

Some time before 1776 one Andrew Morehouse came from the north of England to New York and served as colonel during the Revolution. His great grandson became rector of St. Andrews, Mount Holly, and from him and Martha Read came George Read Morehouse, born at Mount Holly, New Jersey, March 25, 1829. He entered as a junior at Princeton College and graduated in July, 1848, with high honors, matriculating at the University of Pennsylvania. Leaving there at the close of one term for the Jefferson Medical College, he graduated there March, 1850, and in the following year became M. A. at Princeton, taking his M. D., from Pennsylvania in 1875 and an hon. Ph. D. from Princeton in 1895.

From his first settlement in Philadelphia says his friend, Dr. Weir Mitchell, "he had large success as a practitioner and a valued consultant, but all his most important literary work was done in conjunction with other physicians and comprised chiefly laboratory and hospital research. In 1860, I discovered certain facts of novel interest in reptilian physiology and offered him the chance of working out with me the problems presented. This research on the anatomy and physiology of the respiratory organs of chelonia is now in some sense a classical essay. Leidy praised it warmly and Agassiz asked me who was this remarkable young naturalist and why he had never heard of him."

Early in the Civil War, Morehouse served in the Filbert Street Hospital as assistant surgeon, and when the Hospital for Nervous Diseases was instituted Weir Mitchell asked for Morehouse as colleague and these two, with W. W. Keen, spent years of industrious research, being relieved of much red tape routine by order of the surgeon-general and all these papers passed into the "Medical History of the War." Unfortunately an accidental fire in Morehouse's office destroyed many notes on his chosen subjects of "Choreal Spasms from Wounds" and "Epilepsy."

He was a skillful operator and in one case of paralysis removed through the mouth a bullet which had lodged in the cervical vertebræ. "I saw him," adds Weir Mitchell, "trephine the skull and open a cerebral abscess, the first case on record, unless one by Detmold preceded it."

Dr. Morehouse married Mary Ogden, widow of David Ogden, of Woodbury, New Jersey, but had no children. His death occurred through renal disease on November 12, 1905. He became a fellow of the College of Physicians in 1863, and was also on the consultant staff of the Orthopedic Hospital and St. Joseph's Hospital and a member of the American Academy of Medicine.

D. W.

Tr. Coll. of Phys , vol. xxvii., Phila., 1906.

Morrison, Robert Brown (1851–1897).

Robert Brown Morrison was born in Baltimore, Maryland, on March 13, 1851. He went first to Phillips Exeter Academy, Exeter, New Hampshire, in 1869 entered Harvard University, but did not graduate, then continued his studies at the University of Göttengen, Germany, graduating M. D. from the University of Maryland in 1874. Soon after he became a member of the Clinical Society of Baltimore, and of the Medico-Chirurgical Faculty of Maryland, but in 1882 returned to Europe and studied dermatology at Prague under Pick and Chiari.

While there he won distinction by his original investigations, the most important being his extensive and painstaking study of the histo-pathology of the prurigo papule and the application of certain stains in syphilitic tissue.

From Prague he went to Vienna and studied under Neumann and after this to the hospitals of Hamburg and Berlin. Upon his return in 1884, he was elected professor of dermatology in the Baltimore Polyclinic and Post-Graduate Medical School. He was also lecturer on dermatology in the Woman's Medical College, Baltimore.

In 1887 he was elected clinical professor of dermatology in the University of Maryland, but two years later was appointed professor of dermatology at the Johns Hopkins University.

He was president of the American Dermatological Association 1893–4, and was regarded as the pioneer dermatologist of Maryland, his observations and contributions regarding skin diseases of the negro being, perhaps, the most valuable ever written.

He was a gentleman of broad culture, charming personality, and his published writings bear the stamp of an astute student, of a painstaking clinician.

In the last years of his life failing health compelled him to resign his professorships, and in other ways curtail his activities.

His death occurred at Baltimore, September 30, 1897.

J. M. W.

Morton, Samuel G. (1799–1851).

Samuel Morton was the son of George Morton, who came to this country from Ireland at the age of sixteen, and of Jane, daughter of John and Margaret Cummings, of Philadelphia. They had nine children of whom Samuel was the youngest.

The father died when Samuel was but six months old and Mrs. Morton with her three children moved to Westchester, New York, in order to be near her sister.

When Samuel was of school age, he went to various boarding schools conducted near Westchester by members of the Society of Friends, and Morton's early education was derived entirely under their auspices. In 1812 Morton's mother married Thomas Rogers and returned to Philadelphia, and Morton soon afterwards was sent to another Quaker School in West Town, and from there to the private school of John Gummere at Burlingtou, New Jersey, to study the higher mathematics. After studying under John Gummere, Morton was, in 1815, apprenticed to a mercantile house in Philadelphia. He did not take kindly to business life, and after the death of his mother in 1816, he gave it up. According to Wood the friendship formed with several eminent physicians who were in attendance on his mother during her protracted illness helped to turn him towards the study of medicine. In 1817, at the age of nineteen, he commenced this study in the office of Dr. Joseph Parrish, who was one of the most successful practitioners of his day. He had so many office pupils that in order to provide adequate tuition for them, he had associated with himself several young instructors in various branches. Among them was the naturalist, Richard Harlan, who exerted a marked influence in turning Morton's thoughts toward science. In his early school days, Morton is said to have shown a fondness for natural history, and this was fostered by his step-father who was an amateur mineralogist. He was thus prepared to be influenced by Harlan and other young physicians who took delight in the study of nature.

While studying under Dr. Parrish, Morton also attended lectures at the medical department of the University of Pennsylvania, and 1820 took his M. D. there. In the same year he became a member of the Academy of Natural Sciences, an institution subsequently much indebted to him for its development, and of which he was president at the time of his death.

In 1821 Samuel went to Clonmel, Ireland, to visit his uncle, James Morton. He was received with open arms by his relatives, but after a brief visit with them, was persuaded to go to Edinburgh to continue his medical studies. American degrees were not at this time much esteemed in Europe, so that Morton was obliged at Edinburgh to attend the full term of an undergraduate. In 1824 Morton returned to Philadelphia and

began to practise, in 1827 marrying Rebecca Pearsall. Soon after his return he was made auditor and a little later recording secretary of the Academy. In this year he published an "Analysis of Tabular Spar from Bucks County," followed by numerous papers dealing with geology and paleontology. The most important of these were collected and published in 1834, in a volume entitled "Synopsis of the Organic Remains of the Cretaceous Group of the United States," which book at once gave its author a deserved scientific reputation. According to Marcon it is the starting-point of all paleontological and systematic work on American fossils. In addition to his contributions to paleontology Morton at this period published various zoological papers, among them one on "A New Species of Hippopotamus," determined from a skull received from Dr. Goheen, of Liberia. Meanwhile Morton's interest in scientific medicine was likewise advancing. His first published essay was one on "Cornine," a new alkaloid, printed in 1825–1826. His "Illustrations of Pulmonary Consumption," published in 1834, was a credit to American science. He followed Dr. Parrish in recommending the open-air treatment of the disease and in 1835 he edited an American edition of Mackintosh's "Principles of Pathology and Physic."

Morton's chief scientific contributions, however, came from still another direction. He was soon after his return selected by Dr. Parrish as one of his associates in teaching, and lectured upon anatomy in that connection from 1830 to 1835–6. His lectures were characterized by simplicity and clearness without any attempted display, and gave entire satisfaction both to his associates and pupils. In 1839 he was elected professor of anatomy in Pennsylvania College from which his resignation was accepted with regret in 1843. In 1849 he published an elaborate and valuable work on "Human Anatomy," special, general and microscopic, completed with much labor and care. "Among the inducements to this work, not the least," as he states in the preface, "was the desire to be enrolled among the expositors of a science that had occupied many of the best years of my life." It was when he began his career as a teacher of anatomy that Morton received the stimulus which led to the work on which his lasting reputation rests.

Morton* states that "having had occasion, in the summer of 1830, to deliver an introductory lecture to a course of anatomy, I chose for my subject 'the different forms of the skull as exhibited in the five races of men.' Strange to say I could neither buy nor borrow a cranium of each of these races, and I finished my discourse without showing either the Mongolian or the Malay. Forcibly impressed with this great deficiency in a most important branch of science, I at once resolved to make a collection for myself." Although most of the skulls belonging to the collection were contributed by some hundred friends, the cost of collecting to Morton must have been between $10,000 and $15,000. Agassiz, on visiting Philadelphia soon after his arrival in America, wrote that "Dr. Morton's u n i q u e collection of human skulls is also to be found in Philadelphia. Imagine a series of 600 skulls, mostly Indian, of all the tribes who now inhabit or formerly inhabited America. Nothing like it exists elsewhere. This collection alone is worth a journey to America."

The two most important works by Morton based on his splendid collection of skulls are his "Crania Americana" and his "Crania Egyptica," the first published in 1839.

He wrote to Gliddon:

"You will observe by the annexed prospectus that I am engaged in a work of considerable novelty, and which, as regards the typography and illustrations at least, is designed to be equal to any publication hitherto issued in this coun-

*Letter to J. R. Bartlett, Esq., "Transactions of the American Ethnological Society," vol. ii, New York, 1848, quoted by Patterson.

try. You may be surprised that I should address you on the subject, but a moment's explanation may suffice to convey my views and wishes. The prefatory chapter will embrace a view of the varieties of the human race, embracing, among other topics, some remarks on the ancient Egyptians. The position I have always assumed is, that the present Copts are not the remains of the ancient Egyptians, and in order more fully to make my comparisons, it is very important that I should get a few heads of Egyptian mummies from Thebes, etc. I do not care to have them entirely perfect specimens of embalming, but perfect in the bony structure, and with the hair preserved, if possible. It has occurred to me that, as you will reside at Cairo, and with your perfect knowledge of affairs in Egypt, you would have it in your power to employ a confidential and well-qualified person for this trust."

Morton's ethnological studies led him to the conclusion that the human races are of diverse origin. For this he was bitterly assailed by numerous people including several clergymen who claimed that he was denying the authority of the Scriptures by conclusions of this character. Morton's life was made for a time unpleasant by the bitterness of the controversy, but his fine character was too well understood by those nearest him for those who attacked him to do him great injury.

In an essay on "Hybridity," published in "Silliman's Journal" for 1847, Morton showed that there are many examples of fertile hybrids known, and that therefore the fertility of offspring from members of different human races cannot be considered an argument against the distinct specificity of these races. Since Darwin's influence has spread abroad the whole subject would now, of course, be taken up from a different standpoint. Agassiz accepted, in the main, Morton's views. According to Marcon, Morton was second only to Cuvier in his influence on Agassiz's mind and scientific opinion.

Of the opponents of Morton the most

bitter was the Rev. Dr. Bachman, of Charleston, South Carolina, who published a book and several monographs attacking Morton. While they were of no value from the scientific standpoint, they served to stimulate Morton to get and publish new evidence. While in the midst of publishing such evidence in support of his own point of view, Morton was suddenly stricken with mortal illness, and died in Philadelphia, May 15, 1851. The end is thus described by Patterson:

"Never had Morton been so busy as in that spring of 1851. His professional engagements had largely increased, and occupied most of his time. His craniological investigations were prosecuted with unabated zeal, and he had recently made important accessions to his collection. He was actively engaged in the study of archeology, Egyptian, Assyrian, and American, as collateral to his favorite subject. His researches upon hybridity cost him much labor, in his extended comparison of authorities, and his industrions search for facts bearing on the question. In addition to all this, he was occupied with the preparation of his contribution to the work of Mr. Schoolcraft, and of several minor papers. Most of these labors were left incomplete. The fragments published in this volume will show how his mind was engaged, and to what conclusions it tended at the close. For it was now, in the midst of toil and usefulness, that he was called away from us. Five days of illness—not considered alarming at first—had scarcely prepared his friends for the sad event, when it was announced on the fifteenth of May, that Morton was no more. It was too true, he had left vacant among us a place that cannot soon be filled. Peacefully and calmly he had gone to his eternal rest, having accomplished so much in his short space of life, and yet leaving so much undone that none but he could do as well."

Dr. Morton was considerably above the medium height, of a large frame, though somewhat stooping, with a fine oval face, prominent features, bluish-gray eyes, light hair, and a very fair complexion. His countenance usually wore a serious and thoughtful expression, but was often pleasingly lighted up with smiles during the relaxation of social and friendly intercourse. His manner was composed and quiet, but always courteous, and his whole deportment that of a refined and cultivated gentleman. (G. B. Wood.)

Dr. Morton, according to Meigs, was a member of the following societies:

The Academy of Natural Sciences of Philadelphia; Philadelphia Medical Society; College of Physicians of Philadelphia; Massachusetts Medical Society; American Ethnological Society, New York; Medical Society of Sweden; Academy of Science and Letters at Palermo; Royal Society of Northern Antiquaries at Copenhagen; Academy of Science, Letters, and Arts de Zelanti di Arce-reale; Imperial Society of Naturalists of Moscow; Medical Society of Edinburgh.

The following is a list of his principal papers and published works as given by Meigs:

"Observations on Cornine, a New Alkaloid." ("Medical and Physical Journal of Philadelphia," for 1825, 1826.)

Dr. Morton's name is connected, in the "Journal of the Academy," with the following papers and notices:

"Analysis of Tabular Spar from Bucks County, Pennsylvania," with a notice of various minerals found at the same locality, May, 1827. ("Journal of the Academy," vi.)

"Description of a New Species of Ostrea," with some remarks on the Ostrea Convexa of Say, May 1, 1827. ("Journal of the Academy," vi.)

"Geological Observations on the Secondary, Tertiary and Alluvial Formations of the Atlantic Coast of the United States of America," arranged from the notes of Lardner Vanuxem, by S. G. M., January 8, 1828, vi.

"Description of the Fossil Shells which Characterize the Atlantic Secondary Formation of New Jersey and Delaware,

Including Four New Species," December 11, 1827, and January 1, 1828.

"Note, Containing a Notice of Some Fossils Recently Discovered in New Jersey," June 2, 1828, vi.

"Description of Two New Species of Fossil Shells of the Genera Scaphites and Crepidula; With Some Observations on the Ferruginous Sand, Plastic Clay, and Upper Marine Formation of the United States," June 17, 1828, vi.

"Additional Observations on the Geology and Organic Remains of New Jersey and Delaware." January 19, July 6, 1830, vi.

"Notice of Some Parasitic Worms," March 15, 1831, vi.

"Some Remarks on the Ancient Peruvians," June 1, 1841.

"Remarks on a Mode of Ascertaining the Internal Capacity of the Human Cranium," April 6, 1841.

"A Memoir of William Maclure," read July 1, 1841.

"Observations on the Embalmed Body of an Egyptian—*Ibis religios*," May 4. 1841.

"Observations on Eight Skulls from Mexico," July 6, 1841.

"Remarks on the Sutures of the Cranium as Connected with the Growth of the Corresponding Bones," May 17, 1841.

"Description of Fossil Shells from the Cretaceous Deposit of the United States," October 12, 1841.

"On an Albino Racoon," November 6, 1841.

"On the So-called Pigmy Race of People Who are asserted to have Formerly Inhabited a Part of the Valley of the Mississippi," November 15, 1841.

"Description of Two New Species of Fossil Shells from the Lower Cretaceous Strata of New Jersey," November 7, 1841.

"Results of Measurement of Forty-five Adult Negro Crania, in Order to Ascertain the Internal Capacity of the Skull in the African Race," December 14, 1841.

"Description of Some New Species of Organic Remains of the Cretaceous Group of the United States; With a Tabular View of the Fossils Hitherto Discovered in this Formation," October 12, November 7, 1841; January 25, 1842.

"Verbal Communication on an Adult Skeleton from Ticul, Yucatan," May 9, 1842.

"Brief Remarks on the Diversities of the Human Species, and on Some Kindred Subjects," being an introductory lecture delivered before the class of Pennsylvania Medical College in Philadelphia, November 1, 1842.

"Inquiry into the Distinctive Characteristics of the Aboriginal Race of America," second edition, 1844.

"On the analogy which exists between the Marl of New Jersey and the Chalk Formation of Europe,"—a letter to Prof. Silliman, February 14, 1832. ("American Journal of Science and Art," vol. xxiv.)

"Notice of the Fossil Teeth of Fishes of the United States; the Discovery of Galt in Alabama, and a Proposed Division of the American Cretaceous Group." ("American Journal of Science and Art," vol. xxviii.)

"On a Supposed New Species of Hippopotamus," February 27, 1844.

"Remarks on the Skull of a Hottentot," May 21, 1844.

"Description of Head of a Fossil Crocodile from the Cretaceous Strata of New Jersey," August 27, 1844.

"On a Second Series of Ancient Egyptian Crania," October 29, 1844.

"Observations on Mosasaurus of New Jersey," November 24, 1844.

"Measurements of Skulls of Native Africans," December 17, 1844.

"Remarks on the Skulls of a Mexican, a Lenape, and a Congo Negro," May 6, 1845.

"Remarks on the Crania of Two Ancient Peruvians, Two Mound Skulls from Missouri, a Hottentot, a Mozambique Negro, and Four Mummied Egyptian Heads," September 2, 1845.

"Remarks on Two Skulls of Natives of New Holland," November 18, 1845.

"Verbal Remarks on Cretaceous Fossils from Burlington County, New Jersey, March 1, 1846.

"On Peruvian Remains," March 1, 1846.

"Description of Two New Species of Fossil Echinodermata from the Eocene of the United States," May 26, 1846.

"On Two Living Hybrid Fowls between Gallus and Numida," September 29, 1846.

"Address at the First Meeting of the Academy at the New Library and Meeting-room," May 4, 1847.

"Remarks on an Aboriginal Cranium from Chilicothe, Ohio," May 25, 1847.

"Remarks on an Indian Cranium from Richmond, on the Delaware," December 21, 1847.

"Remarks on a Bushman Boy at Philadelphia," February 8, 1848.

"Remarks on an Ancient Peruvian Cranium from Pisco," April 11, 1848.

"Remarks on Four Skulls of Shoshonees," August 8, 1848.

"Observations on the size of the Brain in Various Races and Families of Man," April 25, 1848.

"Biographical Notice of the Late George McClellan, M. D.;" read before the Philadelphia College of Physicians, September 4, 1849.

"Illustrations on Pulmonary Consumption, Its Anatomical Character, Causes, Symptoms and Treatment, with Twelve Colored Plates," Philadelphia, 1834.

"Macintosh's Practice of Physic, With Notes by S. G. Morton."

"Crania Americana," or a "Comparative View of the Skulls of Various Aboriginal Nations of North and South America," to which is prefixed an essay on the "Varieties of the Human Species," illustrated by seventy-eight plates, and a colored map, by Samuel George Morton, M. D., etc., etc., folio; Philadelphia and London, 1839.

"Crania Ægyptiaca;" or "Observations on Egyptian Ethnography," derived from history and the monuments, plates and wood-cuts, Philadelphia and London, 4to, 1845.

"An Illustrated System of Human Anatomy," special, general and microscopic, Philadelphia, 8vo, 1849.

Among other papers not included in the list given above mention may be made of:

"An Inquiry into the Distinctive Characteristics of the Aboriginal Race in America," second edition, Philadelphia, 1844.

"Some Observations on the Ethnography and Archeology of the American Aborigines." "American Journal of Science," 1846.

"Catalogue of the Skulls of Man and the Inferior Animals, in the Collection of Samuel George Morton, M. D." Third edition, Philadelphia, 1849.

"Additional Observations on Hybridity in Animals, etc." A reply to the objections of Rev. John Bachman, D. D., Charleston, 1850.

"Notes on Hybridity," Philadelphia, 1851.

C. R. B.

For biography see
Wood, G. B., Memoir of S. G. Morton. Read before the College of Physicians of Philadelphia, Nov. 3, 1852.
Grant, W. R., Lecture on S. G. Morton. delivered introductory to a course on anatomy and physiology at Pennsylvania College, 1852.
Meigs, C. D., Memoir of S. G. Morton. Read before the Academy of Natural Sciences of Philadelphia, Nov. 6, 1851.
Patterson, H. S., Memoir of S G. Morton in Nott and Gliddon's "Types of Mankind," Philadelphia, 1854.

Morton, William Thomas Green (1819–1868).

The credit of demonstrating the practicability of ether anesthetization must be ascribed to William Thomas Green Morton, dentist, son of a store-keeper farmer in Charlton, Massachusetts. "His first demonstration was made on October 16, 1846, at the Massachusetts General Hospital in Boston, and John Collins Warren, the senior surgeon, was the daring operator to sanction and utilize the experiment. For several years Morton had considered this subject of anesthesia. He had seen nitrous oxide tried and had experimented with sundry substances. C. F. Jackson, the chemist, had encouraged him to employ sulphuric ether which he did by tests on animals, himself and one patient. The achievement was an admirable piece of scientific work for which the man received scant reward. Though he did not discover anesthesia, the profession owes a debt of gratitude to him for seconding the discoverer and risking his reputation and his patient in an unexplored field. Warren died in 1856, having lived to see his son J. Mason Warren associated with himself at the Massachusetts General Hospital."

Morton had his diploma from the Baltimore College of Dental Surgery and entered into dental partnership with Dr. Horace Wells to practise in Boston. In 1844 he married Elizabeth Whitman of Farmington, Connecticut, and that same year studied medicine at Harvard Medical School.

His writings included:

"Morton's Letheon (cautioning those who attempt to infringe on his legal rights)," Boston, 1846.

"Remarks on the Proper Mode of Administering Sulphuric Acid by Inhalation," 1847.

"On the Physiological effects of Sulphuric Ether," 1850.

Surgical Memoirs. J. G. Mumford, 1908.
Trials of a Public Benefactor, N. P. Rice, 1859 (port.).
History of Medicine in the United States. F. R. Packard, 1901.
Historical Material for the biog. of W. T. G. Morton. Benj. Perley Poore, Wash., 1856.
Practitioner, London, 1896, vol. lvii (port.).

Mosher, Jacob Simmons (1834–1883).

Dr. Mosher was born in Coeymans, New York, March 19, 1834. His father of English, his mother of German descent.

In 1853 he entered Rutgers College, where he displayed most remarkable ability; but, owing to various circumstances, he left that institution near the close of his junior year. Shortly afterwards he accepted the position of principal of the Public School No. 1, at Albany, but in 1862, entered the Albany Medical College, from which he graduated in 1863, having made a record in scholarship which has rarely been equalled since. His thesis (on "Diabetes") was original and profound. While still in his student days, he became instructor in chemistry and experimental philosophy in the Albany Academy, and in 1865 was advanced there from the instructorship to the professorship of the same subjects.

1864 saw him surgeon to the Army of the Potomac, and later assistant medical director for the state of New York.

The professorship of chemistry and medical jurisprudence in the Albany Medical College became his in 1865, and, in the same year, the registrarship and librarianship.

To recount the various services of Dr. Mosher would be an almost never-ending task. The operations performed, though many and skillful, constituted only a very small fraction of his service to mankind.

He married, December 30, 1863, Emma S. Montgomery, of Albany, and had four sons and one daughter.

Besides being a man of active life and wide-ranging sympathies, he was an expert in botany, as well as in medicine. A bibliophile, also, he possessed a wonderful library of rare and curious volumes, and was an authority on prints and etchings, of which he had a very large collection. He was also an expert bibliopegist. As an expert witness, he was unsurpassable and yet, busy as he was, his time was ever at the disposal of his friends and the poor.

He died on the morning of August 13, 1883. For several days he had been complaining of pain about his heart, but neither his friends nor himself had suspected anything serious. In the morning, his attendant could not rouse him by the loudest of knocking, and the doctor was found in his bed, dead. A book, one of his cherished volumes, was tightly grasped in his hand. It is related by an intimate friend (and the anecdote is well illustrative of Dr. Mosher's character) that, while the departed doctor's body was lying in state in the parlor of his home, a decrepit woman came into the chamber of death, and "cried to God to bring him back to her and her sick child." "The half crazed woman spoke," this correspondent says, "for thousands who felt the same desolation."

Among the positions held were: surgeon to Gov. Hoffman's staff, with rank of brigadier-general; military superintendent and surgeon in charge of the Albany Hospital for disabled soldiers; surgeon-general for New York; deputy health and executive officer of the port of New York; member of the commission of experts, appointed by Pres. Hays to study the origin and cause of the yellow-fever epidemic; member of the medical and surgical staffs of the Albany and St. Peter's Hospitals; founder, trustee, and professor of the Albany College of Pharmacy; president of the faculty of the same institution; and a member of innumerable medical societies. His most distinguished work by far, however, was done as professor of medical jurisprudence and hygiene in the Albany Medical College. ("Medical Record," New York, 1883, vol. xxiv.)

T. H. S.

Medical Annals, Albany, 1883, iv.
Tr. Med. Soc., N. Y., Syracuse, 1885 (W. G. Tucker, M. D.).

Mott, Alexander B. (1826–1889).

It is always rather a doubtful privilege to be the son of an illustrious father particularly when following in his profession, but Mott the younger was operating with his father when only twenty-four. He was the fourth son and fifth child of Dr. Valentine and Louisa Dunmore Mott and grandson of Dr. Henry Mott, and born in New York City the twenty-first of March, 1826. As a boy he went to Columbia College Grammar School. Then followed five years in Europe with his family, an experience in naval warfare as marine in 1844, and in a mixed pursuance of medicine and business at Havre, France. On returning home he

graduated (in 1850) at the Vermont Academy of Medicine and took his diploma from the New York Medical College. He had been helping his father before graduation and continued to do so, taking charge of and performing most of the operations in the surgical clinics.

In 1851 he married the youngest daughter of Thaddeus Phelps and ten years later, like most doctors, went off to the war as brigade-surgeon, and medical director successively, helping to found the first United States Army General Hospital in New York, in which were received some 4,000 patients. This gave him fine surgical experience—an experience which, coupled to his natural genius, considerably improved the health of New York's citizens. Among other operations, nine times he tied the common carotid; twice exsected the entire ulna, and twice removed the entire lower jaw. He may justly be said to have transmitted to posterity the heritage of a name illustrious in surgery with added memories of fine work. On August 11, 1889, he died at his country house at Yonkers, after a two days' illness from pneumonia.

Among his writings was: "Surgical Operations and the Advantages of Clinical Teaching."

His appointments included: senior surgeon, Mount Sinai Hospital; surgeon, Bellevue Hospital; surgeon, New York State Militia; co-founder and professor of anatomy in Bellevue Hospital Medical College.

There is a portrait in the Surg.-gen. Library, Wash., D. C.
Med. and Surg. Reporter, Phila., 1864-5.

Mott, Valentine (1785–1865).

The dead are often praised more than the living, and many a cry of expostulation, heart-broken sometimes in its appeal for justification, has been uttered by doctors who were allowed no honest joy in their vanquishment of dread disease. So Valentine Mott, a leader in surgery at last, perhaps a little querulously defiantly said: "Men who have never done anything themselves have attempted to rob me of some of my operations, but I stand on the firm and immovable rock of truth, and none of them make me afraid."

He was born at Glen Cove, Oyster Bay, Long Island, on August 20, 1785, son of Dr. Henry Mott. As a schoolboy he had private tuition in Newtown, Long Island, and then attended medical lectures at Columbia College, working as well under his relative Dr. Valentine Seaman. Like all young doctors who could afford it, he straightway, after graduating M. D. in 1806, went to Europe, first to London, where he saw all the best men at work and became a pupil of Sir Astley Cooper. At Edinburgh he consorted with men like Hope, Playfair and Gregory and wanted afterwards to get into France in spite of the Anglo-Franco War and Napoleon's prohibition against foreigners. He had some idea of smuggling himself over on a small fishing boat, but friends dissuaded him. In the spring of 1809, he returned to New York and, feeling the competency of genius, succeeded in getting permission from the trustees of Columbia College to lecture and demonstrate on operative surgery, being the first in New York to give private lectures.

In 1811, although only twenty-six, he was elected professor of surgery at Columbia College and when the medical faculty of that college and the College of Physicians and Surgeons were united he was soon given the post of professor of surgery. Here he continued until 1826, but, difficulties arising between the professors and trustees on principles of college government, he resigned and with his able associates founded Rutger's Medical College.

The vast reputation which Dr. Mott enjoyed was due mainly to his original operations; his bold carefulness when undertaking that which was entirely new and his great success in rescuing from prolonged suffering the victims of a morbid growth. Many a time was he called upon to perform at midnight by the flickering aid of a candle, operations not only difficult in themselves but dangerous to the patient and without any assistance than that of excited relatives or ignorant friends. So intent was the young professor on practical improvement that in the very face of severe penal laws he went one dark night, dressed as a poor workman and driving a common cart, to a lonely graveyard where his confederates unearthed eleven bodies. He drove back all alone to the Medical College with his perilous load, for he jeoparded not only his professional reputation but his life in order to advance scientific knowledge.

He was the first, or one of the first, in the States to give clinical instruction. When but thirty-three he placed a ligature around the bracheo-cephalic trunk only two inches from the heart for aneurysm of the right subclavian artery for the first time in the history of surgery, and the patient survived twenty-eight days, dying from secondary hemorrhage.

In 1828 he exsected the entire right clavicle for malignant disease, where it was necessary to apply forty ligatures and expose the pleura. He has priority, too, in tying the primitive iliac artery for aneurysm successfully, and early introduced his original operation for immobility of the lower jaw in 1832. In 1821 he performed the first operation for osteosarcoma of the lower jaw and was the first to remove it for necrosis. Sir Astley Cooper said "He has performed more of the great operations than any man living." And all this before anesthetics, when stout arms had to hold down the writhing man and firm strength keep proportionally quiet the shrieking child.

When Rutger's Medical College finally closed in 1831, Mott was re-appointed professor of operative surgery in the College of Physicians and Surgeons, but, his health failing a little, in 1834 he traveled in Europe, Asia and Africa. "It was during these travels that, full of love for his profession and always ready for a surgical operation he tied the carotids of a cock in the valley of the Peneus and sacrificed him to Aesculapius. Mott returned to New York after six years' absence, to meet with a very warm welcome and the offer (accepted) of the surgical chair in the University Medical College. "His experience was so vast, his observations so acute, his enthusiasm for surgery so undying that his lecture hall was always crowded with students and physicians anxious to profit by his teaching." But during his whole career he would never sacrifice a limb for the mere éclat of an operation, but would say to his students, "Allow me to urge you when about to perform an important surgical operation to ask yourselves solemnly whether, in the same situation, you would be willing to submit to it."

Distinguished as a great surgeon he was no less eminent as a consistent Christian and a good loyal citizen.

He died of typho-malarial fever and gangrene of the left leg, resulting from occlusion of the arteries, on April 26, 1865, in the eightieth year of his age.

In consideration of his great merit Mott received many honorary titles, among them: LL. D., University of the State of New York; fellow of the Medical Societies of Louisiana, New York, Connecticut, and Rhode Island; fellow of Imperial Academy of Medicine, Paris; of the Chirurgical Society of Paris; of the Medical and Chirurgical Society of London; of Brussels; of Kings College of Physicians, Ireland, etc.

Among his valuable contributions to surgical literature must be noted:

"Relative Anatomy of the Subclavian Arteries within the Scaleni Muscles."

"Memoirs on Tying the Arteria Innominata."

"On Excision of the Lower Jaw."

"Papers on Ligature of Carotids, Subclavians, External and Internal Iliacs."

"Exsection of Clavicle for Enormous Osteo-sarcoma."

"Essay on Treatment of Ununited Fractures."

"On a Peculiar Tumor of the Skin (Perchadermatocele)."

"On Facture of the Penis."

"On the Effects of Admission of Air in the Veins in Surgical Operations."

"Mott's Velpeau," four volumes, New York, illustrated.

"Mott's Cliniques," 1860.

"Hemorrhage from Wounds and Its Arrest."

Gross, S. D., Memoir of Valentine Mott, Phila., 1868 (with portrait).
Post, A. C., Eulogy on the late Valentine Mott, N. Y., 1866 (with portrait).
Boston M. and S. Jour., 1851, vol. xliii.
Lancet, London, 1865, vol. i.
Med. and Surg. Reporter, Phila., 1864, vol. ii.
Tr. Med. Soc., N. Y., Albany, 1866 (S. B. Gunning).
There is also a portrait in the Surg.-General's Library, Wash., D. C.

Moultrie, James (1793–1869).

Dr. Moultrie was born at Charleston, South Carolina, March 27, 1793, a descendant from Dr. John Moultrie, of Culross, Fife, Scotland, who emigrated to South Carolina prior to 1729. His father was Dr. James Moultrie, a scholarly physician. His early education was received at Charleston, South Carolina, and at Hammersmith, England. Upon returning to America, he began to study medicine with Drs. Barron and Wilson, and graduated from the University of Pennsylvania in 1812.

He was a member of his State Medical Societies; the Société de Médecine de Marseilles; Société Phrénologique de Paris.

Dr. Moultrie began to practise in his native city in 1812, but upon the breaking out of war in 1812, he offered his services and was appointed surgeon in charge of a hospital in Hampstead. On May 22, 1813, he was commissioned by Gen. Joseph Alston, physician of the port of Charleston.

The main energies of his life were spent as a teacher of physiology and in furthering the cause of medical education. As early as 1822 he was in correspondence with Dr. Cooper, president of the South Carolina Medical College, with regard to the founding of a medical college in South Carolina. When the college was finally established at Charleston in 1824 Dr. Moultrie declined a chair upon the ground that, failing to secure an appropriation, the venture could not succeed. In 1833 he accepted the chair of physiology under the new charter, which position he held for many years.

He was one of the delegates from the Medical Society of South Carolina who were sent to Philadelphia in 1847 to join in the organization of a National Medical Association. On account of his active work in this connection he was made one of the vice-presidents, and in 1851, at the Charleston session, he was elected president.

Dr. Moultrie was a man of simple and refined tastes, devoted to agriculture, horticulture, music and the fine arts. In his special sphere he exhibited profound thought and a high degree of analytical power. As a lecturer he preferred to sacrifice beauty of diction to the claims of a minute and detailed presentation of his subject.

He married Sarah Louise Shrewsbury, on November 12, 1818, but had no children, and died on May 29, 1869, of "old age" after an illness of only a few hours.

His chief publications were: an article on the "Uses of the Lymph," published in the first volume of the "American Medical Journal," and an essay on the "State of Medical Education in South Carolina," published in 1836 by the South Carolina Society for the Advancement of Learning.

R. W. JR.

Charleston M. J., vol. xii, 1857.
Tr. Amer. Med. Assoc., Phila., vol. xxix, 1878.

Mower, Thomas Gardner (1790–1853).

Graduating in arts at Harvard College he studied medicine under Dr. Thomas Babbit, of Brookfield, and in 1812 was appointed surgeon's mate in the United States Army and served with distinction on the Canadian frontier. After the War of 1812 he was for several years on duty on the upper Missouri. In 1844 he was elected a member of the American Philosophical Society of Philadelphia. Mower was one of those men who labored earnestly and zealously to advance and elevate the medical department of the army. During the last years of his life he was stationed in New York, where he died December 7, 1853.

A. A.

Necrol. Alumni Harvard Coll., Bost., 1864, Brown, Hist. Med. Dep. Army, Washington, 1873.

Muir, David Holmes (1848–1904).

David Holmes Muir, eldest son of Dr. Samuel Allan Muir, was born at Truro, Nova Scotia, in 1848, practised there all his life, and died there March 11, 1904.

His general education was obtained in his native town, and his professional training was first with his father and afterwards at the College of Physicians and Surgeons, New York, from which he graduated M. D. in 1867. He was a member of the Medical Society of Nova Scotia, and its president in 1879. After graduation he became assistant to his father, and soon had a very large practice of his own, which he retained until compelled to relinquish it through ill health. He married Miss Ritchie, daughter of Hon. J. W. Ritchie, judge in equity, and had two sons.

D. A. C.

Muir, Samuel Allan (1810–1875).

Samuel Allan Muir was born in Scotland in 1810. He practised for a time in Glasgow, Scotland, but mainly at Truro, Nova Scotia.

His professional training was had at Glasgow and at Edinburgh, and he graduated in 1834, with the L. R. C. S. (Edinburgh) and L. C. P. and S. (Glasgow).

He was a member of the Medical Society of Nova Scotia, and its president in 1871. After practising for a while in Glasgow, Scotland, he came to America, but his becoming a practitioner in Nova Scotia may be called rather a matter of accident. He first came to this Province in search of his diplomas which had been stolen from him by a young adventurer.

When he observed that the majority of people in the Province owned a horse and carriage, he judged that the country must be prosperous and a good one to settle in. He soon acquired a very extensive practice and was widely sought as a consultant. He was an excellent surgeon, fertile in resource and prompt in action. In dress he was careless, in manner brusque, in speech caustic, but still he was very popular and greatly respected. His knowledge of anatomy was both extensive and accurate, and he was a good teacher and a favorite preceptor. His favorite studies, outside of professional subjects, were history and metaphysics.

He married a Miss Crowe, of Truro, and had three sons and two daughters, and two of his sons adopted medicine as a profession. In 1875 he died in Truro.

D. A. C.

Muir, William Scott (1853–1902).

William Scott Muir, third son of Dr. Samuel Allan Muir, was born at Truro, Nova Scotia, in 1853, and died there in 1902.

After a good education in the public schools of Truro, he began to study medicine with his father, and continued under the medical faculty of Dalhousie College, Halifax, from which he graduated M. D. and C. M. in 1874. After filling the position of house surgeon at the Provincial and City Hospital, Halifax, and a brief period of practice at Shelburne, Nova Scotia, he went to Edinburgh, where he subsequently took his L. R. C. S. and L. R. C. P.

Returning from Edinburgh to Truro in 1877, he soon acquired an ever-increasing practice. He had one of the best libraries in the Province, and kept well abreast with medical progress. No notice of his career would be at all complete without reference to his work for the Medical Society of Nova Scotia, for under his skillful guidance its active membership more than quadrupled. He also found time to contribute frequently to the medical press, and some of his

communications were of unusual interest. The following are the titles of some of his papers published in the "Maritime Medical News," Halifax: "Cocaine, Its Use and Abuses;" "Fracture of Patella;" "Notes on Midwifery Cases;" "Therapeutics," an address before the Canadian Medical Association; "Thrombosis of the Vulva;" "Tuberculosis of the Arm Cured by an Attack of Erysipelas;" "Infectious Pneumonia;" "Typhoid Fever;" "Presidential Addresses" before the Colchester Medical Society, and before the Maritime Medical Association.

He married Catherine, daughter of Walter Lawson, C. E., of Scotland, and had one son, who graduated M. D. and C. M. in 1906.

He was a member of the Medical Society of Nova Scotia; a member of the Maritime Medical Association, and its president in 1901; vice-president of the Canadian Medical Association in 1890; a fellow of the New York State Medical Society.

D. A. C.

Mundé, Paul Fortunatus (1846–1902).

This foreigner, who took root on American soil and dying left behind a record of fine gynecological and obstetrical work both practical and literary, was a native of Dresden where he was born on September 7, 1846, the son of Dr. Charles and Bertha Von Horneman, daughter of a councillor to the King of Saxony. The elder Mundé, becoming involved in the revolution of 1848, came to the States with his wife and three-year-old boy, and settled in Florence, Massachusetts, and opened a sanatorium. The son went to the famous Boston Latin School, afterwards entering the medical side at Yale University. In 1864 he secured a place as acting medical cadet in the Union Army and began a career which led to his taking part in three most important wars.

After six months' service he studied medicine again, this time at Harvard and graduated with high honors in 1866. The succeeding seven years he spent in

Germany, serving in 1866 as assistant surgeon in the Bavarian Army in the war between Prussia and Austria and gaining the medal of honor for services to the wounded. Three years followed as resident physician at the Maternity Hospital in Würzburg as assistant to Prof. Scanzoni whose gynecological work undoubtedly turned young Mundé towards that specialty.

In 1870 the war flame was again lighted in Europe and this time, as battalion lieutenant-surgeon, Mundé served in the Bavarian ranks for Prussia against the French. In the siege of Paris, while away at headquarters, he was told his field hospital was on fire. He rode back to find two inmates in the top story had been cut off by the flames. Instantly he rushed in and rescued both. For this the Emperor William gave him the iron cross. Such was the receiver's innate modesty that I never knew of this or the Austrian medal until after his death.

Again the soldier turned student, at Heidelberg, Berlin, and Vienna where he spent nearly two years and took the degree of master of obstetrics in 1871. Later he was in London, Edinburgh and Paris seeking all that was new in gynecology and obstetrics, and when in 1873 he returned to America he determined, as soon as he could afford it, to devote himself to these specialties. This same year he married Eleanor Claire Hughes, of New Haven, Connecticut.

In order to occupy his time well while practice came in he, in 1874, took over the editorship of the "American Journal of Obstetrics," and held the position eighteen years. Many of his earlier articles appeared in it and had wide influence in shaping the opnion of the day. When he became secretary to the New York Obstetrical Society he had no official stenographer and relied on his own notes for the accurate and full accounts published. At that time the society was dominated by master minds—Sims, Peaslee, Emmet, Thomas, Jacobi and others. Mundé was rather in ad-

vance of his own set and bridged the gulf between the old and the new. The surgical spirit of the times led him early to surgery and I well remember his first laparotomy (1877), an ovariotomy, of course. He did first what was then considered indispensable—drew off some of the fluid for examination, using a needle, probably far from aseptic, and an old stomach pump, the modern aspirator and antiseptic surgery being then unknown. There was a necessarily fatal result when the tumor was removed but his next case was a success. His next appointment was as assistant surgeon to the Woman's Hospital under Dr. Fordyce Barker, but this did not give him enough surgery. He found more when he became gynecologist in 1881 to the Mount Sinai Out-door Department where most of his surgical work was done. When the American Gynecological Society was formed in 1876, he was successively treasurer, vice-president and president. Other honors came upon him. He was president of the New York Obstetrical Society; vice-president of the British Gynecological Society; member of the German Gynecological Society; consulting gynecologist to the St. Elizabeth Hospital, and to the Italian Hospital.

Mundé's valuable literary contributions comprise more than 100 articles on gynecologic and obstetric subjects covering a period of thirty years. His book, "Minor Surgical Gynecology," 1880, had a second edition in 1885. His "Diagnosis and Treatment of Obstetric Cases by External Examination and Manipulation" came out in 1880; his last and greatest work was the re-writing and editing of "A Practical Treatise on the Diseases of Women" by Gaillard Thomas. The articles of which a full list is given by me in the "Transactions of the American Gynecological Society," 1902, vol. xxvii, under his name, included:

"The Diagnosis and Treatment of Obscure Pelvic Abscess in Women, etc.," 1880.

"The Curability of Uterine Displacements," 1881.

"A Year's work in Laparotomy," 1882.
"A Rare Case of Adeno-myxosarcoma of the Cervix Uteri," 1889.
"Flap Splitting Operation for Lacerated Perineum," 1889.
"Premature Delivery of a Dead Child Induced by Acute Appendicitis," 1894.
"Mental Disturbances in the Female Produced and Cured by Gynecological Operations," 1897.
"A Case of Aneurysm of the Uterine Artery Cured by Ligation of the Internal Iliac Artery," 1898.

As a lecturer Mundé was a fluent and interesting speaker, not a great orator, but one who commanded attention by the forceful way in which he put facts founded on personal experience. Dartmouth College appointed him professor of gynecology, a position he held for twenty years, lecturing in the summer. She also gave him her LL. D.

Of his personal character, he was devoted to his family, loyal to his friends, and had a love of truth which dominated all his actions and, through him, all those who were trained under his care.

M. D. M.

Tr. Am. Gynec. Soc., Phila., 1902, vol. xxvii, portrait (M. D. Mann).
Am. Jour. Obstet., N. Y., 1902, vol. xlv. W. M. Polk.
Boston Med. and Surg. Jour., 1902, vol. cxlvi.
Gaz. de Gynéc., Paris, 1902, vol. xvii.
Gynaekologia, Budapest, 1902, vol. xxvi, Temesváry.
N. Y. Jour. Gynec. and Obstet., 1893, vol. iii.
Portrait also in the Surg.- gen. Lib., Wash., D. C.

Munn, William Phipps (1864-1903).

Physician, surgeon, writer, his father, Dougald, of the Clan Campbell, a weaver by trade, came to America in 1845, settling first in Cincinnati and later in Pittsburg. His mother was a McCall; her people emigrated from Dumfries in 1820 and were among the early settlers of Pittsburg. Henry Phipps, founder of the Tuberculosis Institute of Philadelphia, is one of the family.

After a preliminary education in the schools of Pittsburg, Munn entered the medical department of the University of Michigan, whence he graduated in 1886. Slim in figure, sandy in complexion and with unlimited "sand" in his disposition, Munn already showed the bent of his nature.

On November 8, 1888, he married Adelaide E. Barrett, of Pennsylvania. His medical practice in Pittsburg had just become well established when signs appeared of the pulmonary trouble which finally caused his death. He removed to Denver in the fall of 1890. Without friends, or money, or experience, or good health Munn so impressed the influential members of the profession that when, in 1891, the Denver Health Department was reorganized under Dr. Henry K. Steele, he was chosen to be one of two assistant commissioners. Those were great times in the sanitary history of Denver. For the first time the interests of public health were intelligently and conscientiously studied. In the division of duties in the Health Department the department of contagious diseases was assigned to Munn. Dr. Munn was the first physician in Colorado to employ antitoxin in the treatment of diphtheria, and he recognized also the dangers of implanting an indigenous tuberculosis through the presence of invalids seeking Colorado for the benefits of the climate; therefore he led in the organization of a society for the control of tuberculosis long before there was any general national awakening on the subject. In 1893 Dr. Dunn was appointed a member of the Colorado State Board of Health, to serve six years. But time and again it was found that the sanitary recommendations first made by Munn were thought too radical to be practicable, yet were afterwards adopted.

Though devoted to the public health service, Munn found it necessary to give attention to private practice; his chosen field being genito-urinary surgery, in which he secured an enviable distinction. He was elected president of the Denver Arapahoe County Medical Society in

1894 and president of the Colorado State Medical Society in 1900. He paid the cost of the strenuous life, for while his energies were diverted from consideration of his own health, the insidious disease which had first ostracised him to Denver made secret strides and, after a series of hemoptyses, he died, in the flower of his age, on March 12, 1903.

H. S.

Munro, John Cummings (1858–1910).

A Franklin medal scholar and graduate of the Boston Latin School, J. C. Munro entered Harvard University in 1877, graduated in 1881, and received the M. D. from Harvard Medical School four years later. Establishing himself in general practice in Boston, he soon began to specialize in surgery, developing a rare skill which placed him early in his career in the front rank of the profession. Dr. Munro was associated with the Harvard Medical School as assistant in anatomy from 1889 to 1893; assistant demonstrator of anatomy from 1893 to 1894; assistant in clinical surgery from 1894 to 1895; instructor in surgery, 1896 to 1902, and lecturer in surgery, 1903 to 1905. He was keenly interested in the development of surgery, towards which his work was a great contribution. He was surgeon at the Boston City Hospital, 1893 to 1903; consulting surgeon, St. Luke's Home, 1901; special consulting surgeon, Quincy Hospital, 1902; consulting surgeon, Framingham Hospital, 1905; and surgeon-in-chief, Carney Hospital, 1903. He was a member of the Association of American Anatomists, American Surgical Society, Clinical Surgical Society, of which he was president in 1905, and member of the Southern Surgical and Gynecological Association.

He died at his home in Boston, December 6, 1910, from recurrent cancer, for which operation had been performed three years before.

Munro will best be known for his surgical clinic at the Carney Hospital instituted in 1903, which was the first permanent surgical service to be established in New England. His work there served a most useful purpose in various ways. It demonstrated the possibility of doing satisfactory surgery, successful in its results, with simplicity of plant and technic and with a minimum of red tape. In its instruction, it had to do with and reached not so much the undergraduate in medicine as the general practitioner, the worker in the surgical field, the visitor in search of sensible ideas and their application in the field of surgery. Dr. Munro was well known both in this country and abroad. His contributions to the literature of surgery were numerous and on a variety of subjects. His skill as a surgeon was acknowledged by all. ·Back of it, however, and revealed to but few, were qualities of mind and heart that deserve more admiration than his skill and made the man even greater than the surgeon. Munro was keen in observation of men and their methods, he was always charitable in his judgments of both. Traveled, well versed in general literature, appreciative of art in all its aspects, he made a most charming companion. His influence on his fellows was wide and stimulating. A hard worker himself, he incited younger men to action, and his hand was ever ready to aid and to encourage them.

J. Am. M. Assoc., 1910, lv.

Munson, Eneas (1734–1826).

Organizer of the Connecticut Medical Society, clergyman, a physician renowned for knowledge of materia medica and the natural sciences, Eneas Munson was born in New Haven, June 13, 1734, the eldest child of Benjamin Munson, a mechanic and whilom schoolmaster.

He graduated from Yale in 1753, and immediately after taught school in Northampton; studying also divinity, he was soon licensed to preach. In 1755 he acted for a short time as domestic chaplain for the Gardiner family of "Gardiner's Island." Hard study (so-called) and insufficient exercise, however, soon broke his health, so he relinquished the ministry for medicine, studying under the Rev. John Darbe, of Oyster Ponds, Long Island, and first settled in Bedford, New York, as a physician. Two years later he removed to New Haven to spend the remaining sixty-six years of his life as a physician of great eminence in his native town.

He was among the first to endeavor to incorporate the Connecticut Medical Society, which he served as first vice-president for two years, or, until, by the death of its president, he succeeded to the presidency. This office he held for seven years. The degree of M. D. was conferred upon him by the society in 1794. "It is generally believed that, up to the early part of the present century (*i. e.*, nineteenth) Dr. Munson was the ablest physician who ever practised for a long time in New Haven. In the matter of professional learning and scientific information, he ranked with the eminent men of his country."

On account of his knowledge of mineralogy, chemistry, botany and materia medica he had a wide reputation, which led to his selection to fill the chair of materia medica and botany in 1810, in the newly established medical institution at Yale, although he was then seventy-nine years old. He was, consequently, unable to perform the active duties of this office, which he left to his younger associate, Dr Eli Ives.

His quaint dry humor still survives in many amusing anecdotes. Bronson relates that "he was once dining with the Yale corporation at commencement dinner when Pres. Dwight, who was a good trencherman, remarked, preparatory to some observation on diet: 'You observe, gentlemen, that I eat a great deal of bread with my meat.' 'Yes,' said the doctor instantly, 'and we notice that you eat much meat with your bread.'"

He married first Susanna, eldest daughter of Stephen and Susanna (Cooper) Howell, on March 15, 1761, and had nine children, all of whom reached adult life, and one of them practised medicine for a short while. His wife

dying on April 21, 1803, he married again in November, 1804, Sarah, widow of Job Perit, and daughter of Benjamin and Mary Sanford, of New Haven. She survived him three years.

His death was due to an enlarged prostate, and occurred on June 16, 1826, at the age of ninety-two. His portrait is in the possession of Yale University and an engraving from it is to be seen in Thacher's "Medical Biography." His writings consist of a report of two cases in "Cases and Observations by the Medical Society of New Haven County, New Hampshire," 1788, pp. 25–28, 84–86, and "A Letter on the Treatment most Successful in the Cure of Yellow Fever in New Haven," in 1794; on a collection of papers on the subject of " Bilious Fevers," by Noah Webster, New York, 1796.

W. R. S.

Bronson, H., N. H. Colony, Hist. Society's Papers, ii.
Dexter, F. B., Yale Biographies and Annals, ii.
Thacher, J., American Med. Biography, i.
Bacon, F., Some Account of the Medical Profession in New Haven.

Murdoch, James Bissett (1830–1896).

His father was the Rev. David Murdoch, D. D., who came from Scotland to Canada as a missionary of the London Colonial Missionary Society in 1832, his mother, Elizabeth Bissett, of Glasgow, Scotland, himself being born in Glasgow, October 16, 1830, and brought to America when a child.

His boyhood was passed in Bath, Canada, and in Catskill, New York, his early education received in these places and in Kinderhook Academy. Some months were spent in Dr. Doane's drug store in Catskill, New York, and later he studied under Dr. William Wey, of Elmira, afterwards going to the College of Physicians and Surgeons in New York, whence he graduated in 1854 and later served as resident physician in Bellevue Hospital.

Dr. Murdoch was a member of the Oswego County (New York) Medical Society and its president in 1865, also a member of the New York State Medical Society. A member of the Allegheny County (Pennsylvania) Medical Society and its president in 1885, and a member of the Pennsylvania State Medical Society, of which he was president in 1888. After serving as resident physician in Bellevue Hospital, New York, in 1885, he was surgeon on the steamship "North Star," a vessel sailing between New York City and Havre. After a year so spent he practised in Oswego, New York, where he remained until 1872, with the exception of the four years from 1861 to 1865, during which he served in the army, being present at the battles of Bull Run, Falmouth, etc. In 1872, Dr. Murdoch moved to Pittsburg, the scene of his greatest professional activity. From 1872 until his death Dr. Murdoch was attending surgeon to the Western Pennsylvania Hospital. On the organization of the Western Pennsylvania Medical College in 1887, he became clinical professor of surgery and also dean of the college, which positions he held until shortly before his death. In 1861 he married Jane Pettibone, of Oswego, who died four years later leaving him one son. In 1868 he married Jennie Moorhead, youngest daughter of the late Gen. James K. Moorhead, of Pittsburg, by whom he had two sons and two daughters. The only member of the family who followed the profession of medicine was Dr. J. M. Murdoch, of Polk, Pennsylvania. He was a frequent contributor to the medical journals of the country on surgical subjects. Dr. Murdoch was an ardent advocate of the "torsion of arteries" for the arrest of hemorrhage in surgical operations. He died October 29, 1886, at Pittsburg, the cause of death being diabetes.

A. K.

Stone's Biographies of Eminent American Physicians and Surgeons.
A portrait of Dr. Murdoch is in the Western Pennsylvania Medical College and in the rooms of the Allegheny County Medical Society, in Pittsburg.

Murdoch, Russell (1839–1905).

Russell Murdoch was born in Baltimore, February 12, 1839, but much of his early life was spent in Scotland, and his collegiate education received at Edinburgh University (1856–59), yet he returned to this country to study medicine at the University of Virginia, where he graduated in 1861. Soon after, he became resident physician at the Baltimore Almshouse, and later (1862) attending physician to the Baltimore General Dispensary. In 1862 he was appointed surgeon in the Confederate Army and served in the engineer corps until the close of the war. He was with Gen. Lee at the surrender at Appomattox.

After the war he took up the study of ophthalmology in America and abroad, and, returning to Baltimore, became lecturer on diseases of the eye and ear at the University of Maryland (1868–69). About this time Dr. Agnew invited him to come to New York as his associate, but he declined.

He was one of the founders of the Baltimore Eye, Ear and Throat Charity Hospital in 1862, and an attending physician until his death, for several years professor of ophthalmology and otology at the Woman's Medical College of Baltimore (1884–87), and was elected a member of the American Ophthalmological Society, July 21, 1868.

He was married in 1873 and had four daughters, all of whom became medical missionaries to China.

He was in active ophthalmic practice until the time of his death. On March 18, 1905, he performed a cataract operation. After its completion, while speaking to a colleague, he suffered an attack of apoplexy, at first very slight, it increased in severity, and he died in a few hours.

This is a meagre outline of the life of a man who in many ways was remarkable. He was many sided. Well trained in the natural sciences, especially in zoology and botany, he took an active and continued interest in the Maryland Academy of Sciences until his death. His special studies were in the comparative anatomy of the eye, a subject upon which he was an authority.

He had great artistic talents to which his works in sculpture testify. Several reliefs which he executed are well known in his community and highly prized. His inventive skill produced a number of very useful instruments, the best known of which is his eye speculum; an enlarged form of this he devised as a mouth-gag.

He was an able and successful operator, and was one of the few men of his years who was ready to apply rigidly the rules of asepsis. In his relation to patients, public as well as private, his gentleness and kindness and patience were extreme.

He was a spiritual man and a member of the Presbyterian Church, to which he devoted much time. But though intensely religious he was very tolerant of the views of others. His great familiarity with the Bible was a constant source of wonder to his friends.

H. F.

Obit. by Friedenwald, Trans. Am. Ophth. Soc., 1905.

Murphy, John Alexander (1824–1900).

John Alexander Murphy was born in Hawkins County, East Tennessee, January 23, 1824, the son of Patrick and Margaret (McKinney) Murphy. The father, a native of Ireland, came to this country while a young man, and settled in East Tennessee, where he married Margaret McKinney, whose family came to America after the Covenanter's War in the North of Ireland. Murphy received his education in the public schools and in Cincinnati College, in 1843 beginning to study medicine with Dr. John Pollard Harrison, and graduating in the Medical College of Ohio, 1846, serving afterwards as interne in the Commercial Hospital. He was one of the founders of the Miami Medical College, organized in 1852, and professor of materia medica, therapeutics and medical jurisprudence. In 1853 he went to Europe, and studied in the great hospitals.

When in 1857 the Miami Medical

College was united with the Medical College of Ohio, Dr. Murphy was made professor of materia medica and therapeutics, and in 1865 the Miami Medical College was re-organized, Dr. Murphy being appointed professor of theory and practice.

In association with Drs. George Mendenhall and E. B. Stevens he established and edited the "Medical Observer" until its union with the "Western Lancet." He was until near his death on the staff of the Commercial Hospital and for many years a member of the Ohio State Medical Society, and its president in 1880.

He married November 11, 1862, a daughter of Dr. Samuel G. Menzies, of Kentucky, and had two daughters, Nora and Mary Ann, and a son, Archibald. The latter died at the age of three. Dr. Murphy died in Cincinnati, February 28, 1900.

A. G. D.

Murray, Robert Drake (1845–1903).

Robert Drake Murray, naval surgeon, son of Joseph Arbour and Nancy Drake Murray, was born in Ohio, April 21, 1845, and died on the twenty-second of November, 1903. Although a native of Ohio, he became a Floridian by adoption in the early 70's. He was senior-surgeon in the Public Health and Marine Hospital Service, having entered that department of the government in 1872, his first station being Key West, Florida. He came from a family of Revolutionary fame. Entering the army at the early age of fifteen, in the war between the states, he was several times wounded, and in the last encounter, at the battle of Saltville, Virginia, was so seriously injured that he was left on the field for dead, and was captured and imprisoned at Richmond. In 1865 he began the study of medicine in the Tripler United States Army Hospital at Columbus, Ohio, afterwards became a pupil of J. Augustus Seitz, in Bluffton, Ohio, and later studied under John E. Darby, M. D., of Cleveland. Dr. Murray attended the Cleveland Medical College and in 1868 received his degree, and, after one course at the Jefferson Medical College, he graduated M. D. there. In 1871, having been resident physician to the Philadelphia Hospital for fifteen months, Dr. Murray was appointed assistant surgeon of the United States Navy, 1871–72, and did active work in the United States Marine Hospital Service, being senior surgeon of the service since 1896. He encountered yellow fever during twenty-five summers in over fifty towns and in eleven states, besides on board ship, serving in epidemics of that disease at Key West, Florida, in 1875; at Fernandina, 1877; and New Orleans, 1878; and was secretary of the Thompson Yellow Fever Commission of that year. He commanded the first armed cordon sanitaire in the United States, one hundred miles in length at Brownsville, Texas, 1872. He had command of the district of South Mississippi during the epidemic of 1897, and served as an inspector to decide on the character of cases of fever during much of 1898 and 1899. Among the public positions held by Dr. Murray were those of postmaster of Bluffton, Ohio; demonstrator of anatomy, Cleveland Medical College, 1868–70; and in the Philadelphia School of Anatomy, 1869–71; Florida Medical Association (of which he was president in 1873); Medical Society of the State of Tennessee; Medico-Legal Society of New York; Philadelphia Hospital Medical Society (of which he was president in 1870); and Association of Military Surgeons of the United States. He wrote a number of works of value, principally devoted to the specialty which constituted his life work. Among these are the "History of Yellow Fever in Key West in 1875," "Report on the Fernandina Epidemic of Yellow Fever," "Treatment of Yellow Fever," and numerous official reports and tracts. He deserves the credit of writing the first letter in 1873, which led to the organization of the Florida Medical Society in the following year. In 1875 he married Lillie, daughter of the Rev. C. A. Fulwood, D. D., at Key West, Florida. She died at Ship Island Quarantine, 1887, leaving five children, Gillie, Rebah, Karlie, Robert Fulwood and Joseph Arbour. Dr. Murray died on the twenty-second of November, 1903, at Laredo, Texas, from injuries received in a runaway accident, eight days previously. He had been ordered from Key West to Laredo, Texas, in the latter part of September to settle disputes of diagnosis arising over an outbreak of "fever" along the Texan border of the Rio Grande River, and which was variously termed "dengue," "jaundice," and "malaria." His reputation as a diagnostician was worldwide, and because of this knowledge he was always chosen and ordered to points where such skill was demanded, especially was he an expert in his knowledge of tropical diseases, such as yellow fever and malaria. Yellow fever was on the wane, the disease had been conquered and he was at the zenith of fame at the close of a well directed and satisfactorily conducted campaign against a most insidious foe, when he received injuries from which he subsequently died. While his own life from the age of fifteen, when he was wounded in the war, to his death at fifty-eight, was one of constant pain and suffering, yet his own discomforts and troubles were never spoken of by him, for selfishness had no place in his nature. Thus was the man seen by others; to me he was all of that and a great deal more besides, but here more cannot be said without tearing aside a veil of hallowed memories from a friendship, which a close companionship of over thirty years formed; a friendship commencing at the feet of Esculapias. How many loving recollections does the mention of his name bring up?

"For my boyhood friend hath fallen, the pillar of my trust;

"The true, the wise, the faithful, is sleeping in the dust."

J. Y. P.

From the Report of the State Board of Health, Florida, 1904. Memoirs of Florida.

Mussey, Reuben Dimond (1780–1866).

As a surgeon some of Mussey's surgical exploits have become historical and gained the approval not only in the States but in Europe. The ligature of both carotids in the same patient for the cure of an immense nevus in the scalp, also removal of the scapula with a portion of the clavicle after previous amputation at the shoulder-joint were achievements of a high order. He also antedated Sims in the successful surgical treatment of vesico-vaginal fistula.

He was the son of Dr. John Mussey, of Pelham Township, Rockingham County, New Hampshire, and born on the twenty-third of June, 1780. The story of his youth resembled that of many other doctors, short means, long hours of work on a farm or in teaching to get money for fees, and a brave uphill fight which landed him at Dartmouth College, whence he graduated in 1803, and studied medicine under Dr. Nathan Smith. Dartmouth in after years gave him her LL. D. He took his M. B. in 1805, and in the same year began practice in Ipswich, now Essex, Massachusetts, but went on to his M. D. (University of Pennsylvania) in 1809. While in Ipswich he married Miss Sewall, who survived the marriage only three years. On his return from Philadelphia he settled in Salem, Massachusetts, and in his six years there attained a large practice chiefly obstetrical, but he had already distinguished himself as a surgeon and in 1814 was given the chair of medical theory and practice at Dartmouth. From three professorships offered him in 1837 he accepted that of the Medical College of Ohio and lectured there fourteen years. When the Miami Medical College founded by him was opened he lectured on surgery there for six years, resigning in 1857 and going to Boston where he spent the remainder of his life and died there on June 21, 1886. His second wife was Hetty, daughter of Dr. Osgood, army surgeon. Besides some daughters he had four sons—Charles, Reuben B., Francis B., and William H., the last two becoming physicians.

As a man of science he was diligent and deliberate with the most conscientious attention to details. As an operator he was slow and cautious and according to Samuel Gross admitted the human side by praying with and for his patients. He was at issue with Benjamin Rush concerning the non-absorbtiveness of the skin and to prove his theory immersed himself in a strong solution of madder for three hours. He had the satisfaction of detecting madder in the urine for two days, the addition of an alcohol rendering it red. But this bold experimentor nearly killed himself in trying to see whether he could not pass ink by immersing himself in a solution of nutgall and consequently in sulphate of iron. In 1830 and before that Sir Astley Cooper had taught there could be no union after intracapsular fracture, so Mussey set out for England with a specimen showing such a possibility.

His valuable library is now in the Cincinnati Public Library.

His writings included:

"Experiments and Observations on Cutaneous Absorption," 1809, Philadelphia.

"Animalcula in the Atmosphere of Cholera," Cincinnati, 1849.

"Aneurysmal Tumours on the Ear Successfully Treated by Ligation of both Carotids," 1853, and various pamphlets on the subjects of "Drink and Tobacco."

R. D. M.

Address by Dr. A. B. Crosby, 1869, at the Dartmouth Med. Coll.
Life and Times of Reuben D. Mussey, Col. Med. Jour., 1896, vol. xvi.
Jour. Am. Med. Ass., Chicago, 1896.
Cincin. Lancet and Obs., 1866, n. s., vol. ix.
Med. Rec., N. York, 1866, vol. i.
Cincin. Med. Obs., 1866, vol. i.
There is a portrait in the surg.-gen. Collection, Washington, D. C., and a bust, by Frankenstein, over his tomb.

Mussey, William Heberden (1818–1882).

William H. Mussey, surgeon, son of Reuben D. and Hetty Osgood Mussey, was of French descent and born in Hanover, New Hampshire, September 30,

1818. He went as a boy to Moore's Indian Charity Academy, Hanover, and various other schools, then when twenty-nine gave up a grocery business in Cincinnati and entered the Medical College of Ohio, graduating M. D. in 1848, at the same time studying with his father and practising with him three years.

In 1851 he had a profitable two years in Paris as pupil of Ricord, Trousseau and Bernard, and was elected president of the American Medical Society of Paris, returning to Cincinnati in 1853, and during the war acting as surgeon to St. John's Hospital for Invalids. He with Cincinnati business men organized also what was perhaps the first voluntary military hospital in wartime.

After serving in various positions during those dark days he was associated with Gen. I. F. Wilder and in 1862 became medical inspector in the United States Army and lieutenant-colonel. When a year later his health broke down he went back to Cincinnati and held the chair of operative and clinical surgery in the Miami Medical College, being also later surgeon-general for the state of Ohio with the rank of brigadier-general.

Most of his writings were published in medical journals, specially the "Western Lancet" and "Medical Observer," of which he edited the surgical columns. But his best gift to Cincinnati was that of 5,000 volumes and 2,500 pamphlets as a nucleus of the Mussey Medical and Scientific Library as a memorial of his celebrated father.

On May 5, 1857, he married Caroline Webster, daughter of Dr. Harvey Lindsay, of Washington, D. C., and had two children, one of whom, William, became a doctor.

Dr. Mussey's death came very suddenly. He operated at the Cincinnati Hospital on the morning of July 31, 1882, and spent some hours afterwards with his patients. But in the afternoon he was stricken with paralysis and never regained consciousness, but died the next day.

R. D. M.

Hartwell (Edward Mussey). A memorial Sketch of W. H. Mussey, Baltimore, 1883. Repr. from Ann. Soc., Army of Cumberland, 1882.
Repr. Cincin. Hosp. (1883), xxiii, ii, port.

Mütter, Thomas Dent (1811–1859).

A museum bequeathed, a lectureship founded, a life well lived and skill as an anatomist shown make Thomas D. Mütter worthy of remembrance.

He came of German and Scotch ancestry, the son of John and Lucinda Gilles Mütter, his ancestors had settled in North Carolina, in ante-Revolution days. Thomas was born in Richmond, Virginia, in March, 1811. But at eight he was an orphan and a relative had him educated at Hampden Sidney College, afterwards placing him with a Dr. Simms of Alexandria. When twenty he took his M. D. from the University of Pennsylvania, but, it was overwork perhaps, his health failed and he went as surgeon on the corvette Kensington, bound for Europe. He is next seen eagerly studying the methods of master minds at European clinics.

While making a reputation as a public teacher in the medical institute, he achieved a high reputation as a practical surgeon, as attested by his large clientèle among the citizens and the strangers from various parts who sought from his skill the relief which their various sufferings demanded. The subjects of clubfoot and its analogous class of affections about the joints; the deformities resulting from burns, with the institution of a plastic treatment for their relief of a bold, original, and most successful character, and the reparation of the innumerable disfigurations that arise from the loss or distortion of parts, had already administered greatly to his renown as a surgeon, and exercised his abilities as an author.

In the thorough re-organization of the faculty of Jefferson Medical College which took place in 1841, he was promoted to a higher place of usefulness and honor by an appointment to the professorship of surgery in that institution.

From this date began the halcyon

period of Prof. Mütter's career as a surgeon. From year to year his efforts increased, and his ambition expanded with success that followed his elevation. From the vantage ground which he then occupied, he could see that a field for honorable distinction was spread immeasurably before him. The toil of constant preparation, the task of daily appearance before his class in this arena, putting on and off his armor, and his exercise under it in the field, seemed not to oppress or weary him.

Sir William Fergusson, writing in 1867, says " the greatest success recorded before my own views were made public was that achieved by Mütter, of Philadelphia, who operated successfully on nineteen out of twenty cases of harelip."

"After he became a teacher," says in no unkindly tone Dr. S. D. Gross, "Mütter loved to refer to these men (Dupuytren, Louis, Liston) as his 'friends' and to hold them up to the admiration of his pupils. Like most of the young doctors who went abroad he considered one Frenchmen equal to a dozen Americans."

The failing health of Dr. Thomas Harris made him select Mütter as associate in a summer school of medicine called the Medical Institute, and meanwhile his skill in the special diseases studied abroad brought him private practice. 1841 saw him occupying the chair of surgery in Jefferson Medical College. He carefully prepared himself, whether for lectures or cases, even in the minutest points and then with equal skill and firmness, with a sparkling eye and dilating faculties, advanced to his task. He had a beau ideal of the art of surgery. One weakness—though almost a laudable one —was his great desire to lead and to have personal influence. One of his biographers says he would occasionally adopt the old method of being called out of church or of making an appointment for a pseudo operation with his students, by whom he was adored.

In 1856 a complication of gout and lung disease forced him to resign his chair, though at once elected emeritus professor by the faculty. A winter sojourn at Nice did not fulfill his expectations and he returned in 1858 and passed the next winter at the Mills House, Charleston, with his devoted wife, but his disorders returned and he died there in 1859, leaving a young wife but no children.

His generous gift of his museum to the Philadelphia College of Physicians, with $30,000 for upkeep and a lectureship in connection with it will form his best monument now that new men and new methods are in the field of surgery, some of them ignorant of their obligations to the learning and hard work of the men of Mütter's day.

He was not fond of writing and a somewhat loosely written treatise on "Clubfoot" and his edition of "Liston's Operative Surgery" only remain, nor, oddly, did he ever hold any hospital appointment.

Autobiography, S. D. Gross, Phila., 1887.
Hist. of Med. in Phila., F. P. Henry, Chicago, 1897.
Address by Prof. Pancoast on Mütter, Phila., 1859.

N

Nancrede, Joseph Gerrard (1793–1857).

Joseph Gerrard Nancrede was born in Boston in 1857. His father, Paul J. G. de Nancrede, was an officer under Rochambeau. The boy had his early education in a Catholic seminary in Montreal, where he started a lifelong intimacy with Papineau, who afterwards played so conspicuous a part in Canadian politics. Thence he went to Paris, where he received his collegiate education and studied medicine. On returning to his native country he attended the medical lectures at the University of Pennsylvania, and in 1813 obtained his M. D. Thus qualified, he began to practice in Louisville, Kentucky, but soon returned to Philadelphia, where he spent the remainder of his life. In 1822 he married a daughter of Com. Truxton; her death preceded his own by eight years.

At a very early date he was associated with his elder brother, Dr. Nicholas C. Nancrede, in bringing out a translation of Legallois' "Experiments on the Principles of Life," etc.; afterwards he made a translation and abridgment of Orfila's work on "Toxicology." He wrote occasional papers for the medical journals; of these, one was on "Mania a Potu," in the first volume of the "Medical Recorder"; another, "An Account of the Doctrine of Fevers," by Broussais, in the eighth volume of Chapman's "Philadelphia Journal." In the fourteenth volume of this work appeared his Memoir of Dr. Mongez; and in the sixteenth of the "American Journal of Medical Sciences," "Observations on a Case of Cesarean Operation," occurring in his own practice, in which both mother and child were preserved. He was instrumental in procuring the first use to be made here of Monoesia. He was also active in causing trials to be made of the sphygmometer,

and translated an account of its use and application.

Nancrede died on the second of February, 1857, in his sixty-fourth year, of phthisis pulmonalis. He died as he lived, in the communion of the Roman Catholic Church, leaving, in default of issue, his estate to his adopted son, Dr. Samuel J. G. Nancrede.

From the N. Amer. Med.-Chir. Rev., 1857, vol. i.

Neilson, William Johnston (1854–1903).

He was born in Perth, Ontario, March 4, 1854; his father, Cornelius Neilson, emigrated from Ireland in 1818. His mother, Eleanor Moorehouse, was born in Ontario, of Irish parents.

He went as a lad to the Perth public and grammar schools, and his medical course was had in McGill University, Montreal, where he took the M. D., and C. M., in 1878, after a very brilliant career as a student.

He practised for a short time at Parkdale, Ontario, and Hastings, Minnesota, then went to Winnipeg in 1881, where he lived until his death. He was chosen professor of anatomy in Manitoba Medical College in 1888, and was also a member of the staff of the Winnipeg General Hospital from 1892 onwards. He died on the evening of a large political gathering in the Constituency of North Winnipeg of which he was elector, at the Winnipeg General Hospital, July 17, 1903, of pulmonary abscess.

A painting by V. A. Lang hangs in the library of the College of Physicians and Surgeons of Manitoba, in Winnipeg.

J. H.

Newberry, John Strong (1822–1892).

John Strong Newberry, an eminent scientist of New York City, was born in Windsor, Connecticut, December 22,

1822. While he was yet an infant his father, Henry Newberry, removed to Summit County, Ohio, where he founded the present town of Cuyahoga Falls. The son was educated entirely in Ohio, and graduated in 1846 in the Western Reserve College, located at Hudson. He immediately turned his attention to the study of medicine, attended lectures in the Cleveland Medical College, and received his degree of M. D. there in 1848. The next two years of his life were spent in travel and study in both the United States and Europe, a large part of this period being passed in Paris. In 1851, however, he returned to Cleveland, Ohio, and began to practise, but was too much interested in the natural sciences to enjoy the dull routine of medical practice, and in May, 1855, when offered by the War Department, the position of acting assistant surgeon and geologist of the United States Exploring Expedition under Lieut. R. S. Williamson, designed to explore the region between San Francisco and the Columbia river, a c c e p t e d it without hesitation. In 1857-8 he was again assigned by the War Department to accompany Lieut. J. C. Ives on his exploration of the Colorado river, and his report of the results of this exploration was scarcely completed when he was ordered to join Capt. J. N. Macomb, topographical engineer, United States Army, in a further exploration of the San Juan and upper Colorado rivers. Elaborate and valuable reports of these expeditions were published by the War Department, until the outbreak of the Civil War in 1861 turned the attention of the government to more pressing duties. Soon after the close of the war in 1866 he was called to the chair of geology and paleontology in the School of Mines of Columbia College, New York, and this position he continued to fill with entire success until his death, December 7, 1892.

In 1869 he was called to Ohio as state geologist, to direct the geological survey of the state then ordered. He at once organized the work and directed it with energy and success until its completion in 1875, when he prepared and published valuable reports of the results of his labors. In 1884 he was also appointed paleontologist of the United States Geological Survey, with charge of the fossil fishes and plants.

Dr. Newberry was a member of the Ohio State Medical Society, before which he read in 1852 a paper on "The Specific Identity of Typhus and Typhoid Fevers." Most of his writings were of a geological or paleontological character. He was one of the original corporators of the National Academy of Sciences, president of the New York Academy of Sciences and a member of numerous scientific societies of both this country and Europe.

H. E. H.

Cleave's Biographical Cyclopedia of the State of Ohio, Cuyahoga Co.
A History of Columbia University, University Press, New York, 1904.
A catalogue of the most important scientific writings of Dr. Newberry will also be found in Johnson's Cyclopedia, under his name, and also in the Surg.-general's Cat., Wash., D. C.

Nichols, Charles Henry (1820–1889).

Born on October 19, 1820, at Vassalboro, Maine, Dr. Nichols stood long in the front rank of American superintendents of institutions for insane, and was associated with very much of their work.

He went as a boy to the schools of Maine and Providence, Rhode Island, and afterwards to the Universities of New York and Pennsylvania. He held his M. D. from the latter, also M. A., Union College, and an LL. D. from Columbia College, District of Columbia. His tutorage in ministering to the insane was under Dr. Amariah Brigham in the State Asylum at Utica, New York, where he was chosen medical assistant in 1847. In 1849 he was appointed physician to the Bloomingdale Asylum, New York City, and resigned in 1852.

He was mentioned by Miss Dorothea Dix and selected by Pres. Filmore to superintend the construction and take charge of the government hospital for the insane at Washington. It was a great work, demanding a capable, broad man every way, and the manner in which he administered his trust showed that the president had made no mistake in his choice. He had looked to the end to some purpose; an end that justified all his labors of love; that built twenty-five of the best years of his life into those hospital walls. He saw his plan reproduced in Australia, in Newfoundland, and in many state institutions. At considerable pecuniary sacrifice to himself he doubled the hospital land, he extended its accommodations, he kept the institution in everything abreast of the most enlightened, curative treatment of the time, so that when after a quarter of a century they called him back to Bloomingdale Asylum, creating the office of medical superintendent for him, he left St. Elizabeth's a hospital the most perfect of its kind.

He was, for a succession of years, president of the Association of American Superintendents of Institutions for the Insane. He was also an honorary member of the Medico-Psychological Association of Great Britain. He died on December 16, 1889.

In the jurisprudence of insanity, those who remember the Mary Harris case do not need to be told how he stood. But his principle work was in the daily hospital routine.

D. S. L.

Appleton's Biog., 1888.
Med. Record, N. York, 1889, vol. xxxvi.
Amer. Jour. Insanity, 1889, vol. xliv.

Nichols, James Robinson (1819–1888).

James Robinson Nichols, son of Stephen and Ruth Nichols, was born at West Amesbury, Massachusetts, July 19, 1819; the first years of his life being spent on a farm, until, in his eighteenth year he worked with his uncle, a druggist in Haverhill. After three years, he entered the medical department of Dartmouth College. His course here was interrupted by illness and the degree conferred on him was by courtesy in recognition of scientific work. Being, by illness, obliged to

give up active practice Dr. Nichols returned to the drug business in Haverhill and gave his time to lecturing and chemistry. In 1856 he established a laboratory in Boston where for sixteen years he worked successfully. His next venture was an experimental farm near Haverhill. As a member of the Board of Agriculture, Dr. Nichols was able to give practical help to the farmers of the state. He was also a member of the Massachusetts Medical Society. The " Boston Journal of Chemistry," later called the "Popular Science News," was founded by Dr. Nichols in 1866. His writings include: "Chemistry of the Farm and Sea," 1867; "Fireside Science," 1872, and "Whence, What and Where," 1883.

He married Harriet Porter in 1844, and Margaret Gale in 1851. After a long illness from chronic gastric disturbance he died at Haverhill, on January 2, 1888.

M. K. K.

Personal communication, Austin P. Nichols.
Boston Med. and Surg. Jour., 1888, vol cxviii.

Nickles, Samuel (1833–1908).

Samuel Nickles was born in Cincinnati, Ohio, August 8, 1833, the son of Francis and Mary Winkerman Nickles, of Berne, Switzerland, who came to Cincinnati just before his birth. Owing to the death of his father while he was still an infant, Samuel's early years were passed in comparative poverty, but the sterling qualities of his mother, coupled with the lad's insatiable thirst for knowledge led him to gain a good common school education.

Later, while supporting his mother and sisters as an employé in various mercantile houses he devoted all his spare time to studying medicine. German was to him as his mother tongue.

In 1856 he graduated from the Eclectic Medical Institute in Cincinnati; in 1862 he served as surgeon to the Eighty-first Ohio Reserve Militia, and in 1865 graduated from the Medical College of Ohio, and was at once appointed its demonstrator of anatomy, a position held until 1869, when he was made professor of medical chemistry. In 1874 he was given the chair of materia medica and therapeutics. This he held until 1898, when he was made professor emeritus, and retired from active teaching. He was known among the students as "dear old Sammy Nickles." His life was epitomized by his clinical assistant, Dr. T. W. Hays, as follows: "Attention to duty, honesty, conscientiousness." In 1885 he became president of the Academy of Medicine of Cincinnati. While in active practice he contributed to it a great many excellent papers. He was a voluminous writer. In 1868 he translated the second German edition of Emil Siegle's "Treatment of Diseases of the Throat and Lungs." The following articles in the "Reference Handbook of the Medical Sciences" are from his pen:

"Cholagogues," vol. iii.
"Diuretics," vol. iii.
"Emetics," vol. iii.
"Expectorants," vol. iv.
"Hypnotics," vol. iv.
"Laxatives," vol. v.
"Cathartics," vol. vi.
"Tonics," vol. vii.

Of his contributions to periodical literature the "Index Medicus" lists the following:

1881. "The Modus Operandi of Cod-liver Oil." ("Cincinnati Lancet and Clinic," vol. vi.)

"Modern Therapeutics," ibid., vol. vii.

1884. "Digitalis, its Pathological Action." ("American Journal Medical Sciences," n. s., vol. lviii.)

1892. "Calomel as a Diuretic." ("Ohio Medical Journal," vol. iii.)

On August 8, 1858, he married Alice Bilmer, of Cincinnati, and had six children; Mrs. Nickles died December 27, 1869.

Only two children survived their father. On March 15, 1871, Dr. Nickles married Mrs. Caroline (Dick) Weglan, and had two more children. Dr. Nickles died April 21, 1908, the result, primarily, of an attack of influenza in the latter part of January.

A. G. D.

Norcom, William Augustus Blount (1836–1881).

He was born in Edenton, May 24, 1836, the youngest son of Dr. James Norcom, a learned physician of that place. His early education was at home with his father but he afterwards went to the Edenton Academy. He did not receive a college course and graduated in medicine from the University of Pennsylvania in 1857, afterwards settling in his native town. When the Civil War broke out he was appointed assistant surgeon in the hospital at Petersburg, Virginia.

He was president of the Medical Society of North Carolina in 1874, and a member of the Board of Examiners from 1872 to 1878. His presidential address on "Malarial Hemorrhagic Fever" was a valuable contribution to the literature of that disease. Another of his comprehensive papers was "The Modern Treatment of Acute Internal Inflammation" (1868). Dr. Norcom was particularly noted for his scholarly attainments and the wonderful powers of memory. Page after page of his favorite authors he could repeat by heart. He lived in an atmosphere of medical events and was said to be more enthusiastic about medicine than ardent in its practice. He died in St. Vincent's Hospital, Baltimore, February 28, 1881.

H. A. R.

Transactions Medical Society of N. C., 1881. Personal communications from Miss L. T Rodman and Dr. Richard Dillard.

Norris, William Fisher (1839–1901).

William Fisher Norris, born in Philadelphia, January 6, 1839, was the son of Dr. George W. Norris, an eminent surgeon. The son took the degree in arts at the University of Pennsylvania in 1857, and the medical one in 1861, afterwards spending eighteen months at the Pennsylvania Hospital as resident physician. Some phases of his character are well illustrated by a stirring episode occurring during his residency, which he related to me many years later. Hearing an unusual commotion in one of the wards, he entered and found the nurses and many of the patients fleeing in dismay before a stalwart and violent lunatic who had entered the opposite end of the ward with a huge cleaver in his upraised hand. No sooner did he see the young doctor dressed in his ward coat, than he ran violently with this weapon raised to brain him. Dr. Norris awaited calmly his rapid approach and, as the blow descended, with quick eye, firm and accurate hand, grasped the wrist with the unyielding, paralyzing grasp of the trained athlete, and at the same time tripped the feet of the man, pinioned his arms, and so held him until help arrived and he was placed in a straight-jacket.

After this service he became assistant surgeon in the United States Army, and was in charge of Douglas Hospital at Washington, where he served until 1865 with distinguished merit. He visited Europe in 1865, spending most of his time with Arlt, Jaeger, and Mauthner in Vienna. He also worked with Stricker on experimental pathologic histology of the cornea, the results of which were published jointly. In 1870 he returned to Philadelphia, became lecturer in ophthalmology and otology at the University of Pennsylvania, and soon devoted himself exclusively to ophthalmology, becoming clinical professor of this branch. Later he was honorary professor, and in 1876 full professor of ophthalmology. In 1870, elected a member of the American Ophthalmological Society; in 1884, its president, and in January, 1872, a member of the staff of Wills' Eye Hospital. His writings are not numerous, but have scientific mark. His largest work is his "System of Diseases of the Eye," published conjointly with Dr. Oliver, and his greatest influence can be seen in the large number of distinguished ophthalmologists who owe their training to him.

He was thirty-three years of age, of massive frame, well rounded, not corpulent, a large dome-like head, with the blonde hair of a Norseman, trimmed in the conventional form, a full beard, light in color, fine in texture, a complexion ruddy with the tints of perfect, vigorous health, and a calm benignant manner, striking in one of his age, which found expression largely through his clear blue, unhesitating eyes.

He died November 18, 1901, in Philadelphia.

A list of his papers is given in the Surgeon-general's Catalogue, Washington, District of Columbia.

H. F.

Trans. Am. Oph. Soc., vol. x (port.).
Oliver, C. A., William Fisher Norris, Phila., 1901.
Med. Rec., N. Y., 1901, vol. lx.
N. Y. Med. Jour., 1901, vol. lxxiv.
Phila. Med. Jour., 1901, vol. viii.
Tr. Coll. Phys., Phila., 1902, 3. s., vol. xxiv.
There is a portrait in the surg.-gen. library, Wash., D. C.

North, Elisha (1771-1843).

An early vaccinator, author of the first book on epidemic cerebrospinal meningitis, founder of the first eye dispensary in the United States, Elisha North was born January 8, 1771, in Goshen, Connecticut, and was destined to become one of the pioneers in certain lines of medical research. He early showed a predilection for medicine and at the age of sixteen is said to have cared for a broken leg with rare skill and success. Later he studied medicine with his father, Joseph North, who dabbled somewhat in this science, although his chief occupation was that of farming. Feeling the limitations in this preparation for his future career, the son came to Hartford to study under the then renowned Lemuel Hopkins, and later spent, possibly, two years at the University of Pennsylvania. Returning to Goshen he practised there until his removal to New London, in 1812.

While living in Goshen, 1800, he carefully investigated the utility of vaccination. In the use of vaccine virus he met with considerable opposition at first, but seems eventually to have silenced the hostility of the public, although he claimed his practice of vaccination was not profitable, on account of the many, experienced and inexperienced, who undertook to perform it. Besides being one of the pioneers in the study of vaccination, he early took up the investigation of epidemic cerebrospinal meningitis, when this dread disease appeared in this country, in 1807, coming upon Goshen "like a flood of mighty waters, bringing along with it the horrors of a most dreadful plague." The malady completely mystified and baffled all the physicians who tried to cope with it; they found difficulty in giving it an adequate name; they were unable to classify it; they were at variance as to the best methods of treatment. With commendable care North sought to acquaint the public with this new and dread affection, by giving in book form the views of the various authors in this country upon it, as well as his own. His experience with it was very extensive and his treatment most successful, and though he attended more than 200 patients with it, yet he lost only two. The book was the first volume to be written upon this subject, the disease having been first recognized in Geneva in 1805. In the book, North details the symptoms pretty much as we now know them, including the joint affections. Unfortunately he never published the second edition, although he planned extensive alterations for it some thirty years later.

In 1812, when forty-two, he was invited to remove to the city of New London. The offer was too flattering to decline so he accepted and spent the remaining years of his life in practice there. In 1817 he established, in New London, the first eye infirmary in the United States, which he thus refers to: "We had attended to eye patients before that time, but it occurred to us then that we might multiply our number of cases of that description, and thereby increase our knowledge, by advertising the public in regard to an eye institution. This was done, and we succeeded; although not to our wishes in a pecuniary view of the

case. Our success or exertions probably hastened in this country the establishment of larger and better eye infirmaries (i.e., for larger cities)." North was especially proud of his work, in this specialty, and in the title page of his "Outlines of the Science of Life" we find the words, under his own name, "conductor of an eye infirmary;" elsewhere he writes: "I have had the pleasure to prevent total blindness and restore sight to twelve or thirteen persons, during the last three years. These would now probably be moping about in total darkness, and be a burden to society and to themselves, had it not been for my individual exertions." He was active in the work of the State Medical Society, which conferred upon him the degree of M. D. in 1813. In practice he exhibited a remarkable degree of caution, deliberation and careful reflection. "As a physician he enjoyed the confidence and friendship of his brethren, and was much valued for his philosophical habits of mind in cases of difficulty and uncertainty." His quaint humor is yet preserved in numerous, amusing anecdotes. After his death, the following was found in his ledger:

"Mr. Blank, to doctoring you till you died, $17.50."

His writings consist of twelve titles (Bolton's bibliography); nine of them represent papers in the different daily and medical or scientific journals. In one of them he describes his "Operation of Lithotomy, by the Posterior Method;" another paper is of interest as it details an epidemic of "Typhoid Fever in Goshen. During 1807;" others consider "Hydrocele Capitis Infantum," "Cyanetic Trachealis," "Epidemic Cerebrospinal Meningitis," "Fuel and Phrenology." His three volumes are entitled: (1) "A Treatise on a Malignant Epidemic, commonly called 'Spotted Fever;'" (2) "Outlines of the Science of Life," (3) "The Pilgrims Progress in Phrenology."

He married Hannah, the daughter of Frederick Beach, of Goshen, on December 22, 1797, and had eight children. One of his sons, Ford North, studied medicine but forsook it to teach elocution at Yale and gained some prominence also as a microscopist.

Dr North's death occurred when he had reached the age of seventy-three, on December 29, 1843.

W. R. S.

Bolton, H. C., Memoir of Elisha North, Trans. Conn. Med. Soc., 1887, 135–160. Steiner, W. R., Dr. Elisha North, One of Connecticut's most Eminent Medical Practitioners. Johns Hopkins Hosp. Bull., xix. 1908.

Norwood, Joseph Granville (1807–1895). A noted physician and geologist, he was born in Woodford County, Kentucky, December 20, 1807, on his father's farm, about five miles from Lexington. His father, Charles Norwood, was a native of Westmoreland County, Virginia, and the son of John Norwood, an Englishman, who came to Virginia about 1740. From Joseph's birth it was decided by his father and the attending physician (Dr. Ridgley) that he should study medicine. A strongly expressed desire at this time, suggested by association, to become a printer resulted in his being placed with Mr. Jacob Winn, a banker and manufacturer of bale-rope and bagging with whom he remained a year, who entrusted him for three months with the conduct of his banking business while absent in the East.

It happened that a Mr. Snell visited Lexington, giving illustrated lectures in science, chemistry, electricity, etc., and Joseph conceived a love for experimental science, which could only be satisfied by reading and private study. At last, determining to study medicine, he entered Transylvania Medical School of which Dr. B. W. Dudley was dean and graduated in 1836, with special honors; his thesis "On Spinal Diseases" being published in pamphlet form by the faculty. He now entered into practice and was called, in 1840, to the chair of surgery by the Madison (Indiana) Medical Institute and published "Outlines on a Course of Lectures on the Institutes of Medicine."

1843 saw him elected to the chair of materia medica in the University of St. Louis; he found his work and the investigation of geological problems, to which he had already devoted much time and thought, and had thereby become known to the geologists of this and foreign countries, too great a task for even his iron constitution and, resigning most of his private and public work, he accepted in 1847 the position of chief assistant geologist, on the Geological Survey of the Northwest, ordered by congress, under Dr. D. D. Owen as chief. Two reports on the country, then only known to fur traders and Indians, appeared and received due commendation, leading to his appointment in 1851 as state geologist of Illinois. This position he held till March, 1858, when a political upheaval put a new party into power, and an end to his activity as geologist, for they refused the means to publish any of his reports excepting his "Abstract of a Report on Illinois Coals."

Immediately upon his removal from the directorship of the Illinois Survey, Dr. Norwood was offered the position of assistant geologist of the Missouri Survey which he held two years, when, without having made any application, he was elected to the chair of natural science in the University of Missouri at Columbia, where he henceforth rendered important and highly valued services as teacher and investigator till his death in 1895.

Dr. Norwood was a man of broad and deep scholarship, courteous and dignified, much liked, and, aside from his scientific and professional attainments was well versed in foreign literature, reading German, French and Spanish with ease, and even took up in his eightieth year the study of Dutch to afford him a better insight into its literature than translations could furnish.

A partial list of his publications includes:

1838. "Outlines of a Course of Lectures on the Institutes of Medicine."

1839. "Monograph on Club-foot."

1846. "Description of a New Fossil

Fish from the Palaeozoic Rocks of Indiana."

1846. "Description of a Remarkable Fossil Echinoderm from the Limestone Formation of St. Louis."

1847. "Researches among the Protozoic and Carboniferous Rocks of Central Kentucky."

1848. "First Report as Assistant United States Geologist in Survey of the Northwest."

1852. "Second Report."

1851–1857. "State Geologist of Illinois Reports" (written; but not published).

1854. "Two Palaeontological Papers: 1. Producti with Descriptions of Twelve New Species. 2. Notice of the Genus Chonetes, etc., with Description of Eleven New Species."

1868. "Experimental Exercises and Problems in Elementary Chemistry."

O. F.

Nott, Josiah Clark (1804–1873).

Josiah Clark Nott, the first to do extirpation of the coccyx for inflammation, was born March 31, 1804, in Columbia, Richland District, South Carolina, and died at Mobile, Alabama, March 31, 1873, on his sixty-ninth birthday. He was the son of Abraham Nott, a judge and politician, who was born in Saybrook, Connecticut, in 1767 and died at Fairfield, South Carolina, in January, 1830. Dr. Nott's father was a graduate of Yale College, and studied for the ministry, but did not take orders. Dr. Nott commenced the study of medicine in the office of James Davis, M. D., of Columbia, South Carolina, in 1824, and attended his first course of lectures at the College of Physicians and Surgeons, New York, then situated in Barclay street, in the winter of 1825–26, under Profs. Wright Post, Valentine Mott, John W. Francis, David Hosack, Samuel L. Mitchill, William James Macneven, and a second course at the University of Pennsylvania; graduating thence in April, 1827. He was resident student at the Philadelphia Almshouse from September, 1827, to September, 1828, after which he became demonstra-

tor of anatomy in the University of Pennsylvania, under Profs. Physick and Horner. In 1829 he returned to Columbia, South Carolina, and commenced practice. In 1835 he went to Europe and spent that and the next year visiting the hospitals and studying medicine, natural history, and kindred sciences. In the latter part of 1836 he settled in Mobile, Alabama. In 1857 Dr. Nott was called to the chair of anatomy in the University of Louisiana, · but resigned it after one winter's service to resume his profession in Mobile, and in 1858 founded the Medical School in Mobile, where he lectured two years on surgery, when the college was broken up by the war. Soon after the close of the war he left the South, and in 1867 went to Baltimore, Maryland, remaining one year, and in April, 1868, removed to New York City. Here he soon took a prominent position as an able and accomplished physician and gynecologist. Skene, in his "Diseases of Women" says "coccyodynia" was first described by Dr. Nott in the "North American Medical Journal," May, 1844, but it attracted little attention until 1861, when Sir J. Y. Simpson revived the subject and gave it the name of "coccyodynia." Nott has also an article on "Extripation of Os Coccyx for Neuralgia," in the "New Orleans Medical Journal," 1844–5. He was an untiring student and indefatigable worker, ever ready in public or private to advance science. During his short career in this city, he read numerous papers bearing evidence of a well-trained mind and ripe scholarship. Besides contributing extensively on professional and kindred topics in the medical journals of New Orleans, Charleston, Richmond, Philadelphia and New York, he has published several ethnological works, which have attracted great attention in Europe as well as the United States. Among these are "Two Lectures on the Connection between the Biblical and Physical History of Man" (1849); "The Physical History of the Jewish Race" (1850); "Types of Mankind" (1854); and "Indigenous Races of of the Earth" (1857). The last two were prepared in connection with Mr. George R. Gliddon. The object of these works is to refute the orthodox theory of the unity of the human race, by showing that the present types of mankind lived around the Mediterranean 3,000 B. C., and that there is no evidence that during the last 5,000 years one type has been changed into another.

From the Med. Reg., State of N. York, vol xi., 1873–4.

J. Anthro. Soc., Lond., 1868 (H. R. H. Mackenzie).

Tr. Am. M. Ass., Phila., 1878, vol. xxix (W. H. Anderson).

Tr. M. Ass., Alabama, Montgomery, 1877 (W. H. Anderson).

Nourse, Amos (1794–1877).

Destined to be versatile as a man and as a physician, Amos Nourse was born in Bolton, Massachusetts, was educated at Andover Academy, graduated from Harvard in the class of 1812, and studied medicine with Dr. John Randall of Boston. After some years, during which his career is not discoverable, we find him in 1819 a partner of Dr. Ariel Mann of Hallowell. Here he remained practising until 1844, when, having got into the current of politics, he moved to Bath, Maine, where he was collector of customs for several years.

Side by side with this position, he maintained regular consulting hours, kept up his studies, and, as a result, became known as a good obstetrician, and in 1846 was appointed lecturer on that topic in the Medical School of Maine. He lectured steadily until 1854, when he accepted the chair of medicine in the same school, and filled it until the year 1866. After resigning the position of collector at Bath, he was elected judge of probate of Sagadahoc County, and filled that position for twelve years. To show his versatility, and the general esteem in which he was held, we may mention that in 1861 the governor of Maine appointed him to fill a vacancy in the United States Senate, which he might have held permanently for life had he so desired.

Although not educated for the law, his ability, culture and common sense, his ideas of justice and his impartiality combined with strict integrity fitted him for the faithful discharge of his duty as judge of probate. He was a member of the Maine Medical Society, and later on of the Maine Medical Association, with whose interests he was identified from its formation. His address as president of the association in 1865 was on "The Faults and Defects in the Cultivated of our Profession." In 1864 he wrote for the "Boston Medical and Surgical Journal" a paper on "Menstruation."

As a teacher, his instruction was sound, and he was particularly noted for his personal interest in seeing that pupils understood what he said. If he discovered in conversation that he had not been understood, he improved his lecture at the next opportunity.

Amos Nourse had one or more strokes of paralysis at a good old age and died after what might be called an illness lingering but not painful. He passed away at Bath, April 7, 1877, aged eighty-two, revered and honored.

J. A. S.

Trans. Maine Med. Assoc., 1877.

Noyes, Henry Dewey (1832–1900).

Henry Dewey Noyes was born in New York City in 1832 and graduated from New York University A. B., 1851, A. M., 1854, and M. D. from the College of Physicians and Surgeons in 1855. After serving three years on the resident staff of the New York Hospital, and spending a year in study in Europe, he entered upon the practice of diseases of the eye and ear, 1859, in New York. He was assistant ophthalmic surgeon in the New York Eye and Ear Infirmary, 1859 to 1864, surgeon from 1864 to 1900, and executive surgeon from 1875 to 1898; professor of ophthalmology and otology in Bellevue Medical College from 1868; one of the founders of the American Ophthalmological Society in 1864 and president from 1878 to 1884. His special ability lay in his fine teaching powers and his keen clinical observation, to which his very numerous publications from 1860 to 1898 attest. His text-book on diseases of the eye, published in 1890 (second edition in 1894), is one of the best. He died at Mount Washington, November 12, 1900. H. F.

Trans. Am. Oph. Soc., vol. ix.
Journ. Am. A., 1896, vol. xxvi.
Rhode Island Med. Soc., 1896, vol. v.
Knapp's Archives of Ophthalmology, vol. xxv.
Stone's " Biography of Eminent Physicians and Surgeons."
Med. News, 1900, vol. lxxvii.
Med. Record, 1900, vol. lviii.

Noyes, James Fanning (1817–1896).
James F. Noyes was born August 2, 1817, on a farm near Kingston, Rhode Island, a direct descendant of the Rev. James Noyes, Puritan and Nonconformist who emigrated from England and settled in Newberryport, Massachusetts, in 1634. Dr. Noyes went as a lad to the private schools near his home, ill health preventing his taking a college course. In 1842 he began to study medicine with Dr. Joseph F. Potter, of Waterville, Maine, and in 1844 took a course of lectures at Harvard Medical School; and in 1845 one at Jefferson Medical College, Philadelphia, graduating M. D. in 1846. After some post-graduate work in New York City, Dr. Noyes was appointed assistant physician in the United States Marine Hospital at Chelsea, Massachusetts. In 1849 Noyes began active work at Waterville, Maine, where he soon secured a large practice. In 1851 he removed to Cincinnati, Ohio, to form a partnership with his former preceptor, Dr. Potter. 1855 was spent in Europe studying ophthalmology at Berlin, with A. von Graefe and Richard Liebreich. In 1859 he again returned to Europe and studied in Paris with Desmarres and Sichel. In 1863 he settled in Detroit where he remained till his retirement in 1886, being the second regular physician to practise ophthalmology and otology in Michigan. He was a founder of the Detroit Academy of Medicine, president in 1873; member

of the Michigan State Medical Society; of the American Ophthalmological Society and the American Otological Society. He was honorary member of the Texas State Medical Society; member of the Ohio State Medical Society; of the Rhode Island State Medical Society; and of the Maine State Medical Society. In 1869 he was elected professor of ophthalmology and otology in Detroit Medical College, a position held for ten years. In 1872 he was president of the Detroit Academy of Medicine. From 1866 to 1880 he was ophthalmic and aural surgeon to St. Mary's Hospital, Detroit; and from 1863 to 1886, ophthalmic and aural surgeon to Harper Hospital, Detroit; from its foundation to 1886 he was ophthalmic and aural surgeon to the Detroit Woman's Hospital. He took great interest in the Oak Grove Insane Asylum at Flint, Michigan, and erected an amusement building known as "Noyes Hall." Under a gruff exterior, Dr. Noyes carried a warm and sympathetic heart. If a patient gave instant attention and unquestioned obedience, Dr. Noyes was a most delightful doctor. would inculcate proper respect for the To others he gave such attention as profession in general. While in general practice Dr. Noyes had a reputation for daring and skillful surgery and till his death nothing held so much interest for him as a well performed surgical operation. He was among the first to treat strabismus by the tucking method. His first operation was done March 3, 1874, and published in the "Transactions of the American Ophthalmic Society," p. 274. It differed from the modern tucking in that the tendon was divided and the ends sufficiently overlapped to correct the deformity and then stitched together.

Dr. J. F. Noyes never married. He died in Providence, Rhode Island, February 16, 1896, from heart failure.

Papers:
"Extensive Ossific Deposits in Left Eye, with Sympathetic Affection of the Right Eye." ("Detroit Review of Medicine and Pharmacy," vol. i.)

"Temporary Blindness from Lead Poisoning." (Ibid., vol. iv.)

"Dacrocystitis and Lachrymal Obstructions." (Ibid., vol. iv.)

"An Improved Iridectomy Forceps." (Ibid., vol. v.)

"Asthenopia, Causes, Recognition and Treatment." (Ibid., vol. v.)

"Paracentesis Membrane Tympani." (Ibid., vol. vi.)

"Blindness from Intra-cerebral Tumor." (Ibid., vol. vi.)

"Strabismus Convergens a Symptom, not a Primary Affection." (Ibid., vol. viii.)

"Calcification of the Aortic Valves of the Heart." (Ibid., vol. ix.)

"The Ophthalmoscope's Contributions to General Medicine." ("Transactions of the Michigan State Medical Society," vol. i.)

"Sympathetic Ophthalmia." (Ibid., 1870.)

"Embolism of the Central Retinal Artery of the Eye." (Ibid., 1873.)

"Case of Spontaneous Iridocyclitis followed by Sympathetic Ophthalmia." ("Detroit Lancet," 1879.)

"Case of Fatal Rapidly Growing Intraorbital Tumor" (round celled sarcoma). ("Transactions of the American Ophthalmological Society," 1879.)

"New Operation for Strabismus." (Ibid., 1879.)

"On the Use of the Ophthalmoscope." ("Transactions of the Michigan State Medical Society," 1872.)

L. C.

The Phys. and Surg. of U. S. W. B. Atkinson.

Trans. Mich. State Med. Soc., 1896.

Memorial Remarks. James Fanning Noyes, Jour. Amer. Med. Association, May 2, 1896.

O

O'Dwyer, Joseph (1841–1898).

For nearly thirty-five years Joseph O'Dwyer, was on the staff of the New York Foundling Hospital, investigating, discovering and planning for the extinction of those diseases which wrought disaster among his child patients—more especially that of diphtheria, and his name will always be connected with his victorious intubation, destined to save many thousands until antitoxic serum came with stronger help.

He was born in Cleveland, Ohio, 1841, and shortly after, his parents moving to Canada, he was brought up and educated not far from London, Ontario, beginning medical studies under a Dr. Anderson and coming up to New York to attend lectures at the New York College of Physicians and Surgeons, graduating there in 1886 and shortly after obtaining by competitive examinations the post of resident physician at the City Hospital of New York, on Blackwell's Island, and did fine service, twice contracting cholera, when that disease was rife. His next post was examiner of patients for the City Board, so, in partnership with Dr. Warren Schoonover, he settled in New York and in 1872 was appointed to the place where he did his life work, at the Foundling Hospital.

At this time a bad epidemic of diphtheria was in the hospital and forty or fifty per cent. of the children were probably, in those ante-serum days, doomed, doctors and nurses helpless, powerless to alleviate the horrors of asphyxiation.

O'Dwyer, ingenious, reflective, a lover of children began to ponder the situation. He saw the often ineffectivity of tracheotomy introduced by Trousseau in Paris, and began to devise some method of providing a channel for the passage of air through the larynx, and at first devised a small bivalve speculum, which accom-
plished a little but not much; the little patient, however, breathed with comparative ease for sixteen hours before death. An improved tube brought recovery in the second case and O'Dwyer's twelve years of labor and thought were rewarded. But the tubes were full of faults and O'Dwyer continued to work until he had perfected the instrument. His originality has been doubted, yet although there were many others on the same path he was the one to reduce the idea of intubation to practical utility. There was some opposition too in the Foundling Hospital, as he seemed to be adding to the torture of the children by experimentation, and some of the specialists in children's diseases had given the new method a trial and failed. A thorough discussion of the method was held at a meeting of the Academy of Medicine of New York, and it was a source of bitterest disappointment to O'Dwyer that many authorities on children's diseases agreed that his invention was of little service. Little by little, however, the advantages were seen and also in stenotic diseases of the larynx. It was characteristic of the real philanthropist to find O'Dwyer turning with equal eagerness to study and use antitoxin as soon as it was introduced, continuing its use when others were almost discouraged by the difficulty of determining a dose and the complications which followed. A thought which occupied him very much toward the end of his life was a mechanical method of treating pneumonia. He had made a series of experiments on the lungs and hoped to abort the disease in its inception by producing artificial emphysema.

Dr. Northrup, speaking of O'Dwyer, said "In the maternity service he was the expert obstetrician; in intubation an inventor and teacher, in general medical service the constant consulting mind whose opinion in times of clinical difficulties and troubles everyone sought.

For nearly ten years after his wife's death he continued a large practice though never quite the same man again. Naturally, he was of a rather melancholy disposition and loved sad songs and stories. In December, 1897, he began to develop some anomalous symptoms pointing to a serious pathological condition within the skull. The prominent New York consultants could not agree as to the cause and a postmortem did not entirely clear up the doubtful diagnosis. On January 7, after being lethargic for some days, Dr. O'Dwyer died, having reached the maturity of his powers and with the consciousness of having done one good work and of being ready to do more.

He married Catherine Begg, and had eight sons; four of them died when young, of the "Summer Complaint," so says the eldest son. The other four, Joseph, Frank, Launcelot and Victor grew to manhood.

Among his writings, chiefly contributions to medical journals, is: "Analysis of Fifty-six cases of Croup Treated by Intubation of the Larynx," 1888; "Intubation in Chronic Stenosis of the Larynx," 1888.

Makers of Modern Medicine, J. J. Walsh, 1907.
For Biography, see Bókay (J.) Emlék beszéd O'Dwyer, József (etc.) fol. Budapest, 1899.
Budapesti k. orvosegy, 1899—iki évkönyve, 1900.
Am. Gynec. and Obst. J., N. Y., 1898, xii.
Ann. Gynec. and Pediat., Bost., 1897–8, xi.
Ann. di laringol. (etc.), Genova, 1900, i, (F. Massei).
Arch. Pediat., N. Y., 1898, xv (W. P. Northrup).
Med. News, N. Y., 1898, lxxii (W. P. Northrup).
Med. Rec., N. Y., 1898, liii (W. P. Northrup). [Discussion.]
N. York Acad. M. (1896–1901), 1903 (W. P. Northrup).
Boston M. and S. J., 1898, cxxxviii.
Brit. M. J., Lond., 1898, i.
Brooklyn M. J., 1898, xii (G. McNaughton).
Canad. J. M. and S., Toronto, 1898, iii, port.
Janus, Amst., 1897–8, ii, port. (R. Park).
Jahrb. f. Kinderk., Leipz., 1900, n. F., li (J. von Bókay).
München. med. Wchnschr., 1898, xlv, port. (H. von Ranke).
J. de clin. et de thérap. inf., Par., 1898, vi (G. Variot).
Pediatrics, N. Y. and Lond., 1898, v, port. (A. Jacobi).

O'Hagan, Charles James (1821–1900).

The son of a newspaper editor, he was born in Londonderry County, Ireland, September 16, 1821, and attended school at Belfast, completing his course at Trinity College, Dublin, and coming to this country in 1842. He taught school in North Carolina, first at Kinston, then at Hookerton and finally at Greenville, where he afterwards permanently settled.

He received his medical degree from the University of New York in 1847, and was president of the Medical Society of North Carolina in 1870; and during the Civil War served the Confederacy as surgeon throughout the four years, leaving behind him an honorable record. His chief duty was with the Thirtieth North Carolina regiment attached to the brigade of Gen. Matt W. Ransom.

Dr. O'Hagan built up an extensive practice in Greenville and became the leader of his profession in that community. He was widely sought for as a consultant. Many years before the external application of water was advocated in disease he had systematically bathed his fever cases. One of the best of the very few papers he ever wrote was on "Veratrum Viride in Puerperal Eclampsia." ("North Carolina Medical Journal," May, 1879, vol. iii.) He was an important factor in the professional and social life of his time, and might have had high political honors, had he desired them. His personality was striking, his wit racy, of the soil whence he sprung; his sarcasm keen, but genial; his intellect trained and cultivated.

He married twice, first to Eliza Forest in 1864 and who died in 1871, leaving two children, and in 1877 to Elvira

Clark, who bore him one child, and died in 1889.

The doctor himself died at his home December 18, 1900, of apoplexy.

His portrait by Jacques Busbee, and the gift of the North Carolina Medical Society, was presented to the State Library on October 29, 1902, Senator Ransom delivering the oration.

H. A. R.

Carolina Medical Journal, Jan., 1901, vol. xlvii, No. 1.
Transactions N. C. Medical Society, 1901.

Ordronaux, John (1830-1908).

John Ordronaux, medico-jurisprudentist, only son of John and Elizabeth (Charreton) Ordronaux, was born in New York City, August 3, 1830. His father, a Frenchman, served on the American side in our second war with England, at one time commanding the privateer Prince of Neufchatel. The father dying in 1841, the lad was adopted by John Moulton, who owned the property now known as the William Cullen Bryant estate, at Roslyn, Long Island. Ordronaux received his A. B. at Dartmouth in 1850, and his LL. D. at Harvard in 1852. For two years he practised law at Taunton, Massachusetts, then removed to New York. Here he received the M. D. from the National Medical College in 1859. On the breaking out of Civil War he was made examining surgeon for volunteers in Brooklyn, and in 1864 was appointed assistant surgeon of the Fifteenth Regiment, National Guards, State of New York. During his services in these capacities he published the first American work on military hygiene, "Hints on Health in Armies," and also a "Manual for Military Surgeons on the Examination of Recruits and Discharge of Soldiers." His most important works were "Jurisprudence of Medicine" (1869) and "Judicial Aspects of Insanity" (1878), both of which went through several editions. He also wrote copiously for the medical and legal press. But, though Dr. Ordronaux was widely known as a writer on legal medicine, it is chiefly as a teacher of that important branch

that his fame will always rest. For forty-eight years he was professor of this subject in various prominent schools of law and medicine, and probably under his care a larger number of doctors and lawyers have received their medico-jurisprudential instruction than under any other man. His teaching record is as follows: 1860-1906, Columbia Law School; 1864-1908, Dartmouth Medical School; 1865-1873, National Medical College, Washington, D. C., and in the law school of the same (Columbia) University; 1865-1873, University of Vermont, Medical Department; 1872-1889, Boston University Law School.

In 1870 he received the degree of LL. D. from Trinity College, Hartford, Connecticut, and in 1895 the same degree from Dartmouth.

Dr. Ordronaux was a small, slender, frail-looking man ("of the ramrod type," as one of his army comrades expressed the matter) but very well built and wiry. His hair was red, in later life white. His complexion was absolutely pallid, his eyes were keen, luminous, and dark. He was slow, methodical, and thoughtful, except when excited; then he was rapid indeed, and voluble.

He was a timid man physically and socially. He was a bachelor, and for many years lived at Roslyn with a widow and her family, after her death obtaining quarters with a neighbor who continued to take care of him when at home up to the time of his death. He was so very sensitive that the slightest physical hostility, or even opposition which savored of hostility, caused the doctor, like the leaves of a sensitive plant when touched, to fold up within himself. If, when he was testifying as expert in court, the cross-examination became of an overbearing or brow-beating character, he could scarcely (as he often informed his friends) refrain from bursting into tears. He was pertinacious and stuck to his guns, but the mental and emotional strain was unduly great, and sometimes made him ill. He had few friends, in the ordinary acceptation of the word, but everyone who knew him loved him. He was fond of children, but they seemed to stand in awe of him, to feel that here was a being beyond their comprehension; and this was always a matter of great regret to the good doctor. Among his intimate friends were Joseph White Moulton, the historian (with whom he made his home for a number of years) and also William Cullen Bryant and Parke Godwin.

He was a man of simple and most economical life. For years he limited his expenditures for his daily luncheon to twenty-five cents; being remonstrated with upon this matter by his friends, he allowed himself thereafter the princely sum of forty cents. He told these friends, in all seriousness, that the matter had cost him deep and prolonged thought, as well as the extra fifteen cents. When they laughed, he added, with a sheepish grin, that he believed it would be a good rule for him to take warm water and dried apples at luncheon, since it was a fair inference that the former would swell the latter. He denied himself many pleasures for the sake of saving the money they would cost. He used to do his own sewing, and bought the material and made his neckties. Sometimes he bought provisions, and took them to his room and cooked them.

He was fond of books, and was an authority upon them; yet he had not a large library. He had ample means, but motives of prudence and economy would ever cause him to consider the advisability of purchasing.

He was a communicant of the Episcopal church at Roslyn, and a regular attendant at the services, and most earnest in his responses and singing. During the absence of the rector he would occasionally conduct the services himself and read a sermon—usually one of Jeremy Bentham's.

He was a veteran of the Civil War, and, on Memorial Day, and at the funerals of deceased members of his Grand Army post, he would don his uniform and march with the rest.

The doctor was a man of enormous intellectual activity. Not only did he attempt to keep up with all the advances of medicine and law, but he was a profound theologian. He was reported to have, and doubtless did possess, a greater knowledge of theological dogma and ecclesiastical history than the great majority of accredited ministers and professors of theology. He never practised medicine actively, but, in the legal profession, was recognized as a keen, close reasoner, and, though he had but little reputation as a lawyer before the public, was employed to write briefs in many of the celebrated cases which occupied public attention from 1900 back to the early seventies. His work as a lawyer was done in the same way that all of his labor was performed, quietly and without ostentation.

He was a man of great melancholy at times, and on such occasions was well-nigh inaccessible even to his intimates. The depression of spirits was partly temperamental and partly due to the fact that he had never had a real home, or, in fact, a real boyhood. It was also possibly due in part to the gradual decay of medical jurisprudence as a subject for instruction in the medical colleges and law schools. In a number of letters to the present writer the doctor plays upon this theme at (for him) considerable length and with great sadness. To Dr. Ordronaux the subject of medical jurisprudence was not a merely intellectual affair, but something which touched the emotions deeply: he was greatly concerned for the future of legal medicine, and insisted that the colleges did not know what they were doing in rejecting so important a branch.

He died at about 3 A. M., Monday, January 20, 1908. At three the preceding afternoon, he had been stricken with cerebral apoplexy. Inside of sixty seconds he lost consciousness, and then, little by little, he went into a still deeper sleep. He had always greatly feared lest he might some day be a charge on others, and had often expressed the wish to die either suddenly or after a short illness, in order that he might not be the means of giving trouble.

T. H. S.

Long Island Med. Jour., vol. ii, No. 4, April, 1908 (portrait). Who's Who in America, 1908. Jour. Am. Med. Assn., vol. 1, No. 6, Feb. 8, 1908.

Ormsby, John S. (1806–1876).

John S. Ormsby was born on August 23, 1806. He did not limit his practice to any special lines of work but covered the whole field of medicine and surgery as customary in the early days in the West.

He attended school in Greensburg, Pennsylvania, and took his academic degree in 1829 at Pittsburg, Pennsylvania, and his medical one at the University of Pennsylvania.

Dr. Ormsby came of sturdy eastern stock and in 1851 moved from Greensburg, Pennsylvania, to Sacramento, California, where he practised for ten years. From there he moved to Nevada during the early gold excitement, and then to Salt Lake City, Utah, in 1866, where he practised and died at last after a long and busy life, at the home of his son in Logan on October 4, 1876.

Dr. Ormsby married Jane Hindman in 1836, and one son, Dr. O. C. Ormsby, of Rexburg, Idaho, followed in his father's footsteps.

W. B. E.

Orton, George Turner (1837–1901).

Born in Guelph, Ontario, January 19, 1837; he was the son of Dr. Henry Orton, a pioneer of Western Ontario and a scion of a family of doctors, for besides his father and his grandfather, two uncles and three brothers were doctors. The eldest brother was surgeon-major in the British Army, serving in the Crimean War, and the Indian Mutiny.

After receiving his early education in the Guelph public schools he was sent to Trinity College, Dublin, but completed his course at St. Andrew's University, Scotland, where he took his M. D. in 1860,

and in 1861 he was elected member of the Royal College of Surgeons, England.

After completing his medical course, Dr. Orton returned to Canada and began to practise at Fergus, Ontario, in 1862, where he remained till 1879, when he removed to Winnipeg, Manitoba. In Fergus, he soon built up one of the largest practices in the province, and was besides surgeon to the Thirtieth Battalion, Wellington Rifles, and for three years Reeve of the town. His wide influence as a physician undoubtedly made his entrance into political life easier than it would otherwise have been, but his ability as a statesman retained him there.

His interest in public affairs, and the development of Canada in general, was such that he was elected to the House of Commons in 1874, and represented the Constituency continuously for fourteen years. During the Rebellion in the Northwest Territories in 1885, he was brigade-surgeon under Gen. Middleton and was present at the engagements of Fish Creek and Batouche. On his return to the House of Commons at the next session he was given an enthusiastic ovation by members of both sides of the House.

He married Annie Farmer in 1862, by whom he had two daughters.

He died at home in Winnipeg, November 14, 1901, of pneumonia.

J. H.

Otis, Fessenden Nott (1825–1900).

Fessenden Nott Otis, a son of Oran Gray and Lucy Kingman Otis, was born in Ballston Spa, Saratoga County, New York, May 6, 1825. His family came from England to Hingham, Massachusetts, late in the seventeenth century, and his immediate ancestors settled in Ballaston before the Revolution. He was first a pupil at the local public schools, then began to study medicine at the New York University in 1848, finishing at the New York Medical School, where he received his degree in 1852.

After serving as interne at the Charity

Hospital, New York, he became a surgeon to the Pacific Mail Steamship Company, and lived in Panama. He remained in the steamship company's employ until 1859; in 1860 he settled in New York, and took up general practice.

He was first lecturer and in 1871 professor of venereal and genito-urinary diseases in the College of Physicians and Surgeons. His principal writings were upon genito-urinary disease, although he contributed some well-known articles on syphilis. His volume of six hundred pages entitled "Practical Lessons on Syphilis and Genito-urinary Diseases," was.an exhaustive work on the subject.

He was the inventor of the Otis Urethrometer and the Otis Dilating Urethrotome. He was a member of the New York State and County Societies and the New York Academy of Medicine. In 1859 he married Frances H., daughter of Apollos Cooke, of Catskill, New York.

The last few years of his life ill health compelled him to abandon active practice, and he died in New Orleans, May 26, 1900.

J. M. W.

Boston M. and S. J., 1900, cxlii.
Brit. M. J., Lond., 1900, i.
Med. Rec., N. Y., 1990, lvii.

Otis, George Alexander (1830–1881).

George Alexander Otis, surgeon and brevet lieutenant-colonel, United States Army, curator of the Army Medical Museum, and editor of the surgical volumes of the "Medical and Surgical History of the War of Rebellion," died at Washington, D. C., February 23, 1881, at the comparatively early age of fifty years. His great-grandfather, Ephraim Otis, was a physician who practised at Scituate, Massachusetts. The father of Otis, also George Alexander Otis, married Maria Hickman, and George Alexander was born in Boston, Massachusetts, November 12, 1830. In 1846 he entered Princeton College and graduated, with the degree of A. B., in 1849, and she conferred upon him the degree of A. M. in

1852. In the fall of 1849 he went to Philadelphia, and matriculated in the medical department of the University of Pennsylvania. That institution conferred upon him the degree of M. D. in April, 1851. During a stay in Paris Otis made diligent use of the opportunities afforded for professional improvement. Moreover, he took a deep interest in the stirring panorama of French politics, as shown by a series of letters he took time to write to the "Boston Evening Transcript."

In the spring of 1852 Otis returned to the United States. Immediately after his return he established himself at Richmond, Virginia, where he opened an office for general medical and surgical practice, and where his tastes and ambition soon led him to embark in his earliest enterprise in the domain of medical literature. In April, 1853, he issued the first number of "The Virginia Medical and Surgical Journal." Dr. Howell L. Thomas, of Richmond, was associated with him as co-editor, but the financial risk was assumed entirely by Otis; its most striking characteristic was the number of translations and abstracts from current French medical literature which appeared in its pages. Otis had, by this time, become dissatisfied with his prospects of professional success in Richmond, and circumstances led him to select Springfield, Massachusetts, as his place of residence. Another journal, "The Stethoscope," was united with "The Virginia Medical and Surgical Journal," under the title of "Virginia Medical Journal," with McCaw as editor, and Otis as corresponding editor, until 1859. The War of the Rebellion changed the whole tenor of his life. During almost the whole time Surg. Otis accompanied his regiment— the Twenty-seventh Massachusetts Volunteers—and shared its fortunes. January 22, 1864, he was detached and ordered to Yorktown, Virginia, to assume the duties of surgeon-in-chief of Gen. Wistar's command. June 26, 1864, he tendered his resignation and received an appointment as assistant surgeon of United

States Volunteers, to date from June 30, 1864.

At this time he renewed his acquaintance with Surg. Crane, then on duty in the surgeon-general's office, and in 1864 Otis was assigned as assistant to Surg. John H. Brinton, curator of the Army Medical Museum, and engaged in the duty of collecting materials for the "Surgical History of the War of the Rebellion." The first half of the volume was occupied by the "Surgical Report" prepared by Otis. It was a thoughtfully prepared document, which excited the universal admiration of military surgeons in Europe as well as in America. The first was "A Report on Amputations at the Hip-joint in Military Surgery," published as "Circular No. 7," surgeon-general's office, July 1, 1867. An examination of this monograph shows that he had already pretty well begun to emancipate himself from the leading-strings of the French school, and had fully acquired the desire so manifest in his subsequent work to compare and weigh all accessible human knowledge on each branch of his subject before arriving at his own conclusions. The second of the studies was: "A Report on Excisions of the Head of the Femur for Gunshot Injury," published as "Circular No. 2," surgeon-general's office, January 2, 1869. During the interval between the appearance of these two volumes, and subsequently, Otis found time to prepare and publish several valuable reports on subjects connected with military surgery, one of which was: "A Report of Surgical Cases Treated in the Army of the United States from 1865 to 1871," issued as "Circular No. 3," from the surgeon-general's office, August 17, 1871. He was engaged at the time of his death on the third surgical volume, which he left in an unfinished condition; a colossal fragment. Otis received the appointments of captain, major, and lieutenant-colonel by brevet, to date from September 29, 1866, "for faithful and meritorious services during the war." He was promoted to be surgeon in the army, with

the rank of major, March 17, 1880. He was elected a foreign member of the Medical Society of Norway, October 26, 1870; a foreign corresponding member of the Surgical Society of Paris, August 11, 1875, and an honorary life member of the Massachusetts Medical Society in February, 1877. Until his last illness Otis retained much of the fondness for literature which characterized him in early life. Hesitating, often embarrassed, in his manner in ordinary conversation, especially with strangers, he became eloquent when warmed by the discussion of any topic in which he took interest.

J. J. W.

Am. Jour. Med. Sc., 1881, vol. lxxxii (J. J. Woodward).
Brit. M. Jour., Lond., 1881, vol. ii.
Tidskr. i. mil. Helsov., Stockholm, 1882, vol. vii.
Tr. Am. M. Ass., Phila., 1881, vol. xxxii.

Ouchterlony, John Ardid (1838–1908).

He was born in Gothenborg, Smalend, Sweden, June 24, 1838, his father, a captain in the army. He received his early education in Sweden. He came to America alone in 1857, and settled in New York City where he studied medicine with Dr. T. Gaillard Thomas, and completed his medical studies in the medical department of the University of the City of New York, whence he graduated in 1860. During 1861 he entered the United States Army as surgeon, and achieved notable success in his chosen work. In 1862 he was assigned to hospital work in and near Louisville. During his hospital service his skill and learning attracted much attention, and in 1864 he was elected lecturer on clinical medicine in the University of Louisville. He continued his army service in conjunction with his lectureship until the latter part of 1865, when he resigned from the government service and began private practice. He was one of the founders of the Louisville Medical College in which he was professor of materia medica, therapeutics and clinical medicine. He resigned from the

Louisville Medical College in 1876. From 1876 he had no college associations. In 1878 he accepted the chair of principles and practice of medicine in the Kentucky School of Medicine, which he filled with marked success and ability until 1882, when he resigned to accept the chair of principles and practice of medicine and clinical medicine in the University of Louisville. He filled this chair from 1882 until his death. He had been president of the Medico-Chirurgical Society and of the Louisville Obstetrical Society. In 1890 he served as president of the Kentucky Medical Society; in 1891 he received from the Swedish Royal Academy of Sciences the Linnean Gold Medal; in 1891, in recognition of his marked ability and renown, King Oscar of Sweden made him a Knight of the Royal Order of the Polar Star. In 1892 the University of Notre Dame conferred upon him the degree of LL. D. He was an honorary member of the Michigan State Medical Society, and had also served as vice-president of the American Medical Association. In 1894, in recognition of his ability and his devotion to his church, Pope Leo the Thirteenth made Dr. Ouchterlony a Knight of the Order of St. Gregory the Great. As a diagnostician he was preeminent. His extremely wide medical knowledge along with constant and deep study and constant investigation gave him an extremely keen insight into the science of medicine. His contributions to medical literature are numerous and important. Perhaps one of his best known was a treatise in 1887 on the "Preventative Treatment of Tuberculosis." While he did not intend this to be exhaustive it covered in full the delicate character of this morbid process, and with rare precision pointed out many of the present modes of attack on this disease. His studies were not confined to medicine alone, for he was distinguished as a scientist and a linguist, both here and abroad. He spoke five modern languages fluently and was thoroughly conversant with Greek and Latin. In

1863 he married Kate Grainger and had one son.

O. W. D.

Mec. Rec., N. Y., 1905, lxviii.

Owen, William (1788–1875).

This obstetrician was born in Staunton, Virginia, on the twelfth of January, 1788. Three years later his family removed to Lynchburg, then known as Lynch's Ferry, and there he spent his life.

Beginning in a drug store, he pursued at the same time the study of medicine for three years under the guidance of able instructors, afterwards attending a course of lectures in the University of Pennsylvania, but being too poor to take at once the second course, and graduate, he therefore entered upon the practice of medicine, returning some years later to college and completing the course and receiving his degree in 1815, the subject of his thesis being "Mercurial Disease." He was a charter member and an honorary fellow of the Medical Society of Virginia, and the first president of the Lynchburg Medical Association.

He was a man of great vigor and endurance and did an enormous amount of work. He did for many years nearly all the obstetrical and surgical operations in his town and the surrounding country. As early as 1816 he resected the entire shaft of the tibia, preserving the periosteum, the patient recovering with a useful limb. In 1832 he devised an anterior splint for fractured femur, which has ever since been in use in Lynchburg, and known as his invention. A gentle and kind man, he was much beloved by his patients. In spite of his enormous practice, he never forgot nor neglected the poor who needed his services, and died in very moderate circumstances, when he might have left quite an independent fortune, had he been less indulgent. Dr. Owen married Miss Latham, a sister of Dr. Henry Latham, a physician of Lynchburg, and one of his sons, William O. Owen, became a surgeon.

After several years of failing health he

died on the twenty-second of January, 1875, in the eighty-eighth year of his age.

R. M. S.

Dr. J. M. Toner's Lives of Two Thousand Five Hundred Physicians, unpublished.

Owen, David Dale (1807–1860).

David Dale Owen had for father the well known philanthropist celebrated for his co-operative experiments first in Scotland and later at New Harmony, Indiana. His mother was the eldest daughter of David Dale, merchant and Lord Provost of Glasgow. David was born at Braxfield House, New Lanark, Scotland, June 24, 1807.

His early training included a course of architectural drawing and .carpentering and a classical course at the Lanark Grammar School. This was followed by three years at the celebrated institution of Emmanuel Fellenberg, near Berne, Switzerland. David and his brother, Richard, selected chemistry in addition to the usual course and on returning to Scotland in September, 1826, studied under Dr. Andrew Ure at the Andersoniam Institute in Glasgow. Soon after they left Liverpool in a sailing vessel, passed through the West India Islands and reached New Orleans about the last of December and arrived at New Harmony to join their father early in January, 1828. Here they began to practise with the chemical apparatus they had brought from Glasgow, and the two brothers worked together until 1831, when David returned to Europe to further qualify himself in chemistry and geology and worked under Dr. Turner at the London University. On returning the following year he fell a victim to Asiatic cholera and on recovery began to study medicine at Ohio Medical College in Cincinnati, with a view to improve himself in anatomy and physiology, as essential aids in the study of paleontology.

During the summers of these years Alexander Maclure, brother of the noted geologist, William Maclure, engaged Dr. Owen to arrange the extensive collection of minerals and fossils made by his brother and to distribute specific suites to colleges, the residue to form the nucleus of a museum. To this nucleus Owen added largely by purchase, obtaining from Dr. Krantz, of Germany, an ichthyosaurus, larger than the one in the British Museum, from the lias of Wurtemberg. He also obtained a nearly complete megalonyx which he exhumed near Henderson, Kentucky. The entire collection was nearly all consumed by fire after it had been purchased by the Indiana University.

After graduating M. D. in the spring of 1836 he went on a state geological survey with Dr. Gerard Troost, a journey undertaken by Owen, at his own expense, for the sake of practice. But in the next year he turned aside from things purely scientific in order to go to Switzerland to marry Caroline C. Neef, third daughter of Joseph Neef, the coadjutor of Pestalozzi, but he was soon at work again, this time as state geologist of Indiana, publishing his notes in 1838. His merits were recognized at the capital and he was deputed to survey the mineral possibilities of Dubuque and Mineral Point dist icts of Wisconsin and Iowa, some 11,000 square miles. His report was published in 1840. In one month from the time of beginning he had one hundred and thirty-nine sub-agents and assistants; had instructed the former in the elementary principles of geology; organized twenty-four working corps and furnished them with skeleton maps. In all this, Dr. John Locke, of the Medical College of Ohio, was his valued helper.

Such good work caused him to be appointed United States geologist and to be given the direction of the Chippewa land district survey. The preliminary report in 1848 has in it 323 lithographs from his original sketches, also numerous maps. A more full survey of an extended district occupied the next five years, and Congress made a large appropriation for its printing and illustration in finest style. The wood cuts in this volume of six hundred and thirty-eight quarto pages are by his brother Richard, while David for the first time brought the medal ruling style of engraving to bear on fossil specimens.

Gov. Powell, of Kentucky, selected Owen as state geologist in 1854, and the results of his survey occupied four large volumes, with maps and illustrations. Duties came thronging fast, for the Kentucky survey was not completed before Owen was made state geologist for Arkansas, but the second volume for this expedition was not quite finished when he died, though he dictated up to three days of his death. The offer, a second time made, of state geologist for Indiana, had been taken on condition that the work should be carried through by his brother Richard, who had then, because of the war crisis, resigned his professorship of natural science at Nashville, Tennessee. The volume had 368 pages with wood cuts and diagrams by Richard and the last proofs were read by him in camp when he was serving in the Fifteenth Indiana Volunteers.

Great and indefatigable perseverance marked Owen's life work. Although he found that the Arkansas summer surveys, often made in the rich malarial bottoms, injured his health and brought him home in the autumn with a hue denoting strong malarial derangement, he not only continned the surveys but continued his laboratory winter work far into the night. But the unrelaxed strain and attacks of cardiac rheumatism terminated his career on November 13, 1860. His wife, two sons and two daughters survived him.

His work as an artist deserves some mention, for, besides leaving some good paintings in oil of his family he richly illustrated his reports. He also sent to London on canvas in distemper, views of the fossil sigillaria found erect *in situ* twelve miles from New Harmony. These were presented by Sir Roderick Murchison at a meeting of the British Association for the Advancement of Science. Owen subsequently took Sir Charles Lyell to the locality. He was always eager to share his scientific pleasures and built at his own cost (some $10,000) a laboratory fully equipped in every respect, so fine also architecturally that he furnished the design for the Smithsonian buildings and carefully tested the various specimens of stone submitted.

The Am. Geologist, Aug., 1889 (port.).
The History of Am. Geol. G. P. Merrill, 1906 (port.).

Owen, William Otway (1820-1892).

He was the son of Dr. William Owen, a skillful surgeon and obstetrician of Lynchburg, and born in that city, October 20, 1820. He began life as a civil engineer, but yielding to the wishes of his father, he studied medicine, graduating from the University of New York in 1842. Entering immediately into practice in Lynchburg, he was a prominent doctor in that city for half a century.

He was a surgeon in the Confederate Army, and apointed surgeon-in-chief of the hospitals at Lynchburg, a position for which he was particulary well qualified. He was a member of the Medical Society of Virginia.

Dr. Owen was a skillful surgeon and performed many important operations, such as ovariotomies, lithotomies, perineal sections, etc. In his work he was tireless, watchful and faithful, and while always dignified and positive, he was yet warmly sympathetic, and greatly beloved by his patrons.

He married, in 1863, Alice Lynn, and was survived by four sons and two daughters. His oldest son, R. O. Owen, was a physician.

He died at his home in Lynchburg, Virginia, on the fifteenth of February, 1892, in the seventy-second year of his age, his death the result of a severe attack of epidemic influenza, complicated with organic trouble and general physical decline.   R. M. S.

Trans. Med. Soc. of Va., 1892.

P

Packard, John Hooker (1832–1907).

John Hooker Packard was born August 15, 1832, at Philadelphia, Pennsylvania, a son of Frederick A. and Elizabeth Dwight Hooker. He graduated from the department of arts, University of Pennsylvania in 1850, and in the same university, from the department of medicine in 1853. He had for preceptor in medicine Joseph Leidy, the eminent anatomist, to whose teaching he undoubtedly owed his fondness for and skill in anatomical pursuits. After graduation he went abroad and continued his medical studies in Paris.

In 1855 he was resident physician to the Pennsylvania Hospital for eighteen months. He then began private practice and for many years was very active as a teacher, especially in anatomy, surgery and obstetrics. As time went on, however, he limited his work almost entirely to the practice of surgery. During the Civil War he was appointed acting assistant surgeon, United States Army, serving as attending surgeon to the Christian Street and the Satterlee United States Army General Hospitals in Philadelphia, and as consultant to the Haddington Hospital, and to the hospital at Beverly, New Jersey. During the progress of the battle of Gettysburg, he received orders to report at the scene of action and although quite ill at the time, from what subsequently developed into a very severe case of typhoid, he obeyed at once. For three days and nights he labored incessantly and then being utterly unable to continue at work, was sent back to Philadelphia suffering from a nearly fatal attack of the fever.

From 1863 to 1884 he was one of the visiting physicians to the Episcopal Hospital of Philadelphia, in 1884 visiting surgeon to the Pennsylvania Hospital, which position he held until his retirement from active work in 1896. He was also surgeon to St. Joseph's Hospital of Philadelphia.

Dr. Packard was a member of the College of Physicians of Philadelphia, and vice-president from 1885–1888. He was the first Mütter lecturer in that institution from 1864–1866, his lectures being on "Inflammation." He was one of the founders of the Pathological and Obstetrical Societies of Philadelphia, and twice president of each. He was also one of the original members of the American Surgical Association.

Among his noticeable operations were two successful hip-joint amputations and a successful ligation of the internal iliac artery. In 1872 he published the first notice of the primary anesthesia from ether, and in 1880, an article in the "New York Medical Record" of May 22, on the value of an oblique incision in the skin in lessening the disfigurement of scars, which is still frequently referred to.

In 1886, in a paper read before the Medico-Legal Society of New York, he suggested the use of a lethal chamber for the infliction of the death penalty, death to be caused by the abstraction of oxygen from the atmosphere and the introduction of carbonic acid gas.

Dr. Packard was a profoundly religious man, an Episcopalian. Although he rarely talked upon religious subjects, his belief was a vital part of his existence and colored all the important actions of his life. He had very considerable artistic ability and much of his work was illustrated with his own pencil. In 1896 he infected himself in the course of an operation. Following the severe illness which ensued upon this accident, he retired from all active medical work. His culture, geniality and sense of humor endeared him to many friends, both contemporaries and also many of a much younger generation, with all of whom he maintained pleasant social intercourse.

His literary work, besides many contributions to current medical journals was as follows: A translation of "Malgaigne's Treatise on Fractures," 1859; "Handbook of Minor Surgery," 1863; "Lectures on Inflammation," 1865; "Handbook of Operative Surgery," 1870; articles on "Poisoned Wounds" and on "Fractures," in "Ashhurst's International Encyclopedia of Surgery," 1883; and on "Fractures and Dislocations," in "Keating's Cyclopedia of the Diseases of Children," 1889. He also published three editions of the "Philadelphia Medical Directory," in 1868, 1871 and 1873. In 1881 Dr. Packard edited the American edition of "Holmes's System of Surgery."

A handsome oil painting of Dr. Packard was presented by the Ex-residents' Association of the Pennsylvania Hospital to that institution, and now hangs in the hall.   F. R. P.

Page, Alexander Crawford (1829–1899).

Alexander Crawford Page was born at Truro, Nova Scotia, in 1829.

As a boy he went to the schools of his native town, and when a young man set out with but few dollars in his pocket to seek his fortune in the United States. The schooner which was to carry him over the Bay of Fundy and away to Boston got windbound long before reaching that destination. However, he got ashore on the west side of the bay, and completed his journey to Boston on foot. Here he obtained work to support himself, and at the same time studied Latin and Greek and otherwise prepared himself to enter the Medical School of Harvard University, from which he graduated M. D. in 1856.

Dr. Page was from 1888–1899 president of the Provincial Medical Board; examiner in obstetrics and diseases of women and children, in Dalhousie University; president of the Medical Society of Nova Scotia in 1874. Soon after graduation he returned to practise in his native town.

Of studious habits, he was well read in his profession, and alive to all its improvements, fertile in resources, prompt in action, and thoroughly to be depended upon. He was a good all-round practitioner. Obstetrics, however, was his favorite branch of practice, and he was most successful in this. Dr. Page contributed valuable papers of a practical kind to the Nova Scotia Medical Society and the Colchester County Medical Society, some of which have been published.

Dr. Page married a Miss Blair, of Truro, but had no children. He died in Truro in 1899.   D. A. C.

Page, Benjamin (1770–1844).

One of the most remarkable pioneer physicians of Maine was Benjamin Page, born April 12, 1770, at Exeter, New Hampshire, son of the first Dr. Benjamin Page, who after his Revolutionary service practised at Hallowell, and died in 1829, aged seventy-six In Andover, young Page studied medicine first with his father, then with Dr. Thomas Kittredge, after being educated at Philip's Exeter Academy.

He began practice at Hallowell in 1791, but after a year or so went to Boston, was inoculated with the small-pox and he and a friend passed away the time of confinement practising music. He returned to Hallowell and drew up plans for building a small-pox hospital in Winthrop, Maine. This plan, however, fell through, owing to Jenner's discovery of vaccination.

His friends claimed that Dr. Page was the first American physician to vacci nate, but they forgot the prior claims of Dr. Benjamin Waterhouse. The fact remains, though, that Dr. Page vaccinated early in Maine and devoted his time to it zealously for the rest of his life.

Previous to this, in 1790, Benjamin Page married Miss Abigail Cutler, of Newbury Port, and she was a skillful nurse to her husband in times of sickness. They were never separated for a day for over forty years.

Dr. Page was devoted to his profession

and although not ambitious enjoyed with complacency his unrivalled success. His access to the best medical library in New England, that of Dr. Benjamin Vaughan in Hallowell, helped him largely. He made no display of his talent, he did not pretend to be learned, but always filled the exigency. A leader in medicine, he was cautious rather than adventurous and his long experience enabled him to compete successfully with younger men. He was excellent in the management of fevers and injuries, and his success in fractures was noted. He avoided calomel and bleeding when they were everywhere carried to excess. Better not used than abused, was his opinion. He was a remarkable obstetrician and is said to have brought into the world three thousand children without losing a mother or a child. In this branch of medicine he displayed wonderful tact and skill. He rarely used the forceps. Owing to his great diagnostic skill he was an unrivalled physician for children. An epidemic of spotted fever raged in Maine in 1812–14, during which he saved a large proportion of lives. Thacher says that almost all of the cases were attended personally by Dr. Page, and that he is entitled to the greatest honor for his indefatigable industry at this time.

He was well versed in Latin and French, and after attending Talleyrand and other distinguished Frenchmen who were journeying through Maine, Dr. Page was able to discuss their symptoms in their native language. It is averred that Talleyrand was so much pleased with his physician's treatment that he thanked him in French in a letter and enclosed five times the fee suggested. For many years this remarkable physician was at his best, had a very large practice in Central Maine and travelled extensively round about Hallowell. He sometimes went as far as Canada on consultations. His standing with his professional brothers was of the highest, as is proved by the numerous letters received by him asking his advice in emergencies. He was very communicative to his

pupils, many of whom rode with him during his practice. He received from Bowdoin the honorary degree of M. D. in 1843. He was a member of the Massachusetts Medical Society, and Maine Medical Society, and had an excellent medical library. He was a philosopher as he advanced in age, lived economically yet was generous to the poor. A man without rebuke in his own town, he never discussed politics or religion. Dr. Benjamin Page was large in stature, well formed, mild and benignant in countenance, lovely in intelligence and very cheerful. His head was small, his eyes sparkling and his face extremely vivacious. He was very suave, much given in later years to society, and a man very fond of company.

Dr. Page died indirectly from smallpox, January 25, 1844, during an epidemic of this disease, after he had saved all the patients who went to the hospital. He left a son, Dr. Frederick Benjamin Page, who distinguished himself as a physician in the South.   J. A. S.

From Documents furnished by G. S. Rowell. Boston M. and Surg. Jour., 1845, xxxiii.

Pallen, Montrose Anderson (1836–1890).

This gynecologist was born in Vicksburg on January 2, 1836, and had for father a professor of obstetrics in the St. Louis Medical College. Briefly summed up the appointments and writings of the son included: professor of gynecology in the University of the City of New York; the same in the Humboldt Medical College, 1866; the St. Louis College of Physicians and Surgeons, in 1869; in 1873, surgeon-general of Missouri, and during the Civil War medical director.

He took prize essays in 1858 and 1867 for "The Ophthalmoscope" and "Uterine Abnormities," read before the American Medical Association, and wrote also on "Faulty Implantation of the Vagina," "Ovarian Cysts," "Atresia of the Vagina," etc., etc.

Anne Elize, daughter of Louis A. Benoist, was his wife and he had two children.

Med. Rec., N. Y., 1890, vol. xxxviii.

Pallen, Moses Montrose (1810–1876).

This obstetrician was the son of one Zalma Pallen, a Polish officer, who served under Napoleon I, and came to Virginia in 1800 and settled in King and Queens County, where Moses was born on April 29, 1810. The lad was educated at the University of Virginia and went to St. Louis in 1842. Among the professors of the St. Louis Medical College, none was more popular than Dr. Pallen for he was indeed a teacher by nature, who adapted himself perfectly to the student classes of his time.

He was of medium height, stocky build, an exceedingly solid looking man. He had a big head, well shaped, covered with a crop of gray hair; a broad round face, seemingly almost as equally broad as it was long. He wore a close cropped mass of side whiskers, his eyes were small and sparkling, his eyelids large and puffy. He had a strong fat nose, a large mouth with big lips which were constantly relaxed and compressed fitfully at the command of his mind. A student, writing of him in the classroom, says: "His intense mind guides and forms his words, his memory is an ever-ready stock from which he draws capital to enhance the value of his discourse and compel truth itself. He tells you that when you approach the lying-in woman "you are nearer to the throne of God than the stars of heaven are, that living is death and dying is life, and birth is both; that birth into this life is the death of the embryo-life. God grant that our earthly death may be our birth into a glorious new being. Watch this suffering and pained lying-in creature, in her harsh hard hours of dire travail, remember that your patience and gentleness to her must be as boundless as the sea. Your attention should be infallible, study and adapt yourselves to her whims of exceeding great agony, give, yes, keep giving her hope and bless her with your strength. Let your untiring attention to babe and mother be so that a clean conscience can make you undreading face your God. Each pang of pain that she is denied betters the growing soul of progeny."

Moses Pallen's work bore fruit for fifty-eight years, truly a rare cycle of virtued benefit. Every detail of the lying-in period was placed before the student in its most effective light. "Gentlemen," he would say, "as the head presses down upon the pudenda take large flannel cloths, well boiled, and when still generous with their heat keep them to the pudenda. This gracious warmth gives unimagined comfort and relaxes the assailed muscles, thus making an easier passage-way for the head."

"He could say "pudenda" with such volume and import as to make it sound almost like the boom of an explosion. His direction for the fixing of the navel cord and the belly band upon the child was given with all the grave profundity and seriousness as though it was earth's most important affair of state. His direction for the application of a diaper upon the child was inexpressibly scientifically comical. His worth requires no interpreter and duty to him was as the voice of God. He was like necessity, he did everything well, never wild in his assertions, he always acted as he believed —that nothing is impossible to well directed labor.

He held the chair of obstetrics in the St. Louis Medical College over twenty years and was also a founder and one time president of the St. Louis Academy of Science. This later office he also filled with the St. Louis Medical Society. During the Mexican War he held a contract surgeonship in St. Louis for the United States Army.

He died in St. Louis on September 25, 1876. His wife was Janet Cochran, daughter of William Wallace Cochran, of Baltimore. W. B. O.

St. Louis Med. Courier, 1904, vol. xxx (port.).
Tr. Am. Med. Assoc., Phila., 1877, vol. xxviii.

Palmer, Alonzo Benjamin (1815–1887).

Alonzo Palmer was born in Richfield, Otsego County, New York, of Puritan parents; his father, a native of Connecticut, died when he was nine years old. His early education was at the schools and academies of Oswego, Otsego and Herkimer. In 1839 he took his M. D. from Fairfield Medical College, Fairfield, New York. After practising twelve years at Tecumseh, Michigan, he removed to Chicago where for two years he was associated with Dr. N. S. Davis. Meantime he spent two winters in New York and Philadelphia studying in hospitals and clinics. During the cholera epidemic of 1852 he was city physician in Chicago and had charge of the cholera hospital, caring for about fifteen hundred patients yearly. In 1852 he was appointed professor of anatomy, medical department, Michigan University, but from lack of funds never occupied the chair. In 1854 he was given the chair of materia medica and therapeutics and diseases of women and children, in 1869 transferred to the chair of pathology and theory and practical medicine, which he occupied till death. In May, 1861, he was appointed surgeon of the Second Michigan Infantry and surgeon in Gen. Richardson's Brigade, at the first battle of Bull Run, and other operations of his regiment until he resigned in September. In 1864 he was professor of pathology and practise of medicine in Berkshire Medical College at Pittsfield, Massachusetts. In 1869 he was called to a similar position at the medical department, Bowdoin College, Maine, doing the work in the vacations at the other institutions. From 1854–60 he was an editor of the "Peninsular Medical Journal," and the consolidated "Peninsular and Independent Medical Journal," Detroit, and president, in 1872, of the Michigan State Medical Society. In 1875 he succeeded Dr. Abram Sager as dean of the medical department, Michigan University, and except one year held the office till his death. In 1855 the University of Nashville, Tennessee, gave him the honorary A. M., and he had the LL. D., University of Michigan, in 1881. Above everything else he loved to lecture; one year to the same class he delivered one

hundred and ninety-six lectures, half of them new. At any moment he was ready to fill a vacant hour in any course in the department, never regarding it a hardship. In 1867 he married Love M. Root, of Pittsfield, Massachusetts, who survived him and perpetuated his memory by endowing the Palmer Ward at the University Hospital, also by erecting a tower on St. Andrew's Episcopal Church, of which he was a member. They had no children Dr. Palmer died at his home in Ann Arbor, December 23, 1887, from septicemia.

Alonzo B. Palmer's most ambitious publication and towards which all other writings pointed was his "Treatise on the Science and Practice of Medicine, of the Pathology and Treatment of Internal Diseases," two volumes of about nine hundred pages each, published in 1882, followed by "A Treatise on Epidemic Cholera and Allied Diseases," of two hundred and twenty-four pages, Ann Arbor, Michigan, 1885. The following is an incomplete list of his papers:

"Reduction of Inversion of the Uterus after a Lapse of Years." ("Peninsular and Independent Medical Journal," vol. i.)

"Children's Diseases." ("Peninsular and Independent Medical Jounal," vol. i.)

"Pulmonary Tuberculosis in Children." (Ibid., vol. iv.)

"Change of Type in Inflammatory Disease." (Ibid, vol. v.)

"Prostatic Hypertrophy and Urinary Obstructions; Its Treatment without Catheterism." ("Transactions, Michigan State Medical Society," 1884.)

"Climate and Consumption." ("Michigan University Medical Journal," vol. iii.)

"Causes and Treatment of Inflammation of Internal Organs." ("Transactions, Michigan State Medical Society," 1866.)

"The Pathology of Raynaud's Disease." "Transactions Ninth International Medical Congress," vol. iii.)

"Miliary Fever." ("Physician and Surgeon," vol. ii.)

"Law and Intelligence in Nature."

("Transactions, Michigan State Medical Society," 1873.)

"Contrasted Cases of Phthisis." ("Physician and Surgeon," Ann Arbor, vol. i.)

"Remarkable Atrophy of the Abdominal Walls in a Female." (Ibid, vol. i.)

"The Treatment of Malarial Fever." ("Michigan University Medical Journal," vol. ii.)

L. C.

Representative Men in Mich., West. Biographical Co., Cincinnati, Ohio, 1878, vol. ii. History of the University of Mich., Ann Arbor, 1906.

A Memorial Discourse on the Life and Services of Alonzo Benjamin Palmer, M. D., LL. D., by Corydon L. Ford, M. D., LL. D., The University Press, 1888, Medical Age, 1887.

Med. Record, N. Y., 1887, vol. xxxii. Trans. Mich. State Med. Soc., Detroit, 1888, Memorial volume, Alonzo Benjamin Palmer, 1890, Riverside Press, Cambridge, by Mrs. Palmer.

Palmer, James Croxall (1811–1883).

James Croxall Palmer, surgeon-general of the United States Navy, was descended from an old English family. He studied medicine at the University of Maryland and was commissioned assistant surgeon in the navy in 1834. He spent seventeen years of his life in actual sea-cruises. In 1842 he was promoted to the rank of surgeon. Palmer served in the Mexican as well as in the Civil War. He was with Farragut on the Hartford in the famous battle of Mobile Bay. In 1871 he was appointed medical director and on June 10, 1872, surgeon-general of the navy. He retired June 29 of the same year, and died in Washington, April 24, 1883.

A. A.

Stone, Biogr. Em. Am. Phys. and Surg., Indianapolis, 1898.

Palmer, John Williamson (1825–1906).

He was born in Baltimore, Maryland, April 4, 1825, the son of Edward Palmer, a merchant and descended from Edward Palmer, 1572–1625, the Oxford scholar and antiquarian, who in 1624 designed the foundation of the first college of arts in America on Palmer's Island, at the mouth of the Susquehanna.

Dr. Palmer graduated M. D. from the department of medicine of the University of Maryland, in 1846. He practised for some years, being first city physician of San Francisco, 1849–50, and surgeon in the East India Company's service in the second Burmese War, 1851–52. After traveling extensively in China, Hindustan and other far Eastern countries, he returned to the United States in 1853 and abandoned medicine for literature. During the Civil War he was southern correspondent for the "New York Tribune"; attaché of the confederate government charged with singular and hazardous responsibilities skillfully and bravely discharged, and valued volunteer on the staff of Maj.-gen. John C. Breckenridge. After the War he settled in New York City.

The following are the titles of some of his works: "The Queen's Heart," comedy, 1858; "The New and the Old, or California and India," 1859; "Up and Down the Irrawaddi," and "Folk Songs," 1860; "Epidemic Cholera," 1866; "The Poetry of Compliment and Courtship," 1867; "The Beauties and Curiosities of Engraving," 1879; "A Portfolio of Autograph Etchings," 1882; "After his Kind," 1886; "For Charlie's Sake and Other Lyrics and Ballads," 1901. He translated "L'Amour" (Michelet), 1859, "La Femme" (Michelet), 1859, "Histoire Morale des Femmes" (Legouve), 1860. Years before Bret Harte discovered the California of fiction, Palmer had revealed it in such stories as "The Fate of the Farleighs," "The Old Abode," "Mr. Karl Joseph Kraft of the Old Californians," and a number of others. He also contributed to the leading magazines and was one of the editors of the Century and Standard Dictionaries.

Palmer thus had a varied experience as traveler, editor, prose writer and poet, but it was especially in the last-named rôle, that he achieved fame and success. As a lyric poet he shines pre-eminent among Americans. His style is spirited and original, his language full of vigor, grace and pathos. He wielded the pen of a master and remarkable are the word-pictures he dashed off in the moments of his inspiration. His most famous poem was the Confederate war song—"Stonewall Jackson's Way"—composed within sound of the guns on the day of the Battle of Sharpsburg, September 17, 1862, and familiar to all Confederate soldiers. Some of these poems were published in 1901, under the title "For Charlie's Sake and Other Lyrics and Ballads." His poem "King's Mountain," a ballad of the Revolution, was published in the "Yale Alumni Weekly." His mind was clear and active up to his last illness and only about a year before his death he wrote what he considered his best poetic effort, "Ned Braddock."

Dr. Palmer died at Baltimore, from pneumonia, in his eighty-first year, on February 26, 1906. He married Miss Henrietta Lee, also an authoress, of Baltimore, in 1855, who survived him with one son.

E. F. C.

Sketches and portrait of Dr. Palmer appeared in the "Baltimore Sun" of February 27, 1906; in "Old Maryland," vol. ii, No. 3, March, 1906, and in "The Hospital Bulletin" of the University of Maryland, vol. ii, No. 1, same date.

Pancoast, Joseph (1805–1882).

Joseph Pancoast, son of John and Anne (Abbott) Pancoast, was born in Burlington, New Jersey, on the twenty-third of November, 1805, the descendant of an Englishman who came to this country with William Penn. Joseph graduated at the medical department of the University of Pennsylvania in 1828, and began to practise in Philadelphia, making surgery his specialty; in 1831 beginning to teach classes in practical anatomy and surgery. He was appointed physician to the Philadelphia Hospital, Blockley, and head physician to the children's hospital connected with it. In 1838 he was elected professor of surgery in the Jefferson Medical College,

Vol. II—16

and in 1847, professor of anatomy in the same institution. He held the latter chair until 1874, when he resigned and was succeeded by his son, William H. Pancoast. In addition, he was one of the surgeons of the Pennsylvania Hospital from March 27, 1854, until February 29, 1864. Many operations new to surgery were devised by him. Among them was one for soft and mixed cataracts. In this, a very fine needle, turned near the point into a sort of a hook, is passed through the front part of the vitreous humor, between the margin of the dilated iris and the lens, without touching the ciliary body. The advantage of this needle is that the soft part of the lens can be deeply cut and hardened nucleus withdrawn, by a sort of horizontal displacement, along the line of entrance of the needle, the piece being left in the outer border of the vitreous humor. In 1841 he devised the plow and groove or plastic suture, in which four raw surfaces, the beveled edges of the flaps, and the margins of the groove cut by the side of the nose to receive the flaps come together. He used this suture in all his rhinoplastic operations, and union almost invariably followed. He likewise devised an operation for empyema, by raising a semicircular flap of the integuments over the ribs, and puncturing the pleura near the base of the flap; putting a short catheter down to the inner end of the puncture, secured with a strong string, and forming thus a fistulous opening, to which the movable flap served as a valve when the catheter was removed. He demonstrated that often bad cases of strabismus are due to the fact that the oblique muscle is girdled by rigid connective tissue, and that the tendons must be drawn out with a hook and cut. For the occlusion of the nasal duct, in ordinary cases of epiphora, he introduced, by a puncture of the lacrymal sac, a hollow ivory tube from which the earthy matter had been removed and left it to slowly dissolve. He several times restored a voice that was unintelligible by cutting the posterior muscles of the velum palati and loosening any attachment it may have made to the pharynx. He performed four times with success a lumbar operation for large abscesses, lying in the connective tissue between the colon and the cecum and the front of the quadratus lumborum muscle. He originated an abdominal tourniquet, first used in 1860, which, by compressing the lower end of the aorta and by shutting off the arterial blood from the lower limbs, prevented death by loss of blood in amputations at the hip-joint, or even high up on the thigh. In 1862, before the class of the Pennsylvania Hospital, Dr. Pancoast performed for the first time his cure for certain cases of tic douloureux, dividing the trunks of the fifth pair of nerves as they come out of their foramina, at the base of the skull. In January, 1868, he performed for the first time an operation, original with him, for the relief of extrophy of the bladder, by turning down cutaneous flaps from the abdomen and groin over the hollow raw surface of the open bladder.

Dr. Pancoast was a voluminous contributor to the "American Journal of Medical Sciences," the "American Intelligencer," and the "Medical Examiner;" and the author of pathological and surgical monographs; essays and introductory lectures to his class, one of these being "Professional Glimpses Abroad" (1856). He edited "Manec on the Great Sympathetic Nerve," and on the "Cerebrospinal System in Man," and "Quain's Anatomical Plates;" and published an anotated translation from the Latin of Lobstein's "Treatise on the Structure, Functions and Diseases of the Human Sympathetic Nerve" (1831); "Treatise on Operative Surgery" (1844, third edition, 1852), his chief work; and a revised edition of Dr. Caspar Wistar's "System of Anatomy for the Use of Students" (1844). He was a member of the American Philosophical Society; the Medical Society of Pennsylvania, and other scientific organizations.

Dr. Pancoast was married at Philadelphia in 1829 to Rebecca, daughter of Timothy Abbott. He died in Philadelphia, Pennsylvania, March 7, 1882.

C. R. B.

S. D. Gross, Autobiography.
Nat. Encyclo. Amer. Biog., vol. ix.
Boston Med. and Surg. Jour., 1882.
Med. Bull , Phila., 1882, vol. iv.
Med. News, Phila, 1882, vol. xl.
Phila. Med. Times, 1881–2, vol. xii.
There is a portrait in the Surg.-gen. Lib. at Washington, D. C.

Pancoast, William Henry (1835–1897).

William Henry Pancoast was the son of Joseph and Rebecca (Abbott) Pancoast. He was educated at Haverford College, Pennsylvania, where he graduated in 1853. Following in the footsteps of his father, a leading member of the medical profession of Philadelphia, he entered Jefferson Medical College, where he was graduated M. D. in 1856. He then studied two and a half years in London, Paris, Vienna and Berlin Upon his return he settled in Philadelphia and soon acquired a reputation as a brilliant diagnostician, a bold and skillful yet conservative operator. In 1859 he was elected visiting surgeon to the Charity Hospital, a position which he held for ten years, during which time he established a large surgical clinic. On resigning, he was elected consulting surgeon, and placed on the board of trustees. During the Civil War he was appointed surgeon-in-chief and second officer in charge of the Military Hospital, Philadelphia. In 1862 he was appointed demonstrator of anatomy at Jefferson Medical College; this position he held until 1874. He was also a lecturer on surgical anatomy in the Summer School. In 1866 he was elected one of the visiting surgeons to the Philadelphia Hospital. When his father went to Europe in 1867 he was appointed adjunct professor of anatomy in Jefferson College. He also occupied the same position in 1873 and 1874, and upon the resignation of his father in the latter year, he was elected his successor.

Dr. Pancoast was a member of the National Academy of Science; fellow of the College of Physicians of Philadelphia;

JOSEPH PANCOAST.

(By permission of the McDowell Publishing Co.)

member of the Philadelphia College Medical Society (president in 1869), and a member of numerous other medical societies. From 1886 to the time of his death he was professor of general descriptive and surgical anatomy and clinical surgery in the Medico-Chirurgical College of Philadelphia, an institution which he helped to found. He published numerous papers on clinical and surgical subjects.

After the death of the Siamese twins he obtained their bodies, and made an examination under the auspices of the College of Physicians and Surgeons of Philadelphia, and proved that the band could not safely have been cut, except in their childhood.

During the later years of his life Dr. Pancoast suffered greatly from ill-health, and after his resignation in 1874 of his chair of anatomy in the Jefferson Medical College, he gradually withdrew from the active duties of his profession. In May, 1877, the formal opening of the Jefferson College Hospital was, at the request of the trustees, inaugurated by him in an eloquent address, and this was his last official act in the school with which he was connected for more than forty years. At the time of his death Dr. Pancoast was the only survivor of the celebrated faculty of 1841 in the Jefferson Medical College.

He died on the fifth of January, 1897.

C. R. B.

Med. Mirror, St. Louis, 1890, i, (port).
J. Am. Med. Ass., Chicago, 1897, xxviii.
Med. Rec., N. Y., 1897, li.
Tr. Am. Surg. Ass., Phila., 1897, xi.

Parker, Daniel McNeil (1822–1907).

Daniel McNeil Parker, of English and Scottish descent, was born at Windsor, Nova Scotia, April 28, 1822, and died at Dartmouth, Nova Scotia, November 4, 1907. His practice, of half a century, was at Halifax, Nova Scotia.

He had his general education at the Collegiate School, Windsor, and the Academy at Horton, Nova Scotia. In the late thirties he became an indentured student in medicine to Dr. William Bruce Almon,

and in 1841 went to the medical school of Edinburgh University, in 1845 graduating M. D. from the University and also as L. R. C. S. (Edinburgh), taking a gold medal in surgery, the title of his thesis being "The Mechanism and Management of Parturition." He also held the D. C. L. of Acadia College, Wolfville.

Dr. Parker was a member of the Medical Society of Nova Scotia, and its president in 1857 and 1877; a member of the Canadian Medical Association, and in 1870 its second president. He was consulting surgeon at the Provincial and City Hospital, and, later, the Victoria General Hospital, Halifax; as a public-spirited citizen, he was identified with and a co-worker in most of the educational and philanthropic work of the city.

Upon his return to Nova Scotia after graduation, he settled down to practice in Halifax, where he soon had a good reputation. In 1891 he gave up practice in Halifax, in order that he might acquaint himself at first hand with the new Listerian surgery, then in its earlier development in full use at Edinburgh. The next two years were devoted to study and research at Edinburgh and Paris. Upon his return to Halifax in 1873, he limited his practice to that of a consultant in medicine and surgery, and in this he was highly successful. In 1895, after half a century of successful work, he retired.

Dr. Parker travelled considerably on both sides of the Atlantic and thus happened to be in position to witness several notable events, such as Dr. Chalmers leading out the Free Church Ministers in 1843, the bombardment of Fort Sumter in 1861, and the terrors of the Commune in Paris in 1871.

Though always very busy, Dr. Parker found time to deliver many addresses on professional subjects and to write some special papers. "Three Cases of Ruptured Perineum and Sphincter Ani Cured by Operation" ("Edinburgh Medical Journal," 1857, p. 448); "Fatal Cases Resulting from the Habit of Arsenic Eating" ("Edinburgh Medical Journal," 1864, p.

116); "Notes of Some Unusual Cases of Disease Involving Primarily the Skin Covering the Mammary Gland" ("Maritime Medical News," Halifax, vol. i, p. 131) may be mentioned.

Dr. Parker married twice, first to Elizabeth Ritchie, daughter of the Hon. J. W. Johnston, attorney-general, their only child, James J. Parker, dying in Edinburgh while a medical student, and his [second wife was Fanny Holmes, daughter of the Hon. W. A. Black, of Halifax. He was survived by a widow, three daughters and one son.

D. A. C.

Parker, Edward Hazen (1823–1896).

Dr. Edward Hazen Parker was born in the city of Boston, the son of Hon. Isaac and Sarah (Ainsworth) Parker. Dr. Parker graduated from Dartsmouth College in 1846, and received his medical degree from Jefferson Medical College in 1848. After graduation, he was at once appointed lecturer on anatomy and physiology at Bowdoin Medical College at Concord, New Hampshire, and there he undertook also the editorship of the "New Hampshire Medical Journal," which he conducted successfully for nine years.

In 1853, on being called to the chair of physiology and pathology in the New York Medical College, Dr. Parker left Concord and established himself in practice in New York City, his confrères in the college being Peaslee and Barker. During the three years that Dr. Parker held this professorship he established the "Medical Monthly" (1854), which he continued to edit personally for many years with great ability and success, and was co-editor of "The Journal of Medicine," Concord, in 1850.

In 1854 he received the degree of A. M. from Trinity College, and in 1858, by the solicitation of many friends and patients, was induced to remove to Poughkeepsie, New York, where he practised nearly up to the time of his death, a period of some forty years.

Dr. Parker was a physician and a surgeon of signal competency and skill. He was a man of extremely fine fiber, of unusual cultivation, and of high scholarly attainments. The following brief poem was written by him years ago. It has been copied and translated into several languages including Greek and Latin, and the first verse was inscribed on Pres. Garfield's tomb.

Life's race well run,
Life's work all done,
Life's victory won;
Now cometh rest.

Sorrows are o'er,
Trials no more,
Ship reaches shore;
Now cometh rest.

Faith yields to sight,
Day follows night,
Jesus gives light;
Now cometh rest.

We a while wait,
But, soon or late,
Death opes the gate,
Then cometh rest.

Dr. Parker lived in Poughkeepsie, New York, for nearly forty years. He was elected president of the Medical Society of the State of New York in 1862; and held a commission in the corps of volunteer surgeons provided by the state under Govs. Morgan and Seymour; and was also one of the medical board of Vassar Hospital. He died on November 9, 1896, at Poughkeepsie, New York.

J. E. S.

Med. Rec., N. Y., 1896, vol. i.

Parker, James Pleasant (1854–1896).

James Pleasant Parker was born in Alabama, and at first was a pharmacist, but later took up medicine (1882) and graduated at Jefferson Medical College in 1886. He studied ophthalmology and otology in Philadelphia and New York, but in 1887 settled in Kansas City to practise these specialties. Four years later he founded the "Annals of Ophthalmology and Otology," and to this publication and his practice he devoted every moment of his time and his entire energy, being rewarded with marked success. In 1892 he removed to St. Louis where he

WILLARD PARKER.
(Permission of Mrs. W. B. Atkinson.)

continued his work unceasingly and without rest, to which his early death, February 6, 1896, is generally attributed. He was then in his forty-second year.

H. F.

Annals of Ophthalmology and Otology, 1896, vol. v.

Parker, Willard (1800–1884).

Willard Parker, a prominent New York surgeon, was born in Francistown, Hilsborough County, New York, in 1800, of Puritan stock.

The boy worked on his father's farm and with his own earnings paid his way at and graduated from Harvard in 1826, studying medicine in Boston and shortly after taking his M. D. from Cambridge College with a thesis on "Nervous Respiration." Only a few weeks after he was appointed lecturer on anatomy in the College of Physicians and Surgeons, New York. As an operator and lecturer he was always successful. "If you were to select a specialty" asked his friend, Dr. Francis, "what would you choose?" He answered, "Medical treatment and diagnosis as associated with surgical cases, but what I regard as beautiful in its results and satisfactory in its issues, is the cutting down for and ligating arteries." He tied the subclavian artery five times, once performing the operation within the scaleni muscles, also taking the precaution to apply a ligature to the common carotid and right vertebral arteries for the first time in this country.

There are two operations which Dr. Parker may partly be said to have originated, cystotomy, for irritable bladder, first done at the Bellevue Hospital, New York, in 1850, and the operation for perityphlitic abscess, in 1864. Parker was not aware that Mr. Hancock, of London, had done the same operation successfully in 1848. It is curious that Parker's reasoning in favor of the operation was exactly the same as Hancock's.

One of Parker's special claims to public esteem was his untiring work for public hygiene and temperance. When Valentine Mott died in 1865, he became president of the New York State Inebriate Asylum.

He resigned active practice and lecturing in 1870, and was made emeritus professor of surgery. Princeton College gave him her LL. D. that same year,

He did not write much, except articles to the medical journals, and these included: "Cases of Extensive Encephaloid Degeneration of Kidneys in Children;" "Some Rare Forms of Dislocation;" "Trephining the Cranium and Ligature of the Carotid in Epilepsy and Cure;" "Practical Remarks on Concussion of the Nerves;" "Ligature of Subclavian Artery for Axillary and Subclavian Aneurysm;" "Ligature of the Subclavian Inside the Scalenus together with Common Carotid and Vertebral Arteries for Subclavian Aneurysm."

On the establishment of St. Luke's, the Roosevelt and the Mt. Sinai Hospitals he became one of the consulting surgeons and was for many years a most active member of the Pathological Society and of the Medical and Surgical Society.

He may be said to have died in harness, for although prevented by physical suffering during the last two years of his life from working, he was frequently consulted by old patients and professional friends. He could not be called a learned man, but he was what some learned men never become, a wise one. He was not a master in the use of instruments of precision, but he often comprehended the significance of symptoms and their prognostic value more correctly than his younger confrères.

D. W.

Distinguished Living New York Surgeons. Dr. S. W. Francis, N. Y., 1866.
Boston Med. and Surg. Gen., 1884, cx.
Med. News, Phila., 1884, xliv.
Med. Rec., N. York, 1884, xxv.
Med. and Surg. Reporter, Phila., 1865, xiii.
N. York Med. Jour., 1884, xxxix.
Tr. Am. Surg. Assoc., 1884, Phila., 1885.
Tr. Med. Soc., N. York, Syracuse, 1885.
There is a portrait in the Surg-gen. lib., Washington, D. C.

Parker, William W. (1824–1899).

At Port Royal, Caroline County, Virginia, on May 5, 1824, William Parker was born; his early education obtained at Richmond Academy, his medical at the Medical College of Virginia, from which he graduated in 1848, afterwards settling down to practice in Richmond, Virginia. He was a member of the Richmond Academy of Medicine and of the Medical Society of Virginia.

In the Civil War he was captain and, later, major of artillery in the Confederate States Army; he was the founder of the Magdalen Home in Richmond; the Old Ladies' Home, and the Home for Foundlings. He served a term as president of the Academy of Medicine, and was elected president of the Medical Society of Virginia in 1890.

A co-temporary says of him that "He was one of the most unique figures in the profession. He always rode on horse-back and did an enormous practice, chiefly among the poor people in moderate circumstances; and perhaps no man ever did so much work for humanity in Richmond for such poor remuneration. A man of great courage, both physical and moral, he served his country during the Civil War as commander of Parker's Battery of Artillery, winning great distinction by his daring and courage as an officer.

It has been told of him by old war comrades that after hard battles lasting all day, he was wont to lay off his coat and roll up his sleeves and work all night as a surgeon.

From an early period in his life he was an ardent and consistent Christian, carrying the same enthusiasm into his church as he did upon the field of battle. He possessed, too, a well-equipped and well-stored mind, to which was added the fiery enthusiasm of youth.

Dr. Parker married in January, 1862, Ellen J. Jordan, and had three sons and three daughters. One of his sons, Dr. William W. Parker, became a physician in Richmond. The father died at his home in Richmond, on August 5, 1899.

He was a prolific writer for the newspapers on whatever subject was at the time of public interest, and contributed some papers to the Medical Society of Virginia and some to the journals; the titles of most are given below:

"Erysipelas, Treatment of, New Method." ("Virginia Medical Journal," 1857.)

"Burial versus Cremation." ("Transactions of the Medical Society of Virginia," 1886.)

"The Duty of a Doctor to a Patient Suffering under Malignant Disease," ibid., 1888.

Blood Gravitation in Health and Disease," ibid., 1889.

"Rise and Decline of Homeopathy," ibid., 1890.

"Ancient and Modern Physician,"— St. Luke and Jenner, presidential address, ibid., 1891.

"Woman's Position in the Christian World," ibid., 1892.

R. M. S.

Dr. J. N. Upshur's Medical Reminiscences of Richmond, etc.
Trans. Med. Soc. of Va., 1899.

Parkes, Charles T. (1842–1891).

Charles T. Parkes had remarkable success as a teacher of anatomy, and a clear and concise method of demonstration which not only excited enthusiasm and love in all his students, but gained for him a wide reputation.

He was born August 19, 1842, at Troy, New York, the youngest of ten children. His father, Joseph Parkes, an Englishman, came to Chicago in 1860. At that time the son was a student in the University of Michigan, where he afterwards received his A. M. He enlisted in the army in 1862 as a private and was discharged three years later as captain.

At the close of the war he returned to Chicago, and began to study medicine under Dr. Rae, professor of anatomy in Rush Medical College. He graduated from this college in 1868, and was at once appointed demonstrator of anatomy, which position he held until his appointment as professor of anatomy in 1875.

His specialty was abdominal surgery in which he was a pioneer investigator.

The first to advocate uniting severed intestines; he in this antedated Drs. Senn and Murphy. For the purpose of gaining a better knowledge of both the cousequences and treatment of gunshot wounds of the intestine he made a series of experiments on forty dogs. The number of recoveries astounded the medical profession and lead to further experiments in all parts of the world. He made his first report at a meeting of the American Medical Association in Washington, 1884. He took with him three specimens of intestine and a living dog from which he removed five feet of intestine perforated by bullet wounds. His work in the surgery of the gall-bladder, which was then in its infancy, was no less conspicuous in influencing new lines of treatment. Preceding Parkes' there were not twenty-five ideal cholecystotomies. He recognized the practical place of surgery in the relief of common maladies.

Always a student, he read much, loved old books and also kept in touch with the continental medical schools. For several years before his death he had been accumulating material for works on general and abdominal surgery but his sudden death stopped the writing. The writings he left were published under "Clinical Lectures," but there were some fifty or more besides what appeared in the current medical journals and of which a partial list can be seen in "Distinguished Physicians and Surgeons of Chicago," F. M. Speery, 1894.

He married, in 1868, Isabella J. Gonterman and had two children, Charles Herbert and Irene Edna. The son became, like his father, a surgeon. Dr. Parkes was described as a handsome man of splendid physique, over six feet, with a gentle kindly face and a devotion to little children and out-door sports.

Among his appointments he was: attending surgeon to the Presbyterian Hospital; surgeon-in-charge of St. Joseph's Hospital; surgeon-in-chief to the Augustana Hospital; consulting surgeon to the Hospital for Women and Children, and professor of surgery in the Chicago Polyclinic. He held also the presidency of the Chicago Medical Society and of the Chicago Gynecological Society. In 1887 he was elected professor of surgery—successor to Prof. Moses Gunn—and in this position he was gaining wide renown at the time of his death, which occurred after a short illness from pneumonia, March 28, 1891.

There is a portrait in the Chicago publication referred to. D. W.

Trans., The Illinois State Med. Soc., 1891.
Distinguished Phys. and Surgeons of Chicago, F. M. Speery, Chicago, 1904.
Appreciations by various surgeons.

Parkhill, Clayton (1860-1902).

He was born on a farm in Vanderbilt, Pennsylvania, on April 18, 1860, and in 1881 entered Jefferson Medical College (Philadelphia) and graduated in 1883. He was then appointed physician to the Philadelphia Hospital and served one year. In the meantime, he completed a course at the Pennsylvania School of Anatomy and Surgery under Dr. George McClellan, and subsequently became his assistant. Leaving Philadelphia, he settled in Denver in 1885.

He was demonstrator of anatomy in the University of Denver and, the Gross Medical School being organized, was appointed to the same position and also that of professor of clinical surgery, and left here for the chair of surgery in the University of Colorado at Boulder, and was also dean of this school.

About this time he devised his apparatus for cleft palate and jurymast for fractures of the maxilla and clamp for the treatment of fractures of long bones ("Annals of Surgery," May, 1898). By the latter, a valuable apparatus, he is best known to the profession.

In 1898 he was appointed surgeon-general of the National Guard by Gov. McIntire and was re-appointed by his successor, Gov. Adams. During the latter's administration, war broke out between the United States and Spain and Dr. Parkhill became surgeon to the First Colorado Regiment with rank of major.

He went to San Francisco with the regiment, but not to the Philippines. He was promoted to the position of brigade-surgeon and was transferred to the camps of the South and Porto Rico and served on Gen. Miles' staff in Porto Rico, where he rendered splendid service. After the close of the war, he was honorably discharged, returned to Denver and resumed work, though in impaired health. He was a man of splendid address, of genial nature, a fine teacher and brilliant surgeon, scrupulously neat, possessed mechanical ingenuity and his technic was faultless. He died in Denver, January 16, 1902, from acute appendicitis, complicated with nephritis and uremia. Though himself a surgeon, who never shrank from duty, yet, unlike most surgeons, he would not submit to the knife. He married S. Effie Brown, of Redstone, Pennsylvania, April 28, 1886, and had two sons; Clayton, Jr., and Forbes.

His writings included:

"Anatomical Anomalies." ("Denver Medical Times," 1889.)

"A Successful Nephrectomy for Tuberculosis." ("International Journal of Surgery," New York, 1891.)

"A MacEwen Operation for the Radical Cure of Hernia." ("Denver Medical Times," 1891.)

"Linear Craniotomy." ("Medical News," Philadelphia, 1892.)

"The Removal of the Gasserian Ganglion." ("Medical News," Philadelphia, 1893.)

"Linear Craniotomy in Microcephalus." ("International Medical Magazine," Philadelphia, 1893.)

"A New Apparatus for the Treatment of Fracture of the Inferior Maxilla." ("Journal American Medical Association," 1894.)

"Two Abscesses of the Brain Caused by Septic Emboli Resulting from a Gunshot Wound Inflicted Thirty-two Years Before." (Drs. Eskridge and Parkhill in "New York Medical Journal," 1895.)

"A New Instrument for Marking the Skull in Brain Operations." ("Medical News," Philadelphia, 1895.)

"A New Apparatus for the Fixation of Bones After Resection and in the Fractures with a Tendency to Displacement." ("Transactions American Surgical Association," 1897.)

"Pseudo-arthrosis of the Tibia; Union with the Parkhill Clamp." ("Western Medical and Surgical Gazette," 1897.)

"Cases of Cerebral Surgery." ("Transactions Colorado Medical Society," 1893.)

"Further Observations Regarding the Use of the Bone Clamp in Ununited Fractures, Fractures with Malunion, and Recent Fractures with a Tendency to Displacement." ("Annals of Surgery," 1898.)

"A New Treatment Suggested for Fractured Olecranon." ("Denver Medical Times," 1885.)

"Barton's Fracture." ("Denver Medical Times," 1886.)

W. W. G.

J Am. M. Ass., 1902, xxxviii.
J. Ass. Mil. Surg. U. S., Carlisle, Pa., 1902–3, xi.

Parrish, Joseph (1779–1840).

Joseph Parrish was born in Philadelphia, September 3, 1779, and started in life as a hatter, but when he became of age, turned to the study of medicine, and became a student under Dr. Caspar Wistar. He took his medical degree at the University of Pennsylvania in 1805, and in the same year, became resident physician at the yellow-fever hospital. From 1806–12 he held the same post at the Philadelphia Dispensary, from 1816–22, at Philadelphia Almshouse, and 1816–29, at Pennsylvania Hospital. He was associated in the establishment of the Wills' Hospital, and was an active member of the College of Physicians. He was one of the foremost Philadelphia physicians who at that time took an active interest in natural history as well as in scientific medicine. Among other studies which led to considerable popular reputation, was his demonstration that the poplar worm is harmless. It had hitherto been supposed to be venomous and trees were being ruthlessly destroyed because a man was found dead with a worm beside him. In 1807 he gave what was then a novelty, a popular course of lectures on chemistry. He had many private pupils and ultimately established a very large practice.

He was an editor of the "North American Medical and Surgical Journal." According to Dr. George B. Woods, "perhaps no one was known more extensively in the city or had connected himself by a greater number of beneficent services to every ramification of society."

The following brief character sketch of Parrish occurs in Patterson's "Memoir of Samuel George Morton."

"Elevated to his prominent position against early obstacles, and solely by force of character, industry, and probity, he was extensively engaged in practice; and, although unconnected with any institution, his office overflowed with pupils. His mind was practical and thoroughly medical, and so entirely did his profession occupy it that he seemed to me never to allow himself to think upon other topics, except religious ones, in which also he was deeply interested. A strict and conscientious friend, he illustrated all the best points in that character." He died in Philadelphia, on March 18, 1840.

C. R. B.

Geo. B. Wood's "Memoir of the Life and Character of Joseph Parrish," Philadelphia, 1840.

Parry, Charles Christopher (1823–1890).

Charles Christopher Parry, botanist, was born in the hamlet of Admington, Goucestershire, England, August 28, 1823, and descended through a long line of clergymen of the Established Church.

In 1832 the family removed to America, settling on a farm in Washington County, New York. He entered Union College at Schenectady, and graduated with honors, beginning the study of medical botany in his undergraduate years, and subsequently receiving his M. D. from Columbia College.

Coming west and to Davenport in the fall of 1846, he entered into practice, but soon discovered that all his natural tastes

and instincts led directly away to the unvexed, blossoming solitudes of nature.

His earliest collecting had been done in the attractive floral region about his home in Northeastern New York, in the summer of 1842 and the four years following; and now again, he employed much of the season of 1847 in making a collection of the wild flowers about Davenport, of which, with the dates of finding, he has left a manuscript list. Those of us who knew him well in after years can readily picture the brisk, dark-complexioned, though blue-eyed youth, symmetrically but slightly built and somewhat below the medium height, in his solitary quest by riverside and deep ravine, over wooded bluff and prairie expanse, for the treasures which were more to him than gold—for such early friends as "the prairie primrose, the moccasin-flower, and the gentian," which in later years he complained had been quite driven out by "the blue-grass and white clover."

In the course of that summer, also, he accompanied a United States surveying party, under Lieut. J. Morehead, on an excursion into Central Iowa, in the vicinity of the present state capital. From this time on (except for a short time while connected with the Mexican Boundary Survey, when he discharged the duties of assistant surgeon), the physician was merged in the naturalist. He was almost continuously in the field collecting, but Davenport remained his home. Here, in 1853, he married Sarah M. Dalzell, who, dying five years later, left with him an only child, a daughter. But she, too, died at an early age.

In 1859 he married again; to Mrs. E. R. Preston of Westford, Connecticut, who through the more than thirty years of their union, entered helpfully into all his works and plans, assisting him in his study and often accompanying him to the field.

Dr. Parry gives in "Proc., Davenport Acad. of Sci., vol. ii," a succinct, chronological account of his work up to 1878. For more than thirty years the greater part of his time had been spent in observing and collecting—along the St. Peters and up the St. Croix; across the Isthmus to San Diego, to the junction of the Gila and Colorado, along the southern boundary line and up the coast as far as Monterey; through Texas to El Paso, to the Pimo settlements on the Gila, and along the Rio Grande; in the mountains of Colorado, to which and to those of California he returned again and again in the pursuit of his special study, the Alpine Flora of North America; across the continent with a Pacific railroad surveying party by way of the Sangre de Christo Pass, through New Mexico and Arizona, through the Tehachapi Pass, through the Tulare and San Joaquin Valleys to San Francisco; through the Wind River district to the Yellowstone National Park; in the Valley of the Virgen and about Mt. Nebo, Utah; about San Bernardino, California, and in the arid regions stretching to the eastward; and in Mexico about San Luis Potosi, Saltillo, and Monterey.

The winter of 1852-3 was spent in Washington, in the preparation of his report as botanist to the Mexican Boundary Survey; and the years from 1869 to 1871 inclusive, while botanist to the United States Agricultural Department, were also passed chiefly at the capital, employed in arranging the extensive botanical collections from various government explorations, which had accumulated at the Smithsonian Institution. During this period, also, he visited, in his official capacity, the Royal Gardens and herbaria at Kew, England, and was attached as botanist to the Commission of Inquiry which visited San Domingo early in 1871.

In 1879, being called to the East by the illness and death of his father, he did little if any work in the field. In 1880, as special agent of the Forestry Department of the United States Census Office, he accompanied Dr. Engelmann and Professor Sargent in an expedition to the valley of the Columbia and the far Northwest. Wintering in California he spent the following year in that state, making numerous collecting trips north and south, including a trip to the Yosemite in June. In January and February, 1883, he

made two camping trips into Lower California; then, going to San Francisco, made numerous excursions from that point, and returned to Davenport in September. In June, 1884, he sailed a second time for England, returning in August of the following year, after spending much time at Kew, and visiting other herbaria and gardens on the Continent.

The summer of 1886 he spent partly with friends in Wisconsin, partly in the quiet enjoyment of his Iowa home. But even when resting, his mind did not rest —his wonderfully voluminous correspondence went on, and the microscope filled in his otherwise leisure hours. Again the winter was passed in San Francisco, from which city he made numerous collecting trips as before. Remaining in California, chiefly in the vicinity of San Francisco, until September, 1888, he was busily employed making special collections of Arctostaphylos and Ceanothus, and in the study of these and the genus Alnus. His last visit to California was made in the spring of 1889. Returning to Davenport in July, he made a trip to Canada and New England, visited New York and Philadelphia and returned to his home but a few weeks before his death.

Parry was recognized as an authority by botanists everywhere; not only in this country (where he ranked with the first) and in England, but on the Continent as well; and this notwithstanding the fact that he never published a book, had no ambition in the way of authorship, and left most of his discoveries to be described by others. His writings, though sufficient to constitute volumes, and comprising much of great scientific value, are scattered in fragmentary form through various government and society reports, scientific journals, and the daily press.

In 1875 he was made a fellow of the American Association for the Advancement of Science, and kept up a corresponding membership in Philadelphia, Buffalo, St. Louis, Chicago, and California Academies of Science.

His name (bestowed by surveyor-general F. M. Chase) is borne by a peak of the Snowy Range, to the northwest of Empire City.

Besides contributing largely to the collections of his botanical friends and of various societies at home and abroad, he made for himself one of the finest herbaria in the land, a collection, systematically classified and arranged, comprising over 18,000 determined specimens representative of nearly 6,800 species, together with some 1,400 specimens determined only as far as the genus.

To bring the Mexican rose into cultivation, for example, he made an extra trip into Lower California. He was at especial pains to introduce the remarkable Spiræa cæspitosa or "tree moss," found in the Wasatch Mountains. Every region he explored was viewed not alone with the botanist's searching eye, but was studied as well in its topographical and climatic aspects, as affecting its economic possibilities.

Deeply affectionate, almost extravagantly fond of children, and with a sense of humor which often sparkled in his home conversation, he was yet so reticent that only the intimate few were aware of these traits in his character. With no expensive habits and almost no wants save knowledge, he looked on money as of value chiefly for the amount of this it could procure and diffuse.

Dr. Parry discovered during his extensive explorations hundreds of new plants afterwards described by Dr. Gray and by Dr. Engelmann, and his name is firmly fixed in the history of West American botany. While his greatest service has been rendered to botanical science, yet horticulturists will not soon forget that it was Dr. Parry who discovered Picea pungens, the beautiful blue spruce of our gardens; Pinus Engelmanni, Pinus Torreyana, Pinus Parryana, Pinus aristata, and a host of others of beauty and value. Through his zeal and enterprise many plants now familiar to American and European gardens were first cultivated. Zizyphus Parryi, Phacelia Parryi, Frasera Parryi, Lilium Parryi, Saxafraga Parryi,

Dalea Parryi, Primula Parryi, and many other plants of great beauty or utility bear his name in commemoration of his labors and worthily do him honor.

In the vicinity of San Diego, in 1882, as Mr. Orcutt further relates, "he rediscovered the little fern Ophiglossum nudicaule, which he had first found in 1850, and which ever since had been unseen. In the neighborhood of Todos Santos, or All Saints Bay, were discovered the new Ribes viburnifolium, Parry's Mexican rose (Rosa minutifolia, Engelmann), and a dwarf horse-chestnut (Aesculus Parryi) among other new plants;" also, later, in the same region, "the new spice bush (Ptelea aptera, Parry)." The Parry lily (Lilium Parry,) Watson) was discovered in 1876 on the ranch of the Ring brothers in Southern California, near San Gorgonio Pass.

A tolerably full list of his writings can be seen in the "Proc. of the Davenport Acad. of Science," vol. vi.

Parry died on the twentieth of February, 1890, at his home in Davenport.

C. H. P.

Parry, John S. (1843–1876).

John S. Parry, a Philadelphian obstetrician, the only son of Seneca and Priscilla S. Parry, was born on the fourth of January, 1843, in Drumore, Lancaster County, Pennsylvania.

His mother, when widowed, worked her farm and educated her four children well. John was known as a boy as "the little doctor," and when seventeen studied medicine under Dr. I. M. Deaver, then matriculated at the University of Pennsylvania, and took his M. D. there in 1865.

When he became a resident in the Philadelphia Hospital he had an opportunity of studying an epidemic of puerperal fever and gathering notes for a valuable paper. On leaving the hospital in 1866, he married Rachel P., daughter of William and Annie Sharpless, of Philadelphia, and settled to practice in that town, but acted as visiting obstetrician to the Philadelphia Hospital and with his

PARSONS 252 PARSONS

colleague, Dr. E. L. Duer, re-organized the lying-in wards and utilized the valuable clinical material for the students. One result was his "Observations on Relapsing Fever in Philadelphia in 1869–70." As a member of the Pathological Society and the College of Physicians and Surgeons he wrote many papers for the meetings, notably one on "Rachitis," his conclusions as to its equal prevalency in Philadelphia being supported by exhaustive statistics; another paper was on "Inherited Syphilis."

Appointments and honors came rapidly: physician for women's diseases at the Presbyterian Hospital; counsellor of the College of Physicians; president of the Obstetrical Society; vice-president of the Pathological Society, and surgeon to the State Hospital for Women and Infants which he had helped to found. Although in bad health he made a big fight to complete his notable book—"Extra-uterine Pregnancy" (1875)—and many remember how in his library, pale, haggard and racked with cough, he toiled day and night. He was persuaded on its completion to go to Florida, though but little hope was entertained of his return. This proved to be the case, for only the work-battered earthly tent returned for burial, after young Parry finished his pilgrimage, in Jacksonville, on the eleventh of March, 1876.

His biographer, Dr. J. V. Ingham, describes him as a writer never idle, and gives a list of some thirty-five excellent articles, reviews, and his additions to the second American edition of "Leishman's System of Midwifery," notably those on "Forceps" and a whole chapter on "Diphtheritic Wounds of the Vagina."

Tr. Coll. Phys., Phila., 1876, 3. s., vol. ii (J. V. Ingham).
Quart. Tr. Lancaster City and Co. M. Soc., 1881–2, vol. ii (J. Price).

Parsons, Joseph Addison (1815–1886).

The author once asked a man if Col. Joseph Parsons, of Parsonsfield, were a scholarly man, for he had named one of his sons after Sir Charles Grandison, and the other after Joseph Addison. "Oh no," said he, "he was a good farmer and had no great knowledge of books, but as one of twenty-three children himself, and having sixteen of his own, he had to call them something." Now this Joseph Addison, or as he called himself, J. Addison Parsons, was the seventeenth child of Joseph Parsons and Abigail Adams, his second wife. He was born June 30, 1815, and a direct descendant in the fifth generation of Coronet Joseph Parsons, who settled in Springfield, Massachusetts, in 1635.

Joseph and brother Charles went to school together, studied medicine together, graduating at the Medical School of Maine in 1837, and practising side by side for a while. But Charles soon abandoned medicine, leaving Joseph to continue a physician for the rest of his long life. In his prime he was a nice looking man, picturesque, tall, rather long haired, and with a prominent nose, a good humored man, talked well on medicine and at one time was a great hand at making political speeches, although he never went really into politics, or accepted offices.

During the Civil War he promised to attend gratuitously the wives and children of every man in the town who would enlist. Later in life he married Miss Mary Ginn, but had no children. For many years before that event, he was an old bachelor, and kept, literally, an open house for the benefit of his friends. Whenever anybody wanted him in the day time, they would walk in and if at night they would run upstairs and waking him up out of his sleep, make him go with them to a patient.

He was once called out by a man who had the habit of getting pretty "full" to cheer himself when there was sickness in the family. One day he dragged the doctor out into his own team, and started off in haste. Passing through the village, on the way to the farmhouse where the patient lay sick, the man pulled up the horse with a jerk, so that Dr. Parsons was nearly hurled over the dasher. "Why Simms," said he, "are you crazy, what are you stopping the horse for?" "Well," said the man, "I just thought I'd stop at the undertaker's and order a coffin, for your cases never get well."

During the small-pox epidemic in the country, the lone women would often close the doors and windows of their houses, facing the road, opening only the door occasionally to let in a little air. One time Dr. Parsons was passing the house of a friend. As he came near he saw a woman with spectacles and a poke bonnet who had her face close to the window to see who was passing. When she saw it was Dr. Parsons coming from a small-pox case, she closed the shutters and hurried back into the room. Later on when the doctor asked why she had done such a thing, she replied, "Why, I was afraid I would catch the small-pox from you."

Dr. Parsons lived a good life, and did good work as a country physician, and was capable and trustworthy. Hardly a great man, he certainly was a good one, and one of whom one heard more stories than any other physician in Maine.

He practised nearly fifty years, and died after a short illness, June 8, 1886.

J. A. S.

Family Papers.

Parsons, Usher (1788–1868).

Illustrious for his extraordinary medical services on the United States Steamship "Lawrence," at the Battle of Lake Erie under Commodore Oliver Hazard Perry, Dr. Usher Parsons deserves perpetual re-discovery by the medical profession of the United States. For many years after that battle, people talked of "Usher" Parsons, and cheers were given for him whenever he attended a medical meeting. "Who is that"? "Why, that is Dr. Parsons." "What! Usher! Let me know him at once," was another way in which he was mentioned.

He was born in Alfred, District of Maine, August 18, 1788, the youngest of the nine children of William and Abigail (Frost Blunt) Parsons. His father was descended from Joseph Parsons, who came from England and was living in Springfi e l d, Massachusetts, in 1646. His mother was a daughter of the Rev. John Blunt, of New Castle, New Hampshire, and was connected with the celebrated Sir William Pepperell, who captured Louisburg in 1745.

Young Usher was named for a relative, the Hon. John Usher, once lieutenant-governor of the province of New Hampshire. He had an ordinary country school education, and was clerk for a while in shops in Portland and Kennebunk, Maine. It was at the latter place when about twenty years of age that he printed his first literary effort, in the shape of some verses entitled "A Pettifogger's Soliloquy." Having accumulated a little money he began to study medicine with Dr. Abiel Hall, of Alfred, and attended a course of lectures at Fryeburg under the direction of that eccentric yet talented anatomist, Alexander Ramsay. After a few months his funds were so depleted that he was compelled to return home, to discover one night when tramping on the highway that he was an ignoramus and that without general knowledge he could not proceed in the study of medicine.

He therefore devoted the next two years to Greek and Latin with the Rev. Moses Sweat, of Sanford, and then graduated at Berwick Academy. Having now obtained a better understanding of the classics, he resumed medicine with Dr. Hall, continued with Dr. Joseph Kittredge, of Andover, Massachusetts, and finished his medical apprenticeship with Dr. John Warren, of Boston. The catalogue of the Massachusetts Medical Society dates Dr. Usher Parsons as a fellow in 1818, but license for him to practise medicine and surgery issued by this society, February 7, 1812, is still extant.

Leaving Boston he tried for an opening at Exeter, and Dover, New Hampshire. Then he applied for service in the navy, for the War of 1812, declared on the eighteenth of June, and received notice that if he hastened back to Boston he could have the berth of surgeon's-mate on the United States Ship "John Adams," although arriving post haste, he was mortified to find that the ship had sailed without him. He then walked to Salem hoping for a similar appointment on a privateer then fitting out, but some one else had just forestalled him. He set off on foot for Dover, and soon received through the kind efforts of Dr. Joshua Bartlett, then a member of Congress, an appointment as surgeon's-mate in the navy. Curiously enough he was ordered to the "Adams," but knowing that she had sailed he volunteered for a secret expedition to the Great Lakes presumably to be under the command of Commodore Chauncey. Arriving in Buffalo in October, 1812, he found many people suffering from an epidemic of pleuro-pneumonia, and as a sort of graduating thesis, wrote for a local paper suggestions regarding its cause, treatment, and cure.

The winter and spring of 1812–13 were passed in taking care of the sick and wounded in the neighborhood of Buffalo, and when Commodore Perry arrived in June, 1813, Usher Parsons was at once brought into great and unusual intimacy with him, owing to the fact that the other surgeons of superior rank were all on the sick list.

His health was miserable on the tenth of September when the Battle of Lake Erie was fought, but as his good fortune would have it he was the only surgeon on the "Lawrence," against which the enemy concentrated its entire fire with the strategic view that if the commodore's flagship were ruined the entire fleet would be obliged to surrender. Owing to the enormous damage to the "Lawrence," Perry as is well known was compelled to transfer his flag to the "Niagara." Nearly every one on the "Lawrence" was wounded, the ship seemed ready to sink, she actually surrendered. But when after another hour or two Commodore Perry returned victorious and once more hauled aloft his pennant, he was supported on that bloody

deck by Dr. Usher Parsons who had done phenomenal surgery during the famous fight.

The "Lawrence" being shallow built, the wounded were received in the ward room on the level with the water, with the result that the enemy's fire went straight through that improvised operating room measuring about twelve by eighteen feet. A midshipman with a tourniquet applied to his arm was moving away from Dr. Parsons when a cannon ball hit him in the breast and killed him. As Dr. Parsons was dressing a fractured arm another cannon ball injured both of the patient's legs. Almost all that he could do on that day with so many wounded was to give sedatives, to check hemorrhage and to apply the necessary dressings, but amidst that awful cannonading he performed six amputations of the leg above the knee-joint.

In appearance amidst that frightful carnage Dr. Parsons would have been taken for a mere butcher at his work, but he did all that could be done in the narrow space allotted him, saved many lives, and as he often said afterwards, the proudest moment of his life was when he met in Cleveland a man for whom he had successfully amputated an arm at the Battle of Lake Erie some forty years before.

On the next morning the wounded from the entire fleet, including those remaining over on the "Lawrence" from the day before, ninety-six in all, were brought to Dr. Usher Parsons, and before nightfall everything necessary for their recovery was completed, the enemy's surgeons most humanely assisting.

Rewards for such extraordinary surgical work were soon showered upon Dr. Parsons in the shape of the thanks of Congress, a highly commendatory letter from Commodore Perry, a medal for skill and bravery in action, a commission as surgeon in the navy, and prize money, most of which went to liquidate debts incurred in obtaining his medical education.

The next two years were spent in the Mediterranean on the "Java" with Commodore Perry. During a storm while on this ship Dr. Parsons had the misfortune to break a patella. He kept a diary during this voyage and never failed to visit the hospitals and the most celebrated surgeons whenever he happened on shore. Returning in March, 1817, he lectured at the proposed medical school at Brown University, and finally after attending lectures at the Harvard Medical School got his degree in 1818, and his fellowship in the Massachusetts Medical Society.

His next sea service was in the "Guerrière" in which he sailed as far north as Russia and south into the Mediterranean.

Paris was next visited and from Dr. Parson's letters we hear of Dupuytren then at the summit of his career and doing more surgery than all the other surgeons in Paris combined. Dupuytren was savage to his patients. Baron Larrey was overfond of the knife, but operated adroitly and gracefully. He held a clinic every Thursday for visiting medical men, and gave instruction which it was a pleasure to follow. Dr. Parsons was disgusted with the bad treatment of ulcers, and grew tired of seeing flaps stuffed with lint to prevent primary healing. He bought a stethoscope from Laennec, and with it a certificate in his handwriting that it was fit for service.

When in London, Dr. Parsons saw all the leaders of the day and especially mentioned Abernethy as engaging, amusing, yet as impressive a lecturer as he ever had heard. Abernethy's quaint illustrative anecdotes were very instructive. Dr. Parsons made in London the acquaintance and obtained thereby the life-long friendship of Sir Richard Owen the naturalist. Finally he mentioned as the three most quoted American medical books: Benjamin Rush, "On the Mind;" Gorham's, "Chemistry," and Cleveland's "Mineralogy."

Obtaining leave to return home owing to ill health, Dr. Parsons was on his arrival ordered to the Charleston Navy Yard, where he lived some years.

During this time he made a journey to New York where he saw his old friend, Dr. Lyman Spalding, the founder of the United State Pharmacopeia, and the veteran physician, Dr. David Hosack.

After his resignation from the navy in 1823 he settled in Providence, Rhode Island, for the remainder of his life. He married Miss Mary Jackson, daughter of the Rev. Abiel Holmes, of Cambridge, Massachusetts, and had one child, Dr. Charles W. Parsons.

While living in Providence he was chosen to fill important medical chairs, among which may be mentioned the professorship of anatomy and surgery at the Dartmouth Medical School (1820–1822), and the same position at the Brown University Medical School (1823-1828). He also lectured on obstetrics at the Philadelphia Medical School in 1831–1832. Here too is the place to say that he was thrice elected president of the Rhode Island Medical Society (1837–39).

As a physician Dr. Parsons was industrious and faithful. He was rather inclined to be strict in his orders, a habit presumably acquired during his service on shipboard. His judgment was sound, and his diagnostic skill excellent. As a surgeon he was cautious ratner than dextrous or rapid. He was fond of pointing out the house in which he first operated successfully for strangulated hernia an operation which, by the way, he performed fifteen times with eleven successes. He did a good deal of ophthalmic surgery, and paid much attention to orthopedic surgery at that time a speciality much neglected. His results in cleft palate were fine. He ligated the common carotid for a brain tumor, and when at the age of seventy-four, he amputated an arm with perfect success. Before the days of ether, he relied on laudanum and brandy and then by his presence infused his patients with steadiness and calmness equal to his own.

He was a member of various literary societies, and to their meetings contributed papers on the "Genealogy of the Frost and Parsons Families," an account of "The Battle of Lake Erie," and an essay on "Indian Names." He wrote an excellent "Life of Sir William Pepperell," for the completion of which he made the long journey to Louisburg. Finally he delivered the oration at the unveiling of the statue to Commodore Perry at Cleveland, in 1860. He was fond of novels, and wrote one called "The Avenger of Blood," based upon a story which he heard while on board the "Guerrière." He studied the Bible, at times, and thought that the Old Testament was our noblest literature.

Dr. Parsons was prolific in medical writings, carrying off the Boylston prize four times and the Fiske prize once. His subjects were: "Periostitis;" "Cancer of the Breast;" "Cutaneous Diseases;" "Enuresis," and "Spinal Diseases." His excellent book "Physician for Ships" went through five editions of two thousand each. Others of his papers bear such titles as "Gunshot Wounds Through the Thorax;" "Introduction of Medicine into the Veins;" "Anatomical Preparations," and "Removal of the Uterus." His style was as clear and forcible in his writings as in his spoken discourses.

He was the founder of the Providence Medical Society, often its president, and in that position suggested the foundation of the Providence City Hospital. Taking him all in all it would be difficult to find a man of greater merit in American medicine, for he gave of his entire mind for over fifty years to the advance of medical science. October 18, 1868, he exhibited the first symptoms of his approaching end and died easily at the last, December 19, 1868. The postmortem revealed cerebral degeneration and acute inflammation of the cerebellum. Portraits of Dr. Usher Parsons show a genial, handsome man with overhanging brows, deep set eyes, but a winning smile

J. A. S.

Memoirs of Usher Parsons by his son, Dr. Charles W. Parsons, Providence, Rhode Island, 1870.
Spalding Family Letters.

Partridge, Oliver (1751–1848).

Oliver Partridge was born in Hatfield, Massachusetts, April 26, 1751, and died in Stockbridge, July 24, 1848, thus being over ninety-seven years old at the time of death. He practised medicine for seventy-four, approaching the lengthy record of Dr. Edward Augustus Holyoke, of Salem, Massachusetts, who was in practice for eighty.

He was the son of Col. Oliver Partridge and of a daughter of the Rev. William Weston, and was educated in the schools and by private instruction. In 1771 he removed from Hatfield to Stockbridge and studied medicine under Dr. Erastus Sargeant, a physician of western Massachusetts.

Soon after entering upon his profession the Revolutionary War broke out. Partridge was at the Battle of Bennington and gave his professional services to those of the combatants who needed them. He enjoyed a very large practice and did much consulting work, and was a member of the Massachusetts Medical Society from 1785 to 1803, when he retired.

He was never married.

Dr. Partridge published several papers on botanical and on medical subjects in later life, in the "Boston Medical and Surgical Journal."

W. L. B.

S. W. Williams, in Boston Med. and Surg. Jour., 1848, vol. xxxix.
Med. Communicat., Mass. Med. Soc., 1849–54, Boston, 1854, vol. viii.

Patterson, Richard John (1817–1893).

Richard John Patterson, alienist, was born at Mount Washington, Massachusetts, September 14, 1817, and had his early education at the public schools. He received his M. D. from the Berkshire Medical College, at Pittsfield, Massachusetts, in 1842, and that same year became a medical assistant to the Ohio State Insane Asylum at Columbus, until 1847; then became medical superintendent of the Indiana Hospital for the Insane at Indianapolis, which position he held for six years afterwards; from

1866 to 1874, professor of medical jurisprudence in the Chicago Medical College.
He was a large man, five feet ten inches
high and of heavy build. His hair;
brown, his eyes hazel; in manner very
quick. He was a good and ready
talker, but seldom told stories. A little
anecdote of his childhood, however, he
was fond of narrating. One Sunday
morning he ran away from church and
caught a fine string of trout. Not daring
to bring them home on that day, he hid
them. Monday, the time still looked
suspiciously close to Sunday, so he
waited still longer. Tuesday he decided
it would be all right to go and bring home
the fish. Alas! the fish were spoiled.
This very deplorable fact led to inquiry
and detection. His parents dealt with
him after the manner of the real New
Englander of that time. And, as the
doctor was himself wont to say, in all the
affairs of his subsequent life, he was
more inclined to give particular attention
to "prognosis." He was exceedingly
fond of driving a fast horse. "I take my
exercise," said he, "vicariously." He
made friends quickly and was fond of
children, but very seldom played with
them. He married Lucy Clark, of Cincinnati, Ohio, in 1848. He wrote but
little in connection with his specialties
(outside the lectures which he delivered at the Chicago Medical College)
but was wholly absorbed in the work of
teaching and practising. He was an
excellent hand with the knife in more
senses than one, and used to spend long
hours in whittling and joining together
new models for hospital furniture. He
used to say, "Every boy who intends to
be a physician should learn how to
whittle." The clause in the Illinois law
for the commitment of the insane, which
provides for the appointment of a medical
commission by a judge of court, in lieu of
a jury trial, was entirely owing to his
strenuous efforts.

He died at Batavia, Illinois, April 27,
1893, after a few days illness, of
pneumonia.

T. H. S.

Pattison, Granville Sharp (1791–1851).
The youngest son of John Pattison, of
Kelvin Grove, Glasgow, he was educated
at Glasgow, and at seventeen began to
study medicine, being admitted as a
member of the faculty of the Physicians
and Surgeons of Glasgow in 1813. He
acted, in 1818, as assistant to Allan
Burns, the lecturer on anatomy, physiology, and surgery at the Andersonian
Institute in that city, but only held the
office for one year, and was succeeded by
Dr. William McKenzie.

He came to Philadelphia in 1818, and
lectured privately on anatomy, but was
disappointed in not obtaining the chair
of anatomy which had been promised him
by the University of Pennsylvania. In
1820 he was appointed to the chair of
anatomy, physiology and surgery in the
University of Maryland, in Baltimore, a
position he filled for five years. He then
resigned on the ground of ill-health.

During this period he edited the second
edition of Burn's "Observations on the
Surgical Anatomy of the Head and
Neck," which was published in 1823.
Pattison returned to England in July,
1827. He was appointed and for a short
time occupied the important post of
professor of anatomy at the University
of London (now University College),
acting at the same time as surgeon to the
University Dispensary, which preceded
the foundation of the North London
Hospital. This position he was compelled to relinquish in 1831 on account
of a disagreement with the demonstrator
of anatomy. In the same year he
became professor of anatomy in the
Jefferson Medical College, Philadelphia,
where he received the M. D. degree. He
was appointed professor of anatomy in
the University of New York on the re-organization of its medical department in
1840, a position he retained until his
death.

He was the author of "Experimental
Observations on the Operation of Lithotomy" (Philadelphia, 1820), and of
much controversial matter of ephemeral
interest. He edited in 1820 the "Ameri-

can Recorder," and the "Register and Library of Medical and Chirurgical Science," Washington, 1833–36, and was co-editor of the "American Medical Library and Intelligencer," Philadelphia, 1836. He also translated Masse's "Anattomical Atlas," and edited Jean Cruveilhier's "Anatomy of the Human Body."

It is probable that no anatomical teacher of his time attained a higher reputation. His reputation lay in his knowledge of visceral and surgical anatomy, and in applying this knowledge to the diagnosis and treatment of diseases, accidents and operations. His earnest manner and clever demonstrations made him very popular in the lecture room. He possessed a singularly attractive eloquence, that left a lasting impression upon his audience. He had little taste for surgery and abandoned it in his later years. One outline of Pattison's attitude toward the development of an anatomical department is given in the Résumé on anatomy in the introduction to this cyclopedia.

Pattison was actively interested in the establishment of the Grand Opera House of New York City. He was fond of music, hunting and fishing, and had a naturally, somewhat indolent nature and love of ease, or otherwise would probably have attained a much more lasting reputation as an anatomist.

He died in New York, November 12, 1851, leaving a widow, but no children.

C. R. B.

Autobiography Dr. S. D. Gross, 1887.
Dict. Nat. Biog., Lond., 1895, xliv (D'Arcy Power).
N. Y. J. of Med., 1852, n. s., viii.
Lancet, London, 1830–1, vol. ii.
Gent. Mag., 1852, vol. i.

Peabody, James H. (1833–1906).

James H. Peabody's ancestors on both sides were English, his first American antecedent was Lieut. Francis Peabody, who came from St. Alban's, Hertfordshire, in 1865, to New England. George Peabody, the noted philanthropist, was a nephew and reared in the family of John Peabody, the grandfather of the doctor. Dr. Peabody's mother was Amelia Humphries Cathcart, and he was born at Washington, District of Columbia, on the seventh of March, 1833.

After having been a page in the National House of Representatives he was later given a clerkship in 1852 in the Pension office. During his service in the Pension office he completed a seven years' course of study in the University of Georgetown, receiving his diploma in 1860. Towards the end of his course he praetised medicine before and after the regular hours of his other employment.

After being mustered out in 1865, he pursued some special medical study in Bellevue College, New York, and moved to Omaha in the Spring of 1866. Here he served as acting assistant-surgeon in the army with special detail to attend the officers and their families in Omaha, and was eventually made brevet lieutenant-colonel by Pres. Johnson. He also engaged in general practice at that time.

Dr. Peabody occupied many important and influential positions in Omaha and Nebraska. In his office in May, 1868, the Nebraska State Medical Association was organized and he became its second president. He married, on May 26, 1859, Mary Virginia Dent, of Louisville, Kentucky, and a second time, in 1867, to Jennie Yates, of Omaha. His death occurred in Omaha, September 9, 1906. He was professor of surgery for many years in Creighton Medical College and attending physician to St. Joseph's Hospital.

In the early years of the State Medical Association he contributed interesting accounts of important surgical cases. Some of his more important articles are: "Diphtheria." ("Transactions, Nebraska State Medical Association," 1880.)

"Treatment of Diphtheria with Oil of Turpentine."

"Report on Climatology and Prevalent Diseases in Nebraska." ("Transactions, Nebraska State Medical Association," 1873.)

"Report of Nine Cases of Metro-

Edmund R. Peaslee.
(By permission of the American Journal of Obstetrics.)

Peritonitis." ("Transactions, Nebraska State Medical Association," 1873.)

H. W. O.

Morton History, vol. i., also portrait.
West. M. Rev., Lincoln, Neb., 1906, xi.
Another portrait is in the 1882 History of Nebraska.

Peaslee, Edmund Randolph (1814–1878)

Edmund Randolph Peaslee, best known in connection with ovariotomy, was born at Newton, New Hampshire, on January 22, 1814, the son of the Hon. James and Abigail Peaslee.

In 1832 he entered Dartmouth College and five years later began to study medicine under Dr. Noah Worcester, of Hanover, New Hampshire, taking his A. M. from Dartmouth in 1839, and M. D. from Yale Medical College in 1840. After studying abroad for one year he returned to Hanover to take the chair of anatomy and physiology at Dartmouth Medical College, but in 1871 accepted instead that of gynecology and retained it until his death. Several of his winter courses in the seventies included lectures on ovarian tumors and ovariotomy at the College of Physicians and Surgeons, Columbia University.

Dr. Peaslee was a prolific writer. His book on "Human Histology," published in 1854, was a master-piece for that date and the first upon that subject published in the English language. While this and many articles added greatly to his prominence as a pathologist and surgeon, especially in the field of abdominal surgery, it was his magnificent work "On Ovarian Tumors" (1872), dedicated "To the memory of Ephraim McDowell, M. D., the father of ovariotomy, and to Thomas Spencer Wells, Esq., the greatest of ovariotomists" that made his reputation world wide.

He was the first to conceive of and to use the so-called normal salt solution, 3j salt to Oj warm water. It was in February, 1855, and he used it in washing out the peritoneal cavity in cases of septicemia following ovariotomy. He called it "Artificial Serum"—an excellent name. The account is given in his book on "Ovarian Tumors," page 509. He had previously reported it in the "American Journal of Medical Sciences," in January, 1856. Very few medical men at the present day know where and when the normal salt solution originated. Although it was not sterilized it was clean, and its conception and use was a great thing at that time. His cheerful temperament did not allow the cares and burdens of professional work to weigh upon or hinder him, and the amount of work, literary and professional, which Dr. Peaslee did during the thirty-seven years of his professional career was truly amazing and could have been accomplished only by the most absolute devotion to his ideals. It is no wonder that his success from the earliest years, was assured; and as time went on and his field of labor grew larger and more exacting he reaped his reward in the admiration of his brother physicians and the love of many whose lives were entrusted to his care. In his home life, Dr. Peaslee was particularly happy, his devotion to his family great considering the fact that his time was generally so thoroughly occupied.

He was a member of the Presbyterian Church and a constant attendant. His ideal of the life of a physician was derived to a great extent from the deep love and veneration which he at all times felt and so frequently expressed for his Maker. In July, 1841, he married Martha T., daughter of Stephen Kenrick, of Lebanon, New Hampshire, and died on January 21, 1878.

His appointments included: the professorship of anatomy and surgery, Bowdoin College, Maine; of physiology and pathology, New York Medical College; of obstetrics there later; of diseases of women, Albany Medical College, New York; of gynecology, Bellevue Hospital Medical College. He was successively president of the Medical Society of the County of New York; of the New York Academy of Medicine and the American Gynecological Society.

Among his writings are:

"A Monograph on Pathology and Rational Treatment in Infantile Laryngo-tracheitis," New York, 1854.

"A Monograph on the Fetal Circulation," New York, 1854.

"Human Histology in its Relations to Descriptive Anatomy, Physiology and Pathology," Philadelphia, 1857.

"Ovarian Tumours and Treatment (excepting Ovariotomy)," New York, 1864.

"Retroflexion of the Unimpregnated Uterus," Albany, 1866.

"Ovarian Tumours, their Pathology, Diagnosis and Treatment, especially by Ovariotomy," New York, 1872.

J. E. J.

Am. Jour. Obstet., N. Y., 1878, vol. xi.
Med. Rec., N. Y., 1878, vol. xiii.
Tr. Am. Gynec. Soc., 1878.
Michigan Med News, 1878, Detroit, vol. i.
There is a portrait in the surg.-gen. collection, Wash., D C.

Peck, William Dandridge (1763–1822).

William D. Peck, professor of natural history in Harvard University, son of John Peck, was born in Boston, May 8, 1763. His mother, whose original name was Jackson, died when he was seven years old. Though so young he felt it keenly and cherished her memory with fond affection, and it is not improbable that the event contributed with other circumstances, to cast that shade of melancholy over the mind of the son which at times required the best influence of his friends to disperse.

Admitted bachelor of arts at Cambridge in 1782, he was considered one of the best students of his class, being greatly in love with natural history, studies which occupied and delighted him through life. He was, however, destined for commercial pursuits and passed a regular apprenticeship in the counting house of the Hon. Mr. Russell, where his exactitude and industry acquired for him the confidence and lasting friendship of that distinguished merchant.

Mr. Peck's father was a man of very great genius in the mechanic arts. He was the most scientific, as well as the most successful naval architect which the United States had then produced. The ships built by him were so superior to any then known, that he attracted the attention of Congress, and was employed by them to build some of their war ships. But he made very little money and, disgusted with the world, retired to a small farm in Kittery, resolved that his models, founded as his son always affirmed, on mathematical calculations, should never be possessed by a country which had treated him with so much ingratitude. The failure of his father's schemes defeated young Peck's prospects as a merchant; and at an early age, he too, with not a little of his father's discontentedness, went to the same obscure village and kept in touch with the scientific world only by correspondence and occasional visits. For nearly twenty years he led a most ascetic and secluded life, seldom emerging from his hermitage. But his mind, so far from being inactive, was assiduously and intensely devoted to the pursuits to which the bent of his genius and taste inclined him. At a time when he could find no companion nor any sympathy in his studies, except from the venerable Dr. Cutler, of Hamilton, who was devoted to one branch of them, botany, Peck made himself an able and profound botanist and entomologist, under all the disadvantages of very narrow means and the extreme difficulty of procuring books. But his studies extended to zoology, ornithology and ichthyology, in which his knowledge was more extensive than that of any other man in this part of the United States. During Mr. Peck's stay in Kittery and during the two or three years when he lived in a delightful spot in Newbury, where the river Artichoke joins the Merrimack, prior to his removal to Cambridge, he made a most beautiful collection of the insects with which our country abounds, with many fine preservations of aquatic plants and of the more rare species of fish to be found on our coasts, rivers and lakes.

On March 27, 1805, he was elected first

professor of the Massachusetts professorship of natural history at Cambridge. The Board of Visitors wished him to visit the scientific establishments of Europe, so he spent three years abroad, visiting men of science in England and France, but his longest stay was in Sweden. During his absence he collected a valuable library of books connected with his own subjects, together with many exquisite preservations of natural subjects and rare specimens of art, many of which were presented to him by the scholars and men of science in Europe.

Mr. Peck inherited his father's taste for mechanical philosophy and as an artist he was incomparable. His most delicate instruments in all his pursuits were the products of his own skill and handicraft. He was a good classical scholar and a lover and a correct judge of the fine arts, fond of painting and sculpture and architecture, without professing to skill in them. No man who ever saw the exquisite accuracy and fidelity with which he sketched the subjects of his peculiar pursuits in entomology or botany, could doubt the refinement of his taste.

Peck was an incorporator of the American Antiquarian Society in 1812, and one of its first vice-presidents. He was also a warden of Christ Church, Cambridge, from 1816–1819. He died at Cambridge, October 3, 1822, from a third attack of hemiplegia.

Collections of the Mass. Historical Society, vol. x, second series, 1843
Memoir, by Dudley Atkins Tyng.

Peirce, David (1740–1803).

The simple facts of the life of this old-time country practitioner are that he was born in Newbury, Massachusetts, in 1740, settled at Spruce Creek, in Kittery, Maine, about 1760, and practised there until his death in 1803. He wrote no medical papers for there was no magazine in those days in which to print them. He was an ordinary country doctor of an age forgotten and of which few traces remain. He is nevertheless worthy of being mentioned

in every historical work on "American Medicine," because in his three large account books, still extant, we can trace his medical career day by day for nearly forty years in a manner almost unique in the annals of medicine.

Arriving in Kittery about 1760, he studied medicine, possibly with Dr. Sargent, of New Castle, or with some of the Portsmouth practitioners, compounded and sold drugs, practised medicine and did minor surgery extensively. He opened a country store and sold merchandise of every sort, acted as legal adviser to many patients, was town physician, town agent during the Revolution, and at one time postmaster.

Turning now to his books it is an agreeable task to sift from its thousand entertaining facts a few that shall bring before us the work of one of our early American physicians.

Dr. Peirce was chiefly a physician. It is doubtful if he ever performed any capital operations. On one occasion he consulted with Dr. Hall Jackson and Dr. Ammi Ruhamah Cutter, both of Portsmouth, in a case of compound comminuted fracture. He was present and assisted at the operation performed as he quaintly informs us by "The Gentlemen of the Faculty."

He saw many dislocations of the axilla and shoulder, opened abscesses of the breast, stimulated chronic ulcers of the leg, scraped necrosed bones, and did much minor surgery in a careful way. He once charged a patient "For making a large hole in your leg," thirteen shillings. He operated successfully on an axillary abscess. One old scrap of paper gives the names of fourteen patients whom he visited in one day, a good record for a country doctor considering the miles between their homes, and the bad roads to travel. He inoculated patients for the small-pox and "carried them through," as was the phrase, for eight shillings.

He had an excellent reputation as an obstetrician. His usual charge for such cases was one pound and four shillings sterling. In entering these cases on his books he mentioned the sex of the child and the hour of its birth. If a child were born out of wedlock he wrote distinctly: "To delivering your daughter, of a bastard infant." In a few rare instances he called in as consultant in a tedious labor Dr. Hall Jackson across the river. Twins are rarely mentioned in his books, but if they arrived the sex and the birth hour of each was mentioned.

Peirce was of good standing with his medical brethren, for he consulted as needed with the two Portsmouth physicians before mentioned, as well as with Drs. Gilman, Little and Lyman of whom we find no trace elsewhere than in Peirce's books.

Although he used many medicines, he did not use much at a time. He bled a good deal less than most physicians of his day. His first cases were simply treated with phlebotomy. He salivated his patients but little, if any. He used a "Small" purge and a "Large" purge. Emetics were daily employed in his practice. It is amusing to read: "To three emetics for the three children," suggestive at that season of the year of sudden overeating of fruits, in that one family. His charges were moderate. He mentions three sorts of visits, one when called definitely to go at a distance, a second as he was "passing" by, and a third which he calls "accidental." What the last means is hard to tell, as rarely, if ever, is any specific accident mentioned.

During the Revolution he was an active patriot, scouring the country for ammunition and supplies for the Kittery militia. At one time he rode to Concord, Massachusetts, on this service and for the hire of a horse paid in the debased currency of those days the sum of ninety-five dollars. He also acted as surgeon for the Massachusetts Bay Colony Troops, stationed near Kittery.

He was a man of considerable property for those days, owning, for instance, shares in a privateer and in two fishing schooners which sailed in and out of the Piscataqua. Whenever the fishermen came in with a cargo of fish, he would superintend the unloading, charge for his time, and skill, as well as for food and rum for the captain and crew. He also owned a farm, which seems to have been tilled almost wholly by his patients in return for medical services. He also owned wood lots from which the wood was cut by patients every spring and piled into his barns every fall. His cattle and sheep were "pastured out" on the fields of patients, at so much a month. In a word, for years he carried on an enormous business in medicine, merchandise and produce on a basis of barter, he being the physician-in-charge and his patients paying him in produce, labor, merchandise, but rarely in cash.

Scattered along the thousand pages of his old books we read many odd charges a few of which may here find insertion.

A widow with the surname of Philadelphia always has visits to herself charged to "Your Ladyship," but the rank thus suggested diminishes when on the credit side we see these visits paid "by washing," or "by the son digging potatoes" in the doctor's fields. On the one side we read of the attentions given at the birth of a son, and on the credit "by your shingling my porch and mending the garden fence."

Dr. Peirce was a forgetful man, and for months at times his books would remain unposted. Once we read of "To two visits made to you when you were living at home" but not charged until the settlement of the father's estate twenty years later. If he forgot what was due to himself, he was strict to give credit to his patients, as in this way; " By work on my 'mash' two days, not entered at the time, two years ago." If at the time of settlement he owed the patient, he invariably wrote beneath the account: "I owe you the sum of fourteen shillings to be taken out in medical services." He charged a father for two visits to a child and then years later adds: "To two lots of medicine forgotten at the time of visit to your child."

As a speller Dr. Peirce was dreadfully

defective, though spelling was then at a low ebb. But what can we think of "Spinin, Howin, Halin, Sain, digin, Spinin TOE, spinin Linnen"?. The nearest he ever got to the name of "Chisholm," was plain "Chism." "Duzzen, Hetters (heaters), biscates, macrel," and so on were frequent humerons blunders on his books.

Here is something queer, "To a quart of rum and to a pint of rum which your wife pretended to BORROW but never paid any attention to."

A certain patient paid for services in the shape of a "Nice Apple Tree," which Dr. Peirce at once caused to be planted by the man who brought it. A child is born to a certain family not connected with the Sheafes, yet he says "The child is more than 3/4 Sheafe."

Peirce was published to Olive, daughter of Rishworth and Abigail Gerrish Jordan, September 20, 1765, and probably married her soon after. On her death he married Ruth, daughter of Dr. Sargent, of New Castle, or his widow. He had nine children who were well brought up. They wore home-spun suits and occasionally were treated to leather "britches." Their schooling was paid for by patients, and only once in their lives did one of them go to a "Summer Camp" and even that was at the expense of some otherwise unpaying patient. He was a devout man. When his parents or relations died he noted down their departure for a better land and emphasized their decent burial. When his wife died, he mentions the sad fact simply yet bravely. As for himself when his time came he died suddenly, August 25, 1803, and let us hope that after his years of medical practice he received that same decent burial which he had given to his relations gone before him.   J. A. S.

Facts complied from "Old Eliot," by Dr. J. L. M. Willis, Eliot, Maine, and from Dr. Peirce's "Leigers" extending from 1705 to 1801.

Peirson, Abel Lawrence (1794-1853).

Abel L. Peirson, for many years the leading surgeon of Essex County and the first to publish a "Report of Private Surgical Operations Performed with Ether Anesthesia," was a descendant of John Pearson, or Pierson, who settled in Rowley, Massachusetts, in 1643, and the son of Samuel Peirson, of Biddeford, Maine, being born in that town, November 25, 1794.

Entering Harvard College as a sophomore in 1809, he graduated in 1812, and at once began to study medicine with Dr. James Jackson, four years later taking his M. D. from Harvard. Vassalboro, Maine, was the place of his early practice, but he remained there less than a year and a half, removing to Salem, Massachusetts, early in 1818, for a larger field and to be in closer touch with the leading members of his profession with whom he had many ties of friendship.

He married his cousin, Harriet Lawrence in 1819, and in 1832 went abroad and studied medicine in Paris and elsewhere, being among the first of the Americans to become acquainted with Laennec's method of exploring the chest for the physical signs of disease. In his practice he gave chief attention to surgery and acquired a high reputation. From a conversation he had with Dr. Charles T. Jackson in October, 1846, he learned of the properties of sulphuric ether. He was present at the Massachusetts General Hospital on the occasion of the first use of that anesthetic, October 16, having been a consulting surgeon to that hospital since 1839, and November 14, 1846 he made trial of etherization in the removal of a fatty tumor, with complete success. Again, on November 19 he did an amputation of the arm without the patient experiencing pain, and in the next few days did an amputation of the leg and removed a large fatty tumor of the shoulder under ether anesthesia, the ether being administered in each case by a dentist named Fisk. These cases were sent to the "Boston Medical and Surgical Journal" for report. ("Boston Medical and Surgical Journal," December 2, 1846, vol. xxv, p. 362.) This is the first published report of surgical operations performed with the aid of ether anesthesia—the "New Gas"—outside the Massachusetts General Hospital.

He was an active fellow of the Massachusetts Medical Society and was at one time president of Essex South District branch of the society; he was also a member of the American Academy of Arts and Sciences.

While returning from a meeting of the American Medical Association he was killed in a railway wreck at Norwalk, Connecticut, May 6, 1853. His wife and five children survived him, the oldest son, Edward Brooks, becoming a physieian in Salem.

Among his writings are to be mentioned: "Some Account of the Measles Epidemic in Salem in 1821." "The Boylston Prize Essay on Chin-cough in 1824." "Operation for Hare-Lip," 1836, and "A Dissertation on Fractures," 1840 ("Massachusetts Medical Communications, vol. xi, part iv, second series).

W. L. B.

Letters of A. L. Peirson, loaned by his grandson, Dr. E. L. Peirson. Obit. by James Jackson, M. D., Comm., Mass. Med. Soc., vol. viii.

Pendleton, Lewis Warrington (1844–1898).

Named after Com. Warrington, of the navy, his father having been a secretary to that officer for some years; Lewis Warrington Pendleton was born in Camden, Maine, March 18, 1844.

At the age of ten his parents moved to Gorham, Maine, in order that their children might have the benefit of instruction at the local academy. When he was seventeen, young Pendleton returned to Belfast and began to study with Dr. Nathan Parker Monroe.

When the war broke out, he became a hospital steward, and after his return, on account of poor health, renewed his medical studies and graduated at the Medical College of Albany, New York, in 1865. To that institution he always had great allegiance, and ten years later

delivered before its graduating class a remarkable oration on the "Loneliness of the Physician."

He practised in Belfast for fourteen years very successfully and then moved to Portland in 1880, where he at once obtained a fine clientage and much personal favor, so that upon his death he was greatly mourned. At the death of William Warren Greene, he was elected a surgeon to the Maine General Hospital. In that position he did excellent and conscientious work until his resignation in 1895, owing to poor health. He was twice elected president of the Maine Medical Association, and on each occasion delivered an excellent address.

Beside the orations above mentioned, he read papers on "Nephrectomy" and on "Transmitted Tendencies" which were of great literary and medical value.

The death of two lovely children in early married life had apparently been compensated for by the birth of a fine boy but he also was suddenly taken away when ready for college. This was a double shock, and although the doctor attended to his practice in Portland, and even went to the South for vacations, it was plain to his friends that the end could not be very far away.

For all that, the news of his death in Florida, January 13, 1898, from a hopeless disease with which he had been suffering for years, came with a sense of profound grief to his large body of friends.

J. A. S.

Trans. Maine Med. Assoc

Penrose, Richard Alexander Fullerton (1827–1888).

This Philadelphian obstetrician was the son of Charles Bingham and Valeria Fullerton Biddle Penrose, and was born March 24, 1827. He graduated from Dickinson College in 1846 and took his M. D. from the University of Pennsylvania in 1849. For three years before he began to practise in Philadelphia he was resident physician at the Pennsylvania Hospital. In 1854, partly through his efforts, the wards of the Philadelphia Hospital were opened to medical instruction and he was soon after made consulting-surgeon there. He was one of the founders of the Children's Hospital and of the Gynecean Hospital, and was elected professor of obstetrics and diseases of women and children in 1863 in the University of Pennsylvania but retired from active work in 1888 with the title of emeritus professor. Dickinson College gave him her LL. D. in 1875.

His articles to medical journals included:

"Introductory Lecture to a Course on Obstetrics," 1859.

"A Discourse Commemorative . . . of Hugh L. Hodge," 1873.

"Treatment of Post-partum Hemorrhage," 1879.

"A Lecture on the Mechanism and Treatment of Breech Presentations," 1874.

"On the Mechanism of Labor and the Treatment of Labor Based on the Mechanism," 1888.

There is a portrait in the Surg-gen Lib , Wash., D. C.

Pepper, William, Jr. (1843–1898).

The re-formation of medical education, the re-organization of the University of Pennsylvania, the establishment of a great commercial museum and free library are deeds whose fruit is long enjoyed but the author soon forgotten. William Pepper, enthusiastic, persistent, sophistical, set out in life with a breezy determination to effect necessary changes and did so.

He entered life well endowed, being the son of Dr. William and Sarah Platt Pepper, of Philadelphia, who were rich enough to give the boy a good education at the University of Pennsylvania whence he graduated B. A., 1862, and took his M. D. in 1864. Four months after this his father died, but had left the son a vivant ineradicable heritage of thinking and working. In 1865 he was elected a resident physician at the Pennsylvania Hospital and on completion of service was appointed pathologist and

museum curator, a position held for four years. Morbid anatomy became his special study and in 1868 he was appointed lecturer to the University and brought to the work rare skill and untiring energy; the descriptive catalogue of the Pathological Museum issued in 1869 by Dr. Pepper and Dr. Morton gives good evidence of this. But much-needed reforms equally engaged Pepper's attention. How much he was instrumental in the removal of the university to new buildings in West Philadelphia was shown when the vice-provost at the inauguration of Pepper as provost in 1881 said: "To him who has pleaded for mercy to the helpless sick as a lover would plead his own cause, who has touched with a master hand the springs of influence, to him public esteem has given the wreath as the moral architect of our hospital." "It is gratifying to think he lived to see it placed on a solid basis of success, with the maternity department splendidly organized, the Pepper Clinical Laboratory, given in memory of his father, and the new Nurses' Home and the Agnew Wing in full operation. The plan of reorganization was not carried on without much bitterness; indeed, it looked at one time as though the faculty would split." "Then there was the long and painful controversy lasting almost five years over the proposition to again elevate the standard of medical education." But Pepper's plans were crowned with success, also further efforts in the organization of the Association of American Physicians and the first Pan-American Medical Congress of which he was president. He also interested the governments of the South American states in his commercial museum.

When in 1894 he resigned the provostship it was only to return to his first love, the scientific management and promotion of museums. In 1891 he had undertaken to establish the Archeological and Paleontological Museums and the Commercial and Economic Museum, his desire being to see in Pennsylvania "a great group which would serve to illustrate the past and present history of man in every one of his relations"

"I prefer the life of the salmon to that of the turtle" he said once to Prof. Osler, but an arduous life of thirty years began to tell on him in 1898, when he had signs of dilatation of the heart with bronchitis and dyspnea. A visit to the Pacific coast was contemplated. Then came the news of his death in Oakland, California, July 28. "He died" wrote his physician "at eight in the evening with a copy of Stevenson's 'Treasure Island' in his hands. At seven I had left him gazing upon Mt. Diabolo shadowed in the gathering darkness. I was called at eight and found him in the attitude and with the expression of *angor animi* from which he never roused. I have never seen so beautiful a nature in sickness; his conduct and disposition were worthy of Marcus Aurelius."

"As a man," said Osler, his biographer, "he formed a most interesting study. In Athens he would have been called a Sophist and I do not deny that he could when the occasion demanded play old Belial and make the worse appear the better cause to perplex and darken maturest counsel, but how artistically he could do it! He was human, and to the faults of a man he added those of a college president . . . but a man engaged in vast schemes with many clashing interests is sure to be misunderstood and to arouse sharp hostility in many quarters."

Besides appointments named he held: Physician to the Pennsylvania Hospital and to the Children's Hospital; lecturer on clinical medicine, University of Pennsylvania; professor of theory and practice of medicine, University of Pennsylvania; member of the College of Physieiaus, of the Pathological Society of Philadelphia; honorary member of the New Jersey Medical Society; founder and one year editor of "The Philadelphia Medical Times"; LL.D. of Lafayette in 1881 and of Princeton in 1888.

His writings comprise among others: "Lectures on Clinical Medicine"; "The Fluorescence of Tissues (with Dr. E. Rhoad)"; Meigs and Pepper on "Diseases of Children"; "Trephining in Cerebral Diseases"; and editing the "System of Medicine," by American Authors."

D W.

An Alabama Student, Wm. Osler, Frowde, 1908.
Eminent Amer. Phys. R. F. Stone, Indianapolis, 1898.

Perkins, Elisha (1740–1799).

The name of Perkins, son of Dr. Joseph Perkins and born in Norwich, Connecticut, January 1740, marks one of those epochs of credulity which seize men from time to time when any exceedingly novel cure is proclaimed. The terms "Perkinism," "Tractorism," were known both in America and abroad and the wonderful metallic rods which Perkins said and believed to be curative of almost every ill in men (and horses!) certainly wrought psychotherapeutic wonders.

Perkins himself was a magnetic person, handsome, over six feet, of wonderful endurance and self control. He had felt a curious magnetic power in himself in touching anyone and set about finding some combination of metals which might have the same effect in healing disease. These he found and named "tractors," two small rods, one of brass, one of steel, which had to be drawn downwards for twenty minutes over the affected parts. A patent was obtained; doctors, and philosophers gravely approved and professors of three American universities said they believed in it. The tractors came to be used in Copenhagen where twelve well known physicians so favorably reported on them that the records were printed in an octavo volume. In 1803 Benjamin Perkins, the son, established the Perkinean Institution in London with the Right Hon. Lord Rivers as president and Sir William Barker as vice-president, and 5,000 cases were treated. There is reason to think Elisha Perkins was self-deceived or really perceived the real efficacy to lie in the imagination and so

WILLIAM PEPPER.

kept up the outward therapeutic symbols. An imaginative, restless, inquiring man he introduced another remedy for dysentery and low fever "consisting of the vegetable with the muriatic acid in the form of common vinegar saturated with muriate of soda." Believing this to be antiseptic in yellow fever he went to New York during the epidemic of 1799, and after four weeks' unremitting care of the sick he fell ill of the fever and died, aged fifty-nine.

It was owing to the exertions of one Dr. Haygarth of Bath, England, that the idea of any healing power resident in the tractors themselves was refuted, for he and a colleague effected many cures with tractors made of painted wood, and Dr. Fessenden, of London, dealt the idea a final blow in his "Terrible Tractoration' " (1800) by "Christopher Caustic."

Thacher stoutly maintains that Perkins had no intention of deceiving, but perhaps the large fortune made through tractoration hurried on the following act duly registered in the "Archives of the Medical Society" of the state of Connecticut, 1800, "that Dr. Elisha Perkins be expelled from the society as a patentee and user of nostrums."

D. W.

Thacher, Med. Biog., 1828, Boston.
The Med. Repository, vol. i, 1800, New York.
London Med. Rev., vol. iii, 1800, London.
New Cases of Practice with Perkins Metallic Tractors, by Benj. D. Perkins, London, 1802.
Terrible Tractoration, by "Christopher Caustic," M. D., London, 1800.
International Clinics. (D. Waterson).

Perkins, Joseph (1798–1872).

Joseph Perkins, son of Joseph and Patience (Dennison) Perkins, was born in Bridgewater, Vermont, April 1, 1798. He studied under Dr. Joseph A. Gallup, of Woodstock, and Dr. Selah Gridley. He received his M. D. in 1821. Immediately after, he began practice in Castleton, and stayed there fifty-one years. Under Dr. Perkins' guiding hand, the Castleton Medical College, where he was professor of materia medica and obstet-

rics, grew and prospered and during the years 1839 to 1854, there were graduated 854 doctors. In 1857 Dr. Perkins severed his connection with the college and removed his private museum and apparatus to the medical department of the University of Vermont.

He was for many years a prominent member of the Vermont State Medical Society and its president in 1855. He died on January 6, 1872, of congestion of the lungs.

Joseph Perkins was five times married: To Mary Gridley, daughter of Dr. Selah Gridley, of Castleton; to Amelia Cook; to Zilpah Higley; to Cynthia Claghorn; finally to Mrs. Iola (Denison) Guernsey. His oldest son, Dr. Selah G. Perkins, practised in Waterford, New York, and later in Castleton from which place he entered the army as captain of the First Vermont Cavalry. He was killed in a skirmish in 1862. The second son of Dr. Perkins was also a physician, Dr. William C. Perkins. He had three children by his first wife; one by the second; one by the third, and six by the fourth.

C. S. C.

Peter, Robert (1805–1894).

Of good southern English stock and related to the Bathurst Peters, Robert Peter, born January 21, 1805, scientist and eager researcher into everything he could get time for, came over from Cornwall when twelve years old with his parents Robert and Johanna. Six other children came with them and the family settled first in Baltimore, then in Pittsburg, Pennsylvania, where the children soon had to make each a share of the family expenses. Robert went into a drug store and developed a bent for chemistry and medicine, eventually graduating M. D. from Transylvania University in 1834. But after practising for awhile in Lexington, he turned his attention wholly to natural sciences and, being a real amateur (lover), was able as a lecturer and writer to make his students enthusiastic. His chemical work while on the Kentucky Geological

Survey made him known as a delicate and exact analyst and he acquired a local reputation as a toxicologist. When on a summer tour in England in 1839, with his friend, Dr. O. J. M. Bush, he energetically collected books and apparatus for his class teaching and came home the proud owner of a Daguerre photographic outfit—the first in the West. Doubtless his wife, Frances Paca, daughter of Maj. William Dallam, whom he had married four years previously and his children Johanna and Alfred had their "likenesses" taken in every possible position.

After his return he also experimented with the then novel guncotton and with pyroxyline; electricity gaining his delighted attention. He had an ear always alert for new ideas, a trait strikingly displayed even in old age, and would sweep cheerfully aside his most cherished theories when they were shaded by dawning scientific facts. This energetic doctor, along with one Dr. Short, made also some good botanical researches, welcoming anything fresh in zoology or mineralogy which they came across in their travels and cultivating such a fine herbarium at home as to enable them to exchange specimens with European botanists. 1846 saw his memorial in connection with his "Report on the Relation of Forms of Disease to the Geological Formation of a Region," with a map of his own designing.

Peter's whole life was one of self-effacement and advancement of science, thinking only for the students in the energy he showed in all that concerned the Kentucky School of Medicine. When the end came this even-tempered, genial old doctor had his great desire fulfilled—to wear rather than rust out; to preserve his intellect to the last. He had seen eighty-nine years when, at Minton, near Lexington, he died on April 26, 1894.

Among his appointments was that of: lecturer on natural science at the Rensselaer Scientific School, Troy, New York; chemical lecturer in the Western University of Pennsylvania; professor of chemistry, Morrison College, Transylvania University; dean of the faculty, Transylvania University medical department; professor of chemistry, Kentucky School of Medicine.

His writings were chiefly in the way of pamphlets of a scientific turn. Among them should be noted "The Chemical Examination of the Urinary Calculi in the Museum of Transylvania University," Lexington, 1846; "On the Application of Galvanic Electricity to Medicine," Lexington, 1836; also "A Brief Sketch of the History of Lexington, Kentucky and Transylvania Universities," 1854.

V. R.

The Hist. of the Transylvania Univ. contains a biog. of Dr. Peters, also a portrait

Peters, John C. (1819–1893).

John C. Peters, born in New York City in 1819, was educated at the College of Physicians and Surgeons there and the Universities of Berlin and Vienna. He was one of the founders and once president of the New York Pathological Society and for many years edited their proceedings.

He made a special study of Asiatic cholera and his literature on the subject was the most complete in this country. With Dr. Edmund C. Wendt he wrote a "Treatise on Cholera" and in 1866, "Notes on Asiatic Cholera," a standard work. In 1873 he travelled throughout the southern states studying the disease and his "Report" was published by Congress. He also wrote treatises on diseases of the brain and nervous system and helped Dr. Alexander S. Wotherspoon to translate Rokitansky's "Pathological Anatomy" and was a collaborator on "Materia Medica" (1856–60). The "Surgeon-general's Catalogue," Washington, District of Columbia, gives a list of nearly thirty treatises by him.

In 1890 he was stricken with paralysis and died at his Long Island home in 1893.

Med. Rec., N. Y., 1893, vol. xliv.

Phares, D. L. (1817–1892).

William and Elizabeth (Starnes) Phares came to West Feliciana, Louisiana, from Virginia, and their son was born there January 14, 1817. In 1832 he entered the Louisiana State College at Jackson, Louisiana, now Centenary College, and graduated from the Louisiana State College in 1837, and in April, 1839, from the medical department of Louisiana State University. "The day he graduated he was elected a member of the faculty without his knowledge or consent and Dr. Barton introduced him to the other members of the faculty as one of their number." This position he declined and returned home to West Feliciana, from which place he moved to Whitestown, now Newtonia, Wilkinson County, Mississippi, where he practised until 1880. In 1840 the degree of A. M. was conferred upon him by Bacon College.

In 1836, during college vacation, he married Mary Armstrong Nesmith, of Amite County, and had three sons and five daughters.

In 1842 he erected buildings for and opened the Newton Female Institute and in 1852 was largely instrumental in building the Newton College.

During the Civil War, Dr. Phares continued in private work, but in 1863 he was thrown from his buggy and received injuries from which he suffered for the remainder of his life.

In 1878, by request of the State Association, he prepared a report on the medical plants of the state, some seven hundred in number. He was one of the leading spirits in the founding and building of the Mississippi Agricultural and Mechanical College and at its opening in 1880 he was assigned the chair of biology, which he filled until 1889.

In 1881 he married Mrs. Laura Blanche Duquercron, of Starkville, Mississippi, and by her had two sons who died in infancy.

In 1889 he moved to Madison Station, Mississippi, but on May 3, 1891, was stricken with paralysis and had a second attack October 13, 1891, dying on September 18, 1892. "A constant student, an accurate observer, a painstaking physician, temperate in all things save work, a conscientious Christian. He was also recognized as an authority on the medical virtues of indigenous plants of the South. When he discovered and promulgated the value of viburnum prunifolium and gelsemium his name became imperishable and he proved himself greater than the chieftain of many battles by placing in the hands of his comrades two weapons to wage war against the foes of flesh."

J. A. R.

Phelps, Edward Elisha (1803–1880).

Edward Elisha Phelps was born in Peacham, Vermont, April 24, 1803; his father was Dr. Elisha Phelps who moved to Windsor soon after the son's birth. The boy was educated at Norwich University; his first course of medical lectures being taken at the Dartmouth Medical School and his course completed under Prof. Nathan Smith, at New Haven, Connecticut, graduation in medicine following after this at Yale in 1824.

Dr. Phelps' health being poor he spent some time in the South, assisting in a survey of the Dismal Swamp canals, and devoting himself incidentally to botanical studies. He seems always to have been a student of plant life.

In 1828 he commenced to practise at Windsor, making his home there throughout his life. He soon made a reputation for himself in the profession, and was elected professor of anatomy and surgery in the medical department of the University of Vermont, occupying the position for two years. In 1841 he was appointed lecturer on materia medica, medical botany and medical jurisprudence in Dartmouth Medical School, and held the chair of materia medica and therapeutics and lectured on botany until 1849, during this time collecting a very complete museum of medical botany for the college. In 1849 he was transferred to the chair of theory and practice of medicine which he occupied until 1871, when he retired from active college work and became professor emeritus. Afterwards, he collected for the college a museum of pathological anatomy with money furnished him by his friend, Hon. E. M. Stoughton, and 1851 and '52 saw him traveling in Europe. The honorary A. M. was conferred on him by the University of Vermont in 1835 and that of LL. D. by the same institution in 1857.

During the Civil War he was a member of the State Board of Examining Surgeons and in this position earned a high reputation for strict and impartial judgment. In the fall of 1861 he was given active duty on the staff of the commander of the Vermont Brigade, serving during the spring and summer of 1862 in the Peninsula. On account of impaired health, he returned to Vermont and was put in charge of the Military Hospital and Camp at Battleboro. This camp attained a wide reputation for the percentage of recoveries which took place there and the credit for this was chiefly due to Dr. Phelps. During the closing months of the war, he was transferred to a Kentucky hospital from which he returned to his home and practice at Windsor.

Dr. Phelps was one of the founders of the Connecticut Valley Medical Society and also its president. He was also a member of the Vermont State Medical Society. To both of these organizations he presented valuable papers. He was a genuine, sincere man, who hated hypocrisy and quackery of any form.

He married, in 1821, Phoebe Foxcroft Lynn, of Boston, and had one daughter. Phelps died November 26, 1880.

C. S. S.

Tr. Amer. Med. Assoc., Phila., vol. xxxii. 1881.
Tr. N. Hampshire Med. Soc., Concord, vol. xci, 1881.

Physick, Philip Syng (1768–1837).

Some biographers of Philip Syng Physick have attributed his fame as the "Father of American Surgery" to the fact of his having few rivals, but a name is not easily retained if undeserved and the scanty records of Physick show a man who was forceful enough to overcome the physical disabilities which might have hindered his medical work.

He was born in Philadelphia, on July 7, 1768, of Edmund and Abigail (Syng) Physick, daughter of a silversmith, his father, receiver-general of the Province of Pennsylvania and after the Revolution agent for the Penn estates. He intended his son for a doctor and made him one in spite of the lad's expressed objection to studying medicine. From the Friends' School, kept by Robert Prout, the local historian, he went to Pennsylvania University and graduated B. A. in 1785, studying afterwards with Dr. Adam Kuhn. He was, to quote Gross, "a faithful, scrupulous toiling soul, something of a prig and not popular with his mates but readily devouring any mental pabulum offered him, notably when, advised to read Cullen's first lines on the 'Practice of Physic' he learnt by heart all the dreary stuff." His father was determined to give the son every opportunity of learning his profession so sent him in 1789 to London where he was fortunate enough to live with John Hunter and to gain his esteem for his skillful dissections, and his influence to obtain the post of house-surgeon to St. George's Hospital where he stayed a year and, on leaving was made a member of the Royal College of Surgeons.

Five testimonials as to the "medical qualifications and correct deportment" were given young Physick when he left St. Georges, and Hunter offered him a partnership. Why he refused the honor of this collaboration and the opportunity of working with Astley Cooper, Abernethy, Home, etc., Physick, reticent always, does not state. He went instead to Edinburgh and took his M. D. there when twenty-four.

Everything seemed to point to rapid success when the young doctor, fresh from John Hunter and Edinburgh and armed with good recommendations, landed, in 1792, again in Philadelphia, but perhaps for want of "push" he was some

PHILIP SYNG PHYSICK.

three years with scarcely any practice. A terrible epidemic of yellow fever, however, broke out in 1793, and he, volunteering help, was elected physician to the fever hospital at Bush Hill, a work which would have brought him more in contact with those who could be useful to him, only he resigned the next day owing, so it is said, to his objection to serve with one Devèze, a Frenchman. But he did faithful work among the yellow-fever patients, always following his master, making careful notes and frequent autopsies and making a living by taking care of several families for a small annual sum, and in 1794, Devèze being no longer at Bush Hill, he took service there: this, with his surgeoncy at the Pennsylvania Hospital, brought him into prominence. 1800 saw him lecturing on surgery in the University School to certain students, lectures which Rush himself attended and applauded. During thirteen years he was professor of surgery and during that period made his great reputation. "For the first time here students heard something more than theory and a mere setting forth of operations and technic; they were taken to the root of things and made to observe, deduce and record."

In the operating-room his deftness and precision were remarkable and as a lithotomist he was probably without equal in skill or number of operations performed. One of his last was upon the aged Chief Justice Marshall, a remarkable case, nearly a thousand calculi in size varying from a partridge shot to a pea were removed and the patient made a good recovery. In orthopedic surgery his facility and inventive mechanism brought him wide fame, and his treatment of coxalgia is well known and most of the appliances to-day are modifications of his methods. His modification of Desault's splint for fractured thigh is still in use and his appliance for outward displacement of the foot in "Pott's fracture" seems to have anticipated that of Dupuytren. Like Hunter his surgery was conservative—a conservatism often carried to excess. As to general practice

he went by the light of experience of common sense and was intolerant in his practice and teaching of the theories of others. He had great faith in venesection and Dr. Charles D. Meigs tells of a patient of his for whom he consulted Physick. She had a violent attack of conjunctivitis; great pain and threatened destruction of the eye. "She was duly bled, to-day, tomorrow, the next and next morning, and so on until at last she fainted so badly that terror laid hold on us both and we fled for succor to Dr. Physick. He came the next day at ten o'clock, looked at the eye and asked "Who is your bleeder? Send for him and tell him to take twelve ounces of blood from the arm and request him to meet you in the morning and repeat the operation if necessary." Although I was horrified I complied with the request and the next day on looking into the eye could discover only the faintest trace of inflammation. In fact, the woman was virtually cured.

It is a pity Physick's lectures were never printed; they were worth it and we have nothing save a few articles. He was not a great reader even on his own subjects. His lectures, which he often got up at four A. M. to write, were as carefully written as if for publication, he deeming it wrong to trust to memory and to instruct others upon subjects he did not clearly understand. One of his biographers, S. D. Gross, describes him as a cold dyspeptic, pessimistic, unsociable man, but full of sympathy for suffering humanity; strikingly erect and handsome but pallid, his face as if chiselled out of marble, the eyes black and his hair powdered and worn in a queue. Fond of money but never claiming high fees, he yet left nothing of his large fortune to the advancement of medicine. His mind was much troubled on theological matters but what conclusions he came to in the end his reserved nature did not allow him to disclose. Postmortem fears also disturbed him and he left orders for his body to be wrapped in flannel and kept in a warm temperature so that decomposition might be evident, a double coffin, and his grave to be watched for several weeks for fear of bodysnatchers. He died in Philadelphia on December 15, 1837.

He was married in 1800, though little can be gleaned concerning his wife save that she was a Miss Emlen, "highly gifted and talented," and had four children, also that Physick was "a faithful domestic character," allowing his daughters to entertain as much as they liked and only allowing himself recreation towards the end of his life when he loved to go with them to his summer house in Cecil County, Maryland.

He was professor of surgery, Pennsylvania University, 1805–19; professor of anatomy, 1819–31; president of Philadelphia Medical Society, 1824; emeritus professor of anatomy and surgery, Pennsylvania University, 1831–37; member of the Academy of Medicine of France, 1825; honorary fellow, Royal Medical and Chirurgical Society, London, 1856.

D. W.

There is a portrait in the Collection of the Surg.-gen. Lib., Washington.
Autobiography, S. D. Gross.
Review of Dr. Horner's necrologic notice of Dr. P. S. Physick, Phila., 1838.
Notice of Dr. P. S. Physick, W. E. Horner, Phila., 1838.
Amer. Jour. Med. Sc , (J. Randolph,) Phila , 1839.
Maryland Med. and Surg. Jour., (S. Collins,) Baltimore, 1840.

Pickering, Charles (1805–1878).

Charles Pickering, known to the scientific world as an anthropologist and botanist, was of good New England stock, being a grandson of Col. Timothy Pickering, a member of Washington's military family and of his first cabinet. He was born on Starucca Creek, Upper Susquehanna, Pennsylvania, on a grant of land owned by his grandfather. His father, Timothy Pickering, died when 30, leaving Charles and his brother Edward to the care of their mother.

He left Harvard before graduation, but took his M. D. there in 1826. In his earlier years he used to make botanical expeditions with one William Oakes, and when he settled in Philadelphia in 1829, he had a strong bent towards natural science, very soon being appointed one of the curators at the Academy of Natural Sciences, during this time publishing a brief essay on "The Geographical Distribution and Leading Characters of the United States Flora." When the United States Exploring Expedition was organized in the autumn of 1838 to sail for the South Seas, Pickering was elected as the principal zoologist, and the fame of that expedition rests chiefly on the work he then did with Prof. Dana. Although Pickering retained the ichthyology, he went keenly into the geographical distribution of animals and plants; to the latter especially as affected by the operations and movements of the races of man. A year after the expedition, and at his own expense, he visited Egypt, Arabia, Eastern Africa and Western and Northern India, publishing in 1848 his volume, "The Races of Men and Their Geographical Distribution" (vol. ix, Wilkes' "Exploring Expedition Report"). In the fifteenth volume appeared his "Geographical Distribution of Animals and Plants." He had no better luck than many a scientist, for, in the course of printing, Congress appropriations stopped and the publication of further Reports was abandoned. But under privilege, he brought out in 1854 a small edition of the first part of his essay and in 1876 a more bulky one "On Plants and Animals in Their Wild State." These writings and some contributions to scientific journals, notably to the "Smithsonian Contributions to Knowledge," constituted his no mean help to the study of natural science, but he had been long and lovingly working on a book yet unfinished when he died, a book edited afterwards by his wife, Sarah S. Pickering, and appearing in 1879 entitled, "Chronological History of Plants, or Man's Record of His Own Existence."

Prof. Harshberger, whose biography of him I have used, says he was singularly retiring and reticent, dry in ordinary intercourse, but to those who knew him well, communicative and genial. D. W.

The Botanists of Philadelphia. J. W. Harshberger, 1899.
Proc. Acad. Nat. Sc., Phila., 1878 (W. S W. Ruschenberger.)

Picton, John Moore White (1804–1858).

John Moore White Picton, physician, was born in Woodbury, New Jersey, 1804, and died in New Orleans, 1858. Graduating in 1824 from the United States Military Academy, and in 1832 from the medical department of the University of Pennsylvania, he settled in New Orleans, where he practised for thirty-two years, acquiring great reputation as an operator. He served for many years as house-surgeon of the Charity Hospital and as president of the medical department of the University of Louisiana. Founder of the New Orleans School of Medicine in 1856, he was professor of obstetrics there until 1858. J. G. R.

Appleton's Cyc. of American Biography.
The Medical Dept. of Tulane University of La. Med. News, N. Y., 1902.

Piffard, Henry G. (1842–1910).

Henry G. Piffard, author of the first systematic treatise on dermatology in America, was born in Piffard, Livingston County, on September 24, 1842, his paternal ancestors coming from Dauphiné, France, and his mother's being of Dutch extraction.

His studying was done at the University of the City of New York where he took his A. B. and A. M., and his M. D. at the College of Physicians and Surgeons, New York, in which city he specialized in skin diseases. He married, in 1868, Helen H., daughter of Gen. William K. Strong, of New York.

One of his best contributions to medical literature was the translation, from the French of A. Hardy, of the "Dartrous Diathesis" (1868). Following this came "A Guide to Urinary Analysis" (1873); "An Elementary Treatise on Diseases of the Skin" (1876).

His appointments included: surgeon to the New York Dispensary for Diseases of the Skin and professor of dermatology in the University of the City of New York. In 1862 he served for a short time with the Sanitary Commission on the James River, Virginia.

His membership included the Medical Society of the County of New York; the New York Academy of Medicine; New York Dermatological Society, of which he was president in 1876.

Dr. George Henry Fox of New York, in the "Journal of Cutaneous Diseases," for February, 1911, gives some reminiscences of Henry Grainger Piffard. Dr. Piffard began to collect foreign works on skin diseases. He was a fair German and a better French scholar, but knew very little of Italian. To supply this deficiency he at once subscribed for one or two Italian medical journals, selected a teacher, and attacked the language with his customary vigor. Happening to run across an advertisement of some book, entitled something like "Trattato della Pelle et cetera," he gave his book-dealer an order for it. The bookdealer, in a polite note, informed him that this was an expensive work, published by the Italian Government, and that it would take several weeks to import it. Piffard replied in language more vigorous than polite—"Expense be damned"; when he wanted a book he expected his dealer not to talk about it but to get it. In about two months, during which time his knowledge of Italian had rapidly increased, the book arrived and with it a bill for about £12. To his surprise and dismay he discovered at first glance that it was not a strictly dermatological work, but an elegantly bound and elaborate treatise on the tanning of hides.

Jour. of Cutaneous Diseases, Feb, 1911. (George H. Fox.)
Atkinson's Phys. and Surgs. of the United States.

Pinkney, Ninian (1811–1877).

Ninian Pinkney, surgeon, United States Navy, graduated from St. John's College in 1830, and commenced to study medicine with Dr. Edward Sparks. In 1833 he graduated from the Jefferson Medical College, Pennsylvania, and the following year entered the United States Navy as assistant surgeon and continued on active duty until retired as medical director with rank of commodore in 1873. In 1848 he received the vote of thanks of the General Assembly of Maryland, for gallant and meritorious sevices in the Mexican War. He prepared and delivered a series of lectures, some of which were published. Among the best are: "On the Nerves of the Brain and Organs of Sense," (1839); "Life and Character of Admiral Collingwood" (1848); "A Treatise on Asiatic Cholera" (1849); "Home and Foreign Policy of the Government of the United States" (1854). In the same year he also delivered the commencement oration at St. John's College, and made the presentation address at the Naval Academy on the occasion of Commodore Perry's presenting the flag that had been raised on the soil of Japan. Surg. Pinkney was persistent in his advocacy for increased and definite rank for the medical officers in the Navy, and, in 1870, was chairman of a delegation which proposed the medical staff rank and grade for the United States Navy which later, after slight modifications, became the law. He died at his home near Easton, Maryland, in 1877, leaving his widow and a daughter.   C. A. P.

Tr. Am. M. Ass., 1878, xxix.

Pitcher, Zina (1797–1872).

Zina Pitcher, son of Nathaniel Pitcher and Margaret Stevenson, was born April 12, 1797, on a farm in Washington County, New York. When five years old his father died, leaving the mother with four young sons and an unattractive farm. Being Scotch, she had learned the value of education and determined to provide the best possible for her children. Zina worked hard during spring, summer and fall that he might study during the winter in common school or academy.

He began to study medicine at the age of twenty-one with private practitioners and at Castleton Medical College, graduating M. D. from Middlebury College in 1822. While studying medicine he tutored in Latin, Greek and natural sciences—the latter with Prof. Eaton, of Rensselaer Polytechnic Institute at Troy, New York. Soon after graduating, the Secretary of War, John C. Calhoun, sent him a commission as assistant surgeon, United States Army. The responsibility of this position rapidly developed his self-reliance, so that he was soon made surgeon. During his fifteen years of army service he was stationed at different points on the Northern Lakes (then a savage frontier) on the tributaries of the Arkansas, among the Creeks, Cherokees, Choctaws and Osages and at Fortress Monroe. At these places his leisure hours were spent in study of nature about him, observation of the habits of the Indians, their diseases and the means used for their recovery. The results of these studies may be seen in works on botany, in plants named after him; on fossils bearing his name; and in a letter to Dr. Morton on the existence of consumption among the aborigines and in his article on "Indian Therapeutics," printed in the fourth volume, of Schoolcraft's history of the "Conditions and Prospects of the Indian Tribes." In 1835 he was president of the Army Medical Board. In 1836 Dr. Pitcher resigned his commission and settled in Detroit. From 1837 to 1852 he was regent of the University and probably planned most details respecting the medical department. With the appointment of the medical faculty he was made emeritus professor. He was mayor of Detroit in 1840–41–43. Long dissatisfied with the educational facilities of the frontier town, he made an exhaustive study of its schools and laid the results before the Common Council and persuaded it to join him in asking the Legislature to enact a law authorizing the establishment of free public schools in Detroit, which petition was granted. He was city physician, 1847; county physician, 1845; and during Buchanan's administration, surgeon of the Marine Hospital in Detroit. He was elected president of the American Medical Association at its meeting in Detroit, 1856, and was editor of the "Peninsular Medical Journal," 1855–56–58; he was president of the Old Territorial Medical Society during fourteen years; president of the Michigan State Medical Society, 1855–56; a founder of the Sydenham Society; a founder of Detroit Medical Society, 1852–58. Zina Pitcher was versed in the habits of beasts and birds; his contributions to Indian materia medica were classic. His perception of scientific facts was unusually quick and his memory tenacious. In driving through the country he at once detected an unfamiliar plant or animal, secured a specimen and determined its place. While in Texas he collected many fossils and forwarded them to the Philadelphia Academy of Natural Sciences. Studies of these and allied collections were the basis of Dr. S. G. Morton's work entitled "Cretaceous System of the United States." One of the specimens is known as "Gryphœa Pitcheri." In "Gray and Torrey's Flora of the United States" several new species are named after Dr. Pitcher in acknowledgment of his service to botany. So general is the use of hot water in checking hemorrhage that few remember that it originated with Dr. Pitcher. His home was at the service of the sick; he was known to have taken a stranger suffering from small-pox into his home, and both nurse and doctor him to recovery. Moreover, to him the Bible was a guide, a counsellor and inspiration.

In 1824 Zina Pitcher married Ann Sheldon, of Kalamazoo, Michigan, and had a son (Nathaniel) and daughter (Rose), the mother dying in 1864. In 1867 he married Emily Backus, grand-daughter of Col. Nathaniel Rochester, of Virginia, the founder of Rochester, New York, and on the death of DeWitt Clinton, acting governor of New York.

Dr. Pitcher died April 5, 1872, from unoperated stone in the bladder.

His papers included:

1832. "Penetrating Wound of the Abdomen and Section of the Intestinal Canal Successfully Treated on the Plan of Ramdohr." ("American Journal, Medical Sciences," vol. x, p. 42.) (Under the conditions this was a remarkable piece of surgery.)

1852. "Report of Committee on Epidemics of Ohio Indians and Michigan." (By G. Mendenshall and Zina Pitcher; Ibid.)

1853. "Are Typhus and Typhoid Fevers Identical?" ("Peninsular Medical Journal," vol. i, second series.

1853. "Epilepsy Treated by Ligation of the Common Carotid Artery." ("Peninsular Medical Journal," vol. i, pp. 8–10.)

1854. "Medicine of American Indians." (Part 4, pp. 502–519, of Schoolcraft's "Information Respecting the History and Prospects of the Indian Tribes of the United States," Philadelphia, 1854.)

1855. "On the Induction of Puerperal Fever by Inoculation." ("Peninsular Medical Journal," vol. ii.)

1855. "Amputation in Utero." (Ibid., vol. iii.)

1855. "Malformation of the Heart." (Ibid., vol. iii.)

1855. "Report on the Epidemics of Ohio Indians and Michigan for the Years 1852–53." (G. Mendenhall and Zina Pitcher, "Transactions, American Medical Association," vol. vii, presented in 1854.)

1856. "Scurvy from Moral Causes." ("Peninsular Medical Journal," vol. iii.)

1856. "Case of Vicarious Menstruation Showing also the Morbid Relations of the Colon and Uterus." (Ibid., vol. iv.)

1857. "Morbus Coxarius." (Ibid., vol. iv.)

1857. "Alterative Influence of Valvular Heart Disease in Pulmonary Tuberculosis." (Ibid., vol. v.)

1858. "Clinical Instruction." ("Peninsular and Independent Medical Journal," vol. i. Response to A. B. Palmer.)

1858. "On the Influence which Theoretical Opinions in Medicine have Exercised over Therapeutics." "President's Address before Michigan State Medical Society." (Ibid., vol. iii.) 1861. "Contributions to Military Surgery." ("American Medical Times," New York, vol. ii, pp. 351–353.)

L. C.

History University Mich., Ann Arbor, University Press, 1906.
Representative Men in Mich., West. Biographical Co., Cinn., Ohio, 1878, vol. i.
Trans. Mich. State Med. Soc., 1874.
Mich. Univ. Med. Jour., Ann Arbor, 1872, vol. iii.
Richmond and Louisville Med. Jour., Louisville, Ky., 1869, vol. vii.
Trans. Amer. Med. Ass., vol. xxiii.
A portrait, 1851, and bust of Zina Pitcher, 1852, are in the Medical Faculty Room at Ann Harbor, Mich.
Life, Novy, Michigan Alumnus, 1908,

Plant, William Tomlinson (1836–1898).

William Tomlinson Plant, a medico-jurisprudentist, was born at Marcellus, New York, July 27, 1836, of English ancestry, taking his medical degree at the University of Michigan, at Ann Arbor.

At first he settled at Ithaca, New York, later, however, he removed to Susquehanna, Pennsylvania, and, in 1861, joined the United States Navy, holding the positions of assistant and post-assistant surgeon.

In 1866 he married Frances C. Walrath, of Chittenango, New York.

For some years he was professor of clinical medicine and medical jurisprudence in the medical department of the Syracuse University and wrote repeatedly on medico-legal topics, much of his work possessing enduring value.

T. H. S.

Jour. Am. Med. Assn., Nov. 5, 1898.

Pollak, Simon (1816–1903).

Simon Pollak was born near Prague, April 14, 1816, and received his M. D. there in 1835, and for surgery and obstetrics in Vienna, 1836. He arrived in New York in 1838, then spent a short time in New Orleans and in other southern towns, and in March, 1845, settled in St.

Louis, Missouri, where he was one of the founders of the Missouri Institute for the Blind in 1850. In 1859 he went to Europe and spent amost two years in study in Paris, Vienna, Berlin, and London, returning to St. Louis in 1861; but on account of the Civil War he removed to New York and aided in the founding of the United States Sanitary Commission. On behalf of this society he returned to St. Louis, where he joined the Western Sanitary Commission. About this time he organized the first eye and ear clinic west of the Mississippi, in St. Louis. In 1863 he was appointed general hopsital inspector United States Sanitary Commission at a salary of two hundred and fifty dollars a month, which position he accepted, but declined the salary.

One of the early members of the American Ophthalmological Society, he was known as a prominent oculist and teacher, active and very popular throughout his unusually long life. At his last birthday his friends and colleagues tendered him a great ovation at a dinner. He died October 31, 1903.

H. F.

Archives of Ophthalmology, vol. xxxiii.

Pomeroy, Charles G. (1817–1887.)

Charles G. Pomeroy, one of the founders of the New York State Medical Association, was born in Madison County, February 22, 1817.

Shortly after his birth his parents took him to Ontario County, where they settled on a farm, near the village of Canandaigua.

In this village and in Rochester, young Pomeroy attended school until he was seventeen, then studied under Dr. Post. Four years later the censors of Ontario Medical Society granted him a license to practise, then followed a few months' experience in Monroe County, before forming a partnership with Dr. Alexander McIntyre, of Palmyra. Dr. Pomeroy again changed his home to practise for eight years in Fairville; then moved to Newark, Wayne County, New York, where he founded the State Medical Association and was an organizer of the Wayne County Medical Society and many times elected as its president. He was also president of the Medical Association of Central New York. As governor, trustee and resident physician of the New York State Custodial Asylum for Feeble-minded Women Dr. Pomeroy worked until his impaired health obliged him to resign. He married twice. His first wife dying in early life, he married a second time in 1850.

Dr. Pomeroy died of granular disease of the kidneys with cardiac complications, in Newark, December 14, 1887.

M. K. K.

Transactions of the New York State Medical Association, 1888, vol v.

Porcher, Francis Peyre (1825–1895).

A distinguished physician and botanist, he was born December 14, 1825, and was descended from Isaac Porcher, a French Huguenot who emigrated from France at the time of the prosecution of the Huguenots by the Romish Church. He graduated from the South Carolina College in 1844 with the degree of A. B. and took his M. D. from the Medical College of the State of South Carolina in 1847. His thesis, entitled: "A Medico-botanical Catalogue of the Plants and Ferns of St. Johns, Berkley, South Carolina," was published by the faculty of the college. This work proved to be the forerunner and ground work of a very remarkable series of books, as follows:

"Sketch of the Medical Botany of South Carolina," 1849; "Medical Poisonous and Dietetic Properties of the Cryptogamic Plants of the United States," being a report made to the American Medical Association at its sessions held at Richmond, Virginia, and St. Louis, Missouri, 1854; "Resources of the Southern Fields and Forests" (war volume), 1863; second edition, 1869.

In addition to these large works he wrote, in 1860, a prize essay entitled "Illustrations of Disease with the Micro-scope: Clinical Investigations," with upwards of five hundred original drawings from nature and one hundred and ten illustrations in wood. For this, a prize of $100 offered by the South Carolina Medical Association was awarded to him.

The first edition of "The Resources of the Southern Fields and Forests" was published by order of the surgeon-general of the Confederacy and it was also a medical botany of the Confederate States. After graduating in medicine he spent two years in France and Italy, perfecting himself in the refinement of his profession. Dr. Porcher returned to Charleston, South Carolina, and assisted in establishing the Charleston Preparatory Medical School. He was subsequently elected professor in the chairs of clinical medicine and of materia medica and therapeutics in the Medical College of the State of South Carolina. He was for five years one of the editors of the "Charleston Medical Journal and Review," and also assisted in editing and publishing four volumes "new series" after the War between the states.

Dr. Porcher, with his two brothers, served throughout the War, a third being killed in 1862. He was surgeon to the Holcombe Legion; to the Naval Hospital at Fort Nelson, Norfolk Harbor, and at the South Carolina Hospital at Petersburg, Virginia. His contributions to medical literature have been numerous and valuable. Some of his most important contributions have been upon "Yellow Fever," "Diseases of the Heart," ("Wood's Hand-book of the Medical Sciences"), reports of sixty-nine cases of paracentises of the chest walls in case of effusion, on the medical and edible properties of the cryptogamic plants, on gastric remittent fevers," etc., etc. A partial list of Dr. Porcher's works will be found in the "Index Medicus" of the surgeon-general's office in Washington.

Dr. Porcher was an ex-president of the South Carolina Medical Association and of the Medical Society of South Carolina, ex-vice-president of the American Medical Association, member of the Association of American Physicians, and an associate fellow of the College of Physicians of Philadelphia. The degree of LL. D. was conferred upon him in 1891 by the University of South Carolina.

He was first married to Virginia, daughter of the Hon. Benjamin Watkins Leigh, of Richmond, Virginia. His second wife was Margaret, daughter of the Hon. J. J. Ward, of Georgetown, South Carolina. He had five children by his first wife and four by his second. One of his sons became a physician. Dr. Porcher was a man of wonderful capacity for work. He had no higher ambition than the advancement of his profession. It may truthfully be said of him that he "scorned delights and lived laborious days."

During a long illness from paralysis a plant was brought to him which he immediately detected to be a specimen of Trillium Pumilum, and he announced that it had not been seen before in one hundred years. He was supported in this statement by the most distinguished authorities. So great was his ambition to excel as a physician that he almost gave up botany in his latter years fearing that his reputation as a botanist might excel his reputation as a physician. He might easily have acquired wealth had his mind been so directed, for he had stated in his book in 1849 that oil from cotton seed was exceedingly valuable, and in 1870 others began to accumulate enormous sums from this source.

He died November 19, 1895, leaving to his children that great heritage, a name untarnished.   W. P. P.

Tr. South Car. M. Ass., Charleston, 1896.

Porter, Charles Hogeboom (1834–1903).

Charles Hogeboom Porter, medicojurisprudentist, was of Dutch and English ancestry and born at Ghent, Columbus County, New York, November 11, 1834.

His art degree was from Yale in 1857, and his professional one from the Albany Medical College in 1861. Settling in Albany, he devoted especial attention to legal medicine, but throughout the Civil War was assistant surgeon of the Sixth New York volunteer heavy artillery.

He contributed largely to the literature of medical jurisprudence. Among his more important articles are: "Arsenic in Common Life" ("Berkshire Medical Journal," 1856); "Arsenic, and Cases" ("Transactions, Medical Society of New York," 1861); "A Statement of the Case of the People vs. Fere" ("Journal of Psychological Medicine," New York, 1870).

In 1855–6 he was professor of chemistry at the Vermont Medical College, and from 1859 till 1864 professor of chemistry and medical jurisprudence in the Albany Medical College.

Dr. Porter was of medium height and thickly set. His skin was dark, his hair thin and black, and his eyes a deep brown. These eyes were very expressive. A former student of the doctor relates that, once, after a lecture, he went to Dr. Porter to ask him some trivial question, not at all in an earnest way but only to "annoy the professor." Dr. Porter fixed his quiet, steady eyes upon the student, and kept them there for some time without uttering a word. "I slunk away," relates the former student, "most thoroughly ashamed." Dr. Porter was slow and deliberate in speech and action, always weighing his words most carefully. On the witness stand he was admirable, chiefly for the exactness and care of his utterances. He did not have "a host of friends," but to the few he did possess he was just and loyal.

He died after a lingering illness at Canandaigua, New York, November 21, 1903, very much regretted by the very few who had known him well.

T. H. S.

Jour. Am. Med. Assn., 1903.
Albany Med. Annals, 1904, vol. xxv.

Porter, James Burnham (1806–1879).

"Dr. Jim," as he was familiarly known over a wide territory, was one of a medical family famous in Vermont for a century, and greatly missed when he died in 1879.

His father, James Porter, was one of four brothers, all medical men, and was long a Vermont practitioner. James B. Porter was educated at Middlebury College, and had his medical education at Castleton and Woodstock, graduating at the latter institution. He was long a member of the Vermont Medical Society.

He was one of the best types of the country doctor, and widely sought in consultation.

He was called to attend the man injured in the construction of the Rutland Railroad, who became the famous "crow bar case." This case was reported by John Harlow in the "Boston Medical Journal," in November, 1848, and had a wide circulation in medical literature. The patient, who had an iron bar driven through his skull, lived many years, and his skull is still preserved in the Warren Museum at Harvard College.

Dr. Porter married, in 1834, Harriet Griggs, of Brookline, Massachusetts.

Of his four children, one, Charles Burnham, became a surgeon and was a lecturer at Harvard.

C. S. C.

Porter, Robert R. (1811-1876).

Robert R. Porter entered the University of Pennsylvania graduating in 1835, and was soon after appointed resident physician of Frankford Insane Hospital, in 1835. He was a member of Delaware State Medical Society, its president in 1858. His practice was confined exclusively to Wilmington, Delaware, with the exception of one year's residence at the Frankford Insane Hospital.

Dr. Porter was a physician of ability and of high professional honor; in addition, a man of enterprise and of public spirit and took a leading position in every movement for public good.

He married, in 1841, Lucinda, only daughter of Judge Millard Hall, and had five daughters and one son. Dr. Porter died suddenly of apoplexy, April 14, 1876.

He published in the "American Medical Journal" his "Observations on the Condition and Treatment of the Insane,"

and also assisted Dr. Samuel Morton in the preparation of his work on "Phthisis Pulmonalis."

H. M. T.

Scbraf's Hist. of Delaware.

Post, Alfred Charles (1806–1886).

This clever nephew of a clever uncle— Wright Post—began his classical education in Columbia College when only fourteen, but was born in New York City, of Joel H. and Elizabeth Browne Post; his father was a successful merchant. The lad held his B. A. from Columbia and worked under his uncle in 1823, but he took at the same time courses of lectures at the College of Physicians and Surgeons. He also took varoloid, which laid him up for some time until he was able to set to work with new vigor and get his M. D. in 1827. Like most young men of the time, he went to Europe, flitting about from England to Paris and Berlin and Italy. In 1829 he returned to New York and became house surgeon to the New York Hospital and in 1836 visiting surgeon. When in 1851 he became professor of surgery his lectures were very popular, particularly those on ophthalmic, aural, orthopedic and plastic surgery. In 1840 he published a small treatise on "Strabismus" and on "Stammering," having operated for the latter at an earlier period than any other American surgeon. That same year he devised a new method for doing bilateral lithotomy, employing, to divide the prostate, a canula sliding over a rod and armed with two knives one of which projected on each side. No operation was too great or too small, extirpation of the thyroid, paratoid and cervical glands, making an artificial anus, tracheotomy. As an aside from his surgical duties he was keen on missionary work and said, not irreverently, that the two things he most enjoyed were a good operation and a good prayer meeting.

His colleagues say he could not be said to have passed middle life until he was eighty. During the last ten years of his life he performed some of his most delicate operations in plastic surgery and four months before his death did a difficult ovariotomy in forty-five minutes.

In 1831 he married Harriet, daughter of Cyrenius Beers, of New York, and had eleven children, one of whom was Dr. George E. Post, a medical missionary, at Beirut, Syria.

He held among other appointments the professorship of surgery in the medical department of the University of New York; president of the medical faculty there; member of the Berliner Königlich Medizinisch-chirurgishe Gesellshaft.

His writings were chiefly to medical journals and included, among others, "A Case of Blepharoplasty;" "Club Foot;" "Cicatricial Contractions;" "Contraetions of Palmar Fascia."   D. W.

Trans. Med. Soc., State of N. Y., 1887.
Med. Rec. N. Y. 1886, xxix.   (J. C. Peters.)
Med. and Surg Reporter, Phila 1865, xii
(S W. Francis)

Post, George Edward (1838–1909).

One of America's most noted medical missionaries, and equally known as a scientist and author, George Edward Post was born in New York city, December 17, 1838, the son of Dr. Alfred and Harriet Beers Post. He graduated from the old New York Free Academy, now the College of the City of New York, in 1854, taking his master's degree three years later. He then entered the medical department of the University of New York, from which he graduated in 1860. One year afterwards he entered the Union Theological Seminary.

Dr. Post was elected to the professorship of surgery in the Syrian Protestant Hospital at Beirut, which is maintained by the Presbyterian Board of Foreign Missions, and this he held until his death. He was also surgeon to the Johanniret Hospital, in Beirut.

The Protestant Hospital was then a small struggling institute with few students. Dr. Post lived to see it with an enrollment of eight hundred representing some twelve or fourteen nationalities, and Post was equally clever in dealing with their physical, intellectual or moral needs. Not only that, he was a great linguist; could hold Arab scholars fascinated by his graceful speech or draw around him ignorant muleteers and caravan followers by his simple colloquial talk.

He wrote on many subjects, in several languages. He was author, in Arabic, of the "Flora of Syria, Palestine and Egypt;" "Text-book of Botany;" "Text-book of Mammalia;" "Text-book of Birds;" Translations of Butler's Physiology;" "Concordance to the Bible;" "Text-book of Surgery;" "Text-book of Materia Medica;" and "Dictionary of the Bible." Two of these were published in English.

He also wrote, in French and Latin, "Plantæ Postianæ," which was published in Geneva. Dr. Post contributed largely to Smith's, Hastings's, Jacobus', and Barnes' Dictionaries of the Bible.

He was a man of vigorous frame, alert in every action, and endowed with an unusual versatility of gifts, both mental and spiritual, and his place in clinic or chapel was rarely empty. Late in the evening he would often be working in the college herbarium he had presented and which contains some of the rarest oriental plants. He studied the plant and animal life about him to such advantage as to gain membership in European societies and give the schools text-books in Arabic upon the "Botany, Mammals and Birds of Persia," besides treatises on "Surgery and Materia Medica."

For his work in the missionary and medical fields, he received the decoration of Othnanieyh of Turkey, of the Ducal House of Saxony, and of the Red Eagle and Knights of Jerusalem of Germany. He was also member of the Linnaean Society of London, the Torrey Botanical Club of New York, the Botanical Society of Edinburgh, and the Academy of Medicine, New York.

He married Sarah Reed, of Georgetown, District of Columbia, and three children survived him. Of his two sons, Bertram Van Dyck became a professor of biology in Robert College at Constantinople and Wilfred M., surgeon at the American Hospital, Caesarea.

On September 29, 1909, at midnight a long attack of pneumonia gained the victory over the worn body of George Post. He left a place which many could fill for he himself had fitted them so to do.

D. W.

New York Observer, Oct. 7, 1909.
New York Evening Post, Oct. 8, 1909.
The Missionary Review, New York, Dec., 1909, in which there is a good portrait.

Post, Wright (1766–1828).

Wright Post was born at North Hempstead, Long Island, on the nineteenth of February, 1766, and educated at home under a private tutor, Dr. David Bailey, at the age of fifteen, beginning his medical studies with the celebrated surgeon, Dr. Richard Bayley. After four years of hard work, he went to London to continue preparation under Dr. John Sheldon, a celebrated teacher of anatomy and surgery, with whom he lived two years, attending lectures and working in the London Hospital.

In 1786 he returned to New York and began to practise, and in 1787 delivered a course of lectures on anatomy in a spare room of the New York Hospital, where Dr. Bayley was teaching classes in surgery. This course was interrupted by the "doctor's mob," which, excited by some scandalous reports concerning "body snatching," broke into the building and destroyed a valuable collection of anatomical and pathological specimens. In 1792 the professorship of anatomy and surgery in the college medical school, then held by Dr. Bayley, was divided into two parts, and Dr. Post was made professor of surgery. Meanwhile Dr. Post visited Europe and collected materials for a museum. For half a century this remained one of the largest anatomical cabinets in America. Dr. Post performed several important surgical operations, the most distinguished of these was the tying of the subclavian artery above the clavicle. In 1792 Dr. Bayley exchanged chairs with Dr. Post, who

remained professor of anatomy till 1813. When the medical school of Columbia became consolidated with the College of Physicians and Surgeons, he became professor of anatomy and physiology in the new faculty.

He received an honorary M. D. from the University of the State of New York in 1814. His reputation lies almost entirely in his surgical achievements, for he published few papers of importance. He held a surgeoncy to the New York Hospital; was an active officer of the New York County Medical Society; and from 1820–26 was president of the College of Physicians and Surgeons.

The following account of Post by Valentine Mott gives some idea of the character of the man:

"Wright Post was at that time a man of about forty years of age, tall, handsome, and of fashionable exterior, wore long whiskers and his hair powdered and tied back in a queue. Those who recollect his thin worn figure in later years, wrapped in a furred surtout, could scarcely have recognized in him the elegant gentleman of my early days. Dr. Post had at this time attained to the very highest rank in his profession, both as a physician and surgeon, and although equalled in the extent and renown of his surgical practice by his distinguished colleague in the New York Hospital, Dr. R. S. Kissam, he stood, perhaps, alone in its lucrative practice and in the estimation and confidence of the higher walks of society. He was unrivalled as an anatomist, a most beautiful dissector, and one of the most luminous and perspicuous teachers I have ever listened to, either at home or abroad. His manners were grave and dignified; he seldom smiled, and never trifled with the serious and responsible duties in which he was engaged, and which no man ever more solemnly respected. His delivery was precise, slow and clear, qualities inestimable in a teacher, and peculiarly adapting his instructions to the advancement of the junior portion of the class. He was one of the first American pupils (preceding Dr. Physick) of the celebrated John Hunter, of London, from whose lips and those of Mr. Sheldon, he imbibed those principles of practice which he afterwards so ably and usefully applied.

"Two great achievements are on record to attest his powers. He was the first in this country to tie, successfully, on the Hunterian principle, the femoral artery for popliteal aneurysm. On the second memorable occasion, I had the honor to assist him; it was a case of ligature of the subclavian artery above the clavicle, without the scaleni muscles, for an aneurysm of the brachial, involving the axilla. The patient came to me from New Haven, in company with an intimate professional friend of mine, the late Dr. Gilbert; the aneurysm was cracked and oozing, and supported by layers of adhesive plaster, by which its rupture was prevented, and life maintained until the time of the operation. The brother of the patient, a merchant of New York, whose family Dr. Post attended, naturally preferred that he should perform the operation, as I was then quite young. To this wish I cheerfully acceded, but lost thus the chance of gaining a surgical laurel for my brow— the operation never having been performed in this country before, and but once in Europe, and then unsuccessfully, by its first projector, Mr. Ramsden, of St. Bartholomew's Hospital, London. This is now, happily, a well recognized surgical procedure, which six times I have successfully performed. In this operation, the American needle for the ligature of deep-seated arteries was first used in New York, and it belonged to me.

He married Miss Bailey of New York in 1790. After a career of forty years as a professor of anatomy, he retired into private professional life, in which he continned active, with occasional intervals of ill health, until his death, in the sixty-fourth year of his age. He died on the fourteenth of June, 1828, at Throg's Neck, New York, universally esteemed, deeply regretted, and leaving a good posterity."

C. R. B.

Valentine Mott's Address, College of Physicians and Surgeons, New York, 1850. William's Amer. Med. Biog., 1845.

Pott, John (16— -1652(?).

Dr. John Pott being ordained by the London Court to succeed Lawrence Bohune as physician to the Colony of Virginia, sailed with his wife Elizabeth on the George and landed at Jamestown in 1620. Having succeeded to the Council in Virginia it seems natural that Pott should covet the former official's station and emoluments—that of physician-general to the Colony, with five hundred acres of land and twenty tenants. The minutes of the London Company for the sixteenth of July, 1621, show that he was recommended for the position by Dr. William Gulston: "For so much as the phisicans place to the company was now become voyde by reason of the untimely death of Dr. Bohune, slain in the fight with two Spanish shipps of Warr the nineteenth of March last, Dr. Gulstone did now take occasion to recommend unto the company for the said place one Mr. Potts, a Mr. of Artes, well practised in Chirurgerie and Physique, and expert also in distillinge of waters, and that he had many other ingenious devices so as he supposed his service would be of great use unto the colony in Virginia."

The Council ordered that "If Mr. Pott would accept of the place upon the same conditions as Dr. Bohune did, he should be entertained and for his better content should be specially recommended to the Governor to be well accommodated and should have a chest of Physique £20 charge unto the company, and all things thereunto apertaining together with £10 in books of Physique which should always belonge unto the company, which chest of Physique and Books Dr. Gulstone was desired to by, and seeing he intended to carry over with him his wife a man and a maid they should have their transporte freed, and if one or more Chirurgions could be got they likewise should have their passage freed which conditions Me. Pott having accepted of was refferred to the commitees to be further treated and concluded with."

Dr. Theodore Gulstone, graduate of Oxford, died in 1632, bequeathing $1,000 for founding the Gulstonian chair of anatomy in the London College of Surgeons, a lectureship which is still continued.

Dr. Pott became a member of the Council by royal selection on May 24, 1625, and governor by election of the Council on March 5, 1628. After little more than a year as chief executive he was succeeded by Sir John Harvey. Hardly had the latter assumed the reins of government before Dr. Pott's enemies sought his disgrace, charging him with having pardoned and restored the privileges of a wilful murderer, and with holding some cattle not his own. Harvey confiscated his property and ordered him to remain under arrest at his home until the General Court of July 9, 1630, when he was arraigned before a jury of thirteen on the charge of "felony." The doctor declared the evidence against him hypocritical and unreliable but the jury found against him. Gov. Harvey withheld sentence until he could learn the wishes of the King, writing him that the prisoner "was the only physician in the Colony skilled in epidemical diseases," pleaded for his pardon, and the restoration of his estate because of his lengthy residence and valuable service. Mrs. Pott took ship for England to importune the King in person.

Charles appointed a commission to determine the matter, which reported that the condemning of Dr. Pott "for felony" upon superficial evidence was drastic and very erroneous. The King signed his pardon restoring all rights and privileges on July 25, 1631, most particularly for the reason that he was "the only physician in the Colony."

After his pardon by the King, Dr. Pott retired from public life and devoted his time to his profession. He had acquired a grant of three acres on Jamestown Island in 1624, which was increased to twelve acres in 1628, but the unhealthiness of the Island drove him inland. in 1632 he purchased a plantation and erected the first home in Middle Plantation, seven miles from James City, which he called "Harop." The fact that the "Surgeon of the Colony" had moved to Middle Plantation was a convincing argument in favor of its healthfulness. Surveys were quickly made and new homes erected so that there grew up around "Harop" a village which was later given the name of Williamsburg, where in 1693 the College of William and Mary was founded under royal patronage.

Williamsburg, first the habitation of Dr. Pott, became the capital of Virginia in 1698, and here her lawmakers assembled until the exigencies of the Revolution made it advisable to transfer the seat of government to Richmond, in 1779.

It is not known when Dr. Pott died, but his death probably occurred in Virginia, and certainly after March 25, 1651, at which time his son John, styled Jr., signed the test of fealty to the Commonwealth as a citizen of Northampton County.   C. C. M.

From the Interstate Med. Jour., St. Louis, June, 1910. (Caleb C. McGruder.)

Potter, Frank Hamilton (1860-1891).

Frank Hamilton Potter was the only son and eldest child of Dr. William Warren Potter, and born in Cowlesville, Wyoming County, New York, January 8, 1860. Descended from a long line of American physicians, he early directed his attention to medicine and graduated at the Buffalo Medical College in the class of 1882. Prior to his graduation, he served in the Rochester City Hospital for two years. After receiving his degree he settled in Buffalo, and, on the organization of the Medical Department of Niagara University in 1883, was appointed clinical assistant in surgery. He subsequently held the lectureship of descriptive anatomy, in 1884; demonstrator in surgery, and lecturer on botany in 1884–

85; lecturer on materia medica from 1885 to 1888, and lecturer on laryngology from 1888 to May, 1891. In recognition of his active efforts and conspicuous ability, the Niagara University conferred upon him, in 1885, the *ad eundum* degree of M. D. At the close of the session of 1891, he severed his connection with the school with which from its organization he had labored successfully, and accepted the position of clinical professor of laryngology in the Buffalo University Medical College.

At one time he was a member of the surgical staff of the Sisters' of Charity and Emergency Hospitals. He was a member of the Buffalo Medical and Surgical Association; and the Medical Society of the State of New York.

He was a frequent contributor to the medical and literary societies of which he was member, and had clearness of expression as well as beauty of style and diction. The following may be mentioned as some of the titles of his chief contributions:

"The Proper Use of Ergot in Obstetrical Practice." ("Boston Medical and Surgical Journal," vol. xxvi.)

"Tuberculosis of the Nose, Mouth, and Larynx." (Ibid., vol. xxvii.)

"Treatment of Acute Tonsillitis in Children." (Ibid., vol. xxvii.)

"Congenital Bony Occlusion of the Nares." Report of a case. (Ibid., vol. xxviii.)

"The Influence of Oral Irritation in the Production of Disease of the Upper Air-tract." (Ibid., vol. xxix.)

"On the Treatment of Hay-fever." (Ibid., vol. xxx.)

"Croupous Rhinitis." (Two papers.) ("Transactions of the Medical Society, State of New York," 1889 and 1891.)

"Cystoma of the Nasal Passages: with Report of a Case." Candidate's Thesis for Membership in American Laryngological Association. (Unpublished.)

Among the instruments he devised may be mentioned nasal scissors, mechanical nasal saw, self-retaining nasal speculum.

In 1887, after returning from Europe, whither he went for study and travel, he married Eva, daughter of Lars G. Sellstedt, the famous artist, and had two sons. The widow and these children survived him.

T. L.

Buffalo Med. and Surg. Jour., Aug., 1891. (Thomas Lothrop).
Memorial of Frank H. Potter (port.). (William W· Potter.)

Potter, Jared (1742–1810).

An army surgeon during the Revolution and a physician of eminence in his day, Jared Potter was born in East Haven, September 25, 1742; fifth in descent from John Potter, an original settler of New Haven, who signed the "Plantation Covenant."

In 1760 he graduated from Yale College, and immediately after began to study medicine. He devoted the next three years of his life to this, dividing the time equally between Dr. Harpin of Melford and the renowned Rev. Jared Eliot of Killingworth. Then he returned to East Haven and soon acquired an extensive practice. Yielding to some pressing invitations he removed, about 1770, to New Haven, where his "business and popularity as a physician rapidly increased." The ominous signs of an impending struggle between Great Britain and the colonies led him, apprehensive of danger, to remove, in 1772, to Wallingford, because further inland.

He was one of the founders and incorporators of the Connecticut Medical Society in 1792, serving as its first secretary and later, in 1804–05, as its vice-president. He was also a fellow from New Haven County for eleven years and acted as a member of important committees. He declined to become a candidate for the presidency. In 1798 the society conferred upon him the honorary degree of M. D.

During the first year of the Revolution he served as surgeon to the first of the six regiments raised by order of the General Assembly of Connecticut, and in this capacity took part in the expedition against Quebec. In subsequent years he used to describe those terrible times, and the torture he endured on account of his helplessness in the midst of so much misery. At the expiration of two years' service he became surgeon to Col. William Douglas' regiment, in July, 1776, and was present through the campaign around New York City. He was mustered out with the regiment, on December 29, 1776, and then returned home to resume practice. His health, however, was much impaired, during the next two years, by what he had undergone.

He was greatly interested in politics, and was a member of the Lower House of the General Assembly for eighteen sessions (1780–1809). On one occasion he was nominated for the upper house, but was defeated. In his political views he strongly allied himself with the Jeffersonian Democracy, while in his religious belief he was a Universalist. This attitude in politics and religion placed him at variance with the prevailing sentiments of his alma mater, and caused him to speak derogatory words against her.

In the zenith of his fame he was probably the most celebrated and popular physician in the state. And rightly, for he strove by buying the latest books on medicine to keep himself well abreast of the times. This helped, also, to make him a famous medical teacher. The celebrated Dr. Lemuel Hopkins of Hartford was his first student. His consultation practice was very extensive and carried him over most of the state. For "he was an excellent judge of symptoms and specially skilled in diagnosis." "In practice he was particularly fond of alkalies and alkaline earths. The famous 'Porter's powder,' as used by him, was composed of chalk, carbonate of ammonia, camphor and charcoal. He used it largely in dyspeptic and other gastric complaints."

He married Sarah Forbes, on April 19, 1764, and had two daughters. These daughters married two brothers, the younger girl was the mother of Jared P. Kirkland, a physician of Ohio.

His death, which occurred on July 30, 1810, was due to a peculiar accident. As he passed a field of rye on his farm he plucked a head of ripe grain and, on shelling it, threw the kernels into his mouth. Unfortunately, a beard lodged on the uvula, causing inflammatory gangrene and shortly after, death.

W. R. S.

Bronson, H., N. H. Colony Hist. Society's Papers, ii. Dexter, F. B., Yale Biographies and Annals, ii. Thacher, J., American Med. Biography, i.

Potter, Nathaniel (1770–1843).

Author and teacher, Nathaniel Potter, founder of the University of Maryland and for thirty-six years professor of medicine there, was born at Easton, Talbot County, Maryland, in 1770; his ancestors came from Rhode Island, and his father, Dr. Zabdiel Potter, served as surgeon in the Revolutionary Army. He was educated at a college in New Jersey and studied medicine under Dr. Benjamin Rush, of Philadelphia. He graduated M. D., at the University of Pennsylvania in 1796, his thesis being "On the Medicinal and Deleterious Effects of Arsenic." In 1797 he settled in practice in Baltimore and continued in active professional work until his last illness. On the organization of the College of Medicine of Maryland (later the University of Maryland), December 28, 1807, he became professor of principles and practice of medicine and continued in the occupancy of this chair until he died. The other positions which he held were: Dean of the College of Medicine, 1812, 1814; president, Baltimore Medical Society, 1812; president Medical Society of Maryland, 1817; one of the editors of "Maryland Medical and Surgical Journal," 1840–1843. Among his more important writings were: "An Account of the Rise and Progress of the University of Maryland,' 1838; "Memoir on Contagion," 1818; " On the Locusta Septentrionalis," 1839; American editions of Armstrong on "Typhus Fever," 1821, and (with S. Calhoun) "Gregory's Practice," two volumes, 1826 and 1829 (two editions). Prof. Potter was of medium height, full figure and ruddy complexion. There is an oil painting of him at the University of Maryland, pronounced a faithful likeness. He was an implicit believer in the resources of medicine; and relied especially upon calomel and the lancet, carrying the use of both far beyond what would be considered allowable at this day. He did not believe in the *vis medicatrix naturæ*, and is said to have told his pupils that if nature came in the door he would pitch her out of the window. Potter was a man of wonderful skill in diagnosis and of national fame. He showed his courage by making himself the subject of experiments with the secretions of yellow fever patients, thus establishing the non-contagiousness of that disease. In this he combated the view of Rush. His later years were embittered by pecuniary embarrassment and the expenses of his burial were borne by his professional friends. He died suddenly, during a fit of coughing, January 2, 1843, in his seventy-third year. His remains repose in Greenmount Cemetery, unmarked by stone or device. He married twice, but his family is now extinct.

E. F. C.

There are several portraits of Dr. Potter, two in oil, a third a profile by St. Mérwin. Quinan's Annals of Baltimore, 1884; Cordell's Historical Sketch, 1891; Cordell's Medical Annals of Maryland, 1903; and Cordell's History of the University of Maryland, 2 vols., 1907.

Powell, Seneca D. (1847–1907).

Born in Wilcox County, Alabama, he was of colonial descent, his ancestors coming from South Carolina. Powell was a cadet in the University of Alabama at the outbreak of the Civil War when he was in his fifteenth year and served in the southern army until the end of the war, when he began to study medicine and graduated from the University of Virginia in 1869. He then came to New York and graduated in medicine from the University of the City of New York in 1870, serving a year and a half on the house staff of Bellevue Hospital. In 1871–72 he was assistant inspector of the Board of Health, and also an assistant to the Professor of Medicine in Bellevue Hospital Medical College.

He soon became chief assistant to the late Professor James L. Little in the University Medical College, and held that position until the latter accepted the Chair of Surgery in the Post-graduate Medical School in 1882, when he followed his chief. In the latter named place, Dr. Powell was for some years instructor in surgical dressings, then professor of minor surgery and finally of clinical surgery, which position he held until his resignation in 1905. He was also president of the Medical Society of the County of New York in 1893, and of the Medical Society of the State in 1897–98.

Dr. Powell was one of the best teachers in surgery, especially of minor surgery. He had a fine personality, and was a very great favorite. A most important contribution to be noticed in his life is that we owe to him the discovery of the fact that pure alcohol instantly neutralizes the caustic effect of carbolic acid, thus making the acid available for the sterilization of infected areas without risk of systemic poisoning or serious local damage. Powell discovered this fact in the following manner: While at the Postgraduate hospital preparing for an operation, he held out his hands to receive the modicum of 5 per cent. solution of carbolic acid to sterilize them before doing the operation. His resident inadvertently poured his hands full of pure liquefied carbolic acid. Dr. Powell instantly dropped the acid on the floor and immersed his hands in a bath of alcohol, which stood nearby. The skin of the hands was not injured in the least, and in this way the discovery was made. Arguing from this, he introduced the carbolic acid treatment of leg ulcers, the lesion being painted with pure acid and then the acid neutralized when it has acted sufficiently, by the application of alcohol. The Powell treatment of leg and other ulcers has been extensively followed since then, and with gratifying results. He was also greatly interested in the surgery of the skull for the relief of cerebral disease, especially idiocy. Dr. Powell contributed many interesting cases to the medical journals, especially the "Post-Graduate." He resigned from this journal in 1905 of which he had been co-editor since 1887, on account of failing health. He married twice, first a daughter of Robert Irwin, and had one son, Irwin Powell, who died a few months before his father in the vigor of youthful manhood. In 1889 Dr. Powell married Isabelle V. Wilson, who, with twin daughters, Emily and Isabelle, survived him.

Dr. Powell was elected a director of the Post-graduate School in 1890, and served in that capacity until his resignation as a professor, when he gave up his directorship. The school owes much of its success to his skill and popularity in the days of his active work. He was a child of the school, having begun work with it in its infancy and having been actively connected with it for twenty-three years.

He died at his home in Greenwich, Connecticut, on August 24, 1907.

His article on "Carbolic Acid in Surgery" is in the "Transactions of the Southern Surgical and Gynecological Association," 1900, xiii.

Post-graduate, Oct., 1907 (port.)

Powell, Theophilus Orgain (1837-1907).

Theophilus Orgain Powell, a descendant of Englishmen who had come to Virginia in 1609, was born on March 21, 1837 in Brunswick County, Virginia, graduating from the Medical College of Georgia in 1859. He devoted his whole attention to the study of nervous and mental disease, especially when promoted to the superintendency of Georgia State Sanatorium, for being possessed of quick perception and fine tact he was able to

get at the root of many obscure forms of alienation. He also served as president of the Georgia Medical Association and of the Medico-psychological Association. His writings were chiefly for journals dealing with his own specialty. On January 12, 1860 he married Frances Augusta Birdsong of Hancock County, and had two children, Julia and Haller. At the time of his death he had been in ill health for some months and finally died from an attack of acute pneumonia at Tate Springs, Tennessee, on August 18, 1907.

J. G. B.

Atlanta Med. and Surg. Jour., 1885-6, n. s., vol. ii.

Power, William (1813-1852).

A native of Baltimore and born in 1813, his education was obtained at Yale College, which gave him his A. B. in 1832 and later that of A. M. He studied medicine under Dr. John Buckler of Baltimore in 1833, and matriculated at the University of Maryland, and in 1835 graduated M. D., then spent three years in Paris, studying under Louis, Chomel, Andral, Rostan, Grisolle, Barth and Roger. Paris was at that time the medical center of the world, and Power was one of that remarkable group of young Americans who gathered there. In 1841 –42 he delivered at the University Hospital two courses of lectures on physical exploration of the chest; these were the first lectures of the sort given at the university and were well attended. His health now gave way and in 1843 he abandoned work and went to Cuba. In the following year he resumed teaching and in 1845 was appointed lecturer on the theory and practice of medicine, and in 1846, on the resignation of Elisha Bartlett, he succeeded to him. He married in 1847. In January, 1852, in a letter full of pathos, he reluctantly resigned his chair, and on the fifteenth of August following, he died in Baltimore, the victim of consumption, in his thirty-ninth year.

He was the first to teach in his native

city, clearly and impressively, the glorious discoveries of Laennec, and to imbue the students with his own enthusiastic love of science. His strength was in his clinical teaching, and the University of Maryland has never lost the effect of his thoroughness and system. He was not a large contributor to medical literature.

E. F. C.

For list of his writings see, Quinan's Medical Annals of Baltimore, 1884; for sketch and portrait see Cordell's Historical Sketch, 1891, and Medical Annals of Maryland, 1903.

Pratt, Foster (1823–1898).

Foster Pratt was born at Mt. Morris, Livingston County, New York, January 9, 1823. His father, the Rev. Bartholomew Pratt, was of English descent; his mother, Susan (McNair) Pratt, of Scotch-Irish; their ancestors landed in Plymouth, Massachusetts, 1622. Foster Pratt had his early schooling at Franklin Academy, Prattsburg, Steuben County, New York, then, thrown on his own resources at the age of seventeen, he worked as a teacher for seven years. In 1847 he entered the University of Pennsylvania taking his M. D. there in 1849. He began practice at Romney, Hampshire County, Virginia, and soon secured a large clientèle, but removed to Kalamazoo, Michigan, September, 1856.

In 1858 he was sent to the State Legislature on an independent ticket where, in the face of strong opposition, he secured the appropriation of $100,000 for the completion of the Michigan Insane Asylum at Kalamazoo, the first large appropriation ever made. After this no sacrifice of time or convenience was too great for him if the asylum's interests were concerned. At the beginning of the war he assisted in raising the Thirteenth Regiment of Michigan Volunteer Infantry, of which he was appointed surgeon, and remained with it through the war, accompanied Sherman in his march to the sea, and was mustered out at Louisville, Kentucky, August, 1865, resuming practice at Kalamazoo. In 1871, being made president of Kala-

mazoo, and knowing the scanty quantity and poor quality of its water, he made a study of the local geology, finding an inexhaustible supply of the purest water, and also did much for proper drainage. In 1878 he was president of Michigan State Medical Society; and honorary member of the American Medico-psychological Association. In his presidential address of 1877 Dr. Pratt pointed out the defects in the educational agencies of the medical profession and insisted that the only remedy was a more perfect medical organization. Without hope of reward Foster Pratt gave much time to promoting in Michigan of a better preliminary education of medical students; a more thorough technical training; the management of professional affairs by professional men; and such organization as needed to enforce the conditions essential to the best professional evolution. Dr. Pratt was a striking looking man, tall, well proportioned, handsome, a born leader.

In October, 1849, he married Mary Lisle Gamble, of Moorefield, Hardy County, Virginia. He died suddenly at Kalamazoo, Michigan, August 12, 1898, from heart failure following occasional attacks of angina pectoris.

Papers:

"Legal Relations of Insane Patients." ("Transactions of Michigan State Medical Society," 1878.)

"Legal Responsibility of Surgeons for Ununited Fractures." ("Transactions of Michigan State Medical Society," 1882.)

L. C.

The Representative Men of Mich., Cincinnati, O., 1878, vol. iv.
Biographical Record, Kalamazoo, Alleghany and Berrien Co.

Prentiss, Daniel Webster (1843–1899).

Daniel W. Prentiss was born on May 21, 1843, in Washington, District of Columbia, the birthplace of his parents. His father, William Henry Prentiss, was a son of Caleb Prentiss of Cambridge, Massachusetts. The general education of Dr. Prentiss was obtained in the schools of Washington and Columbian University. He married Emilie A. Schmidt, daughter of Frederick Schmidt, of Rhenish, Bavaria, October 12, 1864, and two of his sons became doctors. He held the A. M. of Columbia College, District of Columbia, and the M. D. of Pennsylvania. After graduation Dr. Prentiss engaged in general practice in Washington and held a prominent position in the profession. From 1879 he was professor of materia medica and therapeutics in the medical department of Columbia University; physician in charge of the eye and ear service of Columbia Dispensary from 1874 to 1878; visiting physician to Providence Hospital in 1882; member of the Medical Society, Medical Association, Obstetrical and Gynecological Society. Some contributions to medical literature are as follows: "Croupous Pneumonia"—report of eleven cases occurring in private practice, from February to June, 1878, read before the Medical Society; "Remarkable Change in the Color of the Hair from Light Blond to Almost Black, in a Patient while under Treatment by Hypodermic Injections of Pilocarpine;" "Membranous Croup treated with Pilocarpine;" "Change of Color of Hair," 1881; "Avi Fauna Columbiana," being a list of the birds of the District of Columbia, revised and rewritten by Dr. Elliott Coues and Dr. D. W. Prentiss, 1883; "Gall Stones of Soap," 1889; "Report of Five Hundred Consecutive Cases of Labor in Private Practice," 1888; Case of the Change of Color of Hair of Old Age to Black, Produced by Jaborandi;" a "Paper on Pilocarpin, Its Physiological Actions and Therapeutic Uses."

In the "National Medical Review," 1899-1900, ix, page 542, it is stated that Dr. Prentiss became a member of the National Medical Society in 1864, and was active in its scientific work and a warm promoter of all measures that tended to advance the best interests of the profession. Much of his work was original and his writings all showed his early work in the natural science. The

cases reported by him were usually of rare forms of disease or of conditions before undescribed.

He died on November 10, 1899.

D. S. L.

Atkinson's Physicians and Surgeons, 1878.
Tr. of the Med. Soc., D. C., vol. iv, 1899.
National Med. Rev., vol. ix, 1899-90.

Prescott, Albert Benjamin (1832-1905).

Albert Benjamin Prescott was born at Hastings, New York, December 12, 1832; son of Benjamin and Experience (Huntley) Prescott whose ancestors emigrated from England to Massachusetts in 1640. This ancestor, James Prescott, was the fourth generation from James Prescott, who for bravery was made Lord of the Manor of Derby in 1564 by Queen Elizabeth. When nine years old Albert B. Prescott suffered a severe injury to his right knee which entailed long suffering and permanent disability. His general education was with private tutors and in 1864 he graduated M. D. at the Michigan University Medical Department. In May, 1864, he passed the regular examination for the United States Army and was commissioned assistant surgeon with duty at Totten General Hospital, at Louisville, Kentucky. On August 22, 1865, he was discharged from service with the brevet rank of captain of the United States Volunteers and immediately entered upon his life work at Ann Arbor, in the Laboratory of the University of Michigan with the rank of assistant professor of chemistry and lecturer on organic chemistry and metallurgy. On the organization of the school of pharmacy, in 1868, its management was placed in his hands. He was successively professor of organic and applied chemistry and pharmacy; of organic chemistry and pharmacy; professor of organic chemistry. From 1876, dean of the school of pharmacy; from 1884 director of the chemical laboratory; fellow of the London Chemical Society; in 1886 president of the American Chemical Society; in 1899 president of the American Pharmaceutical Association. In 1886 Michigan University gave him her **Ph. D.**; in 1896 the **LL. D.**; in 1902 Northwestern University also gave him the **LL. D.**

He contributed much to the literature of chemistry, in the form of reports of research work in analytical and organic chemistry; works of reference on these subjects; papers on the education of pharmacists and topics of general interest. His first book "Outlines of Proximate Organic Analysis," greatly promoted this subject. Later investigation concerned the natural organic bases and certain other derivatives.

In 1866 he married Abigail Freeburn who, with a foster son, survived him.

Dr. Prescott died at Ann Arbor, Michigan, February 25, 1905, from Bright's disease.

Papers:

"The Chemistry of Nitrogen as Disclosed in the Constitution of the Alkaloids." (Reprinted from "Transactions of the American Association for the Advancement of Science," Salem, 1887.)

"Pharmaceutical Chemistry in its Relation to Medical Practice." ("Michigan University Medical Journal," vol. i.)

"Should Proprietary Medicines be Required to Give an Account of Contents." ("The Physician and Surgeon," vol. viii.)

"Control of Chemical Operations in the Stomach." (Ibid., vol. i.)

"Contamination of Potable Waters by Lead and Zinc." ("Michigan University Medical Journal," vol. ii.)

"Chemistry of Muscle." ("Michigan Medical Journal," vol. i.)

"Chemical and Microscopical Analysis of the Bark of the Rhamnus Purshiana." ("New Preparations," vol. iii.)

"Outlines of Proximate Organic Analysis for the Identification, Separation and Quantitative Determination of the More Commonly Occurring Organic Compounds," 1875.

"Organic Analysis;" a greatly enlarged second edition of preceding, 1889.

"First Book in Quantitative Chemistry" (through eight editions).

"Qualitative Chemical Analysis;" with

S. H. Douglas, three editions; with O. C. Johnson, fourth to sixth edition," etc., etc.   L. C.

History Univ. of Mich., 1906.
Full-sized portrait in the reading room of the General Library, Ann Arbor.
Memorial by University Senate, Michigan State Medical, and various other scientific bodies.
Albert Benjamin Prescott, Address. Memorials on life of, with bibliography of 126 papers, 76 pages, by Mrs. Prescott, private printing, Ann Arbor, 1906.

Prescott, Oliver (1731–1804).

Oliver Prescott was born in Groton, Massachusetts, April 27, 1731, of the fourth generation from John Prescott, who came from England about the year 1640. His father was a member of the General Court; his mother, Abigail, daughter of Thomas Oliver, of Cambridge, Massachusetts.

Oliver was educated at Harvard College, where he received his degree in 1750. After graduation he was a pupil of Dr. Ebenezer Robie, of Sudbury, Massachusetts. He settled in Groton and soon gained a very extensive practice. It was said of him that he acquired a habit of sleeping while making his rounds on horseback. He was a corpulent man, over six feet in height. His son, Dr. Oliver Prescott, Jr., vouches for the truth of his father's sleeping habit and says he has frequently travelled with him and witnessed it, "the horse continuing the whole time at the usual travelling pace." "He would, when drowsiness came upon him, brace himself in the stirrup, rest one hand on the pommel of the saddle and resign himself without fear, for miles together, to quiet repose."

Dr. Prescott was one of the original members of the Massachusetts Medical Society and was president of the Middlesex Medical Society during the whole period of its existence.

In 1791 Harvard conferred upon him the honorary degree of M. D.

He took a prominent part in the Revolution, having been major, lieutenant-colonel and colonel of militia under the

King, and in 1775 was made brigadier general of militia by the Supreme Executive Council of the Massachusetts Bay. In 1779 on the death of John Winthrop, he was appointed his successor in the office of judge of probate for the county of Middlesex, and gave great satisfaction by the tactful discharge of his duties.

He was the first president of the trustees of the Groton Academy, and a fellow of the American Academy of Arts and Sciences.

In 1756 he married Lydia, daughter of David Baldwin, of Sudbury, by whom he had ten children, four of them surviving him.

W. L. B.

The Physicians of Groton, S. A. Green, Groton, 1890.
Amer. Med. Biog., 1828, James Thacher.

Preston, Ann (1813–1872).

Ann Preston was the daughter of Amos and Margaret Preston, and born at West Grove, Chester County, Pennsylvania. Her reputation as a physician was gained in Philadelphia where she spent the most of her time after leaving her country home.

Being closely confined by grave responsibilities, her early education was not a liberal one.

She took an active interest in the anti-slavery cause and early became known as a forcible writer on the subject. An incident is told of her which illustrates the fearless courage which characterized her actions and the work she did to help those who were fleeing from bondage.

One Sunday morning while her parents were attending a Friend's meeting a fugitive slave woman was forwarded to their house, Miss Preston concealed her in a closet in the garret and made her comfortable, anxiously waiting the time of her removal to the next station. The man at whose house the woman was last concealed came running with the information that his house was being searched by the slave-catchers and they would be there next.

Miss Preston was alone but with great coolness she locked the woman into the closet then went to the pasture and caught a horse, harnessed him to a carriage and after dressing the woman in her mother's Quaker clothes, carefully adding the two veils often worn by Friends when riding, they started in the direction from which the slave-catchers were expected. They soon appeared, riding rapidly toward them but seeing only a young girl and an apparently elderly woman leisurely going to meeting, they rode rapidly on. Miss Preston took the woman to the house which had been recently searched and she eventually reached Canada in safety.

When the Woman's Medical College of Pennsylvania opened in 1850, Miss Preston was one of the first applicants for admission and graduated at the first commencement in 1851–2. The winter after she attended lectures at the college and in the spring accepted the chair of physiology and hygiene then vacant.

At that time it was impossible for a woman to gain admission to any hospital in Philadelphia. So highly did the managers of the Woman's Hospital value Dr. Preston's work at that time that in a report is found the following statement: "To her efforts more than to all other influences may be traced its very origin." She said in speaking of it, "I went to every one whom I thought would give me either money or influence," and when the hospital was opened she was put on the Board and became consulting physician, holding these offices until the time of her death.

In 1866 Dr. Preston was elected dean of the faculty, which position she held for six years. In 1867 she wrote her ever-memorable reply to the preamble and resolutions adopted by the Philadelphia County Medical Society, to the effect that they would neither offer encouragement to women becoming practitioners of medicine nor meet them in consultation. This was one of her ablest literary productions and so completely did she answer the arguments put forth by the society that no reply was attempted.

For years Dr. Preston had looked forward with pleasure to making a home for herself and in 1864 she gathered around her a pleasant family.

In 1871 she had acute articular rheumatism from which she did not completely recover, so when the college opened in the fall she resumed her usual duties with less than accustomed vigor. Another attack made it impossible for her to leave her room and at this time she prepared the Annual Announcement for the college session of 1872–73. It was the last work of her life, performed slowly and painfully, and this exertion brought on the relapse which terminated in complete nervous prostration from which she died April 18, 1872.

Both the college and hospital were remembered in her will, the interest of four thousand dollars being used annually to assist in the education of one good student.

                                    F. P.

Address in Mem. of Ann Preston, Penn ,
1873   (E. E. Judson)

Preston, George Junkin (1858–1908)

George Junkin Preston, neurologist, was born in Lexington, Virginia, 1858. the son of Col. J. T. L. Preston. He graduated A. B. in 1879 at Washington and Lee University and took his M. D. at the University of Pennsylvania, in 1883.

In 1894, as a member of the Medical and Chirurgical Faculty of Maryland, he was the first to suggest the feasibility of establishing a State Bacteriological Department. As chairman of the Faculty Library, he did his utmost to increase its richness and utility.

He made the study of the nervous system his life work, and in 1885 went abroad and studied under Charcot, and, later, worked on the subject at Leipzig. In 1889 he was professor of physiology in the Woman's Medical College, Baltimore and in 1890 entered the Faculty of the College of Physicians and Surgeons of Baltimore as professor of physiology and diseases of the nervous system. He also held the post of neurologist to the city, Bayview, the Hebrew and St. Agnes' Hospitals. In all this work he labored unceasingly to better the condition of the insane and attained high rank as a neurologist for his knowledge and work were of an intensely practical nature.

He died in Baltimore on June 17, 1908.

His writings included:

"The Differential Diagnosis and Treatment of Multiple Neuritis," 1891.

"The Effect of Arterio-sclerosis Upon the Central Nervous System," 1891.

"Traumatic Lesions of the Spinal Cord," 1893.

"Cerebral Œdema," 1894.

And a large volume "Hysteria and Certain Allied Conditions," 1897.

Bull. of the Med. and Chir. Fac. of Maryland
1908–190 , i
Maryland Med. J., 1908.

Preston, Robert J. (1841–1906).

Robert Preston, alienist, was the son of John F. Preston, of Washington County, Virginia, and born in that county in 1841; he was a member of a prominent Virginian family.

He went as a lad to Emory and Henry College, Virginia, taking the A. M., and studying medicine at and graduating from the University of Virginia in 1867.

He was a member of the Tri-State Medical Association of the Carolinas and Virginia; honorary fellowship was conferred upon him by the Boston Gynecological Association, the Lynchburg (Virginia) Academy of Medicine, and the Medical Society of Virginia (1895).

During the Civil War he served his state first as a private and, later, by promotion as a captain in the Twenty-first Virginia Cavalry, and made for himself a record for gallantry. He joined the Medical Society of Virginia in 1871, proved a zealous member, and had the honor of election to the presidency in 1894; had the same honor conferred upon him by the Abingdon Academy of Medicine and the American Medico-psychological Association in 1901–02 of which he was president in 1892. In 1887 he was elected first assistant physician to the Southwestern State Hospital (for the Insane), and in November, 1888, superintendent of the same. which position he filled until his death.

Dr. Preston was a man of high order of intelligence and an excellent physician. As superintendent of the hospital he made a faithful and popular official; a good disciplinarian, using reason and persuasion rather than harshness and force; he was eminently successful in the management of his unfortunate charges.

Dr. Preston married twice; his first wife, whom he married in 1875, was Martha E. Sheffey, and had two children, Ellen F. and Robert J., both of whom graduated in medicine. In 1902 he married Mrs. Elizabeth Gravely (née Stuart), who with a son survived him.

In 1906, while en route for Toronto, Canada, to attend a meeting of the British Medical Association, he was taken ill at Lewiston, New York, and died suddenly at that place on the twentieth of August.

His contributions to medical literature were numerous; some of his more important articles were:

"Rupture of the Uterus, New Symptoms." ("Virginia Medical Monthly," vol. i, 1874.)

"Report on Advances in Diseases of Women and Children." ("Transactions of the Medical Society of Virginia," 1877.)

"Puerperal Fever." ("Virginia Medical Monthly," vol. ii, 1874.)

"Associated Dining-rooms, Their Moral and Curative Effect." (Ibid., vol. xvi.)

"Sexual Vices—Their Relation to Insanity—Causative or Consequent." (Ibid., vol. xv.)

"Mental, Moral and Hygienic Therapeutics in Relation to Home Life and in General Practice," president's address to Virginia Medical Society, "Transactions," 1895.

"Review of the Progress, Care, Maintenance of the Insane in Virginia during the Years 1887–1897, Inclusive."

("Transactions of the Medical Society of Virginia," 1898.)

"Rupture of the Carotid Artery—Successfully Ligated." ("Virginia Medical Semi-monthly," vol., viii.)

R. M. S.

Va. Med. Semi-monthly, vol. xi.
Men of Mark in Virginia, vol. v, with a full page portrait.

Prewitt, Theodore F. (1832–1904).

Theodore F. Prewitt, born in Fayette, Howard County, Missouri, on March 1, 1832, the son of Joel and Mary Trimble Prewitt. Owing to the death of his father, and being one of a family of eleven, he was thrown upon his own resources at the early age of fourteen. He entered the St. Louis Medical College, whence he graduated in 1856, and married Mary Ingram, of Virginia, during the last year of his medical course. After the death of his wife in 1862, he went to St. Louis and again married in 1871, this time to Mary Sowers; and the same year was appointed superintendent of the City Hospital, which position he held for three years. He spent some time at a number of the leading European hospitals.

On his return to St. Louis he accepted the chair of surgery in the Missouri Medical College, and later was elected dean.

On the consolidation of the Missouri Medical College and the St. Louis Medical College to form the Medical Department of Washington University, he was continued in the chair of surgery and held this position until his death.

For twenty-five years he was surgeon to the St. John's Hospital and the surgical clinic at that institution.

United to a desire for knowledge was an endowment of untiring energy, which enabled him to prosecute with vigor whatever matter claimed his attention. While occupied with the cares of a large practice, he at all times had at heart the cause of medical education.

Prewitt was president of the American Surgical Association, of the Missouri State Medical Society, the St. Louis Medical Society, the St. Louis Surgical

Society, and the St. Louis Obstetrical Society, and a fellow of the Philadelphia Academy of Surgery.

Am. Med., Phila., 1904, vol. viii.
Med. Bull., Wash. Univ., St. Louis, 1904, vol. iii.
St. Louis Cour. Med., 1904, vol. xxxi (port.).

Price, Mordecai (1844–1904).

The son of Joshua and Feby Moore Price; Mordecai graduated from the University of Pennsylvania in 1869 and became one of the most eminent abdominal surgeons and gynecologists of Philadelphia and an operator of repute. He was born in Rockingham County, Virginia, in 1844, and came to Philadelphia when a boy and was associated in his work with his brother, Dr. Joseph Price.

He died suddenly at his home in Philadelphia from apoplexy, October 29, aged sixty.

Amer. Med., Phila., 1904, vol. viii.
Buffalo Med. Jour., 1904, n. s., vol. xliv.
J. Am. M. Ass., Chicago, 1904, xliii.
N. York Med. Jour., 1904, vol. lxxx.

Pryor, William Rice (1858–1904).

William Rice Pryor, gynecologist, was born in Richmond, Virginia. His father, the Hon. Roger A. Pryor, was minister to Greece in 1855, and a justice of the Supreme Bench in New York.

Pryor was educated in Virginia, then entered Princeton University and in 1881 took his M. D. from the College of Physicians and Surgeons of New York, being appointed assistant gynecologist in the New York Polyclinic in 1866 and afterwards, in 1895, professor of gynecology, retaining that position till his death, and was also on the staff of the Charity and St. Elizabeth's Hospital. He became a fellow of the American Gynecological Society in 1892.

His principal work consisted in improving the technic of abdominal hysterectomy, advocating more rational methods of treatment in puerperal infection, especially by the vaginal route whenever practicable and devising simple methods of exploring the bladder and ureters. In 1903 appeared his "Textbook of Gynecology," written in his characteristic style, and which gives an excellent resumé of his teaching.

His health began to fail in the spring of 1904 and he died August 25, 1904 iii St. Vincent's Hospital.

My friendship with him grew warmer every year. He was a man of fine presence and cordial manners, boundless enthusiasm. I continue to carry with me the recollection of his work, but above all the example he set us of absolute fearlessness and sturdy manliness.

His writings included:

"Septic Endometritis with Peritonitis and their Treatment," 1892.

"Mr. Lawson Tait and the Germ Theory of Disease," 1894.

"A New Method of Treating Adherent Retroposed Uteri," 1895.

"The Anatomy of the Endometrium and the Technic of Its Removal by Curretage," 1896.

"A Method of Examining the Pelvic Contents which Renders Exploratory Laparotomy Unnecessary," etc., 1896.

"Text-book of Gynecology," 1903, and a complete list, some fifty-eight, is given by his biographer Dr. J. Whitridge Williams in vol. xxx, 1905, of the American Gynecological Society's Transactions.

J. W. W.

Buffalo Med. Jour., 1904–5, n. s., vol. xliv.
Tr. Am. Gyn. Soc., Phila., 1905, vol. xxx (port.).
Tr. South. Sur. and Gyne. Ass., 1904, Birmingham, 1905, vol. xvii.

Purple, Samuel Smith (1822–1900).

There is an old proverb that "A shoemaker should not look beyond his last," but fortunately for medical libraries there was one lad who worked with a book on the bench as he made shoes and who got up at four in the morning to study and looked far beyond his last to being, some day, a doctor.

This boy was Samuel Smith Purple, of English stock who came over in 1674. He was born to Lyman Smith and Minerva Sheffield Purple on June 24, 1822, at Lebanon, Madison County.

The father was a tanner and shoemaker and young Samuel only went to a rural school, and when his father died in 1839 he had to take over the business, pay the many debts and support the family. But he had two relatives who encouraged him to study: his grandfather, Dr. Sheffield and Dr. W. D. Purple, and when twenty-three had so far succeeded in business that he took a course of medical lectures at Geneva Medical College, secured free for him. There were some big teachers there and Purple returned home eager to earn money for more teaching. The gift of a free course at the University of New York from his uncle and the advantage of being under Valentine Mott enabled him to graduate M. D. in 1844 and return home happy.

Whether to be a country practitioner or a city one? He had a poor wardrobe and twenty-five dollars in cash. To the city he went, working on a canal boat part of the way to save fare, and entering the service of the old Marion Street Maternity, New York, until he had an appointment in the New York Dispensary. Patients came slowly, but they did come eventually, also an editorship—of the "New York Journal of Medicine," which he held capably for ten years, and his own papers in it established his reputation as a man who knew what he was writing about. 1875 saw him president of the New York Academy of Medicine and re-elected in 1877. He had worked hard for its interests and used all his influence and most of his money to secure for it a library and a home, and deserved the honor. One man lent a willing ear, this was Dr. John B. Beck, who, himself possessing a valuable library, urged Purple to avail himself of his editorship to collect old medical books, pamphlets, and files of medical journals. Much dealing with old bookstores led him to begin on American historical literature and helped Dr. Henry Stiles in editing "The New York Genealogical and Biographical Record." One of his "finds" he rescued from going to a paper mill. It was Dr. Samuel Bard's "In-

quiry into the Nature and Cure of Angina Suffocativa or Sore Throat Distemper," 1771, a very accurate account of what is now known as diphtheria. To the Academy library he gave that great treasure the serial medical literature of this country, for more than one-fourth of a century ransacking every bookstore and corresponding with every likely person, 5,000 medical journals being his ultimate gift and $75,000 donation won by his influence from Dr. Alexander Hosack.

There was so much he meant to do besides: to write up biographies for his splendid collection of medical portraits and increase the number of valuable works in the Academy library, but in 1899 he had hemorrhage into the posterior chamber of the eye which permanently destroyed its sight, and he knew he had advanced Bright's disease. He had never married, but his roof-tree sheltered his old mother, brother and brother's widow and children. He met death in the same calm dignified way with which he had coped with early poverty, and the shoemaker's son is commemorated on a tablet in the library of the New York Academy of Medicine as its founder and president.

Among the few published papers are found: "Corpeus Luteum; Its Value as Evidence of Conception and Its Relation to Legal Medicine;" "Observations on Wounds of the Heart and Their Relations to Forensic Medicine;" forty-two cases.

He was, among other offices, an honorary member of the Medical Society of the State of New York; corresponding member of the Epidemiological Society, London; physician to the New York and Lying-in Asylum; examining surgeon, New York State Department.

There is an oil painting of Dr. Purple in the library of the Academy of Medicine, New York.   D. W.

Med. Lib. and Hist. Jour., April, 1903. (S. Smith.)

Putnam, Israel (1805–1876).

Israel Putnam was born in Sutton, Massachusetts, December 25, 1805, and a good Christmas present he proved to his parents, for he became a noted physician and citizen, and left one son, Judge William LeBaron Putnam, of Portland, Maine, a jurist noteworthy upon the American bench.

Dr. Putnam's father was Israel Putnam, a cousin of Gen. Putnam of the Revolution; his mother Hannah LeBaron, a descendant of Dr. Francis LeBaron, a great man in colonial days.

Israel Putnam, Jr., graduated from Brown University, Rhode Island, in 1827, studied with Prof. James McKenna of Topsham, Maine, and attended lectures at the Medical School of Maine, graduating in 1830. Instead of remaining in the same town with his preceptor, and trying to compete with him and divide the practice, as is the way in this century, young Putnam moved to Wells, Maine, and began practice there. After staying there four years, he married Miss Sarah Emory Frost, of Topsham, moved to Bath and stayed there for the rest of his life. He soon obtained positions of prominence, as a surgeon to the Marine Hospital, and City Physician; he was a member of Maine Medical Society, and the Maine Medical Association, and did excellent work in each.

In his later years he was often of great help to younger physicians, and once said to a young graduate, "Come and take that house next to me, and when they call me out in the night I will say, 'You had better go to doctor-so-and-so, across the street, he is a first-rate fellow, and wider awake at night than I am in the day time.'"

He, like every other doctor, had a favorite drug, hyoscyamus, a good supply of which he carried around with him in his pockets in the shape of a large black lump. When some patient would meet him in the street and say one of his women folks was "sort of nervous like," he was sure to fish out the hyoscyamus, pinch out enough to make a few pills, roll them around in his hand and fingers as men do tobacco, and hand them to the old patient, who would go off rejoicing.

When a physician can resign a ten years' mayoralty (Bath), then resume his practice, and get all he wants for patients, it proves that he has made a few friends. Looking at the portrait of this well known physician, you see a large face, bright eyes, long lips smiling at you from the corners, and you cannot help feeling that you knew him in real life.

After a prolonged illness of several months, Dr. Putnam died June 30, 1876, highly thought of and greatly missed.

J. A. S.

Trans. Maine Med. Assoc.

Putnam-Jacobi, Mary (1842–1906).

Mary Putnam, born in London, England, August 31, 1842, was the eldest of the ten children of George Palmer Putnam, publisher. She was descended on both sides from New England colonial stock and seven of her ancestors fought at Bunker Hill.

She was educated by her mother and by tutors, but not the least part of her education was gained from her literary environment. Her precocious intellect early set a high goal for her efforts and the study of medicine appealed most strongly, but together with it she wielded then, and always, a most facile pen. Many of Mary Putnam's writings exist from her ninth year on; at seventeen she wrote a story, "Found and Lost," which was later accepted and published by the "Atlantic Monthly." This success almost turned her from her early decision to study medicine. She began to teach at the age of nineteen to earn money for a medical education, and at the same time studied anatomy under private instruction. Gaining admission as its first woman student to the New York College of Pharmacy, she graduated in 1862. The following two years she spent at the Woman's Medical College of Philadelphia, graduating in 1864. After one year spent as interne in the New England Hospital for Women and Children, she taught and wrote in New Orleans to continue medical study in Paris, where she went in 1866. During the first eighteen months she studied in the hospitals, but could not gain admission to l'École de Médecine because of lack of precedent. Her application through a friend to a certain professor for permission to enter his dissecting room was granted on the condition that she attend in male attire, whereupon meeting the professor and looking up at his towering six feet from her short five, she exclaimed "Why, Monsieur, look at my littleness, men's clothes would only exaggerate it. I should never be taken for a man and the objection to mixing with the students would be increased a hundred fold." Struck by her earnestness the good professor agreed, and her enrollment in l'École de Médecine soon followed. "How generously and delicately this brave girl adventurer was treated by the students and the faculty of those days, let this never be forgotten, to the honor of all the Frenchmen who then studied and taught in this great school!" Upon her graduation in 1871 Dr. Putnam received the highest mark for each of her five examinations, and her thesis took the bronze medal, the second prize awarded. She was the first woman ever to take the full course and the second to receive a degree in this institution; Dr. Elizabeth Garrett Anderson being the first.

Dr. Putnam's achievement in opening l'École de Médecine of Paris to women gave her an international reputation and led to many attractive positions being offered her, but she joined the little group of women who were struggling to establish the Woman's Medical College of the New York Infirmary, where she immediately became professor of materia medica and therapeutics. When Mary Putnam returned from Europe with a Paris medical degree and a training in scientific medicine, she was admitted in 1873, without discussion, to the Medical Society of New York County at the suggestion of Dr. Abraham Jacobi, its distinguished president, whom she married a few months later. She also became a member of the pathological, neurological and therapeutic societies, and of the New York Academy of Medicine. In conjunction with Dr. Anna Angell, she founded a dispensary at the Mt. Sina Hospital in 1873; in 1874 the Association for the Advancement of the Medical Education of Women, and in 1876 won the Boylston prize (Harvard University), with an essay on "The Question of Rest for Women During Menstruation." From 1880 she was visiting physician to the New York Infirmary for Women and Children and visiting physician to St. Mark's Hospital from 1893. In 1882 a school for post-graduate instruction was opened in New York City and Dr. Putnam Jacobi was invited to a place on its faculty as the clinical lecturer in children's diseases, the first time such a lectureship in this country had been given a woman.

In 1893 in just recognition of her contributions to neurology she was made chairman of the neurological section of the Academy of Medicine. Dr. James R. Chadwick, of Boston, used to cite as an instance of her wonderful ability to quickly marshal facts from her fund of knowledge, the occasion of her after dinner speech at the Annual Meeting of the Massachusetts Medical Society in 1889. He had invited her, the first woman thus honored, to be the guest of the Society; on their way to the hall he inquired her topic for an after dinner speech and was dismayed to hear she did not understand she was to make one, but more dismayed to have her add, "Oh, well, I will speak on 'Women in Medicine,'" for that hotly discussed, long-mooted subject must not be dragged in. "All right," she said and when her turn came made as he said "a simply stunning and brilliant address on 'Practical Study in Biology,'" calling forth ringing, enthusiastic applause from the men.

Logical, keen and alert in argument, swift to seize upon the kernel of thought and discard the mesh of verbosity, broadminded, retentive of facts, almost to the encyclopedic point, original in her conceptions and strong to follow where reason led; all these were qualities of Mary Putnam-Jacobi's mind, and above and imbuing all was what Dr. Osler called her heliotropic potency, the truly solar gift of calling out the best that was in those about her.

She was always interested in the political conditions of women, and in 1894 took up the gage in behalf of the ballot for women. She was also an early and ardent advocate of the necessity of having a woman physician in every insane asylum.

Dr. Putnam-Jacobi had a dread of becoming a literary physician, feeling that a man who distinguishes himself most highly outside of his profession is rarely a distinguished member of his craft. As a medical writer she made for herself a high and permanent place. She was an active and industrious contributor to medical journals and to the archives of societies; her papers, numbering nearly a hundred, possessing, in addition to original scientific importance, a literary style rare in medical articles. From among her papers may be cited:

"Antagonism of Medicines." ("Archives of Medicine," 1881.)

"Infantile Paralysis," ("Pepper's Archives of Medicine," 1885.)

"Primary Education." ("Popular Science Monthly," 1886.)

"Some Considerations on Hysteria," 1888.

"Acute Mania after Operations," 1889.

"Spinal Myelitis, Meningitis in Children." ("Keating's Cyclopedia," 1890.)

"Brain Tumors." ("Wood's Reference Hand-book of the Medical Sciences.")

Dr. Jacobi died in 1906 of a meningeal tumor pressing on the cerebellum. In the seventh year of her ten years' illness she sent her friend, Dr. Charles L. Dana, a story of her symptoms which he pronounced "so lucid, so objective and yet so human that it would be a classic in medical writing." In January, 1907, the Woman's Medical Association of New York City held a memorial meeting to Mary Putnam-Jacobi at the Academy of Medicine. In all the addresses from men and women eminent in medicine, reform and literature there was one dominant note, "her dedication to the work of helping her fellow mortals." A memorial tablet to her memory has been placed in the main hall of the Woman's Medical College of Pennsylvania. A movement by the Woman's Medical Association of New York City is on foot to establish a fellowship in her honor to be known as "The Mary Putnam Jacobi Fellowship."

A. B. W.

Addresses by Drs. Blackwell, Cushier, Osler, Dana, by Mrs. Florence Kelley and by Richard Watson Gilder, In Memory Mary Putman Jacobi, N. Y. Academy of Medicine, Jan. 4, 1907.
Addresses by Drs. Welch, Galbraith and Mills, in Trans. Alumnæ Assoc., Woman's Med. Col. of Penn., 1907.
N. Y. Medical Journal, June 16, 1906.
Personal knowledge and informations, H. B. B., The Woman's Journal, Boston, June 16, 1906.

Putnam, Sumner (1818–1887).

Sumner Putnam was born February 21, 1818, in East Montpelier, Vermont, the son of Sylvanus and Lucinda (Bancroft) Putnam, a descendant in the sixth generation of John Putnam, who came from England in 1634 and settled in Danvers, Massachusetts.

As a boy he went to the common schools and Montpelier Academy, afterwards studying medicine with Dr. Jared Bassett, of Plainfield, Vermont, and taking his medical degree from the Vermont Medical College at Woodstock in 1842.

Soon after graduation he located at Greensboro, Vermont, and in 1865 removed to Montpelier and practised there until his last sickness.

He was an active member of the Vermont State Medical Society, and its president in 1871. Dr. Putnam was a man of high professional ideals. He was wrapped up in his profession, and to the last kept in touch with the latest happenings in the medical world. He contributed many papers to the Vermont State

Medical Society and medical journals, some of the most valuable being on nervous and mental diseases.

He married in December, 1847, Diana F., a daughter of Dr. Nathaniel and Fanny (Davis) King, of East Montpelier, and had four children, only one of whom, Alice M., lived to adult age.

Dr. Putnam died at Montpelier, August 20, 1887, from chronic cerebral meningitis.   C. S. C.

Tr. Vermont M. Soc., 1888-9.

Q

Quinan, John Russell (1822–1890).

John Russell Quinan, medical historian, was of Irish lineage, one of the six children of the Rev. Thomas Henry Quinan, a native of Balbriggan, Leinster County, Ireland, and Eliza Hamilton (Quinan), native of Enniskillen, Ulster County, Ireland. He was born at Lancaster, Pennsylvania, August 7, 1822, and educated at Woodward High School, Cincinnati, and at Marietta College, Ohio. Studying medicine with Dr. John K. Mitchell, of Philadelphia, he afterwards graduated M. D. at the Jefferson Medical College in 1844, and began practice in Calvert County, Maryland. Here he labored assiduously, as the leading physician of the county, for twenty-five years, achieving much honor, but little profit. He removed to Baltimore City in 1869 where he achieved distinction as the medical historian, *par excellence*, of Maryland.

Dr. Quinan was president of the Medical and Chirurgical Faculty of Maryland in 1885–86. A list of his writings is given in the "Transactions of the Faculty," for 1891. The most important was a work of two hundred and seventy-four pages, issued by the Faculty in 1884 and entitled, "The Medical Annals of Baltimore from 1608 to 1880, Including Events, Men and Literature; to which is Added a Subject Index and Record of Public Services." This work originated in a celebration of the sesquicentennial anniversary of the founding of the City of Baltimore by the Medical and Chirurgical Faculty in 1880. To Dr. Quinan was assigned the part of writing the records of the "Physicians of the City," and, in doing this, he found it impossible to discharge the duty satisfactorily in the brief period assigned him

and asked further time for its execution. The work once undertaken grew under his hands and when it was published four years after its inception, it had grown into a volume. Dr. Quinan received no compensation whatever for these great labors, but in his enthusiasm would have proceeded to issue a second and enlarged edition to constitute the "Medical Annals of Maryland," had not his mind been diverted into other channels by his appointment as one of the editors of Foster's "Medical Dictionary," on which he labored during the last year or two of his life, possessing peculiar qualifications for it in his knowledge of ancient and modern languages. Among other more interesting works of Dr. Quinan are his articles on "Inoculation and Vaccination in Maryland," and "A Key to Questions on Orthography," 1865. He died suddenly November 11, 1890, after attending a case of infantile convulsions, death being probably due to disease of the heart or great arteries.

Dr. Quinan married August 31, 1845, Elizabeth Lydia Billingsley, of Calvert County, Maryland, who survived him with five children.

His greatest pleasure seemed to be in making some historical research in the libraries surrounded by his loved books. In brief, he was a man of the most scholarly tastes, a model physician, a most Christian gentleman.

The only teaching position he ever filled was that of lecturer on medical jurisprudence in the Woman's Medical College, 1883–85.

E. F. C.

For portrait and biographical data see Quinan's Medical Annals of Baltimore, 1884, and Cordell's Medical Annals of Maryland, 1903.

R

Ralph, John (1793–1870).

John Ralph remains the outstanding figure in medical education in Ontario. During the War of 1812 he came over from England, but his ship was captured by an American cruiser and after peace was declared he returned to England and studied law and medicine conjointly at Cambridge; after graduating in Arts he was eventually called to the Bar in 1821. He studied medicine under Sir Astley Cooper and other great leaders and after becoming a member of the Royal College of Surgeons he returned to Canada, settling first as a doctor and lawyer in Norfolk and later in Dundas, frequently bringing into court a pair of saddlebags, one filled with instruments and medicine, the other with briefs. In 1828, incensed with what he considered an unjust decision by Justice Sherwood, he threw off his gown and with it his legal practice, settling wholly to medical work in Victoria, eighty-nine miles from Toronto. A little incident which occurred there gives a glimpse of Ralph's character. Two men had been condemned to death for stealing an ox. The gallows were ready, but Ralph determined to ride into Toronto and intercede with Sir John Calborne, the lieutenant-governor. The swiftest horse in the village was borrowed and after a few words with the officiating minister, John Ryerson, the doctor sped away.

The time of death drew near, the doomed men mounted the scaffold; Ryerson, an old circuit rider was asked to pray. Kneeling, he began softly, to husband his resources; half an hour, an hour, passed and the sun-baked crowd grew restless, the condemned were clearly annoyed.

Murmurings arose, yet still the prayer came in husky voice from parched lips; no one heeded the words; his real prayer was "Hasten Dr. Ralph's coming." At the end of an hour and a half uproar began, when a shout was heard "Here comes Dr. Ralph." Too exhausted to speak Ralph rode to the foot of the scaffold and held up the reprieve.

In 1831 he removed to York, afterwards incorporated as the City of Toronto and went on its Medical Board and in 1834 married Grace Haines, of Kingston. His connection with the Rebellion of 1837 made his hurried flight from Canada a necessity. But in 1843 he was able to return from Rochester and the reward of £500 for his capture was withdrawn.

So he settled down again and opened a medical school for which in 1851 he obtained an act of incorporation. His class and dissecting room outgrew the shed it began in; a church building was taken and the school became the medical department of Victoria College University with Ralph as dean.

When the session of 1856–7 opened, his colleagues, owing to differences which had arisen, resigned in a body and for two weeks Raph was professor-of-all-work supported by the College Board. Later on the chairs were all filled but the seceders obtained a right to retain the title of Toronto School of Medicine and as such continued their work, this college indirectly also owing its origin to Dr. Ralph, and both joining with the Trinity Medical College formed eventually the medical department of the University of Toronto.

Ralph was not a frequent contributor to medical literature, but his fame as a brilliant lecturer and teacher remains undimmed even to this generation. Dignified, handsome, courtly in manner, a profound thinker, with a subtle intellect, equally fitted to cope with the intricacies of legal, political or medical problems, Ralph left a big blank when he died an old man of seventy-seven at Mitchell,

Ontario, on October 19, 1870. The University of Victoria had given him her degrees of M. D. and LL. D.

N. A. P.

Hist. of the Upper Canada Rebellion, J. C. Dent.

Ramsay, Alexander (1754–1824).

In glancing through the medical literature of the early years of the nineteenth century, no name perhaps is more often mentioned than that of Dr. Alexander Ramsay. According to some, he was a compound of personal deformity, immense learning, uncontrollable temper, and inordinate vanity. According to others, he was a wonderful dissector, an unapproachable lecturer on anatomy, and a man who once known could never be recalled without unfailing reverence and deep affection.

It is generally believed that Ramsay was born in 1754, for on his death-bed in 1824 he said that he was just seventy years old. He came of a good family, and one of considerable means, as proved by old title deeds to real estate. He received an excellent academic education, presumably at Aberdeen University, and then studied medicine in London, Dublin, and Edinburgh with the celebrated teachers of that era. Finding it impossible, in Edinburgh, to continue his anatomical studies beyond a certain point, he established an anatomical school and museum of his own, and in that way finally compelled the medical faculty to add an anatomical school to the University. Unfortunately, even at this early age, his temper was bad, and he was constantly embroiled with men of the best standing in the profession, so that his influence was far from what his learning deserved. Besides lecturing, he learned how to draw and to engrave his own plates, and in this way originated his system of anatomy, worthily begun, but never completed.

Although a fine teacher and lecturer, Ramsay was born a wanderer beneath the bands of the Orion, as said before, and could not rest quiet anywhere. Whether the election of one of the Monroes, instead of himself, to the chair of anatomy made him angrier than ever, we do not know, but at this time he began to talk of founding in the wilderness of America an institution which should stand at the head of the world in anatomy. In this way, he talked at the age of thirty-six, but it was not until an epidemic of yellow fever appeared in New York about 1802, that he decided to cross the ocean.

Arriving in Boston, he lectured there, then made his way to New York, and finally betook himself to the small settlement of Fryeburg in Maine, but how he could ever expect in that solitary region to build any institution that could influence American medicine, passes comprehension. While here, at intervals for many years, he lectured on anatomy, had some small attendance at thirty dollars a course, and practised medicine occasionally. Never did he fail at the patient's bedside to express his horror and loathing of other practitioners who were "murderers and vile Hottentots." Here too he became famous for his fever-treatment. After stripping the patient and placing him on a flat board, he would wrap him in blankets wrung out in hot water; keep applying hot water externally for fifteen minutes, then bare the patient again, dash a tumblerful of cold water on his chest and then on his back, and so rush him into a warm bed, a profuse sweat and a rapid cure. With this treatment, and rare doses of brandy, he never lost a patient.

Another epidemic of yellow fever in New York in 1803 set him on his way to that city, but on arriving in Boston, his banker was horrified at the rashness, the risk, the danger, and awful waste of money, enough, he said, to buy a farm. Ramsay, however, not to be diverted from his purpose to study the sickness, went on despite the oppressive weather, found New York a plague-stricken city, did good medical work on the spot and printed his results later in the "Edinburgh Medical Journal" for July, 1812. Ramsay probably returned to Edinburgh in 1805, for he then personally received an honorary degree from Aberdeen, took a look at his property, and continued work on his anatomical plates. Returning to New York, in 1806, he tried to establish a new medical school in connection with Drs. Douglass, Hosack and Miller, but the plan failed. The next year saw him lecturing in various cities, and in 1808 we find him engaged by Dr. Nathan Smith to give his anatomical lectures at the Dartmouth Medical School, where many practitioners and students flocked to listen to his reputed eloquence. Old letters tell us that Dr. Spalding, of Portsmouth, furnished several subjects, carting them across the state in barrels of rum. Others tell us that the only man living who could manage Ramsay was Nathan Smith, who laughed him out of his fits of anger and brought smiles to his face once more. Ramsay offered a gold medal to the best dissection made during the course, and at night lectured on natural history.

The London papers bear witness that Ramsay was there in 1810, and that he traveled about England lecturing and begging money for his school at Fryeburg, District of Maine, until 1816. He also wrote for the medical magazines, articles on "Contractions of the Muscular System from Intellectual Influence," and in 1812–13 published the first parts of his system of anatomy embracing the brain and the heart; truly wonderfully engraved.

Although his temper was notorious, he still had friends, among whom were the Duke of Sussex and his two body physicians, Sir Joseph Banks, and other men of influence. Having decided to sail once more to America, he applied with the endorsement of his friends for a free passage on a government vessel, carrying out the British Ambassador. He claimed that his great services to medicine in studying the yellow fever and publishing his great work on anatomy deserved this reward, but his request was declined.

He lectured in New York in 1816, and then at the medical school at Fairfield, where, although his knowledge was admired, he was soon detested for introducing religious discussions into his medical lectures. 1817 found him in Charleston, South Carolina, and then in Savannah, Georgia. At the one place, he collected a herbarium of medical plants, at the other he carried on a newspaper squabble with an editor who had insulted him on his deformity of body. His expenses on this trip were large, amounting to not less than $3,000.

From this year to the end of his life in 1824, Ramsay was incessantly at work, mostly in New England. In one year he petitioned the New Hampshire Legislature to establish an Institution for Anatomy at Conway in that State. In another year he asked the legislature of Maine to aid him for an institution at Fryeburg. His applications were both in vain. At that time he valued his anatomical museum at $14,000, and threatened in each State to send it back to Europe, unless he were assisted with money. He was elected honorary member of the New Hampshire Medical Society, and read before it his "Personal Experiences from a bite by a Rattlesnake." The topics of his lectures were generally: "The Animal and Intellectual Economy of Human Nature as Founded on Comparative Anatomy," and "Dissection as a Basis of Physiology, Anatomy, Surgery and Medicine." Arriving in a town, he would advertise for money to complete his Academy, from which there should be no appeal in medicine. He asserted that Columbia should ask him to found such an institution, instead of his demeaning himself to beg for it. Dr. Ingalls, of Boston, offered him, at one time, his lecture-room, but the attendance and receipts were small. Ingalls is said to have been one of the few who could manage him, despite his temper.

The winter of 1821 found Ramsay lecturing in Montreal and other Canadian cities. His learning was brilliant, as ever, but the man behind was hard to deal with. 1823 laid him low with a "lung" fever and a similar disease terminated his life at Parsonfield, Maine, in 1824. He was buried at Fryeburg, where by many he was cherished as a teacher, physician and friend.

A man earnest in his intentions, but of so unfortunate a temperament that he was never able to enlist competent assistants to carry out his work, even when living, to say nothing of training them preparatory to his death. His aim in life was to establish in America an Anatomical Museum of which the Nation should be proud. In this he failed. Another purpose of his life was to improve everyone with whom he came in contact, and in this he often succeeded. He was visionary in the extreme. He urged a physician, for instance, to leave his growing practice, to travel five hundred miles to Fryeburg, and after learning Ramsay's system of teaching, to take it up for a living to the entire abandonment of his practice. He must have been more than visionary, to believe that from a country village like Fryeburg, the roads to which were mostly impassable half of the year, he could exercise any permanent influence upon American medicine.

He was as egotistical as he was disinterested. He would make any sacrifice to advance medicine. Yet his friends who might have helped him were few, owing to his sudden fits of anger and almost constant irritability. He was deeply religious, and as deeply conscious of his faults. Upright in his outlook, he was fretted and disappointed in his expectations, and correspondingly embittered with the world. He was genuinely eloquent; his students hung upon his every word.

Personally, he was short, clumsy and mis-shapen, yet he was always referring to the beautiful development of his muscles and the magnificent shapeliness of his head. After his death, his famous collection of specimens and preparations was most unfortunately dispersed.

Some writer has said that Ramsay hated every physician, and saw in every anatomist a rival, but no one, reading the charming letters of recommendation given by him to another anatomist seeking a vacant chair of anatomy in a metropolitan school, would believe this charge, nor can we forget his excellent behavior to physicans at Dartmouth under the gentle handling of Dr. Nathan Smith.

Ramsay was a genius, as his beautifully engraved plates bear witness, and as attested by letters of the past. Like all such, however, he was too eccentric for ordinary humanity to understand or endure. He wrote many medical papers and many letters. His style was quaint and turgid. Too often did the remark of some person "cause the blood to curdle in my veins." He wrote his letters and lectures on large sheets of paper, the upper half covered with a design beautifully engraved, of the sun above, and below it the mottoes "To thy years there shall be no end" and "They die and return to the dust." Below these, three cherubims, one standing, one flying, and one seated weeping over a skull and hour glass. In the extreme lower left-hand corner was a delicate etching of Edinburgh Castle.

We may find the key to Alexander Ramsay's character in his mis-shapen body. Born well-formed, possibly injured for life by careless handling in infancy, may he not have always brooded over that misfortune and fancied that all the world were talking of this, to his great disparagement? J. A. S.

Sketch of Dr. Alexander Ramsay by Dr. George Bradley, U. S. N., in the Transactions of the Maine Medical Association, 1883, vol. viii. Port. in the Surg.-gen. lib., Wash., D. C.
Spalding Family Letters.

Ranney, Ambrose Loomis (1848–1905).

Deserving to be remembered as one who did fine pioneer work in ophthalmology, Ambrose Ranney was born on the tenth of June, 1848, in Hardwick, Massachusetts, one of the thirteen sons of Lafayette and Adeline Eliza Loomis Ranney, seven of whom became doctors. Graduating A. B. and A. M. from Dartmouth College he first studied under his uncle, Prof. Alfred L. Loomis, in New York City, then graduated M. D. from the University of the City of New York in 1870.

Early recognizing the connection of eye strain as a cause of functional nervous disease he paid special attention to and wrote a great deal on this subject, the most important of which writings are given in the "Surgeon-general Library Catalogue" under his name.

Some of his books passed several editions and were translated into French or German. Among these is his chief work: "Essentials of Anatomy," 1880; "Applied Anatomy of the Nervous System," 1888; "Treatise on Surgical Diagnosis," 1884, and "Practical Medical Anatomy," 1882.

Dr. Ranney was for many years a railroad surgeon and there were few physicians more frequently on the witness stand. He was so expert a witness that Chief Justice Van Brunt said, "Any lawyer who attempts to cross-examine Dr. Ranney is a fool"; but a good instance of counsel triumphant over Ranney is given in Wellman's "Art of Cross-examination."

In 1876 he married Marie Celle, of New York City, and had two children, A. Elliott and Marie Bryan. Dr. Ranney died suddenly from heart disease in New York City, December 1, 1905.

He was adjunct professor of anatomy, University of the City of New York; president of the New York Academy of Medicine; professor of nervous and mental diseases in the University of Vermont, Medical Department.

D. W.

Jour. Am. Med. Ass., 1905, xlv.
N. York Med. Jour., 1905, lxxxii.
The Art of Cross-examination, F. L. Wellman, 1908, p. 66.

Rauch, John Henry (1828-1894).

Best known as a natural scientist, John Henry Rauch was born in Lebanon, Pennsylvania, September 4, 1828, and graduated from the University of Penn-

sylvania in 1849. He was great on the subject of sanitation, above all, the cheapest form of it—fresh air. When he settled in Burlington, Iowa, he got marine hospitals established and a large cemetery for the town. Professor Agassiz had his help in collecting material, chiefly piscatorial, for his "Natural History of the United States," from the upper Mississippi and Missouri Rivers, and in 1856, he largely aided in getting a bill through Congress for a geological survey of Iowa, when in Venezula in 1870, he visited the mining districts to see what improvements could be made in the miners' dwellings and made a fine collection of natural objects for the Chicago Academy of Natural Sciences.

Rauch was president of the Iowa State Medical Society in 1858; an organizer of the Chicago College of Pharmacy; professor of materia medica in the Rush Medical College; professor of materia medica and botany in the Chicago College of Pharmacy, and served throughout the civil war as surgeon and medical director.

He found time, like most busy men, to do that to which his genius prompted him. Natural Science was his mistress. At the first meeting of the Iowa State Medical Society he gave an address on, "The Medical and Economical Botany of the State," but during the fire of 1871 his synopsis of "The Flora of the Northwest," his "South American Notes" and his herbarium and valuable notes were all destroyed. He had, however, contributed to the material benefit of his countrymen by his writings on cattle and other plagues, drainage. etc.

He died in 1894.

Rep. Proc. Illinois Army and Navy M. Ass Springfield, 1896, vi (port.).
Tr. Illinois M. Soc., Chicago, 1894, xliv (port.)

Ravenel, Edmund (1797-1870).

Edmund Ravenel physician, chemist, and conchologist, was born at Charleston, South Carolina, Dec. 8, 1797, of Huguenot lineage being descended from René Ravenel, Sieur de la Massais, the emigrant.

His early education was in the schools of his native city; and in 1819, he received his M. D. at the University of Pennsylvania.

He began to practice in Charleston, and in 1824 took an active part in the organization of the Medical College of South Carolina. He was elected to the chair of chemistry in the new college, which position he held for ten years, afterwards removing to his country home where he devoted himself to planting until the close of the war when he returned to Charleston. During the summer months he lived on Sullivans Island where he occupied the leisure hours stolen from his practice with gathering his large and valuable collection of shells. This collection contained 3500 species of land, fresh water and marine shells from all parts of the world. What remains of this collection is now preserved in the Charleston Museum. The catalogue of Dr. Ravenel's collection made in 1834 was interesting as being the first of its kind published in America. He was a contemporary and correspondent of Say, Lea, Conrad, Gould and other pioneers of conchology in this country.

In his later years he lived in his home at Charleston, a victim of almost total blindness, where he died, July 27, 1870.

He married twice: First to Charlotte Ford and afterwards to Louisa C. Ford. By his first wife he had one daughter; and by his second, eight children, one of whom, Edmund, studied medicine.

The following is a partial list of his publications:

"Catalogue of the Echinidæ, Recent and Fossil, of South Carolina." "Pamphlet, Charlestion, South Carolina," 1848.

"Description of Three New Species of Univalves, Recent and Fossil." "Proceedings of Elliott Society of Natural History," vol. i, 1858.

"The Limestone Springs of St. John's Berkeley, and Their Probable Availability for Increasing the quantity of Fresh Water in Cooper River." "Proceedings of Elliott Society of Natural History," vol. ii, 1860.

"Tellinidæ of South Carolina." "Proceedings of Elliott Society of Natural History," vol. ii, 1860.

"Catalogue of Recent Shells in the Cabinet of Dr. Edmund Ravenel." "Pamphlet, Charleston, South Carolina," 1834.

"Description of Two Species of Fossil Scutella from South Carolina." "Journal Academy of Natural Sciences," Philadelphia, vol. viii.

"Description of New Recent Shells from the Coast of South Carolina." "Proceeding Academy of Natural Science Philadelphia," 1861.

"Paper on Some South Carolina Fossils." "Proceeding Academy of Natural Sciences, Philadelphia," vol. ii, 1844.

Dr. Ravenel was Vice-president of the Elliott Society of Natural History, Charleston, South Carolina, from its organization in November, 1853 to his death.

R. W., Jr.

Ravenel, St. Julien (1819–1882).

St. Julien Ravenel was born at Charleston, South Carolina, December 19, 1819. Through his father, John Ravenel, he was descended from René Ravenel, of Bretagne, who emigrated to South Carolina after the revocation of the Edict of Nantes, and through his mother, Elizabeth Ford, of Morristown, New Jersey, he traced descent from the old Gualdo family of Vicenza, Italy.

His boyish education was had in Charleston, South Carolina, and at Morristown, New Jersey, and he began the study of medicine with Dr. J. E. Holbrook, graduating from the Medical College of the State of South Carolina in 1840, and for two years following he studied at Philadelphia and at Paris.

Upon his return in 1842 he was elected demonstrator of anatomy in the Medical College of the State of South Carolina. When the war between the States broke out he entered the Confederate service and was appointed surgeon of the Twenty-fifth South Carolina Regiment. Subsequently he was appointed chemist in charge of the laboratory at Columbia, South Carolina, for the preparation of medical supplies.

Dr. Ravenel began the practice of medicine at Charleston, South Carolina, upon his return from Europe and soon gained an enviable reputation as a skillful diagnostician. But yielding to his fondness for purely scientific work—inspired by Holbrook and Agassiz under whom he studied—he abandoned purely medical practice in 1852 in order to devote himself to chemistry. His diagnostic acumen, however, was called into requisition from time to time throughout his life; and he rendered his profession further service by overthrowing the old calomel treatment of yellow fever. In the field of agricultural chemistry he manifested an extraordinary fertility and his discoveries exercised an immense influence in the rehabilitation of South Carolina after the war. In 1856 he ascertained that lime could be manufactured from marl and established the lime works at Stoney Landing, near Charleston, which furnished most of the lime used in the Confederate States. Much of his life was spent in the study of agricultural chemistry in the effort to improve agricultural conditions of his state. He approached the subject from the point of view of the physiologists and drew his conclusions from experiments in the field. "In doubt, ask the plant" he said, "it alone knows all about it." The principles which he advocated as a result of his investigations resulted in increasing in one section the yield of long staple lint cotton per acre from 100–150 pounds to 300–400 pounds. In 1866, having resumed investigations begun before the war, he discovered the value of the phosphate deposits near Charleston and founded the Wando Phosphate Company for the manufacture of fertilizers. This was the beginning of the industry which figured so prominently in the commercial salvation of South Carolina. At the time of his death he was engaged upon investigations looking to the improvement of rice culture.

During the war his inventive genius produced the famous torpedo boat "Little David" which was built in 1863.

Dr. Ravenel was a man of unassuming manners and great modesty. It is related that his own father did not know the ability of his son until one day at a dinner party when a question pertaining to physiology was asked the young doctor, and his reply manifested an extent of learning, originality of thought, and power of expositon that astonished everybody. His chief fault was that he allowed himself to be too busy to leave a written record of his work.

He married Harriet Horry Rutledge in 1851, and had five daughters and four sons, none of whom studied medicine.

He died of cirrhosis of the liver, November 16, 1882.   R. W., Jr.

Proc. Am. Acad. Arts and Sci , Boston, 1881-2, n. s. ix.

Ray, Isaac (1807–1881).

Isaac Ray, alienist, author of "A Treatise on Medical Jurisprudence" (1839), and superintendent of the Butler Hospital for the Insane, Rhode Island, was born in Beverly, Massachusetts, on the sixteenth of February, 1807, and began to study medicine under Dr. Hart and Dr. Shattuck, settling down to practise first in Portland, Maine, then in Eastport. His first course of lectures had nothing to do with dry legal matter but were botanical, and at one course he met his wife, Abigail May, daughter of Judge Frothingham, of Portland. He had two children, a boy and a girl.

The prevalent views as to treatment and responsibilty of the insane led him to study and write on these subjects and this book ran through six editions.

He spent some time in Europe visiting asylums and on his return devoted himself to the erection of the Butler Hospital and was its excellent and untiring superintendent until ill-health compelled him, in 1867, to resign.

He died at his home in Philadelphia on the thirty-first of March, 1881, from pulmonary disease; his death being hastened by that of his only son, Lincoln, a doctor.

Ray was a grave earnest man; one who reserved his opinion until he had something worth saying, so his words carried conviction, and his testimony in legal-medical cases found attentive hearkening. His writings included:

"Hints to the Medical Witness in Questions of Insanity," 1851.

"Insanity of George III.," 1855.

"A Discourse . . . on Dr. Luther V. Bell," 1863.

"A Contribution to Medical Pathology," 1873.

"The Duncan Will Case," 1875.

A fuller list is in the Catalogue of the Surgeon-general, Washington, D. C.

His appointments and titles included: M. D., Harvard, 1827; LL. D., Brown University; fellow of the College of Physicians of Philadelphia; president, Rhode Island Medical Society; president, Association of Medical Superintendents of America, of Institutions for the Insane.

D. W.

Am. J. Insan, Utica, N. Y., 1881-2, vol. xxxviii (T. S. Kirkbride).
Am. J. Med. Sc., Phila., 1881, n. s., vol. lxxxii (T. S. Kirkbride).
Boston M and S Jour , 1881, vol civ
J. Psych Med. Lond., 1881, n. s , vol vii (W. A. F. Browne).
Med-leg. Jour , N. Y , 1887-8, vol. v (C K. Mills).

Raymond-Schroeder, Aimee J. (1857–1903).

Both general practitioner and editor, Aimeé J. Raymond-Schroeder was born in Montreux, Switzerland, August 21, 1857. Edward Raymond, the original ancestor of the family in America, Capt. Urial Raymond, of the Revolutionary Army, also John Alden and Gen. Southworth, on the mother's side, are names found on the family tree. She was the youngest daughter of Henry J. Raymond, founder and editor of the "New York Times." This brilliant man was a strong supporter of Drs. Elizabeth and Emily Blackwell in their early struggles for the medical education of women, and this doubtless influenced his daughter in her decision to study medicine.

Most of her early life was passed in France and Italy. As her father's daughter she had access to the best society here and abroad, so that although her education was desultory, it was really one of the best and broadest. Her only degree was that taken at the Woman's Medical College of the New York Infirmary, in 1889.

She was a member of the County Medical Society of New York, and for several years held a post in the out-patient department of the New York Infirmary, and was associated with other organizations, being particularly active in agitating and securing the enactment of better laws regulating the conditions for working girls.

Always, regardless of herself when others were in question, her professional work was done with a headlong passion of altruism which her friends found adorably characteristic. Her almost unreasoning generosity in giving herself to others proved too much for her frail body, and upon her marriage in 1893 to Dr. Henry Harmon Schroeder, of New York, she retired from active practice, although remaining an earnest student of medicine and devoting her time to its literary side.

She died December 25, 1903, after an operation for appendicitis.

Dr. Raymond-Schroeder was a valued member of the editorial staff of the "New York Medical Record" and "American Journal of Obstetrics." Her one book was "Health Notes for Young Wives." She did much translation from the French and Italian including Pozzi's "A Treatise on Medical and Surgical Gynecology," and translated numerous articles for "The Twentieth Century Practice of Medicine."

A. B. W.

New York Medical Record, vol lxv. Personal information and personal knowledge.

Rea, Robert Laughlin (1827–1899).

Robert Laughlin Rea, a Chicago surgeon, was born in Rockbridge County,

Virginia on July 1, 1827 and, until fifteen had a scanty education, followed by farm work in Indiana and five years as a teacher. He afterwards studied medicine under Dr. W. P. Kitchen, and in 1855 graduated at the medical college of Ohio, although degreeless, he had previously practised for four years at Oxford, Ohio. He occupied the positions of demonstrator of anatomy in his alma mater; physician to the Commercial Hospital, Cincinnati; for sixteen years professor of anatomy, Rush Medical College, Chicago; the same in the Chicago Med. College, and in 1882, professor of surgery in the College of Physicians and Surgeons of which he was a co-founder. During the war of the Rebellion he served as surgeon in the Federal ranks.

"Surgery was his choice in practice and his knowledge of anatomy made him a skillful and dexterous operator. He seized upon all the rapidly increasing innovations in surgery and adopted them."

He married Permelia Mellie, and at his death made provision for the endowment of the Rea professorship of anatomy in the North-western University and gave $5000 to the College of Physicians and Surgeons.

His death, from a complication of cerebral and kidney disorders, occurred on July 10, 1899.

Distinguished Physicians and Surgeons of Chicago, 1904, F. M Sperry.

Reamy, Thaddeus Asbury (1829–1909).

Thaddeus Asbury Reamy was born in Frederick County, Virginia, April 23, 1829. His father, Jacob A., was of Huguenot extraction, his mother, Mary W. Bonifield Reamy, of Scotch and English. They were natives of Virginia but migrated to Muskingum County, Ohio, in 1832. Here Reamy, the first of eleven children, was brought up on a farm and received a rudimentary education at the district school. As soon as he became of age he taught school himself and, as opportunity afforded, completed his education. He commenced the study of

medicine under Dr. D. L. Crist, and in 1854, after attendance upon two courses of lectures, obtained his M. D. from the Starling Medical College. He practised medicine at Zanesville until 1871, when he moved to Cincinnati.

The honors conferred upon him, and the work he did, indicates the character of the man. With no advantages other than those of nature's endowment, such as a powerful and versatile mentality, a rugged physical organism and a magnetic and winning address, he rose by his own efforts, and often against active opposition, to the highest honors of his profession. He was one of our pioneers and did good work. A self-made man and possessing the self-reliance and resourceful qualities of such men, he held the first obstetric clinic ever held in a college amphitheater in this country. His extensive knowledge, felicity of expression, quickness at repartee, and willingness to fight for his convictions caused him to be feared.

In his days there was no out-door obstetrical clinic and lying-in hospital connected with the Cincinnati Medical College, and Reamy had two or three rooms established in the rear of his amphitheater. He too, introduced into that city the study of pregnancy, labor and confinement in the living human female in an amphitheater.

He was invited to join the American Gynecological Society in 1877, the year after its foundation, and took an active and prominent part in its deliberations until prevented by advancing age and infirmity. He was vice-president in 1881, president in 1886, and was placed on the list of honorary members in 1907 at the age of seventy-eight years.

The degree of A. M. was awarded him by the Ohio Wesleyan University in 1870, that of LL. D. by Cornell College in 1890. He was professor of materia medica and therapeutics in Cincinnati College of Medicine and Surgery from 1858 to 1860. He was surgeon to the Thirteenth Provost Marshal District of Ohio in 1863; professor of diseases of women and children in Starling Medical College from 1864 to 1871; professor of obstetrics, clinical midwifery and diseases of children in the Medical College of Ohio from 1871 to 1888 when he became professor of clinical gynecology. He was also obstetrician and surgeon to the Good Samaritan Hospital, and consulting surgeon to Christ's Hospital. He was an ex-president of the Ohio State Medical Society; of the Cincinnati Academy of Medicine; member of the Southern Surgical and Gynecological Association; the Medico-Chirurgical Society of Philadelphia.

Dr. Reamy died of chronic intestinal nephritis on March 11, 1909, at the home of his niece in Cincinnati.

H. T. B.

Tr. Am Gyn. Soc., 1909, vol. xxxiv (Henry T. Byford) (port.).
The Reamy Birthday Dinner, Cincinnati, 1899.

Redman, John (1722–1808).

The materials for a biography of John Redman are somewhat scanty yet all writers agree he deserved to be remembered as one who did good service in Philadelphia, if only for the share he took in laboriously combating the yellow-fever epidemic there in 1792.

He was born in Philadelphia, February 27, 1722, and went for his education first to a school kept by the Rev. William Tennent and afterwards to study medicine under Dr. John Kearsley, Jr., and soon after he is heard of as in Bermuda practising as a doctor. A somewhat restless energetic man this John, for he is next seen in Edinburgh "walking" the hospitals, then on to Paris to study new methods and from there to Leyden, where he graduated M. D. in 1748. Not content with this amount of experience he returns to England and works some time at Guy's Hospital, so one is not surprised to learn that on returning to Philadelphia he "soon built up a lucrative practice." "Like most doctors of his time he believed in systems and attached himself to the teaching of Boerhaave, although his practice was formed by the rules of Sydenham, all of which means that he trusted in the healing power of nature and used a simple form of therapeutics." His paper "De Abortu" appeared in 1748; in 1751 he was elected a consulting physician to the Pennsylvania Hospital and held the position twenty-nine years, and from 1786 to 1805 was president of the College of Physicians. Redman has not left any writings except his pamphlet on the "Yellow Fever in Philadelphia in 1762" which he read before the College of Physicians in 1793, when a greater epidemic of it was raging, and he was attending some eighteen or twenty new cases daily. He tells he based his treatment on "purgation with Glauber's salts, sustaining the patient with cordials or wine with an antiemetic of tartar vitriolat gr. x and a half or whole drop of ol. cinnamon in a spoonful of simple mint and two spoonfuls of decoction of snakeroot every two hours." In order to lessen danger of contagion he had a bowl of vinegar kept in the room and a hot iron occasionally plunged into it; he himself when there always kept tobacco in his mouth to prevent the swallowing of saliva, the only precaution used, as he found the use of many preservatives to affect his mind "with such fears as I thought were likely to render me more susceptible of infection than the omission of them." The College of Physicians exercised the same mental therapy by ordering the tolling of bells to be discontinued as many died from fear of the fever. Redman had had two attacks of fever and in 1762 developed liver disease and was obliged to restrict his practice, but his pupils, Rush and Shippen and many others always kept a warm friendship for the old doctor.

He died in Philadelphia, March 19, 1808.   D. W.

An Acc. of the Yellow Fever in Phila., 1762, Phila., 1793.
Physiology, Alex. Monro, Notes of His Lectures, 1746.
Phila. Med. Museum, 1808, vol. v.
Universities and Their Sons (Phila.).
An Enquiry into the Origin of Yellow Fever, Rush, Phila., 1793.

Reed, Walter (1851–1902).

Walter Reed, chairman of the United States Army Yellow Fever Commission, and discoverer of the mode of propagation of the disease, was born in Gloucester County, Virginia, on September 13, 1851. His father, Lemuel Sutton Reed, and his mother, Pharaba White, were both of English descent and both North Carolinians by birth, though the greater part of Lemuel Reed's life was spent in Virginia as a Methodist minister.

Walter, the youngest of six children, was educated at different private schools until, at the age of sixteen, he entered the University of Virginia. He did so with the intention of pursuing the usual undergraduate course of study, but at the end of the first year he determined to study medicine and graduated from the medical department of the university in 1869, being the youngest student who had ever done so. On leaving Charlottesville, he went to New York and matriculated at Bellevue Medical College, receiving his M. D. there at the end of a year. He was then associated with several hospitals in New York and Brooklyn among which was the Kings County Hospital, where he was interne.

In 1874 he made up his mind to enter the medical corps of the United States Army and, after passing the required examinations, received his commission as assistant surgeon with the rank of first lieutenant in June, 1875. His first station was at Willet's Point, near New York Harbor, but in May, 1876, he was ordered to Arizona where he began a garrison life of thirteen years on the frontier. These years of life in the far west were tedious and uninteresting in the extreme but they constituted the soil best suited to the development of Reed's talents, and the foundations of his career as a scientist were then laid.

In 1889 he began to feel the necessity for time and opportunity to keep abreast of the time in medical research and obtained an appointment as examiner of recruits in Baltimore with permission to attend the courses just opened to phy-

sicians at the Johns Hopkins Hospital. The science of pathology and bacteriology was then new a field of investigation and it was to these subjects in particular that he devoted himself. His first scientific paper on "The Contagiousness of Erysipelas" was published in 1892 and from that time forward he was a constant contributor to medical periodicals. The papers written during this period witness the indomitable perseverance and industry of the man as well as his usual intellectual endowments, for not only were they all written within a single decade but the scientific researches they record were all executed within the same space of time.

In 1898, when the Spanish-American war broke out, Reed was appointed chairman of a committee to investigate the causation and mode of propagation of the epidemic of typhoid fever among the United States Volunteers, the other members being Dr. V. C. Vaughan of Ann Arbor and Dr. E. O. Shakespeare of Philadelphia. The report of this committee is a most interesting and important work, revealing some points concerning the disease which were not before appreciated, or even known.

Reed's first association with yellow fever was in 1897, when he and Dr. James Carroll were appointed by Surg.-Gen. Sternberg to investigate the bacillus icteroides which Sanarelli claimed to be the specific cause of yellow fever. The investigations carried on by them proved beyond a doubt that the bacillus icteroides is a variety of the common hog-cholera bacillus and if present in yellow fever at all it must be as a secondary invader. In 1899, when the disease appeared among the American troops stationed at Havana, a commission of medical officers from the United States Army was appointed to investigate its cause and manner of transmission, Reed being chairman. The other members were Dr. Carroll, Dr. J. W. Lazear, and Dr. Aristides Agramonte, a Cuban immune.

Shortly after Reed's arrival in Havana,

in June 1900, he had the opportunity to observe an epidemic of yellow fever at the little town of Pinar del Rio, and what he then saw convinced him that the prevailing belief in the transmission of the disease by means of fomites conveyed in clothing, bedding, etc., was erroneous. He determined, therefore, that the search for the specific cause of the disease, upon which up to that time all effort had been concentrated, had better be abandoned, and every energy bent upon discovering the means by which it was transmitted. The line of investigation which, in his opinion, offered most prospect of success was the theory suggested by Dr. Carlos Finlay in 1882 that the disease was conveyed from one person to another by a certain species of mosquito, the *stegomyia fasciata*. Some preliminary experiments showed that there was reason to believe in the truth of this supposition, and an experimental sanitary station, called Camp Lazear, was established by Reed near Quemados, in order that further experiments might be carried on under conditions of absolute security.

The first experiment at Camp Lazear was made upon a young private from the United States Army, John R. Kissinger from Ohio, who volunteered to be bitten by mosquitoes which had bitten a yellow-fever patient. Kissinger was kept in strict quarantine for two weeks and was then bitten by some mosquitoes which had been purposely infected fifteen to twenty days previously. At the end of three and a half days the disease developed and he had it in a typical form. This experiment was confirmed by others of the same nature, proving conclusively that yellow fever is transmitted by the *stegomyia fasciata*.

It was next necessary to prove that the disease is not conveyed by fomites and for this purpose a building was especially constructed by Maj. Reed from which all ventilation was excluded, the temperature being extremely hot and the atmosphere damp. In this building Dr. E. G. Cooke and two private soldiers, Folk and Jernigan, volunteered to sleep for twenty nights surrounded by articles of clothing and bedding used by yellow fever patients and soiled by discharges. Not a single case of the disease developed and the same experiment repeated on several subsequent occasions was followed by the same negative result.

These experiments were succeeded by others for the purpose of investigating various secondary points connected with the mosquito theory of the disease, the facts established altogether being these: The mosquito, *stegomyia fasciata*, serves as the intermediate host for the parasite of the yellow fever.

Yellow fever is not conveyed by fomites, hence disinfection of articles supposed to be contaminated by the disease is unnecessary.

The infection of a building with yellow fever is due to the presence of mosquitoes which have bitten some one with the disease.

Yellow fever can be produced experimentally by the subcutaneous injection of blood taken from the general circulation during the first, second and third days of the disease.

Intervals of at least twelve days must elapse after the mosquito has bitten a yellow fever patient before it is capable of transmitting the disease. The bite of the mosquito at an earlier date after contamination does not appear to convey any immunity against a subsequent attack.

The mosquito is capable of infection for at least fifty-seven days after contamination and possibly longer.

On the conclusion of these experiments, in February, 1901, Maj. Reed returned to his work in Washington, where he was professor of bacteriology and clinical microscopy in the Army Medical School, and of pathology and bacteriology in the Columbian University. His natural aptitude for teaching appears to have been great and as the subjects which he taught were then comparatively unknown, he was compelled to develop his own methods of instruction, a fact which imparted an originality to his lectures

WALTER REED.

and laboratory work which made them peculiarly attractive.

In the summer of 1902 Harvard University showed her recognition of Reed's services to humanity by conferring upon him the honorary degree of M. A. and shortly after the University of Michigan made him an LL. D.

In November, 1902, he was taken ill with appendicitis, for which his old friend and brother officer Maj. Borden operated, finding trouble extending back over some years. The removal of the appendix was followed by sloughing, and unfortunately Reed's general health was so much depreciated by years of over-exertion that he had no strength to make resistance. On the fifth day after the operation symptoms of peritonitis appeared, after which he sank rapidly and died on November 22, 1902. He was buried at Arlington, the monument erected to his memory by his wife bearing this inscription, taken from the address made by Pres. Eliot when conferring upon him the Harvard degree, "He gave to man control over that fearful scourge, Yellow Fever."

Walter Reed married, in 1876, Emilie Lawrence of Murfriesboro, North Carolina. He had two children; a son, Walter Lawrence, became an officer in the United States Army, and a daughter, Emilie Lawrence.

Reed's greatest service to humanity was, of course, his discovery of the means by which yellow fever can be controlled, a discovery which, as Gen. Leonard Wood said, "results in the saving of more lives annually than were lost in the Cuban war and saves the commercial prosperity of the country greater financial losses in every year than the cost of the Cuban war." Aside from his work in yellow fever, however, he accomplished much in the service of his fellow men. His investigations in typhoid fever, in erysipelas, and in cholera did much to improve our knowledge of these diseases; his influence as a teacher was singularly deep and far-reaching; while the good done during the long years of quiet

unrecognized service as a post surgeon brought an amount of health and happiness into many lives which can never be estimated.

His writings included:

"The Contagiousness of Erysipelas." ("Boston Medical and Surgical Journal," vol. cxxvi, 1892.)

"Remarks on the Cholera Spirillum." ("Northwest Lancet," St. Paul, vol. xiii, 1893.)

"Association of Proteus Vulgaris with Diplococcus Lanceolatus in a Case of Croupous Pneumonia." ("Johns Hopkins Hospital Bulletin," Baltimore, vol. v, 1894.)

"The Germicidal Value of Trikresol." ("St. Louis Medical and Surgical Journal," vol. lxvi, 1894.)

Idem. ("Proceedings of the Association of Military Surgeons of the United States," Washington, St. Louis, vol. iv, 1894.)

"A Brief Contribution to the Identification of Streptococcus Erysipelatos." ("Boston Medical and Surgical Journal," vol. cxxxi, 1894.)

"An Investigation into the So-called Lymphoid Nodules of the Liver in Typhoid Fever." ("Johns Hopkins Hospital Report," Baltimore, vol. v, 1895.)

"An Investigation into the So-called Lymphoid Nodules of the Liver in Abdominal Typhus." ("American Journal of Medical Sciences," Philadelphia, n. s., vol. cx, 1895.)

"What Credence should be given to the Statements of Those Who claim to furnish Vaccine Lymph free of Bacteria." (Read before the District of Columbia Medical Society, June 5.) ("Journal of Practical Medicine," New York, vol. v, July, 1895.)

"The Character, Prevalence, and probable Causation of the Malarial Fevers at Washington Barracks and Fort Meyer." ("Report of the Surgeon-general of the Army," Washington, 1896.)

"The Parasite of Malaria." ("Journal of Practical Medicine," New York, vol. vi, April, 1896.)

"Serum Diagnosis in Typhoid Fever." ("Report of Surgeon-general of the Army," Washington, 1897.)

"On the Appearance of Certain Ameboid Bodies in the Blood of Vaccinated Monkeys (Rhoesus) and Children, and in the Blood of Variola," an experimental study. ("Transactions of the Association of American Physicians," Philadelphia, vol. xii, 1897.

"Typhoid Fever in the District of Columbia; Diagnosis: The Value of Widal's test, the Dried Blood Method." ("National Medical Review," Washington, vol. vii, 1897.)

"Experiments with Hollister's Formaldehyde Generator." ("Report of the Surgeon-general of the Army," Washington, 1897.)

"Splenic Leukemia." ("Transactions of the Medical Society of the District of Columbia," October 27, 1897; "National Medical Review," Washington, vol. vii, 1898.)

"Report on the Practical Use of Electrozone as a Disinfectant in the City of Havana, Cuba." ("Report of the Surgeon-general of the Army," Washington, 1900.)

"The Propagation of Yellow Fever; Observations Based on Recent Researches." ("Medical Record," New York, vol. lx, 1901.)

"Recent Researches Concerning the Etiology, Propagation and Prevention of Yellow Fever, by the United States Army Commission." ("Journal of Hygiene," Cambridge, England, vol. ii, 1902.)

Walter Reed and James Carroll.

"Bacillus Icteroides and Bacillus Choleræ Suis," a preliminary note. ("Medical News," New York, vol. lxxiv, April 29, 1899.)

"The Specific Cause of Yellow Fever." A reply to Dr. G. Sanarelli. ("Medical News," New York, vol. lxxv, 1899.)

"A Comparative Study of the Biological Characters and Pathogenesis of Bacillus x (Sternberg), Bacillus Icteroides (Sanarelli), and the Hog-cholera Bacillus (Salmon and Smith)." ("Jour-

nal of Experimental Medicine," Baltimore, vol. v, 1900.)

"The Prevention of Yellow Fever." ("Medical Record," New York, vol. lx, 1901.)

"The Etiology of Yellow Fever," a supplemental note. ("American Medicine," Philadelphia, vol. iii, 1902.)

Walter Reed, James Carroll, and Aristides Agramonte.

"The Etiology of Yellow Fever," an additional note. ("Journal of the American Medical Association," Chicago, vol. xxxvi, 1901.)

"Experimental Yellow Fever." ("American Medicine," Philadelphia, vol. ii, 1901.)

Walter Reed, James Carroll, Aristides Agramonte, and Jesse W. Lazear.

"The Etiology of Yellow Fever," a preliminary note. ("Philadelphia Medical Journal," vol. vi, 1900.)

Walter Reed, and George M. Sternberg.

"Report of Immunity Against Vaccination conferred upon the Monkey by the Use of the Serum of the Vaccinated Calf and Monkey." ("Transactions of the Association of American Physicians," Philadelphia, vol. x, 1895.)

C. W. L.

Am. Med. Phila., 1902, vol. iv.
Brit. M. J., Lond., 1903, vol. i.
J. Am. M. Ass., Chicago, 1902, vol. xxxix.
Med. Rec., N. Y., 1902, vol. lxii.
N. York, N. J., 1902, vol. lxxvi.
Proc. Wash. Acad. Sc., 1903-4, vol. v (G. M. Sternberg).
Kean J. R. The Scientific work and discoveries of the late Major Walter Reed, Wash., 1903.
Kelly, H. A. Walter Reed and Yellow Fever, N. Y., 1906.
In Memory of Walter Reed, U. S. Army, Wash., D. C. (Wash., 1903).

Reese, John James (1818–1892).

John James Reese was born in Philadelphia, June 16, 1818 and took both his liberal and medical degrees from the University of Pennsylvania. Settling in Philadelphia, he soon had an excellent practice.

In 1861 he entered the Federal Army as

volunteer surgeon, in which capacity he was placed at the head of the Christian Street Hospital, in Philadelphia.

He was several years physician at St. Joseph's Hospital, and the Gynecological Hospital and Infirmary for Diseases of Children.

He was a fellow of the College of Physicians, Philadelphia, and honorary member of the New York Medico-legal Society.

Dr. Reese was editor of the seventh American edition of A. S. Taylor's "Medical Jurisprudence." He also wrote well and much on his own account on topics connected with toxicology and legal medicine. In particular, his world-famed text-book entitled "Medical Jurisprudence and Toxicology," went through some seven editions and did much to brighten the luster of his name. This work, small but compact, contained the kernel of toxicology and forensic medicine as it existed in his time. The book was popular in the extreme.

Dr. Reese was a tall, slim man, of dark complexion and with very black hair and eyes. His manner was quick and animated, and he was very copious and pleasant of speech. He was possessed of a magnetic · presence, and his lectures always fell upon attentive ears. He was a member of the Protestant Episcopal church.

He died at Atlantic City, New Jersey, September 4, 1892.   T. H. S.

Journal of the American Medical Association, October 29, 1892. American Universities and Their Sons, 1902, vol. i.

Reeve, James Theodore (1834–1906).

He was born of American parentage near Goshen, Orange County, New York, April 26, 1834, and was educated in the common schools, afterwards studying medicine at Ann Arbor, Michigan, Castleton Medical College, and Jefferson Medical College, receiving his M. D. from Castleton in 1854, and from Jefferson in 1855, and had the honorary A. M. from Ripon College, Ripon, Wisconsin, in 1882. He was a member of the New York Medico-legal Society and president of the Wisconsin State Medical Society.

Dr. Reeve began to practise at the age of twenty-one in Depere, Wisconsin, and practised continuously in the Fox River Valley for fifty-one years, seeing and actively participating in its growth from a primeval wilderness to an important commercial and educational center. When the Civil War broke out he drove with his wife from Green Bay to Madison, Wisconsin, through 150 miles of unsettled country, and enlisted in the army, being appointed second assistant surgeon of the Tenth Regiment. He was soon transferred to Twenty-first Regiment, and served throughout the war, his regiment participating in many severe engagements, notably the battles of Stone River, Perryville, Resaca and Kenesaw Mountain, and Chicamauga. After the latter engagement he remained with the field hospital and was captured and taken to Libby Prison for three months. On being exchanged he returned to the service, marched with Sherman from Atlanta to the sea, and was present at the siege of Savannah, Averysboro and Bentonville. He was promoted to the position of brigade-surgeon, and at the close of the war was acting division-surgeon, with rank of major, and after the war settled at Appleton, Wisconsin.

Besides being, like all good doctors, a sort of father confessor to patients, he was very often sought for aid and comfort wholly aside from professional matters; and the words "the best friend I ever had" were on the lips of many who never called on him in sickness. To others he was fond of sending gifts of money outright in quaint ways, as gold pieces in pill-boxes, marked "take one when necessary." In such ways he gave away considerable sums, while spending on himself practically nothing beyond what was necessary for food and clothing.

He was married in 1857 to Laura Spofford, and had six children, the eldest being associated with him in practice. He died at Appleton, November 4, 1906, at the age of seventy-two, of chronic bowel trouble, complicated with nephritis, the foundation for which was doubtless laid during army service, and aggravated by unremitting toil.

He contributed little to the medical press, but during eighteen years of work as secretary of the State Board of Health he wrote thousands of letters to physicians and members of local boards of health, urging and directing organization for intelligent sanitation, and aiding in mitigating and preventing the spread of epidemics. These, and the editing and writing for the annual reports of the board, constituted no small contribution to the progress of the highest branch of medical science.

J. S. R.

J. Am. M. Assoc , Chicago, 1906, xlvii.

Reiter, William Charles (1817–1882).

William Charles Reiter was a classical family physician but his activity was not confined to the practice of medicine; natural history, and especially botany, in which science he held a foremost position in his locality, were to him an avocation of great interest and enjoyment.

His father, of French Huguenot ancestry, was born in Hessia. His mother was of Hanoverian extraction. Married in Baltimore, Maryland, they removed to Pittsburg, Pennsylvania, about 1812, where William Charles was born March 24, 1817. He attended lectures at Jefferson Medical College during the session of 1834–5 after which he engaged in practice at Pleasant Unity and Mount Pleasant, Pennsylvania, and in 1836, on the death of his preceptor, Dr. A. Torrence, succeeded to his practice. At this time he was married and after four years of professional work he returned to Jefferson Medical College, where he graduated in the spring of 1839. Of a philosophic bent of mind, he took much pleasure in the study of natural history, and was looked upon as a local authority in botany.

On the establishment of the Pittsburg College of Pharmacy in 1880, he was elected to the chair of materia medica and botany, which office he filled for several years till the infirmities of age necessitated his resignation. Previous to this time he also delivered lectures at the Western University of Pennsylvania at Pittsburg on chemistry, geology and physiology.

He was married on November 8, 1836, to Eliza Reynolds, daughter of Capt. William Reynolds, of Westmoreland County, Pennsylvania, and had four children, three daughters and one son.

Reiter died at Edgewood Park, Pennsylvania, a suburb of Pittsburg, on November 20, 1882, of general arteriosclerosis.

At the time of his earlier life the cause of most diseases was purely a matter of speculation and to a man of Reiter's strong convictions and force of mind the need of forming a theoretical etiology based upon experience and observation became almost mandatory. Thus he believed that diphtheria was due to an excess of fibrin in the blood, and in support of this hypothesis and the treatment of the disease with enormous doses of calomel (as much as three or four drams during the course of the attack), he published, in 1878, a booklet on "The Treatment of Diphtheria Based upon a New Etiology and Pathology," which attracted wide attention.

His portrait was in the possession of his daughter, Miss Mary Reiter, at Edgewood Park, Pennsylvania.

A. K.

Rex, George (1845–1895).

Born at Chestnut Hill, Philadelphia, he graduated at the University of Pennsylvania, and during his earlier life was assistant demonstrator of anatomy there. He was also a member of the College of Physicians and Surgeons and became a member of the Academy of Natural Sciences in 1881, serving as conservator from 1890 until his death.

Dr. Rex was considered the highest authority of the myxomycetes in the United States. It was his enthusiastic study of this group which first brought him to the academy and he was the author of a number of species, which owing to his extreme conservatism, will doubtless continue to bear his name. His collection of myxomycetes, presented by his sister, is in the Academy of Natural Science, Philadelphia, but he was also an ardent admirer of everything beautiful in microscopic nature. As a faithful and tireless worker he inspired his co-laborers and as a medical practitioner for twenty-five years in Philadelphia, earned the gratitude of high and low.

During the Civil War he acted as engineer in the United States Navy. He died suddenly on the morning of February, 1895 of heart trouble.

His writings included: "Siphoptychium Casparyi." "Botany Gazette," ix–x. "The Myxomycetes.""Ibid," ix–x. "On the Genus Lindbladia." "Botany Gazette, ibid," vxi. "New American Myxomycetes." "Proceedings of Academy of Natural Science," Philadelphia, 1891. "New North American Myxomycetes," ibid, 1893. "Notes on Cribraria minutissima and Licea minima. " Botanical Gazette," xix. "The Banded-spore Trichias." "Journal of Mycology," ii.   J. W H.

The Botanists of Philadelphia, J. W. Harshberger, 1899.

Reynolds, Edward (1793–1881).

Edward Reynolds was born in Boston, February, 1793, and graduated in arts in 1811 at Harvard College, afterwards studying medicine for several years under Dr. John Collins Warren. In London he studied under Abernethy, Astley Cooper, and William Lawrence (on the eye), and in Paris under Bichat and Dupuytren, devoting himself on his return to America chiefly to general and ophthalmic surgery. In 1824, with John Jeffries, he founded a dispensary, which a few years later developed into the Massachusetts Charitable Eye and Ear Infirmary, and he served the institution continuously until 1870. Elected an honorary member of

the American Ophthalmological Society at its inception, he was one of the founders of the Tremont Medical School, and professor of surgery in this institution.

He died at the end of his eighty-ninth year, 1881, in Boston.   H. F.

Hubbell's "Development of Ophthalmology, etc "
Boston Med. and Surg. Journal, 1882, vol. cvi.

Rice, Ebenezer (1740–1822).

Ebenezer Rice was one of those interesting medical characters who flourished previous to the Revolution, and also one of those who were made or marred by their own actions during that period. Born about 1740, he graduated at Harvard in the class of 1760, studied medicine with some Massachusetts practitioner, and settled in Wells in 1763, and gradually obtained a good practice, but some said that although he had first-rate luck with his patients it was because they suggested to him what they would like to take.

He was an honest, kind, fatherly sort of a physician, but he should have been a clergyman, for in the church and in his position as deacon, he was at home. He was at church invariably, and there everything went well, and it was his guidance, and his money, and the money that he persuaded out of other people that kept the old church in repair and built a new one later on.

This official sort of a position, as a head of the church finally brought other offices, and we find him in May, 1773 on the Committee of Correspondence with the other colonies, when taxes from England were heavily increasing. For a while Dr. Rice held up his head as a brave and valiant member, then he began to vacillate, finally to side secretly with the British, and at a stormy meeting of the Committee, he was asked to apologize for his Toryism.

Concerning this meeting we can perhaps understand why men's tempers were high that night in 1774, when we know that during the meeting the twenty-three members drank twenty-three bottles of "brandy toddy" and "rum punch." Soon after his arrival in town, Dr. Rice married Miss Martha Wells, but she died in 1773, leaving him three or four children. Within a couple of years, he married the Widow Elizabeth Howe, of Marlborough, Massachusetts, and just about that time he began to believe that the colonists had gone too far; that England was too big to conquer, and that all the members of the committee would be hanged on the arrival of the British Army. So taking his new wife and children, he emigrated to Marlborough, where his wife had lived before her marriage, and there, far from the dangers of British invasion, he led a quiet life, not dying until 1822.

Like many other medical men of those days, Dr. Rice had some business as a source of income besides the scanty fees from practice and he had a good deal at one time to do with mining and smelting iron ore in the towns of Kennebunk and Wells.

Just as a pioneer in Maine, at a time when great physicians were few, Dr. Rice deserves praise and mention in a biographical work.

J. A. S.

Trans. Maine Med. Assoc.

Rich, Hosea (1780–1866).

This capable surgeon, the son of Paul and Mary Dennis Rich, was born in Charlestown, Massachusetts, Oct. 1, 1780. His childhood was spent on a farm, where he obtained that sturdiness which lasted through life. He studied medicine with Dr. John Elliot Eaton, of Dudley, Massachusetts (Harvard College 1777), and with Dr. Thomas Babbitt, of Harvard, 1784. He studied medicine for five successive years, thus laying a solid foundation for success. On January 6, 1803, Rich married Mrs. Fannie Burke Goodall, by whom he had eight children, one of whom became a medical practitioner. Soon after marriage Rich tried practice at various places without success and finally set sail

with an expedition for Port au Prince, as surgeon's mate. Two years later, John Burke, a brother-in-law, having moved to Bangor, Maine, then on the edge of the primeval forest, advised his brother-in-law to settle there, so on July 4, 1805, Rich went to Bangor, there to labor successfully nearly sixty-one years.

He was a prominent member of the Maine Medical Society, afterwards president of the Maine Medical Association. The transactions of the latter society not having been printed until Rich was advanced in years, we have no means of knowing what papers he contributed. As he had really no degree, as a reward for his long continued usefulness and excellent standing in the Commonwealth of Maine, Bowdoin College granted him her honorary M. D. in 1851, gratefully acknowledged by Dr. Rich when he was more than seventy years of age as a token of being well thought of.

During the War of 1812 he was surgeon of the Fourth Maine Regiment at the Battle of Hampden, Maine, where some 750 British attacked half the number of Americans. Rich had just extracted a bullet from the hand of a wounded soldier when the enemy entered the hospital. He ran one way, the patient another, and they did not meet again for several years. We can imagine the pleasure, when at that time Dr. Rich was able to show his patient the bullet that he had taken from his hand. It should be added that on the day after the battle, by permission of the invaders, Dr. Rich resumed work at the hospital.

He kept to the truth so far as his conscience would permit and encouraged his patients to the last. As a surgeon he was conservative, studying the anatomy thoroughly before operating, and always trying in every way to avoid operation if possible. The "Dublin Hospital Gazette," February, 1856, reports one of his cases in which a thong forming the nucleus of a calculus was successfully removed July 3, 1855, at Bangor. His patient had foolishly pushed a leather thong into his bladder by means of a broken twig. Nothing happened for a long time until pain set in and an operation became imperative. Rich did the operation, and removed the calculus. In it was the missing leather thong. This calculus was exhibited by Dr. William Brown, of Bangor, who was then at Dublin. He had assisted at the operation, and with the consent of Dr. Rich took the calculus to Europe for exhibition. It was composed of triple phosphate and phosphate of lime and fusible in the blow-pipe.

His first capital operation was an amputation of a leg in 1809. His last was a couching for cataract June 27, 1865, when he restored to a man older than himself a good amount of sight.

On August 14, 1855 he was taken ill with what was to be his only and last illness, for he passed away slowly, week by week, dying finally January 30, 1866.

J. A. S.

Trans. Maine Medical Assoc., Portland, 1866-1868.

Richardson, Alonzo Blair (1852-1903).

Alonzo Blair Richardson, eminent as an alienist and neurologist throughout the United States, and superintendent of the Government Hospital for the Insane at Washington, District of Columbia, died in that city on the evening of June 27, 1903, after but a few hours' illness. Dr. Richardson was born near Harrisonville, Scioto County, Ohio, September 11, 1852. Entering the Ohio University at Athens, Ohio, he remained two years, going thence to the Ohio Wesleyan University at Delaware, Ohio. In the fall of 1874 he attended his first course of lectures at a medical college in Cincinnati, Ohio, and the next year entered the Bellevue Hospital Medical College at New York City, where he graduated in 1876. Returning to Ohio he accepted a position as assistant physician at the State Hospital, Athens, Ohio. In 1880 he was appointed superintendent. He was successively superintendent of the State Hospital, Columbus, Ohio; the State Hospital, Massillon, Ohio, and when occupying the

same post at the Government Hospital, Washington, he obtained government grants for the enlargement and improvement of the latter. In 1892 he was, without solicitation or suggestion on his part, unanimously elected to the superintendency of the State Hospital in Columbus, Ohio, and retained this position until the completion of the new State Hospital at Massillon, Ohio, in 1898. He had been one of the board of constructors of that institution from its first inception, and had largely shaped its plans.

Amid the multiplied demands of his position he continued an enthusiastic student. He must be counted among the foremost of those who have led in the notable amelioration and improvement in the treatment of the insane that has taken place. Despite his busy life in other respects, he found time to contribute to some of the leading journals of the time. Insanity and its causes among the American troops in the Philippines and Cuban campaigns formed some of the subjects from his ready pen. Dr. Richardson was a member of the Columbus, Ohio, Academy of Medicine, the Ohio State Medical Society, the New York Medico-Legal Society, the American Medico-psychological Association, of which he was elected president.

Dr. Richardson was professor in mental diseases in both Columbian and Georgetown Universities, in Washington. He was survived by a widow, Julia Dean Richardson, and four children, Dr. William W., Mrs. W. G. Neff, Edith Harris, and Helen.   C. H. C.

Amer. Jour. of Insanity, vol. lx, 1903.

Richardson, Tobias Gibson (1827-1892).

Tobias Gibson Richardson, son of William A. and Symia Higgins Richardson of Louisville, Kentucky, was a student of Samuel D. Gross, and graduated M. D. from the medical department of the University of Louisiana, 1848, where for some years he was professor of anatomy and later professor of surgery. He was also a member of the College of

Physicians of Philadelphia and of the American Surgical Association. His chief writings appeared in the "North American Medical and Chirurgical Review," the "New Orleans Medical and Surgical Journal," the "Transactions of the American Medical Association," and in those of the American Surgical Association. The chief are:

"Injuries of the Knee-Joint." ("Transylvania Journal of Medicine," vol. x, 2.

"A Case in Which Death resulted from the Thompsonian Practice, with an Autopsy" (ibid.)

"An Essay on Tenotomy with Illustrative Cases." ("Western Journal of Medicine.")

"Report on Statistics of Hernia, with New Operation for the Radical Cure." ("Semi-Monthly Views," vol. i, 1859.)

"Six Operations for Strangulated Hernia, Five of Which had Favorable Issue."

In 1841 he "extirpated successfully the parotid gland. He amputated both legs at the hip-joint at one time in the same subject, and the patient recovered, growing afterwards extremely fat." (This was years prior to the use of anesthetics or antiseptics.)

In 1854, while demonstrator of anatomy in the University of Louisville, Richardson published his work entitled "Elements of Human Anatomy: General, Descriptive and Practical" (1854). This was the first and only systematic treatise of the kind ever published in the valley of the Mississippi. It consisted of one volume, octavo, seven hundred and thirty-four pages and two hundred and sixty-nine illustrations, with several marked improvements in the arrangement of its subjects, and with the unique feature of "substituting English for Latin terms wherever this appeared to be practicable and judicious." Dr. Richardson subsequently became a professor in one of the schools of Philadelphia. He did his best work, however, in New Orleans, where he occupied the chair of surgery in the Tulane University, and was visiting physician to the Charity Hospital.

His first wife was Sarah E., a daughter of Dr. Charles Wilkins Short, a prominent physician of Kentucky, after whom the Shortia was named. Mrs. Richardson on her way up the Mississippi to join her husband was drowned with her three children below Vicksburg through the destruction of the steamboat by fire.

Richardson was elected president of the American Medical Association at Buffalo, in 1878.

Several years after the loss of his wife, he married Cora Slocum, a relative of the Brashear family of Kentucky and after his death in 1892 Mrs. Richardson contributed $100,000 to build a memorial addition to the Tulane University in memory of her husband. A. S.

"Some Reminiscences in the Lives and Characters of the Old-time Physicians of Louisville, by T. B Greenley, M. D " American Practitioner and News, March 15, 1903.
Transactions of the Kentucky State Medical Society, 1875.
Tr. Am. Med. Assoc., Phila., xxix, 1879.
Med. and Chir. Rev., Phila., 1857–61.
T. G. Richardson, in memory of, by various authors, N. Orleans., Tulane Univ., 1893.
N. Ore. M and S. J , 1895–6, n s , vol. xviii

Ricketts, Howard Taylor (1871–1910).

Howard Taylor Ricketts, one of the most notable young workers in the field of medical research, died in the American Hospital in the City of Mexico, May 3, 1910, from typhus fever, contracted while pursuing investigations regarding its cause.

He chose the most dangerous of all positions in the field, when, with a great future before him, he chose first to seek in its favorite jungle the typhus germ in Mexico, and died for humanity. That his heroism was not unique, in fact comparatively commonplace, did not lessen its value.

Born in Findlay, Ohio, on February 9, 1871, he received his literary degree from the University of Nebraska, Lincoln, in 1894; graduating from the Northwestern University Medical School, Chicago, in 1897. He served as interne in Cook County Hospital from 1897 to 1899, then continued his research work, being made fellow in cutaneous pathology in Rush Medical College, and in 1889 instructor in pathology. During this time he pursued his researches on blastomycosis. In 1902 he became associate professor of pathology in the University of Chicago. His next important work in medical research was regarding the Rocky Mountain spotted fever (tick fever), which occupied his attention for several summers. In 1906 his book on "Infection, Immunity and Serum Therapy" appeared, which went through three editions and was a very complete short treatise on the subject. His latest research work concerned the causation of typhus fever (tabardillo), which had been epidemic in Mexico for some time past. When appointed professor of pathology in the University of Pennsylvania, he accepted the position with the understanding that he was to be free to continue his researches during the winter, spring and summer.

Ricketts was for several years a valued editorial writer on "The Journal" and much of his research work was done under grants made by the Committee on Scientific Research of the American Medical Association.

His society membership included the American Association of Pathologists and Bacteriologists, and the Chicago Medical, Clinical and Pathological Societies. He was a persistent, untiring and insatiable worker, and to this his illness and death were probably due, as he was worn out when he died.

A signal honor was shown Dr. Ricketts' memory when Pres. Diaz, of Mexico, directed that the professors and students of the National Medical School be present on the occasion of the removal of the body to Chicago, and that the medical school and institute of bacteriology be draped in mourning three days and the laboratory in which Dr. Ricketts made his investigations named "The Howard T. Ricketts Laboratory."

Jour. Am. Med. Assoc., Chicago, May 14, 1910, in which there is a portrait.
Mexican Herald, May 4, 1910.
Old Penn., Phila., May, 1910.

Ricord, Philippe (1799–1889).

He was born of French parents at Baltimore, Maryland, December 10, 1799, and when twenty years old was sent to Paris to study medicine. He was early appointed interne in the surgical service of Dupuytren, but his mischievous spirit made him lose his position. The misadventure did not prevent him from continuing his medical studies, and he graduated M. D. in 1826. As he had no means he practised for two years in country villages. In 1828 he returned to Paris, became surgeon by concourse of the Central Bureau, but for the next two years was obliged to support himself by courses on operative surgery in La Pitié Hospital. In 1831 he was appointed surgeon-in-chief of the Hospital du Midi for syphilis and continued to hold this position until 1860, when he was obliged to retire on account of age.

He enjoyed a world-wide reputation in his speciality and was regarded as the highest authority upon it, his clinics being followed by students and physicians from all parts of the world. His researches on syphilis established a rational therapy of that disease. In 1834 he announced his theory on the transmission of the disease, the laws of which he laid down in precise terms. He demonstrated that gonorrhea was entirely distinct from syphilis, that constitutional syphilis always starts in an indurated chancre, and that venereal affections are local and general. Medicine is indebted to him also for new methods of curing varicocele and performing urethroplasty, for which he received the Monthyon prize in 1842.

As a teacher he was unequalled but always refused to teach officially. Elected a member of the Academy in 1850, he became its president in 1868. In 1852 he became physician to Prince Napoleon and in 1869 was appointed consulting surgeon to the Emperor. He attended Napoleon III. in 1869–70 for the disease of the bladder from which he died. In 1870–71 he gained fresh laurels as president of the Lazaretto, during the siege of Paris. He was decorated with a great many orders.

Pres. Thiers made him an officer of the Legion of Honor for his services in the F r a n c o-German War. Fournier, his pupil and successor, edited many of his works. During his last years he disappeared almost into oblivion. His brilliant mind gave way and he died at Paris, October 21, 1889.

Of his writings may be mentioned the following: "De L'Emploi du Spéculum," 1833 (of the bivalve speculum invented by him); "De la Blennorrhagie de la femme," 1834; "Emploide l'Onguent Mercuriel dans le Traitement de l'Erysipèle," 1839; "Monographie du Chancre," 1837 (the clearest exposition of his doctrine); "Théorie sur la Nature et le Traitement de l'Epididymite," 1838; "Traité des Maladies Vénériennes," 1838, nouv. éd. 1863, av. 66 pl.; "De l'Ophthalmie Blennorrhagique," 1842; "Clinique Iconographique de l'Hôpital des Vénériens," 1842–63, av. 66 pl.; "De la Syphilisation et de la Contagion des Accidents Secondaires," 1853; "Lettres sur la Syphilis," 1851; 3 éd., 1863; "Leçons sur le Chancre . . . Publ. par Alfred Fournier," 1857, 2 éd., 1860; together with a large number of observations in Richelot's translations of John Hunter's "Traité de la Maladie Vénérienne," 3 éd., 1859, and a great quantity of memoirs, observations, communications, for the most part in the "Mémoires and Bulletins of the Academy of Medicine," 1834–50, verses, etc. All of his productions are distinguished by simplicity of style. E. F. C.

Biographisches Lexikon der Hervorragenden Aerzte aller Zeiten und Völker, von Dr. Aug. Hirsch, Wien, 1887, Bd. v.
Ann. de dermat. et syph., Paris, 1889, 2 s., vol. x (H. Feulard).
Boston M. and S. J., 1889, vol. cxxi.
Edinb. M. J., 1889, vol. xxxv.
Lancet, Lond., 1889, vol. ii.
Progrès Med., Paris, 1889, 2. s., vol. x.
Gazz. med. Ital. Lomb. Milano, 1863, 5. s., vol. ii.

Riddell, John Leonard (1807–1865).

John Leonard Riddell, physician, author and inventor, was born in Leyden, Massachusetts, in 1807, of fine Scotch-Irish ancestry which could be traced back to the eighth century.

He held his degrees of A. B. and A. M. from the Rensselaer School of Troy, New York, and began his career as a lecturer on scientific subjects. In 1835 he was made adjunct professor of chemistry and botany in the Cincinnati Medical College, from which he received his M. D. He published a catalogue of plants in 1835 entitled "A Synopsis of the Flora of the Western States," the pioneer botany of that section of the country, and in 1836 he became professor of chemistry in the Medical College of Louisiana, a distinction which he enjoyed until his death in 1865.

His catalogue of Louisiana plants assures to him the discovery of several new, or unobserved, species, one genus being called for him, Riddellia (Riddellia tagetina, Nuttall).

In 1838 the president of the United States appointed Dr. Riddell melter and refiner for New Orleans, as a recognition of the creditable work just performed in a scientific exploration conducted in Texas; his incumbency in this office lasted until 1849. In 1844 he was one of a commission recommended by the governor and legislature to devise a means for protecting New Orleans from overflow. About this period he became devoted to microscopy and invented the binocular microscope, as noted on page 273, vol. xvi, edition nine, of the "Encyclopedia Britannica." According to Herringshaw's Encyclopedia of American Biography, he was the discoverer of the microscopical characteristics of the blood and black vomit in yellow fever.

Dr. Riddell was a frequent contributor to the "New Orleans Medical and Surgical Journal," among his publications being noted "Probable Constitution of Matter and Laws of Motion, as Deducible from, and Explanatory of, the Physical Phenomena of Nature," 1845, vol. ii, and "Nature of Miasma and Contagion," vol. xvi, 1859.

J. G. R.

N. Orl. M. and S. Jour., vol. xix, 1866–7.

Ridgely, Frederick (1757–1824).

He was born on Elk Ridge, Anne Arundel County, Maryland, May 25, 1757, receiving his academic training at the Academy of Newark, Delaware, and beginning to study medicine in his seventeenth year under Dr. Philip Thomas, of Fredericktown.

His studies were interrupted by the Revolution. At the age of nineteen we find him surgeon to a Corps of Riflemen raised in the upper counties of Virginia and adjoining Maryland. With these he arrived before Boston a few days after the Battle of Bunker Hill, June, 1775. He steadfastly followed the Army of Washington through the trying times of 1776, and in 1777 Maryland honored him by the surgeoncy of the Fourth Maryland Regulars. When the British Army evacuated Philadelphia, he resigned to attend a course of lectures under Drs. Shippen, Kuhn and Rush. His friendship with Dr. Rush, to whom he bore in appearance and manners a striking resemblance, began prior to his matriculation and lasted for life. He was not permitted to remain long enough to obtain his degree for early in 1779 he was appointed surgeon to a vessel about to sail with letters of marque and reprisal from that port. The ship made a short cruise off the coast of Virginia when, falling in with an enemy of superior size, she was chased into the Chesapeake and after a severe engagement, captured. As his vessel struck her colors, he jumped overboard and made his escape by swimming two miles to shore. He re-entered the Army and continued as medical officer until the close of the war.

After cessation of hostilities he began the practice of medicine between Annapolis and Baltimore, but being of an adventurous turn he joined the tide of emigration westward, arriving in Lexington in 1790.

Soon after he began to practice he was appointed surgeon-general to the army commanded by Gen. Wayne and served in the decisive campaign of 1794; finally bidding farewell to military life he again began practice in Lexington, where he remained more than thirty years.

He devoted much of his time to instruction, and his "shop" was thronged with pupils, many of whom afterwards became the most distinguished medical men in the west, among them Benjamin Winslow Dudley, the most successful lithotomist in the State, and Walter Brashear, who did the first successful hip-joint amputation in the world.

To Ridgely is due the honor of having been the first clinical and didactic instructor west of the Allegheny Mountains. He, with Samuel Brown, was the first teacher of "physic" in the Transylvania University. In 1799 he was made professor of materia medica, midwifery and practice of "physic" in the University. Dr. Charles Wilkins Short refers to "His unwearied assiduities in the discharge of his professional duties."

He died while on a visit to his daughter at Dayton, Ohio, on November 21, 1824.

A. S.

Transylvania Journal of Medicine, Lexington, Kentucky, vol. i, 1828, (Charles Wilkins Short).

Riley, John Campbell (1828–1879).

A son of Dr. Joshua Riley, of Georgetown, District of Columbia, he was born there on December 15, 1828, and graduated A. B. (1848) and A. M. (1851) from Georgetown College, District of Columbia.

After receiving his medical degree from Columbian College, District of Columbia, in 1851, he immediately began to practice, and in 1859 succeeded his father in the chair of materia medica, therapeutics and pharmacy in the National Medical College, District of Columbia, continuing to lecture without interruption until within a short time of his death. His text-book on materia medica and therapeutics, with deserved reputation for its conciseness and suitability to the needs of the students, was translated into Japanese (Tokio, 1872). He was popular as a lecturer, and his great familiarity with his subject made his lessons of value and interest to his hearers. For many years he was dean of the faculty; he was a member of the Medical Society and Medical Association of the District of Columbia, and on the Committee to revise the Pharmacopœia of the United States, of which latter he was secretary. He was consulting physician to Providence Hospital, to the Central Free Dispensary and the Washington Eye and Ear Infirmary. His "Compendium of Materia Medica and Therapeutics," Philadelphia, 1869, was translated into Japanese at Tokio in 1872.

Assiduous devotion to duty may no doubt be accepted as one of the causes of his death. Uremic coma and convulsions from Bright's Disease were the final symptoms. He was much esteemed as a useful citizen and had many personal friends when he died on February 22, 1879.   D. S. L.

Minutes of Medical Society, D. C., February 24, 1879. Atkinson's Physicians and Surgeons, 1878: National Medical Review, February, 1879. Appleton's Biog., 1889, v, Transactions, American Medical Association. 1879.

Ring, Charles Augustus (1854–1907).

Charles Augustus Ring, the son of Oren and Elizabeth Sewell Ring, was born in Portland, Maine, February 16, 1854, the eldest of three sons, all of whom became physicians. While a mere lad of sixteen, he enlisted for the Civil War as a drummer boy with the Twenty-fifth Maine Regiment, but was stricken with typhoid fever and soon returned. He entered Bowdoin College and graduated with the class of 1868. Being too young to study medicine then, he worked with the Coast Survey and after a year first became a medical student, and graduated from the Medical School of Maine in 1872. Taking additional courses later he also got a degree from the Columbia Medical College in 1873. He was soon chosen to be lecturer of chemistry and afterwards of obstetrics in the Portland School for Medical Instruction, and finally professor on obstetrics in the Medical School of Maine. He was also distinguished for his fine work as visiting physician to the Maine General Hospital. Resigning from his position owing to his poor health, the directors appointed him obstetrician of the hospital as a proof of his demonstrated skill in this branch of medicine. A very modest man; once in his life he spent much time in equipping himself as a dermatologist but never took the least trouble to inform the profession of his intentions, or to advertise his mastery of that speciality.

Charles Augustus Ring was more of a personality as a physician than as a literary light in medicine. He did not often talk at the debates of the Maine Medical Association of which he was long a useful member, he did not write many papers, but those for the Association as well as for the Portland Clinical Society were unique from a diagnostic point of view. As a teacher he was straightforward, clear and distinct in his remarks and as an obstetrician won great renown.

He married, December 31, 1844, Elizabeth Miller Collier, of Cincinnati, Ohio, but left no children.

About a year before his death, Ring developed the first symptoms of Bright's disease, which carried him slowly to the grave. He suffered greatly at the last, but bore his illness patiently. His sight also became affected from intercurrent degeneration of the retina, and towards the end of his life he could hardly distinguish light from darkness. The faces of those who were dear to him were lost to his view.

He died suddenly July 8, 1903, leaving the memory of a charming and interesting man.   J. A. S.

Trans. Maine Med. Assoc , 1904, xv (port)
F. H G.

Rives, Landon Cabell (1790–1870).

Landon Cabell Rives was born in Nelson County, Virginia, October 24, 1790; the son of Landon C. Rives, and graduated from William and Mary College, Virginia, receiving his M. D. from the University of Pennsylvania in 1821. After graduation he practised in his native State until 1829, when he went to Cincinnati, Ohio, and, until 1860, had a large practice. At this time he retired from active practice.

In May, 1835, when the medical department of Cincinnati College was founded, he was made professor of obstetrics and diseases of women and children. In 1849 Dr. Rives was elected professor of materia medica in the Medical College of Ohio, and in 1850 was transferred to the chair of obstetrics. In 1854 he resigned the professorship. In this year he edited John Lizar's "Anatomy of the Brain."

During the last ten years of his life he rested from active professional work. He was never married. He died in Cincinnati, June 3, 1870. A. G. D.

Trans. Ohio State Med. Soc., 1870. (E. B. Stevent.)

Roberts, William Currie (1810-1873)

William Currie Roberts was born in London, England, in 1810. When about ten years old he was brought to this country, where liberal and democratic ideas were so readily engrafted upon his nature that but few knew he was of foreign birth. He did not have the advantage of a collegiate education, but great attention was given to his mental training and in 1828 he began to study medicine with the distinguished surgeon, Valentine Mott. During the years 1828, 1829, 1830, he attended medical lectures at the Geneva Medical College, Medical Department of Rutgers' University; during the winter of 1830-31 at Philadelphia, and graduated at the college of Physicians and Surgeons, New York, in 1832. The same year he married Matilda. daughter of Martin Hoffman, of New York, who died after seven years, leaving him two sons and a daughter, but the latter died at the age of eleven.

In 1835, in conjunction with several of his medical friends, he founded the New York Infirmary for the Diseases of Women and Children, doubtless the first special institute of its character estab-

lished in New York; but, after a brief though useful existence, its doors were finally closed on account of lack of funds.

In 1839 he served as physician at West Point; in 1844 physician to the Northern Dispensary, having charge of the department of "Diseases of Women and Children and Nervous Disorders." In 1841, for about a year, he edited the "New York Medical Gazette," and in this are to be found two of his papers: "Contributions to the Literary History and Pathology of Cholera Infantum" and "Thymic Enlargement." In 1846 he started the "Annalist," a journal which he continued to edit until 1848. His other literary efforts were the editing of four or five numbers of "Wood's Addenda to the Medico-Chirurgical Review," between July, 1847; and April, 1849, and, in 1834, in connection with Dr. James B. Kissam, he translated Bourgery's "Minor Surgery." In 1835 he translated the work of the Chev. J. Sarlandière, ex-surgeon French Army and of the Military Hospital of Paris, which is entitled, "Systematized Anatomy: or Human Organography, in Synoptical Tables, with Numerous Plates for the Use of Universities, Faculties, and Schools of Medicine and Surgery. Academies of Painting. Sculpture and of the Royal Colleges." This is a large folio volume, beautifully illustrated with fifteen folio plates. Dr. Roberts' first monograph, a popular essay on "Vaccination," appeared in 1835, signed, "A physician."

Roberts died in December, 1873, having suffered for about a year from an organic affection of the heart.

Medical Register N. Y, N. J., and Conn., 1874, xii
Memoir of William C. Roberts, 1874 (G. M Smith).

Robertson, Dr. Andrew (1716-1795).

This army surgeon was born in Scotland in 1716, and graduated from the University of Edinburgh, entering the British Army as a surgeon and serving three years in Flanders, and being present at the battle of Fontenoy in 1745.

Ten years later he came with his regiment to America and went on the disastrous expedition against Fort Du Quesne. He escaped the carnage of Braddock's defeat with twenty men, who made their way, subsisting on acorns alone, to Dunbar's camp, to which the remnant of the Army under Col. Washington had retreated.

Soon after his return he resigned his commission and emigrated with his wife and child to Virginia. He landed at Indian Banks in Richmond County, where he was entertained by a wealthy Scotch merchant, Mr. Glasscock. He prescribed, at the request of her father, for Mr. Glasscock's little daughter, who was then sick with measles, and it is said that this his first patient became his fourth wife in 1771.

Dr. Robertson settled in Lancaster County and for many years enjoyed an extensive practice, acquiring a high reputation. In addition to fame he also acquired wealth, and was specially noted for his charity and attention to the indigent sick. He continued in active practice to the day of his death, which occurred on March 1, 1795.

He made several contributions to medical literature, and some of his articles were published in the "Medical Inquires and Observations," London.

R. M. S.

Robertson, Charles Archibald (1829–1880).

Charles Archibald Robertson was born in Mobile, Alabama, on the fifteenth of October, 1829, being the son of Archibald T. Robertson, of New London, Connecticut, and Sarah Carnico, of Beverly, Massachusetts. His father was of Scotch, his mother of French and English descent.

He studied at the Beverly Academy and Phillips' Exeter Academy, at Exeter, New Hampshire, entering Harvard College in 1846, from which he graduated in 1850. He began his medical studies at the Tremont Street Medical School, and was a special student of diseases of the chest, under Dr. Henry I. Bowditch, when he also took up studies in skin diseases, under Dr. Silas M. Durkee.

He attended lectures at and received his diploma from the Jefferson Medical College, Philadelphia. Returning to Boston, he studied diseases of the eye and ear at the Perkins Institution and Boston Eye and Ear Infirmary, which studies were also pursued at Wills' Hospital in Philadelphia. The next year and a half were spent in Europe for professional study and general travel; four months he was under the instructions of the noted aurist of St. Mark's Hospital in Dublin— Sir William R. Wilde. At Paris he devoted himself to the teachings of Desmarres and Sichel, giving his time and studies to the clinics of these great masters.

Robertson, on his return to this country, began practice with a preparation which is the fortune of few. The department which he selected was the diseases of the eye and ear, commencing at Boston in 1855, and soon after removing to the State of New York.

In 1861 he joined the medical staff of the Army, and was appointed surgeon of the One Hundred and Fifty-ninth Regiment of New York volunteers. He served with distinction in that regiment until 1863, being for a portion of the time division-surgeon in Gen. Grover's Division, at Port Hudson. Owing to ill health he resigned and returned north to resume practice in 1863, settling temporarily at Poughkeepsie, then removing to Albany, where he remained in practice till the time of his death, being the first regular oculist located in this section of the State. He was surgeon in charge of the department of diseases of the eye and ear at St. Peter's Hospital, and ophthalmic and aural surgeon of the Albany Hospital. For years he was attending oculist at the Troy Hospital, and afterwards surgeon-in-chief of the Eye and Ear Relief.

He held ever a leading place among American oculists, and was one of the founders of the American Ophthalmological Society; was a member of the International Ophthalmological Society, also of the American Otological Society; the Medical Society of the State of New York, and president of the Medical Society of the County of Albany. His literary taste was marked and his style clear, vigorous and incisive. His method of thought was simple and direct and moved with independence. His medical writings consist of reports of cases and monographs:

"The Importance of Examining the Dioptric Media in Some Pathological Affections of the Eye," February, 1865.

"Glaucoma and its Cure by Iridectomy," Translated from the French, November, 1866.

"Some Curious Reflex Phenomena after Injuries of the Eye," July, 1870.

"Violent Rupture of Superior Rectus Oculi." "Section and Advancement of Internal Rectus Oculi," 1873.

"Remarkable Perturbation of the Olfactory Nerve following Extraction of Cataract," 1873.

"Diagnosis of Diseases of the Eye," 1874.

"An Eye Case in the Courts," 1874.

"Old Eyes made New, or Injury from Eye Cups," 1874.

"Pigmentation of Retina," 1877.

He died April 1, 1880, of chronic pleurisy, which had confined him to his house and bed for nearly a year. His death was not unexpected, although his remarkable vitality had so resisted disease that hope was not fully extinguished until near the last. His mind was unclouded and he gave his attention to all about him to the end. Dr. Robertson married Ellen A. Fuller, of Cambridge, Massachusetts, in 1853. J. S. M.

Med. Rec., N. Y., 1880, vol. xvii.
Tr. M. Soc. County Albany (1870-80), 1883, vol. iii (port.) (J. S. Mosher).
Tr. M. Soc., N. Y., Syracuse, 1881.

Robinson, William Chaffee (1822-1872).

William Chaffee Robinson was born in Charlton, Connecticut, November 27, 1822. Working hard as a boy, and as the result of the training of poverty, he developed great self-reliance, perseverance, and was powerfully ambitious to succeed. When almost a youth he was a teacher to others nearly all older than himself. At the age of twenty-three he studied medicine with Dr. John Ford, of Norwich, Connecticut, and graduated at the New York University Medical School in 1849. Being then at the age of twenty-seven, Robinson made the acquaintance of a musician in Portland, of the same family name, came to that city, established himself in a very promising locality, taking his chances with the other doctors.

He was then one of the seven physicians there but in the conservative East gaining a practice was slow, and Robinson had to wait long before he made enough for a living.

He obtained the position of City physician, which gave him an opportunity to ensure a large circle of political and influential friends for clients. In that position he had great success, gained in popularity, patronage and renown, and finally became one of the best and most beloved medical men.

After seven years he was able to marry and soon obtained all the practice to which he could possibly attend. In 1866 he was chosen lecturer in materia medica at the Medical School of Maine, and professor in 1868. Two years later he was chosen professor of obstetrics and diseases of women, serving till his death in that position.

In all of these positions he gained great local fame, and his numerous students carried away cheerful and instructive remembrances of his lectures. He was tall and handsome, shaved his upper lip, but wore a long beard and was famous for his witty remarks. He was an active member of the Maine Medical Association, and among his various papers contributed to its meetings may be mentioned "A Case of Lithotomy of a Child of Twelve," and another one on "Materia Medica."

Overwork in the year 1869 brought upon him an attack of paralysis, prostrating him for many months, yet he was finally able to resume practice. After another few months, however, gangrene of the left foot ensued, and the disease made constant progress despite amputation at the knee. With very remarkable fortitude he struggled on, conscious to the last day of his life, which was June 30, 1872. J. A. S.

Trans. Maine Med. Assoc.

Roby, Joseph (1807–1860).

A native of Wiscasset, Maine, he was born in the year 1807. Graduating at Brown University, Providence, Rhode Island, in 1828, he began to study medicine in Boston, under Drs. Jackson and Channing, distinguishing himself as an insatiable reader. He took his M. D. from Harvard University in 1831, and settled in Boston. Roby's happiest days were passed in his "den" at the college, and he lingered around this spot during the last years of his life, as if drawn thither by some fascination, while the deadly consumption was consuming his frail body, until a fatal hemorrhage cut short the slender thread of life on June 3, 1860. He was buried in Mt. Auburn Cemetery, at Boston.

Many important improvements were made during his connection with the Baltimore school, and largely through his efforts, as, the introduction of gas into the dissecting-room, compulsory dissection, and attendance upon clinics, and instruction in histology, pathology and the use of the microscope.

He held the professorship of anatomy and surgery at Bowdoin College, Maine, 1837; of materia medica and anatomy, Dartmouth College, New Hampshire, 1840; of anatomy and physiology, University of Maryland, 1842.

He left a widow and children when he died in 1860. E. F. C.

The Library and Hist. Jour., Brooklyn, 1906
Boston Daily Advertizer, June 7, 1860.

Rockwell, William H. (1800–1873).

William H. Rockwell, alienist, was born February 15, 1800, graduating from Yale College in 1824 and from the medical side of the same in 1830. Soon after, he was made assistant physician to the Retreat at Hartford, Connecticut, and in 1836 superintendent of the Brattleboro Asylum, Vermont. This place had then no money for the erection of buildings, and during Rockwell's administration, largely through his efforts, nearly $200,000 was actually earned and put to this use. His whole medical life was devoted to the most unselfish care of the insane. He died at Brattleboro, Nov. 30, 1873, after having been confined to bed from a fracture of the thigh caused by a fall from a carriage eighteen months previously.

Am J. of Insanity, 1877–78, xxxiv.
Tr. Ver. M. Soc , 1874–6, St. Albans, 1877.
Boston M. and S. J., 1873, lxxxix.

Rodgers, John Kearny (1793–1851).

The eldest son of a physician of Scotch descent, John Kearny Rodgers was born in the City of New York in 1793, and fortunately has a good and kindly biographer in Dr. S. D. Gross, from whom I quote freely.

When Rodgers was a Princeton student under Dr. Stanhope Smith (with whom he was not a favorite) the latter one day told him in a fit of anger that if he did not mend his ways he might as well shut up his books for he could never become useful or distinguished, judging from his present behavior. To this the future surgeon promptly replied "The world shall see, Sir," and indeed the world did see. His ambition was stimulated, his dormant energies roused. His early studies were under Dr. Wright Post, professor of anatomy in the College of Physicians and Surgeons, New York, from which place in 1816 Rodgers graduated, yet even before that, acted as demonstrator of anatomy for his master. After serving as house surgeon to the New York Hospital he went to London to study and became much interested in ophthalmic surgery and very soon after his return established with his friend, Dr. Edward Delafield, and others, the New York Eye Infirmary. In 1818 he was appointed demonstrator of anatomy in the College of Physicians and Surgeons, New York, and four years after, surgeon to the New York Hospital, an office he had much coveted and which he retained up to his death. As an operator his crowning triumph was the ligation, in 1845, of the left subclavian artery on the inside of the scalene muscle on account of a huge aneurysm, a feat which up to that time was universally regarded as impracticable. True, the patient did not recover, but the operation was masterly and nothing left undone to insure favorable results. Conscientious in dealing with his patients, he never operated merely for the sake of operating. In consultations he was the wise counsellor and always a sympathizing and trusted friend and physician.

His death, in 1851, was caused by a rare disease, phlebitis of the liver, followed by peritonitis. It is to be regretted that he left no record of his vast experience save the publication of a few brief medical papers.

He has one or two papers, among them is:

"Ligature of the Left Subclavian Artery within the Scalenus Muscle for Aneurysm," 1846.   D. W.

Autobiography of S D Gross
Biog. Sketch of J. K. Rodgers, Dr. E. Delafield, N. Y., 1852.
N. Jersey Med. Reporter, 1851, vol. v.

Rogers, Coleman (1781–1853).

Coleman Rogers was born March 6, 1781, in Culpepper County, Virginia. In 1787 his father emigrated to Kentucky, and settled in Fayette County, at a place known as Bryant's Station, about five miles from Lexington. Coleman Rogers was the seventh among eleven sons and one daughter. Although six feet two inches in height and weighing usually one hundred and eighty pounds, he was one of the smallest of the family, and in early life suffered from bronchial trouble.

But little is known of his history prior to his twenty-first year, but it is probable he only went to the local schools. At the age of twenty-one he began to study medicine with Dr. Samuel Brown, of Lexington. In 1803 he went to Philadelphia (making the journey on horseback in twenty-three days) where he remained eighteen months for lectures at the University of Pennsylvania. While there he was the private pupil of Dr. Charles Caldwell. Although qualified, poverty prevented his graduating before leaving Philadelphia. On his return to Kentucky he settled in Danville, and formed a partnership with Dr. Ephraim McDowell. On the third of November, 1805, he was married to Jane Farrar, and in 1810 returned to Fayette County, where he remained until 1816, when he again went to Philadelphia and eventually received an honorary M. D. While there he was offered the position of adjunct professor of anatomy in the medical department of Transylvania University; this he declined. In 1818 he removed to Cincinnati, Ohio, where he became associated with Dr. Daniel Drake in practice, and was a colleague of Drake in the Medical College of Ohio, and one of the original incorporators of that institution. He was vice-president and professor of surgery at its organization. In 1821 he removed to Newport, Kentucky, then a village opposite Cincinnati; settling finally, 1823, in Louisville, Kentucky, where he remained. He was for ten years surgeon to the Marine Hospital in Louisville.

In 1832, in connection with Drs. Harrison, Powell and A. G. Smith, he organized the Louisville Medical Institute and was appointed professor of anatomy. For more than fifty years he was in active and successful practice.

He died February 16, 1855, aged seventy-four years.   A. G. D.

Address on Coleman Rogers, M D, 1855. (H. M Bullitt)

Rogers, Henry Raymond (1822–1901).

Henry Raymond Rogers, one of Dunkirk's most prominent citizens and the oldest physician in Chatauqua County, New York, was born in Winslow, Maine, in 1822, and was a graduate of the Jefferson College in Philadelphia. He became distinguished for his scientific investigations, and his original views of matter and the laws which govern it attracted the attention of scientific men. His theory was that all physical phenomena, without exception, are transformations of electrical energy. His articles on astronomy and physics had a wide circulation both in the United States and Europe and provoked much discussion. He was a member of the Chatauqua County Historical Society and the American Association for the Advancement of Science. For some years before his death, however, he left off his practising in order to devote all his time to literary work. He wrote among other papers: "New and Original Theories of the Great Physical Forces." 1878.

"Cholera, Its Nature and Cure," published, 1903.

He died at his home in Dunkirk in 1901 after a short illness.

Med. News, 1901, vol. lxxix.
Brit. Med. Jour., 1901, ii.

Rogers, Joseph Goodwin (1841–1908).

Born in Madison, Indiana, November 23, 1841, he was the son of Dr. Joseph H. D. and Abby Goodwin Lane Rogers. His father was a giant in stature and of great force of character as befitted a pioneer physician in Indiana and Kentucky at an early day. His mother was a gentlewoman of refined and cultivated tastes. From his father he inherited a sturdy, forceful and strong character; from his mother refined tastes, high ideals and an artistic temperament. His education was largely derived from his mother as at the early age of eight he suffered from Pott's disease and for many years was confined to bed. He became a diligent student and an omnivorous reader of good books and was self-taught to a remarkable degree. When eighteen he began to study medicine under his father's dictation, later at the Cincinnati College of Medicine, and Bellevue Hospital Medical College, New York, from the latter receiving his M. D. in 1864. He served as a surgeon in a military hospital until the close of the Civil War, and then went abroad for two years of travel and study. He fitted himself to practice as an ophthalmologist and upon his return, entered upon a successful career at Madison. Indiana for many years.

In 1879 he was offered the superintendency of the Indiana Hospital for the insane at Indianapolis, which, after much hesitation and at great personal sacrifice he accepted as a duty owed to the public. For four years he devoted himself to the reorganization and development of the hospital and freed it from political and partisan interference. He proved to be too much in advance of public opinion and he retired with honor at last rather than to sacrifice his high ideals of right and duty.

His special fitness for hospital management, however, had been proved and in 1883 he was selected by the Governor of Indiana, and a newly appointed commission, medical engineer for the erection of three hospitals for the insane. He entered upon his duties with great enthusiasm and energy and at the end of five years had planned and erected the Northern Hospital at Logansport, the Eastern Hospital at Richmond, and the Southern Hospital at Evansville, Indiana three modern hospitals, fully abreast of the most advanced ideas of hospital construction. Singularly enough they were exponents of three distinct hospital types, the pavilion, the cottage and the radiate plans respectively, and stand to-day as monuments of his ability and versatility.

When he had completed his labors as medical engineer he was offered the choice of the superintendency of whichever one of the hospitals he might prefer. He chose the hospital at Logansport, and from May, 1888 until the day of his death continued in medical charge of it. Under his skilled direction the Northern Hospital, in physical economy, humane methods and medical care, reached the highest development. It rarely falls to the lot of any one man to plan and build a hospital and afterward to direct and develop it for a period of twenty years. He never rested from his labors and was devoted to his work body and soul. The hospital will bear the marks of his genius as builder and director in every part and department and his influence will be felt for many generations.

·Amid all his varied duties and lines of activity, he remained essentially a physician whose professional attainments were of the highest order and he ever kept abreast of the progress of general medicine and psychiatry.

His writings include a long list of reports, state papers and monographs, all of which were carefully prepared, thoroughly treated and adequately expressed in Classic English. In 1885 he received the honorary degree of Doctor of Philosophy from Hanover College. In 1900 he was president of the American Medico-Psychological Association at the Richmond meeting and delivered an illuminating address on " Hospital Construetion." For four years he filled the chair of materia medica and therapeutics at the Indiana Medical College at Indianapolis.

In June 1872, he married Margaret Watson of Bedford, Pa, who with three daughters and two sons survived him. His home life was perfect and in it as husband and parent he found the greatest happiness of his life.

He died April 11, 1908 of nephritic disease after a long illness at the Northern Indiana Hospital, Logansport.

H. M. H.

Condensed from a sketch by Dr. E. F. Muth in Am. Journal of Insanity.

Rogers, Lewis (1812–1875).

Lewis Rogers was born in Fayette County near Lexington, Kentucky, October 22, 1812, the son of Joseph and Anne Early Rogers, and David W. Yandell called Lewis "the most practical of all scientific teachers, the most scientific of all practical teachers" he had known.

He had his B. A. from Transylvania University in 1831 and in that year the same degree from Georgetown College. His M. D. was from the University of Pennsylvania in 1835. The Louisville Medical Institute was opened in 1836–7 and he became assistant to the chair of clinical medicine. In 1839 he married Mary Eliza Thurston and had seven children one of whom, Coleman, became a doctor.

He was also assistant to the chair of clinical medicine in Louisville Medical Institute, 1836–1849; professor of medicine and therapeutics, medical department of University of Louisville (former Medical Institute), 1849–1856–7; professor of theory and practice of medicine, medical department, University of Louisville, 1857–1867; professor of theory and practice of medicine, made vacant by the resignation of Dr. Austin Flint, 1856. The term of 1867–68 he again occupied the chair of materia medica and therapeutics; but resigned at its close on account of an iritis that had troubled him for some time. This iritis finally necessitated iridectomy, which was performed by Dr. Agnew.

His writings included:

"Introductory Lecture before the Medical Class of the University of Louisville," delivered November 4, 1850, Louisville, 1850.

"Facts and Reminiscences of the Medical History of Kentucky" (an address before the Kentucky State Medical Society), Louisville, 1873.

"Climate in Pulmonary Consumption, and California as a Health Resort," 16 pp., 8°, Louisville, 1874.

Lewis Rogers was about six feet two inches tall, but of spare build. He was brilliant, humerons, practical and scientific, a shrug of his shoulder often expressed more than a sentence. His painstaking observation and logical reasoning qualified him for the accurate diagnosing for which he was noted.

His final illness was a malignant disease of the liver; first diagnosed by himself on account of certain nodules that appeared on the ribs. He died the seventeenth day of June, 1875.

Yandell quoted "He left an armor none can wear." His portrait is in the possession of his daughter, Mrs. George Gaulbert, of Louisville.

R. A. B.

See "A Discourse on the Life and Character of Dr. Lewis Rogers." by David W. Yandell, Amer. Pract., Louisville, 1875, xii.

Rohé, George Henry (1851–1899).

His parents, John and Mary Fuchs Rohé were natives of Bohemia of humble origin and their son was born in Baltimore on the twenty-sixth of January, 1851, and educated in the public schools, afterwards studying medicine with Dr. F. Erich and taking his M. D. at the University of Maryland in 1873. For some years after he was connected with the United States Signal Service, but while in Boston studied dermatology under Dr. E. Wrigglesworth, and after leaving the Signal Service became assistant to Dr. Erich, professor of gynecology in the College of Physicians and Surgeons and was also appointed lecturer on dermatology. Appointments followed quickly: the professorship of obstetrics; of therapeutics and mental diseases; superintendent of Springrove Hospital for the Insane; and the same of an asylum which he organized at Sykesville, Maryland.

For a year prior to his death he had symptoms of cardiac trouble and his death came very suddenly on February 6, 1899, while he was attending the National Prison Congress at New Orleans.

He contributed largely to dermatology but his work culminated in the field of psychiatry, and he began the great work of planning a hospital for mental diseases upon the most advanced ideas.

Dr. Rohé's contributions to medical literature were numerous and useful: The most important were his "Textbook of Hygiene," first edition, 1885, third edition, 1894; "Practical Manual of Skin Diseases," 1885–86, and (with Lord) 1892; "Electricity in Practical Medicine and Surgery" (joint author with Liebig), 1890; in addition to these, he was associate editor of the "Independent Practitioner," 1882, and of the "Annual of Universal Medical Science," 1890, and editor of the "Medical Chronicle," 1882–85. Among other offices he was president of American Association of Obstetricians and Gynecologists, 1893–94; president of Medical and Chirurgical Faculty of Maryland, 1893–94; president of Maryland and American Public Health Associations, 1898–99. The honorary degree of A. M. was conferred upon him by Loyola College, Baltimore.

Dr. Rohé possessed a phenomenal memory accompanied by great readiness in applying his knowledge. He was a most industrious reader and acquired a knowledge of several languages. His self-confidence was unbounded and there was no position or duty which he did not consider himself competent to fill. He left a wife, Mary Landeman, and one child, a daughter.

E. F. C.

Journal of Alumni Assoc Coll Phys and Surg , vol ii, No. 1, for Sketch and Portrait; see Idem, vol iv, No 1.
"Robé as Man and Friend," by Prof. Wm Simon.
Cordell's Medical Annals of Maryland, 1903

Romayne, Nickolaus (1756–1817).

The fact that Nickolaus Romayne is described as "often unpopular with the profession" makes one imagine what was really the case, that the said Nickolaus "was a man of very strong intellectuality and vigorous personality." The biographical materials are but scanty; he was born in the City of New York, September, 1756, and had his early education at Hackensack in New Jersey. At the beginning of the Revolutionary War he went abroad and finished his medical studies in Edinburgh, afterwards spending two years in Paris, London and Leyden. "His return from Europe" says Dr. Mitchell, "excited considerable conversation both here and in Philadelphia; he was reported to have improved his opportunities with singular diligence. In London and Edinburgh he went through the course of study required by the university statutes and published a dissertation in Latin on 'De Generatione Puris' which he composed himself 'without the aid of a "grinder," or hired translator.'" Then Thacher goes on to say that when Romayne was appointed trustee of the new medical board formed after the war he found an opening for his talents as teacher, and "his superior attainments in literature and medicine elevated him with high notions and filled him with contemptuous ones of some who had been less fortunate in education."

The first post-bellum faculty of professors did not do much. Romayne had resigned and practised as a private teacher. Anatomy, practice of physic, chemistry and botany were all taught by this extraordinary man with such success that he drew hearers even from Canada. Then he goes to Europe again to get in touch with everything new and is admitted a licentiate of the Royal College of Physicians of Edinburgh, the first American to receive that honor.

There was not much for him to do when he went back, but in 1806 an act was passed for incorporating medical societies. "By a sudden and singular change of sentiment Dr. Romayne was called from his retirement and elected first president of the Medical Society of New York, and next year delegate to the State Medical Society in Albany, afterwards being chosen president. He was in his element planning many reforms, and when the regents of the university were to act under the provisions of the Act for providing a College of Physicians and Surgeons, though Romayne was assisted by numerous and powerful supporters he may be considered as the leading agent and the person without whose urgency the work would not have been completed. He was rewarded by being selected, in 1807, as the first president.

Romayne would have been, says one who knew him well, the most eminent medical man in New York, but he indulged in speculating and became involved in embarrassments detrimental to his profession.

He died in New York, July 20, 1817.

D. W.

Amer. Med. Biog., Thacher, Boston. 1828.
Hist. of Med., S. Wickes, Newark, 1879.
Address on Med , J. Shrady, N. Y., 1888

Roosa, Daniel .Bennet St. John (1838–1908).

Daniel Bennet St. John Roosa was born at Bethel, New York, April 4, 1838. He studied at Yale and under John W. Draper and graduated in medicine at the University of the City of New York in 1860, afterwards for a term serving in the New York Hospital, and in 1861 as assistant surgeon of the Fifth Regiment National Guard in the field.

Subsequently he studied ophthalmology and otology in Berlin and Vienna, but returned to America in 1863 and served as surgeon in the Twelfth Regiment National Guard of New York. In the fall of the same year (1863) he entered upon general practice, but within a couple of years devoted himself exclusively to ophthalmology and otology. He was professor of these branches in the University of the City of New York from 1866 to 1882, and from 1875 to 1880 in the University of Vermont, and later in the New York Post-graduate School, which he helped to found and of which he was president; one of the founders of the Manhattan Eye and Ear Hospital, and for many years surgeon there. He was also a member of the American Ophthalmological and American Otological Societies, and president of the International Otological Society. In 1864 he translated von Troeltsch's text-book on "Diseases of the Ear," and in 1869 appeared his own treatise on the subject. He likewise translated Stellwag's "Treatise on the Eye," and was a very voluminous contributor to periodic literature. He held the honorary M. A. from Yale and the honorary LL. D. from the University of Vermont.

Of sturdy, dominant personality, full, sonorous voice, and forceful expression.

he made himself felt in all affairs in which he took part.

He died on March 8, 1908, in New York City.

H. F.

A tolerably full list of his writings is in the Cat. of Surg.-gen., Wash., D. C. Stone's Biography of Eminent American Physicians and Surgeons. Trans. Am. Otol. Soc., vol. xi, Part i.

Ross, George (1845–1892).

He was born in Montreal, March 11, 1845, the second son of Arthur Ross, Seigneur of Beau Rivage, who was son of David Ross, King's Counsellor.

He was vice-dean and professor of medicine in the medical faculty of McGill University from 1889 to 1891, professor of clinical medicine from 1872 till 1889, and professor of hygiene from 1871 till 1873. In 1862 he began the study of medicine at McGill, having previously graduated in Arts with honors and the Chapman gold medal. In 1866 he graduated in medicine, and won the Holmes gold medal for general proficiency. His connection with the Montreal General Hospital began in 1866, when he was appointed apothecary. Among other places to which he was elected were those of president of the Medico-Chirurgical Society of Montreal; of the Canadian Medical Association; vice-president of the American Association of Physicians, and governor of the College of Physicians and Surgeons of Quebec. He died, unmarried, in November, 1892.

George Ross was an authoritative teacher, a wise clinician with a keen instinct for diagnosis, and implicit confidence in his judgment once it was formed. He had skill and experience, literary taste and niceness of expression, and courtesy for all.

Dr. Ross wrote extensively upon aneurysm. He was co-editor of the "The Medical and Surgical Journal," Montreal, and "The Medical Journal," Montreal. A. M.

Montreal, M. J., 1892–3, xxi. Med. News, Phila., 1892, lxi.

Ross, Joseph Presley (1828–1890).

Joseph Presley Ross, founder of the Presbyterian Hospital in Chicago, was born in Ohio, 1828, and after school and a short experience in business he worked under Dr. G. V. Dorsey, and graduated in medicine at the Ohio Medical College, Cincinnati, in 1853. His appointments included: physician to the City Hospital and professor of clinical medicine and diseases of the chest, Rush Medical College. When the great fire of 1871 utterly destroyed the latter his energy in getting plans and funds for a new college and hospital was the main factor in their re-erection. Yet he felt the city hospital accommodation was not sufficient.

Especially was this true of private hospitals for a better class of patient than the paupers housed in the County Hospital. He resolved that his own religious denomination should possess a hospital like those already maintained by the Presbyterians in the older cities of this country. He secured a donation of $10,000 from his father-in-law, Tuthill King; another, of $15,000, from the faculty of Rush Medical College, to which he afterwards added $5,000 dollars from his own pocket. At last, largely through the influence of Dr. Hamill, a legacy of $100,000 from the estate of Daniel Jones insured the completion of the edifice. After a prolonged illness he died on the fifteenth day of June, 1890.

Early Medical Chicago, J. N. Hyde.

Rosse, Irving Collins (1847–1901).

Irving Collins Rosse, alienist, author, and medical jurisprudentist, was born at East New Market, Dorchester County, East Shore, Maryland, October 2, 1847, of Anglo-Scotch descent.

He attended St. John's College, Annapolis, for three years, then West Point Military Academy for one. Turning his attention to medicine, he left the Academy, and studied for a time with Dr. Alexander H. Bayley, of Cambridge, taking his medical degree in 1866 from the University of Maryland.

For a time he studied in London,

Berlin, and Paris, and received an honorary A. M., in later life, from Georgetown University, and a rather large number of honorary degrees from various institutions in Europe.

His life as a doctor began with his entry into the position of clinical assistant in the Baltimore Infirmary, where he served with marked distinction, but resigned to enter the United States Army wherein as army surgeon he lived at various posts throughout the west and south. Once he was quarantine officer for Georgia, and in this capacity was present on Tybee Island during the outbreak of cholera there. A little later he was appointed quarantine officer at Brazos, Santiago, Texas, and also saw much service on the staff of Gen. Henry Hunt, in North Carolina, during the troubles with the Ku Klux Klan.

Rosse was at one time professor of nervous and mental diseases in the Georgetown University. He was also vice-president of the Medico-legal Society of New York, and a member of numerous social, literary, and scientific clubs and associations.

He married, when forty-seven years of age, Florence James, of New York, a granddaughter of Gen. Worth, and had one child, a son.

Dr. Rosse died of ptomaine poisoning at Washington, District of Columbia, May 3, 1901.

Dr. Rosse was an extensive writer, and his literary work was valuable both for its contents and its form. He assisted in the preparation of the "Medico-Surgical History of the Rebellion." Later, he had in charge the force which compiled the "Index-Catalogue of the Surgeon-general's Library," doing much personal work on the latter. He wrote voluminously, too, as correspondent for the "New York Herald" and the "San Francisco Examiner," and contributed numerous scientific articles to the press of this and of various foreign countries. He was one of the crew on the famous ship Corwin, which sailed in 1881 to the relief of the Jeanette. While on this cruise he ascended the supposedly inaccessible Herald Island, and was the first human being in history to set foot on Wrangle Island. For these and other exploits he was created a fellow of the Royal Geographical Society of England. On his return he wrote two books: "The Cruise of the Corwin" and "The First Landing on Wrangle Island." One of the most remarkable of Dr. Rosse's writings is an article on "Personal Identity," contributed to volume i, of Witthaus and Becker's "Medical Jurisprudence, Forensic Medicine, and Toxicology." This article displays the widest range of scholarship combined with profound and original research. As he was interested greatly in lego-medical matters, he wrote very much on this topic. No list of all, or even the most, of his writings, could possibly be given within the bounds of this sketch.

He was a great athlete and once, when crossing the Atlantic, persuaded the captain of the steamer to stop the vessel while he took a plunge in the ocean. On another occasion, when quarantined in a small boat for a number of days, with only a single companion, he used, to relieve the tedium, to stand upon his hands. He had very little to say to those who did not interest him, but was affable and communicative in the presence of those whose tastes were similar to his own. He did not like animals, and was not fond of children. He loved books, but did not collect, or keep, them. He used to say he had his library in his head, and, certainly, whatever he read he stored in his mind most carefully. He delved but little in other fields than the scientific, but, in that realm of never-ending spaces, his range was wide indeed. In the field of mental and nervous diseases, and in the field of medical jurisprudence, and in the field of geographical exploration, and, most of all perhaps, in the field of editing and general authorship, Dr. Rosse's work possesses much of a high and enduring value.

Some of his other articles were: "Reversive Anomalies in the Studies of the

Neuroses," 1888; " Borderland Insanity;" Neuropathic States Involving Doubt," 1890; "The Neuroses from a Demographic Point of View;" "Washington Malaria and Politics as Genetic Factors," 1889; "Triple Personality;" "Sexual Hypochondriasis and Perversion of Genesic Instinct," 1892. T. H. S.

Atkinson's "A Biographical Dictionary of Contemporary American Physicians and Surgeons," Philadelphia, 1880, Supplement. Stone's "Biography of Eminent American Physicians and Surgeons," Indianapolis, 1894 Minutes of Med Soc , D C , 1901 Tr. Med Soc , D C , 1901, vol vi

De Rosset.

This family furnished North Carolina with six members of the medical profession, all living for the most part in the City of Wilmington, and descendants of Armand De Rosset (1695–1760), M. D., University of Basel, who emigrated with his wife and three children before 1735.

Of these there were three who distinguished themselves as physicians.

De Rosset, Armand John, the elder (1767–1859), graduated from Princeton, then the college of New Jersey, in 1785 and received his medical degree in 1790 from the University of Pennsylvania. He was a pupil and a great friend of Benjamin Rush; there is preserved an interesting correspondence between them. Dr. De Rosset entered on an extensive practice in Wilmington and kept in active service for sixty-nine years. His reputation extended over the south. His last work was attending a woman of sixty-one years in confinement. For many years he was port physician of Wilmington.

De Rosset, Moses John, the younger (1796–1826), had his academic degree from the University of North Carolina in 1816 and his medical diploma from the New York (?) Medical College in 1820. He practised medicine in co-partnership with his father. In the yellow-fever epidemic of 1821 he was particularly active and skillful. Though he practised but six years before his untimely end, he left a splendid reputation.

De Rosset, Moses John (1838–1881), who lived in more modern times, was born in Pittsboro, North Carolina, July 4, 1838. His early schooling was in the city of Geneva, Switzerland, in Diedrich's Academy. After three years he spent six months in Cologne and returned from Europe in 1857, having chosen medicine as his profession. At the age of twenty-one he received his M. D. from the University of New York (1859). He was resident physician in Bellevue Hospital until the Civil War broke out, when he became assistant surgeon in the Confederate Army. After the war he settled in Baltimore where he was appointed adjunct to the professor of chemistry in the University of Maryland and professor of chemistry in the Dental School. In 1873 he removed to North Carolina to practice in diseases of the eye and ear, but in a few years went to New York, where he lived until just before his death in 1881. Dr. De Rosset was a remarkable student, possessing a retentive memory and high intellectual talents. He was a voluminous writer. He translated Bouchardat's "Annuaire" (1867) and contributed freely to journals. His last paper appeared in the "American Journal of the Medical Sciences," October, 1878, and was entitled "The Muscle of Accommodation and its Mode of Action." The other two were Moses John De Rosset (1726–1767) and Armand John De Rosset (1807–1897). H. A. R.

James Sprunt Historical Monograph No. 4, by K. P. Battle.
North Carolina Med. Jour., May, 1881.

Rothrock, Abram (1806–1894).

Abram Rothrock was born on April 19, 1806, in Derry Township, Mifflin County, Pennsylvania, in what was then a heavily wooded and wild part of the state. He was accustomed from his early childhood to the hard work of an outdoor life, being well acquainted not only with farm work, but also the duties in his father's tannery.

One winter's morning at three A. M., Dr. Edmund Burke Patterson, of Lewistown, was returning from a long call and noting the light in a farm house stopped in to warm himself. He found the young lad lying on the floor in front of the huge old fire place and studying by its light an English grammar. The doctor asked him if he understood it and receiving an affirmative, gave him a sentence to parse and being pleased with his ability to do so he questioned him further concerning his work.

The outcome was that he asked him to come and make his home with him in Lewistown and become his office boy. After a consultation with his parents the offer was accepted and he worked for the doctor and went to school. In 1826 he studied under Dr. Patterson remaining with him until his death, when he continued his medical work under Dr. James Culbertson. In the winter of 1828–29 he attended a course of lectures at the University of Pennsylvania and then, owing to a lack of the necessary funds, returned to Mifflin County. At this time the canal, which for many years served as the great artery of traffic till the railroad rendered it obsolete, was in process of construction and the young student served for a couple of years as a sort of contract surgeon for the workmen, earning in this way the money for the continuance of his medical education. He then re-entered the University of Pennsylvania and in 1835 graduated and started in on his life work in Mifflin County, settling down to a general practice in McVeytown where he continued almost to the day of his death, on September 9, 1894.

Two years after coming to McVeytown, in 1837, the doctor married Phoebe Brinton, daughter of Joseph and Jane Trimble, of Concord, Delaware County, Pennsylvania, and had three children, two daughters, Ann Amanda and Mary, and one son, Dr. Joseph Trimble Rothrock, who rendered great service, not only in medical but also in scientific work.

Dr. Rothrock was in the habit of sending his cases of incipient tuberculosis to the "Coalings," as the coal hearths were called, where the charcoal was burned. Anyone who has seen the most primitive of cabins occupied by the charcoal burners, can readily see that it must have been the life in the open air far more than the smoke of the smoldering charcoal that effected the cure. Built either round or square at their base and with the roof running to a single point, like an Indian wigwam, they were constructed of a layer of logs covered over with leaves and dirt as a thatch with one side left open for the huge stone fireplace and with a door resting up against another side. Within, a crude platform served as bed; table and chairs, windows there were none and the only other articles of furniture were the cooking utensils and the tools of the occupants. An excellent shelter they made for snakes, too, and the custom of the wood choppers was to leave a toad in the cabin when they left. If on their return the little tenant was at home it was a good sign, but if he was not to be seen a careful search was next in order to get rid of the snake that had killed it. It can readily be seen that patients sent to such sanatoria were apt to take the fresh air cure most faithfully and many cures were the result, though they were in those days generally supposed to be due to some particular virtue of the smoke from the burning pits.

Of magnificent health and unusual muscular strength, he worked with a persistance and energy that would have killed or broken down the average individual. And this life he continued to lead, until death called him as he was nearing his eighty-ninth year. A most devout member of his chosen church (the Presbyterian) it was remarkable to see how so busy a man found time to go there regularly.

He was a member of the State Medical Society, holding the position of first vice-president of this latter organization in 1878.

A. M. R.

Row, Elhanon W. (1833–1900).

Elhanon W. Row, surgeon, was born in Orange County, Virginia, on November 8, 1833, and after a common school education, taught in a school in Alexandria, Virginia. He read medicine under Dr. David Pannill, of Orange County, then entered the University of Pennsylvania and graduated in 1858, settling in his native county.

At the beginning of the Civil War he joined the Orange Rangers as a private, but was soon commissioned surgeon of the Fourteenth Virginia Cavalry, which position he filled until the surrender at Appomattox. In 1883–84 he was a member of the State Legislature and did noble work in accomplishing the passage of the act creating the Medical Examining Board. In 1888, as the well earned reward for his work in the Legislature, he was elected president of the Medical Society of Virginia, and the following year was made an honorary member of the society.

Returning home after the war, he settled at his county-seat, where he continned to practise until his health failed. The writer was intimately acquainted with Dr. Row and can give testimony as to his real worth as a friend, a citizen and a physician.

He married about 1880, a Miss Newman of Orange County, and an only daughter survived him, his wife and two infant children dying some years before his own decease.

For the last two years of his life he was in failing health and unable to do much work. In May, 1900, his strength gave way entirely and on the twenty-third of that month, he rested from his labors.

He was not a writer; his only contributions to medical literature that we are aware of is his address as president of the State Society, entitled "Medical Reform," "Transactions of the Medical Society of Virginia," 1889, and a paper, "Case of Bowel Obstruction, Profound Shock, Death," ibid., 1899.

R. M. S.

Trans. Med. Soc. of Va., 1900.

Ruschenberger, William Samuel Waithman (1807–1895).

Ruschenberger was born on a farm near Bridgeton, New Jersey, September 4, 1807, educated in New York and Philadelphia and at the age of nineteen entered the United States Navy as surgeon's mate and was ordered to the Pacific Coast. But after a short stay he returned east and entered the medical department of the University of Pennsylvania, whence he graduated in 1830. In the following year he was commissioned surgeon in the navy. As surgeon he made a number of cruises to various parts of the world. Ruschenberger was an able writer. In 1834 he published "Three Years in the Pacific" and in 1838, 'A Voyage Around the World." These, books were widely read and were republished in England. In 1854 appeared "Notes and Commentaries During Voyages to Brazil and China." One of his best known works is "An Account of the Institution and Progress of the College of Physicians of Philadelphia During 100 Years," which appeared in 1887. His "First Books on Natural History," a series of eight small volumes, were very popular in their time and contributed more than any other work to popularize the natural sciences in this country.

Ruschenberger was a member of the American Philosophical Society, of the College of Physicians of Philadelphia, of the Academy of Natural Sciences of Philadelphia, and of a number of other societies. He died in Philadelphia, March 24, 1895. His portrait is preserved in the hall of the College of Physicians of Philadelphia.   A. A.

Tr. Coll. Physicans, Phila., 1896, xviii.
Proc. Am. Philos. Soc., Phila., 1895, xxxiv.

Rush, Benjamin (1745–1813).

The "American Sydenham," as he was termed by Lettsom, was born in Byberry Township, Philadelphia County, on December 24, 1745. His family were English Quakers, but, curiously enough, both his father and grandfather were gunsmiths. After going as a boy to the

WILLIAM S. W. RUSCHENBERGER.
(By permission of the Surgeon-General, Washington, D. C.)

academy kept by the Rev. Samuel Finley, later president of Princeton College, at Nottingham, he entered Princeton, where he received the degree B . A. in 1760. He spent the subsequent six years as an apprentice to Dr. John Redman, one of the most prominent physicians of Philadelphia, and during this time translated the "Aphorisms of Hippocrates" into English and kept a medical notebook from which was subsequently derived the only account written by an eyewitness, of the yellow-fever epidemic which occurred in 1762 in Philadelphia. He also was one of the ten pupils who attended the first course of lectures on anatomy given by Dr. William Shippen, Jr.

In 1766 he entered the medical school of Edinburgh University and took his M. D. there in 1768, his graduation thesis being called "De Coctione Ciborum in Ventriculo." Thacher says it was written in classic Latin, and adds quaintly "and I have reason to believe without the help of a grinder of theses." While he was at Edinburgh, Pres. Finley, of Princeton College, died, and the trustees elected the celebrated Dr. Witherspoon, of Paisley in Scotland, as his successor. The latter at first declined the appointment, but the trustees appointed young Rush as their deputy, and his solicitations at length prevailed on the eminent Scotchman to accept the position. From Edinburgh, Rush went to London and from thence to France to study, returning to Philadelphia in 1769. In the same year he was elected professor of chemistry in the college of Philadelphia, thereby rendering complete the medical faculty of the first medical school established in what is now the United States. The other teachers were John Morgan, William Shippen, Jr., and Adam Kuhn. Clinical lectures in association with their teaching were also given at the Pennsylvania Hospital by Dr. Thomas Bond.

Upon the death of Dr. John Morgan in 1789, Rush succeeded him as professor of the theory and practice of medicine in the College of Philadelphia. When, in 1791, that institution was merged with the University of the State of Pennsylvania to form the University of Pennsylvania, Dr. Rush was appointed professor of the institutes of medicine and clinical medicine. In addition to his public teaching Dr. Rush had a large number of private students, and it has been estimated that in the course of the forty-four years in which he was actively engaged in teaching he instructed 2,250 pupils. His lectures, judging from the notebook of his pupils and from the statements of those who heard them, were models of lucidity and comprehensiveness. He had the gift of imparting to his students some share of his own wonderful . enthusiasm and thirst for knowledge. The prevalent medical teaching of his day was that of Cullen. Diseases were classified and every disease was supposed to possess an appropriate specific treatment. Underlying principles were entirely disregarded in an effort to build up a purely artificial classification of diseases and their treatment. Rush attacked the prevalent theories of medicine at once. He proclaimed the importance of the principles upon which a correct knowledge of the practice of medicine could only be based. "In his public instructions, the name of the disease is comparatively nothing, but its nature everything. His system rejects the nosological arrangement of diseases, and places all their numerous forms in morbid excitement, induced by irritants, acting upon previous debility. It rejects, likewise, all prescriptions for the names of diseases, and by directing their application wholly to the forming and fluctuating state of diseases, and of the system, derives from a few active medicines all the advantages which have been in vain expected from the numerous articles which compose European treatises upon the materia medica. This simple arrangement was further simplified by considering every morbid state of the system to be of such as neither required depletion or stimulation."

The author of the above quotation then goes on to state in pathetic terms what an advantage this has given the students who have studied under Benjamin Rush over those who, like himself, had been obliged to learn by the old methods.

One marked peculiarity in Rush was his readiness to acknowledge an error and retract opinions proven erroneous by subsequent researches or events. One of his active and enquiring mind, continually employed in original researches and constantly by his writings and teaching endeavoring to advance medical science, was bound to err sometimes, and it redounds to his credit that when such mistakes were seen, he promptly acknowledged the fault.

His therapeutic standbys were the lancet and calomel. The latter he called Sampson, and his enemies in derision were wont to say " because it has slain its thousands." It was in the yellow fever of 1793 that Rush had the efficacy of these two therapeutic agents especially impressed upon him and the lesson he then learned as to their value he never allowed himself to disregard. He states that he and the other physicians of Philadelphia had been completely nonplussed in their efforts to find a method of treatment which seemed in any way to control the course of the disease. In this extremity he found among some papers in his library a manuscript which had been prescribed to him by Dr. Franklin years previously. It was an account of the yellow fever of 1741 in the Province of Virginia, written by a Dr. Mitchell. In it the latter put forth the strongest claims of the value of free purgation in the treatment of yellow fever, even where the disease was accompanied by an extreme degree of debility, and a very feeble pulse. Rush, upon reading Mitchell's manuscript, reasoned that the feeble pulse seen in so many cases was the result of debility from " an oppressed state of the system." He proceeded to immediately put his ideas into effect by administering enormous doses of calomel and jalop to all his patients. In addition to this he practised copious venesection, put the patient upon a low diet and used applications of cold water to the surface of the body, combined with the drinking of large quantities of water. He also advised that the temperature of the sickroom be low.

Rush hastened to impart his ideas to his fellow practitioners, and, indeed, to the public at large. The results achieved by his methods were certainly most gratifying. An oft-quoted statement is contained in his notebook for September 10. "Thank God! out of one hundred patients whom I have visited or prescribed for this day, I have lost none." He was overwhelmed with patients, and at length was himself taken ill and underwent a course of his own treatment. After his recovery he resumed his labors and remained at them until the epidemic was ended.

He shared the common fate of the famous in stirring up detractors. By his proclaiming his belief that the yellow fever was the result of filth in the streets of their city and not an importation, he caused the greatest anger among the citizens of Philadelphia. His most infamous assailant was William Cobbett, in his "Peter Porcupine's Gazette." Rush sued him for defamation of character, and, having won his suit, gave the $5,000 which the law awarded him to the poor. Another famous quarrel in which Rush was involved occurred in the yellow-fever epidemic of 1797. Rush again published and adhered to his views on the efficacy of bleeding and purgation and also to the claim that the disease arose from the filthy condition of certain parts of the city. The "United States Gazette" published a very severe article on Rush, which he supposed had been written by a Dr. Ross. John Rush, son of Benjamin, wrote a bitter reply to Dr. Ross and after some further interchange of literary hostilities proceeded to cane him. Dr. Ross challenged Dr. Benjamin Rush to a duel, as he declared him responsible for his son's actions. Rush refused the

Benjamin Rush.

challenge and published the whole correspondence in the newspapers. One result of the controversy over the yellow fever of 1797 was the founding of the "Academy of Medicine of Philadelphia" by the adherents of Dr. Rush. The latter resigned from the College of Physicians, but always protested that he bore no ill-will towards that body. Dr. Physick was the first president of the new society.

In 1783 Dr. Rush was elected physician to the Pennsylvania Hospital, a capacity in which he served until his death. During that time he never missed a daily visit and was never more than ten minutes late. Morton's "History of the Pennsylvania Hospital" contains a most interesting account of his many services to that institution, particularly the reforms and advanced methods advocated by him in the treatment of the insane.

Dr. Rush served in a number of important political and military capacities. He was a member of the Provincial Congress of 1776, and as such signed the Declaration of Independence. On April 11, 1777, he was appointed by Congress, surgeon-general of the middle department of the Continental Army. Of his military services but little information is ascertainable. He became involved in the Conway cabal, being an ardent partisan of Gates and Samuel Adams in their criticism of what they termed the Fabian policy of Washington. With the downfall of the cabal Rush realized that his prospects for advancement in the Army were shattered, and wisely retired to the field of professional activity in which he had occupied so prominent a position. One invaluable result of his military experience remains in his pamphlet entitled "Direction for Preserving the Health of Soldiers," which was published by order of the Board of War. It is an excellent exposition of the rules of military hygiene and camp sanitation. He refused to draw any salary for his military services. In 1799 he was appointed Treasurer of the United States Mint, a position which he held until his death, when his son was appointed to succeed him.

Among his many activities may be mentioned his membership in the American Philosophical Society, before which he read a number of communications and of which he was at one time vice-president. He was chief among the founders of the Philadelphia Dispensary in 1786, the first dispensary established in this country. He assisted in founding the institution now known as Franklin and Marshall College, at Lancaster, Pennsylvania, and also in the founding of Dickinson College, at Carlisle, Pennsylvania.

Three subjects which were particularly near to his heart were the freeing of the negroes, the abolition of the death penalty, and the restriction of the immoderate use of alcohol and tobacco. On all these subjects he wrote many disquisitions and delivered frequent addresses.

He was very active in founding the Bible Society, and also in many other projects for the furtherance of religion. St. Thomas' Church, a large negro place of worship, was founded through his activity.

When he was a young man he wrote in stilted phrase to Dr. Ramsey: "Medicine is my wife; science is my mistress; books are my companions; my study is my grave; there I lie buried, the world forgetting, by the world forgot." In the latter part of his life he had put away this preternatural gravity and after having married a wife and begot thirteen children by her he writes in treating of the causes of insanity "celibacy is a pleasant breakfast, a tolerable dinner, but a very bad supper. The supper is not only bad, but, eaten alone, no wonder it sometimes becomes a predisposing cause to madness." His wife, whom he married in 1776, was Miss Julia Stockton, of a New Jersey family.

In addition to his printed works, which were published in seven volumes, Rush edited editions of some of the most famous English works on medicine, including those of Sydenham. Among his writings, besides those which have been already mentioned, there are several worthy of special note. He wrote of the disease we now term thermic fever, describing it with great accuracy in "An Account of the Disease occasioned by Drinking Cold Water in Warm Weather." There are also a number of other treatises by him on climatic affections, all possessing distinct value. Probably his best known book is his "Medical Inquiries and Observations on the Diseases of the Mind." Pepper stated that "His more elaborate address and orations are admirable, and some of them, as those on Cullen and on Rittenhouse, and his address on 'The Influence of Physical Causes on the Moral Faculties' are splendid performances."

In Ramsay's sketch is included the accompanying letter, written by Mrs. Rush to Dr. Mease, shortly after her husband's death, describing his last illness.

"At nine o'clock in the evening of Wednesday, the fourteenth of April, 1813, Dr. Rush, after having been as well as usual through the day, complained of chilliness and general indisposition, and said he would go to bed. While his room was preparing and a fire making, he became so cold that he called for some brandy and drank it; he then went to his room, bathed his feet in warm water, got into a warm bed, and took some hot drink; a fever soon came on, attended with great pain in his limbs and in his side; he passed a restless night, but after day-light a perspiration came on, and all the pains were relieved except that in his side, which became more acute. He sent for a bleeder, and had ten ounces of blood taken from his arm, with evident relief. At ten o'clock Dr. Dorsey called and saw him, heard what had been done, and approved of the treatment; observed that his pulse was calm, but rather weak, and advised him to drink plentifully of wine whey, which

was immediately given to him. He remained the rest of the day and on Friday with but little apparent disease, though never quite free from fever, and always complaining when he tried to take a long breath. On the morning of Saturday he awoke with an acute pain in his side, and desired that the bleeder might be sent for; to this I objected on account of the weak state of his pulse. I proposed sending for Dr. Dorsey, but Dr. Rush would not consent to his being disturbed; he reminded me of his having had a cough all the winter, and said 'this disease is taking hold of my lungs, and I shall go off in a consumption.' At eight o'clock Dr. Dorsey saw him and, upon feeling his pulse, objected to his losing any more blood, and called in Dr. Physick, who agreed in the opinion that bleeding was improper. The pain in his side, however, continuing, and his breathing becoming more difficult, Dr. Physick consented to his losing three ounces of blood from his side by cupping; this operation relieved him so that he fell into a refreshing sleep, and towards the evening of Saturday his fever went off, and he passed a comfortable night, and on Sunday morning seemed free from disease. When Dr. Physick saw him, he told me that Dr. Rush was doing well, that nothing now appeared necessary but to give him as much nourishment as he could take; he drank porter and water and conversed with strength and sprightliness, believing that he was getting well, until about four o'clock in the afternoon when his fever returned, but in a moderate degree. At five o'clock Dr. Physick and Dr. Dorsey visited him, and found him not so well as in the morning, but did not appear to apprehend what so soon followed, for at that time nothing was ordered different from the morning. At nine o'clock they again visited him, when they found him so low as to apprehend a fatal termination of his disease. Stimulants of the strongest kind were then administered; you, my friend, know with how little effect!"

A detailed list of his writings can be seen

in the "Surgeon-general's Catalogue," Washington, District of Columbia.

F. R. P.

Thacher's American Medical Biography, Art., Benjamin Rush.

Benjamin Rush, Address before the American Medical Association, June, 1889.

Gross, S. D. Lives of Eminent Am. Phys., Phila., 1861.

Lettsom, J. C. Recollections of Dr. Rush, London, 1815.

Mitchell, T. D. The Character of Rush, Phila., 1848.

Ramsay, D. An. Eulogium on Dr. Rush, Phila., 1813.

Am. M. and Phil. Reg., N. York, 1813–14, iv.

J. Am. M. Assoc., Chicago, 1890, xiv.

N. Eng. J. M. and S., Boston, 1813.

There is a portrait in the surg.-gen. collection, Wash., D. C.

Russell, John Wadhams (1804–1887).

His grandfather was Capt. John Russell, who commanded a privateer brig in 1778; his father, the Hon. Stephen Russell, of Litchfield County, Connecticut; his mother, Sarah Wadhams, of Goshen, Connecticut. John Wadhams was born in Canaan, Litchfield County, Connecticut, January 28, 1804.

As a boy he went to the common schools of Litchfield, then entered Hamilton College in 1821 with the intention of taking a complete course, but in 1823 health failing, he was compelled to go to South Carolina, where he recovered and began the study of medicine under Dr. Sheridan. In 1824 he attended a course of lectures in the medical department of Yale Collegé, and the year following a course in Berkshire Medical College of Pittsfield, Massachusetts. The following year he studied medicine with Dr. George McClellan, of Philadelphia. In 1826 he entered Jefferson Medical College, and in 1827 took his M. D. there. In 1827 he began to practise at Litchfield, Connecticut, in partnership with Dr. Abbey, filling meantime the office of demonstrator of anatomy in the medical department of Yale College. In 1828, by the advice of his physician, he removed to Ohio, with the hope "that the malarial climate might ward off a tendency to consumption." He settled first in Sandusky,

Erie County, but finding the lake winds too harsh, moved during the same year to Mt. Vernon, in Knox County, where he remained constantly engaged in practice until 1887.

He was one of the founders of the Ohio State Medical Society, of which he became president in 1862; the State of California Medical Association.

Dr. Russell was of medium height and rather stout. He was lame, a disability resulting from an injury in childhood. He had dark hair, dark complexion, aquiline features, and piercing black eyes. In manner he was cheerful. A fine conversationalist, but inclined to be abrupt and rather positive. He had the caution of the proverbial Connecticut Yankee, and before performing a dangerous operation, to avoid suits, made it a custom to have the patient sign a proper instrument dividing responsibility and assuming for himself no more than he considered just.

He was in active practive from 1827 until 1887, and during that long period performed many of the capital, and most of the minor operations of surgery, operating for stone in the bladder more frequently than any other surgeon of Ohio of his day, and, though his facilities were meagre as compared with those of the present, he never lost a case. He preferred the suprapubic operation, and used it in several cases, but, swayed by custom, more frequently chose the lateral.

During the early years of his practice it was impossible to obtain necessary instruments, and he was often compelled to devise such as he needed. He made models of dough for special purposes, and forged them himself, or had silversmiths copy them in silver or other metal. Some of these home-made instruments are now in the possession of his grandson, Dr. John E. Russell, and it is remarkable how closely they resemble in form those now in use, especially the instruments for the removal of stone and those for tracheotomy.

In the early fifties he treated successfully a case of spina bifida involving cervical vertebræ. This operation and its results were considered so remakable that the father, Hon. C. P. Buckingham, took the patient, a child, to New York, where it was exhibited to the most renowned surgeons of that city. They reported it to the Society of Surgeons in London, England, and it was published in the London "Lancet."

In 1828 he married Eliza Beebe, daughter of the Hon. William Beebe, of Litchfield, Connecticut. They had five children, William B.; Sarah, who died in infancy; John Wadhams, Jr.; Ann Eliza; Isaac Wadhams. All of the sons were at some time partners of their father, but died early. His grandson, Dr. John E. Russell, was his partner during the last six years of his life.

Dr. Russell died of uremia March 22, 1887, in Mt. Vernon, Ohio.

He wrote and delivered many addresses before the State Medical and other societies, but, from lack of appreciation of his own ability and learning, published few or none. In 1876 at the meeting of the International Congress of Physicians and Surgeons, Prof. Gross introduced him as "the man, who, but for his extreme modesty, would have been the leading surgeon of the world."

A portrait is in possession of his grandson, Dr.John E. Russell.

S. L.

Tr. Ohio M Soc Columbus, 1887 (F. C. Larrimore)

S

Sager, Abram (1810–1877).

Abram Sager was born at Bethlehem, Albany County, New York, December 22, 1810. His father, William Sager, was a farmer of German ancestry, who settled in New York at an early age. Abram studied medicine with Profs. Marsh and Ives at Albany and New Haven, Connecticut, but graduated M. D. from Castleton Medical College, at Castleton, Vermont, in April, 1835. For a time he practised in Detroit, Michigan, then at Jackson, but finally settled at Ann Arbor. In 1837 he was made chief of the botanical and zoological departments of the Michigan Geological Survey. The zoological specimens which formed the basis of his report laid the foundation for the present zoological collection of Michigan University Museum. The Sager Herbarium in the University Museum contains 1,200 species and 12,000 specimens. He also prepared and placed in the museum of the medical department a valuable collection illustrating comparative craniology, neurology and embryology of the vertebrata. From 1842 to 1855 he was professor of botany and zoology in Michigan University; in 1848 he was made professor of theory and practice of medicine; in 1850 professor of obstetrics and diseases of women and children—a place occupied till made emeritus professor in 1874. He resigned his chair because he disapproved of the actions of the regents in connecting homeopathy with the medical department. For several years before his resignation Dr. Sager was dean of the medical department. In 1852 the University gave him the honorary M. A. In 1874 Dr. Sager was elected president of the Michigan State Medical Society, and was a member of the Obstetrical Society of Philadelphia, and the New York State Medical Society. Dr. Sager's success as a teacher was gained in spite of natural defects in the way of an inferior physical appearance, an unpleasant voice and a temperament shrinking from publicity, but the intrinsic merit of his subject matter and weight of character fixed the attention of his audience.

In 1838 he married Sarah E. Dwight, of Detroit, Michigan, and had eight children, five of whom survived him.

He died in Ann Arbor, Michigan, August 6, 1877, from phthisis pulmonalis.

Papers:

"Notes on the Anatomy of the Gymnopus Spiniferus." ("Peninsular Medical Journal," vol. iii.)

"Observations on the Hirundei in Michigan." (Ibid., vol. iv.)

"Observations on the Development of a New Species of Helminth." (Ibid., vol. ii.)

"Case of Amaurosis of Pregnancy Connected with Albuminuria." (Ibid., vol. x.)

"Report on Obstetrics." (Read before the Michigan State Medical Society, 1868, Ann Arbor, 1869.)

"Cases of Floating Kidney." ("Peninsular Medical Journal," vol. ix.)

"Cases of Delivery by Cesarean Section." ("Michigan University Medical Journal," vol. ii.)

"Experiments on the Respiration of Various Cases." (Ibid., vol. i.)

"Case of Simultaneous Intra- and Extra-uterine Pregnancy." (Ibid., vol. i.)

L. C.

History of the Univ. of Mich., Ann Arbor, The Univ. Press.
Trans. Amer. Med. Ass., Phila., Pa., 1878, vol xxiv.
Trans. Mich. State Med. Soc., Lansing, 1878.
Life, Huber, Michigan Alumnus, Feb., 1903

Sargent, Joseph (1815–1888).

Joseph Sargent, founder of the Worcester Society for Medical Improvement and instrumental in the building of the Worcester Lunatic Hospital and the Washburn Memorial Hospital, was the son of Col. Henry Sargent, and born in Leicester, Massachusetts, December 15, 1815.

After graduating from Harvard College in 1834 he studied medicine one year with Dr. Edward Flint, of Leicester, and three years at a private school in Boston, of which Dr. James Jackson was the head, also attending lectures at the medical schools of Harvard University and of the University of Pennsylvania, Philadelphia. After receiving his M. D. from Harvard in 1837, he spent one year as house doctor in the Massachusetts General Hospital, two years in study in Paris, and in 1840 opened an office in Worcester, but in 1850 spent another year in Europe, and again in 1868.

For forty-eight years Dr. Sargent was a leader in the medical profession, holding in turn all the offices in the district Society. He was councillor in the State society for a long time, and in 1874–76 vice-president. He was one of the original members of the Boston Society for Medical Observation. To his exertions also is largely due the present prosperity of the City Hospital, of which he was trustee from 1871 to 1886, serving at the same time as a member of the consulting staff.

He married Emily Whitney, September 27, 1841.

Dr. Sargent brought to Worcester a store of knowledge and skill, which made him pre-eminently the most conspicuous member of the medical profession in Central Massachusetts. He died in Worcester, October 13, 1888.

L. F. W.

Satterlee, Richard Sherwood (1798–1880).

Richard Sherwood Satterlee, surgeon, United State Army, son of Maj. William Satterlee, was born December 6, 1798, at Fairfield, Herkimer County, New York. After graduating in medicine Satterlee began to practise in Seneca County, New York, but soon went West and settled at Detroit. In 1822 he was appointed assistant surgeon in the United States Army. He served during the Seminole war in Florida and rendered notable services during the Mexican one, being present in the battles of Cerro Gordo, Cherubusco, Molino del Rey and Chapultepec. In 1853 he was appointed medical purveyor, which office he held until the close of the Civil War. In 1866 he was made brevet brigadier-general as a reward for faithful and meritorious services. Under Pres. Johnson he retired from active service, and his death took place in New York November 10, 1880. He married in June, 1827, Mary S. Hunt, of Detroit, Michigan.

A. A.

Stone, Biogr. Em. Am. Phys. and Surg. Indianapolis, 1898.
Port. in Sur.-gen. Collection, Wash., D. C.

Sarrazin Michel S. (1659–1736).

Michel S. Sarrazin, physician and naturalist, was born in 1659, and came to Canada in 1685. Becoming noted both as a doctor and a scientist, he had the honor of being elected member of the French Academy. Moreover, several years after his arrival in Canada he was appointed King's physician for the country, the only bearer of that title in all New France. His salary was a bare 600 livres, without recompence from his patients. Sarrazin was also a member of the Supreme Council of Quebec.

About 1712 he married Marie Anne, the daughter of Francois Hazeur, fils, and had seven children. He died in Quebec, September, 1734 and his widow received a pension from the King; his sons, who were regarded as protéges of the State, were then studying medicine in Paris.

There seems to be some confusion among the botanists as to which Sarrazin the plant Sarracenia was named for. It was first named and described by J. B. Tournefort in "Institutiones rei herbariæ," second edition, Paris, 1700, thus: "Sarracena Canadensis foliis cavis et auritis. Saracenam appelavi a Clarissimo D. Sarrazin, Medicinæ Doctore,

Anatomico et Botanico Regio insigni, qui eximiam hanc plantam pro summa qua me complectitur bene volentia e Canada misit." Linnaeus in his Genera Plantarum, 1753, established the genus ascribing it to Tournefort. The latter (on pp. 37, 38) gives great credit to Dr. Jean Antoine Sarrazin for his magnificent edition of Dioscorides and his notes on plants. As no initials are given to this Dr. Sarrazin, many writers have assumed that Dr. Jean Antoine is the one meant. But he was born in Lyons, France, April 25, 1547, and died there Nov. 29, 1598, ten years before Tournefort was born. It was impossible, therefore, for him to have sent the plant to Tournefort.

The Jesuit Relations, vol. lxvii.
Montreal M. J., June, 1908 (M. Charlton).
"Nicholas" erroneously given for "Michel."
Biog. Lex. der Hervorr., Aerzte, vol. v.
Enclo. Britt., vol. xiii, ed., 1878.

Sayre, Lewis Albert (1820-1900).

Lewis A. Sayre seems to have regarded the world as a valley of dry bones and himself specially commissioned as a re-creator. His collection of writings concerns all things osseous; tho the writer himself is full of warm throbbing interest in all the ways of osteological reformation and improvement. He was born February 29, 1820, at Bottle Hill, now Madison, New Jersey, the son of Archibald and Martha Sayre, his father a prosperous farmer. As a little boy, Lewis was prepared for school by John T. Derthick at Madison for the Wantage Seminary at Deckertown, S u s s e x County. From there he went to Lexington, Kentucky, graduating at Transylvania University in 1839. Soon after he settled in New York as pupil of Dr. David Green, graduating M. D. at the College of Physicians and Surgeons in 1842 and straightway forging ahead and doing operations generally considered the work of matured surgeons. Appointed prosector of surgery in the College of Physicians and Surgeons he, as early as 1841, did an operation for strabismus which

had only been twice before attempted. Having charge of Willard's clinic he opened an abscess connected with chronic disease of the knee-joint and propounded the principle then new of opening by free incision all joints where there is suppuration with destruction of synovial membrane and erosion of the articular cartilage. Some severe criticisms did not deter him from firmly declaring similar cases not necessarily constitutional seeing local treatment and free incisions produced so marked improvement. In 1852 he exsected the head and neck of the femur and a portion of the acetabulum with perfect success. When Bellevue Hospital Medical College, of which he was an organizer, was inaugurated, Sayre was given the chair of orthopedic surgery, the first for the science in this country.

In 1854 he performed the difficult operation, without any resultant deformity, for morbus coxarius, being the first to do it in America. In 1871 he, by special invitation, lectured on hip disease before several medical societies in Europe, and was created a Knight of the Order of Wasa by Charles IV of Sweden for his success in treating one of the royal family. When, a delegate to the International Medical Congress in Philadelphia in 1876 he read a paper on the subject and did the operation. Lord Lister said on its conclusion "I feel this demonstration would of itself have been sufficient reward for my journey across the Atlantic." A year later, as a delegate to the British Medical Association, he again lectured and demonstrated. A formal resolution thanking him was passed by the Association. He invented a number of important instruments used in his practice and wrote exhaustively. His "Illustrative Treatise on Spinal Disease and Spinal Curvature," was written while abroad and dedicated to the medical profession of Great Britain.

He married January 25, 1849, Eliza Ann Hall, of Harlem, New York, and had four children: Mary Hall, and three sons who all became doctors, Charles H. Hall,

Lewis Hall and Reginald Hall, the two former dying before their father.

Among his many writings may be mentioned:

"Exsection of the Head of the Femur and Removal of the Upper Rim of the Acetabulum for Morbus Coxarius," 1854.

"A New Operation for Artificial Hipjoint in Bony Anychlosis," 1863.

"A Practical Manual on Club-foot," "Lectures on Orthopedic Surgery." These two volumes, with the one mentioned, passed through a great many editions and were translated into several languages, including Japanese. For a fuller list the Surgeon-general's Library at Washington can be consulted.

Among his memberships and appointments was membership of the Medical Society of the State of New York; New York Academy of Medicine; New York Pathological Society; honorary member, Medical Society of New Brunswick; the British Medical Association; Medical Chirurgical Society of Edinburgh; the Surgical Society of St. Petersburg.   D. W.

Living New York Surgeons, S. W. Francis, N. Y., 1866.
Boston M. and S. Jour., 1900, vol. cxliii.
Brit. M. J., Lond., 1900, vol. ii.
Med. Rec., N. Y., 1900, vol. lviii.
Med. News, N. Y., 1900, vol. lxxvii.
N. Y. Med. Jour., 1900, vol. lxxii.
There is a portrait in the Surg.-gen. Lib., Wash., D. C.

Schadle, Jacob E. (1849–1908).

Jacob E. Schadle was of German ancestry and born at Jersey Shore, Pennsylvania, June 23, 1849, graduating from Jefferson Medical College in 1881, and practising first in a Friend's settlement at Pennsdale, in central Pennsylvania. After two years he moved to Shenandoah, Pennsylvania, and six years later came to St. Paul.

It was during his residence in Shenandoah, and while acting as lazaret physician, that he made a record by the skill and courage which he displayed in the handling of a widespread epidemic of small-pox and stamping out the disease.

In 1885 he reported the successful treatment of three cases of mushroom poisoning by administering large doses of atropine. This was the first instance of the use of atropine as an antidote for amanitine poisoning.

Schadle had, for years, been the leader in his specialty in the Northwest. He was remarkably deft in the manipulation of instruments in the throat and nose, and as an operator he had few superiors, and invented a number of surgical instruments which are now in general use. Schadle was a frequent and highly valued contributor to the medical journals of this country. His articles include:

"Empyema of the Accessory Sinuses of the Nose."

"Erosions and Ulcerations of the Triangular Cartilage of the Septum."

"Adenoid Growths in Children."

"Relationship Between Diseases of the Nose and Throat and General Diseases."

"History of Medicine."

"Pica."

"Treatment of Syphilitic Cicatricial Adhesions Between the Soft Palate and Posterior Wall of the Pharynx."

"The Relation of Hay-fever to the Antrum of Highmore."

"Membranous Laryngitis, a Complication of Influenza."

"The Relation of Antral Sinusitis to Hay-fever and Asthma."

He had for several years been engaged in the study of the etiology and treatment of hay-fever, and had advanced an entirely new theory as to the cause of this disease, which he had hoped to elaborate at the meeting of the American Medical Association. He was an enthusiastic student of those diseases connected with his special line of work and had done much original work.

He was a member of the Minnesota State Medical Association, the American Rhinological Laryngological and Otological Association, of which he was president of the Western section in 1888, and was for many years professor of diseases of the throat and nose in the medical department of the University of Minnesota.

He married the daughter of Dr. D. H. Miller, of Mifflinburg, a physician of Central Pennsylvania. He died at St. Joseph's Hospital in St. Paul, May 29, 1908, of cerebral thrombosis followed by general paralysis, after an illness of several weeks' duration.

St. Paul's Med. Jour., July, 1908

Schmidt, H. D. (1823–1888).

H. D. Schmidt was born at Marburg, Prussia, receiving the usual education of a German boy, then was apprenticed to an instrument-maker at the age of fifteen, which training in after-life enabled him to conceive and construct various pieces of apparatus for the benefit of his scientific investigations (his microtome and injector, employed in his researches into the histology of the liver). During his apprenticeship he visited the large cities of Europe and came to Philadelphia in 1848, where he began the study of anatomy and constructed papier maché models of such correctness and beauty that several are still preserved in the medical department of the University of Pennsylvania. Attracting the attention of Leidy and Jackson, he became prosector to Dr. Jackson and assisted Prof. Leidy in many of his physiological investigations. After studying five years, he graduated in medicine in 1858 (University of Pennsylvania) and devoted himself to histology. By his own contrivance of an injecting apparatus, he was able to solve the question of the termination of the bile ducts of the liver and to demonstrate their origin in the intercellular capillaries. In 1860 Dr. Schmidt went south, first to the Medical College of Alabama, in Mobile, and thence to New Orleans, succeeding Penniston as demonstrator of anatomy in the New Orleans School of Medicine. During the Civil War he served the South as a military surgeon. At the close of the struggle he returned to New Orleans and was installed as pathologist to the Charity Hospital, a position which he occupied for twenty years. He was known as a man of strong convictions, honest and

earnest; never cynical nor prejudiced in regard to the opinions of others. (See article in "New Orleans Medical and Surgical Journal," December, 1888, vol. xvi, n. s.) He contributed to literature:

"On the Minute Structure of the Hepatic Lobules." ("American Journal of Medical Sciences," January, 1859.)

" Researches into Pathology and Cause of the Present Epidemic . . . Yellow Fever." ("Southern Journal of Medical Sciences," November, 1867.)

"Microscopical Anatomy of the Human Liver." (" New Orleans Journal of Medicine," October, 1869, and January and April, 1870.)

"Origin and Development of the Colored Blood Corpuscles in Man," read before Royal Microscopical Society of London. (" Monthly Microscopical Journal," 1874.)

"Construction of the Dark or Double Bordered Nerve Fiber," read before Royal Microscopical Society of London. (Ibid., July, 1874.)

"Development of the Smaller Bloodvessels in the Human Embryo," read before the Royal Microscopical Society of London. ("Ibid.," January, 1875.)

"Principal Facts elicited from a Series of Microscopical Researches upon the Nervous Tissues," read before Royal Microscopical S o c i e t y of London. ("Ibid.," July, 1874.)

"Structure of the Nervous Tissues and Their Mode of Action." (" Transactions, American Neurological Society," vol. i, 1875.)

"Development of the Nervous Tissues of the Human Embryo." ("Journal, Nervous and Mental Diseases," July, 1887.)

"Structure of the Colored Blood-corpuscles of the Amphiuma Tridactylum, the Frog and Man," read before Royal Microscopical Society of London, published May and July, 1878.

" Repeated Attacks of Apoplexy with Aphasia." ("Journal, Nervous and Mental Diseases, 1878.)

"Structure and Function of the Ganglionic Bodies of the Cerebro-spinal

Axis." ("Journal, Nervous and Mental Diseases," 1879.)

"Pathology of Yellow Fever." (" New York Medical Journal," February, 1879.)

"Nature of the Poison of Yellow Fever and Its Prevention." (" New York Medical Journal," May, 1879.)

"Destructive Lesion of the Left Hemisphere with General Pachymeningitis," read before American Neurological Association, June 15, 1881.

"Pathological Anatomy of Leprosy." ("Archives of Medicine," December, 1881.)

"Is Bacillus Lepræ a Reality or Fiction?" ("Chicago Medical Journal and Examiner," 1882.)

"Influence of the Structure of the Double-contoured Nerve Fiber upon the Production and Conduction of Nerve Force." ("Proceedings, American Society for Advancement of Sciences," 1881.)

"Case with Tumor in Fourth Ventricle of the Brain, Unaccompanied with Special Symptoms." ("Journal, Nervous and Mental Diseases," July, 1822.)

"Microscopical Research into the Nature of the So-called Bacillus Tuberculosis," read before New Orleans Medical and Surgical Association, November 6, 1882.

"Pseudo-bacillus Tuberculsois," New Orleans Pathological Society, 1883.

"Pathological Anatomy of the Cerebrospinal Axis of a Case of Chronic Myelitis of Nineteen Years' Standing." ("Journal, Nervous and Mental Disases," July, 1883. J. G. R.

N. Orl. M. & S. J., 1884 and 1888, n. s. xii, xvi.

Scott, Upton (1722-1814).

A founder and first president of the Medical and Chirurgical Faculty of Maryland, he was the son of Francis Scott, of Templepatrick, near Antrim, Ireland, where he was born in the year 1722. After a literary training, probably at the University of Dublin, he began to study medicine and early in 1747 purchased for £60 a surgeon-mate's position in one of

the oldest of the British regiments, that of Lord George Sackville, and was stationed in Scotland. This was the regiment commanded by Wolfe. He accompanied his command in the ensuing campaign in Flanders. During the winter the regiment came down into the lowlands and Dr. Scott availed himself of the opportunity to attend lectures at Edinburgh and Glasgow, taking his M. D. from the latter, April 10, 1753, and having secured an engagement with Mr. Horatio Sharpe, the new governor of Maryland he disposed of his commission and sailed for Annapolis the ensuing summer.

Favored by the patronage of Gov. Sharpe, he became the court physician of the Maryland capital, and secured a large practice. He also held the sheriffship of Anne Arundel County in 1759 and secretaryship of the Council or Upper House of Assembly. On his return to Maryland, after the war, he seems to have recovered his property and to have enjoyed the confidence of the community, as though no differences had ever existed.

In 1760 Dr. Scott built a handsome brick house. Here, in the exercise of a generous hospitality, he passed a green old age and died on the twenty-third of February, 1814, aged ninety-one.

Various relics of him have been preserved besides his letters. Among these are his diploma, his medicine chest, a miniature painted on ivory, a pair of pistols presented to him by Col. Wolfe, a portrait of Dr. Cullen, the gift of that great physician and a letter from him, in which he speaks of Scott as one among his first pupils, and a "List of Flowers that Grow in the Vicinity of the Cape of Good Hope," which was handed in the form of an order to his nephew, Lieut. D. Murray, of the United States Navy, at Annapolis in 1807. Dr. Scott wanted to bring to Maryland for planting purposes near Annapolis all seeds and bulbs of Cape of Good Hope plants that could possibly be obtained, and as Lieut. Murray attended to this order for him it is probably a fair assumption that many of the flowers of Colonial Maryland sprang from this origin.

Dr. Scott was a close observer, taking a deep interest in medical progress and frequently ordering new books through his agent in London.

Shortly after his arrival in Maryland he married Elizabeth Ross, an heiress, with a large landed estate, but died without direct descendants.

E. F. C.

For picture and Memoir of Dr. Scott. Cordell's Medical Annals of Maryland, 1903. Also Upton Scott of Annapolis. Maryland. Med. Jour., Balt., 1092, vol. xlv (E. F. Cordell).

Schultz, Sir John Christian (1840–1896).

John C. Schultz, of Norse and Irish descent, son of William Schultz, of Bergen, Norway, and Elizabeth Riley, of Bandon, Ireland, was born at Amherstburg, Ontario, January 1, 1840, and received his education at Oberlin College, Ohio, and Kingston, Ontario, then took his medical course at Victoria College, Toronto, graduating in 1861.

The life of Sir John Christian Schultz is intricately woven into the early history of the Canadian North West, formerly called Rupert's land. His first trip there was made at the age of twenty, before he graduated in medicine. He returned to his home in 1861 to take his degree, but immediately went back to the land of his adoption where he successfully practised till public duties claimed all his time.

In 1863 he assisted Gov. MacTavish and the right Rev. Bishop Anderson in forming the Institute of Rupert's Land, of which he became secretary, taking an active part in the founding of its museum and contributing papers on prevailing diseases of Rupert's Land and on the plants, minerals and other natural resources of the country. In this year, after reading a paper on the "Flora of the Red River Valley Country" before the Botanical Society of Kingston, he was elected a fellow of that Society.

While a member of the House of Commons, he impressed on the Government the vast resources of the new province, pointing to what he termed "Greater Canada" as having the largest extent of arable and grazing land and the greatest coal measures in the Dominion; and he also advocated a trans-continental railway to bind the Dominion together.

In 1867 he married Agnes, daughter of James Farquharson, Esq., of British Guiana. In 1984 the degree of LL. D. had been conferred upon him by Queen's University, Kingston. He died in April, 1896. An incident of his early life in the Northwest illustrates alike the adventurous side of life there in the sixities, and the ready and resourceful character that ever marked Sir John Schultz. As a boy he had lived near the old scenes of the life of the great Indian chief Tecumseh and the stories of the noble life of the red man had a profound influence on the lad. Throughout his life he was dauntless and forceful, yet kind and gentle. His natural sagacity stood him in good stead on many occasions. On one of his early trips from Ontario to Fort Garry, he went by way of St. Paul, Minnesota, from which place he drove all the way, a distance of four hundred and fifty miles. The Indians throughout the northern central states were all on the war path, and the young doctor was advised not to try to make the journey. He, however, secured a companion and set forth. After some days' journey they were surprised by a band of warriors and immediately piled up their kit as a barricade. A parley ensued between the two men and the forty Indians, when a shout came from behind an elm tree, demanding "by what right the white man passed through their country?" The barricade answered "I am a Segenash Mushkekewenene (English medicine man) travelling to the wigwams of the English people at the English fort." The "Elm Tree" answered "We saw you as you crossed the ford and you were dressed like the people we have just driven from our hunting grounds." The barricade answered, "Clothes do not differ among the whites and we are not 'Kitchemokomans' (Americans) but 'Sagenash' (English) who have passed this trail for years in peace." Yet it became apparent that the Indians would have to be convinced of these assertions if these two travellers were to leave the spot alive, and the slight knowledge of the Indian language possessed by the doctor's companion, with a few phials of medicine and a pocket surgical case were now used in this behalf. The "barricade" engaged not to fire if the chief would send one of his braves across the ford to examine and report. The "Elm Tree" engaged on behalf of his followers to let the travellers pass if the envoy's examination was satisfactory. The young Indian brave, with full war paint and more feathers than clothes, came over, and his quick eye took note that the trappings and equipage were of St. Paul make, but the sight of the rows of bottles and curious surgical instruments seemed to satisfy the warrior, who returned to his band, and after a hurried consultation the "Elm Tree" announced that they "will come over and shake their English brothers' hands." The handshaking over, the two hosts entertained their guests in such royal style that they were in danger of leaving themselves hungry for ten days. As they were about to proceed on their way the chief gave them an invitation, that sounded more like a command, to spend the night at his camp some four miles away. Of necessity the invitation was accepted and a tent was assigned to the two travellers. All night long they lay awake to hear conversations in a nearby "tepee" during which frequent references were made to "Segenash" and "Kitchemokomans." In the morning a squaw who was suffering from smoke irritated eyes, and who had received an ointment in the evening, ing, was considerably improved. The Indians were now thoroughly convinced, and the chief displayed the medal his grandfather had received from George the III; the squaws brought corn for their horses and pounded maize and fish for the travellers. Their journey was then continued and they reached their destination without further molestation.

J. H.

Parliamentary Companion, 1890. The making of the Canadian West, 1898. Three paintings are in possession of Lady Schultz, two by Forbes and one by Hatch, and a portrait hangs in Government house, Winnepeg.

Schuppert, Moritz (1817–1887).

Moritz Schuppert, surgeon, was born in Marburg, Germany, in 1817, where he received a good education, studied medicine, married, and then came to New Orleans. Poor and unfriended but endowed with great native ability and a knowledge of the science of medicine far in advance of that possessed by most American physicians of that day, these advantages soon made themselves felt. In 1853 he distinguished himself in the yellow-fever epidemic and became visiting surgeon to the Charity Hospital, where for years he continued to serve with enthusiasm and exactness. In 1854 he was city physician; in 1859 he established in conjunction with Dr. Choppin, an orthopedic institute. He rapidly rose to be one of the most prominent surgeons and citizens of the city. He performed many surgical operations, was skillful in the treatment of deformities, a vigorous writer, a thinker and an inspirer of thought in his associates. His biographer compares him to the Luther of his native home, stern, simple, outspoken, rugged. A lover of candor, a hater of meanness, of rough exterior and tender heart, a loyal friend, a strong man.

He died May 2, 1887.

His contributions to literature add many valuable pages to the "New Orleans Medical and Surgical Journal," and are, notably: "Facial Neuralgia;" "Vesico-Vaginal Fistula;" "Biniodide of Mercury in Syphilis;" Resuscitation from Death by Chloroform" "Excision of Entire Scapula with Preservation of a Useful Arm (1870);" "Penumatometry: Results of Lister's Antiseptic Treatment of Wounds in German Hospitals and Remarks on the Theory of Septic Infection"

(1875-6); "Lister's Antiseptic Treatment of Wounds" (1878-9); "Bloodletting and Kindred Qusetions" (1881-2); "Tetanus and Tetany" (1884-5).

He was the first to introduce Lister's practice into the South and is rightly regarded as the father of antiseptic surgery in Louisiana.   J. G. R.

Seaman, Valentine (1765-1817).

Valentine Seaman, a New York physician, was the fourth son of Willet Seaman, a merchant, and descendant from John Seaman who arrived from England and settled in Hempstead about 1660.

The City Almshouse was the only institution where medical instruction could be had and Valentine after studying with Nicholas Romayne, entered there as resident physician. In 1791, he took his M. D. at the University of Pennsylvania, and was made one of the surgeons to the New York Hospital, which post he held until his death.

He was very active in introducing vaccination into his city and vaccinated his own son and a number of citizens, and in 1816, published a discourse on the subject. In 1810-11 he, with several other doctors, formed a new medical institution whch was associated with Queen's College, New Brunswick, but it only lived three years. The manumission of slaves and the mental improvement of midwives were two other things concerning which this active enthusiast was very keen.

In the winter of 1815 he had inflammation of the lungs and developed consumption which ended his life in June, 1817. He married the second daughter of John Ferris, of Westchester and had nine children.

He wrote: "An Account of the Epidemic Yellow Fever as it Appeared in New York in 1795" (New York, 1796); "The Midwife's Monitor and Mother's Mirror," etc. (New York, 1800); "Pharmacopeia Chirurgica in usum nosicomii Novi Eboracensis" (New York, 1811), and many other articles for the "New

York Medical Repository" in 1798 and 1808.

Biog. Lex. der Hervorragenden Aerzte, Wien., 1887.
William's Am. Med. Biog.

Seguin, Edward Constant (1843-1898).

Edward Constant Seguin was born in Paris in 1843, the son of Edouard Seguin, well known for his researches on idiocy and his work in training the feebleminded. The elder Seguin came to America in 1848; the son studied at the College of Physicians, New York, where he graduated in 1864. In 1862 he was appointed. a medical cadet in the regular army and served two terms, later at Little Rock, Arkansas, and was post-surgeon at Forts Craig and Selden, in New Mexico. The winter of 1869-70 was spent in Paris under the teaching of Brown-Séquard, Cornil and Charcot, which deeply interested him in diseases of the nervous system. In 1871 he became connected with the College of Physicians and Surgeons and founded a clinic for these diseases.

But while his chief work was in the direction of such healing it must not be forgotten that to him in great part was due the introduction of medical thermometry into the United States. In a footnote to the first article in Seguin's "Opera Minora," called "The Use of the Thermometer in Clinical Medicine" ("Chicago Medical Journal," May, 1886,) Amidon said: "this article and the observations leading to it form the starting-point of medical thermometry in the United States." The work was done by Dr. W. H. Draper and Dr. Seguin and is interesting as presenting probably the first temperature chart on record in this country. It is called "A Record of Vital Signs" and gives a chart of the pulse, respirations and temperature. His papers on aphasia, infantile paralysis, on tetanoid paraplegia, and, above all, his lectures and admirable series of papers on localization of brain-lesions did a great deal to stimulate the study and practice of neurology. His work on spastic paraplegia, his lectures and series of papers preceded those of Erb and Charcot. To him is due what is known as the American method of giving potassium iodide in enormous doses.

Though a specialist, he had very wide sympathies in the profession and threw himself with great enthusiasm into literary ventures. Thus, in 1873, he joined with Brown-Séquard in the editorship of the "Archives of Scientific and Practical Medicine and Surgery," a journal which did not, however, survive a year. Between 1876–8 he edited a series of American clinical lectures, but his most pretentious venture was the "Archives of Medicine" (1879), in which an attempt was made to supply the profession with a high-class journal. But it was not a financial success and lapsed after the twelfth volume.

From the shock of an awful domestic tragedy in 1884, Dr. Seguin never fully recovered. After staying abroad for two years he resumed practice in New York, but did not teach again. Many years before his death he lost one of his fingers, the result of a spindle-shaped growth. In 1896 a growth appeared in the abdomen and there were, later, signs of diffuse metastases. From a long and trying illness he was released on February 19, 1898.

From an obituary in the Philadelphia Medical Journal, 1898, vol. i.

Selden, William B. (1773–1849).

Born in 1773, he was the son of the Rev. William Selden, pastor of the Episcopal Church at Hampton, Virginia, and received a good education, afterwards studying medicine for several years under Drs. Taylor and Hansford of Norfolk, and then attending a course of lectures at the University of Pennsylvania. After two years in Edinburgh, he had not received a degree as he had to return home on account of lack of funds.

He then settled in Norfolk and was associated with Dr. Alexander Whitehead. In 1779 he obtained some vaccine virus from Dr. Jenner and with this proceded to vaccinate, and kept up a con-

tinuous supply for nearly fifty years. He declared that all this time he could see no variation in the appearance of the vesicle, nor any failure in its power to protect. From the beginning of his practice he used the bark in the treatment of malarial fevers without waiting for the fever to subside, and in severe cases, anticipated the paroxysms by full doses of camphor and opium. Long before Graves wrote on the subject, he treated typhoid fever by careful nursing and proper medicines, rather than with drastic remedies. He was one of the first in this country to use calomel in the treatment of the summer diarrhea of children, trying it first in 1807 in the case of his own child. He had a large obstetrical practice, and was one of the best accouchers of his day, and was probably the first to perform the operation of decapitation of the fetus. This he did in the case of a woman with a shoulder presentation, who had been in labor for two days. The shoulder was forced so low in the pelvis that the neck was easily reached, and the doctor decided to sever the neck, rather than attempt to turn. This he did with a pruning knife with a curved blade which he happened to have in his pocket. The body was then easily delivered by pulling down the arm and the head was expelled by the uterine contractions. The woman recovered.

Dr. Selden was a scholarly man, an earnest student and a close observer. From the beginning of his career it was his habit to write down every morning his observations on the climate and weather, and to record briefly any noteworthy case he had seen. These records were lost during the Civil War when his son's library was plundered by the Federal troops.

He married in 1802 Charlotte Colgate, of Kent, England, and several children were born. Three sons and a daughter survived him and two of the sons, William and Henry, became physicians.

He died on July 18, 1849, his last illness presenting the symptoms of cancer of the stomach. R. M. S.

Selden, William (1808–1887).

Born in Norfolk, Virginia, August 15, 1808, he was the son of Dr. William B. Selden, a noted physician of that city. He attended lectures and graduated from the University of Pennsylvania in 1830, after which he spent two years in London and Paris, then, returning to this country, he settled in his native city, and soon built up a large practice.

He was a member of the Medical Society of Virginia, of which he was twice elected vice-president.

In May, 1863, he was commissioned surgeon in the Confederate Army, and served to the end of the war in army hospitals. The rest of his professional life was spent in his native city, where he accomplished much good through his great ability and valuable counsel. He was one of that band of heroic physicians who stood steadfast at the post of duty during the terrible epidemic of yellow fever which visited Norfolk and Portsmouth in 1855, being chairman of a committee appointed by the city council to investigate the cause and origin of the epidemic. This committee, which consisted of six physicians, submitted a full and valuable report, with the correct conclusion that the disease was introduced by the steamer Ben Franklin. This report is from his pen, and few more valuable contributions to medical literature have been given the profession.

It is said of him that his abilities were so diversified and various that it is difficult to say in what branch of the profession he most excelled, and still harder to determine in which, if any, he was deficient.

He married Lucinda Wilson, the daughter of Dr. Daniel Wilson, of Louisville, Kentucky, and died at his home in Norfolk, Virginia, November 7, 1887.

An able writer, he made some very valuable contributions to medical literature; the titles of some are:

"Report on the Origin of Yellow Fever in Norfolk in 1855." (" Virginia Medical Journal," vol. iv.)

"Gunshot Wound of the Axillary Artery." ("Confederate States Medical and Surgical Journal," vol. i.)

"Opium Poisoning Relieved by Scalding Water." (" Virginia Medical Journal," vol. v.)

" Bony Union of Fracture of the Neck of the Femur, with Report of Cases and Comments Thereon." ("Transactions of the Medical Society of Virginia," 1877.)

"Autopsy of a Case of Bony Union of an Intra-capsular Fracture of the Neck of the Femur." ("Transactions of the Medical Society of Virginia," 1879.)

R. M. S.

Trans. Med. Soc. of Va., 1888.
Med. and Surg. Reporter, Phila., 1887, vol. lvii.

Sellman, John (1764–1828).

John Sellman was born in the city of Annapolis, Maryland, in 1764, and belonged to an old family of that state; he received a good preparatory education and entered the army as surgeon's mate, reaching Cincinnati with Gen. Wayne in the spring of 1793. The war being over, he resigned his commission in 1794, and lived on Front Street, Cincinnati, where he practised until his death.

On November 1, 1799, Drs. Sellman and Hall formed a partnership. They stated in their card to the public that corn, rye, oats, corn-fed pork, and merchantable wheat would be taken in payment for services. Early in the nineteenth century the government established the arsenal and barracks at Newport, Kentucky. Dr. Sellman was employed for many years as citizen surgeon.

He lived in Cincinnati thirty-five years, and was, at the time of his death, the oldest resident physician.

He died Jannary 1, 1828.

A. G. D.

Semmes, Alexander Jenkins (1828–1898).

Alexander Jenkins Semmes was born December 17, 1828, in the District of Columbia; graduated A. B., 1850; A. M.,

1852, Georgetown College. District of Columbia: M. D., 1851, Columbia College, District of Columbia.

He was the son of Raphael Semmes, Esq., of Nanjemoy, and Matilda Neal Jenkins, of Cobneck, Charles County, Maryland; his paternal and maternal grandfathers were officers of the Maryland line of the Revolutionary Army, and came to Maryland between 1636 and 1650. He studied medicine three years with Grafton Tyler, and after graduating at the National Medical College, District of Columbia, settled in New Orleans, Louisiana, where he was a resident physician of Charity Hospital, New Orleans, in 1860. He was appointed surgeon of the Eighth Louisiana Volunteers, June 19, 1861, and July 4 was commissioned a surgeon in the confederate Army, serving from 1861 to 1863 as surgeon and brigade surgeon in Hay's Louisiana brigade, of Stonewall Jackson's corps, in the army of Northern Virginia, and was surgeon in charge of the third division of the Jackson Military Hospital at Richmond, Virginia.

After the close of the war he returned to New Orleans, then removed to Savannah, Georgia, and from 1870 to 1876 was professor of physiology in the Savannah Medical College. Subsequently he took orders in the Roman Catholic Church and in 1886 became president of the Pio Nono College, Macon, Georgia.

He was the author of "Medical Sketches in Paris," 1852; "Poisoning by Strychnine," 1855; "Medico-Legal Duties of Coroners," 1857; "Gunshot Wounds" 1864; "Notes from a Surgical Diary," 1866; "Surgical Notes of the Late War," 1867; "Medical Reviews and Criticisms," 1860–61; "Revaccination; Its Effects and Importance," 1868; "Preparations of Manganese," 1868; "Evolution of the Origin of Life," two papers read before the Georgia Medical Society, 1873; "The Influence of Yellow Fever on Pregnancy and Parturition," paper read before the Georgia State Medical Association, 1875; and other papers both numerous and important.

He also wrote frequently for literary and other non-professional periodicals. He married October 4, 1864, at Savannah, Georgia, Sarah Lowndes, daughter of John Macpherson Berrien, attorney-general of the United States in the cabinet of Pres. Jackson, and for many years United States Senator from Georgia.

He died September, 1898, at New Orleans.

D. S. L.

Atkinson's Phys. and Surgs of the U. S., Appleton's Biography.
Stone's American Phys. and Surgs.

Semmes, Thomas (1778–1833).

The eldest son of Edward and Sarah Middleton Semmes, of Prince George County, Maryland, he was born on August 13, 1778. The Semmes family was of French origin, and the first to receive a grant of land in the colony of Maryland was one Joseph Semmes, as shown by a record now in the state archives.

His family were Roman Catholics and it was the intention of his parents that he should become a priest, but their design was frustrated by the death of both parents before the boy was twelve. After having acquired a good classical education, he read medicine with Dr. Elisha C. Dick, of Alexandria, District of Columbia, and, later, attended lectures at the University of Pennsylvania, graduating in 1801. His inaugural thesis on the general effects of lead, and the nature and properties of lead acetate, presented many striking and original observations.

After graduating he went abroad and spent a year studying in Paris and St. Petersburg, after which he returned home and settled in Alexandria, District of Columbia, where he continued to live and practise until his death.

He soon obtained in the highest degree the confidence of the public, and his success was almost unprecedented. He repaid that confidence by untiring assiduity, especially in times of calamity, as when the epidemics of 1803 and 1822 visited his people. In both of these years yellow fever came, and in 1832 there occurred one of Asiatic cholera, so-called. His success as a practitioner was remarkable, as was well evinced in the latter epidemic, as is shown by the fact that while there were hundreds of deaths from the disease in Washington and Georgetown, there were only about thirty in almost an equal number of cases in Alexandria.

In 1808 he married Sophia Wilson, the daughter of John P. and Eliza Ramsey, and six children survived their parents.

Towards the close of his life he was attacked by a wasting disease, the result of incessant toil, and in July, 1833, was taken with a fever which he was unable to successfully combat, and on the last day of that month (July 31, 1833) he passed away.

A portrait of Dr. Semmes is now in the possession of a grand-daughter.*

*Mrs. S M. Slaughter, Mitchells, Culpepper County, Virginia. There is also a portrait of him in the collection in the library of the surgeon-general of the United States Army.

R. M. S.

An unpublished sketch by one of his daughters. Amer. Jour. Med. Scs., vol. xvii
William's Medical Biography.

Senkler, Albert Edward (1842-1899).

Albert Edward Senkler was an Englishman by birth, having been born at Docking, Norfolk, England, March 8, 1842. When he was still a boy his father, a clergyman of the Church of England, came to Brockville, Ontario. His early education was obtained under the tutelage of his father, who was a fellow of Caius College, Cambridge and a scholar, one who gave him at home an education and an intellectual start in life, such as few boys have. Being naturally of a scientific bent, Albert decided to study medicine, and at an early age entered McGill University at Montreal, where he received, when only twenty-one, his M. D., and that of Master of Surgery in 1863. Two years later he began to practise at St. Cloud, Minnesota, where he soon had a large clientèle. From 1873 to 1876 he was a member of the Minnesota State Board of Health and made the first meteorological observations in the State of Minnesota. 1880 saw him at St. Paul, where he lived up to the time of his death. He was president of the Minnesota Academy of Medicine, and professor of clinical medicine in the medical department of the Minnesota State University, also at the time of his death on the staff of every hospital in St. Paul. Indeed it may be said that his profession, recognizing and appreciating his character and distinguished ability had conferred upon him every honor within its power. He married Frances Isabella Easton, at Brockville, Canada, August 28, 1867. Two children were born; the son, George E., became a doctor.

Dr. Senkler, after a lingering illness, which for nearly a year prevented him from attending to his practice, died at his home in St. Paul, Sunday morning, December 10, 1899. A gentleman of the noblest type; a scholar in medicine, an accomplished physician who loved his profession and all that was best in it.

B. F.

Senn, Nicholas (1844-1908).

Nicholas Senn, justly termed by his contemporaries the greatest surgeon, medical authority and writer the West had ever produced, was born in Buchs, Canton of St. Gall, Switzerland, on October 31, 1844, but his parents came to the United States in 1852 and settled in Ashford, Wisconsin. Nicholas became a student at the Chicago Medical College in 1868, and after graduating there returned to Europe and devoted his time to research and pathological studies. His early experimental work on abdominal surgery, later carried into practice, made him foremost in this field. His decalcified bone plates for intestinal anastomoses, given to the profession after an astounding number of experiments, revolutionized intestinal surgery and were the forerunners of all modern mechanical intestinal devices. His researches on intestinal perforation, especially by gunshot wounds, in which he introduced the hydrogen gas test, were the work of a master. Surgical tuberculosis was for some time his especial study and he developed and practised many of our modern ideas on the surgical aspect of this condition. His studies on tumors including the first comprehensive writing on the subject in this country, were enough to make him famous.

In military surgery his record was especially brilliant, for his contributions to improve first aid on the battle field and his extensive experiments which developed our modern conservative methods in the treatment of bullet wounds commanded the attention of the surgical world.

Senn's experimental work on dogs, "Intestinal Anastomosis by means of Decalcified Bone Plates" brought this department of surgery into notice throughout the civilized world and became the foundation of that brilliant and wonderful work that is being performed in every quarter of the globe. Another brilliant conception was the "Inflation of the Gastrointestinal Tract with Hydrogen Gas as a Means of Detecting Perforation."

Yet the world knows little of his unselfish labors. In a laboratory constructed under the sidewalk by his Milwaukee house, night after night he carried on his original investigations. In 1902 he spent five months becoming acquainted with the hospitals of Europe, Asia Minor and Egypt. At the outbreak of the Spanish-American War he left a large practice and hurried south doing heroic service in the face of usual inefficiency of the ambulance supplies. Once, escorting Spanish wounded to Santiago as exchange prisoners he made friends with the young surgeon, Rodondo, in charge of the Spanish ambulance. "Not Nicholas Senn of Chicago?" asked the Spaniard. "Then if the army is composed of men such as you we certainly cannot hope for success." The acquaintance ripened into friendship and Rodondo translated Senn's "Practice of Surgery" into Spanish.

Of his liberality, the Senn collection of books in the Newberry Library, on which collection he spent $50,000, is a lasting memorial. This was not his only gift. The Senn Memorial building for scientific purposes; the Senn professorship; Senn fellowship and the Senn rooms in St. Joseph's Hospital for the perpetual use of sick members of his own profession represent in all an outlay of $50,000 and an endowment of $75,000.

The ultimate cause of his death on Jannary 2, 1908, was chronic interstitial myocarditis, though the end was hastened by his ascending a peak of the Andes, some 16,000 feet high when on a trip round the coast of South America. His wife, Aurelia S. Muehlhauser, survived him.

His appointments included: resident physician to Cook County Hospital, Wisconsin; attending physician, Milwaukee Hospital, Wisconsin; professor of surgery, College of Physicians and Surgeons, Chicago; professor of surgery and clinical surgery, Rush Medical College: and he was founder of the Association of Military Surgeons of the United States. Member of the Royal Medical Society, Buda-Pest; Glasgow Academy of Medicine; Imperial Royal Medical Society of Vienna.

Some of the results of his research were given to the world in the following: "Experimental and Clinical Study of Air Embolism;" "Fractures of the Neck of the Femur with Special Reference to Bony Union after Intra-capsular Fractures;" "Surgery of the Pancreas based on Clinical and Experimental Researches;" "Experimental Enquiry concerning Elastic Constriction as Hemostatic Measure;" "Surgical Treatment of Intestinal Obstruction;" "Experimental Contribution to Intestinal Surgery;" "Surgical Bacteriology;" "Principles of Surgery;" "Tuberculosis of Bones and Joints." The list of his writing occupies three pages in the Catalogue of the Surgeon-general, Washington, D. C.

D. W.

Compiled from: Obituary Notices, Nicholas Senn, by Dr. S. M. Wylie, Ill., 1908.

NICHOLAS SENN.

Sewall, Lucy (1837–1890).

Lucy Sewall, a pioneer woman physieian, descended from a · long line of Puritan ancestors, belonged to the Sewalls of Massachusetts. She was born in Boston, April 26, 1837, the daughter of Samuel E. Sewall, lawyer and reformer. While in her youth, coming under the influence of Dr. Marie Zackrewska, she was drawn to study medicine. She seems to have been the first girl of fortune and family to study medicine in the United States. She entered the only college then open to women, the New England Female Medical College of Boston, graduating in March, 1862, then went to Europe where women were admitted to hospitals only by favor, but such was her ability and personality that she not only gained favors, but proved herself eminently worthy of them in her work with Dr. A. Chereau, whose lectures she attended in Paris.

Upon her return in 1863 she became resident physician of the New England Hospital. Her romantic and enthusiastic friendship for Dr. Zackrewska, while yet her pupil, led the young Boston girl to devote her life, her fortune and the influence she could command from a wide circle of friends to the building up of the hospital. In 1869 she resigned the position of resident physician to become attending physician, serving until 1886, and considered an expert obstetrician. The Maternity Building at the New England Hospital is named after her, Sewall Maternity.

Through her influence the Massachusetts Infant Asylum was founded, the first effort made in Massachusetts to save the lives of infants who would otherwise have gone to the almshouses or the "baby-farms."

The latter years of her life were those of enforced semi-invalidism, because of organic heart disease, but she took up the study of mineralogy as a diversion.

She died of valvular disease of the heart, February 13, 1890, having well achieved the purpose of her life, that of creating confidence in women as physicians and surgeons.

A. B. W.

Personal communication, The Nat. Cyclopedia of American Biography, vol. x. A. Chereau, L'Union Medicale, Paris, vol. xix. Woman's Journal, Boston, vol. xxi. Jex Blake, Medical Women, 1872.

Sewall, Thomas (1787–1845).

Thomas Sewall was born April 16, 1787, at Augusta, Maine, the son of Thomas and Priscilla (Cony) Sewall, and married Mary Choate, sister of Rufus Choate, November 28, 1813. There was but one child, Thomas, born April 28, 1818. After receiving his M. D. at Harvard, Dr. Sewall studied under Rush and others at the University of Pennsylvania. He was given to original research and published possibly the first monograph on the postmortem appearance of the gastric mucosa in alcoholics, shortly following the work of Beaumont on digestion. He was the first or one of the first opponents of phrenology and wrote a monograph, "The Errors of Phrenology Exposed." He also published papers in the current medical journals.

He was the author of "Lectures Delivered at the Opening of the Medical Department of Columbia College," etc., Washington, 1825, 1826. "Eulogy on Dr. Goodman," Washington, 1830, 1832, 1840; "Examination of Phrenology," etc., Washington, 1837, 1839. "The Enquirer; Pathology of Drunkenness," 1841; this was later translated into German and established his reputation both at home and abroad as an original investigator. D. S. L.

Minutes of Med. Soc., D. C., Apr., 1845. Appleton's Med. Biog., 1889. The Med. Exam., Phila., 1845

Seymour, William Pierce (1825–1893).

William Pierce Seymour did not leave much written work, but was one of those who, a generation ahead of the profession, seem to care little or nothing about posthumous reputation but devote themselves entirely to mastering every subject for the sake of exact knowledge and teaching. He was one of the three sons of Israel and Lucinda Pierce Seymour who were among the early settlers of Troy, New York, where William was born October 17, 1825. He worked as a schoolboy under Prof. Charles H. Anthony and, graduating from Williams College in 1841, studied medicine with Dr. Alfred Wotkyns, whose daughter he afterwards married in 1852. He graduated from the University of Pennsylvania in 1848 and the following year began to practise in Troy. After filling many appointments, 1870 saw him professor of obstetrics at the Albany Medical College, and, added to this three years later the professorship of gynecology. A student of Hodge, he yet corrected errors of that time and recognized in the human pelvis three straits or planes having their appropriate diameters and their axes decussating at a similar angle of 130 degrees to the planes of entrance, rotation and exit, leaving the teaching of Levret as to the two straits and axes to the lower animals, where it belongs.

His statement as to the infectivity of pneumonia, made in 1868 before the Rensselaer County Medical Society, met with strong opposition, and ten years before his strong advocation of operation for appendicitis, then called typhlitis, was deemed impossible. Those who knew him best, however, and were educated to follow him, appreciated his ability and mental worth.

He died on April 7, 1893, passing away quietly as if falling asleep. He left two sons, Alfred W. and William Wotkyns, the latter following his father's profession.

Stone's Eminent Amer. Phys. and Surgs.

Shakespeare, Edward Oram (1846–1900).

Edward Oram Shakespeare was born May 19, 1846, in Delaware, and graduated at Dickinson's College in June, 1867, taking his M. D. at the University of Pennsylvania in 1869. After practising

in Dover, he removed to Philadelphia in 1874. He was made lecturer on operative surgery at the University of Pennsylvania and wrote a number of ophthalmological papers.

He investigated the cause of a great epidemic of typhoid fever in Wyoming Valley near Wilkesbarre, Pennsylvania, and discovered the cause in the contamination of the mountain water, which report was of great value. In 1885 he was sent as United States representative to Spain to investigate cholera, and made an elaborate report to Congress. During the war with Spain he was appointed brigade-surgeon.

He died June 1, 1900.   H. F.

Stone's Biography of Eminent American Physicians and Surgeons.
Journal Am. Med. Assoc., June 9, 1900.

Shapleigh, Elisha Bacon (1823–1892).

Best known as an expert in forensic medicine, Elisha Bacon Shapleigh was born in York County, Maine, on November 6, 1823, a descendant of one Nicholas Shapleigh who emigrated from England in 1630.

His A. B. was from Yale in 1846, his M. D. from the University of Pennsylvania, in 1849.

Immediately after graduation he settled in Lowell, Massachusetts, but in 1851, removed to Philadelphia, where he married in June, 1864, Anna, daughter of William Lloyd.

He was a copious writer for the medical press, especially on subjects connected with toxicology and legal medicine.

Dr. Shapleigh was a man of medium size, but heavy build. He had dark skin, hair and eyes, and wore a full beard. He was slow and deliberate in speech, but fond of telling stories; he was ever saying "that reminds me." He was read almost as widely in law as in medicine.   T. H. S.

Memoir, J. Collins, 1893.

Shattuck, Benjamin (1742–1794).

Benjamin Shattuck was a descendant of William Shattuck, who was born in

England and died in Watertown, Massachusetts, August 14, 1672, aged fifty-eight. Benjamin was born in Littleton, Massachusetts, November 11, 1742, the grandson of the Rev. Benjamin Shattuck, first minister of Littleton, and son of Stephen Shattuck, farmer, a man of great physical and mental powers and a warm patriot. On the memorable April 19, 1775, after he was sixty-five, he shouldered his gun and marched to Concord and followed the retreating enemy to Cambridge. Benjamin's grandmother was a grand-daughter of the celebrated John Sherman, clergyman and metaphysician.

He was fitted for college by Jeremiah Dummer Rogers and graduated A. M. from Harvard College in 1765. After studying medicine with Dr. Oliver Prescott, of Groton, Massachusetts he settled, in Templeton, and practised there until his death in that town, January 14, 1794.

April 12, 1772, he married Lucy, daughter of Jonathan Barron, a brave provincial officer who was killed in "Johnson's Fight" at Lake George, September 8, 1755. They had seven children.

Dr. Shattuck was settled in a region with but few inhabitants; instruments and books were scarce. By perseverance and sagacity coupled with unremitting labor he built up a large practice and was accounted the foremost physician of the county.

W. L. B.

Shattuck Memorials, 1855, Lemuel Shattuck.
Discourse by Ebenezer Sparhawk, A. M., Boston, 1882.
Genealog. Dict. of the First Settlers of New Eng., James Savage, 1861.
Hist. Har Medical School, T. F. Harrington. Amer. Med Biog., James Thacher, M. D., 1828

Shattuck, George Cheyne, Senior (1784–1854).

George Cheyne Shattuck was born in Templeton, July 17, 1784, the youngest son of Dr. Benjamin Shattuck, and Lucy Barron, and was named for George Cheyne, an old London and Bath physician who lived between 1671 and 1743.

He was educated at Dartmouth College, where he received his A. B. in 1803; M. B. in 1806; the honorary M. D. in 1812, and LL. D. in 1853, meanwhile receiving the M. D., from the University of Pennsylvania in 1807, and the honorary A. M. from Harvard in the same year. He was a fellow of the American Academy of Arts and Sciences, and began to practise in Boston in 1807, and continued there until his death, March 18, 1854.

He married Eliza Cheever Davis, daughter of Caleb Davis, and lived and died in his house at the corner of Staniford and Cambridge Streets in the West End. He had a very large family practice and was noted for his benevolence. Dr. Edward Jarvis relates of him that upon many occasions he was called upon to treat the needy students at Andover and Cambridge. After hearing their complaints and prescribing for them, he would hand the sufferer a prescription and say courteously, "Now, sir, will you be good enough to carry this prescription to the apothecary 134 Washington Street, and while he is putting up the medicine, will you do me the favor to carry this note to Mr. K., No. 5 Congress Street?" The grateful student wishing to make some return for a free consultation and for the kindly interest in his case, gladly took the note to Mr. K. only to learn that it was an order to K., the tailor, for a suit of clothes for the bearer of the note.

Shattuck was president of the Massachusetts Medical Society from 1836 to 1840 and delivered the annual discourse in 1828. He was, many years before the establishment of the Board of Health, one of the consulting physicians of the City of Boston. He avoided public office as a rule. He was a man of strong religious convictions. Rev. Cyrus A. Bartol said of his last hours, "'Pray with me,' was commonly his first salutation as I entered his sick chamber. 'I want your prayers, they are a great comfort and consolation. Pray not for my recovery, I am going to God. I wish in your prayer to go as a sinner.' "

At various times he gave Harvard College over $26,000. His donation of $7,000 made the foundation of Dartmouth College Observatory, and he gave many books and portraits to the college library.

The year before he died he established the Shattuck professorship of pathological anatomy in the Harvard Medical School by a gift of $14,000. Of his six children all but the oldest son, George Cheyne, died when young. Shattuck assisted Dr. James Thacher with his American Medical Biography, as mentioned in the preface by Thacher.

W. L. B.

Shattuck Memorials, Lemuel Shattuck, 1855.
Memoirs by Edward Jarvis, M. D. aud Discourse by Rev. C. A. Bartol, 1854.
History Harvard Med. School, T. F. Harrington.
Port. in the Surg.-Gen. Lib., Wash., D. C.

Shattuck, George Cheyne, Junior (1813–1893).

George Cheyne Shattuck was born in Boston, Massachusetts, July 22, 1813, the son of Dr. George Cheyne and Eliza Cheever Davis Shattuck, and grandson, on his mother's side, of the Hon. Caleb Davis, all of Boston.

His early education was obtained at the Boston Latin School and at the famous "Round Hill School" at Northampton, Massachusetts. It was there, probably, that the interest in educational matters began which led him in later life to found St. Paul's School in Concord, New Hampshire. In his early life his love of study was, perhaps, over-stimulated by his father, so that he was inclined to work beyond the strength of a not too rugged constitution. He received his A. B. from Harvard College in 1831, and after spending a year at the Harvard Law School he entered the Harvard Medical School, took his M. D. in 1835 and then went abroad for study. In common with his friends, Bowditch, Stillé and Metcalfe, he was much influenced by the methods, the teaching and personality of Louis, with whom he kept up an intimacy

until the latter's death forty years later. Shattuck and Stillé read papers before the Paris Society for Medical Observation, in 1838, that served to mark out the distinction between typhus and typhoid fevers.

On April 9, 1840, having settled to practise in Boston, he married Anne Henrietta Brune of Baltimore.

For nearly twenty years he was a professor in the Harvard Medical School; from 1855 to 1859, professor of clinical medicine, and from 1859 to 1873, professor of the theory and practice of medicine. In 1849 he succeeded Oliver Wendell Holmes as visiting physician to the Massachusetts General Hospital and served in this capacity for thirty-six years. He was president of the Massachusetts Medical Society from 1872 to 1874, and a fellow of the American Academy of Arts and Sciences.

He died March 22, 1893. He was survived by a daughter and two sons, one of the latter being Frederick Cheever Shattuck, who became professor of clinical medicine in the Harvard Medical School, and the other, George Brune Shattuck, the editor of the "Boston Medical and Surgical Journal." An oil painting of Dr. Shattuck is in the Boston Medical Library.

W. L. B.

Shattuck Memorials, Lemuel Shattuck, 1855.
A Brief Sketch of the Life of Dr. George Cheyne Shattuck, by Caleb Davis Bradlee, D. D., 1894.
A Sermon by Henry A. Coit, D. D., LL, D., 1893.
Boston Medical & Surg. Jour., vol. cxxviii

Shaw, Charles H. (1875?–1910).

Charles H. Shaw, botanist, was born about 1875 in Delaware, Ohio, where he received his early education. He graduated from the Ohio Wesleyan University, and later came to the University of Pennsylvania, where he entered the Graduate School, receiving the Ph. D. in 1901, electing botany as his major subject. His doctor's thesis, published in "Contributions from the Botanical Laboratory, University of Pennsylvania," vol. ii, No. 2, pages 122–149, was entitled "The Comparative Structure of the Flowers of Polygala polygama and P. pauciflora with Observations on Cleistogamy." After graduation he was elected to the chair of biology in Ursinus College, Collegeville, Pennsylvania. Later he became professor of botany in the Medico-Chirurgical College where he continued to serve until June, 1910, when he resigned to become professor in the university. Shaw loved an outdoor life and open air pursuits, and a few of his summer vacations were spent in exploring the Catskills, the Adirondack Mountains and the Alps of Europe. Lured by the greater attractions of the mountains of British Columbia, he led organized camping parties to visit the wilds of a country unrivaled on this continent for scenic beauty and grandeur. On one of these trips (the summer of 1904) Dr. Shaw made a large collection of mountain and Alpine plants which were distributed to the herbaria of the world. He also contributed a number of papers to botanic journals, among which should be mentioned "The Development of Vegetation in the Morainal Depression of the Vicinity of Woods Hole " (1902); "Causes of Timber Line in High Mountains" (1909); "The Teaching of Respiration in Plants." One summer was spent by Dr. Shaw in study abroad with Prof. C. Flahault at the University of Montpellier, France. Shaw remarked to the writer in June of this year that he had planned to make this the biggest campaign yet.

He left in high spirits to meet a party of ten persons, men and women, with Mrs. Shaw as one of the party. Their permanent camp was located on the delta of one of the streams emptying into that part of the Columbia river known as Lake Timbasket, British Columbia, when his death by drowning occurred, the details of which will never be known, as he was alone in a canoe, returning to camp after seeing two of his university colleagues to the trail on August 8, 1910.

J. W. H.

Old Penn. Weekly Review, Phila., 1910.

Shaw, Charles Stoner (1856–1899).

Charles Stoner Shaw was born in Pittsburg, September 13, 1856, the second son of Thomas Wilson and Catherine Stoner Shaw. His early education was obtained at the Ward and high schools of Pittsburg.

He graduated in medicine at the University of Pennsylvania in 1879 and returning to Pittsburg was associated with his father and devoted himself to general practice for several years, gradually, however, restricting himself to the treatment of diseases of children. In 1894 he was elected to the chair of diseases of children in the medical department of the Western University of Pennsylvania, in Pittsburg, which position he held until his death. His wide knowledge coupled with his scholarly attainments, exceptional for his age, at once attracted the students and made his lectures a marked feature in the college course.

He was a member of the County, State and National Medical Societies. At the time of his death he was the unanimous choice for the presidency of the Allegheny County Medical Society.

Shaw was a man of high ideals, and stood for all that is best and highest in the medical profession. With a view to do battle in its cause and to stimulate the observance of the Code of Ethics, the more especially as to its bearings on nostrums and nostrum advertising in the medical press, he, with some half dozen others of the younger physicians of Pittsburg, organized in December, 1885, "The Pittsburg Medical Review," a monthly periodical owned and controlled entirely by the editors. Dr. Shaw was recognized as editor-in-chief of this publication and under his vigorous efforts, directed especially at the "Journal of the American Medical Association," the board of trustees of that journal gradually eliminated the more obnoxious advertisements, until its pages were practically free from all advertisements which the code of ethics forbids.

Dr. Shaw was not married and died in

Albuquerque, New Mexico, of pulmonary tuberculosis, December 28, 1899.

His contributions to medical literature partook largely of the nature of editorials together with papers on general medicine and pediatrics.

His portrait is in the hall of the Assembly Room of the Pittsburg Free Dispensary. A. K.

Shaw, John (1778–1809).

John Shaw was born at Annapolis, Maryland, May 4, 1778, and entered St. John's College on its opening in 1789 and took his A. B. there in 1796. He began the study of medicine under Dr. John Thomas Shaaff, of Annapolis. In 1798, while attending his first course of lectures at the University of Pennsylvania, he received an appointment as surgeon in the United States Navy, and sailed to Algiers. He spent about a year and a half in North Africa, holding a position which was partly medical and partly consular. While there he learned to speak Arabic, and became physician to the Bey of Tunis, Secretary of Legation and Chargé d'Affaires. He returned home in the spring of 1800, but in July, 1801, left America for medical studies in Edinburgh. But early in 1803, before he had obtained his medical degree there, he was induced to go to Canada by the Earl of Selkirk, who had founded a colony. He remained in the Earl's service until 1805, when he returned to Annapolis, to practise. In February, 1807, he married and removed to Baltimore, where he joined with Davidge and Cocké in founding the College of Medicine of Maryland (University of Maryland), in which he held the chair of chemistry. He was treasurer of the Medical and Chirurgical Faculty of Maryland from 1807 to his death, which occurred at sea, January 10, 1809, at the age of thirty, from consumption. Dr. Shaw published a number of poems, and left a manuscript of his travels and life in Africa. The former were collected and republished in a volume in 1810, preceded by a biographical memoir. ("Poems by John Shaw,"

Philadelphia, 1810.) His prose style is sprightly and entertaining, his poetry is chiefly sentimental and patriotic and is sweet and graceful. E. F. C.

Cordell's Historical Sketch, 1891.
Medical Annals of Maryland, Cordell.

Shaw, John Cargyll (1845–1900).

John Cargyll Shaw, a New York alienist, was born September 25, 1845 at St. Ann's Bay, Jamaica, and died in Brooklyn January 23, 1900. His parents were John and Christiana Drew Shaw. After education in the local schools he came to the United States with his mother and sister when seventeen. After serving with a wholesale druggist in New York, and attending lectures on chemistry, he studied medicine under Dr. George K. Smith and in 1874 took his M. D. from the College of Physicians and Surgeons. He took great interest in studying the histology and pathology of the nervous system in the laboratory of Dr. Satterwaith and Prof. Seguin and became clinical assistant to the latter at the College of Physicians and Surgeons.

He was appointed neurologist at St. Peter's Hospital, Brooklyn, New York, and filled the position of medical superintendent of the Lunatic Asylum of Kings County, where he instituted and carried out many needed and praiseworthy reforms. He was appointed lecturer on the diseases of the nervous system at the Long Island College Hospital, and advanced to the position of clinical professor of the mind and the nervous system, increasing his reputation in the field of clinical instruction. Twice president of the New York Neurological Society, he was also elected president in 1893 of the Medical Society of the county of Kings and consulting physician to the State Hospital for the Insane, Poughkeepsie, New York and occupied the position of neurologist in: St. Peter's Hospital, the Long Island College Hospital, the Brooklyn Hospital, St. Catherine Hospital, the Long Island Throat Hospital, the Brooklyn Eye and Ear Hospital, and the Kings County Hospital. He held membership in: The New York Neurological Society, the Brooklyn Pathological Society, the American Neurological Society, the Medical Society of the County of Kings, the Neurological Society of Brooklyn, the Medical Society of the State of New York and the Brooklyn Anatomical and Surgical Society.

Dr. Shaw contributed many valuable papers on subjects relating to the nervous system, reading them before medical societies and publishing them in medical journals. The following may be mentioned: "Muscular Atrophies in Locomotor Ataxia;" "Hemiplegia in Children"; "Progressive Muscular Atrophy and its Pathology;" "Anomalous Cases of Locomotor Ataxia;" "General Paralysis of the Insane;" "The Practicability and Value of Non-Restraint Treatment of the Insane;" "Raynaud's Disease;" etc., etc. He contributed to "International Clinics" and for a time was an associated editor of the "American Medical Digest, and he wrote "Essentials of Nervous Diseases and Insanity." Moved by the kindness of his heart, and dominant by insight and reason, his efforts were directed and applied to the more humane treatment of the insane. The commissioners of Charity, moved by his persistent importunities, gave the good doctor all their aid to improve the condition of the poor who had become insane from want, anxiety, hard work and improper food. There was a praiseworthy effort to transform the modern "Bedlam," as it were, back into the Home of Bread, the "Bethlehem," in which the better emblem of sanity might come with hope and peace. Chains, shackles, handcuffs and strait-jackets were taken off. Occupations and amusements were provided. Cottages were built for the less violently insane, and better sanitary conditions were established.

Shaw set out on his life work with ambition, industry, perseverance and high aims and made himself master in every department of his specialty.

Am. J. Insan., Balt. 1900–1, lvii (B. Onuf).
Brooklyn M. J., 1900, xiv.

Shecut, John Linneus Edward Whitridge (1770–1837).

This physician was born at Beaufort, South Carolina, December 4, 1770, descended from French Huguenots who sought refuge in Switzerland, near Geneva, whence his parents, Abraham and Marie Barbary Shecut, emigrated to South Carolina in 1768–9.

He began to study medicine under Dr. David Ramsay, and in 1791 graduated from the University of Pennsylvania.

He was a member of the Literary and Philosophical Society of South Carolina, which he organised in 1813, first as the Antiquarian Society. He was first president of the American Homespun Company, the first cotton factory in the state, which he himself founded in 1820.

Dr. Shecut began to practise at Charleston immediately after graduation and continued in active duty until death. He was one of the pioneers in the therapeutic application of electricity, and in 1806 exhibited a machine which he had designed for its administration. In his discussion of the yellow-fever epidemic of 1817 he advanced the theory that the cause of this malady was "a peculiar derangement of the atmospheric air" depriving it of "a due proportion of the electric fluid," acting in conjunction with "a peculiar state or diathesis in the animal economy particularly pre-disposing to disease."

Dr. Shecut's interests were not limited by medicine, as shown by his activity in scientific, literary and industrial fields. His work on the flora of Carolina was written for the purpose of stimulating an interest in the study of botany and to simplify the Linnaean system. In later life he became actively interested in theology and organized the body of Trinitarian Universalists. This organization seems to have been rather short-lived, for the founder became allied with the Methodists, of which denomination he was a member at the time of his death.

He married Sarah Cannon, January 26, 1792, and had four children, one of whom, William Harrel, studied medicine.

He married his second wife, Susannah Ballard, on February 7, 1805, and had five children more by this marriage.

He died at his home at Charleston, June 1, 1837, of paralysis. A voluminous writer, the following are among his chief works:

"Flora Carolinensis, an Historical, Medical and Economical Display of the Vegetable Kingdom," Charleston, South Carolina, 1806.

"Medical and Philosophical Essays," Charleston, South Carolina, 1819, containing topographical, historical and other sketches of the city of Charleston; "An Essay on the Prevailing Fever of 1817;" "An Essay on Contagions and Infections;" "An Essay on the Principles and Properties of the Electric Fluid;" "The Elements of Natural Philosophy and a New Theory of the Earth;" "The Eagle of the Mohawks," a novel, New York; "The Scout, or the Fort of St. Nicholas," a novel of the seventeenth century, New York.

There is also in possession of his descendants a manuscript work entitled "Trinitarian Universalists."

R. W., JR.

Sherman, Benjamin Franklin (1817–1897).

The youngest of five brothers, all physicians; he was a descendant of one Henry Sherman, born in Devonshire, England, in 1516, and John Sherman, who came to Connecticut in 1634. Benjamin was born in Barre, Vermont, May 241 1817, graduated at the Albany Medical College and finally settled down to prac, tise in Ogdensburg where he married Charlotte C. Chipman of Waddington and had five children two of whom became doctors. He began practice when medical education was hard to obtain.

Taking long journeys by stage and sailing vessels to reach recognized teachers, he fitted himself to be one of the best men around. He eagerly kept pace with every advance, so that, in his eightieth year, younger men came to him to take advice and borrow books and instruments. Often he had to mount at sunrise, fill his saddlebags with home manufactured drugs and set out on a long tour not knowing whether a major operation or a delicate piece of eye surgery would be required en route. As physician and chemist he was also called on for evidence in important trials and litigations. Among his appointments were: presidency of the New York State Medical Society; presidency Northern New York Medical Society, and of the St. Lawrence County Medical Society.

Mem. by Dr. J. M. Mosher in Tr. Med. Soc. State of N. York, 1898.

Shipman, Azariah B. (1803–1868).

It seems a little curious that more than once the sons of a farmer, brought up in absolutely healthy surroundings, should turn to the study and cure of disease. Daniel and Sarah Eastman Shipman looked for one of their five boys to manage the farm but away they all went, Parson, and John, Daniel and Joseph and Azariah. Azariah was born on March 22, 1803, and helped till he was seventeen on a new farm at Pitcher, Chenango County. Then, without money or influential friends, doing farm work in summer and teaching in winter, he determinately gave his odd leisure to studying medicine, two years later working under his eldest brother who had become a doctor in Delphi, New York, and in 1826, with a license from the County Medical Society, he too practised in that county, successfully it may be presumed, as he was able to marry, in 1828, Emily Clark, step-daughter of a Mr. Richard Taylor. In Cortland, in Syracuse, as professor of anatomy in the University of Laporte, Indiana, he had a fine reputation for surgery and his reputation led to his doing nearly all the important operations for miles around, some, such as removal of tumors, tracheotomy, lithotomy, under difficult circumstances. Three years as army surgeon during the war broke down his health, and a tour in Europe in 1868 was disappointing in recuperatory results. He landed in Paris after the trip, failing under a pulmonary affection and on September 15, 1868, he sank rapidly and died.

His keen desire for knowledge of all kinds was starved in his boyhood, and his library, with its old books and curiosities, told how one day he meant to enjoy a learned leisure which, long expected, never came.

D. W.

Tr. M. Soc., N. Y., 1869. (H. O. Jewett.)

Shippen, William, Sr. (1712-1801).

Plodding through old medical biographies—works of the never-was-and-never-will-be such another man type and wherein every doctor seems to have had "few equals and no superiors," readers may glean that William Shippen, after being born in Philadelphia Oct. 1, 1712, studied medicine in his youth with Dr. John Kearsley, Jr., and soon after became "uncommonly successful and rose to a high reputation." He was one of the founders of the College of New Jersey towards which he donated large sums and bequeathed an annuity, and was first physician to the Pennsylvania Hospital, also a trustee of the College of Physicians, Philadelphia.

"He never in the course of his whole life" says the biographer "was once heard to swear profanely and never drank wine or spirituous liquor," which two facts were certainly worthy of record in those old times. He wore "a ruffled shirt" and had an unruffled temper, was a firm friend of Whitefield the Methodist reformer, and departed this world on November 4, 1801, "being buried by the side of his six grandchildren, followed by a large train of his mourning relatives and friends."

D. W.

Thacher, Med. Biography.
Morton and Woodbury, Hist. of the Penn. Hosp.

Shippen, William, Jr. (1736-1808).

He was born in Philadelphia October 21, 1736, and went as a boy to an academy kept by the Rev. Samuel Finley, Not-tingham, in which John Morgan and Benjamin Rush were also pupils. He received the degree of A. B. from the College of New Jersey (Princeton) in 1754. He was the valedictorian of his class, and the great preacher Whitefield, who was present, is said to have declared that he had never heard better speaking and urged Shippen to go into the ministry. He, however, returned to Philadelphia, where he devoted himself to the study of medicine with his father, Dr. William Shippen, Sr., until 1758, when he went abroad to finish his medical education. Watson[1] quotes a letter written by the father to an English correspondent, in which he writes, "My son has had his education in the best college in this part of the country, and has been studying physic with me, besides which he has had the opportunity of seeing the practice of every gentleman of note in our city. But for want of that variety of operations and those frequent dissections which are common in older countries, I must send him to Europe. His scheme is to gain all the knowledge he can in anatomy, physic, and surgery."

In London young Shippen studied anatomy with John Hunter and midwifery with William Hunter and Dr. McKenzie. He also had an opportunity of seeing much of the work of Sir John Pringle and Dr. William Hewson. He also became upon friendly terms with Dr. John Fothergill, the famous Quaker physician, a friendship which was fruitful in great benefit to medical education, as Fothergill became greatly interested in the Pennsylvania Hospital, and in the medical department of the College of Philadelphia. To the hospital he sent a series of crayon pictures illustrating the anatomy of the human body, which he had especially made by Remsdyck. The pictures are still there and in a good state of preservation.

Before returning to his native land Shippen obtained his M. D. from Edinburgh University, his thesis being "De Placentæ cum Utero Nexu." In Edin-

[1] Annals, vol. ii, p. 378, Edited 1844.

burgh he had sat at the feet of Munro *primus* and Cullen.

Upon finishing his studies in London and Edinburgh he wanted to continue them in France, but, as England and France were then at war, he only managed it by the friendly interest of Sir John Pringle. This great authority on military surgery secured him the position of travelling physician to a tuberculous lady who having court influence, had got George the Second to procure for her a special passport through the south of France. In this capacity Shippen went over and met some of the celebrated physicians of Paris.

In 1762 he returned to Philadelphia, bringing with him the Fothergill pictures, and full of schemes to establish courses in anatomy and midwifery for the instruction of his fellow-countrymen. These plans soon took form and he announced his first course of lectures in a newspaper letter dated the eleventh of November, 1762, in which he stated "that a course of anatomical lectures will be opened this winter in Philadelphia for the advantage of the young gentlemen now engaged in the study of physic in this and the neighboring provinces, whose circumstances and connections will not permit of their going abroad for improvement to the anatomical schools in Europe; and also for the entertainment of any gentlemen who may have the curiosity to understand the anatomy of the human frame. In these lectures the situation, figure, and structure of all the parts of the human body will be demonstrated, their respective uses explained, and as far as a course of anatomy will permit, their diseases, with the indications and methods of cure briefly treated of. All the necessary operations in surgery will be performed, a course of bandages exhibited, and the whole concluded with an explanation of some of the curious phenomena that arise from an examination of the gravid uterus, and a few plain general directions in the study and practice of midwifery. The necessity and public utility of such

a course in this growing country, and the method to be pursued therein, will be more particularly explained in an introductory lecture, to be delivered on the sixteenth instant, at six o'clock in the evening, at the State House, by William Shippen, Jr., M. D.

"The lectures will be given at his father's house in Fourth Street. Tickets for the course to be had of the doctor at five pistoles each; and any gentleman who may incline to see the subject prepared for the lectures and learn the art of dissecting, injecting, etc., is to pay five pistoles more."

His first course of lectures was attended by ten pupils but it was not long before larger numbers came. The public was greatly opposed to dissection at that time and Shippen met with violent opposition on the part of the populace, who stoned him and smashed on several occasions the windows of the house in which the dissections were performed. To allay this prejudice he announced in letters to the newspaper that the bodies he used were those of persons who had committed suicide or been legally executed, except "now and then one from the Potter's field."

In 1765 Dr. Shippen began his lectures on midwifery, the first systematic instruction given in obstetrics in this country. He himself engaged actively in the practice of that branch although it was still customary to leave the management of labor cases chiefly in the hands of female midwives. Shippen's lectures were illustrated by the "anatomical plates and casts of the gravid uterus at the hospital."

In connection with his midwifery lectures he also established a small lying-in hospital "under the care of a sober, honest matron, well acquainted with lying-in women."

In May, 1765, the Board of Trustees of the College of Philadelphia had voted to establish a medical school in connection with the College and had elected John Morgan professor of medicine in it. In September, 1765, Dr. Shippen was elected professor of anatomy and surgery. In

WILLIAM·SHIPPEN, JR.

(From a portrait in the College of Physicians, Philadelphia.)

the introductory lecture to his course of anatomy lectures in 1762 the latter had referred to the importance of establishing a medical college in the colonies and this statement of Shippen's is sometimes quoted to show that the credit of being the founder of the department of medicine of the College of Philadelphia should belong to him rather than to Morgan. There is no doubt, however, that this was merely an expression of opinion and should not be taken as proving the existence of any definite plan for such an institution in Shippen's mind. To John Morgan belongs the sole credit of drawing up the scheme of the first organized medical school in this country.

When in 1779 the Legislature repealed the charter of the College of Philadelphia and recreated them in the newly-created University of Pennsylvania, Shippen was the only member of the faculty who at once accepted a professorship in the new school. In 1783 the friends of the college succeeded in having its charter restored, whereupon the trustees re-elected the professors in the medical school to the chairs they had previously occupied. It is curious to note that Shippen was a professor in both the college and the university, despite the rivalry between them, but in 1791 the College of Philadelphia and the University of the State of Pennsylvania agreed to combine and form one body under the title of the University of Pennsylvania, and Dr. Shippen held the chair of anatomy, surgery, and midwifery, with Dr. Caspar Wistar as adjunct professor in the same branches.

Shippen served as physician to the Pennsylvania Hospital in 1778 and 1779. He seems to have resigned because of his necessary absence on military affairs. In 1791 he was re-elected to the staff of the hospital and served until 1802, when he resigned.

He was a member of the American Philosophical Society and one of the founders of the College of Physicians of Philadelphia, being president of the latter from 1805 to 1808.

Dr. Shippen's first military position during the Revolution was that of medical director of the Flying Camp in the Jerseys, and as such he was directly subject to the authority of Dr. John Morgan. When Morgan was dismissed from the position of director-general of the military hospitals and physician-in-chief of the American Army, Shippen was appointed by order of Congress, October 9, 1776, director of the hospitals on the west side of the Hudson River. He was by this order placed on an equal footing with Morgan, whose authority was henceforth to be limited to the hospitals on the east side of the Hudson. Shippen was ordered to report directly to Congress, thus ignoring Morgan, through whom such reports had hitherto been made. Morgan, in his "Vindication" directly accuses Shippen of being the cause of his overthrow, and of aiming at securing the position of head of the department for himself. If this were so Shippen's efforts were crowned with success, for, on April 11, 1777, he was appointed to succeed Morgan as director-general of the Military Hospital and physician-in-chief of the American Army. This position he held until his resignation in January, 1781. In August, 1780, he was courtmarshalled on charges affecting his financial integrity. He was acquitted and, as stated above, continued in his position.

In 1798 Shippen suffered a terrible blow in the death of his son, a young man of great promise. Dr. Caspar Wistar, in his Eulogium of Shippen delivered before the College of Physicians shortly after his death, says that this loss seemed to destroy his interest in every remaining object. He seldom lectured and his practice declined. He died in Germantown, a suburb of Philadelphia, on July 11, 1808.

Wistar gives a delightful pen picture of Shippen: "His person was graceful, his manners polished, his conversation various, and the tones of his voice singularly sweet and conciliatory. In his intercourse with society be was gay without levity, and dignified without haughtiness or austerity. He belonged to a family which was proverbial for good temper. His father, whom he strongly resembled in this respect, during the long life of ninety years had scarcely ever been seen out of humor. He was also particularly agreeable to young people. Known as he was to almost every citizen of Philadelphia, it is probable that there was no one who did not wish him well."

F. R. P.

C. Caldwell, Extract from an Eulogium in the Med. Coll., Phila., 1818.
C. Wistar, Eulogium delivered by Dr. Wistar before the Coll. of Phys, Phila., 1809.
Phila. Jour. Med. Sci., vol. v, 1822.
Med. Repository, N. York, 1802.
Henry's Standard Hist. of the Med. Profession in Phila.
Carson's Hist. of the Med. Dpt. of the Univ. of Penn.
Morton's Hist. of Penn. Hospital.

Shoemaker, John Veitch (1858–1910).

Born in 1858, he graduated A. B. and A. M. from Dickinson College and M. D. from Jefferson in 1874. He was a member of the American Academy of Medicine; Association of Military Surgeons of the United States; British Medical Association and London Medical Society; president of the American Medical Editors' Association and president of the American Therapeutic Association; demonstrator and lecturer on anatomy, and lecturer on cutaneous affections in Jefferson Medical College from 1874 to 1886; professor of cutaneous diseases and materia medica and therapeutics since 1886 in the Medico-Chirurgical College, and president of the institution since 1890; senior physician to the Medico-Chirurgical Hospital; founder of the "Medical Bulletin" in 1879, and "Medical Register" in 1887; and editor of the "Medical Times and Register."

He was surgeon-general of the State of Pennsylvania from 1898 to 1902; and during the Spanish-American War raised the necessary funds and presented to the State of Pennsylvania a fully-equipped hospital train for the transportation of its sick soldiers from Camp Alger, Virginia. He was commissioned first lieutenant, Medical Reserve Corps, United States Army, in 1898.

Dr. Shoemaker was a prolific contributor to the literature of dermatology, materia medica and therapeutics. He died at his home in Philadelphia, October 11, 1910, from acute nephritis, aged fifty-two.

J. Am. Med. Ass., 1910, vol. lx.

Short, Charles Wilkins (1794–1863).

Charles Wilkins Short was born in Woodford County, Kentucky, on October 6, 1794. His father, Peyton Short, emigrated there from Surrey County, Virginia, and his mother was Mary, daughter of John Cleves Symmes. He acquired his literary education at Transylvania University, Lexington, Kentucky, where he graduated in 1810. In 1813 he entered the University of Pennsylvania as a private pupil of Dr. Caspar Wistar and thence graduated in 1815, first settling in Lexington, Kentucky. He remained only a short time, moving to Hopkinsville, Kentucky, where he practised until 1825 when he was called to the chair of materia medica and medical botany in the Transylvania University where he served as dean of the faculty for ten years.

With his colleague, Dr. John Eston Cook, he founded the "Transylvania Journal of Medicine and the Associate Sciences" in 1828. The University of Louisville, then an Institute but one year old, called him to the chair of materia medica and medical botany in 1837. He remained in active service in this institution until 1849, when he retired from active life. Dr. Short was never a voluminous writer and confined his publications mainly to botanical subjects. Among his most prominent writings were "Notices of Western Botany and Conchology," a paper published jointly by himself and Mr. H. Halbert Eaton (1830). "Instructions for the Gathering and Preservation of Plants in Herbaria" (1833); a "Catalogue of

CHARLES WILKINS SHORT.
(By permission of Dr. Gross.)

the Plants of Kentucky;" "The Bibliographia Botanica" (1836); "Sketch of the Progress of Botany in Western America;" "Observations on Botany in Illinois" (1845).

An industrious botanist, and an effectual promoter of botany in this country, his great usefulness in this field was mainly owing to the extent and the particular excellence of his personal collections, and to the generous profusion with which he distributed them far and wide among his fellow-laborers in this and other lands. He and the late Mr. Oakes, the one in the West and the other in the East, but independently, were the first in this country to prepare on an ample scale dried specimens of uniform and superlative excellence and beauty, and in lavish abundance for the purpose of supplying all who could need them."

The name of Short is commemorated by a number of plants: the Genus Shortia, Vesicaria Shortii, Phaca Shortiana, Aster Shortii, Solidago Shortii, Carex Shortiana.

The little story in connection with the Shortia is that when Dr. Gray was in Paris in 1837 he saw in the herbarium of the elder Michaux a mutilated plant whose label simply stated that it came from "les hautes montagnes de Carolinie." He tried in vain on his return to find the plant, but unsuccessfully. Two years later he described the plant and dedicated it to C. W. Short, and it became the object of all botanists visiting the Carolinas to find it. In 1877 it was found accidentally by G. M. Hyams, a boy who had picked it up on the banks of the Catawba River near the town of Marion in McDowell County, North Carolina. (Letter from Asa Gray to Prof. Sargent, dated September 17, 1886.)

He was married to Mary Henry Churchill in November, 1815, and had one son and five daughters. Dr. Short died in Louisville, Kentucky, March 7, 1864, of pneumonia.

T. L. B.

Tr. Amer. Phil. Soc., Phila., 1865.
S. D. Gross, Biographical Sketch of Charles Wilkins Short, Philadelphia, 1865.

Shotwell, John T. (1807–1850).

John Shotwell was born in Mason County, Kentucky, January 10, 1807, to which place his parents had emigrated from New Jersey at an early period in the history of the West.

The boy's early love of literature determined his father to give him a liberal education, so the family moved to Lexington, Kentucky, and the son entered Transylvania University in 1822, and graduated in 1825, with so high a reputation that Dr. Drake persuaded him to take up medicine. He began to study with Dr. Drake in 1826, and became his partner in 1830. In 1832 he received his M. D. from the medical College of Ohio, and was immediately appointed adjunct professor of anatomy to his friend, Dr. Jedediah Cobb.

In 1832 he married Mary Ward, daughter of John P. Foote of Cincinnati.

He was demonstrator of anatomy in the Medical College of Ohio from 1836 to 1838 and in the latter year succeeded Dr. Cobb as professor of anatomy, occupying this chair, with the exception of the session of 1849–50, until his death.

In 1842 he went to Europe, to visit the great medical centers.

During the cholera of 1850 his strength was overtaxed, and, a victim to the importunities of his patients, and his desire to relieve the suffering, he died July 23, 1850.

A. G. D.

Cincin. Med. Observer, 1857, vol. ii.
Tr. Ohio Med. Soc. Columbus, 1851

Shrady, George Frederick (1837–1907).

George Shrady, no less known as a medical journalist than a surgeon, was born in New York on the fourteenth of January, 1837. He was educated at New York College and graduated from the College of Physicians and Surgeons, New York, and from the surgical division of the New York Hospital. Yale College gave him her M. A. in 1869 for promoting the interest of medical literature. He made his début as associate editor of the "American Medical Times" and became known in its columns during the War of Secession. Then he founded and became editor-in-chief of the "Medical Record." His leaders were much appreciated in the States and their influence was felt in the medical world. He was one time surgeon to the Presbyterian Hospital, New York, and member of the chief New York medical societies. In 1860 he married Mary, daughter of John Lewis of Ulster County, New York, and died on the twenty-ninth of November, 1907, in the City of New York. A short list of his writings shows the journalist-surgeon to have done good work:

"Ligation of the Lingual Artery near Its Origin, as a Preliminary Procedure in the Extirpation of Cancer on Diseases of the Tongue," 1878; "A New Subcutaneous Saw, Knife and Bone Rasp," 1879; "The Curved Flap in Plastic Operations on the Face," 1879; "Reproduction of the Shaft of the Humerus, after Excision for Acute Necrosis," 1880; "Intraparietal Hernia," 1881; "Surgical and Pathological Reflections on Pres. Garfield's Wound," 1881; "Removal of the Large Nasopharyngeal Tumor, with Extensive Attachments to Base of Skull; an Expected Brain Complication; Death," 1882; "Successful Tracheotomy for Diphtheritic Croup in a Child Eleven Months Old," 1882; "Case of Strangulated Hernia with Remarks on Treatment," 1884; "The Surgical and Pathological Aspects of Gen. Grant's Case," 1895; "The Curability of Cancer by Operation," 1887; "Some Observations on Cancer of the Breast," 1892; "Operative Relief for Deformity after Pott's Fracture," 1893; "A Simple Method of Closing Large Operation Wounds by Sliding Skinflaps," 1893; "Dr. J. Marion Sims, Surgeon and Philanthropist," 1894; "Shock in Modern Surgery," 1889; "Early Diagnosis of Mammary Tumors," 1901; "Hip and Thigh Amputation for Sarcoma of the Femur," 1904., etc.

D. W.

Revue de Chir., Jan. 10, 1908.
Boston M. and S J., 1907, clvii
Med Rec , N. Y , 1907, lxxii.

Shuler, Lawrence S. (1790–1827).

Lawrence Shuler, a noted Indiana surgeon, was born in New York State in 1790 and graduated M. D. from the College of Physicians and Surgeons, New York. A scientific and skillful surgeon, many operations, more difficult in those days, were done by him. He operated on a little girl of eleven for congenital blindness with perfect success, and removed a very large abdominal tumor from a woman seven months' pregnant. One case was that of a false joint in a man who had had his humerus fractured; Shuler followed the practice of Charles Bell and Physick and nine months after a complete union was formed. His fellow townsmen predicted a great career for their clever young surgeon, but he caught cold while visiting Annapolis one winter and tuberculosis supervened and finally killed him. He was twice president of the Indiana State Medical Society.

The Med. Hist. of Indiana. Kemper.

Shumard, Benjamin Franklin (1820–1869).

Benjamin Franklin Shumard was born in 1820 and graduated in 1841, and shortly after he received his degree, began practice in the country at some distance from Louisville.

The frequent and prolonged excursions which this enthusiast made around Louisville and into the interior of Kentucky soon resulted in a large and interesting collection of prehistoric remains, which in due time were systematically arranged and described; and as not a few of these specimens were unknown, his fellow-naturalists, as a just tribute to his labors and researches, bestowed upon them the name of their discoverer, a practice usual with scientists.

Dr. David Dale Owen, engaged in the geological survey of the Northwestern Territories, under the direction of Congress, selected as his assistant the young scientist, whose fitness for the position had been shown by his previous labors. Conjointly with his friend, the late Prof.

Lunsford C. Yandell, he furnished, in 1847, for the "Western Journal of Medicine and Surgery" an elaborate paper entitled "Contributions to the Geology of Kentucky," in which he attempted to show the connection between certain geological formations and particular diseases. The paper attracted much attention, and was widely copied by the medical and secular press.

Other positions of trust and honor awaited Dr. Shumard. In 1850 he assisted in making a geological survey of Oregon; and soon after his return home he was employed on the palaeontology of the Red River country, in continuation of the explorations commenced by his brother, Dr. George G. Shumard. In 1853 he was appointed assistant geologist and palaeontologist in the Missouri Survey. Five years afterwards he was commissioned as geologist for Texas. But, after he had been busy at work for two years, and was almost ready to publish his report, he was suddenly, in consequence of a change in the governorship of the State, superseded, and of course obliged to retire from the field. This proved to be his last effort as a public geologist.

He then began practice in St. Louis and in 1866 was elected professor of obstetrics in the University of Missouri, thus adding somewhat to his slender income. After some time, however, his health broke down, and he was obliged to abandon, not only his chair, but his practice.

On the fourteenth of April, 1867, he died of pulmonary trouble, in the forty-ninth year of his age.

At the time of his decease he was president of the St. Louis Academy of Science. All of his contributions to scientific journals, which were numerous and varied, had a bearing more or less direct upon geology and palaeontology, with the history of whose progress on this continent his name will live.

S. D. G.

Autobiography of S D Gross, Phila., 1887.

Silliman, Benjamin, Sr. (1779–1864).

Benjamin Silliman, born in Connecticut on August 8, 1779, had his A. B. and A. M. degree from Yale in 1796 and 1799; his A. M. and M. D. from Bowdoin College, both in 1818, and the LL. D. of Middlebury College in 1826. From 1802–1858 he was professor of natural science at Yale, and edited the "American Journal of Science and Arts" from 1818 until his death at New Haven on November 13, 1864. A bronze statute to his memory stands in the grounds of Yale University.

An Address commen of Benjamin Silliman, New Haven, 1865 (Theo D. Woolsey)
Leading American Men of Science   D. S. Jordan.

Silliman, Benjamin, Jr. (1816–1885).

This son of Benjamin and Harriet Trumbull Silliman, who was born on December 4, 1816, followed his father along the road of natural science for, after graduating from Yale in 1837, he became assistant teacher on this subject at Yale and associate editor with his father of the "American Journal of Science and Arts," until the close of the first fifty volumes in 1845, when the chief editorship devolved on him, with James D. Dana. In 1849 the University of Charleston gave him her honorary M. D. and that same year he was made professor of medical chemistry and toxicology at Louisville University, but after five years resigned to take his father's chair of chemistry at Yale.

Editorial duties engrossed him in 1853 when, in connection with the Crystal Palace exhibition, he worked up "The World of Science, Art and Industry," and in 1854 "The Progress of Science and Mechanism." His "First Principles of Natural Philosophy or Physics," 1858, had a second edition in 1861. Yale benefited considerably by his generosity and the results of his mineralogical researches in California. In 1868 he presented the whole of his collection to the Museum.

He married, in 1840, Susan H.,

daughter of William J. Forbes, and had seven children.

Atkinson's Phys. and Surgs. of the United States.
The relation of Yale to Medicine. W. H. Welch, Yale Med. Jour., Nov., 1901.

Sims, James Marion (1813–1883).

James Marion Sims was on his father's side English, on his mother's of Scotch-Irish descent. His paternal grandfather, John Sims, was born December 27, 1790, and married Mahala Mackey in 1812. Of the father, his distinguished son left a record that "he was one of the best of men and best of husbands." He was sheriff of Lancaster County, South Carolina, from 1830–1834. His mother was the daughter of that Lydia Mackey, wife of Charles Mackey, a revolutionary soldier, who having been taken within the British lines, was tried by court-martial and sentenced to death as a spy by Col. Tarleton, and she successfully interceded with this British officer for the commutation of the death sentence, and ultimately obtained her husband's liberty.

Marion Sims was born in Lancaster District, South Carolina, January 25, 1813. He attended the common schools there, entered the Franklin Academy in 1825, and later was sent to the South Carolina College at Columbia, from which he graduated in December, 1832. Speaking of himself at this time he says: "I never was remarkable for anything while I was in college except good behavior. Nobody ever expected anything of me, and I never expected anything of myself." What a mistake of the youth concerning the man who was to achieve the greatest reputation ever accorded to an American surgeon.

On the twelfth of November, 1833, he matriculated at the Charleston Medical School, where he attended lectures for one year, and in 1834 became a student at Jefferson Medical College, Philadelphia, from which he graduated in 1835. In May of that year he settled as a practitioner in Lancaster, but after a

short period of discouragement removed in the fall of 1835 to Mount Meigs, Montgomery County, Alabama, where he was soon recognized as a clever doctor. While living here he volunteered in the Seminole War and in an expedition against the Creek Indians. Returning from this public service, and ambitious for a larger field, he established himself in Montgomery, the capital of the State, in December, 1840.

The boldness and success of his operations in general surgery soon attracted a large clientèle, which encouraged him to establish a private hospital, and within a few years he startled the professional world by the announcement of the cure, by an original method, of a series of cases of vesico-vaginal fistula. Up to that time there was not an authenticated successful treatment for this important surgical lesion, and when the science of obstetrics was in its infancy, there were thousands of women who, as a result of unskillful attendance in childbirth, were left in the most deplorable and loathsome condition by reason of injuries to the bladder; they were, in fact, among the most wretched and pitable of human beings, and attracted the sympathy and attention of the enterprising young surgeon. He sought out a number of these helpless women, gave them shelter and free treatment in his hospital, and after several years of patient, anxious and persistent effort, finally succeeded in curing them. In the evolution of this operation he invented the silver-wire suture and the duck-bill speculum, the announcement of these successful cases attracting world-wide attention, and in many quarters being received with incredulity.

The invention of the speculum came about in this way: Early one morning in 1845, a countrywoman riding on horse-back into Montgomery was thrown from her horse and suffered a displacement of the uterus. Sims was called to see her, and found her in bed complaining of great pain in her back and a sense of tenesmus in both bladder and rectum.

JAMES MARION SIMS.

(By permission of the American Journal of Obstetrics.)

A digital examination revealed a retroversion of the uterus. He placed the patient in the knee-elbow position, inserting two fingers into the vagina in the effort to push the womb into place. To his great surprise there was an inrush of air which dilated the vagina and exercised pressure enough to carry the displaced organ into position. The ballooning of the vagina by atmospheric pressure brought all parts of this hitherto inaccessible surgical region into full view. Forgetting everything for the moment except the value of this important revelation, he jumped into his buggy, and drove hurriedly to a hardware store in Montgomery, where he bought a set of pewter spoons of different sizes. Bending the bowl and part of the handle of one of these at a right angle, he placed one of his patients suffering from vesicovaginal fistula in the genupectoral position, inserted the improvised speculum, and atmospheric pressure accomplished the rest. The fistulous opening was clearly seen. He says:

"Introducing the bent handle of the spoon, I saw everything as no man had ever seen before. The fistula was as plain as the nose on a man's face; the edges were clear and well defined, and the opening could be measured as accurately as if it had been cut out of a piece of plain paper. The speculum was perfectly clear from the very begnning. I soon operated upon the fistula, closing it in about an hours' time, but the operation failed."

He did not then know the cause of failure, but later discovered that it was due to infection from the use of silk ligatures. Not long after this, in walking from his home to his office, he noticed upon the ground a bit of spiral wire, such as was used to give elasticity to suspenders before the days of India rubber. He picked up the wire, uncoiled it and it came over him at once that he had found a suture which, if made of a pure metal, would not only hold, but be less apt to induce infection. He carried the wire immediately to a silversmith in Mont-

gomery, gave him a half-dollar silver piece, and asked him to beat that into a wire of the size of the brass wire he presented. This was skillfully done by the smith, and with this wire and the speenlum was done the first successful operation for vesico-vaginal fistula, and Marion Sims had taken the first great step towards the immortality which awaited him. Of this instrument the illustrious Thomas Addis Emmett said:

"From the beginning of time to the present, I believe that the human race has not been benefited to the same extent and in a like period by the introduction of any other surgical instrument. Those who did not fully appreciate the value of the speculum itself have been benefited indirectly to an extent they little realize, for the instrument in the hands of others has probably advanced the knowledge of the diseases of women to an extent which could not have been done for a hundred years or more without it."

But it was not alone in this particular line that he achieved distinction, but also in other departments of surgery.

In 1835 he performed a successful operation for abscess of the liver; in 1837 one for removal of the lower jaw without external mutilation, the operation of excision being done entirely from within the mouth, and a successful removal of the superior maxilla for tumor of the antrum. He performed originally the operation of cholecystotomy, without the knowledge of the fact that Dr. Bobbs, of Indiana, to whom he always accorded full credit, had preceded him by a few months.

To him it may well be said that mankind is indebted for the surgical invasion of the peritoneal cavity. In his great paper entitled: "The Careful Aseptic Invasion of the Peritoneal Cavity for the Arrest of Hemorrhage, the Suture of Intestinal Wounds and the Cleansing of the Peritoneal Cavity, and for all Intraperitoneal Conditions," before the New York Academy of Medicine, on October 6, 1881, quoting from his own experience as surgeon-in-chief of the Anglo-American Ambulance Corps in the Franco-Prussian War, Dr. Sims courageously promulgated these rules:

1. The wound of entrance should be enlarged sufficiently to ascertain the whole extent of the injuries inflicted.

2. These should be remedied by suturing the wounded intestine and ligating bleeding vessels.

3. Diligent search should be made for extravasated matter, and the peritoneal cavity should be thoroughly cleansed of all foreign matter before closing the external wound.

4. The surgeon must judge whether the case requires drainage or not.

In 1853 he established himself in New York City, and in February, 1855, organized the State Hospital for Women, with this becoming the founder of the great science of gynecology. From the temporary structure at 83 Madison Avenue, the hospital was removed to the block of ground donated to it by the city on 50th Street and Lexington Avenue, whence after nearly a half century it was removed to the magnificent new building at 110th Street and Morningside Heights.

In 1861 Dr. Sims for the first time visited Europe, and on the eighteenth of October of that year, at the Hotel Voltaire, successfully demonstrated his operation for vesico-vaginal fistula. Among those who witnessed this operation were some of the greatest surgeons of that age, Nélaton, Velpeau, Civiale, Baron Larrey, Sir Joseph Olliffe, Huguier and others. By this and other cases, his presence in Paris created a *furore* in medical circles. So great was the reputation achieved that he was called to all parts of Europe, not only to operate, but in consultation, and to treat various maladies in the department of gynecology; in fact, a short time saw him enjoying a most lucrative practice among the best people in European capitals. Upon one occasion, in attendance upon an important case, he became for several weeks the guest of the Emperor Napoleon at St. Cloud.

After the close of the Civil War in America Dr. Sims returned to New York, but upon the outbreak of the Franco-Prussian War in 1870, he sailed for Europe, and there organized and became surgeon-in-chief of the Anglo-American Ambulance Corps. He rendered such distinguished professional services, especially at and after the battle of Sedan, that the French Republic conferred upon him the order of Commander of the Legion of Honor. From this time until his death, November 13, 1883, he lived alternately in Europe and America, busily engaged in practice of his profession wherever he found himself.

Dr. Sims contributed extensively to professional literature, not only as it related to obstetrics and gynecology, but to medical and surgical science in general. His most important professional work was entitled "Clinical Notes on Uterine Surgery."

Among the many official positions which he occupied was that of the president of the American Medical Association, in 1876.

Near the close of his long and eminent career as a practitioner and teacher of gynecology, Prof. T. Gaillard Thomas, in an address to the graduating class of the medical department of Cornell University, delivered at Carnegie Hall, said:

"If I were called upon to name the three men who in the history of all times had done most for their fellow men, I would say George Washington, William Jenner and Marion Sims."

Immediately after his death a movement for the erection of a statue in his memory was inaugurated in Europe and in his native country, and in 1894 there was unveiled in Bryant Park, New York City, a statue in bronze, a life-like image of the great teacher, the spontaneous gift from his brothers in the profession throughout the civilized world, and from many of the unfortunate beings his genius and skill had benefited. In brief yet comprehensive phraseology, the inscription tells the story of his career:

J. MARION SIMS, M. D., LL. D.
BORN IN SOUTH CAROLINA, 1813. DIED IN NEW
YORK CITY IN 1883.
SURGEON AND PHILANTHROPIST.
FOUNDER OF THE WOMAN'S HOSPITAL OF THE STATE
OF NEW YORK.
HIS BRILLIANT ACHIEVEMENTS CARRIED THE FAME
OF AMERICAN SURGERY
THROUGHOUT THE CIVILIZED WORLD.
IN RECOGNITION OF HIS SERVICES IN THE CAUSE OF
SCIENCE AND MANKIND
HE RECEIVED THE HIGHEST HONORS IN THE GIFT OF
HIS COUNTRYMEN
AND DECORATIONS FROM THE GOVERNMENTS OF
FRANCE, PORTUGAL, SPAIN, BELGIUM, AND ITALY.

On the reverse:

PRESENTED
TO THE CITY OF NEW YORK
BY
HIS PROFESSIONAL FRIENDS,
LOVING PATIENTS,
AND
MANY ADMIRERS
THROUGHOUT THE WORLD.

Marion Sims possessed a striking personality. With all his long and bitter struggle with poverty and for professioual recognition, and in his early days for health and life itself, time had dealt gently with his form and face, whereon nature had set in unmistakable lines the stamp of greatness. Although he had rounded well the years allotted by the psalmist, his step was still quick and firm, his carriage erect, dignified and graceful. The frosts of age had not tinged the rich abundance of his dark-brown hair, which fell straight back from off the massive forehead, for the ever-active brain and the deep-seated, searching eyes of brown, asked always for the light! The brows were arched and unusually heavy and prominent; the nose beautifully proportioned and of Grecian type; the mouth well shaped, lips usually compressed, which, with the prominent chin, bespoke courage and firmness of purpose, His face was oval, clean-shaven and smooth, and the usual expression was of almost womanly sweetness, yet it was quick to vary in harmony with whatever emotion was predominant. Away from excitement and in the home-life, his expression and actions were almost boyish. He never seemed to have for-

gotten that he was once a boy, and he would throw himself into a household frolic with all the abandon of his early days. He was courageous to a degree, and, although he rarely lost control of his temper, yet he was at times imperious and aggressive. When occasion demanded he was a good fighter, and fought his enemies with right good will; but he was quick to forgive, and just before his death he said one day, "I have forgiven all who ever did me wrong, with one exception." As said of him by a gifted orator, he possessed qualities ideal in the make-up of a truly great surgeon, "the brain of an Apollo, the heart of a lion, the eye of an eagle, and the hand of a woman."

A full list of his writings may be seen at the end of "The Story of my Life," New York, 1884; they include: "On the Treatment of Vesico-vaginal Fistula," Philadelphia, 1853; "Silver Sutures in Surgery," New York, 1858; "Clinical Notes on Uterine Surgery," New York, 1866.   J. A. W.

Tribute to Jamet Marion Sims (W. O. Baldwin), 1884.
In Memoriam, Austin Flint, James Marion Sims (W. M. Carpenter), 1866.
Am. J. Obstet., N. Y., 1884, vol. xvii (P. F. Mundé).
Boston M. and S. Jour., 1883, vol. cix.
Galliard's M. Jour., N. Y., 1883, vol. xxxvi (autobiography).
Med. Rec., N. Y., 1883, vol. xxiv.
Tr. Am. Gyn. Soc., 1884, N. Y., 1885, vol. ix.
Tr. Am. Surg. Ass., 1884, Phila., 1885, vol. ii.
Port. in the Surg.-gen. Lib., Wash., D. C.

Simons, Benjamin Bonneau (1775–1844).
Benjamin Bonneau Simons was of French extraction, being descended from the Merovingian Kings, and originally named Saint Simon. The first colonist, Benjamin, came to this country in 1685 and became the progenitor of the whole Simons family in the South. Benjamin Bonneau Simons was born in Charleston, September 16, 1775, and graduated at Brown University, Rhode Island, and immediately went abroad to study medicine.

He attended the schools of Edinburgh, London and Paris, and was the pupil of

John and Charles Bell and did the dissections for their famous anatomical plates.

So greatly were his capabilities held in estimation that he was told, did he remain in Europe he would be able to pave his street with gold.

Returning to America, he began to practise in his native city in 1801, as a surgeon; he drew much of his practice from the northern states. He was considered the leading surgeon of the South, some of the medical profession even coming there to hear him lecture.

He was the first man to trephine bone for abscess and did the first successful operation in South Carolina for stone in the bladder, and was said to be the only man in America who cured goiter. He treated thirteen cases of bone necrosis and first recognized the condition and treatment.

Dr. Simons was a member of the Medical University of Edinburgh; fellow of the Royal Society of London, and one of the early presidents of the Charleston Medical Society.

He was professor of chemistry and the author of a valuable treatise on the bones, as well as several other medical works. He married Maria Vanderhorst, daughter of Gov.-gen. Arnoldus Vanderhost and Elizabeth Raven, and had two daughters.

There is a picture of him by Bowman in the board-room of the Roper Hospital; the same artist also painted him in another position, and so good was the likeness that it is said his old negro servant on seeing it exclaimed, " lor! massa's in dere, " indicating the room in which the portrait stood. Simons was fond of drawing his friends around him and entertained lavishly at his house on East Gay in Charleston, where he died of apoplexy September 27, 1844.

R. W., Jr.

Carolina Jour. Med, Sci. and Agricul., 1825, vol. i.

Skene, **Alexander Johnson Chalmers** (1837–1900).

In the death of Dr. Skene, on July 4, 1900, at the age of sixty-two, American gynecology lost one of the last of its famous pioneers. He was born in Fyvie, Aberdeenshire, Scotland, June 17, 1837, of a family that had made its name known in Scotch history for nine centuries. His schooling was in Aberdeen and Kings College. He came to America at the age of nineteen, began the study of medicine three years later at Toronto, matriculated at the University of Michigan in 1861, and was graduated from the Long Island College Hospital in 1863. In that year and the following he served as acting assistant surgeon in the United States Volunteers at Port Royal, Charleston Harbor, and David's Island, prominent in plans for army ambulance work. He kept up his interest in military matters in the National Guard of the State as surgeon to the Twelfth Regiment and First Division, and as lieutenant-colonel on the staff of General Molineux (1884–1885.)

In 1864 Dr. Skene entered practice in Brooklyn, and within a year had begun his college and hospital work in obstetrics. Professor of both branches of gynecology at thirty-one, he gave his best strength to the Long Island College Hospital, as teacher, as operator, and as dean and president (1886–1893), until the last year of his life. It was he who was most active in securing practical and beautiful plans giving adequate expression to the great Polhemus gift of a college and clinic building. The college owes its most famous alumnus a debt it can never repay.

Dr. Skene was professor of gynecology in the New York Post-graduate Medical School, 1883–86, and consultant to various hospitals and dispensaries. He was one of the founders of the American Gynecological Society and its tenth president (1886), and founder and honorary president of the International Congress of Gynecology and Obstetrics. He had been president of the Medical Society of Kings County, of the New York Obstetrical and of the Brooklyn Gynecological Society, and was a corresponding or honorary member of many foreign societies, such as those of Paris, Leipzig, B r u s s e l s, Edinburgh, London, etc. Aberdeen University conferred on him the degree of LL. D. in 1897.

He was the author of "Diseases of the Bladder and Urethra in Women," 1878 and 1887; "Treatise on Diseases of Women," 1888, 1892 and 1898; "Education and Culture as related to the Health and Diseases of Women," 1889; "Medical Gynecology," 1895, and "Electro-hemostasis in Operative Surgery," 1899, and he wrote from a large experience and with great diligence. He wrote in the hours before breakfast to avoid interruption, and in writing, as in teaching, his method was clinical, detailed, practical. His huge capacity for work was due to a magnificent physique—his chest girth was forty-four inches. His eyes always twinkled with the memory of "last in class, first in field sports." Thus he was able to carry the burdens of college teaching, hospital operating, medical society duties, the large private sanitarium, and an extensive practice. Two days before he died sixty patients came to the office.

Dr. Skene married Annette Wilhelmine Lillian Van der Wegen, of Brussels, Belgium, who survived him. They had no children.

His country home was at Highmount, in the Catskills, where his love of the mountains had full scope, and where he could indulge his affection for animals. There he had more leisure for modelling. His life-size portraits in marble are indeed noteworthy, in view of the scantiness of the time he could give to sculpture.

If one were to attempt an appreciation of Dr. Skene's work one might select certain items, such as the insistence on gynecologic and surgical methods in obstetric work (1877); the well-known observations on the urethral glands, a source of intractable trouble until recognized (1880); the many new instruments devised, the systematic hemostatic treatment of blood-vessels and pedicles by heat of moderate degree that dries and does not char (1897).

In him progressiveness and originality were balanced with caution and clear sense. Two instances will suffice. In the days when we planned to cure most pelvic pain by removing the ovaries, he was credited with timidity because of his careful restriction of this universal remedy. Again, he was said to be behind the times during the epidemic of vaginal hysterectomy. Yet the profession has come back to the conservatism from which he would not swerve.

Breadth of view was his. From the early days when he was Austin Flint's assistant he studied his patient as an individual, and overlooked nothing in the general condition nor any detail of constitutional treatment. Such detailed care prepared the patient for operation (or avoided the necessity). His technic was so quiet and seemingly simple that only a brother surgeon appreciated its speed and thoroughness.

Few men concealed more generous deeds. Strong in his likes and dislikes, tenacious of purpose, keen of insight, full of apt anecdote, tactful, discreet, hopeful, inspiriting, his impress was strong on those about him. Personal magnetism eludes biographies. The impress of vigor and simplicity, the attraction of kindliness and heartiness—these things may not be written.

A full list of his most important pamphlets can be seen in the "Surgeon-general's Catalogue," Washington, D. C.

R. L. D.

Tr. Am. Gynec. Soc., Phila., 1901, vol. xxvi.
Amer. Gyn. and Obstet. Jour., N. Y., 1900, vol. xvii.
Albany Med. Ann., 1901, vol. xxii.
J. Am. Med. Ass., Chicago, 1900.
Med. Record, New York, 1900.
Med. News, New York, 1900.
Post-graduate, New York, 1900.

Skillman, Henry Martyn (1824–1902).

Henry Martyn Skillman was the youngest child of Thomas T. and Elizabeth Farrer Skillman. His father, a native of New Jersey, came to Lexington in 1809 and founded there the largest publishing house in the Mississippi Valley. Sprung as Dr.

Skillman was from Puritan and Presbyterian ancestors, he inherited the stern sense of duty and principle that characterized them, and passed a long life without departing from the tradition of his forebears. He began life by spending two or three years at Lexington as an apothecary, but determined in 1844 to study medicine and after three years' diligence graduated from Transylvania University, March, 1847.

Early appreciated, he was appointed in 1848 demonstrator of anatomy in the medical department of his alma mater, a position he filled so ably for three successive years that he was appointed to the chair of general and pathological anatomy and physiology in 1851, which position he retained until elected to the chair of physiology and institutes of medicine in 1856, lecturing before large classes, in these branches until the close of the institution in the summer of 1857.

He was distinguished for the accuracy and clearness of his teachings, was painstaking and apt in his instructions, and his knowledge of the branches which he taught was abreast of his day and generation. He was the last surviving member of the medical department of Transylvania University.

On October 30, 1851, he married Margaret, daughter of Matthew T. Scott, president of the Northern Bank of Kentucky.

Among his other appointments he was contract surgeon for the United States Government; president of the Kentucky State Medical Society, 1869. He was the first president of the Lexington and Fayette County Medical Society, in 1889, and it is claimed that he was the first physician in Lexington to administer anesthesia.

He contributed many papers on topics particularly pertaining to medicine and materia medica to the "Transactions of the Kentucky State Medical Society." His knowledge of practical therapeutics was marvelous, which made him an accurate clinician, and his skill in surgery was great, his office being always an attraction for medical students.

The confidence of the people was unbounded. Some of his admirers said, with Calvinistic logic, if "we're tae dee, we're tae, and if we're to live, we're to live," but all said this for the doctor, "that whether you are to live or die, he can aye keep up a sharp moisture on the skin."

Dr. Skillman was active in all public matters and greatly interested in everything pertaining to the growth and prosperity of his native city. He died at Lexington in March, 1902.

S. B.

Slack, Elijah (1784–1866).

Elijah Slack was both M. D. and LL. D. and was born in Bucks County, Pennsylvania, November 6, 1784, graduating at Princeton in 1810 and soon after taking charge of an academy at Trenton, and subsequently being professor of natural sciences, and Vice-president in Princeton College.

In 1817 he went to Cincinnati and in 1819, when the Medical College of Ohio was organized, was appointed professor of chemistry, which position he held for fourteen years.

He was also a minister of the Presbyterian Church. During the whole of his active life he was a teacher. Dr. Slack was the first president of the Cincinnati Medical Society, which was organized in 1819. He was also first president of Cincinnati College, incorporated the same year. He died May 29, 1866.

A. G. D.

Cinn. Lancet and Observer, 1866, n. s., vol. ix.

Slayter, William B. (1841–1898).

William B. Slayter was born in Halifax, Nova Scotia, in 1841, and died there in 1898.

He practised for a few years in Chicago, and subsequently in Halifax for upwards of thirty years, then having taken his Arts' course at Trinity College, Toronto, he took his professional training there, and continued his medical and surgical studies in Chicago, London and Dublin. His degrees were: M. D., Chicago; M. R. C. S. and L. R. C. P., London; F. O. S., Dublin. He was also a member of the Medical Society of Nova Scotia, and president of that Society in 1878.

For many years previous to his death he was professor of obstetrics in the Halifax Medical College, and surgeon at the Victoria General Hospital, Halifax.

After completing his medical course at London, Dr. Slayter served a term as house surgeon at the Westminster Hospital and subseqeuently was assistant to Forbes Winslow, the eminent English alienist. He began practice in Chicago and became assistant to Dr. Brainard on the surgical staff of Rush Medical College, and acquired a good practice. On the death of his brother, the heroic Dr. John Slayter, in 1866, he removed to Halifax, and became one of the leading practitioners. His kindly and genial manner and generous disposition gained for him a host of friends, and his musical talents, which were of a high order, won him a still larger circle of admirers.

He married a Miss Clarke, of Chicago, and had a large family. Two of his sons entered the profession—Dr. John Slayter, of the Royal Army Medical Corps, and Dr. Howard Slayter.   D. A. C.

Small, Horatio Nelson (1840–1886).

He was eldest of the three sons of Richard and Abigail Jose Small, of Buxton, Maine, and was born there November 10, 1840, receiving his early education in Guildhall, Vermont, whither his parents had removed during his childhood, and ultimately graduating at the Dartmouth Medical School in 1862.

He immediately joined the army as assistant surgeon of the Seventeenth Regiment New Hampshire Volunteers. In August, 1863, he was made a full surgeon of the Tenth Regiment New Hampshire Volunteers, serving as brigade-surgeon in the Ninth, Eighteenth and Twenty-Fourth Army Corps and received an honorable discharge at the end of the war as a soldier and officer.

Directly after the war Dr. Small came to Portland, associated himself with Dr. William Chaffee Robinson, took up the latter's practice during his last illness and at his death had all that he could possibly attend to as physician and obstetrician.

He was chosen visiting physician to the Maine General Hospital, lecturer on obstetrics at the Portland School for Medical Instruction, surgeon on the governor's staff in 1879. Although his contributions to medical literature were not many, he read before the Maine Medical Association one or two memorable papers, one of which was on " Nasal Catarrh, " "Extra-uterine Pregnancy" (Maine Medical Association, 1893). He was quick in diagnosing and accurate and extraordinarily skillful and bold as an obstetrician and in the use of forceps, of which he was rather overfond. He could see no need for delicate women to wait dangerous delivery when with his skillful forceps he could rapidly terminate labor with safety to mother and the child. Ready in emergencies, in one case he was called in consultation, and upon entering the room and seeing the patient comatose, paid no attention to the consultant, but whipped out his lancet and opened a vein and when the patient was showing symptoms of rallying he began to talk about the case.

To see Dr. Small riding along during a procession was to see something noble, for he was a perfect picture of human skill on horseback and himself and his horse made an ideal picture. The blographer recalls him as being very kind to him, a stranger in a strange place, helping without question to money, to friends, and advancement in medicine when few were thinking of even offering any aid. Dr. Small was married November, 1862, to Harriet Newell, of Burke, Vermont, who survived him several years, but had no children. In 1884 he began to show signs of failure and was obliged to rest. On his return he seemed relieved, but although his disease was checked it was too serious to be cured, and he was compelled to abandon practice again. He died rather suddenly at the last, on the morning of December 29, 1886.

J. A. S.

Trans. Maine Med. Assoc., 1887.

Small, William Bryant (1862–1904).

This interesting man was born in Lewiston, Maine, the son of Addison and Florence Wyman Small. He was educated at Bates College, graduating in 1885, and studying with Dr. Wedgewood, of Lewiston, at the Medical School of Maine for two years, graduating in medicine at the Belleview Hospital Medical College in 1888.

His examinations were passed so remarkably well that he gained by merit alone the position of attending physician at the Randall's Island Hospital in New York, where he remained more than a year. He soon moved to Lewiston, where he practised until his death.

In the fourteen years of practice, he became a marked man, noted for his keen diagnosis, his excellent surgery, and his interesting contributions to the meetings of the Maine Medical Association, of which he was one of the leading members. He always had something of interest to say and was a first rate speaker. Forcible, earnest, and argumentative, yet free from any pugnacity.

Among Dr. Small's medical papers was a very able discussion on "Appendicitis," and another on "Accidents as a Cause of Appendicitis," and a careful paper on "Artificial Feeding." Each paper that Dr. Small contributed to the meetings of the Maine Medical Association seemed a better one than the preceding. He married in September, 1892, Maud Ingalls, who, with a young son, survived him.

He died in 1904 at the time of his greatest influence from a complication of diseases; probably due to too much work and too little recreation. He was said to have died from cardiac exhaustion.

J. A. S.

Trans. Maine Med. Assoc., 1904.

Smart, Charles (1841–1905).

Charles Smart, surgeon, United States Army, graduated in medicine at the University of Aberdeen in 1862, and immediately after came to America and joined the Sixty-third New York Infantry as assistant surgeon, rendering faithful and meritorious service during the Civil War. In 1864 he was transferred to the regulars and in 1866 was promoted to the rank of captain, in 1882 to that of major. In 1897 he was made lieutenant-colonel and deputy-surgeon-general, and in 1901 colonel and assistant surgeon-general.

From 1882 to 1902 Smart was on duty in the office of the surgeon-general at Washington and was one of the co-editors of the well-known "Medical and Surgical History of the War." For several years he was a member of the faculty of the Army Medical School. During the Spanish-American War he did important work inspecting the camps of the American troops. In 1902 he was sent to the Philippines as chief surgeon, but a stroke of apoplexy compelled him to return to the United States. He died at St. Augustine, Florida, April 23, 1905.

He wrote the "Handbook for the Hospital Corps of the United States Army and State Military Forces" (1889), a most excellent book, which was in use in the army for many years. "He combined with brilliant scientific attainments a great capacity for hard work together with an unfailing loyalty to duty."

A. A.

J. Ass. Mil. Surg., Carlisle, Pa., 1906, xix.
J. Am. Med. Ass., Chicago, 1905, xliv.

Smith, Albert (1801–1878).

Albert Smith was born in Peterborough, New Hampshire, June 18, 1801. He fitted for college at Groton, Massachusetts Academy. His father was unable to send him to college and he went to work in his cotton mill where he remained five years, and saved enough to put him through his college course, graduating in 1825, and after working several years more he entered the medical department of Dartmouth, and took his M. D. in 1833. He began to practise at once in his native town and in 1849 was appointed professor of materia medica and therapeutics in the Dartmouth Medical School, where he continued to lecture until he resigned in 1870, and became emeritus professor. In 1857 he delivered his course of lectures at the University of Vermont and also a course at the Bowdoin Medical School in 1859.

The honorary LL. D. was conferred on him by his alma mater in 1870, and the honorary M. D. by the Rush Medical College of Chicago in 1875. He was also president of the New Hampshire Medical Society.

Dr. Smith married February 26, 1828, Fidelia Stearns of Jaffrey, New Hampshire, and had three children, Fred. Augustus, Susan S., and Catherine B.

As a medical instructor he was included among the first in New England. He devoted the leisure in the later years of his life to the preparation of " A History of Peterborough," which book was published in 1876. He published a lecture on "Hippocrates" and another on "Paracelsus," besides various articles in the medical journals and in the transactions of the state society.   He died in Peterborough, February 22, 1878.

I. J. P.

Tr. N. Hampshire M. Soc. 1878 (H. M Field).
Tr. Am. M. Ass., Phila., 1878.

Smith, Albert Holmes (1835–1885).

Dr. Smith's biography resembles many others of energetic, clever doctors in that it ends with detailing all the fame he might have acquired had he lived. "His ambition lay in the direction of capital operations in gynecology and, had he lived, it is likely he would have acquired as much skill and reputation in this as in obstetrics."

Descended from Quaker ancestors who had emigrated from Yorkshire, England, in 1685, and who were among the earlier settlers of Pennsylvania, Albert Holmes was the third son and seventh child of Dr. Moses B. and Rachel Coate Smith, and born July 19, 1835, in Philadelphia. As a lad he went to the Westtown School and Gregory's Classical School, entering at thirteen the freshman class in the University of Pennsylvania. He entered the University in 1849 and took his bachelor's degree in 1853; graduating M. D. in 1856 and studying under Prof. G. B. Wood.

When he left the Pennsylvania Hospital in 1859 he soon entered on a busy practice and in 1860 married Emily, daughter of Charles Kaighn of Kaighn's Point, New Jersey. As a practitioner he was extremely popular, but his highest skill lay undoubtedly in obstetric manipulations, and as a teacher in the practical character of his teachings and the large amount of information he imparted.

To pass over the part played by him in connection with the admission of women doctors to the County Medical Society would be to ignore an important chapter in his life. He became consulting physician to the Women's Hospital in 1867, a time when the acceptance of such a position meant strong moral courage. A resolution was offered to the College to expel any doctor consulting with women—a resolution aimed at those who were on the staff of the Women's Hospital. After a heated debate this was rejected, but many of Smith's confrères were alienated from him.

His powers of physical endurance were wonderful, but an attack of typhoid in 1880 formed a prelude to five years of work often carried on in physical weariness. A visit to Sir Henry Thompson, London, in 1883 benefited and encouraged him, and he returned to active practice but the following year destructive adenoma of the prostate gland from which he had suffered for some time compelled him to give up work, though his interest in the world outside continued until three days before his death on December 14, 1885.

He held many appointments and

memberships, notably resident physician to the Pennsylvania Hospital; visiting obstetrician to the Philadelphia Hospital; consulting physician to the Woman's Hospital. One of the founders of the Philadelphia Obstetrical Society, he was its president in 1874–76; also a founder of the American Gynecological Society and its president in 1884, fellow of the College of Physicians, Philadelphia; president of the County Medical Society, Philadelphia, and honorary member of the British Gynecological Society.

Among his pamphlets are:

"Retarded Dilatation of the Os Uteri in Labor," 1877.

"Pendulum Leverage of the Obstetric Forceps," 1878.

"An Improved Speculum," 1869.

"The Present Aspect of the Puerperal Diseases," 1884, and others descriptive of surgical appliances of his own invention.

There is a portrait in the album of the American Gynecological Society, 1876–1900, Philadelphia, 1901.

Am. Jour. Obstet., vol. xix, N. York, 1886 (W. Savery).
Med. News, vol. xlvii, Phila., 1885.
Tr. Am. Gyn. Soc., vol. xi, N. Y., 1887 (T. Parvin).
Proc. Am. Phil. Soc., vol. xxiii, Phila , 1886.
Tr. Call. Phys., Phila., 1887.

Smith, Andrew Heermance (1837–1910).

Andrew Heermance Smith, for more than fifty years a medical practitioner in New York City and author of many monographs on medical subjects, was born at Charlton, Saratoga County, New York, in 1837, and educated at Ballston Spa Institute, Union College, College of Physicians and Surgeons and the Universities of Göttingen and Berlin. At the close of the Civil War, in which he served with credit, Dr. Smith resumed the practice of medicine. He was physician to St. Luke's and Presbyterian hospitals and surgeon to the Manhattan Eye, Ear and Throat Hospital. At the time of his death he also was consulting physician to several other hospitals.

Dr. Smith was president of the New York Academy of Medicine in 1903–04, and had affiliations with numerous other societies and clubs. He died at his home in New York City on April 8, 1910, of arteriosclerosis.

Among his writings should be noted:

"Oxygen Gas as a Remedy in Disease" (Prize Essay), New York, 1870.

"The Effects of High Atmospheric Pressure, Including the Caisson Disease" (Prize Essay), New York, 1873.

"Supplementary Rectal Alimentation and Especially by Defibrinated Blood," 1879.

"The Influence of Barometric Changes upon the Body in Health and Disease," 1881.

"The Physiological, Pathological and Therapeutical Effects of Compressed Air," 1886, etc.

Boston Transcript, April, 1910.
Surg.-gen. Cat., Wash., D. C.

Smith, Henry Hollingsworth (1815–1890).

He graduated M. D. at the University of Pennsylvania in 1837, serving afterwards as resident physician in the Pennsylvania Hospital for two years, after which he studied abroad, finally settling in Philadelphia to practise in 1841. He was one of the surgeons to the St. Joseph's Hospital, Episcopal Hospital and the Philadelphia Hospital (Blockley), also professor of surgery in the University of Pennsylvania from 1855 to 1871 when he became professor emeritus, but in 1861, on the outbreak of the Civil War, was appointed to organize the hospital department of Pennsylvania with the title of surgeon-general of Pennsylvania.

At the first battle of Winchester, Virginia, he originated the plan of removing the wounded from the battlefield to large hospitals in Reading, Philadelphia, Harrisburg and other large cities, and established the custom of embalming the dead on the battle ground. He organized and directed a corps of surgeons with steamers as floating hospitals at the siege of Yorktown, and served the wounded after the battles of Williamsburg, West Point, Fair Oaks, Cold

Harbor and Antietam. After thoroughly organizing the department of which he was in charge, he resigned his commission in 1862. In 1883 he was elected president of the State Medical Society.

Dr. Smith was the author of many important medical publications, which include "An Anatomical Atlas," to illustrate William E. Horner's "Special Anatomy" (Philadelphia, 1843); "Minor Surgery" (1846); "System of Operative Surgery, with a Biographical Index to the Writings and Operations of American Surgeons for 234 Years" (2 Vols., 1852); "The Treatment of Disunited Fractures by Means of Artificial Limbs" (1855); "Professional Visit to London and Paris" (1855); "Practice of Surgery" (2 Vols., 1857–63); and numerous surgical articles in medical journals. And he translated from the French "Civiale's Treatise on the Medical and Prophylactic Treatment of Stone and Gravel" (Philadelphia, 1841); and edited the "United States Dissector" (1844) and "Spencer Thompson's Domestic Medicine and Surgery" (1853). In October, 1843, he married Mary Edmunds, eldest daughter of Prof. William E. Horner who had been his preceptor in the study of medicine. He died April 11, 1890.

F. R. P.

Tr. Phila. Co. Med. Soc., 1890.
Med. News., Phila., 1890.
Med. Rec., N. Y., 1890, vol. xxxvii.
A Memoir of H. H. Smith by B. Lee., Phila., 1890.

Smith, James (1771–1841).

He was born at Elkton, Cecil County, Maryland, in 1771. He was a master of arts of Dickinson College, 1792, and a pupil of Dr. Rush. He attended the University of Pennsylvania and is thought to have graduated there in 1794. He was a founder and attending physician of the Baltimore General Dispensary, 1801–1807; on March 25, 1802, he opened a private vaccine institute in Baltimore; in 1809 became state vaccine agent, and in 1813 United States vaccine agent. He held this position until 1822, when the office was abolished. He edited

"The Vaccine Inquirer," 1822, and was treasurer of the Medical and Chirurgical Faculty of Maryland from 1811 to 1817. He died at Pikesville, Baltimore County, Maryland, June 12, 1841.

Dr. Smith's reputation rests upon his connection with vaccination. Although not the first to introduce it into Maryland his use of it began at the Almshouse with the second supply received in Baltimore, and the date of his first case was May 1, 1801. The virus was put up for greater security in three different ways, on the blade of a lancet, or between small plates of glass, or on thread charged with it, but in any case confined in a vial well corked and sealed. Says Dr. Smith. "The physicians of Baltimore generally were invited to inspect these cases and offers were made to furnish them with virus, but no one could be prevailed on to make any use of it beyond the walls of the almshouse during the whole summer, notwithstanding the small-pox was then prevailing in the city." A full account of these cases was published in the "Baltimore Telegraph." An accident cut short his activities in May, 1822.

Dr. Smith received no salary for his services as United States vaccine agent, and the expenses of the institution were met by subscriptions and donations. While he had charge he supported twenty special agents who were furnished with horses and they rendered 6750 days' services vaccinating and distributing matter gratuitously for rich and poor, and securing the lives of more than 100,000 persons. (Quinan.)

There is preserved in the archives of the Medical and Chirurgical Faculty, at Baltimore, a patent for "an improvement in the art of vaccination," obtained by Dr. Smith from the government in 1822. The "improvement" consisted in moistening the crust and grating upon it small pieces of glass or ivory, to which it would adhere when dry and might thus be transmitted by letter to remote points. Dr. Smith speaks of the crust as "a cryptogamous plant of the order of fungi."

E. F. C.

There is a fine oil portrait of Dr. S. in the family of Gen. Felix Aguus, of Baltimore which has been reproduced in Cordell's Medical Annals of Maryland, 1907. For Quinan's vindication of Smith from the responsibility of the North Carolina outbreak of Small-pox, see Maryland Medical Journal, x, 1883.

"The Introduction of Inoculation and Vaccination into Maryland Historically Considered."

For writings see Quinan's Medical Anuals of Baltimore, 1884.

Smith, John Lawrence (1818-1883).

J. Lawrence Smith was born near Charleston, South Carolina, December 17, 1818, and died in Louisville, Kentucky, October 12, 1883. At an early age he manifested great taste for mathematics; when four years old he could do sums in addition and multiplication with great rapidity. This was some time before he could read. At eight years he was doing algebra, and at thirteen was studying calculus. As a boy he went to the best private schools of Charleston; afterwards to the University of Virginia, where later he devoted himself to the higher branches of physics, mixed mathematics and chemistry, studying the latter rather as a recreation. He selected civil engineering as a profession and was employed as assistant engineer on the road projected at that time between Cincinnati and Charleston, but this not proving congenial to his scientific tastes, he determined to study medicine and after three years' study, graduated M. D. at the Charleston Medical College. Three years in Europe followed. He studied physiology under Flourens and Longet; chemistry under Orfila, Dumas and Liebig; physics under Pouillet, Desprez, and Becquerel; mineralogy and geology under Elie de Beaumont and Dufrenoy, and prosecuted original researches on certain fatty bodies. His paper on "Spermaceti," in 1843, at once stamped him as an experimental inquirer. On his return to Charleston in 1844, he began to practise and delivered a course of lectures on toxicology before the students of the Charleston Medical College, at which time he established the

"Charleston Medical and Surgical Journal," which proved a success.

But the state needing his services as assayer of bullion coming into commerce from the gold-fields of Georgia, North and South Carolina, he relinquished his practice and also gave a great deal of attention to agricultural chemistry. The great beds of marl on which the city of Charleston stands early attracted his attention. He first pointed out the large amount of phosphate of lime in these marls, and was one of the first to ascertain the scientific character of their immense agricultural wealth. Dr. Smith also made a valuable and thorough investigation into meteorological conditions, character of soils and culture affecting the growth of cotton. His report on this subject was so valuable that in 1846 he was appointed by Sec. Buchanan, in response to a request of the Sultan of Turkey, to teach the Turkish Agriculturists the proper method of cotton culture in Asia Minor. On arriving in Turkey, Dr. Smith was chagrined to find that an associate on the commission had induced the Turkish Government to undertake the culture of cotton near Constantinople. Unwilling to associate his name with an enterprise which he felt satisfied would be a failure —the event justified his judgment—he was on the eve of returning to America, when the Turkish Government tendered him an independent position as mining engineer, with most liberal provisions, so he worked in this position for four years with such signal success that the Turkish government heaped upon him decorations and costly presents. Since 1846 the Turkish government has continued to receive large revenues from his discoveries of emery, chrome ores, coals, etc. His papers on these subjects, read before learned societies and published in the principal journals of Europe and America, gave him a high position among scientific men. His discovery of emery in Asia Minor destroyed the rapacious monopoly of this article at Naxos, in the Grecian Archipelago, extended its use and greatly reduced its price. His studies on emery and its associate minerals led directly to its discovery in America and in Massachusetts and North Carolina a large industrial product of emery is now on. To him justly belongs the credit of having done almost everything for these commercial enterprises by his successful researches on emery and corundum, he also investigated a great many Turkish resources, and his paper on "The Thermal waters of Asia Minor," is of great scientific value. In 1850 he invented the inverted microscope. This instrument, with its ingenious eye-piece micrometer and goniometer is an important improvement. ("American Journal of Science and Arts," New Haven, 1852, 2 s., xiv.) This instrument has been unjustly figured and described in some works as Nachet's chemical microscope.

After Dr. Smith's return to America, his alma mater, the University of Virginia, called him to the chair of chemistry, in which, with the help of his assistant, George J. Brush, he performed the valuable work of revising the "Chemistry of American Minerals." Having married a daughter of the Hon. James Guthrie of Louisville, Kentucky, Prof. Smith resigned his chair in the University of Virginia, and adopted Louisville as his home and in 1854 was made professor of chemistry in the medical department of the University of Louisville, but he finally resigned it to devote his time to scientific research.

In 1855 he published a valuable memoir on "Meteorites," his private collection of which was one of the largest in the world.

In 1873 he issued an interesting work containing the more important of his scientific researches and he contributed a large number of valuable papers to various scientific journals. Prof. Smith was very ingenious in devising new apparatus and methods of analysis. While much of his work was of a practical kind, he yet preferred original research in the less cultivated fields. While studying samarskite he discovered what he thought

to be a new element which he named mosandrium. In 1878 he published an account of his researches on this subject, which attracted much attention among scientists.

Prof. Smith was a most indefatigable worker; his more important original researches number nearly one hundred and fifty. He co-edited "The Southern Journal of Medicine and Pharmacy," Charleston, 1846.

In 1879 he was elected corresponding member of the Academy of Sciences of the Institute of France to succeed Sir Charles Lyell. Prof. Smith received honors from the principal scientific bodies of the world. He was a member of the following societies: The American National Academy of Sciences; Membre Correspondant de l'Institut de France (Académie des Sciences); the Chemical Society of Berlin; of the Chemical Society of Paris; of the Chemical Society of London; of the Société d'Encouragement pour l'Industrie Nationale; of the Imperial Mineralogical Society of St. Petersburg; American Association for the Advancement of Science. He was Chevalier de la Légion d'Honneur; member of the order of Nichan Iftahar of Turkey; member of the order of Medjidiah of Turkey; chevalier of the Imperial Order of St. Stanislas, of Russia.

Prof. Smith was of imposing presence and great dignity, strong, pure-hearted, withal one of the most modest and unostentatious of men. He was most generous with his apparatus, and anyone manifesting an interest in science was sure of help and encouragement.

J. B. M.

Pop. Sci. Month., N. Y., 1874–5, vol. vi (port.).
Louisville Med. News, 1879, vol viii.
In Memoriam (M. Michel) Charleston, S. C., 1884.
Year Book City of Charleston, S. C., 1883.

Smith, Joseph Mather (1789–1866).

"Forty years a public teacher in medicine, forty-six years constantly concerned in the active duties of public hospitals; for more that thirty years a consulting physician whose practical advice was widely sought by his confrères" is a good introduction to the child who was born to Dr. Matson Smith and his wife in New Rochelle, 1789; graduated at the New York College of Physicians and Surgeons in 1815 and served as surgeon's mate during the War of 1812. In 1824 he published his fine treatise on the "Elements of the Etiology and Philosophy of Epidemics," which Sir James Johnston, reviewing in the "Medico-Chirurgical Review," described as characterized not only by great talent and force of argument but also by candour and talent, doing honor to American medicine."

Four years as visiting physician to the State Prison; fighting the typhus which broke out there and in the Bellevue Almshouse in 1825 and three outbreaks of yellow fever, gave him a good and valued experience in epidemics. When, in 1831, an outbreak of cholera was announced in Europe, Dr. Smith set to work preparing to prevent or combat it, should it reach America. He traced its progress and elimination in all parts of the world, so that, when come it did in 1849 he and his confrères, Beck and Moore, were all ready. Record word was done in fighting the pestilence and every day the doctor met the municipal committee to confer. The following year Dr. Smith gave to the American Medical Association a lengthy and valuable report on "Hygiene and Preventive Measures in Case of Possible Epidemics," and 1860 saw his exhaustive treatise on the "Medical Topography and Epidemics of the State of New York," in which geology, geography, botany, hydrology, and meteorology are made to throw all possible light on the subject.

Even when seventy years had passed he, with faculties untouched by time, worked away at all hygienic reforms and everyone knows what cheerful work that is and the dull-headed opposition it provokes. Specially he encouraged and honored the sanitary inspectors and never failed to be present at their meetings.

On the morning of April 22, 1866, seventy-eight years old, he completed an earthly career of useful deeds. The Bible had for many years been his daily counsellor and sanctified the fireside.

In 1831 he married Henrietta M. daughter of Henry Martin Beare of New York and had two daughters and three sons, the eldest of whom, Gouverneur M., became a physician in New York.

His writings included:

"Elements of the Etiology and Philosophy of Epidemics," 1824; "Epidemic Cholera Morbus of Europe and Asia," 1831; "Influence of Diseases on the Intellectual and Moral Powers," 1848; "Illustrations of Mental Phenomena in Military Life," 1850; "Puerperal Fever; Its Causes and Propagation;" "Medical Topography and Epidemics of the State of New York," 1860; "Therapeutics of Albuminuria," 1863; "On the Identity of Typhus and Typhoid," 1846; "On Yellow Fever," 1859.

His appointments included professor of theory and practice of medicine, New York College of Physicians and Surgeons; visiting physician New York Hospital; president New York Academy of Medicine; president of the Council of Hygiene; and many others.

D. W.

Eulogium on (W. C. Roberts) N. Y., 1867.
Trans. N. York State Med. Soc., 1867.
Med. Rec., N. Y., 1866, vol. i.

Smith, Nathan (1762–1829).

Nathan Smith, professor of physics in the Medical College of Yale and the second to perform ovariotomy in America (1821), was a farmer's son and born in Rehoboth, Massachusetts, September 30, 1762. His father and mother settled in Chester, Vermont, then a wild district, and the boy, after a desultory education, taught other boys, himself untaught, but unconsciously gaining much from the country life and a little exciting experience in the state militia on the Canadian border. He was twenty-one when Josiah Goodhue of Putney, Vermont, did an operation near Chester and young Smith

NATHAN SMITH.

saw it and wanted to know more concerning this craft of surgery. He asked Dr. Goodhue to teach him, but, "What has been your education? enquired the surgeon, "Until last night I have labored daily with my hands." Goodhue advised him to study one year then enter at Harvard, and, perhaps being used to ambitious young countrymen, thought he should see no more of him, but he turned up later at Putney, studied three years with Goodhue, then settled down, diplomaless, to doctor the people of Cornish, New Hampshire.

But ambition would not rest. He knew how little he knew and went to Harvard. There John Warren the surgeon saw there was good stuff in him and helped him. In 1790 he graduated M. B. with a thesis on "The Circulation of the Blood" and returned to Cornish, where the crudity of the local doctors became to him even more apparent than before. His earliest idea was to establish a small school of medicine, but he first asked the encouragement and approbation of Dartmouth College and on their deciding to postpone giving help he went straight on to accomplish his purpose. Perhaps part of this purpose was to perfect himself still more, for he went to Edinburgh, Glasgow and London and from Edinburgh sent home thirty pounds worth of medical books and, bringing with him apparatus for teaching anatomy, and chemistry established the Medical Institute in connection with Dartmouth College, getting appointed professor of anatomy and surgery and chemistry, and getting also the A. M. degree. The lectures excited the greatest interest, and Pres. Wheelock, Smith's greatest helper, returned from a lecture to lead evening prayer in the old chapel and began by saying "O Lord, we thank Thee for the oxygen gas; we thank Thee for the hydrogen gas and for all the gases. We thank Thee for the cerebrum; we thank Thee for the cerebellum and for the medulla oblongata."

In 1813 Yale determined to have a medical college, and Nathan Smith.

"The New Hampshire Medical Institute," was out of swaddling clothes, so Smith left his foundling and became professor of the theory and practice of surgery, addin to this the work of practitioner and consultant and giving occasional lectures at Dartmouth and Burlington.

Like most able workers he was always being asked to do a little more and from 1821–1826 he is found giving *all* the lectures, save chemistry and anatomy, in the new medical school at Bowdoin College, Maine, which he had been asked to organize.

But in 1828 the burden began to tell, a severe but short illness left him debilitated yet still he worked on until in 1829 attacks of giddiness and a slight indistinctness of speech troubled him and on the twenty-sixth of January this good worker died.

In some of his methods he was fifty years in advance of his time. His clear-headedness in investigation is best shown in his essay on typhus fever in which the gist and germ is contained of all that which Louis in Paris enunciated many years later. His operations were brilliant and successful, especially in lithotomy, then a comparatively new operation here, and he is credited with first operating in the States for staphylorrhaphy. His ingenuity was also displayed in the maneuver method for reducing dislocations of the hip-joint. With regard to his ovariotomy, Dr. Gilman Kimball says "in point of absolute merit Nathan Smith is entitled to the same honors as McDowell. His first operation was not, as intimated, an accidental one, but the result of deliberate study, and done in ignorance of McDowell's first operation twelve years previously."

His writings are practically included in his "Medical and Surgical Memoirs" (1831) in which is also the one on typhus fever. For two years, 1825–6, he was co-editor of the "American Medical Review."   D. W.

Nathan Smith, by Gilman Kimball, Trans. Am. Gyn. Soc., vol. viii, 1884.

A Narrative of Medicine in America, J. G. Mumford.
American Medical Biography, S. W. Williams.
Medical and Surgical Memoirs, Nathan Smith (port.).
A Eulogium on . . . . . pronounced at his funeral, New Haven, 1829 (J. Knight).

Smith, Nathan Ryno (1797–1877).

Nathan Ryno Smith was the second of the four sons of Dr. Nathan Smith, the distinguished New England surgeon and founder of Dartmouth and Yale College Medical Schools. The name "Ryno" was derived from the Poems of Ossian, a favorite author of his mother. He was born on the twenty-first of May, 1797, in the town of Cornish where his father had been practising for ten years. After having received a preliminary training at Dartmouth, he entered Yale as a freshman in 1813 and graduated A. B. in 1817, at the age of twenty and in 1823 received from Yale College the degree of doctor of medicine, in his inaugural thesis defending the view that the effects of remedies and diseases are due to absorption into the blood and not to an impression on the nervous system, as many eminent writers then maintained. He continued his experiments on this subject, and his publications in 1827 are referred to by Dr. Alfred Stille in his work on "Therapeutics," vol. i, p. 51.

He began practice at Burlington, Vermont, in 1824, and in the following year he was appointed to the professorship of surgery and anatomy in the University of Vermont.

While in Philadelphia he met Dr. George McClellan, an able anatomist and surgeon, who was then giving private instruction in that city to large classes. This gentleman and others were then engaged in organizing a new medical school, the Jefferson Medical College. Being impressed by the ability and acquirements of Dr. Smith, they invited him to join with them and offered him the chair of anatomy, and he accepted.

In 1825 he published at New York an "Essay on Digestion" of ninety-three pages and after his settling at Philadel-phia, edited in 1825–26, with the cooperation of his father, the "American Medical Review." In June, 1827, he founded a medical periodical entitled the "Philadelphia Monthly Journal of Medicine and Surgery," which was continued into the following year and then merged into the "American Journal of the Medical Sciences."

In 1827 Dr. Smith's connection with Jefferson Medical College was severed by his acceptance of the chair of surgery in the University of Maryland, made vacant by the withdrawal of Granville Sharp Pattison. With this event commenced Dr. Smith's long and eventful career of fifty years at Baltimore, terminating only with his death in 1877.

In 1829 appeared his work on "Diseases of the Internal Ear," being a translation from the French of J. A. Saissy, with a supplement of twenty pages by himself, on "Diseases of the External Ear." The latter is written in the most concise and simple manner and covers most of the inflammatory affections of the auditory canal, congenital deformities, injuries as well as the treatment of foreign bodies, insects and indurated wax in the auditory canal. In 1830 he issued a journal, entitled "The Baltimore Monthly Journal," the first number of which appeared in February. It continued until the end of the year, when it ceased on account of lack of support. In the September and October numbers appeared a noteworthy article, entitled "Description of an Apparatus for the Treatment of Fractures of the Thigh and Leg, by Smith's Anterior Splint." One-half of the original matter of the volume of 510 pages consisted of contributions by Smith. The Medical and Surgical Memoirs (of Nathan Smith, his father), appeared in 1831 with a memoir by N. R. Smith.

He was also for many years a collaborator and frequent contributor to the "American Journal of the Medical Sciences." He also wrote many articles for a journal published at Baltimore by Prof. E. Geddings of the University of

Maryland, from 1833 to 1835; for the "Maryland and Virginia Medical Journal," 1860–61, of which Dr. W. Chew Van Bibber was a co-editor, and for the "Baltimore Medical Journal," founded in 1870 by Drs. Howard and Latimer. In 1832 appeared his great work on the "Surgical Anatomy of the Arteries," quarto, of which a second edition appeared in 1835.

In 1867 he published a small volume of seventy pages, giving a description of the method of using his "Anterior Suspensory Apparatus in the Treatment of Fractures of the Lower Extremity, with Cuts and Diagrams." And finally he issued a little duodecimo in 1869, which he called "Legends of the South, by Somebody Who wishes to be Considered Nobody." Early in his career at Baltimore he conceived the idea of writing a work on "Surgery" with good cuts, and did from time to time compose a large part of it, but it remained at his death among his unfinished papers.

In 1867, when eighty years old, he made his first and only visit to Europe. Although he sought in it only relaxation from his labors and amusement, he naturally visited many of the great European hospitals. His reputation had preceded him everywhere and he was received with the greatest deference, Sir James Paget in London being particularly attentive and the French surgeons giving him the title of the "Nestor of American Surgery."

He continued his active work at the University for two years longer, when he resigned and was made emeritus professor and president of the Faculty. In 1870 he was elected president of the Medical and Chirurgical Faculty, and the following year was re-elected to the same office, special provision being made in his case for this unusual honor. Not long after this, painful disease and infirmities of age began to oppress him. He still attended to office consultations, he wrote upon his surgery, he found pleasure in reviewing the classics, especially Homer and Virgil, and, above all, he found that

satisfaction and peace in the Christian religion which philosophy and science had been unable to secure for him. Thus engaged, the painful disease of the bladder from which he suffered slowly advanced and finally mastered his vigorous constitution on the third of July, 1877, a few weeks after he had passed his eightieth year.

He always lectured without notes and in slow, deliberate fashion. His voice was of medium pitch and distinct, though not strong. He indulged in story and humor whenever the opportunity permitted, although he was never coarse, profane or obscene. The portrait of him at the university is an admirable likeness, and represents him in his characteristic attitude while lecturing.

He was among the first to perform subcutaneous section of the tendo Achillis for club-foot (1836); Strohmeyer introduced it in Germany in 1831. Smith's reputation must rest chiefly on his lithotome and anterior splint. The former was first made known in the "Medical and Surgical Memoirs," 1831. By 1834 he had operated with this instrument with complete success in every instance, twenty-three times. By 1860 he had operated with it over one hundred times. In all, he performed the operation about 250 times, all except the first three or four being done with it, and with a relatively small mortality. A picture of this instrument is given in the "Memoirs" and also in the "Transactions of the Medical and Chirurgical Faculty," 1878.

But the invention which he regarded as his chief contribution to surgery was his anterior splint. He was engaged in perfecting this instrument for over thirty years and it was not completed until 1860. In 1867 he published his work on "Treatment of Fractures of the Lower Extremity by the Use of the Anterior Suspensory Apparatus." In this he claimed that his invention was applicable to all fractures of the thigh and leg.

Smith was the founder of the Medical

Department of the University of Vermont; President of the Medical and Chirurgical Faculty of Maryland. A. B. and M. D. of Yale, and LL. D., Princeton. E. F. C.

Cordell's Med. Ann. of Maryland, 1903.
An Address Commemorative of (Chew S. C.), 1878.
Maryland M. J., Balt., 1877, vol. i.
Tr. Am. Ass., Phila., 1878, vol. xxix.
S. D. Gross, Autobiography, 1887, vol. ii.

Smith, Peter (1753–1816).

Peter Smith, who wrote a "Dispensatory," the first of its kind in the West, was a son of Dr. Hezekiah Smith, of the "Jerseys," "a home old man, or Indian doctor." Peter was born in Wales, February 6, 1753, from whence this branch of the Smith family came. He was also a relative of Hezekiah Smith, D. D., of Haverhill, Massachusetts. Educated at Princeton, he was married in New Jersey to Catherine Stout, December 23, 1776. He seems to have early, under his father, given some attention to medicine, and became familiar with the works of Dr. Rush, Dr. Brown, and other writers of his day on "physic," as well as with the works of Culpepper. and acquired much information from physicians whom he met in New Jersey, Pennsylvania, Virginia, North and South Carolina, Georgia, Kentucky, and Ohio. He called himself an "Indian doctor," because, as he said, he relied in his practice much on herbs, roots, and other remedies known to the Indians, though he did not confine himself to botanical remedies. He seems to have been an original investigator, availing himself of all opportunities within his reach for acquiring knowledge, especially acquainting himself with domestic and tried Indian remedies, roots, herbs, etc.

Starting from New Jersey about the year 1780, he commenced his wandering, emigrating life with his wife and "some" small children. He lingered for a time in Virginia, then in the Carolinas, and "settled" in Georgia. He sought out people from whom he could gather knowledge of "the theory and practice of medicine," and preached the gospel, possibly in an itinerant way. He was a devout Baptist of the old school. A strong anti-slavery man, even in that early day, he could not be content with his Georgia home, as he put it, "with its many scorpions and slaves." Accordingly, he took his family on horseback—little children, twin babes among them, carried in baskets suitable for the purpose, hung to the horns of the saddle ridden by his wife—and thus, without roads to travel, crossed mountains, rivers, and creeks. The wilderness was not free from danger from Indians, but he traversed the woods from Georgia through Tennessee to Kentucky, intending there to abide. But, finding that Kentucky had also become a slave State, the dogmatic old man and his family bid good-bye to Kentucky and went to Ohio. He left that State with a parting shot to the effect that it was the home of "headticks and slavery," and emigrated to Ohio, settling on Duck Creek, near the Columbia Old Baptist Church, now adjacent to Norwood village, and near the limits of Cincinnati, reaching there about 1794.

He became, with his family, a member of the Duck Creek congregation, and frequently preached there and at other frontier places, still pursuing the double occupation of farming and the practice of medicine. In 1804 he again took to the wilderness with his entire family, then numbering twelve children, born in the "Jerseys and on the line of his march through the wilderness, the States and the Territories." He finally settled on a small, poor farm on Donnel's Creek, Ohio, in the midst of rich ones, where he died December 31, 1816. It seems from his book (p. 14), published while there, that he did not personally cease his wanderings and search for medical knowledge, as he states that he was in Philadelphia July 4, 1811, where he made observations as to the effect of hot and of cold air upon the human system.

In "The Dispensatory," it is to be regretted that Dr. Smith neglected the use of botanical names. His plants are all employed under common names, but he describes the appearance and habitat of each specimen so carefully as to enable the experienced reader to identify most of them. Rafinesque, who credits Dr. Smith's work, objects to his common names, which, however, are very interesting in connection with the text. The pains he takes to credit authorities from whom he obtained information is very refreshing, the relationship of these names to the substances used being useful to us to-day in connection with many drugs.

J. U. L.

Smith, Philip Greth (1810–1879).

Philip Greth Smith was born in Bern township, Berks County, Pa., in 1810 and educated at Mt. St. Mary's College, Maryland, reading medicine with his brother-in-law, Dr. Daniel Deppen, of Bernville. In the fall of 1835 he married Louisa G. Allgaler, of Reading, and moved to Lebanon, where he engaged and continued in practice for forty-four years. In 1850 he purchased the rights of Lebanon County for "Coad's Patent Graduated Galvanic Battery," and thereafter confined his practice almost exclusively to chronic diseases. While belonging to the old school, he largely used botanic remedies which, in earlier life, he himself gathered. He cultivated valerian in his garden, producing some of the finest, equalling if not excelling the English root in appearance and medical virtues. He was familiar with the medicinal plants growing in Lebanon and the adjoining counties, and with assistants spent several weeks every autumn in gathering and curing them. From these he made his tinctures, decoctions and extracts.

He was a faithful member of St. Mary's Roman Catholic Church, companionable, courteous and pleasant and greatly respected by all with whom he came in contact. He died December 4, 1879, aged sixty-nine years. Of a numerous family, two sons survived, one of whom, Dr. W. C. J. Smith, became a physician in St. Clair, Schuylkill County.

J. H. R.

From an account read before the Lebanon County Historical Society, October 19, 1900, by J. H. Redsecker.

Smith, Samuel Mitchell (1816–1874).

Samuel Mitchell Smith was born in Greenfield, Highland County, Ohio, on the twenty-sixth of November, 1816. Definite information in regard to his parents is not obtainable, but it appears that his father was a minister of the Presbyterian church.

The boy's early education was obtained from his father and in private schools. Before his majority he obtained a position as teacher in the district schools of Greenfield and vicinity, by economy accumulating sufficient funds to enter Miami University, Oxford, Ohio, and after the usual course took his M. A., afterwards becoming a pupil of Dr. John Morrison and matriculating in Jefferson Medical College in Philadelphia, from which he received his M. D., and within a year was appointed assistant physician to the Central Ohio Hospital for the Insane in Columbus.

On August 3, 1843, he married Susan Evans Anthony, daughter of Gen. Charles Anthony, of Springfield, Ohio, and very soon afterwards resigned his position in the State Hospital and began to practice on East Rich Street, near the corner of High, in the city of Columbus.

In the autumn of 1846 he was appointed professor of materia medica and therapeutics in Willoughby Medical College, transferred in that year from Willoughby, Lake County, Ohio, to Columbus. In 1847 Starling Medical College war founded and Willougby merged into it, most of the teachers becoming members of the faculty of the new school, Dr. Smith retaining his chair with medical jurisprudence added. There was no change in his relations to the school until 1850, when he was transferred to the chair of practical medicine, and in 1851 elected dean of the faculty. In 1860 he declined re-election to the deanship, but retained the chair of practice until 1874.

In 1859 Gov. Salmon P. Chase appointed Dr. Smith surgeon-general of the state; he held this post also under Gov. Dennison and Gov. Tod. In 1872 he sustained a slight attack of cerebral hemorrhage, which caused incomplete hemiplegia from which, though not wholly disabled, he never recovered. In January, 1874, he sustained a second attack, which completely disabled him and caused his death November 30, of the same year. He was very familiar with the Bible, and was seldom at loss for a quotation therefrom. He knew Shakespeare equally well, and liked Scott and Longfellow and had great fondness for Isaac Walton. His lectures were concise and very clear. His clinical lectures were especially good, and no one was surprised at his popularity with students, who never "cut" his hour.

While he allotted more time to general practice, he was an enthusiastic and very successful obstetrician, and was the first in Columbus to administer choloroform in labor.

He had four children, Elizabeth, Frances, Manette and Charles, all of whom survived their father. About twenty years ago his family had a bronze statue with a drinking fountain, designed by the artist, William Walcutt, placed at the southeast corner of High and Broad streets in the city of Columbus, where it still stands.   S. L.

> Tr. Ohio Med. Soc., Cincin., 1876, vol. xxxi (T. A. Reamy).

Snow, Albion Parris (1826–1898).

This man, one who was always ready to advance the profession as a whole, was born in Brunswick, Maine, March 14, 1826, the son of poor parents, and like the children of many other such was all the more eager for knowledge and improvement.

It is said of the Snow family that the wife brought into the world four male children inside of one year, one being born on the twenty-fifth of December, 1833, and triplets, December 2, 1834. By his perseverance and determination, young Albion studied medicine with Dr. Edmund Randolph Peaslee, then at the Medical School of Maine, and at the Dartmouth Medical College, finally graduating from the Medical School of Maine in 1854. During this time he was well thought of as an anatomist, and was made demonstrator in both of his schools in succession. He married Matilda Sewall, of Winthrop, and settled in that town, directly after graduating. After six busy years practising in Winthrop, he went abroad, and upon his return offered his services to the State, but did not go to the War. He joined the Maine Medical Association in 1865, and soon became an active member, was elected president at one time, and in his inaugural address strongly advocated a State Board of Health. The association following his advice saw it ultimately established. He also formed the Kennebec County Medical Society, and joined the American Medical Association. He collected statistics of prevalent diseases during many years in Kennebec county.

He was tall, dignified, had a polite yet firm voice, and was listened to with pleasure, both at home and at the discussions at the State Association. He was in favor of a medical Registration Law, he worked zealously for it before the Legislature, but it fell through and he failed to bring about its establishment, which later on occurred under other hands. He died October 25, 1898, failing gradually at the last.

Thinking back some years, I recall a little incident. Dr. Snow called me in consultation some twenty years ago, and I advised the hypodermatic use of pilocarpin, for a certain disease of the eyes. Not knowing how to use the syringe, I handed it to Dr. Snow, and asked him to perform the little act. But he, not knowing any more about it than I did, handed it back, and said he never had seen it before; so I was caught in my own trap, and had to make my first hypodermatic injection for a disease of the eyes.

J. A. S.

Trans. Maine Med. Assoc.

Snow, Edward Sparrow (1820-1892).

Edward Sparrow Snow was born in Austinburg, Ashtabula County, Ohio, July 5, 1820. His parents, Sparrow, and Clara (Kneeland) Snow were natives of Massachusetts, of English descent, living on a farm near Austinburg, Ohio, in 1817. Edward S. Snow graduated at Grand River Institute, Ohio, in 1842. During his student days he served two years as adjutant of First Rifle Regiment, Second Brigade and Twenty-first Division under Col. Tracy and Gen. Stearns of Ohio. He studied medicine with Dr. O. K. Hawley, of Austinburg, Ohio, and in 1847 took his M. D. from the medical department of Western Reserve College, Cleveland, Ohio. After practicing a brief period at Plymouth and Dearborn, Michigan, he was appointed acting assistant-surgeon of Detroit Arsenal. After a year he was displaced, but in 1852 reinstated by Jeff Davis, and continued to serve till the Arsenal was abandoned by the United States Ordinance Department. Dr. Snow was a founder of the Wayne County (Michigan) Medical Society, both in its first and second epochs; founder of the first Detroit Medical Society; founder of the Michigan Medical Society. Dr. Snow was a large man, fully six feet tall and weighing over two hundred pounds. His face was smooth, ruddy, rather full, hair sandy, gracious expression, thoughtful manner, deliberate in speech. He died in Dearborn, Michigan, July 18, 1892, from apoplexy.   L. C.

Representative Men in Mich., West. Biographical Co., Cinn., O., 1878.

Solly, Samuel Edwin (1845-1906).

An Englishman, who spent his active life in Colorado. A general practitioner, devoting himself to diseases of all kinds, especially to chest diseases seeking an arrest in that climate, and a restless

pioneer in the now prevalent climatic treatment of tuberculosis. Such in brief was Dr. Solly.

Born in London, May 5, 1845, he was educated at Rugby and later at St. Thomas' Hospital. His father was a distinguished London surgeon. His grandfather, a financier, joined with others in building the "Sirius," one of the first steamships to ply between England and America.

In 1874 Solly cast his lot with the infant Colorado (being driven to it by disease) and with others was so insistant on its climatic virtues as to compel the world to hear. His principal writing was the "Handbook of Medical Climatology," though he published a large number of monographs on various diseases as they were affected by climate, and principally that of Colorado. His last important work was to build, with funds provided by the late Gen. Palmer, Cragmor Sanatorium overlooking Colorado Springs. He lived to conduct this institution through the first year of its existence. He was a fellow of the Royal Medico-Chirurgical Society of London; ex-president of the American Climatological Association, of the American Laryngological, Rhinological, and Otological Society; Colorado State Medical Society, and the El Paso County Medical Society. He received the honorary M. D. from the University of Denver. He was a director of the National Society for the Study and Prevention of Tuberculosis.

He married in 1872, in London, England, Alma Helena Sandwell, who died in 1875, leaving two daughters, Lillian and Alma, and in 1877(?) in Philadelphia, Pennsylvania, Mrs. Elizabeth Meller Evans, of Philadelphia, a widow with two children, Helen and William. On the nineteenth of November, 1906, Dr. Solly died in Asheville, North Carolina, of heart disease, complicated with Bright's disease.   S. A. F.

Somers, John (1840-1898).

John Somers was born in St. John's, Newfoundland, in 1840, and died in

Halifax, Nova Scotia, in 1898, after practising in Halifax most of his professional life.

His general education was obtained at St. Mary's College, Halifax, his professional training at Bellevue Medical College, New York, from which he graduated M. D. in 1866.

Dr. Somers was a member of the Medical Society of Nova Scotia, of which he was president in 1883.

He was for a time assistant-surgeon in the United States Army, and, for years, a visiting physician of the Victoria General Hospital, Halifax, and professor of physiology in the Halifax Medical College. Dr. Somers led a life of great activity, was engaged in many matters of social and public interest, and was a warm supporter of the Halifax Medical College. He was an ardent student of botanical science, did much to extend the knowledge of the flora of Eastern North America, and presented a large number of papers on this subject to the Nova Scotia Institute of Natural Science, which may be found in that Society's printed Transactions.

Dr. Somers married a Miss Brown, of Halifax, and left several sons and daughters.　　　　　　　D. A. C.

Somervail, Alexander.

Born in Scotland and probably educated at the University of Edinburgh. He emigrated to America in the early years of the nineteenth century and settled in Essex County, Virginia, and practised there until his death.

He was a very skillful and observant physician, and evidently a student of diseases and a contributor to medical literature. In a paper on "The Medical Topography and Diseases of a Section of Virginia" he shows that he recognized as a distinct variety of continued fever, the disease we now term Typhoid Fever, which in that day was confounded with continued Malarial Fever. He was one of the first to recognize Typhoid Fever as a distinct disease.

In his early life, though brought up in the Scottish Kirk, he was an avowed infidel, but later became an earnest Christian and was noted for his high moral character and charitable works, being a physician of the poor as well as the rich.

He married the daughter of the Rev. John Mathews, of St. Anne's Parish, Essex, and was the brother-in-law of John Baynham, the noted surgeon.

The following articles are known to have been published by him: "The Medical Topography and Diseases of a Section of Virginia," and "Cases Illustrative of the Use of Muriate of Lime in Palsy from Diseased Vertebræ" ("Philadelphia Journal of Medical and Physical Sciences," vol. vi, 1823).

He died at his home in the seventy-sixth year of his age.　　　R. M. S.

Spalding, Lyman (1775–1821).

The interesting career of this studious physician and anatomist has never been properly described owing to lack of material, to say nothing of the fact that at the time of death at the youthful age of forty-six, his children who might have written something to rescue his memory from oblivion, were too young to appreciate what he had done in so short a life.

Lyman Spalding was born in Cornish, New Hampshire, June 5, 1775. His father was Lieut.-Col. Dyer Spalding who had been in the Indian Wars and who, moving from Plainfield, Connecticut, settled in Cornish in 1763. His mother was Elizabeth Parkhurst from that same Connecticut town. When young Lyman had arrived at the age of eleven years, Nathan Smith, M. D., one of America's most celebrated medical men, settled in Cornish, and was early attracted by the studiousness of the boy. At Dr. Smith's suggestion he was sent to the Charleston Academy near by, and later on again at Smith's advice to the Harvard Medical School where he formed with the professors a personal intimacy which lasted for life.

Graduating in 1797, Dr. Spalding's help was at once enlisted by Dr. Smith in the foundation of the Medical School at Dartmouth where the young man lectured on chemistry for two years and acted as anatomical demonstrator when subjects offered. Finding at the end of 1799 that he could not earn a living by lecturing alone, Spalding moved to Walpole, New Hampshire, for a short time and thence to Portsmouth in the same State. Here he found a galaxy of physicians, including Drs. Ammi Cutter and Hall Jackson, while Joshua Brackett was but a few miles away. Nothing daunted, he began an active campaign of vaccination, just introduced from England, and was the first in America to test publicly the efficacy of this procedure against small-pox, at the pest house in Portsmouth Harbor in July, 1801.

Besides proving his medical worth in this way, he printed yearly bills of mortality, and sent them to many prominent physicians of the day in order to induce them to study the diseases of the towns in which they lived. In this way he became acquainted with the leaders of American medicine, especially in the larger cities. He studied anatomy zealously, during the cool weather dissected in a specially arranged cellar in his own house, and soon formed an anatomical museum. In the summer he cultivated medicinal plants, and at the local medical society exhibited personally grown and prepared opium. He was active in the New Hampshire Medical Society and served for eight years as its secretary. He established a County Medical Society. He wrote to the authorities in Washington of the unsanitary conditions of the fort in the harbor and obtained a commission as contract surgeon for the troops around Portsmouth.

He continued his correspondence with Nathan Smith, but although Dr. Smith wished him to return to the Dartmouth Medical School as lecturer he could not see his way clear to leave his practice for two months in the year. He early became noted as a surgeon and did all of the operations of the day over an extent

of country of fifty miles from Portsmouth as a center. He was interested in the yellow-fever scourge, and after introducing his vaccination, his next move was to get appointed to the town Board of Health, and then to improve the sanitary condition of its dwellers. He constructed a fine galvanic machine and used it for the treatment of his patients.

In 1802 he married Elizabeth, daughter of Peter Coues, who was in the Royal Navy and on the "Royal George" when she went down "with twice four hundred men," as Cowper sang.

Hearing in 1808 from Dr. Smith that the famous Alexander Ramsay was to lecture on anatomy at Dartmouth, Dr. Spalding set out with a precious cargo of dissecting material for Hanover, and delivered it at last safely to the delighted Smith who after inviting Ramsay had been looking around in vain for subjects for the lectures. During this course Spalding dissected and prepared everything for Ramsay, and received abundant thanks.

Returning to Portsmouth for another year of study and practice he spent the winter of 1809–10 in Philadelphia under the instruction of Rush, Caldwell, Physick, and Dorsey, but chiefly he devoted weeks and months to anatomy in company with Caspar Wistar.

The result of his public dissections and preparations at Philadelphia, where we read from old letters, "The whole medical world of Philadelphia is talking of Spalding's beautiful anatomical demonstrations and preparations of the lymphatics," was a most unlooked-for invitation to the chair of anatomy at the Fairfield Medical School in New York. He was diffident at first of his ability to lecture, but accepted and for seven years did most excellent work. It has been said that his prognostications concerning this school did not prove true, but keeping his eyes fixed on medicine, he failed to comprehend, until too late, the ruin inflicted on his plans by meddlesome politicians, at that time rampant in New York State.

From the Fairfield School he resigned in 1817, but previously he had removed from Portsmouth, as too small a place for his talents and established himself in practice in New York City in 1812.

During the eight years of practice between this date and his early death in 1821, Dr. Spalding exhibited the same medical energy that had always characterized him. He made the acquaintance of the best men in medicine and in literature, belonged to the leading societies, and obtained a good practice though not very remunerative. Among his labors in this period are his studies regarding yellow fever, renewed papers on vaccination, extensive investigations into hydrophobia, and the foundation of the United States Pharmacopeia. He was accused of unduly praising scutellaria as a cure for hydrophobia, but he replied that he had written his paper only to show what others claimed for it. Eagerly as he studied yellow fever, he failed to solve the cause.

As early as 1815 he had written to friends urging the establishment of a National Pharmacopeia, but several pronounced it an impossible and useless task. He kept hold of his idea, however, and in 1817 read his paper before the New York County Medical Society. It was received in silence, referred to a committee and, though favored, yet it was nearly buried in innumerable clauses and resolutions through which the human mind finds it to-day a hard road to travel; three long years of endless letter writing to physicians between Eastport, Maine, and New Orleans followed, often receiving no reply, often getting rebuffs, postponements, or promises. Although a work of national importance it was very difficult to get a committee together even for the two meetings, one at Philadelphia and one at Washington. Travel was slow, progress in the work was impeded and heartbreaking. At last he had his reward, at the end of 1820 the work appeared in Latin and English on alternate pages. Dr. Lyman Spalding was the originator, founder and almost single-handed worker upon the original Pharmacopeia of the United States.

About this time Dr. Caspar Wistar died and Dr. Spalding made every endeavor to obtain his vacant chair. He had to work against local influence, but many favored him for the place; a temporary candidate was placed in the lecture room, but the actual appointment seemed sure for Dr. Spalding, when he met with an accident from a blow on the head, fell rapidly ill, with what seemed to be traumatic meningitis, and despite every care grew rapidly worse. Finding death drawing near he asked to he taken back to Portsmouth, and died there a few days after his arrival.

In summing up the character of this man we find him versatile in many branches of medicine; yet always having the advance of medicine his dearest aim in life. He wrote many medical papers at a time when literature was scant and turgid with verbiage. His papers were brief, clean-cut and to the point, he loved anatomy, as proved by using his own cellar for dissecting purposes and his own house for a museum.

Although devoted to medicine, yet he took an active part in the public schools of each place in which he lived. Nature too he loved, often writing on her phenomena wherever they seemed to relate to the human race. Foreign languages he studied in order to read medical books in which they were written and was a good botanist, so far as experiments with medicinal plants. As a letter writer he was rather laconic, but carried on a large and interesting correspondence with the leading medical lights of the world. He made many friends and retained them to the end of his life. Taking him all in all, it cannot be denied that he was a shining light in medicine, that he died too early, yet even in the short twenty-five years of his active medical life he did more than his share of careful, scientific medical work.

J. A. S.

Family papers and letters resurrected after a century of forgetfulness and neglect.

Spence, John (1766-1829).

He was born in 1766 in Scotland, receiving his education at Edinburgh University, where he spent five years. Fully qualified to graduate in medicine, he was prevented from doing so by reason of the development of pulmonary tuberculosis, and having been advised by his preceptors to take a long sea voyage, he came to Virginia. Being in straightened circumstances, he accepted a position as tutor in a family living in Dumfries, then a thriving town with an extensive trade with Scotland. In 1828, in consideration of his well merited distinction, the honorary M. D. was conferred upon him by the University of Pennsylvania.

The voyage to and sojourn in Virginia so restored his health that at the expiration of his engagement in 1791 he began to practice medicine, for which he was well prepared and soon attained, in the region in which he lived for nearly forty years, a high reputation as a judicious and sucessful practitioner. When vaccination was introduced into the United States he gave his attention to the subject, and satisfying himself of its great prophylactic power, did much to inspire the public, both in Virginia and the adjoining states, with confidence in it. Having imbibed his first principles under the immediate instruction of Cullen, they were never obliterated from his mind and were ever to him infallible evidences and tests of medical truths.

He made numerous contributions to medical literature, one of which was a valuable one on the efficacy of digitalis in pulmonary hemorrhage. He was an earnest advocate of the use of digitalis in pulmonary affections and dropsies.

In 1806 he carried on an interesting correspondence with Dr. Benjamin Rush on the successful treatment of puerperal mania, which was published in the "Medical Museum" of Philadelphia. He was one of the collaborators of the "American Journal of Medical Sciences," and contributed to it a good paper on the efficacy of a sea voyage in arresting pulmonary consumption in his own case.

He left many manuscripts in which the results of his professional experience were recorded.

The last two or three years of his life were spent in combating a disease, the exact nature of which is not known. Its chief symptoms were ascites and anasarca which followed a violent attack of bilious fever succeeded by attacks of gout. He kept himself alive long beyond the time at which his disease threatened to end his existence by the use of his favorite remedy, digitalis, and by trips in summer to watering places. His last days were saddened by the death of a favorite son.

He died at his home on May 18, 1829, aged sixty-three years, leaving a widow and several small children.

R. M. S.

W. E. H. in the American Journal of Medical Sciences, vol. v, Phila., 1829.
Medical Biography, Williams.

Spencer, Pitman Clemens (1793-1860).

Known as a surgeon and lithotomist, he was born in Charlotte County, Virginia, the son of Gideon and Catherine Spencer, his father, a lieutenant in the state service in the Revolution. Pitman Spencer had few early advantages and began to study medicine with his brother, Dr. Mace C. Spencer, in 1810, remaining with him until 1812, when he volunteered and acted as surgeon's mate to a detachment of troops located at Norfolk. He attended lectures at the University of Pennsylvania, graduating in 1818.

He settled in Nottoway Court House, and, associated with Dr. Archibald Campbell, practised until 1827, when he went abroad, passed some time in London and Paris, and made a tour of Switzerland and Italy. While in Paris he studied under Dupuytren and afterwards always used the latter's doubled, concealed lithotome.

Dr. Spencer was a member of the (old) Medical Society of Virginia. A contemporary said of him that he was a born surgeon, but cared more for the art than the science. He was bold to recklessness in operating, but had marvellous success

This was attributable to the great care with which he prepared his patient; to freedom in the use of soap and water, rendering both himself and patient as nearly aseptic as possible, and to the care of his patients after operation. He used in his operations a solution of creosote in alcohol, an excellent antiseptic. His operations of all kinds were well done, and generally successful, and his prognoses of traumatisms seldom erred.

He paid special attention to lithotomy, discarding lithotrity as not comparable in results, a conclusion arrived at only after a thorough trial of both operations. He spent much time practising the crushing operation upon the cadaver while in Paris, and possessed a fine set of instruments. He did the operation of lateral lithotomy twenty-nine times, losing only his first two patients. Less than a year before his death, he operated successfully upon an eight-year-old boy, removing a calculus weighing 580 grains. He protested against the use of the catheter after operation, and tying the legs together awaited the passage of urine by the natural channel.

His reputation as a lithotomist was very extended, indeed, almost world-wide, which fact and a similar one in the case of his greater surgical co-temporary, Dr. J. P. Mettauer, show what a positon may be obtained in a provincial town, or even in a small village, unaided by metropolitan or academic advantages. He was far ahead of his time in the use of both asepsis and antisepsis without knowing it. His practice extended over southside Virginia and far into North Carolina, and his name was a household word, and his word the law in things surgical.

He never married, although a great beau, and assiduous in his attentions to ladies, especially young ladies.

He died in Petersburg on the fifteenth of January, 1860, in the sixty-seventh year of his age.

So far as I have been able to discover the following articles are all that he contributed to medical literature:

"A Case of Calculus successfully treated by Lithotrity." ("American Journal Medical Sciences," 1832.)

"Report of the Successful Removal of an Enormous Tumor of the Neck." ("American Journal Medical Sciences," 1844.)

"Case of Irritable Uterus." ("The Stethoscope," vol. i, April, 1851.)

"Report of Fifteen Cases of Lithotomy." ("The Stethoscope," vol. i.)

"Empyema Successfully Treated by Paracentesis Thoracis." ("Virginia Medical and Surgical Journal," vol. iv.)

"Results of Twenty-four Operations for Lithotomy." ("Virginia Medical and Surgical Journal," vol. iv.)

"Report of Twelve Cases of Lithotomy."

R. M. S.

Maryland and Virg M. J., Richmond, 1860, xiv.
N. Am M. and Chir. Rev., Phila., 1860, iv.

Spencer, Thomas (1793–1857).

Thomas Spencer was born in Great Barrington, Massachusetts, October 22, 1793. His father, Eliphalet Spencer, wheelwright, was a man of more than ordinary intellectual strength and physical energy who served during the Revolutionary War in the Connecticut regiment, and fought at the battle of Saratoga, and witnessed the surrender of Burgoyne. An elder brother taught Spencer arithmetic and in 1806 he had three months' schooling for the purpose of studying English grammar, and never forgot the mortification of being outstripped by one of the school girls somewhat older than himself.

When nineteen he was taught surveying by his brother, Gen. Ichabod Spencer, and about the same time began to study medicine with Dr. Dix, of Delphi. By his surveying and school teaching, he was enabled to earn the fees for his medical course, and in 1816 received a license to practise from the Medical Society of the County of Herkimer.

Dr. Spencer at once began to practise in the town of Lenox. He was elected to the several offices of the Medical Society of the County of Madison in 1820, and attended a second course of lectures at the Medical College at Fairfield, and received his M. D.

In 1824 Spencer was elected to the Assembly from the Legislature of New York State. In 1832 curious as it might seem to us now, during his presidency of the Medical Society of the State of New York in 1822, he attended a course of lectures at the University of Pennsylvania, going occasionally to the lectures of the Jefferson Medical College. His article on "Cholera" was written in Philadelphia in ten days, just preparatory to its delivery in that city. It was well received and noticed in Cincinnati, Philadelphia and other medical journals of the day. At the suggestion of the Hon. John C. Spencer, late Secretary of War (not a relative), to Drs. Spencer and Morgan, a medical college under the powers of the Geneva College was founded. The first course of lectures was delivered in 1835, Dr. Spencer filling the chair of theory and practice of medicine for fifteen years. Through his energy large endowments were obtained for the literary and also for the medical department. He removed to Geneva in order that he might be more convenient to the college. In 1847, when the Mexican War broke out, Dr. Spencer was appointed surgeon of the Tenth Regiment of New York and New Jersey Volunteers, he served for nearly one year and a half on the northern line of the Army; at Matamoras he organized a field hospital and brought everything in connection with it, its appliances and appurtenances, to a great degree of perfection.

Soon after his return Dr. Spencer removed to Milwaukee, in order to be near the Rush Medical College, Chicago, where he became professor of theory and practice of medicine. Owing to ill health he was obliged to resign and return to Syracuse. The Board of Trustees, however, elected him emeritus professor. Dr. Spencer relinquished his practice in Syracuse to accept a professorship in the Philadelphia College of Medicine about

1852, and accordingly removed to that city, where he continued to reside until the period of his death which took place on May 30, 1857.

M. K. K.

Abridged from a biography by Dr. James J. Walsh. Tr. M. Soc., N. Y., Albany, 1858 (S. D. Willard).

Squire, Truman Hoffman (1823-1889). When a general practitioner like T. H. Squire with evident talent for surgery remains a practitioner, one regrets a loss to both sides of the profession, but commonplace hindrances often keep a man tied while ambition soars. Truman Squire was born to John Graham and Rhoda Smith Squire in Russia, March 31, 1823. He went as a lad to the Fairfield Academy and graduated from the College of Physicians and Surgeons, New York, in 1848, settling eventually in Elmira and practising there all his life with the exception of a term of service during the War. He married Grace, daughter of Dr. Nathaniel Smith, of Bradford County, Pennsylvania, and had two daughters and a son, the latter, Charles L., practising with his father.

Dr. Squire possessed a reputation in skillful surgery appreciated by his colleagues and, added to this he had a fine talent of invention, one result of which was an instrument for easy admission to the bladder through the natural channel, an invention which culminated in the soft rubber catheter of Nélaton. Squire's was designed for cases of enlarged prostate and consisted of the employment at the distal extremity of a metallic catheter of a number of ball-and-socket joints in the form of a continuous tube which admitted of much mobility and readily found entrance through a sinuous canal to the cavity of the bladder. In 1876 the Arguentieul Prize from the Academy of Medicine of Paris of 1500 francs was awarded him for his contribution to surgical appliances for use in genito-urinary disease. Dr. Squire died on November 27, 1889, at his home in Elmira.

Trans. Med. Soc. State of N. York, 1890 (Wm. C. Wey).

Staples, Franklin (1833–1904).

Franklin Staples was one of the best known and most generally respected physicians in Minnesota, and through his writings, especially upon subjects relating to the history of medicine, his name was known throughout the country.

Born in Raymond (now Casco), Cumberland County, Maine, November 9, 1833, he began to study medicine under Dr. C. S. D. Fessenden, of Portland, Maine, in 1855, and attended lectures at Bowdoin College in 1856. He was head instructor of the old Center Grammar School, Portland, Maine, for some four years, but upon his retirement entered the College of Physicians and Surgeons, New York, and graduated in March, 1862, subsequently being appointed demonstrator of anatomy in the medical department of Bowdoin College.

In the summer of 1862 he established himself as a general practitioner in Winona and married, June 4, 1863, Helen M. Harford, of Portland.

Dr. Staples was one of the founders of the Winona Preparatory Medical School. In 1871 he was elected president of the Minnesota State Medical Society. From 1883 to 1887 he held the chair of the practice of medicine in the medical department of the University of Minnesota.

His writings on medical and surgical subjects have from time to time been published in scientific and professional journals, and from their marked ability, attracted the attention of the medical profession. Among the first of his writings in this line was his report on "The Influence of Climate on Pulmonary Diseases in Minnesota," and "A Report on Diphtheria," "The Treatment of Fracture of the Femur," besides many other articles pertaining to medicine and surgery, and particularly to the history of medicine.   B. F.

Staughton, James Martin (1800–1833).

Born in Bordentown, New Jersey, in 1800, he was the son of the Rev. William Staughton, a most distinguished Baptist divine, of Coventry, England, who came to America in 1793, and of Maria Hanton Staughton. He received his education in Philadelphia and while still a boy gave lectures on chemistry in the Female Seminary in Bordentown, which school his father kept. He graduated from Jefferson Medical College, Philadelphia, in 1821, and after graduation practised for a short time in Philadelphia, but moved to Washington, District of Columbia, where his father was placed at the head of an institution in that city. Staughton was soon appointed professor of chemistry in Columbia College and when the medical department was added was made professor of surgery. In preparing for this position he spent two years in Europe.

In the spring of 1831 an attempt was made to establish in Cincinnati a medical department of Miami University, and Dr. Staughton was elected professor of surgery. Before the beginning of the first session, this school was united with the Medical College of Ohio, and Staughton held the same chair. In 1832 Cincinnati was visited by the cholera and he was stricken with the disease when it reappeared in 1833. He married in 1828, Mrs. Louisa Patrick of England and had five children.   A. G. D.

Stearns, Henry Putman (1828–1905).

Born in Sutton, Massachusetts, April 28, 1828 of a family prominent in the history of Massachusetts since 1630, his preparatory studies were at Yale College which he entered in 1849, and from which he received the degree of A. B. in 1853. He received his medical education at Yale and Harvard and was made an M. D. at the former in 1855. He went for post-graduate study in the same year to Edinburgh and became an interne in the Royal Infirmary, later studying in Paris and returning to America in 1857. He settled at Marlboro, Massachusetts and practiced until 1859, when he removed to Hartford, Connecticut. In 1861 upon the outbreak of the Civil War he was commissioned a surgeon in, the First Connecticut Volunteers, and as such participated in the first battle of Bull Run. He was later made a surgeon of the United States Medical Corps and was detailed as brigade surgeon to the army of Gen. Fremont at St. Louis. Later he was assigned to the staff of General Grant and was with him throughout his service in the south-west except for a short period when he served as medical director of the right wing of the army of Gen. Mc-Clellan. He subsequently was appointed medical inspector of hospitals on the staff of Col. R. C. Wood, assistant surgeon general and later superintended the building of the Joseph Holt Hospital at Jeffersonville, Ind. Afterward he became medical director of the United States general hospital at Nashville, Tennessee where he had continuously under his charge at least 10,000 patients.

In September 1865 he was mustered out of the service at his own request with the rank of brevet lieutenant-colonel, and returned to Hartford, Connecticut to resume practice.

In 1874 at much pecuniary sacrifice, he accepted the superintendency of the Hartford Retreat because the demands of his large practice had proven too great for his health and strength. The remainder of his professional life consequently was devoted to the care of the insane, in which branch of medicine he proved himself a diligent student, a skillful physician and a sagacious, conscientious and able administrator. He practically rebuilt the Retreat and added cottages and other subsidiary buildings. He also made marked improvements in the medical care and treatment of the patients under his charge. He acted frequently as a medico-legal expert in court, and his services as a consultant were highly prized by his brother physicians.

A prolific writer, he wrote many books and papers. The following is a partial list: Parts 1 and 2 medical volumes and parts 1, 2, and 3 surgical volumes of the "Medical and Surgical History of the War and Rebellion;" "Classification of the Insane;" "The Relations of Insanity to Modern Civilization;" "The Insane Diathesis;" "Phases of Insanity;" "The Care of Some Classes of the Insane;" "Expert Evidence in the Case of the U. S. vs Guiteau;" "Insanity, Its Causes and Prevention;" "Progress in the Treatment of the Insane;" "General Paresis and Senile Insanity;" "The Classification of Mental Diseases;" "The Importance of Cottages for the Insane;" "Some Notes on the Present State of Psychiatry;" "Lectures on Mental Diseases" and "Commissions in Lunacy."

He was lecturer in psychiatry at Yale University from 1875 to 1897, and resigned because of ill-health.

His memberships included: the American Medico-Psychological Association (President in 1891); the New England Psychological Association; Connecticut Medical Society; City Medical Society, serving each society as both vice-president and president.

He remained in active charge of the Hartford Retreat until failing health compelled him to resign March 31, 1905, after a service of thirty-one years.

He married at Dumfries, Scotland, in 1857, Annie Elizabeth Storrier who died in 1903, after nearly forty-six years of ideal married life. .

After a brief and painless illness he died May 27, 1905.   H. M. H.

N. Eng. M. Month., Conn , 1884-5, iv (port.).

Stearns, John (1770–1848).

John Stearns was born in Wilbraham, Massachusetts, on the sixteenth day of May, 1770. He was early fitted for college, and graduated at Yale with distinguished honor in 1789. He studied with Dr. Erastus Sergeant of Stockbridge until 1792, when he went to Philadelphia and attended the lectures of Shippen, Wistar, Rush, and others at the University. The year following, in 1793, he entered upon practice, near Waterford in the county of Saratoga, New York, where in 1797 he married a daughter of Col. Hezekiah Ketchum.

The inception of the Medical Society of the State of New York was received from John Stearns, and he was elected its secretary at the first meeting in 1807, and continued to fill the office for several years. In 1807, Dr. Stearns communicated to the profession through Dr. Ackerly, in an article published in the eleventh volume of the "New York Medical Repository," his observations on the medical properties of ergot in facilitating parturition. Whatever may have been known of this substance before, Dr. Stearns was the first to elicit attention to it in the United States, and his observations were doubtless original.

In 1809 he was elected to the Senate of the state of New York, and served as senator for four years until 1813. He removed to Albany in 1810, and for nine years was actively engaged in practice, enjoying largely the public confidence. The Regents of the University conferred upon him the honorary degree of doctor of medicine in 1812. In 1817 he was elected president of the Medical Society of the State of New York, and was deservedly re-elected in 1818, 1819 and 1820.

In 1819 Dr. Stearns removed to New York, where he practised for many years, and contributed largely to the medical periodicals of the day. Upon the organization of the New York Academy of Medicine in 1846, its first president was John Stearns, then venerable in professional life.

A little more than one year later, on the eighteenth of March, 1848, Dr. Stearns died a martyr to the profession in which he had so long lived, his death occurring as the result of a poisoned wound, in the seventy-ninth year of his age.   S. D. W.

From Albany Med. Annals and Biographies, Sylvester D. Willard, 1864.

Stebbins, Nehemiah Delavan (1802–1888).

Nehemiah Delavan Stebbins was born in Beekman Town., Dutchess County,

New York, February 27, 1802; the eldest son of Lewis and Sarah (Delavan) Stebbins, a lineal descendant of Rowland Stebbins who emigrated from Yorkshire, England, on the ship Francis and settled at Northhampton, Massachusetts, in 1634. The boy had a common school education and in 1820–21 worked as a civil engineer in the construction of the Erie Canal, between Rochester and Lockport. After this he studied medicine with Dr. A. F. Oliver, in Penn Yan, Yates County, New York. Later he attended the College of Physicians and Surgeons of New York City, and was licensed to practise by the New York State Medical Society. He first settled at Hammondsport, Steuben County, New York, and eventually in Detroit until 1868, when he settled in Southern California. He was a member of the first and second epochs of the Wayne County Medical Society, and a founder of each; a founder of the first and second epochs of the Michigan State Medical Society, and president in 1857–58. He was six feet tall, of spare build, long legs, short body. Pleasant, penetrating blue eyes showed from deep sockets and overhanging dense brows; he was quick in movement, gracious in manner, firm in his convictions. He was a lover of all kinds of knowledge for its own sake, as well as for what practical good it accomplished. In his frequent visits to the writer, while staying in Detroit, his first question after being seated was, "What is new within your field of observation?" If anything could be given, he was as delighted as a boy with his first pants. Dr. Stebbins' sanguine, cheery disposition, indefatigable industry, devotion to friends and profound faith in God, Bible and church, were important factors in his success. On June 28, 1832, he married Emily White in Rochester, New York. She died in 1859. Of their three children, one, Dwight Delavan Stebbins, became a physician, but died young from typhoid infection while serving the soldiers of the Rebellion. The father died at his brother's home in Dowagiac, Michigan, May 31, 1888. He went to bed well, but never woke to his earthly friends.

Papers:

"Medical Practice in the Bible." ("Transactions American Medical Association," vol. ix.)

"Deep Seated Ulcer of the Os Uteri as a Cause of Abortion." ("Detroit Review of Medicine and Pharmacy," vol. i.)

"Medicine and Inductive Science." (President's Address Michigan State Medical Society, 1858, "Peninsular Medical Journal," vol. v.)

"Scriptural Evidence of a General System of Medical Practice being taught in the Bible, and a Comparison of this Practice with Rational Medicine and Homeopathy." (Reprint from "Peninsular Medical Journal," 1857.) L. C.

Transactions Mich. State Med. Soc., 1888, Detroit, Mich.

Steiner, Lewis H. (1827–1892).

Dr. Steiner, librarian of the Enoch Pratt Free Library, Baltimore, was born in Frederick City, Maryland, May 4, 1827. He was descended from German ancestors who settled in western Maryland early in the eighteenth century. He attended Marshall College, at Mercersburg, Pennsylvania, and took his B. A. there in 1846. The degree of A. M. was conferred upon him three times; by his alma mater in 1849, by St. James College in 1854, and by Yale in 1869. His M. D. he had from the University of Pennsylvania in 1849. In 1852 he removed to Baltimore, where he held the chairs of chemistry in the Maryland Medical Institute (a preparatory school) and in the Maryland College of Pharmacy. He also held the same chair later in Columbia College and the National Medical College, at Washington, District of Columbia, and lectured at times on natural history, physics and pharmacy. In 1861 he returned to Frederick City.

During the Civil War he was chief inspector of the United States Sanitary Commission in the Army of the Potomac. After 1868 his time was given up mostly to literary and scientific pursuits.

Dr. Steiner's death took place suddenly in his library, of apoplexy, February 18, 1892. He was a member of the Reformed Church, and always took an active interest in its affairs. He left a widow, three daughters and two sons. He was a close student, an eloquent speaker, and a ready writer. At the age of twenty-four he published his first work, entitled "Physical Science." He later translated "Will's Chemical Analysis." He was assistant editor of the "American Medical Monthly." He was a member of the Medical and Chirurgical Faculty of Maryland. He was also a member of the American Academy of Medicine and its president in 1879. "No brighter example," says Prof. Raddatz, his biographer, "of high and earnest ardor in his country's cause, of manhood, integrity and energy, shines in the galaxy of sterling citizens which the sturdy race from which he sprang has given to our state." (For portrait, see Cordell's "History of the University of Maryland," 1907, vol. i. For list of writings, see Quinan's "Medical Annals of Baltimore," 1884.) E. F. C.

Stephen, Adam (—— –1791).

A native of Scotland, Stephen was educated at Edinburgh University where it is said he studied six years, the last two "in different physical classes," and that Donald Munroe, Gregory and Stephen took away the palm in all classes of philosophy, mathematics and physic." Leaving college he passed the examination for the position of naval surgeon, "but discovering that officers and men were a parcel of bears," he went as hospital-ship surgeon for the army in the expedition against Port L'Oriente. After various adventures he finally settled in Virginia.

He took part in the French and Indian War, and with another physician of Scottish birth, Dr. James Craik, accompanied Washington on that perilous journey which terminated at Fort Necessity. The Revolution found him on the side of his adopted country. In her preparation for the struggle with the mother-country, Virginia raised nine regiments of infantry, the first six of which were placed on the continental establishment and their officers commissioned by Congress. The third and fourth of these were commanded respectively by Hugh Mercer, also a physician and a native of Scotland, and Adam Stephen. Stephen took an active part in the war, and became a general in the Continental Army, also filling the position of peace commissioner to the Indians. The town of Martinsburg in Berkeley County (now West Virginia) was founded and laid out by Stephen.

The following quaint mention of two operations done by him are from a curious old manuscript endorsed in the hand-writing of Dr. Rush in 1775, and read: "Stephen made himself known by making an incision into the liver of Mrs. Mercer of Stafford County, cleansing and healing the ulcers there, contrary to the opinion of all the faculty employed to cure the lady." It would seem probable that this was a case of abscess of the liver which was cured by operation. He also did an operation on one Abraham Hill for aneurysm, "restoring him the use of his arm and hand."

Dr. Stephen was noted for his talents, energy, learning, and skill in his professional work. He died at an advanced age, at his home in Martinsburg, November, 1791. R. M. S.

Stephenson, John (1797–1842).

John Stephenson was born in Montreal, in 1797, and received his early education from the Sulpicians although he was not a Catholic. He was apprenticed to William Robertson as a medical pupil in 1815, for which privilege he paid fifty pounds and in 1817 went to Edinburgh and took his degree in 1820. He also became a member of the Royal College of Surgeons of England and studied under Roux in Paris. He returned to Montreal in 1821, where he obtained the distinction of being the first to organize medical education in Canada. He married Isabella

Torrance in 1826 and died in 1842, and was survived by a son who was at one time professor of astronomy in Calcutta, and a member of the English bar.

The first official announcement of medical education in Canada is contained in the minutes of the Montreal General Hospital under date August 6, 1822. The entry reads: "That Dr. Stephenson be allowed to put in advertisements for lectures next winter that they will be given at this hospital." Out of these lectures arose McGill Medical faculty, and Stephenson was the first registrar. He was first occupant of the chairs of surgery, anatomy, and physiology, and he occupied all three at the same time. A. M.

Stevens, Alexander Hodgdon (1789–1869).

The Stevens family came originally from Cornwall, England, Alexander being the third of the six sons born to Ebenezer and Lucretia Ledyard Stevens. He came into the world in New York City on September 4, 1789. Private teaching, and in 1803 Yale College completed his early education which was afterwards followed by medical study under Dr. Edward Miller and the taking of his M. D. in 1811. The next year he voyaged to Europe as a despatch bearer but was captured by an English cruiser and detained prisoner at Plymouth, England. When freed, he went up to London and attended the lectures of leading surgeons, especially Abernethy and Astley Cooper. Then followed Paris and an interne service under Boyer whose clinical lectures he translated into English on returning to New York. Again made prisoner after embarkation, he was soon liberated and on reaching America took an appointment as army surgeon while the war lasted. In 1813 he lectured as professor of surgery in Rutger's College, New Jersey, and married that same year Miss Ledyard of New Jersey. While surgeon to the New York Hospital he introduced the practice of bedside instruction. 1825 saw him again in London and Edinburgh, correcting an error of the great Liston before an operation on a man for supposed hard tumor. In London, he was called in consultation by Mr. Lawrence of St. Bartholomew's regarding a case of tibia fractured near the malleolus. He recommended sawing off the projecting end of bone to ensure reduction; thus introducing at St. Bartholomew's a procedure common in New York.

When cholera broke out in New York in June, 1832, carrying off 2996 in two months, Dr. Stevens and his colleagues did gallant work. In 1815 after years of strenuous work he retired to his country home on Long Island and went in largely for agriculture. He married twice after the death of his first wife, a Miss Morris of Morrisiana and afterwards to a lady of Long Island. His own death occurred 1869. A firm believer in the great truths of Christianity he said to his daughter a few days before he died, "I have spent this whole morning in scientific reading, but I come back to my Bible. It contains all I need; there is no book like it."

The Stevens Triennial Prize ($1000) for the best essay on a medical or surgical subject was one of his kindly last acts.

He held many other appointments and memberships: fellow of the College of Physicians and Surgeons; surgeon, New York Hospital; president, College of Physicians and Surgeons; president, American Medical Association; honorary LL. D. of Columbia College, New York City; president and co-founder of New York Academy of Medicine.

He was co-editor of the "Medical and Surgical Register," New York, and the "New York Medical and Physical Journal."

D. W.

Med. Record, May, 1869–70, vol. iv.
Med. Reg. of N. York City, 1869, vol. vii, Same biog.
Med. and Surg. Reporter, Phila., 1865, vol. xiii (S. W. Francis).
Discourse Commemorative of, J. G. Adams, N. York, 1871.
A portrait by Henry Inman is in the Gallery of the New York Hospital.
Memoir by Dr. G. Adams, Tr.: Med. Soc. St. of. N. York, 1874.

Stevens, **Edward B.** (1823–1896).

Edward B. Stevens was born in Lebanon, Ohio, in 1823. He received his literary education at the Miami University, Oxford, Ohio, and graduated at the Medical College of Ohio, in 1846, first settling in Monroe, Ohio, but after a few years he went to Cincinnati, where with George Mendenhall and John A. Murphy he founded the "Medical Observer" in 1856. He was managing editor and continued as such after the consolidation of the journal with the "Western Lancet." In 1860 he was appointed demonstrator of anatomy in the Medical College of Ohio, but resigned at the end of the term, in 1865 accepting the chair of materia medica in the Miami Medical College, which he held until he was offered the same chair in the large medical school, created by the merging of the Geneva Medical College into the College of Medicine of Syracuse University, when he resigned his position in the Miami College, sold the "Lancet and Observer," and left for Syracuse. The new position did not come up to his expectations, so after a few months he returned to Lebanon, his native town, where he became well-known as a gynecologist and obstetrician. In 1878 he started the "Obstetric Gazette," in the columns of which he did his best work as medical editor. On account of poor health he was unable to attend to his professional duties for several years before his death in 1896.

Taken from "Daniel Drake and His Followers," Otto Juettner.

Stevenson, Henry (1721–1814).

He was born at Londonderry, Ireland, in the year 1721, and educated at Oxford, England. With his brother, John, also a physician, he emigrated to Baltimore about the middle of the eighteenth century. According to George W. Archer, he and Dr. Alexander Stenhouse settled in the sixth decade of the century in Bush River Neck, Baltimore County, and there married sisters. In 1756 he erected a stone mansion, which he called "Parnassus," but which his neighbors called "Stevenson's Folly," on the banks of Jones Falls, just north of the present city of Baltimore. This was connected with the town by a long trestle bridge over the meadow or marsh. Here he maintained, at his own expense, an inoculating hospital from 1768 to 1776, and again after the Revolution, from 1786 to 1800. In 1765 he was styled "the most successful inoculator in America." He did not confine his operations to Baltimore but went out into the counties to inoculate the people of the state. Among those who submitted to inoculation at his house was Gen. James Wilkinson, afterwards commander-in-chief of the American Army, and he has left an account of the event in his "Memoirs," i, p. 11. It may be interesting to note that his charge for inoculation was two pistoles, and for board and lodgings, twenty shillings a week. At the outbreak of the Revolution he espoused the royal cause and left Baltimore on the declaration of independence. His brother John left with him although he had founded the trade of Baltimore and had the title, "Romulus of Baltimore." Henry, however, after holding office as surgeon in the British Navy from 1776 to 1786, returned in the latter year and continued to practise in Baltimore until his death, March 31, 1814. He, Henry Stevenson, was one of the founders of the Medical College and Chirurgical Faculty of Maryland in 1799. In his treatment of yellow fever during the epidemic of 1797, he reported sixty-seven cases of the disease in his practice from July to October in that year with but six deaths. In the treatment he used no venesection, and little calomel but tonics freely. Dr. Stevenson left numerous descendants in Maryland. He was married three times; first, to Miss Stokes of Harford County, and had a son and daughter, George and Martha; second, to Anna, daughter of the Rev. John Henry, and had two sons and two daughters, Cosmo, Gordon, Anna, Julia; third, to Ada C. Bondell, no issue.

E. F. C.

In the Maryland Medical Journal, Centennial Number, April 29, 1899, there is a picture of Dr. Stevens, also of his house "Parnassus."
Cordell's Med. Annals of Maryland, 1903.

Stevenson, **Sarah Hackett** (1849–1910).

This pioneer woman physician, was the daughter of Col. John Stevenson, and born at Buffalo Grove, Illinois, February 2, 1849, of Scotch-Irish ancestry. Her grandfather, Charles Stevenson, came to this country after the Irish Rebellion of '98, purchasing large tracts of land in Ohio and Illinois. Her grandmother was Sarah Hackett of Philadelphia. She took her degree from the Woman's Medical College of the Northwestern University and in 1874 went to Europe for two years' study and was fortunate in having a biological training under Huxley and Darwin, fitting her to fill the chair of physiology in the Woman's Medical College to which she was later appointed. Upon her return to Chicago in 1876, she began to practise. She became a member of the Illinois State Medical Society and was sent as its delegate to the Annual Meeting of the American Medical Association held in Philadelphia in 1876; to the association, which five years before had laid on the table, without a vote, the hotly discussed motion of admitting women as members.

She was the first woman to serve on the staff of the Cook County Hospital, and was admitted to the International Society of Obstetricians and Gynecologists at Brussels, became vice-president of the Pan-American Congress at Washington, was a member of the Chicago Medical and Chicago Medico-surgical Societies, was president of the National Temperance Hospital; a consultant of the Woman's Hospital, of Bellevue Hospital, and professor of obstetrics at the Woman's Medical College of Northwestern University. She was instrumental in establishing the Maternity Hospital, the Illinois Training School for Nurses and the Home for Incurables.

Dr. Stevenson was the author of a "Text-book on Biology," for beginners which had an extensive sale and is used in the schools.

In 1904 Dr. Stevenson had a cerebral hemorrhage and after six years' illness, died August 13, 1910, at St. Elizabeth's Hospital, Chicago, where she had been a patient for several years. The gathering in the hospital chapel for her funeral services was a notable one, men and women, prominent in every walk of life from East and West came to pay their last tribute to the woman whom they had admired and honored. A. B. W.

N. Y. Med. Record, June 10, 1876.
Jacobi-Putman, Mary, in Woman's Work in America.
Waite, Dr. Lucy, in "Distinguished Physicians and Surgeons of Chicago."
The New World, Chicago, August 21, 1910.
Personal Information.

Stewart, David (1813–1899).

He was born at Port Penn, Delaware, February 14, 1813, the son of Dr. David Stewart, and was educated at Newcastle Academy, Delaware, settling in Baltimore about 1831. He was a member of the state senate in 1840 and on June 8 of that year represented the Pharmacistry of Baltimore in the founding of the Maryland College of Pharmacy. He was the first independent professor of pharmacy in the United States and lectured at the University of Maryland on that branch until 1847, where he took his M. D. in 1844. With Drs. Frick, Theobald and C. Johnston, he founded and lectured at the Maryland Medical Institute, 1847. He was chemist to the State Agricultural Society and professor of chemistry and natural philosophy and vice-president of St. John's College, Annapolis, 1855 to 1862. He removed to Port Penn, Newcastle County, Delaware, 1862, and died at that place September 2, 1899.

Dr. Stewart was one of the most enlightened and public-spirited pharmacists of his day. To him the profession of Maryland owes the introduction of many valuable remedial agents, as collodion, cod liver oil, glycerine, gutta percha, etc. Through a committee of which he was chairman, the Medical and Chirurgical Faculty has the distinction of having been the first society in America (June 8, 1855) to propose the substitution of the decimal system of weights and measures for those then in use. ("Journal and Transactions of Maryland College of Pharmacy," 1860.)

E. F. C.

Cordell's Medical Annals of Maryland, 1903

Stewart, David Denison (1858–1905).

David Denison Stewart, noted among his contemporaries for his improvement in the technic of electrolytic wiring in the operative treatment of aneurysm was the son of Franklin and Amelia Jacques Stewart, and born on October 10, 1858. He was a student of medicine at Jefferson Medical College and took his M. D. there in 1879. Both clinical and acquisitive instincts were highly developed and in later years he devoted himself specially to aneurysms and to diseases of the stomach and intestines. He came early into notice when in Kensington, Philadelphia, by his skillful diagnosis in some cases supposed to be cerebrospinal meningitis which he found to be lead encephalopathy caused by the local bakers using chrome yellow in cakes largely sold to children. His preeminence in his special field was fully recognized by his colleagues.

His writings included many very original papers, notably a third communication on "The Occurrence of an Hitherto Undescribed Form of Chronic Nephritis unassociated with Albuminuria," which appeared in "The Lancet" (London), September 4, 1897, after being read before the Association of American Physicians, May, 1897.

Dr. Stewart never married, but he was genial and beloved and specially fond of music. As to his appointments he was clinical lecturer on medicine at Jefferson Medical College; professor of clinical medicine in the Philadelphia Clinic; physician to St. Christophers Hospital for Children; member of the Association of American Physicians, and fellow of the University of Pennsylvania.

His most lengthy contributions to medical literature are articles on "Diseases of the Stomach," in Hare's "System of Practical Therapeutics;" Diseases of the Spinal Cord," in Loomis' "System of Practical Medicine;" "Diseases of the Kidneys and Lithuria," in Keating's "Cyclopedia of Diseases of Children," and "Diseases of the Stomach," in Sajous' "Cyclopedia." His most important papers were on "Some Phases of Gallstone Disease;" on "Primary Tuberculosis of the Kidney with Special Reference to a Primary Miliary Form," and the three already noted in which he called attention to a condition which had been unnoted in medical literature.

D. W.

Trans. Coll. Phys., Phila., 1906, vol. xxviii.

Stewart, Jacob Henry (1829–1884).

Jacob Henry Stewart was born at Peekskill, New York, January 15, 1829, and attended Phillips Academy in his native town, entering Yale College later. He graduated in medicine at the University of the City of New York in 1851, and from that date until 1855 practised with his father, Dr. Phylander Stewart, at Peekskill. In May, 1855, his health being impaired, he came to St. Paul, Minnesota. Through his skill and learning he soon gained a leading position and in 1856 was appointed physician of Ramsey County, and in 1857 elected state senator. He received his commission as surgeon of the First Minnesota Regiment, from Gov. Alexander Ramsey, April 29, 1861. Dr. Stewart was captured at the first battle of Bull Run, while in the act of attending a wounded Confederate soldier. He was roughly handled by some of the members of the famous Virginia Black Horse Cavalry, but proved such a good fellow, that they afterwards did well by him. He established a field hospital at Bull Run in Sudley Church, using the pews as beds, and the pulpit (with one of the church doors on its top) as an operating table. He was slightly but painfully wounded in the foot, when the engagement opened, but worked unremittingly, until taken prisoner. Dr. Stewart remained in attendance upon the wounded on the battlefield, when he might have escaped with the retreating troops, and was detained a prisoner at Libby Prison. His skillful care of the wounded doubtless saved many lives and he was treated with marked consideration by the Confederates during his captivity, as they allowed him to look after the suffering soldiers. When Surg. Stewart was exchanged, and parolled at Richmond, Virginia, Gen. P. T. Beauregard called him to him, and asked if he had a son— upon receiving an affirmative reply, the general returned the doctor's sword (which had been taken from him) saying: " when your son is old enough, to understand, give him this, and tell him, Gen. Beauregard gave back his father's sword, in recognition of his bravery, in remaining at his post of duty, when the Union Army retreated." Dr. Stewart did not return to his regiment, as his place was filled before he was released.

Gov. Alexander Ramsey, upon Dr. Stewart's return to St. Paul, appointed him surgeon-general of the state of Minnesota, which office he filled during the remaining mustering of troops.

In 1864, although a Republican, he was elected mayor of the Democratic city of St. Paul. In 1879, he was surveyor-general of Minnesota, a position he retained for four years. He died on August 25, 1884.

Dr. Stewart married on October 1, 1857, Miss Katharine Sweeny of Philadelphia, Pennsylvania. Three children survived them; Mrs. Charles A. Wheaton, Dr. J. H. Stewart and Robert D. Stewart.

B. F.

Stewart, James (1799–1864).

James Stewart was the son of Charles Stewart, a wealthy merchant of New York City, and was born April 7, 1799. He began life as a wholesale druggist in Maiden Lane, New York, afterwards studying medicine and graduating from the College of Physicians and Surgeons about the year 1824.

He soon afterwards entered upon practice. He first practised in the city of New York, and married a Miss Cushing, and had four children; one son and three daughters who survived him.

In the year 1827 he founded the Northern Dispensary of New York.

He paid special attention to the most obscure affections of the heart and lungs during several years of dispensary practice, and it is believed that no practitioner of New York City for many years excelled him in accuracy of diagnosis. His essay on "Cholera Infantum," which was crowned by the New York Academy of Medicine with their highest prize, is simply a record of facts and experiences gathered at the bedside through a long series of years.

In the year 1839 Stewart first became known to the profession as an author, by the publication of his translation of M. Billard's treatise on "The Diseases of Children," with an appendix of nearly one hundred pages of original matter. Stewart's treatise on "The Diseases of Children," was first published in 1841, and a second edition in 1843. His next work was entitled "The Lungs, Their Uses, and the Prevention of Their Diseases, with Practical Remarks on the Use of Remedies by Inhalation."

He used every opportunity of making himself acquainted with the effects of various professions, arts, trades, and callings on the respiratory organs, and presented the results to the profession in this work. He was also the author of several able articles and reviews in different medical journals, in particular his essay on "Dropsy Following Scarlatina," in the third volume of the "New York Journal of Medicine"; and his paper on "Animal Food in Cholera Infantum, and the Summer Complaints of Children," and his "Remarks on the Resuscitation of Persons Asphyxiated from Drowning," in the same journal.

About the year 1853 Dr. Stewart originated a plan for the establishment of a hospital for children, and the institution was opened in 1854, under the name of the "New York Nursery and Child's Hospital."

Though able to attend to his duties as medical examiner until July, 1864, chronic dyspepsia compelled him to retire to the country to recruit for a few weeks, but he died September 12 of that year, 1864, aged sixty-five.

·   C. A. L.

Tr. Med. Soc. State of New York, 1865 (C. A. Lee).

Stewart, James (1846–1906).

James Stewart was the son of Alexander Stewart by his wife, Catherine McDiarmid, and was born at Osgoode, County Russell, Ontario, on November 19, 1846. He was educated in the public school and at the Ottawa Grammar School, and in 1865 entered the Faculty of Medicine of McGill University, and graduated in 1869. He began to practise medicine at L'Original, afterwards Varna, Brucefield, then Winchester. In 1883 he went to Scotland, where he obtained the qualification of Licentiate of the Royal College of Physicians and Surgeons of Edinburgh. In the same year he returned to Montreal and was appointed professor of materia medica and therapeutics in the Medical Faculty of McGill University. In 1884 he became registrar of the Faculty, a post which he held till 1891, and in 1891 was appointed to the chair of clinical medicine; in 1893, to the combined chair of medicine and clinical medicine.

In addition to these university appointments he was physician to the Royal Victoria Hospital since its foundation; and in 1903 was president of the Association of American Physicians, and co-editor of the "Montreal Medical Journal." He died in Montreal on the sixth of October, 1906, in the sixtieth year of his age. At the time of his death he was professor of medicine in McGill University, and physician to the Royal Victoria Hospital. As well known in Vienna as in Montreal, he was the recipient of many honors which were not of his seeking, but were a tribute to the esteem in which he was held by the profession in Canada and the United States.

"His reputation was further enhanced by numerous and valuable contributions to the literature, particularly in the domain of neurology, to which he devoted special attention. A. M.

The Montreal Med. Jour., Nov., 1906 (port.).

Stewart, Morse (1818–1906).

Morse Stewart was born at Penn Yan, New York, July 5, 1818, of Scotch-Irish ancestry who had lived more than a hundred years in Connecticut ere moving to the then wilderness of West New York. His general education was obtained at a preparatory school in Pittsfield, Massachusetts, and Hamilton College, New York, where he completed the regular course at the age of twenty. He began medical studies with Dr. Samuel Foote, of Jamestown, New York, took three courses at Geneva Medical College, at Geneva, New York, and took his M. D. in 1841. After doing some post-graduate work he settled in Detroit, Michigan, in 1842. The same year he was licensed to practise by the Michigan Medical Society. He was a founder for the first and second epochs of the Wayne County (Michigan) Medical Society; a founder of the Sydeham Medical Society of Detroit; a founder of the Detroit Medical Society (1835–59) and its first president. Stewart was very active during the epidemics of Asiatic cholera, 1849–54 and recognized the first case of cerebrospinal meningitis occurring in Detroit. Stewart was about five feet nine inches tall, of spare and slender build, large head covered with abundant hair to the end, high forehead, prominent nose, firm, sensitive mouth and chin, always a smooth shaven face, fine blue eyes protected by projecting bone and eyebrows. His carriage and manner were characteristic of an old-time educated gentleman. He was crippled in many ways by deafness, and a temper which occasionally got the best of him. Dr. Stewart married twice; first to Miss Hastings, by whom he had no children; second to Isabella, daughter of the Rev. George Duffield. She died in 1888 leaving three sons and two daughters. Two of the sons, Morse, Jr., and Duffield, became physicians. Stewart and his second wife were large factors in the founding and conduct of the Detroit Home for the Friendless; the Thompson Home for Old Ladies; and Harper Hospital (Detroit). Except for them the money for Harper Hospital would have gone to endow the First Presbyterian Church. Dr. Morse Stewart practised till October 3, 1906, when feeling weary he lay down to rest; and on October 9, quietly passed to the unknown. Most of his papers and addresses were never published, for, in the period of his greatest productiveness, the facilities for publication were meager and he had an extreme modesty.

"Epilepsy from Undeveloped Uterus." ("Detroit Review of Medicine and Pharmacy," vol. i.)

"Criminal Abortion." ("Detroit Review of Medicine and Pharmacy," vol. ii.)

"Case of Poisoning by Strychnia." ("Peninsular Medical Journal," vol. iv.) L. C.

The Phys. and Surg. of the U. S., W. B. Atkinson, Phila., Pa.
Biographical Cyclopedia of Mich., West Publishing Co., N. Y. and Detroit, 1900.

Stiles, Richard Cresson (1830–1873).

Richard Cresson Stiles was born in West Chester, Pennsylvania, in 1830, and was educated at Yale College, where he graduated in 1851. He studied medicine with Dr. Turner, at the Kings County Hospital, Flatbush, Long Island, and took his M. D. at the University of Pennsylvania in 1854. During the next two years he continued his medical studies in Europe, chiefly in Paris. While abroad he married an American lady whom he met in Leghorn, a daughter of Dr. Thomas Wells, of New Haven, Connecticut. On his return to this country, he was appointed professor of physiology in the

University of Vermont, at Burlington. He had made assiduous preparation for such a position by a long course of physiological study and investigation during his residence in Paris, and entered upon his course of instruction with a great promise, which was abundantly fulfilled. In 1858 he accepted the chair of physiology in the Berkshire Medical Institution, Pittsfield, Massachusetts. In these positions his life was eminently to his taste. He was a student, and his time was constantly devoted to study and instruction. His microscope and his laboratory had a large part of his heart. In 1859 he settled in Pittsfield, and in 1860 established, in conjunction with Dr. W. H. Thayer, the "Berkshire Medical Journal," a monthly publication, which was issued for one year. The presence of war made it an unfavorable time for a new literary enterprise, and it was discontinued at the close of the first volume. In 1862 he was impelled by patriotism to enter the United States service. His desire for service in the field was gratified early in 1863 by his being transferred to the Army of the Potomac as surgeon-in-chief of Caldwell's Division of Hancock's Corps. He left the service in 1864 and, going to Brooklyn, received the appointment of resident physician at King's County Hospital. Dr. Stiles resigned his office after about a year's service, and went to Brooklyn to practice medicine; he was, however, made one of the Consulting Board of the hospital, and retained that position during life.

His lectures at Burlington were continued with the interruption of his two years' service in the army, until 1865. In Brooklyn he took an active part in the operations of the County Medical Society and was twice elected president. It was on his suggestion that the Pathological Section was formed in 1870, and until his sickness he was a constant attendant upon its semi-monthly meetings. He had a succession of private classes in histology during his residence in Brooklyn, which were attended by young physicians who were drawn to him by his high reputation in the Society. He was a fluent writer, but the papers which he left were produced in the latter period of his life. They include several monographs on physiological and pathological subjects, a memoir of Haller, which was the oration for 1868 before the Medical Society of the County of Kings, and very valuable contributions to the Annual Reports of the Metropolitan Board of Health, especially those for 1868 and 1869. That for 1868 contains an elaborate report on the "Texas Cattle Disease," then prevailing to an alarming extent in New York, to which he contributed the results of his careful microscopic examinations. In the course of them he discovered in the bile of the infected animals a vegetable parasite which became further developed there, and which was in his opinion the cause of the disease. His enthusiasm over what promised, in its wide suggestions, to be a discovery of great value to medical science will be remembered by all his friends. He says, "The fungus origin of zymotic disease is now conceded by the highest authorities in mycological research, and the Texas fever is one which points with unusual clearness to this mode of propagation." His conclusions were confirmed by Prof. Hallier, of Jena, to whom Dr. Harris sent specimens of the infected bile. He pronounced the parasite a new discovery, and named it in honor of the discoverer, Coniothecium Stilesianum.

He never was idle, and his labors continued long past the hours that belong to sleep. This was his ruin. Early and late he labored at his engrossing science, until his mental powers began to give indications of disorder, and in the summer of 1870 a grave form of insanity was developed, from which he never recovered. His general health, however, was good, and he attended more or less to practice at different times. In 1872 he travelled again in Europe. During the latter part of winter and early spring his mental disease grew more serious; and early in April, 1873, he went home to his mother's house in West Chester, Pennsylvania. There he was attacked with pneumonia of a grave form, and died after ten days' illness.

From the Med. Reg. of the State of N. York, vol. xi, 1873-4.

Stillé, Alfred (1813-1900).

Born in 1813, the son of John and Maria (Wagner) Stillé, early Swedish immigrants, Dr. Stillé began his lifework with the generation which saw the new pathology and the new clinical methods. After joining in the "conic section" rebellion at Yale, which led to the retirement of one-half of the class, he seems to have had for a time a leaning toward the law. "During the years of probation," he says, "I tested the strength of my partiality for a medical career by some medical reading, including Bell's "Anatomy" and Bichat's "General Anatomy," and attending the anatomical instruction at the Jefferson Medical College.

The best of luck awaited him when, in 1835-36, he became house physician at "Blockley," under W. W. Gerhard, a clinical teacher of the very first rank, and fresh from the wards of the great French physician, Louis.

While still a medical student two of his fellow-townsmen returned from abroad glowing with the fire they had caught in Paris, the then acknowledged center of medical science. Gerhard and Pennock were the apostles of the school of observation under whose preaching he became a zealous convert and, as soon as it was possible, hastened to the enchanted scene of their European labors.

Method and accuracy were from the first characteristic of Dr. Stillé's work. He played an interesting part in that splendid contribution of American medicine to the differentiation of typhus and typhoid fever. I will let him tell the story in his own words. In a manuscript he says: "The year 1836 is memorable for an epidemic of typhus (t. petechialis) which prevailed in the district of the city which is the usual seat of epidemics caused or aggravated by crowding, viz.,

south of Spruce and between Fourth and Tenth Streets. A great many of the poor creatures living in that overcrowded region and who were attacked with typhus were brought to the Philadelphia Hospital, where I had charge of one of the wards assigned to them. I had the great good fortune to study these cases under Dr. Gerhard. His permanent reputation rests upon the papers published by him in Hays' 'Journal,' in which he fully established the essential differences between this disease and typhoid fever. Every step of my study of typhus in the wards and post-mortem revealed new contrasts between the two diseases, so that I felt surprised that the British physicians should have continued to confound them. I was very diligent in making clinical notes and dissections, spending many hours every day in the presence of the disease. "In an unpublished memoir of Dr. Stillé read before the Medical Society of Observation (September 14 and 28, 1838); the two diseases are compared, symptom by symptom and lesion by lesion; and, apart from the phenomena of fever common to all febrile affections, the opposite of what is observed in the one is sure to be presented in the other." (Valleix, "Arch. gen.," February, 1839, p. 213.)

Between two and three years of study in Europe gave Dr. Stillé a fine training for his lifework. Returning to Philadelphia, he began practice, wrote for journals, taught students, and gradually there came to him reputation and recognition. After lecturing on pathology and the practice of medicine in the Philadelphia Association for Medical Instruction he was elected, in 1854, to the chair of practice in the Pennsylvania Medical College. In 1864 he succeeded Dr. Pepper (primus) in the chair of medicine at the University of Pennsylvania. While always a student, he was no hermit, but from the start took a deep interest in the general welfare of the profession. He was the first secretary of the American Medical Association, and president in 1867. The local socie-

ALFRED STILLÉ.
(By permission of Dr. F. P. Henry.)

ties recognized his work and worth, and he became president of the Pathological and of the County Medical Societies, and in 1885 he took the chair of our ancient and honorable body. He was from the outset of his career a strong advocate for higher medical education, and from 1846 —the date of his first address on the subject—to 1897—the date of his last— he pleaded for better preliminary training and for longer sessions. No one rejoiced more in the new departure of the the University in 1876, and he was a consistent advocate of advanced methods of teaching.

His medical writings show on every page the influence of his great master. His first important work, "The Elements of General Pathology," 1848, was based on the modern researches, and every chapter echoed with his favorite motto, *Tota ars medica est in observationibus.*

Apart from numerous smaller articles in the journals, there are two important monographs by him—one on "Cerebrospinal Meningitis" and the other on "Cholera." In addition, two minor studies were on "Dysentery," in the publications of the United States Sanitary Commission, and on "Erysipelas."

Estimated by bulk, the most important of Dr. Stillé's works are the "Materia Medica and Therapeutics" and the "National Dispensatory." It was always a mystery to me how a man with his training and type of mind could have undertaken such colossal and, one would have thought, uncongenial tasks.

Dr. Stillé was not only a booklover, but a discriminating and learned student. Our shelves testify not less to his liberality than to his taste for rare and important monographs, while the Stillé Library of the University of Pennsylvania will remain a monument to his love of the literature and history of our profession. It interested me greatly, and I only knew him after he had passed his seventieth year, to note the keenness of his mind on all questions relating to medicine. He had none of those irritating features of the

old doctor, who, having crawled out of the stream about his fortieth year, sits on the bank, croaking of misfortunes to come, and, with less truth than tongue, lamenting the days that have gone and the men of the past. Hear the conclusion of the whole matter—the lesson of a long and good life. It is contained in a sentence of his valedictory address: "*Only two things are essential; to live uprightly and to be wisely industrious.*"

Dr. Stillé was twice married; but his first wife had to be kept in an asylum and when she died he married an old and intimate friend.

He died in Philadelphia, on September 24, 1900.   W. O.

Abridged from a paper by Dr. Wm. Osler in the Univ. of Penn. Med. Bull., June, 1902.

Trans. of the Coll. of Phys. of Phila., 1902.

Stillé, Moreton (1822–1855).

Moreton Stillé, medicojurisprudentist, youngest son of John and Maria Stillé, was born in Philadelphia, October 27, 1822. On his mother's side he was descended from Tobias Wagner, who was appointed chancellor of the University of Tübingen in 1662; by his father he was chiefly of Swedish descent. Taking his preparatory training at the Edgehill Seminary, Princeton, he entered the University of Pennsylvania, in 1838, whence he graduated in 1841, in 1844 receiving his medical degree from the same university. His preceptor was his brother, the equally famous Dr. Alfred Stillé. He went abroad, studying in Dublin, London, Paris, and Vienna, then, returning home, entered into practice and became, in 1848–9, resident physician at the Pennsylvania Hospital. Recognition came slowly and not till 1855—the year of his death—was he elected to a professorship, or rather lectureship, that of internal medicine in the Philadelphia Association for Medical Instruction.

He wrote frequently and well, his most important writings relating to matters connected with the subject of medical jurisprudence. His journal articles are to be found chiefly in "The American Journal of the Medical Sciences." Together with the distinguished attorney, Francis Wharton, he composed "A Treatise on Medical Jurisprudence"—a masterpiece both of science and of literary style. This work—the first, without doubt, on the subject, produced in America by a lawyer and a doctor working conjointly—passed through several editions, and was highly esteemed by both the legal and the medical profession. The parts of this work written by Dr. Stillé were the second, third, fourth, and fifth books, those on the "Fetus and New-born Child," on "The Sexual Relations," on "Identity," and on the "Cause of Death."

Dr. Stillé was a very ambitious, as well as an able, man. On going to Europe, he wrote to his brother: "Indifferent to the present, I live only for the future; upon it my most earnest gaze is fixed, and I strive to enter its ever receding portals, to grasp its cloudy phantoms, its beckoning illusions. If I know myself, I shall not be content with a place in the crowded middle ranks of the profession." He was one of those who "toil terribly," and the result of this trait is plainly apparent in his remarkable book. He was a man of such distinguished and charming presence that he became at once the recipient, while abroad, of marked attention from such men as Drs. Stokes, Graves, Churchill, Hamilton, Law, and McDonnell. Dr. Stokes, in particular, was very fond of him, and the two were much together on the former's rounds and at his house. Of a generous and self-sacrificing nature, it is related that, during the epidemic of cholera in 1850, he offered his services to the Blockley Hospital free of charge, and remained personally in the building day and night, working both as a physician and as nurse till himself stricken down by the terrible disease. He was one of the few that recovered.

He married, in 1850, Heloise, daughter of S. Destouet, of Philadelphia, and had several children.

Early in July, 1855, he was attacked by the disease from which he was to die. For the sake of his health he went to Cape May, and was at first greatly benefited. One night, however, after bathing, he thoughtlessly slept in a draught, and this exposure produced an attack of pleurisy which, though slight, he was not quite able to recover from, owing to his enfeebled condition. August 20, 1855—the year in which Theodric Romeyn Beck died—he passed away, only thirty-three. He never even saw a copy of his remarkable volume—for the work was not in type till some months after his death—yet he left a name which will never be erased from the annals of medical jurisprudence in America. T. H. S.

"A Treatise on Medical Jurisprudence," by Francis Wharton and Moreton Stillé, Phila., 1855, (Francis Wharton).
Gross's "American Medical Biography," Phila,. 1861.
Memoir of Moreton Stillé, M. D., by Samuel L. Hollingsworth, M. D., Phila., 1856 (port.).

Stites, John, Jr. (1780–1807).
The first physician who arrived in Cinciunati after the beginning of the nineteenth century was John Stites, Junior, a native of New York. He studied medicine three years in Philadelphia under Dr. Caldwell. He reached Cincinnati in 1802, and brought with him the published works of his preceptor, as well as those of Dr. Rush. Before his arrival scarcely anything of the kind had reached the town; so he had the distinction of introducing the young medical science of our country. Entering into partnership with Dr. Goforth, he became one of Dr. Daniel Drake's preceptors. In less than a year, however, he removed to Kentucky, where he died in 1807, aged twenty-seven. A. G. D.

St. John, Samuel (1813–1876).
Samuel St. John, an eminent chemist of New York City, was born in New Canaan, Connecticut. Of his early education there is no information; that it was thorough we know from the fact that he was the valedictorian of his class in

Yale College, where he graduated in 1834. The two years succeeding were devoted to the study of law, and a third to the duties of a tutor in Latin, when a sudden attack of hemoptysis warned him of the necessity of rest and a change of climate. Accordingly he traveled for a year in Europe, and immediately upon his return in 1838 was elected to the professorship of chemistry, geology, and mineralogy in the Western Reserve College, at Hudson, Ohio. In 1851 he was called to the chair of chemistry and medical jurisprudence in the Cleveland Medical College, a position which he filled with eminent success until called in 1857 to the chair of chemistry in the College of Physicians and Surgeons, New York City. This latter position he occupied continuously until his death at New Canaan, in the house in which he was born, September 6, 1876.

St. John received no special medical education, and was never a practising physician, but received the degree of M. D. from three distinct institutions, viz.: the Vermont Medical College, in 1839; the Cleveland Medical College, in 1851, and the College of Physicians and Surgeons of New York, in 1857. He was likewise honored with the degree of LL. D. by the Georgetown College of Kentucky.

While a man of thorough scientific education and attainments, Dr. St. John was extremely modest and reserved. Dr. John C. Dalton, his colleague and friend, has described him as "a man whom no breath of suspicion ever touched, and whose integrity was a natural and essential part of his organization. "His son, Dr. Samuel B. St. John, became an ophthalmologist in Hartford, Connecticut.

H. E. H.

An excellent portrait of Dr. St. John is preserved in the faculty room of the Medical Department of the Western Reserve University.

The College of Physicians and Surgeons, New York. A History, edited by John Shrady, A. M., M. D., 1903.

Stockbridge, Tristrim Gilman (1806–1871).

Any life of this capable physician would be incomplete if we did not first say something about his father, John Stockbridge, of Bath and Topsham, Maine. Dr. John Stockbridge was born in Hanover, Massachusetts, April 16, 1780, and studied with Dr. Gad Hitchcock, of Pembroke, Massachusetts. He practised in Topsham in 1804, and was very intimate with Dr. Isaac Lincoln, the well known physician of Brunswick. Dr. Stockbridge was so well thought of that Dartmouth College gave him an honorary M. D. in 1822. He moved to Bath, Maine, and practised there extensively, until his death May 3, 1849. During his lifetime he was an active member of the Massachusetts Medical Society, as well as of the Maine Medical Society. He married Theodosia Gilman, the daughter of the Rev. Tristrim Gilman, of North Yarmouth, Maine. The eldest son of this marriage, Tristrim Gilman, was born in Bath, Maine, and studied medicine with his father and also at the medical school of Maine where he graduated in 1827.

Instead of dividing practice with his father, he established himself in Winslow, Maine. His first year of experience was tremendous, but he proved his medical stamina by competing with several other physicians of that region in taking care of a widespread epidemic of small-pox which ravaged the population, and which was one of the causes leading to a large depopulation of the surrounding towns, the people going West. After a few years of practice here, he decided to return to Bath and assist his father, who lived for some years later, but did not continue practice after the return of his capable son to the homestead.

The young Dr. Stockbridge of Bath soon gained as extensive a practice as he had previously had at Winslow, and was considered about the best man to be found thereabouts as physician and especially as surgeon. His personality won him many friends and clients. He was tall and commanding in person, very affable in manner and had a kindly word for everyone with whom he came in contact. He was also, as we have said, a good surgeon for those times, and being of a large figure, he inspired the confidence of those who were obliged to submit themselves to the knife, as most people generally feel more safe in the hands of someone who is robust, rather than slender. He was rather distant in his ways to strangers and his prejudices were very strong whenever he had been deceived in any way. The health of Stockbridge began to fail in August, 1870. but he continued practice until December, when he was obliged to give up work. His death was due to inflammation of the liver which had troubled him in a slight degree for a number of years. He suffered greatly at the last, and died from asthma, January 20, 1871.

J. A. S.

Trans. Maine Med. Assoc.

Stockwell, Cyrus M. (1823–1899).

Cyrus M. Stockwell was born in Colesville, New York, June 20, 1823, and had his general education in Oxford, New York, beginning to study medicine at Binghamton, New York, and graduating M. D. at Pittsfield Medical College, Pittsfield, Massachusetts, in 1850. After practising for a couple of years in Pennsylvania he settled in 1852 in Port Huron, Michigan. At the outbreak of the Civil War he became surgeon of the Twenty-Seventh Michigan Infantry, and for a time after was assistant surgeon at Fort Gratiot, Michigan. In 1863 he resigned from the army and resumed civil practice. He was a founder of the Michigan State Medical Society and its first president, in 1866. From 1865 to 1872 he was regent of Michigan University. Like other pioneer physicians, his early life was a succession of long rides over bad roads or no road; forty to sixty miles travel his daily task. Dr. Stockwell usually selected horses with bad tempers. One was so vicious that he had to shackle its feet when descending a hill, to prevent his dashboard from being kicked to pieces. The endurance of some of these animals was remarkable. His son, Dr. C. B., relates the following: "One day he and a druggist started for Detroit at 4 A. M. They went to Detroit, transacted their business and reached Port Huron at 12 midnight, making a distance of at least one hundred and twenty miles, yet on the following day the horse was as lively as ever." In making his long rides he drove a sulky with wheels seven feet in diameter. When he came to a tree, fallen across the way, he would unhitch his horse, lead it around the tree, then drag the sulkey over and re-hitch his horse and move on. He married twice and died at Port Huron, December 9, 1899, from arteriosclerosis, leaving a widow, two daughters and one son, Dr. C. B. Stockwell, of Port Huron. Among his papers are:

"Cholera." ("Transactions, American Medical Association," vol. viii.)

"Dysentery in Michigan." ("Transactions, American Medical Association," vol. viii.)

"Criminal Abortion." ("Transactions, American Medical Association," vol. xv.)

"Report on Diseases in Northeastern Michigan." ("Peninsular and Independent Medical Journal," vol. i.)   L. C.

The History of Mich. Univ., Ann Arbor, 1906.

Stone, Alexander Johnson (1845–1910).

Alexander Johnson Stone, gynecologist, was born in Augusta, Maine, September 7, 1845. He received his education in the public schools, then took up the study of medicine and graduated from Berkshire Medical College, Pittsfield, Massachusetts, in 1867. After spending a few months abroad, chiefly in Paris, he returned to Boston, where he served as an assistant of Horatio R. Storer for about a a year, during which he received special training in the then rapidly developing specialty of gynecology. Coming to Minnesota some time in 1868, he first settled in Stillwater, where he engaged in general practice. But his cherished ambition to practice his chosen specialty made him remove to St. Paul in 1870.

In 1871 he founded the first medical publication in the Northwest, "The Northwestern Medical and Surgical Journal," of which he was editor and proprietor, and to which he was a large contributor. After a career of three or four years this rather pretentious publication was, for some reason, discontinued. He did not again enter the field of medical journalism until 1886 when he became editor and proprietor of "The Northwestern Lancet," which continued under his guidance and management until 1901.

He loved to teach, and was a fluent speaker, with ability to impart knowledge in an interesting and impressive manner. He was the pioneer of medical teaching in the Northwest, having organized the St. Paul Medical School, preparatory, in 1871. It was intended by this preliminary course, merely to supplement the instruction given by preceptors in those days. The success of this undertaking led to the establishment of the St. Paul Medical College in 1879 where a full course of medicine was offered. From this time on he was identified with practically every venture in medical teaching in the Twin Cities up to the establishment of the College of Medicine of the University in 1888. In this school he ably filled the chair of diseases of women from its organization to the time of his death, on July 16, 1910.

He served as president of the State Medical Association, the Association of Medical Editors, the Association of Military Surgeons, and as vice-president of the American Medical Association. In 1887 the Iowa State University conferred upon him her LL. D. At the time of his death he was surgeon-general of the State of Minnesota, and with dignity filled that position.

He was also much interested in matters of public health. In 1895 he was appointed Commissioner of Health of the city of St. Paul, and under his administration was established and organized the public bacteriological laboratory.

J. L. R.

St. Paul Med. Jour., vol. xii, 1910.

Stone, Robert King (1822–1872).

Robert King Stone was born in 1822, in Washington, District of Columbia. His ancestors were among the earlier settlers of Washington; both contributing to its progress and prominently identified with its establishment and prosperity. At an early age he entered Princeton College and ranked among its brightest scholars. After receiving his A. B. he returned to Washington, and worked under Dr. Thomas Miller. Dr. Miller selected Stone as his assistant in the dissecting room, considering him a close and minute dissector, good in anatomical studies and especially in minute anatomy. After attending a course of lectures in the National Medical College, District of Columbia, Stone went to the University of Pennsylvania, where he took his M. D., in 1849 that of the University of Louisville and in 1851 the University of New York. Soon afterwards he went to Europe and walked the hospitals of London, Edinburgh, Vienna and Paris, paying particular attention to ophthalmic surgery and ear diseases. He was the private pupil of the celebrated Desmarres, assisting him in operations. At the same time he did not neglect his favorite studies of comparative anatomy and operative surgery.

Returning to Washington in 1847 he began general practice and became assistant to the chair of anatomy in the National Medical College and was in 1848 appointed adjunct professor of the chair of anatomy and physiology, and afterwards professor of anatomy, physiology and microscopic anatomy. A ready and fluent lecturer, he always illustrated his lectures by the most beautiful drawings and diagrams made by himself. Having a decided preference for ophthalmic and aural surgery, he was appointed to that chair, earning enduring laurels in the position, but he was thrown from his carriage and his thigh was fractured. He never afterwards engaged in active practice. Resigning his position in the college, he devoted himself to private patients principally for ophthalmic and aural surgery. He died suddenly in Philadelphia on April 23, 1872, from apoplexy.

In 1849 he married a daughter of Thomas Ritchie, the founder, in 1804, of the "Richmond Enquirer," and in 1845 of the "Washington Union."

D. S. L.

Trans. Amer. Med. Ass., vol. xxiv, 1873.
Busey, Reminiscences.
Address before the Med. Soc., Wash., D. C., by Dr. Thomas Miller.

Stone, Warren, Sr. (1808–1872).

Warren Stone, one of New Orleans most noted surgeons was born in St. Albans, Vermont, on February 3, 1808, the son of a farmer, Peter Stone, who married Jerusha Snow. As a lad young Warren inclined to study medicine and left home to do so under Dr. Amos Twitchell in Keene, graduating M. D. from the Medical School at Pittsfield, Massachusetts, but patients proving scanty he went off in the Amelia to New Orleans. Cholera broke out and the passengers were landed on Folly Island by Charleston, and housed there. Stone helped with the cases but had cholera also and when landed in December at New Orleans was sick, poor, and insufficiently clothed. He had a very wearying time but faithfully fulfilled the duties of any, even a minor, position, which came along. A Dr. Thomas Hunt, who had nursed him at Folly Island and previously seen his good work, got him at last the post of assistant surgeon at the Charity Hospital. In 1836 he became resident surgeon, then lecturer on anatomy and finally professor of surgery in the University of St. Louis, which post he held until his resignation in 1872.

In 1843 he married Malvina Dunreath Johnson, of Bayou Sara, and one son, Warren, became a surgeon.

Stone was noted as much for his diagnostic skill as his surgery; his judgment in cases properly surgical was unequalled. He did much to inculcate the propriety of opening diseased joints and improving surgical technic. He was the first to advise thoracotomy in cases of empyema with drainage and the removal of rib in cases of liver abscess. As a writer too he was good, and ably edited "The New Orleans Medical and Surgical Journal" for ten years, his articles appearing chiefly in that and the "New Orleans Monthly Medical Register." They included: "Ligature of the Femoral Artery," "Ligature of the Carotid Artery," "Operation and Removal of One-half of the Inferior Maxilla," "Comminuted Fracture of the Thigh," etc. He had a most wonderful memory and never used any notes or forgot any fact he read and remembered patients who had been to him years before. He died in New Orleans on December 6, 1872, of Bright's disease.

Stone's Eminent Physicians and Surgeons.

Stone, Warren, Jr. (1843–1883).

Warren Stone, surgeon, was born in New Orleans, Louisiana, in 1843, and was not only known as his father's son but also for his own good work. Educated at the Jesuit College, New Orleans, he afterwards served during the war in the Confederate Army and when he went home settled down to study medicine graduating at the University of Louisiana in 1867 and getting the appointment of professor of surgical anatomy when the Charity Hospital Medical College was opened in 1874. Just a year before he made what he thought to be the first recorded cure of traumatic aneurysm of the subclavian artery by digital pressure. Like his father, he gave great attention to the subject of yellow fever. When it was epidemic in Brunswick, Georgia, and the Southwest, he travelled about from one village to another healing and comforting the sick. He did not long survive the death of his father, dying on January 3, 1883, in New Orleans of Bright's disease, his death a distinct loss to the city for he was justly regarded as one of her most accomplished and promising surgeons.

D. W.

Stone's Eminent Physicians and Surgeons

Storer, David Humphreys (1804-1891).

David Humphreys Storer, medico-jurisprudentist and obstetrician, son of Chief Justice Storer, of Maine, was born at Portland, Maine, in 1804. His B. A. was from Bowdoin College in 1822, and, in 1825, his M. D. from the Harvard Medical School.

Settling in Boston, he soon had an excellent practice. The annual discourse at the Massachusetts Medical Society was delivered by him in 1851, his subject being "Medical Jurisprudence." He was one of the founders of the Tremont Street Medical School (1837). Later he accepted the chair of obstetrics and medical jurisprudence in the Harvard Medical School, a position held from 1854 till 1868. Everything he did was marked by thoroughness and accuracy.

In the realm of general science his work was equally distinguished as in the more restricted field of medicine. His discoveries in natural history were numerous and important. In the field of ichthyology his writings at the present day are still esteemed most highly. The chief of these writings are: "A Synopsis of the Fishes of North America" (1846), and "A History of the Fishes of Massachusetts" (1867). Among many positions held he was fellow of the American Academy of Medicine; member of the Massachusetts Medical Society, of the Obstetrical Society of Boston; honorary member of the Medical Society of the State of New York; visiting physician at the Massachusetts General Hospital from 1849 till 1858, and to the Boston Lying-in Hospital from 1854 till 1868, and dean of the Harvard Medical School from 1855 till 1864.

He married, April 30, 1829, Abby Jane Brewer, and had five children. Of these, Horatio Robinson was one of the pioneers in gynecology, and another son, Francis Humphreys, was professor of agricultural chemistry, at Harvard University.

Dr. Storer was tall, slender, and handsome. He was fond of wearing a long black waistcoat and a long black coat, yet he was careless in dress and negligent of social conventions. His voice was very pleasant, but occasionally cracked when he grew excited—a trifling defect which only the more endeared him to his students. He was always exceedingly earnest in his manner, whether lecturing or conversing, and was horrified at the beginnings of willful abortion as practised by the women of well-to-do American families, or no families. Concerning this matter of willful abortion he frequently wrote and spoke. He was one of the first to show a medical stereoscopic picture (1870), in Boston.

He died at Boston, September 10, 1891, regretted by all who had known him.

An excellent portrait of Dr. Storer is to be seen in the Boston Public Library.

T. H. S.

Boston of To-day.
Scudder, Biographical Notice, Proc. Am. Acad., xxvii.
Universities and Their Sons, vol. ii.
Cleveland, History of Bowdoin Coll.
In Memoriam D. H. S. (Meeting Suffolk Dist. Med. Soc., Jan. 20, 1892).
Harrington and Mumford, The Harvard Medical School, vol. ii.

Stoy, Henry William (1726-1801).

Henry William Stoy was born in Herborn, Germany, March 14, 1726, and first studied theology, being ordained for that work in America in 1752. He first settled in Lebanon County, Pennsylvania, but in 1756 removed to Philadelphia on account of his health, where he married Maria Elizabeth Maus. The marriage caused a great deal of dissatisfaction in the congregation, and resulted in his resignation and removal to Lancaster in October, 1758. In the early part of 1763 he resigned and returned to Europe, the Amsterdam classes reporting that he attended their meeting May 3, 1763. It is reported that he went to Leyden and studied medicine, but the matriculation books do not reveal his presence there, but that he went to his native town, Herborn, and studied medicine with Prof. John Adam Hoffman, who was professor of the university untll 1773. He returned to America, probably in 1767, for in November of this year he wrote to Holland that he had returned, had had several calls and concluded to accept Tulpehocken, the present Host church in Berks County. He was, however, not in good standing with the church authorities in Pennsylvania, who declined again to receive him as a member of the Coetus, or Synod, not for any moral delinquencies, but because of his disputation with many of the ministers and for the further reason that he was regarded as a "stirrer up of strife." He left the Host church about 1772 or 1773 and moved to Lebanon and began the active practice of medicine.

While practising, he also preached at various places, and was pastor to several country congregations. Like some of the doctors of more modern times, he rated himself as a statesman and took an active part in politics. In 1779, during the Revolution, he wrote a letter addressed to Joseph Reed, president of the Supreme Executive Council of Pennsylvania, on "The Present Mode of Taxation," advocating a single tax on land, and he has the honor of being the first single tax man in the country, though his ideas differed from the single tax theories of the present day and were impracticable. He was elected to the Pennsylvania Legislature in 1784, and wrote frequently on political subjects for the papers. Highly educated, he was fluent in German, Latin, and English, but it was as a physician that he gained greatest prominence and came to be known far and wide, not as a preacher, but as a doctor. His cure for hydrophobia and his hysteric drops, or "mutter tropfen," gave him great notoriety, and people sent long distances for the remedies. In Gen. Washington's account book, sold at Birch's auction sale, in 1890, and bought by Mr. Aldrich for $400, appears this record:

"Oct. 18, 1797. Gave my servant, Christopher, to bear the expenses to a person at Lebanon in Pennsylvania celebrated for curing persons bit by wild animals, $25.00."

Whether Dr. Stoy's success in curing the disease was due to the remedy or to the fact that possibly only a small per cent. of the so-called rabid dogs are afflicted with rabies, we are unable to say, but from the ingredients it contained we are led to believe there was not much virtue in it. The remedy consisted of one ounce of the herb, red chickweed, four ounces of theriac and one quart of beer, all well digested, the dose being a wine glassful. Red chickweed is supposed to be antivenomous, nervine and stimulating.

For the information of the medical fraternity I can say his noted hysteric drops, or "mutter tropfen," were made of opium, castor, saffron and maple seed, each one dram, and Lisbon wine four ounces, and possessing anodyne and antispasmodic properties, were doubtless beneficial in nervous disorders. That Dr. Stoy was a progressive physician, keeping abreast of the times, is shown by the fact that he was active in introducing inoculation for the smallpox, although there was a great prejudice against it as an attempt to thwart Providence.

After an eventful life, he died in Lebanon, September 14, 1801, and was buried at the Host Church, in Berks County.

F. R. P.

From an account read before the Lebanon County Historical Society, October 19, 1900, by J. H. Redsecker, Ph. M.

Stribling, Francis T. (1810–1874).

Francis T. Stribling, alienist, was born near Staunton on the twentieth of February, 1810, and after receiving a good education, was for some years employed in assisting his father, clerk of Augusta County. He then took a course of lectures at the University of Virginia, and another in the University of Pennsylvania, taking his M. D. from the latter in 1830 and settling to practice in his native town. In 1836, when only twenty-six, he was elected physician to the Western Lunatic Asylum of Virginia, and in 1840, superintendent. He was one of the prime movers in the organization of the Association of Medical Superintendents of Institutions for the Insane in 1844, and was a member during the rest of his life. He was an honorary member of the Medical Society of Virginia. His entire time was devoted to the management of the asylum and the care of his unfortunate patients, the number of whom increased during his administration from seventy-two to more than 350. Possessing great professional ability, extensive knowledge of mental disorders, together with evenness of temper, and inflexible firmness, he was peculiarly fitted for the position. He entered most heartily into that spirit of reform, then growing in strength, that the insane were the subjects of disease rather than demoniacs possessed of an evil spirit, and was an ardent advocate of the modern humane and rational methods of treatment. His success gained for him an extended reputation, and he was regarded as an authority in his native State on all questions connected with his speciality.

He took, also, an active interest in the establishment of a State institution for the deaf, dumb and blind, and was one of those influential public men who effected the founding of one at Staunton. As early as 1845 he began to urge the establishment of a hospital exclusively for the colored insane, and never ceased to bring it to the attention of the Legislature until his object was accomplished. He married Henrietta F. Cuthbert, of Staunton, in 1833, and had three daughters and a son.

He died at his home in Staunton on the twenty-third of July, 1874.

His only known writings are his annual reports, which were considered models of their kind. He was also the author of some valuable laws governing the hospitals for the insane, which were passed by the Legislature.

The Western State Hospital owns a portrait of him.

R. M. S.

Stringham, James S. (1775–1817).

James S. Stringham, the earliest professor of medical jurisprudence in America, and the earliest American writer on that subject, was born in New York City, where his parents gave him the foremost educational facilities of the time. Some time after taking his degree from Columbia College in 1793, he began later to study theology, but, by reason of delicate health, ceased for a time all study and afterwards his liking and attention both turned in the direction of science and medicine. To Edinburgh, therefore, the medical Mecca of the time, he went, and there received in 1799 his medical degree.

Shortly after his return to New York (in 1804) he was appointed professor of chemistry in Columbia College, and prepared and delivered a course of lectures on medical jurisprudence, the first in America. When, in 1813, the medical faculty of Columbia was merged with the faculty of the College of Physicians and Surgeons, Dr. Stringham was very naturally appointed to the chair of legal medicine. His lectures were always clear, forceful, and interesting, and were greatly enriched by his wide and varied learning. These lectures were published in the "American Medical and Philosophical Register" in the following year (1814) and are highly prized at the present day by all interested in the deveopment of American medical jurisprudence.

For the greater part of his life Dr. Stringham was a sufferer from organic heart-disease. On several occasions he was obliged on this account to cease his professional work. In 1817, on the advice of his friends, he proceeded to the island of St. Croix, seeking relief from his terrible infirmity. But no relief came except death, which occurred on June 29, of the same year. T. H. S.

Thacher's American Medical Biography, 1828, vol. ii.
Witthaus and Becker's Medical Jurisprudence, Forensic Medicine, and Toxicology, vol. i (R. A. Witthaus).
Trans. Internat. Med. Congress, Phila., 1876 (Stanford E. Chaillé).

Strong, Nathaniel (1783–1867).

Born of English parentage in Northampton, Massachusetts in 1783, he served as surgeon in the War of 1812, and before coming west made a trip around the world, presumably as ship's surgeon. The printed announcement of the Censors of the Seventh District Medical Society shows that he was licensed to practice November 6, 1817, and located in Centerville, a small village in Montgomery County, Ohio, but available details of his professional life are meager, his special claim for recognition resting upon a paper written in 1818.

This essay, which discusses the whole subject of reproduction, and displays the alert observer and a remarkable familiarity with comparative anatomy, is still in existence. In it the modern doctrine of ovulation and menstruation is distinctly and clearly taught, thus antedating by four years Doctor Powers, of London, who is credited with the discovery, although it was not generally accepted until Négrier, in 1831, proved its truth by his beautiful anatomical preparations. When written (1818), Dr. Strong's manuscript was sent to a prominent medical journal, but was rejected, presumably on account of the obscurity of the author. But for this rejection, this man of genius and original thinker, though only a backwoodsman, would to-day stand before the world as the discoverer of one of the fundamental facts in the physiology of generation.   W. J. C.

Strudwick, Edmund (1802–1879).

Edmund Strudwick was born in Orange County, North Carolina, on the twenty-fifth day of March, 1802, at Long Meadows, about five miles north of Hillsboro, the county seat. His lineage was ancient and long-established in the community, his father being an important political factor and distinguished for those qualities which afterward graced his son.

His medical studies began under Dr. James Webb, and he graduated as a doctor of medicine at the University of Pennsylvania on April 8, 1824. He served for two years as resident physician in the Philadelphia Almshouse and Charity Hospital.

Of the North Carolina State Medical Society he was a charter member and the first president.

All kinds of surgery attracted him and he sought for it. Scores of operations for cataract were performed by him, according to the now obsolete needle method, without losing an eye. Once as he was driving homeward after a long trip in the country, he saw an old man trudging along being led by a small boy at his side. Dr. Strudwick stopped, ascertained that the man had been blind for twelve years, made him get up into carriage and took him to his (the doctor's) home. One eye was operated on first and the other the next week, sight being restored to each. This case, as did all other similar ones, appealed to Dr. Strudwick very greatly.

If there was any special operation for which Dr. Strudwick was famous, it was that of lithotomy. Certainly he was the leading lithotomist of his time in North Carolina. There is no record of the exact number he performed, but it was large and his mortality low. Dr. Strudwick lived in a section of the State where this affection abounded. His custom was always to do the lateral operation and to introduce no tube or other drainage unless there was hemorrhage. It is said that he did twenty-eight consecutive lithotomies without a death. One case in particular has come down to us—a very large stone, wedged into the trigone and assuming its shape. On the posterior surface grooves had formed along which the urine trickled down from the ureteral openings. After making the incision and finding that the calculus was too large to extract entire, Dr. Strudwick sent to the blacksmith's, secured his tongs and crushed it. Fortunately, the stone was of the soft phosphatic variety.

Many breast amputations were done by Dr. Strudwick. In all cases he cleaned out the axilla, thus anticipating most of the surgeons of a later period. His after-results were in some cases quite surprising and were uniformly better than was the rule in those days.

He performed the operation for lacerated perineum several times, invariably using silver wire, but undertook no trachelorrhaphies. His practice was always to sew up a perineal tear immediately after confinement and his success in these recent cases was noteworthy. Another anticipation of modern methods was his habit of never employing applications to the interior of the uterus, but of advocating and using intrauterine injections of salt solution.

The most important operation of Dr. Strudwick's career was one about which, unluckily, the record is meager. It was, however, probably in 1842, that he successfully removed from a woman a large abdominal tumor, weighing thirty-six pounds.

Dr. Strudwick was married in 1828, two years after beginning practice, to Ann Nash, whom he survived but two years. They had five children—two girls and three boys. The girls died in infancy, and two of the boys became doctors.

He was exceedingly active and actually up to his final hours his energy was comparable to that of a dynamo. His fine condition of health was aided also by his simple habits. He was not a big eater, and was extremely temperate. He also had the gift of taking "cat naps" at any time or place—a habit that William Pepper, the younger, did so much to celebrate. Dr. Strudwick frequently slept in his chair. He was an early riser, his life long, the year round. And one of his invariable rules—which illustrates the sort of stuff of which he was made—was to smoke six pipefulls of tobacco every morning before breakfast. He was a most insatiate consumer of tobacco, being practically never free from its influence.

He bought all instruments and books as they came out. In a flap on the dashboard of his surry he kept a bag in which were stored a small library and a miniature instrument shop. And often he would return with his carriage full of cohosh, boneset, etc., indicating his familiarity with medical botany.

He was once called to a neighboring county to perform an operation. The night was dark and cold; the road was rough; the horse became frightened at some object, ran away, upset the buggy and threw the occupants out, stunning the country doctor who had met him, and who, it was afterwards learned, was addicted to the opium habit, and breaking Dr. Strudwick's leg just above the ankle. As soon as he had sufficiently recovered himself, Dr. Strudwick called aloud, but no one answered and he then crawled to the side of the road and sat with his back against a tree. In the meantime the other physician, who had somehow managed to get into the buggy again, drove to the patient's home where for a time he could give no account of himself or his companion. When the doctor's buggy came back again at sunrise, he got in, drove to the house, without allowing his own leg to be dressed, and sitting on the bed, operated upon the patient for strangulated hernia with a successful result.

The going out of this great man's life was as tragic and unusual as his career had been brilliant and useful. In possession of his customary good health, at the age of seventy-seven, he succumbed to a fatal dose of atropine taken by mistake from drinking a glass of water in which the drug had been prepared for hypodermic employment in an emergency.

N Carolina M. J , 1880, v.
Abridged from a memoir by H. A. Royster.

Sutherland, Charles (1831–1895).

A son of the Hon. Joel Barlow Sutherland, a physician, soldier, statesman and jurist, the first president of the Society of the War of 1812; he was educated in the private schools of Philadelphia and at Jefferson Medical College, and received his M. D. in 1849. He entered the military service in October, 1851, as acting assistant surgeon and, when commissioned, served at various stations, chiefly throughout the west, engaging in numerous expeditions against the Indians, and was promoted surgeon-major April 16, 1862. He was with Gen. Halleck's forces at Columbus, Kentucky, and Memphis, Tennessee, fitting out numerous large general hospitals and equipping extensive forces with medical supplies, also serving as assistant medical director and inspector with Gen. Grant and participating in the siege of Vicksburg, besides holding afterwards many army appointments, being in 1876 promoted colonel and surgeon, serving as medical director and promoted to surgeon-general of the army by Pres. Harrison, December 23, 1890. He retired to Washington two years before his death, on May 10, 1895, having fulfilled the duties of his many offices with fidelity and ability.

J. E. P.

Pilcher, James Evelyn, Journal of the Association of Military Surgeons of the United States, vol. xvi, 1905 (port.).
The Surgeon-generals of the United States Army, Carlisle, Pa., 1905 (port.).

Sutton, George (1812–1886).

George Sutton, of Aurora, Indiana, who wrote a considerable number of papers on epidemics and made them a special study, was born in London, England, on June 16, 1812, and came with his parents to America in 1819. As a lad he went to the village school and in 1828 to the Miami University, afterwards studying medicine with Dr. Jesse Smith in Cincinnati. In 1836, he graduated from the Ohio Medical College with a thesis on the "Relation between the Blood and Vital Principle," in the spring of the same year beginning practice in Aurora, Indiana, where he married Sarah Follre and had five children, four sons and one daughter.

In 1843 an epidemic of erysipelas broke out in Aurora and Sutton's paper on it in the "Western Lancet" was, for its excellence, practically all incorporated into Copland's Medical Dictionary. He also wrote on "The Medical History of Cholera in Indiana"; in 1856 another report on erysipelas and the same year a careful study on hog cholera, which was then ravaging the State, he was one of the first to study the disease in a systematic way. These studies were published in in the Cincinnati "Gazette" 1857, and more extended, in the "American Medico-Chirurgical Review," 1858. He was instrumental in organizing the Dearborn County Medical Society which met first at his house and was president of this society, and of the Indiana State Medical Society.

He served the American Medical Association for two years as Chairman of the Committee on Meteorology and Epidemies and compiled the reports.

Keenly interested, also, in natural science, the antiquities of the west early attracted his attention, and he wrote articles concerning a large collection of geological and other specimens he had collected. One of his papers was "Evidences in Boone County, Kentucky, of Glacial or Ice Deposits of Two Distinct and Widely Distant Periods"; and an address before the Association for the Advancement of Science. A tolerably full list of his writings may be seen in J. M. Toner's "Address before the Rocky Mountain Medical Association" (biographical section), 1877, from which this biography is gathered.   D. W.

"The Med Hist. of Indiana," G. W. H. Kemper, 1911.

Sweat, Moses (1788–1865).

The portrait of Moses Sweat shows us a handsome looking man with long flowing patriarchal beard and hair, the latter pushed back from his forehead, a clean-shaven upper lip, and a placid face. He was the eldest son of Jonathan and Sarah Ayer Sweat, and was born in Portland, Maine, March 15, 1788.

He had a career of over half a century as physician and surgeon, though he made no specialty of surgery, but cases of this sort for fifty miles around fell into his hands and he worked mostly in that line the best part of his time.

In the beginning of his life he was a plain mechanic, but not liking manual labor, began to study medicine at first during his work, and later on with Dr. James Bradbury, of Parsonsfield, an early member of the Maine Medical Society. He also studied at Dartmouth with the celebrated anatomist, Alexander Ramsay in 1808 and, later on, at Ramsay's Medical School in Fryeburg, Maine. He was demonstrator of anatomy at Dartmouth while a student there, and also at Fryeburg, so that the knowledge of anatomy then gained made him remarkable as a surgeon.

He was a member of the Massachusetts Medical Society, and afterwards of the Maine Medical Society, and as his fame increased, he received an honorary M. D. from the Medical School of Maine in 1823, and from the Castleton, Vermont, Medical School in 1846. He was an expert in reducing fractures, and in setting dislocations, and was often called to great distances for accidents of this sort in which he possessed an extraordinarily acute power of diagnosis, and skill in manipulation.

He performed during his life time all of the operations of the day and had no superior in Maine. He married Elizabeth Wedgewood, of Portland, in 1811, and had eleven children, the youngest of whom became a doctor.

Unfortunately, however, for the hopes of his father, this promising son who was beginning to take the drudgery of long journeys from his shoulders, died very early. From this shock Dr. Sweat never actually rallied to do his work as of old. His bright hopes were crushed; his interest for work was destroyed. The pleasurable contemplation of his former success in surgery was embittered, and became like Dead Sea fruit.

This manly physician and skillful surgeon passed gently away August 25, 1865.   J. A. S.

Trans. Maine Med. Assoc.

Sweetnam, Lesslie Matthew (1859–1901).

Lesslie Matthew Sweetnam, surgeon, son of Matthew Sweetnam, Post Office inspector, was born in Kingston, Ontario, on August 1, 1859.

As a lad he went to the Upper Canada College, Toronto, graduating M. B. from the University of Toronto and M. D. from Victoria College in 1881, afterwards doing post-graduate work in Great Britain, Europe, New York, Philadelphia and Baltimore, and in 1885 marrying Margaret Victoria, daughter of C. H. Goodesham of Toronto, by whom he had one daughter who, to his great sorrow, died before him.

An untiring worker, he faithfully attended to the incessant demands of a large general practice, often making routine calls into the small hours of the night, yet building up a large surgical practice, paying visits to other clinics and quick to adopt the best methods. An original thinker, he worked out a number of improvements in surgical technic. He showed that cases of extreme tympany might sometimes be relieved by posture alone. In one instance he placed a patient who appeared to be in a dying condition in the knee-breast posture with prompt relief to the accumulation of gases. He also devised the inflatable rubber balloon contained in a silk bag as a means of dilating rectal strictures without risk. Personally, he fearlessly followed duty wherever it led. He went to Colorado with a relative troubled with laryngeal tuberculosis who was most careless in his habits, confidently expecting to lose his own life in devotion to duty. The nurse, whom he warned of the risk, took the disease and died.

Sweetnam practically wore himself out in incessant labors for the sick. He contracted nephritis with attacks of extreme pain and hematuria and had but partially recovered when he was poisoned in amputating an arm of a tramp infected with the gas bacillus. This added burden was too much for the crippled kidneys and he died suddenly in a uremic convulsion on December 11, 1901.

He had rare surgical judgment, was a

deliberate operator and obtained excellent results. In many ways he was years ahead of his time. As a man he at once inspired confidence and as a friend was as true as steel.

Sweetnam was on the staff of the Toronto General Hospital; surgeon to St. Michael's Hospital, and the House of Providence and was a professor in the Ontario Medical College for women. His articles included:

"Concurrent Morbilli or Rötheln and Vaccination." ("Canadian Journal Medical Society," vol. vii, 1882.)

"Pseudo-hypertrophic Muscular Paralysis," idem.

"Subiodide of Bismuth in the Treatment of Wounds." ("Canadian Practitioner," 1887, vol. xii.)

"The Treatment of Varicose Veins of the Lower Extremities." (Idem., vol. xviii, 1893.)

"Urethral Carbuncle." (Idem., vol. xx, 1895.)

"Relief of Tympanites by Posture." ("Annals of Surgery," vol. xxiii, 1896.)

H. A. K.

Canad. Pract. and Rev. Toronto, vol. xxvi, 1901.
Canad. Jour. Med. and Surg., vol. xi, 1902.
Methodist Mag. and Rev., Toronto, vol. lv, 1902 (port.).

Swett, John Barnard (1752–1796).

John Barnard Swett was born in Marblehead, Massachusetts, June 1, 1752, the son of a merchant and the grandson of Joseph Swett, who introduced foreign commerce into Marblehead, probably a descendant of John Swett, Newbury, freeman, May 18, 1642, first settlers by that name (Savage). John Swett went to Harvard College, where he graduated in 1771. It had been intended that he should follow the ministry, but being present accidently at the autopsies "on the bodies of some persons who had come to a violent death" he determined to study medicine and did so in spite of opposition on the part of his preceptor. On graduating he studied medicine in Edinburgh, Scotland, for three years under Dr. William Cullen. He shipped

as fleet surgeon in an expedition of merchant vessels to the Falkland Islands on completing his studies in Edinburgh and with the funds acquired in this way finished his medical education in the hospitals of France and England, returning to America in 1778 in season to enlist as surgeon in the Continental Army, and take part in the expedition to Rhode Island under Gen. Sullivan. During the war he lost his valuable library and surgical instruments which he had collected abroad at great expense.

In 1780 he settled in Newburyport, Massachusetts, as an active practitioner and during the succeeding sixteen years did a large part of the surgery of this town and the surrounding country. Being naturally of a social disposition and possessed of polished manners and good humor, he was a great favorite.

He died of yellow fever contracted in the summer of 1796 when there was an epidemic in Newburyport. He threw himself into the work of caring for the sick and died a martyr to the cause.

Dr. Swett married Charlotte Bourne of Marblehead soon after settling in Newburyport. They had four sons.

He was an original member of the American Academy of Arts and Sciences, and of the Massachusetts Medical Society, of which he was the first corresponding secretary, 1782–1789.

W. L. B.

A Genealog. Dict. of the First Settlers of N. E., James Savage, 1860.
Amer. Med. Biog., 1828, James Thacher, M. D.

Swinburne, John (1820–1889).

John Swinburne's early life presented the not unusual spectacle of a clever lad, one of a large family with small means, doing uncongenial work cheerfully until he could conscientiously tread the path of inclination. The ninth child and sixth son of Peter and Artemesia Swinburne he was born in Denmark, Lewis County, New York, on May 30, 1823. From boyhood he attended the county district school and afterwards acted as teacher, subsequently studying at Fairfield, Herkimer County.

In the spring of 1843 he became interested in medicine and chemistry, fortunately studying the latter under Prof. Mather and in 1844 taking up medicine under Dr. Griffin Sweet and afterwards under Prof. J. H. Armsby. He graduated from Albany Medical College in 1846, with a thesis on "The Anatomy of the Neck."

During the first years of his practice in Albany he gave all his leisure to practical anatomical studies and the careful preparation of specimens. After graduating M. D. he was obliged, owing to a serious attack of pleurisy, to take up country practice, but was in a short time appointed demonstrator of anatomy at Albany Medical College. Three years he held this post, giving loving care to the arrangement of a private anatomical museum, where pupils attended, till 1851. The skeleton of the celebrated Dr. Enson who was exhibited on account of his remarkable attenuation, was prepared by Swinburne for this museum. While almshouse physician Swinburne attended 800 cases of ship fever in one year with only fifteen deaths, he himself being attacked by the disease. In May, 1862, he became medical superintendent of the New York wounded troops at the front, a post which was no sinecure, for the victims of disease increased more rapidly than the government could provide accommodation. He succeeded in improving the surgical appliances of that day and published his ideas in two valuable pamphlets. His first official visit was paid to the Peninsula in 1862 when he helped as surgeon after the battles of Williamsburgh and West Point, and he was one of the eight surgeons who organized the hospital at White House. His report on the battles and the soldiers he subsequently attended, induced Gov.

Morgan to appoint him superintendent of the New York State Troops and soon after he was the means of preparing an asylum for 2500 patients in Virginia.

After the war he served six years as quarantine health officer at the port of New York, doing fine service and obviating many epidemics by his careful supervision.

War seems to have held attractions for him, because after these six years he went abroad and served with the French Army during the Franco-Prussian War, organizing the American Ambulance Corps in Paris and taking care of it during the siege for which he had the Cross of the Legion of Honor.

By 1873 he was back again in Albany taking an active share in politics as well as medicine and doing much work as a good citizen. He maintained a free dispensary, treating thousands of cases, chiefly surgical, and was professor of clinical surgery in Albany Medical College; consulting surgeon to Albany Hospital and a member of various important medical societies. Among his writings are:

"Treatment of Fracture of the Femur by Extension," 1859; "Introduction of Air into the Uterine Veins during Criminal Aborton," pronounced by Dr. Dalton the only case on record; "Compound and Comminuted Gunshot Fractures of the Thigh and Means for Their Transplantation;" "Treatment of Fractures of the Long Bones," 1861; "Reports on the Peninsular Campaign," 1863, and other pamphlets.

He married in 1848 Henrietta Judson of Albany and had four sons.

He died in Albany on March 28, 1889.

Med. Rec., N. Y., 1889, vol. xxxv.
Med. and Surg. Rep., Phila. 1864-5, vol. xii.
Tr. Med. Soc., N. Y., Albany, 1864.
The case of Swinburne (Edit.), Med. Gaz., N. Y., 1880, vol. vii.

T

Tackett, John (1815-1891).

John Tackett was born in Huntsville, Alabama, November 27, 1815, and began to practise at Cooksville, Mississippi, the spring after his graduation at Louisville Medical College in 1844 and two years later moved to Richland. His wife was Bettie Dulaney, and he had five children.

In 1847 he performed Cesarean section successfully alone. This case was reported to the "New Orleans Medical and Surgical Journal" by Dr. B. Harvey, and the operation was quoted by Dr. Paul F. Eve in his book of "Remarkable Surgical Cases," in very complimentary terms.

In 1861 he enlisted in the Confederate army as surgeon, but was subsequently called home by a petition to the governor from the fathers and the husbands of families in and near Richmond, who wished him to remain and provide for the health, comfort and protection of their wives and children.

He died in Richland, Mississippi, December 3, 1891 of pneumonia.

Transactions of the Mississippi State Medical Association, 1892.

Taliaferro, Valentine Ham (1831-1887).

Valentine Ham Taliaferro, gynecologist, born in Oglethorp County, Georgia, on September 24, 1831, was a descendant of one Zachariah Taliaferro an early colonial and the son of Charles B. and Mildred Meriwether. As a boy he went to the local schools and Kellog Academy then graduated M. D. from the University of New York in 1852, soon after marrying Mary A., daughter of his old preceptor, Dr. B. O. Jones of Atlanta. He had four daughters and two sons one of whom, Valentine Ham, became a doctor. During the Civil War he was surgeon to the Second Georgia Cavalry and organized the Tenth Brigade of the same. At the end of the war he was brevet brigadier-general.

In 1857 Dr. Taliaferro became professor of materia medica in Oglethorp College, Savannah, and successively professor of diseases of women and children in the Atlanta Medical College; of obstetrics and diseases of women and children and dean in 1876. In 1881 he successfully started a private infirmary for the diseases of women, the first of its kind in the South.

As a writer he did good work, co-editing and writing for the "Medical and Literary Weekly," "The Hygienic and Literary Magazine," and the "Oglethorp Medical and Surgical Journal," Savannah.

Among his writings are: "Medication by the Use of Uterine Tents in the Diseases of the Body and Cavity of the Uterus," 1871; "The Application of Pressure in Diseases of the Uterus, Ovaries and Peri-uterine Structures, "1882; "Intrauterine Tampon for Dilating the Uterus and Securing Better Drainage in Diseases of the Endometrium," 1884.

Between the years 1882-1886 Dr. Taliaferro made a valuable contribution to gynecological literature in a paper on "Intrauterine Tampon," for purpose of Dilating the Uterus, Securing Better Drainage, and Treating Diseases of the Endometrium." This paper was published in the "Atlanta Medical and Surgical Journal."

He was known as a skillful gynecologist and one keenly interested in medical progress and his fellowmen. In the autumn of 1887 he was persuaded by his friends to take a rest at Tate Springs, Tennessee, but, too ill to operate just before leaving, he took with him some patients, among them a charity case and the last operation he ever did was for her.

He died on the seventeenth of September, 1887, of valvular heart trouble. His wife survived him only a few months.

J. A. R.

Atlanta Med. and Surg. Jour., 1884, n. s., vol. i.
Atkinson's Phys. and Surgs. of the U. S.

Taliaferro, William J. (1795–1871).

William J. Taliaferro was born in Newington, Orange County, Virginia, in 1795. He was of Italian extraction; his ancestors came to this country long before the Revolution. His father, Col. Nicholas Taliaferro, served in that war, and at its close settled in Kentucky. The son inherited his father's patriotism. In the War of 1812 he served as a volunteer in Ball's Kentucky Light Dragoons, which formed part of the left wing of Gen. Harrison's army. At Camp Seneca he enlisted in Com. Perry's fleet, and took part in the battle of Lake Erie. Soon thereafter he rejoined the army and served in the battle of Moravian Town, Canada West, October 5, 1813. For these services he received seven hundred dollars prize money, and a gold medal from the state of Kentucky. On his return from the army he began to study medicine with Dr. Keith, of Augusta, and in 1818 attended lectures at the University of Pennsylvania, where he witnessed for the first time the operation for cataract. He returned to Kentucky, and began practice in Washington, Mason County.

In 1823 he operated successfully for cataract on a boy five years old who had been blind from birth. After a few years he moved to Maysville, Kentucky, where his success as an oculist attracted patients from all parts of the south and west.

About this time Mr. Hitchcraft, a man of wealth and influence became blind, and spent much time and money, but refused to try Taliaferro and went east, and finally to Europe seeking relief from oculists. He returned home without improvement and disheartened, but, at the instance of friends, visited Dr. Taliaferro, who said he could cure him. An agreement was drawn up by his friends that he was to pay the doctor five thousand dollars if cured; if not, the doctor was to forfeit four thousand. The result was a perfect success, and Mr. Hitchcraft sent for the doctor, and said to him, "You have fulfilled your part of the engagement, now I will fulfill mine, and pay you the five thousand dollars." The doctor was astonished, and refused to accept so large a sum. In 1841 he moved to Cincinnati, and in 1843 married the widow of James Ramsey, of Hamilton, Ohio. No children were born. Late in life Dr. Taliaferro accepted the chair of ophthalmology in the Cincinnati College of Medicine and Surgery, and lectured there until within a short time of his death, March 22, 1871.

A. G. D.

Tate, John Humphreys (1815–1892).

John Humphreys Tate, obstetrician, was born near Harper's Ferry, Charleston, Virginia, in 1815, and practised for fifty years in Cincinnati, Ohio. He came of good old stock; Magnus Tate, the elder, came from the Orkney Isles and landed in Philadelphia, May 20, 1696.

John H. was educated at Hanover College, South Hanover, and graduated there. He then studied with Prof. John Morehead of Cincinnati, matriculated in the Medical College of Ohio and graduated in 1840. After practising a few years Tate went to Paris to further his education in medicine and surgery and remained abroad for two years, most of the time being spent in Paris.

In 1856 he was elected to fill the chair of physiology, hygiene, and medical jurisprudence in the Medical College of Ohio, and to serve on the staff of the Commercial Hospital. After serving two years he resigned, and in 1870 became a member of the faculty of the Cincinnati Medical College, and in 1873 was elected president of the Cincinnati Academy of Medicine and from 1873 to 1875 served as obstetrician and gynecologist to the Cincinnati Hospital. Dr. John Tate was a gentleman of the old school, very studious, endowed with a most remarkable memory, occupied the highest positions in the gift of his profession and had the respect and friendship of all. His record in obstetrics is somewhat unique in that he attended more confinements than any practitioner in Cincinnati. He originated a special method of restoring an inverted uterus to its original position (known as Tate's method) and cured the longest standing case of inverted uterus on record.

Tate introduced the following resolution in the Cincinnati Academy of Medicine which passed it, and then went to Columbus and presented it before the state legislature and secured its adoption. All money received from the sale of tickets to medical students witnessing operations and attending lectures in the amphitheater of the Cincinnati Hospital shall go to the establishment and maintenance of a medical library and museum. In this way Dr. Tate became the founder of the Cincinnati Hospital Library. He married Margaret Kincaid Chenoweth in 1853 and had nine children, John Chenoweth, Abbie Humphreys, Lizzie Polk, William Ross, George North, Thomas Orkney, Magnus Alfred, Frank McCormack, Ralph Booth Tate. Two, Magnus and Ralph, selected medicine as a profession.

John Humphreys Tate died of cerebral hemorrhage when seventy-six years old, on February 7, 1892, at Cincinnati, Ohio.

A. G. D.

Taylor, Charles Fayette (1827–1899).

Charles Fayette Taylor, orthopedic surgeon, and inventor, was born and brought up on a farm in Williston, Vermont, April 25, 1827. His grandfather, John Taylor of Williston, was a great-grandson of the Rev. Edward Taylor (1642–1727) of Westfield, Massachusetts, who came to this country from England in 1669.

After taking his M. D. at the University of Vermont in 1856, he went to London and studied therapeutic exercises under M. Roth, a pupil of Ling.

On returning he settled in New York City and introduced the so-called "Swedish movements" into this country. His book on the "Theory and Practice of the Movement Cure" (Lindsay and Blakiston) was published in 1861. His experience with therapeutic exercises soon directed his attention to the neglected state of sufferers from chronic joint and spinal troubles and other deformities, and he studied with enthusiasm the problem of improving their treatment, being a pioneer in the application of local rest and protection by proper splinting, and in the abundant use of fresh air. To these ends he devised a series of corrective and protective appliances, many of which are still standard. In this work he made use of everything which seemed of service, adding whatever of value his own original mind could suggest regardless of tradition.

He also devised a system of exercising machines for the weak and paralytic, many of which were worked by power like the Zander apparatus. He proved his mastery in three fields, therapeutic exercises, mechanical orthopedics, and a common sense psychotherapy, somewhat on the lines now practised by Dubois of Bern, and which enabled him to effect many striking cures in bedridden neurasthenics and others.

In 1866 Dr. Taylor called the attention of Howard Potter, Theodore Roosevelt, James Brown, John L. Aspinwall, and others to the need of a place where crippled and deformed poor might receive treatment. Becoming interested, these friends with Dr. Taylor, founded the New York Orthopedic Dispensary, afterwards the New York Orthopedic Dispensary and Hospital, which Dr. Taylor served for eight years as surgeon-in-chief.

Dr. Taylor's originality, thoroughness, self reliance and enthusiastic devotion to the welfare of his patients won the confidence of the profession and gave him a remarkably successful practice, until his health began to fail in 1882. After extensive travels in foreign countries he settled in Southern California, where he died January 25, 1899. He had married Mary Salina Skinner of Williston on March 7, 1854, who with four children survived him.

He was honored with medals or diplomas at Paris in 1867, at Vienna in 1873, and at Philadelphia in 1876. He was made corresponding member of the Imperial Medical Society of Vienna on Billroth's nomination, and charter member of the American Orthopedic Association; a fellow of the New York Academy of Medicine; a member of the New York County Medical Society; a fellow of the American Geographical Society, and of the New York Academy of Sciences.

His published work includes between forty and fifty titles, mostly on orthopedic subjects. Those on the "Mechanical Treatment of Angular Curvature or Pott's Disease of the Spine" (1863), and its German translation (1873); "Spinal Irritation or the Causes of Backache among American Women" (1864); "Infantile Paralysis" (Lippincott, 1867); on the "Mechanical Treatment of Disease of the Hip-joint" (William Wood, 1873), and its German translation in the same year; and "Emotional Prodigality" (Dental Cosmos, July, 1879) are still classic. His largest work was on "The Theory and Practice of the Movement Cure," 1861.

Though not opposed to the use of drugs when definitely indicated, he found no use for them in his practice and never wrote a prescription. He was a tireless worker and always felt that he could have accomplished more except for his meager schooling, poor eyes, and ill health in early manhood. Writing in 1887 he says, "I acknowledge that deficiency of early training left me more free from bias and less hemmed in than is often the case after special training. But it has always seemed to me that I could have managed the bias if I could have had the training."

How completely Dr. Taylor overcame through his own exertions the defects in his schooling is evident from these recol-

lections as well as from his other writings. His mind was fertile in original ideas and stored with information, from his constant habit of informing himself in regard to everything with which he came in contact. He was particularly interested in processes of manufacture, in machinery and in people as individuals, especially those engaged in productive occupations, and those in need of help, mental, physical, moral, or material, and his interest was not theoretical; he was one of the most helpful of men.

H. L. T.

Memorial by E. H. Bradford, M. D., and autobiographical reminiscences, Transactions American Orthopedic Association, 1899. Obituary in Pediatrics, No. 5, 1899; Year Book, New York Orthopedic Dispensary and Hospital, 1899. American Physical Educational Review, vol. iv, No. 3, 1899.

Taylor, Isaac Ebenezer (1812–1889).

Isaac E. Taylor was one of the eight children of William and Mary Taylor of Philadelphia where he was born April 25, 1812. Educated at Rutgers College he afterwards took his M. A. and M. D. at the University of Pennsylvania, settling down to practice in New York in 1839 with his wife Eliza Mary, daughter of Stuart Mollen.

In 1840 he visited Paris and studied under Cazeaux and at Dublin and on his return to New York had charge of the gynecological section in the city, Eastern, Northern and Demilt dispensaries, taking a private class of four in each, which really was the origin of the gynecological clinic there. He will be remembered chiefly for his demonstration of the non-shortening of the cervix during pregnancy ("American Medical Journal," 1862), in which he anticipated Muller, to whom credit is generally given. As a literary contributor to the "Transactions of the New York State Medical Association," of which he was a founder and ex-president, he did valuable work and also helped forward the cause of medicine by being the founder and lifetime president of the Bellevue Hospital Medical College. In 1839, he with

Dr. James A. Washington, introduced to the medical profession in the New York Dispensary the hypodermic treatment by morphia. The story of his life might seem uneventful but he did earnestly and honestly much of the foundation work on which the success of medical science depends. On October 30, 1889, he died in New York.

Among his appointments were: president of New York County Medical Society; vice-president and fellow of New York Academy of Medicine; president obstetrical section of the Academy of Medicine; vice-president American Gynecologists; honorary member Medical Society of Christiana; physician Bellevue Hospital.

His numerous articles included: " Cases of Diseases Peculiar to Females and Nervous Diseases," 1841; " Rheumatism of the Uterus and Ovaries," 1845; " Labor with Anteversion of Uterus in that State," 1856; "Mechanism of Spontaneous Action of Uterine Inversion," 1872, etc. A list is given in the " Transactions New York Medical Association," 1890, vol. vii.

Am. J. Obstet., N. Y., 1890, vol. xxiii (W. T. Lusk).
Gaillard's Med. J., N. Y., 1890, vol. 1 (J. Shrady).
Med. and Surg. Reporter, Phila., 1866, vol. xv.

Taylor, John Winthrop (1817-1886).

John Winthrop Taylor, surgeon-general of the United States Navy, was the son of Charles Williams Taylor, of New York, and Cornelia, daughter of Francis Bayard Winthrop and prepared for college at Mr. Sears' school in Princeton, New York, graduating from Princeton College. He studied medicine with Dr. Thomas Harris, of the navy, in Philadelphia, and took his medical degree from the University of Pennsylvania. He entered the naval service as assistant-surgeon on March 7, 1838, and was promoted to the rank of surgeon, May 1, 1852, serving as surgeon on the Pensacola, West Gulf Blockading Squadron from 1861–63, as fleet surgeon of the

Gulf Squadron from 1866–67, as fleet surgeon, north Pacific Squadron 1867–69. He was appointed surgeon-general of the navy, October 21, 1878, and retired August 19, 1879, having reached the age of sixty-two years. Sur.-Gen. Taylor died almost instantly in Boston, January 19, 1880. He married in 1842, but had no children.

C. A. P.

Tr. Am. M. Ass., 1882, xxxiii.

Taylor, Robert William (1842-1908).

Robert William Taylor was born at Coventry, England, August 11, 1842. His family came to the United States in 1850; and his father who died soon after arriving in America, was an Oxford graduate and had had considerable means.

Dr. Taylor had good educational advantages until he was fourteen years, then, so that he might not be a burden on his widowed mother, he left school and entered the employ of a retail druggist; his ability was such that at the early age of twenty-one he was placed in full charge of one of the largest retail drug stores in New York City.

But the wish to follow a profession more in keeping with the traditions of his family made him enter as student under Dr. Willard Parker and he graduated from the College of Physicians and Surgeons in 1868, when he settled in New York City, and for the first few years devoted himself to general practice. Early in his career becoming acquainted with Dr. Freeman J. Bumstead, which association turned his attention from general practice to the study of skin, venereal and genito-urinary diseases.

In 1871, only three years after graduation, he published a paper on " Dactylitis Syphilitica" which was of such signal merit that it attracted widespread attention, and at once placed him in the front rank of medical observers.

In 1879, in collaboration with Dr. Bumstead, he published a notable textbook, "The Pathology and Treatment of Venereal Diseases." This book ran through many editions, the last one, rewritten by Dr. Taylor, and with the title changed to, "A Practical Treatise on Genito-urinary and Venereal Diseases," appeared in 1904.

In 1887 he edited "A Clinical Atlas of Venereal and Skin Diseases," and in 1899 "A Practical Treatise on Sexual Disorders of the Male and Female."

In addition to these larger works Dr. Taylor frequently contributed to medical journals, articles on venereal and dermatological subjects, all of his writings being of marked value, his statements being always carefully thought out and concisely expressed. Helpful with his books, he was none the less so to all who knew him, and particularly to the young and struggling physician.

During his professional life he collected one of the most valuable libraries on syphilology and dermatology in this country and was a generous donor to the New York Academy of Medicine of rare books on these subjects.

In 1891 he was appointed clinical professor of genito-urinary and venereal diseases in the College of Physicians and Surgeons, New York; he resigned this professorship in 1905. Prior to his connection with the College of Physicians and Surgeons he was professor of dermatology in the Woman's Medical College of the New York Infirmary, and in the medical department of the University of Vermont.

He was one of the founders and once president of the American Dermatological Association, and one of the founders of the New York Dermatological Society, also a member of the American Association of Genito-urinary Surgeons, the New York Academy of Medicine, and the Medical Society of the State and County of New York. With but little education and no money, he succeeded in reaching the topmost pinnacle of medical fame, and when he died in New York, January 4, 1908, his reputation was international.

J. M. W.

A full list of his writings is given in the Cat. of the Surg.-gen. Office, Wash., D. C.

Tebault, Alfred George (1811–1895).

Evidently of Huguenot origin, this physician was born in Charleston, South Carolina, on February 23, 1811, and educated in the best schools in his native city, then having decided to devote his life-work to medicine; he studied with Thomas Y. Simons, after which he matriculated in the South Carolina Medical College, from which he graduated in 1831. In company with his friend, Dr. H. B. Phillips, he settled in Macon, North Carolina. He went to Norfolk, Virginia, in 1832, when that city was visited by Asiatic cholera. In that, or the following year, he settled in Princess Anne County, Virginia, where he spent the greater part of his life.

He was a member of the Medical Society of Virginia, and was in 1873 elected president, and was made an honorary member the next year. He was also honorary member of the Norfolk Medical Society. He was offered a professorship in two medical colleges, but declined both.

He married in 1833 Mary H., daughter of Maj. C. Cornick, of Princess Anne County, Virginia, who died about 1840. By this marriage he had three children, who survived him; Dr. A. George Tebault, of Louisiana, and two daughters. After the death of his first wife, he went West and spent about a year in travelling, after which he returned home and married Elizabeth A. Murray, of Princess Anne County, and had one son, who survived him. His second wife dying, he married Eliza A. Bonney, and had several sons and daughters. One son was a physician—Dr. W. P. Tebault, of Norfolk.

In his declining years he removed to Norfolk, at his home in which city, he died in his eighty-fifth year, of marasmus, on the twenty-seventh of August, 1895.

Notwithstanding he was a man of such extensive information, he wrote little for the benefit of his fellow practitioners. The titles of such of his writing as we have been able to find are:

"Epidemics of the Tide-Water District

of Virginia," the report of a committee of which he was chairman. ("Transactions, Medical Society of Virginia," 1872.)

"Is Drinking Water a Cause of Malarial Fevers?" (" Virginia Medical Monthly," vol. i.)

[ ]"The Mission of the Physician," Presidential Address. ("Transactions, Medical Society of Virginia," 1874.)

"Case of Intussusception." (" Virginia Medical Monthly," vol. i.)

"Cases in Midwifery." (" Virginia Medical Monthly," vol. ii.)

"Rachiotomy in Transverse Presentations." (" Virginia Medical Monthly," vol. iii.) R. M. S.

Trans. Med. Soc. of Va., 1895.

Tennent, John (Eighteenth Century).

Though he was a distinguished physician and writer, little is known of Tennent, and what little we have is chiefly through his contributions to medical literature. He is said to have been born at Port Royal, Virginia, where he practised later. There seems little doubt that he was a well known doctor, and as far as known, was probably the first native physician to make contributions to professional literature.

He was a correspondent, and probably a relative, of Dr. Richard Mead, of London, as his articles were first communicated to him, with the title "Epistles to Dr. Richard Mead." These epistles were written in the years 1736 to 1738, and in one of them, published in Edinburgh in 1742, he described the epidemic diseases and climate of Virginia. He was the first to describe the plant polygala Seneca, or the Seneca snake-root, and to make known its therapeutic properties, commending most highly its value in the treatment of pleurisy, pneumonia and the bite of the rattle-snake. His "Essay on Pleurisy," another of the epistles, was published at Williamsburg, Virginia, in 1736, and republished in New York in 1842. An epistle "Respecting the Bite of a Viper and its Poison," was published in Edinburgh in 1742, also that on the "Epidemic Diseases of Virginia."

Another paper, "Observations on Seneca Snake-root," was published in London in 1741. He also published a paper in the "Medical and Physical Inquiries," of London, in 1742, condemning the use of vinegar, as advocated by a Dr. Ward, in the treatment of the fevers of the West Indies and other subtropical regions, which were so fatal to Britons in that day.

It is not known in what year or at what age he died.

R. M. S.

Tewksbury, Samuel Henry (1819–1880).

Jacob Tewksbury, the father, of Hebron, Maine, was a very clever practitioner for his time, and an active member of the Maine Medical Society. He married Charlotte Nelson, of Paris, Maine, and Samuel Henry was born in Oxford, Maine, March 22, 1819. He studied medicine with his father and at the Medical School of Maine, graduating in 1841. He then attended lectures at the Harvard Medical School and at the College of Physicians and Surgeons of New York.

He began practice at Frankfort, Maine, but after marrying Miss Diana Eaton, of Paris, Maine, rejoined his father in practice. In 1850 he moved to Portland, w h e r e he practised thirty years Among the great things which Dr. Tewksbury did for medicine in Maine was the introduction of the practice of gynecology, resection of the knee-joint, the successful operation for stone in the bladder by the new method, and using the first flexion and extension in the re-setting of a hip-joint dislocation. He was also active in clinical exhibits before the Maine Medical Association as far back as 1855, showing his early knowledge of successful surgery especially in cases of resection.

He was twice elected president of the Maine Medical Society and in his addresses called special attention to the need of the formation of the Maine General Hospital. It was later on a deep disappointment to him that the rules could not have been made so as to permit any reputable physician to put

JAMES THACHER.

atients into private rooms or in beds ot then occupied.

In this respect he was far sighted, for ith such an arrangement things would ave been much better. Tewksbury rote a large number of medical papers of reat value, largely upon excisions and n gynecology. He was a man of noble gure, handsome face and markedly tall. determined and successful man, he was ctive but impulsive, a good anatomist nd a clever, neat and skillful operator. Iis style in conversation was terse, but a his papers he was inclined to be oquacious. Most of these were published for many successive years in the Transactions of the Maine Medical association."

He often used invectives which were ometimes more convincing than polite. ienerally brusque and apparently uncivil at times, he concealed beneath arsh words a very kind heart.

After a long and successful carrer of early forty years he died suddenly July 8, 1880. J. A. S.

Trans. Maine Med. Assoc., 1880.

Thacher, James (1754–1844).

Chiefly known for his contributions to American medical history, James Thacher vas born in Barnstable, Massachusetts, iis mother the daughter of a Mr. Norton of Martha's Vineyard. He studied medicine under Dr. Abner Hersey, and in 1775 entered the army as assistant surgeon. He says: "Not less than one thousand vounded and sick are now in this city Albany) . . . . Amputating limbs, repanning fractured skulls and dressing he most formidable wounds have familarized my mind to scenes of woe." Thacher was at West Point in 1780 at the ime of the treason of Arnold and the apture of the ill-fated André, concerning which events he gives a thrilling account in his military "Journal During the American Revolution," 1826. The war over, he settled in Plymouth, Massachusetts and gave a large share of his ime to antiquarian research and joining he American Academy of Arts and

Sciences. He also joined the Massacuhsetts Medical Society and received an hononary M. D. from Harvard in 1810.

He seems to have taken an interest not only in medical history, but in all that served to promote civic health and happiness. Gross says "he was small in statue, light and agile in his movements, fond of social intercourse, yet regular and studious in his habits. During a few of his last years he was afflicted with a difficulty of breathing." In May, 1844 he died, serenely, in his ninety-first year.

He wrote "The American New Dispensatory, 1810," 4th edition, 1821, and wrote "Observations of Hydrophobia," 1821; "Modern Practice of Physic," 1817; "American Orchardist," 1822; "American Medical Biography," 1828 in two volumes, a most readable work, especially for its prefatory history of medicine. His "Essay of Demonology, Ghosts, Apparitions and Popular Superstitions," appeared in 1831 and the "History of Plymouth," in 1822. Besides all this, he wrote much for the medical journals of his day.

Boston M. and S. J., 1891, cxxiv (J. B. Brewster).
"Lives of Eminent American Physicians," S. D. Gross.
Med. Communicat. Mass. M. Soc., Boston, 1844, vii, pt. 3.

Thacher, Thomas (1620–1678).

Thomas Thacher, preacher and physieian, author of the first publication on a medical subject, in America, was the son of the Rev. Peter Thacher, rector of St. Edmunds, Salisbury, England, and born in England, first of May, 1620, coming to this country when fifteen years old with his uncle, Anthony Thacher, in the "James" and landing in Boston, third of June, 1635. In that same year he went to Ipswich with his uncle.

In a letter published by Anthony Thacher we learn that Thomas had a narrow escape from shipwreck, for Anthony, with the Rev. John Avery and a party of friends, twenty-three in all (even then it would seem an unlucky number), sailed from Ipswich to Marblehead where Mr. Avery was to be settled. Thomas preferred to go by land. A violent storm arose and Anthony's pinnace was cast away on a desolate island off the top of Cape Ann, and he and his wife alone were saved. The island carrying two lofty granite lighthouses and lights of the first class, bears the name of Thacher's Island to this day.

Before coming to America Thomas received a good school education, his father planning to send him to Oxford or Cambridge. He was educated for the ministry by Charles Chauncy, the second president of Harvard College, and, it is probable, received something of a medical education from the same source, for Channey was skilled in the medicine of the day. At all events Thacher was learned in many things. He was a scholar in Arabic and composed a Hebrew lexicon. Dr. Mather tells us that according to Eliot, he was a great logician, and, understanding mechanics in theory and practice, could do all kinds of clock work to admiration. He was ordained as pastor in Weymouth, second of January, 1645, and removing to Boston in 1667, was installed as the first minister of the Old South Church, February 16, 1670. The last sermon he preached was for Dr. Increase Mather.

Dr. Thacher married a daughter of the Rev. Ralph Partridge, of Duxbury, eleventh of May, 1643, by whom he had two daughters and three sons, one of the latter a noted minister. He married a second time, June, 1664, Margaret, widow of Jacob Sheafe and daughter of Henry Webb. He died of a fever, October 15, 1678, following a visit to a sick person.

The title of the publication, issued by Dr. Thacher, in the year 1677, was "A Brief Rule To guide the Common People of New England how to order themselves and theirs in the Small-Pocks, or MeaSels." A reprint of this dated 1702 is a little pamphlet of eight pages, 5½ x 3½ inches, and signed, "I am, though no PhySitian, yet a well wiSher to the Sick; And therefore intreating the Lord to turn our hearts, and Stay His hand, I am, A Friend; Reader to thy Welfare, Thomas Thacher, 21, 11, 1677, 8." The reprint is marked, "Boston, Reprinted for Benjamin Eliot, at his Shop under the WeSt-End of the Exchange, 1702," and may be found in the Boston Medical Library.

W. L. B.

A Biographical Dictionary of the First Settlers in New England, by John Eliot, D. D., Salem and Boston, 1809.
A Genealogical Register of the First Settlers of New England, John Farmer, 1829.
A Genealog. Dictionary of the First Settlers of N. E., James Savage, 1861.
American Medical Biog., 1828, James Thacher, M. D.
Hist. of Medicine in the U. S., to 1800, Francis R. Packard, M. D., 1901.

Thayer, Proctor (1823–1890).

Proctor Thayer, a surgeon, Cleveland, Ohio, was the son of Daniel Thayer, a farmer, and born in Williamstown, Berkshire County, Massachusetts, October 16, 1823. The death of his father in 1830 compelled his mother to break up her home in the East, and accept the invitation of her eldest son to live with him in Aurora, Portage County, Ohio. Here the son, Proctor, received such education as was attainable and was designed to be apprenticed to a shoemaker of the town; but the boy rebelled and positively refused to learn this humble trade. By dint of industry and economy he succeeded in working his way through the Western Reserve College, at Hudson, Ohio, in the scientific department of which he graduated in 1842, and eventually studied medicine with Dr. Delamater, of Cleveland. Here he attended medical lectures in the Cleveland Medical College, until his graduation there in 1849. In 1849 he was appointed to the charge of the cholera hospital in the city of Cleveland, and won many encomiums for his courage, skill and success. In 1852 he was appointed demonstrator of anatomy in the Cleveland Medical College, in 1856 elected to the chair of anatomy and physiology, and this was exchanged in 1862 for that of the principles and practice of surgery, to which was annexed, at his own request, the chair of medical jurisprudence. During the Civil War Thayer was active as an examining surgeon, and in the volunteer medical service in South Carolina and at Pittsburg Landing and Corinth. On returning to Cleveland he resumed duties in the college, until, in 1890, failing health compelled him to claim a few months of rest. Unfortunately neither rest nor medical treatment sufficed for his restoration, and he died in Cleveland October 1, 1890.

On June 27, 1861, Dr. Thayer married Mary Ellen Mesury, and had two boys and two girls. One of these boys, Joseph M., became a physician.

Dr. Thayer was a prudent and skillful surgeon of bluff and hearty manners and a ready and caustic wit, which won him both friends and enemies. As an expert witness upon the witness stand he was at his very best, and woe to the unwary lawyer who aspired to entangle or confuse him in the toils of medico-legal ambiguities. As a teacher he was distinguished by positiveness and a clearness of statement, which rendered him very popular among students. If we add to this that Dr. Thayer is said to have been the first teacher in the Cleveland Medical College to discard written lectures and even notes, and to deliver his lectures extempore, his popularity in college circles is readily understood. Dr. Thayer was a member of the Ohio State Medical Society and of the Cuyahoga County Medical Society.

A good portrait (crayon) of Dr. Thayer will be found in the parlors of the Cleveland Medical Library Association.

H. E. H.

Cleave's Biographical Cyclopedia of Ohio, Cuyahoga County. Philadelphia, 1875.

Thomas, Amos Russell (1826–1892).

Amos Russell Thomas, dean of the Hahnemann Medical College of Philadelphia, was born in Watertown, New York, on October 3, 1826, the son of Col. Azariah Thomas, whose Welsh ancestors were among the earliest settlers in Massachusetts.

At first Thomas tried being a business man, but soon began to study medicine instead at the Syracuse Medical College, graduating in 1854, and practising that same year in Philadelphia, studying, meanwhile taking his medical degree at the old Pennsylvania Medical College. In this college he was first demonstrator and afterwards professor of anatomy for ten years. Soon after going to Philadelphia he became a convert to homeopathy and in 1867 was made professor of anatomy in the Hahnemann Medical College.

Besides scientific papers to the journals of his school, Thomas wrote a valuable book on "Post-Mortem Examinations and Morbid Anatomy," also "Diseases of the Pancreas," "History of Anatomy," "Evolution of Earth and Man," and edited the "American Journal of Homeopathy," four years, and was co-editor of the "Hahnemannian Monthly."

Early in life he married Elizabeth Bacon, of Watertown, and one son, Charles M., followed his father's profession. His only daughter, Florence, died in 1880, fifteen years before her father, who died at his house in Devon of carcinoma of the bladder December, 1895.

From data supplied by Dr. T. L. Bradford. Hahnemann. Month., Phila., 1892, vol. xxvii. Port. in the Surg.-gen. Lib., Wash., D. C.

Thomas, Charles Widgery (1816–1866).

Judge William Widgery, of Portland, was a sagacious man, who had been in turn lawyer, judge of common pleas, officer of a privateer in the Revolution, member of the Massachusetts General Court, and of the United States Congress. He had a daughter, Elizabeth, who married one Elias Thomas, of Portland. Their son, Charles Widgery Thomas, was born February 14, 1816, graduated from Bowdoin in 1834, and delivered the salutatory address in Latin.

He excelled so much in foreign languages that after his graduation he was offered a tutorship in German, but preferred to practice medicine, so studied with Dr. John Taylor Gilman, attended lectures at the Medical School of Maine; at the Berkshire Medical College in Massachusetts, and finally obtained his degree from the Medical School of Maine in 1837. He settled in Portland, and labored there the rest of his life with the exception of a winter spent at a post graduate course in Philadelphia.

He was chosen city physician and practised in that post for several years, gaining a deep knowledge of the diseases attached to poverty, and attaining the best medical skill. In 1863 in conjunction with Dr. Theodore Harmon Jewett, of South Berwick, he examined all the recruits in the Portland District and was very shrewd in his detection of malingers. When Dr. Jewett resigned, Dr. Thomas took entire charge of this onerous work, which gradually broke down his health. Thus enfeebled, he had an attack of tonsillitis, with diphtheritic exudation, which passed away so soon that he was apparently on the road to health, when he was suddenly attacked with diphtheritic paralysis, and died, to the sorrow of a large clientage and of his numerous friends. Leaving behind him a father aged ninety-seven: he was gone like a flash.

Thomas was known always as a wise, safe and discreet physician, as a courteous and honorable man. He was good to the younger physicians. Inheriting the fun and humor of his family, he was cheerful and mirthful to a high degree. He was a very versatile man, fond of music, had a fine voice and with his brother, George, made music fit for the gods. He was a witty man, like many others of his family. He was epigrammatic on occasions. His brother George had an enormous and finely cultivated basso voice. When Dr. Thomas heard that George was to sing in St. Stephen's Church, he said as if by inspiration:

"Ye Bulls of Bashan now retire:
"For Brother George has joined the choir."

Calling upon a patient, he found her worrying in an old fashioned, four-post bed. Believing that she had an exanthem, which would not break out by the aid of the usual remedies, he set out to accomplish this miracle by startling the patient in a most extraordinary fashion. Taking off his coat and waistcoat, he gave an enormous jump, caught hold of one of the bed posts, and, with a herculean effort, vaulted across the bed, patient and all, and landed safely on the other side. "Why, what is the matter with you. doctor, are you crazy?" cried the patient. "Nothing is the matter with me, madam, but you have now got the measles." In point of fact, the rapidly advancing redness of her face and neck soon convinced her that Dr. Thomas was right, and that mental excitement often has curious effects upon the bodily frame.

J. A. S.

Trans. Maine Med. Assoc., 1866–8, Portland, 1869.

Thomas, Theodore Gaillard (1831–1903).

T. Gaillard Thomas, gynecologist, was born on Edisto Island, Charleston, South Carolina, November 21, 1831, a lineal descendant of the Rev. Samuel Thomas, who in 1794 was sent by the Church of England as a missionary to establish the Episcopal Church in South Carolina. His father, was the Rev. Edward Thomas, a clergyman of the Episcopal Church. Through his mother he was descended from Joachim Gaillard, a Huguenot, who went to South Carolina after the revocation of the Edict of Nantes.

Educated in the Charleston, South Carolina, College, he left there in the senior year to enter the Medical College of the State of South Carolina, where he graduated in 1852.

After completing his internship at Bellevue Hospital (which began during the epidemic of typhus fever) and Ward's Island, New York Hospital, he went to Europe, going over on a sailing ship and returning on a large emigrant vessel as surgeon. He remained in Europe nearly two years, visiting and serving as interne in the different hospitals, giving special attention to obstetrics in the Rotunda Hospital at Dublin.

Upon his return to New York he established, with Dr. Donoghue, a quiz class in connection with the University of New York, which was very successful and attracted much attention. Later he formed a partnership with Dr. J. F. Metcalf, who was then the leading general practitioner of the city. This association continued for fifteen years.

He devoted himself especially to obstetrics, being professor of that specialty in the University Medical College for eight years, succeeding Dr. Bedford in 1855. In 1863 he was appointed professor of obstetrics, diseases of women and children, at the College of Physicians and Surgeons, until the chair of diseases of women was established, when he was elected to fill it. In 1870 he did a vaginal ovariotomy.

In 1872 he was elected attending surgeon to the Women's Hospital, when he practically gave up general practice to devote himself to gynecology.

He married Mary Willard, of Troy, New York, in 1862.

From 1872 until 1887 he was attending surgeon of the Women's Hospital in the State of New York, when he resigned and continued to operate in private practice until 1900. He was consultant at the Presbyterian, French, the New York Lying-in, Skin and Cancer and Memorial Hospitals.

He was a member of the New York City Medical Society, New York Pathological Society, New York Academy of Medicine, New York Obstetrical Society, New York State Medical Association, and American Gynecological Society, corresponding fellow of the Obstetrical Societies of Philadelphia, Louisville and Boston, and honorary fellow of the British Gynecological Society.

He died February 28, 1903; a widow, with two sons, J. Metcalf and Thomas Gaillard, Jr., survived him.

His largest writing was the "Practical Treatise on the Diseases of Women,"

Philadelphia, 1868, which was translated into French, German, Italian, Spanish and Chinese and of which over 60,000 copies were sold. His articles included: "A History of Nine Cases of Ovariotomy," 1869. "Gastro-elytrotomy, a Substitute for the Cesarean Section," 1870; "Comparison of the Results of Cesarean Section and Laparo-elytrotomy in New York," 1878; "A New Method of Removing Interstitial and Sub-mucous Fibroids of the Uterus," 1879, etc.

A tolerably full list is given in the "Surgeon-general's Catalogue," Washington, District of Columbia.

P. F. C.

Am. J. Obstet., 1903, vol. xlvii (port.).
Tr. Am. Gyn. Soc., 1903, vol. xxviii.
N. Y. Jour. Gyn. and Obstet., 1891-2, vol. i.

Thomas, Willam George (1818–1890).

He was born March 23, 1818, in Louisburg, North Carolina, where he received a common school education and studied medicine with Dr. Wiley Perry, taking his medical degree at the University of Pennsylvania in 1840 and first practising in Tarboro, North Carolina, where he remained until 1850, then removed to Wilmington, North Carolina.

He was a founder of the State Medical Society, and one of the first vice-presidents and later president. His writings are few. The only lengthy paper is an account of the yellow-fever epidemic in Wilimington (1862), prepared in reply to Dr. E. K. Anderson. From the beginning Dr. Thomas became dominated in his practice by two ideas; first, to study climatic diseases, and second, to pay attention to obstetrics and diseases of women. He was bold in the use of quinine, giving five grains every two or three hours in the remission stage of marlarial fever—a practice unheard of at that day (1852); and in his frequent application of the obstetric forceps.

Dr. Thomas was a pioneer in gynecology. Before Marion Sims, he actually employed wire sutures for a vesico-vaginal fistula, his "duck-bill" speculum having been made by a local blacksmith.

He was diligent in his labors and skill-ful—sympathetic in manner and hand-some in appearance, his physical vigor enhanced by much horse-back riding. His marked characteristics were truth and moral courage.

He married, in 1843, Mary Summer Clark, and had three children. One of these, Dr. George Gillett Thomas, became a surgeon.

Dr. Thomas died of laryngeal diph-theria in 1890.   H. A. R.

Eminent Men of the Carolinas.
In memoriam,North Car. M. J., Wilmington, 1890, vol. xxv.
Obituary. Tr. M. Soc., N. Car., 1890, Wilmington, 1891 (port.).
Portrait also in the Surg.-gen. Lib., Wash., D. C.

Thompson, Jesse **C.** (1811–1879).

The parents of J. C. Thompson were of Scotch-Irish extraction, natives of Frank-lin county, Massachusetts. Jesse C. was born in Heath, in the same county, January 9, 1811. His father owned a farm, on which Dr. Thompson passed his boyhood.

He had mapped out for himself the study and practice of medicine as a life work, and in the summer of 1834 he began to read medicine with Drs. Bates and Fitch, at Charlemont, near his home, attending his first course of lectures at Berkshire Medical College, Pittsfield, Massachusetts. He graduated at Berk-shire Medical College and practised in Bloomfield, Pickaway County, forty-two years.

A keen observer and close student, his many years' experience gave him a prominent place in the counsels of all neighboring practitioners, who regarded his advice and opinion with great respect. In surgery he ranked as a wise, careful, and successful operator. He success-fully performed the operation of exsec-tion of the head of the humerus, leaving the patient—a young laboring man— with a useful hand and arm; besides many others demanding the greatest skill and surgical knowledge. It was his pride and profound satisfaction that in

a career so long and practice so varied, he left no cripples behind. On June 6, 1838, he married Emily Sage, and had five children. He died January 7, 1879. Once he did a Cesarean section under most difficult circumstances. The pa-tient lived in a small cabin on a farm several miles distant from Circleville and from Bloomfield. The doctor was called late at night, found his patient, who had been in labor many hours, in a state of collapse. Knowing it to be impossible to obtain professional assistance in time, he deemed it necessary to operate with-out delay, and, with no help except that of a few women of the neighborhood, and only the poor light of two or three tallow candles, be proceeded with the instru-ments in his pocket case to make the necessary incision. He encountered no difficulty, and the patient made an unin-terrupted and speedy recovery. The child was alive and grew into a strong and lusty youth.   R. B. W.

Thompson, **Mary Harr**is (1829–1895).

The first woman who specialized in surgery and remarkable for her splendid organizing and administrative ability. Little is known of her early life beyond the simple fact of her birth at Fort Ann, New York State, and of her education at West Poultney Academy, Vermont.

In 1859, at the age of thirty, she began to study medicine at the New England Female Medical College. Dr. Zakrz-ewska, at that time professor of obstetrics there, wrote, "Dr. Thompson commenced her studies with me in 1859. She gradu-ated from the Woman's Medical College of Pennsylvania, serving a year as interne with Dr. Emily Blackwell. She was the first woman surgeon who performed capital operations entirely on her own responsibility."

Mary Thompson began to practise in Chicago in 1863 and two years later founded a hospital for women and chil-dren. The building which housed this work was swept away in the fire of 1871 and within twenty-four hours the Relief and Aid Society sent an appeal to Dr.

Thompson to re-establish it, the Society offering to provide means; during this period of tremendous emergency, first a house and later a barracks was utilized and the sick, maimed and burned were brought to the building before beds could be put in. In 1873 when the erection of permanent quarters was contemplated, the Relief and Aid Society gave $25,000 on condition that twenty-five patients should be cared for constantly. Dr. Thompson also visited Boston; her appeal there meeting with generous response, and the institution which bears her name, the Mary Thompson Hospital of Chicago for Women and Children, was soon an accomplished fact. Thirty years Dr. Thompson labored there, doing all the surgical work, with wonderful precision and dexterity of manipulation.

But professional eminence was not her only claim to remembrance; her philanthropy was catholic, and she was also a firm suffragist and agitated the question among her pupils.

The Chicago Medical College Department of North West University conferred a degree on Dr. Thompson in recognition of her work, the only one it had ever granted to a woman. She also became a member of the Internation Medical Association in 1887, and of the Chicago Medical Society.

Dr. Thompson passed away in the midst of her activities after an illness of only twenty-four hours on May 21, 1895.

Several years after her death a memorial bust of Dr. Thompson, the work of the well-known sculptor, Daniel C. French, was presented by her friends to the Art Institute of Chicago.

A. B. W.

Woman's Journal, Boston, vol. xxvi, p. 229.
Chicago Medical Rec., Feb., 1905.
Personal communication

Thompson, Robert (1797–1865).

Robert Thompson, a physician of Columbus, Ohio, was born in Washington County, Pennsylvania, September, 1797. His literary education was slight, his medical instruction acquired with Dr. George McCook, of New Lisbon, Ohio. He was licensed to practise medicine and surgery in 1824 by the Fourteenth District Medical Society of Ohio, and in 1834 received from the Medical College of Ohio the honorary M. D. He married, in 1824, Ann M. Seeber, of New York State, and settled first at Pleasant Hill, Muskingum, County, Ohio, but removed thence to Washington, Guernsey County, and finally, in 1834, settled in Columbus.

In 1831 he was elected to the State Senate, and was for many years physician to the State Asylum for the Deaf and Dumb.

Dr. Thompson was one of the founders of the Ohio State Medical Society, and its president in 1847.

He is said to have been a very competent surgeon and extremely ingenious in the invention of new surgical instruments and apparatus. Among the latter were a bone forceps, a tonsillotome, uvula scissors, a cornea knife, a cataract needle, a tourniquet, a trephine and a popular and useful abdominal supporter.

He was a fluent and ready writer, and numerous contributions from his pen will be found in the "Transactions of the State Medical Society." Among these, the more important are:

"On Mesmerism." ("Western Lancet," 1843, vol. ii.).

"Resection of the Left Superior Maxillary Bone." ("Transactions of Ohio State Medical Society," 1849.)

"Choloroform, Gutta Percha and Collodion." (Ibid., 1849.)

"Report on Medical Literature." (Ibid., 1851.)

"Nitrate of Silver in Diseases of the Lungs." (Ibid., 1855.)

"Chloroform." (Ibid., 1857.)

"Cataract." (Ibid., 1859.)

"Report on Fractures." (Ibid., 1859.)

He died in Columbus, Ohio, August 18, 1865.   H. E. H.

Cincinnati Lancet and Observer, vol. ix, 1866.
Transactions of the Ohio State Medical Society, 1867.
Transactions of the American Medical Association, 1867.

Thomson, **Adam** (———— -1767).

He was born and educated in Scotland; the date of birth has not been ascertained. In his memorable and eloquent "Discourse on the Preparation of the Body for the Small-pox," he refers to "the Famous Monro of Edinburgh" as one of his first masters in the healing art.

He settled in Prince George's County, in the Province of Maryland, early in the eighteenth century. In 1748 he went to Philadelphia where he continued to practice, his services being in demand throughout the colonies because of his eminence and success as an inoculator.

In 1738 he began his method of preparing the body for small-pox. It consisted of a two weeks' course of treatment or "cooling regimen" preparatory to inoculation, to wit: a light, non-stimulating diet, the administration of a combination of mercury and antimony, and moderate bleeding and purgation. He[1] admitted that Boerhaave's Aphorism No. 1392 advanced the "hint" that mercury and antimony properly prepared and administered "might act as an antidote for the variolous contagion." Dr. Thomson's phenomenal success with the method convinced him that "mercury under proper managment is more of a specific agent against the effects of the variolous than the venereal poison." He was careful to give it within the bounds of salivation and to modify the regimen to suit the patient's age and constitution.

In his "Discourse" he says: "On every occasion for the space of twelve years where I have been called to prepare people for receiving the small-pox, either in the natual way or by inoculation— having prepared many for both—I have constantly used such a mercurial and antimonial medicine as Boerhaave has described, and I can honestly declare that

[1] Boerhaave's 1392'd Aphorism. Some success from antimony and mercury prompts us to seek for a specific for the small-pox in a combination of these two minerals reduced by art to an active, but not to an acrimonious or corrosive state.

I never saw one so prepared in any danger under the disease."[1]

His explanation of the manner in which immunity is acquired against small-pox is most interesting, and suggests to readers of to-day Pasteur's exhaustion hypothesis. He states: "It seems to me highly probable that there is a certain quantity of an infinitely subtle matter which may be called the variolous fuel, equally, intimately and universally diffused through the blood of every human creature; in some more, in others less, that lies still and quiet in the body never showing itself in any manner hitherto discovered until put in action by the variolous contagion, at which time it is totally expelled by the course of the disease."

He found the average medical practitioner of America poorly educated, and therefore a source of danger in the community. He recommends in the discourse that the Legislature interpose in behalf of the safety of the people and appoint proper persons to judge of the qualifications of those permitted to practise.

Dr. Thomson delivered his "Discourse on the Preparation of the Body for the Small-pox" before the trustees and others in the Academy of Philadelphia, on Wednesday, the twenty-first of November, 1750.[2] It was published by Benjamin Franklin, and was reprinted in London in 1752, and in New York in 1757. It met with favorable reviews in America, England and France. Dr. Thacher ("American Medical Biography," vol. i, p. 66, 1828) refers to the "Discourse" in the following manner: "This production was highly applauded both in Ameria and Europe, as at that period (1750) the practice of inoculation was on the de-

[1] Dr. Thomson makes a similar assertion in a letter which appeared in the Md. Gaz., Nov. 25, 1762.

[2] An original Franklin print of the Discourse is on file in the Library of the surgeon-general's office, Washington, D. C. Copies of it may be seen in the Libraries of the Johns Hopkin's Hospital and of the Medical and Chirurgical Faculty of Maryland.

cline. The author states that inoccula-
tion was so unsuccessful at Philadelphia
that many were disposed to abandon
the practice; wherefore, upon the suggestion of the 1392'd Aphorism of Boerhaave, he (Thomson) was led to prepare
his patients by a composition of antimony
and mercury, which he had constantly
employed for twelve years, with unin-
terrupted success."

Drs. Redman and Kearsley, of Philadelphia, and others, first opposed the
method, but later it was universally
adopted in the colonies and was favorably
received in England. It soon became
known as the American method for inoculation and was introduced as routine procedure in the first Inoculating Hospitals
which were established near Boston,
Massachusetts, in February, 1764. Dr.
William Barnett was called from Philadelphia to supervise the work because of
his reputation there as a successful inoculator. He used Dr. Thomson's method,
but was not generous enough to admit
the fact. (See address, Quinan, "Maryland Medical Journal," vol. x, p. 115,
1883.) In England the method was
highly recommended by Huxham, Woodward and others.

Woodville in "History of the Inoculation of the Small-pox in Great
Britain" (p. 341, 1796) quotes from Dr.
Gale's "Dissertation on the Inoculation
of the Small-pox in America," as follows:
"Before the use of mercury and antimony in preparing persons for inoculation one out of one hundred of the inoculated died, but since only one out of eight
hundred," and (ibid., p. 342) by last
accounts, 3,000 had recovered from inoculation in the new method by the use of
mercury and antimony and five only had
died, viz.: children under five years of
age." Dr. Gale and others conceded
Dr. Thomson to be the most successful
inoculator in America.

Thomson married the widow of James
Warddrop, of Virginia. She was Lettice
Lee, daughter of Philip Lee, of Virginia,
a great granddaughter of Richard Lee,
the emigrant. After Thomson's death

she married Col. Joseph Sims. She had
issue only by Dr. Thomson, Mary Lee and
Alice Corbin.

Dr. Adam Thomson died in New York
City on the eighteenth of September, 1767.
The following notice of his death ap-
peared three days later in the "New York
Mercury:"

"On Friday morning early, died here,
Adam Thomson, Esq., a physician of distinguished abilities in his profession, well
versed in polite literature, and of unblem-
ished honor and integrity as a gentleman."   H. L. S.

Dr. Adam Thomson (H. Lee Smith), Johns
Hopkins Hosp. Bull., 1909, vol. xx.
Amer. Med. Biography (Thacher), vol. i,
1828.
Condamine. Discourse referred to in Hist.
de. inoc. in Mem. de l'Acad., p. 521, 1765.
Cordell, Dr. E. F. The Med. Annals of
Maryland, 1903.
Gale, Dr. Benjamin. Trans. Philos. Soc.,
London, vol. lv.
Hamilton, Dr. Alexander. A Defense of
Dr. Thomson's Discourse on the Preparation
of the Body for Small-pox, Annapolis. Pub.
by Bradford, Philadelphia, 1751.
Lee of Virginia. By Edmund Jennings
Lee, M. D., Franklin Printing Co., Phila.,
1895.
Monthly Review of London, Apr., 1752.
Med. and Phys. Journal, London, 1752
Norris, Dr. George W. The Early Hist. of
Med. in Phila., 1886.
Quinan, Dr. Jno. R. The Med. Annals of
Md., 1885. Md. Med. Jour., vol. x, 1883.
Smith, James. Address to Mem. of Leg. of
Md., vol. viii, 1818.
Smith, Margaret Vowell. Capt. John Haw-
kins' American Monthly Magazine, May,
1895.
St. Andrew's Soc. of the State of N. Y. His-
torical Sketch, Centennial Celebration, 1856,
N. Y.
Thomson, Adam. A Discourse on the
Preparation of the Body for the Small-pox,
and the manner of receiving the Infection,
as it was delivered in the Publick Hall of
the Academy, before the Trustees and others,
on Wednesday the twenty-first of November,
1750, Phila. B. Franklin and D. Hall, 1750.
Woodville, Hist. of Inoc. of the Small-pox in
Great Britain, 1796.

Thomson, Samuel (1769-1843).

Associated with a system called the
Thomsonian and as having implicit
faith in steam and in lobelia as curative
agents Thomson should not by any

means be deemed a quack if the term means a vain and tricky practitioner, for he told all he knew in as plain a manner as possible and acquired much knowledge of hitherto unknown virtues of plants. He experimented on himself, then published the results, leaving others to form their own opinions.

He was born on February 9, 1769, in Olstead, Cheshire County, New Hampshire, the son of John and Hannah Cobb Thomson. He began early as an herbalist for, discovering by self experimentation when four years old the emetic properties of lobelia, he amused himself inducing boy friends to chew it, and made further researches as a boy by associating with an old woman herbalist, the only "doctor" in that wild region. When sixteen he offered himself as a pupil to a "root doctor," one Fuller of Westmoreland, but owing to deficient education was refused. Later, he bought a farm in Surrey and married. In 1796 his second child having scarlet fever and the doctor (Bliss) practically giving up the case, Thomson made his first experiment with steam and saved the girl. After that, wise in herbal lore, particularly that relating to lobelia he became a traveling doctor riding on horseback through New Hampshire, Maine, Vermont and Massachusetts, first patenting his remedies at Washington. He finally settled down to practise in Beverly, Massachusetts, and naturally met with opposition among the faculty though he also made converts to his system who, as he did, used lobelia emetics, sweating, capsicum, composition powder and hot drops. The author was once in jail on a charge of murder by lobelia poisoning but was acquitted and afterwards opened an office and infirmary in Boston. For twenty years the Thomsonian System flourished in New England, such men as Benjamin Waterhouse and Samuel L. Mitchill, in their private correspondence approving with reservations of the System and unreservedly of the author's frankness and zeal.

Thomson passed from life on October 4, 1843, heroically partaking of his own remedies to the very end.

"His New Guide to Health" was first issued in 1822 and, passing through various editions with enlargements, became "Thomson's Materia Medica or Botanic Family Physician," which reached a thirteenth edition edited by Dr. John Thomson, his son. Two journals were started, "The Botanic Watchman," in 1834, and the "Thomsonian Recorder," 1833, which furnish curious and amusing reading.   D. W.

Bull. of the Lloyd Library, Reproduction Series, No. 7, 1909.
History of the Healing Art, Dr. Gardner C. Hill, 1904.
The Botanic Watchman, vol. i, 1834.

Thomson, William (1833–1902?).

William Thomson was born in Chambersburg, Pennsylvania, January 28, 1833, one of the three sons of Alexander Thomson, judge of the Sixteenth Judicial District of the State, and Jane Graham. He studied medicine at the Jefferson Medical College, and graduated M. D. in 1853, and early attracted the attention of Dr. John Kearsley Mitchell, being led by him to take over the practic of Dr. Clark, of Merion, on the Pennsylvania Railroad, where he settled as a country physician. Four years later he married Rebecca George, a member of a well-known family of Friends then living on the original grant of land from William Penn to their ancestor.

In the summer of 1861, as assistant surgeon, with rank as lieutenant, he entered the regular service, just before the disaster of Bull Run. He served in this position in the Army of the Potomac and in Washington and Alexandria until, in 1862, he joined Gen. McClellan's headquarters as chief of staff to the medical director, Jonathan Letterman. He was present throughout the Peninsula campaign and at Antietam.

In 1863 he was placed as surgeon in charge of the Douglas Hospital, Washington, and in 1864 made medical inspector at Washington, which contained in its various hospitals over 23,600 beds. In

1866 he organized a hospital for the treatment of cholera, and had charge of the Post Hospital.

After a brief stay on duty in Louisiana, he resigned in 1868 and was elected a fellow of the College of Physicians of Philadelphia in April, 1869. ˋ While in Washington he was largely interested in the Army Medical Museum, —the creation of John H. Brinton—and was the largest contributor to the first published catalogue, for which he wrote valuable descriptions of osteomyelitis and wounds of joints.

With his friend, William Norris, he had utilized photography in the study of wounds, and had induced the surgeon-general to establish, in connection with the museum, a photographic bureau. Thomson and Norris were the first to make negatives by the wet process of the field of the microscope with high and low powers, and led the way to the splendid success obtained later through the resources of the surgeon-general's office. These studies in optics finally dominated the future of Thomson and Norris, and led to their practice and teaching of ophthalmic surgery.

Dr. Thomson, thus led by his mastery of photography to a close study of optics, began soon to display that facility of resource in ophthalmic medicine which characterized all he did.

Early in his career, his attention was directed to the subjective methods of determining the static refraction of the eye, and in 1870 he described a test for ametropia based on the experiment of Scheiner, and later in the same year brought his method to the notice of the members of the American Ophthalmological society.

In 1902 he brought before this society a new apparatus for the correction of ametropia, and upon its constant improvement he spent much time during the last years of his life, working at it almost until the day of his death. In 1896 he wrote his important article on "The Detection of Color Blindness."

Two institutions in Philadelphia are especially indebted to one work of William Thomson, namely, the Wills Eye Hospital, with which he became connected in 1868, and the Jefferson Medical College, with which he was identified from 1873 until 1897, first as lecturer on diseases of the eye, later as honorary professor of ophthalmology, and finally, in 1895, as full professor of ophthalmology, with a seat in the faculty.

He was a member of the Philosophical Society, the Academy of Natural Sciences, honorary member of the New York Neurological Society, sometime physician to the Episcopal Hospital.

A list of his ophthalmic papers is given in the "Transactions of the College of Physicians," of Philadelphia, 3 s., 1909, vol. xxxi. They include: Chapter on Diseases of the Eye in Gross' "Surgery" (fifth edition); "Test for Diagnosis of Ametropia, with Instrument;" "Ophthalmoscope in Diagnosis of Intracranial Lesions;" "History of First Case of Tumor of Brain Diagnosticated with the Ophthalmoscope in Philadelphia;" "Astigmatism as a Cause of Persistent Headache" (with Mitchell); "Connection between Posterior Staphyloma and Astigmatism;" "Correction of Conical Cornea by Sphero-cylindrical Glasses;" "Rapid Diagnosis of Refraction with a New Instrument;" "System Adopted by the Pennsylvania Railroad in 1880 for Examination of Employees for Color-blindness, Vision and Hearing, with Instruments, Color-stick, etc.;" "Supplement to Nettleship on Diseases of the Eye;" "Edition of Ophthalmological Part of Annual of Medical Sciences" (1889); "New Wool Test for Detecting Color-blindness;" "Normal Color Sense and Detection of Color-blindness in Norris and Oliver's System;" Chapter on Diseases of Eye in "American Text-book of Surgery;" "Relation of Ophthalmology to Practical Medicine;" "Use of Circles of Diffusion for Correcting Ametropia, with an Instrument."

S. W. M.

Tr. Coll. of Phys. of Phila., 1909, vol. xxxi (S. W. Mitchell).

Tr. Am. Ophth. Soc., Phila., 1909, vol. xii.

Thornton, Matthew (1714-1803).

The last name to be signed to that memorable document, the Declaration of Independence, was that of Matthew Thornton, born in Ireland in 1714. His father emigrated to this country in 1717, and settled in Wiscasset, Maine. From there they removed to Worcester, Massachusetts, where Matthew received his education. Here he studied medicine and settled in Londonderry, New Hampshire, where he acquired an extensive practice and became conspicuous for professional skill as well as the distinction of being an aggressive and public-spirited patriot.

Dr. Thornton shared in the perils of the expedition against Louisburg as surgeon of the New Hampshire Division of the army.

When the political crisis arrived, Thornton abjured the British interests. He was a member of the convention which declared New Hampshire to be a sovereign state, and was elected its president.

He served in the Continental Congress from 1776-1778 and in the latter year resigned to accept the chief-justiceship of Hillsborough County. He held this position only two years, resigning to accept a position on the supreme bench of the state. In 1783 Thornton was elected a member of the State House of Representatives and the next year a member of the State Senate.

In 1780 he purchased a farm on the banks of the Merrimac near Exeter and spent the remainder of his life there, dying in Newburyport, Massachusetts, while on a visit to his daughter, on June 24, 1803.

I. J. P.

Biog. of the Signers to the Declaration of Independence, Phila., 1849.

Thornton, William (1761-1828).

Born on Tortola Island in the West Indies, May 27, 1761, he held the Edinburgh M. D. and after graduation continued his medical studies in Paris and traveled extensively through Europe, then came to the United States, married in 1790 and returned to Tortola. In 1793 he returned to Washington and that same year published his "Elements of Written Language," and afterwards many papers on other subjects, including medicine, astronomy, philosophy, finance, government and art. He was also associated with Fitch in early experiments in running boats by steam. Always inventive, he was wisely put in charge of United States patents from the passage of the Act of Congress 1802 till his death; and during the War of 1814 was the means of preserving the records of the Patent Office from destruction by the British. He was the first architect of the Capitol, as also its designer; and of many buildings in the District of Columbia and elsewhere.

In 1794 he was appointed by Washington one of the three commissioners of the District of Columbia. He died March 27, 1828.

D. S. L.

Appleton's Medical Biog., 1889.
Hist. of the U. S. Capitol, Glenn Brown, 1900.

Tilden, Daniel (1788-1870).

Daniel Tilden was born in Lebanon, Grafton County, New Hampshire, August 19, 1788. The boy was compelled to share in the general work of the family. Nevertheless, by perseverance he was able to secure the A. B. from Clinton College, New York, and in 1807 began to study medicine with Dr. Joseph White of Cherry Valley, New York. His first course of medical lectures was taken in the College of Physicians and Surgeons of the Western District of New York, just organized at Fairfield, Herkimer County, and his M. D. he received from the medical Department of Dartmouth College in 1812. In the same year Dr. Tilden was examined by the State Board of Regents of the State of New York and received their diploma; in 1827 he was granted an honorary M. D. by the Berkshire Medical College of Massachusetts. In 1817 he removed to Ohio and settled first in Erie County at a place now known as Cooke's Corners, but in 1825 removed to Norwalk, Huron County, and in 1839 to Sandusky, where he continued in practice until a short time before his death.

Dr. Tilden was a fine specimen of the doctor of the old school as developed on the western reserve, ready, staunch, faithful to duty. He was president of the Ohio State Medical Society in 1856, president of the Erie County Medical Society for many years, and an honorary member of the New York State Medical Society. He also served in the State Senate from 1828 to 1835. He died full of years and honors May 7, 1870.

H. E. H.

Transactions of Ohio State Medical Society, 1870. Obituary by Dr. E. B. Stevens. No portrait of Dr. Tilden is known to the writer, nor have any literary productions from his pen been preserved.

Tilton, James (1745–1822).

James Tilton, surgeon-general of the army, was one of the first recipients of M. D. from the Philadelphia School of Medicine. Practitioner in Dover, Delaware, he entered the army in 1776 as surgeon of the Delaware Regiment, with which he saw much service until his promotion in 1778 to the grade of hospital surgeon, in which capacity he proved of much value, strenuously opposing the combination of purveyor and director-general in one person and the overcrowding of hospitals; from the latter cause he himself acquired typhoid. While commanding hospitals at Trenton and New Windsor he introduced the hut system, and upon the reorganization of the medical department in 1780 was appointed senior hospital physician and surgeon. Perhaps he is best known by his untiring efforts to secure army medical organization reform. While serving with the forces in Virginia he was present at the capitulation of Yorktown and mustered out in 1782. This was followed by one term in Congress and many re-elections to the Legislature, during which period he was engaged in civilian practice with horticulture as a recreation. 1812 saw his

brochure upon "Economical Observations on Military Hospitals, and the Prevention and Cure of Diseases Incident to an Army," which made so deep an impression as to cause his appointment as physician and surgeon-general of the army in 1813. By personal inspection and supervision he enormously improved the sanitary conditions of the army and materially reduced the sick rate. He served several times as president of his State Medical Society.

During the latter part of his service as physician and surgeon-general he developed malignant growths which prevented further active service until mustered out at the close of the war. One of these growths affected his lower extremity, necessitating its amputation, during the course of which the patient supervised and directed the operation with unexampled fortitude. He died at his home near Wilmington, at the ripe age of seventy-seven.   J. E. P.

Pilcher, James Evelyn, Journal of the Association of Military Surgeons of the United States, vol. xiv, 1904, portrait, and The Surgeon-Generals of the United States Army, Carlisle, Pa., 1905, portrait.

Toland, Hugh H. (1806–1890).

Hugh H. Toland has been styled by some "the great surgeon of the Pacific slope." He was born on his father's plantation, Guilder's Creek, South Carolina, April 6, 1806, the fourth of ten children. His father, John Toland, emigrated from the north of Ireland, and came to South Carolina after the War of Independence. Hugh read medicine under Dr. George Ross, and helped in the doctor's drug store, afterwards going to Transylvania University of Lexington, Kentucky, taking his degree while barely of age. In 1829 he settled in Pageville, South Carolina, and during this time performed several important operations which gave him considerable reputation in the neighborhood. This circumstance gave the young doctor a desire to perfect himself in surgery, and, determining to go to Paris, he utilized his time. During the two years at Pageville Dr. Toland saved about three thousand dollars, and in the spring of 1833 he sailed for France and sought quarters in Rue de l'École de Médicine, Paris, where he lived economically for the next two years and a half, and applied his time in constant attendance under illustrious surgeons in the hospital clinics.

During the succeeding twelve years, Dr. Toland practised alone, and married Mary Goodwin, who lived only a few years. In 1844 he married Mary Avery, of Columbia, who in 1852 accompanied him to California.

Early in 1852 the doctor purchased a quartz mill and had it shipped to San Francisco but his mining ventures never succeeded, so he settled in San Francisco. Until 1860 Dr. Toland included obstetrical cases in his practice, but determined to give this up on account of the disturbance of his night's rest. At this time he married his third wife, Mrs. Mary B. M. Gridley. On the breaking out of the Civil War in 1861, Dr. Toland's annual income was over forty thousand dollars. He had been appointed surgeon to the Marine Hospital in 1855, and the appointment was renewed yearly until the establishment of the City and County Hospital, where Toland was appointed visiting surgeon. Patients from the entire Pacific Coast sought the San Francisco City and County Hospital for treatment.

In 1866 he founded a college of Medicine, known for the next six years as "Toland Medical College." He had secured a suitable lot on Stockton, near Chestnut Street. He alone supplied the funds necessary to erect a substantial brick building and to furnish it with the adjuncts deemed requisite.

Toland had, for some years previously, been publishing the "Pacific Medical Journal," and in 1872 it was re-named the "Western Lancet."

Although Dr. Toland was accredited with some sternness of manner when dealing with men patients, his manner toward women and children was exceedingly gentle and sympathetic.

During the seventies there was much written about the power of the iodides in the cure of the later symptoms of syphilis. Dr. Toland vigorously combated this idea and insisted that mercury, and mercury only, was really curative in syphilis at any stage.

As a surgical operator Dr. Toland was rapid, direct and abundantly resourceful in the presence of unexpected developments. To the disinterested witness he perhaps might not appear to be particularly dexterous, but he always knew exactly what he meant to do, and did it in the most direct way. Toland took especial pleasure in operating for urinary calculus, and he always used the lithotome cache double of Dupytren.

He had often expressed the hope that he would not die a lingering death. This hope was realized, for when the final summons came, he was about to go down stairs to begin his daily round of work, when he fell to the floor, expiring at once. Although no autopsy was performed, it was understood that a fainting fit had caused him to fall, striking his forehead violently upon the floor, and causing cerebral hemorrhage. His death caused sincere mourning in many a home.

R. A. McL.

From a sketch of his life, written by Mr. A. Phelps after the doctor's death; and from recollections of personal communications during the last ten years of his life, when the writer was associated with him in practice and in college and hospital work.

Tolmie, William Fraser (1812–1886).

Born at Inverness, Scotland, and educated in Glasgow, from which university he held his L. S. P. and S., he left Scotland for America in 1832, in the service of the Hudson's Bay Company, coming around Cape Horn on a sailing vessel and arriving at Fort Vancouver on the Columbia River, then the chief trading post of the company, in the spring of 1833.

In 1834 he joined the expedition under Mr. Ogden, which traded along the Northwest coast as far as the Russian boundary, establishing trading posts at different points for the Hudson's Bay Company, and after five years as surgeon in Fort Vancouver he visited his native land, and the following year was placed in charge of the Hudson's Bay Company's posts on Puget Sound. He took a prominent part during the Indian war of 1855–56 in pacifying the Indians, being an excellent linguist.

Dr. Tolmie was known to ethnologists for his contributions to the history and linguistics of the native races of the west coast. In 1884 he published, in conjunction with Dr. G. M. Dawson, a nearly complete series of short vocabularies of the principal languages met with in British Columbia. He retained to the day of his death accurate recollections of the stirring events of the early Colonial days, and there was no one so intimate with the Indian affairs of the province.

O. M. J.

Toner, Joseph Meredith (1825–1896).

Toner, himself a faithful biographer of his medical confrères, well deserves that his own biography should be written. He was born on April 30, 1825, in Pittsburg, Pennsylvania, and went as a lad to the Western University, and Mt. St. Mary's College, Maryland. His M. D. was from the Vermont Academy of Medicine, and his A. M. from the Jefferson Medical College. He practised successively at Summit and Pittsburg, Pennsylvania, Harper's Ferry, Virginia, and finally at Washington, District of Columbia, where he established himself in November, 1855. He was president of the American Medical Association; a member of the Medical Society and Medical Association of the District of Columbia; an honorary member of the New York and California State Medical Societies, and of the Boston Gynecological Society. He was a founder of Providence Hospital and St. Ann's Infant Asylum, Washington, to which he was visiting physician, and from 1856 was attending physician to St. Joseph's Orphan Asylum, Washington. In consideration of the perishable character of much of the early medical literature of this country, Dr. Toner devised a scheme for a repository of medical works that should be under the control of the medical profession of the United States and located at the National Capitol. His resolution on that subject was adopted by the American Medical Association in 1868 and resulted in the establishment of the library of that organization. The collection was placed in the Smithsonian Institution and reached the number of several thousand volumes, including pamphlets.

In 1871 Dr. Toner founded the Toner lectures by placing $3000 (which afterwards increased to nearly double that amount) in the hands of trustees charged with the duty of annually procuring two lectures containing new facts valuable to medical science; the interest on the fund, save ten per cent., which was added to the permanent fund, was paid to the authors of the essays. These lectures were included in the regular list of publications of the Smithsonian Institution. It was the first attempt in this country to endow a course of lectures on such conditions. Dr. Toner devoted much time and research to early medical literature, collected over a thousand treatises published before 1800, and besides publishing numerous monographs, had in preparation a "Biographical Dictionary of Deceased American Physicians," of which more than four thousand sketches were completed. He was an authority on the medical, biographical and local history of the District of Columbia and devised a system of symbols of geographical localities adopted by the United States Post Office Department. A member of numerous medical, historical and philosophical associations, he published more than fifty papers and monographs upon subjects of interest to the medical profession.

His more important publications are: "Abortion in a Medical and Moral Aspect;" "Arrest of Development of the Cranial Bones—Epilepsy," 1861; "Maternal Instinct of Love," 1864; "Propriety and Necessity of Compelling

Vaccination;" "History of Inoculation in Pennsylvania," 1865; "Anniversary Oration before the Medical Society of the District of Columbia;" "The Portability of Cholera and Necessity for Quarantine," 1866, joint paper with Charles A. Lee, M. D.; "History of Inoculation in Massachusetts;" "Medical Register of the District of Columbia," 1867; "Address at Dedication of Medical Hall, Washington," 1869; "Necrology of the Physicians of the Late War," 1870; "Medical Register of the United States," 1871; "A Sketch of the Life of Dr. Charles A. Lee;" "Facts of Vital Statistics in the United States, with Diagrams," 1872; "Free Parks, Camping Grounds or Sanitariums for the Sick Children of the Poor in Cities;" "Statistical Sketch of the Medical Profession of the United States;" "Statistics of the Medical Associations and Hospitals of the United States," 1873; "Dictionary of Elevations and Climatic Register;" "Annals of Medical Progress and Education in America;" "Contributions to the Study of Yellow Fever in the United States— Its Distribution; with weather maps," 1874; "Annual Oration before the Medical and Chirurgical Faculty of Maryland," 1875; "Biographical Sketch of Dr. John D. Jackson;" "Medical Men of the Revolution," an address before the Alumni of the Jefferson Medical College, 1876; "Sketch of the Life of Dr. T. M. Logan;" "Biography of Dr. John Morgan, of Philadelphia;" "Address on Biography before the International Medical Congress," 1876; "Rocky Mountain Medical Association;" and a "Memorial Volume with a Biography of Its Members," 1877; also addresses before various societies and colleges.

In 1874 he placed a gold medal, struck at the United States Mint and bearing his likeness, at the disposal of the Faculty of Jefferson Medical College to be awarded annually to the student producing the best thesis based upon original research. In the same year he established a medal to be granted annually by the faculty of the University of Georgetown, District of Columbia, to the student who should collect and name the greatest number of specimens in any department of the natural sciences. In 1882 he gave his entire library, including manuscripts, to the United States Government. It consisted of 28,000 books and 18,000 pamphlets.

Parvin ("Transactions of the seventy-fifth Anniversary, of the Medical Society of the District of Columbia," 1894, p. 22) says of Toner:

"He was one whose genial manners, generous heart and kindly deeds have endeared him to all who have known him; one who had made for himself a name in the profession by important historical researches, and by his large and valuable collection of medical works donated to the public," Congress, in acknowledgement of the doctor's present to the nation of 28,000 books and pamphlets, ordered both his bust and portrait to be made and placed in the Library of Congress—a just and honorable recognition of his great and generous gift. He should be held in honored rememberance as the faithful historian, who through years of painstaking and laborious investigations collated the early history of the profession in this district, from municipal and national records, newspaper publications, family reminiscences, legend and tradition. He verified and arranged these data with such accuracy and completeness in an address delivered September 26, 1866, that it is now and always will be accepted as the standard history of the medical profession of this district prior to 1866."

"No one ever approached, much less equalled him, in the painstaking collection of data, of personal history that might prove of interest, and it was a mystery to many how he managed to have his facts apparently within immediate reach whenever the occasion called for them."

He died at Cresson Springs, Pennsylvania, on July 30, 1896.   D. S. L.

Minutes Medical Society, D. C., October 14 and 21, 1896. Atkinson's Biog., 1878.

Northwestern Medical and Surgical Journal, St. Paul, Minn., 1872-3, iii; Appleton's Biog. 1889, vi; National Medical Review, Washington, D. C., 1896-7, vi. Antisell T. Biographical Sketch of J. M. Toner, Wash., D. C., 1877.

Torrey, John (1798-1873).

John Torrey, best known as a botanist, was the son of Capt. William Torrey, a Revolutionary soldier.

John graduated M. D. in 1818 with a thesis on "Dysentery," and, although eminent as a chemist and mineralogist, it was as a botanist that his fame reached the highest point. Throughout the world he was regarded as one of the foremost in this department of science. His faith in the Holy Scriptures found a firm foundation in the study of nature. The God of the one was the God of the other. If there were difficulties, he knew, if not immediately, they would in time be reconciled. The more closely they were studied, the more positive would be the mutual confirmation.

Among his good works should be mentioned the gift of his valuable and extensive herbarium and his botanical library to Columbia College.

In 1824 he was appointed professor of chemistry, geology, and mineralogy at the Military Academy at West Point. From 1827, when he resigned this position, to 1855, he was professor of chemistry and botany in his alma mater, and subsequently was emeritus professor. From 1830 to 1854 he was professor of chemistry and natural history in the College of New Jersey, Princeton, New Jersey, and in 1853 assayer in the United States Assay Office, and no political change in war or peace disturbed him in this position, to which a son succeeded. He was one of the earlier presidents of the New York Lyceum of Natural History. His published works are numerous and of the highest value. A catalogue of his works, which may be imperfect, is as follows: "Catalogue of Plants Growing Within Thirty Miles of New York," published in 1819; "A Flora of the

Northern and Middle States of North America; or, a Systematic Arrangement and Description of all the Plants Hitherto Discovered in the United States of North America," 1824; "Compendium of the Flora of the Northern and Middle States," 1826; "Cyperaceæ of North America," 1836; "Flora of the State of New York," 2 vols., 1843-4; " Botanical Reports of the Various Land Exploring Expeditions of the United States from 1822 to 1858;" "Appendix to Dr. John Lindley's Introduction to Botany," 1831; "Flora of North America," 1838; This work was edited jointly with Dr. Asa Gray.

Yale College gave him the honorary M. A., in 1823, and Amherst, that of LL. D., in 1845.

Torrey will be remembered by the students of the College of Physicians and Surgeons as an excellent teacher. No man had a better understanding of their character. Were they uproarious—he joined in their glee, and they soon lent an attentive ear. Were they stupid—he was patient and painstaking. Were they rude—he was always a gentleman, and at once commanded respect. He quietly pursued his course, giving us the plain truth in a simple and comprehensive manner. The boys always had a good time in his room, for he relished a joke as much as any of them. In a serious and quiet manner he was closing a lecture with some remarks upon formic acids, when he was interrupted by the reception of a note from one of the students. His eye twinkled, and his benevolent face changed to a smile as he glanced at the question asked. "Is not formic acid an *ant*-acid?" He at once dismissed the class amid shouts of laughter, remarking that he was not prepared to give an immediate answer, but they should have the rest of the hour to themselves.

Torrey's knowledge of old New York was great and interesting. He botanized along the stream which passed from the Collect across Broadway under a bridge to Hudson river, and many a stately mansion now stands in what he knew as a pasture or a wild wood. The city was but a hamlet when he first knew it, and as late as 1831, in the notice of his father's death, the friends are informed that "carriages will be in waiting at St. Paul's church until half-past four o'clock" to take them to 402 Hudson Street to attend the funeral at 5 o'clock.

John Torrey himself died at his house in the grounds of Columbia College on March 10, 1873.

He married a daughter of William Shaw, who came from Dublin, Ireland, by whom he had several children. The first knowledge we have of the Torrey family is that it was known in Spain under the name of Torre. From thence there was an emigration to England. Religious troubles brought a branch to Plymouth, Massachusetts, and the way to New York was found out by a descendant.

From the Med. Reg. of the State of N. York, 1873-4, vol. xi.

Touatre, Just Charles (1838–1901).

Just Charles Touatre, born at Puycasquier, department of Gers, France, on September 2, 1838, received his early education and his degrees of bachelier és lettres and bachelier és sciences, at the Lyceum of Auch, graduating in medicine from La faculté de Paris, March, 1868. Prior to receiving his diploma, he served as auxiliary surgeon and later as surgeon-major on the frégate "Admiral Belloc" and the transport "Polikart."

Soon after graduation, he decided to seek his fortunes in America, which he had visited while serving as marine surgeon. He was attracted naturally to Louisiana by the large element of French speaking people there and though reaching New Orleans while that unfortunate city was still in the throes of the Reconstruction Era, following the war of Secession, he built himself a most prosperons clientèle among the Franco-Louisianan element.

A thoroughly educated man, a physician of ability, he was also a splendid diagnostician. Besides being an excellent physician, he was a delightful *raconteur* and a most pleasant companion at table, or at a medical meeting. When he came to Louisiana, he brought the first clinical thermometer ever used in our state. This was a French naval centigrade thermometer and it became of great use in 1869 when the next yellow fever epidemic appeared. It was by the use of this that his colleague and contemporary, Dr. Charles Faget was able to establish as proven, an observation, which he had made some years previous on the loss of correlation of pulse with temperature in cases of yellow fever.

Later in the severe epidemic of 1878 he rendered such signal services to his compatriots of French birth and origin, that the French Republic recognized these services, by decorating him as an Officer de la Légion d'Honneur. He remained many years after this in Louisiana and it was the pleasure and great advantage of the writer of these notes, to consult with him in 1897 during a small epidemic of yellow fever, which broke out in New Orleans.

His literary work, which is very extensive, was published for many years in different journals. In 1898 Dr. Charles Chassaignac, the editor of the "New Orleans Medical and Surgical Journal," compiled and translated from his articles, a most complete work or monograph on "Yellow Fever," which was published in book form and has remained to this day, a most valuable clinical report. It is specially useful in diagnosis and in treatment, for it proves the theory of absolute rest and horizontal position with no food on the stomach, except flushing the kidneys with water, and that, principally by Vichy water. This book he dedicated to the profession in New Orleans, and was his last serious work.

Feeling the fatigue of practice and having saved an ample competence, in 1898 he left the land of his adoption "la seconde mère," as he loved to call Louisiana, to go and finish his days in la belle France.

He retired from practice, bought a little farm in the country of his birth and became a gentleman farmer. There he died September 21, 1901, away from the friends and admirers in the far-away land, who still remembered him and bitterly mourned his loss.

L. G. L.

Towles, William B. (1847–1893).

This anatomist was born in the County of Fluvanna, Virginia, March 2, 1847, the second son of Dr. W. B. and Harriet Johnson Towles, and was educated in the schools of Buckingham County, studying medicine at the University of Virginia, graduating 1867, within one year after matriculation, a feat admissible in that day, attempted by many but accomplished by very few, as it required great proficiency and stamina. When about seventeen he volunteered in the Confederate Army, and served in a Virginia regiment until the close of the war. He was a member of the Medical Society of Virginia from 1872 until his death.

After graduating he settled in Carroll County, Missouri, and practised successfully for five years, when, at the urgent request of Dr. John S. Davis, professor of anatomy and materia medica at the University of Virginia, he accepted the position of demonstrator of anatomy in the university, and on the death of Dr. Davis in 1885, was elected to succeed him. During the latter years of his life he also filled the chair of anatomy in the University of Vermont, his lectures there being given in the spring after the completion of the course at the University of Virginia. He was repeatedly invited to accept the chair of anatomy in other schools, but always declined.

He was a profound anatomist, and as a demonstrator has never been surpassed in facility and ability to instruct. As a professor he was second only to that great teacher of anatomy, John S. Davis, whose most efficient style of teaching he acquired in a marked degree. His knowledge was not confined to anatomy, for he was well informed in all branches of medicine, and general subjects.

He married in 1880 Mary E. Thompson, of South Carolina, who, with two sons and a daughter, survived him.

He died on September 15, 1893, from hemorrhage of the stomach, after a few hours' illness, having been taken while delivering his first lecture of the session.

He was the author of Towles' "Notes on Anatomy," which were based upon Dr. Davis' lectures, "Syllabus of Notes on Osteology" and "Syllabus of Notes on Materia Medica."

R. M. S.

Trans. Med. Soc. of Va., 1893.

Townsend, David (1753–1829).

David Townsend, son of Shippie and Ann (Balch) Townsend, was born in Boston, June 7, 1753 and died in the same city April 13, 1829. He was descended in the fourth generation from Thomas Townsend of Norfolk, England, who came to Massachusetts in 1637.

He graduated from Harvard College in 1770 and received her honorary M. D., in 1813. He studied medicine under Gen. Joseph Warren and accompanied him as surgeon in Buner's regiment to the battle of Bunker Hill; he was commissioned surgeon to the sixth regiment of foot commanded by Col. Asa Whitcomb, January 1, 1776; was senior surgeon to the General Hospital, Northern department, in March, 1777, and was with the army under Washington during the winter at Valley Forge. On October 9, 1781, he was made surgeon-general of the hospital department. For many years and up to the time of death he was physician in charge of the U. S. Marine Hospital of Massachusetts, in Chelsea.

Dr. Townsend was an active member of the Massachusetts Medical Society from 1775 to 1824, when he retired.

He married Elizabeth Davis, May 24, 1785. Their son, Solomon Davis Townsend, became a noted surgeon of the Massachusetts General Hospital, and there were six other children.

Dr. David Townsend was an ardent Universalist in religion and published a book entitled, "Gospel News," in 1794. He was a Mason and was buried according to their rites, in Revere Beach, at low tide.

W. L. B.

Memorials of the Townsend family, through Charles W. Townsend, M. D., a grandson.
Medical Men of the Revolution, J. M. Toner.

Townsend, Solomon Davis (1793–1869).

Solomon Davis Townsend, performer of the second operation under ether anesthesia in America, was the son of Dr. David and Elizabeth Davis Townsend, and born March 1, 1793. He died September 19, 1869.

He married his cousin, Catherine Wendel Davis, October 5, 1819, and had four children. Charles Wendel Townsend, a grandson, son of Thomas Davis, became a physician in Boston and a noted ornithologist and author.

Solomon Davis graduated from Harvard College in 1811, and took his M. D. there in 1815 after he had served three years as naval surgeon, chiefly in the Mediterranean in the "Independence" under Com. Bainbridge. Here he became a friend of Farragut, then a midshipman, afterwards admiral, and a warm friendship began which lasted through life.

Townsend was a member of the surgical staff of the Massachusetts General Hospital and was present at the first operation performed under ether in 1846.

His home was at 18 Somerset Street, at present occupied by the New England Historic Gynecological Society, of which he was once a member.

W. L. B.

Memorials of the Townsend Family, through Charles W. Townsend, M. D.
Medical Com. Mass. Med. Soc., vol. ii.
Bost. Med. and Surg. Jour., vol. lxxxi.
Portrait in possession of Charles W. Townsend.

Trask, James Dowling (1821–1883).

James Dowling Trask, a fine obstetrician and a co-founder of the American Gynecological Society, was born at Beverly, Massachusetts, on August 16, 1821. He graduated at Amherst College in 1839 and took his A. M. in 1842, and his M. D. from the University of the City of New York in 1844, immediately after beginning practice in Brooklyn. In 1845 he married Jane Cruickshank, daughter of Thomas O'Darrell, K. C. B. of Belfast, Ireland.

From 1847 to 1859 he practised in White Plains, Westchester County, New York, then settled in Astoria, New York City, and became for a few years professor of obstetrics and diseases of women in the Long Island College Hospital until ever increasing private practice compelled him to speak to the medical world through his writings and at the various societies. His writings showed most painstaking labor and fine intellectual quality. His first, "On the Nature of Phlegmasia Dolens" ("American Journal of the Medical Sciences," January, 1847), met with high commendation from O. W. Holmes, and the second, on "Rupture of the Uterus," in the same journal in October, 1847, presented a summary of 303 cases; followed in July, 1856, by a sequel with over one hundred more cases. His "Occlusion and Rigidity of the Os Uteri and Vagina" ("American Journal of the Medical Sciences," July, 1848), was a valuable showing, from sixty-eight cases, that in obstinate rigidity of the os uteri, that incisions are not fraught with danger to the adjacent organs. "Statistics of Placenta Previa" ("Transactions, American Medical Association," 1855), received the prize from this Association and fills ninety-four pages of the "Transactions," and other articles were contributed to the "New York Medical Journal" and the "American Journal of Obstetrics." He was always longing for leisure to write more, but was not very strong during the last five years of his life and died on Sunday morning, September 1, 1883, after an illness of only five days' duration.

Tr. Am. Gyn. Soc., 1883, N. Y., 1884, vol. viii (port.) (F. Barker).

Trevett, Samuel **R.** (1783–1822).

Samuel R. Trevett, surgeon of the United States Navy; educated at Harvard University, and graduated in 1804. He studied medicine under Dr. Holyoke, of Salem, and Dr. John Warren and entered the United States Navy as surgeon's mate. He had a great liking for this service, his heart and soul belonged to it. "His imagination," says Thacher, "was prolific in calling up the brightest visions of the future glories of the American Navy." He served on the "Constitution" during the last year of the War of Independence. During the War of 1812 he was on duty on the same ship and later on the "President." At the close of this war he was appointed surgeon of the Charleston Navy Yard, and in 1822 was ordered as surgeon on the sloop of war "Peacock," but was seized with yellow fever and died at Norfolk, Virginia, November 4, 1822. Trevett was a most able, conscientious and amiable gentleman, an enthusiastic servant to his country and a model of an American naval officer.   A. A.

Thacher, Am. Med. Biogr., Bost., 1828.

Trimble, **James** (1818–1885).

He was born in Tyrone, Ireland, 1818, but little is known of his early life and antecedents except that he studied medicine and having obtained his M. D., entered the British Navy as a surgeon, then resigned his commission and settled in California in 1849—the year of the great gold rush. He practised very successfully in the Golden State until 1858, when he moved to Victoria, then the capital of the Crown Colony of Vancouver Island. No doubt he was induced to take this step by reason of the rich discoveries of gold in the bars of the Fraser River. At this time thousands of miners and adventurers were flocking to Victoria from California, on their way to the new gold fields. He succeeded in the new Colony and soon became well known and popular. For two years he was mayor of Victoria, and when the Crown Colony of British Colum-

bia entered the Dominion of Canada, he again entered the political arena, 1874. Greatly respected and trusted by his fellow members, he was unanimously elected Speaker of the first provincial parliament after Confederation, presiding over the debates with dignity and impartiality. He achieved an enviable reputation as a successful practitioner and for many years was one of the leading members of the profession. Many of the men and women now eminent in British Columbia were ushered into this world by the kindly and learned physician who did so much to uphold the honor of the profession in these early days in Vancouver.

He was a fine example of the pioneer physician and surgeon. It should be remembered that in his day there were none of those medical conveniences which now abound in the Province of British Columbia. In common with all other pioneer medical men he had to depend entirely upon his own exertions and that he was eminently successful speaks volumes for his resourcefulness.

Dr. Trimble died on New Year's Day, 1885, after a short illness, from gangrene, complicated by heart disease.

O. M. J.

Tripler, **Charles Stuart** (1806–1866).

Charles S. Tripler, army surgeon, was born in New York, 1806, and graduated M. D. at the College of Physicians and Surgeons, New York City, 1838. He at once entered the army as assistant surgeon but July 2, the same year, was made full surgeon. During the first years of his practice he was situated at various posts about and within Michigan. In the Mexican War he was medical director of Gen. Twiggs' Division. After the war he was on duty at various posts throughout the West. In 1861 Dr. Tripler was first appointed medical director of Gen. Patterson's Army in the Shenandoah Valley. Upon Gen. McClellan's assuming chief command, he was made general director of the Army of the Potomac and organized the medical service in that department. After the battles of the Peninsula, he was appointed to duty in Michigan and soon brevetted colonel for meritorious service; shortly before his death he was promoted to brevet brigadier-general, and was chief medical officer of the department of Ohio and lived with his family in Detroit. In 1849 he was president of the Michigan Medical Society.

He died in Cincinnati, Ohio, 1866, from epithelioma, leaving a wife and one daughter.

Papers:

"Gunshot Wounds of the Stomach." ("Peninsular Medical Journal," vol. iv.)

"Tripler and Blackman; Handbook for the Military Surgeon," 1861.

"Report on Rank of Medical Department of the Army." ("Transactions, American Medical Association," vol. xvi.)

"Remarks on the Irritative Fever of Drunkenness," 1827.

"Delirium, its Nature and Treatment." (Reprint from "Western Lancet," Cincinnati, Ohio, 1857.)

"The Causes, Nature and Treatment of Scurvy." (Reprint from "Cincinnati Lancet and Observer," 1858.)

"Manual of the Medical Officers of the Army of the United States," Part I; "Recruiting and Inspection of Recruits." (Cincinnati, Ohio, 1858.)

"The Duties of Physicians in Relation to Medical Delusions," 1859.

"An Epitome of Tripler's Manual for the Examination of Recruits." (Prepared by Maj. Charles R. Greenleaf), Washington, Government Printing Office, 1884.   L. C.

Trans. Amer. Med Ass., Phila., vol. xviii.
Detroit Review of Medicine and Pharmacy, vol. i.
Med. Dep. U. S. Army, Wash., 1873.

Triplett, William Harrison (1836–1890).

William Harrison Triplett was born September 15, 1836, at Mt. Jackson, Virginia, and took his M. D., 1859, from Jefferson. He was acting assistant surgeon, U. S. A.

W. H. Triplett, surgeon, on the paternal side was descended from an old Virginia family of English extraction, represented in the war of the Revolution by Col. Triplett, of Middleburg, Virginia, and on the maternal side was the grandson of Dr. J. Irwin, a refugee from the Irish rebellion of 1788. After graduating in medicine Dr. Triplett settled first at Harrisonburg, Virginia, staying one year, then to Woodstock, Virginia, from which, February 3, 1873, he removed to Washington. His specialty was surgery. He was a member of the Medical Society and Medical Association of the District. In the "Boston Medical and Surgical Journal," he discussed the "Improper Treatment of Wounds in the United States Hospitals," "Transposition of Thoracic and Abdominal Viscera, with Hydro-encephalocele, in an Infant Living Thirty Days," and "Glanders in the Human Subject;" while to the "Richmond and Louisville Medical Journal," he contributed papers on "Hodgkin's Disease," on "Syphilitic Arteritis, with Occlusion of both Subclavian Arteries," and on "Three Forms of Bright's Disease." He also wrote "The Laws and Mechanics of Circulation," 1885. He was professor of anatomy in the Georgetown Medical School, 1875. He married on June 1, 1867, Kathleen McKoy, and died at Woodstock, Virginia, on March 27, 1890.   D. S. L.

Atkinson, Eminent Phys. and Surgs. of the U. S.
Min. of Med. Soc., D. C., April, 1890.

Tucker, David H. (1815–1871).

Professor of theory and practice of medicine in the Medical College of Richmond.

David H. Tucker was the eldest son of St. George Tucker, professor of law at the University of Virginia, graduated in medicine from the University of Virginia in 1836, and in the following year from the University of Pennsylvania. The next two years he spent in Paris, perfecting himself in medicine. Returning to the United States he began to practise in Philadelphia. A few years later he married Elizabeth, daughter of George M. Dallas, subsequently vice-president of the United States. With a number of friends Tucker founded the Franklyn Medical College, in which he took the chair of obstetrics, to which branch he had devoted particular attention during his studies in Paris. A few years later Tucker accepted the chair of theory and practice of medicine in the Medical College of Richmond. In this city he soon acquired a name as one of its most distinguished practitioners. In his later life he suffered from ill health and his vision became seriously impaired. He died March 17, 1871.

Tucker possessed a brilliant mind and profound learning. He was sincere and true in his friendship and singularly frank and candid in his manners.   A. A.

Trans. Am. Med. Assoc., Phila., 1872, xxiii. "Incidents of my Life," T. A. Emmet.

Tufts, Cotton (1734–1815).

Cotton Tufts was the eldest son of Dr. Simon and Abigail (Smith) Tufts, and born in Medford, the thirtieth of May, 1734.

Early in life Cotton evinced a studious disposition and was admitted to Harvard College when only fourteen years old. Here he took his A. B. in 1749, and in 1785 the college conferred on him her honorary M. D. Thacher says he went through a regular course of medical education and settled in Weymouth.

He married Lucy, daughter of Col. John Quincy, of Braintree, and had a large practice in and about Quincy. It is related that he introduced a new and original treatment for the putrid sore throat, which was very prevalent and mortal. This was most successful and helped to increase his popularity and extend his fame.

He was an original member of the Massachusetts Medical Society and its fourth president from 1787 to 1795. In 1780 he was one of the incorporators of the American Academy of Arts and Sciences, and was a member of the Constitutional Convention. In 1765 he

wrote the spirited and patriotic instructions to the representatives of the town of Weymouth against the Stamp Act. For more than forty years he was deacon of the church.

His death occurred the eighth of December, 1815. A very quaint portrait of Dr. Tufts is in the Fifield Room in the Boston Medical Library.   W. L. B.

American Medical Biog., 1828, James Thacher.
Biographical Dictionary of the First Settlers of N. E., John Eliot, 1809.

Tufts, Simon, Sr. (1700–1747).

Simon Tufts, Sr., the earliest physician in Medford, was born the thirty-first of January, 1700, in Medford, the youngest son of Peter Tufts the second, son of Peter Tufts the first, who came to Charlestown from England in 1650. Simon was the ninth child of Peter and his second wife, Mary, daughter of the Rev. Seaborn Cotton. As there were twelve children by this wife and four by the first it is plain that there was no aiding of race suicide in this family.

He graduated A. B. from Harvard College in 1724, probably studying medicine at the same time, for he began practice in Medford the year of his graduation.

He married Abigail Smith and had seven children, the fourth child being the eminent Cotton Tufts, M. D.

He had an extensive practice and was called often to visit the sick at Harvard College, refusing to receive fees, however, from the students. The doctor was a justice of the peace and a special justice.

He died on his birthday, the thirty-first of January, 1747. Funeral sermons were preached in his honor in Medford, Boston, Cambridge and Charlestown.   W. L. B.

A Genealog. Dict. of First Settlers of N. E., James Savage, 1860.
Early Physicians of Medford, C. M. Green, 1898.
Amer. Med. Biog. James Thacher, M. D., 1828.

Tully, William (1785-1859).

William Tully was born in Saybrook, Connecticut, February 18, 1785, and died in Springfield, Massachusetts, February, 1859. He graduated from Yale in 1806, studied medicine with Drs. M. F. Cogswell and Eli Ives, attended two courses of medical lectures at Hanover, and in 1819 received the honorary M. D. from Yale. In 1811 he began practicing at Enfield, thence removing to Middletown, becoming, in 1824, professor of theory and practice in the Vermont Academy of Medicine, where he was elected president of the college. In 1825, together with Prof. Alden March, he removed to Albany, New York, where he practised until 1829, when he was appointed to the chair of theory and practice of the medical department of Yale University. Here he lectured for twelve years, including in his courses the subject of botany. His lectures were inspiring to his students, with whom he was a great favorite and he was actively engaged to the time of his death in both practice and teaching.

In 1823, in connection with Dr. Thomas Miner, he issued a volume of "Essays on Fevers and other Medical Subjects," comprising 484 pages and contributed many papers to medical and other journals, also assisted Drs. Webster and Goodrich in compiling Webster's "Dictionary of the English Language," editions 1840 and 1847. At the time of his death he was engaged in writing a work on "Materia Medica, Pharmacology, and Therapeutics," vol. i, 1,534 pages, in twenty-four parts, appearing between November, 1857, and February, 1858.

There is a portrait in Yale University.

From the Bull. of the Lloyd Library, No. 12, 1910.
Boston M. and S. J , 1861, lxv.

Turnbull, Lawrence (1821-1900).

Lawrence Turnbull was born September 10, 1821, in Scotland, and came to America when twelve years old. He studied at the Philadelphia College of Pharmacy, from which he graduated. Several years were spent in this profession, in which such able work was done as to gain him an award of merit from the Franklin Institute. He then studied medicine with Prof. John K. Mitchell and graduated at the Jefferson Medical College in 1845, when he relinquished his chemical work, though he remained for sometime a lecturer at the Franklin Institute on chemistry applied to the arts.

He served for a term as resident physician at the Blockley Hospital in Philadelphia, and in 1857 was elected one of the physicians in the Western Clinical Infirmary (later Howard Hospital) in the department of diseases of the eye and ear, and served until 1887. In 1859 he visited Europe, travelled extensively, devoting himself to the study of diseases of the eye and ear. He served during the Civil War in Emory Hospital and at Fortress Monroe. His chief work has been in ophthalmology and otology, to the literature of which branches he has contributed richly. In 1878 he was elected aural surgeon of the Jefferson Hospital. Dr. Turnbull's writings are permeated with a true scientific spirit, and recorded marked advances in their day. A fairly full list is in the surgeon-general catalogue, Washington, District of Columbia.

He died in Philadelphia, October 24, 1900.   H. F.

Stone's Eminent American Physicians and Surgeons.

Turney, Daniel (1786-1827).

Daniel Turney was born in Shepherdstown, Virginia, April, 1786, of old Huguenot stock. He was a man of great mental grasp and a dominant factor in any movement in which he took part. He is said to have studied medicine with a prominent surgeon of Philadelphia, shortly before his removal to Ross County, Ohio, in 1800. He was one of the band of pioneers who founded the town of Circleville in 1810, and there he practised until 1823, when he removed to Columbus, where he died four years later. During his years of practice he was a leading man, not only in his profession, but as a citizen in whatever community he lived. His wife, Janet Sterling Denny, long survived him, and his two sons, Wilson Delano Turney and Samuel Denny Turney, became prominent men of their time, the former as a man of affars and politician, the latter as a physician. C. A.

Turney, **Samuel** Denny (1824–1878). The son of Dr. Daniel Turney and Janet Sterling Denny, he was born in Columbus, Ohio, on the twenty-sixth of December, 1824.

Kingdon College, Gambier, Ohio, had completed his education pro tem, when he went to Circleville, Ohio, to be a druggist's assistant to support his mother.

Shortly after, he studied medicine with Dr. P. K. Hall, and in 1857 graduated from the University of Pennsylvania, then returned to Circleville until the Civil War began, when he was successively surgeon to the Thirteenth Ohio Volunteer Iufantry; staff colonel and medical director of Van Clave's Division of the Army of the Cumberland and medical director-general of the hospitals at Murfreesboro. He was very keen on the erection of blockhouses, but, as usual in war time there was a great deal of inefficient medical aid. A medicine chest was furnished each house, but knowledge to use its contents was often lacking. Turney wrote a semi-official and amusing pamphlet to go with each chest entitled " Blockhouse Surgery for Block-heads."

He returned to private practice after the war and became professor of physiology and pathology in the Starling Medical College. After a visit to European clinics he became professor in the same college of diseases of women and children.

As an operator he was, at the beginning of an operation, somewhat nervous, but afterwards rapid and brilliant. He kept well up with the times both in work and reading and his writings included:

"History of the War of the Rebellion."

"A New Principle in the Application of the Obstetric Forceps."

"The Use of Esmarch Bandages in Chronic Ulcers."

"Solid Food in Typhoid Fever."

Turney died after an attack of inflammation of the brain on January 18, 1878.

C. A.

Memoir of S. D. Turney (J. H. Pooley), Cincin., 1878.
Ohio M. and Surg. Jour., Columbus, 1878, n. s. vol. iii.
Tr. Ohio Med. Soc., Columbus, 1878, vol. xxxiii (B. B. Leonard).

Turner, **Edward** Kitchen.

Shadowy gossip from old documents makes us long for more about Edward Turner and to wish we knew him better.

Graduating from Harvard in the year 1771, he came to Kennebunk and from there went to the Port or the place where the river empties into the sea below the main village of Kennebunk of to-day. In a short time he vanished into the darkness of the wild and desolate sea. Coming to Kennebunk, shortly after graduation, he soon showed himself a stalwart man. When Dr. Ebenezer Rice, of that time, began to show the white feather, Turner stood up and took the lead in opposition to the tyranny of King George. How it happened that he is found remaining so long in this neighborhood, instead of going to the front, we do not know, unless he thought that he could do better work at home, raising funds, drilling men, and getting them pushed along into service. His turn came when a privateer sailed into Port, or perhaps was fitted out there, and Turner was made surgeon's mate. Everybody round about had liked him for his busy ways for he had done good medical work during his short stay.

So he set sail on a privateer, but of all who saw him go, no one ever heard another word of Edward Kitchen Turner.

His was a brief, bold and generous career, promising greater things had time allowed. J. A. S.

From Old Papers.

Turnipseed, Edward Berriam (1829–1883). This surgeon was born in Richland County, South Carolina, on October 29,

1829, of English and German parentage in a house built on land granted to his family in Richland. He graduated M. D. from South Carolina Medical Collge, Charleston, in 1852, then studied medicine in Paris and afterwards went to St. Petersburg and entered the Russian Army as surgeon-major, doing fine work during the siege of Sevastopol, getting knighted by the Emperor and receiving other orders; not returning to America until 1856, when, after three years in New York, he settled in Richland, taking up his army practice again on the outbreak of Civil War as brigade-surgeon and afterwards resuming private practice, this time in Columbia, South Carolina. His wife's name was Clara M., daughter of J. T. Hendrix, of Lexington, South Carolina.

In the "Transactions of the South Carolina Medical Association" for 1875–77, Turnipseed is shown as an inventor of some useful surgical instruments, among them some for staphylorraphy, a quadrilateral urethrotome, a speculum, also a cotton chopper, and a beehive which shows he was always on the inventive track wherever he happened to be. His writings include:

"Gossypium Herbaceum and Viscum Album, used by Negro Women to Procure Abortion," 1852; "Superior Maxillary Section of Malar and Pterygoid Process of Sphenoid Bone," 1868; "Modification of Syme's and Pirogoff's Operation of Ankle-joint," 1868; "Facts Regarding the Anatomical Difference Between the Negro and White Races (locality of Hymen)," 1868; "Why Should we Support the Perineum During Labour at All," 1877.

He belonged to the American Medical Society of Paris, the New York Pathological Society, and the South Carolina Medical Association.

D. W.

Med. News, Phila., 1883, vol. xlii (P. P. Porcher).
Obit. J. Am. Med. Assoc., Chicago, 1883, vol. i.

Twitchell, Amos (1781–1850).

Amos Twitchell was born in the town of Dublin, on the slopes of that grand old mountain, Monadnock. He was the son of Samuel and Alice Willson Twitchell and born April 11, 1781. His childhood was characterized by his great love of reading and at the age of seventeen be journeyed on horseback and rapped for admittance at Harvard but was refused on account of the lack of preliminary education. Nothing daunted, he turned his face to the North and came to old Dartmouth's door, which graciously swung open to him in 1798; so Harvard lost one whom Dr. Bowditch describes as one of "the most honest and intellectual men this country has produced." His life at College was a struggle with poverty; he graduated in 1802 and at once entered on medical studies under Dr. Nathan Smith. Both men were strong characters, singular in their strength and of similar tastes, so that they were drawn together, and a life long friendship resulted that was strong and mutually helpful.

At that time material for dissection was hard to obtain, but Amos Twitchell possessed all he needed. In 1805 he graduated and first practised in Norwich, Vermont, then in Marlborough, New Hampshire. He entered partnership here with his brother-in-law, Dr. Carter, intending to devote his whole attention to surgery. About the time of his removal to Marlborough he performed an operation which if then published would have given him an international reputation. October 8, 1807, he was called to Sharon, New Hampshire, over forty miles distant, to see a lad named John Saggart, whose jaw had been shattered in a skirmish at the muster of the State Militia. All the adjacent parts were severely bruised and extensive sloughing took place. On the tenth day after the injury, while dressing the wounds, Dr. Twitchell observed that one of the sloughs lay directly over the carotid. The aged mother of the lad stood near as the sole attendant, and he said to her, "If that spot goes through the coats of the vessel, your son will bleed to death in a few moments." He dressed the wound and was unhitching his horse when the old lady frantically called, "it is bleeding." The doctor went in and found him deluged with blood. The dressings were removed and the blood jetted forcibly in a large stream for a distance of two or three feet. With his left thumb he compressed the artery; the patient had fainted: keeping his thumb on the vessel, he cut down with a scalpel more than an inch below where the external branch was given off. The mother separated the sides of the wound with her fingers and at length they succeeded in separating the artery from its attachments and the aged mother passed a string under the vessel and tied it while Dr. Twitchell controlled the hemorrhage and held the candle. The lad recovered.

Sir Astley Cooper's claim of priority has been generally acknowledged, but he did not tie the common carotid until June, 1808, eight months after Dr. Twitchell's case.

Cooper's was the first case published, but in 1817 was published a case that occurred October 17, 1803, when Mr. Fleming, of the British Navy, tied the vessel for a servant on ship board, who had attempted suicide. Twitchell's case was not published until 1838.

In 1810 Dr. Twitchell removed to Keene, New Hampshire, where he practised until he died.

He joined the New Hampshire Medical Society in 1811 and was its president, 1827–1830. Although always busy he found time to attend its meetings and was the idol of the society.

He was an indefatigable worker with such a practice so extensive that he had an arrangement of post-horses at country inns, so that he was enabled to travel at the rate of eight or ten miles an hour.

In 1838 he removed successfully the arm and clavicle for malignant disease.

In 1840 he had diagnosed and operated upon three cases of suppuration in the medullary canal. He frequently operated for stone in the bladder, did excisions of joints, and had performed several ovariotomies before McDowell's case was published.

Although offered professorships at Dartmouth, Vermont, and Brunswick Medical Colleges, he declined them all.

In 1816 he was elected an overseer of Dartmouth College, and in 1838 became honorary member of the Massachusetts Medical Society, and was one of the founders of the American Medical Association.

Dr. Twitchell was an abstainer in regard to the use of alcohol and was a vegetarian for many years.

He married Miss Elizabeth Goodhue in June, 1815, but they had no children.

He died of heart disease May 26, 1850.

I. J. P.

Med. Communicat., Mass., Med. Soc., 1850.
N. Hamp., Jour. Med., Concord, 1850-1.

Tyler, John (1763–1841).

The son of Samuel and Susanna Tyler, whose people came from England and France about 1600; this ophthalmist was born in Prince George County, Maryland, June 29, 1763, and began to study medicine under Dr. Smith, of Georgetown. He was a pupil at St. Bartholomew's Hospital, London, in 1784, where he received his diploma and studied also with John Hunter, Fordyce, Baillie and Pott. He began practice in Frederick City, Maryland, 1786, and was, according to Quinan, the first oculist in America, acquiring great reputation in ophthalmology and being one of the first in the United States to operate for cataract. Patients came long distances, even from adjoining states to obtain the benefit of his skill in couching. It is recorded that he was an officer in the "Whiskey Insurrection" in Pennsylvania, and his name figures as a co-founder of the Medical and Chirurgical Faculty in Baltimore, and an elector of Pres. Jefferson. Being possessed of a competency, he retired from practice as his hearing became dull from age and disease. He died unmarried in Frederick City, October 15, 1841. Dr.

Charles Frederick Wiesenthal mentions him in a letter to his son, Andrew, then pursuing his medical studies in London. After urging him to seek to acquire skill in surgical operations, especially in lithotomy and extraction of cataract, he says: "There is a young man returned lately, Mr. Tyler, who is settled in Frederick and has successfully couched two or three persons, which has at once made him very conspicuous and he has made a considerable good match on the strength of it (June 5, 1787)."   E. F. C.

Hist. of Western Maryland, Scarff.
Toner's Ms. Biographies, Nat. Lib., Wash., D. C.

V

Van Buren, Peter (1801–1873).

Peter Van Buren, the son of Barent and Catherine (Vosburg) Van Buren, was born at Ghent, Columbia County, New York. He had his preliminary education at the Academy, in Lenox, Massachusetts and at Hudson, New York. Under Dr. Thomas Broadhead he studied medicine, and his name appears in the catalogue of the College of Physicians and Surgeons as a graduate in the class of 1823. He married Mary, daughter of his instructor, Dr. Broadhead and for one year practised in Herkimer, Herkimer County, New York, then removed to Clermont, Columbia County, where he formed a partnership with Dr. Broadhead. After fourteen years at Clermont, he removed to Albany, and from 1854 until his death lived in New York City. He was the victim of many ills during the latter years of his life, his constitution having been impaired by typhoid fever and in 1873 he died of consumption and was buried in Woodlawn Cemetery, leaving four children.

He filled the position of president in the Medical Societies of the Counties of Columbia and Albany, was also vice-president of the Medical Society of the State of New York and filled in all these societies most of the subordinate positions. After his removal to the latter city, he became a member of the medical societies there. He was at one time military surgeon on the staff of the governor, and in 1829 a member of the legislature. The Transactions of the Medical Society of New York contain several of his articles.

Dr. Van Buren was for many years an active member of the Dutch Reformed Church.

Medical Register, N. Y., N. J., and Conn., 1874, xii.

Van Buren, William Holme (1819–1883).

I came across a notice of Van Buren in the "Autobiography" of Samuel D. Gross and have freely transcribed:

"This (March 25, 1883) ought to be a sad day for me," says Gross, "one of our most distinguished men has dropped out of our ranks. Van Buren died this morning at his house after protracted illness in which he endured much suffering from softening of the brain attended by paralysis and albuminuria."

Born in New York in 1819 of rather poor parents of Dutch descent whose people had come over in 1700, Van Buren entered Yale, and attended medical lectures in the University of Pennsylvania, but, before taking his M. D. there in 1840, he went to Paris and studied under Velpeau. On his return he wrote his thesis on "The Use of the Immovable Dressing in the Treatment of Fractures." His was the first attempt to introduce this practice, and the thesis made a strong impression on the profession. The first five years of his post-graduate life were spent in the Army, chiefly with Gen. Winfield Scott, but in 1845 he began practice in New York, for a time acting as prosector to his father-in-law, Valentine Mott. Seven years later he became professor of anatomy in the University of New York and held the post for fourteen years, and for sixteen years that of professor of the principles of surgery in the Bellevue Hospital Medical College, lecturing also on clinical surgery, particularly in following out the complicated affections of the genito-urinary organs, and becoming, in the abstract sense of the word, a specialist.

The active part he took in the organization of the United States Sanitary Commission should be remembered, for he spared neither time nor money and the sacrifice he incurred from loss of practice must have been considerable. He did some good writing too, translating Bernard and Huette's "Operative Surgery" and Morel's "Histology," and writing on "Diseases of the Rectum." With his assistant, Dr. Keyes, he made an exhaustive treatise on "Diseases of the Genito-urinary Organs:" a valuable paper on "Aneurysms" attracted some attention and an erudite article on "Inflammation," in the "International Encyclopedia of Surgery" also came from him.

In 1842 he married the daughter of Valentine Mott.

Abridged from Autobiography of Dr. S. D. Gross.
Distinguished living New York Surgeons, S. W. Francis.

Vance, Reuben Aleshire (1845–1894).

A physician and surgeon of Cleveland, Ohio, he was born in Gallipolis, Ohio, August 18, 1845. His father, Alexander, was of Virginia extraction, his mother, Eliza Shepard, of Puritan, and this combination produced a character unique and striking. The son was educated in the schools of Gallipolis and in the Gallia Academy, and even while a lad was precocious. At the age of nine he was an expert typesetter, and when the Civil War burst upon the land, at the age of sixteen he enlisted as a private in the Fourth Virginia Infantry, a regiment commanded by his brother; saw much active military service, and was distinguished for a gallantry bordering upon recklessness. At the close of the war he decided to study medicine and matriculated in the Bellevue Medical College, and graduated there in 1867; after the usual hospital service he settled down to private practice in New York City. In 1868 he was attending physician to the New York Central Dispensary; then assistant to the chair of the diseases of the mind and nervous system in Bellevue Hospital Medical College; assistant physician to the New York State Hospital for diseases of the nervous system; attending physician to the Bellevue

Hospital Dispensary; physician-in-chief to the New York Institution for Epileptics and Paralytics. In 1870 he was called upon, as an expert witness, to testify in the famous murder case of Daniel McFarland. In 1873 he went to Europe for purposes of travel and study, and on his return, in 1875, married Anna Cooper, daughter of Dr. James Cooper, of New York. In 1879 he removed to Cincinnati, where for two years he lectured on pathological anatomy in the Cincinnati College of Medicine and Surgery. On the reorganization of the medical department of Wooster University in 1881, Dr. Vance was given the chair of clinical and operative surgery, and removed to Cleveland. He had been interested in St. Alexis Hospital, of Cleveland, almost from its inception, and at the time of his death was president of the hospital staff. He died of cerebral hemorrhage, following an attack of the grippe, March 19, 1894.

He was a member of the Ohio State Medical Society. A frequent contributor to the medical journals of his day, he was a graceful, clear and forcible writer. Of contributions it will be sufficient to notice: "The Ophthalmoscope in the Treatment of Epilepsy." ("New York Medical Journal," vol. xiii, 1871.) "Writer's Cramp or Scrivener's Palsy." ("Boston Medical and Surgical Journal," vol. lxxxixi, 1873.) "Trichina Spiralis," an inaugural address before the Ohio Valley Medical Society ("Cincinnati Lancet and Observer," vol. xx, 1877), and "Vesico-vaginal Fistula." ("Cleveland Medical Gazette," 1888.)

He left a library of some five thousand volumes, ranging from the "Chirurgical Treatise" of Richard Wiseman and the "De Curtorum Chirurgia" of Taliacotius, to the first edition of the most obscure poet of the Elizabethan period, and reflecting in its contents both the ability and eccentricity of its collector. An excellent half-tone picture will be found in the "Cleveland Medical Gazette" (vol. ix, 1894).   H. E. H.

Cleveland Medical Gazette, vol. ix, 1893–4.

Vander Poel, Samuel Oakley (1824–1886).

Samuel Oakley Vander Poel came of a fam ly long distinguished in the affairs of New York. His father was also a physician at Kinderhook, Columbia County, New York, which was the doctor's birthplace on February 22, 1824. He took a course at the University of the City of New York, of which Theodore Frelinghuysen was then chancellor, then returned home, and for a while studied medicine with his father. This prepared him for entrance to Jefferson Medical College, in Philadelphia, from which he graduated in 1845. The ensuing two years he passed with his father, and in 1847 went to Paris. In 1850 he came home and settled in Albany, where he married.

Vander Poel had acquired a large practice when, in 1857, Governor King appointed him on his staff as surgeon-general. In 1860 he became President of the Albany County Medical Society. The duties of surgeon-general had been barely more than nominal during Governor King's administration, but in 1861, when Governor Morgan selected him for that place on his staff, the requirements and responsibility of the position were great. After the war he resumed private practice and in 1867 was chosen to the chair of general pathology and clinical medicine at the Albany Medical College, and was elected president of the State Medical Society, in 1870. While still devoted chiefly to his private practice, Governor Hoffman appointed him in 1872 health officer for New York. Quarantine matters were then in a deplorable state, and Dr. Vander Poel's powers of organization were again called into play.

During his term he filled, in 1876, the chair of the theory and practice of medicine in the Albany Medical College. In 1883 he was elected to a Professorship of public hygiene in the University of New York, and had an LL. D. from there in 1884.

He died in Washington, on March 12, while on the way South for his health.

Med. Rec. N. Y., 1886, vol. xxix.
Albany M. Ann., 1886, vii.
Tr. M. Soc. N. Y., Syracuse.
Portrait in Surg.-gen. Lib., Wash., D. C.

Van de Warker, Ely (1841–1910).

Ely Van de Warker, gynecologist, was born in West Troy, New York, November 27, 1841. He had his early education at a private school under Mr. Arthur, father of Mr. Chester A. Arthur. He attended the Troy Polytechnic, and later had medical training at the Albany Medical College.

On graduation, he entered the 162nd Regiment of the New York Volunteers and served as surgeon until the close of the Civil War, attaining the rank of major. He began practice in Troy, New York, in 1865, and in the same year married Louise Gardner of Hancock, Massachusetts, who died the following year. He moved to Syracuse about the year 1870 and in 1872 married Helen A. Adams of that city who lived until 1907. In 1908 Dr. Van de Warker retired from active practice on account of failing health, and died in 1910. He was survived by two daughters and three grandchildren.

Van de Warker should be reckoned among the pioneers in American Gynecology as he spent a particularly useful life in diffusing the benefits of modern surgery over a wide area of middle New York. One of the founders and most active members of the American Gynecological Society; he was also for a considerable time a prolific writer and zealous in promoting the advance of his specialty from that stage which it occupied in the 70's and 80's to its present status. His writings for the most part appear in the "Transactions of the American Gynecological Society;" the "American Journal of Obstetrics" and the "New York Medical Journal." He was particularly forceful and happy as a writer, and the Gynecologists of his day well remember the great interest excited by the elaborate consideration of the "Mechanical Treatment of Versions and Flexions of the Uterus," a theoretical and practical study of the pessary, which is to be found in the "Gynecological Transactions" for 1883.

The paper which excited most attention was "A Gynecological Study of the Oneida Community," ("American Journal Obstetric," New York, 1884). He also wrote on the "Treatment of Extrauterine Pregnancy by Electricity" a much mooted subjected at that time.

His literary interests were not confined to a specialty alone, as he wrote a paper on the "Abandoned Canals of the State of New York" illustrated by seven artistic photographs which appeared in the "Popular Science Monthly," September, 1909. He also wrote a book of 225 pages entitled "Woman's Unfitness for Higher Co-education," December, 1903, written when he was Commissioner of Schools at Syracuse, New York.

But he really began his work a decade too early to take any active part in the working out of the larger problems of gynecologic surgery. He was the founder of the Syracuse Hospital for Women and Children where he served as surgeon-in-chief for more than twenty years. He is said to have performed over 2000 laparotomies.　　　　H. A. K.

Album of the Fellows, Amer. Gyn. Soc., Phila., 1901.
Albany Medical Annals, Oct., 1910.

Vander **Weyde**, **P**eter H. (1813–1895).

Peter H. Vander Weyde, scientist, editor, writer and physician was born in Nymegen, Holland, in 1813, and graduated from the Royal Academy at Delft. He was a scientific writer and teacher in Holland, and professor of mathematics and natural philosophy at the Government School of Design. In 1842 he founded a journal devoted to mathematics and physics, and in 1845 received a gold medal from the Society for the Promotion of Scientific Knowledge for a text-book on natural philosophy. At the same time he was the editor of a liberal daily paper, which waged vigorous warfare against existing abuses in the government.

In 1849 he came to New York, and graduated from the New York University Medical College in 1856, and practised medicine until he was appointed professor of physics, chemistry, and higher mathematics at the Cooper Institute. He was also professor of chemistry in the New York Medical College. In 1864 the chair of industrial science was expressly created for him at Girard College, Philadelphia. This last professorship he resigned a few years later, and returning to New York became the editor of "The Manufacturer and Builder," a scientific journal. He contributed many valuable articles of a scientific nature to "Appleton's New American Cyclopedia," of which he was an editor. He had more than two hundred patents on inventions of his own, mostly electrical. Besides these attainments he displayed much merit as musician, composer and painter.

Med. Reg. of N. York, 1895, xxxiii.

Van Dyck, Van Alan **C**ornelius (1818–1896).

This erudite medical missionary was born in Kinderhook, Columbia County, New York, on August 13, 1818, of Dutch parentage, and by dint of hard work managed to get a medical education at Jefferson Medical College, Philadelphia, and when only twenty-one was appointed medical missionary in Syria and Palestine. From June, 1843, he taught in the newly founded Abeih Seminary, yet making long journeys to attend the sick and translating medical and religious text-books into Arabic for the students. He was equally learned in philology, mathematics, astronomy and medicine, and in certain branches of science gave the Arabs a scientific terminology before unknown. From 1851 his life was given more exclusively to religious work though he found time for his well-known Arabic geography. He set out in 1857, editing and completing an Arabic Bible on which a colleague had labored eight years, and after another eight years' work by Van Dyck it was published in 1865. He spent some two years in New

York superintending its electrotyping and teaching Hebrew, then on his return to Beirut supervised the printing of Bibles; conducted an Arabic journal and was professor of the theory and practice of medicine in the Syrian Protestant College; also helping to found the Astronomical Observatory and working hard in the Greek and St. John's Hospital.

He died on November 13, 1896, at four in the morning after a useful life of nearly seventy-eight years, just before his last brief illness translating Wallace's "Ben Hur" into Arabic.

D. W.

Van Rensselaer, Jeremiah (1793–1871).

Jeremiah Van Rensselaer was born in Greenbush, Rensselaer County, New York, in 1793. He was a descendant of the old Dutch settlers who, in 1637, founded the colony of Rensselaerwyck. After completing his academic studies at Yale College, he, in 1813, went to New York and worked under his uncle, Dr. Archibald Bruce, where he acquired that taste for the natural sciences, for which in after years he was distinguished. After getting his M. D. in 1817, he went abroad and spent three years in attendance upon the lectures and hospitals in Edinburgh, London and Paris. Upon his return to New York he practised extensively. He was for many years corresponding secretary of the New York Lyceum of Natural History, and during 1895 delivered a course of lectures before the New York Athenaeum with great success. In 1852 he retired from active pursuits to the care of his estates at Greenbush. He returned to New York after a visit abroad in feeble health, and a few months later, in 1871, died of pneumonia.

The Med. Register of N. Y., 1871, vol. ix.

Vattier, John Loring (1808–1881).

He was the son of Charles Vattier, of Le Havre, France, who emigrated to this country and came West as a member of Gen. St. Clair's Army, locating here and amassing a fortune dealing in real estate. His mother was Pamela Loring, of Balti-more, Maryland, and he was born on October 31, 1808, in a little house at the corner of Front and Eastern Row, now Broadway, Cincinnati, Ohio. After going to the best schools of that day, but principally to private preceptors, he entered into the services of an apothecary, with the object of becoming a physician and in 1827 took up medicine and matriculated in the Medical College of Ohio, under Prof. Whitman, Slack, and Cobb; between terms he devoted his time to the steamboat traffic, reading medicine in spare moments of long trips. He was a clerk on the "Alexander Hamilton," at the time it made the first through trip of any steamboat between Cincinnati and St. Louis. He finally graduated in 1830 and settled in Aurora, Indiana, but the field not being attractive enough, he returned to Cincinnati and embarked in the wholesale drug business, the firm name being Ramsay and Vattier, which venture of about four years' duration became unprofitable and the firm dissolved, and in 1863 he returned to practise medicine in his native city, which he did to the time of his death, enjoying a successful career. At one time he was a partner of the renowned Dr. John T Shotwell.

At the time of the Seminole War and trouble leading up to the Mexican War, he was appointed by Maj. Melancthon J. Wade as surgeon of the First Regiment, third brigade of first division, Ohio Militia.

In 1853 Vattier was appointed postmaster at Cincinnati by Pres. Pierce and continued in office until May, 1858, and again in 1859 he was appointed to the same office by Pres. Buchanan and remained there until the administration of Pres. Lincoln.

At different times he was trustee and director of many institutions, among the public ones may be stated, the City Hospital, Longview Asylum, Cincinnati College of Medicine and Surgery and the Medical College of Ohio; with the latter he was identified closely and did much towards bringing it into prominence.

He was president of the Academy of Medicine in 1867.

A curious history may be read in connection with Vattier in the "Transactions of the American Medical Association for 1881" concerning his membership in the Society of the Last Man, organized in Cincinnati during the cholera.

The year 1832 was a fatal one in the history of the United States through the ravages of Asiatic cholera. The dreadful scourge had secured a footing in New Orleans, and was cutting a deadly swath northwards in the Mississippi Valley, its advance guard reaching St. Louis, where as it spread to the east and to the west, the victims fell by hundreds. The thirtieth of September of that year was a gloriously bright Sunday, and on the afternoon of that day, in Cincinnati, were gathered in the studio of Joseph R. Mason, a prominent young artist, Dr. J. L. Vattier, Dr. James M. Mason, Henry L. Tatem, Fenton Lawson, William Disney, Jr., William Stanbery and the artist. Conversation naturally turned upon the plague and the havoc it was causing, the stalking and unconquerable phantom being the one topic everywhere.

One of the number in a spirit of levity suggested the formation of a society to be known as the Society of the Last Man, and proposed that on each recurring anniversary of the organization a banquet should be held, at which the survivors were to attend, and when but one living representative remained he was to open a bottle of wine provided at the first meal.

They came together for the first time on the night of October 6, 1832, and lots were drawn for the custody of the charge. In 1855 Henry Tatem and Dr. Vattier alone faced each other. The casket was now in the possession of the former, and two months later the fell destroyer seized him and in his delirium, he cried " Break open that casket and pour out the wine. It haunts me." The next year Dr. Vattier was alone at a banquet set for seven.

Vattier died in Cincinnati in 1881 and no writings with the exception of a few controversial tracts, can be traced.

O. J.

Cincinnati Lancet and Clinic, n. s., vol. vi, 1881 (J. H. Buckner).

Tr. Am. Med. Assoc., Phila., vol. xxxii, 1881 (J. M. Toner).

The Century Magazine, June, 1908 (H. D Ward).

Vaughan, Benjamin (1751–1835).

This man, the only member of the British Parliament who ever adorned medicine in Maine, was born in the Island of Jamaica, April 19, 1751, the eldest son of Samuel Vaughan, a merchant of London, who came to Boston, and ultimately married Sarah Hallowell of that city. Benjamin was educated at Cambridge, England, and then at Edinburgh, and was appointed private secretary to Lord Shelbourne. Wishing to marry Sarah Manning, of London, her father objected because Vaughan had no profession. In order to gain his consent, Vaughan studied medicine in Edinburgh, and after obtaining his medical degree was married, but instead of practising medicine, he went into business with his father-in-law. Dr. Vaughan had early become acquainted with Benjamin Franklin and Laurens, and after the Revolution, was an active participator in the transactions for peace with America. He was a secret messenger, carrying notes and messages which it was not advisable to send by an ordinary carrier; during a change in agents, he was made the secret one for Britain in France. King George did not think so highly of Dr. Vaughan as others did, and mentioned him in one letter as playing too much into the hands of Franklin, whom the King considered a low sort of man. Four times Vaughan went to Paris, and spent several months. He was a tried friend of Franklin, edited the first edition of his works in England, and later on, in America, edited another and new edition in 1806.

Up to the year 1794 Vaughan lived mostly in London, while there writing "The Calm Observer," became a member of Parliament, traveled to France again, and predicted negro insurrections in San Domingo owing to the emancipation of slaves by the French. During the French Revolution he was an active participator and became entangled with liberators who wanted to establish in England a republic like the French Republic. Upon these conspirators some of Vaughan's letters were found, so that Vaughan alarmed for his safety escaped to France, and took refuge with the American Consul, Gen. Skipwith, in Paris.

William Pitt being consulted regarding the return of Vaughan said that he did not consider him dangerous, but only an enthusiast; that he could return and take his seat in Parliament if he desired, and that the government would take no notice of what he had said or done. Vaughan, however, was afraid of Pitt's veracity, and never returned to England. He remained in France a year, and entered the field of hard work. In order to avoid arrest as an Englishman, he went by the name of Jean Pusey. In 1795 the Committee of Safety discovered and arrested him, but after a month in the Carmelite Monastery Prison, he was released. It is reported that he was once mobbed in the streets of Paris, as a spy of William Pitt. It has also been said that he was very intimate with Robespierre. Leaving France, he arrived at Geneva, but reading of the probable fall of Robespierre, he ultimately returned to Paris on the very day on which this monster was guillotined.

Vaughan again escaped to Strasburg, and wrote a panegyric upon the Directory. He also wrote a pamphlet, saying that the prophet Daniel predicted the French Revolution, but this was suppressed. Finally he went to America to join his brother Charles.

About 1797, Benjamin Vaughan and his brother Charles settled in Hallowell, Maine, which was named for his maternal grandfather, Benjamin Hallowell. He had a fine medical and literary library, loaned the books from it freely, and on his death left some of them to the Insane Asylum at Augusta, to Harvard, and to Bowdoin College. He practised medicine in Hallowell, but not very extensively. We hear of him occasionally as consulting with Gen. (doctor) Henry Dearborn and it must have been curious to see in a country town like Hallowell, the former member of the British Parliament and the former major-general of the United States Army discussing the symptoms of some poor farmer on an out-lying country road. Vaughan also gave much time to agriculture. He wrote frequently for publication. He was a learned writer and a profound thinker and many of his writings and essays are unknown as he did not print in his own name. He offered his services to Jefferson, but they were not accepted. Harvard gave him the LL. D. degree in 1801, and Bowdoin in 1812. He died after a short illness, December 8, 1835, aged eighty-five.   J. A. S.

Trans. Maine Med. Assoc.

Vermyne, J. B. B. (1835–1898).

J. J. B. Vermyne was born in Holland, and studied in the universities of his own native land, later becoming a surgeon in the Dutch Army. For a time he served in Surinam, then practised medicine in Holland. With his wife, an American, he joined the Red Cross Society, and served during the Franco-Prussian War, for which he received the Order of the Legion of Honor from the French Government. He then settled in New Bedford, Massachusetts, the home of his wife, and devoted himself for a short time to general practice, afterwards more exclusively as an ophthalmist and auralist. In 1873 he was elected a member of the American Ophthalmological Society, and in 1875 of the American Otological Society. He displayed great ability in his special lines of work. He was one of the founders of St. Luke's Hospital, New Bedford. He was a man of culture, especially in art and music.

He died in 1898 at the age of sixty-three at Francestown.   H. F.

Trans. Am. Ophth. Soc., vol. viii.

W

Wagner, John (1791–1841).

After studying at Yale he took his A. B. there in 1812 and his A. M. three years later, then began to work at medicine under Dr. Post of New York. When the latter went to Europe for his health, Wagner, dissatisfied with his opportunities, resolved to visit the schools of London and Paris, and unexpectedly ran up against his preceptor in Liverpool who gave him a letter to Sir Astley Cooper. A year as "dresser" in Guy's Hospital followed and plenty of eager attendance at Sir Astley's lectures, two large folio volumes in manuscript testifying to his interest. "America," wrote Sir Astley in his testimonial, "who is making rapid progress in professional science, will be proud to rank among its citizens a man so clear in his intellect, highly informed in his profession, and so kind and gentle in his manners."

Wagner settled down and married in New York, but after a few years went to Charleston, South Carolina. With his advent a new era in surgery began. Many of his confrères remember the exhibition of surgical ability in a case of osteo-sarcoma of the lower jaw in which nearly half that bone was removed, the third operation of the kind in the States, two of them by Charleston surgeons. Other operations of importance were undertaken—the amputation of the arm at the shoulder joint, the tying of the artery in popliteal aneurysm with many others which showed his masterly skill in using the knife and his intimate acquaintance with the human structure. Practice rapidly increased and in the winter of 1826 he began a course of dissections and demonstrations in practical anatomy with the art of preserving specimens, in which latter he was rarely excelled.

In 1829 he was appointed professor of pathological and surgical anatomy in the medical college of South Carolina. Such a professorship was new, and treated of topics necessitating much research and practical information. The syllabus published by Wagner showed his large views and personal resources.

Elected to the chair of surgery in 1832 he continued as professor until his death on May 22, 1841, often doing his work in great bodily pain, suffering from rheumatism early contracted.

He married (date undiscoverable) a Miss Breact and had eight children.

D. W.

Am. Med. Jour., 1841.

Wales, Philip Skinner (1837–1906).

Philip Skinner Wales, surgeon-general of the United States Navy, was born at Annapolis, Maryland, and graduated from the University School of Medicine, Baltimore, in 1856. The same year he entered the navy as assistant surgeon, was promoted to surgeon in 1861, and served during the Civil War at the Naval Hospital at Norfolk and on the steamer Fort Jackson. He became a member of the board of Examiners in 1873, and later occupied the posts of medical inspector, chief of the Bureau of Medicine and Surgery, and medical director, also served as surgeon-general of the navy from 1879 to 1884. He retired from active service on account of age February 27, 1896, and spent most of his time in Washington. He died suddenly from cancer of the intestines in a hospital in Paris, September 15, 1906.

He wrote "Mechanical Therapeutics," 1867, and several valuable articles for the medical journals. C. A. P.

Med. Rec., N. Y., 1906, lxx.
J. Am. M. Ass., Chicago, 1906, xlvii.

Walker, Thomas (1714–1794).

Thomas Walker was born in King and Queen County, Virginia, a grandson of Maj. Thomas Walker, a burgess from Gloucester in 1662. While it is not known whether or not he was a graduate in medicine, he was certainly a practitioner of note. He is, for instance, credited by Ashhurst ("Principles and Practice of Surgery") with having trephined bone for suppurative osteomyelitis in 1757, making him one of the first known to have done that operation.

He lived at Castle Hill in Albemarle County, and during his life, filled many important positions of trust, and was the guardian of Thomas Jefferson. It is believed that he was the first to explore Kentucky, which he visited in 1745 and again in 1750.

He was commissary general of the Virginia troops in the French and Indian War; a member of the house of Burgesses of the Virginia Convention of 1775; commissioner to treat with the Indians after their defeat by Andrew Lewis; and also a Commissioner to run the boundary line between North Carolina and Virginia, which was known as Walker's line.

He died on the ninth of November, 1794, in the eighty-first year of his age.

R. M. S.

Wallace, William B. (1833–1897).

William B. Wallace, president of the Kings County Medical Society, received his early education in Rothesay, Scotland. Later he returned to his native country (Ireland) and attended Doyle College in Londonderry. He studied medicine in Edinburgh and graduated from the Royal College of Surgeons in 1856, and from the Royal College of Physicians in 1860. During the Crimean war he was acting assistant surgeon in the Royal Navy. After the war he entered the service of the Cunard Steamship Company as surgeon. In 1864 he came to the United States and practised in Brooklyn. In 1867 he married Ella Louise Ladd. He became actively identified with the educational and charitable institutions of the city and was visiting physician to several hospitals.

"There was no sacrifice within his power he was not only willing to make, but did make for the cause of Ireland and to the detriment of his professional advancement. His death was pathetic and within a few hours of that of his son, a young physician whom he had looked forward to helping him as a breadwinner."

A. A.

Brooklyn Med. Jour., 1897, xi.
"Incidents of my Life," T. A. Emmet.

Walter, Albert G. (1811–1876).

Albert G. Walter was a pioneer surgeon and one of the first to open the abdomen deliberately for traumatism, and one of the earliest American orthopedic surgeons, having up to the time of his death cut more tendons in one patient than any other surgeon; added to all this he gained distinction as a skillful lithotomist and operating oculist.

He was born in Germany in 1811; studied medicine in Koenigsberg, where he received his degree, then took a postoperative course of one year at Berlin. He was pupil and assistant of the celebrated Dieffenbach, by whom he was advised to emigrate to America. On the way he was shipwrecked upon the coast of Norway and lost all his effects. He was brought with the other passengers and landed in London, without friends or means, but procured a situation as clerk in a law office, where he remained one year to secure means to continue his journey, during which time he attended medical lectures and especially those of Sir Astley Cooper, who afterwards remained his friend. Afterwards he crossed to America and began practice in Nashville, Tennessee, remaining there two years, when he went to Pittsburgh and practised there until his death in 1876.

In 1867 he published a work entitled "Conservative Surgery," advocating the thorough drainage of crushed limbs by very long and deep incisions to release the imprisoned products, demonstrating that in this way only could crushed limbs be saved when the presence of imprisoned fluids under high tension would result in infection or interference with blood supply.

On January 12, 1859, he was called to attend a patient who had been kicked in the suprapubic region and sustained an intraperitoneal rupture of the bladder. He made the correct diagnosis and, with a courage peculiar to the man, opened the peritoneal cavity widely, sponged away the effused urine, drained the bladder and his patient recovered. This was not only the first case in which the abdomen had been opened for rupture of the bladder, but was also the first case of deliberate laparotomy for injury which has been recorded. Although this case was published by Dr. Walter in the "Medical and Surgical Reporter," of November 16, 1861, it received scant notice till the publication of a similar successful case by Dr. R. F. Weir, in 1884.

Dr. Walter was a man of wonderful industry, taking the most minute notes of his cases, making plaster casts of his orthopedic cases and sketches of his operative work. He enjoyed good health until his death from pneumonia, in 1876.

J. J. B.

Ward, Thomas (1807–1873).

Thomas Ward was born in New Jersey, and died April 13, 1873. He was the son of Gen. Thomas Ward, of Newark, New Jersey, of Revolutionary fame, who represented his district in the First Congress of the United States. Dr Ward was educated at Princeton College and spent two years in Paris, studying in the medical colleges. He returned to this country in 1828, and continued at the Rutgers Medical College, taking his M. D. there in 1829. Dr. Ward about this time married the second daughter of Jacob Lorillard. Though distinguished as a physician and a man of literary culture and attainments, he was best known as a patron of art and a warmhearted philanthropist. Ward devoted himself to music, poetry and the fine arts,

and had a finely cultured musical taste, ranking among the first amateurs of the day. He composed many ballads and comic operas, which were familiar to old New Yorkers. As a lover of fine arts and antiquities he was widely known, and his library and music rooms in Forty-seventh Street were richly stored with valuable objects of rarity and beauty. Dr. Ward has a place among the "American Poets." He published a volume in 1842, entitled "Passaic and Other Poems, by Flaccus," the signature so familiar to the old readers of the "New York American." During the war Dr. Ward's muse was active in writing "war lyrics," which won much admiration when written, but are difficult to come across now.

D. W.

Med. Reg. State of N. Y., 1873.

Warder, John A. (1813–1883).

John A. Warder was born in Philadelphia in 1812. He absorbed a deep love for nature in his father's house when a boy, where Audobon and other famous naturalists were daily visitors, and at the time of his death had risen to national prominence as a naturalist. His family moved to Springfield, Ohio, in 1830, and in 1834 young Warder returned to Philadelphia to attend Jefferson Medical College, graduating in 1836. The following year he located in Cincinnati and entered enthusiastically and successfully on medical practice. He was a publicspirited and energetic citizen, and gave much time to the study of school construction and educational systems. He was an active member of most scientific societies in his part of the country, especially the Cincinnati Natural History Society, and served as a member of the Ohio State Board of Agriculture. He was particularly interested in forestry and landscape gardening, and in 1853 enriched botanical science by his description of the Catalpa Speciosa, one of the most beautiful and valuable forest trees, as a separate species. In 1857 he moved to North Bend, Ohio, where he established a home surrounded by a model garden and farm. In 1873, as United States Commissioner to the Vienna Exposition, he submitted an official report on forests and forestry which gave a tremendous impetus to the forestry movement in this country. Most of his writings pertained to botany and practical forestry, but to the profession he gave his translation of Trousseau and Belloe's "Larangeal Phthisis."

In him the Medical College of Ohio had a loyal friend at the time they most needed help and support. He held the chair of chemistry for three terms (1854–1857). His active and useful life ended in 1883.   O. J.

Taken from "Daniel Drake and His Followers," Otto Juettner.
J. Am. M. Ass., Chicago, 1883, i. (J. M. Toner)

Ware, John (1795–1864).

John Ware was born in Hingham, Massachusetts, December 19, 1795, the son of the Rev. Henry Ware, who was minister in that town for eighteen years, and later Hollis professor of theology in Harvard College from 1805 to 1840, serving also as acting president of the college in 1810 and in 1828–29. The immigrant ancestor of the family was Robert Ware, who "came from his English home to the colony of Massachusetts Bay sometime before the autumn of 1642," and settled in Dedham, where he married and brought up his family, and was "the progenitor of a long line of moral teachers." John Ware's mother was the daughter of the Rev. Jonas Clark, "the patriot parson of Lexington," and the granddaughter of the Rev. John Hancock of that town.

Graduating from Harvard College in 1813, John Ware entered the Harvard Medical School and received his M. D., in 1816. He began his medical career in Duxbury, Massachusetts, but in 1817 returned to Boston, where he acquired an extensive practice. In his diary he says: "I had always a great many patients, but for many years a very small income, and was obliged to have recourse to other means besides my profession for the support of my family. Some of my receipts were from dentistry, which I practised about ten years."

From his diary it is learned that he also eked out his income by keeping school and by taking private "scholars." In 1820 he records the receipt of the "Boylston Premium of fifty dollars." In 1823–25 he was physician at the Boston Almshouse, which paid a small stipend. He also gave two courses of lectures and wrote for the "North American Review." With Dr. Walter Channing he was editor of the "New England Journal of Medicine and Surgery," from 1824 to 1827, and on the establishment of the "Boston Medical and Surgical Journal" in 1828, he served for a year as its first editor. This literary work was a valuable training, it gave him a good literary style and put him in touch with medical progress with which he was so closely identified in the succeeding years. After twenty years of unremitting effort he wrote, "My success in life, professionally, is, as often I reflect upon it, a matter of surprise to me. I came to Boston with no advantages of friends, or relations, or purse."

In 1852 Ware was appointed adjunct professor to Dr. James Jackson; Hersey professor of the theory and practice of physic in the Harvard Medical School. Four years later he succeeded Dr. Jackson in the professorship, which he held until 1858. In 1839, with Drs. Jacob Bigelow, and Enoch Hale he founded the Boston Society for Medical Improvement, a medical organization with a most honorable history. In 1842 Dr. Ware published a "Contribution to the History and Diagnosis of Croup." He pointed out that "the only form of croup attended with any considerable danger to life is that distinguished by the presence of a false membrane in the air passages." This may be regarded as one of the earliest recognitions of the characteristics of diphtheria. He also published essays on delirium tremens and on hemoptysis. He was much interested in natural science, and he enlarged with original matter and re-published Smellie's "Natural History" under the title of "Philosophy of Natural History," by Ware and Smellie. He also wrote a memoir of his brother, the Rev. Henry Ware, Jr. Dr. Ware was a member of the American Academy of Arts and Sciences and from 1848 to 1852, president of the Massachusetts Medical Society. For a short time he was a visiting physician to the Massachusetts General Hospital, and on the organization of the Boston City Hospital in 1864, was appointed to the consulting staff. For the last twenty years of his life his health was somewhat impaired, and he spent his summers and leisure moments on his country place in Weston, although continuing in practice as a consultant. He died of apoplexy in Boston, April 29, 1864.

Dr. Jacob Bigelow said of him: "A favorite term used by Dr. Ware in enumerating the various causes of mortality was 'hyper-practice.' He had an instinctive aversion to over-drugging. His prescriptions were simple, seldom containing more than one, two or three articles."

Dr. Ware married April 22, 1822, Helen Lincoln, daughter of Desire Thaxter and Dr. Levi Lincoln, of Hingham, and had eight children. One of his sons was Maj. Robert Ware, A. B., (Harvard) 1852, M. D. 1856, surgeon of the Forty-fourth Massachusetts Infantry, who lost his life in the War of the Rebellion. Mrs. Ware died in 1858 and in 1862, Dr. Ware married Mary Green Chandler, of Lancaster, Massachusetts, who survived him.

Dr. Ware's portrait may be seen in the Boston Medical Library in John Ware Hall, which was dedicated to his memory by his son-in-law and daughter, Dr. and Mrs. Charles M. Green. Dr. Ware's memory is perpetuated in the Harvard Medical School by the endowment, in 1891, by William Story Bullard, of the John Ware Memorial Fellowship. At the same time Mr. Bullard established similar fellowships in memory of Dr.

George Cheyne Shattuck and of Dr. Charles Eliot Ware (half-brother of John Ware).

At a meeting of the Massachusetts Medical Society held May 25, 1864, shortly after Dr. Ware's death, Dr. Oliver Wendell Holmes read a poem in memory of John and Robert Ware, father and son. One stanza referring to John Ware, but applicable alike to his son, runs:

"A whiter soul, a fairer mind,
    A life with purer course and aim,
A gentler eye, a voice more kind,
    We may not look on earth to find.
The love that lingers o'er his name
    Is more than fame."
                            W. L. B.

Ware Genealogy; Robert Ware of Dedham, Massachusetts, 1642—1699, and his Lineal Descendants, Boston, 1901.
Family records and Dr. Ware's Dairy, through his daughter, Mrs. Charles M. Green
Boston Medical and Surgical Journal, Communications of the Massachusetts Medical Society. Dr. Edward H. Clarke in a Century of American Medicine, 1876.
History of the Boston City Hospital, 1906.
The Poetical Works of Oliver Wendell Holmes.

Warfield, Charles Alexander (1751–1813).

He was the son of Azel Warfield, and was born in Anne Arundel County, Maryland, December 3, 1751. He is credited with having been a graduate (M. B. ?) of the College of Medicine of Philadelphia, but his name does not occur in the catalogue, and he signs a diploma of the College of Medicine of Maryland as Praêses in 1812, without degree. He early took sides against England in the disputes with the American colonists. In 1774 we find him major of a battalion in his county and wearing a label bearing the dangerous inscription: "Liberty and Independence or Death in Pursuit of It." In October of the same year, hearing of the arrival of the Brig "Peggy Stewart," in the harbor of Annapolis, loaded with forbidden tea, on the nineteenth of the month he placed himself at the head of the "Whig Club," of which he was a prominent member, and marched to the capital with the determi-

JOHN WARREN.
(From a painting by R. Peale.)

nation to burn vessel and cargo. When the party arrived opposite the State House, they were met by Judge Samuel Chase, who had been employed as a lawyer by the owner of the vessel, a Scotch merchant. This gentleman proceeded to harangue them in the interest of his client, and was making some impression, when Warfield interrupted him, upbraiding him for inconsistency, for he had previously inflamed the whole country with patriotic speeches, and declaring it submission or cowardice in any member of the club to stop short of their object. As the party marched on, they met Stewart who put on a bold front and threatened them with the vengeance of his king and government. They erected a gallows in front of his house and gave him his choice, either to swing by the halter or go with them on board and set fire to the vessel. He chose the latter and the doctor accompanied him with a chunk of fire. In a few moments the whole cargo and vessel were in flames, and were soon entirely destroyed.

In 1812 he was president of the College of Medicine of Maryland at Baltimore (University of Maryland), a position which he held till his death, which occurred at his place " Bushy Park," on January 29, 1813. At the meeting held in June following a committee of five members of the state faculty was appointed to prepare a testimonial to his life.

Dr. Warfield was a founder of the Medical and Chirurgical Faculty of Maryland in 1799 and from 1803 to 1813 was also on its Board of State Examiners. He had a wide reputation as a physician and an extensive practice and taught many medical students in his office. He married Miss Eliza Ridgely, a daughter of Maj. Henry Ridgely. He has left many descendants in Maryland. There is an oil portrait of him extant which has been reproduced with sketches in Cordell's "Medical Annals of Maryland," 1903, and Cordell's "History of the University of Maryland," 1907, vol. i; see also appendix to latter. The portrait represents a short person of perhaps forty-five with a full suit of gray hair, a full face and regular features and a most determined expression.   E. F. C.

Warren, John (1753–1815).

He was born in the family homestead in Roxbury, Massachusetts, July 27, 1753, and graduated at Harvard in 1770, after which he studied medicine for two years with his brother, Joseph, then practised in Salem. He was at the Battle of Bunker Hill, attending the wounded on the field and coolly exposing himself to the fire of the British. He received a bayonet wound in endeavoring to pass a sentry in order to see his brother and after the battle was appointed hospital surgeon, and in 1776 accompanied the Continental Army to New York and New Jersey. He was at Trenton and Princeton, where he rendered distinguished service.

For nearly forty years John Warren occupied the foremost place among the surgeons of New England. He was recognized as the leading medical expert and surgical scientist of the times. In 1780 he demonstrated anatomy in a series of dissections before his colleagues, and in 1783 was appointed professor of anatomy and surgery in the newly established medical school at Harvard. When the Massachusetts medical society was organized he was chosen as its first president, an office which he held continuously from 1804 until his death in 1815.

Dr. Warren's avocations outside of his profession of medicine and surgery were pursued with the same intelligence and zeal that characterized his regular work. Warren was the author of "Mercurial Practice in Febrile Diseases," a volume that had a wide vogue among the fraternity. In addition he wrote "Memoirs," addressed to the American academy, "Communications," published by the Massachusetts Medical Society, and numerous articles in "The Journal of Medicine and Surgery." He died in Boston, April 4, 1815.   G. F. B.

Lives of Eminent American Phys., S. D. Gross.

Am. Jour. of Clinical Med., June, 1909 (George F. Butler).

Warren, John Collins (1778–1856).

Among the men of past generations few led more steadily laborious and useful lives than John Collins Warren. He was born in Boston in 1778, on the first of August, the eldest son of that interesting John Warren who served in the Revolution and founded the Harvard Medical School.

Warren was intended by his father for a mercantile life, but passed a couple of years at French and the pretended study of medicine, as he himself says. Then he went to Europe and settled down to serious work, in 1799. London claimed him first, where he became a pupil of William Cooper, and later of William Cooper's nephew, Astley Cooper. Warren secured a dresser's position at Guy's Hospital—it was merely a matter of money down—and served at such work and dissecting for something more than a year, then went to Edinburgh for a year, where he received his medical degree, and for a final year to Paris. In the two latter places he studied hard—going in for chemistry, general medicine and midwifery, as well as anatomy and surgery. He lived in Paris with Dubois, Napoleon's distinguished surgeon, and studied anatomy with Ribes, Sabatier, Chaussier, Cuvier and Dupuytren; medicine with Corvisart, and botany with Desfontaines. That was a brilliant gathering for the edifying of a young gentleman from Boston.

In 1802, Warren came home, and found his father in very poor health. In order to relieve him he immediately assumed a great part of his practice.

The years between 1802 and 1810 were important years to Warren. To begin with, he married, in 1803, a daughter of Jonathan Mason, and began the rearing of his many children. With Jackson, Dixwell, Coffin, Bullard and Howard, he formed a Society for Medical Improvement. In 1806 he was made adjunct to his father in the chair of anatomy and surgery at Harvard, and succeeded to the full professorship, upon his father's death, in 1815.

Warren's name will always be associated with two important facts: the founding of the Massachusetts General Hospital and the introduction of ether anesthesia. These two events were separated by an interval of twenty-five years, but around them both are grouped nearly all that is conspicuous in Boston medicine during the first fifty years of the last century.

In 1809, while still comparatively fresh from European teachers, he published a valuable paper on organic diseases of the heart, a subject, which until then was little understood in this country; and in 1811, together with Jackson, Gorham, Jacob Bigelow and Channing, he assisted in founding the "New England Journal of Medicine and Surgery." This publication was ably edited and in 1828 was united with another, under the title, "The Boston Medical and Surgical Journal."

As a writer, Warren was lucid and strong. He had a great many things to say and he said them well.

He was a very able surgeon of the painstaking type. In those days all operations, even the most inconsiderable from our point of view, were serious matters.

With all care and method, Warren was not a timid operator. His amputations were bold and brilliant; he removed cataracts with great success; taught and practised the operation for strangulated hernia—the first surgeon in this country to do so, and against strong professional opinion here; introduced the operation for aneurysm according to Hunter's method. His excisions of bones for tumor, especially of the jaw, became famous and are classics—for are they not recorded in volumes of the "Boston Medical and Surgical Journal"? In 1837, when fifty-nine years old, he published his magnum opus, "Surgical Observations on Tumors," a thick octavo with plates—a great collection of cases and remarks, interesting and instructive to-day. But all this gives only a very faint idea of his ceaseless literary activity. He was always writing; reports, memoirs, essays, lectures poured from his pen. It was a fiuent pen, and had behind it a brain stored with keen thoughts and abundant information.

Always greatly interested in comparative anatomy and paleontology, he was able to secure, among other trophies, the most perfect skeleton of the mastodon which exists—the monster still preserved in the old building on Chestnut Street which has been known for sixty years as the Warren Museum. All through his life he devoted himself, like Hunter and Cooper before him, to the collection of anatomical specimens. This collection, together with the treasures of the Medical Improvement Society, passed years ago to the Harvard Medical School and formed the nucleus of the fine "Warren Museum" of that institution.

He was prominent also in the establishment of the American Medical Association, and there was that other great event with which his name is most conspicuously connected; the first public use in surgery of ether anesthesia. This was in October, 1846, when he was approaching his seventieth year. It is needless here to enter upon that most interesting and confused chapter of American surgery. Suffice it to admit as Jacob Bigelow admitted years afterwards, that to Warren belongs the credit, in his old age, of allowing his name and position to stand sponsor for this courageous and revolutionary experiment.

The old man lived on until 1856. Fifteen years before his death his wife died, leaving him with six grown children, and two years later he married a daughter of Gov. Thomas Lindall Winthrop, who also died before him.

He kept busy almost to the end of his life, especially with his writing. His last surgical paper was published in May, 1855, just a year before his death, which closed a brief and painful illness.

Among his writings are: "Cases of Organic Diseases of the Heart," Boston, 1809; "A Comparative View of the Sensorial and Nervous Systems in Men and Animals," Boston, 1822; "Surgical Observations on Tumors," Boston, 1837; "Inhalation of Ethereal Vapor for the Prevention of Pain in Surgical Operations," Boston, 1846; "The Mastodon Giganteus of North America."

J. G. M.

Johns Hopkins Hosp. Bull., July, 1903 (J. G. Mumford).
Mem. of John C. Warren (H. P. Arnold), Cambridge, 1882.
Lives of Eminent Am. Phys., S. D. Gross.
Hist. and Genealog. Register, 1865.
Life of John C. Warren (E. Warren), Boston, 1860, in which there is a portrait and also in the Surg.-gen. collection, Wash., D. C.
Reminiscences of an Old New England Surgeon, J. C. Warren, Jr., Maryland Med. Jour., 1901, vol. xliv.

Warren, Joseph (1741–1775).

Joseph Warren was born at Roxbury, June 11, 1741, and after graduating at Harvard, in 1759, was appointed master of the Roxbury grammar school. He studied medicine under Dr. James Lloyd, and at the age of twenty-three established himself permanently as a physician in Boston. By his successful treatment of small-pox patients, during the epidemic that scourged the New England cities at that period, he acquired a high reputation among the faculty. One of his most illustrious patients was John Adams, afterwards president of the United States, who was so favorably impressed with the young doctor that he retained him as his family physician.

In 1764, he married Elizabeth Hooton, a young lady who inherited an ample fortune.

His zeal in the cause of patriotism rendered him indifferent to bright prospeets of professional advancement, and he soon gave himself heart and soul to American freedom. At every town meeting held in Boston, from the arrival of the British troops in October, 1768, to their removal in March, 1770, his voice was heard and his influence felt. On the morning of June 17, 1775, he met the committee of Safety at Gen. Ward's headquarters on Cambridge Common. Hearing the British had landed at Charlestown he mounted his horse and rode over to Bunker Hill. He asked for the place of greatest need and danger, and, near the end of the battle when the Americans were retreating and he was trying to rally the militia he was struck by a ball in the head and instantly killed. A monument was erected by his brother masons twenty years after, but the Bunker Hill Monument now stands in its place.

G. F. B.

Abridged from a paper in the Am. Jour. of Clin. Med., June, 1909. Portrait in the Surg.-gen. lib., Washington, D. C

Washburn, Cyrus (1774–1859).

Cyrus Washburn was born November 5, 1774, at Hardwick, Massachusetts, the son of Ebenezer and Dorothy (Newhall) Washburn. Ebenezer Washburn was for forty years a school teacher and employed his time, while serving in the army of the Revolution, in teaching the soldiers. Cyrus had a common school education and at seventeen was apprenticed to a cabinet-maker, but an accident so disabled him, that he changed his plans and engaged in school teaching. While so doing he secured the means of studying medicine, with Dr. Spencer Field of Oakham, Massachusetts. His credentials for practice consisted of a certificate from his preceptor, but, twenty-nine years later, he received his M. D. from the Medical College of Castleton.

He began practice in Hardwick, Massachusetts, in 1800 and three years later removed to, and stayed in, Vernon, Vermont.

He held a commission as justice of the peace for fifty-five years and during this time he is said to have performed the marriage ceremony about eight hundred and fifty-three times. His popularity was enhanced by certain legal restrictions in the neighboring states. During the first half of the last century

there was a law in both New Hampshire and Massachusetts that all persons desiring to be married must have such desire and intention published at three public meeting days or three Sabbath days in their respective towns. Sometimes the parties so desiring to be joined in marriage resented this publicity, so they crossed the border to Vernon and sought Dr. Washburn's services. Thus the good doctor acquired a certain fame outside his profession which remains to this day. The marriage ceremony invariably used by Dr. Washburn follows: "The marriage ceremony of Dr. Cyrus Washburn, Esq.:

Parties and relatives being agreed,
To solemn rites we will proceed,
Worthy and much respected groom and bride
That you by nuptial ties may be allied
In preparation for the endearing bands
In token of united hearts; join hands.

"Considering this union of hands, expression of a reciprocal change of heart and affection, do you mutually espouse and avouch, each the other, to be your betrothed, your married companion for life, etc.," the service ending in verse.

" Let no discordant jars your bliss destroy,
But virtue, peace and love your lives employ;
May Gospel faith and works be well combined,
Adorn your lives and educate your mind,
Where'er you dwell let virtue be your guide,
And God above will bless both groom and bride
To good old age may Heaven protract your span
The kind assuagers of each others pain;
Remember, too, all earthly joys must end,
And each be severed from your dearest friend;
But death itself which earthly joys removes
Still heightens virtue and true love improves
Then keep the goal of happiness in mind,
And what you lack on earth, in Heaven you'll find;
Where none are married, none in marriage given,
But are, as are the angels, pure in Heaven."

Dr. Washburn married first, Electa Stratton and had two children. His second wife was Rhoda Field by whom he had six children. His third wife was Lucy Hathaway. Dr. Washburn died at the ripe age of eighty-five.   C. S. C.

Washington, James Augustus (1803–1847).

James Augustus Washington was born in the town of Kinston, North Carolina,

July 31, 1803. His father, John Washington, came to North Carolina from Virginia, and was of the same family as *the* Washington, though of this fact Mr. Washington never made especial mention. His mother, Elizabeth Cobb, of a prominent North Carolina family, was a humanitarian in the broadest sense; her life-long custom was to visit the sick and distressed, one of her children usually accompanying her with a bountiful basket to relieve the hunger and pains of poverty. From this source Dr. Washington inherited his great love for mankind and tender sympathy for all forms of suffering.

After finishing a very creditable course at Chapel Hill, the University of North Carolina, he studied medicine with Dr. Parker, a physician of Kinston, and afterwards attended medical lectures at the University of Pennsylvania. Graduating there, he went to Paris, where, through an acquaintance with LaFayette, he obtained the favor of Louis Philippe, thereby gaining access to all the French institutes and academies, the then centers of medical science. His stay in Paris was probably from 1830 to 1832.

On his return to America, Washington settled in New York City, where he soon won distinction. The people would come in great numbers from far and near to procure the benefit of his marvellous skill and kindness. It was told that on one of these visits, he was called to see a very poor woman who was desperately ill. Finding no one in the house of an age to assist him, he went out, cut the wood, filled a pot with water, heated it, and, using an old hogshead in lieu of a tub, gave her a bath himself. It is needless to say that she recovered.

He was noted for his courtly manners and great personal magnetism. Although such a scholarly man, he never wrote anything. He spent most of his time in getting up improved instruments and in investigating the nature of disease; this latter seems to have interested him from his earliest years.

His fame was great in the south and

west, also in Europe. It is probable that he had more patients from a distance than any other physician of that period. A grateful Scotch patient had the celebrated sculptor David, make a beautiful bronze medallion of him, which, within recent years was in the possession of his family.

Washington became deeply interested in the experiments with crude morphine begun by LaForgue in 1836. He would cure neuralgia by scraping the skin and dusting the sore with morphine. In 1839, he used a morphine solution and injected it under the skin with an Anel's eye syringe. This was four years prior to the invention of Dr. Wood of Edinburgh, and Dr. C. B. Woodley of Kinston says Prof. A. Smith used to tell his students at the old Bellevue Hospital Medical College that Washington invented the hypodermic syringe.

December 2, 1834, he married Anna W. Constable of Schenectady, New York. He died in 1847, survived by six children. A relative tells that in his last illness, which was some form of stomach trouble, he said to those surrounding his bed that if he could only operate on himself he could be cured, as he knew the exact location of his disease.

L. T. R.

From a newspaper sketch of Dr. Washington published in Kinston, N. C , October, 1892, Dr. H. O. Hyatt, Editor.

Waterhouse, Benjamin (1754–1846).

Benjamin Waterhouse, founder of the Harvard Medical School, first vaccinator for small-pox in America, by vote of the London Medical Society dubbed the "Jenner of America," was born in Newport, Rhode Island, March 4, 1754, the son of a tanner, Timothy Waterhouse, who lived in Portsmouth and removed to Newport, a man of considerable weight in the community as he was made a judge of the Court of Common Pleas and a member of the Royal Council of and for the colony of Rhode Island and Providence Plantations. His mother, Hannah Proud, was a niece of the illustrious John Fothergill, of England. She, like Dr. Fothergill, was born in Yorkshire, England, and both were Quakers.

Benjamin went to the same school in Newport as Gilbert Stuart, the celebrated portrait painter, and at the age of sixteen studied medicine with Dr. John Halliburton, of Newport, remaining there until he sailed for Europe in 1775. He arrived in London in April of that year and became a member of Dr. Fothergill's family. He remained about three years in England, part of the time attending lectures in Edinburgh and elsewhere and also visiting the London hospitals and some of Dr. Fothergill's own patients.

In 1778, he was sent to the University of Leyden, at that time the most noted medical school in the world, to complete his education. There he remained four years, taking his degree in 1781 and attending courses of lectures on additional subjects not included in the college curriculum, for another year. At Leyden he was thrown in contact with John Adams, who had been sent to Holland to court an alliance with America, and Waterhouse lived in Adams' family for a while. Finally in June, 1782, after an absence of more than seven years, Waterhouse, twenty-eight years old, probably the best educated physician in America, returned to his native town and began to practise. His old preceptor, Dr. Halliburton, had just removed to Halifax, so Waterhouse stepped into his shoes.

In the following year Harvard University invited him to assist in forming a medical school in Cambridge and to take the chair of theory and practice of medicine. This he did and removed to Cambridge, Massachusetts, where he spent the rest of his life. Benjamin Waterhouse (theory and practice of medicine); John Warren (anatomy and surgery), and Aaron Dexter (chemistry) formed the entire faculty of the new Harvard Medical School. Waterhouse delivered the inaugural oration, a scholarly and well written address in Latin.

In the years 1786 and 1787 he delivered a course of lectures on natural history in the Rhode Island College at Providence, and in succeeding years these lectures, touching chiefly on mineralogy and botany, were repeated and continued in Cambridge. They were really the first systematic instruction in these branches in America. Having obtained a large and valuable collection of minerals from his friend, Dr. Lettsom, of London, Dr. Waterhouse formed the nucleus of the present fine collection at Harvard and was instrumental in forming the Botanical Garden at Cambridge, in order to have specimens with which to illustrate his lectures. In 1786 Harvard conferred on him her honorary M. D.

Having helped to found a medical school, his next great life work was the introduction into America of the vaccination of cow-pox as a preventative against small-pox. In the year 1799 he received from his old friend, Dr. Lettsom, a copy of Edward Jenner's "Inquiry into the Causes and Effects of the Variolæ Vaccinæ, or Cow-pox," published by Jenner in 1798. It was thought that this was the first copy to reach the new world. It produced a profound impression on Waterhouse and he straightway published in the "Columbian Sentinel," of Boston, March 12, 1799, a short account of the new inoculation, under the title, "Something Curious in the Medical Line." "This publication," he says, "shared the fate of most others on new discoveries. A few received it as a very important discovery, highly interesting to humanity; some doubted it; others observed that wise and prudent conduct which allows them to condemn or applaud, as the event might prove; while a greater number absolutely ridiculed it as one of those medical whims which arise to-day and to-morrow are no more." Dr. Waterhouse about this time received from London the second publication in vaccine literature, Dr. George Pearson's book entitled, "An Inquiry Concerning the History of the Cow-pox Principally with a View to Supersede and Extinguish the Small-pox." Shortly he read a paper on the new inoculation before a meeting of the American Academy of Arts and Sciences, held in Cambridge. The academy was presided over by his old friend, John Adams, then president, and was composed of many eminent literary men. The communication was received with great acclaim by the Academy and especially by the president. Very soon Waterhouse received the third publication on vaccination, namely, William Woodville's "Reports of a Series of Inoculations for the Variolæ Vaccinæ, or Cow-pox, etc." published in 1799. He spared no pains to receive the fullest and most reliable information on the subject. In June, 1800, he succeeded, after many futile attempts, in procuring some vaccine virus on threads, from Dr. Haygarth, of Bath, England, all of the previous shipments having been spoiled during the long journey over the ocean. With this virus, on July 8, 1800, he vaccinated successfully his little five year old son, Daniel Oliver Waterhouse, the first person to be so treated in America. The result being satisfactory he vaccinated two others of his children, and in addition a nurse maid and a servant boy. The phenomena were carefully described by him. He refused to vaccinate others until he had ascertained whether vaccination was really protective. To determine this he made application to Dr. William Aspinwall, physician to a private small-pox hospital in Brookline, Massachusetts, to submit his children to the disease. This Dr. Aspinwall did gladly and the children were not only exposed to small-pox, but inoculated with the variolous matter. The results were entirely satisfactory and put Waterhouse in a position to advance the crusade. As he truly remarked—"One fact in such cases is worth a thousand arguments."

Waterhouse was a prolific writer and something of a controversialist. In his early work with vaccine he made the same mistake as Woodville; he not only vaccinated with cow-pox, but within a few days, inoculated with small-pox as

well, consequently many of the patients had variola as well as vaccinia. Later he recognized the mistake, also the reason that much of the virus was without virtue was because Jenner's golden rule was broken, namely, "Never to take the virus from a vaccine pustule, for the purpose of inoculation, after the efflorescence is formed around it." In 1801 Waterhouse sent Pres. Thomas Jefferson some infected threads and such books and drawings as would enable a physician to perform vaccination properly. This was in answer to a letter from Jefferson showing interest as a result of reading Waterhouse's publications. This virus proved to be inert, but later some fresh virus was sent him with which Dr. Wardlaw, of Monticello, vaccinated the president's family, August 6, 1801. Thus was vaccination popularized in Monticello, and before long in Washington through virus sent there to Dr. Gant. In like fashion virus was sent to New York and Philadelphia. Finally, at Waterhouse's request, the Boston Board of Health, after many refusals to act, appointed a committee of seven of the most reputable physicians in the town to investigate the subject. They vaccinated nineteen children in August, 1802. In November of the same year these same children were inoculated two different times with variolous matter and exposed for twenty days to the contagion of small-pox at the small-pox hospital on Noddle's Island (East Boston). The experiment proved conclusively "that cow-pox is a complete security against the small-pox," as not one of the children took the disease. Thus was the practice of vaccination fixed forever in Boston and its vicinity. Waterhouse kept in touch with practitioners throughout the county and furnished them with fresh virus from England while supporting vaccination with his pen, his friendships formed in England putting him in possession of the latest and best information on the subject.

He was peculiarly well fitted to fight for a worthy cause and he fought long and earnestly, encountering much obliquy and abuse, but doing as much for his native country and for humanity as he would had he foregone a lengthy foreign education and served during the Revolution either as an army surgeon or in the ranks, as did many of his contemporaries.

At this late day it is hard to appreciate the awful ravages made by the small-pox. According to Moore (James Moore, "The History of the Small-pox," London, 1815), the annual loss of life had been progressively augumented until in the last thirty years of the eighteenth century it was estimated by Sir Gilbert Blane and Dr. Lettsom (who reported their investigations to a committee of the House of Commons), that the number of deaths from this disease in Great Britain and Ireland was between 34,000 and 36,000 annually. It is glory enough to have made permanent the practice of vaccination and thus saved countless thousands of lives.

In Dr. Waterhouse's middle life and later years he was beset by professional jealousies and intrigues among the physicians connected with the medical school, so in 1812, when only fifty-six years old, he felt constrained to resign his professorship. His time from now on was devoted mainly to literature. Pres. Madison gave him the medical supervision of nine medical posts in New England, thus providing for the family a means of support, for Waterhouse's long-continued efforts to make known the true doctrines of Jennerian vaccination had impoverished him. This position he held seven years. Appeals to the Massachusetts Legislature were in vain. Intrigues had deprived him of his position as physician to the United States Marine Hospital with a stipend of £500 a year and he felt himself too old to take up a new means of gaining a livelihood.

Waterhouse wrote the first work on vaccination published in this country, entitled, "A Prospect of Exterminating the Small-pox," published in 1800. In 1802 he published a larger pamphlet on the same subject. At the close of the course of lectures in the Medical School in 1804, he delivered to the students of the university a lecture on "Cautions to Young Persons Concerning Health," containing the general doctrine of chronic disease, showing the evil tendency of the using of tobacco upon young persons, more especially the ruinous effects of smoking cigars, with observations on the use of ardent and vinous spirits in general." This lecture won great fame, much to Dr. Waterhouse's pleasure. During the next fifteen or twenty years, six editions were printed and the lecture was translated into several foreign languages.

Dr. Waterhouse married twice, the last time to a daughter of Thomas Lee, of Cambridge. In personal appearance Dr. Waterhouse was of medium height, compactly built and destitute of any superfluous flesh; quick and alert in all his movements, he seemed at all times to be prepared both bodily and mentally, for immediate action or speech. Being of Quaker origin he was scrupulously nice in his attire, dressing always in the English medical style in fine black broadcloth, and carrying a gold headed cane. When speaking he gesticulated freely and enunciated strongly. In conversation he was full of information and of anecdote, and very entertaining."

He died in Cambridge, October 2, 1846, at the advanced age of ninety-two years and seven months, having been in poor health for many years before the end.

The following are the titles of some of his publications: "The Botanist;" "Lectures on Natural History with a Discourse on the Principle of Vitality;" "Circular Letter to the Surgeons in the Second Military Department of the United States Army (on dysentery)," Cambridge, 1817; "Dissertatio Med. de Sympathia," Lndg. Bal., 1780; "An Essay Concerning Whooping Cough, with Observations on the Diseases of Children," Boston, 1822; "Essay on Junius and his Letters; Life of W. Pitt, etc.," Boston,

1831. "Journal of a Young Man of Massachusetts Captured at Sea by the British, May, 1812," Boston, 1816; "Oratio Inaug. Quam in Academia Harvardiana Habuit., 1783," Cantab, 1829; "Rise, Progress and Present State of Medicine," Boston, 1786. W. L. B.

The Jenner of America, W. M. Welch, An Address, Phila., 1885.
Jefferson as a vaccinator, Henry A. Martin, Bull. Har. Med. Alumni Asso., 1902–3.
The History and Practice of Vaccination, James Moore, Lon., 1817.
Reports of a Series of Inoculations for the Variolæ Vaccinæ, or Cow-pox, by William Woodville, M. D., London, 1799.
Bos. Med. and Surg. Jour., vol. xxxv., Oct. 7, 1846.
Hist. Har. Med. School, vol. i (T. F. Harrington.) Port. in the Van Kaathoven Coll., Surg.-gen. Lib., Wash., D. C.

Waterman, Thomas (1842–1901).

Thomas Waterman, a prominent expert in mental diseases, was the son of Thomas and Joanna (Twole) Waterman, and born in Boston, December 17, 1842. He was the grandson of Col. Thomas Waterman and of the eighth generation from the English ancestor who settled in New Hampshire.

As a lad he went to the Brimmer Grammar School, Boston Latin School and Harvard College, where he graduated in 1864. He began the study of medicine with Jeffries Wyman, at that time professor of comparative anatomy and physiology in Harvard University. Waterman received his M. D. from the Harvard Medical School in 1868 and practised medicine in Boston from that time until his death, December 14, 1901. After 1883 he devoted much of his time to mental diseases and was examining physician to the commissioners of public institutions of Boston. He also appeared in the courts of law as an expert in mental disease. His honesty, self-possession and carefully weighed testimony made him an excellent witness. He was a member of the Massachusetts Medical Society; Boston Society for Medical Improvement, and Boston Medico-Psychological Society.

During his medical training he was house surgeon at the Massachusetts General Hospital and from 1870 to 1881 physician and surgeon to the Boston Dispensary; surgeon to St. Joseph's Home from 1871 to 1878; instructor in comparative anatomy and physiology, at Harvard University in 1873 and 1874; and assistant demonstrator of anatomy in the Harvard Medical School from 1879 to 1882.

He married Harriet Henchman, daughter of Edward Howard, maker of the famous Howard clocks, December 4, 1872, and had two daughters.

Dr. Waterman was much interested in the exposure of pseudo-spiritualism and mediumistic impostors.

W. L. B.

Bos. Med. and Surg. Journal, vol. cxlvi.
Physicians and Surgeons of America, I A. Watson.

Watson, Beriah André (1836–1892).

Beriah André Watson, surgeon, was born near Lake George March 26, 1836, the third son of Perry and Marion Watson. He attended the local schools and the State Normal School, Albany and studied medicine with Dr. James Reilly at Succasunna, New Jersey, matriculating at New York University in 1859, and taking his M. D. there in 1861.

He served as surgeon during the Civil War in the United States' service and after the battle of Gettysburg was commissioned surgeon with the rank of major. After this he settled in Jersey City and was instrumental in the formation of the New Jersey Academy of Medicine, and was one of the organizers of the Jersey City Hospitals, where he became surgeon in 1869. In 1873 he was surgeon to St. Francis' Hospital and, later, to Christ Hospital.

Even with all his work as surgeon he managed to get through a great deal of writing in his library—one of the largest medical libraries in the State. He took a great interest in mineralogy also, and had a good collection. A keen sportsman he had many trophies hanging on his walls and wrote a volume in 1888, "The Sportsman's Paradise."

His death was the result of exposure and fatigue while in pursuit of game. This happened on December 22, 1892. His wife and one daughter survived him.

His writings, of which there is a fairly long list in the catalogue of the Surgeon-general's Library, Washington, District of Columbia, included: "A Case of Facial Neuralgia treated by Extirpation of the Superior Maxillary Nerve." ("Medical Record," 1871.)

"Woorara in Rabies." ("American Journal of Medical Science," vol. lxxiii.)

"Gunpowder Disfigurements." ("St. Louis Medical and Surgical Journal," vol. xxxv.)

"Pyemia and Septicemia." ("New York Medical Journal," vol. xxvi).

"Disease Germs, Their Origin, Nature and Relation to Wounds." ("Transactions of American Medical Association, vol. xxix.)

He translated several medical essays from the French and German, and wrote one large volume "Amputations and Their Complications" (1885) and left an unfinished work on "Surgery of the Spine." He contributed "Pyemia and Septicemia to Pepper's "American System of Practical Medicine" and a chapter on "The Operative Treatment of the Spleen" to Keating's "Diseases of Children." A short "History of Surgery" was one of his contributions to medical history and he also wrote a brochure on "Experimental Study of Lesions Arising From Severe Concussions."

In 1882, Rutgers College gave him her honorary M. A. D. W.

The Annals of Surgery, 1893, xvii (Roy Inglis).

Trans. Amer. Surg. Ass., Phila., 1894, xii, xxiii.

Wanghop, John Wesley (1839–1903).

John Wesley Waughop, medicojuris-prudentist, was born October 22, 1839, near Peoria, Illinois, and had his medical degree from the Long Island College in 1865.

Settling in Chicago, he practised for a number of years, then, on account of health, removed to Olympia, Washington, where, soon after his arrival, he was made superintendent of the Western Washington Hospital for the Insane. While in Washington he was very active in medical society work, the old Medical Society of Washington Territory being organized in his house. He was president of the State Medical Society; vice-president of the Medico-legal Society of New York, etc., etc. In 1897 he removed to the Hawaiian Islands, where he practised for six years. A part of this time he was superintendent of the Koloa Hospital. He did much special work on tuberculosis for the Hawaiian Board of Health, and wrote a good deal on lego-medical topics, and was an experienced and careful anesthetist, having, according to report, administered chloroform, in Washington and Hawaii combined, over ten thousand times without one single death.

Dr. Wangbop was a tall and heavily-set man, of dark complexion and with brown hair and black eyes. He was very fond of general, as well as of scientific, literature, and his favorite authors were Shakespeare, Dickens, Tennyson, Schiller, Goethe. He was given to translating from the German by way of recreation, and would frequently drop down in his chair during a spare twenty minutes, and, taking up his quill (which he always preferred to any other pen) would write out the translation to a couple of paragraphs from some German author. In this way he translated numerous German stories which were published in the newspapers, as well as one or two German historical works.

Two little anecdotes paint his character in adversity. When a boy, while at play on the ground near the old family mare she accidentally stepped on him, laying open a large portion of his scalp. Though the injury must have been painful, he did not go to his parents about it; and they were shocked when they came upon him to find him still at play with the great gash over his forehead, a scar which persisted all his life. So again when he almost severed his great toe while splitting kindling one winter's eve. He stole off to bed without telling anyone of the occurrence, and it was only when his good mother was drying her children's stockings that night before herself retiring, that the tell-tale cut and blood in his sock betrayed the mishap.

In 1866 he married Eliza S. Rexford, of Chicago, by whom he had one child, Philip Rexford, who became a physician in Seattle, Washington.

Dr. Waughop died at sea off Cape Flattery, Washington, enroute per steamship "Noana" from Honolulu for Vic toria, British Columbia. He had been gradually sinking in the Hawaiian Islands, with pernicious anemia, and in order to seek relief from this affection he was on his way to the healthier climate of the North.

T. H. S.

Medico-Legal Journal, Sept , 1906, vol. xxiv, No. 2 (Dr. E. S. Goodhue).

Wayne, Edward S. (1818–1885).

Edward S. Wayne, of Quaker origin, was born in Philadelphia in 1818, and in his early years was apprenticed to a drug firm. Here he became proficient not only as a chemist, but as a mechanical engineer, and while a mere boy superintended the erection of a white lead factory, of which he had the charge for some years. After several years Wayne became partner in a firm of chemists and afterwards had an analytical laboratory, where he remained until his health failed, when he returned to Philadelphia, dying in that city December 11, 1885.

He was awarded a degree by the Ohio Medical College, serving therein as professor of chemistry, and becoming an authority with the medical profession, as well as in all things pertaining to pharmacy. He was active in the organization of the Cincinnati College of Pharmacy, holding the chair of chemistry therein until a year or so before his death, when his failing health led him to resign this for a position in the State Board of Pharmacy.

He was an easy writer, and, between 1855 and 1870, contributed numerous papers to the "American Journal of Pharmacy," and to the American Pharmaceutical Association, the titles of these being recorded in these publications, among them being one on "The Gizzard of the South American Ostrich," from which he first showed that a preparation thus obtained could be used as a remedy for dyspepsia. In 1860, when Nicholas Longworth became enthusiastic over the possibility of the Ohio hillsides becoming a national source of grape and wine culture, Professor Wayne united with him, and instituted experiments for making therefrom cream of tartar and tartaric acid. He actively engaged in assaying minerals, and showed that a quicksilver mine in North Carolina yielded 150 pounds of mercury to the ton.

During the early days he was one of the first to manufacture coal oil from bituminous coal, a business that was wrecked on the opening of the kerosene fields.

I remember Professor Wayne as a medium-sized man of charming personality, easy in manner and a ready conversationalist, exceedingly neat and up-to-date in dress, even to the verge of being dandified. His work as an educator brought him into contact with the young, with whom he was always a favorite, by reason of his delightfully pleasant address his unquestioned knowledge, his invariable courtesy to all, and his helpful encouragement. J. U. L.

Bull. of the Lloyd Lib. Pharmacy Series No. 2, 1910 (port.).

Webster, James (1803–1854).

James Webster was born in Washington, Lancashire, England, December 24, 1803. His parents emigrated to this country while he was still a small boy, and settled in Philadelphia, where his father became an eminent book-seller and publisher, and established the "Medical Recorder," of which his son later became an editor. Webster's father meant him to study law, but the boy's inclinations led to the study of medicine, which he took up first in Baltimore and then in Philadelphia, graduating at the University of Pennsylvania in 1824, at the age of twenty. He was a private pupil of Dr. J. D. Godman, and when the latter went to Rutgers College in 1826, he was succeeded at the Philadelphia School of Anatomy by Webster, a post retained for four years. He was a good teacher and excellent anatomist, although not so talented and energetic as some of the others who had had charge of the Philadelphia School of Anatomy. He made a practice of performing all dissections before his classes. He was thoroughly devoted to the interests of his class, and according to Dr. W. W. Keen, at one time, when there was greater difficulty than usual in getting subjects, he sat up night after night, watching that neither the University or any private room should obtain them till he was supplied, and gaining his point.

His literary efforts while in Philadelphia were limited to editing the "Medical Recorder," in 1827–29, when it was merged into the "American Journal of the Medical Sciences." Dr. Keen also states that he believes that Webster was the editor of another rather pugilistic journal, which, however, was short-lived. In 1835 Webster moved to New York, where he acquired a reputation as a surgeon, especially of the eye and ear. In 1842 he went to Rochester as professor of anatomy in the Geneva Medical College.[1] In 1849 he took the chair of anatomy in the University of Buffalo, which he resigned in 1852. He was one of the most popular surgeons in western New York, cautious, yet bold. In character he is said to have been a man of gentle instincts, generous to a fault, and thoroughly likeable. At the time of his death July 19, 1854, he was emeritus professor of anatomy at the Geneva Medical College.   C. R. B.

[1]Keen states that Webster was appointed to this professorship in 1830; the writer in the "Boston Medical and Surgical Journal" gives 1842 as the date when Webster went to Rochester.

W. W. Keen, Philadelphia School of Anatomy.
Boston Medical and Surgical Journal, vol. li, 1854.
Tr. Med. Soc. N. York, 1855 (C. B. Coventry)
N. Y. Jour. Med., 1854, n. s., vol. xiii.

Webster, Noah (1758–1843).

The writer whose published contributions in the eighteenth century are of the greatest permanent value to medicine was not a physician, but a useful and versatile man, Noah Webster, who graduated from Yale in 1788, and who was the first epidemiologist this country produced. In 1796 he published "A Collection of Papers on the Subject of Bilious Fevers Prevalent in the United States for a Few Years Past," and in 1799 a two volume work known to all students of epidemiology entitled "A Brief History of Epidemic and Pestilential Diseases," which is of unusual interest and on account of its records and observations of epidemic diseases in this country has an enduring value. There are scattered papers by him on various medical subjects, and one of these is buried in the "Medical Repository," .2 s. vol. ii, and should be rescued from forgetfulness. In this critique of Erasmus Darwin's "Theory of Fever," Noah Webster gives a well reasoned, clear and definite presentation of that modern theory associated with Traube's name which explains febrile elevation of temperature by the retention of heat within the body.

Webster was admitted to the bar in 1781, and in 1788 settled in New York as a journalist. He was a co-founder of Amherst College, Massachusetts, and lived in Amherst in 1812. His other writings included the well-known "Spelling Book," 1783–5; "Dissertation on the English Language" (1789); "A Compendious Dictionary of the English Language" (1806); "American Dictionary of the English Language" (1828); "Rights of Neutrals" (1802); "A Collection of Papers on Political, Literary and Moral Subjects," and "A Brief History of the United States" (1823).

In 1789 he married Rebecca, daughter

of William Greenleaf, of Boston. He died in New Haven on May 28, 1843, when eighty-five years old.

W. H. W.

Yale in Relation to Medicine, Wm. H. Welch, 1901.
Am. J. Med. Sciences, 1876, vol. lxxii.
A History of the Pennsylvania Hospital, T. G. Morton, Phila., 1895.
The Century Cyclopedia of Names
Noah Webster, H. E. Scudder, 1882.

Wellford Beverly Randolph (1797–1870).

The son of Dr. Robert Wellford, of Fredericksburg, Virginia, he was born in that town on July 29, 1797. Both father and grandfather were doctors. His father was a native of England, and a licentiate of the Royal College of Surgeons. The son studied medicine under his father and then attended two courses of lectures in the University of Maryland, taking his M. D. in 1817.

He was a member of the Medical Society of Virginia (ante-bellum), in 1851–2, president of the State Society and president American Medical Association. In 1854, professor of materia medica and therapeutics in the Medical College of Virginia; he continued to fill the position until the infirmities of age caused his retirement in 1868, when he was made professor emeritus. After graduation he began practice in conjunction with his father in his native place, where he remained until called to Richmond.

His first wife was Betty Burwell Page, whom he married in 1817. She died the next year, leaving one daughter. His second wife was Mary Alexander, whom he married in February, 1824, by whom he had five sons and a daughter, all of whom survived him, except the second son, Dr. Armistead N. Wellford, of Richmond, who died in 1884. The oldest son, Dr. John S. Wellford, succeeded his father in his chair in the Medical College of Virginia. Beverly Wellford died after a protracted illness following a stroke of paralysis, in Richmond on December 27, 1870. He does not seem to have been a contributor to medical literature. We can find no record of any article by him, except his presidential addresses to the American Medical Association in 1853 ("Transactions, American Medical Association," 1853), and the Medical Society of Virginia in 1852.

R. M. S.

From data furnished by Dr. Wellford's son, Mr. Beverley R. Wellford, Jr.

Wellford, Robert (1753–1823).

Robert Wellford, a surgeon in the British Army, was the son of William Welford (the name was spelled in England with a single l), a surgeon of the town of Ware in Hertfordshire, where he was born on April 12, 1753, and most probably pursued his professional studies in London, as he was a licentiate of the Royal College of Surgeons, London.

Soon after he began practice in Ware a traveler who was passing through sustained a fracture of the thigh, and in the absence of Wellford's father, who was urgently summoned, the treatment of the case fell into the son's hands, and so successfully did he manage that the patient became a friend and through this friend, who had influence at court, the young surgeon was tendered an appointment in the medical service of the British Army, either in India, or with the troops then preparing for service in America. Choosing the latter, he came to this country as surgeon of the First Royal Grenadiers for service in the War of the Revolution.

The battles of Brandywine and Germantown threw many prisoners into the hands of the British; these who were held in Philadelphia, receiving the most unkindly, if not brutal, treatment at the hands of the British surgeon and many valuable lives were unnecessarily lost in consequence. This condition of affairs caused Gen. Washington to remonstrate forcibly with Gen. Howe, with the result that the latter upon investigation removed the surgeon, and in his place appointed Dr. Wellford. His administration proved a great success, for by his careful attention a marked change for the better was brought about in the physical condition of the prisoners, and was much appreciated by them, their friends, and by Gen. Washington, who, with many others, became his life-long friend. But, it also made for him some bitter enemies in the persons of certain of his superior officers—notably of the Tory and Hessian contingents of the British Army—and by their conduct towards him his position was rendered intolerable, and he resigned from the service, and determining to make this country his future home, he settled down to practice in Philadelphia.

One of his patients among the prisoners was Col. John Spotswood (a grandson of the old colonial governor of Virginia), whose brother came to Philadelphia to carry the colonel home, as soon as the way was opened by the retreat of the British troops. Upon the solicitation of the Spotswoods, and following the advice of Gen. Washington that he adopt as his American home the vicinity of Fredericksburg, Dr. Wellford accompanied them to Virginia. He brought with him to his new home on the banks of the Rappahannock letters of earnest commendation and of introduction from Washington, and in addition, possessed the affectionate appreciation and good will of all the Spotswood clan. Settling in Fredericksburg, he soon had a good practice, and married a grand-daughter of Edward Randolph, the youngest of the seven sons of William Randolph, of Turkey Island, Catherine Yates by name.

When, in 1794, the so-called "Whiskey Insurrection" in Pennsylvania broke out and assumed so serious an aspect that troops were mobilized by the federal government to subdue it, the president appointed Dr. Wellford surgeon-general of these troops. His services, however, were not required, as the raising of forces was sufficient in itself to quell the uprising.

He lived and practised in Fredericksburg until his death in Fredericksburg on April 24, 1823. His son, Dr. Beverly R. Wellford was a physician, and from 1854 to 1868 professor of materia medica and therapeutics in the Medical College of Virginia.   R. M. S.

The foregoing sketch is based upon data furnished by his grandson, B. R. Wellford.

Wells, **Ebenezer** (1801–1879).

Prof. Wells, a renowned lecturer on obstetrics at the Medical School of Maine, although gossip says that he gained his appointment more by petticoat government than medical worth, deserves mention as a worthy doctor. He did good work and was a teacher in medicine in the proper sense of that word at a time when learning was at a low standpoint. Born in Warren, Maine, March 9, 1801, he was educated by the Rev. Mr. Weldon, of that town, studied medicine with Dr. Joel Stockbridge, of Bath, and graduated at the Medical School of Maine in 1823, afterwards settling in Freeport, Maine, and practising there about fifty-six years.

He married first, October 19, 1823, Lydia Sewall, of Bath, and had three children, and afterwards Mary Angier, daughter of Dr. John Angier Hyde, a practitioner of Freeport. He was often called to assist our learned professor on obstetrics in difficult labor cases, when knowledge from practice was far ahead of book-learning.

Ebenezer Wells was probably one of the best educated men of his time in Maine. He was a good lecturer and well thought of by his patients and brother practitioners. He was early a member of the Maine Medical Society, and attended its meetings with great regularity. After a while he got into politics. Clinging, however, to his practice and professorship, he was given a position as post-master as a reward for political skill with the Whigs. This he held for eight years, then joined another party and was post-master for twelve years more. He was also on the State Legislature for several years, and held various positions of trust, being in fact, a very popular man of the past, and working always for the improvement of the community in which he lived.

He died after a brief illness, October 23, 1879.

J. A. S.

Trans. Maine Med. Assoc.

Wells, Horace (1815-1848).

The credit of first using inhalation of an effective anesthetic for surgical purposes is generally assigned to Horace Wells, a dentist of Hartford, Connecticut. He had seen a person made insensible to pain at a lecture by Dr. G. O. Colton in December, 1844, and himself had a tooth extracted next day under the influence of the nitrous oxide gas. He at once began to use it in dentistry.

In January, 1845, he went to Boston, where Dr. Morton gave him an opportunity of experimenting. For some reason this experiment ended fatally and this had such a depressing effect on Wells that he withdrew from practice and finally ended his own life.

"Wells was the first to take the step to which the finger of Humphry Davy had pointed forty-five years before and the results and claims of Wells were familiar to his friend and former partner, Morton." ("A Consideration of the Introduction of Surgical Anesthesia," W. H. Welch, Boston, 1906.)

A History of the Discovery of the Application of Nitrous Oxide Gas, Ether, and Other Vapors to Surgical Operations, J. G. Wells, Hartford, 1847.
Discovery by the Late Dr. Horace Wells, Hartford, 1850
Dr. Wells, the Discoverer of Anesthesia, New York, 1860.
Richmond and Louisville Medical Journal, Louisville, 1877, vol xxiv.
Galignani's Messenger, February 17, 1847.
New York Tribune, August 2, 1858.
An Examination of the Question of Anesthesia, Truman Smith, New York, 1858.
Trials of a Public Benefactor (T. G. Morton) as Illustrated by the Discovery of Etherization, N. P. Rice, 1859.

Wells, John Doane (1799-1830).

He was born in Boston, March 6, 1799, and graduated in the academic department at Harvard, in 1817, afterwards entering on the study of medicine and serving an apprenticeship with Dr.

Shattuck, who offered special advantages for the study of anatomy. "It was the custom among the young men, with whom he associated, for each one, having dissected a part, to give a lecture thereon to his fellow students. In this useful exercise Wells took much pleasure, and he would often give an exposition, which for accuracy of knowledge, clearness of arrangement and facility of expression would not have been discreditable to an older and much more experienced lecturer." Wells received his M. D. from Harvard in 1820, when his dissertation—on cancer—is said to have been a very good one.

In 1821 he went to Brunswick, Maine, as assistant dissector to Nathan Smith. He frequently took Smith's place in the lecture room, and in the following May was appointed professor of anatomy and surgery. He then went to Europe, and visited France, England and Scotland to prepare for his work. He returned in 1822, and commenced work in 1823 at Brunswick, where his great success as a lecturer served to establish a high reputation for the school. He spent much time in building up a library and a museum. The yearly course of lectures in medical schools in his day was short. After completing his course of lectures, he returned to Boston to establish a practice and in 1823 was appointed physician to the Boston Dispensary, but continued his work each year at Brunswick, and became the most popular lecturer on anatomy in New England. In 1826 he was elected professor of anatomy and surgery in Berkshire Medical Institute at Pittsfield in which the course of lectures was held at a different time of the year from that at Brunswick. In 1829 he received a call to the University of Maryland, at Baltimore. Overwork in connection with the two New England schools, as well as in Baltimore, is said to have sapped his strength so that tuberculosis gained a rapid hold on him, and he died in Boston, the twenty-fifth of August of the following year. Wells, while not gifted with an original mind, was both brilliant and eloquent.   C. R. B.

Boston Medical and Surgical Journal, vol. iii, 1831.

Balt. Month. Jour., Med and Surg., 1830–31, vol. i, Nathan R. Smith, Eulogium, ibid.

Wesselhoeft, Conrad (1834–1904).

Conrad Wesselhoeft, a prominent homeopathist, was born in Weimar, Germany, March 23, 1834, and came to America with his parents, Robert and Ferdinanda E. Wesselhoeft, when a boy.

He graduated from the Harvard Medical School in 1856 and at once began practice in Boston, soon becoming one of the leading homeopathists. As physician and trustee of the Massachusetts Homeopathic Hospital for nearly the entire period of his professional life, he was unremitting in his labors for the cause of homeopathy. In 1879 he was president of the American Institute of Homeopathy and in later years president of the Massachusetts Homeopathic Medical Society, and also of the Boston Homeopathic Medical Society. He filled the chair of pathology and therapeutics in the Medical School (Homeopathic) of Boston University for many years, with distinguished ability.

As a medical author his work covered a wide range, the most notable of his writings being a translation of the "Organon" of Hahnemann. He was one of the committee for preparing the "Cyclopedia of Drug Pathogenesy," also on the committee for publishing the "Pharmacopeia of the American Institute of Homeopathy," and his writings for journals and medical societies have been very numerous.

Dr. Wesselhoeft married Elizabeth Foster Pope, who survived him. In March, 1904, more than two hundred of his friends and associates celebrated his seventieth birthday by a banquet, and presented him with a loving-cup and a purse of $2,000.

Dr. Wessehoeft had closer relations with the members of the regular profession than most homeopathists. He

lectured on one occasion at least to the students of the Harvard Medical School explaining the principles of homeopathy, and it was his aim to bring into closer touch all practitioners of the healing art.

His death occurred in Newton Centre, Massachusetts, December 17, 1904.
                    W. L. B.

Bulletin Harvard Med. Alumni Asso., April, 1905.

West, Hamilton Atchison (1830–1903).

Hamilton Atchison West was born in Russell's Cave, Fayette County, Kentucky, the second child and eldest son of James N. and Isabella Atchison West. His father was a native of Georgia and his grandfather, Dr. Charles West, a physician of Georgia and a member of the legislature.

He went as a boy to the common schools and entered the medical department of the University of Louisville, graduating in 1872 with first honors— the faculty medal—for the best thesis, his subject being the "Thermometry of Disease."

In 1873 he moved to Galveston, Texas, where he lived till his death. It was largely through his efforts that the medical department of the University of Texas was located in Galveston, and upon its organization he was elected to the chair of general and clinical medicine.

He was a vice-president of the American Medical Association in 1898.

Dr. West's first wife was Sallie Mason Davenport, of Virginia, and his second Mrs. Ella May Fuller. Five children survived him.

His death was due to acute suppression of urine, occurring in the course of chronic interstitial nephritis, which was further complicated by pneumonia.

He had gone to New York City in the hope of getting relief, but within a week after his arrival he rapidly succumbed, dying at the home of his brother, December 30, 1903.

Dr. West was a good writer and contributed largely to medical literature. He wrote the articles on "Dengue," and "Dysentery" in the "American System of Medicine," and the article on "Yellow Fever" in Gould and Pyle's "Cyclopedia of Medicine." H. E. H.

West, Henry S. (1827–1876).

Died at Sivas, in Turkey in Asia, April 1, 1876, Henry S. West, M. D., a missionary physician, formerly of Binghamton, New York, aged forty-nine years, three months.

Such was the announcement which reached the friends of Dr. West, causing the most profound regret throughout a large circle.

He was born in Binghamton, New York, January 21, 1827, the only son of Silas West, M. D. He entered Yale College in the class of 1844. He graduated at the College of Physicians and Surgeons in New York city, March, 1850. Immediately after graduation he began to practise in Binghamton, in company with his father, and so continued for a number of years. In 1858 he accepted an appointment as missionary physician from the American Board of Commissioners for Foreign Missions. The field of service assigned him was Turkey in Asia, and, accompanied by his wife, he sailed from Boston to join that mission in January, 1859. He was stationed at Sivas, a city containing a population of 35,000 or 40,000 inhabitants, situated about 450 miles southeast of Constantinople.

On reaching the station assigned him, Dr. West entered at once upon his duties and his services soon became in great demand. The center of his practice was at Sivas and the numerous towns and villages by which it is surrounded. There were other important cities in Asia Minor into which the practice of Dr. West extended—the nearest of these being Tokat, about fifty miles to the northwest, containing about 30,000 people, and Kaisarieh, 100 miles to the southwest, embracing, with its suburbs, a population of 150,000. In giving a description of the extent of his practice, the doctor remarks: "My practice was largely in these cities also, therefore I had frequent occasion to visit them professionally, when I was always thronged with patients, and many came to me to be treated from those places, at Sivas. I was frequently called also to other important towns and cities of Asia Minor, distant from 150 to 300 miles."

Many of these calls were to surgical cases, and in treating them the doctor developed a tact and an operative ability, of which he himself was probably unaware until they were brought out by the emergencies of his position. Of the surgical cases, affections of the eye, and of the urino-genital organs, were largely predominant.

In 1868 he re-visited the United States and reported upward of sixty-eight operations for stone in the bladder. He read before the Medical Society of the State of New York a paper "Medical and Surgical Experience in Asia Minor," published in the "Transactions," of that year. In 1870 he was elected an honorary member. G. B

Obituary Notice of Henry S. West, M. D., by George Burr, M. D., Trans. of the Med. Soc. State of N. York, 1877.

Westmoreland, John Gray (1816–1887).

Born in Monticello, Jasper County, Georgia, in 1816. When John was about five years of age his father removed to Fayette County, near the Pike County line, when that county was inhabited principally by a friendly tribe of Indians. As soon as the Westmoreland family arrived, these Indians with a couple of negro men, which the old gentleman owned, built him a two-room house out of logs, which they cut and hewed to proper shape. John Gray was the second son of a family of eight, raised on this pioneer farm, working on the farm in the summer and going to school in the winter, till at the age of eighteen, he finished his education at the Fayetteville Academy, and studied medicine with a neighboring country doctor, graduating at the Medical College of Georgia in March, 1843, and directly commencing to practise in Pike county, afterwards settling in Atlanta, where he continued in active practice for at least forty-five years.

To his brain is due the conception and putting into existence of the Atlanta Medical College, to-day known as The Atlanta College of Physicians and Surgeons, and to this college Dr. Westmoreland gave much time and hard work, at the same time contributing very liberally out of his own funds to build it up. From the beginning he held the chair of materia medica and therapeutics for at least forty years, at the same time being dean of the faculty for that length of time. From an humble beginning at its first session in the summer of 1855, with only a very few students, to-day as the Atlanta College of Physicians and Surgeons, it has in actual attendance in its various departments several hundred students.

In connection with the Altanta Medical College, Dr. Westmoreland originated the Brotherhood of Physicians. Each member upon joining this society was given a beautifully engraved certificate of membership, to which was attached an engraving of his then five year old son, Robert W., who following the footsteps of his father became an active practitioner of medicine of Atlanta.

From this Brotherhood has sprung the Atlanta Society of Medicine, of which at least two hundred leading physicians of high civic and professional standing are among its members.

Together with his brother, Willis F., Dr. Westmoreland established the "Atlanta Medical Journal."

When the Civil War came on and the sessions of the college suspended there were several subjects on hand in the anatomical department. T h e s e Dr. Westmoreland embalmed and carefully stored them away. Several years after the war, Dr. Westmoreland turned them over to the college in such good condition that they were used as fresh subjects. Dr. Westmoreland established the first hospital in the city of Atlanta,

for many years maintaining it principally at his own expense. During the early part of the war he sold $100,000.00 worth of Atlanta city property, lending the entire amount to the Southern Confederacy. Of course this was to him an entire loss.

Long before the pestiferous, stegomyia fasciata, and his cousin, culex, began to buzz in medical circles, Westmoreland took the position that yellow fever was non-contagious and to convince the public and medical profession of the correctness of his position, he often took his yellow fever patients into the inner room of his office and slept with them, and at no time ever contracted the disease.

The only public office Dr. Westmoreland ever held was in 1855 when elected member of the House of Representatives of Georgia, going there solely for the purpose of getting a donation from the state to help build the Atlanta Medical College. In this he succeeded to the extent that the state granted the college $15,000.00, in return for which the college has ever since that time gratuitously educated some young man every session from each of the congressional districts of the State of Georgia.

Dr. Westmoreland married Annie Buchanan, a near relative of Pres. James Buchanan, and had two children, Louisa, and a son, Robert W.

Dr. Westmoreland on his paternal side was of English ancestry, a lineal descendant of Lord Westmoreland. In 1740 three Westmoreland brothers emigrated to America, first settling in Virginia. Of these, one, William, came to North Carolina, and one of his descendants coming to Georgia, settled in Fayette County, long before the Indians had left that part of the State. This gentleman was Dr. Westmoreland's father.

R. J. M.

Westmoreland, Willis Furman (1828–1900).

Willis Westmoreland, surgeon, was born in Pike County, Georgia, June 1,

1828. He was a descendant of Lord Westmoreland of Westmoreland County, England, from whom Westmoreland County, Virginia, was named about three centuries ago. In 1740 three Westmoreland brothers emigrated from England to Virginia, settling at Jamestown. They were Robert, William and Thomas. Robert settled in Virginia, William in North Carolina, and Thomas in South Carolina. Willis Furman was the great-grandson of William, one of whose descendants came to Georgia and settled at that time in Fayette County, known as Pioneer Georgia, coming here long before the Indians had left that part of the State.

Young Willis went to the best country schools and like most farmer boys alternated between farm and schoolhouse till about twenty years old. He then read medicine with his brother, Dr. John Gray Westmoreland, at that time practising in Pike County.

His first course of lectures was in the Georgia Medical College during the winter of 1848 and 1849. The next session of lectures, he graduated at the Jefferson Medical College in Philadelphia in 1850. In 1851 he went to Paris where he spent three years making himself proficient in his favorite department, surgery. Returning home, he first settled in his native county in 1854, but soon removed to Atlanta and from the very beginning fully identified himself with surgery. Together with his brother, John G., he established the "Atlanta Medical and Surgical Journal," to-day one of the leading medical journals. He joined the Georgia Medical Association in which he held during his life many important positions. For fifteen years he was president of the Atlanta Association of Medicine. His contributions before these organizations, and in many medical journals on surgery stamp him as one of the ablest men of the age.

Dr. Westmoreland was an active, energetic man, capable of undergoing much physical labor. Wishing to visit Texas in his youth, he rode all the way on horseback from Pike County, Georgia, to middle Texas. Remaining a short time, he returned, each ride taking him about thirty days to make it. At present the same distance can be traveled over in as many hours by rail.

As a monument to the memory of this energetic man, his old neighbors in Pike County point with pardonable pride to a plain, two room frame building, still standing at a neighboring cross-road. In 1851 when he determined to start country practice, there was no room to be had fit to see patients in. He had no money to build one, so he went to the woods, cut down and hauled the timber to the nearest sawmill, had the lumber sawed and with his own hands built the rooms himself.

Aside from being a leading surgeon, during the late Civil War he ranked as general, by special appointment from Pres. Davis himself, in the Confederate service.

Being an ardent supporter of the Atlanta Medical College from its very beginning, he occupied the chair of surgery for at least thirty years.

In 1856 he married Maria Jourdan, of LaGrange, the daughter of a leading politician; they had two children, the second being Willis F. Jr., who became a surgeon and after the death of his father, occupied the same chair (surgery) at the Atlanta College of Physicians and surgeons.

In June, 1890, Dr. Westmoreland died of apoplexy.   R. J. M.

Atlanta M. and S. J., 1884–5, n s. i port.

Wey, William C. (1829–1897).

The Wey family had lived for sometime in Catskill; the great-grandfather of William C. was a physician there, his father a druggist, and William was born on January 12, 1829, graduating from the Albany Medical College, 1849, settling in Elmira that same year to practise. He did good work for forty-eight years for the State and the medical profession as manager of the State

Reformatory; manager of the State Inebriate Asylum; senior-consultant of the Arnot Memorial Hospital and president of the State Medical Examination and Licensing Board.

On November 15, 1853, he married Mary Bowman, daughter of Dr. Edward Covell, of Wilkesbarre, and had two children, the boy, Hamilton D., becoming a doctor.

A scholarly man, accomplished in other arts besides medicine, Dr. Wey was a leading doctor in the Chemung Valley and when he died on June 30, 1897, Elmira lost not only a friend but a clear-headed adviser. His paper on "Medical Responsibility and Malpractice," read as president of the Medical Society of the State of New York in 1871, showed him to be well above the average.

Memorial, by Dr. W. W. Potter in Tr. Med. Soc. of the St. of N. York, 1898.

White, Charles Abiathar (1826–1910).

Charles Abiathar White, natural scientist, was born at Dighton, Bristol County, Massachusetts, January 26, 1826, the second son of Abiathar White and his wife Nancy, daughter of Daniel Corey, of Dighton. The first of this line in America was William White, who established himself at "Wind-mill Point in Boston about 1640."

When Charles was twelve years old his father's family removed to Burlington, but he revisited his old home in Dighton in 1847, and married a school mate, Charlotte R. Pilkington, daughter of James Pilkington, of Dighton. Eight children were born, six of whom survived him. It was at Burlington that his first scientific papers were written. He made many journeys to various parts of the great Mississippi Valley for geological study, and in the years 1862 and 1863 assisted Prof. James Hall in his paleontological work for New York state.

In pursuance of his long-cherished purpose, he studied medicine under Dr. S. S. Ransom, and afterwards graduated M. D. from Rush Medical College, now the medical department of the University of Chicago. In 1864 he removed with his family from Burlington to Iowa City and there began to practise.

While practising medicine at Iowa City he was appointed state geologist of Iowa. He conducted that survey until 1870, when two volumes of reports were published, devoted mainly to structural and economic geology.

In 1866 he received the M. A. from Iowa College at Grinnell, and in 1867 was appointed professor of natural history in the Iowa State University. He became first member, then fellow of the American Association for the Advancement of Science in 1868, and closed his work upon the Iowa survey in 1870, when he assumed the full duties until 1873, when he was called to a similar chair in Bowdoin College, Brunswick, Maine.

In 1874, at the request of Maj. (then Lieut.) G. M. Wheeler, he undertook the publication of the invertebrate paleontology of the government survey west of the one-hundredth meridian, then under his direction. In 1875 he removed with his family to Washington, and joined the United States Geological Survey of the Rocky Mountain Region, in charge of Maj. J. W. Powell.

In 1876 he joined the United States Geological Survey of the Territories in charge of Dr. F. V. Hayden and remained with it until its suspension in 1879. He was appointed curator of paleontology in the United States National Museum in 1879, and geologist to the reorganized United States Geological Survey in 1882.

In 1882 he was commissioned by the director of the National Museum of Brazil to prepare for publication the cretaceous invertebrates which had been collected by members of the geological survey of that empire. The results of this work were published at Rio de Janeiro in both Portuguese and English.

The degree of LL. D. was conferred upon him by the State University of Iowa in 1893, and he was one of the founders of the Geological Society of America, and elected to corresponding membership in the Geological Society of London; Isis Gesellschaft für Naturkunde, Dresden, Saxony; the R. Accademia Valdarnese del Poggio, Montevarchi, Italy; the k. k. Geologische Reichsanstalt, Vienna, Austria; the Kaiserliche Leopoldinisch-Carolinisch. Deutschen Akademie der Naturforscher, Halle, on the Saale.

An annotated list of his papers was published in Bulletin thirty of the United States National Museum in 1885, a continuation of it in the "Proceedings" of the same, vol. xx., in 1897, some 220 in all. They embrace subjects pertaining to geology, paleontology, zoology, botany, anthropology, local history, medicine and domestic science.   M. B.

Science, vol. xxxii., n. s., 1910.

White, Frances Emily (1832–1903).

Frances Emily White was graduated from the Woman's Medical College of Philadelphia in 1872, and appointed demonstrator in anatomy and instructor in physiology in her alma mater, being promoted in 1876 to the professorship of physiology, a position held until ill health forced her to resign in 1903.

Dr. White was widely known throughout the United States. A woman of scientific mind, clear headed, and logical she also had the quality of making her students reach to the standard set for them. She was one of the first women to lecture before the Franklin Institute of Philadelphia and was delegate to the International Medical Congress in Berlin in 1890, being the first woman to act in that capacity. She was a member of the Philadelphia County Medical Society.

She died at Jamaica Plain, Massachusetts, December 29, 1903.

Dr. White wrote frequently on scientific subjects. Some of the more important writings being:

"Woman's Place in Nature." ("Popular Science Monthly," 1875.)

"Persistence of Individual Consciousness.' '("Pennsylvania Monthly," 1878.) Also, contributions to the "International Journal of Ethics."

"Relations of the Sexes." ("Westminster Review," 1879.)

"Protoplasm." ("Popular Science Monthly," 1883–84.)

"Blood, is it a Living Tissue?" ("New York Medical Record," vol. xxxiii, 1883.)

"Matter and Mind." ("Popular Science Monthly," 1887.)

"Hygiene as a Basis of Morals." ("Popular Science Monthly," 1889.)
                                          A. B. W.

Woman's Medical Journal, Toledo., May, 1904. (Eliza H. Root.)
Personal Information.

White, James Platt (1811–1881).

Of Puritan ancestry, descendant of one Peregrine White, the first child born in the Plymouth colony, he was the son of David Pierson White and born on March 14, 1811, at Austerlitz, Columbia County. With a fair classical education he attended medical lectures at Fairfield, New Jersey and Jefferson Medical College, taking his degree from the latter in 1834 and the next year marrying Mary Elizabeth, daughter of Henry F. Penfield New York. Practice came to him before graduation in the shape of a cholera epidemic at Black Rock, Buffalo, an emergency doctor being required. The establishment of the medical school in Buffalo was largely due to his exertions and his work as professor of obstetrics and gynecology went on until his death. He was the first to introduce into the states the custom of clinical illustration of labor and the innovation roused a storm of abuse from the enemies of the college and in the medical and lay press, Dr. White being obliged to bring a suit for libel in self defence, which suit he gained. One of his important improvements in obstetrics was the restoration of the inverted uterus in cases where this condition had existed for a long period, even for fifteen or twenty-five years. Two of his cases were reported before the first publication by Tyler Smith of London, on behalf of whom priority has been claimed. As an ovariotomist he was very expert, doing over 100 the last twenty years of his life.

His death was unexpected, following a brief illness; but he was weakened by overwork and this cheery, kindhearted, skillful healer died in the autumn of 1881.

His appointments included: president of the New York State Medical Society, 1870; president of the Buffalo Medical Association.

His chief contributions to medical literature were published in the " Buffalo Medical Journal" and the "Proceedings of the New York State Medical Society." He was also the author of the articles on "Pregnancy" in Beck's "Medical Jurisprudence."

"A Report of the Reduction of Two Cases of Chronic Inversion of the Uterus." ("Transactions New York Medical Society," Albany, 1874.)

"Chronic Inversion of the Uterus." ("Transactions International Medical Congress," 1876, Philadelphia, 1877.)

"Hints Relative to Intrauterine Medication." ("Transactions American Gynecological Society," 1879, Boston, 1880, vol. iv.)

D. W.

Amer. Jour. Insan., Utica, N. Y., 1881–2.
Amer. Jour. Obstet., N. Y., 1882, xv.
Med. Record, N. Y., 1881, xx.
Tr. Amer. Gyn. Soc., 1882.
Memoir. Austin Flint in Tr. Med. Soc., St. of N. York, 1882.

White, Samuel Pomeroy (1801–1867).

The son of Dr. Samuel White, this surgeon was born the eighth of November, 1801, in the city of Hudson, New Jersey, and went as a lad to Middlebury College, Vermont and Union College, Schenectady where he received an honorary graduating diploma when recalled by his father to work under him. Later, two years at the University of New York and the University of Pennsylvania well fitted him to be his father's partner.

In 1827 he had his attention called to a case of gluteal aneurysm for which he ligated the internal iliac artery, this being the second time on record of doing the operation for this disease.

Successful in ligating the internal iliac

artery, which he termed his "darling operation," it seemed a fit reward that he should be invited to the chair of surgery and obstetrics in the Medical Institute, Berkshire, Massachusetts, and in 1830 that of theoretical and operative surgery. In 1823 the Medical Society of the County of Columbia had granted him an honorary diploma on account of his high abilities.

But he coveted a wider field and three years later went to New York and there was equally successful.

He was singularly reluctant to appear before the public even in writing and never yielded to those who wanted some of his valuable lectures printed, yet at all times he gladly helped anyone by conversation.

About ten days before death he was seized with a violent chill, the prelude to typhoid fever and he died on June 6, 1867, when sixty-six years old. He married Caroline Jenkins of Hudson, who with three sons and four daughters, survived him.   D. W.

The Med. Reg. of New York City, 1869, vol. vii.

White, William Thomas (1829–1893).

William Thomas White was born in Richmond, Maine, in 1893, the eighth in descent from John Howland and Tristam Coffin, both of the Mayflower, and the eighth also from Christopher Hussy and George Bunkor. He obtained his medical education in the Medical School of Maine, and at the New York Medical College, graduating from the latter in 1855. He served as interne in the hospitals on Ward's and Blackwell's Islands, during that year and the next and became demonstrator of anatomy at the former school under Dr. E. R. Peaslee. He served three and a half years as surgeon-in-chief of the Panama Railroad, acquiring a critical knowledge of the Spanish tongue, by reason of which he afterward became a leading physician in the Spanish and Cuban colonies of New York, whereunto he removed in 1865. He was attending surgeon to the Dermilt Dispensary for fifteen years, visiting surgeon to the Presbyterian Hospital for three and a half, and to the City Hospital on Blackwell's Island for seventeen years, also edited the "Medical Register, New York, New Jersey and Connecticut," for fifteen.

In May, 1860, he married Evaline J., daughter of Jeremiah Springer, of Litchfield, Maine, who died in 1885, leaving three daughters. Two years later he married Mary A., daughter of Captain James D. Barstow, of Bath, Maine. He died in 1893 of cardiac hypertrophy, from degeneration of the heart walls.

For many years he was a Fellow of the New York Academy of Medicine; also a member of the New York County Medical Society, and one of the founders of the New York State Medical Association, and of the New York County Medical Association.

Med. Register of New York, 1894, vol. xxxii (port.).

Whitehead, William Riddick (1831–1902).

Born at Suffolk, Virginia, December 15, 1831, he was the son of William Boykin Whitehead of Southampton County, Virginia, of English descent and kinsman of William Whitehead, poet laureate of England, who emigrated during the reign of Cromwell. His father was a sugar planter in Louisiana, his mother was Miss Riddick of Suffolk, Virginia, descendant of Col. Willis Riddick of the Revolutionary War.

He married his cousin, the daughter of Thomas Benton of Suffolk.

In 1851, he graduated at the Virginia Military Institute at Lexington, studied medicine one year at the University of Virginia and graduated from the University of Pennsylvania in 1853 after which he studied medicine in Paris. Thence he went to Vienna and applied to Gortchakoff, the Russian Ambassador to the Austrian Court, for a position as surgeon in the Russian Army, then engaged in war with France, England and Turkey. The minister received him most graciously, secured him a Russian passport and gave him letters to his cousin, Prince Gortschakoff, the commander-in-chief of the armies of Southern Russia. His diploma was sent to St. Petersburg and he was appointed staff surgeon and sent to Odessa where, for several months he remained enjoying the gay, fashionable life of officers in his position. At his request, he was assigned to active duty with the army at Sevastopol. On arrival, he found Dr. Turnipseed, of South Carolina, ill with typhus fever and in the same room with the body of Dr. Draper of New York City, who had just died of the same disease, both in the service of Russia. Here Dr. Whitehead was under the guidance and teaching of the great surgeon, Pirogoff, who treated the young American surgeon with much kindness and consideration. On Pirogoff's recommendation at the close of the war, Dr. Whitehead was given, by order of the Emperor, the cross of Knight of the Imperial Russian Order of St. Stanislaus. Shortly before the treaty of peace, he was honorably discharged and returned immediately to Paris and resumed his duties in its hospital and dissecting room.

In 1860, he received the degree of M. D., de la Faculté de Paris; then returned to New York and was elected professor of clinical medicine in the New York Medical College.

After the fall of Fort Sumter, he returned to his native state, Virginia, and was subsequently appointed by Mr. Davis, surgeon of the Forty-fourth Virginia Infantry. He was present at the battle of Chancellorsville and put the wounded "Stonewall" Jackson in the ambulance and sent him to the rear. After the battle of Gettysburg he took charge of the wounded of Jackson's old corps, and on the retreat of the Confederates, the camp fell into the hands of the Federals who permitted Dr. Whitehead to remain in charge and furnished him with necessary supplies for the wounded.

A month later, he, with others, was sent to Baltimore and imprisoned at Fort McHenry, instead of being exchanged as he anticipated. In the meantime, his cousin, to whom he was afterwards married, was living in Brooklyn, and obtained permission from Sec. Stanton to cross the lines into Virginia. Dr. Whitehead was informed of this and one dark night made his escape in citizen's clothes, scaling the brick walls across the peninsula, and the following night was in Brooklyn, at the home of his betrothed. He left the next morning for Canada, visiting Toronto, Montreal and Quebec, and on to Bermuda, where he met Maj. Walker of Petersburg, Virginia, Confederate quartermaster, who gave him a passage on a blockade runner destined for Wilmington, North Carolina, which was reached in safety. He went to Richmond and, after short leave of absence, during which time he was married, was appointed by Surg-gen. Moore, president of the Board for examination of recruits and disabled soldiers.

At the close of the war he returned to New York and practised, chiefly as a surgeon, until 1872, when he went to Denver and spent the balance of his life, making occasional trips to Europe with his family.

He had three children, Charles B., Frank and Florence.

He was a prolific contributor to medical periodicals and the inventor of the well-known, useful mouth-gag, which goes by his name.

His writings included:

"De l'Oedème et de ses variétés." "Thèse de Paris," 1860.

"On Excision of the Superior Maxilla;" etc. (Nos. xv and xvii of "New York Medical Journal," vol. iii, 1866.)

"Extirpation of an Osseous Tumor of the Upper Jaw." ("Medical Record," June 1, 1867.)

"The Prevention of Fatal Anesthesia from Chloroform, by the Previous Use of Alcoholic Stimulants," 1867.

"Perineal Urethrotomy." ("Medical Record," January 1, 1867.)

"Case of Muco-periosteal Uranoplasty." ("American Journal Medical Sciences," July, 1868.)

"Account of a New and Very Successful Operation, for the Worst Forms of Cleft of the Hard and Soft Palate." ("American Journal Medical Sciences," October, 1868.)

"Ancient Specula, and the Conical or Cylindrical Speculum of the Moderns." ("New York Medical Journal," March, 1868.)

"Surgical Treatment of Cleft of the Hard Palate, with an Illustrative Case, Colored Illustrations." ("New York Medical Journal," April, 1869.)

"Report on the Best Methods of Treatment of Different Forms of Cleft Palate." ("Transactions American Medical Association," 1869.

"Remarks on the Physiological Action of the Interossei Muscles of the Hand, with an Easy Method of Strengthening the Fourth Finger of the Pianist." ("New York Medical Journal," October, 1869, illustrated.)

"Cases of Rare Cystic Tumors." ("American Journal Medical Sciences," April, 1869.)

"Results of the Operation for Cleft of the Hard and Soft Palate;" with a tabular statement of cases. ("Medical Gazette," 1870 or 71.

"Remarks on the Reproduction of Bone," 1870.

"Remarks on a Case of Extensive Cleft of the Hard and Soft Palate, Closed at a Single Operation.'' ("American Journal Medical Sciences," July, 1871.)

"Cases of Fibrous Stricture of the Rectum, Relieved by Incisions and Elastic Pressure; with Remarks." ("American Journal Medical Sciences," January, 1871.)

"Cases of Cleft of the Hard and Soft Palate, Closed by Operation." "Reproduction of Bone in the Palatine Vault." ("American Journal Medical Sciences," January, 1872.)

"Cases of Stricture of the Rectum Treated by Different Methods; One of Them by Electrolysis." ("American Journal Medical Sciences," July, 1872.)

"Remarks on the Management of the Inner-maxillary Bone in Double Harelip (three cases)." ("Transactions Colorado Territorial Medical Society for 1873.")

"Remarkable Mode of Union in a Case of Cleft Palate." ("Transactions Colorado State Medical Society," June, 1877.)

"Absence of the Uterus, with a Previous History of Chronic Inversion of This Organ, which was Mistaken for Polypus, and Removed with Ligature; with Remarks." ("American Journal Medical Sciences," January, 1877.)

"Rupture of Posterior Tibial Muscle; also a Description of a New Apparatus for Making Extension and Counter Extension at the Ankle-joint, in Diseases of This Joint." ("Denver Medical Times," December, 1885.)

"The Closure of Cleft of the Hard and Soft Palate, at a Single Operation, with a Brief Report of a Recent Case." ("Medical Record," August 7, 1886.)

"The Operative and Mechanical Treatment of Some Joint Diseases and Injuries; with Special Reference to Hip, Knee and Elbow-joints; with Illustrative Cases." ("Transactions American Orthopedic Association," vol. i, 1889), etc, etc.

W. W. G.

Whiting, Joseph Bellamy (1822–1905).

Descended from New England ancestors, he was born in Barkhamsted, Litchfield County, Connecticut, December 16, 1822. When seventeen he began teaching school, studying medicine and several years later, graduated from the medical college at Berkshire, Massachusetts in 1848. He began to practise at Wolcottville, Connecticut and married there in 1850 Frances Hungerford. In 1852 he removed to Brooklyn, New York, where his wife died in 1854. A few years later he removed to Janesville, Wisconsin, where, in 1860, he married the widow of Chief Justice Whiton.

During the Civil War he was surgeon-in-chief of the Military Hospital at Milliken's Bend, opposite Vicksburg, surgeon-in-chief of hospitals in the Military District of Natchez, Mississippi. His arduous duties, especially onerous during a very severe outbreak of small-pox, so undermined his health that he was compelled to resign and return to Janesville, where in 1865 he resumed practice.

Dr. Whiting found time for other duties as well as giving faithful devotion to his professional career; in 1889 Pres. Cleveland appointed him a member of the Chippewa Indian Commission to buy lands of that tribe in the White Earth, Red Lake and Leech Lake reservations in northern Minnesota, and in 1895 he was surgeon-general of the Grand Army of the Republic.

The illness and death of his only son, Dr. Joseph Whiting, Jr., a month preceding his own death was a great blow, from which he failed to rally, and he died at Janesville, Wisconsin, March 27, 1905, from the infirmities of old age.

S. B. B.

Whitman, Marcus (1802–1847).

To the pioneer medical missionary is due a great part of the knowledge of strange countries and diseases and when Marcus Whitman with his wife, Narcissa Prentiss went some 4,000 miles into Oregon he began a work the fruits of which we reap. Practically, by his quick recognizance of the possibilities there and his famous ride in winter to Washington to avert its sale he largely helped to save Oregon to the United States. Daniel Webster, in the Senate, had openly said he would never vote a cent to bring the Pacific Ocean an inch nearer Boston, and even then the British were treating for the State.

Marcus Whitman was born at Rushville, Yates County, New York, on September 4, 1802, the third son of Beza and Alice Whitman, the family line going back to John Whitman, who came from Hereford, England, in 1602. Marcus held his medical diploma from Fairfield, and after practising in Canada for four years and for a while at Wheeler, New York, he offered himself as medical missionary to the American Board of Foreign Missions and was commissioned to explore Oregon.

So, the first physician on the Pacific coast of the states and the first to carry physical and spiritual help to the Indians there, Whitman and a band of co-laborers worked until 1846. But the British Fur Company, partly in revenge for losses, stirred up the Indians to suspect Whitman of ulterior motives in befriending them. In 1847, attacked by measles they would not submit to the same treatment as the whites and they died by hundreds, "Whitman has poisoned us!" A plot was laid, and on the twentieth of November, Whitman, his wife and twelve others were killed and scalped, some other forty-six being taken captives. Today Whitman College stands at Walla Walla, Washington, to perpetuate his memory, and the Baird professorship, founded for the advance of natural science is doing much to make known the richness of Oregon.

D. W.

The Whitman Coll. Quarterly, Jan., 1897.
Marcus Whitman, M. Eells, 1909.
How Marcus Whitman saved Oregon, O. W. Nixon, 1896.
History of Oregon, W. H. Gray.

Whittaker, James Thomas (1843–1900).

The son of James and Olivia S. Lyon Whittaker, he was born in Cincinnati, March 3, 1843, and was educated in Covington, Kentucky, graduating in 1859, in September of that year entering Miami University, Oxford, Ohio, and graduating in 1863.

While in the navy, 1863–65, he received leave of absence to attend the medical lectures at the Medical College of Ohio.

He graduated from the University of Pennsylvania in 1866; and from the Medical College of Ohio in 1867.

In 1868, going to Berlin, he attended the lectures of Langenbeck, Martin and others. He went also to Prague to study clinical obstetrics and in January, 1869, to Vienna.

In 1870, he received the A. M., and in 1891, the LL. D. from Miami University.

Whittaker was acting assistant surgeon in the United States Navy; member of the American Academy of Medicine;

Association of American Physicians; fellow of the College of Physicians of Philadelphia; fellow of the Chicago Academy of Medicine.

In 1869 he was assistant professor of obstetrics and diseases of children in the Medical College of Ohio, and pathologist to the Good Samaritan Hospital. In 1870, professor of physiology, and in 1879 professor of theory and practice of medicine, which position he held until his death.

Quite a linguist, he would while studying a language in his busy years, take his teacher with him in his carriage, reading and conversing in the intervals between visits.

He was much interested in Koch's work of the bacillus tuberculosis, and introduced tuberculin into Cincinnati.

He edited the "Cincinnati Clinic" from its foundation in 1871 until July, 1876, and later was an associate editor of the "International Medical Magazine."

Dr. Whittaker married three times; to Mary Box Davis, in 1873, who died 1883, leaving no children. In 1884, to Ella M. Harrison, who died 1888, leaving three children, James, Alice and Hugh. In 1890, he married his third wife, Virginia Lee Joy, who survived him; by this marriage there were two children, Wallace and Virginia.

Dr. Whittaker died in Cincinnati on June 5, 1900, of carcinoma of the rectum.

His more important works are: "Morbid Anatomy of the Placenta," prize essay, New York, 1870; "Text-book on Physiology," Cincinnati, 1879; "Theory and Practice of Medicine," 1893; "Exiled for Lèse Majesté," 1898 (a novel).

A. G. D.

See, In Memoriam by A. G. Drury, Cincinnati, 1900.

Whittier, Edward Newton (1841–1902).

Edward Newton Whittier was born July 2, 1841, at Portland, Maine. He entered Brown University in 1858, but before he graduated the Civil War had begun and Whittier left his books, and did not return until peace was restored.

With characteristic zeal and energy he sought early opportunity to enter the service of the Union; and his first term was of three months with the First Rhode Island Volunteer Regiment. Immediately upon his return from duty he joined the Fifth Maine Battery, and was commissioned a second lieutenant; and presently became first lieutenant. At the battle of Gettysburg this battery, then under his command, won conspicuous distinction by resisting effectually a night attack by the enemy upon the Union troops stationed at Culp's Hill. For this service he received the special medal of honor conferred by Congress for "faithful, gallant, and meritorious services," with brevet rank of captain of volunteers.

He resumed student life at Providence after his discharge from the army. then went to the Harvard Medical School, from which he graduated in 1869, and in 1873 was on the visiting staff of the Massachusetts General Hospital, a position he held many years. In 1877 he was assistant in clinical medicine; and his teaching service in the Harvard Medical School continued until 1888, when he held the position of assistant professor in clinical medicine. Whittier was a remarkably able teacher of the elementary branches of clinical medicine and many a man now living remembers his public clinics at the Massachusetts General Hospital. "Gentlemen," he would say, "The patient who came to us this morning is peculiarly fitted by reason of his intelligence to tell us all what is the matter with him." Meanwhile, Pat Mahoney, a good deal frightened at being the center of interest to some two score pairs of eyes ranged around the ample amphitheater, blinks and gasps, "Mr. —— What is your name? Yes, Mr. Mahoney is not content with the diagnosis of one man, he wishes to have the combined wisdom of all these doctors." And then Dr. Whittier, erect and military in bearing, would sweep his arm in a semicircle towards the seats. By this time Pat felt he was getting more attention

than the average patient and showed signs of returning confidence. After a little further buoyant treatment he was quite ready to have any number of stethoscopes applied to his chest and submit to an unlimited amount of percussion.

A differential diagnosis by the aid of tables and schedules written on the board and a summary of the treatment were parts of every clinic.

After resigning his appointment in 1888, Dr. Whittier devoted himself with great success to private practice; and it is fair to say that at no period of his life was he more widely esteemed than at the time of his last sickness.

He died at his home in Boston, June 14, 1902, aged sixty-one, the end coming suddenly, as a result of sclerosis and obstruction of the coronary artery.

W. L. B.

Bulletin Har. Medical Alumni Asso., July, 1902.
Bos. Med. and Surg. Jour., vol. cxlvi.

Widner, Christopher (1780–1858).

Christopher Widner was one of the clever young army surgeons whom warfare caused to settle in a new country. He had taken his membership and fellowship degree at the London Royal College of Surgeons and joined the Fourteenth Light Dragoons as surgeon when the war of 1812 broke out and he was sent to Canada and elected to stay in Toronto (then York) when peace was declared.

The recognized leader of the profession, the life and soul of the General Hospital, he gave to the earlier practitioners of the province an enormous impulse towards scientific surgery, and was equally skilled in surgical diagnosis and in operative technic. In 1833 he founded and was the first president of the Medical and Chirurgical Society of Upper Canada, and was also president of the Board of Health and contended for a high degree of proficiency.

In person he resembled Lord Roberts, though his military service had not engendered a perfectly controlled temper and he had a lurid gift in the use of expletives when things did not go right. But he was just and honorable and full of charity for the poor.

He was twice married: the first union an unhappy one, the second not ideal because of wide difference in social rank. His death was tragic. Deeply affected by the loss of a much loved son he walked to the cemetery and fainted on the grave, and though promptly carried home he never quite recovered consciousness and died the following morning.

N. A. P.

Wiesenthal, Andrew (1762–1798).

Andrew Wiesenthal, anatomist, was the only son of Dr. Charles Frederick Wiesenthal, of Baltimore, and born in the year 1762. Having received a good education in his native city, he began to study medicine in his father's private school, then studied anatomy under Shippen and attended lectures in Philadelphia and London. He spent three years in the latter city, 1786–1789, as interne in St. Bartholomew's Hospital, studying under John Sheldon, Crnikshank, John Marshall, and Percival Pott. Returning to Baltimore in the summer of 1789, shortly after the death of his father, he began instruction, the ensuing winter, in anatomy, physiology, pathology, operative surgery and the gravid uterus, to a class of fifteen. He attempted with Dr. George Buchanan to found a medical college, but while he failed in this, he continued instruction in anatomy and surgery in his private school up to the time of his death, which occurred in Baltimore December 2, 1798. In 1789 he married Sarah Van Dyke, of Eastern Shore, Maryland. They had one son, Thomas Van Dyke Wiesenthal, who also became a doctor in the United States Navy.

In the "London Medical and Physical Journal," vol. ii, No. 8, October, 1799, it is said that Andrew made an important pathological discovery in Baltimore, in 1797. The account of it is conveyed in a letter from him dated May 21, 1797, and it is sent to the editors of the above journal for publication by "Andrew Marshall, Bartlet's Building, September 10, 1799." The discovery was that the deadly epizoötic in fowls and turkeys—known as syngamosis, a verminous tracheobronchitis (vulgarly "the gapes") was due to a cylindrical worm, since known as Syngamus Trachealis. This worm infests the trachea, choking the young chicks. He gives an illustration of it, of natural size and as magnified under the microscope. This probably represents the first discovery of an organism producing an epidemic or infectious disease ever made. Dr. Wiesenthal's priority is well established. The worm was seen in England for the first time by Montagu, in 1806–1808, and did not figure in French publications till well into the latter half of the nineteenth century. See L. G. Neumann, "Traité des Mal. Parasitaires," translation by Fleming, London, 1892. The letter, which was published, as seen, after Andrew's death, is reproduced in "Old Maryland," vol. ii, No. 4, April, 1906.

E. F. C.

Wiesenthal, Charles Frederick (1726–1789).

He was born in Prussia in 1726, but of his family and life there is nothing known. Family tradition asserted that he was physician to Frederick the Great, and the knowledge of the details of the military service in Prussia, as displayed in his correspondence, favors the view that he was connected in some way with the army. It is not known whether he possessed a medical degree or not. He arrived in Baltimore, which was first settled chiefly by Germans, in 1755, and for thirty-four years thereafter, was in active practice. Shortly after his arrival he married a lady of York, Pennsylvania, and had one son and three daughters. Naturalized in 1771, he warmly espoused the cause of the patriots and his services and advice were of the greatest value during the Revolution. In January, 1775, he was made a member of the Committee of Observation of Baltimore

County; March 2, 1776, he was commissioned surgeon-major of the First Maryland (Smallwood's) Battalion; in 1777 he was surgeon-general of the Maryland troops, having general charge of the medical interests of the government in Baltimore, including the hospital which he established. Dr. Wiesenthal erected buildings for a medical school and dissecting room on the rear of his lot, and these buildings are still standing. He taught many students of his time, and in 1788 while they were dissecting the body of a murderer a mob gathered and broke up the proceeding. He was a leader among the Lutherans and secured the building of the first church of that denomination in Baltimore (1762).

Keenly desiring a law for the regulation of medical practice in the state he headed a movement for professional organization, which resulted in the formation of a medical society on November 27, 1788, of which he was elected president. His death took place on June 1, 1789, during the absence of his only son Andrew, then a student of medicine in London. He was the first physician in Baltimore to drive a four-wheeled carriage; on this was inscribed his crest and motto—"a horse's head bridled and bitted, with two crossed arrows beneath and the words Premium Virtutis." His rare and singular virtues and his nobility of character earned him the title "The Sydenham of Baltimore." His coat of arms, mortar and pestle, and much of his correspondence are still extant.

E. F. C.

A sketch of C. F. Wiesenthal with portrait and extracts from his letters. E. F. Cordell. Johns Hopkins Hospital Bulletin, Nos. 112–113, July–Aug., 1900. Medical Reports, Idem, No. 177, Dec., 1905. Cordell's Medical Annals of Maryland, 1903.

Wigglesworth, Edward (1840–1896).

Edward Wigglesworth, dermatologist, was born in Boston, December 30, 1840, and educated in Chauncey Hall and the Boston Latin School, afterwards graduating from Harvard College in 1861, and from the Harvard Medical School in 1865.

He then studied in London, Paris and Vienna for five years, devoting especial attention to dermatology. On returning to this country there were but few exclusive practitioners of this branch of medicine, and he became one of the pioneers, devoting his life to it. It was his ambition to collect the best and rarest books, the most perfect models, and other costly means of illustrating this subject. This collection was later given to the Harvard Medical School, but his library was always freely open to those who could make it useful. At his own charge he opened a dispensary for diseases of the skin, at which he continued to minister, regardless of time and expense until special departments for such treatment were made part of the leading medical institutions of Boston. He was for sometime one of the physicians for diseases of the skin in the Boston City Hospital, and later became head of that department. For several years he was one of the instructors of the Harvard Medical School, and impressed upon the students the importance of the details necessary for the successful treatment of the repulsive and distressing maladies which they encountered.

He was a member of a number of medical societies, including the American Dermatological Association, also corresponding member of the New York Dermatological Society.

His contributions to the literature of dermatology were many and valuable, especially in the earlier part of his professional life, and though later partially disabled by failing health he was still keenly interested in the work of his colleagues and in the progress of his specialty. Among his earlier publications were papers on "Alopecia," read before the Massachusetts Medical Society in 1871; contributions to the "Archives of Dermatology," of which he was a founder, on "Fibromata of the Skin," and on "Sarcoma of the Skin," in 1875; on the "Auto-inoculation of Vegetable Parasites," and on "New Formations," in 1878; and on "Faulty Innervation as a Factor in Skin Diseases," in the "New York Hospital Gazette," in 1878. In 1882, in conjunction with Dr. E. W. Cushing, he published in the "Archives of Dermatology," a paper on "Buccal Ulcerations of Constitutional Origin"; in 1883 a communication on "Purpura from Quinine" appeared in the "Boston Medical and Surgical Journal"; and in 1896 he delivered the annual address before the American Dermatological Association.

Throughout his active career there was but little medical work of general importance to his community in which he was not a participant. He devoted considerable time and money unsuccessfully to the popularizing of the metric system, and was a founder of the Boston Medical Library Association. He did active service as one of the committee to raise the large sum necessary to establish the Harvard Medical School and was actively interested in the early attempts to secure registration of physicians in order to protect citizens of his native state against quackery and extortion. As a member of the health department of the American Social Science Association he spent years of faithful and persistent effort in promoting its unselfish objects. Although through inheritance he might have lived solely for his own pleasure, his life was one of continued devotion to the welfare of others. A hater of shams and uncompromising in his own sense of right, he was nevertheless tolerant of the views of others.

While still in practice, and apparently still fit for years of continued usefulness, he died at the age of fifty-five. Death came as he would have wished, swiftly and surely, without suffering. A preliminary brief attack of unconsciousness, followed by such slight discomfort that the few intervening days were rather those of rest than prostration, and the final apoplectic stroke, so immediate and so beneficent that to him at least, the blow was surely full of mercy. He died in January, 1896, of apoplexy following Bright's disease.

In 1882 he was married to Sarah Willard Frothingham, who with two children survived him.

P. A. M.

Wilbur, Hervey Backus (1820–1883).

This philanthropic physician, educator of the idiot, was born in Wendall, Massachusetts, August 18, 1820; his father was a Congregational minister and known as a lecturer on natural history, and the author of a popular work on astronomy.

The son graduated from Amherst College in 1838, and from the Berkshire Medical College at Pittsfield, Massachusetts in 1842, then practised medicine at Lowell and Barre and married Elizabeth Holden. After her death he married Emily Petheram of Skaneateles, New York, and was survived by two sons by his first wife, Charles H. and Harry, and by his second wife and two sons, Hervey and Dr. Fred Petheram Wilbur.

Hearing of Dr. Edward Seguin's success in the teaching of idiots at Bicêtre, he became interested and eagerly read Seguin's book on the subject. Later, his preceptor at Lowell left his practice temporarily in his charge. In this duty he visited the County Home where he found a man, idiot, only possessing a good memory for dates. The belief that from this one faculty the man's mind could have been educated to a certain degree, took possession of him, and in 1848, at Barre, Massachusetts, in his own house, he opened the first school for idiots in this country. A physician, Dr. Frederick F. Backus, of Rochester, New York, then a member of the New York Senate, became interested in Dr. Wilbur's work in Massachusetts and succeeded in having the state open an experimental school at Albany in 1851. Dr. Wilbur was called to the charge of it, and, in 1854 it was made a permanent charity of the state under his care and removed to Syracuse.

He died suddenly on May 1, 1883, of rupture of the heart.

A tablet in the wall of the main building of the New York State Institution for the Feeble-Minded says: "The first in

America to attempt the education of the feeble-minded, and the first superintendent of this Asylum. By his wisdom, zeal, and humanity he secured its permanent establishment."

J. V. D.

Arch. Med., N. York, 1883, vol. ix (C. W Brown).
Jour. Amer. Med. Assoc., Chicago, 1883, vol. i (J. M. Toner).

Willard DeForest (1846–1910).

DeForest Willard, orthopedist, was a native of Newington, Hartford County, Connecticut and born March 23, 1846, son of Daniel H. and Sarah Maria (Deming) Willard, both his parents descendants from families closely identified with the development of America in the Colonial period. Dr. Willard was in the ninth generation from Major Simon Willard, the founder of Concord, Massachusetts (1632). He went to Hartford High School and entered Yale in 1863, and afterwards to the University of Pennsylvania, whence he took his M. D. in 1867. He received the degree of Ph. D. from the University in 1871, and the honorary A. M. from Lafayette in 1882. Dr. Willard early selected surgery as his chosen branch of medical practice and from the time he graduated in 1867 up to this date he was continuously connected with the anatomical and surgical departments of the University. Prior to his graduation in medicine, during the Civil War, he served under the United States Sanitary Commission at City Point and Petersburg. In 1867–1868 he was resident physician at the Philadelphia Hospital and from 1881 to 1907, served as surgeon to the Presbyterian Hospital. He was consulting surgeon to the Home for Incurables, and the State Hospital for the Chronic Insane at South Mountain. In 1887 Dr. Willard was appointed lecturer on orthopedic surgery in the University, and was clinical professor of orthopedic surgery from 1889 to 1903; and professor of orthopedic surgery since 1903. In this subject his interest was always most enthusiastic. It was he who organized

this department at the University and secured the erection of the orthopedic ward in the Agnew wing of the University Hospital. He was president of the American Orthopedic Association in 1890, of the Philadelphia County Medical Society in 1893–1894, and of the Philadelphia Academy of Surgery in 1900. He was fellow of the Philadelphia College of Physicians and of the American Surgical Association, in which latter society since 1895 he held the office of recorder.

The strenuous professional career which Dr. Willard had and the high regard which his professional brothers had for him is evinced by the following partial list of offices he held.

At the University he was demonstrator of surgery from 1870 to 1877; demonstrator of anatomy from 1867 to 1870; attending orthopedic surgeon to the University Hospital; surgeon to the orthopedic out-patient department from 1877 to 1889. He was president of the American Surgical Association in 1901; Fellow of the American Orthopedic Association; of the Philadelphia Academy of Surgery; the Philadelphia County Medical Society: of the Pennsylvania State Medical Society; the Philadelphia Pathological Society; and the Philadelphia Obstetrical Society.

Dr. Willard married in 1881 Elizabeth M. Porter, a daughter of the Hon. William A. Porter, a granddaughter of Governor D. R. Porter, and had one son Dr. DeForest Porter Willard.

He was perhaps one of the most eminent orthopedic surgeons. He specialized in this branch of surgery long before it was recognized as a special branch, and was in every sense a pioneer who should rank with Andry, Potts, Stromeyer, Mutter and Sayre. His special course of lectures given in 1887 at the University, was the first delivered on this subject.

Beginning in 1887, in the out-patient department, Dr. Willard organized the Orthopedic Department in 1889, and with the assistance of the Ladies' Auxiliary raised $150,000 for the department within the last eighteen years, which made it possible to establish the Children's Orthopedic Ward and Orthopedic Clinic, and special gymnasium and machine shop, rendering the department the most efficient of the sort connected with any teaching institution. He died shortly before eleven o'clock, Friday night, October 14, at his home in Lansdowne, Pa. He had been ill only a few weeks, and his condition was not considered serious until he developed double-pneumonia.

His writings, of which there is a tolerably full list in the catalogue of the surgeon-general, Washington, District of Columbia, included:

"Club-foot. Is Excision of the Tarsus Necessary in Children?" 1884.

"Nephrectomies for Gunshot Wound and Tuberculous Kidney," 1889.

"Osteotomy for Anterior Curves of the Leg," 1889.

"Spinal Caries: Operative Treatment," 1889.

"Arthrectomy in Diseases of the Joints," 1890.

"Operative Treatment of the Deformities Resulting from Infantile Spinal and Cerebral Spastic Paralysis," 1891.

"Experiments in Pneumonotomy and Pneumonectomy: Suturing of Lung," 1892.

"Nerve Suturing—Neurorrhaphy, Nerve-grafting," 1894.

Old Penn. Weekly Review, Oct., 1910 (port.).

Willard, Sylvester David (1825–1865).

Sylvester Willard's ancestors came over to Massachusetts from England in 1634, he himself being the son of one David Willard, physician, and Abby Gregory, daughter of Lieut. Matthew Gregory of Albany. Sylvester Willard's name is worthy of perpetuation because of his industry in writing biographies of his medical predecessors and his great efforts to ameliorate the condition of the insane.

He went first to school in his native town, and he graduated at the Albany Medical College in 1848. By 1852 he was making headway as a young doctor

in New York. Ten years later patriotism led him to work as a volunteer surgeon among the soldiers in the battle of West Point, nor did his efforts for their relief cease with the war, but the sum of $200,-000 voted for the disabled was chiefly incoming by his urgency.

Perhaps Sylvester Willard is best known by his determined and well-planned investigations as State Commissioner into the condition of the insane. He chose upright men who would not hesitate to reveal unpleasant truths and the result was a report which contained details of misery and wretchedness, and which led ultimately to the building of better asylums; greatly deserved, therefore, was the surgeon-generalship of New York, bestowed on him as the successful candidate in 1865.

The historical medical literature would have been greatly enriched had time allowed Dr. Willard to carry out his plan of writing biographies and records. As it was, he did much, but the daily calls of his profession, his duties as surgeon-general and solicitude for his bill in the Legislature concerning the insane told too much on a man not over strong. As he was leaving home on Sunday evening, March 26, he felt a chill and went to bed. Typhoid fever supervened and death came a week later.

In 1861 he married Susan Ellen Spence, daughter of Mirmion Spence. Two children were born, Margaret and Sylvester David.

Among his appointments were: presidency of the Albany County Medical Society; and the surgeon-generalship of New York.

In addition to some fifteen biographies and the "Annals of the Medical Society of the County of Albany," he wrote "Suicide and Homicide," 1861; and "Conservative Surgery," 1861.

D. W.

Trans. Med. Soc., of N. Y., Albany, 1866 (Franklin B. Hough).
Med. and Surg. Reporter, Phila., 1865, vol. xiii. Trans. M. Soc., County Albany, 1851–70, Albany, 1872, vol. ii.

Williams, Elkanah (1822–1888).

Born in Lawrence County, Indiana, December 19, 1822, Elkanah Williams was one of the thirteen children born to Isaac and Amelia Gibson Williams, both of Welsh extraction, and born in North Carolina.

In 1819 the father moved from Tennessee and settled near the village of Bedford, Indiana, and made a fortune in farming. His older sons were satisfied with the education they could get at home, but Elkanah had higher aspirations and preferred study to farm work.

He matriculated at the State University at Bloomington, Indiana, 1843, then went to De Pauw University, where he took his degree in 1847. Bishop Simpson was president while Dr. Williams was at Asbury, and a strong personal attachment was formed between them, which only ended when the former passed away. It was his intention to study medicine, but before doing so he taught school for a short time. He matriculated at the University of Louisville, Kentucky, and took his M. D. in 1850.

While a medical student he married Sarah L. Farmer in December, 1847, and practised in Bedford until the death of his wife in 1851. Against the advice of many of his friends, he determined to make diseases of the eye a specialty, and to that end went abroad, in 1852, to study in the eye clinics of Europe. He chose a most auspicious time, so far as ophthalmology was concerned. A new light was dawning, for the ophthalmoscope was about to enlighten the unseeable fundus oculi and explain many things hitherto only matters of conjecture. He learned the use of this valuable instrument in Berlin, Vienna and Paris, and was one of the first to demonstrate its practical use at the Moorfield's Hospital in London.

The following is from a sketch of Williams, in the "Transactions of the American Ophthalmological Society." "Before his return to America he had contributed a paper of exceptional interest, in which he gave a practical demonstration in London, England, in July, 1854, on the use of the ophthalmoscope. Mention is made of this in the "Medical Times Gazette," page 7, linking his name with a praiseworthy effort, for which he also received the appreciation of the English ophthalmologists."

When Williams returned from abroad in 1855, he settled in Cincinnati. His specialty was quite an innovation at that time; the operative part of ophthalmology was within the province of the surgeons, and ordinary eye diseases were treated by all practitioners. It was discouraging work at first, but he steadily held on and his charming personality won him friends from the first. Above the average height, with broad shoulders, slightly stooped, his genial face and his kind eyes inspired confidence in his clients. In time, clients from Kentucky, Indiana, Illinois and from all the towns and cities of Ohio came to seek advice and to have him operate on important eye cases. His fame spread abroad over Ohio and the contiguous states, and in time he had a practice which taxed his endurance. As an operator he was careful, prudent and skillful, and spared no pains to gain the best results.

In 1865 Williams was elected professor of ophthalmology of the Miami Medical College. While there were teachers of eye diseases in the east at this time, yet to him belongs the honor of first filling a chair devoted to this specialty. He was an entertaining and instructive lecturer, presenting his subject in an attractive manner.

He filled the chair of ophthalmology in a most acceptable manner until failing health compelled him to quit. He served for twelve years on the staff of the Cincinnati Hospital. His clinical lectures were always very attractive to students, and from the large material at his command he was able to make his lectures practical and instructive.

He was one of the founders of the Academy of Medicine of Cincinnati which was organized in March, 1857. He was also president of the state society in1875, and president of the International Ophthalmological Congress in New York City, 1876. He was also a member of the American Otological Society, and an honorary member in 1888.

He was not only honored at home, but abroad; in 1880 being made an honorary member of the Athens Medical Society, and of the Ophthalmological Society of Great Britain in 1884.

During his last trip to Europe the International Ophthalmological Congress met in London. In the discussion on some important subject he made a speech in English. Then the Germans wanted to hear it in their language, and he delivered it in German. There were calls from the Frenchmen, and he repeated it in French. Dr. Williams frequently said that if he had a talent for anything it was for languages.

His second wife was Sally B. McGrew, whom he married April 7, 1857. She was a beautiful and attractive woman and a devoted wife. Dr. Williams had two daughters by his first wife, one of whom survived him.

For many years Dr. Williams was associate editor of the "Lancet and Observer," his articles reflecting his careful observations. His best article was that on "Injuries of the Eye," in Ashhurst's "System of Surgery."

Among his other contributions were the following, published in the "Cincinnati "Lancet and Observer," 1856; ".Cases of Keratoconus," 1857; "Kyklitis or Inflammation of the Corpus Ciliare, Trachoma and Pannus Treated by Inoculation." In 1858, "Excision of a Cicatrix in the Cornea for the Relief of Neuralgia in the Eye and Face;" Cases of Parasites in the Human Eye," 1859; "Cataract Operated on by Linear Extraction;" "Obliteration of the Lachrymal Sac by Actual Cautery;" "Diseases of the Lachrymal Sac;" "Iridectomy in Glaucoma;" 1860, "Exophthalmos with Goiter and Functional Derangement of the Heart;" 1861, "Fluid Cataract;" 1862, "Vesicles on the Cornea," "Sepa-

ration of the Retina;" 1863, "Trachoma Causes and Mode of Propagation;" 1864, "Treatment of Trachoma," "Phlyctenular Ophthalmia;" "Hypopyon;" "Keratitis;" 1865, "Aqua Chlori, or a Collyrium;" "Diseases of the Eye," "The Ophthalmoscope, Construction of the Instrument and Method of Using It;" "Reutes Ophthalmoscope;" 1864, "Caries of the Orbit;" "Ectropion;" "Inoculation and Syndectomy;" "Discharge of Vitreous in Flap Extraction;" "Modified Linear Extraction;" "Extraction of Cataract without Opening the Capsule;" "Hemeralopia or Night Blindness;" "Retinal Detachment, Operation and Result;" "Sarcoma of the Choroid;" "Thread Operation to Relieve Secondary Divergent Strabismus;" "Basedow's Disease;" "Anesthesia Retinæ;" "Binocular Temporal Hemiopæ;" "Strabismus with Rigidity of the Muscles;" "Stricture of the Nasal Duct;" "The Unguentum Citrium Rubrum or Brown Citrine Ointment," 1869, "Tumor of the Brain with Optic Neuritis;" 1876, at the meeting of the International Medical Congress, he presented a very interesting paper entitled "Orbital Aneurysmal Disease and Pulsating Exophthalmos, Their Diagnosis and Treatment", 1879, "Symptomatology of Optic Neuritis."

He died at Hazelwood, Pennsylvania, on October 6, 1888, of cerebral apoplexy.

A. G. D.

Sattler's: Trans. Am. Oph , Soc., vol. v. (port.).
Hubbell's, Development of Ophthalmology. New York Med. Jour., 1888, vol. xlviii.
Trans. Ohio Med. Soc , 1889.

Williams, Henry Willard (1821–1895).

Henry Willard Williams was born in Boston, December 11, 1821, and after a Latin School education, entered a counting-room, later becoming secretary and publishing agent of the Massachusetts Anti-slavery Society. At the same time he began to study medicine at Harvard in 1844, afterwards spending three years in Europe. Besides his general medical and surgical studies he became greatly interested in ophthalmology, studying under Sichel and Desmarres in Paris, Friedrich and Rosas in Vienna, and Dalrymple, Lawrence, Dixon and Critchett in London. He then returned to America and graduated at Harvard in 1849. From 1850 to 1855 he was instructor in the theory and practice of medicine in the Boylston Medical School, and in 1850 organized a class of Harvard students for the study of eye disease and after a few years of general practice, limited himself to ophthalmic work. He was one of the first to introduce etherization in cataract operations (1853) and the suturing of the flap (1865). In 1856 he read a most important paper "On the Treatment of Iritis without Mercury." His first literary work was a translation of Sichel's "Spectacles: Their Uses and Abuses in Long and Short-sightedness," (1850). In 1862 his "Practical Guide to the Study of the Diseases of the Eye," appeared and in 1865 his essay, "Recent Advances in Ophthalmic Science," won the Boylston prize. In 1881 his most important work appeared, "The Diagnosis and Treatment of Diseases of the Eye," (second edition, 1886). These works presented the science and practice of ophthalmology in the clearest manner and in accordance with the most advanced thought of the day, and their popularity was attested by the demand for new editions.

His greatest influence was exercised as a teacher and lecturer (1869) and later (1871) as professor of ophthalmology in Harvard Medical School, also in the medical societies in which he took an active and leading part.

He impressed his strong personality on his medical brethren, as he lived and worked largely for them. He was, all in all, a doctor first, and other things afterwards. . . .

Of large stature and strong character, he was a conspicuous figure on all medical occasions and proved a frequent and forcible and persuasive speaker. Conservative to a fault, he was yet kindly and thoughtful of his professional brothers.

He did not grow old, but retained his enthusiasm to a remarkable degree.

In 1864 he was one of those who founded the American Ophthalmological Society, and was for many years its president. On retiring in 1891 from the chair of ophthalmology, on account of ill health, he endowed the professorship. His son, Charles, followed his father as an ophthalmologist; another son, Francis Henry, likewise became a physician.

Dr. Williams died June 13, 1895.

H. F.

Trans. Am. Oph. Soc., vol. vii.
Boston Med. and Surg. Journal, June 27, 1895.
History of Boston City Hospital.
Knapp's Archives of Ophthalmology, xxiv.

Williams, Stephen West (1790–1855).

Stephen West Williams, second son of Dr. William Stoddard Williams of Deerfield and a lineal descendant of Rev. John Williams, the first minister of that town, was born in Deerfield, March 27, 1790. The family furnished many eminent physicians to New England, and Stephen early showed a studious turn of mind. When sixteen he had read the five volumes of Rush's "Enquiries," "Darwin's Zoonomia," Thornton's "Medical Extracts" in five volumes, and other lengthy works, and two years later began an apprenticeship in medicine under his father. Like Rush, he early formed the habit of taking notes on matters that particularly interested him and in this manner and by reporting cases for the medical journals acquired facility in writing. His first medical publication was an account of the two remarkable cases of suicide of the brothers Clap, which was published by Rush in his "Diseases of the Mind," and subsequently quoted by Esquirol in his works on insanity.

In the winter of 1812–13, he attended a term of lectures at Columbia College by Post, Hosack, Mott and others, and in 1853 settled as a doctor in Deerfield, moving in 1853 with his family to Laona, Illinois. In his early years he practised surgery, but later in life devoted himself to an extensive consultative practice. He became a member of the Vermont State Medical Society in 1815, and of the Massachusetts Medical Society in 1817. In the latter he was an influential member, being orator at its annual meeting in 1842, with a scholarly address, "Medical History of the County of Franklin in the Commonwealth of Massachusetts." He was instrumental in the formation of the Franklin District Society, one of the branches of the Massachusetts Medical Society, in 1851.

In 1816 he published a volume on the indigenous plants of Deerfield and its vicinity and subsequently wrote numerous papers, which were published in the periodicals of the day upon the medicinal properties of plants. In 1817 he read a "Traditionary and Historical Sketch of the Aboriginal People of the Country" before the New York Historical Society, published in the "Society's Transactions."

From 1823 to 1831 he held the chair of medical jurisprudence in the Berkshire Medical Institution and in 1838 delivered a course of lectures on the same subject in the College of Physicians and Surgeons in New York, supplying a chair made vacant by the illness of Professor Beck, subsequently for two years he served as lecturer upon medical botany and jurisprudence in Dartmouth College and professor of materia medica, pharmacy and medical jurisprudence in Willoughby University, during this period delivering over four hundred lectures, carefully written out in full.

Dr. Williams's most noted work was his modest, dun-colored octavo of some 400 pages on American Medical Biography, published in 1845, in which he continued James Thacher's pioneer biographical writing in a manner most satisfactory to the student of early medicine and at the same time showing a more careful regard for facts than Thacher. Previous to this he wrote an "Indigenous Medical Botany of Massachusetts" and a "Catechism of Medical Jurisprudence," and in 1847 appeared the "Genealogy of

the Williams Family in America." Many more of his writings are to be found in the medical journals of the time and a list of his published minor works is in Allibone's "Dictionary of Authors." Dr. Williams was the author of the first report of the American Medical Association on medical biographies and the originator of a practice on the part of the Association of collecting biographies of deceased medical men of the country who had attained prominence.

In 1824 the Berkshire Medical Institution gave him her honorary M. D., and in the same year Williams College made him an Honorary A. M. He was an honorary member of the New York Historical Society, The Royal Society of Antiquarians at Copenhagen, the State Medical Society of Wisconsin.

Dr. Williams was simple and unostentatious in his habits and, owing to an inborn timidity, was never a polished public speaker. He suffered at times with angina pectoris which disqualified him in a degree from the performance of major surgical operations. After moving from Deerfield to Laona, Illinois, in 1853 he was not altogether happy in his changed surroundings. His strength failed during the spring of 1855, but he was able to visit patients until a week before his death, which occurred from heart disease on July 7, 1855. The last entry in his journal made shortly before had reference to the annual meeting of the Massachusetts Medical Society, of which he was an ardent member, held on June 27 of that year. It was as follows: "Today the Medical Society meets at Springfield, my heart is with them."

W. L. B.

Boston Medcical and Surgical Journal, Aug. 9, 1855, vol. liii (James Deane, M. D.).
Tr. American Medical Ass., 1878, xxix (J. M. Toner, M. D.).

Williams, Thomas Henry (1822–1904).

Thomas Henry Williams was born in Dorchester County, Maryland, in March, 1822, the son of Isaac F. and Rebecca R. (Stuart) Williams. The early years of his life were spent in Cambridge, Maryland, and he studied medicine under Dr. Alexander Hamilton Bayly, later graduating from the University of Maryland in March, 1849. He was commissioned assistant surgeon in the United States Army and was stationed at various western posts. At the beginning of the Civil War he resigned from the United States Army and went to Richmond, where he was appointed surgeon in the Confederate Army. During the war he was medical director and inspector of hospitals in Virginia. He organized the Confederate Medical Corps of brigade and division surgeons and under his supervision nearly all of the large hospitals in Virginia, outside of Richmond and Petersburg, were established. He held the position of assistant to the surgeon-general of the army at Richmond for some time prior to the close of the war and did effective service. In 1865 he returned to Cambridge and later went to Richmond to practice. He passed the last years of his life in Cambridge, where he died on September 22, 1904. Dr. Williams married Bettie Hooper, daughter of Dr. John H. and Anna C. Hooper, of Cambridge.

Dr. Williams was noted for his hospitality and kindness and no man in the county was more respected for his uprightness; he had a large circle of friends. He was very active in organizing the Cambridge-Maryland Hospital and after his death, the operating room in the hospital was equipped by his wife as a memorial to him.

B. W. G.

Williams, Obadiah (1752–1799).

This pioneer physician of central Maine was born in Antrim, New Hampshire, March 21, 1752, and after studying medicine with some physician of that town, started off as surgeon's mate to the battle of Bunker Hill, and did his share of medical work throughout the Revolution. He seems to have served as a surgeon for some years, but his record is dusky through the mist of a

century or more, and traces of him are hard to find, until we first actually meet with him at Sydney, Winslow and Waterville about 1792. It is, however, possible that Dr. Williams came to Winslow and Waterville on hearing that the death of Dr. John McKechnie had left that settlement without any physician.

At all events, we hear of his building a log cabin in 1792. Owing to the increasing practice he soon put up a one-story frame house, the first in the town, now known as the old Parker House. The next three years brought more business, and he built the first two-story frame house, which later became a hotel. He married Hannah Clifford, and had seven children. Williams was very kind and generous to Dr. Moses Appleton, who settled in the same town as Dr. Williams grew older.

In this same generous spirit, Williams gave a good deal of his land to the town for a park, and for putting up a church and school house. The church was afterwards changed into a Hall, while the school house was often used as a church in which young Dr. Appleton officiated when parsons were scarce.

Dr. Williams was a pioneer in that part of the country, did much work in the out-lying districts, and had an excellent reputation as physician and surgeon, doing his operations with poor instruments and no anesthetics.

The exact date and month of his death are unknown, but he seems to have died suddenly in 1799, leaving a good memory for kindness and for trying to make his patients believe that his successor, Dr. Appleton, would do even better for them than he himself had done.

J. A. S.

Waterville Centenary, Dr. F. C. Thayer.

Williamson, Hugh (1735–1819).

In the year 1730, a clothier, one John Williamson, from Dublin, emigrated to America and settled in Chester County, and the next year married an Irish girl, Mary Davison, from Derry, who in coming over as a little child was captured by Theach, known as the pirate Black-beard. After this little bit of romance in her life she settled down with John, the clothier, and had four girls and six boys, Hugh being the eldest one, a most studious lad, with a great liking for mathematics. His father gave him a very good education and meant him to go to Europe, but the College of Phila-delphia receiving its charter, he was sent there and took his B. A. when twenty-two.

His first idea was to be a minister and he went as far as to become a licentiate, but a delicate chest and church disputes made him turn to another favorite study, medicine, which science he still pursued when, having taken his M. A. from his old college he became professor of math-ematics there. Three years after, this serious, determined young man found his way to Edinburgh University, studying medicine there and in London and finally getting the M. D. of Utrecht. Then followed a very diversified life, writing with others concerning the transit of Venus in 1769, individually propounding original theories concerning the comet of that year and so on to a pamphlet on the "Variation of Climate in North America," a remarkably observant paper which brought him honorary memberships from Holland and an LL. D. from another foreign university. Arrayed in new honors he took a new rôle, that of col-leeting with some colleagues funds from the West Indies and Britain for the Academy of Newark, Delaware. The King of England gave a liberal donation "notwithstanding his great displeasure towards his American subjects," for Williamson was the first to report the tea party in Boston Harbor and advise the Privy Council to use conciliatory measures. Directly after, the war began and Williamson hearing of a clandestine correspondence detrimental to America being carried on between Hutchinson and leading members of the British Cabinet, by a bold ruse obtained the letters and sent them to Franklin, taking care to leave London the next day.

But in the midst of these exciting events he found time for scientific experimenta-tion with John Hunter and Franklin and read a paper before the Royal Society in London "On the Gymnotus Electricus or Electric Eel." On the declaration of independence he went back to Phila-delphia and finding no army surgeonship open bought a trading sloop and did a little mercantile voyaging to the West Indies along with his brother from South Carolina, and while in the latter state was invited to Newbern to inoculate with the small-pox. In 1779 the merchant again became the doctor in real earnest as surgeon to the North Carolina Militia, doing valiantly for both conquerors and prisoners.

Peace, and three years as a Represent-ative; eloquent always and sent to Annapolis as delegate to amend the Con-stitution. This piece of civic doctoring accomplished he married Maria, daughter of the Hon. Charles Ward Apthorpe, but she died when the younger of his two sons was only a few weeks old. The widower now devoted himself to his little boys and the writing of a big work on "Climate from a Medical Point of View" and on "The Fevers of North Carolina," and in 1812 appeared his big two-volumed "History of North Caro-lina," all this done along with endless scientific papers and a "Report as Commissioner to Inquire into the Origin of the New York Yellow Fever Epidemic in 1805."

The death of his beloved elder son in 1811 did not abate the zeal of a nearly heart-broken father for everything that could help his country and state. He took refuge among his books when weary, yet with unabated intellectual vigor he reached the first month of his eighty-fifth year "the punctuality and ability he had brought to his never decreasing duties being a continual source of sur-prise to his juniors."

On May 22, 1819, while taking his customary ride, the heat of the day being unusually great, "he suddenly sank into a deliquium" and was dead before aid could be summoned. So ended the life of this man who was preacher, philosopher, scientist and doctor. His biographer gives a little portrait of him as very .tall, dignified, in some respects eccentric, and to people who displayed wilful ignorance or disregard to religious truth "his language and manners possessed a degree of what might be denominated Johnsonian rudeness." Fortunately the Johnsonian genius was his also.

D. W.

Essays on Various Subjects, N. York, 1824.
A Biographical Memoir of Hugh Williamson, D. Hosack, N. York, 1820.
Portrait in the Surg-general's Library, Wash., D. C.

Wilson, Ellwood (1822–1889).

The son of a farmer in Bucks County, Pennsylvania, Ellwood Wilson, gynecologist and obstetrician, was born in that county on February 4, 1822, and had for early education the village school and library. After acting as druggist's apprentice he graduated from the Jefferson Medical College in 1845 and went that same year on the staff of the Philadelphia Dispensary, a place which furnished him plenty of obstetrical and gynecological cases, his ability leading Charles D. Meigs to take him as assistant, and, when Meigs retired, a good deal of the practice fell to Wilson; also he succeeded Dr. Warrington in the Philadelphia Lying-in Charity, and when associated with him founded and conducted the first training school for nurses, and was also a founder of the Philadelphia Obstetrical Society. It is believed he was the first to establish a dispensary there for the exclusive treatment of women and the first to clinically lecture on their diseases. As he was instrumental in helping some 34,000 babies into the world he did not get much time to write about any abnormalities in them or their mothers. He entered into a discussion with Dr. William Goodell upon the relative value of podalic version and forceps delivery in narrow pelves, advocating the forceps

as a wiser procedure. He was one of the earliest members of the American Gynecological Society, its vice-president, and member of the College of Physicians of Philadelphia.

He died on July 14, 1889, at his country house near Philadelphia.

D. W.

From the Trans. Amer. Gyn. Soc., 1889, vol. xiv (W. H. Parish).
Also Am. Jour. Obstet., N. Y., vol. xxii, 1889.

Wilson, Henry Parke Custis (1827–1897),

Practically the founder of gynecology in Maryland, Henry Parke Custis Wilson was born on March 5, 1827, in Somerset County, Maryland, and died in Baltimore, December 27, 1897. His father's ancestor, Ephriam, came over from England and settled on the eastern shore in the early part of the eighteenth century and Henry was the son of Henry Parke Custis and Susan E. Savage Wilson.

He was educated at Princeton, whose A. B. and A. M. he held and graduated M. D. from the University of Maryland in 1851, settling afterwards in Baltimore and practising there until his death in 1897.

For some years he was the only gynecologist in Baltimore and was the second in his state to do a successful ovariotomy and the first there to remove the uterine appendages by abdominal section. Report makes him the second in the world to remove a large uterine tumor, this patient recovering. He also invented a number of instruments for use in gynecological surgery.

In 1858 he married Alice Brewer Griffith, of Baltimore, who with five children survived him: Robert Taylor, William Griffith, Alicia Brewer, Emily Griffith and another daughter. The elder son became a doctor.

Wilson was a founder and president of the American Gynecological Society; the Medical and Chirurgicial Faculty of Maryland; member of the British Medical Association; vice-president of the British Gynecological Society and honorary fellow of the Edinburgh Obstetrical

Society and the Washington Obstetrical and Gynecological Society; surgeon to the Hospital for Women of Maryland and consulting surgeon to the Johns Hopkins Hospital.

His chief papers were: "Ovariotomy During Pregnancy;" "Division of the Cervix Backward in Some Forms of Anteflexion of the Uterus, with Dysmenorrhea and Sterility;" "Hysterectomy with a New Clamp for Removal of large Uterine Fibroid Tumors;" "Twin Pregnancy, one Child in the Uterus, Another in the Abdomen;" "Retro-Displacements of the Uterus," etc.

D. W.

Trans. Am. Gyn. Soc , 1898, vol. xxiii. (B
B. Browne).
Cordell's Med. Annals of Maryland, 1903.

Wilson, John ("Capt. Thunderbolt") (1784–1847).

The early history of this character is wrapped in mystery. It is supposed he came from Scotland and had studied medicine at Edinburgh. He appeared in Brookline and Dummerston about 1820. In these towns he taught school, and studied medicine at the "Academy of Medicine," at Castleton, afterwards practising very successfully, but in 1836 going to Brattleboro, where he spent the rest of his life. Dr. Wilson was associated with one, Arnold, at Brattleboro in building a steam saw mill, on the site of the present railroad station. This was an unprofitable venture, but the doctor continued to live at this point. Hence he made professional visits to the rural districts "in a rather inferior carriage, accompanied by a little boy." In his prime, he was a gentleman in appearance and bearing, and apparently well educated. He was reputed a skillful practitioner. During his last years, however, he fell into intemperate habits and his practice dwindled.

A certain air of mystery and romance seems to have followed him during his life, and gained general belief after his death. Two years after Dr. Wilson's appearance in the Connecticut Valley, a certain highwayman, Michael Martin, popularly known as "Lightfoot," was hung at Cambridgeport, Massachusetts, for highway robbery. While awaiting execution, "Lightfoot" made a "Confession," which found its way into print.

In this, he described his career as a robber and desperado, and showed himself to have possessed unusual talent in this rôle. He had operated with great daring and no mean success in Scotland, England, and Canada, until he was finally brought to justice in this country.

In this "Confession," Martin frequently mentions a companion and leader, whom he designates as "Captain Thunderbolt." Together they had pursued an eventful career in Great Britain, and later in America. He describes certain wounds received by "Thunderbolt," among which were a cut from a saber thrust on the neck, and a shortened and wounded leg, from the effects of a musket ball. It is related that "Thunderbolt" once held up a stage coach on its way to London, and holding a pistol to a man's head, said, "Give me your money, or I'll blow your brains out," to which the man replied, "Blow away, I'd as soon go to London without brains as without money." "Thunderbolt" seems to have appreelated the joke or the man's nerve, for it is said he left him with a laugh. There is little doubt that the bold highwayman, "Captain Thunderbolt," and the Brattleboro doctor, John Wilson, were the same man. There are many facts corroborative of this supposition. Dr. Wilson led a secluded life, with few acquaintances and no intimates. His necessary errands to grocery and other stores seem to have furnished about the only opportunities for his neighbors to get acquainted with him. He is said to have become greatly excited, whenever "Lightfoot's Confession" was mentioned, and once, when he saw a copy at a patient's house, he threw it into the fire. Summer and winter, he always wore a large muffler about his neck, and it was hinted, that during the delirium preceding his death, those who were present, heard events described very similar to those mentioned in "Lightfoot's Confession."

Dr. Wilson married a Brattleboro lady, the daughter of Seleh Chamberlain, who secured a divorce from him on the ground of cruelty, and she is reported to have said she would not live with a robber. The last of his life was passed in seclusion with a young son, on the banks of the Connecticut River. A marble slab marks his grave in the Brattleboro Cemetery.

C. S. C.

Wilson, Thomas Bellerby (1807–1865).

He was born in Philadelphia, January 17, 1807, and educated there, afterwards settling there and acquiring a practice which became one of the most extensive in the city. In his later years he retired from the practice of medicine and devoted himself wholly to ornithology and kindred branches of natural science. He made an extensive collection of birds, including nearly every known American species, which for size and variety is said to have ranked third in the world at the time. He presented it to the Philadelphia Academy of Natural Sciences. He became a member of the Academy in 1832, and its president in 1863, and participated actively and enthusiastically in all its affairs, contributing extensively to its library, and securing numerous gifts from others. Dr. Wilson, although a tireless student of nature and the author of several letters and monographs, left little or nothing in published form. He died in Newark, Delaware, March 15, 1865.

C. R. B.

Winslow, Caleb (1824–1895).

He was born in Perquimans County, North Carolina, January 24, 1824. His father was Nathan Winslow, of that county, his mother, Margaret Fitz Randolph, of Virginia, both Quakers.

When about twenty he graduated from Haverford College, Pennsylvania, and in

1849 took his M. D. from the University of Pennsylvania, settling in Hertford the same year, becoming widely known as a skillful surgeon. His work consisted largely of amputation of limbs, breast excisions, cataract operations, trephining and removal of external tumors.

In the operation of lithotomy he became especially expert and his record of ninety-nine operations with but one death was for a long time the best in the world. A report of these cases is published in the "Maryland Medical Journal" for February 23, 1884 (vol. x). It is stated that he had never seen an operation for stone until after he had performed many himself. He also did a trephining for epilepsy and cured the patient.

In 1866 he removed to Baltimore, Maryland, where, finding the surgical field already occupied, he developed a large general practice and died on June 13, 1895. His widow and three children survived him. Two sons, John R. and Randolph, became medical men in Baltimore.

H. A. R.

North Carolina Medical Journal, Aug., 1892.
Personal communications from R. Winslow.

Winthrop, John, Jr. (1606–1676).

This scholar, statesman and sometime doctor was born at Groton, Suffolk, England, on February 12, 1606, and prepared for college in the Free Grammar School at Bury St. Edmunds and completed his education at Trinity College, Dublin. Subsequently he studied law and was admitted as a barrister of the Inner Temple, but a thirst for travel and adventure sent him seaward as secretary to Capt. Best of the ship of war, Repulse in the fleet under the Duke of Buckingham. After the failure of the expedition of this fleet to relieve the French Protestants of La Rochelle, Winthrop spent the next fourteen or fifteen months in European travel, visiting, during that time, Italy, especially Padua and Venice, Constantinople and Holland. He followed his father to this country in 1631 and shortly thereafter was made an assistant in the Massachusetts Colony. A year later he led a company of twelve to Agawam (now Ipswich), where a settlement was made. In about a year, he returned to England and received a commission to be governor of the river Connecticut, for one year. On coming back to America he built a fort at Saybrook, Connecticut, and lived there part of that time. Then making no effort to have the commission renewed, he returned to Ipswich and became one of the prudential men of the town. Subsequently, he moved to Salem, established some salt works, made another trip to England, and finally, receiving Fisher's Island as a grant from the general court of Massachusetts, went there in the fall of 1646. This grant was, subsequently, confirmed by both Connecticut and New York. In the spring of the following year he removed to Pequot (now New London), but, after a residence of eight years, moved to New Haven. From here he was called to dwell in Hartford on being elected governor of Connecticut, in 1657. He had previously (September 9, 1647), been given a commission to execute justice "according to our laws and the rule of righteousness," and in May, 1651, was elected an assistant of Connecticut. He served as governor one year, then became deputy governor on account of a law which prevented his reëlection. This law being repealed the next year, he served continuously as governor from 1659 until his death in 1676, although in 1667, 1670 and 1676 he requested to be relieved of this office.

He was always an omnivorous reader and much given to scientific studies. The taste for medicine came naturally to him as his father was well versed in it as well as other members of his family. "The scarcity of physicians in the colonies and Winthrop's willingness to give advice free of charge —so far as his studies enabled him to do so"—caused him to be much consulted. Many letters are still extant, coming from all parts of New England, seeking aid for

various ailments and Cotton Mather declares: "Wherever he came, still the diseased flocked about him, as if the Healing Angel of Bethesda had appeared in the place." Winthrop's sovereign remedy, Rubila, was much sought after. It appears to have been composed of diaphoretic antimony, nitre and "a little salt of tin." In one of his son's letters, we find the directions "but remember that Rubila be taken at the beginning of any illness," and Roger Williams elsewhere writes: "I have books that prescribe powders, but yours is probatum in this country." Besides Rubila, Winthrop prescribed nitre, iron, sulphur, calomel, rhubarb, guaiacum, jalap, horse-radish, the anodyne mithrodate, coral in powder form, elecampane, elder, wormwood, anise, unicorn's-horn and an electuary of millepedes. He was made a member of the Royal Society of England shortly after its incorporation, on January 1, 1662, and during his stay of a year and a half in England, at that time, he took an active part in the society's proceedings, read a number of papers on a great variety of subjects and exhibited many curious things.

He married first, in 1631, his cousin, Martha Jones, who died at Ipswich, Massachusetts, three years later. In 1635 he married Elizabeth, daughter of Edmund Reade of Wickford, county Essex, and step daughter of the famous Hugh Peters. She died at Hartford, in 1672. By her Winthrop had two sons and five daughters. The sons, Fitz John (Governor of Connecticut, 1698–1707) and Wait Still (Chief Justice of Massachusetts) had both a very laudable knowledge of medicine.

Winthrop died on April 10, 1676, and is buried at Boston, in the King's Chapel Burying Ground. A portrait of him, copied from a painting in the possession of the family, is to be seen in the library of the State Capitol at Hartford. It has been often reproduced, being most accurately given in Water's sketch of Winthrop's Life.

W. R. S.

Waters, A Sketch of the Life of John Winthrop, the Younger. Privately printed, 1900.
Steiner, Governor John Winthrop Jr., of Connecticut, as a Physician, John Hopkins Hosp., Bull , xiv, 1903.

Wislizenus, Frederick Adolphus (1810–1889).

In the ' Lancet," London, 1889, ii, p. 936, it is stated that the romance of medicine might well claim Wislizenus as one of its heroes. He was born in Koenigsee, Germany, in May, 1810, and at the usual age left the gymnasium for the university to study medicine and took his M. D. in 1834 from Zürich University. He worked at Göttingen, Jena, and Würzburg, until, shortly before graduation, he became compromised in the famous "Frankfürter Attentat," and had to flee the country.

In the spring of 1833 a conspiracy had been formed in Frankfurt-on-the-Main, to avenge itself on the Federal Diet which by its severely restrictive press laws had roused the citizens, particularly the younger portion, including many students in the several faculties, to something little short of madness. In this conspiracy Wislizenus, with Matthiä and others of the medical "Burschenschaft," took a leading part—the design being to blow up the Diet. On April 3, 1833, the attempt was made. The guard house was carried by storm, and the conspirators were within an ace of effecting their purpose when the military appeared in the nick of time, arrested nine of the youths, and put the others to flight. Among those who, after hairbreadth escapes, eluded arrest was young Wislizenus, who found his way to Switzerland, where, at the University of Zürich, he resumed his studies and graduated M. D. with distinction, and in 1835 came to the United States. Ultimately settling in practice at St. Louis, he rapidly formed an extensive clientèle, of which his compatriots were the nucleus, and was enabled to give time to pure science and also to travel in and beyond the States. He made memorable visits to Mexico and the Rocky Mountains, and published most interesting records of his observations and experiences. By all classes he was looked upon as an enthusiastic and large minded reformer, an honest and benevolent survivor of the " Vor Achtundvierziger" men, as the precursors of the revolution of 1848 are familiarly called.

He died in St. Louis, Missouri, on September 22, 1889.   D. S. L.

Smithsonian Institution, Ann. Report, 1904.

Wistar, Caspar (1761–1818).

The parents of Caspar Wistar were of German extraction, and belonged to the Society of Friends, of which they were highly respected members. His grandfather, Caspar Wistar, founded at Salem, New Jersey, the first glass works in this country; Wistar was born in Philadelphia, September 13, 1761, and went as a boy to the well-known Friends' School, founded by William Penn, in Philadelphia. The school at that time was in charge of Mr. John Thompson, an able teacher of Latin and Greek. Wistar is said to have acquired a desire for medical study during the battle of Germantown, October 4, 1777, when he helped to care for the wounded. He became a private pupil of Dr. John Redman, and also attended the practice of Dr. John Jones, at the same time going to the medical lectures of Drs. Morgan, Shippen, Rush and Kuhn, at the recently organized medical school of Philadelphia. Such teachers aroused in Wistar an ambition to pursue his medical study in Europe, where he went after attaining the degree of bachelor of medicine. Tilghman relates the following story of Wistar's examination in medicine:

" There was a singularity in this examination of which I have been informed by a gentleman who was present. The faculty of medicine were not all of one theory, and each professor examined with an eye to his own system; of this Wistar was aware, and had the address to answer each to his complete satisfaction, in his own way. Of course the degree was conferred on him."

Wistar spent a year in England and then went to Edinburgh, and in 17 ٠٦ graduated doctor of Medicine there, publishing and defending a thesis called " De Animo Demisso."

Wistar was initiated into the practice of medicine and surgery under the patronage of Dr. Jones, then the most distinguished surgeon in Philadelphia. Dr. Hosack relates the following story: " Dr. Jones, having occasion to perform a very important operation, invited Dr. Wistar to accompany him. When the patient was prepared, Dr. Jones, addressing Dr. Wistar as having better sight than himself, at the same time presenting him his knife, requested it as a favor that he would perform the operation. Dr. Wistar immediately complied; and such was the skill and success with which it was performed, that it at once introduced him to the confidence of his fellow-citizens.

He was appointed physician to the Philadelphia Dispensary, established in 1787, and in 1789 to the professorship of chemistry and physiology in the College of Philadelphia. From 1793–1810, he was physician to the Pennsylvania Hospital. He became in the meantime a fellow of the College of Physicians, and a member of the " American Philosophical Society," and its president in 1815.

In 1788 he married Isabella, daughter of Christopher Marshall, of Philadelphia. She died in 1790, and in 1798 he married Elizabeth Mifflin. By his second marriage he had several children, three of whom were living at the time of his death.

Wistar was largely instrumental in effecting the union of the medical school attached to the University of Pennsylvania and its rival, the College of Philadelphia. Upon the consolidation of the two rival schools, in 1792, he was associated with Dr. William Shippen, as adjunct professor of anatomy, midwifery and surgery in the University of Pennsylvania. Subsequently surgery and midwifery were separated from anatomy. After the death of Shippen in 1808, Wistar was made professor of anatomy. As a teacher he at once exhibited distinguished qualifications: fluency of utterance, unaffected ease and simplicity of manner, perspicuity of expression, animation, earnestness, and impressiveness.

He published a " System of Anatomy," which was primarily designed as a text-book for his classes. It is an excellent work, and shows a good knowledge, for that time, both of anatomy and physiology. He published several memoirs in the " Transactions of the American Philosophical Society," and made a contribution to the anatomy of the ethmoid bone, thus described by Tilghman.

" Anatomy has been so much studied both by the ancients and moderns, and so many excellent works have been published on the subject, that any discovery, at this time of day, was scarcely to be expected. Yet, it is supposed to be without doubt, that Wistar was the first who observed and described the posterior portion of the ethmoid bone in its most perfect state, viz.: with the triangular bones attached to it. Of this he has given an accurate description in the volume of our transactions now in the press. On the subject of that discovery he received, a few days before his death, a letter from Prof. Soemmering, of the kingdom of Bavaria, one of the most celebrated anatomists in Europe, of which the following is an extract: 'The neat specimen of the sphenoid and ethmoid bones are an invaluable addition to my anatomical collection, having never seen them myself, in such a perfect state. I shall now be very attentive to examine these processes of the ethmoid bone in children of two years of age, being fully persuaded Mr. Bertin has never met with them of such a considerable size, nor of such peculiar structure.' "

" Wistar played an active part in the cultured society of Philadelphia. His house was the weekly resort of the literati of the city of Philadelphia, and at his hospitable board the learned stranger from every part of the world, and of every tongue and nation received a

CASPAR WISTAR.
(By permission of Dr. Thomas Wistar.)

cordial welcome. His urbanity, his pleasing and instructive conversation, his peculiar talent in discerning and displaying the characteristic merits or acquirements of those with whom he conversed will be remembered with pleasure by all who have ever enjoyed his society and conversation." (Hosack).

In 1816, he was elected president of the American Philosophical Society, and in 1813 he succeeded Benjamin Rush as president of the Society for the Abolition of Slavery.

Tilghman thus describes the chief characteristics of Wistar:

"The understanding of Wistar was rather strong than brilliant. Truth was was its object. His mind was patient of labor, curious in research, clear, although not rapid in perception, and sure in judgment. What is gained with toil is not easily lost.

He died in Philadelphia, January 22, 1818.

Wistar's memory is splendidly perpetuated by the Wistar Institute of Anatomy and Biology, established in Philadelphia by Gen. Wistar, and in the corallorhiza Wistereana, the Wisteria frutescens the well-known and beautiful vine Wisteria named after the doctor by his friend Nuttall, the botanist.   C. R. B.

Hosack, D., A Tribute to the Memory of Caspar Wistar, Hosack's Medical Essays, New York, 1824.
Tilghman, W., An Eulogium in commemoration of Dr. Caspar Wistar. In an appendix to John Golder's Life of William Tilghman, Philadelphia, 1829.
Caldwell. An Eulogium on Caspar Wistar Phila., 1818.
Some Amer. Med. Botanists, H. A. Kelly.
Communications from the Wistar family.

Witt, Christopher (1675-1765).

Dr. Christopher Witt, or DeWitt, as he is occasionally named, was born in Wiltshire, England, in the year 1675; he emigrated to America in the year 1704 and joined the theosophical colonists on the Wissahicken. He was then in his twenty-ninth year, and in addition to being a thorough naturalist and skilled physician, was well versed in the mystic sciences and in astronomy. He was esteemed highly by his fellow-mystics, his services as a physician were constantly called into requisition. Shortly after the death of Kelpius, Dr. Witt, together with Daniel Geissler, moved to a small house in Germantown upon the land owned by Christian Warmer, who, with his family, looked after the welfare of their tenants.

Dr. Witt was a good botanist, and upon moving to Germantown, he started a large garden for his own profit and amusement. It is probably the first botanical garden in America, antedating Bartram's celebrated garden by twenty years. Dr. Witt corresponded for many years with Peter Collinson, of London, whose letters to some of the leading men in the province mention the high esteem and regard in which Dr. Witt was held by the English naturalist. In later years there was a friendly intercourse between Dr. Witt and John Bartram.

Besides being an excellent botanist, Dr. Witt was an ingenious mechanic, constructing the first clocks made in Pennsylvania, and probably in America. He was an artist and a musician, possessing a large pipe organ said to have been made by his own hands. He also practised horoscopy and would cast nativities using the hazel rod in his divination.

When the Doctor was eighty years old his eyesight failed him, resulting finally in blindness. His slave, Robert, carefully looked after his wants until his death in the latter part of January, 1765, at the age of ninety. He was buried in the Warmer burial-ground in Germantown. This spot became known as Spook Hill, as tales were told which have survived to the present time, how upon the night following the burial of the old mystic, spectral flames were seen dancing around his grave.   J. W. H.

The Botanists of Philadelphia, 1899, John W. Harshberger.
Sachse, "The German Pietists of Provincial Pennsylvania, 1895.

Wolcott, Erastus Bradley (1804–1880).

Erastus Bradley Wolcott was born in Benton, Yates County, New York, October 18, 1804. His father, Elisha Wolcott, having removed to that section from Salisbury, Connecticut, in 1795. The first of the family in this country was Henry, second son of John Wolcott, of Galdon Manor, Tolland, Somersetshire, England, who came to Massachusetts in 1630 and to Connecticut in 1638 where his descendants made the name historic, it having been borne by officers of the colonial army; by deputies, senators, by several governors of the State, by the secretary of the treasury under Washington, and by a signer of the Declaration of Independence.

The ancestry of Jane Allyn, wife of Lieut. Henry Wolcott, a direct ancestor of Dr. Wolcott, has been verified in twenty lines.

High ideals, industry, wholesome living and adaptability to the conditions of life in a new country were manifest in the colonists from Connecticut who settled in western New York. A Godfearing folk, their first care was to provide schools for their children, who were well trained in gentle, courteous manners and not only in the ordinary branches, but in physical exercises, in music and in study of the English classics, with which Dr. Wolcott had an unusual acquaintance. He and his brothers and cousins became so proficient upon various musical instruments that they were asked to play at a reception to La Fayette in Rochester in 1826. Erastus Wolcott began his medical training under Dr. Joshua Lee, practitioner of the time.

After three years of study and practical experience with Dr. Lee, Ontario, the Medical Society of Yates County licensed him as a practising physician in 1825.

To obtain means for further study he accepted a position as surgeon with a mining company in North Carolina, practising there and in Charleston, South Carolina, until 1830. Returning to New York, he entered the College of Physicians and Surgeons at Fairfield and completing the course with distinction, especially in anatomy, received his M. D. and was urged by professors to settle in New York City; however, wishing to see the Western country he entered the United States Army as surgeon in 1836, and after accompanying the command removing the Cherokees west of the Mississippi, he was ordered to Fort Mackinac, where he met and married Elizabeth J. Dousman. Resigning in 1839 he settled in Milwaukee where his practice became so exacting as to leave him no time for writing nor even for reporting his own cases. The illiberal rules of the medical societies of that day excluded Dr. Wolcott from membership because he would extend his surgical and consultative aid to homoeopathic physicians.

From 1860 until his death he was surgeon-general of Wisconsin, organizing medical service for the state, selecting and nominating all the surgeons. With a staff of assistants he was sent to the field whenever any number of Wisconsin regiments became engaged. In 1850 he was appointed regent of the State University.

His boyhood in country life made him an athlete of unusual proficiency, and developed unfailing physical stamina. His father possessed the bow of Red Jacket "made of hickory backed with deer sinews, only a very vigorous man could draw it to its maximum power. With it Erastus Wolcott sent a blunted arrow through the siding of an abandoned house from a distance of several rods." (Cleveland History, Yates Co.).

Dr. Wolcott was also an expert shot with rifle and gun, and could use a sling with the accuracy of aim of a David. His hands were models of nervous energy and accuracy of touch, the left hand being almost equal in dexterity to the right. Clark Mills, the sculptor, took a cast of the head of Dr. Wolcott in Washington and stated that it was the only one in his collection of five hundred that measured mathematically the same on both sides.

He was tall and straight as an arrow

and an accomplished horseman. His physical perfection, his gentleness, generosity ·and unfailing courtesy, with his professional attainments made him a prominent figure in the community and his death was felt as a great public loss.

Married in 1836, his wife died in 1860, having lost three children in infancy and leaving two.

In 1869 Dr. Wolcott married a second wife, Laura J. Ross, M. D., one of the earliest women graduates.

Dr. Wolcott died January 5, 1880, of pneumonia after an illness of five days, the result of prolonged exposure to very severe cold.   .

Although he never reported his work, to him is due the credit of having performed the first nephrectomy, which was recorded by C. L. Stoddard in the "Philadelphia Medical Reporter," 1861–62, vol. vii, p. 126.

His surgical activities were fostered by his accurate knowledge of anatomy, his nerve, clear judgment and great deftness.

Working as he did in pre-antiseptic days he was aided by his own scrupulous cleanliness of hands and instruments and by the comparative freedom from bacteria of a newly settled community. He had few trained and frequently no assistants, often administering his own anesthetic, therefore his success in plastic surgery, in that of the head and abdomen including oöphorectomy, lithotomy and in Cesarean section must be considered remarkable.   M. W. Y.

History of Wisconsin, p. 760, C. R. Tuttle.
Wolcott Memorial, Congressional, Yale College, Hartford, Conn., and other libraries.
U. S. Biographical Dict.
History of Milwaukee, photograph, and remarks by Drs. Kempster and Marks.
The first Nephrectomy, M. B. Tinker, M. D., in Johns Hopkins Bulletin, 1901, vol. xii.
Portraits in possession of E. B. Wolcott Post.

Wood, Edward Stickney (1846–1905).

Edward Stickney Wood, professor of chemistry in the Harvard Medical School, was born in Cambridge, Massachusetts, April 28, 1846. About the time of the formation of Harvard College, one Jonathan Wood and William Stickney settled in Essex County, Massachusetts. In 1841 Alfred Wood, a grocer of Cambridge, a descendant of Jonathan, married Laura Stickney, a descendant of William. Their second son was Edward Stickney Wood.

He was fitted for college in the public schools of Cambridge and graduated from Harvard College in 1867, and from the Harvard Medical School in 1876, during the course serving as house pupil in the United States Marine Hospital in Chelsea, and as surgical interne in the Massachusetts General Hospital. In 1872 he spent six months studying physiological and medical chemistry in laboratories in Berlin and Vienna, and was made full professor of chemistry in the Harvard Medical School in 1876, holding the position until the time of his death, which occurred at Pocasset, Massachusetts, of cancer of the cecum, July 11, 1905.

He married Irene E. Hills, December 26, 1872, who died leaving a daughter. On December 24, 1883, he married Elizabeth A. Richardson, who survived him without children.

He was a fellow of the Massachusetts Medico-legal Society, Boston Society for Medical Improvement, and Massachusetts Medical Society and made many contributions to medical literature. He translated Neubauer and Vogel on "Urinary Analysis," and with Dr. Robert Amory, revised that portion of Wharton and Stillé's work devoted to medical jurisprudence. There was hardly a case for trial for capital crime in New England for twenty years where his knowledge of chemistry and especially his skill in the demonstration of blood stains, was not required.   W. L. B.

Bos. Med. and Surg. Journal, vol. cliii.
Bulletin Har. Med., Alumni Asso., July, 1905.
Harvard Graduates' Magazine, Sept., 1905, (port.).

Wood, George Bacon (1797–1879).

Seen through the eyes of his generous biographer Dr. S. D. Gross, George

Bacon Wood is known as a rather uncommon man, a puzzle to the ordinary mortal, a delight to his intellectual equals. Dignified, somewhat formal, loving books and science more than society, giving loyally of his substance to men and institutions in need.

His family came over from Bristol, England, in 1682 and George was born at Greenwich, a small village in New Jersey, March 12, 1797, his father, a prosperous farmer there and able to give him a good education. He studied medicine under Dr. Joseph Parrish and when made professor of materia medica and pharmacy at the University of Pennsylvania he characteristically spared nothing that would make his teaching clearer. A large conservatory in his garden furnished medicinal plants, native and exotic, and he spent $20,000 on diagrams, casts and models. Such efforts to instruct had never been known before in this country. In the University of Pennsylvania he established at an expense of $50,000 what is known as the auxiliary department for instruction in botany, chemistry, geology, mineralogy and zoology. To the College of Physicians he gave his library and $15,000. Though adding nothing new to our knowledge of the nature and treatment of disease he wrote and taught with such fidelity, such scrupulous exactness, with such reprimanding of slovenly work and recognition of effort that hundreds of students incurred a debt of gratitude. He was one of the most voluminous medical writers of the age. The first edition of his big " Dispensatory," written with Franklin Bache, appeared in 1833, and with the assistance of his nephew he lived to revise the fourteenth edition. His other two large works mentioned at the end of this sketch both reached many editions, his "Practice of Medicine" being largely used as a text-book in some of the English and Scotch schools. Most of his writing was done in the small hours, he often working till four in the morning.

For some months before his death he became unwieldly and was obliged to keep his bed. He died at his house in Arch Street, on March 30, 1879, aged eighty-two, his wife having died twelve years before; children he had none.

He was the author of many works which rendered good service; among them may be noted: "The Dispensatory of the United States" written in conjunction with Dr. Franklin Bache, 1833; "A Treatise on the Practice of Medicine," 1847; "A Treatise on Therapeutics and Pharmacology," 1856; "History of the Pennsylvania Hospital;" "History of the University of Pennsylvania;" "History of Christianity in India."

He was A. B., University of Pennsylvania, 1815 and M. D., 1818; LL. D., Princeton, 1858; professor of chemistry in the Philadelphia School of Pharmacy from 1822–1831; of materia medica from 1831–35; professor of the same in the University of Pennsylvania, 1835–1850; of the theory and practice of medicine at the same, 1835–59; president of the College of Physicians of Philadelphia for thirty-four years; president of the American Medical Association.

D. W.

Sketch in Dr. S. D. Gross's Autobiography.
Am. J. M. Sc., Phila., 1879, n. s., lxxviii (W. S. W. R.).
Med. Rec., N. Y., 1879, vol. xv.
Proc. Am. Phil. Soc., Phila., 1880, vol. xix (H. Hartshorne).
Tr. Am. M. Ass., Phila., 1879, vol. xxx (J. H. Packard).
Tr. Coll. Phys., Phila., 1881, 3 s., vol. xxv, lxxvi. (S. Littell.)

Wood, Isaac (1793–1868).

His father Samuel Wood came to New York in 1803 with his wife, Mary Searing and ten children and opened a bookstore where three more editions of the parent volume appeared, Isaac being the fourth son and sixth child of the original ten. Four of his brothers helped the father enlarge the business into a publishing house and printed the American edition of the "Medico-chirurgical Journal" and the "Medical Record."

Isaac was born in Clinton Town, Nine Partners, Dutchess County, New York State, on August 21, 1793, and attended

GEORGE B. WOOD.

(From a painting in the College of Physicians, Philadelphia.)

various schools, getting his classics from a Scotch minister. There is no mention of his going to college, but he studied medicine with Dr. Valentine Seaman and was licensed to practise by the New York State Medical Society in 1815. The medical apprentice in those days had plenty to do, and Isaac, besides cleaning the consulting rooms and collecting the bills, had to compound medicines and find time for study. He used to sit up till two or three in the morning studying and studying with special zeal after he had had success as a "resurrectionist," for not only was it against law and popular opinion to obtain a body, but dangers were incurred before a thorough examination could be made. One night he went out with two other students and having secured a body from the cemetery tied its hands and feet together and fastening it (a small subject) round his neck so as to be suspended in front, threw a large cloak over all and walked down Broadway at night, locking arms with his two friends and passing within three yards of the night watchman who looked upon them and their singing as the pranks of gay youths returning from a party. On two occasions he was forced to flee the city, having been betrayed by his colored assistant.

So eager was Wood to study each dissection when he was surgeon at the New York Hospital that he would often go without food all day and scale the hospital gate at 4 A. M. to study with his colleague Dr. J. C. Bliss. He received his M. D. in 1816 from Rutger's College, New Jersey; his thesis being "Carditis and Pericarditis."

When in 1832, the cholera broke out in New York, Dr. Wood predicted its ravages at Bellevue Hospital and in confirmation of his apprehension out of 2,000 inmates 600 died, Wood, at that time physician there, was himself one of the first to fall ill; the dead and the dying were often in the same room and coffins could not be made fast enough.

While at Bellevue, Wood performed nearly all the surgical operations that were required. It is generally conceded that he was the first to remove the ends of the bone in lacerated injury of the elbow-joint. His first case succeeded so well that the patient could use his arm during ordinary labor, not having lost the power of flexion.

When there was talk of founding a New York Academy of Medicine, Wood entered with great zeal into its organization and was twice its president and among other appointments he was consulting physician to the New York Dispensary and Bellevue Hospital; consulting surgeon to the New York Ophthalmic Hospital; member of the American Geographical Society and fellow of the College of Physicians and Surgeons.

Dr. Wood married three times and had four children.

D. W.

Distinguished Living New York Physicians, S. W. Francis.

Med. and Surg. Reporter, Phila., 1866, vol. xv.

Wood, James Rushmore (1813–1883).

The sports of the boy often determine the vocation of the man, and James Wood industriously making skeletons to stock a boy's "museum" at his aunt's farm is seen afterwards as one of America's big surgeons and the childish collection has grown into the "Wood Museum" of Bellevue Hospital. His father, Elkanah Wood, was a miller, who, with his wife, Mary Rushmore, were Quakers and when they moved from Mamaroneck to New York City to set up a leather store, James, their only child, spent his summers at Half Hollow Hills on Long Island, for his winter schooling going to a small Quaker school, and from there to study medicine with twelve other lads under Dr. David L. Rogers. His first course of lectures was at the College of Physicians and Surgeons, New York, and in 1834 he graduated at Castleton, Vermont, soon after being appointed demonstrator of anatomy and beginning private practice a year or two later.

As a hospital surgeon Dr. Wood had

a most enviable reputation. His operations were brilliantly successful, the results mainly due to the unflagging interest, unfaltering energy and untiring watchfulness. Nothing done escaped his notice and, though strict, every member and student at the hospital conceded his right to dictate and his kindly control. In the periosteal reproduction of bone he had an international reputation. The president of the German Congress of Surgeons invited him to send some specimens of bone reproduction to Berlin for exhibition with similar specimens. Langenbeck greatly admired the regenerated lower jaw and said he did not believe another specimen existed. In nerve surgery Wood was equally successful, his best operation, performed four times consecutively with ultimate cure, was the removal of Meckel's ganglion with the superior maxillary division of the trigeminus for the relief of tic douloureux. He was the first in America (1840) to divide the masseter muscles and, as far as his biographer was aware, the first to devise division of the peronei muscles in chronic dislocation of the tendon and to treat acute and chronic knee inflammation by division of the ham strings and tendo Achilles. He had in his collection six fine specimens of osseous union of the femur with the tibia after resection. Report also gives him the credit of first curing aneurysm by digital pressure, and he tied for aneurysm the external iliac eight times in succession with only one failure.

Two rather amusing stories are told of Wood: once when making the valedictory address he said fervently, "Gentlemen, as you go out into the world remember the eyes of the *vox populi* are upon you." On another occasion, before his anatomy students, he said, holding up that stumbling block, the sphenoid bone, "Gentlemen, this is the sphenoid bone; damn the sphenoid bone."

With Drs. Parker, Payne and Mason he had much to do with the Act which granted for anatomical teaching "the bodies of all vagrants dying unclaimed."

His work also on behalf of the Bellevue Training School for Nurses did a great deal to systemize this valuable science.

Death came in the hey-day of a full professional life when almost half a century had left untouched his health and skill. As an instructor he brought clinical and didactic information together in fruitful union; tradition will preserve his unsurpassed skill at the operating table, and his contributions to surgical science are permanent.

He married in 1853, Emma, daughter of Mr. James Rowe, of New York, and had one son and two daughters besides a child who died in infancy.

His literary contributions, though not numerous were all of value, and included: "Strangulated Hernia," 1845; "Spontaneous Dislocation of the Head of the Femur into the Ischiatic Notch During Morbus Coxarius," 1847; "Ligature of the External Iliac Artery Followed by Secondary Hemorrhage," 1856; "Phosphorus-necrosis of the Lower Jaw," 1856; "Early History of Ligation of the Primitive Carotid," 1857.

Among his appointments one finds: professor of operative surgery and surgical pathology, Bellevue College Hospital; emeritus professor of the same; demonstrator of anatomy at Castleton Medical College; consulting surgeon, New York Academy of Medicine; twice president of the New York Pathological Society; member of the New York Academy of Medicine, honorary member New York and Massachusetts State Medical Societies. D. W.

Boston Med. and Surg. Jour., 1882, vol. cvi.
Med.-Leg. Jour., N. Y., 1883-4, vol. i (port).
Med. Record, N. Y., 1882, vol. xxi.
Med. and Surg. Reporter, Phila., 1884-5, vol xii.
N. Y. Med. Jour., 1884, vol. xxxix (F. S. Dennis).

Wood, Thomas (1813–1880).

Thomas Wood was born in Smithfield, Jefferson County, Ohio, August 22, 1813, the son of Nathan and Margaret Wood, and the youngest of five children.

The family for three generations were

natives and inhabitants of West Chester, Pennsylvania, his great-grand parents having been born there in 1750. The family were Quakers. Dr. Wood's father was a farmer in very moderate circumstances, so that the boy's early education was an exceedingly limited one; he seems, however, to have obtained through his own exertions, good schooling. In 1835 he began to study medicine with Dr. W. S. Bates, of Smithfield.

In June, 1838, he went to Philadelphia, preparatory to entering the University of Pennsylvania. His letters home show that in this he suffered many privations, and the answers indicate many doubts as to the wisdom of the undertaking, but the lad went steadily on his way. In April, 1839, he received his diploma, and immediately an appointment in the Friends' Asylum for the Insane, near Philadelphia. There he remained three years. In 1842, he returned to Smithfield, and began practice, but in 1844 went to Europe and on his return in 1845, went to Cincinnati, and began a career which certainly justified all his former privations and longings. The Ohio College of Dental Surgery was chartered January 21, 1845, but did not begin operations until November, 1846. Dr. Wood was professor of anatomy and physiology there, which position he held for a number of years.

Among his appointments he was demonstrator of anatomy in the Medical College of Ohio, 1853; professor of anatomy; professor of surgical anatomy; editor and owner of the "Western Lancet," in connection with Dr. L. M. Lawson, from 1853 to 1857; on the staff of the Commercial (now Cincinnati) Hospital from August 15, 1861, to March 15, 1867; and again in 1870 and 1871, a member of the Academy of Medicine of Cincinnati.

Dr. Wood was a versatile genius; in 1839, before he graduated in medicine, he invented an instrument designed to facilitate the calculation of areas, which received the highest praise from a committee appointed by the Franklin Institute of Philadelphia. It was called the "arealite."

At the same time he presented to the same body a fountain pen, which was likewise highly commended.

Subsequently he invented an instrument for determining the length of lines, and to find the horizontal of a line when it ascends or descends a hill. This was called "The Lineal Mensurator;" a patent was granted July 22, 1839.

In an old scrap-book of the doctor's is a drawing of a balloon which could be driven in any direction.

For many years the doctor kept a scrap-book, in which are found a great number of poems, some of considerable merit, none of which were ever published.

Dr. Wood married, March 14, 1843, Emily A. Miller, at Mount Pleasant, Jefferson County, Ohio, and had two children, Edwin Miller, born January 30, 1844, who became a doctor. A second son, Samuel S., died in infancy. In 1855 he again married, this time to Elizabeth J. Reiff, of Philadelphia, and had six children. Charles Reiff Wood, born May 9, 1857, became a doctor, but died in 1891. Mrs. Wood died July 27, 1871, and Dr. Wood, undaunted, made a third venture with Carrie C. Fels, of Cincinnati, on July 27, 1876, but had no children.

Dr. Wood died November 21, 1880, in Cincinnati, from blood-poisoning acquired while treating some of the injured in a railroad collision, October 20, 1880.

A. G. D.

Cincinnati Lancet and Clinic, 1880, n. s., vol. v.

Wood, William (1810–1899).

Destined to be known as a scientific, thorough and deliberate man, of the highest character in medicine, this physician was born in Scarboro, Maine, October 2, 1810, the son of William and Susan Simonton Wood. The young boy received his first instruction at the hands of the mother of the well-known John Neal, of Portland, and after passing beyond her skill in teaching, attended the public schools. Being unusually bright, he learned with great rapidity, entered Bowdoin when less than fifteen, and graduated in the class of 1829. He then studied medicine at the Medical School of Maine and took his M. D. in 1823, soon afterwards going to Europe and spending most of his time in the hospitals of Paris for nearly three years. He set out for home in the winter of 1836 and encountered many storms, so that the voyage lasted seventy-two days, and the ship with all on board was given up for lost.

He began practice upon his return, and with his inherent zeal and large acquirements in medicine, ultimately obtained a large clientèle. A skilled diagnostician, he made daily use of the microscope, and by this means gained an insight into the diseases of many patients who had been given up by others who had failed to make microscopic examinations of excretions. One case in particular, towards the end of his medical career is worth reporting; a gentleman highly thought of by his fellowmen was suffering hopelessly, and Dr. Wood was called in consultation. The minute that he looked at the patient, he exclaimed to the family physician, "Sir, can you not see that your patient is dying from uremia?" "How long since, in the name of God, did you use the catheter?" This patient died, for he was too far gone for relief, but this incident shows the diagnostic skill of William Wood.

All that he wrote, or had in the way of operations or what he said in discussions at the meetings of the Maine Medical Association, are lost because the transactions were not then deliberately printed.

It would not do to pass unnoticed Dr. Wood's great love for natural history. To this branch of science he gave much time and in it he was an expert. He was the founder of the Maine Natural History Society. He was fond of botany, and had a collection of medicinal plants in his fine garden. In the second story of his house he had a large room looking out on the garden and round about it books were piled with great profusion. He had more than one microscope and I have heard him say that he had as much enjoyment out of a microscope costing him a few dollars, as from one of the more expensive, costing hundreds.

Dr. Wood married Mrs. Mary Stanwood Jordan and had four children, and it was a matter of regret to him that his son did not become a doctor.

To sum up the character of this well-known physician, we should say that he represented all that was best in medicine, an excellent practitioner, careful student, a rare diagnostician, and a genial painstaking man; fond of books, and always ready to look on the hopeful side of disease at the patient's bedside.

He died simply from old age, in 1899, after a brief illness, leaving a most charming and agreeable memory among natural history students and medical men.

J. A. S.

Trans. Maine Med. Assoc.

Wood, William Maxwell (1809–1880).

The father of this surgeon-general of the United States Navy, was Gen. Wood, a prominent merchant of Baltimore, who had come to this country at a very early age. His son William, the eldest of eight children went to the Bel Air Academy, Harford County, Maryland, and graduated in medicine at the University of Maryland in 1829. He at once entered the medical corps of the navy and served as surgeon in four wars, the Seminole, the Mexican, the Chinese and the Civil. As surgeon on board the Minnesota, he witnessed the famous battle between the Merrimac and Monitor. He was commissioned medical director and surgeon-general of the navy May 21, 1871, and retired March 3, of the same year. He died at Owing's Mill near Baltimore March 1, 1880. Gen. Wood wrote "Wandering Sketches of People and Things in South America," "Polynesia," "California and Other Places" (1849); and "Fankwei or the San Jacinto in the Seas of India, China and

Japan" (1859); besides numerous essays, lectures, etc.

A. A.

Tr. Am. M. Asso., Phila., 1882, xxxiii.
Med. Rec., N. Y , 1880, xvii.

Woodward, Joseph Janvier (1833–1884). This noted surgeon was born in Philadelphia, October 30, 1833. He was educated in his native city and obtained the A. B. and A. M. from the Central High School of Philadelphia, graduating in medicine at the University of Pennsylvania in 1853 and practising medicine in his native city until 1861, when, at the outbreak of the great war, he offered his services to the Union and served as assistant surgeon with the Army of the Potomac. In 1862 he was assigned to duty in the surgeon-general's office at Washington. After having organized several military hospitals in that city he was put in charge of the Army Medical Museum. While in this position he collected, in conjunction with Col. Otis, the material for "The Medical and Surgical History of the War." Woodward had charge of the medical part. The first volume of the medical history appeared in 1870, the second in 1879. In the meantime Woodward did valuable work in microscopy and photo-micrography and his publications in these fields made his name famous among scientists throughout the world. His papers fill some four columns in the catalogue of the surgeon-general's library at Washington, District of Columbia. His unceasing labors gradually undermined his constitution so that, in the summer of 1880, he was compelled to go to Europe for his health. He returned the same year somewhat improved. In July, 1881, he was called to the bedside of Pres. Garfield. This, too, was a great strain on his constitution and he never completely recovered. He died August 17, 1884.

Besides the great work mentioned, Woodward published "The Hospital Steward's Manual" (1862) and "Outlines of the Chief Camp Diseases of the United States Armies, as Observed During the

Present War" (1863). He also published numerous articles on microscopy, photomicrography, cancer and other subjects. In 1881 he was elected president of the American Medical Association. Woodward was an honorary member of the Royal Microscopical Society and of the Queckett Club of London, of the Liverpool and Belgian Societies of Microscopy and many other societies at home and abroad.

There is a portrait in the surgeon-general's library, Washington, District of Columbia.

A. A.

Med. News, Phila., 1884, xlv.
Med. Rec., N, Y.. 1884, xxvi.
Memoir, J. S. Billings, 1885.

Woodward, Rufus (1819–1885). Rufus Woodward was the son of Dr. Samuel B. Woodward, and was born in Wethersfield, Connecticut, October 3, 1819.

He was fitted for Harvard College in the Worcester schools. After graduating from college in 1841 he began to study medicine with Dr. Joseph Sargent, of Worcester, and in 1842 entered the Harvard Medical School, where he graduated three years later. For three years he was assistant physician at the State Lunatic Hospital in Worcester, and then spent two years in study in Europe, devoting much time to the study of insanity, with the intention of assisting his father in a private asylum for mental diseases in Northampton. His plans were changed by the latter's sudden death in 1850, and on his return to this country soon after, he established himself in general practice in Worcester. For thirty years he devoted himself to his profession, seeing patients even on the very day of his sudden death, December 30, 1885, at the age of sixty-six.

He was a member of the local and state medical societies and during the war of 1861–65 was examining surgeon for volunteers. From 1863 to 1866 he was city physician and again in 1877 he held this position, and from 1871 to 1880 visiting surgeon to the City Hospital. In natural history and botany he was always greatly interested and was one of the founders and for many years president of the Worcester Natural History Society. Much of his spare time was spent in his garden, and any wild flower of the neighborhood of Worcester, he did not know, was rare indeed.

His son Lemuel F. Woodward became a doctor.

W. L. B.

Phys. and Surg. of the United States, W. B. Atkinson.

Woodward, Theodore (1788–1840).

Theodore Woodward was born in Hanover, New Hampshire, July 17, 1788, and died in 1840. At the age of twenty-one he began to practise and remained all his life in Castleton, Vermont. By the aid of his colleague Dr. Selah Gridley and some friends of the enterprise he succeeded in founding and establishing the Vermont Academy of Medicine at Castleton, Vermont, which became associated with Middlebury College. He was a member of the Corporation of the Vermont Academy of Medicine from 1818 to 1840, and professor of surgery and obstetrics there from 1818 to 1824 and the same in 1822 with diseases of women and children added. In 1824 he was registrar of the Academy and made professor of the principles and practice of surgery, obstetrics and the diseases of women and children, continuing this work until 1838, when he became incapacitated by the disease that terminated his life.

He was a laborious student of everything which related to the nature and cure of disease, and blended with unusual symmetry the characters and avocations of the student and the physician.

Woodward was distinguished for quickness of apprehension and acute discrimination when investigating disease, and great shrewdness in the expediency and adaptation of remedies.

During the course of his practice he performed most of the operations of surgery which are regarded as critical and was distinguished for his fortunate selection of the proper time and medical treatment.

He married Mary Armington, and had three sons and three daughters. One son, Adrian Theodore Woodward, studied medicine and became distinguished as a general surgeon.

J. H. W.

Boston Med. and Surg. Jour., 1841, vol. xxiii.

Wooten, Thomas Dudley (1829–1906).

Thomas Dudley Wooten was born in Barren County, Kentucky, March 6, 1829. His parents were Virginians. He graduated from the medical department of the University of Louisville in 1853, and settled in Springfield, Missouri, in 1856. At the outbreak of the Civil War he enlisted as a private, but later was made surgeon of Foster's regiment, Second Missouri Infantry. In August, 1861, he was appointed chief surgeon of McBride's Division, and a little later surgeon-general of all the Missouri forces. Afterwards he was made medical director of the First Army Corps of the West, commanded by Gen. Sterling Price. In 1865 he practised in Paris, Texas, and in 1876 moved to Austin, in both places achieving considerable reputation as a surgeon.

He was a member of the county and state medical societies in 1885. He married in 1853 Henrietta Goodall of Tompkinsville, Kentucky, and had four children. Two of his sons, Goodall and Joseph S., became physicians.

Dr. Wooten did at Eureka Springs, Arkansas, August 1, 1906, of acute gastro-entero-colitis, after an illness of four days. G. M. D.

Daniel's Texas, N. J., Austin 1887-8, iii (port.).

Worcester, Noah (1812–1847).

Noah Worcester, an early dermatologist, Cincinnati and Cleveland, Ohio, was born in Thornton, New Hampshire, July 29, 1812, the son of a teacher of very moderate estate. He was compelled to provide largely for his education by teaching, and in this way struggled through Harvard College after an interrupted course of study of five years, 1827–1832; then settled in Hanover, New Hampshire, studied under Dr. R. D. Mussey, matriculated in the medical department of Dartmouth College, and graduated there in 1838. He was at once appointed demonstrator of anatomy in his alma mater, and invited by Dr. Mussey to became his assistant. When, in the same year, Dr. Mussey accepted the chair of surgery in the Medical College of Ohio, Worcester was invited to accompany him and be his partner. Soon after his arrival in Cincinnati he received the chair of physical diagnosis in the Medical College of Ohio and in 1841 visited Europe and renewed his studies in London and Paris. On his return to the United States in 1842 he married Jane Shedd, of Peacham, Vermont, an old sweetheart, well advanced in pulmonary tuberculosis, a disease which terminated her life in the following year. Grief at her loss, and the intimate association and anxiety which preceded her death, wore heavily upon the health of her husband, and from this time Dr. Worcester was always an invalid and soon developed signs of undoubted tuberculosis. He was himself a firm believer in the infectiousness of that disease. In spite of waning health and strength, he struggled bravely to fulfil the duties of his profession, and in 1843 even accepted the chair of general pathology, physical diagnosis and diseases of the skin in the newly organized medical college of Cleveland. He was, however, never able to perform the work in spite of the generous and hearty aid afforded by his medical colleagues. For a year or two he lectured on diseases of the skin, but soon even this labor proved too great and he retired to Cincinnati, where he died of tuberculosis in March, 1847.

We have from his pen "A Synopsis of the Symptoms, Diagnosis and Treatment of the more Common and Important Diseases of the Skin," Philadelphia, 1845.

H. E. H.

From an Address by Jacob J. Delamater, M. D., Cleveland, November 3, 1847.

Wormley, Theodore George (1826–1897).

Theodore George Wormley, toxicologist and legal physician, was born at Wormleysburg, Pennsylvania (a town named after his ancestors) on the first day of April, 1826. His people were of German descent. They were also very poor, and Wormley not only had to furnish the means for his education, but also to support his mother.

When sixteen years old, he went to Dickinson College, for three years devoting himself to his work with the utmost assiduity, then after studying medicine with Dr. John J. Meyers, he entered the Philadelphia College of Medicine, in Philadelphia, where he received his doctorate in 1849.

For a while he had some difficulty in finding a suitable practice. Spending almost a year in Carlisle, Pennsylvania, then a few months in Chillicothe, Ohio, he eventually settled (in 1850) in Columbus, where he remained twenty-seven years, rising to the top of the profession. During most of this time he was professor of toxicology in the Starling Medical School.

In 1877 he removed to Philadelphia, because elected to the chair of chemistry and toxicology in the University of Pennsylvania. It is interesting to note that for this position he competed with the famous Dr. John James Reese. This position he held almost twenty years.

Wormley was a very extensive writer, his magnum opus being a large volume entitled, "The Micro-chemistry of Poisons," 1867. Of this world-famous book it is well-nigh impossible to speak in terms of too high praise. Though the work is extensive (the second edition contains almost 800 pages) it is very concisely written, and is characterized throughout by the ripest and fullest scholarship and the most painstaking accuracy. Never before perhaps had toxicological subjects been handled with quite the high degree of literary skill and the miraculous care for detail and truth which appear in this volume. The work soon became known throughout the lego-medical world. This famous work is dedicated "To my wife, who, by her skillful hand, assisted so largely in its preparation, this volume is affectionately inscribed." In the back of the book are fifteen pages of steel engravings, numbering ninety-six engravings in all, each of the utmost fineness and accuracy. At the bottom of each page we read, "Mrs. T. G. Wormley, ad nat. del. et sculp." It is told by Dr. John Ashhurst, Jr., that, when the manuscript of the book was handed to the publishers, the latter declared that it would be impossible to find a draughtsman capable of reproducing the illustrations by which the manuscript was accompanied, so great was their exquisite delicacy. In fact, a number of engravers, to whom the matter of reproducing these illustrations was submitted, declared (according to the "American Literary Gazette") that the work, assuming that it could be done at all, would cost the engraver who did it, his eyesight. Thereupon Mrs. Wormley set herself to work to acquire the difficult art of engraving on steel. This feat she accomplished to such a degree that the desired engravings were produced by her hand and remain to this day a marvel of the steel engraver's art. Further engraving of a highly accurate sort was done for the second edition of the book, by Dr. Wormley's elder daughter, Mrs. John Marshall.

Dr. Wormley was a man of medium height, always smooth-shaven, and had brown hair and blue eyes. He was a healthy, vigorous man, and delighted to pass the winter through without an overcoat.

He was not merely a scientist of superabounding energy, but also a man of strong and sincere affections and sentiments, a lover of nature, of music, and his home.

His love of nature was more than mere enthusiasm for dry-as-dust science. This fact is shown by his wide-ranging investigations in other fields than that of his own particular specialty. He was interested in ornithology and icthyology, in crystallography, in infusorial earth and diatoms. He discovered a species of fish (of brilliant coloring) to which he gave the name of Etheostoma Iris. He mounted many birds and fishes, which are to be found at the present moment in the Smithsonian Institution at Washington. And birds and fishes, crystals and diatoms, were to him but parts of a very great and very beautiful world which he loved, and which he tried to comprehend for the reason that he loved it.

During the summer of 1896, Prof. Wormley began to be attacked by the disease which eventually ended his life. At that time he was on a farm in Berks County, working among plants and flowers, as he very much loved to do. In the fall he went back to the city and his customary teaching, but soon it became apparent that he was seriously affected with chronic Bright's disease, and the end of the great worker arrived one quiet Sunday morning, January 3, 1897. The world of legal medicine lost perhaps its clearest mind; while a very much larger and broader world was undoubtedly the poorer for the dropping out of one of the very finest examples of a quiet, unassuming scholar and gentleman.

He was co-editor of the "Ohio Medical and Surgical Journal," from 1862–4 and a tolerably full list of his writings is in the the Surgeon-general's Catalogue, Washington, District of Columbia.

T. H. S.

Journal of the Am. Chemical Soc., xix, No. 4. April, 1897 (port.), Edgar F. Smith; Trans. Coll. of Phys. of Philadelphia, 1897. John Ashurst; Univ. Med. Magazine, 1896–97, Alumni Notes; Universities and Their Sons (Univ. of Penna.) vol. i (port).

Wright, John (1811–1846).

John Wright was born in Troy, February 2, 1811, the son of John Wright. His early education was secured at Allen

Fish's School in Troy, where he was prepared for admission to the Rensselaer Institute where he graduated. His education was further completed at Yale College where he graduated in 1834 and also from the College of Physicians and Surgeons of New York.

He was an ardent student in, and a great lover of Natural History. At one time he had quite a museum of birds and animals which he had procured and mounted himself. Rafinesque and Audubon were his friends and each visited him at Troy. He referred in after years to Mount Rafinesque which he named in honor of his friend, but which is known now as Bald Mountain, about five miles northeast of Troy. Dr. Wright had a pet raccoon, a remarkably fine specimen of which Audubon made a sketch while on his visit to Troy, reproducing it in his great work on the animals of North America.

Dr. Wright was professor of natural history in the Rensselaer Polytechnic Institute from 1838–1845 and published a Flora of Troy and vicinity, and was associated with Prof. Amos Eaton in publishing the "North American Botany," (eighth edition).

He was also on the state survey of Michigan in 1837 as state botanist and continued in that work about 2 years.

For several years he was associated in practice with Dr. Thomas C. Brinsmade of Troy, a combination of talent that gave them the best kind of practice. Dr. Wright attended to the surgical cases.

On April 11, 1838, he married Mary Cottrell who died April 10, 1841. They had one son who died September 18, 1841. He married again, Catherine Wyant, December 5, 1844. He died of tuberculosis of the lungs, April 11, 1846, at Aiken, South Carolina. He was a member of the Rensselaer County Medical Society.

The full title of his book was:

A catalogue of "Plants growing without Cultivation in the Vicinity of Troy," by John Wright, M. D., and James Hall, A. M., Troy, 1836. S. E. J.

Wright, Joseph Jefferson Burr (1801–1878).

A surgeon, United States Army, he graduated in arts at the Washington College in 1821, obtained the M. D. degree at the University of Pennsylvania in 1825, and practised medicine in his native town until 1833 when he was appointed assistant surgeon in the Army of the United States, in 1844 to the rank of surgeon. Wright served with distinction during both the Mexican and the Civil War. In 1865 he was made a colonel "for faithful and meritorious service during the war." He retired in 1876 and died two years later. A. A.

Trans. Am. Med. Ass., Phila., 1879, xxx

Wright, Marmaduke Burr (1803–1879).

Marmaduke Burr Wright, a physician and medical teacher of Cincinnati, Ohio, was born in Pemberton, New Jersey, November 10, 1803. His early education was acquired in the Trenton Academy, and at the age of sixteen began to study medicine with Dr. John McKelway, of Trenton, an alumnus of the University of Edinburgh. After attending three courses of medical lectures in the University of Pennsylvania he received his M. D. there in 1823 and in the same year he settled in Columbus, Ohio, and speedily established his reputation as a skillful physician and surgeon. In 1835 he married Mary E. Olmstead, of Columbus. In 1838 he held the chair of materia medica and therapeutics in the Medical College of Ohio, and two years later was transferred to the chair of obstetrics in the same institution. From this position he was removed by the action of the trustees of the college in 1850, a step which occasioned no little controversy and bitterness of feeling, but he was reelected to the same chair in 1860, and continued to hold this position until his retirement, with the title of professor emeritus, in 1868. During a large portion of his term of service in the Medical College of Ohio Dr. Wright filled the office of dean of the faculty.

Dr. Wright was one of the founders of the Ohio State Medical Society in 1846, president of this society in 1861, corresponding member of the American Society of Physicians of Paris, an honorary member of the American Gynecological Society, president of the Cincinnati Academy of Medicine in 1864, a member of the Cincinnati Obstetrical Society, and for thirty years held a position on the staff of the Commercial and Cincinnati hospitals.

He was an early and persistent advocate of cephalic version in obstetrics, "American Practitioner," March, 1876, and of the establishment of asylums for the care and cure of inebriates. A fluent and logical writer he contributed numerous papers to the journals and societies of his day. Among the more important of these were:

"Difficult Labors and Their Treatment." ("Transactions of the Ohio State Medical Society," 1854); the "Prize Essay of the Ohio State Medical Society," for the year 1854; "Drunkenness, its Nature and Cause or Asylums for Inebriates." ("Transactions of the Ohio State Medical Society," 1859); "Report of the Committee on Obstetrics to the Ohio State Medical Society." ("Transactions of Ohio State Medical Society," 1860).

He died in Cincinnati, August 15, 1879.

H. E. H.

Transactions of the American Medical Association, vol. xxxi, (1880) (S. Loving).
Transactions of the Ohio State Medical Society for 1880.
Am. Pract., Louisville, 1879, vol. xx (T. P.).
Obstet Gaz., Cincin., 1879–80, vol. ii (A. G. Drury).
Tr. Am. Gyn. Soc., 1879, Boston, 1880, vol. iv (port) (T. Parvin).

Wyman, Jeffries (1814–1874).

This doctor, who did so much to advance the knowledge of natural sciences, was the third son of Dr. Rufus and Ann Morrill Jeffries, and born at Chelmsford, Massachusetts, on August 11, 1814. As a lad he went to the local academy; in 1826 to Phillips Exeter Academy and graduated from Harvard in 1833, he was not remarkable as a student, although he showed a liking for chemistry and anatomy. Some of his class-mates remember the interest which was excited among them by a skeleton which he made of a mammoth bull-frog from Fresh Pond, probably one which is still preserved in his museum of comparative anatomy. His skill and taste in drawing, which he turned to such excellent account in his investigations and in the lecture room, as well as his habit of close observation of natural objects met with in his strolls, were manifested even in boyhood.

He began the study of medicine under Dr. John C. Dalton at Chelmsford and at Lowell, also studying under his father and taking the regular courses at Harvard Medical School. Elected house-student in the medical department at the Massachusetts General Hospital in his third year, the position offered him good opportunities for the study of disease. He graduated in 1837. His graduation thesis, which was not published, was entitled "De Oculo." He started practising in Boston, and at the same time was made demonstrator of anatomy in the Harvard Medical School under Dr. Warren, a position bringing but scanty returns, but his life was abstemious. He was unwilling to accept more from his father who out of his moderate income had provided for the education of two sons, so he often went without things he really needed and to get a little ready money he joined the Boston Fire Department.

Fortunately in 1840 he was offered the curatorship of the Lowell Institute by Mr. John A. Lowell. He gave a course of twelve lectures upon comparative anatomy and physiology in the winter of 1840-41, and earned enough from this course of lectures to spend a short time in study in Europe. In Paris he studied human anatomy in the school of medicine, and comparative anatomy and natural history at the Jardin des Plantes, attending the lectures of Flourens,

Majendie, and Longet on physiology, and of de Blainville, Isidore St. Hilaire, Valenciennes, Dumeril, and Milne-Edwards on zoology and comparative anatomy. He took a walking trip along the Loire and another along the Rhine, whence he went through Belgium to London. In London he made a study of the Hunterian collections at the Royal College of Surgeons, but was called home by the illness of his father, who died before he reached America. On his return to Boston he spent most of his time in scientific work, but without adequate remuneration. In 1843 he was offered a professorship of anatomy and physiology in the medical department of the Hampden-Sidney College, established at Richmond, Virginia. The work in the medical college lasted merely during the winter and spring months, and the rest of the year he spent in Boston. In 1847 he resigned this professorship to accept the Hersey professorship of anatomy in Harvard College, a chair at this time transferred from the medical school to the college at Cambridge, while a new professorship, the Parkman, was established at the medical school in Boston and conferred upon Oliver Wendell Holmes. Wyman began his work at Harvard in Holden Chapel, a small building not well fitted to the purpose. The upper floor was made into a lecture room while the lower floor contained the dissecting room and museum of comparative anatomy, which was a mere rudiment when he took charge of it, but rapidly enlarged under his activity. He gave two annual courses of lectures and lessons, each for twenty weeks. One was on embryology, the other on anatomy and physiology. In addition to teaching undergraduates he directed numerous special pupils in advanced work and was loved as a simple, unaffected, attractive, stimulating teacher.

Wyman's museum was one of the first of its kind in the country to be arranged on a plan both physiological and morphological. "No pains and labors were spared, and long and arduous journeys and voyages were made to contribute to its riches."[1] (Gray.)

Among these expeditions, the following are the more important: In the summer of 1849 he accompanied Capt. Atwood, of Provincetown, upon a fishing voyage up the coast of Labrador. In the winter of 1852, while in Florida for his health, he began a fruitful study of this district. In 1854, accompanied by his wife, he travelled extensively in Europe, and visited many of the best museums. In the spring of 1856, with his pupils Green and and Bancroft as companions, he sailed to Surinam, made canoe trips far into the interior, where they got many interesting collections, but also got the fever from which Wyman suffered severely. In 1858–59 he accompanied Capt. J. M. Forbes on a voyage to the La Plata, ascended the Uraguay and the Parana, and then with George Augustus Peabody, as a companion, crossed the pampas to Mendosa, and the Cordilleras to Santiago and Valparaiso, returning home by way of the Peruvian coast and the Isthmus.

Wyman's museum was made up of specimens gathered largely by himself and at his own expense, and in the main prepared by his own hands, but Agassiz by his personal enthusiasm got many to aid him. In Dr. Wyman "we have an example of what one man may do unaided, with feeble health and feebler means, by persistent and well-directed industry, without éclat, and almost without observation. While we duly honor those who of their abundance cast their gifts into the treasury of science, let us not, now that he cannot be pained by our praise, forget to honor one who in silence and penury cast in more than they all." (Gray).

Although Wyman's salary was small, he adapted his wants to his means, yet was not one to complain when, in 1856, Dr. William J. Walker, a friend of his father's, sent him ten thousand dollars to aid him in his work. In the same year

---

[1] Holmes in a biographical sketch of Wyman in the Atlantic Monthly for November, 1874, has given an interesting description of the museum.

Thomas Lee, another friend, supplemented the endowment of the Hersey scholarship with an equal sum, stipulating that the income should be paid to Prof. Wyman during life, whether he held the chair or not. The aid given Wyman by these two gifts did much to enable him to continue scientific work in comfort. In 1866 Wyman was made one of the trustees of the Museum and had the Professorship of American Archeology and Ethnology, founded by George Peabody, of Harvard University. By the other trustees he was made curator of the museum. After taking charge of the museum, he devoted himself mainly to ethnology.

"With what sagacity, consummate skill, untiring diligence and success, his seven annual Reports, the last published just before he died, his elaborate memoir on shell-heaps, and especially the "Archeological Museum in Boylston Hall, abundantly testify. If this museum be a worthy memorial of the founder's liberality and foresight, it is no less a monument of Wyman's rare ability and devotion." (Gray).

In 1850 Wyman married Adeline Wheelwright, who died in June, 1855, leaving two daughters and in 1861, Anna Williams Whitney, who died in 1864 shortly after the birth of a son.

Wyman suffered throughout most of his life from consumption, which grew worse as time went on, so his winters were usually spent in Florida. During the earlier years he did much to build up the museum of which he had charge. "The record shows that he has made here one hundred and five scientific communications, several of them very important papers, every one of some positive value.

He was a member of the Faculty of the Museum of Comparative Zoology, and was chosen president of the American Association for the Advancement of Science for the year 1857, but did not assume the duties.

His scientific papers embrace a wide range of studies including human and comparative anatomy, physiology, microscopic anatomy, paleontology, ethnology, archeology, and studies of the habits of animals. He also wrote several capital biographical sketches of fellow scientists.

In human anatomy, his most important paper is entitled, "Observations on Crania," published in the "Proceedings of the Boston Society of Natural History," for 1868. This contains considerable valuable information. Wyman also made a careful study of the skeleton of a Hottentot, was one of the first to investigate the arrangement of spongy bone in relation to the uses to which the bone is put; compared the spicula of bone in the neck of the human femur with that in the femurs of animals which do not stand upright; gave a careful description of the brain and cranial cavity of Daniel Webster, and important evidence concerning the effect of heat on the structure of bone.

A master in the field of comparative anatomy and paleontology, he achieved some popular, as well as scientific reputation by showing the Hydrarchus Sillimani publicly exhibited as the remains of a gigantic extinct sea-serpent, to be in fact made up of fossil bones belonging to several animals and these animals mammals, not reptiles. He also showed that some, at least, of the so-called paddles exhibited with this skeleton were casts of chambered cells. Wyman made numerous valuable studies of fossil remains including those of a fossil elephant and of a megatherium and of the cranium of a mastodon. In comparative anatomy the most important publication is probably that on the nervous systems of Rana Pipiens published in the "Smithsonian Contributions to Knowledge," 1852. In this he gives a full description of the peripheral nervous system of the bull-frog and of the changes undergone during metamorphosis. His theoretical summaries are particularly valuable. His paper on the embryology of the skate (Raia Batis) in the "Transactions of the American Academy of Arts and Sciences," 1864, is also important. In

1843 he published an account of the anatomy of the chimpanzee and in 1847 the first account of the osteology of the gorilla ("M e m o i r. Boston Society Natural History"). To him is due the name of this animal which was discovered by Dr. Thomas S. Savage. This name was adopted from a term used by Hanno, the Carthaginian, in describing the wild men found on the coast of Africa, probably one of this species of the Orang. This term was adopted at the suggestion of Dr. A. A. Gould. Gray wrote in 1874: "Nearly all since made known of the gorilla's structure, and of the affinities soundly deduced therefrom, has come from our associate's subsequent papers, founded on additional crania brought to him in 1849, by Dr. George A. Perkins, of Salem; on a nearly entire male skeleton of unusual size, received in 1852, from the Rev. William Walker, and now in Wyman's museum; and on a large collection of skins and skeletons placed at his disposal in 1859, by Du Chaillu, along with a young gorilla in spirits, which he dissected. It is in the account of this dissection that Prof. Wyman brings out the curious fact that the skull of the young gorilla and chimpanzee bears closer resemblance to the adult than to the infantile human cranium."

In the "Boston Medical and Surgical Journal," for 1866, he published a valuable paper on the "Symmetry and Homology in Limbs." In this he took the standpoint that the limbs of each side are reversely symmetrical. In a paper "Notes on the Cells of the Bee," ("Proceedings of the American Academy for January," 1866), he shows clearly that the structure of the honeycomb is far from being ideally perfect. Of the development of organisms in boiled water, enclosed in hermetically sealed vessels and supplied with pure air, he reported in the "American Journal of Science and Arts," for 1862, the second in the same journal for 1867, in the first paper showing infusoria could develop even after prolonged boiling of the water and when air admitted came through red-hot

tubes. In the second paper he showed that when the boiling was carried up to five hours no organisms develop.

Wyman's studies of Unusual Methods of Gestation in certain Fishes ("Silliman's Journal," 1859), were likewise valuable. He gave a careful account of the development of Surinam toads in the skin of the back of their mother, and showed that developing ovum is nourished at the expense of materials derived from the parent.

His interpretations according to Wilder, were either teleogical or purely morphological; that is, they either illustrated function or the relations of single parts without reference to the entire organism. "He would not allow his imagination to outstrip his observation."

Gray gives the following account of Wyman's character:

"His work as a teacher was of the same quality. He was one of the best lecturers I ever heard, although, and partly because, he was the most unpretending. You never thought of the speaker, nor of the gifts and acquisitions which such clear exposition were calling forth—only of what he was simply telling and showing you. Then to those, who like his pupils and friends, were in personal contact with him, there was the added charm of a most serene and sweet temper. He was truthful and conscientious to the very core. His perfect freedom, in lectures as well as in writing, and no less so in daily conversation, from all exaggeration, false perspective, and factitious adornment, was the natural expression of his innate modesty and refined taste, and also of his reverence for the exact truth.

Of Wyman's mode of work in the laboratory, O. W. Holmes gives the following description:

"In his laboratory he commonly made use, as Wollaston did, of the simplest appliances. Give him a scalpel, a pair of forceps, a window to work at, and anything that ever had life in it to work on, and he would have a preparation for his shelves in the course of a few hours or days, as the case might be, that would illustrate something or other which an anatomist or a physiologist would find it a profit and pleasure to study. Under a balanced bell-glass he kept a costly and complicated microscope, but he preferred working with an honest, old-fashioned, steady-going instrument of the respectable, upright Oberhaueser pattern. His outfit for happy employment was as simple as John the Baptist's for prophecy."

To Holmes we are likewise indebted for the following personal description of Wyman:

"Jeffries Wyman looked his character so well that he might have been known for what he was in a crowd of men of letters and science. Of moderate stature, of slight frame, evidently attenuated by long invalidism, with a well-shaped head, a forehead high rather than broad, his face thin, his features bold, his expression mild, tranquil, intelligent, firm as of one self-poised, not self-asserting, his scholarly look emphasized by the gold-bowed spectacles his near-sightedness forced him commonly to wear; the picture of himself he has left indelibly impressed on the memory of his friends and pupils is one which it will always be a happiness to recall."

He died at Cambridge, Massachusetts, on September 4, 1874, of pulmonary tuberculosis.

C. R. B.

A nearly complete bibliography of Wyman's works is given in the Biographical Memoirs of the National Academy of Sciences, vol. ii, 1886, pp. 77–126. It is reprinted in "Animal Mechanics," 1902.

Jeffries Wyman. Address of Prof. Asa Gray at a memorial meeting of the Boston Society of Natural History, held October 7, 1874.

Prof. Jeffries Wyman. A memorial outline, by Oliver Wendell Holmes. "Atlantic Monthly," vol. xxxiv, July–December, 1874.

Jeffries Wyman. By Burt G. Wilder. Old and New, November, 1874.

Jeffries Wyman, by Burt G. Wilder. "Popular Science Monthly," January, 1875 (with portrait).

Prof. Wilder, one of the most devoted and most distinguished of Wyman's pupils, also has an account of Wyman in Holt's "American Naturalists."

The Scientific Life, by S. Weir Mitchell, "Lippincott's Magazine," March, 1875.

Jeffries Wyman. By Frederick W. Putnam Proceedings of the American Academy of Arts and Sciences. N. S. vol. x. Contains a bibliography.

History of the Lowell Institute. By Miss Harriette Knight Smith, 1898, (port.).

Wyman, Morrill (1812–1903).

Morrill Wyman, son of Rufus Wyman, a physician of Chelmsford, Massachusetts, was born in that town July 25, 1812.

He graduated from Harvard College in the same class as his brother Jeffries in 1833, and received the M. D. from the Harvard Medical School in 1837. He studied with Dr. William J. Walker, of Charlestown, before graduating from the school and after graduation served as house officer at the Massachusetts General Hospital. He began and continued practice in Cambridge in 1838 until a few years before his death, which occurred January 31, 1903, at the ripe age of ninety-one.

For a few years during his early life he was adjunct Hersey professor of the theory and practice of physic in the Harvard Medical School. From 1875 to 1889 he was an overseer of the University and in 1885 was given the LL.D. of Harvard. He was consulting physician to the Massachusetts General Hospital, to the Cambridge Hospital, in the establishment of which he was especially prominent, and to the Adams' Nervine Asylum in Jamaica Plain, a part of Boston.

In 1839 he married Elizabeth Aspinwall, daughter of Capt. Robert S. Pulsifer, a Boston shipmaster. He was survived by a son and daughter.

In 1846 he published a volume of 400 pages on ventilation which was an authority for many years.

On February 23, 1850, he removed a large quantity of fluid from the chest of a patient suffering from pleural effusion, making use of an exploring needle and a stomach pump. He repeated the operation a few days later with success, and on April 17, of the same year, operated on a patient of Dr. Henry Ingersoll Bowditch.

Bowditch was convinced of the value of the operation, described it and gave it popularity, assigning, however, the credit of the discovery of thoracentesis to Wyman.

Wyman is chiefly known for his brochure on "Autumnal Catarrh (Hay Fever)," published in 1872.

He was dearly beloved by many generations of students at Harvard College to whom he was not only the college physician, but adviser, helper in time of need.

W. L. B.

Harvard Graduate's Magazine, June, 1903.
Memoir by H. P. Wolcott, Bos, Med. and Surg. Jour., vol. clxviii.
Memorial meeting, Bos. Med. and Surg. Jour., vol. clxix.
Bulletin Har. Med. Alumni Asso., April, 1903.
History Har. Med. School, T. F. Harrington. Bos. Med. and Surg. Jour., vol. clxviii.

Y

Yale, Milton LeRoy (1841–1906).

LeRoy Milton Yale, pediatrist, and known also for his good etching, was born at Holmes Hole (Vineyard Haven), Massachusetts, on February 12, 1841, the son of LeRoy Milton and Maria Allen Yale.

He brought the same exactitude to his surgical as to his artistic work, and dealt with children with equal carefulness.

As an etcher he produced several hundred plates. The best of his work had the qualities demanded of a painter-etcher and he took an active interest in founding the New York Etching Club.

He graduated from Columbia College in 1862 and from Bellevue Hospital Medical College in 1866, lecturing there for some time on orthopedic surgery, and afterwards on obstetrics in the University of Vermont, also holding successively a surgeonship in the Charity, Bellevue, and Presbyterian Hospitals. He was co-editor of the "Medical Gazette;" medical editor of "Babyhood" and wrote "Nursery Problems," 1893; "The Century Book of Mothers;" "Phimosis," 1877; "The Mechanical Treatment of Chronic Diseases of the Hip-joints," 1878; "Remarks on Excision of the Hip," 1885; "The Diagnosis of Early Hip-joint Disease from Rheumatism, Neuralgia and So-called 'Growing-pains,'" 1893.

He died on September 14, 1906.

D. W.

Arch, of Pediatries, vol. xxiii, 1906.

Yandell, David Wendel (1826–1898).

He was M. D., LL. D. (University of Louisville); soldier of the Civil War (South Carolina); medical director of the Department of the West; professor of clinical surgery University of Louisville; editor and founder of the "American Practitioner"; president of the American Medical Association; surgeon-general of the troops of Kentucky; president of the American Surgical Association; pioneer in clinical teaching in the west; honorary fellow, and corresponding member of the Medico-Chirurgical Society of Edinburgh; fellow of the Medical Society of London. He was born at Craggy Bluff, Tennessee, on the fourth of September, 1826. The ancestors of the Yandells came from England and settled in South Carolina, in Colonial days. His father, was Lunsford Pitts Yandell, a pioneer in medical education in the West; his mother was Susan Juliet Wendel, a daughter of David Wendel, of Murfreesboro, Tennessee. He studied medicine at the University of Louisville, and graduated in 1846. That year he went to Europe, where he continned his studies, and wrote two series of letters (one secular, the other medical) which established his reputation as a writer. In 1850 he was made demonstrator of anatomy in the University of Louisville. About this time he established the "Stokes Dispensary," the first clinical institution in the west, and later was elected to the chair of clinical medicine in the University. When the Civil War was on Yandell became a soldier in the Confederate Army, and was made medical director of the department of the West, by Gen. Albert Sidney Johnston, and was in the battles of Shiloh, Murfreesboro, and Chickamauga. In 1867 he was elected to the chair of the science and practice of medicine in the University of Louisville, and in 1869 took there the chair of clinical surgery. As a teacher of clinical surgery he had few rivals.

In operating he cut to the line and required depth with precision. His dissections were artistic, and he found his way through the labyrinthine surgical spaces with certainty and safety. His dressings were beautiful, while his treatment of wounds, surgical and accidental, was characterized by a scrupulous cleanliness, which in post bellum days was prophetic of aseptic surgery. In 1870, in conjunction with Dr. Theophilus Parvin, he established "The American Practitioner," which held high place in medical literature for sixteen years (1886), when it was combined with the "Medical News," under the name "American Practitioner and News." He was editor-in-chief of this journal till the year of his death. All his writings were forceful, terse, and condensed. One of his own papers, published in the second volume of the "Practitioner," is a classic. This is an analysis of 415 cases of tetanus.

His nature was gentle and affectionate; his liberality and benevolence conspicuous. He married Francis Jane Crutcher, of Nashville, Tennessee, in 1851 and had four children: a son and three daughters. He died in Louisville, Monday, the second of May, 1898, of arterio-sclerosis, his last illness stretching over a period of five years. During the last two years his mind was a blank.

His contributions to literature include: "Notes on Medical Matters and Medical Men in London and Paris," Louisville, 1848; "Reply to the Attack of Dr. E. S. Gaillard," "American Practitioner," Louisville, 1871); "A Clinical Lecture on the Use of Plastic Dressing in Fractures of Lower Extremity," 1876; "Pioneer Surgery in Kentucky;" a sketch, 1890; "Temperament," an address, 1892; "Battey's Operation," 1875.

H. A. C.

Yandell, Lunsford Pitts (1805–1878).

Briefly summed up the professional life of Lunsford P. Yandell is that he graduated M. D. from the University of Maryland, 1825, and was professor of chemistry, Transylvania University, 1831–1837; founder of Louisville Medical Institute, 1837, which became University of Louisville, 1846; professor of chemistry, materia medica, and physiology, in the University of Louisville 1837–1858; geologist; minister of the gospel (Presby-

terian), 1862; editor "Transylvania Medical Journal," Lexington; editor "Western Medical Journal," Louisville; president Kentucky State Medical Society, 1878.

He was born July 4, 1805, on his father's farm near Hartsville, Sumner County, Tennessee; his father, Dr. Wilson Yandell, was a native of North Carolina. Of Lunsford's childhood and early school days nothing is known. He began to study medicine under his father, attended one course of lectures at the Transylvania University, Lexington, Kentucky, and another at the University of Maryland. After six years' practice in Tennessee, he was called to the chair of chemistry in the Transylvania University. This chair he held until 1837, when he came to Louisville, where he was a founder of the Medical Institute which in 1846 became the University of Louisville. During the war he was for a time in the hospital service of the Confederacy. In 1862 he was licensed to preach by the Memphis Presbytery, and served as pastor of a church in Dancyville, Tennessee, but in 1867 he returned to Louisville and resumed practice, though preaching frequently, as occasion offered. He devoted much time to literary work and geological research, in which science he was a pioneer in the West. He made many valuable contributions to paleontology, preparing numerous papers and enriching the science through not a few discoveries in fossil life. As early as 1847 he published, with Dr. B. F. Shumard, "Contributions to the Geology of Kentucky." In 1848 a note by Prof. Yandell concerning the discovery of calcareous arms in Pentremites Florealis was published in the "Bulletin of the Geological Society of France." In 1855 he discovered a new genus of Crinoidea, which he named Acrocrinus Shumardi. Sir Charles Lyell, Prof. Owen, and other masters in paleontology recognized the value of his work, and his name stands memorialized and immortalized in fossils as follows: Platycrinus Yandelli (Owen and Shumard); Actinocrinus Yandelli (Shumard); Chonetes Yandellana (Prof. James Hall); Amplexus. Yandelli (Edwards and Haime); Trachonema Yandellana (James Hall); Phillips astrea Yandelli (Dr. C. Rominger).

In all the years of his busy life, he was unresting in the labors that he loved. They were diversified, but such was the skill he displayed in each department which he adorned, that in looking at any one specimen of his work we might have supposed that one was his vocation. Whether he wrote history, essays upon geology, on medical themes, biography, the advancement of education, or the wisdom, the power and beneficence of the Creator in His works, he seemed to make each theme his own, and he adorned it with life and beauty. Independently of his lectures, he wrote fully one hundred papers on the various subjects that he had studied, and they are papers of profound interest. Among his medical- and general-literature papers, the best known are: "History of American Literature;" "History of Kentucky Medicine;" A Review of the Last of the 'Idyls of the King," Tennyson; "The Diseases of Old Age" (completed and sent to the printer a few days before his death). He married twice: first to Susan Juliet Wendel and had six children. His second wife was Eliza Bland by whom he had none.

His death on the fourth of February, 1878, was caused by pneumonia, after a few days' illness. Being in pain he asked his son for a portion of opium, and when laudanum was given him, in the Latin of his favorite, Sydenham, he said: "Magnum donum Dei," and these were his last words.

His writings included: "An Introductory Lecture on the Advantages and Pleasures of the Study of Chemistry," 8° Lexington, 1831; "An Account of Spasmodic Cholera, as it Appeared in the City of Lexington, in June, 1833," Lexington, 1833; "Chemistry, as Affording Evidence of the Wisdom of God," an introductory lecture, Lexington, 1835; a prize essay on "Bilious Fever," Louisville, 1841; "A Reply to a Critique on Liebig's Animal Chemistry," Louisville,

1843; "On Etherization," 36 pp., 8°, Louisville, 1848; "On the Progress of Etherization," Louisville, 1849; "A Reply to the Attack of Dr. Charles Caldwell," 9 pp., 8°, Louisville, 1850; "On the Distribution of the Crinoidea in the Western States of America," Louisville, 1852 (reprint, "Proceedings American Association of Advanced Science," Washington, "History of the Medical Department of the University of Louisville," an introductory lecture, Louisville 1852; "Biographical Sketch of Dr. B. F. Shumard," Indianapolis, 1870; "A Memoir of Dr. Benjamin W. Dudley," 16 pp., 8°, Louisville, 1870; "Epidemic Cholera; Its Origin and Treatment," Louisville, 1871; "Recollections of the Medical Society of Tennessee," published by permission from "Lindsley's Medical Annals of Tennessee," Louisville, 1872; "On Puerperal Convulsions," Louisville, 1871; "Medical Literature of Kentucky," Louisville, 1874; "Address on American Medical Literature," Philadelphia, 1876; "Notes on the Life and Writings of Dr. Benjamin Rush," "Indianapolis Journal Co.," 1876; "Old Age, Its Diseases and Its Hygiene," 14 pp., 8°, Louisville, 1878, (Reprinted from "American Practitioner," Louisville, 1878, xvii).

H. A. C.

Biography (J. M. Toner). Also Tr. Amer. M. Assoc., Philadelphia, 1878, xxix (T. S. Bell), Tr. Kentucky Med. Soc., 1878, Louisville, 1879, xxiii (R. O. Cowling). Amer. Prac., Louisville, 1878, xvii (T. S. Bell), Louisville M. News, 1878, vol. v (R. O. C.), Nashville Jour. M. and S., 1878, xxi.

Yates, Christopher C. (1778(?)–1848).

Christopher C. Yates was born in Rensselaer County, studied medicine with Dr. Samuel Stringer, a veteran in the profession, and was probably licensed by the Supreme Court of the State, in the year 1802 or 1803. For many years he lived in Albany and at one time created great excitement in the community by exhuming, for dissection, a half-breed Indian who had died there. The public were incensed by such sacrilege, and Dr.

Yates braved the storm almost at the risk of his life.

In 1812, a bilious epidemic fever appeared in Albany, upon which Dr. Yates wrote an article which was published in the "American and Philosophical Register," in 1813. He attributed the prominent characteristics of the disease to derangement of the liver and regarded the malady as purely inflammatory, and the treatment adopted as of the old heroic practice. The article was reviewed by Drs. Hosack and Francis. In 1820, he took an active and decided part in the controversy on yellow fever.

In 1832 he published an article on "Epidemic, Asiatic or Spasmodic Cholera, Prevailing in the City of New York, with advice to planters in the south on the medical treatment of their slaves."

He also discussed cholera in a letter to Dr. Barent P. Staats, the health officer of Albany in 1832, and gave an account of the disease as observed by French authors. These articles are preserved in the State Library. While living in New York, Dr. Yates lost a son, Winfield Scott, a lad of eighteen, extraordinarily proficient in the various branches of learning.

Yates gave his attention to the cure of stammering, as a professional specialty, but there remains no evidence that he was particularly skillful in such cases.

He returned to Albany about 1840, but went eventually to Parishborough, in Nova Scotia, where he passed the rest of his days, and died September 23, 1848.

In personal appearance, he was tall, with a slender figure, an intelligent face, and prepossessing address. Though a man well read in his profession, and of considerable intellectual ability and culture, it is truthful to add, that in his character and example, there was nothing to admire but everything to avoid; and that his influence upon the profession and upon society was demoralizing.

Ann. of the Med. Soc. of the County of Albany, (1806-1851). Sylvester D Willard.

Young, Daniel S. (1827-1902).

Daniel S. Young, surgeon, artist and inventor, was born in New York in 1827 and graduated in medicine at the Albany Medical College, New York, in 1855, settling in Cincinnati. During the war he was surgeon of the 21st Regiment Ohio Volunteer Infantry, afterward lecturing on surgery in the Cincinnati College of Medicine and Surgery. He contributed some valuable papers on military surgery to the "Cincinnati Journal of Medicine," which was edited by G. C. Blackman, accompanying them with beautiful colored illustrations, all his own work, he being an expert draftsman, painter, engraver, lithographer and wood-cutter. Young was engaged in writing a "Surgical History of the Civil War, but abandoned the work when the War Department announced the preparation of such a work by the surgeon-general's office. He was for some years connected with the surgical staff of the Cincinnati Hospital and had a wide reputation as a surgeon and obstetrician. He died in 1902.

Dan Young, as he was known, was a versatile man. Years ago he discovered that zinc plates might be used for engraving but never thought of patenting his invention. He was a master of the art of etching and modelling; and some beautiful samples of his work are to be found in the library of the Cincinnati Hospital. He was also a violin-maker; in fact, there was hardly any kind of handiwork in which he did not excel. In making splints or dressings of any kind he was quick as he was resourceful and artistic. It is but natural to suppose that he possessed the eccentricities of genius to a liberal extent.

Young in 1867 reported a case of gangrene of the heart, a pathological curiosity. In 1880 he made a drawing within twelve hours after the shooting of President Garfield, showing the exact location of the bullet; and the autopsy, made many weeks later, proved the correctness of Young's diagram.   O. J.

Taken from "Daniel Drake and His Followers," Otto Juettner.

Z

Zakrzewska, Marie Elisabeth (1829–1902).

Berlin, Prussia, was the birth-place of Marie Zakrzewska, a pioneer woman physician, her father an officer in the Prussian Army was a descendant of a Polish family of high rank which shared their country's downfall. Her mother traced descent from a gipsy queen of the tribe of Lombardi. The greatgrandmother went through the events of the Seven Years' War as assistant-surgeon to her father, an army-surgeon, her daughter was a veterinary surgeon and Marie's mother studied and followed the profession of midwife when her husband was dismissed from the army on account of his revolutionary tendencies.

Marie was the eldest of a family of five sisters and one brother.

When eleven years old she was taken by a doctor to the dead house of a hospital to see the corpse of a young man whose body had turned green from poison; she was left to roam at will in the dissecting rooms and later was forgotten and locked alone in the dead house until late at night.

She was, also, about this time given two books to read, "The History of Surgery" and "History of Midwifery," and her school days ended when she was thirteen.

The mother's practice was by this time arge and increasing and Marie assisted her mother wherever possible. Marie, when twenty was admitted as student in the Berlin School of Midwifery, but only after a direct appeal to the King by Dr. Schmidt, a prominent physician of the school, himself in failing health. It was planned that Marie should eventually be chief accoucheur in the Hospital Charité and professor of midwifery when he resigned. Marie met with untold opposition, which was only overcome through Dr. Schmidt's tenacity of purpose and the desire of his colleagues to fulfill his dying wishes.

The appointment was granted on May 15, 1852, but enmity was insidious, and in November of the same year she relinquished her position.

The first report of the Pennsylvania Female College had been sent to Dr. Schmidt, and Marie planned to emigrate, a project not executed until March, 1853. The parting from a home to which she was never to return, was, she writes, the hardest moment of her life. A sister accompanied her and after a voyage of forty-seven days the two girls reached New York with the sum of one hundred dollars between them. It was a blow to learn from Dr. Reisig, a friend, that in America, women physicians were of the lowest rank, and her limitations in the English language prevented her from getting in touch with members of the medical profession. Nevertheless, after securing suitable rooms Marie put out her sign but practice did not come. Then Marie turned heroically for a time from her chosen work and started in the trade of supplying embroidered work to the wholesale houses. She was soon able to give work to as many as thirty girls and thus earned sufficient to keep in comparative comfort a family of four, for in September a second sister and a friend joined them. From her work girls she gained a lasting impression of the almost hopeless struggle they waged against a life of shame. The wolf being now a reasonable distance from the door, Marie turned again to her cherished project, and obtained an interview with Dr. Elizabeth Blackwell, whereby the gates, so long closed, began to swing slowly open to the kingdom of hope.

Dr. Elizabeth Blackwell invited Marie to assist in her dispensary, offered to give her lessons in English and obtained admission for her to the Cleveland Medical College. The two years at this college gave her considerable pecuniary distress and in 1855, when joyfully expecting the arrival of her mother, a despatch brought her the crushing news of her death and burial at sea. Returning to New York Dr. Zakrzewska with Drs. Elizabeth and Emily Blackwell bent every effort to the task of bringing into existence the "New York Infirmary for Women," which was opened in May, 1857, with Dr. Zakrzewska as first resident physician.

In 1857 the New England Female Medical College of Boston invited Dr. Zakrzewska to fill the chair of obstetrics. Dr. Zakrzwseka consented with the provision that a hospital for chemical work should be opened with the college; after three years, finding growth impossible either in college or hospital, she resigned to begin the foundation of a hospital for women and children, where nurses might be trained and women receive the same practical medical training as men. Friends were ready to aid and a small ten-bed hospital was started in Pleasant Street; rapidly the work increased and eventually land was purchased in Roxbury and a thoroughly equipped building built, which became the New England Hospital for Women and Children. For nearly forty years she was the guiding inspiration.

Though she did not marry, her roof sheltered two sisters and the family of a German reformer, Karl Hinzen, a Republican exile. She wrote much on important and vital questions.

In 1899 Dr. Zakrzewska, now seventy years old, retired. She had been suffering for some time from a nervous trouble which took the form of noises, which she described to a physician as a steady sound of falling rain preventing sleep, which evoked the comment "Well, we do

fall asleep even if it rains hard, and so you will." With fortitude and cheerfulness she awaited the last sleep and this release came on May 12, 1902.

Among the papers she has left are most interesting and valuable talks upon: "Climate; Its Influence upon Health;" "The Woman's Club;" "Amusements; The Value of the Theatre;" "The Dormitory System in Schools and Colleges;" "The Poor; How Best to Help Them;" "The Duty of the Physician to Give Moral as Well as Physical Aid to Her Patient;" "The American Woman" (a series of able articles sent to an English woman's journal). A. B. W.

Obituary. The Woman's Medical Journal, Toledo, vol. xii., p. 134-137. C. W., Woman's Journal, Boston, vol. xxxiii, p. 162-163. Memoir, Issued by New England Hospital for Women and Children, Boston, 1903, 30 pp. Autobiographical letter to Miss Mary L. Booth of New York, incorporated in "A Practical Illustration of Women's Right to Labor," Ed. Caroline H. Dall, 1869.

Zollickoffer, William (1793-1853).

The available material for a life of William Zollickoffer, botanist, proved very scanty. He graduated M. D. at the University of Maryland, 1818 and at the Washington University, 1838. He was one of the earliest in the states to write a materia medica and his, entitled "A Materia Medica of the United States," came out in 1819, and was re-issued in 1827. He also wrote, in 1822, a pamphlet on the "Use of Prussiate of Iron in Intermitting and Remitting Fevers." He was lecturer on medical botany, materia medica and therapeutics at the University of Maryland. It is said the Zollikoferia, one of the *asteraceae*, was named after him by De Candolle. His death took place in Newmarket, Virginia, in 1895.

Medical Ann. of Maryland, E. F. Cordell, 1903.
The Vegetable Kingdom, J Lindley, ed., 1846.

CPSIA information can be obtained
at www.ICGtesting.com
Printed in the USA
BVHW071051290119
538944BV00018B/555/P

9 781331 057